American Political Science Series

GENERAL EDITOR
EDWARD S. CORWIN
Professor of Jurisprudence in Princeton University

American Political Science Series

Under the Editorship of
EDWARD S. CORWIN

Representative Government
By HENRY JONES FORD

American City Government
By WILLIAM ANDERSON, University of Minnesota

International Relations (REVISED EDITION)
By RAYMOND L. BUELL, Foreign Policy Association

New Governments of Central Europe
By MALBONE W. GRAHAM, JR., University of California at Los Angeles

New Governments of Eastern Europe
By MALBONE W. GRAHAM, JR.

American Parties and Politics
By HAROLD R. BRUCE, Dartmouth College

International Law
By ELLERY C. STOWELL, American University

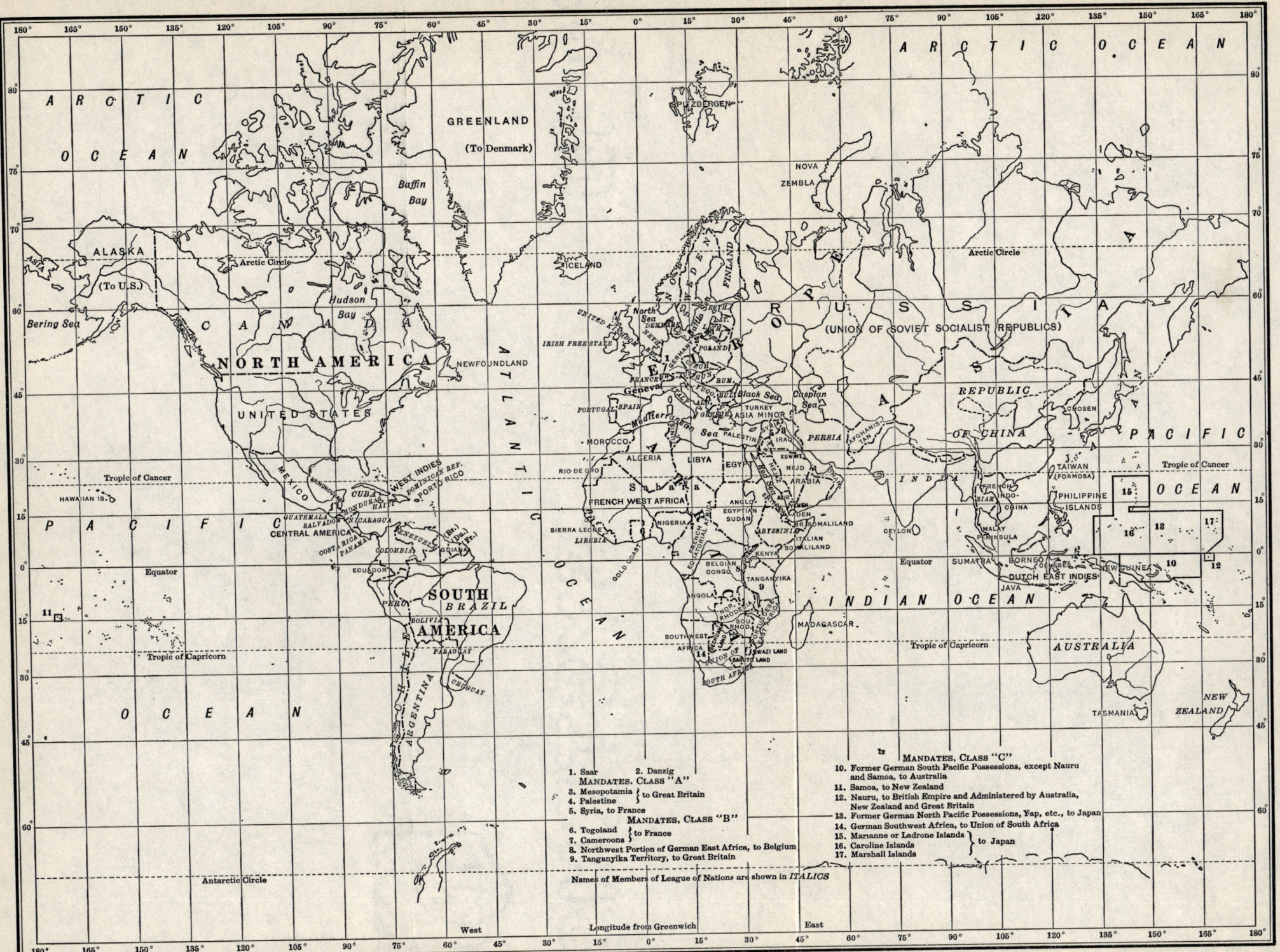

INTERNATIONAL RELATIONS

REVISED EDITION

BY

RAYMOND LESLIE BUELL

RESEARCH DIRECTOR OF THE FOREIGN POLICY ASSOCIATION
FORMERLY ASSISTANT PROFESSOR IN GOVERNMENT
AT HARVARD UNIVERSITY

NEW YORK
HENRY HOLT AND COMPANY

COPYRIGHT, 1925,
BY
HENRY HOLT AND COMPANY

COPYRIGHT, 1929,
BY
HENRY HOLT AND COMPANY, INC.

November, 1929

PRINTED IN THE
UNITED STATES OF AMERICA

TO

F. D. B.

PREFACE

Lord Morley's statement that "Political Science is wider than law, because its work may be said to begin where law ends," applies particularly to international relations. For many years our universities and colleges have devoted considerable attention to the study of cases involving international law. While this subject is important, its appeal must be primarily to the expert; much international law, moreover, never gets into a court. On the other hand, international relations—the discussion of policies which result in the clash of national interests and of methods by which these clashes can be avoided and peace preserved—should be of interest to every educated man and woman.

I have attempted to approach the subject of international relations, not from the viewpoint of contemporary events, diplomatic history, personal politics, or even international organization, but to approach it from the viewpoint of political science—to begin where international law leaves off. The hypothesis upon which I have proceeded is that a field of international relations exists which is almost as distinct from international law as the study of American government is from constitutional law.

I have taken the liberty to draw on certain paragraphs in my articles, published in recent years, in *Asia*, *The Atlantic Monthly*, *Current History Magazine*, *Foreign Affairs*, *Forum*, and *The Yale Review*, for which acknowledgment is made.

I am under a great debt to Edward S. Corwin, the editor of this series, and also to Archibald Cary Coolidge, Arthur N. Holcombe, Stanley K. Hornbeck, Manley O. Hudson, George Grafton Wilson, Allyn A. Young, Herbert Feis, Lindsay Rogers, John Dickinson, Raphael Demos, Robert R. Wilson, Walter R. Batsell and my father, whose criticism of manuscript or proof has been of the highest value. Needless to say, no one but myself is to blame for the errors in fact or in judgment which inevitably creep into a book of these pretensions.

R. L. B.

PREFACE TO SECOND EDITION

Since this volume first appeared in 1925, a number of important international transactions have occurred. The Locarno agreements, the International Economic Conference, the Geneva Naval Conference, the Pan American Conference at Havana, and the Young Plan are all events with which the student of international relations should be familiar.

This book is already of such proportions that it is impossible to mention every international agreement entered into during the last four years. I have attempted to limit this revision to those changes in international relations and organization which show some concrete advance. Thus it is impossible to review every dispute which has come before the League Council or the World Court, but I have described in some detail such controversies as the Greco-Bulgarian incident of 1925, the Hungarian-Rumanian Optant question, and the Bolivia-Paraguay dispute, which are illustrations of the strength as well as the weakness of existing international machinery.

In bringing this book up to date I have relied heavily on the Information Service of the Foreign Policy Association.

R. L. B.

August, 1929.

CONTENTS

PART I

PROBLEMS OF NATIONALISM AND INTERNATIONALISM

CHAPTER PAGE

I. THE SENTIMENT OF NATIONALITY................... 3
1. The Human World.—2. National Characteristics.—3. The Influence of Geography and Language.—4. Religion—the Vatican.—5. History.—6. Education.—7. The Value of Small Nations.—8. Cultural Internationalism.—9. Educational Conferences—the Committee of Intellectual Coöperation of the League of Nations.

II. SELF-DETERMINATION............................ 28
1. The Causes of Self-Determination.—2. Self-Determination in History and International Law.—3. Self-Determination at the Peace Conference.—4. Plebiscites—Abuses.—5. Where to Draw the Line.—6. Who Should Draw the Line?—The Aaland Islands Case.—7. The Problem of Frontiers.

III. THE CONFLICT OF COLOR......................... 56
1. An Inter-racial War?—2. Causes of Race Prejudice.—3. Necessity for Racial Segregation.—4. Treatment of Orientals in the West.—5. The Demand for Racial Equality.—6. Racial Homogeneity v. Racial Equality.—7. The Kenya Dispute.—8. The Gentlemen's Agreement.—9. The Problem of Democracy in Inter-racial Communities.

IV. PAN-NATIONALISM............................... 73
1. Aryan, Teutonic and Nordic Supremacy.—2. Difficulties with Racialism.—3. Pan-Germanism.—4. Pan-Slavism.—5. The Norden Movement.—6. The Pan-Angle Movement.—7. Pan-Latinism and Pan-Hispanism.—8. The Pan-African Movement.—9. The Pan-Islam Movement.—10. The Pan-Turanian Movement.—11. The Pan-Arab Movement.—12. The Pan-Asiatic Movement.—13. The Prospects for Racial Nationalism.

CONTENTS

| CHAPTER | PAGE |

V. ECONOMIC NATIONALISM.......................... 96
    1. The Demand for Economic Self-Sufficiency.—2. The Diversity of Natural Resources.—3. Tariffs and International Relations.—4. Tariff Discriminations and "Wars."—5. Export Taxes and Embargoes.—6. The Monopoly of Raw Materials.—7. Trusts and Foreign Trade.—8. National Aid to Shipping.—9. Results of Economic Nationalism.—10. The Economic Motive and War.—11. The Example of the Saar.—12. The Justification of Economic Nationalism.

VI. ECONOMIC INTERNATIONALISM..................... 123
    1. The Commercial Treaty.—2. Most-Favored-Nation Treatment.—3. National Treatment.—4. Freedom of Transit.—5. Free Access to the Sea.—6. Freedom of Navigation.—7. Limitations on Tariffs.—8. International Control over Communications.—9. Unfair Competition.—10. Coöperation in Agriculture.—11. Economic Coöperation during the War and through the League of Nations.

VII. LABOR AND THE WORLD.......................... 154
    1. The Labor Internationals—Treaties against Propaganda.—2. International Labor Legislation Before the War.—3. The International Labor Organization.—4. Its Accomplishments.—5. The Labor Office.—6. The Enforcement of Labor Treaties.—7. International Aspects of Immigration—Immigration Treaties—Emigration Conferences.—8. Emigration and Over-Population.

VIII. THE PROTECTION OF MINORITIES.................. 179
    1. The Minorities of Europe.—2. The Difficulty with Internal Guarantees.—3. Treaties Protecting Minorities before the War—the Defects of These Treaties.—4. The New Minorities Treaties.—5. The League of Nations and Minorities—the German Settlers' Case.—6. Criticisms of the Minorities Principle—the "Little Protocols."—7. Recent Minority Developments.—8. The Exchange of Minorities.

IX. MULTI-NATIONAL STATES......................... 203
    1. The Alternative of Autonomy.—2. The British Empire as a Multi-National State.—3. The Dominions and Foreign Affairs—the Halibut Treaty—Imperial Conferences—Veto over Imperial Treaties—the Need for Consultation.—4. Zionism.—5. Finland and Poland.—6. The Soviet Government and Autonomy.—7. Autonomy in Austria, Hungary and

CONTENTS

CHAPTER PAGE

Turkey—The Lebanon.—8. Iceland and Quebec.—9. Centralization v. Autonomy.—10. Guaranteed Autonomy—The Ruthenes—The Aaland Islands.

X. THE CONFEDERATION OF NATIONS 231
1. Confederations and Federations.—2. Their International Advantages.—3. Imperial Federation.—4. Balkan Federation—5. The Little Entente.—6. Baltic Federation.—7. The New Russian Federation.—8. Pan-Europa.—9. Coöperation in Central America.—10. The Pan-American Movement—the Monroe Doctrine.—11. Regional Groups and the League of Nations.

XI. INTERNATIONAL ASPECTS OF THE DRUG AND LIQUOR TRAFFICS 255
1. The Drug Habit.—2. The World's Opium Supply.—3. Internal Attempts at Control—Poppy-Growing in India.—4. Opium Treaties.—5. The Hague Convention of 1912.—6. Opium and the League.—7. The Proposals of the United States.—8. Opium Smoking in the Far East.—9. The Opium Conferences of 1924–25.—10. Control of the Liquor Traffic in Africa and the North Sea.—11. Controversies between "Wet" and "Dry" Countries.—12. Liquor Smuggling.

XII. INTERNATIONAL HUMANITARIANISM 275
1. The Slave Trade—The Brussels Act—The League of Nations. —2. The Arms Traffic.—3. The Traffic in Women and Children.—4. Obscene Publications.—5. Catching Criminals.—6. Safety of Life at Sea.—7. International Protection of Animals.—8. International Health—The Health Organization of the League—The Red Cross and Rockefeller Foundation.—9. International Refugee Work—Disasters.—10. Free Legal Aid.—11. "National Interests" and Humanitarianism.

PART II

PROBLEMS OF IMPERIALISM

XIII. THE CAUSES OF IMPERIALISM 305
1. Nationalism and Imperialism.—2. Disputes Caused by Imperialism.—3. The Economic Cause of Imperialism.—4. Over-Population and Expansion.—5. The Military

Cause of Imperialism.—Buffer States—Troop Reservoirs.—6. The Nationalistic Spirit and Imperialism.—7. The White Man's Burden.—8. Missionaries and Imperialism.—9. Is Imperialism Justified?

XIV. THE POLICY OF EXPLOITATION................... 324
    1. The Two Kinds of Colonies.—2. Colonial Empires of To-day.—3. Imperialism and the Native.—4. Forced Labor.—5. Imported Labor.—6. Confiscation of Native Lands.—7. Brutality and Discrimination.—8. Tariffs and the "Drain."—9. Debauchery.

XV. THE POLICY OF TRUSTEESHIP................... 344
    1. Adolescent Peoples.—2. The Trusteeship Principle Applied to Land.—3. Native Farms in West Africa.—4. Coolie Treaties.—5. The Basel Trading Company.—6. Education of Native Peoples.—7. The Berlin Act.—8. The Mandates.—9. Their Legal Status.—10. Guarantees to the Natives.—11. The Mandates Commission.—12. The Ruanda Frontier.—13. The Bondelzwarts Affair.—14. The Extension of the Mandate Principle.

XVI. SELF-DETERMINATION AND BACKWARD PEOPLES.... 370
    1. Imperialism and Force.—2. The Demand for Independence.—3. The Attempt at Assimilation.—4. Autonomy and Indirect Administration.—5. Colonial Legislatures.—6. Communal Representation.—7. Prevention of Deadlocks.—8. The Peaceful Emancipation of Colonies.—9. The Example of Mesopotamia.—10. The Example of Syria.—11. International Intervention.

XVII. CAPITAL AND THE BACKWARD REGIONS........... 396
    1. Foreign Investments.—2. Concessions.—3. Capitalistic Abuses in Backward Regions—the Putumayo Affair.—4. The Revolt Against Foreign Capital.—5. Disputes over Vested Interests.—6. The Control of Foreign Investments —American Policy.

XVIII. FINANCIAL CONTROL........................... 413
    1. Non-Recognition of Defaulting Governments.—2. Temporary Intervention.—3. Financial Control.—4. Cuba, Haiti, Santo Domingo, Nicaragua.—5. Bolivia and Salvador.—6. Liberia and Persia.—7. Dangers of this Type of

CONTENTS

Control.—8. International Financial Control—Egypt—Turkey—Greece—China.—9. The League Plan in Austria and Hungary.—10. The International Adviser.—11. Merits and Demerits of International Control.

XIX. THE OPEN DOOR............................ 437
1. Economic Rivalries of Governments.—2. The Navy and Business.—3. The Closed Door.—4. Effect of the Closed Door.—5. The Open Door Defined.—6. Open Door Agreements.—7. Ineffectiveness of These Agreements.—8. International Coöperation and the Open Door.—9. Necessity of International Control.

XX. INDIRECT FORMS OF IMPERIALISM................. 463
1. Danger Zones.—2. The Leasehold.—3. The Sphere of Influence.—4. Protectorates.—5. Semi-protectorates.—6. Financial Control.—7. Tariff Control.—8. Exterritoriality.—9. Informal Control.—10. Joint Government.—11. National v. International Control.

PART III

THE SETTLEMENT OF INTERNATIONAL DISPUTES

XXI. WAR, ALLIANCES AND ARMAMENTS............... 499
1. Material and Spiritual Costs of War.—2. Warfare in the Future.—3. "Defensive" Alliances.—4. The Balance of Power.—5. Secret Diplomacy.—6. Competition in Armaments—Naval Rivalry—Aircraft and Submarines.—7. The Private Manufacture of Arms.—8. Force and International Society.

XXII. REPARATIONS AND INTER-ALLIED DEBTS........... 523
1. Reparations and the Peace Treaty.—2. The Reparations Commission and Germany's Bill.—3. Germany's Failure to Pay.—4. The Legality of the Occupation of the Ruhr.—5. Germany's Capacity to Pay.—6. The "Dawes Plan" (1924)—Raising Reparations—Getting the Money out of Germany—Foreign Control over Germany—Arbitration and Default.—7. The Inter-Allied Debts.—8. The "Young Plan" (1929).—9. The Bank of International Settlements.

CONTENTS

CHAPTER	PAGE

XXIII. THE LIMITATION OF ARMAMENTS 554

    1. Limitation of Armaments before the War—The Rush-Bagot Agreement—The Argentina-Chile Agreement.—2. The Washington Conference.—3. The Moscow and Latin-American Conferences.—4. The Geneva Conference.—5. The Disarmament of Germany.—6. The Demilitarization of Territory.—7. The Control of Private Manufacture of Arms.—8. Armaments and the League.—9. Obstacles to Disarmament.—10. The Limitation of Alliances.

XXIV. SECURITY AND SANCTIONS 582

    1. Neutralization Agreements.—2. "Territorial Integrity" Agreements.—3. Agreements as to the Status Quo.—4. Non-Aggression Agreements.—5. The Demand for "Guarantees."—6. Article Ten.—7. Four Kinds of Sanctions—Trial of the Kaiser—Blockades.—8. The Sanctions of the League Covenant, Economic, Military, Political.—9. The Attack against the Sanctions.—10. Financial Assistance in Case of Aggression.

XXV. WORLD COURTS 606

    1. Voluntary and Compulsory Arbitration.—2. Arbitration and "Vital Interests."—3. The Permanent Court of Arbitration at The Hague.—4. The Central American Court.—5. The Permanent Court of International Justice.—6. The United States and the World Court.—7. The Settlement of "Non-Legal" Disputes.—8. "Non-Legal" Disputes and the League Covenant.—9. Conciliation Commissions.

XXVI. THE RENUNCIATION OF WAR 647

    1. The Geneva Protocol.—2. The Locarno Agreements.—3. Germany and the League.—4. The "Outlawry of War."—5. History of the Anti-War Pact.—6. What Wars are Renounced?—7. The Greco-Bulgaria Case.—8. The Anti-War Pact and the League.

XXVII. INTERNATIONAL CONFERENCES 676

    1. The Making of International Law.—2. International Legislation before the War.—3. The Supreme Council.—4. International Legislation and the Equality of States.—5. Modifications in the Equality Doctrine.—6. The Lack of a Conference System.

CONTENTS

CHAPTER	PAGE
XXVIII. THE LEAGUE OF NATIONS	693

1. The "Legislative" Function of the League.—2. Membership in the League.—3. The Assembly: Organization and Powers.—4. The Council: Organization and Powers.—5. Relation of the Council to the Assembly.—6. The League's Finances.—7. The League and the Equality Doctrine.—8. The Secretariat.—9. The Amendment and Interpretation of the Covenant.

XXIX. THE CONTROL OF INTERNATIONAL POLICY....... 727

1. Are Democracies Pacific?—2. Control of Foreign Affairs in Japan.—3. Constitutional Checks on the Conduct of Foreign Affairs.—4. Legislative Checks on Foreign Policy.—5. Political Checks on Foreign Policy.—6. Democracy and Secret Treaties.—7. Committees on Foreign Affairs.—8. Public Opinion and Foreign Affairs.—9. A "League of Peoples."—10. The American Constitution and Foreign Affairs.

COVENANT OF THE LEAGUE OF NATIONS................... 758

BIBLIOGRAPHY... 775

INDEX.. 821

ABBREVIATIONS

A. J. I. L.—*American Journal of International Law.*
Cmd. and Cd.—British Parliamentary Papers.
O. J.—*Official Journal of the League of Nations.*
Martens.—Martens, *Recueil Générale des Traités,* in three series.
R. D. I. P.—*Revue Générale de Droit International Public.*
R. D. I. C. L.—*Revue de Droit International et de Législation Comparée.*
T. S.—*Treaty Series of the League of Nations.*
Treaties of the United States.—*Treaties, Conventions, International Acts, Protocols and Agreements between the United States and other Powers,* in three volumes.
U. S. For. Rel.—*Papers Relating to the Foreign Relations of the United States,* published annually or thereabouts by the Government Printing Office, the last volume being for the year 1915.
I. S.—Information Service of the Foreign Policy Association.

INTERNATIONAL RELATIONS

PART I

PROBLEMS OF NATIONALISM AND INTERNATIONALISM

CHAPTER I

THE SENTIMENT OF NATIONALITY

1. The Human World.—2. National Characteristics.—3. The Influence of Geography and Language.—4. Religion—the Vatican.—5. History.—6. Education.—7. The Value of Small Nations.—8. Cultural Internationalism.—9. Educational Conferences—the Committee of Intellectual Coöperation of the League of Nations.

If the Man in the Moon should turn his telescope upon that relatively insignificant speck in the universe, the Human World, he would find much to astonish him. He would see an ocean covering nine-twelfths of the globe, the remainder of which is occupied by the "World Island" of Europe-Asia-and-Africa, as well as the Smaller Islands such as North and South America.[1] If the Man in the Moon peered closely, he would see ant-like men, numbering about 1,700,000,000, scurrying hither and thither on land and sea. He would find that seven-eighths of this population inhabit the great continents, one-fourth being huddled up in the continent of Europe, although it contains only one-seventeenth of the area of the world.

1. THE HUMAN WORLD

If this other-world spectator is not color-blind, he would find that these men are of different hues—in Europe and America, what are called "white men," but in oriental Asia, 825,000,000 beings who mostly are yellow and brown. Beneath the dense foliage of the mysterious continent of Africa, he would see the home of the black man—in one of the richest and largest continents in the world, but inhabited only by about 130,000,000 people. If the Man in the Moon should gaze long enough, he would find that these ant-like men differ not only in physical characteristics, but in material and mental accomplishments. He would find Europe and North America studded with sky-scraper cities, steaming ships, roaring railways, blasting furnaces, soaring air-

[1] Cf. H. J. MacKinder, *Democratic Ideals and Reality* (1919), p. 82.

planes, honking automobiles and greasy gas-stations. In Asia or in Africa he would find little of this quick-lunch bustle, but in its stead, the more pleasant, or at least, the more leisurely life of the shepherd, the farmer, the huntsman and the nomad; darker skinned peoples who fret, not so much about elevators, movies, mah jong or taxicabs, as about sleeping sickness, pugnacious neighbors, beasts of the jungle, the terrors of nature—whether comets or thunderstorms—and the grasping exactions of the white man.

If this mythical visitor should put on his spectacles and take a look at the human history books, he would learn that these ant-like men do not think the same thoughts about government, culture or religion; and that they do not even speak the same language. Some of these men have no "civilization," as that word is used in the human world. Others firmly believe in "western civilization"—a system of ideas and a social organization which has issued from the European factory system and the Jewish-Christian system of morals. Still others, particularly the peoples of Asia, believe in "oriental civilization"—a contemplative system which thinks more of the ends of life than the wherewithal, in which a man is less concerned about his physical miseries than the future welfare of his soul.[1]

If the Man in the Moon had a political bent, he would soon learn that mankind had split itself into a large number of groups, some of which are called states, others, nations, and still others, races. Upon consulting the historians he would learn that in the past the outstanding group in the human world has been the state. However, there is not a single world state, he would be told, but a large number of states, each of which has certain legal and metaphysical attributes upon which the international lawyers are fond to dwell. Perhaps he would be mystified to learn that states are "corporate juristic bodies possessing a unity or moral personality by reason of certain ends that hold their individual members together."[2] But he should be impressed with the fact that these states have "the right of existence" and the "right of independence"; and that each full-grown state is "sovereign"—that is, it has full power over all the ant-like men which it shelters, and is to-

---

[1] Cf. A. M. Rihbany, *Wise Men from the East and from the West* (1922), pp. 35 ff.; B. Russell, *The Problem of China* (1922), p. 185.
[2] C. G. Fenwick, *International Law* (1924), p. 84.

tally free, when it wishes to be, from outside control. Nobody tells these states what to do. As Sir Robert Filmer said several centuries ago, "Where there is no Supreme Power over many nations, their Customs cannot be made legal." [1] Nevertheless, while these states may at one time or another be juridically isolated, they cannot be economically or culturally isolated, because of the complex interdependence of the world. Consequently, when their interests come into conflict, a violent time may result unless both agree to mutual compromise.

For the last several centuries the fundamental unit in international relations has been the state, about fifty five or sixty of which exist in the world to-day. One state is legally similar to the other, since each is looked upon as equal in the eyes of international law. Nevertheless, one state may act quite differently from another; it may be quite dissimilar from another, in the extent of its territory and the characteristics of its people. The actions of a state may be controlled by economic considerations or by racial factors, to be discussed in later chapters. But to-day perhaps the most of these actions are influenced by a force, vaguely known as "nationality" and "nationalism," which this and the following chapter will discuss.

Before the partitions of Poland and the French Revolution, European peoples had thought something of the state and something of the individual; but the conception of a nation apart from either of these factors was unknown.[2] The revolutions of the 18th and 19th centuries, however, were based on the idea that mere governments were accountable to groups existing apart: back of the monarch stood the "people" or the nation. Out of this idea came this new conception of nationality, "A corporate sentiment, a kind of fellow feeling or mutual sympathy, relating to a definite home-country, and binding together the members of a human group, irrespective of differences in religion, economic interests, or social position, more intimately than any other similar sentiment." [3] A body of people united by this sentiment is called a Nation.

---

[1] Filmer, *Observations on Grotius* (in *The Freeholders*, etc., 1699), p. 209.
[2] Lord Acton, *History of Freedom and other Essays* (1909), p. 277.
[3] A. N. Holcombe, *The Foundations of the Modern Commonwealth* (1923), pp. 133–134.

2. NATIONAL CHARACTERISTICS

However vague the conception may be, unmistakable differences in national characteristics exist. These are illustrated by the story of the international conference delegates who were invited to write about the Elephant. The Englishman chose as his title: "Elephant-hunting under the British flag"; the Frenchman "L'éléphant et ses amours"; the German (in three volumes of 1000 pages each) "Einleitung in die Beschreibung des Elephants"; the Pole "L'Eléphant et la question polonaise"; the American "How to make bigger and better elephants"; and the Russian "The elephant, does it exist?"[1]

Purely external differences may mark out one people from another. The costumes of the Slovak, the Magyar, or the Pole have been in the past marks of national distinction. Flags serve the same purpose. So important did Germany regard the flag as a symbol of nationality that she prohibited the use of the French tri-color in Alsace-Lorraine and the Danish flag in Schleswig.[2] In Transylvania—a district inhabited chiefly by Roumanians—Hungary forbade even the use of the three Roumanian colors of blue, yellow and red—the police being instructed to tear up women's dresses displaying them.

Likewise, governments stimulate a national consciousness through national holidays celebrating the historic events of their past—most of which have been battles. Although Sweden has no national anthem, most nations help to maintain their identity by hymns of this nature, some of which, such as the Star Spangled Banner, commemorate hard-fought victories over tyrant foes. Different systems of writing may mark out one nation from the other, although their racial origin is the same—such as the Croats from the Serbs, or the Poles who write in Latin letters from the Russians who use the Cyrillic alphabet.

While these differences in national characteristics exist, they are by no means inalterable. Many of them are due to environment.

[1] S. de Madariaga, *Englishmen, Frenchmen, Spaniards* (1928); cf. K. Francke, *The German Spirit* (1916), p. 91; E. Boutmy, *The English People* (1904); P. G. Hamerton, *French and English* (1889), p. 238; R. B. Perry, *The Present Conflict of Ideals* (1918), Part I.

[2] A. van Gennep, *Traité comparatif des nationalités* (1922), Vol. I, pp. 54 ff.

They change when surrounding conditions change. Before the Revolution of 1789, the French were regarded as stolid and indifferent to political rule or misrule. After the Revolution, they came to be regarded as excitable and unstable in their political ideas. In 1660 Milton referred to the "fickleness which is attributed to us as islanders." [1] But England later came to be regarded as a slow-moving and hard-headed country of merchants. The Germans before the days of Fichte had none of the strutting patriotism of the German in the time of Nietzsche and Bernhardi. As the historian Michelet declared, "In the span of a single lifetime a thorough discipline in patriotism had converted a naturally docile population from being one of the least politically minded races in Europe into an acceptance of the State as being the source of all authority, and the be-all and end-all of life." [2]

While one nation may differ from another in language or in culture, there are certain attributes which every nation has in common. This is a group-consciousness which in theory subordinates the individual to the group by infusing in him the sentiment of "nationality." One aspect of this sentiment is called "patriotism"—the love of country, the desire for its good and a willingness to serve it.[3] However, for the last fifty years patriotism, instead of being cultural, has been largely materialistic, seeking to win for the nation increased wealth and power. These ends have created competitions between nations which have not only led to conflicts of material interests, but have converted love of country into fulsome praise, attributing to the nation virtues superior to the rest of the world and a morality which is above reproach. As a result, this type of patriotism has often degenerated into hatred and intolerance of foreigners. [4]

Properly conceived, there is no finer sentiment in the world than patriotism. As long as its desires remain cultural, patriotism does not involve one nation in conflict with other nations; on the contrary, increasing the culture of one nation enriches the culture of the world. Patriotism means, moreover, the sacrifice of the individual to a larger good. While perhaps men should accept obli-

[1] H. J. Ford, "The Anglo-Saxon Myth," *American Mercury*, Sept., 1924.
[2] Quoted by H. A. L. Fisher, *The Common Weal* (1924), p. 96.
[3] Cf. J. L. Stocks, *Patriotism and the Super-State* (1920), pp. 14 ff.
[4] Cf. Carlton J. H. Hayes, *Essays on Nationalism* (1926), Chaps. IV and VIII.

gations world-wide in scope, in practice they inevitably confine their service to those about them, whom they know. As Karl Pearson once said, "Patriotism is the acknowledgment that we owe duties to our fellowmen and cannot adequately perform them to the human race."[1] In other words, the nation is a link between the individual and humanity.

This quality of national self-consciousness has, entirely apart from its chauvinistic aspects, been of considerable importance in international relations. Nations resent insult more quickly than individuals, and they are less capable of self-control. When men think in the mass, they are apt to throw off all the checks which surround an individual, thinking or acting alone.[2] It is improbable that France would have gone to war against Germany in 1870 had it not been for the Ems dispatch, or that the United States would have gone to war with Spain over Cuba, had it not been for the blowing up of the Maine—an incident which added a deep and burning sense of national injury to the more impersonal humanitarian interest which we had previously manifested over the fate of Cuba. The passage of the Japanese exclusion legislation in 1924 by the American Congress likewise profoundly injured the *amour propre* of Japan.[3] Courtesy is an essential of human intercourse, whether between individuals or nations. While such bywords as "national honor" have been seized upon by jingoes in the past for illegitimate ends, too much attention cannot be paid to satisfying the amenities which the self-consciousness of every nation requires.

A nation, according to one writer, is a "body of people who feel themselves to be naturally linked together by certain affinities which are so strong and real for them that they can live happily together, are dissatisfied when disunited, and cannot tolerate subjection to peoples who do not share these ties."[4] This psychological definition has been widely accepted. But it does not explain why it is that certain peoples associate themselves into

[1] *National Life and Character, a Forecast* (1893), p. 187.
[2] For a proposed International Court of Honor, cf. L. Perla, *What is "National Honor"?* (1918), Ch. X, also cf. C. E. D. Martin, *The Behavior of Crowds* (1920), Chs. III, V.
[3] Cf. p. 68.
[4] R. Muir, *Nationalism and Internationalism* (1917), p. 38. Cf. W. B. Pillsbury, *The Psychology of Nationality and Internationalism* (1919), Ch. II.

GEOGRAPHY AND LANGUAGE 9

one nation and not into another—why there is a French nation and a German nation, instead of a single French-German nation. We must try to bear in mind the factors which help to formulate such differences, even though they are psychological in nature, if the exact relations between nations are to be understood.

3. THE INFLUENCE OF GEOGRAPHY AND LANGUAGE

Geography probably is as important a factor as any in explaining the differences between the nations of Europe and America to-day.[1] The three southern peninsulas of the Balkans, Spain and Italy became the home of different nations partly because of natural configuration. The insular position of England and Japan has likewise left a nationalistic mark. Torrential rivers explain the differences between Spain and Portugal, while a great barren mountain range separates the racially similar peoples of Norway and Sweden. The whole history of Russia is "that of its three great rivers,"[2] while the frigid tyranny of nature has helped produce the patience and mysticism which has so often crept into Russian art and literature.[3] The viciousness of the Kurd and of the Arab has been explained by the droughty oppressiveness of local climate.[4] The absence of natural boundaries has caused Brazil, a country sixteen times as large as France, to remain a single nation.[5] The French wars on the continent "as well as our enterprises on foreign soil, find their cause and their reason for existence in the geographic situation of France."[6]

Geography has also molded American nationality. "The frontier is the line of most rapid and effective Americanization. The wilderness masters the colonist. It finds him a European in

[1] Cf. L. Dominion, *Frontiers of Language and Nationality in Europe* (1917), p. 317; E. A. Freeman, *The Historical Geography of Europe* (3d ed., 1903), pp. 7–11; J. Fairgrieve, *Geography and World Power* (1915); H. J. Fleure, *Human Geography in Western Europe* (1919); M. I. Newbigin, *Geographical Aspects of Balkan Problems* (1915).
[2] A. Rambaud, *Histoire de la Russie* (7th ed., 1918), p. 11.
[3] L. Beaulieu, *The Empire of the Tsars and the Russians* (1893), pp. 161 ff.
[4] E. Huntington, *World Power and Evolution* (1919), p. 216.
[5] Bryce, *South America* (1912), p. 401.
[6] L. Vignon, *L'Expansion de la France* (1891), p. 15; cf. also R. von Jhering, *The Evolution of the Aryan* (1897), Ch. 12.

dress, industries, tools, modes of travel, and thought. It takes from him the railroad car and puts him in a birch canoe. It strips off the garments of civilization and arrays him in the hunting shirt and the moccasin. . . . Little by little he transforms the wilderness, but the outcome is not the old Europe. . . . The fact is, that here is a new product that is American." [1]

So strong is the geographic factor that one of the strongest and finest aspects of patriotism is "love of the soil." The late Maurice Barrès once said that nationality was the love of a material thing, "of an extended space upon the globe, of a land of ploughs, corn, and meadows, shaded with trees, watered with streams, flowery with blossom. . . ." [2] Those suggestive phrases, Love of Country, Vaterland, and La Patrie, express the swelling sentiment which the physical environment of a beautiful Nature may produce amongst a people.

A common language is probably as important as geography in producing a nation. Language is the medium by which men exchange ideas; as one writer has said, "it is the clearest and best characteristic by which a nation is distinguished." [3] When statistics record the nationality of people, language is usually employed as the criterion. A nation struggling for political freedom, inevitably revives its ancient dialects—witness the revival of Celtic in Ireland.

While there are about 3,500 languages and dialects in the world, in Europe and America only about thirty main languages are spoken. Of the three main language families—Indo-European, Semitic and Bantu—Indo-European is dominant among western peoples. The Indo-European family is divided into three principal sub-groups—Romanic, Germanic and Slavic. To the first sub-group belong French, Italian, Portuguese, Spanish and Roumanian. Of these Spanish and French are most widely spoken, the former being used not only in Spain but in Latin America. In the Germanic group are found German, English, Dutch and Scandinavian. The Slavic group embraces Russian, including the three dialects of Great, Little, and White Russian, the western

[1] F. J. Turner, *The Frontier in American History* (1920), p. 4.
[2] Quoted by H. A. L. Fisher, *Studies in History and Politics* (1920), p. 157.
[3] A. Meillet, *Les Langues dans l'Europe Nouvelle* (1918), p. 96. It is very difficult to distinguish between dialects and languages, cf. A. C. Coolidge, "Nationality and the New Europe," 4 *Yale Review* (1915), 447.

GEOGRAPHY AND LANGUAGE 11

Slavic tongues of Polish and Czech, and the southern tongues of Bulgarian and Serb-Croat. The extent to which the leading languages of the world is spoken is as follows:

Languages	Number of People
Chinese	445,000,000 [1]
Indo-Aryan	220,000,000
English	160,000,000
Russian	100,000,000
German	85,000,000
French	70,000,000
Japanese	60,000,000
Spanish	55,000,000
Italian	40,000,000
Portuguese	30,000,000

While language is an important factor in nationality, it is not in every case decisive. A number of languages may be spoken by the same nation. In France, Provençal is spoken, and in Spain, Basque and Catalan. In Alsace people speak a dialect of German but have considered themselves French. Four languages are freely used in Switzerland; while in Belgium, Flemish and Walloon are spoken. In 1914 the Germans seized upon this linguistic difference in an effort to destroy the sentiment of Belgian nationality. The country was divided into northern and southern Belgium, and a Council of Flanders was established to curry favor with Flemish-speaking peoples.[2] Following the War, the separatist spirit engendered by this movement lingered. In June, 1923, a ministerial crisis arose over whether the University of Ghent should continue to give instruction only in French or whether it should change to Flemish. Discussion became so bitter that the separation of Flanders from Belgium was actually proposed.[3] A compromise was finally worked out, providing for two "language régimes" in the University; in one, courses are given two-thirds in French and one-third in Flemish, while in the other, the opposite policy is followed.[4] Language was similarly employed by the Austro-Hungarian Empire. The government cultivated

[1] The Chinese and the Indo-Aryan languages are divided into a number of groups.
[2] Cf. H. Langerock, "The Flemish Demand for Autonomy," *Current History*, August, 1923.
[3] *Ibid.*, Sept., 1923, p. 1057.
[4] *Moniteur Belge*, August 1, 1923.

a literary Slovenic tongue in order to break up the unity of the southern Slavs.[1]

Moreover, there are many distinct nations who speak a common language. English is spoken among the different nations of the British Empire and by the United States. Portuguese is spoken in Portugal and in Brazil. Spanish is spoken by some twenty different nations. All of the peoples of Europe have changed their language one or many times.[2] Thus a nation may exist apart from language. But language is nevertheless a powerful fact in holding together men subject to other unifying influences.[3]

4. RELIGION

In the past religion has been more important in dividing up the peoples of the world than at present. Most religions, especially Christianity and Islam, profess to be world-wide in scope, as the following table would indicate:

Leading Religions of the World

Christians		682,000,000
Roman Catholics	331,000,000	
Orthodox	144,000,000	
Protestants	207,000,000	
Non-Christians		940,000,000
Mohammedans	209,000,000	
Buddhists	150,000,000	
Hindoos	230,000,000	
Confucianists, Taoists	351,000,000	

Less than half of the world is Christian, primarily the countries of Europe and America, as well as the kingdom of Abyssinia. Of the Mohammedans of the world, only about 8,000,000 are found in Turkey, the majority being scattered throughout European colonial empires. Hindooism appears to be more of a national religion than any other, since most of the Hindoos are found in India.

Although religion leaps across national boundaries, there are nevertheless many cases where the force of religion has preserved the vigor of nationality. The religious influence of John Knox

[1] Meillet, p. 243.
[2] *Ibid.*, p. 89.
[3] Cf. Buck, "Language and the Sentiment of Nationality," 10 *Pol. Sci. Review* (1916), 44.

probably saved this sentiment in Scotland from extinction; while Roman Catholicism kept the national light flickering in a politically divided Poland from the partitions down until 1918. Among the Zionists at least, Jewish nationality is a matter of religion.[1] On the other hand, religious differences have sometimes hindered national development. Protestant Ulster has complicated the Irish situation, since the vast majority of Irishmen are Catholic, and the fact that the Croats are Romanists while the Serbs are Orthodox has created a problem in Jugoslavia. Nevertheless, the growth of religious toleration is gradually taking the religious factor out of national as well as international politics.

In the Middle Ages the western Christian church was probably the strongest international organization the world has ever seen. But with the rise of Protestantism, national churches came into existence which have in many cases come to the support of the political state. German churches supported Germany in the last war, while Allied churches, whether Catholic or Protestant, supported Allied countries—both on the same ground that this was a holy war against unholy opponents. In the Balkans the national church has been particularly used to advance national ambitions. "The Greeks have always exploited the Orthodox church as a political expression of their national unity, instead of uniting it to express the spiritual catholicity of eastern Christianity."[2] Many churches are now awaking to the fact that religion has a higher function than to give a pious sanction to nationalistic excesses. In a speech of June, 1922, Mr. Lloyd George said that if the League of Nations was to perform a useful work, it would have to be based on a real spirit of peace, arising out of the heart of each nation. The creation of this spirit, in his opinion, was a task for the churches. The great anti-war movement which swept across the world in the five years following 1918, was primarily a religious movement, fostered by religious organizations. In 1923–24 a dozen national religious bodies in America condemned aggressive war as unchristian. The Federal Council of the Churches of Christ in America issued three calls to 150,000 churches to support the Washington Conference. Of the 13,878,671 names affixed to petitions sent to the President in regard to the Con-

[1] Cf. p. 216.
[2] G. Young, *Nationalism and War in the Near East* (1915), p. 27.

ference, 12,500,000 asked for Divine Guidance.[1] The Council likewise issued two calls for the churches to support the World Court, and one call to support the movement to outlaw war. The active interest of such bodies in international policy shows, whatever else one may say for it, that the churches will not serve as the unthinking instruments of political jingoes in the future. On the contrary, the church organizations in the United States are taking the lead in the movement for a liberal internationalism.

The Vatican.—While the force of nationality has made inroads upon the Roman Catholic church, that organization still maintains an international organization and influence of great importance. Before 1870, the Pope, as ruler over certain Roman states, was treated as a temporal sovereign by all Catholic powers. But in that year the newly formed state of Italy took over Rome for its capital, despite the protests of the Vatican. In 1871 the government exacted the Law of Guarantees safeguarding the independent position of the Pope. The Vatican, however, did not recognize this law, apparently insisting that its position in Rome be placed under treaty guarantee.[2] On February 11, 1929, the Vatican and the Italian government signed a treaty of conciliation, a concordat and a financial convention—thus settling their differences. The treaty recognizes the exclusive jurisdiction of the Pope over the "City of the Vatican." Italy will be represented at the Vatican by an Ambassador. Catholicism is declared the state religion, and marriage is regarded as a sacrament regulated by canon as well as civil law. Italy pays 1,750,000,000 lire as a final settlement of the 1871 difficulties. The Vatican recognizes the existence of the Italian government; and declares that the Roman question is definitely settled.

Despite its change in status, the Vatican has maintained an interest in national and international politics. In a famous encyclical, Leo XIII urged French Catholics to rally to the

[1] Cf. the pamphlets, "The Churches of America Mobilizing for World Justice and World Peace," and "The Churches of America and the World Court of Justice," issued by the Commission on International Justice and Goodwill, of the Federal Council of the Churches of Christ in America. Cf. Gulick and MacFarland, *The Church and International Relations*, 3 vols.; R. J. Cooke, *The Church and World Peace* (1920), Ch. IX.

[2] For different proposals, cf. P. Fauchille, *Traité de droit international* (8th ed., 1922), p. 740; cf. Livre II.

republic. Upon a number of occasions the Vatican has arbitrated disputes, such as the boundary dispute between Haiti and Santo Domingo in 1895. In the year following the Pope asked the King of Abyssinia to release the Italian prisoners of war. About the same time Pope Leo XIII prevented the King of Portugal from visiting the King of Italy whom the Pope refused to recognize—which led to a diplomatic rupture between the two countries. In 1904 the President of France refused to obey a similar injunction, following which relations between the Vatican and France were broken off until 1920, and the position of Catholicism as a state religion in France brought to an end by the Separation Laws of 1905 and 1907.[1] During the World War, particularly in 1917, the Vatican attempted to bring about peace. In 1919 it recognized the independence of the Ukraine—before the latter had been recognized by the European powers. At the Genoa Conference of 1922 Pius XI exercised his influence in an unsuccessful attempt to consummate a settlement of the Russian question.

Because of the great influence which the Pope exercises on world politics, many nations, whether Catholic or non-Catholic, maintain diplomatic representatives at the Vatican. In 1922, twenty-seven governments were thus represented. At present sixteen have made concordats regulating the position of the Catholic church in their respective countries. The only important countries which do not recognize the Vatican in this manner are Russia, Sweden, Norway, Japan and the United States. The participation of the Vatican in international diplomatic conferences has been proposed. Although Russia communicated to the Vatican its proposals for the first Hague Conference, the Pope was excluded from the conference, at the insistence of Italy. In the secret treaty of London of 1915, the powers promised Italy that the Vatican would not be admitted to the Paris Peace Conference. However, in the German plan for a League of Nations, provision was made for Vatican membership.

While those who rigorously believe in the separation of church

[1] In May, 1920, Pope Benedict XV issued an encyclical, *Pacem dei munus pulcherrimum*, abrogating the rule that prevented Catholic sovereigns from visiting the King of Italy. G. Goyau, "Sur l'Horizon du Vatican," *Revue des Deux Mondes*, February 15, March 1, 1922. Perhaps the best book on this general subject is M. Pernot, *Le Saint-Siège, l'Église Catholique et la Politique Mondiale* (1924). Cf. "The Lateran Accord." *I. S.* Vol. V, No. 7.

and state look askance upon the diplomatic activities of the Roman Catholic church, most of the efforts of the Vatican to influence opinion have been similar to those of the Protestant bodies. Both organizations have been animated by a sincere desire to see peace established throughout the world.

5. HISTORY

Moreover, history has had a tremendous influence in molding peoples into national groups. The mighty deeds of kings in unifying disjointed peoples so as to enlarge their empires, unconsciously laid the groundwork of a nation. Such was the work of William the Conqueror in England and the Capets in France. The common efforts—the common successes or the common sufferings—of such a group bind together its members in a spiritual tie, much closer than mere physical or linguistic similarity can forge. The historic record does not have to be one of success. In awakening the members of a nation to their mutual dependence, defeat may be more powerful than victory in stimulating national self-consciousness. The feeling of nationality, in common with many other psychological traits, is strongest when attacked. The aggressions of Napoleon Bonaparte created tremendous national movements in Germany and Spain, as did the aggressions of Japan —a century later—in China. The attempted intervention of the outside world in Soviet Russia, in 1918–19, served to rally a people to the support of a communist régime, when otherwise they might have early driven it from power. In the United States, the national spirit became strongest following our entrance into the World War. Some sacrifice was demanded of every citizen, whether or not under arms. He was required to submit himself to the wishes of the nation. The exploits of our military forces upon the battlefields of Europe still further fostered the national spirit. On the other hand, the contact with foreign customs and foreign peoples—which frequently was unpleasant—often increased the American soldier's boastful pride in his own country.

Almost as important as the events of history are its memories. In his famous definition, Ernest Renan declared, "A nation is a soul, a spiritual principle. Two things which are really only one, constitute this soul, this spiritual principle. One is the past; the other is the present. One is the common possession of a rich legacy of memories; the other is the actual consent and desire to live together, and the will to continue to take advantage of the undivided heritage which has been received." [1]

This knowledge of a common national past is perpetuated and quickened by literature, historic and poetic, and by the schools. Bismarck is reported to have said that next to the Prussian army, the German history professors did most to create the new Germany. Here national sentiment was stimulated by Dahlmann, Droysen, Sybel and Treitschke. In France, it was vivified by Henri Martin's *Histoire de France* and by the works of Thierry and Michelet. In Italy, national unification was preceded by such works as Botta's *Storia dell' Italia*. The state of Czechoslovakia probably owes its creation to Franz Palacky's *History of Bohemia*, which recalled the glorious days of Huss and Ziska; while Alexander Xempol's *History of Roumania* was a tremendous force in stimulating the Roumanians to create a nation-state.[2] When historians recalled to the Poles the great days of the Jagellon dynasty, or to the Serbs the times of Stephen Dushan, or to the Filipinos the fragmentary glories of the Mallalos republic, or to the Indians the oriental splendors of the Mogul Empire, they instinctively—through weaving this bond of common memories—summoned them to renewed national effort.

Imaginative literature is also of great importance in molding national character. German patriotism was quickened by the study of the Niebelungenlied; the French are still stirred by the Chanson de Roland; Finnish nationalism has been stimulated by the Kalevala. "Great literature is an emanation, a projection of the social soul, revealing its profundities to itself. And it is by literature rather than by any other means that the men of one generation stamp the impress of their personalities on the generation that succeeds them." Chaucer expresses that jovial good humor, that delight and satisfaction in high spirits, which reappears again and again throughout the centuries in Shakespeare, Dickens, and Mr. Gilbert Chesterton. Langland, the author of *Piers Plowman*, shows that quality of moral earnestness, of hunger and thirst

---

[1] Ernest Renan, "Qu'est-ce Qu'une Nation?" *Discours et Conférences* (1887), p. 276.
[2] H. M. Stephens, "Nationality and History," 21 *American Historical Review* (1916), 225.

after social righteousness, which has since marked the best litera‚ ture of the English people.[1] Just as in modern times the poets inspired the imperial spirit, so in former times did such poets as Shakespeare stimulate the national idea. What Englishman could not but feel himself more an Englishman after reading that passage from Richard II:

> This royal throne of kings, this scepter'd isle,
> This earth of majesty, this seat of Mars,
> This other Eden, demi-paradise,
> This fortress built by Nature for herself
> Against infection and the hand of war;
> This happy breed of men, this little world;
> This precious stone set in the silver sea,
> Which serves it in the office of a wall,
> Or as a moat defensive to a house,
> Against the envy of less happy lands;
> This blessed plot, this earth, this realm, this England. . . .

6. EDUCATION

It is in the schools that most people learn their history and that patriotism is first taught. In their zeal to promote what they consider to be the interests of the fatherland, teachers sometimes exalt the past glories and virtues of a nation, or of a particular group within a nation, without paying strict attention to the truth. Under Napoleon III, the French schools extolled the monarchy, while under the Third Republic, they preached democracy and *revanche*. In Germany teachers exalted the German Kaiser and the German race. In Japan schools have taught Emperor Worship. In the United States they have taught "Americanization" and the almost divine perfection of a government founded on "The Constitution."

Ordinarily, patriotic teaching has taken an anti-foreign bent. Before the World War, the school children of France were taught that "if there were no army, France would be conquered, and become German or Russian." They were taught to believe that the Rhine was the natural boundary of France. One writer of a school textbook said, "My son, be the soldier of the humiliated Fatherland

---

[1] S. Herbert, *Nationality and Its Problems* (1919), p. 47. Cf. John Drinkwater, *Patriotism and Literature* (1924).

which must be avenged—of France which must be regenerated." Other text-books advocated a "patient hatred of the invader."

In Germany the educational system was used to develop national egotism and to deprecate foreign achievements. One school history stated that the Germans had never been defeated except when fighting Germans; a school geography said that "The Germans are *the* civilized people of Europe, and all real civilization elsewhere . . . is due to German blood." German children were taught that the Fatherland was never wrong, that its wars were always for defense, that "France is the hereditary foe." [1]

In the United States school histories have emphasized Stephen Decatur's remark, "My country, right or wrong," and for many years they not only ignored the British side of the American Revolution, but they perpetuated ill-feeling against the British on account of it. A prominent historian said in 1916, "Americans are taught from childhood to hate Britishers by the study of American history, and not only the descendants of the men who made the Revolution, but every newly arrived immigrant child imbibes the hatred of the Great Britain of to-day from the patriotic ceremonies in the public schools. Germans were taught to hate Frenchmen by the study of German history, and the reply made by Ranke to Thiers in 1871, when the French historian visited Berlin after the overthrow of Napoleon III, and asked why the Germans were bent upon continuing the war with France, was the simple truth that 'The Germans were fighting against Louis XIV.' Hymns of hate are the inevitable outcome of national patriotism based upon national histories. Family blood-feuds, the vendettas of the Corsicans and the Kentucky mountaineers, are considered proofs of a backward civilization, but national hatreds are encouraged as manifestations of national patriotism." [2] When school histories in the United States finally began to say that the right was not all on one side in the American Revolution and other Anglo-American controversies, politicians, many of whom were Irishmen, at once started a campaign to drive such books out of the public schools.

[1] J. F. Scott, *Patriots in the Making* (1916), pp. 46, 58, 68, 73, 74, 173, 174. Cf. A. B. Hart, "School Books and International Prejudices," *International Conciliation*, January, 1911, No. 38.
[2] H. M. Stephens, cited.

When this type of vindictive, swaggering patriotism is engendered in the elementary schools, it soon spreads throughout the nation as a whole. And when patriotism takes this form in the leading nations of the world, an atmosphere is created which makes international good-will and coöperation impossible. Even if all the great economic disputes between nations should be peacefully settled, this would not bring about world peace, as long as the sentiment of nationality garbs itself in braggadocio and conceit, thirsting for dominion, prestige and power.

In the Balkans this type of nationality has been seen at its worst. "There is no region of the earth where the national idea has wrought such havoc or rioted in such wantonness of power as in Macedonia. It poisons and secularizes religion. It sanctions murder, excuses violence, and leaves more kindliness between man and beast than between the adherents of rival races. In its name peoples have done great deeds which liberty should have inspired, and perpetrated oppressions of an iniquity so colossal that only an idea could have prompted them. The miseries of ten centuries have been its work, and the face of the Balkans to-day, furrowed with hatreds, callous from long cruelty, dull from perpetual suffering, is its image and memorial. One turns from a survey of these races and their rivalries, asking what future of peace and common work there can be while the curse of this national idea still teaches men that the vital fact in their lives is the tradition, or the memory, or the habit of speech which divides them from one another." [1]

Sickened by the vices of a perverted nationalism, many outstanding men have condemned the ideal as a whole. Tolstoy called patriotism "an immoral feeling." Tagore said that nationalism is sure to lead to "moral degeneracy and intellectual blindness." [2] Santayana has declared that nationality is "the one eloquent, public, intrepid illusion." [3] In Lord Acton's opinion, the theory of nationality is a retrograde step in history.[4] Bertrand Russell has recently said, "A man who murders one man with his own hand is executed by the law, but a man who, by preaching patriotism,

[1] H. N. Brailsford, *Macedonia* (1906), p. 107.
[2] *Creative Unity* (1922), p. 148. Cf. his *Nationalism* (1917), Ch. I.
[3] *Winds of Doctrine* (1913), p. 6.
[4] *History of Freedom and Other Essays*, p. 298.

causes millions to kill millions, is universally respected and has statues put up to him when he dies. Those of us who do not wish to see our whole civilization go down in red ruin have a great and difficult duty to perform—to guard the door of our minds against patriotism." [1]

Nevertheless it would be difficult to attain a higher ideal than that preached by the greatest nationalist of the 19th century—the Italian, Mazzini. He taught that nations existed to serve mankind. "Nationality ought only to be to humanity that which the division of labor is in a workshop—the recognized symbol of association; the assertion of the individuality of a human group called by its geographical position, its traditions, and its language, to fulfil a special function in the European work of civilization." [2] While German and now American statesmen may advocate the goal of national self-interest, such a narrow ideal was repudiated by the Italian prophet. In his essay on the Duties of Man, Mazzini said, "Ask yourselves whenever you do an action in the sphere of your Country, or your family, *If what I am doing were done by all and for all, would it advantage or injure Humanity?* and if your conscience answers, *It would injure Humanity*, desist; desist, even if it seems to you that an immediate advantage for your Country and your family would ensue from your action." [3]

7. THE VALUE OF SMALL NATIONS

The disappearance of nations from the world in favor of one drab grouping of all the peoples of the globe is neither possible nor desirable. Differences between groups of people cannot be obliterated any more than between individuals. The whole progress of civilization has been away from a barren uniformity to a rich social complexity. As Mazzini taught, each nation may contribute some distinctive social good to the welfare of the world. These contributions cannot be developed unless each national group leads its own life, unobstructed by the outside. Mr. H. A. L. Fisher has pointed out that some of the most precious things in our civilization have come from small nations—the Old Testament, the Ho-

---

[1] "If We Are to Prevent the Next War," *Century*, May, 1924.
[2] Cf. his essay, "Europe: Its Condition and Prospects" (1852).
[3] *The Duties of Man and Other Essays* (Everyman), p. 49. Cf. G. F. Nicolai, *The Biology of War* (1918), Ch. X.

meric poems, the Attic and the Elizabethan drama, the art of the Italian Renaissance, the common law of England.[1] Moreover, some of the most valued social and political experiments, such as plural and compulsory voting, the initiative, referendum and proportional representation, were first developed in the small states.[2] The two best governed nations in the world, according to Lord Bryce, have been the Orange Free State before 1899 and Switzerland.[3] It was the small nations who produced such men as Demosthenes, Dante and Machiavelli. Norway and Sweden have given more writers and artists to the world than has America, while the little country of Denmark, with a population of 2,775,000 souls, has received seven of the Nobel prizes, tying with the United States with its population of 100,000,000 people. As for athletics, the tiny state of Finland ran a fighting second to America at the Paris Olympic games of 1924. It is conceivable that in the future other and smaller cultural groups will promote individual development more successfully than nationality has in the past, and will call forth greater individual sacrifice to a common good. Until that time comes, however, the nation-state is likely to remain the basis of the modern world.

As long as the nation-state remains agitated with fear, its cultural gifts will never be forthcoming. The evils of nationality in the past have been largely due to the fact that each nation believed that its existence depended on force and that its neighbors were eager to see its destruction. If a nation must depend upon force for its existence, there is no hope for the small nation. Nationality will flower at its fullest only when its existence is guaranteed by a type of internationalism which will remove war from the world. "A good international world means a world of nations living at their best." [4]

If this sort of a national world is to be achieved, the old ideas of rivalry must be displaced with new ideas of coöperation—the old hates with a new love. This can be done through two means: (1) by a changed moral and spiritual point of view, which will create a will-to-peace; (2) by removing the political, economic and

---

[1] *Essays on History and Politics*, p. 166.
[2] Baron Beyens, *L'Avenir des petits états* (1919), p. 41.
[3] *Modern Democracies* (1922), Vol. II, p. 457.
[4] A. E. Zimmern, *Nationality and Government* (1918), p. 85.

CULTURAL INTERNATIONALISM

racial causes which now provoke disputes between the nations of the world.

8. CULTURAL INTERNATIONALISM

Since this will-to-peace is primarily an intellectual and spiritual matter, it will be attained not only by changed governmental policies, but by the efforts of the schools and the churches. The virtues of national culture can never be realized until they are compared with foreign cultures. Consequently, the international intercourse of ideas is more important to the peace of the world than freedom of trade.[1] Patriotism may be taught in the schools and practiced in public places without perversion of the truth or without attacking the achievements or questioning the motives of a country's neighbors.

Some people have believed that the diversity of tongues between nations is an obstacle to international intercourse and understanding, and that if we returned to the time when the "whole earth was of one language and of one speech," international peace would be realized. With such ideals in view, they have devised a number of international languages.[2] Probably the most successful international language is Esperanto—an artificial language based on elements common to all European tongues.[3] In Europe this language is spoken by many intellectuals and by a number of labor groups. The third Assembly of the League of Nations asked the Committee on Intellectual Coöperation to study the problem of an international language. But after investigation, the Committee did not feel able to recommend the adoption of an artificial tongue of this character, believing that the League could better direct its efforts toward encouraging the study of living languages and modern literature.[4] Some linguists believe that instead of uniting the people who used it, an international language would tend to sepa-

[1] Cf. the convention of March 15, 1886, for the international exchange of official documents, scientific and literary publications, etc. *Treaties of the U. S.*, Vol. II, p. 1959.

[2] Cf. A. L. Guérard, *History of the International Language Movement* (1922), Couturat and Leau, *Histoire de la langue universelle* (1903).

[3] Cf. *Amerika Esperanto*, the organ of the Esperanto Association of North America.

[4] Supplementary Report to the Fourth Assembly of the League, A. 10 (A) August 27, 1923, p. 45.

rate them because of the difficulty of conveying thought through such an artificial means. If it were possible for such a language to be widely used, it "would be one in which no man could utter what he really meant or express to himself or to others the characteristic features of his personal experience or of the world that surrounds him." [1] More success is likely to come from the international exchange of scholars, artists, and writers. [2]

9. EDUCATIONAL CONFERENCES

Realizing the international importance of education, the Dutch government, at the suggestion of the United States, called an International Conference of Education in 1914, at which it was hoped to discuss improved methods of education and to establish an international Bureau. While seventeen powers accepted the invitation, the conference never met because of the outbreak of the World War. At the Paris Peace Conference, educational associations wished to insert in the League Covenant a provision for an international bureau of education and for the promulgation of educational ideals consistent with the principles of the League. But more pressing considerations prevented the insertion of such an amendment.[3]

In June, 1923, a world Conference on Education was held in San Francisco which was attended by more than thirty distinct racial groups and fifty nations. This conference did not "seek to destroy national identity, but rather to increase national consciousness as

[1] J. A. Smith in Marvin (ed.), *Western Races and the World* (1922), p. 36. A "linguistic" treaty has been proposed between France, Great Britain and the United States whereby English would be obligatorily taught in France, while French would be likewise taught in England and North America, not only in the universities and colleges, but in certain primary schools. P. Otlet, *Les Problèmes Internationaux et les Guerres* (1916), p. 255.

[2] In 1920 the French government officially invited Mr. James K. Hackett, the American actor, to appear in Paris, under the auspices of its Ministry of Fine Arts. At that time, the State Department sent a cablegram expressing the hope that this might be the forerunner of many such interchanges. In the spring of 1924 a world's Authors' League met in New York, while in August, 1924, an International Mathematical Congress was held at Toronto, attended by representatives of three bureaux of the Department of Commerce of the American government. A large number of scientific unofficial international conferences have also been held.

[3] *Eleven Year Survey of the Activities of the American School Peace League* (1919), pp. 7–10; 28–31.

to responsibility in the progress of all. We should not erase national or racial lines, but conserve the variety of taste and talent necessary to the world's advancement. In other words, we would increase the respect of each nation for its flag as well as for the flag of other nations and make the national flag a real symbol of national worth . . . to bring about a world-wide tolerance of the rights of all nations, regardless of race or creed. . . ."[1] The conference hoped to secure more accurate and satisfying information in text-books as to foreign countries, and to emphasize the essential unity of mankind in regard to the evils of war and the necessity of universal peace. These objects should be attained by the teaching of international civics, universal education, and the exchange of teachers. Another such conference met in Geneva in 1929.

Likewise, the League of Nations realizes that its future "depends upon the formation of a universal conscience," and that this conscience can only be created by the propagation of ideas and mutual understanding by scholars and writers in every country, through mutual contact with each other. To accomplish this end, the League set up a Committee of Intellectual Coöperation in August, 1922, composed of scholars from eleven countries, including the United States. This Committee inquired into the conditions of intellectual life in Europe, rendered particularly difficult during the reconstruction period; it organized assistance for those countries where intellectual life was especially endangered; while it encouraged the formation of national committees on intellectual coöperation. Intellectual coöperation has two aspects. The first and more limited one is to promote the joint study and practical achievement of means of coördinating and promoting intellectual life, as illustrated by the establishment of an International Museums Office, the coördination of libraries and agreements reached in regard to scientific property. The wider purpose is to inspire writers, artists and scientists with the conviction that their interests and duties are everywhere identical, and to inspire them with a spiritual and intellectual harmony, reaching over all boundary lines.[2] In 1924 the French government offered to subsidize an International Institute of Intellectual Coöperation at Paris. After

---

[1] *Addresses and Proceedings*, National Education Association, San Francisco, 1923, pp. 402 ff.
[2] Report of the Committee, A. 28, 1928, XII.

making sure that this Institute would be really international in character, the Council accepted the offer "in principle," while the fifth Assembly recommended that the Institute be administered by the League Committee on Intellectual Coöperation who should appoint five persons of different nationalities to act as a Committee of Directors.

In 1927 the Assembly and Council accepted the offer of the Italian government to establish and maintain at Rome, under the guidance of the Council, an International Educational Cinematographic Institute. The object of the Institute is to encourage the production and exchange between the various countries of films on education, art, industry, health and other matters.

The importance of education was recognized by the League Assembly at its 1923 meeting when it passed a resolution urging members of the League to "arrange that the children and youth in their respective countries where such teaching is not given, be made aware of the existence and aims of the League of Nations and the terms of the Covenant."[1] The fifth Assembly resolved that further steps should be taken to promote these objects. These proposals were carried out by a large number of countries. At the suggestion of the Groupement Universitaire for the League of Nations, the French Ministry of Education instructed school teachers to set aside one hour on Armistice Day to explain the work of the only international organization now actively working for the peace of the world.[2]

In August, 1927, an international conference of Press Experts was held at Geneva, delegates being present from thirty-eight states. It adopted a number of resolutions, one of which recommended

[1] *O. J.*, June, 1924, p. 886.
[2] *News Bulletin*, Foreign Policy Association, May 30, 1924. The winner of the Filene French Peace Award proposed that a European League of Nations establish a Bureau of Truth having in each nation representatives to report all false information in regard to foreign countries, disseminated with a view to creating false opinions, etc. "The most powerful wireless station in the world" should be placed at the disposition of this Bureau. *N. Y. Times*, Sept. 1, 1924. Likewise, the Herman award for the best education plan calculated to maintain world peace, won by Dr. David Starr Jordan, called for the coöperation of school teachers throughout the world to inculcate a spirit of international amity among their pupils. The appointment of twelve committees was proposed; one of which was to investigate the teaching of patriotism and one, the present teaching of history. The establishment of a Government Peace Council was also proposed. *N. Y. Times*, Dec. 8, 1924.

equality of treatment as regards the issuing of news from official sources; another advocated the abolition of peace-time censorship; another favored the establishment in newspapers of a special section on the work of the League.

One of the most encouraging signs of the present times is the growth of the "will-to-peace" idea throughout the nations. Nevertheless, many unsettled political and economic problems still confront the world. They cannot be solved by mere sentiment. Warm-heartedness alone will not save us from war. The more one reads of diplomatic history, the more he is likely to be convinced that few statesmen and still fewer private citizens have ever consciously wanted war. They have nevertheless blindly supported domestic policies and national ambitions which made war inevitable. If mankind lacks the intelligence and the imagination to handle the political aspects of the problems of the world, the "will-to-peace" will never be converted into a reality. The present chapter has discussed a few of the non-political aspects of nationality which account for differences between national groups and form potential causes for misunderstanding. The following chapters will discuss the political, racial and economic forces accompanying this sentiment of nationality which still further complicate the international relations of the world.

CHAPTER II

SELF-DETERMINATION

1. The Causes of Self-Determination.—2. Self-Determination in History and International Law.—3. Self-Determination at the Peace Conference.—4. Plebiscites—Abuses.—5. Where to Draw the Line.—6. Who Should Draw the Line?—The Aaland Islands Case.—7. The Problems of Frontiers.

The sentiment of nationality does not become a problem in international relations until it seizes upon political means to advance its cultural ends—when it becomes known as nationalism. It is possible to conceive of a nation, such as the Jews, without a political state of its own. But for the last one hundred and fifty years, every vigorous nation, including the Jews, has demanded the right to govern itself, usually within the walls of a politically independent nation-state. Many writers have assumed that each state should comprise a single nation and that each nation should form a separate state.[1] As long as a nation remains under the control of an alien power, it usually spends its energies in trying to become free. It seeks political means to safeguard a cultural existence—a search which results, in many cases, in losing sight of the cultural end.

"National independence" was the watchword of Poland, of Bohemia, and of Ireland before the War.[2] However laudable such an ideal may be, such demands to become politically free at once create grave problems in international relations. Complete independence for "subject" nations has meant the destruction of multi-national empires, who have naturally resisted such demands

---

[1] Cf. J. S. Mill, *Representative Government* (1861), Ch. XVI.

[2] Since the 17th century the word "self-determination" has been used as synonymous to the theological doctrine of "free-will." It became current in a political sense as a result of the Russian revolution of 1917. Cf. W. A. Phillips, "Self-Determination," *Encyclopedia Britannica* (new vols., 1922). For a discussion of the idea, cf. K. Renner, *Das Selbstbestimmungsrecht der Nationen in besonderer Anwendung auf Oesterreich* (1918).

THE CAUSES OF SELF-DETERMINATION

at the point of the sword. The watchword of nationalism in many cases, therefore, has been the watchword of revolution.

This doctrine not only led oppressed nations to demand their independence, but it led nation-states, already in existence, to struggle for the recovery of "unredeemed" territories, held by other powers. Denmark regarded the territory ceded to Germany still as Danish soil. France never regarded Alsace-Lorraine as permanently lost. Italian irredentism aimed to unite the Italians under Austrian rule to Italy. Roumania longed to bring within its embrace the Roumanians of Transylvania, Bukowina and Bessarabia. Bulgaria likewise wanted to extend its borders to include the Bulgarians of Macedonia and of Dobrudja. Serbia wished to rescue the Serbs and Croats and Slovenes from Hapsburg control. Greece dreamed of the days of the Byzantine Empire, with Constantinople as its capital. Altogether about 54 million people lived under alien governments in Europe in 1914. About fifteen nationalities demanded either political independence or the recovery of "unredeemed" territory.[1]

1. THE CAUSES OF SELF-DETERMINATION

There are many reasons why the sentiment of nationality should acquire a political bent. Probably the strongest cause for the demand for self-determination is the instinctive wish of each national group to govern itself, through its own representatives, without being responsible to any outside authority. But this wish has been fortified by more practical considerations. In the past nations have been led to believe, through sad experience, that the only guarantee of national existence is political independence from alien control.

When an empire or when a nation-state succeeds in establishing its authority, usually by force, over another nation, it ordinarily attempts to destroy the national characteristics of the latter by attempting to merge it with itself. Toward this end it adopts the policy of *assimilation*. This policy aims to obliterate the cultural characteristics of all minorities and to force upon them the characteristics of the dominant nation. The vast majority of states in Europe followed this policy before the World War, on the theory

[1] Cf. C. Seignobos (ed.), *Les Aspirations autonomistes en Europe* (1913), p. xiii.

that since the sentiment of nationality is cultural, it was possible to impose a new nationality upon a minority by force.

In Germany this policy was called Germanization. In German Poland and in Alsace-Lorraine, the government attempted to force the inhabitants to give up their national customs and become Germans. In Alsace-Lorraine French was banished from the elementary schools; pro-French newspapers were suppressed; French clubs were closed; French business names were changed; natives were excluded from local administrative positions; French visitors in many cases were banished from the provinces.[1] France adopted much the same policy upon the retrocession of Alsace-Lorraine after the War, especially in the suppression of German legislation and the elementary instruction in German language.[2] In May, 1928, four Alsatian autonomists were convicted at Colmar and imprisoned.

In Posen the Germans followed even more harsh tactics toward the Poles. Beginning with 1830 a policy of rigorous repression was applied. German was made the only official language and, after 1873, it was made the language of the schools. Shortly afterwards, the Germans attempted to forbid the use of Polish at public meetings. In 1886 the government resorted to a drastic land policy, which was carried still further in 1907 by a law providing for the compulsory expropriation of Polish landowners.[3]

In Hungary the policy of Magyarization was followed toward the minorities.[4] When these minorities were "redeemed" at the end of the World War, the government of Prague in retaliation pulled down the statue of the Magyan poet Petofi, while the government of Bucharest likewise overturned the statue of Kossuth and thirteen other national Hungarian heroes.[5]

When Roumania acquired part of the Dobrudja in 1913, it adopted a policy of Roumanization. Although only one-fortieth of the population was Roumanian, the Roumanian officials sup-

[1] C. Philipson, *Alsace-Lorraine* (1918), pp. 163–168.
[2] T. Corcoran, "The Language Campaign in Alsace-Lorraine," *Studies* (an Irish quarterly), June, 1924. A. Hallays, "En Alsace et Lorraine, la protestation contre les lois laiques," *Revue des Deux Mondes*, August 15, 1924.
[3] W. A. Phillips, *Poland*, Ch. XI; R. Butler, *The New Central Europe* (1919).
[4] Cf. S. Viator (R. W. Seton-Watson) *Racial Problems in Hungary* (1908), Ch. V, and N. Iorga, *Les Hongrois et la nationalité roumanie* (1909).
[5] L. Brun, *Le Problème des minorités* (1923), p. 196.

pressed the two hundred Bulgarian schools, confiscated the Bulgarian endowments, and closed all churches which refused to use the Roumanian language.[1]

Russia followed the policy of Russification by attempting to impose the Russian language on the Baltic provinces, the Poles and the Caucasus.[2] In Turkey, the policy of assimilation—called Turkification—was carried to its most brutal extreme. Minorities such as the Armenians were ruthlessly massacred, while the leaders of the Arab autonomy movement were persecuted.[3] Chile followed a policy of Chilenization toward the Peruvians living in the disputed area of Tacna-Arica, after 1883. Italy has been following a policy of Italianization in the Tyrol.[4] The Czechs have been accused of a policy of Czechization toward the nationalities in the revived nation of Bohemia. In the United States, alien minorities have been subject to a leveling process, called Americanization.[5] Confronted by the rigors of this policy of assimilation, "subject" nations have naturally demanded freedom. A fearful history has led them to believe that their only salvation lay in the establishment of, or association with, a nation-state of their own.

In the third place, simple misgovernment has fortified the demands of nations for political independence. The incredible incompetence of the Turkish administration was a powerful incentive to revolt on the part of the more civilized Christian populations in the Balkans. Usually, a dominant state, addicted to the policy of assimilation, even excluded minorities from local offices, placing them in the hands of officials from the central government and of the dominant nationality. Minorities were likewise excluded from a fair representation in legislative bodies. In other words, they did not govern themselves even in local matters and they did not participate equally in the government of the state as a whole. A revolt against such conditions was not so much a revolt in favor of nationalism as it was a revolt against autocracy.

According to one writer, the Italian Risorgimento was primarily a movement directed against "definite social and political abuses,

---

[1] G. Young, *Nationality and War in the Near East* (1916), p. 285.
[2] Butler, cited, pp. 23-29; Phillips, cited, Ch. X.
[3] Cf. p. 90.
[4] Cf. p. 181.
[5] Cf. H. Kallen, *Culture and Democracy in America* (1924).

and had as its end the creation of responsible government on liberal lines. . . . This is equally true of the Greek War of Independence, which was rather a war for the overthrow of a system of religious, social, and political oppression than for the affirmation of a nationality's right to existence."[1] If the four empires of Europe had been genuinely democratic and if they had been governed efficiently and honestly, it is doubtful whether the doctrine of self-determination would have brought about their overthrow.

2. SELF-DETERMINATION IN HISTORY AND INTERNATIONAL LAW

While nationalism did not reach its height till the 19th century, appeals to the principle of self-determination were made as early as 1526, when the separation of Burgundy from the Crown of France was opposed on the ground that "according to law, no cities or provinces can be transferred to another power against the wishes of the inhabitants or subjects, but only with their express consent."[2]

Despite this 16th-century example, the principle of self-determination did not receive its vogue until the days of the French Revolution and its Declaration of the Rights of Man.[3] So impressed with this doctrine did the Tsar Alexander become that he declared, "the sovereign, elected by God for the welfare of peoples, should not divide up populations, contrary to their wishes and their interests."[4] In 1831 Mazzini, the great Italian nationalist, founded the society of Young Italy, the members of which were willing to shed their blood in defense of the national idea. Napoleon III, Emperor of France, likewise championed the national idea in Poland, Italy and the nations of the Balkans. During the course of the 19th century nationalism or self-determination gave to Europe the two great nation-states of Germany and Italy, and the five smaller nation-states of Greece, Belgium, Serbia, Roumania and Bulgaria. With the exception of Germany, all of these nations relied upon the support of sympathetic powers to achieve their political independence.[5]

---

[1] Herbert, *Nationality and its Problems*, p. 115.
[2] H. Hauser, *Principe des Nationalités* (1916), p. 15.
[3] Cf. W. Mitscherlich, *Der Nationalismus Westeuropas* (1920), pp. 62–115.
[4] F. Duparc, *La Protection des minorités de race, de langue, et de religion* (1922), p. 114.
[5] R. Muir, *Nationalism and Internationalism* (1917), p. 87.

SELF-DETERMINATION IN HISTORY 33

Except in the Balkans and Hungary the movement for self-determination was at a standstill between 1848 and the World War. Four great empires challenged its validity and rigorously suppressed all attempts to put the principle into force. The Russian Empire embraced a number of subject nations—such as the Poles, the Lithuanians, the Finns, the Georgians and the Ukrainians, each of whom was distinct from the Russians proper. The German Empire embraced the Danes of Schleswig, annexed in 1866, the French of Alsace-Lorraine, taken in 1871, and the Poles of Posen. The majority of the population of the Austro-Hungarian Empire was composed of subject nationalities—the Czechs, the Slovaks, the Poles, the Ruthenians and the Southern Slavs. The Turkish Empire, containing only 8,000,000 Turks, ruled 13,000,000 alien peoples—Arabs, Armenians, Greeks and Kurds. For at least three of these empires, self-determination meant suicide. Consequently they smothered the mutterings of subject peoples. The movement for self-determination had apparently reached an impasse, especially since the modern instruments of warfare and great standing armies made impossible isolated revolts.

These nations could receive no help from the principles of international law, to which the principle of self-determination was unknown.[1] Cessions of territory were made during the 19th and 20th centuries by practically all the great European powers without consulting the wishes of the peoples concerned. In 1897 the United States declined the suggestion of the Japanese minister that a plebiscite should be held in Hawaii to determine the wishes of the people in regard to annexation of the territory by the United States.[2] In the following year, the American commissioners, negotiating a peace treaty with Spain, declared that a state could relinquish its sovereignty over part of its territory without the consent of the local inhabitants.[3] In 1861 the United States opposed with all its force the efforts of the South to secede from the Union. European powers, the United States and Japan rigorously attempted to suppress revolts, whether in Poland, Hungary, Ireland, Canada, Korea, Egypt or the Philippines. When a nation did

---

[1] Cf. The Report of the Jurists, and also of the Rapporteurs, Aaland Island question, p. 47.
[2] J. B. Moore, *Digest of International Law* (1906), Vol. I, p. 274.
[3] *Ibid.*, p. 368.

achieve its political independence, it was not by virtue of law but of force.

Upon the outbreak of the World War, the fifteen odd subject nationalities of Europe had an opportunity to redress the wrongs of centuries. Because of military necessity as well as of sympathy, the Allies brought their combined military support to the cause of many nationalities which, single-handed, could never have achieved their aims. In June, 1915, an International Conference of Nationalities was held in Paris, under French auspices, where a permanent commission of delegates, representing every nationality, was established. Later conferences were held at Paris and Lausanne. The Declaration of the Rights of Nationalities, approved by this organization, stated in its preamble that "the diversity of nationalities is a precious factor in progress." It went on to declare that "Nationalities, whether they are founded on a community of origin, language, or tradition, or whether they result from an association freely entered into by different ethnic groups, have the right freely to dispose of themselves. There should be no annexation or transfer of territory contrary to the interests and wishes of the population." The political status of subject nationalities should, in the opinion of this organization, be determined by such a body as the arbitration court at The Hague.[1]

Allied statesmen were quick to pick up the appeal. In a speech in December, 1914, Mr. Asquith, the British prime minister, said that England would not sheath its sword until the rights of the small nationalities of Europe, particularly Belgium and Serbia, had been placed on an impregnable foundation. In their reply of January 12, 1917, to the request of President Wilson that they state their war aims, the Allies declared they were fighting for the "independence of peoples," for the restoration of Belgium, Serbia, and Montenegro, and for the liberation of the Italians, Slavs, Roumanians, Poles and the Czechoslovaks from foreign domination.[2] In a number of fervent speeches, President Wilson proclaimed the right of self-determination. In February, 1918, he

[1] Documents préliminaires, *IIIme Conférence des Nationalités*, June 27, 1916, p. 8.
[2] For a review of these war aims, cf. V. Blagoyévitch, *Le Principe des nationalités et son application dans les traités de paix de Versailles et Saint-Germain*, Part II. According to this writer (p. 155), this was the first war where governments had officially stated their war aims.

declared to Congress, "Peoples and provinces are not to be bartered about from sovereignty to sovereignty as if they were mere chattels and pawns in the game. . . . Peoples may now be dominated and governed only by their own consent. Self-determination is not a mere phrase. It is an imperative principle of action, which statesmen will henceforth ignore at their peril." Commenting on the Treaty of Versailles, the German government declared that no territory should be detached from Germany which formed incontestably an integral part of the German state, or whose population had not requested or consented to be separated.[1] A majority of the Senate of the United States voted in favor of a reservation to the effect that "in consenting to the ratification of the treaty with Germany the United States adheres to the principle of self-determination," particularly in regard to the Irish! However, the Soviet government of Russia probably went further than the other powers in recognizing the principle of self-determination. It recognized it not only in the nationality decree of November, 1917,[2] but in a number of treaties with the new states which had formerly been part of Russia's territory. The treaty between Russia and Esthonia of February 2, 1920, was made "on the basis of the right of all peoples freely to decide their own destinies, and even to separate themselves completely from the state of which they form part, a right proclaimed by the Federal Socialist Republic of Soviet Russia."[3] Likewise in the treaty between Poland, Russia and the Ukraine of March 18, 1921, the contracting parties, "in accordance with the principle of national self-determination, recognize the independence of the Ukraine."[4]

3. SELF-DETERMINATION AT THE PEACE CONFERENCE

During the World War, the principle of self-determination was invoked to bring about the demolition of the Austro-Hungarian Empire and the amputation of parts of Russia and Turkey. In the treaties of peace, the independence of the new nation-states of Poland, Czechoslovakia, Austria and Hungary was recognized.

[1] *Les Contrepropositions de l'Allemagne au projet du traité de paix de Versailles* (1919), p. 31.
[2] Cf. p. 220.
[3] T. S. 289.
[4] T. S. 149.

36 SELF-DETERMINATION

Following the Peace Conference, Europe recognized the existence of the new nation-states of the Baltic, the Ukraine, Egypt and Albania. Likewise, they recognized, as semi-independent, Syria, Mesopotamia and Palestine. The King of the Hejaz, formerly a vassal of Turkey, was also recognized as sovereign over Islam's Holy Land.

By virtue of this principle, France also recovered Alsace-Lorraine; Denmark, Schleswig; Roumania, Transylvania and Bukowina; while Serbia merged its identity with 5,000,000 Slavs formerly living in Austria and Hungary, and with the little kingdom of Montenegro.[1]

While the principle of self-determination was thus recognized to a greater extent than ever before, it was violated in a number of cases where the interests of the Allies would be served, or where other considerations required a different solution. The most striking violation was in forbidding Austria to join Germany.[2] It was also violated in the case of Memel and Danzig, cities with German majorities, as well as in Moresnet, Leobshitz, the German Tyrol and the German colonies. The Conference declined to hear the claims of the Koreans, Filipinos, Egyptians and Irish for independence, and it declined to pass favorably on the demands of such tiny peoples as the Lems, the Neo-Chaldeans, the Armenians, the Aalanders, the Dodecanesians and the Ukrainians.

It was not pure hypocrisy which led the Allied statesmen to reject the principle of self-determination in these instances. When confronted with such cases, they met with difficulties of an economic, political, strategic and racial nature which often made the application of this principle impossible. They were obliged to determine whether every unit of people, no matter how small, was entitled to independence merely for the asking. They were also confronted with the problem of determining just what the wishes of the people concerned were.

4. PLEBISCITES

At recent peace conferences, the nationality of the peoples in dispute has been usually determined by consulting statistics. That is, if the statistics showed that 60% of the people of Posen were

[1] Cf. p. 222. For the case of Bessarabia cf. p. 238.
[2] Cf. M. H. Boehm, *Europa Irredenta* (1923), pp. 247 ff.

Polish, the territory would be given to Poland. But ordinarily, statistics merely tabulate the language spoken by the inhabitants, and as we have seen, language may not be an exact criterion of nationality. Moreover, nationality statistics are often misleading or openly dishonest. They are usually collected by governments antagonistic to the nationality concerned.[1] In some countries no statistics, according to nationality, have been collected. In contested regions, therefore, it is usually impossible to determine the wishes of the peoples concerned by this means.

Inasmuch as self-determination is supposed to mean the consent of the governed, peace conferences have often believed that the best means of ascertaining the wishes of the inhabitants in dispute is by direct consultation—the plebiscite. Since the French Revolution, the plebiscite has been frequently employed, particularly in the latter part of the 19th century. It was employed in the Italian revolution of 1848 to determine the wishes of the Italian duchies as to union. Napoleon III utilized it in bringing about the annexation of Savoy and Nice to France. Following the Crimean War, it was utilized in the union of Moldavia and Wallachia. In 1866 Prussia promised that a plebiscite should be held in Northern Schleswig, a promise which, however, was not carried out until after the World War—and then by the Allies.[2] In 1905 a plebiscite determined whether or not the kingdom of Norway and Sweden should be separated. Plebiscites have also been held to determine the wishes of insular peoples, as in the Ionian Islands, St. Bartholomew, and the Danish West Indies. In the New World the most important provision for a plebiscite was contained in the Treaty of Ancon of 1883, between Chile and Peru. This treaty authorized Chile to hold the district of Tacna-Arica for ten years, after which a vote should determine its future status. But this plebiscite was not carried out, nominally because of a difference of interpretation as to who should vote. The issue caused a bitter dispute which

---

[1] Cf. van Gennep, *Traité comparatif des nationalités*, Vol. I, Ch. V.
[2] Prussia made this promise in the Treaty of Prague, of August 23, 1866 (Art. 3), with Austria. Bismarck later contended that Prussia's obligation was one toward Austria and that no government except Austria could demand the fulfillment of the obligation. In the Treaty of Oct. 11, 1878, between Austria and Prussia, the parties abrogated the provision of the Treaty of Prague in regard to the plebiscite. For the texts of these two treaties, cf. 18 Martens (1st series), 345; 3 Martens (2d series), 531.

was finally referred to the arbitration of the President of the United States in November, 1923, who decided that the plebiscite should be held.[1] In the treaties following the World War, provision was made for nine plebiscites—in Schleswig—territory disputed between Denmark and Germany; in Allenstein, Marienwerder, and Upper Silesia—territory disputed between Poland and Germany; in Eupen and Malmedy—territory disputed between Belgium and Germany;[2] in Klagenfurt—territory disputed between Austria and Jugoslavia; in Burgenland—territory disputed between Austria and Hungary; and in the Saar—territory disputed between Germany and France, where a plebiscite will be held after 15 years.

Abuses.—While in theory the plebiscite should be an accurate means of determining the wishes of the inhabitants, it is subject to many abuses in practice. It appears that many plebiscites have been farcical so far as determining the real wishes of the people is concerned. The plebiscites of the French Revolution were looked upon merely as disguised annexations. Corruption and fraud were likewise charged in the Italian plebiscites of 1848 and of Nice and Savoy; while in the plebiscite at Rome in 1870 some voters cast as many as thirty ballots apiece.[3]

Unless carefully restricted by treaty, voters may be dumped into the district in dispute to cast their ballots for an interested government and then straightway leave the country. Troops and officials of an occupying power may also intimidate the inhabitants. From this standpoint, the plebiscite provided for in Eupen and Malmedy by the Treaty of Versailles was extremely defective. Although Germany renounced all her rights in this territory to Belgium, the inhabitants were allowed to record their desire to have the territory remain under German sovereignty,[4] the results of which the

---

[1] Cf. *Arbitration between Peru and Chile*, on "The Question of the Pacific," Washington, 1923. But the plebiscite was not held. Cf. p. 39. For a history of plebiscites, cf. S. Wambaugh, *A Monograph on Plebiscites with a Collection of Official Documents* (1920), pp. 33–172; J. Mattern, *The Employment of the Plebiscite in the Determination of Sovereignty* (1920), Ch. II; cf. also "Plebiscites," *Peace Handbooks*, British Foreign Office, 1920, No. 25; hereafter cited *Peace Handbooks*.

[2] Cf. Arts. 109, 94, 96, 88, 34, 50 (sec. 34 of annex), Treaty of Versailles; Art. 49, Treaty of St. Germain; Burgenland, Protocol of Venice, Oct. 3, 1921, between Austria and Hungary, *T. S.* 254.

[3] Wambaugh, pp. 83 ff.; Mattern, pp. 85 ff.

[4] Art. 34, Treaty of Versailles.

PLEBISCITES

Belgian government was obliged to communicate to the League of Nations and accept its decision. Since those who wished to protest against Belgian sovereignty were merely allowed to sign an open register, it is not surprising that only 271 out of a population of 63,000 were, under these circumstances, bold enough to vote. A large number of charges by Germany were made as to the conduct of Belgian authorities, which, however, the Council, set aside on the ground of lack of evidence; and in September, 1920, confirmed Belgium's title to the territory.[1] Perhaps this action was justified. But since no provision had been made for secret ballots or for neutral supervision of the polls, this type of plebiscite was of little value in registering the real wishes of the people.[2] A vivid illustration of the difficulties involved in holding a plebiscite is found in the attempted plebiscite in Tacna-Arica. In the 1923 arbitration President Coolidge ruled that a plebiscite should be held but failed to provide for any system of neutral police. A Plebiscitary Commission, composed of American, Chilean and Peruvian members, worked for ten months to hold the plebiscite, but finally voted in June, 1926, to abandon the attempt, amidst tense feelings in Chile and Peru, and throughout South America. In his report, General Lassiter, the American member of the commission, stated that a fair plebiscite could not be held because Chile occupied the territory and had followed obstructionist and terrorist policies toward the Peruvian electorate.[3] The dispute remained unsettled. But in May, 1929, a settlement by negotiation was made in which the province was divided in two, Tacna going to Peru, Arica remaining with Chile. Peru was given certain rights in the port of Arica and a payment of $6,000,000 from Chile. Thus the attempt to hold a plebiscite was abandoned.

More care was taken to secure a fair vote in other plebiscites, such as those authorized in the Treaty of Versailles. As a rule it was provided that troops of the interested parties should evacuate the disputed territory and that the plebiscite area should be placed under the control of an international commission, usually of five

---

[1] *O. J.*, June, 1920, pp. 119, 157; Oct., 1920, p. 404.
[2] Cf. Dugdale, "Eupen and Malmedy: The League's Responsibility," 16 *New Europe* (1920), 201; "Eupen and Malmedy: a Belgian Rejoinder," Cammaerts, *ibid.*, 235.
[3] "American Mediation in the Tacna-Arica Dispute," *I. S.*, Vol. II, No. 11.

members.¹ This commission "shall take all steps which it thinks proper to ensure the freedom, fairness and secrecy of the vote."² In some cases, this commission was supported by neutral troops. Some such provision for neutral supervision appears necessary if a plebiscite is to be fairly conducted.³

Likewise, voting qualifications should be carefully defined. As a rule the right to vote in the plebiscites of the Paris Conference was limited to persons over twenty, born in the territory or who had been domiciled there before a certain date—1900 in the case of Schleswig, and 1919 in the case of Upper Silesia. Under such a provision, Poles or Germans born in Upper Silesia, but living in America, could return and vote. It was charged that 190,000 Germans returned to Upper Silesia and 8,000 to Schleswig, for this purpose.⁴ In the case of the Saar where the plebiscite will not be held for fifteen years, only those domiciled there at the beginning of the period may vote. In order to ascertain who these people are, the Saar commission in 1923 compiled voting registers.⁵ To determine the real wishes of a district, it would appear that bona fide domicile rather than birth should be a voting requirement.

But even if the most intricate machinery is devised for limiting the number of voters and of policing the polls, the plebiscite will still be open to a great number of disadvantages. Such elections will always be accompanied by propaganda and by forms of pressure which it will be difficult for any neutral umpires to control. In the Schleswig plebiscite the Danes sent in loads of butter, pork, tea and coffee, to be distributed to the people free; while sick German children were invited to Denmark for a week's outing. After the election, this "charity" suddenly came to an end! In the Klagenfurt plebiscite, the Slavs took advantage of a famine in Austria to distribute milk and eggs among the Austrians in the district.⁶ Moreover, neutral troops themselves may take sides;

[1] These commissions were usually composed of representatives of Allied governments, but in Schleswig, representatives of Norway and Sweden, with three Allied representatives, constituted the Commission. Art. 109, Treaty of Versailles.
[2] Cf. for Upper Silesia, Art. 88 (sec. 3 of annex), *ibid.*
[3] Cf. "Nécessité du contrôle international," J. Giroud, *Le Plébiscite international* (1920), pp. 164 ff.
[4] S. Wambaugh, "Frontiers by Plebiscite," 107 *Century* (1923), 69.
[5] Cf. Report of Provisional Records Commissioner, *O. J.*, Jan., 1924, p. 109.
[6] Wambaugh, cited.

thus in Upper Silesia, French troops were accused of supporting the Poles, while British troops were accused of supporting the Germans.

Regardless of the outcome, a plebiscite in a district under dispute will inevitably embitter the feelings of one nationality toward the other. A plebiscite campaign inevitably accentuates differences which previously may have slumbered; and whatever disposition may be made of the territory, the fate of minorities is likely to be worse than before. Decision is usually made by a bare majority of the voters, at a time of feverish discussion and propaganda, but binding the future of the area indefinitely.[1] Moreover, people may cast their votes because of temporary economic considerations, such as an inflated currency in one country, which later may lead to regret. In a plebiscite the choice before a voter is many times too limited. Instead of wishing to join either of two states, the inhabitants of an area may simply wish autonomy. Such appears to have been the case of many inhabitants of Upper Silesia.[2]

Before the World War, the plebiscite was largely limited to corporate units of government, such as Nice, Savoy and Parma, which voted, not upon the division of the unit, but upon its relation *as a whole* to another government which it was thought desirable to join.[3] But following the war, the plebiscite was used to divide local units, which at once created a large number of geographic and economic difficulties.

The Paris peace treaties attempted to modify the rigidity of the plebiscite by providing that the votes should be counted by communes rather than by the district as a whole. The boundary commission could, it was hoped, draw a line according to communes which would not upset economic ties so much and which would not leave behind so many minorities as if the whole district had been involved. In Upper Silesia the district as a whole cast 707,000 votes for Germany and 479,000 votes for Poland. But in

[1] Cf. F. Lieber, "De la valeur des plébiscites dans le droit international," 3 *R. D. I. L. C.* (1871), 139.

[2] Certain inhabitants in the second plebiscite zone in Denmark petitioned the Council of Ambassadors for internationalization under the League of Nations. T. Galitza, *Du Droit de voter dans les plébiscites contemporains* (1921), p. 24n.

[3] Cf. Headlam-Morley, "Plebiscites," 236 *Quarterly Review* (1921), 213.

the southern and central districts the Poles had a majority; in the north and west districts the Germans had a majority, the vote being 341,000 to 90,000. In the industrial basin the Germans received 258,000 and the Poles 205,000.[1] The Council of the League, to which the question of drawing the boundary was finally referred, came to the conclusion that the industrial region should be divided. "It endeavored to find a system which, when applied, would assign to each State a number of electors not differing appreciably from the total number of votes given to its favor, and which would, at the same time, as far as possible equalize and reduce the minorities."[2] While the Silesian award was bitterly criticised by both sides, Poles and Germans at first coöperated in the development of the region as they did before the war. But in 1927–1928 the situation over minorities became tense.[3]

Although the plebiscite possesses a great many disadvantages, it does offer one practical means of giving effect to the principle of self-determination. It acts as a check on statistics which in most controversial cases are "doctored," and which may judge nationality upon a linguistic basis, but not determine the actual wishes of the people. According to the statistics, about 88% of the population of Klagenfurt—a district in dispute between Austria and Jugoslavia—was Slovene and therefore supposedly pro-Serb. But in the plebiscite, 60% of the electorate voted to remain with Austria, probably because of economic considerations.[4]

Likewise the plebiscite may serve as a check to the victor or to the exorbitant demands of any particular ally. In five of the plebiscites of the Peace Treaties—in Allenstein, Marienwerder, Klagenfurt, Upper Silesia and one of the two zones of Schleswig-Holstein,—the vote went in favor of the defeated power. If it had not been for the plebiscite, the whole of Upper Silesia would have been Polish to-day. In fact, such was the provision in the original treaty, a plebiscite being authorized only after Germany's protest.

---

[1] For the official figures, cf. H. W. V. Temperley (ed.), *History of the Peace Conference at Paris* (1924), Vol. VI, p. 619.

[2] Cf. *O. J.*, Dec., 1921, p. 1224. In drawing the boundary line, the Allies should have regard "for the wishes of the inhabitants as shown by the vote and to the geographical and economic conditions of the locality" (Art. 97), a provision again making for flexibility.

[3] Cf. p. 199.

[4] Temperley, cited, Vol. IV, p. 379.

Thus a plebiscite is one means of making a victor pay more than lip service to the principle of nationality.

When a plebiscite is not to be held for a term of years after the occupation of territory by a foreign power, many abuses may arise. During this period the foreign government may move in thousands of its subjects, thus transforming a minority into a majority by the time the vote is to be cast. This is apparently what happened in the district of Tacna-Arica, occupied by Chile in 1883. Eighty per cent of the population of this district in 1894 was Peruvian, when the plebiscite should have been taken according to the Treaty of Ancon; but Chile, Peru charges, wilfully prevented the plebiscite until she could bring in enough Chileans to constitute a majority.[1]

Following the World War, Germany demanded that a plebiscite be held to determine whether Alsace-Lorraine should be ceded to France. But this demand was resented by France because Alsace-Lorraine had been annexed by Germany in 1871, without a plebiscite, which the fifteen Alsatian deputies in the Reichstag demanded in 1874. To hold a plebiscite now would, in the opinion of France, recognize the annexation of 1871 as legitimate.[2] In this, as in the above cases, it would have been possible for Germany to settle the territory with her own subjects so that if a vote should be taken later the wishes of the original inhabitants would have been set aside by interlopers. Treaties, as in the case of the Saar, usually provide that only those living in the territory at the time it was originally transferred should be allowed to vote.[3]

Although the Paris Peace Conference recognized the plebiscite to a greater extent than any previous conference, the more important territorial changes, such as the territorial reorganization of Central Europe, Alsace-Lorraine, Danzig, and so forth, were not settled by plebiscite but by diplomatic means. In some of these cases, there was no need of a plebiscite. In others a plebiscite was first attempted and then discarded because of the difficulties in-

---

[1] "The Case of Peru," *Arbitration between Peru and Chile*, cited, pp. 206–251.

[2] Cf. E. Gonssollin, *Le Plébiscite dans le droit international actuel* (1921), pp. 77 ff.

[3] But it is feared by some writers that the population will be forced to vote in favor of France because of the economic control which France will have established over the territory. S. Osborne, *The Saar Question: A Disease Spot in Europe* (1923), Chs. VI and VII.

volved. Such was the case in the district of Teschen, where in September, 1919, the Supreme Council decided to hold a plebiscite to determine whether it should go to Poland or to Czechoslovakia. But the danger of still further inflaming opinion was so great that the territory was divided up between the two countries by the Conference of Ambassadors.[1] In one amusing case, Hungary demanded a plebiscite before ceding certain territory to Austria; while Austria, unwilling to take over territory inhabited by non-Germans, made the same demand, only to have it rejected by the Allies![2] The League of Nations has also been slow to resort to the plebiscite. While it made such a provision originally in an attempt to solve the dispute between Poland and Lithuania over Vilna, it later gave it up because of the hard feeling likely to be stirred up by the procedure. In other cases, the Council of the League has settled boundary disputes by arbitration and conciliation rather than by resort to a popular vote.[3] The establishment of an impartial set of nationality statistics will make it easier in the future to determine the actual composition of a given territory, without the use of a plebiscite; and, as will be pointed out later, the protection of minorities and freedom of trade will diminish the demands for boundary readjustments. In a few great cases, it may even then be necessary to invoke the plebiscite. But it is not an instrument of political science which is likely to rouse the enthusiasm or win the confidence of either peoples or experts.

5. WHERE TO DRAW THE LINE

Literally interpreted, the doctrine of self-determination would sanction the resistance of any minority to the will of a majority.

[1] Cf. Decree of Conference of Ambassadors with regard to Teschen, Spisz and Orava, Aug. 5, 1920, *T. S.* 46.
[2] Temperley, cited, Vol. IV, p. 387.
[3] Cf. the boundary disputes between Hungary and Czechoslovakia, and Hungary and Jugoslavia, *Report to the Fourth Assembly of the League on the Work of the Council*, June 28, 1923, A. 10, 1923, pp. 28–29. In the Mosul dispute before the Council in September, 1924, the Turkish government offered to settle the disposition of this territory by plebiscite. The British delegate, as had Lord Curzon at the Lausanne conference, said that while a plebiscite might choose a ruler, it could not determine a frontier; a neutral army would be required to keep order; since a large part of the population was nomadic, it would be difficult to decide who should vote; a majority of the Kurds were illiterate and did not know how to vote. For the arguments cf. *O. J.*, Oct., 1924, pp. 1319, 1577.

WHERE TO DRAW THE LINE

Extended still further, it would authorize any individual to resist the law. Where should the line be drawn between a real nation and mere particularism? As some doctrinaires would interpret it, the doctrine of self-determination would mean that the province of Catalonia could become independent of Spain; that Brittany and even the Ile Saint Louis could become independent of France;[1] that Scotland and Wales, not to mention Ireland, could revolt from England; that Vorarlberg could leave Austria; that Slovakia could set up a state of its own in Czechoslovakia; that Croatia could leave Jugoslavia; Yucatan—Mexico; Quebec and the Maritime Provinces—Canada;[2] and the southern states—the United States. In all of these instances the inhabitants possess certain characteristics distinguishing them from the nation of which they are a part; and in most of them there has been a demand for independence or autonomy. Nevertheless, if they could invoke the doctrine of self-determination in order to become "free," the world would become Balkanized.

From the social standpoint the creation of a large number of small nation-states may have advantages.[3] On the other hand, small nation-states create a large number of political problems. There is likely to be more bitterness and internal faction in small than in large states. Hatred between small nations is more intense and personal than between larger ones.[4] The establishment of small nation-states means the duplication of governmental machinery, oftentimes at needless expense and at the sacrifice of efficiency. Small nations frequently have difficulty in finding competent and honest officials. When an empire is split into five nation-states, five governments become necessary in place of one. There must now be five presidents or kings and five diplomats to each

---

[1] In the spring of 1924 the Ile Saint Louis, located in the Seine river at Paris is said to have appealed to the League of Nations for autonomy, saying "High Magistrates of the Planet, Great Judges of the World Court, Guardians of the Pact of Nations, Protectors of all small oppressed peoples forgotten or wronged, l'Ile Saint-Louis hurls toward you a cry of appeal and protestation." Cf. Rice, "The Free Isle of St. Louis," *N. Y. Times Magazine*, August 24, 1924.

[2] Cf. Armstrong, "Forces of Disunion in Canada," *Current History*, July, 1924.

[3] Cf. E. A. Freeman, *History of Federal Government from the Foundation of the Achaian League to the Disruption of the United States* (1863), Vol. I, pp. 37 ff. Cf. p. 21.

[4] Cf. James Madison, *The Federalist*, No. 10.

one under the old régime. There are probably twice as many customs officials in Europe now as before the War; ten times as many transport officials, and twenty times as many diplomats.[1] As a result of the Paris Peace Conferences, the frontiers of Europe have about doubled. And this means larger armies and armaments to defend them from conceivable attack. The establishment of new states, whether large or small, leads to boundary disputes and to economic complications of a most serious nature.[2] In the 19th century, self-determination was an integrating force, bringing about the creation of single and coherent nation-states, such as Germany and Italy, out of a mass of smaller, snarling units. But in the 20th century, self-determination has become a disintegrating force, which, uncontrolled, will lead to very serious consequences for the peace of the world and for the welfare of the nations themselves.

That some limitations must be placed upon self-determination has been recognized by the League of Nations. In its report on the dispute between Finland and Sweden over the 16,000 Aaland islanders, who demanded union with Sweden, the Committee of Rapporteurs declared, "To concede to minorities, either of language or of religion, or to any fractions of a population the right of withdrawing from the community to which they belong, because it is their wish or their good pleasure, would be to destroy order and stability within States and to inaugurate anarchy in international life; it would be to uphold a theory incompatible with the very idea of the State as a territorial and political unity." In the opinion of the committee, the separation of a minority from the state of which it is a part can only be considered as an altogether exceptional solution,—"a last resort when the State lacks either the will or the power to enact and apply just and effective minority guarantees." But Finland, a country with a well-developed national life, had not misgoverned the islands or abused their cultural institutions. To recognize the legitimacy of the demands of the Aalanders would be to create animosity between the Finns and the 350,000 Swedes living in Finland proper, which would accentu-

[1] Lord Raglan, "Armaments and Frontiers," 92 *Nineteenth Century* (1922), 17. Cf. E. Wittmann, *Past and Future of the Right of National Self-determination* (1919); R. Lansing, *The Peace Negotiations* (1921), Ch. VII; *ibid.*, *Self-determination* (1921), reprinted from the *Saturday Evening Post.*
[2] Cf. Ch. V.

WHO SHOULD DRAW THE LINE? 47

ate rather than relieve the ill-feeling which the problem had created.[1] The League of Nations Assembly likewise refused to admit as members such states as Lichtenstein, San Marino and Monaco, on the ground that they were too small to fulfil the duties required of full-fledged states. The Supreme Council took a similar decision in the case of Vorarlberg, a province of Austria, having a population of 133,000. In November, 1918, this district proclaimed its independence and later voted to petition the Peace Conference in favor of joining the neighboring state of Switzerland. But this request was denied, apparently on the ground that these peoples presumably wished to separate themselves from Austria in order to escape the obligations imposed on the defeated powers.[2]

It is manifestly impossible to grant independence to so-called enclaves, or little islands of alien peoples living in the midst of a foreign nationality. And even in the case of nations which have had a historic past, such peoples must have a real desire to be free and a population and territory capable of sustaining the economic and political framework of a nation; they must also be capable of governing themselves to the extent of meeting certain minimum obligations toward the outside world.[3] Whether or not a nation should be given political independence depends, not upon universally applicable theories, but upon the facts in each case, which must be determined independently as they arise. Thus in the opinion of the Allied powers, the necessary tests could be met by such states as Poland or Czechoslovakia, but they could not as yet be met by the Ruthenes or by the non-white peoples of the tropics under colonial control.[4]

6. WHO SHOULD DRAW THE LINE?

It is not only important to decide just where to draw the line in these cases; but also to inquire *who* is to draw the line—who is to decide when a particular people should be given their freedom. According to international law, "the grant or refusal of the right to a portion of its population of determining its own political fate by

[1] "The Aaland Islands Question," Report of Commission of Rapporteurs, April 16, 1921, *Council Document B. 7*, pp. 28–30.
[2] Giroud, *Plébiscite*, p. 134.
[3] Cf. B. Lavergne, *Le Principe des nationalités et les guerres* (1921), pp. 17 ff.
[4] Cf. Ch. XVI.

plebiscite or by some other method" is exclusively "an attribute of the sovereignty of every State which is definitely constituted." [1] Nevertheless as long as each state remains the judge whether or not part of its population should become independent or join another state, it is likely to decide the question in favor of what it regards as its own interests. In such cases, a subject nation must resort to force, which is a very inadequate criterion of a nation's capacity to govern itself. Moreover, as long as force remains the only criterion of national independence, civil wars will be perpetual.

President Wilson realized the need of working out a peaceful solution of such questions when he suggested in an early draft of the League Covenant, that while the Contracting Powers should guarantee to each other political independence and territorial integrity, it should be understood between them that "such territorial readjustments, if any, as may in the future become necessary by reason of change in present racial conditions and aspirations or present social and political relationships, pursuant to the principle of self-determination . . . may be effected if agreeable to those peoples." [2] But this provision was omitted from the final draft of the Covenant, which contains no mention of this principle. As at present constituted, the League of Nations has no power to determine whether or not certain territory should be given its independence or transferred to another nation, regardless of the wishes of the inhabitants concerned, in the case of a definitely constituted state. But at the same time, the procedure of the League of Nations may peacefully compromise disputes between nations over the right of self-determination, as it did in the Aaland islands case.

The Aaland Islands Case.—These tiny islands in the Baltic Sea, inhabited by Swedish people, formed part of the kingdom of Sweden until 1809. In that year they were annexed by Russia, and until 1917 were administered by Russia as a part of the Duchy of Finland, also under Russian control.[3] Following the Russian revolution, Finland acquired its independence along with the Aalanders whom it continued to administer. While the Aalanders

---

[1] "The Aaland Islands Question," Report of the Committee of Jurists, O. J., Oct., 1920, Special Supplement No. 3, p. 5.
[2] Cf. R. Lansing, *The Peace Negotiations* (1921), p. 55.
[3] "The Aaland Islands Question," O. J., Spec. Supplements Nos. 1 and 3.

WHO SHOULD DRAW THE LINE? 49

united with the Finns in demanding freedom from Russia, they repeatedly expressed a desire to be reunited with the kingdom of Sweden. In two plebiscites, in 1918 and 1919, the people voted in favor of such reunion. And the Swedish government, adopting the cause as its own, asked the Paris Peace Conference as well as the Finnish government to arrange an official plebiscite to determine the fate of the islands. When the Finns declined this request, relations between the two countries became tense. In June, 1920, the British government brought the dispute before the Council of the League of Nations, under Article XI of the Covenant.[1] It was the contention of Finland that the question thus submitted to the Council fell under her "domestic jurisdiction" which, if true, meant that the Council could not investigate the situation. In order to settle whether or not this was an international question in which the League could be legitimately interested, the Council appointed an international Committee of Jurists, which reported that in the absence of express provisions in international treaties, a state which was recognized as independent and a member of the family of nations could decide for itself whether it should cede territory to another power. Ordinarily, the League could not intervene. But "the formation, transformation and dismemberment of States as a result of revolution and wars create situations of fact which, to a large extent, cannot be met by the application of the normal rules of positive law. . . ." If the state, as was true of Finland, was not yet fully formed, the situation particularly as regards territorial sovereignty was still obscure. "The transition from a de facto situation to a normal situation de jure cannot be considered as one confined entirely within the domestic jurisdiction of a State. It tends to lead to readjustments between the members of the international community and to alterations in their territorial and legal status; consequently, this transition interests the community of States very deeply both from political and legal standpoints." Under such abnormal circumstances, the rights of nationalities could be regarded as of international concern which the League could proceed to investigate.[2] Acting upon this recommendation, the

---

[1] *O. J.*, July–August, 1920, p. 250; for a discussion of Article XI, cf. 629.
[2] Report of the Committee of Jurists, cited, p. 6; cf. the Fisher report, *O. J.*, Oct., 1920, p. 394.

Council decided that this was not a "domestic" question, and appointed a Commission of Rapporteurs to make a recommendation as to the case.[1] As a result, while the Council did not propose to decide the fate of these islands by plebiscite because they were too small and had not been misgoverned, it did make recommendations, strengthening the guarantees of the local inhabitants and providing for the demilitarization of the islands.[2]

At the third Assembly (1923) the Six Nations of the Iroquois, Indian tribes in Canada, distributed through unofficial channels a paper appealing for protection under the League of Nations if Great Britain would not grant their claims.[3] Inasmuch as the protest was not made officially, the League paid no attention to the appeal. Even if the proper procedure had been followed, there is no doubt but that the League would have decided that this case, where the situation was clearly defined, was of purely domestic concern to the British Empire.

It would be manifestly impossible to give the League power to establish new nation-states or transfer territory from one state to another, according to the principle of self-determination, without making it an all-powerful super-state, which is undesirable. Nevertheless, the League's existence will probably reduce the number of wars over self-determination and gradually do away with force as the chief criterion of statehood. This is because of its power to discuss nationalistic disputes and to air such grievances before the world. The mere existence of a forum where these issues may be discussed, even though no action can be taken, will formulate an international conscience which will exert strong pressure upon a state that, under the old system, could misgovern subject nationalities without restraint. When alien nationalities are given no opportunity to voice their grievances, these naturally are magnified. Exposed to the air, they become rarefied; thus in the hearings on the Aalander question, the League Council admitted two inhabitants of the islands, along with representatives of Sweden and Finland. The League is doing even more toward removing nationalistic disputes, by working out measures satisfying the

[1] *Ibid.*, p. 396.
[2] *Ibid.*, Sept., 1921, p. 699.
[3] Cf. the reply of Canada to the Appeal of the Six Nations, *O. J.*, June, 1924, p. 829.

THE PROBLEM OF FRONTIERS 51

desire for self-determination short of independence, namely, by the protection of minorities and by autonomy, developments discussed in later chapters.

7. THE PROBLEM OF FRONTIERS

In achieving political independence, a nation at once becomes involved in the international problem of frontiers. The task of drawing boundary lines is by no means simple. "The majority of the most important wars of the century have been Frontier wars."[1] Following the World War, there were at least thirty boundary disputes between European nations. Until recently half a dozen boundary disputes between South American countries kept on edge the peace of a continent. Disputes of this nature have arisen out of conflicting national interests and conflicting frontier principles; and they have usually created intense bitterness among peoples who, before being inoculated with the virus of nationalism, had lived peacefully side by side.

Many nations have insisted on the principle of *historic* frontiers. They gaze with longing eyes on territory which, in the dim past, was under the domain of the nation. At the Paris Peace Conference Poland fought for the frontiers of the old Kingdom. Serbia dreamed of the days of Stephen Dushan; Czechoslovakia aimed at the frontiers of the ancient kingdom of Bohemia; Greece aimed to restore the boundaries of the Byzantine Empire, which would have given her Constantinople and Asia Minor. France spoke of the frontiers of "1789" and "1792". But despite the force of historic tradition in nationalism, the historic frontier is full of dangers. It disregards the wishes of the present inhabitants, and consequently disregards the principle of self-determination. The historic argument would lead England to demand the annexation of Calais, and France to demand the boundaries of the Napoleonic Empire, which included Holland. As long as this doctrine is supported, international disputes are inevitable.

Other nations have insisted on the economic frontier [2] and on the

---

[1] Lord Curzon, *Frontiers*, The Romanes lecture (1907), p. 5. The dispute over the boundary between Northern Ireland and the Irish Free State, while it did not lead to war, showed the great difficulties involved in drawing new frontiers.

[2] Discussed on p. 116.

strategic frontier. Some writers believe in "the obvious necessity for dividing self-governing states or nations into separate geographical units in such a manner as to set definite and scientific barriers between countries liable to mutual aggression."[1] One military man says, "With secure frontiers, peace would prevail between the sundered worlds."[2] In the past nations have believed that the best way to protect themselves from attack is by setting up frontiers which are physically difficult for an outside power to cross. From the strategic standpoint, frontiers have been divided into *natural* and *artificial* frontiers. Natural frontiers interpose geographical obstacles to invasion. England was able to protect herself from Europe for so many centuries because of the "inviolate sea." Napoleon Bonaparte regarded deserts while other generals have regarded mountain ranges as excellent barriers. Some nations aim to secure a mountain ridge for a defensive frontier, but others go further and attempt to secure not only the ridge but the slope of the other side. Following the Austro-Italian War of 1866, Austria drew the frontier with Italy so that Austria received not only the ridge of the Alps but the far slope. An attack upon Italy could therefore be easily made; Italy, however, could not successfully attack Austria because the latter power held not only the ridge but the slope running up to it.[3] As a result of the World War, Italy was able to rectify the frontier by annexing the Brenner Pass; but in doing so, she acquired territory inhabited by a great majority of Germans. Strategic considerations led the Peace Conference to give Moresnet to Belgium, and a strip of German territory to Czechoslovakia.[4] The Ruthenes were not allowed to establish an independent state, because they lay on the southern slope of the Carpathians where they would be a dagger, so it was said, in the heart of Czechoslovakia. Finally, rivers have been regarded as a good natural frontier. In 1838 Victor Hugo wrote a book, entitled the *Rhine*, in which he said that France would

---

[1] T. H. Holdich, *Boundaries in Europe and the Near East* (1918), p. 5; *ibid.*, *Political Frontiers and Boundary Making* (1916), p. 46.
[2] Vestal, *The Maintenance of Peace* (1920), p. 66.
[3] C. B. Fawcett, *Frontiers, A Study in Political Geography* (1918), p. 85. Cf. S. C. Gilfillan, "European Political Boundaries," 39 *Pol. Sci. Quarterly* (1924), 458.
[4] Cf. Johnstone, "The German Problem in Czechoslovakia," *Foreign Affairs*, June, September, 1923.

THE PROBLEM OF FRONTIERS 53

only be complete when it gained the Rhine as a natural frontier—a sentiment which was repeated at the Paris Peace Conference. Although this argument was rejected, the peace treaties did authorize Allied troops to occupy the Rhineland for fifteen years.[1]

When it has been geographically impossible for a nation to erect natural frontiers, it has been obliged to set up artificial frontiers, drawn according to some astronomical line, or to purely arbitrary considerations, or to the wishes of the local inhabitants.[2] As an artificial frontier is geographically exposed to attack, a nation usually feels that this weakness must be offset by proportionately greater armaments and fortifications. Thus the frontier between France and Germany was lined with forts.[3] Poland, a state without natural barriers against either Russia or Germany, has attempted to offset this weakness by a policy of alliances and large military establishments.

As a matter of fact, the distinction between natural and artificial frontiers is largely fictitious. None of these natural frontiers, whether the sea, rivers, or mountains, has proved impregnable in modern warfare. The greatest river in the war area, the Danube, was crossed by Mackensen in November, 1916, in the face of the Roumanian army.[4] British faith in sea defenses has also been disturbed by the submarine and aircraft. Deserts and mountains are no longer impassable—automobiles now cross the Sahara.

All of these strategic considerations are based on the unhealthy idea that a nation will be attacked unless it is physically able to defend itself. The struggle for strategic frontiers thus becomes part of the competition in armaments which, as we shall see, irritates national feelings and provides a cause for war. Since natural frontiers overlook ethnic considerations, they result in the annexation of peoples against their wishes, and thus create irredentas which again provoke international disputes. This is another example of the workings of the military system: a policy which, adopted to prevent war, inevitably leads to war.

Wherever possible it is desirable that frontiers should be drawn

[1] Cf. p. 531.
[2] Cf. Curzon, cited, p. 34.
[3] Cf. H. B. George, *The Relations of Geography and History*, (4th ed. 1910), p. 327, and Ch. III.
[4] Brunhes and Vallaux, *La Géographie d' Histoire* (1921), p. 357; Vallaux, *Le Sol et l'État* (1911), pp. 367–374.

not according to economic, historic or strategic considerations, but according to considerations of nationality. Probably the most satisfactory frontiers have been "zones of distinct natural barriers or obstacles to human movement and occupation . . . [which] form a break in the distribution of the people." [1] But a frontier which deliberately violates ethnic and linguistic considerations in order to pass through such a zone, is likely to provoke more trouble than it saves.

So many complications are involved in changing boundary lines that much is to be said in favor of the principle of the *status quo*. Unstable boundaries accelerate the fear which so strongly grips the life of the small nation and which leads it to build up large armaments. The Peace Conference of 1919 proceeded on the theory that, in so far as possible, boundaries should be readjusted by balancing the principle of self-determination against other factors and then that these boundaries should be guaranteed against forcible change in the future.[2] Idealists condemned this solution because some frontiers violated the national principle. But unless these violations are flagrant and unless the inhabitants involved are denied the right to retain their national traits, there is little justification for the violent alteration of boundary lines.[3]

---

[1] Fawcett, cited, p. 102.

[2] Cf. p. 587.

[3] In the peace treaty with Hungary, a pacific means of changing frontiers was authorized by Article 29 which provided that Boundary Commissions might, at the request of one of the states concerned, revise certain boundary lines, endeavoring to follow as nearly as possible the descriptions given in the treaties, and "taking into account as far as possible administrative boundaries and local economic interests." In a note to Hungary the President of the Supreme Council stated that should the Delimitation Commissions decide that unjust boundaries had been drawn, they could submit a report to the Council of the League, and the Council, at the request of one of the parties concerned, could "offer its services to obtain by a friendly settlement" the rectification of the frontier. Cf. *O. J.*, Nov., 1922, p. 1426. Hungary thus appealed to the Council in the case of the Jugoslav and also of the Czechoslovak frontiers. In the first case, neither party was satisfied with the proposed alterations. In the second case, minor alterations were suggested by the Council, which were unsatisfactory to Hungary. *O. J., ibid.*, also June, 1925, pp. 602 ff. For a criticism, cf. F. Kellor, *Security Against War* (1924), Vol. I, Ch. XIV.

A more noteworthy settlement of a frontier dispute was the Mosul controversy between Great Britain and Turkey, the former contending that it should be included within Mesopotamia; the latter contending that it should be recognized as Turkish territory. The Treaty of Lausanne provided (Art. 3) that if Turkey and Great Britain could not agree as to the frontier between

Turkey and Mesopotamia within nine months, the dispute should be referred to the League of Nations. The governments promised that, pending a decision, no military movements should take place which might modify the *status quo*. In Sept., 1924, Great Britain placed the dispute before the Council, which appointed a Commission to study the question. *O. J.*, Oct., 1924, p. 1360. A dispute then arose between the two governments as to the territories which their troops could respectively occupy pending final settlement. To settle this dispute, they asked the Council to hold an extraordinary session, at which, in October, 1924, a provisional boundary was drawn. *O. J.*, Nov., 1924, p. 1660. The Council then sent out a Commission of Inquiry to Mosul. In July, 1925, it made a report recommending the union of Mosul with Iraq, provided it remain under the mandate of the League of Nations for 25 years, and that the Kurds should be employed in the administration of their country. Pending a decision and following further frontier incidents the Council dispatched General Laidoner of Esthonia to Mosul to keep the Council informed of the situation. The question now arose whether the Council merely had the power of mediator or could lay down a binding decision. When the World Court ruled, in an advisory opinion, in favor of the latter, the Turkish government protested. (Cf. Advisory Opinion No. 12.) Nevertheless the Council decided at its meeting of December to award Mosul to Iraq subject to the conditions laid down by the Commission of Inquiry. *O. J.*, February, 1926, p. 187.

CHAPTER III

THE CONFLICT OF COLOR

1. An Inter-racial War?—2. Causes of Race Prejudice.—3. Necessity for Racial Segregation.—4. Treatment of Orientals in the West.—5. The Demand for Racial Equality.—6. Racial Homogeneity *v.* Racial Equality.—7. The Kenya Dispute.—8. The Gentlemen's Agreement. 9. The Problem of Democracy in Inter-racial Communities.

Important as national groups have been in modern history, their supremacy is being attacked by a new alignment based on "race." It has been estimated that in 1916 there were 710 million whites, 510 million yellows, 420 million browns and 100 million blacks in the world.[1] While it is almost impossible to define what is meant by "race" as far as groupings within the whites are concerned, there are certain definite physical characteristics which distinguish the Negro, the Indian and the Mongolian from the white man of Europe and North America, even more sharply than cultural traits distinguish one "nation" from another.

Three hundred years ago there was no racial problem as we know it to-day. With the exception of the slaves imported to America, one race remained segregated from the other. China and Japan both sternly banned intercourse with foreigners. When as a consequence of the establishment of colonial empires, the whites came in contact with the darker races, the chief result was an attitude of arrogant supremacy toward peoples not strong enough to resist the white man's rule. European nations who asserted that dealings between themselves should be based on equality and justice, declared that in dealings with the peoples of Africa and Asia, White Supremacy should be the only guide. Nevertheless, as long as the darker peoples remained submissive, unconscious of their power, the racial question did not become acute.

[1] E. M. East, *Mankind at the Cross Roads* (1924), p. 111. A sensational writer puts the number of whites at only 550,000,000 and the non-whites at 1,150,000,000. L. Stoddard, *The Rising Tide of Color* (1920), p. 6.

AN INTER-RACIAL WAR? 57

1. AN INTER-RACIAL WAR?

At the present time, however, the situation is changing. With the growing interdependence of the world, races remain segregated only with difficulty. The intellectual classes of one race now migrate from country to country; while the pressure of population in some countries inhabited by the darker peoples is furthering the demand, whether justified or not, for unrestricted emigration of the laboring classes.[1]

Moreover, the non-white peoples are rapidly developing a national life and a military power, which also threatens the principle of White Supremacy. Japan never did succumb to complete foreign control; at the present time she is the only non-Western nation to be recognized as a great power. India and Egypt are clamoring for complete independence. Recently the whole of North Africa threatened to revolt against the White Man's Rule.

While in the Middle Ages wars were fought over religion, and while in the last century they were fought over nationalism, there is a danger that in the coming century they will be fought over race. Prophecies of such a struggle are as frequent as they are ominous. The future relations of the white to the non-white races is one of the most important problems which students and statesmen have to solve.

At the present day, the existence of deep-seated racial prejudices cannot be denied. Although in France the doctrine of racial equality is practiced as it is preached, in the United States and in the Dominions of the British Empire, there is a widespread animosity among the rank and file against the Oriental and the black man. On the other hand, the Chinese and the Hindoo look with lofty contempt upon the materialism and the militarism of the West. There are those who believe that this racial prejudice is instinctive and therefore ineradicable. Racial irritations, according to this opinion, are bound to continue until an inter-racial war is inevitable. As Mr. Graham Wallas says, "The future peace of the world largely turns on the question whether we have, as is sometimes said and often assumed, an instinctive affection for those human beings whose features and colour are like our own, combined with an instinctive hatred for those who are unlike us."[2]

[1] Cf. p. 175.
[2] *Human Nature in Politics* (3d ed., 1921), p. 77.

The answer which he and others give to this crucial question is that racial prejudice is not due to a universal and single instinct, but is the result of several instincts, heightened by environmental causes. Young children seldom exhibit signs of race or color prejudices: white and black youngsters play together with the utmost abandon. Moreover, Lord Bryce has pointed out that before the days of the French Revolution there was very little self-conscious race feeling in any country or at any time.[1] In communities where the Chinese, Japanese or Indians are few, as in American university circles, they are received upon a basis of social equality. But when the percentage of such racial groups increases, this attitude of friendship gradually gives way to one of aloofness and dislike. If racial prejudice is thus a variable factor, it cannot be wholly instinctive and immutable.[2]

2. CAUSES OF RACE PREJUDICE

Much of the antagonism between racial groups may be due to other than racial causes. Of these, probably the most important is economic. When such races as the Negroes, Hindoos, Chinese or Japanese enter a white community they ordinarily bring with them an inferior standard of living, and hence are willing to work for a lower wage than the white man. While the white farmer and the white capitalist may welcome cheap labor, the Hindoos, Chinese and Japanese have shown a tendency to work for themselves, thus competing with the white farmer and white capitalist, which makes racial animosity, because of economic causes, more intense than ever. Since the Negro and the Mexican are content to remain wage-earners, they have not aroused as much hatred as have the more energetic non-white races. Social dissimilarities have also been of great importance. The Oriental is the product of an Asiatic as opposed to a European civilization. He speaks a language utterly divorced from a European tongue. Moreover, the political fact that the whites have ruled colored peoples for the last two centuries has given them an air of superiority which any autocrat would bear toward his subjects, regardless of their race. The mere fact that the Oriental is "brown" or "yellow" and that

---

[1] Cf. his Creighton Lecture, *Race Sentiment as a Factor in History* (1915), quoted by J. H. Oldham, *Christianity and the Race Problem* (1924), p. 34.
[2] Oldham, cited, Ch. XVI.

the European and American is "white" adds a visual difference, which makes the wholesale assimilation of one race by another virtually impossible. Nevertheless, if the races are kept separate, there is no reason why with the disappearance of these non-racial causes of friction, racial prejudice will not also disappear.

Two great political problems have arisen out of the contact of the white with the colored races: (1) the problems which have resulted from the extension of the white man's rule to countries inhabited by non-whites—the problems of imperialism elsewhere discussed; (2) the problem of discrimination against non-whites who have entered or who wish to enter the white man's country. Both of these problems have been created by the restless energy of Caucasian peoples; in the one case, by the search for new markets; in the other, by the demand for cheap labor.

3. NECESSITY OF RACIAL SEGREGATION

One of the most acute problems before the world to-day is the problem of the treatment of Orientals. Once admitted in wholesale numbers into a country inhabited by whites, conflicts inevitably arise. While it is possible to adjust a limited number of educated Orientals or blacks to the civilization of a white country, this task of assimilation is impossible when the entrance of such races is unrestricted. Experience seems to show that if a racial group is to merge its identity with the predominant ethnic group in the community, intermarriage must take place. If intermarriage is forbidden by law or custom, racial friction, caused by the perpetuation of distinct racial groups, is created, while irregular sexual relations will spring up. The results of interracial marriages in the past have not been regarded as satisfactory. Although scientists do not yet appear agreed as to whether these results have been due to racial or to social causes, the fact remains that inter-racial marriages would produce a hybrid population which would have great difficulty in perpetuating the characteristics of either a white or non-white civilization.[1] Inter-racial marriages would break down those traits of nationality which have enriched the culture of the world, replacing them with a mélange of negative characteristics, without a social heritage or background upon which

---

[1] East and Johnson, *Inbreeding and Outbreeding* (1919), p. 252.

to build. Japanese laborers in America bring with them little of the beauty which is characteristic of Japan; the Indians in British Columbia likewise appear to have left behind the cultural traits of the homeland, and yet to have acquired none of the traits of their pseudo-adopted country. From the strictly national standpoint, each nation is entitled to decide for itself whether or not to maintain the traits which have distinguished it in the past. From the strictly international standpoint, racial mixtures would probably confound the national cultures of the world to the detriment of mankind. Because of the fear of racial marriages, white communities usually impose an inferior social status upon alien races, making the formation of acquaintances between the two sexes difficult. When colored races are thus definitely marked with a social stigma, racial controversies become more acute than ever. If peace between the races is to be maintained upon a firm and friendly basis, and if each race is to contribute its distinctive gifts to the civilization of the world, the segregation of races, as far as the great masses of toilers is concerned, appears essential.

4. TREATMENT OF ORIENTALS IN THE WEST

Instinctively fearing submersion by more energetic or lower-standard colored races, the white countries have enacted laws excluding such races or subjecting them, once admitted, to discriminatory treatment. Within the British Empire, the Hindoos, the Chinese and the Japanese have been subject to various restrictions. While the Dominions have received European immigrants, all of them, with the exception of Newfoundland, have excluded Orientals by one means or another. In certain of the states of the Commonwealth of Australia, Asiatics are disqualified from voting and from obtaining leases in certain irrigated lands. Under certain circumstances they cannot receive mining rights or pensions. While in New Zealand the discriminations against Asiatic residents are insignificant and while in Canada the chief discrimination is that in British Columbia Asiatics are denied the franchise, in the Union of South Africa the discriminations are of fundamental importance. In two provinces—Transvaal and the Orange Free State—the franchise is frankly restricted to whites. In 1913 the Union passed an act forbidding Asiatics to acquire land, while different attempts to establish residential segregation of Asiatics from whites have been made.[1]

In the United States Orientals are excluded by various laws. The Chinese are excluded by exclusion laws, the first of which was enacted in 1882.[2] The Hindoos are excluded by the Immigration Law of 1917 enacting a "Barred Zone" clause, which bans aliens coming from within certain degrees of latitude and longitude on continental Asia, as well as from the islands of southern Asia.[3] The act thus applies to India, Siam, Indo-China, Afghanistan and parts of Russian Turkestan and Arabia. The Immigration Act of 1924 excludes all aliens ineligible to citizenship, a classification which in view of the previous exclusion by law of Chinese and Hindoos, is aimed at the Japanese. Moreover, in 1921 the United States adopted the "quota" system which restricted the number of each national group who could enter the country annually to 3% of the foreign-born persons living here in 1910.[4] In 1924 this figure was reduced to 2% of those living here in 1890. Since the bulk of the foreign-born population here in 1890 had come from northern Europe, the effect of this act was to admit a proportionately large number of "Nordics" as compared to the darker-skinned peoples from southern Europe. According to the House Committee of Immigration, this plan was adopted to preserve the "racial *status quo*" of the United States.[5] This legislation "is perhaps the first example in the history of immigration legislation of a law designed expressly to restrict the number of immigrants admitted."[6]

In the United States, moreover, only "free white persons" and Africans are eligible to citizenship by naturalization—a phrase which the Supreme Court has interpreted to mean that neither Chinese, Japanese nor Hindoos may become naturalized. In several states on the Pacific Coast such aliens—those ineligible to citizenship—cannot acquire any interest in farming property,

---

[1] Cf. L. F. Rushbrook Williams, *India in 1922–23*, a statement presented to Parliament (1923), pp. 5 ff.
[2] 22 Stat. 58.   [3] 39 Stat. 874.   [4] 42 Stat. 5.
[5] House Report 350, 68th Cong., 1st sess., p. 6. In 1929 the National Origins Plan went into effect. An annual number of 150,000 immigrants is now admitted in accordance with the number of each national group resident here.
[6] *Emigration and Immigration: Legislation and Treaties*, International Labor Office, Geneva (1922), p. 214.

which means that they must become wage-earners if they remain on the land.

While the United States refuses to allow Orientals to become naturalized, their children born in this country automatically become citizens, under the Fourteenth Amendment. Moreover, African negroes, Lapps, Finns, Magyars, Turks, Armenians and Mexicans have all been naturalized by American courts. Indians are now citizens of the United States as well as the dark-skinned inhabitants of Porto Rico[1]—inconsistencies in policy which further aggravate racial feeling.

5. THE DEMAND FOR RACIAL EQUALITY

Neither Japan, China nor India demands an unrestricted right of emigration to countries abroad. They accept the principle of national homogeneity, a principle which Japan at least rigorously practices.[2] Although they accept this principle, they also insist just as strongly upon the principle of national or, in this case, racial equality. They object to exclusion from white men's countries only when they are singled out for treatment not accorded to other alien groups. When one race is deprived of privileges freely granted to others, it naturally feels aggrieved. In its eyes such a discrimination immediately brands it as an "inferior" race; and in view of the struggle of the non-white races, especially the Japanese, Chinese and Indians against the supremacy of the white man, such a brand is particularly resented. When Japanese are subjected to discriminatory treatment they suspect that, though the other great powers of the world have been forced to

---

[1] McGovney, "Race Discrimination in Naturalization," 7 *Iowa Law Bulletin* (1923), 121, 211; Buell, "Some Legal Aspects of the Japanese Question," *A. J. I. L.*, Jan., 1923; McClatchey and Buell, "Shall We Naturalize the Japanese?" *Forum*, Sept., 1924.

[2] The Japanese in Hawaii intermarry to a lesser extent than any other racial group. McCaughey, "Race Mixture in Hawaii," *Journal of Heredity*, January and February, 1919. The over-population problem has little fundamentally to do with the emigration question, cf. p. 176. Mr. C. F. Andrews, an authority on India, also states that the Indians have no desire to emigrate. Quoted in Oldham, cited, p. 130.

In Japan laborers, unprotected by treaty, may be excluded by administrative decree, under Imperial Ordinance No. 350. The ordinance is not, however, discriminatory. For text and the rights of foreigners in Japan, cf. R. L. Buell, *Japanese Immigration* (World Peace Foundation, 1924), Vol. VI, Nos. 5–6.

THE DEMAND FOR RACIAL EQUALITY 63

recognize the position of Japan because of the strength of her army and navy, they still cherish feelings of "racial superiority."

This problem has become particularly acute in the British Empire in regard to the Indians. If India is to remain within the Empire, it must not only be given responsible government, according to Indian leaders, but Indians must also be given equal treatment when abroad. One Indian paper inquires, "Where is the consistency in asking India to take a seat at the Council table if an Indian—and not only that, but *no* Indian—is fit to live side by side with an Australian or a Canadian?" [1] As a result this question has been repeatedly before the Imperial Conference.

Japan is the only independent country of non-white people strong enough to protest effectively against discriminatory racial treatment. Consequently the relations between Japan and the United States have been recurrently strained between 1906 and the present time because of legislation, either local or national, which singled out Japanese for treatment not accorded other aliens. In 1906 the San Francisco school board passed an ordinance excluding Japanese children from the general public schools, which led to a bitter protest and to the intervention of President Roosevelt, as a result of which the ordinance was set aside. Following the passage of the anti-alien land law by California in 1913, excluding aliens ineligible to citizenship from owning land, the Japanese government sent a series of notes to the United States, saying that the "measure is unfair and intentionally racially discriminatory." It would not protest to the American government as long as Japanese ineligibility to citizenship was not used to deprive Japanese of rights of a civil nature. But when California resorted to this fact to prevent Japanese from acquiring land, the Japanese government wished "to express frankly their conviction that the racial distinction, which at best is inaccurate and misleading, does not afford a valid basis" for discrimination. [2] In protesting against the Immigration Act of 1924, the Japanese government declared, "International discriminations in any form and on any subject, even if based on purely economic reasons, are opposed to the principles of justice and fairness upon which the friendly intercourse between nations must, in its final analysis, depend. . . . Still

[1] Quoted, in Oldham, p. 133.
[2] Cf. *U. S. For. Rel.* (1913), pp. 633, 653; *ibid.* (1914), p. 434.

more unwelcome are discriminations based on race. . . . It is not denied that, fundamentally speaking, it lies within the inherent sovereign power of each state to limit and control immigration to its own domains; but when, in the exercise of such right, an evident injustice is done to a foreign nation in disregard of its proper self-respect, of international understandings or of ordinary rules of comity, the question necessarily assumes an aspect which justifies diplomatic discussion and adjustment." [1] At the Paris Peace Conference the Japanese delegation unsuccessfully attempted to secure the adoption of an amendment to the League Covenant indorsing the "principle of the equality of Nations and the just treatment of their Nationals." Upon the failure to establish the open door in the Class C mandates, the Japanese government made a declaration saying that it would not acquiesce "in the submission of Japanese subjects to a discriminatory and disadvantageous treatment in the Mandated territories." [2]

European countries have also protested against the "discriminatory" features of the American Immigration Law. In February, 1924, Roumania protested to the American State Department against the "practical elimination of immigration from southern and southeastern Europe," by the "quota" legislation then being discussed. The Italian government also protested against "an unjustified discrimination, de facto if not de jure, enacted to the detriment of a friendly nation," a measure which harshly affected "the interests and pride of the Italian nation." [3]

In the past, the United States, as far as the actions of other countries are concerned, has also protested against a policy of racial discrimination. In 1882 it protested against a law prohibiting the entrance of foreign negroes into Cuba as "imposing a race discrimination." [4] On a number of occasions the United States protested to Russia against its discriminatory treatment of the Jews. In December, 1911, the House of Representatives passed a resolution for the termination of our treaty of 1832 with Russia, asserting that the rights of American citizens abroad should not be impaired "because of race or religion." Before the Senate

---

[1] Note printed in Buell, *Japanese Immigration*, p. 372.
[2] *O. J.*, Jan., Feb., 1921, p. 95.
[3] House Report 350, cited, p. 14.
[4] Moore, *Digest of Int. Law*, Vol. IV, pp. 109, 113.

HOMOGENEITY VERSUS EQUALITY 65

could adopt the resolution, President Taft had terminated the treaty.[1] In 1902 John Hay, Secretary of State, vigorously protested against the treatment of the Jews in Roumania. In a note of August 11, he declared, "The political disabilities of the Jews in Roumania, their exclusion from the public service and the learned professions, the limitations of their civil rights, involving as they do wrongs repugnant to the moral sense of liberal modern peoples, are not so directly in point for my present purpose as the public acts which attack the inherent right of man as a bread winner in the ways of agriculture and trade. The Jews are prohibited from owning land or even from cultivating it as common laborers. . . ."[2]

6. RACIAL HOMOGENEITY vs. RACIAL EQUALITY

Many of the newer countries, such as the British Dominions and the United States, wish to receive white immigrants but they do not wish to receive Oriental immigrants, and for obvious reasons. Consequently these countries do not feel that they need treat the white and the colored men upon the same basis. This task of reconciling the two principles of racial homogeneity with racial equality has therefore seriously perplexed the world. The British Empire has gone much further in reconciling these two principles than the United States. Asiatic immigration has been excluded from the different Dominions. But in the case of the Japanese, it has been done in each case only after negotiations with Japan and by means not offensive to the Japanese people. When the Prime Ministers of Australia attempted to extend the anti-Chinese exclusion laws to the Japanese in 1896, they met the opposition of the British Secretary of State for the Colonies, who said that they should "bear in mind the traditions of the Empire, which make no distinction in favor of, or against race or color."[3] After negotiations with the Japanese ministers, Australia adopted a dictation test, which New Zealand later adopted, under which no immigrant is admitted who fails to write out fifty words in a language dictated to him by the officials. As the authorities may ask the Japanese to

---

[1] *Japanese Immigration*, p. 304.
[2] *U. S. For. Rel.*, (1902), p. 42.
[3] Cd. 8596, p. 13.

read Russian or Sanscrit, they are effectively excluded. After correspondence with Japan in 1905 the Australian government decided to exempt from this test Japanese students, merchants and travelers. In Canada a Gentlemen's Agreement was entered into in 1907 by which the Japanese government undertook to limit the number of domestic and agricultural laborers going to Canada to 400 a year, a figure which was reduced to 150 in 1924. Between 1897 and 1907 the Canadian Governor-General set aside more than half a dozen anti-Japanese bills, passed by the British Columbia legislature, many of which were protested against by the Japanese Ambassador. Thus the British Dominions have effectually excluded the Japanese but after negotiations with Japan and in a way which saved the "face" of the Japanese people. Once admitted into Canada and New Zealand, Japanese are allowed to become citizens and to hold property upon the same basis as anyone else. In Australia, it appears, however, that they are debarred from citizenship.

The Indian being a British subject, his status in the Empire has been of even more serious concern. At the Imperial War Conference of 1918 a resolution was adopted stating that it was an "inherent" function of each of the Dominions to exercise complete control over the composition of its own community, but that British citizens should be admitted from one community to the other for purposes of pleasure, trade or education; and Indians permanently domiciled in other British communities should be allowed to bring in their wives and minor children. At the Imperial Conference of 1921 a further resolution was passed reiterating the power of each "community" within the Commonwealth over immigration. But recognizing the "incongruity between the position of India as an equal member of the Empire and the existence of disabilities upon British Indians lawfully domiciled in some parts of the Empire," the Conference was of the opinion that "the rights of such Indians to citizenship should be recognized." [1] As a result of this resolution, some of the Dominions enacted laws removing discriminations against Indians.

A long controversy between India and South Africa was temporarily relieved by the passage by the South African Parliament in 1914 of the Indians Relief Act which repealed discriminatory

[1] South Africa was unable to accept this resolution. Cd. 1474, p. 8.

and license legislation applied to Indian residents in the past. Following the War the South African government drafted legislation to check competition of the Indian trader with the white, but as a result of a Round Table Conference at Cape Town the two governments signed a Gentlemen's Agreement, on February 21, 1927. Both governments affirmed the right of South Africa to maintain western standards of life. But the South African government dropped the pending legislation and announced its intention to organize a system of assisted emigration in which it agreed to furnish free passage and a bonus of twenty pounds to any Indian in South Africa wishing to be repatriated. It also agreed to take certain steps to improve the conditions of those Indians remaining in South Africa.[1]

7. THE KENYA DISPUTE

A serious controversy has also arisen in regard to the status of the Indians in the British Crown Colony of Kenya, in Africa, where in 1926 there were about 12,500 Europeans, 30,000 Indians and about 3,000,000 negroes. More racially self-confident than ever because of the Government of India Act of 1919 promising them eventual Dominion status,[2] the Indians in 1920 demanded the franchise, the right to hold land, and to enter the colony upon the same basis as the whites. The British settlers naturally resisted the demands, on the ground that the Indians would gain full control of the colony. After a protracted correspondence, the British Colonial Office declared that the interests of the African negroes were paramount to either the whites or the Indians, and that for that reason control over the colony would be retained in the British Foreign Office. In a statement it declared, "Only in extreme circumstances could His Majesty's Government contemplate legislation designed to exclude from a British Colony immigrants from any other part of the British Empire. Such racial discrimination in immigration regulations, whether specific or implied, would not be in accord with the general policy of His Majesty's Government. . . ." Nevertheless, economic considerations demanded the restriction of immigration; while high sanitary qualifications would be demanded of all wishing to reside in the

[1] For the text, see R. L. Buell, *Native Problem in Africa*, Vol. I, p. 155.
[2] Cf. p. 386.

Highlands.[1] Provision was made for five elected Indians in the Legislative Council, compared with eleven elected Europeans. The government has not, moreover, introduced any legislation restricting Indian immigration. While here the British government again attempted to reconcile conflicting racial interests upon a basis of fairness, Indian opinion declined to accept the solution adopted.

8. THE GENTLEMEN'S AGREEMENT

In 1907 President Roosevelt attempted to reconcile the two principles of national homogeneity and racial equality through the Gentlemen's Agreement, by which Japan voluntarily promised not to issue passports to laborers wishing to go to the United States with the exception of those returning from a temporary visit to Japan, and of the wives and minor children of laborers living in the United States. Thus this agreement secured the exclusion of Japanese laborers, while it solved the question of discrimination—Japan voluntarily kept her laborers at home, without any discriminatory legislation being passed by the United States. The Gentlemen's Agreement lasted from 1908 to 1924 when it was abruptly terminated by an act of Congress which substituted in its place an act excluding "aliens ineligible to citizenship." This action was defended on the ground that under the agreement the Japanese population in the United States had increased and that Japan alone was responsible for its administration, the United States being virtually obliged to accept passports issued by the Japanese Foreign Office. While the statistics showed that the Agreement operated very effectively to prevent the admission of laborers—the annual increase by immigration being 578—it was based upon a psychologically bad principle. It was an agreement which had never been submitted to the Senate and the complete text of which had been kept secret. Worst of all—from the popular standpoint—Japan instead of the United States was responsible for its administration.

While the Agreement thus presented defects, these should have been removed by diplomatic means. The action of Congress injured the national pride of Japan—to an extent which the

[1] "Indians in Kenya," Cmd. 1922 (1923). Cf. Rice, "The Indian Question in Kenya," *Foreign Affairs* (N. Y.), Dec. 15, 1923.

American people have never realized. Congress not only enacted what was regarded as a discriminatory measure, but it brought to an end an agreement which Japan had lived up to in good faith, without observing the courtesies of international intercourse.

Upon the relations of Japan and the United States the future of the Pacific and of Asia largely depends. Too much consideration cannot be given to the amenities of race. The best means of securing exclusion and at the same time of satisfying the demand for racial equality would be by a treaty excluding Japanese laborers from the United States and American laborers from Japan, to be jointly enforced at the port of debarkation, and by giving those Japanese permanently resident here, the right to become citizens provided they can pass an individual naturalization test required of all applicants. No danger would result from conferring such rights upon the limited numbers of Orientals now living in white countries. In 1920 there were only some 580,000 Japanese living abroad, of which 111,000 lived in the continental United States, 112,000 in Hawaii, 17,000 in Canada and 5,000 in Australia.[1] While there are more than 8,000,000 Chinese abroad they are found, for the most part, in Formosa, Java, Siam, etc., there being only 61,000 in the United States, 23,000 in Hawaii, 35,000 in Australia and 12,000 in Canada.[2] Many of these Orientals are American citizens by birth, and it is inconceivable that the naturalization of the remainder would imperil white society. On the other hand, it would be a long step toward solving the irritation now existing between East and West. As long as the United States follows its present policy toward its Oriental residents, the friendship of Japan and America will never be what it should be. Moreover, the time will come when China, again strong enough to reassert herself in international affairs, will join Japan in protesting against what both countries consider humiliating treatment. A diplomatic solution, as outlined above, would protect the interests of the white countries, while it would at the same time satisfy the demands of the East, thus diminishing the possibilities of a future "conflict of the Pacific."

[1] *Japan Year Book* (1923), pp. 45–46.
[2] Chen, "Chinese Migrations, with Special Reference to Labor Conditions," *Bulletin of the U. S. Bureau of Labor Statistics* (1923), No. 340, p. 15.

9. THE PROBLEM OF DEMOCRACY IN INTER-RACIAL COMMUNITIES

The conflict of color has become acute not only when the colored races have invaded the homeland of the whites, but also when the whites have attempted to establish settlements of their own in lands dominated by colored peoples. In his *Representative Government*, J. S. Mill pointed out that it was well-nigh impossible to build up a democracy out of intermingled groups of men of different races. While this thesis may have been disproved as far as different "races" among whites are concerned, it has been demonstrably true as regards a mixed community of whites and blacks. Originally the whites solved this problem by ignoring the wishes of the blacks. Even to-day, while in Algeria there are four natives to one European, and in the Union of South Africa, four blacks to one white, the whites control the "representative" assemblies in both countries. In South Africa the whites have even refused to admit the principle of communal representation—a limited number of seats for the negroes as a group. They are afraid that, once this principle is admitted, the negro will eventually gain the upper hand and drive the white man out. Consequently the native is rigorously excluded from politics. In three out of the four provinces, native negroes are excluded from the ballot. Nearly 3,000,000 out of the 4,000,000 people in South Africa have no voice in the government,—a condition which cannot last indefinitely without bringing forth violent protests, especially as the education of the negro increases.

But the problem is by no means solved merely by granting natives and Europeans representation in the same legislature. The racial gulf between white and black is so deep that the association of both races in a single legislature is unworkable. At the same time, it is neither possible nor desirable to withhold political rights from natives in their own country for an indefinite period.

In an effort to solve this knotty problem, France has adopted the policy of native and of foreign sections in legislative assemblies. There are three such sections in the Financial Delegations of Algeria, the first two representing Frenchmen, and the last representing Algerians. In the Grand Council of Tunis there is also a

THE PROBLEM OF DEMOCRACY 71

French and a native section, each deliberating separately, and avoiding, therefore, inter-racial friction.

In South Africa, even more radical steps have been taken. In the Transkei, "a government within a government" has been set up—a native legislature apart from the white legislature, but having power over native affairs, subject to certain British control. A district council has been created in each of the eighteen districts of this territory, along with a Transkeian Territories General Council, composed of a chief magistrate, eighteen resident magistrates and 54 native members. This body discusses such matters as native education, marriage legislation and the disease of stock.[1] The Native Affairs Act of 1920 authorizes the extension of the Native Council plan to all of the native areas throughout South Africa. Each Council may provide for the administration of roads, water, improvement in agriculture, hospitals and education facilities. It is given power to levy taxes on natives to the extent of five dollars per head.

In 1927 the Hertzog government introduced a bill providing for the election of seven European members to the Union Assembly by eligible natives throughout the Union. These members should not vote on matters of non-confidence in the Ministry except on twelve different matters of direct concern to the natives. The government also introduced a bill providing for the establishment of an annual Union Native Council which, subject to government control, should eventually pass laws governing native communities. These bills as yet (1929) have not been enacted into law.

The object of this legislation is to train the native in self-government. Only experience will determine how much responsibility the native may successfully assume, or how much responsibility the white man will be willing to delegate to him. The white man hesitates to increase the political power of the native population out of fear that the native will use this increased strength eventually to drive the white man out of the country. But if conces-

[1] R. L. Buell, *The Native Problem in Africa* (1928) chap. 6; "The Colour Problem," *Round Table*, No. 44 (1920), p. 949; Native Affairs Act, 1920; *Statutes of the Union of South Africa* (1920), No. 23; Natives(Urban Areas) Act, 1923, Sec. 10. For every native village under control of an urban local authority, there shall be a native advisory board of 3 natives. *Statutes of the Union of South Africa* (1923), p. 156. The Governor-General may also convene conferences of chiefs, etc., to ascertain native sentiment.

sions are not made to this legitimate demand of the native for self-rule conflict is inevitable.[1]

[1] The theory has been advanced that the colored races are increasing much more rapidly than the whites. Stoddard, *Rising Tide of Color*, p. 7. But other writers, disproving this idea, have shown that the white race is increasing faster than the colored races. "Over two-thirds of the total yearly increase of world population is white. To 8 million additional whites, there are only 4 million additional non-whites. Before 1950, therefore, unless some radical and relatively permanent overturn of world affairs occurs, the white race will have a true majority instead of a plurality." East, *Mankind at the Cross Roads*, p. 115. Mere climatic conditions make the domination of the world by the colored peoples unlikely; they appear unable to flourish in the temperate zones. Cf. E. Huntington, *Civilization and Climate* (1915); W. Pitkin, *Must We Fight Japan?* (1921), Ch. 23.

Cf. the following table:

Races	Population Millions	Annual Increase per thou.	Annual Increase, Millions	Number of Years to Double
White, European origin	650	12.0	7.80	58
White, non-European	60	8.0	.48	87
Brown	420	2.5	1.05	278
Yellow	510	3.0	1.53	232
Black	110	5.0	.55	139
	1,750		11.41	

CHAPTER IV

PAN-NATIONALISM

1. Aryan, Teutonic and Nordic Supremacy.—2. Difficulties with Racialism.—3. Pan-Germanism.—4. Pan-Slavism.—5. The Norden Movement.—6. The Pan-Angle Movement.—7. Pan-Latinism and Pan-Hispanism.—8. The Pan-African Movement.—9. The Pan-Islam Movement.—10. The Pan-Turanian Movement.—11. The Pan-Arab Movement.—12. The Pan-Asiatic Movement.—13. The Prospects for Racial Nationalism.

Racial disputes have not only arisen between white and colored peoples, but they have divided "white" men among themselves. It is a striking fact that upon becoming powerful a nation as a rule tends to regard itself as racially pure and racially distinct from its neighbors. This was certainly true of the German and of the French Nationalists, and of such Italians as D'Annunzio who, in apologizing for the seizure of Fiume, said, "Religion was for me the persistence of race and virtue of the blood [of] Italy which alone is great and alone is pure." [1] When a nation acquires this attitude, it comes to regard its character as a "soul" which has sprung out of racial origins,[2] and as a result it gains a fatalistic confidence in a triumphal destiny. A nation thus regarding itself as a race usually feels superior to all other races. Once it adopts a physical basis of existence, it substitutes instinct for intelligence and reason as its guide. The nation is no longer the product of a people's will: its acts have now become naturalistic and beyond control. However inconsistent the attitude may be, a nation intoxicated with racial theories is tempted to impose its racial "superiority" upon the remainder of the world, or to re-organize the existing national groups upon the basis of a common racial origin. Thus one German wrote, "We desire, and must desire, a world-

---

[1] Quoted by H. A. L. Fisher, *The Common Weal* (1924), p. 96.
[2] G. Le Bon, *The Psychology of Peoples* (1899), Ch. I. Cf. Le Fur, *Races, Nationalités, États* (1922), Ch. I.

empire of Teutonic stock;"[1] while Treitschke declared, "It makes for health that the nobler race should absorb the inferior stock." On the other hand, the feeling of similarity produced by common physical characteristics has led different members of the colored races to advocate a united movement directed primarily against the dominance of the white man.

1. ARYAN, TEUTONIC AND NORDIC SUPREMACY

It seems that the first ideas of racial superiority started with the doctrine of Aryanism. Professor Max Müller in 1861 set forth the doctrine that there was an original Aryan language which must have been spoken by an Aryan race. In his *Evolution of the Aryans*, Von Jhering asserted that the national character of the Aryans, once formed, was transmitted without change to later generations by heredity.[2] Great impetus to the belief in the superior virtues of this branch of the white race was given by the publication of a work by a Frenchman, Comte de Gobineau, on the *Inequality of the Human Races*, in which he said that the downfall of societies did not depend upon irreligion, bad morals, luxury, or the collapse of institutions, but upon the mixture of races. To him civilization was a matter of race, and in rather labored chapters, he attempted to show that the ten great human civilizations issued from the initiative of the "Aryan" race of which the Teuton was the modern representative. Stagnation set in when the Aryan blood was exhausted. "I say that a people will never die as long as it remains eternally composed of the same national elements."[3] Gobineau's work found its most welcome reception in Germany, where in 1893 a Gobineau society was founded, while in 1906 a collection of Gobineau relics was placed in the university of Strassburg.[4] An English Canon, Isaac Taylor, carried the doctrine to extreme lengths in a book on *The Origin of the Aryans*, in which he says that "the energy, the self-will, the fondness of adventure

---

[1] W. Archer, *Gems of German Thought* (1917), p. 110.
[2] Cf. Ch. 12 on the "Origins of Nationalities."
[3] *Essai sur l'inégalité des races humaines* (2d ed., 1884), Chs. II, III, V, and p. 32. For a criticism, cf. the chapter by F. H. Hankins, "Race as a Factor in Political Theory" in Dunning, *A History of Political Theories, Recent Times* (1924).
[4] M. S. Wertheimer, *The Pan-German League, 1890–1914* (1924), p. 18.

ARYAN, TEUTONIC, NORDIC SUPREMACY

and the love of combat which has enabled the Teutonic peoples to extend their rule over the world, come from the dolichocephalic race; but the intellect and genius of Europe, the great writers, and more especially the men of science, belong to the brachycephalic race." Race is even responsible for differences in religion. "The dolichocephalic Teutonic race is Protestant, the brachycephalic Celto-Slavic race is either Roman Catholic or Greek Orthodox. In the first, individualism, wilfulness, self-reliance, independence, are strongly developed; the second is submissive to authority and conservative in its instincts." [1] The author does not state whether Henry VIII changed the shape of his skull upon turning Protestant!

It was but a step from Aryanism to the doctrine of Teutonism— a confused theory, some of the proponents of which held that the Teutons were the only modern descendants of the Aryan and that all virtue would die with them. The leading exponent of this theory was an Englishman, Houston Stewart Chamberlain who said, in *The Foundations of the Nineteenth Century:* "Our whole civilization and culture of to-day is the work of one definite race of man, the Teutonic." [2]

In France, the Aryan doctrine was developed, in conformity with French racial pride, into a doctrine of Gallicism and Celtism. In America it took the form of elevating Anglo-Saxonism.[3] Each race, it was held, had a certain "genius," and the highest talent for political organization lay with the Teuton. While the racial idea was thus promulgated in the United States before 1914, it did not reach its height until the end of the World War. At that time a large number of books appeared, advocating ideas in many respects similar to the racial theories promulgated in Germany by Gobineau and Chamberlain. Dividing the whites into the Nordic, Alpine and Mediterranean "races," these writers assert that the greatest progress has come from the Nordics, or fair-haired peoples who originally populated America. In perhaps the most forceful of these books, Mr. Madison Grant, a lawyer, says, "The Nordic race is domineering, individualistic, self-reliant and jealous of their [sic] personal freedom both in political and religious

[1] Quoted, J. Oakesmith, *Race and Nationality* (1919), p. 28.
[2] Cf. the Introduction, p. lxvii of the English translation (1910), also Chapters 6 and 9.
[3] Cf. Burgess, *Political Science and Comparative Constitutional Law* (1890), Vol. I, pp. 36–48; also Homer Lea, *Day of the Saxon* (1912).

systems and as a result they are usually Protestants." [1] Elsewhere he says that if the Nordic race is extinguished—with "its capacity for leadership and fighting,"—civilization will pass away.[2] This disaster can be averted only "if the Nordic race will gather itself together in time, shake off the shackles of an inveterate altruism, discard the vain phantom of internationalism, and reassert the pride of race and the right of merit to rule." Another writer says that the term nationalism should "include all peoples who are united by pride in a common race and culture," [3] while the richness of this culture should be developed by shifting many of the burdens which the whites now carry onto the backs of other races. A more spectacular scribe, picturing America's entrance into the World War, says, "With its Nordic heritage ennobled by three centuries of miraculous achievement, the young giant of the Western World heard the call to guide, rehabilitate, and set its example to backward nations throughout the earth." [4]

2. DIFFICULTIES WITH RACIALISM

Despite the assurance with which these writers speak of racial purity and of racial superiority, it is significant that virtually none of the racial proponents have been scientists. On the contrary, it appears that few outstanding scientists to-day maintain that there is such a thing as a pure race, or that one "race" among white men is inherently superior to another.[5] Probably no nation in the world to-day rests upon a solid racial foundation. The Italian nation is made up of twenty different racial groups;

[1] Madison Grant, *The Passing of the Great Race* (new ed., 1918), p. 228.

[2] In his introduction to L. Stoddard's *Rising Tide of Color* (1920), p. xxix; cf. the latter's *Revolt Against Civilization* (1922); and *Racial Realities in Europe* (1924).

[3] C. C. Josey, *Race and National Solidarity* (1923), p. 51.

[4] C. S. Burr, *America's Race Heritage* (1922), p. 216. Cf. C. W. Gould, *America, A Family Matter* (1922); for the difference between ethnic groups and races, cf. J. Deniker, *The Races of Man* (2d ed.), p. 280.

[5] A. H. Keane, *Man: Past and Present* (1899), p. 448; Roland B. Dixon, *The Racial History of Man* (1923); Oakesmith, cited, Ch. IV; Ellsworth Huntington, *The Character of Races* (1924), Ch. VI; G. H. Johnston, *Views and Reviews, From the Outlook of an Anthropologist* (1912), p. 227; Pearson, "The Problem of Anthropology," *Scientific Monthly*, November, 1920; E. G. Conklin, *The Direction of Human Evolution* (1921), p. 41; W. Z. Ripley, *The Races of Europe* (1899), p. 107. Cf. F. Boas, *The Mind of Primitive Man* (1911), Ch. I, and pp. 131 ff; also Jean Finot, *Race Prejudice* (new ed., 1924).

DIFFICULTIES WITH RACIALISM

the French nation of thirteen; the Spanish nation of six; the German nation of five. The population of Great Britain contains three types of Stone Age races, two kinds of Celts, as well as Jutes, Angles and Saxons.[1] Anyone with the slightest knowledge of the history of the Italian Renaissance or of the Christian religion must realize that the finest fruits of civilization have come from the darker branches of the white "race," or in areas having a mixed racial population. While the "Nordics" or the inhabitants of England may possess greater skill in organization than the inhabitants of Italy, it is impossible to say that one is superior to the other, any more than one may say that the winner of a hundred-yard dash is superior to the winner of a marathon race. If racial ties held men together, the World War would never have been fought. While physical heredity is of great importance to mankind, social heritage, which does not depend upon race, is of more importance still. Although there are differences between racial groups, there are even greater differences between individuals within the group. As a recent writer has said, "As between white and negro in this country or North European and South European in this country, there can . . . be no longer doubt of differences in average mental capacity. But the average differences are slight in contrast with the wide variation of abilities in each group. Even the group with the lowest average shows a greater or less proportion of its members above the average of the highest group. Moreover, while some groups reach higher levels than that attained by any members of other groups, the lower limits in all cases reach down through imbecility to idiocy. Thus throughout most of the range of variation there is overlapping. In consequence, the fundamental questions become less those of race than of the relative rates at which the different levels in each race or nationality group are adding to the next generation." [2] In other words, some individuals in the Nordic group may be inferior to individuals in the Alpine group; moreover, differences between groups may be due to social as much as to racial causes.

As a result of these doctrines of racialism, race prejudice is nat-

---

[1] Report of M. Otlet, *Documents préliminaires, IIIme conférence des Nationalités*, Lausanne, June 27, 1916, p. 14. Cf. Olivier, "Colour Prejudice," 124 *Contemporary Review* (1923), 448.

[2] F. N. Hankins, in Dunning, cited, p. 547.

urally intensified, a fact once illustrated by the anti-Semitism of Henry Ford's *Dearborn Independent*, and the activities of the Ku Klux Klan. On the one hand, racialism attacks the doctrine of internationalism, saying that coöperation with "inferior races" upon a basis of equality is quite impossible. On the other, it fervently supports the doctrine of imperialism, justifying the supremacy of a particular race over the remainder of the world because of its inherent physical or "racial" virtues. Furthermore, it subscribes to the theory of racial nationalism—namely, that the real basis of national life is not cultural but physical, and that all members of the same "race" should be united under a common flag. Acting under this stimulus, the racial proponents have from time to time launched a large number of "Pan" movements which have recurrently agitated the waters of world politics.

3. PAN-GERMANISM

Before 1914 the most widely known of these movements was Pan-Germanism. There are about 90,000,000 Germans in the world, but only less than 60,000,000 of which are within the German Reich. The remainder are in Austria, Hungary, Switzerland, Luxemburg, Belgium and the Netherlands. The Pan-German movement had as its aim the association of all these German peoples under one government. When Prussia excluded Austria from the German Empire, a blow was given the idea. But it was revived with the formation of the Pan-German League in 1894. According to its constitution, "The Pan-German League strives to quicken the national sentiment of all Germans and in particular to awaken and foster the sense of racial and cultural kinship of all sections of the German people." [1] The League carried on extensive propaganda, especially in Austria where it would annually distribute Christmas trees to the children of Vienna.[2] During the World War the word Pan-Germanism became synonymous with German imperialism, aiming to dominate the whole of Central Europe from the Baltic to the Ægean.[3]

That the fear of this movement was real at the Paris Peace

---

[1] M. S. Wertheimer, *The Pan-German League, 1890-1914*, pp. 95, 98.
[2] G. Drage, *Austria-Hungary* (1909), p. 533.
[3] Cf. F. Naumann, *Central Europe* (1916); R. Usher, *Pan-Germanism* (1913); A. Chéradame, *The Pan-German Plot Unmasked* (1917).

Conference was shown by Article 80 of the Treaty of Versailles in which Germany not only acknowledged the independence of Austria, but agreed that this independence should be inalienable, except with the consent of the Council of the League of Nations. The German constitution (article 61) originally provided that Austria should be represented in the Reichsrath, with a deliberative vote, until union was achieved. But this provision was stricken out at the demand of the Allied Supreme Council on the ground that it violated the treaty. This violation of the principle of self-determination was justified by the Allies on the ground that the union of Austria and Germany would create a state of 67,000,000 people which, next to Russia, would be the largest state in Europe.[1]

The dissolution of the Austro-Hungarian Empire increased the activities of the Pan-German party which vigorously agitated for the union of German Austria, despite the attitude of the Allies.[2] The economic disintegration of Austria following the War increased Pan-German sentiment. But with its financial reconstruction, under the auspices of the League of Nations, and with the growing plight of Germany, this feeling abated, temporarily at least.

Nevertheless, in the summer of 1928 a great popular demonstration of Germans and Austrians in favor of *Anschluss* took place in connection with the Schubert musical festival in Vienna, which brought forth vigorous protest from a portion of the French press.[3]

4. PAN-SLAVISM

Europe has been the home of another racial movement, called Pan-Slavism. There are about 140,000,000 Slavic peoples scattered about Europe—of which only 110,000,000 were found in the old Russian Empire.[4] The aim of the Pan-Slavist movement varied with its different proponents. It insistently agitated for

---

[1] As a matter of fact, Germany, apart from Russia, is already the largest state in Europe. The Treaty with Hungary (art. 73) also provided that the independence of Hungary is inalienable otherwise than with the consent of the Council of the League of Nations.

[2] Von Sosnosky, "The New Pan-Germanism," 240 *Quarterly Review* (1923), p. 308; Expertus, "Neutralisierung Deutsch-Österreichs?" 6 *Südöst* (1919), p. 97.

[3] R. L. Buell et al., *Europe: A History of Ten Years* (1928), p. 304.

[4] L. Niederle, *La Slave race* (2d ed., 1916), p. 217.

the liberation of the Slavs, whether in Poland or in Austria, held under the subjection of foreign powers, and some of its leaders proposed a confederation of Slavic peoples, under the hegemony of Russia. Such a confederation would extend from the Baltic to the Balkans, thus dominating Europe—which explains why the movement was sponsored by Russia. The father of Pan-Slavism was a Croat by the name of Krijanitcha, who lived in the 17th century. On the political side, he advocated a union of all Slavic peoples under the "very gentle and very illustrious Lord of Russia." He also sponsored the development of a Pan-Slavonic literature, ideas which were carried forward in the 19th century by the great Slovak poet, Kollár. A number of Pan-Slavic congresses were also held, in 1848, in 1867 and in 1908.[1] While the southern Slavs, under the iron rule of Austria-Hungary, welcomed a movement for their deliverance, they did not relish any development that would place them under Russia, which, many believed, would merely be substituting one despotism for another. The ties of race were too intangible to give this positive aspect of the Pan-Slavic movement popular support. And the creation of Czechoslovakia, Poland, and a unified Serbia, following the World War, dealt further blows to an idea made more impracticable than ever by Bolshevism.

5. THE NORDEN MOVEMENT

At the present time, about 11,000,000 Scandinavian peoples live in three neighboring countries, Sweden, Norway and Denmark, who have exhibited a "power of racial endurance rarely found among other European peoples."[2] Originally of one stock in race and language, these peoples were also politically united in 1397 under the Union of Kalmar. The Union was very loose, however, and in 1523 Sweden regained its independence, while Denmark was separated from Norway during the Napoleonic wars. By the Act of Union of 1814 Norway and Sweden were united in a personal union, which was finally dissolved by plebiscite in 1905, following a dispute over foreign affairs. By this time modern nationalism had succeeded in dividing the allegiances

---

[1] L. Leger, *Le Panslavisme et le intérêt français* (1917), Chs. XIII, XV and XVIII.
[2] H. G. Leach, *Scandinavia of the Scandinavians* (1916), p. 1.

of all three of these countries: neither Norway nor Sweden protested against Prussia's annexation of Danish Schleswig in 1866. In the last twenty years, however, a movement has arisen to bring about closer association between these three countries. Beginning in 1903 officials from each government came together to discuss economic problems and to work out joint legislation, such as the Scandinavian marriage law. Since 1909 different members of the Scandinavian parliaments have met together annually.[1] When the World War broke out, common measures were taken to insure the neutrality of the three governments, the three kings holding a conference at Malmo for this purpose in December, 1914. In 1917 the Swedish parliament passed a resolution saying that the time had come for closer economic coöperation between the three countries; while in 1924 a conference was held in Stockholm between the three countries, together with Finland, where an arbitration commission was established.[2]

In 1919 the Norden movement proper was launched by the formation of a Norden society in each of the countries, the object of which was "to deepen the sense of fellowship among the nations of the North, to extend their line of intellectual and economic contact, and to promote practical coöperation among them." So far the movement has been educational and cultural rather than political, based on the belief, apparently, that political coöperation can succeed only after a cultural foundation has been laid.[3] Apart from this movement, an alliance, a tariff union, and the establishment of an international commission or parliament for these countries has frequently been proposed.

6. THE PAN-ANGLE MOVEMENT

Another development among the "light-skinned" peoples is the Pan-Angle movement, which would draw more closely together the English-speaking peoples of the world. Such an association, if carried out, would be of supreme political importance. It would embrace a combined population of 180,000,000 people and such

[1] O. Höijer, *Le Scandinavisme* (1919), p. 31; H. Aall, *Das Schicksal des Nordens* (1918), pp. 45, 349.

[2] Wuorinen, "The Efforts to Form a Union of Baltic States," *Current History*, July, 1924.

[3] "Norden," *American-Scandinavian Review*, August, 1923; cf. "Beretning om Den Danske, Den Norske Og Den Svenske Forening 'Nordens'" (1922).

important nations as the United Kingdom, the Dominions and the United States. An association of this nature could absolutely command the Seven Seas, and because of its great economic resources, it could dominate the Western World. Since the War of 1812, all of the disputes between the Empire and the United States have been peacefully settled, many of them being referred to arbitration. Lord Balfour recently said, "I am moved by a feeling, especially patriotic in its character, for the subgroup [of nations] which speaks the English language, and whose laws and institutions are rooted in British history. . . ." Despite past misunderstandings between the different branches of the English-speaking peoples, "they are capable, when they like, of a mutual comprehension which neither can attain to the same degree in their relations with other great nations of the European continent." [1]

Opinions differ as to the form which Anglo-American coöperation should take. Such organizations as the *English Speaking Union* of the United States and of the British Empire have no definite political policy; but they carry on educational campaigns for the purpose of promoting good feeling. The *Magna Charta Day Association*, an American organization, aims "to arouse the consciousness of our race everywhere to the necessity of holding more closely together and of permitting no enemy to sow seeds of trouble amongst us."

Some statesmen and writers have gone further and advocated a definite political understanding. In May, 1898, Joseph Chamberlain, the British statesman, made a striking speech, advocating an Anglo-American alliance. Probably in view of England's isolation in Europe and America's difficulties with Spain, this idea won the approval of many statesmen and publicists as a result of which the Anglo-American League was formed. While no alliance resulted, the political coöperation between these countries in foreign affairs was considerably closer thereafter than before.[2] The late George Louis Beer advocated a definite alliance between England and the United States, which, in his opinion, would save China from disintegration, hasten self-government in India, and

---

[1] *The Landmark*, June, 1923. Cf. E. Demolins, *Anglo-Saxon Superiority* (1898).
[2] B. A. Reuter, *Anglo-American Relations during the Spanish-American War* (1924), Ch. VII.

keep the peace in Central and South America.¹ On his American tour in 1923, Lloyd George advocated an "understanding" that the United States and England "will stand together for a rational peace." ²

7. PAN-LATINISM AND PAN-HISPANISM

There are 119,000,000 members of the Latin "race" in Europe—26.3% of its total population; while a good many more millions are to be found in Central and South America. Because of this racial affinity some discussion has arisen, not only in favor of a Pan-Iberian movement uniting Spain and Portugal, but for closer coöperation between France, Italy and Spain.³ Within recent years, this development has been confined, as far as Europe is concerned, to Italy and Spain. When the King of Spain paid the King of Italy a visit at Rome, in November, 1923, writers pointed out that at the time when Latin civilization was at its height—during the Renaissance—the Italian states were either under the rule of or in alliance with Spain. Moreover, thousands of Italian emigrants are living peacefully side by side with Spanish peoples in South America, forming another basis of racial sympathy.⁴

In the New World, the Pan-Latin movement has been of more importance. Pan-Hispanism, one phase of this movement, aimed to unite all the Spanish-speaking peoples of the world into one confederation, under the direction of Spain. It would thus include South and Central America, and according to some proponents of the idea, Porto Rico, Cuba, the Philippines, the Falkland Islands and Gibraltar.⁵ While this movement originated shortly after the American war with Mexico of 1846, it did not prosper until Spain had been driven out of its American colonies—in the war of 1898. In 1900 a congress of Spanish peoples was held at Madrid, which was followed by Hispanic-American meetings of

[1] *The English-Speaking Peoples* (1916), Ch. VIII.
[2] *N. Y. Times*, October 12, 1923.
[3] Cf. M. Barrès, "Les Liens spirituels de la France et de l'Espagne," *Revue des Deux Mondes*, June 15, 1924.
[4] *N. Y. Times*, Nov. 21, 1923; "La approximación Latina-Americana," *La Nueva Democracia*, March, 1924.
[5] Rippy, "Pan-Hispanic Propaganda in Hispanic America," 37 *Political Science Quarterly* (1922), 395. For an attack on the idea, cf. R. E. Garrigo, *America para los Americanos* (1910), Chs. V and VI.

one sort or another in 1908, 1911, 1912 and 1914, where the idea of restoring the old colonial empire of Spain, but upon a democratic basis, was discussed. In Madrid a Royal Hispanic-American Academy was founded to work for this end.[1] A number of special arbitration and commercial treaties have been made between Spain and Latin-American countries. Although an attempt to get King Alfonso XIII of Spain to tour South America to arouse enthusiasm for the movement was unsuccessful, an official mission was sent out in 1920 under the leadership of the Infante Don Fernando.[2] So taken with the idea of a rapprochement with Spain was the Mexican Board of Education that in March, 1921, it issued a circular to teachers, saying that heretofore the old Spanish rule in Mexico had been painted in too black colors and that a more kindly attitude toward Spain should be encouraged.[3]

Despite these efforts, the Pan-Hispanic movement did not arouse much popular enthusiasm. The Latin-Americans realize that whatever racial affinities they may have with Spain, no strong edifice can be erected upon the rotten structure of Spanish political life. At the present time, therefore, a more extended idea of Pan-Latinism seems to have engulfed the Pan-Hispanic movement. In 1922 a group of South American intellectuals joined in a demand for a Latin-American, as opposed to a Pan-American Union. This would not be a union of Latin-American governments or politicans, who, it is said, are under the control of the United States. But it would be a union of intellectuals who should aim to develop a new conscience among Latin-American peoples, as a preliminary step toward a confederation of a political nature.[4] After achieving a cultural union, the League proposes as a first political step, the creation of a Latin-American High Tribunal and a Supreme Economic Council. One of the first objects of any confederation must be to extinguish "foreign loans which mortgage the independence of peoples."[5] The movement is frankly directed against the United States. The Latin-American League

[1] F. Berenguer, *El Hispano-Americanismo* (1918), p. 17.
[2] A. Mousset, *L'Espagne dans la politique mondiale* (1923), p. 293.
[3] F. B. Deakin, "Spain and Hispano-Americanism," *Contemporary Review*, May, 1924.
[4] Cf. speech of Dr. José Ingenieros, *La Nueva Democracia*, Feb., 1923.
[5] Cf. p. 417.

advocates a "continental and pacifistic nationalism," [1] and it now publishes a periodical, *Renovación*, in which these principles are voiced.

8. THE PAN-AFRICAN MOVEMENT

Within recent years, racial self-consciousness has flourished more vigorously among the colored peoples than the white. One of its most recent and interesting manifestations has been the Pan-African movement. There are about 150,000,000 negroes in the world, practically all of whom are governed by white powers. The position of the negro is similar to the Jew—he has no real national state for his home, with the exception of such countries as Liberia, Haiti and Abyssinia. The radical wing of the Pan-African movement has adopted the slogan, "Africa for the Africans," and advocates the return of negroes scattered throughout the world to their native homeland, from which European powers must be ejected.[2]

In 1914 the leader of this movement, a picturesque Jamaican negro, Marcus Garvey, organized the Universal Negro Improvement Association with headquarters in New York. This association "advocates the uniting and blending of all negroes into one strong, healthy race. It is against miscegenation and race suicide. It believes that the Negro race is as good as any other, and therefore should be as proud of itself as others are. . . . It believes in the social and political physical separation of all people to the extent that they promote their own ideals and civilization with the privilege of trading and doing business with each other. It believes in the promotion of a strong and powerful Negro nation." Garvey took upon himself such titles as "President General," "His Supreme Highness the Potentate," "The Provisional President of Africa," the "Commander-in-Chief of the African Legion," and the "Head of the Distinguished Service Order of Ethiopia." [3] He also established negro orders of nobility,

---

[1] Cf. *Renovación*, July, 1923. See also J. F. Rippy, *Latin America in World Politics*, Chap. XII.

[2] De Warnaffe, "Le mouvement pan-nègre aux États-Unis et ailleurs," *Congo*, May, 1922.

[3] W. Pickens, "The Emperor of Africa," *Forum*, August, 1923; W. E. Dubois, "Back to Africa," 105 *Century* (1923), 539; M. Garvey, "The Negro's Greatest Enemy," *Current History*, Sept., 1923.

such as the Dukes of Uganda and Knights Commander of the Nile, as well as a corps of Black Cross nurses and a Black Star Steamship line. His "Nation" adopted a flag of Red, Black and Green, and an African National Anthem, while the Improvement Association held supposedly annual conventions. At the 1924 convention it unanimously approved the "idea of God as a creature of imaginary semblance to the black race;" and decided that the picture of Christ as a black man be immediately circulated among the Negro peoples of the world, and that steps be taken to have a crayon picture of the Virgin Mary as a black woman to be subsequently circulated. . . ."[1] Garvey claimed to have 6,000,000 negroes enrolled in his movement—undoubtedly an exaggerated figure. The failure of the Black Star line after expending $800,000 contributed by negroes, and Garvey's conviction in a lower court for fraud, gave the movement a temporary check. Undaunted, Garvey continued his agitation while on bail, especially through his paper, the *Negro World;* he also organized a new steamship company, called the Black Cross Navigation and Trading Company, while in the summer of 1924 he magnificently presided over another "International" convention in New York. He finally was sentenced to five years in a federal prison, but was pardoned before the end of his term and deported.

Some response to the Pan-African movement came from certain regions in Africa, where outbreaks against the whites were made.[2] Ethiopian Churches—native churches accepting Christian theology but retaining native morals—were also founded and became a center of political agitation.[3] On the other hand, the government of the negro republic of Liberia, in August, 1924, vigorously protested to the United States against Garvey's plan to colonize Liberia; it also instructed Liberian consuls not to visé passports of members of the Association going to Liberia from America.

Apparently the more conservative and better educated negroes had nothing to do with the Garvey brand of Pan-Africanism. They believe that the negro problem must be solved by working out a plan of coöperation with the whites, rather than by impos-

---

[1] *Negro World*, August 16, 1924.
[2] Delafosse, "Les points sombres de l'horizon en Afrique Occidentale," *Afrique française* (1922), p. 271, also p. 47.
[3] W. C. Willoughby, *Race Problems in the New Africa* (1923), p. 235.

sible efforts to get the negroes back to Africa where they would be confronted by all manner of hardships, if not starvation. But they have, nevertheless, believed that the relation between whites and blacks might be improved through an international racial organization. Consequently in February, 1919, the first Pan-African Congress was held, with delegates from about fifty countries. This Congress meets in an European or American city, where the color problem is discussed. The control of the Congress is in the hands of a permanent committee of three members from the three states having the largest number of negroes—Great Britain, France and the United States. While the Congress does not demand the creation of a negro state, the Garvey wing having been defeated, it does advocate the principle of racial equality, and an international code of law protecting natives throughout the world.[1]

9. THE PAN-ISLAM MOVEMENT

In the Near East, a number of racial movements have agitated, not only such independent countries as Turkey and Persia, but the colonial world. Pan-Islam, while essentially a religious movement, was also a racial movement inasmuch as it aimed to bring under a single theocratic government the colored peoples controlled by European powers. Of the 227,000,000 Mohammedans in the world, nearly half are under British rule, 30,000,000 are in the Dutch East Indies, and about 25,000,000 are subjects of France. All Orthodox Mohammedans were supposed to look to the Caliph at Constantinople, as their spiritual head. As Mohammedanism advocates a theocracy, in which the Caliph should exercise supreme spiritual and temporal power, this theory was plausibly seized upon by political leaders to agitate for the political union of all Moslems with Turkey—the home of the Sultan.

About 1876 the modern Pan-Islamic movement was started by Abdul Hamid, in order to increase his power. He constructed a railway to the Hejaz, which promoted Moslem pilgrimages to the Holy Places, and also increased Turkey's strategic hold over the Arabs. In 1903 a Pan-Islam society was founded in London, to

---

[1] Delafosse, "Le Congrès panafricain," *Afrique française* (1919), p. 53. Cf. also the *Crisis*, January and February, 1924. The Congress also advocated a negro member on the Mandates Commission.

For the resolutions of the second Congress, cf. *La Vie Internationale*, Nov., 1921.

establish a bond of unity between the Moslems throughout the world. If this movement had been successful, it would have destroyed many colonial empires. Consequently, European powers studiously attempted to wean the sympathies of their Mohammedan populations away from Constantinople. In some districts, such as the Sudan, Christian missions were rigorously excluded for the benefit of Islam. In 1921 Great Britain hesitated to enforce drastic peace terms upon Turkey out of fear of arousing the animosity of the Moslems in India.[1]

At no time, however, did the fears of Europe toward the Pan-Islamic movement materialize. The Moslems themselves are divided into a large number of sects, the two largest ones being the Sunni or Orthodox Mohammedans and the Shiahs, who refused to recognize the Ottoman Caliphate. Moreover, the Sultan of Morocco, the Mahdists of the Egyptian Sudan, the Senussi of the Libyan Desert, the Wahabis of Central Arabia, and the King of the Hejaz, never recognized the Caliph at Constantinople.[2] The final blow to the Pan-Islamic idea came in November, 1922, when the revolutionary Angora Assembly abolished the temporal power of the Caliph—that is, abolished the position of Sultanate. In March, 1924, the Caliphate was abolished altogether, and church and state in Turkey rigorously separated. Although the heads of different Oriental countries put in claims for the honor of being the "Pope" of Islam, no Caliph has since been recognized by any considerable body of Mohammedans. Whatever may be the outcome of the movements to establish the Caliphate outside of Turkey, the Western World may rest assured that Pan-Islam will not menace it, because of the hopelessly divided condition of Islam.[3]

10. THE PAN-TURANIAN MOVEMENT

As early as 1895, a new movement arose in Turkey, which directly challenged the Pan-Islam programme. This was the movement to unite all members of the Turanian race—the 10,000,000

---

[1] Mr. Montague, the secretary of state for India, was obliged to resign from the Lloyd George cabinet because he allowed the publication of a protest from India against the Treaty of Sèvres.

[2] I. Bowman, *New World* (1921), p. 441. Cf. *Moslem Schisms and Sects* (1920), tr. by K. C. Seelye; D. S. Margoilouth, *Mohammedanism*, Ch. V.

[3] Cf. S. M. Zwemer, *The Disintegration of Islam* (1916), Ch. III; E. Insabato, *L'Islam et la politique des Alliés* (1920), pp. 155 ff.

Turks, and 16,000,000 peoples who inhabit parts of Siberia, Mongolia, Manchuria, Turkestan, the Caucasus—under Turkish rule.[1]

Deserting the Pan-Islamic goal of Abdul Hamid, the Young Turk revolution of 1908 veered toward Pan-Turanianism. The Committee of Union and Progress adopted a policy of assimilation, and proceeded to stamp out the autonomy previously enjoyed by the non-Turanian peoples—the Arabs. In 1914 many Turks advocated joining the Central Powers in the war, because of the common racial origin of the Magyar and the Turk—both belonging to the Finno-Ugrian or Turanian race. Turkey was probably also influenced by the consideration that the destruction of the Russian Empire would free the Turanian peoples in Central Asia. But while the Turkish government acquired great strength following its defeat of Greece in 1922–1923, it apparently did little to stimulate the Pan-Turanian idea.

11. THE PAN-ARAB MOVEMENT

Before the World War, the Arabs were scattered about in Syria, Mesopotamia, Arabia and North Africa, separated from each other, but under Turkish or European control. Following the disastrous Russo-Turkish war of 1877, nationalist agitators took advantage of Turkey's weakness to propose a confederation of Arab peoples, headed by an Arab religious chieftain. However, the moderate policy of the Turkish Sultan, Abdul Hamid, and the construction of a railway from Turkey to the Hejaz, strengthened Turkish influence and caused Pan-Arabism to die out. Nevertheless, agitation from abroad continued, and in 1895 an Arab national committee was formed at Paris. Ten years later an insurrection broke out in the Hejaz and Yemen, Arab principalities, which the Turks had great difficulty in suppressing. In 1906 the Arab national committee proposed an Arab empire which would extend from Mesopotamia to the Isthmus of Suez, under the political and religious leadership of the Sherif of the Hejaz.[2]

[1] "Pan-Turanianism," *Encyclopedia Britannica*, 12th ed., vol. 33; Stoddard, "Pan-Turanism," 11 *Am. Pol. Sci. Review* (1917), 12; "X," "Le Panislamisme et le Pan-Turquisme," 22 *Revue du Monde Musulman* (1913), 179; Snouck-Hurgronje, "Islam and Turkish Nationalism," *Foreign Affairs* (N. Y), Sept.15, 1924.

[2] Stoddard, *The New World of Islam* (1922), pp. 169 ff.; E. A. Powell, *Struggle for Moslem Power in Asia* (1923), Ch. IX.

As a result of the repressive policy of the Young Turks, the Arab nationalist movement was stimulated. The demands of an Arab national congress held in Paris in 1913, were answered in Turkey by a reign of terror, spies, police and hanging. Following the outbreak of the War, the Turkish general, Djemal Pasha, executed a number of Syrian revolutionary leaders.[1]

When Turkey entered the War the Allies seized the opportunity of supporting the Pan-Arab movement as a means of striking the enemy. There were two outstanding Arab leaders, the Emir of the Nejd, Ibn Saud, and the Emir of the Hejaz, Hussein, a descendant of Mohammed. Because the latter Emir was more friendly to the British and because he ruled over the Holy Places of Islam, the British decided to give him their support. In a treaty of October 24, 1915, they promised to support Arab claims to independence in the territories outlined by Hussein, except in districts where previous agreements had been made with the French.[2] This meant that in return for revolting against Turkey, the Arabs would be given a state extending from the Suez Canal to Mesopotamia and as far north as Asia Minor, but apparently not including Syria and Palestine.

Despite this treaty, the aspirations of the Arab chieftains were not realized at the end of the War, partly because of the "imperialism" of the Allies, and because of a dispute over the terms of the treaty of 1915. Great Britain contended that it had exempted Syria and Palestine from the Arab state which it had promised to support. The Arab nationalists, on the other hand, contended that Syria was the heart of Pan-Arabism. Nevertheless, the Allies placed Syria under French mandate and Palestine—the home of Zionism—under British mandate; the only part of Arabia which was recognized as really independent was the Hejaz.[3]

As a consequence of the failure to fulfill the Pan-Arab ideal, revolts broke out in Syria and in Mesopotamia. England tried to mollify the Arabs by placing two sons of King Hussein upon thrones—Feisal in Mesopotamia (Iraq) and Abdullah in Trans-

---

[1] Djemal Pasha, *Memories of a Turkish Statesman*, p. 213.

[2] Apparently the British government has not published the official text; what purports to be a copy is found in Djemal Pasha, p. 210.

[3] In July, 1920, the French drove Feisal—Hussein's son—out of Damascus when he was carrying on his propaganda in favor of a united Arab state. Cf. R. Grousset, *Le Réveil de l'Asie* (3d ed., 1924), p. 51.

jordania, each under British control.¹ In 1923–1924 negotiations were carried on in an effort to link up these different Arab kingdoms into a confederation, to which it was hoped Syria would eventually adhere.² But these plans came to an untimely end, not only because of disagreement over the question of Palestine, but also because of renewed fighting in the fall of 1924 between the tribes of the Nejd and of the Hejaz, as a result of which King Hussein was obliged to flee from his capital. In the Treaty of Jeddah of May, 1927, Great Britain formally recognized Ibn Saud as ruler of the Hejaz.³

12. THE PAN-ASIATIC MOVEMENT

No part of the world seems to be immune from the contagion of racial nationalism. In the Orient, as well as in Africa, in Latin-America, or in Europe, propaganda has been circulated in favor of a union of color, for the purpose either of offering resistance to the whites or of dominating the world.

In 1913 a White Peril campaign was started in Japan by a distinguished editor, Mr. Tokutomi, in which he said, "We colored people must combine and crush Albinocracy. We must make the whites realize that there are others as strong as they." In a speech of May, 1913, Count Okuma declared that the "white races regard the world as their property and all other races as greatly their inferiors." ⁴

Anti-foreign sentiment has periodically expressed itself in China. The Boxer revolt of 1899 was a protest against foreign domination. A Boxer proclamation said, "The foreigners shall be exterminated; their houses and temples shall be burned; foreign goods and

---

¹ Article 25 of the Palestine mandate authorized Great Britain to withhold application of such provisions of the mandate as it deemed inapplicable to the territories lying between the Jordan and the eastern boundary of Palestine—Transjordania—subject to stipulations in regard to religious freedom and the open door. On September 23, 1922, the British government sent a memorandum, asking the Council to pass a resolution exempting certain provisions of the Palestine mandate from Transjordania. But "His Majesty's Government accept full responsibility as Mandatory for Trans-Jordan," *O. J.*, Nov., 1922, p. 1390. For Mesopotamia, cf. p. 388.

² *Asie française*, No. 212, June, 1923, p. 198.

³ Cf. "Political and Economic Trends in the Near East, 1927," *I. S.* Vol. III, No. 26.

⁴ A. M. Pooley, *Japan's Foreign Policies* (1920), p. 16.

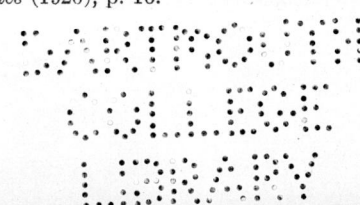

property of every description shall be destroyed. . . ."[1] The revolution of 1911 was partly a protest against the foreign "devils" who coveted China's wealth. In 1922 further anti-foreign demonstrations occurred, taking the form of an anti-Christian movement. Christianity was attacked on the ground that it was superstitious and linked up with imperialism and capitalism.[2]

After the repeated diplomatic defeats of China, whether at the Paris Peace Conference or the Washington Conference on the Pacific, many Chinese realized that Western powers would never save China from the clutches of her own revolutionists or from Japan. And some of them came to believe that perhaps China's best salvation lay in some form of political understanding with Japan.[3]

Many Japanese statesmen have advocated a Chino-Japanese Alliance, as the first step toward the "Fédération des Jaunes." Baron Hayashi, Ambassador to London, and M. Takahashi, at one time Prime Minister, were proponents of this idea. Following the passage of the Japanese exclusion law by the American Congress in 1924, journalists in Japan advocated the convocation in Tokyo of a Conference of Colored Races, and the formation of a League of Yellow Peoples.[4] Still more significant was the fact that at the fifth Assembly (1924) of the League, Japan supported China's demand for a seat at the Council—in striking contrast with her previous opposition to such a demand—and also the fact that Japan supported China at the Opium Conference in the fall of 1924. The subsequent rise of the Nationalist government at Nanking seems to have brought to an end immediate hopes of rapprochement.

But the Federation of Yellows, in the minds of some of its prophets, is not to be merely an association of China, Korea and Japan. It is to be all-Asiatic. In 1920, Soviet Russia seized upon the idea to convoke a Pan-Asiatic Conference at Baku, which was attended by 1,800 delegates from all parts of the Oriental world. The Congress spent most of its time preaching a Holy War against England. It adopted a Manifesto which reads:

[1] Quoted, H. A. Gibbons, *World Politics* (1922), p. 147. Cf. P. H. Clements, *The Boxer Rebellion* (1915), p. 72; P .Weale, *The Conflict of Color* (1910), p. 145.
[2] "The Anti-Religion Movement," 53 *Chinese Recorder* (1922), p. 145.
[3] A. Duboscq, *L'Évolution de la Chine, 1911-1921* (1922), pp. 133 ff.
[4] Buell, *Japanese Immigration*, p. 314.

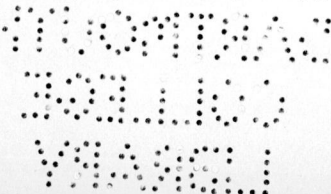

PROSPECTS FOR RACIAL NATIONALISM 93

"Arise, men of India, who live prostrate from starvation and slave labor!

"Arise, peasants of Anatolia, groaning under taxation, bled white by the userers!

"Arise, men of Arabia and Afghanistan, lost in your sandy wastes, and cut off the English from the rest of the world!

"Arise against the enemy of the human race, against imperialistic England!"[1]

Following the agreement of June, 1924, in which Russia gave up all its rights in China acquired under the old Tsarist government, it appeared as if Russia wished to lead a Pan-Asiatic movement. At any rate, the Russian Ambassador to China, Karahan, spoke of China as "an imposed-upon state, taking its rightful place in the world, with a true friend to help it, instead of cynically rude hypocrites to hinder." Moreover, the passage of the Japanese exclusion law brought Japan and Russia together, as illustrated by the treaty of January, 1925. A year previously, the Indian National Liberal party, passed a resolution in favor of a Federation of Peoples "for the emancipation of Asia."[2] The legend of the "King of the World," a yellow sovereign with divine power who is to come and rule over the world in the name of the yellow peoples, may possibly give popular support to this enterprise.[3] Russians were particularly active in assisting the Nationalist government in China.[4]

13. THE PROSPECTS FOR RACIAL NATIONALISM

Such are the movements to create racial "nationalities" or looser groupings. If they should pass from the stage of discussion to action, they would affect international relations vitally. Most of them, such as the Pan-German or the Pan-Slavic movements, would cut across the boundaries of existing states. The Pan-Hispanic movement seeks to wrench from the United States its colonial empire in Cuba, Porto Rico and the Philippines. To be realized, these movements would therefore necessitate a war.

---

[1] Sarolea, "Bolshevism and World Revolution," *Current History*, Feb., 1924.
[2] *N. Y. World*, Jan. 1, 1924.
[3] Ossendowski, "King of the World," *Century*, Nov., 1923.
[4] Cf. "The Rise of the Kuomintang," *I. S.*, Vol. IV, No. 8.

Agitation based upon racial distinctions, whether in peace-time or in war, would intensify ill-feeling and bitterness, to a greater extent even than that provoked purely by economic or nationalistic causes. There can be no more fearful prospect than an interracial war.

It is unlikely that any of these movements will go to the extent of upsetting existing nations and states. Few of them rest upon a genuine cultural desire for association under one government. In the case of the Scandinavian countries or the English-speaking peoples, it is conceivable that some form of association may be worked out. Nevertheless, if this proves so, it will be based not upon racial similarities but upon common ideals and institutions, which the mere physical factor of race cannot explain. The only thing in common which many of these peoples have, apart from a common racial origin which in itself is to be doubted, is antagonism to an outside foe. The colored movements of the world—the Pan-African, Pan-Islam, Pan-Arab, Pan-Turanian and Pan-Asiatic movements—owe what little strength they have at times possessed to resentment toward European and American imperialism, and exploitation by the white man. The recent recrudescence of the Pan-Asiatic movement is due to the unseemly way in which the American Congress handled the Japanese immigration question. The Pan-Latin movement in South America is directed against the "imperialism" of the United States.

In Europe, these racial combinations have been provoked by the same fears. The Scandinavian countries were drawn together during the World War out of fear that, isolated, they would fall prey either to the Central Powers or the Allies. Likewise Pan-Slavism was advocated as a means of resisting the "mounting flood of Germanism," throughout Europe.[1]

Should these artificial props be removed, it is improbable that such racial movements would attract a following. In view of the past aggressions of Japan in Asia, the Chinese will be always loath to enter into a combination subjecting themselves to Japan.[2] The Arab nomad of the Hejaz has little in common with his agricultural "brother," the Syrian peasant. On the other hand, the

[1] Leger, *Panslavisme*, cited, p. 317.
[2] Cf. Liang Shih-Yi, "China Faces the Modern World," *Current History*, Sept., 1924.

American negro is probably more different in culture from the Bantu of Africa than he is from the white man. The Japanese finds himself more at home in Paris or in London than he would in Lhasa or Delhi, or in any other capital which might be proposed for a Pan-Asiatic state.

Viewed from this standpoint, racial nationalism is a gross violation of the principle of self-determination and of democracy. Theories basing the state upon racial similarities would force peoples under one government simply because some psuedo-scientist, journalist or politician believed that in the distant past they had a common racial pedigree. The racial theory cares nothing about the present needs or wishes of these people—it looks only to a dim ancestry.

From whatever angle it be approached, race proves to be a totally unsatisfactory criterion of nationality. For that reason it is most likely to be abused for imperialistic ends. Back of the Pan-Slavic movement lurked Russia; back of the Pan-German movement lurked Germany; back of the Pan-Asiatic movement lurked Japan. When these movements have won the support of governments, it has been not for the purpose of fostering the cultural life of peoples, but of disguising illicit gains by euphemistic terms.[1]

[1] Some students nevertheless feel that recognition should be given to broad racial divisions. They therefore advocate, in place of or in addition to a League of Nations based on a "fictitious divergence of political interests," a League of Races. Snouck-Hurgronje, "L'Islam et le problème des races," 50 *Revue du Monde Musulman* (1922), p. 23.

CHAPTER V

ECONOMIC NATIONALISM

1. The Demand for Economic Self-Sufficiency.—2. The Diversity of Natural Resources.—3. Tariffs and International Relations.—4. Tariff Discriminations and "Wars."—5. Export Taxes and Embargoes.—6. The Monopoly of Raw Materials.—7. Trusts and Foreign Trade.—8. National Aid to Shipping.—9. Results of Economic Nationalism.—10. The Economic Motive and War.—11. The Example of the Saar.—12. The Justification of Economic Nationalism.

Nationalism has been accompanied by a demand not only for political but for economic independence. The nation-state has ordinarily believed that its existence in a jungle-world depends upon economic self-sufficiency—upon sources of raw materials and markets securely under its political control, so large and so diversified as to provide for its own needs, without reliance upon foreign countries. When a nation is fortunate enough to reach this stage, when it gets into the envious position of being able to supply its own needs and of having a surplus as well, it may venture into foreign markets. But if guided by the more extreme conceptions of nationalism, it does not do this in a spirit of exchanging international goods or services, but of "capturing" foreign markets and establishing "favorable" balances of trade.[1]

1. THE DEMAND FOR ECONOMIC SELF-SUFFICIENCY

Pure sentiment has brought much support to the idea of economic self-sufficiency. Nationalists advocate the patronage of home instead of foreign products, even if inferior in quality and higher in price, because of "patriotic" reasons. They have bolstered up such arguments with appeals to self-interest. If foreign competition is rigorously excluded, domestic business men may

---

[1] C. D. Burns, *Government and Industry* (1921), Chs. X and XI.

automatically increase their prices—which explains why many capitalists have been strong nationalists. Although the domestic consumer, of course, foots the bill, he is mollified by the argument that the importation of foreign goods, manufactured by cheap labor, would injure his own high standard and would mean cheap wages at home. In other words, economic self-sufficiency means the full dinner-pail. The nationalists—sometimes out of a false conception of self-interest—overlook the argument made by practically every economist since the days of Adam Smith, that instead of increasing the productivity of a nation, the policy of self-sufficiency decreases it because it means the production at home at a high price of some goods which may be produced, whether for geographic or labor conditions, more cheaply abroad. Or if they do not overlook it, they attempt to answer it by saying that if international trade were unrestricted, one nation, either because of its high standards, its geographic sterility or its industrial inefficiency, might find itself outdistanced in the production of *all* its wants by foreign powers. Yet such an unhappy *dénouement* is inconceivable. As we shall see, the raw materials of the world are so unevenly divided that each nation has certain geographic advantages which it pays to develop to the highest point of productivity. If the United States can produce steel more cheaply than Japan, Japan should buy from the United States. But if the United States devotes itself to the manufacture of steel, it cannot fill all its other needs. If Japan does not manufacture steel because it is unprofitable to do so, she will produce some more profitable commodity, such as silk. She will exchange her surplus silk for the surplus steel. Human wants are unbounded. They cannot be satisfied by gold; they can only be satisfied by goods. As long as this remains true, one nation will always be in the position of contributing certain goods not obtainable as cheaply in other parts of the world.

Other nationalists insist, with a great deal of reason, that if a nation should depart from the policy of economic self-sufficiency in favor of economic internationalism, it would be exposed to (1) exploitation by foreign monopolies of essential raw materials, in time of peace, (2) starvation in time of war. Suppose that Japan were dependent for its food upon China. If war should break out between the two countries, this food supply would automatically

98   ECONOMIC NATIONALISM

be cut off, and the nation without the necessary resources would go down to quick defeat.

So numerous and so bitter have been the commercial conflicts between nations that the division of the world into fifty odd airtight economic units, each isolated from the other, and each representing a nation, might be desirable. In fact, this is the aim of the economic nationalist, as far as his own country is concerned—complete economic independence from the outside world. Whatever theoretical advantages such a solution may have, it is subject to certain very fundamental limitations. Nature has not rationed out raw materials to the world with any regard for the needs of the nations inhabiting it. But with a prodigal want of symmetry, she has distributed these materials haphazardly, giving certain products in superabundance to one part of the globe, yet failing to provide it with products of equal or greater importance. This unevenness of materials and differences in aptitudes partly explains why, despite the nationalism of the present age, the total foreign trade of the world amounts to the stupendous sum of 65 billion dollars a year.[1]

2. THE DIVERSITY OF NATURAL RESOURCES

There are two kinds of raw materials, those, such as tin, which cannot be replenished by the efforts of man, and those, such as wheat, which may be reproduced. Naturally, nations regard the control of the first kind as more important than that of the second. There are minerals which are used for fuel and those which are used for construction purposes. The chief mineral fuels are coal and oil. Coal is especially important in connection with smelting iron. It has been popular to say that the nations possessing coal and iron rule the world.[2] The United States is the richest coal country in the world, having about one-half of the supply, and furnishing two-fifths of the world's annual production. Great Britain is second. On the other hand, such countries as Italy, Belgium, and, to a lesser extent, Spain, have virtually no coal and are obliged to import a supply from abroad.

For many purposes, oil has come to take the place of coal, particularly as locomotive fuel. At present about 98% of the oil

[1] In 1913 this figure was 42 billion.
[2] Tower, "The Coal Question," *Foreign Affairs*, September 15, 1923.

DIVERSITY OF NATURAL RESOURCES

in the world is produced in the United States, Russia, Mexico, the Dutch East Indies, Roumania, India, Persia and Galicia. Most of the oil of the world is under either British or American control. The remainder of the world, including most of Europe, must buy oil from those districts blessed with a supply.

Iron is the chief construction metal, the supply of which has been controlled by four countries—the United States, Germany, France and Great Britain. About fifty per cent of the world's iron comes from the Lake Superior region and Lorraine. The iron and steel industry is concentrated in three geographic units—the United States, England and Franco-Germany.[1] The United States leads the world also in the production of copper and of lead. On the other hand, it is dependent upon the outside world for such materials as copra, tin ore, platinum, antimony and asbestos. It imports manganese—necessary for the manufacture of steel—from Russia, India and Brazil; nickel from Canada. In normal times, the United States consumes one-third of the chromite produced in the world, relying upon Rhodesia and New Caledonia for its supply. While the United States consumes over half of the tin of the world, it produces less than one-fifth of one per cent of its requirements, relying upon Bolivia and Singapore for most of the remainder. Canada supplies the world with 85% of its asbestos.[2]

If we turn to the second type of raw materials, we find that the most important products are those from which we obtain our food and clothing. Although these products may ordinarily be reproduced, an intolerant nature has decreed that some of these products can be grown only in certain parts of the world. Two of the most important agricultural products are cotton and rubber. Of the 24 million bales of cotton used by the world annually, the United States produces about 60% and Egypt 20%. The people of Europe are dependent upon non-European sources of cotton, while Japan takes half the crop grown in India. Europe's supply of wool also comes mostly from South America and the British

---

[1] Leith, "The World Iron and Steel Situation in Its Bearing on the French Occupation of the Ruhr," 1 *Foreign Affairs* (1923), 136.

[2] J. E. Spurr, *Political and Commercial Geology and the World's Mineral Resources* (1923), Ch. XXXII; Gini, *Report on the Problem of Raw Materials and Foodstuffs*, the League of Nations, pp. 108, 133; G. O. Smith (ed.), *The Strategy of Minerals* (1919), Chs. I, III, V, VI, VII, VIII; Todd, "The World Crisis in Cotton," *Foreign Affairs*, Dec. 15, 1923.

Dominions. Sixty-eight per cent of the world's silk comes from Asia, most of which is consumed in the United States. Until recently Chile has supplied the world with nitrates.[1]

Rubber is also a commodity of the first importance, whether to the man who drives an automobile or to the more humble man who merely wears a pair of overshoes. In 1923 the world's export of rubber was $240,000,000, 77% of which went to the United States.[2] Ninety-five per cent of the rubber of the world comes from southeastern Asia, territory under the control of Great Britain, Holland and France.

Many nations of the world are obliged to import food. With the exception of Russia, Hungary, Roumania and Bulgaria, no country in Europe is in this respect self-supporting. Before the War, Europe consumed about three-fourths of the wheat exports of the world, the largest producer of which was the United States, and the second, Russia. The fact that Russia is the granary of Europe explains why the internal condition of this country will always be of international concern.[3]

Because of the varying resources of different countries, a great system of integrated exchange grew up in Europe before the War. In 1914 Germany was the best customer of Russia, Norway, Holland, Belgium, Switzerland, Italy and Austria-Hungary. She was the second best customer of Sweden, and Denmark, and the third best customer of France. She was the largest source of supply to Russia, Norway, Sweden, Denmark, Holland, Switzerland, Italy, Austria-Hungary, Roumania and Bulgaria. She was the second largest source of supply to Great Britain, Belgium and France.[4] Germany was the center of European industry, whether because of the peculiar commercial aptitudes of her people, or because of her raw materials. This position gave her political power and military strength. When, to weaken this influence,

[1] Curtis, "Fertilizers: The World Supply," *Foreign Affairs*, March 15, 1924; Bain and Milliken, "Nitrogen Survey," Part I, *Trade Information Bulletin*, No. 170 (1924), Supplement to U. S. Commerce Reports.

[2] Whitford, "The Crude Rubber Supply," *Foreign Affairs*, June 15, 1924; "Crude Rubber Survey," Part I, *Trade Information Bulletin*, No. 180, p. 1.

[3] Before the War, Russia contributed about one-fourth of the wheat, one-half of the barley, and nearly one-third of the oats to the world's trade. Rew, "The World's Grain Supplies as Affected by the Situation in Russia," *Reconstruction in Europe* (*Manchester Guardian Commercial*), August 17, 1922.

[4] J. M. Keynes, *Economic Consequences of the Peace* (1920), p. 17.

DIVERSITY OF NATURAL RESOURCES

the Paris Peace Treaties struck at Germany's economic system, they seriously affected the economic condition of Europe as a whole.

Although the United States is more nearly self-sufficient, because of a bounteous nature, than any other country in the world, it too is vitally dependent upon foreign markets, especially in regard to agricultural products. Our agricultural exports average over a billion dollars a year. Sixty per cent of our cotton, 20% of our wheat, and 40% of our tobacco is normally shipped abroad.[1] About 80% of our agricultural exports go to Europe; while our foreign trade constitutes about 14% of our total domestic trade.[2] Although it is popular to say that the United States has an especial interest in South America and the Pacific because of trade, statistics show that Europe is still our best customer. In 1928 our total trade with Europe was about $3,624,000,000, while with South America it was only $1,051,000,000, and with Asia, $1,823,-000,000.[3] In this year we did nearly twice the business with Europe that we did with Asia and three times as much as with South America. As long as this condition exists, the United States will always be affected by political conditions in Europe which impair Europe's purchasing power.

In the 17th and 18th centuries it was more possible for nations, living in an under-populated and undeveloped world, to live unto themselves than at the present day. In that period of history, international law did not clearly recognize the right of one nation to trade with another. To-day, however, every nation in the world admits merchants from other countries and recognizes the principle of international trade.[4] But despite the great diversity of commodities in the world and the manifest advantage of international trade, most nations still impose restrictions on such trade in an attempt to defy geography for the supposed benefits of their own merchants and national life, and out of respect for the still powerful dogma of national self-sufficiency.

---

[1] G. Nourse, *American Agriculture and the European Market* (1924), p. 283.
[2] Estimate of B. M. Anderson, *The Annalist, Annual Financial Survey and Business Forecast*, Jan. 5, 1925, p. 11. In 1898 the ratio rose as high as 22.6 and in 1919, 19.5. Cf. also H. M. Strong, "Distribution of Agricultural Exports from the U. S.," *Trade Information Bulletin*, No. 177.
[3] Department of Commerce Reports, Feb. 25, 1929.
[4] Cf. P. Fauchille, *Traité de droit international public* (8th ed., 1922), Vol. I, sec. 285.

3. TARIFFS AND INTERNATIONAL RELATIONS

The most common means of artificially stimulating domestic sources of supply is through the tariff—a tax levied on imports. Every important government in the world imposes tariffs, either for the purpose of revenue or for protection. In the first case, the tariff is imposed so as to produce the greatest amount of money; in the second case, it is imposed with a view to increasing the price of foreign goods so they will not compete so readily with domestic products. The tariff-for-revenue system was followed before the War by five European governments—Great Britain, Belgium, Denmark, the Netherlands and Turkey. The protective system was followed by the remaining countries of Europe, the United States, Japan and the British Dominions.[1]

Apart from tariff treaties,[2] international law imposes no limitations upon the height of tariff duties. Nevertheless, when these duties are so high as virtually to prohibit international intercourse, hardship to foreign merchants or consumers, and consequently international ill-feeling, results. European nations threatened to retaliate against the United States because of the excessive rates of the Dingley tariff of 1897; while much ill-feeling was aroused among Canadian and Japanese merchants over the Fordney tariff of 1922 which killed part of the trade of these merchants with the United States. The Allied debt to the United States can be paid only by exporting goods and services; the high tariff policy of the United States operates to exclude goods, and thus makes the payment of this debt very difficult.[3] Likewise the high tariff policies of most of the countries of the world, who do not wish to receive German imports, make difficult the solution of the reparation problem, since the reparations can in the long run be paid only in exports.

Whatever the social advantages of the small and poor nation-state may be, it presents many disadvantages from the economic standpoint. In the old empires of Germany, Russia and Austria-Hungary, 300,000,000 people lived and worked, and within the

---

[1] *Reciprocity and Commercial Treaties*, U. S. Tariff Commission (1919), p. 463. Cf. T. E. G. Gregory, *Tariffs: A Study in Methods* (1921), Ch. II.
[2] Cf. p. 135.
[3] Cf. p. 546.

borders of each of these empires trade was free, currency was uniform, and trade was stable and secure. When the empires of Russia and Austria-Hungary were broken up into nation-states following the World War, each, influenced by the doctrine of economic nationalism, immediately set up a high tariff wall,[1] making trade across the border virtually impossible. Railways were now cut in two, and traffic, which before the war had been subject to no interruption, found itself at a standstill. In some cases, a farmer who milked his cow in his pasture was obliged to pay an import duty on taking his milk to the barn! Merchants were obliged to do business in three or four different currencies and go through endless formalities in order to move trade.[2] As a result of such restrictions, the commerce between Hungary and Austria and Bohemia decreased from $300,000,000 before the War to $16,000,000.[3] Before the War Hungary had a boundary of 3,000 kilometers in length which was cut by 23 railways and 79 highways; but following the War, its reduced boundary of 1,450 kilometers was cut by 46 railways and 107 highways.

In the new Baltic states tariff rates also interposed obstacles to exchange which had been free under the old Russian Empire. After winning the Greek war of 1921, Turkey threw off the restraints imposed on her by treaty [4] and imposed duties ranging as high as 75% and 100% on flour and other commodities.[5] As soon as its status as a Free State was recognized, Ireland erected a tariff not only against English goods but against Northern Ireland. Great geographic areas such as the United States and Russia may follow a protective policy toward the outside world with comparative impunity because internal resources are so diversified and great. But when such a policy is adopted by tiny nations, having a population less than New York or Boston, it leads to suicidal consequences.

Great Britain wished to retain control over India partly because

[1] During a transitional period, all exports and imports were stopped except by special agreement, cf. p. 109.

[2] Cf. Hodac, "The Tariff Arrangements of the Succession States," *Reconstruction in Europe*, July 27, 1922.

[3] Teleki, *The Evolution of Hungary and Its Place in European History* (1923), pp. 188 ff.

[4] Cf. p. 481.

[5] "Le nouveau tarif douanier turc pour l'Anatolie," *L'Asie française*, April, 1923, p. 117.

it wished to prevent India from excluding British goods. Under free trade which the British government imposed on India, Lancashire merchants could market their goods in India at a price which feeble Indian manufacturers could not meet. It was not until 1917 that Great Britain finally agreed to the protection of Indian cotton manufacturers.[1] The question of tariffs likewise affects the attitude of the United States toward Philippine independence. At present trade between these two territories is free. Granted their freedom, the Filipinos would probably erect a high tariff which would interfere with the profits of American business interests, many of whom are consequently opposed to freeing these islands. But the argument works both ways, because the United States would also erect a tariff wall against Filipino goods, which might lead merchants in the Philippines to oppose independence. In either case, the independence issue is affected by the question of trade obstructions.

Excessive tariffs may also make the population problem more acute. The population of some states is naturally larger than that of others; and in some cases a state with a large population has a very small territory, as in the case of three world powers—Great Britain, Italy and Japan. The over-populated and the under-populated countries of the world may be listed as follows:

Over-populated	Density per square mile	Under-populated	Density per square mile
Netherlands	517.54	Canada	2.24
Belgium	666.22	Australia	1.8
Great Britain	389.57	United States	30.18
Germany	332.78	Brazil	9.29
Italy	332.01	Argentine	7.40 [2]
Japan	383.67	Russia	21.97

[1] *Colonial Tariff Policies*, U. S. Tariff Commission (1922), p. 334; P. Banerjea, *Fiscal Policy of India* (1922), Chs. III and IV. Cf. p. 340.

[2] *Statistical Abstract of the United States, 1921*, p. 907. The following table illustrates the increase in population of states (in millions):

	Population 1788	Rank		Population 1914	Rank
France	25	1st	United States	100	1st
Russia (in Europe)	25	2nd	Russia	90	2nd
Italy	15½	3rd	Germany	65	3rd
Germany	15½	4th	Austria	51½	4th
Great Britain	12	5th	Great Britain	45½	5th
Austria	11½	6th	France	40	6th
United States	3½	7th	Italy	35½	7th

Otlet, *Les Problèmes internationaux et les guerres*, p. 403.

TARIFF DISCRIMINATIONS AND "WARS" 105

Many of the over-populated countries have been able to support their people by following the policy of industrialization. They have imported most of their raw materials and exported manufactured goods in return. Under-populated countries are ordinarily agricultural countries, whose natural advantage it should be to produce raw materials. On the other hand, over-populated countries possess a natural advantage in labor and industrial efficiency. Exchange therefore should spring up. This process, however, comes to an abrupt end when an under-populated and agricultural country such as Canada, Australia or the United States erects excessive protective tariffs which divert domestic efforts from agriculture to manufacture and which exclude the foreign manufactured products of over-populated countries. If the latter cannot sell their manufactures they cannot buy food. If under-populated countries artificially divert capital from agriculture into manufacture, their supply of food for foreign consumption will decline. It is conceivable, therefore, that the growing population of the world will force tariff questions into great international prominence in the future. Confronted by impassable tariff walls, over-populated countries will have no other alternative than to starve to death or to fight for political control over agricultural regions.[1]

4. TARIFF DISCRIMINATIONS AND "WARS"

In many countries it has been customary to discriminate in favor of the goods of certain countries as against goods from elsewhere, in return for similar concessions. Most of the European countries have entered into special tariff agreements for this purpose. Many of them follow what is called a multiple-schedule tariff system, in which the legislature enacts a general tariff which applies to all countries with which special commercial treaties have not been made. Lower duties, usually called "conventional" rates, may be granted to countries in return for similar concessions as fixed by treaty.[2] In France, the maximum tariff rates are about four times the minimum. Since the United States has been unable to make special concessions to France, our trade has been

---

[1] Cf. p. 311 for over-population as a cause of imperialism.
[2] G. M. Fisk and P. S. Peirce, *International Commercial Policies* (1923), p. 121; *Reciprocity and Commercial Treaties*, pp. 505-10; W. S. Culbertson, *Commercial Policy in War Time and After* (1919), Ch. X.

subject to heavy discriminations. In 1919 34% of the total imports of American goods into France was discriminated against by tariff charges which goods from more favored countries did not have to pay. Following the signature of a commercial treaty with Germany in August, 1927, France attempted to subject still other imports from the United States to maximum duties. The American State Department registered a protest, and following promises of modifications in the administration of the American tariff in regard to French goods, the French government allowed the status quo to remain.[1] Haiti has a reciprocity treaty with France according heavy reductions to French goods, thus placing American products at a disadvantage. Other commercial nations include the cost of transportation in the value of goods assessed for ad valorem duties, thus discriminating against goods from a distance. Venezuela requires a fee of five cents for handling packages brought in from foreign countries, except the United States, where the duty is thirty cents. Spain follows a policy of special bargaining, and for some years it has given special favors to certain imports from Colombia, Ecuador, Portugal, Andorra and Italy.[2]

A large number of "tariff wars" have occurred between European countries which did not wish to enter into tariff treaties either for political or economic reasons, or who objected to discrimination. In 1888 Italy and France fought such a war, each applying retaliatory duties to the other. At the end of ten years, Italian exports to France had declined 57%, while French exports to Italy had declined 50%.[3] A similar war between France and Switzerland broke out in 1893, which lasted for two and a half years, with disastrous consequences to trade. In 1891 Russia and Germany got into a similar controversy in which Germany imposed a duty on Russian breadstuffs 115% higher than on like products imported from America, Hungary, Roumania and Argentina.[4]

---

[1] Cf. "The Franco-American Tariff Dispute," *I. S.* Vol. III. No. 17. In October, 1928, the French government protested that the United States had not lived up to its agreement. *New York Times*, October 28, 1928.

[2] W. McClure, *A New American Commercial Policy* (1924), pp. 36, 205 ff. 276.

[3] Culbertson, cited, pp. 264 ff.

[4] P. Ashley, *Modern Tariff History* (3d ed., 1920), pp. 71, 334. Also "Report on Tariff Wars between certain European States," Cd. 1938 (1904), Vol. XCV, p. 701.

In 1905 Austria and Serbia also fought a "Pig War" over tariffs.[1] Similar tariff wars have been fought between France and Roumania, Germany and Canada, and Germany and Spain.

Bargaining for special favors by means of commercial treaties has been a well-known method of world diplomacy. In November, 1908, Portugal signed a treaty with Germany, in which Portugal received most-favored-nation treatment for her wines, and a monopoly of the German market of "Port" and "Madeira." Germany also agreed to cancel the Hohenlohe concession which Portugal had granted to the detriment of British interests, in the Madeira islands. In return for these concessions, Germany was given special concessions in the Portuguese market.[2] For a number of years the United States also followed this bargaining policy. Under the tariff act of 1890 the President was authorized to penalize certain imports, otherwise free, from countries which levied on produce of the United States duties which were "unequal and unreasonable."[3] By virtue of this power, the President made ten agreements which, however, were terminated in 1894. The tariff act of 1897 gave the President virtually a free hand in negotiating for special concessions. Under its authority the President entered into a number of "Argol Agreements" which, however, are not in force to-day. In 1854 the United States entered into a treaty with Great Britain providing for the reciprocal admission free of 28 articles between the United States and Canada—a treaty which was in force eleven years.[4] In 1875 the United States entered into a similar reciprocity agreement with Hawaii.[5] In 1904 the United States threatened to impose a penalty duty of three cents per pound on coffee, otherwise admitted free, if Brazil did not make special concessions to American flour. As a result of this threat, Brazil reduced her duties on American flour, through an arrangement which lasted until 1923. This led to a protest from Argentina on the ground that her flour trade with Brazil was hindered by this preference to the United States. The

---

[1] G. P. Gooch, *History of Modern Europe, 1878-1919* (1923), p. 417.

[2] G. Young, *Portugal, Old and New* (1917), p. 329. Cf. the protocol of the treaty of Nov. 30, 1908, 4 Martins (3d Series), 896.

[3] Cf. F. W. Taussig, *Tariff History of the United States* (7th ed., 1922), p. 279, for comments.

[4] Convention of June 5, 1854, *Treaties of the U. S.*, Vol. I, p. 668.

[5] Convention of Jan. 30, 1875, *ibid.*, p. 915.

only reciprocity agreement to which the United States is now a party is with Cuba. Under a convention of 1902, articles from Cuba are admitted to the United States at 20 per cent less duty than charged on other foreign goods, and vice versa.[1]

In 1916 the Allies held an economic conference in London at which they mapped out plans to carry on a commercial struggle against Germany, after the close of the war, with the object of keeping Germany out of the world markets by different forms of discriminations. During the reconstruction period, the Germans were to be denied most-favored-nation treatment. But because of the Fourteen Points the Allies were only partially successful in carrying out this programme at the Paris Peace Conference.[2]

Such discriminations cause more immediate trouble in international relations than excessive tariffs which apply equally to all. When one nation is given economic preference over another, unless in return for an economic quid pro quo, international animosity is bound to result. Moreover, the constant changing of tariff rates, oftentimes without notice, means great hardship to foreign business men: each modification of a tariff schedule may mean the failure of a foreign firm.

5. EXPORT TAXES AND EMBARGOES

Restrictions are imposed by nation-states not only upon imports but upon exports. The most common form of the latter restriction is the *export tax*. Sometimes this tax may be legitimately imposed for revenue purposes and to conserve resources; at other times, it may be imposed to extort large sums from foreign consumers totally dependent upon the materials upon which the tax is levied. While import duties are ordinarily paid by the home consumer, the export tax usually is paid by the foreigner, a fact which explains why such taxes figure so prominently in diplomatic relations. Ordinarily, undeveloped countries impose export taxes on raw materials. With the exception of Venezuela, all the South American countries impose such taxes.[3] Chile's export tax, which is principally on nitrates, provides more than half her total customs

---

[1] Convention of Dec. 11, 1902, *ibid.*, p. 353; there are certain exceptions; for the provisions of the Act of 1922, cf. p. 123.

[2] Cf. p. 126.

[3] F. R. Rutter, *Tariff Systems of South American Countries*, U. S. Tariff Series, No. 34 (1916), *passim*.

EXPORT TAXES AND EMBARGOES

receipts. In Bolivia, the export taxes, chiefly on tin, comprise one-third of the customs. The export tax imposed by Yucatan on sisal increased the price of sisal to the American farmer; and the export taxes imposed by the Mexican government in 1920–1922 on oil decreased the profits of American oil producers to such an extent that the American government protested against the tax on the ground that it was confiscatory.[1] In Europe, France imposes export taxes on cast iron; while Roumania, Spain, Czechoslovakia, Portugal, Jugoslavia and the Baltic states impose such taxes on certain raw materials. Because of these various restrictions the imports of raw material by Italy declined from what was considered the minimum requirement of 16 million tons to 8 million tons in 1920.[2]

Commenting on such practices, the Economic Committee of the League of Nations declared, "Doubtless, as a general principle, the tariff policy of States is one of their sovereign rights, and there are no doubt circumstances in which export duties or other restrictions may be necessary, *e. g.*, in cases where other sources of revenue are lacking, or where they are an indispensable element in the economic system. Nevertheless, it is undesirable as a matter of principle to employ measures of this kind under normal conditions as weapons of economic warfare."[3] A similar declaration was made by the International Chamber of Commerce.

Sometimes nation-states entirely prohibit the export of products by means of *embargoes*. During the War, this form of control was exercised by belligerent states to prevent trading with the enemy. And in the case of the new states of Europe, it was followed after the war, with the result that trade across new frontiers was nearly at a standstill. In some instances, the hardships resulting from this policy were attenuated by special "compensation" agreements under which a limited amount of products peculiar to one country would be exchanged for particular products in another.[4] While most of these embargoes eventually were lifted, some nations utilize them as a permanent policy. Canada prevents the exportation of pulp-wood from Crown lands, and in 1923 the

[1] Cf. p. 405.
[2] Tittoni, *Modern Italy* (1922), p. 174.
[3] *Report on Raw Materials*, C. 10 M. 7, 1923, II, p. 9.
[4] Cf. E. M. Friedman, *International Commerce and Reconstruction* (1920), pp. 78 ff.

parliament empowered the government to impose an embargo on such exports from private sources—to the detriment of the American paper industry which is dependent upon Canadian pulp.[1]

6. THE MONOPOLY OF RAW MATERIALS

Finally, governments have established *export-controls*—sometimes for the purpose of exacting monopoly prices from the foreign consumer. In Formosa the Japanese government controls a camphor monopoly upon which the outside world is dependent. The Italian government rigidly controls the production of citric acid in Sicily—which furnishes the United States with 95% of its supply—through an organization called the Camera Agrumaria. Likewise, the Yucatan government controls the export of sisal to the United States. Seventy-five per cent of the world's sisal—a product from which binding twine is made—comes from the state of Yucatan in Mexico. In 1915 the Yucatan government fixed a production tax on sisal and authorized the establishment of a "Reguladora"—a commission which was given a monopoly of the sisal trade. Assisted by an American banking group, this commission increased the price of binding twine to the American farmer several hundred per cent. When the Reguladora went bankrupt in 1920, through over-extension, it was succeeded by a new control agency, called the "Exportadora," likewise financed by American banks.[2]

Ever since 1870, the government of Brazil has controlled similarly the price of coffee through a system called "valorization." Under this system several states of Brazil buy up and hold the coffee crop until foreign prices for coffee reach the level at which they desire to sell.[3] In two years, they increased the price of coffee on the New York exchange one hundred per cent. Ecuador has also followed the "valorization" plan in the case of cacao beans, while Greece rigorously controls the production of currants.

[1] W. S. Culbertson, *Raw Materials and Foodstuffs in the Commercial Policies of Nations*, Annals of the American Academy of Political and Social Science, March, 1924, p. 38. The embargo has also been used to prohibit the entry of foreign goods. One of the most flagrant examples was the Canadian cattle embargo imposed by England nominally to protect England against diseased cattle, but really to protect the English farmer; W. P. Neal, "The Canadian Cattle Embargo," 92 *Nineteenth Century and After* (1922), 221.

[2] L. Crosette, "Sisal," *Trade Information Bulletin*, No. 200.

[3] "Valorization of Brazilian Coffee," *Trade Information Bulletin*, No. 73.

In 1919–1920 the price of rubber in the East Indies dropped to 10d., compared with its average price before the war of 5s. 6d. This led the British government to pass the Stevenson Restriction Act of 1922, the purpose of which was to control the production and export of rubber so as to raise the price to about 1s. 3d. As most of the rubber was purchased by the United States, this act so agitated American manufacturers that they persuaded Congress to appropriate money to discover new sources of rubber supply.[1]

In some cases, these export controls, as in the case of the Stevenson Restriction Act, have been for the legitimate purpose of protecting the domestic producer from over-extending himself or of conserving a limited source of supply. But in other cases, the export control has been adopted for the purpose of bleeding foreign consumers.[2] The most extreme form of foreign trade monopoly is practised by the present government of Russia. All purchases or sales of goods relating to Russia must take place via the medium of the Foreign Trade Monopoly. In the United States, one branch of this monopoly is the Amtorg Trading Corporation.

7. TRUSTS AND FOREIGN TRADE

Many governments not only control imports and exports for the purpose of developing a self-sufficient nation, but they also give political support to domestic business interests for the purpose of capturing the foreign markets of the world.[3] In many countries, the organization of combinations is encouraged for this purpose. Before the War there were 600 cartels in Germany, combinations embracing practically every industry in the Empire, which dominated the export trade and prevented the competition of German producers in the foreign market. In France and

[1] Whitford, "The Crude Rubber Supply," *Foreign Affairs*, June 15, 1924. The Stevenson act was terminated in November, 1928.

[2] In 1924 an attempt was made in the American Congress to establish an export-control over wheat. The McNary-Haugen bill (S. 2012) would establish an Agricultural Export Corporation which should purchase certain agricultural commodities when their price fell below the level to which prices have generally risen since the war. The purpose of this bill was to separate the export surplus from the domestic crop, and to hold up the exports until the desired price could be obtained. For a discussion, cf. *Congressional Digest*, May, 1924, pp. 263–277. The proposal was finally vetoed by President Coolidge, in May, 1928.

[3] " Trade promotion," government rivalry for concessions, etc., is mentioned in the section on Imperialism. Cf. p. 431.

Belgium, similar syndicates of iron and steel, coal, glass and other industries operated. The silk-ribbon manufacturers of France and Germany conducted their export business under a joint agreement. In Japan an export organization of textile manufacturers is dominant in the cotton goods trade of China; while the Japanese tea trade is controlled by a national "tea council." In Great Britain, large export combinations have also arisen. A coal trust has given British coal a monopoly of South American markets. British cement and machinery manufacturers have formed a combination to carry on an aggressive campaign for foreign trade. Four London firms fix the price of silver throughout the world.

In 1905 the Baltic and White Sea Conference, consisting of the shipowners of eleven different countries, was organized to control competition in the shipping of northern Europe.[1] In 1883 an international rail syndicate was formed, which divided up the rail business of Europe between British, German and Belgian firms. An international cartel of glass factories also controlled the glass trade.[2] The Stinnes steel interests embrace mines and furnaces throughout the whole of central Europe. Some writers fear the formation of a sulphur trust between American, Italian and Spanish interests.[3] European steel and chemical cartels were formed in 1926–1927. Nitrates and iodine are controlled through a British selling agency acting through Chile. Potash is controlled by combinations of German producers. Crude rubber and gutta-percha are controlled by combinations of producers in the British and Dutch colonies; quinine is controlled by a combination of Dutch planters; tin is controlled by a combination of British producers; mercury is controlled by a common selling agency of Spain and Austrian mines; coffee and sisal are likewise controlled by the governments of Brazil and Yucatan. Quebracho—used for tanning purposes—is controlled by another combination.[4]

In many cases these trusts are international. A combination of

[1] Cf. *11th Annual Report*, The Baltic and White Sea Conference, 1921.
[2] L. Woolf, *International Government* (1916), pp. 328 ff. international armament combinations are discussed on p. 521.
[3] Tittoni, *Modern Italy*, p. 178.
[4] Letter of Secretary of Commerce Hoover to Senator Capper, March 6, 1924. Cf. S. 2843, 68th Cong., 1st sess., a bill to exempt from the anti-trust laws, associations engaged in purchasing raw commodities in foreign countries for importation into the United States.

buyers in Holland, Denmark and Germany have a strong influence on the cotton-seed market.[1] Before the War, an international "shipping ring," the Atlantic Shipping Trust, controlled ocean transportation; while international oil trusts, such as the Royal Dutch Company, a Dutch-British concern, have had tremendous influence upon the price of oil. Moreover, many great oil trusts, such as the Royal Dutch Shell and the Standard Oil Companies, have entered into price-fixing agreements.[2]

Perhaps the most important international organization of this type is the European steel cartel, composed of the steel manufacturers of Germany, France, Belgium and Luxemburg—countries which contain a third of the world's steel capacity. This cartel was established in April, 1926, and was to run for five years. Under this cartel each country is assigned a quarterly production quota, as determined by a three-fourths vote of an administrative board composed of one member from each country. Members of the syndicate agree to pay monthly into a common fund the equivalent of $1.00 a ton of raw steel produced; and any country which exceeds its quota must pay an additional $4.00 per ton for each extra ton. Any country which falls below its quota will be paid for each ton short, a rebate equivalent to $2.00 a ton, but this rebate is restricted to ten per cent of the quota. It was stated that the German quota was fixed at 43.5 per cent of the total, France 31.19, Belgium 11.56, Luxemburg 8.55 and the Saar 5.20. These quotas were based on each country's rate of operations during the first quarter of 1926. Apparently each country agreed to respect the home markets of the others. Some arrangement for dividing sales on foreign markets was apparently also made.[3]

International cartels for the purpose of eliminating competition between national groups, or fixing prices, etc., also exist in the case of European rails, potash, and rayon. The potash agreement exists between French and German producers, and it is interesting to note that the French government owns a large share of the French mines.[4]

---

[1] *Coöperation in American Export Trade*, Report of the Federal Trade Commission (1916), p. 5
[2] P. E. de la Tramerye, *The World-Struggle for Oil* (1924), p. 67.
[3] W. S. Tower, "The New Steel Cartel," *Foreign Affairs*, January, 1927.
[4] Domeratzky, "The International Cartel Movement," *Trade Information Bulletin*, No. 556. U. S. Department of Commerce (1928).

While international agreements of this character remove rivalries between different business groups, such agreements may work hardships upon countries not represented in the cartel in question and upon the consumer generally. Sooner or later therefore some form of control, perhaps of an international nature, may be placed over such organizations.

Sometime trusts have been guilty of "unfair competition" in foreign markets, chief of which is dumping. Either for the purpose of keeping up domestic prices or for the purpose of freezing out foreign competitors, they have sold their products upon the foreign market at a cheaper price than they do at home. While trusts in Germany and in the United States followed this practice before the War more widely than trusts in other countries, dumping was also practiced by firms in Belgium, France, Austria and Japan.[1]

Many nationalistic governments deliberately encourage the formation of trusts to engage in foreign trade. Although the United States prohibits unlawful combinations in restraint of trade at home, it passed an act in April, 1918, called the Webb-Pomerene Act, which declared that the Sherman Anti-Trust law did not apply to trusts organized to carry on foreign trade.[2]

8. NATIONAL AID TO SHIPPING

Many governments also assist this movement to capture foreign trade by granting ship subsidies to domestic companies. This policy is followed by France, Belgium, Holland and Italy,[3] and was adopted indirectly by the United States in the White-Jones bill in 1927. Other countries have given bounties—or cash sums—to merchants for exporting certain commodities.

Still other countries, such as the United States, Spain, France and Sweden, reserve coastwise trade for their own vessels.[4] Foreign ships putting into Portugal are obliged to pay dues in gold, which means they must pay about forty times as much as a Portuguese vessel paying in Portuguese currency. Any vessel calling at a Spanish port, which has not sailed from a Spanish point of origin, must pay a double tonnage tax. Roumania imposes an

[1] J. Viner, *Dumping: A Problem in International Trade* (1923), Chs. IV, V.
[2] 40 Stat. 517.
[3] *National Restrictions on Marine Transportation*, International Chamber of Commerce Brochure No. 28, March, 1923, p. 49.
[4] *National Restrictions on Marine Transportation*, cited.

export tax on freights, from which, however, the Roumanian state line is exempt. Materials required by French government departments, if imported, must ordinarily be carried in French vessels. Across the Atlantic, Chile and Peru recently reserved the coasting trade to national vessels. The result was the monopoly of shipping by one Chilean firm, and an increase of one hundred per cent in freights. A ton of wheat can be carried from Chile to England, 7000 miles, for 30 shillings; but it now costs 36 shillings to carry a ton 700 miles from one Chilean port to another.[1] Other countries, such as Italy and Czechoslovakia, require that emigrants going abroad be transported in national ships.

9. RESULTS OF ECONOMIC NATIONALISM

These measures of economic nationalism are of two types, the *defensive*, such as a protective tariff which immediately affects the domestic consumer more than the foreigner; and the *aggressive*, such as the export tax which usually falls on the foreigner, and those other devices by which governments lend their support to private enterprise for the purpose of capturing foreign trade. As we have seen, the defensive type of economic nationalism, while more legitimate from the standpoint of international solidarity than the aggressive type, has led to a number of international disputes. But when a government grants its merchants engaged in *foreign* trade cheap banking facilities, exemption from taxation, preferential railway rates, subsidies, and other forms of support, international commercial competition ceases to be private and becomes political and diplomatic. In this type of aggressive competition, the nation which is the strongest, in the political and military sense, will probably win.[2]

[1] A. Hurd, "Open Seas and Closed Ports," *Fortnightly Review*, Jan., 1924.
[2] As a committee of the International Chamber of Commerce at its Rome session in 1923 declared, "This Congress notes with regret a growing tendency on the part of some nations to view the exports from and imports to their countries as national commerce and so to claim the right to discriminate in favour of vessels of the national flag against vessels of an alien flag, in regard to the marine transportation of such goods and passengers.

"The Congress considers that such action is contrary to international rights because international commerce is not, and cannot be the exclusive concern of any individual nation and that while every nation is entitled to subsidize its own shipowners or traders . . . no nation is entitled to claim exclusive rights in connection with its international commerce. . . ."

Confronted by foreign monopolies, many countries have attempted to enact protective legislation, such as anti-dumping laws. Domestic legislation of this sort has, however, usually proved ineffective. International monopolies have so many ramifications that they usually escape the control of any one nation.[1] Foreign selling monopolies may also be matched by domestic buying combinations; or domestic monopolies may be encouraged to go out and give battle to foreign concerns. This is the policy which recent administrations have proposed as the best solution for the United States. Yet it is a policy of commercial warfare, to which will be added the bitter competition of governments, each backing a private business concern. Such methods of control are typical of the whole doctrine of economic nationalism. They certainly will not keep the peace.

10. THE ECONOMIC MOTIVE AND WAR

Extreme economic nationalism not only supports the doctrine of commercial warfare but also of political warfare. It strives for the annexation of territory containing materials and markets which it needs, and of seaports giving it access to the sea.[2] This factor explains many of the wars of the last century. Boundary disputes have arisen, not so much over the nationality of the inhabitants of the district in question, as over the control of raw materials in the district. When Germany won the war of 1870 against France, German scientists insisted that the boundary be drawn so as to give to Germany the most valuable iron-fields in Europe—located in Lorraine. While through an error, the line was drawn so as to include only half of these fields, the annexation nevertheless placed Germany in control of about one-third of the iron of Europe[3] which together with the coal of Silesia and the Ruhr made her a great industrial power. Germany's military supremacy was based on iron and coal.

Just before the outbreak of the war in 1914, French troops were withdrawn ten kilometers from the German frontier, as evidence

[1] In his letter to Senator Capper, Secretary Hoover said, "Such combinations cannot of course be effectively reached under the Sherman Act, as they are or can be seated outside of our jurisdiction." Cf. *American Banana Company v. United Fruit Co.*, 213 U. S. (1909), 347.

[2] W. Sombart, *Krieg und Kapitalismus* (1912).

[3] Eckel, *Coal, Iron and War* (1920), p. 329.

of French good faith. Whatever the diplomatic justification of the act, the economic result was almost disastrous. Before the war the Allies had a combined annual capacity of 22,500,000 tons of iron as against 21,500,000 for the Central Powers. But as a result of the French withdrawal and the German occupation of Belgium, great mines and factories fell into the hands of Germany which increased her iron capacity to 27,500,000 tons and decreased Allied capacity to 16,500,000. Only the intervention of the United States turned the balance.[1]

At the Paris Peace Conference a dominant motive of the Allies was to destroy this supremacy of Germany in coal and iron, and her commercial supremacy generally. This was done by confiscating all her foreign property, by compelling her to make certain coal deliveries to the Allies, and also by annexing certain territories.[2] The return of Alsace-Lorraine transferred to France the iron supremacy of Europe, while the Saar and Silesia settlement weakened Germany's coal supply. To-day Germany needs about 20 million tons of iron more than she produces, while France has an exportable surplus of 18 million tons. If she is to operate her blast-furnaces, France needs German coke. Exchange of some sort must therefore spring up—either voluntarily or by compulsion. France apparently decided to adopt the latter method when in January, 1923, she occupied the Ruhr, the great mining center of Germany. With the conclusion of the commercial treaty of August 17, 1927, between Germany and France, the opposite policy of voluntary economic coöperation seems to have been adopted.

11. THE EXAMPLE OF THE SAAR

At the Paris Peace Conference, the problem of reconciling ethnic principles with economic claims arose in the case of the Saar valley. This valley had been an integral part of Germany and at least 90% of its population of 650,000 are Germans. Nevertheless, France desired to annex the territory because it contains coal resources of about 18 billion tons. The one outstanding argument against this annexation was that it would repeat the German seizure of Alsace-Lorraine. Moreover, under a system of international

[1] Eckel, p. 80.
[2] Cf. p. 535.

exchange, Germany could have been obliged—as in fact she was elsewhere—to make coal deliveries, a provision which, however, was too insecure for France who insisted on having some definite form of political control over the mines.

A compromise between the principles of economic and ethnic nationalism was finally worked out and embodied in the Treaty of Versailles. "As compensation for the destruction of the coal mines in the north of France and as part payment toward the total reparation," Germany ceded to France the full ownership of the coal mines of the Saar basin. To-day these mines are operated by the Mining Administration of the French government. While Germany did not cede the territory as such to France, she did renounce in favor of the League of Nations, in the capacity of trusteeship, the government of this area.[1] But the inhabitants retain their German citizenship, while the existing laws and judicial system are maintained, unless the Commission decides that change is necessary. After fifteen years—or in 1935—a plebiscite by communes shall determine whether the population wishes to continue under the League régime, or be united with either France or Germany.[2]

Meanwhile the territory is governed by a Commission of five, appointed by the Council of the League of Nations.[3] According to the treaty, this Commission must include one citizen of France, one native of the Saar not a citizen of France, and three members belonging to three neutral countries. They are appointed for one year, but they are eligible for reappointment. This Governing Commission has all the powers in the Saar which belonged to the German Empire, Prussia or Bavaria. Nevertheless, while this form of government may be more desirable from the standpoint of the local inhabitants than annexation to France, and while, theoretically, the Commission is responsible only to the League of Nations Council, during the first three years of existence it was practically under the control of the French foreign office. One of the so-called neutral members was said to be a Dane who had lived most of his life in

[1] Arts. 45–49, Treaty of Versailles. Apparently Germany retains sovereignty but cedes jurisdiction, as in a lease. Cf. p. 464.
[2] Art. 50, Ch. III, of annex, Treaty of Versailles.
[3] The constitution of the Commission, *O. J.*, March, 1920, p. 50, declares that it has no interest except the welfare of the Saar people.

THE EXAMPLE OF THE SAAR

Paris, and one member appointed to represent the Saar was not only unpopular with his own people, but was obliged to resign after being charged with perjury. The Treaty of Peace authorized the incorporation of the basin within the French customs union, and also the use of French money in the territory, in connection with the mines. Although the treaty provided for a local police force to maintain order, the Commission allowed French troops to occupy the territory. Following the protest of the German government, these troops were reduced in number.

While the Saar is in many respects thus under French influence, the native inhabitants have been given some protection. They may send in petitions to the Council of the League through the Governing Commission,—a right which they frequently invoked to criticise the economic and political policy of the Commission on the ground that it was pro-French. The Treaty of Peace provided that the Commission should secure the views of the elected representatives of the district before changes in the old German laws could be made, or new taxes imposed. Before 1922 the Commission consulted only the local councils; in March of that year an Advisory Council was established, composed of thirty representatives, elected by the inhabitants of the territory. A small technical committee to advise the Commission was also set up.

Discontent in the Saar came to a head in the early part of 1923. Following a strike, which was probably occasioned by economic grievances but which the Commission interpreted to be political—occurring at the same time as the occupation of the Ruhr—a "provisional decree" was issued severely punishing any criticism of the Commission, the League of Nations, or the Treaty of Versailles.[1] This decree was so drastic that at the request of the British government, the Council held an inquiry as to the general administration of the Saar at its meeting of July, 1923. Although the decree in question had been withdrawn, the Council inquired at great length into the Saar administration. The president of the Saar Commission was questioned as to conditions in the Saar, as a result of which a resolution was finally passed reminding the world that the Commission is collectively responsible to the League for the execution of its duties. It also said that the withdrawal of

[1] Text, *O. J.*, 1923, p. 421.

the foreign garrison was desirable as soon as the local force was strong enough to maintain order.[1]

In April, 1926, the French chairman of the Saar commission was succeeded by a Canadian—a change which reduced somewhat French influence. In the following year the Council, of which Germany was now a member, voted to establish an international Railway Defense force of 800 men to take the place of the French garrison which should now be withdrawn.[2]

From the economic standpoint, the Saar has been better off than Germany and probably most other parts of Europe. From the beginning the budget has been balanced, except during the 1923 strike. The Commission has also been successful in operating the railroads. Although the Commission is now more responsible to the Council than originally, French influence still appears strong. Even if the Commission's responsibility to the League should become absolute and exclusive, the system of government established in the Saar would violate the principle of self-determination because it is a system in which the local inhabitants do not directly participate, and which has been imposed from the outside. While the Saar system is better than the extreme nationalistic solution of annexation, it imposes a disagreeable task upon the League. If saddled with other tasks of a similar nature in the future, the League will have a burden which will be extremely difficult to carry.

Other territorial settlements at the Peace Conference were similarly influenced by economic considerations. Poland demanded Upper Silesia and Teschen because of their mineral wealth; she demanded Galicia because of its oil, and Danzig because of its great importance as a port. Czechoslovakia and other of the Succession States demanded territory, not so much on ethnic grounds as in order to gain lands which would enable them to be economically self-sufficient. Jugoslavia wanted the Banat because of its food supply. Likewise Lithuania demanded the port of Memel in order to have a secure access to the sea. Italy demanded the port of Fiume, so as to prevent it from taking trade

---

[1] *O. J.*, 1923, p. 930.
[2] *O. J.*, April, 1927, p. 417. For an excellent general discussion of the Saar, cf. F. M. Russell, *The International Government of the Saar*, University of California Press, 1926.

JUSTIFICATION, ECONOMIC NATIONALISM

away from the Italian port of Trieste. Greece demanded western Thrace because of its agricultural resources. Whenever possible, these economic claims are hidden under appeals to labored statistics showing that the nationality of the inhabitants justifies annexation. In many of these cases, however, the powers want to control the territory, not out of sympathy for its inhabitants, but because of its resources. If trade were free and secure across boundary lines, this scrambling for territory—which sooner or later leads to war—would become unnecessary. Until the economic is divorced from the political frontier, permanent peace will not become a reality. Probably half of the international disputes in which the world is perpetually involved would be eliminated if it were possible freely to trade between one part of the world and the other.

12. THE JUSTIFICATION OF ECONOMIC NATIONALISM

In view of the fatal consequences to which the policy of economic nationalism leads, why do nations refuse to give it up? As a matter of fact they are beginning to desert this policy, to an extent which will be discussed in the next chapter. More progress has not been made in this direction chiefly for four reasons:

I. In the absence of foreign competition, the policy of economic nationalism has tended to establish monopolies in every country following such a policy, out of which a few capitalists may extract large profits from the consumer. These capitalists therefore advocate the continuance and extension of nationalistic policies under the name of "patriotism."

II. A nation fears that if it became dependent on foreign sources of supply, it would be more than ever at the mercy of the foreign monopolies described above.

III. It may also fear that the free interchange of goods produced in a country having a high standard of labor with the goods of a country having a low standard, would pull down the high-standard country to a coolie level. It seems, however, to be generally agreed by economists that the high wages in the United States are not due so much to the protective tariff as to mass production and to labor efficiency. Wages in England, morever, are much higher than on the continent, although England is a free-trade country.

IV. A nation fears that in case of war, economic internationalism would leave it at the mercy of a foe having control of the resources essential for victory.

There is something to be said in favor of each of these last three arguments. Nevertheless, the policy of economic nationalism has proved a poor means of meeting the danger. It has not prevented foreign monopolies of essential raw materials from exploiting the consuming world; and instead of averting wars, it has increased their number in order to secure control of "necessary" sources of supply. The best solution of all these problems, therefore, must be international. Until the institution of war is banished from the world, nations will probably cling to the policies of economic nationalism, despite their fundamental weaknesses. While the third part of this book will point out the extent to which war is being banished, the next two chapters will discuss the means which have already been taken to guarantee and to control international trade, and of improving the conditions of labor in backward countries so that they will not compete unfairly with high-standard-labor countries.

CHAPTER VI

ECONOMIC INTERNATIONALISM

1. The Commercial Treaty.—2. Most-Favored-Nation Treatment.—3. National Treatment.—4. Freedom of Transit.—5. Free Access to the Sea.—6. Freedom of Navigation.—7. Limitations on Tariffs.—8. International Control over Communications.—9. Unfair Competition.—10. Coöperation in Agriculture.—11. Economic Coöperation During the War and Through the League of Nations.

It has been impossible for one power to annex the whole world or even to annex territory enough to supply all of its wants. International trade has therefore leaped over tariff walls. The sheer necessities of geography have tended to break down the more extreme forms of economic nationalism. In fact, it is the practice of such protectionist countries as the United States to impose very low duties on goods, especially raw materials, which it is impossible to produce at home.[1] A vast skein of commercial treaties, most of which have been made between two countries but many of which are multinational, has attempted to regularize international trade, giving the merchants of one nation the right to trade in another nation, subject to the protection of its laws. These treaties have begun to embody principles of economic internationalism, the extension of which eventually may lead to a unified world.

1. THE COMMERCIAL TREATY

As a rule, the ordinary commercial agreement provides that "there shall be reciprocally full and entire freedom of commerce and navigation between the territories and possessions of the two High Contracting Parties." The treaty of commerce between the United States and Germany of December 8, 1923,[2] is one of the most interesting treaties the United States has ever made. It

[1] Cf. Culbertson, *Raw Materials*, cited, p. 21. Also Fisk and Peirce, *International Commercial Policies*, Ch. XI.
[2] Cf. for text, 68th Cong., 1st sess., Executive D.

guarantees to the nationals of each party the right to carry on a wide range of activities in the territory of the other, including the right to lease land for certain purposes. Corporations and associations of either country shall have their status recognized in the other. Elaborate provisions are made for the licensing of commercial travelers. Most interesting of all, the treaty gives the nationals of one country the same right to recover for injuries or death in the other country, as the citizens of that country themselves enjoy. The treaty also guarantees religious freedom.

While foreign merchants may thus enter a country to carry on trade, the ordinary commercial treaty of the United States does not limit the tariff duties which may be imposed on foreign goods. Such treaties do nevertheless attempt to abolish different forms of discrimination, whether between different foreigners, or between foreigners and nationals.

2. MOST-FAVORED-NATION TREATMENT

Most-favored-nation treatment means that no discrimination will be made against the trade of one foreign nation in favor of another,—one nation will be given the same treatment as the most favored. For example, under a most-favored-nation treaty between France and England, France would automatically receive the same reduction in duties which England granted to Italy. In the past the most-favored-nation principle has been subject to two different interpretations. The unconditional interpretation, followed, at least until recently, by European nations, says that when one party to a most-favored-nation treaty makes a concession to a third party, whether gratuitously or for compensation, it must be automatically extended to the other party. Under this interpretation, no exclusive tariff favors are permissible as long as the treaty is in force. But in Europe this rule has been violated, in spirit, by the practice of European governments to grant a low tariff on certain articles so minutely defined that articles of the same general type from another country could not profit by it under the most-favored-nation clause. For example, Italy imposes a higher duty upon cottonseed oil than upon other oils used for the same purposes, but which do not come from the United States. Another country imposes a high duty on a certain brand of hats, which come primarily from the United States. This rather

MOST-FAVORED-NATION TREATMENT 125

dishonest practice, as well as the fact that most-favored-nation treaties are not always in force between European nations, makes possible the special bargaining and the tariff wars described in the last chapter.

The second, or conditional interpretation, on the other hand, openly holds that the most-favored-nation clause applies only to gratuitous concessions, and that if, for example, Cuba should reduce her duties on American goods in return for similar reductions by the United States, no third power could claim such reductions, even though, in the absence of a treaty provision, it offered to make the same concessions.[1] This interpretation, followed by the United States until recently, would not prevent the signature of tariff preference and reciprocity agreements granting special favors to some nations, described in the last chapter.[2] In other words, conditional most-favored-nation treatment did not make for perfect international equality.

A step toward the elimination of discriminatory tariff agreements was taken by the United States in October, 1923, when in an exchange of notes it terminated its preference arrangement with Brazil and accepted the principle of unconditional most-favored-nation treatment, except in the case of Cuba and our dependencies.[3] A similar provision was written into other commercial agreements. It appears that the United States has now adopted, in practice, the European policy of the unconditional most-favored-nation treatment which, if it becomes universal, will prevent all tariff discriminations, as long as such treaties are in force.

A second step—aggressive in nature—and aimed to prevent the imposition of discriminatory duties on American goods by foreign countries—was taken in section 317 of the Tariff Act of 1922.[4] This section provides that when the President finds that a country discriminates against the commerce of the United States, he may impose additional duties on imports from such a country, and if this procedure is not effective in removing the discrimina-

---

[1] Cf. J. B. Moore, *Digest of International Law*, Vol. V, pp. 257 ff.; *Reciprocity Agreements*, cited, Ch. 9; Fisk and Peirce, Ch. XII; Culbertson, *Commercial Policy in War Time and After*, pp. 192 ff.
[2] Cf. p. 106.
[3] *U. S. Treaty Series*, No. 672.
[4] 42 Stat. 944. Cf. W. McClure, *A New American Commercial Policy as Evidenced by Section 317 of the Tariff Act of 1922* (1924), pp. 26 ff.

tion, he may prohibit the entrance of its goods into this country entirely. For example, if France continues to discriminate against American salmon, the President may impose discriminatory duties on French imports into America.

Any form of retaliation is a dangerous mode of procedure in international relations. In the case of the American tariff act this danger is increased by the act's inconsistency. The act makes it possible to penalize even colonial preferences practiced by foreign countries, despite the fact that the United States grants such preferences in its own dependencies.[1] The act in effect condemns certain acts when practiced by foreign powers but by implication sanctions them when practiced by ourselves. The only advantage of this act is that it gives the United States a club with which it may force nations to remove tariff inequalities. A more effective method of removing discriminations would be by negotiating an international most-favored-nation treaty, providing for unconditional equality of treatment throughout the world. It is especially necessary that disputes over the interpretation of such a treaty should be determined by an international tribunal, in order to do away with the evasions of the most-favored-nation principle which have been so numerous in the past. It is doubtful, however, whether states will ever accept such a treaty unless it is accompanied by some limitation on the height of tariffs. As the recent controversy between France and the United States shows, state A may not be willing to grant most-favored-nation treatment to state B if state B severely restricts the entrance of the goods of state A by means of a high if non-discriminatory tariff.

In the Treaty of Versailles, Germany was obliged to grant most-favored-nation treatment to the Allies, who however undertook no similar obligation to Germany. These obligations were to last only five years unless extended, twelve months previously, by the Council of the League.[2] As the Council failed to take this action, these one-sided obligations came to an end in January, 1925. If the Allies now wish to receive most-favored-nation treatment from Germany, they must be prepared to accord her the same rights in return.

[1] Cf. p. 443.
[2] Articles 264–280, Treaty of Versailles.

3. NATIONAL TREATMENT

A second principle of non-discrimination, which goes much further, is called the principle of *national treatment*. This means that there shall be no discrimination between foreigners and citizens, in the exercise of certain rights specified in the treaty concerned. In many treaties it is customary to provide that foreigners shall not be subject to higher shipping charges or general taxes than citizens.[1] The commercial treaty between Germany and the United States contains such provisions. It guarantees that charges for warehousing, tonnage, pilotage, lighthouse, quarantine, and internal taxes generally shall not be higher for Germans than for Americans. In the Treaty of Versailles, Germany was obliged not to tax aliens (from Allied countries) higher than her own citizens. The economic commission of the Genoa Conference recommended that this principle be extended generally.[2] In the A and B mandates, foreigners are given the same right to trade, and so forth, as the nationals of the mandatory power.[3] Probably the most important step toward establishing the principle of national treatment was taken at the Geneva conference on communications, held under League auspices, where a convention and statute on the International Régime of Maritime Ports was signed. In this statute each party agrees reciprocally to grant the vessels of every other contracting state "equality of treatment with its own vessels" in regard to freedom of access to the ports under its control. Except for special reasons, a state may not levy customs duties in a maritime port higher than at any other part of its customs frontier.[4] While this as well as other agreements exempts coastwise trade, its ratification nevertheless would remove much of the bitterness which shipping discrimination has caused in the past.

While the acceptance of unconditional most-favored-nation treatment, as well as national treatment in fiscal and shipping matters, would go far toward establishing commercial peace, it

---

[1] Cf. for shipping, Art. II, Treaty of July 3, 1815, between Great Britain and the United States, *Treaties of the United States*, Vol. I, p. 624.
[2] *International Economic Conference at Genoa*, April–May, 1922, Cmd. 1667, p. 73.
[3] Cf. p. 453.
[4] Agreement of December 9, 1923, *O. J.*, January, 1924, p. 271.

would not prevent a country from locking up its resources unnecessarily, blocking the passage of goods across its territory or extorting monopoly prices from a needy, outside world. The questions of high tariffs and excessive export taxes, which do not discriminate between different foreign countries, would still remain unsolved.

4. FREEDOM OF TRANSIT

An indirect approach to these problems has been through the principle of *freedom of transit*. This does not mean freedom to import goods for consumption within a country without the payment of duty. But it means freedom to ship goods to a third country across the territory of an intervening state. This principle was embodied in the treaty of 1846 between the United States and Colombia, in regard to the Isthmus of Panama; it was accepted by Bulgaria, Serbia and Roumania in the Treaty of Berlin of 1878; it was also recognized in a treaty of 1904 between Chile and Bolivia, in a treaty of 1905 between Sweden and Norway, in an agreement of 1908 between Germany and Portugal, and in an agreement of 1914 between Greece and Serbia. It has been applied in about a dozen treaties in regard to colonies in Africa.[1]

In his Fourteen Points, President Wilson advocated the suppression, as far as possible, of international economic barriers and the establishment of equal commercial conditions,—a principle recognized in Article XXIII of the Covenant, where members of the League agree "to make provision to secure and maintain freedom of communications and of transit and equitable treatment for the commerce of all Members of the League." The same principle was embodied in the peace treaties, in which Germany, Austria, Hungary and Bulgaria promised to give freedom of transit across their territories to the Allies.[2] It was also recognized in a large number of separate agreements following the War, particularly by the Succession States at the Portorose conference;[3] and in the "minority" treaties, where the Allies were granted freedom of

---

[1] For the Treaty of Berlin provisions, cf. Arts. 8, 37, 48, 69 *State Papers*, 749; cf. the Anglo-German agreement of July 1, 1890, Hertslet, *Map of Africa by Treaty*, Vol. II, p. 647; and British-Belgian convention of March 15, 1921, Cmd. 1327; and Fauchille, cited, p. 489. For the Chile-Bolivia Treaty of Oct. 20, 1904, cf. 98 *State Papers*, 763.

[2] Cf. Part XII of the different treaties.

[3] "The Portorose Conference," *International Conciliation* (1922), No. 176.

transit across Poland, Czechoslovakia, Jugoslavia and Roumania. Soviet Russia may ship goods across the Baltic states to the sea,[1] while Germany has the privilege of shipping goods from east Prussia across Polish territory to Germany.[2]

In March, 1921, the League of Nations convened a conference at Barcelona, attended by 44 governments, which produced an international Freedom of Transit Convention.[3] In it the signatory powers agree to treat equally all goods in transit across their territory, and not to impose duties upon the act of transit. A declaration was also signed, recognizing the right of a state having no seacoast to a maritime flag.[4] As a result of these different agreements, one European country may now securely ship its goods to another European country, in peace time, without being obstructed by the tariff walls of a third state.[5]

5. FREE ACCESS TO THE SEA

One phase of the problem of freedom of transit has demanded special attention—the problem of *free access to the sea*. Excluded from the great thoroughfares of the world's trade, the markets of an inland nation may be fatally curtailed. As a result of the World War, the number of landlocked states in Europe was increased from two to six, each of which clamored for a seaport. That this demand was legitimate was recognized by President Wilson in the case of Poland; and by the Treaties of Peace in which Austria and Hungary were guaranteed free access to the Adriatic, and in which Bulgaria was insured "an economic outlet" to the Ægean.[6] Under the old diplomacy there was only one method of satisfying this aspiration and that was by annexation,—a method which Poland proposed to follow in the case of Danzig; Lithuania, of Memel; Italy, of Fiume; and Bulgaria, of Kavala or Dedeagatch.

[1] Cf. annex to Art. 16, convention of February 2, 1920, between Lithuania and Russia, *T. S.* 289; Art. 8, treaty of Oct. 14, 1920, with Finland, *T. S.* 91.
[2] Treaty of April 21, 1921, *T. S.* 308.
[3] Convention and Statute on Freedom of Transit, Barcelona, April 20, 1921, *T. S.* 171.
[4] *T. S.* 174.
[5] The Geneva Conference of 1923 extended freedom of transit to electric power. For the convention, cf. *O. J.*, January, 1924, p. 283.
[6] Art. 311, Treaty of St. Germain; Art. 294, Treaty of Trianon; Art. 48, Treaty of Neuilly.

If free access to the sea can be obtained only by the annexation of ports regardless of the wishes of the inhabitants, irredentist movements will continue to trouble the world. Fortunately, statesmen have been able to work out schemes which will give landlocked states a secure access to the sea, unobstructed by the tariff walls of foreign states, but by means which recognize the ethnic principle involved. These schemes have taken two forms, (1) the internationalization of ports, (2) free zones.

Danzig.—While Danzig has a population of more than 200,000, the great majority of which is German, it is also a Baltic port upon which Poland is dependent for access to the sea. In an effort to satisfy both of these conflicting considerations, the Peace Conference declared Danzig should be a Free City under the protection of the League. Its people could draw up a constitution in agreement with a High Commissioner, who would be the permanent resident representative of the League. The economic interests of Poland are safeguarded by provisions which assure to Poland, not only a passive freedom of transit, but active participation in control of the port. A Danzig Port and Waterways Board, with an equal number of Polish and Danzig members, and a neutral chairman, has control of the ports, waterways and railways of the Free City, in order to insure to Poland the free use of the port for economic purposes.[1] Poland also has control of the foreign relations of the Free City, while she has been allowed to establish a naval base at the entrance of the harbor. Disputes between Poland and Danzig are settled if possible by the High Commissioner; although both parties retain the privilege of appealing to the Council of the League.[2]

Between 1921–1924 a great many initial difficulties arose in working out this arrangement to the satisfaction of both Poland and Danzig. A large number of disputes were referred to the High Commissioner, a majority of which were later appealed to the League Council. In the summer of 1923 the League cleared up most of these disputes; and the Council session of March, 1924, was the first meeting in its history at which the Danzig question did not arise. Despite these disputes the commerce of Danzig

[1] Danzig-Polish convention of Nov. 9, 1920, *T. S.* 153.
[2] For the Constitution of the Free City of Danzig cf. *O. J.*, Spec. Sup., July, 1922.

FREE ACCESS TO THE SEA

in 1923 was 75% greater than it had been in 1912 when the port was in German hands. One-quarter of the commerce in 1922 was German, one-quarter Danzig, one-eighth British. Half of the goods transported out of Danzig by rail in 1921 went to Poland.[1]

While this system of an international protectorate has not been followed as far as other ports are concerned, the same end has been accomplished by other means. Many countries have voluntarily established free ports or zones into which foreign goods might be imported without the payment of duty. By this means great commercial centers have been built up; and in many cases materials have been imported into a free port, manufactured and then reshipped. Trieste and Fiume were free ports of this nature under the Austro-Hungarian régime. The Hanseatic cities of Lübeck, Bremen and Hamburg maintained free zones after entering the German Empire. The free zones in Germany on August 1, 1914, were maintained by the Treaty of Versailles; while Germany was obliged to lease to the Czechoslovak State areas in Hamburg and Stettin.[2] Copenhagen and Gibraltar have likewise been free ports.[3] Outside of Europe, free ports will be found in such flourishing centers as Singapore, and Haifa, in northern Palestine. The establishment of free zones in Mexico and the United States for the purpose of building up foreign trade, has also been proposed.

Salonika.—Not only in the case of Hamburg and Stettin but in Salonika, free zones have been placed under the guarantee of treaty. In 1914 landlocked Serbia demanded an outlet to the Ægean. While Greece would not give up the political control of the territory concerned, she signed a convention giving to Serbia a perpetual lease in a certain district in Salonika which, for customs and administrative purposes, was to be considered Serbian territory. This district was to be under Serbian administration; and Greece promised not to burden this commerce with any charges nor to interfere with Serbian commerce entering or leaving the port. While the War prevented the signature of this con-

---

[1] *Saar Basin and Free City of Danzig*, Information Section, League of Nations (1924), p. 23.
[2] Articles 328, 363, Treaty of Versailles.
[3] Fisk and Peirce, *International Commercial Policies*, pp. 153 ff.

vention, a new treaty was finally concluded in May, 1923.[1] A new agreement enlarging the Jugoslav Free Zone was signed on October 11, 1928. By this means Serbia is given practically the same use of Salonika as if she had full political control.

Memel.—A solution combining some of the principles applied in Danzig and in Salonika was applied to the port of Memel— inhabited by a majority of Germans, but upon which Lithuania, as well as Poland, nevertheless depended for access to the sea. After a long controversy, the disposition of this port was finally referred by the Conference of Ambassadors to the Council of the League of Nations. A commission, headed by an American, Mr. Norman H. Davis, drew up a convention, which provided for the transfer of Memel to Lithuania, but guaranteed the city an autonomous form of government,[2] and also declared Memel to be a port of international concern, subject to the Barcelona freedom of transit convention. The control of the port was placed in the hands of a Harbor Board under the direct control of the city. To it is attached an Economic Supervisory Committee consisting of three members representing the economic interests dependent on the port, a member from Memel, one from Lithuania, and one from Poland, appointed by their respective governments. This Committee supervises the management of the port. If its recommendations are disregarded, appeal may be had to the Council of the League. Moreover, the city of Memel undertakes to lease to the Polish government for 99 years areas necessary for its shipping, which shall be placed under the régime of a free zone.[3]

6. FREEDOM OF NAVIGATION

For many years the world has ceased to tolerate obstructions in the navigation of rivers running through more than one state. The principle of freedom of navigation was laid down in the Euro-

---

[1] "Die servische freizone in Saloniki," *Neue Zürucher Zeitung*, Jan. 30, 1924. At the first Lausanne conference, Greece offered Bulgaria the same facilities at Salonika as had been granted Serbia. But Bulgaria refused to accept such a lease on the ground that her control would be too weak. No further steps have been taken to fulfill the promise to give Bulgaria an "economic outlet" to the Ægean sea. Cf. Minutes, *Lausanne conference*, Cmd. 1814 (1923), p. 457. For text of Convention of May 10, 1923, cf. *Europe Nouvelle*, August 16, 1924.

[2] Cf. p. 229.

[3] Cf. draft convention, Arts. 38–48, *O. J.*, January, 1924 (Part II), p. 137.

pean peace conferences of 1814 and 1815 in regard to the Rhine, Danube and Scheldt. In 1859 the principle was extended to the Po. The Treaty of Versailles declared "international" the Elbe, the Oder, the Niemen and a part of the Danube not affected by previous agreements.[1] On these international rivers Germans and foreigners must be given equal treatment. The principle has also been applied, if in varied forms, to the Congo and Niger in Africa, and to the St. Lawrence, Amazon, Rio Grande and Mississippi in the Americas. At the Barcelona conference a convention was signed applying these principles of free navigation to all "navigable waterways of international concern" under the jurisdiction of the contracting parties.[2] In 1868 provision was made for a Central Commission of the Rhine; while a part of the Danube river has been under the control of an international Danube Commission—an extremely interesting experiment in administration.[3] The Elbe and Oder were also in 1919 placed under international commissions, on which Germany is outvoted; and a new international commission was set up to administer navigation on the newly internationalized part of the Danube.

At least three canals of international importance have been internationalized. In 1888 eight powers signed the convention of Constantinople providing that the Suez Canal shall always be open in time of war as in peace, to every vessel of commerce or of war, without distinction of flag.[4] In the treaty of 1901 between the United States and Great Britain, the Panama Canal was placed under a somewhat analogous régime.[5] Germany was obliged to make similar provisions in regard to the Kiel Canal in the Treaty of Versailles.[6] In 1921 the German government refused to allow the passage through this canal of a French ship carrying contraband to Poland in its war against Russia, on the ground that such pas-

---

[1] G. Kaeckenbeeck, *International Rivers* (1920), Peace Handbooks, No. 149, Art. 331, Treaty of Versailles.
[2] *T. S.* 172, 173.
[3] J. P. Chamberlain, *The Régime of the International Rivers: Danube and Rhine;* and Hostie, "Les actes du Danube et de l'Elbe," *R. D. I. L. C.*, 1923, p. 247; F. B. Sayre, *Experiments in International Administration* (1920), p. 84 ff.
[4] Convention of Oct. 29, 1888, 79 *State Papers*, 18; E. A. Whittuck, *International Canals*, Peace Handbooks, No. 150.
[5] Treaty of Nov. 18, 1901, *Treaties of the U. S.*, Vol. I, p. 482.
[6] Arts. 380–386, Treaty of Versailles.

sage would be a violation of German neutrality. The dispute was placed before the World Court which decided against Germany on the ground that the treaty applied equally in war as in peace and that the canal was analogous in this respect to the Straits.[1] The striking thing about these canal treaties is that the canals were built, with the exception of the Suez Canal, by a single nation and upon national territory; yet because of their great importance to the world, they have been placed under some kind of international servitude.

Likewise freedom of navigation has been guaranteed through straits, located partly within the jurisdiction of one or more powers. In a treaty of 1881 Chile and Argentina guaranteed free navigation in the Straits of Magellan,[2] and the United States and Great Britain applied the same principle to the Straits of Fuca in 1846. Among the most important straits are the Bosphorus and the Dardanelles, connecting the Black and the Mediterranean Seas. Russia has been dependent upon this outlet to market its grain in Europe. Conventions of 1856 and 1871 attempted to internationalize the Straits; but their weakness was illustrated in 1914 when Turkey closed the Dardanelles to Allied commerce. In the Straits convention of July 24, 1923, the Allies attempted to strengthen the international position of the Straits by obliging Turkey to agree to their free use by neutral merchant vessels in time of peace and of war.[3] A Straits Commission, with a Turkish president and representatives of France, Great Britain, Italy, Japan, Bulgaria, Greece, Jugoslavia, Roumania and Russia, a total of nine members, supervises these guarantees; it must make an annual report to the Council of the League of Nations.

Under the old theories of the nation-state, those countries deprived of ports, rivers, canals or straits would simply have to do without, unless they chose to fight. Under the newer theories of economic internationalism, those countries blessed with these natural or even artificial sources of communication share them with the remainder of the world. The economic frontier is thus gradually being divorced from the political frontier.

[1] Case of the S. S. Wimbledon, Series A, *Collection of Judgments*, No. 1, Publications of the Permanent Court of International Justice, June, 1923.
[2] Treaty of July 23, 1881, 72 *State Papers*, 1103.
[3] Cf. F. de Visscher, "Le Régime nouveau des détroits," *R. D. I. L. C.*, 923, No. 6.

7. LIMITATIONS ON TARIFFS

A few steps have also been taken to remove difficulties arising out of tariffs. In 1890 an International Union and Bureau for the Publication of Customs Tariffs was established.[1] This Bureau publishes the changes in tariff duties of the different states, as quickly as possible, so that merchants are not caught unawares. A number of nations accepted more stringent obligations of this nature in a convention on Customs Formalities, drawn up at a League conference in October, 1923. This convention provides for the elimination of excessive and arbitrary customs formalities, and imposes on each state the obligation of publishing its customs duties.[2] While this development does not attack the real tariff question, it removes many of the irritations indirectly produced by nationalistic customs administration.

A similar problem has arisen in connection with the establishment of sanitary quarantines to exclude certain animals or plants from entering a country, for hygienic reasons. An exporter in one country may not know of such a quarantine until his product reaches the ports of the country imposing the quarantine. Moreover, such quarantines may really be an indirect form of embargo for protective purposes.

In order to remove some of these abuses as far as livestock is concerned, the Economic Committee of the League appointed a committee of experts on veterinary questions in 1928 to study the question.[3]

Occasionally commercial treaties will embody "conventional" tariffs, limiting the height of duties. By means of a net of commercial agreements trade between the different Succession States of Austria, at first stagnated by independence, was eventually resumed.[4] The peace treaties provided that the defeated powers could not charge duties on Allied goods higher than those imposed in 1914.[5] They also provided that Czechoslovakia and Poland

[1] Convention of July 5, 1890, 82 *State Papers*, 340.
[2] Convention and Final Act, Nov. 3, 1923, *O. J.*, Dec., 1923, p. 1571.
[3] *O. J.*, December, 1928, p. 1963. The Sixth Pan-American Conference at Havana adopted a resolution in favor of a Pan-American Conference to bring about uniformity and coöperation in quarantines. *I. S.* Vol. IV, No. 9, p. 217.
[4] A. Mousset, *La Petite Entente* (1923), Ch. V.
[5] Article 206, Treaty of Trianon; Article 224, Treaty of St. Germain.

could not impose discriminatory export taxes on coal exports to Austria for fifteen years. No export taxes may be imposed on mining products from the Saar into Germany. In the international treaty in regard to Spitzbergen, signed by nine powers in 1920, the right of the Norwegian government to levy an export duty on minerals was limited to 1% of their maximum value.[1]

Customs Unions.—A number of countries have also entered into customs unions entirely wiping out the economic frontier separating them and establishing free trade. The greatest example in the world of such a tariff union is the United States, the constitution of which completely insures free trade between its different states. Another example of a tariff union—one in which the states retained, for a time, their political independence—was the German Zollverein, created in 1833. Until the end of the War the principality of Luxemburg was a member of this union, a relationship which was terminated in the Treaty of Versailles (Article 40). Luxemburg thereupon entered into a customs union with Belgium.[2] In 1851 Austria and Hungary formed a customs union, renewed every ten years.[3] In 1852 Austria entered into such a union with the little principality of Lichtenstein. But this union was terminated following the War, and Lichtenstein entered into a tariff union with Switzerland. In 1897 Italy entered into a union with the tiny republic of San Marino, and France followed the same policy toward Monaco.[4]

Free trade has also been established by treaty between the Central American republics, between several of the Baltic states, and between Peru and Ecuador.

In an effort to mitigate the economic disorders which follow boundary readjustments, the peace treaties imposed the principle of free trade upon many disputed areas. A customs union was established permanently between Poland and Danzig, and another

---

[1] Up to 100,000 tons, beyond which the duty will be diminished. Art. VIII, Treaty of Feb. 9, 1920, *T. S.* 41.

[2] Convention of July 25, 1921, *T. S.* 256. This convention established a Joint Commission to insure equality of conditions as regards the supply of raw materials and the export of manufactured products, etc.; and also a Mixed Administrative Council to insure uniformity in the administration of customs.

[3] Treaty of March 29, 1923, *T. S.* 545.

[4] G. Lippert, *Das Internationale Finanzrecht* (1912), par. 46.

between France and the Saar.[1] For five years, certain goods from Alsace-Lorraine and the Saar were admitted into Germany without the payment of duty.[2] The mandates may also be incorporated in a customs union with adjoining colonies; a customs union between Syria and Palestine, for goods originating within the territory of each, has also been established.[3] Virtual free trade exists between the Polish and German parts of Silesia. Likewise the railways of this area are being administered as a single unit, under the control of a Common Superior Committee and of a Polish and German direction in their respective territories.[4] Moreover, Poland must permit the exportation of the products of the mines in Polish Silesia to Germany, for a period of fifteen years.[5]

"The Free Zones" Controversy.—In 1815 the customs union idea was adopted for the French districts of Gex-Savoy and the Swiss city of Geneva,—which is economically dependent upon French territory. Between 1815 and 1920 this territory constituted a single economic unit—called the "free zone." In the Treaty of Versailles it was stated, however, that these zones "are no longer consistent with present conditions" and that France and Switzerland would come to an agreement as to their status.[6] In July, 1921, an agreement was signed by the two governments, abolishing the zones, which, however, was rejected by a referendum vote of the Swiss people.[7] A difference of opinion arose between the two governments over the question whether the Treaty of Versailles had abrogated these zones. After a considerable delay an agreement for arbitration was signed on October 31, 1924, asking the Permanent Court of International Justice to deliberate on this question. However, at the end of its deliberations and before the formal decision, the Court is to give the parties an opportunity to effect a conciliatory settlement, in accordance with the treaty. If agreement proves impossible, the Court will make a decision as to the law involved and as to the nature of the new

[1] Art. 104; annex to Art. 50, Sec. 31, Treaty of Versailles.
[2] Art. 68, Treaty of Versailles.
[3] *Report on Palestine Administration*, 1920–1921, p. 24 ff.
[4] Titre VIII, Convention of May 15, 1922.
[5] Art. 90, Treaty of Versailles.
[6] Art. 435 and annex, Treaty of Versailles.
[7] Cf. p. 752.

régime.[1] The French government withheld ratification until the spring of 1928. The case had not been decided by July, 1929.

Proposals looking to the establishment of customs unions for the Americas, for Europe and for the British Empire have frequently been made. Unless, however, such unions become worldwide, they eventually are apt to compete fiercely with each other for trade. If they resort to political weapons, international animosities will become greater than ever. For this reason, universal free trade has been advocated as the chief panacea for the troubles of the world. Undoubtedly the removal of tariff barriers would automatically remove many international difficulties. Nevertheless, it is extremely unlikely that this end will ever be accomplished, except incidentally by the establishment of small confederations, because of the need of revenue and the strength of nationalism. Even under free trade, the international control of commerce would appear necessary in view of the growing complexity of the world. More progress in international relations will come from movements for international agreements limiting the height of import and export duties, especially upon raw materials of which certain states have a monopoly, than from necessarily academic arguments for the universal abolition of tariff barriers.[2]

An important step in removing political obstructions to trade was taken in a League of Nations conference at Geneva in October, 1927, which produced a convention for the abolition of prohibitions and restrictions upon imports and exports.[3] This convention, while it does not affect customs duties, wipes out the various embargoes and prohibitions which grew up especially in Europe immediately following the World War. Certain reservations were made by various states in regard to embargoes on dye-stuffs, coal and scrap iron; but if these reservations are not waived during the next three years, any party may denounce the treaty. This is the first inter-

[1] For the treaty cf. *Journal de Genève*, Nov. 1, 1924. Paulus, "Les zones franches autour de Genève," *R. D. I. L. C.*, 1924, Nos. 1-2.

[2] Cf. Zimmern, "Fiscal Policy and International Relations," *Journal of the British Institute of International Affairs*, January, 1924. Groups of nations have also formed monetary unions to insure the free circulation of a common unit of money. Cf. P. Reinsch, *Public International Unions* (1911), p. 76.

[3] "International Conference for the Abolition of Import and Export Prohibitions and Restrictions," C. 559. M. 201, 1927. II.

CONTROL OVER COMMUNICATIONS 139

national economic agreement to be negotiated under League auspices.[1]

This agreement was followed by two further conferences at Geneva as a result of which 17 states agreed in a convention of July 11, 1928, to abolish, subject to certain conditions, export duties on hides and skins. The preamble of this convention stated that the parties were "desirous of removing the obstacles which at present hinder trade in certain raw materials." [2] The acceptance of this principle of abolishing export duties in the case of one raw material may later be followed in the case of other raw materials. The convention is therefore of great importance.

International coöperation has also become necessary in the field of finance. The reliance of some states upon foreign loans is discussed elsewhere; but a mutual interdependence has also recently grown up in connection with the gold supply. During the World War many governments departed from the gold standard and resorted to inflated currency. When they attempted to return to the gold standard in the reconstruction period, they found that the gold supply of the world had to a large extent migrated to the United States. For a time the accumulation of gold in this country depressed commodity prices throughout the world. In an attempt to solve these and other problems, an international bankers' conference was held in New York in July, 1927, following which the United States Federal Reserve Banks provided easier credit conditions for the facilitation of a gold movement to London. The banks did this by lowering interest rates, and by purchasing large quantities of government securities.[3] The establishment of an international bank to aid in the stabilization of prices, as well as the creation of an international currency, are possibilities for the future.

8. INTERNATIONAL CONTROL OVER COMMUNICATIONS

These efforts to remove discriminations, to limit the height of tariffs, and to secure freedom of transit, free access to the sea and

[1] The United States was a party to this treaty.
[2] "Second International Conference on Hides and Skins and Bones," C. 524. M. 154. 1928. II. A second international agreement limiting the height of the export duties on bones was also signed.
[3] Cf. C. P. Howland, *Survey of American Foreign Relations* (1928), Chap. IV.

freedom of navigation, have had a destructive object—they have aimed to wipe out actual political obstacles to international trade. Economic internationalism has, however, progressed beyond the negative stage; it has become constructive and positive. A large number of international treaties have been made, formulating international rules and establishing international agencies to promote the economic prosperity and welfare of the whole world. Some of these treaties establish bureaus which merely collect information and give advice. At the present time, about forty-five international bureaus are in existence, most of which are limited to these objects. Other treaties, such as the sugar convention, have given a committee certain more positive powers. Still other treaties provide for uniformity in national legislation in regard to such subjects as copyrights or weights and measures. Others again provide for the common observance of international rules and the application of certain penalties when these rules are violated.[1]

The Postal Union.—When nations lived unto themselves in the international state of nature which the old doctrine of sovereignty presupposed, the problem of sending a letter or a cablegram or even a railway train to a foreign country did not arise. But with the growth of economic and cultural activity, international intercourse became inevitable; and if foreign vehicles of communication were not to be arbitrarily obstructed at national boundaries and subjected to discriminating and changing charges, international agreements became necessary. Thus before the establishment of the Universal Postal Union in 1874, five different rates of postage were charged between Germany and Australia; while a letter from the United States to Australia sometimes cost a dollar.[2]

In order to provide for a uniform and secure international postage, 180 postal administrations have associated themselves in the Universal Postal Union.[3] Throughout the territory embraced by these administrations—which now includes practically the whole world—the right to transmit letters and other forms of mail is guaranteed at a uniform maximum charge. The expense of trans-

---

[1] I. Kazansky, *Théorie de l'administration internationale* (1902), Reprinted from *R. G. D. I. P.*
[2] P. S. Reinsch, *Public International Unions* (1911), p. 21.
[3] It took this name only in 1878.

porting this mail may in some cases amount to more than the postage. Consequently, under the postal convention, each government promises to pay the cost of its first-class foreign mail, on the theory that for every letter sent abroad a foreign letter is received.[1]

A Congress of Plenipotentiaries meets at least every five years to consider amendments to the convention, the last congresses being held in Stockholm in 1924 and in London in 1929. In the interval, three postal administrations may place propositions in regard to the postal régime before the members. To be adopted, some amendments require unanimity, and others, a lesser majority, depending on the part of the convention involved. An International Bureau is maintained at Berne, which acts as a clearing house for the settlement of accounts, distributes information, publishes the *Union Postal*, and generally supervises the administrative work of the Union. Under this postal convention, virtually every state has surrendered its "sovereignty" over foreign postage rates; but nobody has worried about it, simply because this method of coöperation has advanced the interests of every country in the world.

The Telegraphic Union.—Telegraphic communications are perhaps as important as postal mail. Consequently in 1865, an International Telegraphic Union was formed. The telegraphic convention, as revised in 1875 and in 1908, insures the transit of telegrams from one country to another, provides special wires for the international telegraphic service, and even stipulates the hours which telegraph offices should keep.[2] Periodic conferences for the purpose of revising the agreement are held, while administrative matters are handled by an International Bureau.

Since this Union did not apply to submarine cables, a special conference, held in 1884, was necessary to protect this means of communication. As a result of this conference, a convention was signed making the willful or culpably negligent breaking of cables punishable.[3] Although violations of the convention may be tried

[1] For the convention of 1874, cf. 65 *State Papers*, 13; for the convention of Nov. 30, 1920, 114 *State Papers*, 294. For a good historical summary, cf. address of M. Zemp, 25th anniversary, *Documents du Congrès Postal de Berne*, 1900.
[2] Convention of May 17, 1865, 56 *State Papers*, 294.
[3] Convention of March 14, 1884, *Treaties of the U. S.*, Vol. II, p. 1949.

only in national courts, any vessel of war may make reports, which may be used as evidence against a ship suspected of violating the convention or legislation enacted to carry it into effect.

With the invention of wireless telegraphy, international action again became necessary, especially in view of the attempt of Great Britain to establish a radio monopoly of the world.[1] The British Marconi Company had made an exclusive contract with the British Lloyd and with the Italian government, under which the wireless stations in England and Italy would refuse to receive or send messages of any other than the Marconi system. Despite the great military advantages of a radio monopoly, the British government finally consented to the freedom of international wireless communication by signing a convention in 1906 establishing a Radiotelegraphic Union. Wireless stations on the coast and on shipboard must exchange radiograms without distinction of the system; and radiograms from one ship to another must be similarly exchanged. Conferences to revise the convention may be held periodically, while the Bureau for the International Telegraphic Union also looks after the administrative work connected with the wireless treaties.[2]

Special agreements for electrical communications have been made by American countries. In accordance with a resolution of the fifth Pan-American conference, an Inter-American Committee on Electrical Communications met in Mexico City in August, 1924, and drew up a convention establishing an "Inter-American Union of Electrical Communications to the end of establishing uniform rules for the exchange of correspondence by electricity." As the United States objected to several features of the convention, it declined to sign. In the fall of 1927 an international radio convention was signed in Washington.

Railways.—Through railway traffic, across national political frontiers, has become another essential of international life. If the United States should stop trains from Canada in the same fashion as it stops immigrants at Ellis Island, the economic life of the continent would be thrown into turmoil. As early as 1840,

---

[1] Reinsch, p. 128. Cf. Convention of Nov. 3, 1906, *Treaties of the U. S.*, Vol. II, p. 1949.

[2] Convention of July 5, 1912, *Treaties of the U. S.*, Vol. III, p. 3048; J. Devaux, *Le Télégraphie sans fil dans les rapports internationaux* (1914), Pt. II.

Belgium came to depend on coal from Germany, while Germany looked to Belgium as a market for her manufactured goods.[1] With a view to facilitating traffic across boundary lines in Europe, where life is especially intricate, nine states signed a convention in 1890 in regard to the transport of merchandise, which authorized through bills of lading and obliged every railway to accept merchandise going from one country to another. Railways may be held responsible for damages to and delay in transporting such goods which are ascertained by the court of the country in which the railway is domiciled.[2] Subsequent conferences were held in 1906 and 1907 at which conventions regulating the maximum gauge, the construction of rolling stock and the loading of cars were signed.[3]

A further development took place at the League's conference on communication, held at Geneva in the fall of 1923, at which a convention and statute on the International Régime of Railways was signed. In this statute the parties promise to provide through service on their railways for international traffic and to facilitate traffic formalities at frontiers. Agreements between different railway administrations for the exchange of rolling-stock should be encouraged, while agreements to secure the uniformity of railways and through tickets for passengers and freight should also be made. The states promise to apply to international traffic "tariffs which are reasonable both as regards their amounts and the conditions of their application, and undertake to refrain from all discrimination of an unfair nature" against the other contracting states or their nationals. Disputes over the interpretation of the statute should be submitted to the League organization on Communications and Transit for an advisory opinion, before resort is had to arbitration.[4]

Even the automobile has been the subject of diplomacy. In 1909 sixteen states signed a convention prescribing the conditions on

---

[1] L. G. McPherson, *Transportation in Europe* (1910), p. 136; cf. G. Eger. *Das Internationales Ubereinkommenüber den Eisenbahn-Frachtverkehr* (1909); cf. *The Proceedings of the International Railway Congress* (1911), 8th sess.

[2] Convention of Oct. 14, 1890, 82 *State Papers*, 771. In case of delay the road may be penalized.

[3] 2d additional Convention of Sept. 19, 1906, 3 Martens (3d series), 920. Final Protocol, May 18, 1907, 2 Martens (3d series), 878.

[4] Agreement of Dec. 9, 1923, *O. J.*, Jan., 1924, p. 239.

which drivers might be given certificates allowing them to drive "internationally." [1] A new convention was signed in 1926. Moreover, upon the advent of the airplane and the establishment of air-routes encircling the globe, difficulties arose when one nation attempted to prohibit a foreign plane from flying over its territory. In order to settle such controversies, the powers signed an Air Navigation Convention in 1919 in which freedom of innocent passage above the territory of states is guaranteed. Airplanes, however, must be provided with a certificate of airworthiness from their respective states; and they must observe certain stipulated rules in regard to departure, flight and landing. The administration of the convention is in the hands of an International Air Commission.[2] An international aviation conference was held in Washington in December, 1928.

9. UNFAIR COMPETITION

Thus whether in the case of letters, telegrams, railway traffic, radio or airplanes, many of the nations of the world, in these different agreements, have frankly admitted that their own interests can best be advanced by accepting certain limitations upon "their right to do as they please." However, while a large number of treaties have been made in regard to international communications, very few have so far been made regulating the activities of international commerce as such. Nevertheless a few steps have been taken to do away with "unfair competition," such as the counterfeiting of foreign goods, stealing trade-marks and dumping. That an inventor or an author should be given part of the proceeds resulting from his labors has been recognized in every country in the world as elementary justice. Yet in the absence of an international agreement (or domestic legislation), an American publisher may bring out a paper edition of Lafcadio Hearn or Bernard Shaw or Joseph Conrad and appropriate the entire profits and royalties to himself. This type of "pirating" has become especially pernicious with the increasing interest in foreign art and literature. An attempt to stop the stealing of patents and trade-marks was made in 1883 when an international convention was signed, establishing a Union of Industrial Property. This conven-

[1] Convention of Oct. 11, 1909, 102 *State Papers*, 64.
[2] Convention of October 13, 1919, *T. S.* 297.

UNFAIR COMPETITION 145

tion, as revised in 1900 and 1911, provides that the citizen of a contracting state who has an industrial establishment in the territory of another state, shall enjoy the advantages which the laws of that state accord to its own nationals.[1] That is, the citizen of State A will receive the same protection in State B for copyrights and patents as State B accords to its own citizens—the principle of national treatment.

Encouraged by the protection thus given to industrial property, authors and artists urged their governments to extend the same principle to works of literature, music, art and photography. As a result of their efforts, an international conference was held in 1886 which formed a Union of Literary and Artistic Property, based on the same principle as the Union of Industrial Property —the principle of national treatment.[2] A joint Bureau of Industrial, Literary and Artistic Property exists at Berne to collect statistics and to do the preparatory work for conferences, held to revise the conventions. It publishes a number of monthly journals, such as "La Propriété industrielle," "Les Marques internationales" and "Le Droit d'Auteur." While the United States is a member of the Union of Industrial Property, it has not become a member of the Union of Literary and Artistic Property, apparently because it regards the "interests" of American publishers of greater value than those of authors.[3]

The campaign against international unfair competition was carried on by the Economic Committee of the League. In May, 1924, a conference of experts was held at Geneva where the revi-

[1] Cf. *Treaties of the U. S.*, Vol. II, p. 1935; Vol. III, p. 2953. In this convention the "contracting parties agree to assure to the members of the Union an effective protection against unfair competition." For the Inter-American patent, copyright and trade-mark conventions of August, 1910, cf. *Treaties of The U. S.*, pp. 2930 ff. Cf. Pelletier and Vidal-Naquet, *La Convention d'union pour la protection de la propriété industrielle* (1902).

[2] Convention of Sept. 9, 1886, 77 *State Papers*, 22. While the convention of 1911 insures only "national treatment," three "restricted" unions have been formed by some of the states signatory to the convention of 1911, the first of which provides for the international registration of trade-marks, and the second for the prevention of fraudulent indications of the place of origin of merchandise—both unions being established at Madrid in 1891; the third is the arrangement of Berne of 1920, providing for the conservation or restoration of rights of industrial property injured by the World War. Cf. *Handbook of International Organizations* (1921), p. 53.

[3] Cf. Reinsch, p. 41.

sion of the existing international convention for the protection of industrial property was discussed. Here the possibility was suggested of allowing representatives of a state to bring an action in the territory of another state when abuses covered by the convention occur. Its suggestions were for the most part embodied in a new convention convened at the Hague in November, 1925.[1] The fourth Assembly also expressed the hope that the Economic Committee would discuss the possibility of international action with a view to the protection of the consumer against fraud not covered by existing conventions.[2] At the request of the League Council the Committee on Intellectual Coöperation has considered a convention to protect the right to scientific discoveries.[3]

10. COÖPERATION IN AGRICULTURE

While it is difficult to conceive of anything more "domestic" in nature than agriculture, here also international treaties have been made. In 1905 fifty-five states signed a treaty establishing an International Institute of Agriculture at Rome. The purpose of the Institute is advisory and informational in character. It collects facts concerning agricultural conditions throughout the world, such as the wages of farm labor and the diseases of vegetables. It studies questions concerning agricultural coöperative organizations and the reconciliation of farm workers and their employers. It may submit to the governments concerned measures for the promotion of agricultural interests. The Institute is organized into a General Assembly of the signatory members, who are divided into different groups; while the executive work of the Institute is in the hands of a permanent committee.[4]

[1] T. S. 1743.
[2] Report to the Fifth Assembly, etc., A. 8, 1924, p. 49.
[3] "Report on Scientific Property." A. 21, 1928, XII.
[4] Convention of June 7, 1905, Treaties of the U. S., Vol. II, p. 2140; Pantaro, "L'Istituto Internazionale d'Agricoltura, La sua vita ed I suoi problemi," Nuova Antologia, Maggio, 1924; O. R. Agresti, David Lubin (1922), Chs. XII–XIV. As this book shows, the Institute falls far short of the idea of Lubin who founded it. For the voting arrangements in this and other international organizations, cf. p. 687. The 1924 Assembly adopted a resolution aiming to coördinate all societies interested in agriculture into some form of International Association, Actes de la Septième Assemblée Générale (1924), p. 853.
In 1915 the United States invited different nations to send delegates to an International Dry-Farming Congress to be held at Denver. U. S. For. Rel.,

COÖPERATION IN AGRICULTURE 147

The Case of Sugar.—In order to promote domestic sugar production, a number of states addicted to the habits of economic nationalism, at one time granted bounties to sugar-producers. As a result, competition between sugar-growing governments ensued which was costly, wasteful, and injurious to international goodwill. Despite the efforts made to stamp out bounties by binational treaties, no progress was made until the signature of the international Sugar Convention of 1902.[1] In this treaty a number of European states formed a union in which they promised to do away with sugar bounties, and to impose a special tax on the imports of sugar from countries, not parties to the convention, which granted such bounties. A Sugar Commission was established to determine whether bounties were being granted; and when the Commission ascertained by a majority vote their existence, the treaty powers were bound to impose a countervailing duty. The Commission was assisted by a permanent bureau located at Brussels, which collected and published information in regard to sugar legislation throughout the world. Its purpose having been largely accomplished, the Sugar Convention was finally denounced in 1920.[2] During its existence, it constituted one of the most extreme forms of international government ever attempted—in which a power could be obliged to change its tariff duties by the majority vote of an international body. An international treaty embodying this countervailing duty idea might be utilized to meet the problem of dumping—to prevent surplus products from being sold abroad at cheaper prices than at home.[3] In May, 1928,

---

1915, p. 17. In 1909 a conference of the United States, Canada and Mexico was held at Washington to discuss the conservation of natural resources. Following this conference, invitations were issued for a world conservation conference at the Hague which, however, did not materialize. *U. S. For. Rel.*, 1909, pp. 1–3.

[1] Convention of March 5, 1902, 95 *State Papers*, 6.
[2] *T. S.*, Vol. I, p. 400.
[3] Cf. J. Viner, *Dumping, A Problem in International Trade* (1924), p. 166, Chs. XI and XII. Another agreement indirectly aiding commerce is the international convention of May 20, 1875, establishing an International Bureau of Weights and Measures, *Treaties of the U. S.*, Vol. II, p. 1924, which has standardized measures; the work is in charge of a bureau, while general conferences are held every six years. This treaty was amended by the convention of Oct. 6, 1921, *Treaties of the U. S.*, Vol. III, p. 3088.

The Secretariat of the League of Nations also publishes a Monthly Bulletin of Statistics. In September, 1923, a Conference of the International Institute

the League Economic Consultative Committee was asked, in view of the new crisis in the sugar industry, to make a new treaty along the lines of the 1902 convention.[1] As a result of this request, the League Economic Organization undertook a study of the question of sugar.

Vineyards and Refrigerators.—About 1860 whole departments of France were inundated by a pest called phylloxera which devastated the vineyards, and caused losses calculated to be twice as great as the German indemnity of 1871. This pest had supposedly come from America, and it soon began to spread to Austria, Spain and other parts of Europe. In order to insure a "common and efficacious" action against the introduction and propagation of phylloxera, a number of governments promised to enact legislation to watch vines with a view to suppressing the disease, and to regulate transportation of articles in which phylloxera might be concealed.[2]

Even the refrigerator has become the concern of the diplomats. In 1920 a number of countries signed a convention for the Foundation at Paris of an International Institute of Refrigeration, the purpose of which is to promote the study of the best solution of the problems relating to the preservation, transportation and distribution of perishable goods. A general conference meets every two years, while the administrative work is handled by an Executive Committee.[3]

11. ECONOMIC COÖPERATION DURING THE WAR AND THROUGH THE LEAGUE OF NATIONS

When an accurate history of the World War is written, we shall probably learn that it was as much an economic as a military struggle. It was the purpose of Germany to shut England off from her food supply, while it was the purpose of the Allies to starve Germany into surrender. To accomplish this end, the Allies were obliged to resort to the highest degree of international economic coöperation the modern world has ever seen. In 1917 a Wheat

of Statistics was held. An International Bureau of Commercial Statistics, based on a convention of December, 1913, is working out a common nomenclature for statistics of international importance, a work which is being assisted by the Economic Committee of the League of Nations.

[1] See "The Question of Sugar," C. C. E. 13.
[2] Convention of Nov. 3, 1881, 73 *State Papers*, 323.
[3] Convention of June 21, 1920, *T. S.* 207.

ECONOMIC COÖPERATION DURING WAR

Executive was formed of representatives of Great Britain, France and Italy which rationed out food to the respective Allied countries according to their needs and to the available supply. Upon the entrance of America into the war, the Allied Maritime Transport Council was formed, which rationed shipping. At various times thereafter twenty Programme Committees were established, covering the whole range of commodities. These Committees determined the amounts needed by the different Allied countries, and the Transport Council recommended the allotment of shipping accordingly. By this means duplication was avoided, unnecessary submarine risks averted and commodities distributed where they would do the most good. An Allied Food Council, Munitions Council, Blockade Council and Finance Council were also established.[1]

When the League of Nations was established in 1920, it was necessary to choose between the type of international administration which would intrust a specific task to an international body, or the type which would merely bring national governments together to coöperate in the promotion of certain ends, undertaken, however, by each government individually. While the first type of administration was followed in the case of the Saar, the second type was adopted for more generally important economic activities. At the present time, no government is willing to give to an international body the authority to regulate important economic matters, such as tariffs or the distribution of raw materials. Fifty-five governments of the world have, however, been willing to participate in periodic conferences, where such matters may be discussed upon the basis of studies made by international experts.[2]

The Technical Organizations.—With a view to the formation of an advisory organization in regard to economic and commercial matters, the first Assembly (1920) authorized the establishment of two Technical Organizations, (1) an Advisory and Technical Committee on Communications and Transit, (2) the Economic and Finance Committee, divided into two sections.

[1] Cf. Cotton and Morrow, in S. P. Duggan (ed.), *The League of Nations* (1919), Ch. III.
[2] Cf. J. A. Salter, *Allied Shipping Control, an Experiment in International Administration* (1921), pp. 253 ff.; cf. also p. 704 this book.

The Committee on Communications and Transit is composed of representatives of the four great powers, Great Britain, France, Italy, and Japan, and about fourteen other members, appointed by the Communications Conferences which are held under the auspices of the League.[1] This committee prepares the ground for the Communications Conferences, the first two of which—the Barcelona conference held in 1921, and the Geneva conference held in 1923—led to conventions and recommendations in regard to freedom of transit, waterways, railways, etc. When these conventions are ratified and go into effect, they are placed under the supervision of this Committee. Serious disputes as to the application or interpretation of these conventions are first submitted to the Committee for an advisory opinion. If necessary the dispute is then referred to arbitration.[2]

The Organization for Communications and Transit established a Permanent Committee on Road Traffic, which is trying to bring about uniformity in traffic regulations between different countries. The Organization is working to unify private law in regard to inland navigation, and to draw up a convention on the penal consequences of collision at sea. It has worked out a scheme to standardize the buoyage and lighting of coasts; it is studying the problem of international air navigation. Under its auspices two international Passport Conferences have been held, the last one taking place at Geneva in May, 1926.[3] This conference adopted recommendations looking to the establishment of an international type of passport, and asking for the suppression of visas.

This Organization has also appointed a special committee to study the question of Reforming the Calender, and especially to work out an arrangement whereby Easter may come on the same date or same Sunday each year.

The second Technical Organization is the Economic and Finance Committee, divided in two sections, each working independently of the other. Up to the present the Finance Committee has held more than 31 sessions, while the Economic Committee has met

[1] Resolutions, First Assembly, *O. J.*, Spec. Supp., Jan., 1921, p. 15.
[2] Cf. Art. 35, Statute on the International Régime of Railways, *O. J.*, Jan., 1924 (Part II), p. 259. A third conference was held in 1927.
[3] *O. J.*, August 1926, p. 1088.

about 25 times. The Finance Committee was largely responsible for the organization of the International Financial Conference convened in Brussels by the Council in 1920. The recommendations of this Conference had an important influence upon European financial policy. The Finance Committee worked out plans for League loans to Austria, Hungary, Greece, Bulgaria, Danzig and Esthonia.[1] As a result of its studies an international conference on double taxation was held in Geneva in 1928. It has drafted a convention relative to counterfeiting.

The Economic Committee has studied the question of the equitable treatment of commerce, unfair competition, the treatment of aliens, letters of exchange, commercial arbitration, abolition of import and export prohibitions, economic crises and unemployment, the unification of statistics, and the simplification of tariff formalities.[2] A conference for the unification of statistics was held in Geneva in the fall of 1928. As a result, an international convention was signed on December 14, 1928, in which the parties agreed to compile statistics in regard to external trade, a return of the population according to occupations, censuses of agriculture, returns of mining, statistical surveys of industry, and index numbers. Methods of compilation were also laid down.[3]

Largely as an outgrowth of the work of the Economic Committee, the Council called an International Economic Conference, which met at Geneva in 1927. Forty-six members of the League, the United States, Turkey and Russia sent delegates. It passed resolutions in regard to liberty of commerce, tariff questions, commercial policy and treaties, subsidies, dumping, discrimination in transport, the rationalization of industry, international cartels, agriculture and other subjects.[4]

To follow up the application of these recommendations the Council created a Consultative Committee, which will work

[1] Cf. p. 426. Cf. also "Financial Committee," *Report to the Council*, C. 613. M. 190. 1928. II.

[2] For the Convention of 1923, cf. p. 135.

[3] The League Council shall appoint a Committee of Technical Experts which shall also contain one delegate from each state not a member of the League to make any suggestions for the purpose of improving the principles of the Convention. "International Conference Relating to Economic Statistics." C. 606(1). M. 184(1). 1928. II.

[4] The World Economic Conference, Final Report. Cf. below.

alongside of the Economic Committee. As far as possible the Consultative Committee is a reproduction of the preparatory committee of the Economic Conference. It contains about 45 members.

This Committee met in May, 1928, and examined world economic conditions in the light of the recommendations of the international conference. It recommended that investigations be carried out in regard to sugar and coal. It met again in January, 1929.

The two technical organizations—the Committee on Communication and Transit, and the Economic and Finance Committee—together with the Consultative Committee, may very readily grow into an advisory international commerce commission, such as the American Congress instructed the American delegate to the Institute of Agriculture to advocate in 1914.[1] Such a body would constantly study the economic troubles of the world, and under its auspices periodic conferences would be held, with a view to arriving at policies, after full and voluntary discussion, to which all might subscribe.

Much of the value of any gathering such as the International Economic conference lies not only in the agreements immediately drafted but also in the expression of sound international economic principles as an ideal which nations may later put into practice. In the resolutions framed by the Conference the statement was made that "each nation's commerce is to-day being hampered by barriers established by other nations resulting in a situation, especially in Europe, that is highly detrimental to the general welfare." The solution must take the form of concerted action. Under the heading of Liberty of Trading, the Conference condemned the system of import and export prohibitions; and it was as a result of its expression that a League conference on this subject was subsequently held.[2] It also declared that when a government carries on any commercial enterprise it should not be treated as entitled to any sovereign rights or immunities. In regard to tariffs, it declared that one of the most formidable obstacles in the way of developing permanent trade relations was the instability of tariffs. It recommended that states should refrain

---

[1] This resolution advocated a commission on merchant, marine and ocean freights, with consultative, deliberative and advisory powers, 38 Stat. 779.
[2] Cf. p. 138.

ECONOMIC COÖPERATION DURING WAR

from making frequent or sudden changes in their schedules. Consular fees should be a charge rather than an additional source of revenue.

In regard to Commercial Policy and Treaties it declared that "the time has come to put a stop to the growth of Customs tariffs, and to reverse the direction" either by individual action or by treaty. The free circulation of raw materials and articles of consumption should not be unduly hindered by export duties. Commercial treaties should contain the unconditional most-favored-nation clause in its most liberal form. The Conference expressed the hope that governments would refrain from subsidies, direct or indirect, to assist home industry or export trade. Dumping should be reduced to a minimum.

The Conference declared that the rationalization of industry possessed benefits, both in the lowering of costs and prices and in expanding markets, but it also had temporary unfavorable consequences upon certain types of workers, which should be avoided.

International cartels possessed the benefits of acting as a check on uneconomic competition and reducing the evils resulting from fluctuation; they might also assure to the workers greater stability of employment and aid the consumer by reducing costs. Nevertheless the Conference believed that such agreements, if they encouraged monopolistic tendencies, involved dangers. Such agreements should not lead to an artificial rise in prices nor restrict the supply of raw materials to any particular country. The Conference did not believe it feasible to establish any international system of supervision over such agreements. But they should be closely observed by the League of Nations, and publicity given to their operation.

CHAPTER VII

LABOR AND THE WORLD

1. The Labor Internationals—Treaties against Propaganda.—2. International Labor Legislation Before the War.—3. The International Labor Organization.—4. Its Accomplishments.—5. The Labor Office.—6. The Enforcement of Labor Treaties.—7. International Aspects of Immigration—Immigration Treaties—Emigration Conferences.—8. Emigration and Over-population.

With the rise of modern industrialism, the nation-state has found its unity shaken by economic groupings of world-wide sympathies. Not infrequently capital and labor have fought a war within the walls of a nation with a bitterness almost the equal of contests between political states. "The struggle of the classes," like the struggle of the races and of the religions, cuts across national boundary lines, and attempts to divide the whole world.

1. THE LABOR INTERNATIONALS

Labor has been a pioneer in internationalism, some of its organizations being not only economic, but political and even revolutionary in purpose. In 1864 the first International Workingmen's Association was founded at London in response to the famous communistic manifesto, "Workers of all countries unite." Under the influence of Karl Marx it gradually became socialistic; and it disappeared in 1873 because of the struggles between socialism and anarchism and the stigma fixed upon such movements by the Paris commune. A second "International" was finally created in 1889. This organization was successful in bringing about the coöperation of labor groups in thirty nations through its congresses, which were often composed of a thousand delegates. The International had hoped to prevent wars by means of an international strike. Its plans failed in 1914, because of the strength of nationalism,—the socialist parties which hitherto had been associated in an international movement against war now split up, each supporting its own government.[1] During the course of the World War, the Second International held a labor conference in Stockholm to define what the peace terms should be and to press for an end of the war. The effort was abortive, partly because of the opposition of the governments concerned. At the close of the war, the Second International held a conference at Berne (1919) at which an attempt was made to clear up the wreckage which the war had caused. This meeting was also a failure; there was only a small attendance, and the discussions were marked by lukewarmness and indecision. No agreement between the revolutionary and the reformist elements could be reached.

Meanwhile the Bolsheviks of Russia, dissatisfied with the nationalistic and reformist nature of the Second International, organized the Third or Communist International at Moscow, in 1919. Many of the radical socialist parties of European countries became affiliated with this body. In the 1920 Congress of this International, Twenty-One Points were adopted as conditions for membership. The members must advocate the dictatorship of the proletariat "in such a way as to make its necessity apparent to every plain worker, soldier, and peasant." Since the class struggle is entering upon the phase of civil war, Communists can have no confidence in bourgeois legality; so it is their duty to create "a parallel illegal organization machine which at the decisive moment will be helpful to the party in fulfilling its duty to the revolution." Special propaganda must be carried on in the army, legally or illegally. All parties before joining this International must renounce all "reformist" tendencies, for world peace is impossible "without the revolutionary overthrow of capitalism." These parties must also expel from their ranks "all unreliable elements." "The Communist International has declared war upon the whole bourgeois world."[2]

Active propaganda in favor of communism was carried on in different European, American and Asiatic countries by means of groups affiliated with the Third International at Moscow.[3] Many

[1] This was not true, however, of the Italian socialists. For the history of the Internationals, especially the First, cf. R. W. Postgate, *The Workers' International* (1920).
[2] For the 21 Points, cf. *The American Labor Year Book*, 1923–24, p. 312.
[3] C. Sarolea, "Bolshevism and the World Revolution," *Current History*, February, 1924.

governments regarded this agitation for the overthrow of capitalist governments as being officially prompted by the Soviet government and for this reason a deliberately unfriendly act. Following the disclosure of a plot "To hoist the Red Flag on the White House," Secretary Hughes dispatched a note to the Soviet government, in January, 1924, saying that the United States would not recognize any government engaged in such activities. In reply the Soviet government declared that this propaganda was the work of the Third International, with which it had no connection. The distinction, however, appeared rather fictitious.

Treaties against Propaganda.—In an effort to stop this revolutionary propaganda, different European and Asiatic governments exacted pledges from Russia as a condition of resuming business with her. In the Trade Agreement of March 16, 1921, between Great Britain and Russia, each party agreed "to refrain from conducting outside of its own borders any official propaganda direct or indirect against the institutions of the British Empire or the Russian Soviet Republic respectively;" more particularly "the Russian Soviet Government refrains from any attempt by military or diplomatic or any other form of propaganda to encourage any of the peoples of Asia in any form of hostile action against British interests or the British Empire, especially in India, and in the Independent State of Afghanistan."[1] Despite such promises, charges were made that the Russian government continued to agitate for the violent overthrow of British institutions. These charges came to a climax in the election campaign of 1924 by the publication of a remonstrating letter from the British Foreign Office to the Soviet government. The incident appeared to contribute to the defeat of the MacDonald government which had just signed an important agreement with Russia, because of the belief that its confidence in the Soviet government had been misplaced.[2]

Following the war, therefore, the radical socialistic parties had affiliated with the Third International, while, for a time, the

[1] 114 *State Papers*, 374. An interesting precursor of this type of agreement was an international convention concerning measures to be taken against the anarchist movement, signed by ten states on March 4, 1904. 10 Martens (3d series), 81.

[2] For the alleged instructions of the Soviet government to the Communists in England in the Zinovieff letter, cf. *Manchester Guardian Weekly*, Oct. 31, 1924.

THE LABOR INTERNATIONALS 157

moderate parties remained with the Second International. In 1921 several national groups opposed to both Internationals came together in Vienna and formed what was popularly called the International Two and a Half, but officially entitled the International Working Union of the Socialist Parties. This body negotiated with both the Second and Third Internationals with a view toward bringing about unity among the workers of the world. While agreement proved possible on several minor points, the differences between the Moscow group and the European and American socialists were too broad to be reconcilable. However, as a result of several conferences in 1923, the Vienna International and the Second International united in a "Labor and Socialist International." A constitution was drawn up providing for international congresses at least once every three years. The most recent Congress was held in Brussels in the summer of 1928. The object of this organization is "the establishment of the Socialist Commonwealth" by means of the class struggle and the independent political and industrial action of the workers.[1] An elaborate administrative machinery of executive and administrative committees, as well as a bureau, is in charge of the work.

The international labor movement is composed of the socialists and the trade unionists, following a similar division in the labor movement of each country. There are about 28 Trade Internationals, such as the International Miners' Federation, with a membership of 2,000,000, and the International Metal Workers' Federation, the most powerful of all such bodies, with a membership of 3,200,000, and the International Transport Workers' Federation, having 2,200,000 members. These trade unions have come together so as to provide mutual help in wage controversies, and to prevent strike-breakers from being transported from one country to another.[2] In 1919 the International Federation of Trade Unions was formed as an alliance of national and international trade federations. It has a membership of about 15,000,000. Dissatisfied with the "conservative" tendencies of this Interna-

[1] Cf. *Labor Year Book*, p. 296.
[2] A recent article advocates the establishment of an International Labor Bank, so that the British, French and German miners would not "suffer defeats from want of capital," in times of strike, etc. Wagner, "The Economic International," *The International Trade Union Review*, Jan.–March, 1924.

158   LABOR AND THE WORLD

tional Federation, the Bolshevik government in 1920 organized a Red International of Labor Unions. An International Confederation of Christian Trade Unions also exists.[1] In view of the great difficulty which the laboring groups of the world have experienced in presenting a united front to capitalism, it is rather surprising that nation-states have been able to coöperate to the extent which they have.

2. INTERNATIONAL LABOR LEGISLATION BEFORE THE WAR

From another standpoint—that of international labor legislation—labor has been important in the field of world relations. The protection of the workingman, as of other classes, has long been recognized as a duty of governments. Practically every country in the world has passed some legislation in regard to the hours and conditions of labor. Oftentimes the enactment of this legislation has been due to strong labor organizations. Its effective administration also depends upon the existence, national or international, of such organizations. While the duty of protecting labor standards has been recognized in theory, the more socially advanced countries have been held back from enacting labor legislation by the fear of unfair competition from industries in states which still allow the exploitation of the workingman or who refuse to adopt humanitarian legislation elsewhere recognized as necessary. For a long time governments allowed matches to be manufactured of white phosphorus, despite the fact that it exposes workmen to a terrible disease. Matches could be manufactured equally well from red phosphorus which is not poisonous. Yet since red phosphorus is more expensive than white, one state alone hesitated to compel the change since its match industry would have been driven off the international market. An international remedy was the only remedy. Moreover, if foreign capital is uncontrolled in undeveloped countries, labor will probably be exploited as it was during the early period of the Factory System in England.[2] By means of international labor legislation,

---

[1] An effort has also been made to establish a Pan-American and Central American Federation of Labor, *Labor Year Book*, p. 289.
[2] Cf. p. 400.

such labor may be protected and its standards raised by the combined strength of the outside world. Thus new countries may be given the benefit of the experience of the old, and unfair competition may be systematically eliminated.

In 1890 the first international labor conference was held in Berlin. It drew up a number of recommendations in regard to mining, child labor and Sunday employment. It was followed by a number of unofficial conferences; but the next governmental conferences were not held until 1905 and 1906.[1] The first important labor treaty was signed between Italy and France in 1904.[2] This treaty granted to nationals of either country laboring in the other, reciprocal banking and insurance accommodations and also guaranteed them the mutual protection of national labor legislation. The most interesting feature of this treaty was the promise of Italy to establish a system of labor inspection which would guarantee the application of labor laws as effectively as in France. The Italian government also declared its intention of realizing gradually the reduction of the working-day for women. Both governments undertook to make an annual report on the application of labor laws to women and children. By means of this treaty, labor conditions in Italy were definitely improved. About twenty-five similar labor agreements were later made between different countries in Europe.

At the international labor conference in Berne (1906) two labor conventions were signed. The first prohibited night-work in industrial employment for all women in industry, subject to certain exceptions.[3] The second prohibited the use of white phosphorus in the manufacture of matches, because of its poisonous nature.[4] The impetus to social reform which such treaties may give is shown by the fact that before 1906 only five European governments had laws prohibiting the use of white phosphorus, but as a result of the treaty a total of eleven governments adopted such a limitation. Likewise, before the convention only four or five

[1] B. E. Lowe, *The International Protection of Labor* (1921), p. xxxiii, Chs. II, III. A large number of unofficial conferences was also held by the International Association for Labor Legislation.
[2] Treaty of April 15, 1904, 98 *State Papers*, 457.
[3] Convention of September 26, 1906, 100 *State Papers*, 794.
[4] For the white phosphorus convention of the same date, cf. 2 Martens (3d series), 872.

states had laws prohibiting night-work for women; but twelve states agreed to the principle in this convention, while four other states enacted the principle into legislation.[1]

Before the War these were the only two international labor conventions in effect. They were, moreover, defective, because no means of deciding differences in interpretation had been provided for. In order to clarify such conventions, reward Labor for its support of the Allies during the World War and prevent the spread of bolshevism, the Treaty of Versailles contained a section (Part XIII) which is a veritable Magna Carta for the workingman.

In the preamble it is declared that universal peace must be based on social justice and that to this end labor conditions should be improved, as for example by regulation of hours of work, prevention of unemployment, provision for an adequate living wage, protection of women and children and the worker against sickness and old age. Moreover, in the Covenant, members of the League agree to "endeavour to secure and maintain fair and humane conditions of labour for men, women and children, both in their own countries and in all countries to which their commercial and industrial relations extend." [2]

3. THE INTERNATIONAL LABOR ORGANIZATION

To carry these principles into effect, a permanent International Labor Organization has been established, composed of the members of the League of Nations, which has two bodies: (1) a General International Labor Conference, meeting annually, and (2) an International Labor Office. Each member state is represented at these conferences by four delegates, two representing the government, one labor, and one capital. The latter two representatives are named by the government "in agreement with the industrial organizations which are most representative of employers and workpeople." [3] These delegates, however, vote individually,

[1] Lowe, pp. 114, 126, 129.
[2] Art 23 (a).
[3] A difference in interpretation over this clause was referred by the League Council to the World Court for an advisory opinion in 1922. It was the contention of a Dutch labor union that the government, in selecting a labor delegate, was bound to consult the largest employees' organization, even

INTERNATIONAL LABOR ORGANIZATION

so that, for example, the labor delegates may cast a united vote against the employers' delegates of every country.

Considerable difficulty has been experienced with "incomplete" delegations,—*i. e.*, only about half of the governments appoint representatives of industrial groups as well as of themselves. The failure to appoint workers' delegates led a committee of the Washington Conference to the conclusion that governments were under a positive obligation to appoint such delegations, but that no action on the part of the Conference seemed possible against a government which did not fulfill this obligation.[1] Apparently only the pressure of opinion, particularly of labor groups, can bring this about. Nevertheless, unless labor representatives are appointed, the purpose of these conferences will certainly not be fulfilled.

Although membership in the International Labor Organization is limited to members in the League of Nations, a special ruling of the first conference admitted Germany as a member. In 1923 the question arose whether or not the Saar Territory could participate in the organization. The question raised a serious issue as to the international status of the Saar which the Governing Body decided that it did not have the power to solve. It was finally decided to allow the Territory to take part in the work of the conference in an advisory capacity, just as states such as Finland had done before becoming members of the League.[2]

Despite the failure of the United States to ratify the Treaty of Versailles, the Labor Conference hoped to secure the collaboration of American industrial organizations. At the Washington session it decided to invite representatives of the workers and employers in the United States to send delegates to the Conference. In 1922 the Director of the Labor Office, M. Albert Thomas, paid a visit to the United States where he was received by representatives of the government and of the industrial groups. When it learned that the American government would approve the

though other labor organizations total more members. This interpretation was rejected by the Court, which was of the opinion that in these circumstances "the most representative organizations" meant those having the largest numbers altogether. Series B, No. 2, *Advisory Opinions*, Permanent Court, August 12, 1922. But the Court finally ordered alternate representation of the two labor organizations concerned.

[1] *Report of the Director*, International Labor Conference, 1924, p. 40.

[2] It is understood that Mexico and the Philippines at one time made overtures to the International Labor Organization as to membership.

participation in the International Labor Conference of industrial representatives, the United States Chamber of Commerce decided to send, at first, not delegates but a representative body of observers, the appointment of which was actually made. But for some reason this decision was later reversed.[1]

The International Labor Conference adopts proposals, by a majority of two-thirds, either as recommendations or as draft conventions, subject to the ratification of the governments concerned. In accepting these conventions governments promise to enact legislation carrying their principles into effect as domestic law. While there is, of course, no obligation to ratify such conventions, each member state is under an entirely novel obligation to place before the proper authority in the home government all draft conventions and recommendations, even though the representatives of that particular government may have voted against them at the conference. These conventions go into effect when two or three parties ratify, depending on the treaty, as between the ratifying states.

4. ITS ACCOMPLISHMENTS

International Labor Conferences were held annually between 1919 and 1928.[2] In the first nine conferences a total number of 27 conventions and twenty recommendations were agreed upon. The first conference, held in Washington, D. C., limited itself to industry; the conference held in 1920 was concerned exclusively with the regulation of conditions of labor at sea; the 1921 conference attempted to adapt to agricultural workers the decisions of the first conference in regard to industry. In 1922 the conference examined constitutional questions relating to the working of the International Labor Organization. In 1923 it discussed "General Principles for the Organization of Factory Inspection." The 1924 conference adopted a draft convention concerning equality of treatment of national and foreign workers in regard to workmen's compensation for accidents; a weekly day of rest in glass-manufacturing processes where tank furnaces are used; and night-work in bakeries.[3]

[1] *The Report of the Director*, 1924, pp. 20 ff.
[2] G. A. Johnston, *International Social Progress* (1924), Chs. IV–VII.
[3] *Report of Director*, 1924, pp. 96–109; cf. *Industry, Government and Labor*, World Peace Foundation, 1928.

The 1926 conference related to conditions of work at sea. The 1927 and 1928 conferences related to minimum wage fixing machinery.

Up to 1928 all of the 27 draft conventions had been ratified and placed in force by some countries, a total of 207 ratifications having been authorized and 992 recommended. Up to October, 1928, Argentina, Bolivia, Brazil, China, Paraguay and Uruguay had not ratified any labor convention.

Among the agreements are an eight-hour day and 48-hour-week convention; an unemployment convention providing for the establishment of free employment agencies; a convention prohibiting the employment of women until six weeks after childbirth; a convention prohibiting night-work by women; a minimum age convention, prohibiting the employment of children under fourteen, and a weekly rest convention, for 24 consecutive hours.

It would be obviously unfair to fasten upon the whole world the same set of labor regulations. For this reason, labor conferences "shall have due regard to those countries in which climatic conditions, the imperfect development of industrial organisation or other special circumstances make the industrial conditions substantially different and shall suggest the modifications, if any, which it considers may be required to meet the case of such countries." [1] Acting upon this principle, the eight-hour day and forty-eight-hour week convention made an exception in the case of Japan where a fifty-seven-hour week was authorized, and in the case of India, where a sixty-hour week was authorized. The convention did not apply to Persia and China. In the minimum age convention the minimum age for children was fixed at fourteen; but in the case of Japan it was only twelve; while in the case of India, children under twelve were prohibited only from working in mines, factories, and transportation.[2] The members also undertake to apply labor conventions which they have ratified to their colonies, except when local conditions make them inapplicable. Up to 1929 the powers had applied these treaties only to a few of their possessions. While exceptions may be necessary in the backward parts of the world, there is obviously the danger that these exceptions may be exploited for the benefit of foreign capitalists residing there, unless an impartial arbiter keeps open a vigilant eye.

This position has already been filled by the International Labor Office. The representative of the Labor Organization on the Per-

[1] Art. 405, Treaty of Versailles.
[2] *Report of Director*, 1924, pp. 291.

manent Mandates Commission has exercised a considerable influence. Following correspondence with the Labor Office, the Chinese government established several bureaus dealing with labor questions, and, in March, 1923, promulgated Factory Regulations, which were the first rules issued in China in regard to modern industry and which embodied all of the suggestions of the Committee on Special Countries of the first Labor Conference, except the principle of a weekly rest. These Regulations were of great importance, therefore, because they signified "the first introduction into that country of modern principles of labor protection," and because this introduction had been brought about at the kindly suggestion and with the assistance of the International Labor Organization.[1]

In Persia—another "backward country"—the International Labor organization was also helpful. Following the friendly representation of the International Labor Office concerning the condition of labor in the carpet-weaving industry of Kerman, the Persian government brought about reforms prohibiting the employment of children under the age of ten. The Japanese government—in control of a country whose industrial development is in its early stages—"has been active in adopting legislation in conformity with the decisions of the Conference"; and "especially as regards the protection of children, great progress has been made in the last two years."[2] By October, 1928, India had ratified 11 labor conventions. In fact, it appears that greater progress in international labor legislation has been made in Oriental than in European countries.

5. THE LABOR OFFICE

In order to supervise the execution of these conventions, an International Labor Office has been established. It is under the control of a Governing Body of twelve government representatives; six representatives of capital, elected by the employer-delegates at the labor conferences, and six representatives of labor, elected by the employee-delegates. Of the twelve governmental representatives, eight represent the states of "chief industrial importance,"

---

[1] *Report of Director*, 1924, p. 287. China has not, however, ratified any convention.
[2] *Ibid.*, p. 291.

THE LABOR OFFICE

which the League Council has decided are Belgium, Canada, France, Germany, Great Britain, India, Italy and Japan. The other governmental representatives are elected by the governmental delegates, with the exception of the eight governments above, at the labor conference. The members of the Governing Body serve for three years.[1]

Under the supervision of a Director, appointed by the Governing Body, the International Labor Office collects international labor information which it publishes in several forms, prepares the agenda for the annual conferences, urges states to effect ratification of labor treaties, and supervises their administration.

In this follow-up work of the labor conferences, the International Labor Office has also been effective. Although the treaty provided that each member must submit draft conventions to the appropriate legislative authority within one year (or in exceptional circumstances, within 18 months), some powers failed to fulfill this obligation. This neglect was made the subject of study by the early sessions of the conference, while the Labor Office continually calls the attention of governments to this obligation.

So closely is the ratification of a treaty in one country connected with the fate of such a treaty in another, that one government, at least, has requested the International Labor Office for information on the way other states had fullfilled their obligations to submit proposals. Likewise, some countries have conditionally ratified treaties. Thus the French Chamber of Deputies approved the ratification of the conventions relating to night-work and unemployment, on condition that Germany, Great Britain, Italy, Poland, Czechoslovakia and the United States ratify. The International Labor Office drew the attention of the Conference to the dangers which might arise if this doctrine of conditional ratification were extended.[2] France delayed ratification of some other conventions until 1924, partly because of constitutional reasons. Likewise, South American countries held back, partly because of difficulties of communication with Geneva, disorganized politi-

---

[1] An amendment to increase the size of the Governing Body so as to increase the non-European membership was introduced in 1922 but had not by 1928 received sufficient ratifications to enter into force.

[2] *Report of Director*, 1924, p. 113.

cal situations, and the weakness of labor organization. In all of these cases, the International Labor Office worked to smooth out difficulties so that ratification would be possible. When treaties are the product of specially convened conferences, such as the Berne Labor Conference of 1907 or the Washington Arms Conference of 1922, they may be pigeonholed by the respective governments, because there is no administrative body responsible for their fate. This weakness, as far as labor legislation is concerned, has been overcome to a certain extent by the Labor Office which, while it has no power to compel ratification, acts as a gentle reminder that such ratification would advance the interests of the world. The Labor Legislation Section of the Office is also performing an extremely important service in translating and bringing together social legislation.

6. THE ENFORCEMENT OF LABOR TREATIES

In supervising the enforcement of treaties, when once ratified, the work of the Labor Office is also very important.

The Office receives annual reports from each member as to the measures it has taken to give effect to the conventions which it has ratified.[1] A committee of the International Conference studies these reports. The Office has assisted in the interpretation of the texts of the labor conventions. Governments or industrial associations of workers or employers may complain to the Office that a labor convention has been violated. If complaints from private organizations are made, the Governing Body may ask the government to make a statement. When complaints are made by one government against another, the Governing Body takes the matter under consideration. When any such matter is considered by the Governing Body, the government complained against may send a representative to sit on the Body, unless already represented. If no agreement is reached, the Governing Body may refer the dispute to a Commission of Inquiry. Upon entering the Labor Organization, each government is obliged to nominate three persons of industrial experience, one a representative of capital, one of labor, and one of independent standing, to form a panel from which the members of this Commission may be chosen, as the need

---

[1] Art. 408, Treaty of Versailles. Cf. *Report of Director*, 1924, Part II.

THE ENFORCEMENT OF LABOR TREATIES

arises. If the Governing Body decides that a dispute should go to such a Commission, the Secretary General of the League nominates three persons, one from each section of this panel; but none of the persons nominated may come from a government directly interested in the complaint. This Commission then proceeds to investigate the complaint, following which it makes a recommendation. It may also recommend measures of an economic character which may be taken against a government which has violated a convention. If a member fails to accept the recommendation of this Commission, it may refer it to the Permanent Court of International Justice, whose decision shall be final.[1] If a member fails to carry out the recommendation of the Commission or the decision of the Court, any other member may take the economic measures recommended in the report.[2]

So far it has not been necessary to refer disputes to such a Commission. And it is possible that through a process of conciliation the Labor Office may not only settle disputes between nations over the application of a convention but also international strikes voluntarily submitted to it by the parties concerned. At the Genoa conference a deadlock arose over whether a 48- or a 56-hour week at sea should be adopted. Following the failure of the conference to adopt the 48-hour week, the International Seafarers' Federation started an agitation in favor of a general seamen's strike. Fortunately it was first decided to ask the International Labor Office to arrange an arbitration with the shipowners. This task was undertaken by the Director of the Office, with the result that in January, 1921, measures were adopted which stopped an international strike from being called.

Thus the Treaty of Versailles has really revolutionized the international relations of labor. It has created an international labor

---

[1] Despite the strong sanctions embodied in these provisions of the treaty, the International Labor Organization has no power of constraint, in itself, and is not therefore a super-state. Cf. Vilallonga, "The Legal Character of the International Labor Organisation," 9 *International Labor Review* (1924), 196, answering an opposite point of view, expressed in M. Guerreau, *Une nouvelle institution du droit des gens. L'organisation permanente du travail* (1923).

[2] Cf. Articles 408–420, Treaty of Versailles; members of the U. S. Senate objected particularly to these provisions in the Treaty. And in our special treaty with Germany, August 25, 1921, the U. S. assumed no obligations under Part XIII of the Treaty. Cf. Article II, *Treaties of the U. S.*, Vol. III, p. 2598.

"legislature" whose recommendations each country is bound to study; and it has established an administrative body to look after the enforcement of labor conventions, and to study general labor conditions.

As a result of the activities of the International Labor Organization an international conscience concerning social conditions is gradually being built up. Any backward step on the part of a state belonging to this organization would at once become subjected to the inquiry of other states. While the abstention of the United States from the organization has hindered the development of such a conscience, the great debate at the sixth conference over the failure of the large industrial powers to ratify the eight-hour day convention, shows that a new moral force has come into existence.[1] Moreover, this organization gives to laboring groups within a country an opportunity to air their grievances against their own government before an international assembly. At the 1924 conference, the Japanese Workers' Delegate declared that while "freedom of association" was guaranteed to laborers in the Treaty of Versailles, in some oriental countries, especially in Japan, this right had not yet been legally recognized.[2] Although the Government Delegates denied that this statement was true, and although the Labor Organization has no power to compel a state thus to change its legislation, the mere existence of this forum will make it morally difficult for any government to enact or maintain legislation which does not accord with the prevailing social sentiment of the world.

At a conference in Washington in 1923, the five republics of Central America signed a convention for the unification of protective laws for workmen which prohibited forced labor; the employment, within school hours, of children under fifteen, or the employment in factories of children under twelve; night-work for women and males under fifteen; and certain Sunday work. The governments also promised to enact laws establishing compulsory insurance for sickness, maternity and old age, and to

[1] Cf. *Provisional Record*, International Labor Conference, sixth session, 1924, No. 9. For a discussion of the whole problem, cf. Feis, "The Attempt to Establish the Eight-Hour Day by International Action," 2 parts. 39 *Political Science Quarterly* (1924), pp. 373, 624. By 1928 Chile had ratified 8 conventions and Cuba 16.

[2] *Provisional Record*, Nos. 1 and 5.

INTERNATIONAL ASPECTS, IMMIGRATION

establish employment agencies.[1] The Pan American Conference of 1928 made certain recommendations in regard to labor.[2]

7. INTERNATIONAL ASPECTS OF IMMIGRATION

Immigration questions have ordinarily been considered "domestic" in nature. Each nation, it is urged, has the "right" to determine for itself what its ethnic composition should be. Nevertheless, when nations attempted, as did China, Japan, and Korea for several centuries, to exclude all foreigners from their midst, the powers of Europe and America battered down the door.[3] At the present time, no nation, leaving out such places as Tibet, pursues such a policy of complete exclusion. Merchants, travelers, students, and officials from every country are welcomed in foreign lands, and ordinarily guaranteed a right of entry by treaty.

Nevertheless, a number of countries now follow the practice of excluding or limiting foreign immigrants of the laboring classes,—fearing unfair competition or the difficulty of assimilation. The "right" to do this has been generally recognized by international law. The Supreme Court of the United States has said, "It is an accepted maxim of international law that every sovereign nation has the power, as inherent in sovereignty, and essential to self-preservation, to forbid the entrance of foreigners within its dominions, or to admit them only in such cases and upon such conditions as it may see fit to prescribe. . . ."[4] These limitations have been imposed because of race, literacy, or simply group interests.[5] Canada and New Zealand authorize the executive authorities to exclude any group considered undesirable for racial, national or economic reasons.[6] While this legislation has been considered strictly internal in character, it has nevertheless provoked a number of international incidents. Of these, the most important has concerned the discrimination against certain countries, such as China and Japan, or, under the quota system, Italy and Roumania—a

---

[1] *Conference on Central American Affairs*, Washington, 1923, p. 367.
[2] *I. S.* Vol. IV, No. 9, p. 221.
[3] P. Fauchille, "The Right of Emigration and Immigration," 9 *International Labor Review* (1924), 317.
[4] *Ekiu* v. *U. S.*, 142 U. S. (1891), 651, 659.
[5] Cf. p. 61.
[6] Act of 1910, 9–10 Edw. VII, Ch. 27; New Zealand Statutes, 1920, No. 23.

question considered elsewhere.¹ Apart from the question of discrimination, international irritations have occasionally been caused by the summary treatment of aliens presenting themselves for admission. Emigrants may be induced to go to a foreign country by fraud, and they may be subjected to unhealthy traveling conditions. Emigrants are usually detained in immigrant stations, where they may sometimes be subjected to uncomfortable or even unsanitary conditions.² After being kept in confinement for a number of weeks or months under such conditions, aliens have then been sent back home, on the ground that they are ineligible for admission. Under the quota legislation those immigrants who present themselves after the quota is filled are obliged to return. In some cases, families have been separated because of the operation of the laws. While treatment of this sort may be exceptional, it may have an irritating effect on public opinion at large. As a result of the harsh administration of the Chinese exclusion laws, in which even the most distinguished Chinese were impounded, ill-will in China led to a boycott of American goods in 1905–1906 which caused cotton imports from the United States to decline one-half.³ Another agitation over the administration of these laws took place in 1921–1922.⁴

One obvious solution of many of these difficulties would be to examine emigrants at the point of origin with a view to determining their eligibility—a provision inserted in the Immigration Act of 1924. Although this task might be exercised suitably by American consular officials, its effectiveness would be increased by coöperation with emigrant nations. Some such coöperation also appears necessary to prevent the smuggling of aliens across frontiers, just as it has been necessary to prevent the smuggling of opium and liquor. According to Secretary of Labor Davis 85,000 aliens surreptitiously entered the United States in 1923–1924.⁵ The value of coöperation in these matters was recognized in the Immigration Act of 1917 which authorized the President of the United States

[1] Cf. p. 62.
[2] Cf. the report of the British Ambassador, Sir Eric Geddes, on Conditions at Ellis Island Immigration Station, Cmd. 1940 (1923).
[3] M. R. Coolidge, *Chinese Immigration* (1909), p. 483.
[4] H. F. McNair, "Treaty Rights of Chinese Merchants and Free Laborers Abroad," *Chinese Social and Political Science Review*, January, 1924.
[5] *N. Y. Times*, Nov. 30, 1924.

to convene an international immigration conference and to make agreements with foreign countries to facilitate the enforcement of the immigration laws.[1]

Immigration Treaties.—A number of treaties have been made regulating immigration, and laying down conditions as to the recruiting and protection of workers. The principal agreements of this nature are the Franco-Polish convention, the Franco-Italian convention, both of September, 1919, and the Franco-Czechoslovak convention of 1920. The Franco-Polish convention provides that workers shall be recruited for emigration through public employment exchanges; and that immigrant workers shall receive equal pay for equal work, and equality of treatment in other respects. The governments undertake to control emigration in such a manner as not to prejudice the economic development of the other country. If necessary, they shall "mutually determine" the number of workers each country may absorb. The supervision of such matters is placed in the hands of a Joint Commission.[2]

In 1921 Italy and Brazil made an emigration treaty in which Brazil recognized labor contracts made in Italy by Italian workers, to be carried out in Brazil, and in which Brazil promised to assist coöperative societies among Italian emigrants.[3] Following the signature of the treaty, a model contract was drawn up for Italian agricultural workers taken to Sao Paulo, which laid down the conditions of recruiting and free transport of the workers and family. The Italian Consul is to be consulted as to the location of these settlers. The planters must open free schools for the settlers' children where the teaching of the Italian language, history and geography is compulsory.[4]

[1] 39 Stat. 874, Sec. 29. This provision was also contained in the Immigration Act of 1907. Similar legislation in Austria, Spain, Hungary, Honduras, Italy, Japan and Czechoslovakia, authorizes the executive to engage in international emigration conferences or to make emigration treaties. *Emigration and Immigration*, p. 363.
[2] Convention of September 3, 1919, *T. S.* 28; the Franco-Czechoslovak convention of March 20, 1920, is very similar—cf. *T. S.* 95.
[3] Convention of Oct. 8, 1921, *T. S.* 401.
[4] *Emigration and Immigration*, p. 352. In 1924 the Imperial Economic Council of Japan made a report on Immigration, saying that appropriate diplomatic measures should be taken to secure the entry of Japanese immigrants and capital in undeveloped countries. *Japan Weekly Chronicle*, June 15, 1924. For the treaties in regard to coolie labor, cf. p. 350.

While the labor provisions of the Treaty of Versailles are silent in regard to immigration, the International Labor Organization has nevertheless paid some attention to this question because of the belief that emigration is connected with unemployment and because of the social and industrial needs of emigrants. The Washington Conference (1919) passed a resolution asking the Governing Body to appoint an International Commission "which, while giving due regard to the sovereign rights of each State, shall consider and report what measures can be adopted to regulate the migration of workers out of their own States and to protect the interests of wage-earners residing in States other than their own. . . ." Nine European and nine non-European countries were represented on this committee, seven of which were countries of emigration, seven of immigration, and four of mixed interests. After studying this problem, the Commission concluded that there were some seventeen abuses to which immigration and emigration gave rise and suggested remedies accordingly.[1] At a session of the Commission, the Brazilian delegate proposed that a permanent International Emigration Commission be established "with a view to directing the migratory current, in a reasonable manner from countries where work is scarce to countries where labor is required."[2] This commission should also act as a conciliatory body in conflicts between governments over emigration. While sympathy was expressed by some delegates for this idea, it was believed that such a commission would be considered as an infringement upon the sovereignty of states. The Commission did adopt a resolution that "whereas the question of emigration is of immediate interest to many nations and to the future peace of the world," the advisability of creating a commission should be considered, which would follow "from day to day with full moral authority the development of this question."[3]

At the 1922 Labor Conference a recommendation was unanimously adopted providing for the communication to the International Labor Office, periodically, of all available information con-

---

[1] *Report of the International Emigration Commission*, 1921, pp. 3–8; cf. the arrangement in Johnston, *International Social Progress*, p. 162.
[2] *International Emigration Commission*, p. 57.
[3] *Ibid.*, p. 6. At the Havana Emigration Conference (1928), Cuba unsuccessfully proposed the establishment of an International Bureau of Migration.

cerning emigration.¹ The recommendation also urged members to conclude agreements uniformly defining the term "emigrant." ² While these recommendations in regard to international migration statistics do not fundamentally attack the problems of migration, they provide the basis for any action which may be taken later.

In 1924 the Governing Body established the Permanent Migration Committee, composed of 102 members.

Emigration Conferences.—Partly because of some doubt as to the constitutional power of the Labor Organization to discuss questions of immigration, partly because of pique at the League over the Corfu affair and partly because of the Italian emigration problem, the Italian government convened an International Emigration and Immigration Conference at Rome in May, 1924. While the International Labor Office coöperated with this conference, the Governing Body made it clear that the holding of this conference did not challenge the power of the Labor Office to deal with emigration problems.

Delegates from fifty-nine states, including the United States, were present at this conference, as well as the President of the Council of the League of Nations and the Director of the International Labor Office. In opening the conference, the Italian Prime Minister, M. Mussolini, said that "emigrants could not be considered as mere commodities. They had a right to find easier conditions of life in the immigration countries, and should, as far as possible, enjoy the same rights as the nationals of those countries, in view of the fact that they share with them the risks and dangers of labor." ³

The conference adopted a number of resolutions, the first relating to Transport and Hygiene. It recommended the compilation of an international sanitary code, the insurance of emigrants, a thorough medical inspection, the laying down of minimum requirements for emigrant ships, and other means of safeguarding the interests of emigrants during the voyage. A second resolution related to Assistance for Emigrants, which recommended

[1] Cf. *Methods of Compiling Emigration and Immigration Statistics*, I. L. O., 1922.
[2] "The Fourth Session of the International Labor Conference," 6 *International Labor Review* (1922), 881.
[3] *Industrial and Labor Information*, International Labor Office, May 26, 1924, p. 22.

state supervision of emigrants' lodging houses, legal aid, state control of emigrant agents, and so forth. A third resolution concerned Immigration and the Demand for Labor Abroad; and dealt with measures concerning undesirable emigrants, simplification of passport formalities, principles underlying labor contracts, measures against secret emigration, and the exchange of labor information. A final resolution in regard to Principles of International Agreements dealt with the definition of the term "emigrant"; and the principles of international agreements concerning equality of treatment of emigrants, and the admission of foreign workers to conciliation and arbitration committees.[1]

A Second International Emigration Conference was held in Havana, Cuba, in the spring of 1928. It was attended by representatives of 19 European and 18 American governments (including the United States) and also China, Japan and two African states. The work of the Conference was devoted to elaborating the principles set forth in the 1924 Statute of Emigrants. The proceedings were marked by suspicion among immigration countries toward the emigration countries, the votes on many resolutions dividing sharply along these lines.[2] It was voted to hold a third Conference at Madrid if so desired by a majority of the governments. The general sentiment was expressed that the Conference should be transferred to Geneva and work in close coöperation with other existing international bodies.[3] In view of the fact that the Italian government who originally sponsored this Conference no longer follows a vigorous emigration policy, the driving force behind this movement for emigration conferences may have already come to an end.

[1] *Ibid.*, June 16, 1924, p. 11. Believing that European conferences in regard to immigration inevitably reflect the point of view of emigrant-exporting countries, proposals have been made for a conference of immigrant-receiving countries, "to agree upon the common rights, duties, interests, and policies of the immigrant-receiving nations." This should be followed by a general migration conference of all nations, both emigrant-sending and immigrant-receiving. Dr. H. H. Laughlin, *Europe as an Emigrant-Exporting Continent and the United States as an Immigrant-Receiving Nation*, Hearings before the House Committee on Immigration and Naturalization, 68th Cong., 1st session (1924), p. 1433.

[2] Cf. "La conférence internationale de la Havane," *L'Europe nouvelle*, October 13, 1928.

[3] The word Geneva was not used, however, out of deference to the United States.

EMIGRATION AND OVER-POPULATION

The sixth Pan American Conference which met at Havana in January 1928 passed a resolution to the effect that no immigration treaty could withdraw an emigrant from the jurisdiction of the country in which he resides; that the equality of civil rights between foreigners and nationals should be recognized; that American states reserved the right to restrict immigration from other continents in accordance with economic, political and social interests; and that the proposal be considered that no American state should place obstacles in the way of emigration from other American states, and vice versa.[1]

8. EMIGRATION AND OVER-POPULATION

As we have seen, a number of countries, such as Italy, Japan, and Germany have been confronted with the over-population problem. All of them at one time have resorted to emigration as a possible solution. Italy has subsidized merchantmen carrying emigrants, and the government also subsidizes Italian schools in South America.[2] Japan follows a similar policy of subsidizing shipping companies so they can offer correspondingly cheap rates to emigrants, who may be provided with additional financial aid. There are some countries who are desirous of receiving immigrants. The Dominions welcome immigrants of the white race. A few South American countries welcome the entrance not only of Italians, but also of Chinese and Japanese. On the other hand, the great under-populated portions of the world, such as the Dominions and the United States, are determined to exclude oriental labor. The United States is also determined to exclude many categories of Europeans who wish to enter the country.

Apart from the question of discrimination, each country, according to international law, may decide for itself what aliens it will admit as permanent residents. While increasing negotiation in regard to immigration is being carried on, no nation is disposed to

---

[1] The United States declared in connection with this resolution that the control of immigration is a matter of purely domestic concern and that as far as the United States is concerned, the authority of its Congress in immigration is exclusive. Cf. "The Sixth Pan American Conference," Part II, *I. S.* Vol. IV, No. 9.

[2] R. L. Foerster, *The Italian Emigration of Our Times* (1919), pp. 272, 467.

place in the hands of foreign countries or of an international body the power to determine what and how many immigrants it shall receive. Nevertheless over-populated countries such as Italy and Japan may raise so-called ethical considerations. If their people do not emigrate, will they not starve? [1] They may feel that the solution of their over-population problem depends upon a vigorous emigration policy.[2] If the under-populated and under-developed portions of the world refuse to receive these emigrants, the imperialists in over-populated countries will declare that they must fight to obtain control of territory so that emigrants may freely enter it. While this argument may make a strong popular appeal, it has been repeatedly demonstrated that emigration is not a solution of the population problem. Despite the energetic efforts to make a settlement colony out of southwest Africa, in 1914 there were only 18,000 Germans in the whole of Africa.[3] The French have attempted to convert their possessions in North Africa into a second homeland without any great degree of success.[4] Despite the colonization efforts of Japan, there are only 332,000 Japanese in Korea, whose total population is 17,500,000. Likewise, Italy's colonies have been admittedly a failure as an outlet for population. Even within the British Empire, emigration from the mother country has been inconsiderable. It is estimated that Canada and Australia are capable of supporting 200 million people, but at present they have a combined population of only 12 million.[5] Following the World War, England attempted to stimulate emigration to the Dominions by an Empire Settlement Act which, however, also failed of its purpose. Emigration to most colonies has failed partly because the white races cannot thrive in a tropical climate. As a solution for the population problem generally, it has failed because while emigrants leave a temporary gap at home, oncoming generations soon fill it up. In fact, in those districts in Ireland and in France from which emigration has been

[1] The average annual increase of population in Japan and Italy is about 500,000.
[2] Cf. the statement of A. Cabrini, "Emigration there has got to be. This has become unmistakably the motto of Italian national life. But—whither?" *Reconstruction in Europe*, Nov. 16, 1922, p. 640.
[3] Beer, cited, p. 10.
[4] Cf. V. Picquet, *Colonisation française dans l'Afrique du Nord* (1914, 2d ed.), Chs. V and VI.
[5] "The Migration of Races," 42 *Round Table* (1921), 270.

EMIGRATION AND OVER-POPULATION

greatest, the birth rate has been higher than in districts whose inhabitants were content to stay at home.[1] In view of these considerations and also the determination of under-populated countries to exclude great masses of immigrants in the future, it appears that the migratory period of the world's history is coming to an end.

As a result, such over-populated countries as England, Germany and even Japan are apparently giving up emigration as a remedy for over-population and have resorted to industrialization—the development of manufactures which should be exchanged for raw materials produced abroad.[2] The success of this solution will depend, however, in part upon the abolition of excessive tariff walls. Moreover, many writers and scientists since the time of Malthus have feared that the food supply would eventually become exhausted, with the result that an industrialized country dependent upon rapidly diminishing foreign sources of food may starve.[3] This fear has been dramatically revived since the War. Many writers and scientists—in imitation of an old school of theology—even fix the exact year for the biological end of the world! Despite these forebodings, it is doubtful whether any calculations as to a future food shortage, for the next century at least, are worth serious consideration, in view of the inventive genius of mankind, the great stretches in the tropics and elsewhere which have been really untouched, as well as the possibilities of reducing our standards and changing our modes of living. Whether this fear of a food shortage be realized or not, the struggle for territory, either

---

[1] Cf. A. M. Carr-Saunders, *The Population Problem* (1922), pp. 297–304; Leroy-Beaulieu, *Colonisation chez les peuples modernes*, Vol. II, p. 441. Cf. H. Wright, *Population* (1923), p. 143.

[2] Cf. p. 104.

[3] E. M. East, *Mankind at the Cross Roads* (1923), Ch. IV. An international agreement between governments to limit population has been suggested. H. Cox, *The Population Problem* (1923), p. 105. Such an agreement might obligate the governments to distribute information in regard to birth control.

In September, 1927, a World Population Conference, held in Geneva and attended by scientists from a number of countries, discussed the various aspects of this question from the purely scientific point of view. Cf. *Journal of the World Population Conference*. Geneva, August 31,–September 3, 1927.

One writer who has made a careful statistical study states that with fertility and mortality rates as they prevail at present, the population of France, England and Germany is doomed to die out. R. R. Kuczynski, *The Balance of Births and Deaths*, Vol. I, (1928), pp. 4, 62.

as an outlet for emigrants or a source for food, will not solve the problem. The real solution is the restriction of numbers—the adjustment of the birth to the death rate—a solution which comes about automatically, so it appears, with the progress of education and the increased standard of living.

Nevertheless from the standpoint of practical politics, the population problem may have serious repercussions in the future. While emigration will not afford a permanent relief, it will act as a temporary safety-valve. And it is the weakness of men that they will ordinarily prefer a temporary to a permanent solution. At first glance, it may seem unjust for a country having a great stretch of comparatively unoccupied territory to exclude emigrants from over-populated countries. While a little study will show that this attitude is fundamentally sound even from the standpoint of international solidarity, provided such countries really develop their agricultural resources,[1] the great masses of people may not think the argument through; but instead, succumb to superficial arguments of jingoism and demand the annexation of more territory as a matter of life or death. If the problem of over-population is not to become the cause for war, peoples must be educated to the fact that emigration is not a relief for their difficulties.

[1] Cf. p. 104.

CHAPTER VIII

THE PROTECTION OF MINORITIES

1. The Minorities of Europe.—2. The Difficulty with Internal Guarantees.—3. Treaties Protecting Minorities before the War.—The Defects of These Treaties.—4. The New Minorities Treaties.—5. The League of Nations and Minorities—The German Settlers' Case.—6. Criticisms of the Minorities Principle—The "Little Protocols."—7. Recent Minority Developments.—8. The Exchange of Minorities.

There is probably no country in the civilized world whose inhabitants are of a single language, race or religion. The complete segregation of one nationality from another has been made impossible by history, by geography and by economics. Like the poor, ethnic minorities are always with us, and the treatment accorded them constitutes a very important problem in international life.

When countries have tried to solve this problem by a policy of compulsory assimilation, failure has been their lot. Separatist movements have been intensified and the relations between states have become embittered. Much of the hostility between Balkan nations has been due to the mistreatment of minorities. Macedonia is still a cockpit of nationalistic rivalries.

1. THE MINORITIES OF EUROPE

At the Paris Peace Conference an honest attempt was made to establish real nation-states from which irredentism would be eliminated. In a few cases this attempt was thwarted by strategic or economic considerations, notably in the Trentino, a district inhabited by Germans but which was given to Italy. Yet as a result of the boundary lines established following the World War, minorities in Europe were reduced from 54,000,000 to 16,800,000; and greater devotion to the nationality principle might have reduced this latter figure by several million. But however meticulously boundary lines might have been drawn, minorities would

180   THE PROTECTION OF MINORITIES

have inevitably remained. The ethnic minorities in Europe today, affected by the peace treaties, are as follows:

Germans	7,594,000
Magyars	2,803,000
Bulgarians	1,339,000
Jugo-Slavs	480,000
Ruthenes (Czechoslovakia)	432,000
Ruthenes (East Galicia)	3,700,000
Ruthenes (Roumania)	300,000
Poles (Czechoslovakia)	167,000
	16,815,000 [1]

About one-fourth of the population of Jugoslavia, one-third of the population of Roumania, two-fifths of the population of Czechoslovakia, and nearly one-half of the population of Poland (including Vilna and East Galicia) consist of ethnic minorities. As a result of the Peace Conference, 400,000 southern Slavs and 220,000 Germans were placed under the Italian flag.[2]

If these minorities should be left to the tender mercies of nationalistic governments, addicted to the policy of assimilation, Europe would continue to ferment in conspiracies, making a stable peace impossible. It was just as essential for the Peace Conference to solve the problem of minorities as it was to set up new nation-states.

2. THE DIFFICULTY WITH INTERNAL GUARANTEES

Minorities may be protected either by internal legislation or by treaty. The constitutions of most modern states guarantee to all persons, regardless of race or religion, certain rights before the law. In 1867 the polyglot state of Austria adopted a constitution which provided that the nationality and language of each people in the country should be conserved. The following year Hungary enacted a Law of Nationalities which guaranteed the use of native tongues in legislative bodies and in schools.[3] In the United States ethnic minorities are protected by the fifth and fourteenth amendments to the Constitution which provide for

[1] N. Buxton and T. P. Conwil-Evans, *Oppressed Peoples and the League of Nations* (1922), p. 82.
[2] J. F. Duparc, *La Protection des minorités de race, de langue et de religion* (1922), p. 332; J. Lucien-Brun, *Le Problème des minorités* (1923), p. 126.
[3] Text, G. Drage, *Austria-Hungary* (1909), Appendix.

DIFFICULTY WITH INTERNAL GUARANTEES 181

the equal protection of the laws, and by the fifteenth amendment which provides that no citizen shall be denied the right to vote on account of race, color, or previous condition of servitude. In Soviet Russia, minorities are under the protection of a Commissariat of Nationalities with a branch for each minority.[1] Turkey has made super-abundant promises to its subject nationalities, as in the decrees of 1839, 1856, 1876 and 1908. At the Paris Peace Conference, Italy promised to follow a policy of toleration toward the Germans in the Trentino.[2]

In some cases these internal guarantees have been observed. It appears that Denmark is following a liberal policy toward the German minority living in Schleswig returned to Denmark after the War.[3] In many cases, however, these guarantees have been shamefully violated. Domestic legislation in Austria, Hungary and Turkey brought little protection to minorities simply because it was not enforced. The Constitution of the United States has not prevented discriminatory legislation against Orientals and it has not prevented the indirect exclusion of the negro from the ballot. Several Italian ministries kept the pledge given by M. Tittoni at the Peace Conference that the Germans in the Trentino would be protected in their ethnic rights. But with the accession of the Fascisti government this policy was changed to one of open Italianization. Local assemblies were dissolved and German property confiscated. The use of German in public services or even in public notices was almost entirely prohibited; while Italian was made the language of instruction in the schools, despite the fact that only ten per cent of the people in the district speak Italian.[4] Italy had signed no treaty agreeing to protect minorities. A minister had merely made a declaration which a later government could disregard, without fear of being called to account by the outside world.

---

[1] Cf. Klimov, "The Jewish Commissariat in Soviet Russia," 5 *Soviet Russia* (1921), 167.

[2] H. W. V. Temperley (editor), *A History of the Peace Conference of Paris* (1922), Vol. V, p. 143.

[3] "Dänemark," *Neue Zürucher Zeitung*, May 15, 1924; Denmark declined Germany's proposal for a minorities treaty, "Dänemark," *ibid.*, May 12, 1924. Cf. also *The German Minority in South Jutland*, Danish Ministry for Foreign Affairs (1924).

[4] Count Toggenburg, a South Tyrol deputy, *Neue Zürucher Zeitung*, Dec. 7, 1923; R. Dell, "Fascist Terrorism in the Tyrol," *Nation*, May 28, 1924.

3. TREATIES PROTECTING MINORITIES BEFORE THE WAR

Because of this weakness in domestic legislation and because of the international interest created by this problem, a large number of treaties in regard to minorities have been made. Before 1815 the principle of religious toleration had been written into at least seven treaties, the most important of which was the Peace of Westphalia of 1648.[1] In consenting to the union of Holland and Belgium in 1815 the European powers affirmed the necessity of insuring "equal protection and favor to every sect," and guaranteeing "the admission of all Citizens, whatever their religious belief may be, to public employments and offices."[2] Similar guarantees were given to the subjects of the Duke of Savoy ceded to the Republic of Geneva. In the following century a number of minority treaties were imposed upon the Balkan states and upon the Turkish Empire. As a condition of recognizing the independence of Greece in 1830, the powers exacted a pledge similar to that given by Holland in 1815. When Greece was given Thessaly in 1881 it was provided that the inhabitants of the ceded territory should enjoy the same civil and political rights as Greeks.[3] At the famous Conference of Berlin in 1878 the principle was laid down that new states would be recognized only on condition that differences in religion should not be made the basis of discrimination in civil and political rights. This principle was recognized in the treaty of Berlin by Bulgaria, Montenegro, Serbia, Roumania, as well as by Turkey.[4]

In 1858 a treaty between Turkey and the powers provided that in Roumania (Moldavia and Wallachia) taxes should be equal and that as between Christians there should be no discrimination in political rights.[5]

An attempt to insert new minority guarantees in the treaties of

[1] Duparc, p. 6.
[2] Annex to Article 8, Treaty of May 31, 1815, 2 *State Papers*, 391. For the guarantees in regard to Poland, cf. p. 208.
[3] Art. III, Convention of Constantinople, May 24, 1881, 72 *State Papers*, 384.
[4] Articles 5, 27, 35, 44, and 62, Treaty of Berlin, July 13, 1878, 69 *State Papers*, 749.
[5] Article 46, Convention of Paris, August 19, 1858, 48 *State Papers*, **77.**

peace, following the Balkan Wars of 1912–1913, was blocked by Serbia.[1] Nevertheless, notes were exchanged in August, 1913, between Roumania and Bulgaria, and Greece and Serbia, promising autonomy to the Kutso-Vlachs—Roumanian nomads who live in various parts of the Balkans—in so far as schools and churches were concerned, which might be subsidized by the Roumanian government, subject to the supervision of the government involved.[2] Moreover, the rights of Moslems in the Balkan countries were safeguarded also in the treaties of peace.[3]

In Turkey the problem of minorities has been even more acute than in the Balkan countries. The recurrent massacres of Christians in this Moslem country have aroused the indignation of the outside world. Between 1774 and 1856 Russia maintained the right to protect Orthodox Christians in Turkey, while France maintained similar rights in regard to Catholics.[4] But beginning with the Treaty of Paris down to the present time, the protection of minorities in Turkey has been regarded as of international concern.

Under the pressure of European powers, Turkey issued a decree in 1856, reiterating a promise made in 1839 of equality of religion, language, and race, which the powers took note of in the Treaty of Paris. At the failure of the Turkish government to enforce these decrees, the consuls of France, England, Austria and Russia in Constantinople instituted an inquiry. In 1875 the Porte issued another firman repeating past promises. But this did not satisfy the powers, representatives of which held a conference at Constantinople and later at London to discuss the problem. At the latter conference, held in March, 1877, they signed a protocol stating that if the reforms were not soon carried out, they would

[1] For the proposal of an American representative, and also of Greece and Bulgaria, cf. *Report of the International Commission to Inquire into the Causes of the Balkan Wars* (1914), p. 185.

[2] 107 *State Papers*, 670–2.

[3] Arts. 8–10, Bulgaria-Turkey, Sept. 29, 1913, 107 *State Papers*, 706; Greece-Turkey, Art. 11, Nov. 14, 1913, 107 *State Papers*, 893; Serbia-Turkey, Art. 8, March 14, 1914, 8 Martens (3d series), 643.

[4] A. Mestré, "Le protectorat catholique de la France en Orient," *L'Europe Nouvelle*, August 9, 1924. This protectorate gives France the right to intervene before Turkish authorities in defense of Catholic interests in Turkey, and the right to decide certain cases involving Catholic communities there. This right has been recognized by the Vatican in 1909 and, apparently, France still holds the protectorate.

consult in common as to the means to be taken to safeguard the welfare of these minorities.[1]

In the Treaty of Berlin of 1878 the powers again permitted the Sultan to make another declaration in regard to religious liberty. He also promised to carry out certain reforms in regard to the Armenians and to inform the powers periodically as to their progress.[2] Instead of carrying out these reforms, however, Turkey staged the frightful Armenian massacre of 1894–1895, which led to another investigation by the powers. This time they presented to Turkey a plan calling for the European supervision of Christian minorities.[3] But the antagonism between England and Russia prevented joint action in forcing this project on Turkey.

Again defying the European powers the Turkish government allowed more Armenian massacres—those of 1904 and 1909—to take place. The terrible conditions surrounding this minority finally led the Conference of Ambassadors at Constantinople to propose a plan in 1914, which would divide eastern Anatolia into two parts; at the head of each should be placed a foreign inspector-general having control of the administration and police, representing the great powers, though technically appointed by the Sultan. This plan was embodied in a Russo-Turkish agreement of February 8, 1914.[4] But when the European war broke out these inspectors were summarily dismissed by the Sultan. Further Armenian massacres occurred in 1915 and 1922.

In 1903 Turkish oppression provoked another insurrection in Macedonia—at that time still Turkish territory—which led the European powers to intervene. They obliged the Sultan to nominate a Christian inspector-general for Macedonia, to be assisted by two civil agents, one Russian and one Austrian, representing the European powers. Foreign experts were to reorganize the police and a Financial Commission representing six European powers was to supervise revenues.[5] This control to some extent ameliorated the conditions of Christians in Macedonia. But it was terminated following the Young Turk Revolution of 1908, because

[1] Protocol of March 31, 1877, 68 *State Papers*, 823.
[2] Art. 61, Treaty of Berlin, cited.
[3] G. P. Gooch, *History of Modern Europe, 1878–1919* (1923), pp. 234 ff.
[4] Text in A. Mandélstam, *Le Sort de l'empire ottoman* (1917), p. 236; cf. J. de Morgan, *Histoire du peuple arménien* (1919), p. 257.
[5] "Affairs in Southeastern Europe," Cd. 1532 (1903), p. 84.

TREATIES PROTECTING MINORITIES

of the belief that Turkey's policy would now be more liberal. But this did not prove to be the case. And the systematic extermination of Christians in Macedonia led the Balkan states—now unsupported by the great powers because of European dissensions—to make remonstrances. Alarmed at these protests, the great powers finally urged Turkey again to carry out the reforms promised in the Treaty of Berlin. But this was "old stuff" to the Balkan states who, in a note of October 12, 1912, demanded that Turkey place the supervision of these reforms in the hands of a Superior Council, composed equally of Christians and Moslems, controlled by the diplomatic representatives of the great powers and the four Balkan states, at Constantinople. Upon the failure of Turkey to reply to this request, the Balkan states declared war.[1] As a result of the Balkan wars, Macedonia was divided up between the Balkan states, but it is doubtful whether the condition of minorities there has been much improved, at least until recently.

The Defects of These Treaties.—Very few of the international treaties providing for the protection of minorities before the War proved effective. Differences in interpretation arose, for the impartial solution of which no provision had been made. Despite the provisions in the treaties of 1858 and 1878, the Jews in Roumania were subjected to discriminatory treatment which brought forth the protests not only of European powers in 1880 but of the United States in 1902.[2] It was the contention of Roumania that her treaty obligations did not extend to Jews, and that these treaties did not give the outside world the right to intervene. Roumania also refused to admit Jews to Roumanian citizenship and thus automatically barred them from rights which the treaties guaranteed to citizens. There was no impartial tribunal to determine whether or not such an interpretation of these obligations was correct.

Secondly, no satisfactory means for enforcing these obligations upon a power, such as Turkey, or as Russia in the case of the Poles,[3] existed. During the latter half of the 19th century the Concert

[1] Cf. Mandélstam, "La Société des Nations et les puissances devant le problème arménien," *R. G. D. I. P.* (1922), 301.
[2] Cf. p. 65; also L. Wolf, *Notes on the Diplomatic History of the Jewish Question* (1919), p. 35.
[3] Cf. p. 219.

of Europe acted together in regard to Turkish affairs. But thereafter the division of Europe into the Germanic and the Allied camps prevented coöperation even for humanitarian purposes. Undoubtedly many interventions in Turkey had been prompted by disinterested considerations. At the same time, the minority treaties gave "to the Great Powers, either individually or in combination, a right to interfere in the internal constitution of the States affected which could be used for political purposes." [1] Turkey accused the European powers of fomenting insurrections among its minority populations so as to justify intervention.[2]

4. THE NEW MINORITIES TREATIES

Whatever the weaknesses of these treaties may have been, the fact remained that the protection of minorities was essential for European peace and that these minorities could be adequately protected only by international treaties. The Paris Peace Conference attempted to work out a system of treaties which would satisfy this purpose and would also evade the difficulties of the past.[3] In 1919–1920 ten treaties with this purpose were drawn up—four with the defeated powers and six with Allied states. They were between the five Principal Allied and Associated Powers, on the one hand, and Poland, Czechoslovakia, Jugoslavia, Roumania, Greece, Armenia, Austria, Bulgaria, Hungary and Turkey on the other.[4]

[1] Clemenceau to Paderewski, covering letter to the Polish Minority Treaty, June 28, 1919; Temperley, *History of the Peace Conference*, Vol. V, p. 139.
[2] Statement of Ismet Pasha, Dec. 12, 1922, Minutes, *Lausanne Conference* (1923), Cmd. 1814, pp. 190–204.
[3] The question had been diligently studied during the War by the Office of Nationalities at Lausanne and by the Central Organization for Durable Peace at The Hague. Duparc, p. 143.
[4] Treaty with Poland, June 28, 1919, placed under the guarantee of the League of Nations, February 13, 1920; Treaty with Czechoslovakia, Sept. 10, 1919, placed under League guarantee, Nov. 29, 1920; Treaty with Jugoslavia, Sept. 10, 1919, placed under League guarantee, Nov. 29, 1920; Treaty with Roumania, Dec. 9, 1919, placed under League guarantee, August 30, 1921; Treaties with Greece and Armenia, August 10, 1920; Treaty of Peace with Austria, Arts. 62–69, Sept. 10, 1919, placed under League guarantee, Oct. 22, 1920; Treaty of Peace with Bulgaria, Arts. 49–57, Nov. 27, 1919, placed under League guarantee, Oct. 22, 1920; Treaty of Peace with Hungary, Arts. 54–60, June 4, 1920, placed under League guarantee, August 30, 1921; Treaty of Peace with Turkey, Arts. 37–45, July 24, 1923. Cf. *The League of Nations and Minorities*, Information Section, League of Nations Secretariat (1923), pp. 13–14.

These treaties impose two general types of obligations. First, all inhabitants, whether citizens of the state or not, are entitled to the protection of life and liberty, and to the free exercise of religion. Secondly, all citizens or nationals of the country, belonging to a racial, religious, or linguistic minority are guaranteed equality in civil and political rights, that is, they can vote and hold office upon the same basis as the dominant nationality. They may freely use their mother language in business, in religious services, in publications, in public meetings and in courts of law. They may establish at their own expense, religious, educational or charitable institutions. In districts where a minority constitutes a "considerable proportion" of the population, instruction in the primary public schools shall be given in its language, and the minority shall receive a fair share of the sums provided by the state and local budgets for educational and religious purposes.

While this second group of rights is guaranteed only to citizens or nationals of a state, every person may become a citizen if he has been born or lived in the territory concerned. If he does not choose to accept this nationality, he must transfer his place of residence to the state whose allegiance he wishes to retain.[1] In other words, all Germans living in territory given to Poland or Czechoslovakia must become citizens of these countries or leave the country, and if they choose to become citizens of the new state, they must be given the same rights as Poles or Czechs, and at the same time be allowed to preserve their national traits unless they should wish voluntarily to change them.[2]

[1] Cf. Arts. 3-9, Treaty with Czechoslovakia, Sept. 10, 1919.
[2] Some of these treaties go still further. Poland and Greece both promise not to hold elections on Saturday, since it is the Jewish Sabbath. Jugoslavia and Greece guarantee special rights to Moslem minorities, while Greece grants special rights to the Vlachs.

In view of the particularly bad record of Turkey toward minorities, an attempt was made to impose unusually severe limitations upon her in the Treaty of Sèvres of August, 1920. This treaty not only exacted more rigid guarantees than did the other minority treaties, but it placed their enforcement, not in the hands of the League Council which was the case elsewhere—but of the Principal Allied Powers, after consultation with the Council.

The Treaty of Sèvres, however, was never ratified; and following the Turkish victory over Greece, Turkey at first refused to accept any international obligations whatever in regard to minorities. At the Lausanne conference, 1922–1923, the Allies attempted to secure the exemption of minorities from military service in return for a compensatory tax, and also to establish a special minority commission at Constantinople. Turkey refused to accede to

Each state recognizes the obligations in these minority treaties as "fundamental laws," not to be overturned by subsequent legislation or administration.[1] They can be changed only with the consent of a majority of the League Council.[2] Each state also recognizes these obligations as of "international concern" which shall be placed under the guarantee of the League of Nations. Instead of being enforced by the haphazard and rudimentary methods of the great powers, themselves divided by diplomatic jealousies, these treaties are to be enforced by a semi-judicial procedure. A member of the League Council may bring the attention of that body to any infraction or danger of infraction of the minority treaties. But a government charged with violating these treaties may sit as a member of the Council and defend itself. If the Council finds that an infraction has taken place, it may "take such action and give such direction as it may deem proper and effective in the circumstances." Moreover, all differences of interpretation of these treaties between the government accepting these obligations and any state which is a member of the Council, is recognized as a dispute of an international character, which may be referred to the Permanent Court of International Justice whose decision shall be final.

Through the instrumentality of the League, the principle of protection of minorities has been extended to other states. In 1920 the first Assembly adopted a resolution requesting that in the event of Albania, the Baltic and the Caucasian states being admitted to the League, they should respect this principle. Considerable difficulty, however, was experienced in getting the Baltic states, especially, to accept these obligations. While in May, 1922, Lithuania signed a declaration before the Council almost identical to the provisions of the Polish Minorities Treaty, Esthonia and Latvia held back. Latvia finally came to terms in July, 1923, by signing a Declaration the terms of which are much more these demands, but finally accepted the same type of minority obligations as imposed on the other powers of eastern Europe, except that they are limited to *Non-Moslem* minorities. Art. 151, Traité de paix entre les puissances alliées et associés et la Turquie. Minutes, *Lausanne Conference*, Cmd. 1814 (1923), August 10, 1920, pp. 175–227; 290–302; 303–313, and Part III, Treaty of June 28, 1923, cited.

[1] Cf. Art. 1, 12, Treaty with Poland, June 28, 1919.

[2] But to change the terms of a mandate, a unanimous vote of the Council is necessary.

vague than that made by Lithuania.¹ The Council here merely has the "right to take up the question anew" if the minorities situation in Latvia does not correspond with the principles laid down in the minorities treaties.² In September, Esthonia finally made a Declaration even more vague than that of Latvia.³ The Council may, however, request information from the Esthonian government in regard to minorities.

A number of binational treaties protecting minorities have also been signed. In settling the Upper Silesian question, the Council of the League decided that the minority principle should be extended to a district where Poles and Germans are inextricably entangled. In the convention of May 15, 1922, Germany and Poland both accepted these obligations in Upper Silesia for a period of fifteen years.⁴ This treaty is noteworthy because it is apparently the first instance where a great power—Germany— assumes such obligations. In 1920 Austria and Czechoslovakia signed a treaty providing for the mutual protection of minorities.⁵ In 1922 four Baltic states, including Poland, signed a treaty to the same effect. Similar provisions were contained in the Treaty of Dorpat between Finland and Soviet Russia, of October, 1920; in the Angora agreement of October, 1920, between Turkey and France, and in the treaty of alliance between Irak and England of October, 1922.

These binational treaties are advantageous in that both parties have an equal interest in seeing that their terms are enforced. There is no such incentive for the states who signed the original ten treaties placed under the guarantee of the League. On the other hand, the binational type is weak if it is not placed under some such international supervision. This was illustrated in a dispute which arose between Russia and Finland over Finnish minorities in eastern Carelia which Finland alleged had been mistreated by Russia in violation of the Dorpat treaty. Unable

---

¹ *O. J.*, 1922, p. 524. Albania signed a similar declaration in 1921, while the Council also "took note" of information submitted for Finland in regard to minorities at its session of October 2, 1921.
² *O. J.*, 1923, p. 993.
³ *O. J.*, 1923, p. 1311.
⁴ Cf. p. 137.
⁵ Part II, Convention of June 7, 1920, *T. S.* 98. Disputes are settled by a Mixed Commission or an Arbitration Court.

to arrive at an agreement with Russia, Finland appealed to the Council of the League in November, 1921. But the Soviet government contended that this was a purely domestic question and that it could not accept any outside intervention. In April, 1923, the League Council asked the World Court for an advisory opinion as to whether or not these provisions constituted an international engagement. The Court ruled that since Soviet Russia had declined to submit to its jurisdiction, it could give no opinion.[1]

5. THE LEAGUE OF NATIONS AND MINORITIES

The obligations assumed in the treaties placed under the guarantee of the League cannot thus be lightly set aside. Each party to these treaties promises to submit to the supervision of the League.[2] However, according to these treaties only states that are members of the League Council may call upon the League to intervene when these treaties are violated. Literally interpreted, this would bar the complaints of the forty states not on the Council, some of whom are most interested in having minorities protected.[3] But the League has adopted a procedure which is more liberal than the treaties. Any state or any minority may send a petition to the League in regard to infraction of these treaties; the Secretariat, after determining whether the petition fulfils the five conditions required,[4] is obliged to transmit it to the state against whom the charge is made. Its reply is communicated with the petition to the Committee of Three, appointed by the Council, which decides whether the petitions are worth bringing to the attention of the Council as a whole.

Thus any minority may petition the League, but the Council

[1] Cf. p. 636.

[2] Cf. report of M. Tittoni, Oct. 27, 1921, *O. J.*, Nov.–Dec., 1920, p. 8.

[3] However, any member of the League may, under article XI of the Covenant call the attention of the Council to any circumstance threatening to disturb international peace. By this means Hungary took a dispute with Roumania to the Council, cf. p. 192.

[4] These conditions are as follows: the petitions (1) must have in view the protection of minorities in accordance with treaties; (2) must not be submitted in the form of a request for the severance of political relations between the minority in question and the state of which it is a part; (3) must not emanate from an anonymous or unauthenticated source; (4) must abstain from violent language; (5) must contain information not recently the subject of a petition. *O. J.*, Nov., 1923, p. 1426.

is under no obligation to invoke the machinery set up in the treaties, unless a member of the Council really believes that the treaties have been violated. Of course, its judgment may be controlled by political considerations.[1] One state may hesitate to bring action against another state, when it has no immediate interest involved. Once a minority has submitted its petition to the League Secretariat, its rights end. If it has no friends on the Council—a body now limited to 14 powers—it has no assurance that its case will be fairly and thoroughly considered. The establishment of a Minorities Commission, similar to the Mandates Commission, has been proposed.

The German Settlers' Case.—Probably the most typical minorities case involved several thousand German farmers in Poland. In November, 1921, the Secretary-General of the League received a telegram saying that the Polish government had ordered these farmers to give up their property, which had been leased to them by the German government following the armistice but before the Treaty of Versailles went into effect. Making use of an emergency procedure, the Secretary-General communicated with the Polish government, as a result of which it promised to refrain from acting against the settlers until the League Council could examine the matter. As the dispute involved the interpretation of certain articles in the Polish minorities treaty, the Council, with Poland's consent, referred it to a committee of jurists. When Poland declined to accept its report, the Council, on February 3, 1923, requested the World Court for an advisory opinion as to whether or not Poland's action involved international obligations and whether Poland had acted in conformity with these obligations. The Court unanimously answered the first question in the affirmative and the second in the negative. It said that private rights were unaffected by changes in sovereignty and that therefore these German leases must be respected. It held that "the facts that no racial discrimination appears in the text of the law of July 14, 1920, and that in a few instances the law applies only to non-German Polish nationals who took as purchasers from original holders of German race, make no substantial difference. . . . There must be equality in fact as well as ostensible legal equality

---

[1] Cf. Heyking, "Racial Minorities and the League," *Foreign Affairs*, June, 1924.

in the sense of the absence of discrimination in the words of the law."¹ Following this opinion, Poland proposed to settle the question by compensating the colonists who had been dispossessed and in refraining from further expulsions. This proposal was accepted by the Council.²

6. CRITICISMS OF THE MINORITIES PRINCIPLE

As the German Settlers' Case shows, a vast improvement has been made in the execution of minority obligations. Despite recent progress, however, the protection of minorities still presents many difficulties, the chief of which arises out of the fact that only members of the Council may invoke the procedure set up in the treaties. In April, 1923, Hungary and Roumania were involved in a minorities dispute, arising out of agrarian legislation passed by Roumania, the effect of which was to confiscate the estates of foreigners, including Hungarians, which Hungary asserted was a violation of the treaty which Roumania had signed in 1919.³ While Hungary could not invoke the procedure laid down in this treaty, it did lay the dispute before the Council under Article XI of the Covenant—which provides simply for conciliation.⁴ The *rapporteur* of the Council suggested that since the dispute involved the interpretation of a treaty, it be referred to the World Court for an advisory opinion.⁵ Although the Hungarian government

¹ *Collection of Advisory Opinions*, Publications of the Permanent Court of International Justice, Series B, No. 6, 1923, p. 24. On September 15, 1923, the Court handed down another advisory opinion arising out of the same dispute. It was the contention of the Polish government that it was obliged to treat as Polish nationals only those persons whose parents were habitually resident in the territory, both on the day of the birth of the person concerned, and on the date of the entry into force of the treaty, January 10, 1920. The treaty of June 28, 1919, said merely "parents habitually resident there." But the Court decided that this meant only at the time of the birth of the person involved, and not at the date of the entry into force of the treaty. *Advisory Opinions*, No. 7. The third Assembly recommended that the Council members appeal without unnecessary delay to the World Court in case of differences as to questions of law or fact arising out of the treaties.

² *O. J.*, Feb. 1924, p. 359; April, 1924, p. 548; July, 1924, p. 926. A second case was brought before the Council by representatives of Belgium, Spain and China in September, 1922, involving the Jews in Hungary.

³ Treaty of Dec. 9, 1919, *Treaties of the U. S.*, Vol. III, p. 3724.

⁴ Cf. p. 628.

⁵ *O.J.*, June, 1923, p. 608. Cf. the criticism of Count Apponyi, *Verbatim Records*, 5th Assembly, Sept. 9, 1924, and the reply of M. Hymans, *Ibid.*, Sept. 10.

CRITICISMS OF MINORITIES PRINCIPLE 193

agreed to this suggestion, Roumania objected; and as no member of the Council invoked its right to refer the case to the World Court, Hungary had no further means of redress.

Nevertheless this dispute, called the Optant Question, has remained before the Council (July, 1929). In 1923 the Council appointed a *rapporteur* to bring about a direct settlement. Negotiations were conducted at Brussels where an understanding between Hungary and Roumania was arrived at on certain points. The Hungarian government declined, however, to ratify the understanding, and the League Council was confronted by another deadlock. The Council in July, 1923, passed a resolution discharging the case and expressing the hope that the Roumanian government would remain faithful to the peace treaty. Following this failure to secure a decision from the Council or the World Court, Hungarian landowners brought suits against Roumania in the mixed arbitral tribunal established by the Treaty of Trianon to hear claims arising out of the peace settlement. In January, 1927, the tribunal finally decided that it had jurisdiction to hear the case. But before it could proceed to an examination of its merits, Roumania withdrew its arbitrator, despite the promise in the Treaty of Trianon to accept the decisions of the tribunal "as final and conclusive." Under article 239 of this treaty the duty had been imposed on the Council of appointing a substitute arbitrator when a national arbitrator was not forthcoming. Instead of executing this duty the Council authorized the Committee of Three to study the problem as a whole. The Committee drew up a report to the effect that the parties should agree to a set of principles governing the case; that, if both parties accepted these principles, the Council should ask Roumania to reinstate its judge on the mixed arbitral tribunal. These principles proved unacceptable. The Council therefore ignored its duty of appointing a judge and allowed Roumania to escape from the obligation of arbitration.[1] Since then the Council has induced both governments to reopen direct negotiations, but by 1929 no result had been obtained.[2]

Now the Council is a political body, and its reluctance to appoint

---

[1] For a documented study of this case, cf. Francis Deák, *The Hungarian-Rumanian Land Dispute*, New York, 1928.
[2] See *Monthly Summary of the League of Nations*, January 15, 1929, p. 412.

the judge to the tribunal was apparently due to a desire not to offend Roumania, which was an ally of France. This case, which cannot help but be damaging to League prestige and to the cause of arbitration, shows the defects in present minority procedure.

Although France, Belgium, Denmark and Italy received territory as a result of the World War, they did not sign minority treaties; and no great power, with the exception of Germany in Upper Silesia, has signed such a treaty. These powers have defended such a discrimination on the ground that the independence of the new states of Europe and the increased territory of other states in the Balkans was due to the armies of the Allies, who were therefore justified in insisting that these states follow policies which would not precipitate war in the future. It is manifestly impracticable to place the Indians and Asiatics in the British Dominions or the negro and the Japanese in the United States under international protection. If the application of minority obligations is suspended until they become universal, it is safe to say they will never be applied. Nevertheless, while there may be some justification for limiting minority treaties to the smaller countries of the world, it is manifestly unfair, for example, to compel Jugoslavia to protect Italian minorities without placing Italy under similar obligations toward Jugoslav minorities. This fact was recognized by the third Assembly (1922) of the League which expressed the hope that states not bound by legal obligations should nevertheless treat their minorities at least as well as required of other countries by treaty.

Likewise, the minorities system has been criticised on the ground that it rests upon a bad principle. According to these critics, it tends to create a state within a state, which will ultimately lead to national disintegration. Instead of insuring social peace, we are told that the system will intensify ill-will.[1] According to others, these treaties have accentuated the differences between Jews and Gentiles rather than smoothing them out.[2] Some minorities have taken advantage of these treaties, such as the Hungarian minorities in Czechoslovakia and Roumania, or the Bulgarian minority in Greek Macedonia, to agitate against the

---

[1] Blociszewski, "La constitution polonaise du 17 Mars, 1921," 45 *Revue des sciences politiques* (1922), p. 54.

[2] P. Mignot, *Le Problème juif et le principe des nationalités* (1923), p. 85.

state of which they are a part. Obviously, the minority treaties should not protect such action. This fact was emphasized by the third Assembly which declared that while the minorities should be protected from oppression, it was their duty to "coöperate as loyal fellow-citizens with the nations to which they belong." In regard to the fear of national disintegration, it may be said that the minority treaties, properly interpreted, do not prevent the voluntary merging of minorities and majorities. They do not, moreover, prevent a state from obliging all minorities to learn the dominant language. But these treaties merely say that in addition to learning such language, the minority language must also be tolerated. The treaties merely prevent assimilation by force—which has always failed of its purpose and which has frequently provoked rebellion and war.

It is undesirable to have minorities constantly appealing to an outside authority for the redress of real or imaginary grievances—a practice which, if indulged in to the extreme, would merely intensify ill-will. "Populations protected solely by means of foreign intervention would soon become an object of hatred on the part of the majority in the countries in which they lived. Moreover, the friction produced by diplomatic intervention between the two governments concerned would be entirely incompatible with a spirit of good understanding and coöperation between States."[1] If a system of protecting minorities is to succeed, some means of *preventing* the infraction of minority rights must be devised. Recognizing this fact, the third Assembly recommended that, while the Council should retain full power in cases of grave infraction of the treaties, good relations could best be promoted by "benevolent and informal communications" with governments accused of mistreating minorities.

The establishment of administrative machinery on the spot, to air minority grievances, composed of representatives of the governments concerned, would also prevent many petitions from going to the Council. In the Polish-German convention of May 15, 1922, in regard to Upper Silesia, the two governments promised to set up in each part of the territory a Minorities Office.[2] If a

---

[1] M. Politis, *Verbatim Record*, 4th plenary meeting, 5th Assembly, Sept. 3, 1924.

[2] Convention Germano-Polonaise relative à la Haute Silesie, Arts. 64–158;

minority cannot obtain satisfaction from the highest administrative authority, it may petition the Minorities Office of its state. If the Office does not bring about an agreement, it may transmit the petition to a Mixed Commission, composed of two Germans and two Poles, with a neutral chairman—an organ of conciliation. If the minority is not satisfied with the opinion of this Commission, it may appeal through the proper channels to the Council of the League. An Arbitral Tribunal also exists to interpret the convention in cases where individual rights are involved.

The Permanent Court of International Justice has handed down a number of judgments and advisory opinions in regard to Upper Silesia.[1]

The "Little Protocols."—A further development of the idea of having League representatives on the spot took place in the so-called "Little Protocols," signed by Greece, Bulgaria, the President of the League Council, and the Secretary-General, in September, 1924. In these protocols, two members of the Mixed Emigration Commission are designated as special representatives of the League, to assist Bulgaria and Greece in the execution of their minority treaties. They may make inquiries on the spot and jointly submit reports to the government concerned on the measures to be taken. They may also receive petitions from minorities who believe that their rights have been infringed. The League representatives will make a recommendation as to settlement, which will be forwarded to the government concerned. However, the League representatives have only advisory powers, and the Council retains its power to settle disputes over minorities as provided in the treaties.[2] Nevertheless, by means of this agreement, which came from the initiative of the Greek and Bulgarian governments, many disputes may be peacefully settled on the spot. The creation of mixed commissions similar to that established in

Art. 562; and Part VI. A significant illustration of the method by which the minorities system operates, especially in connection with the Upper Silesian convention, is found in a communication to the League from certain German minorities in Poland, with the observations of the President of the Mixed Commission, as a result of which the Polish government made provision for instruction in the German language at the schools. *O. J.*, April, 1924, p. 686.

[1] Cf. p. 618.
[2] *O. J.*, October, 1924, p. 1349. The idea of government representatives apparently originated with Professor Gilbert Murray who advanced the idea at the Third Assembly.

CRITICISMS OF MINORITIES PRINCIPLE 197

Upper Silesia or the appointment of advisory League representatives, as in Greece and Bulgaria, in other countries having minorities, might lead governments to settle disputes amicably between themselves without resorting to outside authority.[1]

Finally, the minorities treaties have been attacked on the ground that their provisions are inadequate and that they have not been enforced.[2] The violation of these treaties has been inevitable in view of the fierce nationalistic hates engendered during the War. Many persecutions of minorities, moreover, have taken place in territory whose status has not been fixed and to which these treaties could not therefore apply.[3] Nevertheless, the existence of these treaties gives minorities a peaceful means of airing their grievances before the public opinion of the world. While reparation may not always be made, these treaties, imperfectly enforced, are better than no treaties at all. The negotiation of regional agreements with local machinery will help to iron out differences. And with the stabilization of frontiers, the settlement of other

[1] Cf. resolution for "Commissions paritaires," Interparliamentary Union, August, 1923, *Bulletin Interparlementaire*, July–August, 1923, Part IV.

[2] Cf. *La situation des minorités en Slovaquie et en Russie-Subcarpathique*, Mémoire à la Société des Nations, 1923. Ludwig, "Le Sort des Minorités en Hongrie et en Tchécoslovaquie," and "La Tchécoslovaquie, la grande Roumanie, La Yougoslavie, que seraient-elles sans la signature des traités de Minorités," *Revue de Hongrie*, January 15, April 15, 1923; Duparc, Part III; Lucien-Brun, pp. 194–195; *Manchester Guardian Weekly*, March 28, 1924, p. 260, which reports the introduction of a government bill in Poland giving an extra vote to those who can read and write Polish; S. Munz, "Czechoslovakia under Masaryk," 123 *Contemporary Review* (1923), p. 598; F. Maxwell, "The Treatment of Hungarian Minorities," *Fortnightly Review*, July, 1924.

In Jan., 1923, the Polish government addressed a memorandum to the Council stating that the minority treaties should be interpreted and "applied in a restricted and not an extended sense," and suggesting the partial abolition of the procedure set up for the enforcement of these obligations: no petition should be communicated to the Members of the League except in virtue of an express resolution of the Council; the investigations of the Committee of Three should be "regarded purely as internal routine work;" no question should be laid before the Council except upon the deliberate motion of a Member of the Council. It wished also to do away with petitions of third parties, on the ground that such petitions "constitute an unwarrantable interference . . . in the internal affairs of a sovereign and independent State."

At its meeting of Sept., 1923, the Council, while making some minor changes in the procedure, rejected the main propositions of Poland.

[3] Cf. the Assembly resolution of Sept. 27, 1921, requesting the Council to call the attention of the Allied Powers to the desirability of fixing the status of Eastern Galicia. The Council took such action also, on April 21, 1923, in regard to Thrace. *Report to Fourth Assembly*, A. 10, 1923.

disputes, and the development of the authority of the League, the minorities system is likely to become more and more effective, until most "irredentist" movements are wiped off the map of Europe.

At the same time, no minority treaty will silence the demands of a nationality whose group consciousness is suppressed by a foreign state. No minority treaty would have silenced the demands of Alsace-Lorraine for reunion with France or at least for political autonomy. Minority treaties can never whitewash imperialism. They will succeed only when the minorities to whom they apply are genuine minorities, inextricably part of the state having jurisdiction over them.

7. RECENT MINORITY DEVELOPMENTS

Although quite a number of petitions from dissatisfied minorities were transmitted, the Council between 1920 and 1926 was not very active in considering them. Up to 1925 only three minority cases were deemed worthy of official attention. Even when the evidence indicated that obligations had been violated, the Council did not consider it wise to intervene to the extent of asking a state to withdraw measures contrary to its obligations. It usually merely "expressed confidence" that the state would not continue to enforce such measures.[1] The admission of Germany, as well as other of the former Central Powers, to the League of Nations and the election of Germany as a permanent member of the Council has, however, changed the situation. States solicitous of the welfare of minorities now participate in the minorities machinery. During 1928 the Committees of Three, appointed by the Council to examine minority questions, dealt with twenty-three petitions which were judged to be receivable, coming from eight countries.[2]

While Germany demanded a more rigid enforcement of minority obligations, Poland and other interested countries have attempted to resist any such development. They have advanced the theory that the minority treaties are a temporary expedient until the time when the minority will be assimilated with the majority.

[1] Duparc, "L'État de la protection des minorités à la veille de la 4e assemblée de la Société des Nations," *R. D. I. L. C.*, 1923, Nos. 4–5.

[2] Address of M. Briand to the Council, *Monthly Summary of the League of Nations*, April 15, 1929.

RECENT MINORITY DEVELOPMENTS

From the international standpoint an acute situation in regard to minorities arose in 1927–1929 in Polish Upper Silesia. At the Lugano session of the Council in December, 1928, eight petitions from the Germans in this area were heard. At one meeting, M. Zaleski of Poland declared that members of the German organization in Upper Silesia, the *Volksbund,* had been guilty of treason to Poland. The provisions of the minorities treaties could not be used as a legal basis for the activities of a minority whose objects were directed against the state. The activities of the *Volksbund* were "a real danger to peace." In reply, Herr Stresemann of Germany declared heatedly that the Polish speech had been prompted by a "spirit of hatred toward the German minority." Poland could not deny the duty to protect German minorities in accordance with the Upper Silesia convention.[1] The President of the Council closed the discussion by stating that there was no possibility of the League's becoming "indifferent to the sacred cause of minorities." After this exchange Herr Stresemann declared that Germany would ask to have the entire minorities question placed upon the agenda of the next session of the Council.

At the March, 1929, session Senator Dandurand of Canada proposed a change in the existing minority procedure as follows: (1) all petitions concerning minorities should, except in cases of extreme urgency, be addressed in the first instance to the government concerned, and if the government were unable to satisfy the petitioners, the petition, together with the attached correspondence, should be forwarded to the Secretariat of the League; (2) such petitions should be examined by a committee composed of all the members of the Council or their substitutes; (3) the committee might refer the question to the Council and if neither the committee nor any member made a report to the Council, the committee should decide in what circumstances a public communication thereon should be made.[2]

The purpose of these proposals, which were supported by Germany, was twofold: First to induce a minority to attempt to settle a dispute with the government on the spot, before appealing to Geneva. Second, when an appeal is finally taken to Geneva,

---

[1] Minutes, 53rd session, P. V. 6. Cf. "German-Polish Relations," *I. S.*, Vol. III, No. 12.

[2] For the plan see C. 51. (1) M. 36. (1). 1929. I.

to give greater publicity to the action taken. At present a minority is left ignorant of the action of the Council; moreover petitions are heard not by all the members of the Council, but only by the Committee of Three, from which a state interested in a particular minority is excluded.

In supporting these proposals, Herr Stresemann repudiated the idea that the minority treaties were a temporary expedient. He referred to the establishment of a Permanent Minorities Committee. The Council finally referred the Canadian and German proposals to a committee. According to the press, this committee recommended to the Council at its June session that these proposals should not be adopted.[1] According to the press, the Council adopted a compromise.

8. THE EXCHANGE OF MINORITIES

Adopting a more drastic solution of the minorities problem, some governments have signed treaties providing for the bodily return of minorities to their home countries. In an exchange of notes in 1914, Turkey and Greece provided for the voluntary exchange of minorities left in the territory of each power as a result of the changes made following the Balkan wars. A mixed commission with some neutral members was to see that the exchange was humanely carried out. Provision was also made for the protection of property rights.[2] The execution of the plan was prevented by the outbreak of the World War.

This same principle was adopted in 1919 by Greece and Bulgaria, in signing a treaty providing for reciprocal and voluntary emigration of minorities. A Mixed Commission was established of four members, one Greek, one Bulgarian, and two appointed by the League Council. This Commission supervises emigration and is responsible for the liquidation of the property of emigrants. It makes advances, out of available funds, to these emigrants according to the value of their property.[3]

In January, 1923, Greece and Turkey signed a convention providing for the compulsory exchange of their respective minorities, except the Greeks in Constantinople and the Moslems in western

[1] *New York Times*, May 24, 1929.
[2] A. J. Toynbee, *The Western Question and Greece and Turkey* (1922), p. 141.
[3] Treaty of Nov. 27, 1919, T. S., 9. Cf. article 56 of the Treaty of Neuilly.

THE EXCHANGE OF MINORITIES

Thrace. A mixed commission was set up, of four Turkish and four Greek members, with three members chosen by the League Council from powers which were neutral during the World War. The treaty provides that Turks returning to Turkey shall receive property there to the value of their property left in Greece, and that Greeks returning to Greece shall similarly receive Turkish property. If the total value of Greek property does not equal the value of Turkish property (and vice versa), the balance shall be paid by the debtor government.[1]

This agreement had been negotiated at the suggestion of Dr. Nansen, the Refugee Commissioner of the League, on the ground that Turkey was already expelling minorities and that some such means of control must be established if suffering was to be diminished.[2]

While the policy of voluntary exchange followed in the Bulgarian-Greek convention has some commendable features, compulsory exchange, as set up in the Greek-Turkish convention, appears justifiable only as a last resort. The emigration of Greeks resulted in a great economic loss to Turkey without a corresponding gain to Greece, since it was obliged to take in about one million refugees —one-quarter of its population. Despite the treaty, the expulsions of Greeks from Turkey and of Turks from Greece were accompanied by unspeakable inhumanities, and created that great refugee problem which the League attempted to solve.[3] The compulsory exchange of minorities not only defies economic laws, but it es-

---

[1] Convention Concerning the Exchange of Greek and Turkish Populations, January 30, 1923, Cmd. 1929, pp. 175-187.

[2] Cf. his statement, Minutes, Lausanne Conference, Cmd. 1814 (1923), pp. 113-117; for the protest of the American representative, cf. *ibid.*, p. 187. Also Zekeria, "Solving Greco-Turkish Blood Feuds by Migration"; Lane, "Why Greeks and Turks Oppose Being Exchanged," *Current History*, March and April, 1923.

[3] Cf. p. 297. The existence of the League has, however, prevented atrocities which otherwise would have certainly occurred. In October, 1924, the Turkish government ordered a large number of Greek residents to leave Constantinople despite the fact that the Exchange Treaty stated that the exchange should not apply to Constantinople. The Turkish government refused to submit the question to the Mixed Commission, whereupon Greece placed it before the League Council, at whose intervention the Turkish government agreed to a settlement following an advisory opinion of the World Court interpreting the convention. See Advisory Opinion, no. 10.

For the exemption of Moslems of Albanian origin in Greece from the exchange, cf. *O. J.*, August, 1924, p. 1066.

tablishes a dangerous precedent which may act as an incentive to nationalistic oppression. It cannot by any means be regarded as a substitute for the protection of minorities.

The large number of international conventions entered into in regard to the subject of minorities shows that internal social conditions in sovereign states may be of great consequence and interest to the outside world. By means of such principles the old idea of an exclusive intolerant nationalism is being modified. The next two chapters will point out how the old conception of a nation-state is being further changed by the conception of a multi-national state capable of tolerating a large number of nationalities, upon a basis of autonomy or of federation.

CHAPTER IX

MULTI-NATIONAL STATES

1. The Alternative of Autonomy.—2. The British Empire as a Multi-National State.—3. The Dominions and Foreign Affairs—The Halibut Treaty—Imperial Conferences—Veto over Imperial Treaties—The Need for Consultation.—4. Zionism.—5. Finland and Poland.—6. The Soviet Government and Autonomy.—7. Autonomy in Austria, Hungary and Turkey—The Lebanon.—8. Iceland and Quebec.—9. Centralization v. Autonomy.—10. Guaranteed Autonomy—The Ruthenes—The Aaland Islands.

However effective the protection of individual minority rights may be, such a policy will not quiet the demand of a real nation for independence unless its existence as a political group is also recognized. In cases where ethnic minorities are scattered in insignificant groups through a country, minority treaties will be a sufficient safeguard. But in other cases a nationality, in a minority considering the country as a whole, may be a majority within a restricted district. Taking Germany as a whole, the French in Alsace-Lorraine were in a distinct minority; considering only Alsace-Lorraine, they constituted a majority.

1. THE ALTERNATIVE OF AUTONOMY

If the policy of self-determination were literally applied, all such units should either be given their absolute political independence or be joined to a state of which they are ethnically a part. In the case of a large number of such units, this, however, may be impracticable from the economic standpoint, and otherwise undesirable from the standpoint of the ethnic group as well as of the world at large. Mere representation in the central government will not satisfy such groups, any more than mere minority treaties. The people of Canada would not be satisfied, for example, merely with sending representatives to the British parliament at London, if London insisted on sending out British officials to govern Canada's internal affairs. The people of Catalan—who are in many respects distinct from the Castilians—now send deputies to the Spanish Cortes; they nevertheless resent being governed by Castilian and not Catalonian officials, and paying their taxes into a central treasury, to be disbursed by officials whom they do not control.[1]

If the only choice for such nations were between extreme centralization and absolute independence, the latter alternative would probably prevail, despite its disadvantages. There is another alternative—the establishment of a number of national governments, each autonomous in local affairs, but subject to the control of a central authority in affairs of common concern. The nationalities within such a state would have a common allegiance, a common citizenship, sometimes a common flag, and a common monetary and commercial system. Each national group would, however, be given a legislature of local representatives with power over local affairs, such as schools or taxation. Local officials would be appointed from the people on the spot and would be responsible for the administration of local affairs. Taxes, for the most part, would be devoted to local purposes. Such a policy recognizes the *group* consciousness of a minority-nation, in contrast with the protection-of-minorities policy which guarantees only the rights of *individuals*.

2. THE BRITISH EMPIRE AS A MULTI-NATIONAL STATE

In an attempt to preserve their self-existence and at the same time to satisfy the demands of divergent nations, many states have adopted this policy of autonomy. The most famous example, of course, is the British Empire. The people of Ireland are culturally distinct from the people of England. Who doubts the existence of an Irish "nation"? Even in Great Britain the people of Scotland and Wales differ from the people of England proper. There are still greater differences between the English, on the one hand, and the Canadian, the South African and the Australian.[2] The British Union Jack flies over eight distinct "nations."

At the present time, eight of these nations are self-governing in local affairs—the five Dominions of Canada, Newfoundland,

[1] Joad, "The Spanish Separatists," *Foreign Affairs*, May, 1924.
[2] Tracquair, "The Canadian Type," *Atlantic Monthly*, August, 1923. Also R. Jebb, *Studies in Colonial Nationalism* (1905), pp. 1–2, 8.

BRITISH EMPIRE: MULTI-NATIONAL STATE 205

Australia, New Zealand and South Africa; as well as the Irish Free State, the newly constituted government of Southern Rhodesia,[1] and to a lesser extent Northern Ireland. Each of these nations has a constitution, usually drafted by itself and formally approved by the British government. None of them sends representatives to the parliament at London, but each has a legislature of its own. The only representative of the British Crown in these countries is an official usually called the Governor-General. A figurehead, he "governs" through a ministry of local representatives responsible to a local parliament. If the ministry does not retain the confidence of parliament it must go out of office, and the Governor-General must select another ministry which has the confidence of that body. Each nation has not only a representative but also a responsible government—fully controlling its "national" affairs.

Certain legal links, however, still bind these nations to the mother country at home. The assent of the British Governor-General is necessary before a bill of a Dominion parliament may become law; and the Governor-General may either withhold his assent or he may reserve the bill for the consideration of the home government. Within a certain period of time the home government may also disallow colonial laws.[2] Certain constitutional limitations may also be imposed on Dominion legislatures. The Dominion of Canada must recognize certain rights of the Catholics in Quebec; the Irish parliament cannot abridge freedom of religious opinion; and the Union of South Africa is limited in its control over native affairs. In case a colonial legislature passes an act which violates a statute of the British parliament it is invalid and may therefore be set aside by the Judicial Committee of the Privy Council.[3] Although the supremacy of the mother country is thus upheld, as

---

[1] Between 1889 and 1923 Southern Rhodesia was governed by the British South Africa Company, subject to the control of the Colonial Office. The charter of this company having expired, the people of Southern Rhodesia voted in October, 1922, whether to join the adjacent Union of South Africa or to have a responsible government of their own. They voted in favor of the latter proposition, and responsible government was extended by Letters Patent, Sept. 1, 1923, subject to certain limitations in regard to the natives and the mining and railway rights of the British South Africa Co. *Statutory Rules and Orders*, 1923, p. 1078.

[2] Cf. Arts. 54–57, British North American Act, 1867, 30–31 Vict., c. 3.

[3] Colonial Laws Validity Act, 1865, 28–29 Vict., c. 63.

a matter of practice the Governor-General to-day never vetoes legislation, although laws may occasionally be reserved; moreover the Judicial Committee seldom declares Dominion legislation unconstitutional.[1] The British parliament imposes no taxes on the Dominions and it rarely legislates for the Empire as a whole.[2]

At the present time, the Dominions also exercise powers which might be considered of more than local importance. With the exception of Canada, they may amend their constitutions. They also regulate their tariffs—an extremely important power. All of the Dominions impose duties on British imports, although they usually give a preference to British goods.[3] The Dominions may regulate immigration.[4] In the matter of internal defense they are virtually free. Before the War, Australia, New Zealand and the Union of South Africa enforced a system of compulsory military training. Dominion troops were responsible for internal order, and as long as they remained at home they were under Dominion control. They may likewise maintain local navies.[5]

Although under the policy of autonomy these various nations are virtually free in matters of local concern and have great liberty in other matters which indirectly affect the Empire as a whole, they have had no direct influence until recent years upon the foreign policy of the Empire. The Dominions have no control over the British ministry or the British parliament which may legally involve the whole Empire in war. The only way they may escape the legal liabilities of belligerency is by secession.[6]

England has attempted to mitigate the severity of this autocratic control, first, by relieving the Dominions of the obligations of participating actively in a war for which they are not responsible and in which they are not interested; and secondly, by as-

[1] A. B. Keith, *Responsible Government in the Dominions* (1912), pp. 1002 ff. "Imperial Statutes in Force," Ch. VI; C. J. Tarring, *Laws Relating to the Colonies* (4th ed., 1913).

[2] Cf. "An Act for removing all Doubts and Apprehensions concerning Taxation," 18 Geo. 3, c. 12, which declared, "From and after the passing of this Act the King and Parliament of Great Britain will not impose any Duty, Tax or Assessment whatever" on the colonies, except for purposes of commerce, the revenues of which to be kept in the colony.

[3] *Colonial Tariff Policies*, U. S. Tariff Commission (1922), Chs. XII–XVIII.

[4] Cf. A. B. Keith, *Responsible Government in the Dominions*, pp. 1074–1100, but cf. p. 65.

[5] Keith, *Imperial Unity and the Dominions* (1916), Ch. XV.

[6] "The Imperial Conference," 13 *The Round Table* (1923), 683.

DOMINIONS AND FOREIGN AFFAIRS 207

suming full responsibility for the defense of the Dominions from outside attack. During the World War, it is true, New Zealand and Canada passed conscription acts, while Dominion troops generally played a heroic part on European battlefields. However, these troops were there, not at the command of the British parliament, but of the Dominions who sent them voluntarily.[1] England does not tax the Dominions for the maintenance of a navy which has guarded their communications in the past and protected them from the outside world.[2]

Despite such concessions, this system eventually became unsatisfactory. At the most, it was a benevolent despotism, which ignored the wishes of the Dominions in matters which might mean life or death. The last war, moreover, demonstrated that England could not possibly continue to bear the defense of the Empire alone. If it had not been for the assistance of the Dominions, England might have been defeated. Regardless of the legalities involved, the Dominions cannot stand idle when the very existence of the Empire is at stake. Realizing that they must bear the burden, they have consequently demanded a share in determining what kind of a burden it should be.

3. THE DOMINIONS AND FOREIGN AFFAIRS

This demand of the "nations" of the British Empire to participate in the formulation of Imperial foreign policy, has taken two forms, somewhat inconsistent with each other. The first has demanded freedom to formulate Dominion foreign policies, independent of Great Britain. The second has demanded some participation in the formation of a policy common to the Empire as a whole.

In the domain of treaty-making, the Dominions have been given considerable independence. Commercial treaties signed by Great Britain now contain a clause saying that they shall not apply to the Dominions except upon notice of accession.[3] The Dominions may also withdraw separately from British treaties

---

[1] Keith, *War Government of British Dominions* (1921), Ch. V.

[2] However, following a special defense conference, in 1909, the Dominions began to build up local navies to lighten England's load.

[3] Cf. Article 26, Treaty of April 3, 1911, British Empire and Japan, 104 *State Papers*, 159.

of commerce to which they may have adhered. In 1907 the Dominions were authorized to negotiate separate commercial agreements through their own representatives, but such treaties nevertheless required the signature of a British representative and ratification by the British Crown.

The "Halibut" Treaty.—In 1923 a further step was taken when Canada was allowed to sign a treaty *alone*,—the "Halibut" treaty of March 2, 1923, with the United States.[1] The parties to this treaty were the United States of America and "His Majesty the King of the United Kingdom of Great Britain and Ireland and of the British Dominions Beyond the Seas, Emperor of India." But "His Britannic Majesty" named as his plenipotentiary: "The Honorable Ernest Lapointe, K. C., B. A., LL. B., Minister of Marine and Fisheries of Canada." While he was named by His Britannic Majesty (who may be the King of Canada, according to some Canadians), he was nominated and instructed by the Canadian government. The treaty, however, required the ratification of the British Crown.[2]

However, in making such treaties, a Dominion should give due consideration to its effect upon the remainder of the Empire. At the Imperial Conference of 1923, this principle was adopted, in a formal resolution which also provided that bilateral treaties affecting one part of the Empire only should be signed by a representative of the government of that part, and ratified by the Crown "at the instance of the government" concerned.[3]

Furthermore, the Dominions, India and Ireland are members of the League of Nations, where in the Assembly each has the same vote as Great Britain, and where their representatives act

[1] *Treaties of the U. S.*, Vol. III, p. 2659. Also cf. Correspondence, "Halibut Fisheries Treaty," *Canadian Sessional Paper* No. 111a, 31 Geo. V. A. 1923, for the demands of Canada, to which the London government finally acceded.

[2] Cf. Marriott, "Empire Foreign Policy," 119 *Fortnightly Review* (1923), 788; also Lowell, "Canada's Treaty-Making Power," *Foreign Affairs*, Sept., 1923. The Senate of the United States originally attached a reservation to this treaty, saying that none of the nationals and inhabitants and vessels of any other part of Great Britain (sic) shall engage in halibut fishing contrary to the treaty. While Canada declined to accept the reservation, which would have apparently denied her power to make a treaty, she accomplished the same end by legislation. It appears that the Senate withdrew its reservation, whereupon the treaty was ratified in December, 1924.

[3] Summary of Proceedings, Imperial Conference, 1923, Cmd. 1987, IX.

DOMINIONS AND FOREIGN AFFAIRS 209

under the instructions of their own governments.[1] The Dominions are eligible to election on the League Council upon the same basis as any other member. Three Dominions hold mandates from the League of Nations, transmitting their annual reports directly to Geneva. Canada was elected to the League Council in 1927.

Finally, the Dominions may have certain diplomatic representation of their own abroad. In May, 1920, the British government announced that Canada might nominate a minister to the United States. Ireland "appointed" such a minister to the United States in June, 1924. While he is accredited by "His Majesty the King," in matters affecting the Irish Free State he is not subject to the control of the British Ambassador. Any question, however, whether a subject falls within the Irish minister's sphere, would be determined by consultation between him and the Ambassador. This arrangement thus "would not denote any departure from the principle of the diplomatic unity of the Empire." [2]

Imperial Conferences.—While the Dominions have been given a certain autonomy in international affairs in regard to treaties, membership in the League, and diplomatic representation, they also have acquired some control over Imperial policy as a whole. This control has taken two forms (1) through the Imperial Conference, (2) participation in the making of treaties affecting the Empire as a whole. While a number of colonial conferences had been held before 1907, the first "Imperial Conference" was held in London in that year. This Conference is composed of the prime ministers of the Dominions and of Great Britain (including Ireland), together with other officials. According to the constitution of 1907, this Conference should meet once every four years.[3] Before the World War, these gatherings confined themselves almost wholly to such dreary subjects as cables, judicial appeals, naturalization and preferential tariffs. However, in 1911, the British

---

[1] A number of disagreements between the Dominions and Great Britain at the Assembly have arisen. Cf. Keith, *The Constitution, Administration and Laws of the Empire* (1924), p. 50.

[2] "Correspondence between His Majesty's Government and the United States respecting the appointment of an Irish Free State Minister." Cmd. 2202 (1924).

[3] "Colonial Conference, 1907," Cd. 3404, p. 14. Cf. R. Jebb, *The Imperial Conference, a History and a Study* (1911), 2 vols.

government did inform the Dominions what the foreign policy of the Empire was. Because of the loyal support of the War by the Dominions, a revolutionary change now took place in their relations to Great Britain. From 1917 to the end of the War, the prime ministers of the Dominions were in London almost continuously. Sitting as an Imperial War Cabinet, they were really the supreme executive of the Empire until the peace treaties were signed.

At the Imperial Conference of 1921 it was evident that the Dominions had a great deal more influence over Imperial foreign policy than before the War. In 1911 they had merely been *informed* as to what the foreign policy was; in 1921 they were *consulted* as to what it should be. The theory apparently followed was that Imperial policy was now the product of the whole Commonwealth, as expressed by the Imperial Conference and communications in the interval, but that the machinery for carrying this policy into effect was still the British Foreign Office.[1] Between conferences, no Dominion could be expected to support new actions of the British Foreign Office of which it did not approve.

Veto over Imperial Treaties.—In the second place—the Dominions have exercised a certain veto over Imperial foreign policy by participation in the making of Imperial treaties. When such treaties are drawn up in international conferences, it is customary to give the Dominions some form of representation. In 1912 they were represented separately at the Radiotelegraphic Conference, where their representatives acted under Dominion instructions. This precedent was followed in the Conference on Safety of Life at Sea in 1914. The first political conference at which they were given separate representation was the Paris Peace Conference of 1919. In addition to five delegates for the British Empire proper, Canada, Australia and South Africa had two delegates

---

[1] At the Imperial Conference of 1921, the Upper Silesia and the Japanese Alliance questions were discussed. Cf. *Summary of Proceedings*, Imperial Conference (1921), Cmd. 1474, p. 3. According to a memorandum circulated by Sir Robert Borden at the Paris Peace Conference, in behalf of the Dominion Prime Ministers, "The Crown is the supreme executive in the United Kingdom and in all the Dominions, but it acts on the advice of different Ministries within different constitutional units." *Canadian Sessional Paper*, No. 41j, cited, p. 6.

DOMINIONS AND FOREIGN AFFAIRS 211

each, while New Zealand had one.¹ Much to the displeasure of some of the Dominions, this precedent was not followed at the Washington Conference of 1921–1922, to which the United States invited only the British Empire. However, as no limitation on the number of delegates each power might have was imposed, it was arranged that Australia, South Africa, Canada, New Zealand and India should each have a member on the "British Empire Delegation." ²

Treaties negotiated at such conferences are now signed by Dominion representatives, on behalf of the Crown. The form of the preamble to the treaties recommended by the 1926 Imperial Conference, is as follows:

> His Majesty the King . . .
> for Great Britain and Northern Ireland and all parts of the British Empire which are not separate Members of the League of Nations   A   B
> for the Dominion of Canada   C   D
> for the Commonwealth of Australia   E   F
> for the Dominion of New Zealand   G   H
> for the Union of South Africa   I   J
> for the Irish Free State   K   L
> for India   M   N

Finally, treaties "imposing obligations on more than one part of the Empire" are ratified by the Crown after consultation with the different Dominions. "It is for each government to decide whether Parliamentary approval or legislation is required before desire for, or concurrence in, ratification is intimated by that government." ³ In practice it appears that Dominion parliaments approve Imperial treaties before the Dominion government concerned notifies the British government that it is in favor of ratification.

---

¹ Cf. "Correspondence and Documents Relative to the Representation of Canada at the Peace Conference," etc., *Canadian Sessional Paper*, No. 41j, 10 Geo. V. A. 1919.
² Cf. "Report of Canadian Delegate, Conference on Limitation of Armament," *Sessional Paper*, No. 47, 12 Geo. V. A. 1922, p. 145. General Smuts, prime minister of South Africa, wanted the Dominions to boycott the Conference until the United States granted them separate representation.
³ *Summary of Proceedings*, Imperial Conference, 1923, Cmd. 1987, IX.

From the strictly legal standpoint, it would appear that the ratification of a treaty by the Crown, without the signature of Dominion representatives or the approval of Dominion parliaments, would nevertheless bind the Empire as a whole.[1] In practice, however, it looks as if the Empire will contract no serious political obligations without the consent of the various Dominions. If this rule should be rigidly followed in the future, a single Dominion might veto a treaty which Great Britain and the remaining Dominions desired.[2]

The Need for Consultation.—Despite the changed nature of the Imperial Conference and the participation of the Dominions in treaties affecting the Empire as a whole, the control of Imperial for-

[1] Cf. Keith, *Constitution, Administration, and Laws of the Empire*, p. 45. In the proposed alliance with France of 1919 and also of 1922, there was a provision stating that it should impose no obligation on any Dominion unless and until it was approved by the Parliament of the Dominion concerned. *Documents relatifs aux négociations concernant les garanties de sécurité contre une aggression de l'Allemagne* (1924), pp. 58, 111. *Documents Diplomatiques, Ministère des Affaires Étrangères*. The insertion of this provision implied that in its absence, the alliance would have applied to the Empire as a whole. Thus the Baldwin government, in December, 1924, asked the Council of the League to postpone discussion of the Protocol, until the Dominions could be consulted.

At the Lausanne conference in regard to the Turkish peace treaty, no Dominion representatives were present. At first the Canadian authorities did not recommend approval of the treaty to the Canadian parliament. But the British government insisted that when ratified, the treaty must "be binding on the whole Empire." Cf. "Correspondence with the Canadian government on the subject of the Peace Settlement with Turkey." Cmd. 2146 (1924). Since the British Foreign Office had *consulted* the Dominions in regard to the Lausanne treaty, the Canadian authorities finally changed their minds.

[2] "As the Empire must be either at war or at peace as a whole, it is clear that unless there is a unanimous decision of the self-governing parts of the Empire in favour of ratifying the Protocol, no one part, whether it is Great Britain or a Dominion, can ratify it." "The Geneva Protocol: An Analysis," *Round Table*, Dec., 1924, p. 57.

In July, 1924, the Irish Free State registered with the League its treaty with Great Britain. In December, the British government sent a note to the League Secretariat to the effect that his Majesty's Government "has consistently taken the view that neither it [the Covenant] nor any conventions concluded under the auspices of the League are intended to govern the relations—*inter se*—of various parts of the British Commonwealth." And therefore that Article 18 of the Covenant did not apply to the Irish treaty. In reply the Irish government dissented from this view, stating that it could not accept the "contention that the clear and unequivocal language of that article is susceptible to any interpretation compatible with the limitation which the British Government now seeks to read into it." For the notes, cf. *Manchester Guardian*, Dec. 16 and 24, 1924.

DOMINIONS AND FOREIGN AFFAIRS

eign policy still remains in a critical state. It is doubtful whether an Empire, the treaties of which can be blocked by the vote of a single Dominion, will be able to play a successful part in world affairs. On the other hand, in matters falling short of treaties, and which arise between Imperial Conferences, the Dominions have little control, as was illustrated in the Turkish crisis of 1922. In this crisis, the Turks were stopped from carrying their war into Europe only by the warning of Lloyd George, who also appealed to the Dominions to support Britain's position. According to Mr. Bonar Law, who followed Lloyd George as prime minister, this was the first time in British history that an appeal for help to the Dominions had been made.[1] In such incidents, illustrated also by the French occupation of the Ruhr and the Italian seizure of Corfu, the British Foreign Office alone decided Imperial policy.

In other words, the present problem before the British Commonwealth of Nations is the creation of consultative machinery between England and the Dominions, in the intervals between Imperial Conferences. In 1918 the British government proposed that the Dominions should each keep one Cabinet minister in London for this purpose. Moreover, more frequent Imperial Conferences would make possible the thorough airing of foreign problems before representatives of the Empire as a whole.[2]

However, the most effective guarantee that the Dominions will not be drawn into a war declared by England against their wishes, lies in their membership in the League of Nations. Under the

[1] Allin, "International Status of the British Dominions," *Amer. Pol. Science Review*, Nov., 1923. In July, 1923, more than a hundred Liberal and Labor members of parliament sent a communication to members of the Dominion parliaments stating, "The Dominion governments were invited to send contingents to the Near East, without any preliminary warning that the situation was such as these messages indicated. If war had ensued, it would have been a war decided upon by certain British Ministers without any sort or kind of national or imperial consultation." *Foreign Affairs*, August, 1923.

[2] The Imperial Conference of 1921 resolved that "(a) Continuous consultation, to which the Prime Ministers attach no less importance than the Imperial War Conference of 1917, can only be secured by a substantial improvement in the communications between the component parts of the Empire.

"(b) The Prime Ministers of the United Kingdom and the Dominions and the Representatives of India should aim at meeting annually, or at such longer intervals as may prove feasible.

"(c) The existing practise of direct communication between the Prime Ministers of the United Kingdom and the Dominions, as well as the right of the latter to nominate Cabinet Ministers to represent them in consultation

Covenant and under the Protocol, it is legally impossible for England to declare war on any member of the League without referring the dispute to some form of arbitration or to the Council. If such a dispute should go to the Council, it has been suggested that the Dominions could claim the right to sit as "specially interested" members, thus imposing a check on England's action which, in the absence of the League, they would not have.[1]

In 1926 an Imperial Conference was held in London and adopted a report on inter-Imperial relations which placed in writing the developments of the last few years. This report declared that Great Britain and the Dominions are "autonomous Communities within the British Empire, equal in status, in no way subordinate one to another in any aspect of their domestic or external affairs, though united by a common allegiance to the Crown, and freely associated as members of the British Commonwealth of Nations."[2] It declared that the Governor-General should occupy the same position in a Dominion as did the King in Great Britain; and that consequently in the future communication might be between government and government direct, rather than through the Governor-General. Despite the constitutional provisions in regard to the disallowance and reservation of legislation, the Committee declared that "it would not be in accordance with constitutional practice for advice to be tendered to His Majesty by His Majesty's Government in Great Britain in any matter appertaining to the affairs of a Dominion against the views of the Government of that Dominion." Moreover, parliament at Westminster should not apply legislation to a Dominion without its consent. Changes in the existing system in appeals to the Privy Council might be made after full consultation.

As far as the negotiation of treaties is concerned, it was declared that the principles adopted at the 1923 conference should be followed.

with the Prime Minister of the United Kingdom, are maintained." Cmd. 1474, pp. 9–10.

[1] Cf. Roth Williams, *The League of Nations To-day* (1923), pp. 167–78. It is possible to interpret Article 10 of the Covenant to the effect that the Dominions guarantee the territorial integrity of England against attack—a pledge which they had never given before. Cf. Keith, *Constitution of the Empire*, p. 49.

[2] "Imperial Conference, 1926. Summary of Proceedings." Cmd. 2768 (1926), p. 13.

In the conduct of foreign affairs generally it was frankly recognized that here, as in the sphere of defence, the major responsibility lay with the government of Great Britain. But neither Great Britain nor the Dominions could be committed to the acceptance of active obligations except with the definite assent of their own governments. Some system of personal contact between London and the Dominions should be established. With this end in view Great Britain during 1927 and 1928 appointed High Commissioners to each Dominion.

While there are individuals in the Dominions who advocate the dissolution of the Empire, it is doubtful whether this demand will ever become widespread. The population of South Africa or of New Zealand or of Australia is less than that of a third or fourth rate power. Independent, these countries could have little influence on international affairs. Participating as they did at the Paris and Washington Conferences, they now exercise an influence out of all proportion to their strength.[1] An independent South Africa would probably lead to a revolt of Natal, and it would leave the whites confronted with a black population outnumbering them four to one. The fear of Japan will probably keep Australia and New Zealand within the Empire, while the fear of the United States may have a similar effect upon Canada. As long as the Empire is maintained these fears are allayed and peace between the Dominions is maintained. This is accomplished not by suppressing but by encouraging the sentiment of nationality. "So far from repressing any national diversification otherwise possible, the British Empire is proving itself the fruitful parent of new nationalities; not only safeguarding their infant growth, but offering them, as they reach maturity, a career of national utility in imperial partnership as an alternative to the barren impotence of self-centered isolation."[2] The British Empire is the only successful example, to date, of a real partnership of nations, maintained not by coercion but by good-will, working together for the achievement of common ends. It is a token of what the League of Nations may become.

---

[1] In the last election campaign, the Nationalist party of South Africa gave up its secession plank. Campbell, "South Africa Before the Elections," *Foreign Affairs*, June 15, 1924.

[2] Jebb, *Studies in Colonial Nationalism*, p. 102.

4. ZIONISM

Within the British Empire will be found a still more unique attempt to develop a cultural nationalism apart from a political nationalism—the Jewish national home in Palestine. The Jews have been the only great nation—and there is no mistaking their national characteristics—who have not had a home they could call their own. About fifteen million of them have been scattered throughout the world where thousands have been made the objects of anti-Semitic movements. Moreover, many Orthodox Jews interpret the Old Testament to mean that they shall be restored to the Holy Land.[1] Out of these different factors, the idea of Zionism —the return to Palestine—has arisen as a solution for the Jewish question. The founder of the Modern Zionist movement was Herzl, the author of a book called "The Jewish State." Beginning in 1898, Zionist congresses, attended by Jews from every part of the world, were held annually. Any Jew was eligible to membership in the Zionist organization upon the payment of one shekel a year.[2] About 1911 a divergence arose between the *political* Zionists and the *cultural* Zionists. The former emphasized the establishment of a state under complete Jewish control; they wanted to make Palestine as Jewish as England is English. The latter— realizing the great difficulty in establishing such a state since nine-tenths of the population of Palestine are Arabs—demanded merely a "national" home where Jewish culture and religion could flourish unmolested.

In view of the savage persecution which had been accorded Jews by Russia and Roumania and of such incidents as the Dreyfus affair in France, there was little reason why the Jews of the world should support the Allies in the World War. In an effort to win over the powerful influence of Jewry, and also with a view to the strategic value of Palestine as regards the Suez Canal, the British government, followed by the other Allies, indorsed the idea of cultural Zionism in the Balfour declaration of November 2, 1917. Here it was declared, "His Majesty's Government view with favor

---

[1] Cf. Amos 9, v. 15, "And I will plant them upon their land, and they shall no more be pulled up out of their land which I have given them, saith the Lord thy God."

[2] Cf. E. Cohen, *La Question juive devant le droit international public* (1922), Ch. V; Mignot, *Le problème juif,* cited, pp. 89–135.

the establishment in Palestine of a national home for the Jewish people, and will use their best endeavors to facilitate the achievement of this object, it being clearly understood that nothing shall be done which may prejudice the civil and religious rights of existing non-Jewish communities in Palestine or the rights and political status enjoyed by Jews in any other country."[1] This pledge to the Jews was supposedly fulfilled in the peace treaties which made Palestine a class A mandate under the tutelage of Great Britain.[2] In the mandate, approved by the Council of the League of Nations in July, 1922, the mandatory is made responsible for placing the country under such political, administrative and economic conditions as will lead to the establishment of a Jewish national home; but it is also responsible for safeguarding the civil and religious rights of all the inhabitants of Palestine, regardless of race or religion. The Zionist organization was recognized as an appropriate Jewish agency to advise and coöperate with the administration in matters affecting the establishment of a Jewish national home. The immigration of Jews and their settlement on the land was authorized, subject to British control. The mandatory was made responsible to the League of Nations for maintaining the Holy Places. Complete freedom of conscience and religion, and the right of each community to maintain its own schools were guaranteed.

A great many difficulties confronted the British government in carrying out this guarantee. Arab riots broke out in 1920 and 1921, while a Palestine Arab Delegation protested that the British had placed the government in the hands of a sect which had only one-tenth of the population. They also protested against the immigration of the Jews for the apparent purpose of driving out the Arabs.[3] On the other hand, some Jews protested that they had not been given a large enough share in the government and that a real Jewish political state had not been established. The British attempted to work out a system which would safeguard the interests of the Arabs and at the same time allow the Jews to live in a country made sacred to them by history. With this in

[1] "Zionism," *Peace Handbook*, No. 162, p. 44.
[2] *O. J.*, August, 1922, p. 1007.
[3] "Correspondence with the Palestine Arab Delegation and the Zionist Organisation," Cmd. 1700 (1922).

view they set up a Legislative Council, the majority of the unofficial members being Arabs. But this did not satisfy the Arabs who really desired the complete destruction of the Zionist idea. In an effort to appease both elements the British Secretary of State for Colonies in June, 1922, made a new declaration, saying that his government did not aim to create "a wholly Jewish Palestine." Nor did it contemplate the "disappearance or the subordination of the Arab population, language or culture." The Balfour declaration merely said that a Jewish National Home should be founded *in* Palestine.[1]

Up to the present time, however (July, 1929), the Arabs have boycotted the proposed Legislative Council with the result that no elective assembly has been established for the whole of Palestine.

Zionism thus presents some of the most perplexing problems in self-determination and nationality. Fifteen million Jews have no national home, apart from Palestine to which they are bound by ties of sacred memories. But at the present time, Palestine is inhabited by a population nine-tenths of which is Arabs, who will have nothing to do with the Jews. Left alone, the Arab will do little to develop the country. Under Jewish guidance, the country is likely to flourish, provided coöperation with the Arabs can be secured. The British government cannot withdraw from Palestine without bringing the hopes of the Jews to an end. If it succeeds in working out a modus vivendi between Arab and Jew, it will have achieved a startling reconciliation of two nationalities within the walls of a single political state.

5. FINLAND AND POLAND

The Russian Empire has also attempted to conciliate the demands of nationalism with those of imperialism through the policy of autonomy. When Finland came into the Empire in 1809, the maintenance of her Fundamental Laws was guaranteed by the Act of Assurance of the Emperor Alexander I. While these promises were not at first observed, a constitution was granted Finland in 1863,[2] and in 1869 an Organic Law in regard to the

[1] Cf. Cmd. 1700, p. 18. Also the Palestine Order in Council, *Statutory Rules and Orders*, 1922, No. 1282; also *Report on Palestine Administration*, 1922.

[2] *Peace Handbooks*, No. 47, pp. 13 ff.; A. Rambaud, *Histoire de la Russie*, pp. 837, 1904.

Landtag was proclaimed.[1] As long as the policy of autonomy was followed, Finland appeared content. But in 1899 Nicholas II suspended the constitution, which resulted in the passive resistance of the Finns, culminating in the great strike of 1905. As a result of this opposition, the Tsar granted a new constitution. Despite the protests of members of different foreign parliaments, a bill was passed in the Russian Duma virtually abolishing this constitution; and partly also because of the outbreak of the War, the Finnish Diet did not assemble after 1914. It is little wonder that, shorn of its autonomous powers, Finland should declare its independence from Russia in December, 1917.

In Poland, the history of autonomy was similar, except that it was placed under international guarantee. In the Final Act of Vienna of 1815, the Russian Poles were guaranteed the "institutions, which will insure the conservation of their nationality." Russia carried out this act by granting Poland a very liberal constitution, establishing a Diet and reserving all public employments to Poles. Russia was represented in Poland merely by a Viceroy. It appears, however, that Poland's autonomy was only nominal, while after the revolution of 1830 the constitution was suppressed altogether and the Polish army dissolved. Following further repressive measures in 1863, the French, British and Austrian governments protested to Russia against the violation of the Act of 1815, and asked the restoration of Polish as the official language and the employment of Poles in the administration. They also asked that a conference of the powers should discuss the situation. But Russia protested against what it called interference, such as "no great Power would admit." Diplomatic considerations prevented the three foreign governments from exercising further pressure.[2] When the Tsarist régime fell in 1917, Poland naturally proclaimed its independence.

6. THE SOVIET GOVERNMENT AND AUTONOMY

While the provisional government of Prince Lvoff (1917) refused to recognize the right of self-determination, it nevertheless promised autonomy to the different nationalities of Russia. The

---

[1] F. R. Dareste, *Les Constitutions modernes* (1883), Vol. II, p. 221.
[2] Duparc, *La Protection des minorités*, pp. 125 ff.

Bolshevik government, which came into power in November, 1917, went further and proclaimed the right of the peoples of Russia to dispose of themselves. In a famous declaration, it promised "free development of national minorities and ethnic groups living within Russian territory."[1] As a result of the revolution, the old Empire was dissolved into three groups. First were the bourgeois and absolutely independent republics of Poland, Finland and the other Baltic states. Second was the Russian republic proper, composed of eight autonomous republics, such as Bashkir, Tartar, Kirghiz, Daghestan, Grosky, Turkestan and Crimea, and ten autonomous provinces. These republics were represented at Moscow by delegations attached to the Commissariat of Nationalities.[2] Although the autonomy granted these different republics varied, as a rule military, foreign and commercial affairs were directly controlled by Moscow. Likewise about nine important commissariats in each of these republics, relating to food, finance, labor, communications, public economy, posts and telegraphs, were under the supervision of corresponding secretariats at Moscow. What activities remained were left to the local authorities, who were nevertheless responsible to the Central Executive Committee of Russia.[3]

While this "autonomy" may have been shadowy, the policy of "Russification" which had been followed in Asiatic Russia before the War was dropped; the use of local languages for official as well as unofficial purposes was tolerated, and administrative officials chosen from the peoples on the spot.[4]

Third were eight "independent" republics, of Soviet sympathies, the Ukraine, Khiva, Bokhara, Georgia, Armenia, Azerbaijan, White Russia and the Far Eastern Republic. Between 1920 and 1922, the Soviet government of Russia contracted military and economic alliances with most of these republics, which provided for the joint administration of certain affairs. For example, the

[1] Castagné, "Le Bolshévisme et l'Islam," 51 *Revue du Monde Musulman*, (1923), 6.
[2] Cf. p. 181.
[3] Cf. pars. 4–9, sec. f, "Constitution for the autonomous republic of the Kirghizes," *Revue du Monde Musulman*, cited, p. 179; see *passim* for the other constitutions.
[4] Chamberlain, "Asiatic States in the Soviet Union," *Current History*, June, 1924.

treaty of December 28, 1920, between the Ukraine and Russia provided for joint commissaires of War and Marine, National Economy, Foreign Trade, War, Finance, etc. The remaining departments were left to the Ukraine. Many of these republics had diplomatic representatives at Moscow. They also readily acceded to "friendly" requests that they adopt Russian legislation, such as codes of criminal and civil laws. By the policy of autonomy, Soviet Russia held together some thirty-two republics, autonomous provinces and labor communes.[1]

7. AUTONOMY IN AUSTRIA, HUNGARY AND TURKEY

Less successful were the efforts of Austria, Hungary and Turkey in satisfying the divergent nationalities within these empires. In 1868 Hungary granted the Croats a limited form of autonomy in which they were allowed to retain their flag and coat of arms. Croatia was given a separate Diet as well as forty deputies in the Hungarian parliament. Although taxes were levied by Hungary, 45% of the amount collected in Croatia went for local purposes. The only representative of Hungary there was a "Ban" who communicated to the Hungarian Crown through a Croat member of the Hungarian ministry.[2]

But in Transylvania Hungary followed the opposite policy. While before 1858 this principality enjoyed a considerable degree of autonomy, it was fully incorporated into Hungary by the acts of 1868 and 1876.

Realizing the necessity of granting real autonomy to its different nations, Hungary passed a deathbed law, in 1918 and 1919, granting the "right of self-disposal" to the Ruthenians and Germans, a gesture which, however, came too late, especially in view of Hungary's record of oppression in the past.[3]

In Galicia and Bosnia-Herzegovina Austria also followed the

---

[1] Cf. *Russian States*, compiled from materials furnished by the British Trade Mission to Moscow, 1922; Nazaroff, "Soviet Russia's Advance toward Federation," *Current History*, March, 1923; this system was to be succeeded, however, by a federation; cf. p. 240.

[2] Statute No. 30 of the Year 1868, printed in G. Drage, *Austria-Hungary*, p. 725. For other laws, cf. Dareste, *Constitutions*, cited, Vol. I, pp. 416–437; cf. R. Redslob, *Abhängige Länder* (1914), pp. 174–201.

[3] For texts, see A. de Hevesy, *Nationalities in Hungary* (1919), p. 225.

policy of autonomy before the War. In an effort apparently to defeat the Pan-Slavic movement, Austria granted Galicia (Austrian Poland) a constitution in 1861 which established a Galician Diet but which allowed Galicia also to send deputies to the Austrian parliament. This constitution, however, did not satisfy the Poles, and at the rejection of their proposals in 1868, the Polish representatives withdrew from the Austrian parliament.[1] Later, however, the Poles adopted a more conciliatory attitude toward this régime.

In 1910 Austria granted the recently annexed provinces of Bosnia-Herzegovina a constitution, which provided for a Diet having authority to legislate upon some twenty-seven subjects. A national council of nine members was to be elected by the Diet, whose duty was to present the views of the Diet to the Austro-Hungarian government.[2] Further plans to grant autonomy to the remaining national groups failed because of the attitude of the Magyars. But during the War, the Austrian statesman, Karl Renner, made a plea for autonomy, which he would extend to the smallest governmental units. He proposed the formula of a "double commune," a council of Nation A and a council of Nation B with a political council of both nationalities to handle joint affairs. A similar plan was proposed by Austria's representatives at the Peace Conference.

Recognizing that the principle of self-determination could be served in many cases as well by autonomy as by complete independence, the Conference of Nationalities in 1915 and 1916 advocated "the right of autonomy" in the midst of a state. And in his Fourteen Points, President Wilson advocated, not complete independence, but "the freest opportunity of autonomous development" for the peoples of Austria-Hungary. In a belated attempt to carry this principle into effect, an Imperial Manifesto was issued in October, 1918, declaring that each nationality might form its own commonwealth.[3] The announcement came too late to stop the creation of new states in Central Europe.

Turkey is another empire to experiment with the principle of

[1] W. A. Phillips, *Poland*, p. 213.
[2] Cf. *Bericht Über die Verwaltung von Bosnien und Der Hercegovina, 1913*, published by the Ministry of Finance, Vienna, p. 7.
[3] Temperley, *History of the Peace Conference*, Vol. IV, pp. 101, 264.

autonomy. Since the fifteenth century, each non-Moslem community—Greek Orthodox, United Greek, Armenian and Jewish—was left free not only in religion but in administrative matters which did not concern Mohammedans.[1] Most of these communities were headed by a patriarch, the most important of which was the Greek patriarch at Constantinople. In 1856 the Sultan invited each "non-Moslem community" to draw up a constitution of its own. In 1860 a constitution for the Greek community was actually proclaimed. Three years later a constitution was given the Armenians; but the general assembly thus established did not meet after 1892, although some of the provincial assemblies continued to meet thereafter.[2] It appears that the Christian communities within Turkey proper lived upon a fairly satisfactory basis, until under the influence of western nationalism, they engaged in political intrigues, and until Turkey, under a similar stimulus, began to apply the doctrine of "Turkification," as shown by the Armenian massacres, the suppressions of the Arabs in Syria in 1913–1914, the denunciation of the Statute establishing autonomy in the Lebanon in 1915, and by the removal of the Greek patriarch from Constantinople in January, 1925.[3]

The Lebanon.—One of the most interesting as well as successful cases of autonomy within the Turkish Empire was in the Lebanon—a district in Syria inhabited by two bitterly antagonistic peoples, the Druses and the Maronites. After repeated massacres, the European powers decided to intervene. In a convention of September, 1860, they authorized the dispatch of an expeditionary force of 12,000 men, half of which might be furnished by France, to reëstablish order, but to occupy the territory only for six months. These troops were followed by an International Commission which, in coöperation with the Sultan, drew up a plan for reform. As a result of the work of this Commission, Lebanon was placed under the control of a Christian governor, appointed by Turkey, but actually controlled by the European Conference of Ambassadors at Constantinople. This governor was assisted by a Lebanon

---

[1] A. H. Lybyer, *The Government of the Ottoman Empire in the Time of Suleiman the Magnificent* (1913), p. 34.
[2] C. R. Johnson, *Constantinople Today* (1922), p. 92.
[3] A. J. Toynbee, *The Western Question in Greece and Turkey* (1922), p. 17; A. Mandélstam, *Le Sort de l'empire ottoman* (1917), p. 336; Minutes, Lausanne Conference, Cmd. 1814 (1923), pp. 317–337.

assembly, in which the different religious sects were given equitable representation. The whole administration was placed under the guarantee of the European powers, whose consent was necessary before any organic change could be made. As a result of this system of guaranteed autonomy, peace was maintained, and the country appeared better governed and more content than other parts of Turkey.[1]

8. ICELAND AND QUEBEC

Democracies as well as monarchies have experimented with the policy of autonomy—witness the cases of Iceland and Denmark and of Canada and Quebec. The sturdy inhabitants of the Land of the Sagas have possessed an ancient history and intellectual history, known throughout the world. In the year 930 the Icelanders established one of the first representative assemblies in Europe—the Althing—under which Iceland was governed until 1264 when it entered into an agreement for Union with Norway, whereby it retained its local institutions but received a Norwegian governor-general. A century later, Norway along with Iceland fell under the control of Denmark. Although Norway became separated from Denmark in 1814, Iceland remained under the latter's rule. There followed a period of stern monarchism, during which the Althing did not assemble; Iceland was ruled by Denmark without regard to the national institutions or culture of the people. Following a literary renaissance at the first of the 19th century, the Icelanders began a movement for autonomy. As a result of this agitation, Denmark reëstablished the Althing in 1843. But the powers of this body were limited and Iceland continued to be regarded as an integral part of Denmark. Further agitation led Denmark to grant another constitution in 1874, under which, however, the governor of Iceland was still responsible to Denmark, and the king retained an absolute veto over legislation. Additional concessions were made in 1903, establishing responsible

---

[1] For the text of the Convention of Sept. 5, 1860, cf. 118 Martens (1st series), 224. For the *Réglement* of Sept. 6, 1864, cf. *ibid.*, p. 221. Cf. Protocol relative to the nomination of the Governor of the Lebanon, August 14, 1897, 8 Martens (3d series), 653. Cf. A. Pasha, *Le Liban après la guerre* (1919), pp. 87 ff.; Jouplain, *La Question du Liban* (1908), pp. 250 ff. An autonomous régime was also forced upon such parts of Turkey as Moldavia and Wallachia, Samos, Crete, Bulgaria and Eastern Rumelia.

government in Iceland.¹ But the Icelanders refused to be satisfied until the basis of the old historic agreement with Norway—acknowledging the separate personality of Iceland—was recognized. These demands were finally granted by Denmark in the Act of Union of 1918, approved by both parliaments and a plebiscite in Iceland. This Act recognizes that Denmark and Iceland are "free and sovereign states united by a common King." Although Denmark has charge of Iceland's foreign affairs, Icelandic representatives will be attached to the foreign ministry; and agreements entered into by Denmark shall not be binding on Iceland without its consent. An advisory body of at least six members, half from Iceland and half from Denmark, deals with bills introduced in either parliament affecting the Law of Union. Affairs of common importance such as communications, trade, customs, and shipping, shall be determined by arrangement between the proper authorities. A commission of four members, two from each country, settles differences of opinion arising out of the Law of Union. The agreement may be abrogated by a two-thirds vote of each parliament, which, however, must be confirmed by a three-fourths majority at the polls.² A plebiscite on the Union is to be held in 1940. In 1928 all three political parties in Iceland agreed that in 1940 the Danish control over the foreign affairs of Iceland should come to an end.³

Within the Dominion of Canada, the autonomous province of Quebec serves as a monument of the days of New France which were abruptly terminated by the Peace of Paris of 1763. It is a province inhabited by the French-Canadian who, while loyal to Great Britain, "clings to his language, to his laws, and to his faith. He lays stress upon eternal values. He loves every instrument of his survival—his schools, his colleges, his universities, his social life, his literature, his art—and is second to none in philanthropy. He has less money than Anglo-Canadians, but more contentment."⁴ Under the federal system in Canada, Quebec is virtually autonomous; while certain rights in regard to the Church are guaranteed by the British North America Act of 1867. Canada,

[1] K. Gjerset, *History of Iceland* (1924), pp. 33, 220, 375 ff.
[2] Act of Union of Nov. 30, 1918, 111 *State Papers*, 703.
[3] V. Stefansson, "Icelandic Independence," *Foreign Affairs*, January, 1929.
[4] J. C. Bracq, *The Evolution of French Canada* (1924), p. 53.

alone of the Dominions, does not have the right to amend its constitution because of the fear of London that the remaining provinces would encroach upon Quebec's privileges. While there have been many conflicts between the French-Canadians and the remainder of Canada, the policy of autonomy and toleration appears to have reduced these conflicts to a minimum and paved the way for a sound basis of coöperation.

9. CENTRALIZATION v. AUTONOMY

If a nation would be satisfied with a policy of autonomy, many of the difficulties connected with self-determination would be removed. Boundary disputes, tariff difficulties, and the duplication of armies and much governmental machinery would be set aside. In the case of small nations wholly within an empire, such as the Finns of Russia or the Czechs in Austria-Hungary, a policy of autonomy might have quieted their demands for independence, if it had been really enforced. Such a policy would not, however, have quieted the demands of the Poles or the Slavs, who, divided among a number of states, wished to preserve their national unity. Nevertheless, if the policy of autonomy had been genuinely followed in Russia, Austria and Turkey before the War, it is possible that these empires, organized upon a democratic and autonomous basis, would be in existence to-day.

In fact, it seems that great states hesitate to grant autonomy, believing that it is an indication of weakness, which will be followed by imperial decay. This vicious circle has operated in four European states since the World War. Upon incorporating Transylvania and Bessarabia in 1918, Roumania promised them some form of autonomy, a provision which was omitted from the Roumanian constitution of 1923.[1] In Czechoslovakia, the Slovaks, under Father Hlinka, have complained that previous promises as to autonomy have not been observed;[2] while in Jugoslavia, the Croats, under the late Stephan Raditsch, have made similar complaints.[3] In Spain, many Catalonians, a people with a history and

[1] Mitrany, "The New Roumanian Constitution," *Journal of Comparative Legislation and International Law*, Feb., 1924. The text of the constitution is printed in *Current History*, September, 1923.
[2] *La Situation des minorités en Slovaquie*, cited, vii, p. 36.
[3] "Interview mit Stephan Raditsch," *Neue Züricher Zeitung*, Feb. 22, 1924; E. Lengyel, "The New Gandhi of the Balkans," *Nation*, June 4, 1924.

GUARANTEED AUTONOMY

a language of their own, have demanded the "creation of an autonomous Catalon State," while the Basques have also protested against the oppressive centralization of an inefficient and corrupt central government.[1]

If the autonomy of such groups is not recognized, the spirit of political nationalism may arise to destroy those states which insist on the policy of rigid centralization. Nevertheless, despite the advantages of autonomy, subject nations have often refused to accept it because of the belief that it will never be observed by the dominant power, while states have hesitated to grant it because of the belief that it is a step toward independence. Both of these difficulties are to a certain extent removed by placing autonomy under international guarantee, as was done in the case of Poland and of the Lebanon before the War.[2] In the one case, the guarantee proved worthless because of diplomatic rivalries; in the other case, it provided an effective administration. In neither case, however, did judicial machinery exist to supervise the guarantee.

10. GUARANTEED AUTONOMY

These defects were to a certain extent removed in treaties following the World War, which provided for an internationalized autonomy in several cases, the most important of which was that of Czechoslovakia which was obliged to grant autonomy to 450,000 Ruthenes living south of the Carpathians.

The Ruthenes.—In a treaty of September, 1919, between Czechoslovakia and the Allies, Czechoslovakia promised to constitute the Ruthene territory as an "autonomous unit" with a special Diet having power in all linguistic, scholastic and religious matters and questions of local administration. The Governor shall be appointed by the Czechoslovak President but shall be responsible to the Ruthene Diet. Officials should be chosen "as far as possible" from the inhabitants. The Ruthenes are guaranteed "equitable" representation in the Czechoslovak parliament, but they can vote only on matters not assigned to the Ruthene Diet.

---

[1] F. B. Deakin, *Spain Today* (1924), Ch. VI; Marquis de Olivart, *La Cuestión Catalana ante el derecho internacional* (1909); Davies, "Spain and the Basques," *Fortnightly Review*, Jan., 1924. The Catalonians made an appeal to the League of Nations, upon which, however, no action was taken. *Le Courrier Catalan*, July 15, 1924.

[2] Cf. pp. 219, 223.

These provisions for autonomy are placed under the guarantee of the League of Nations, to be supervised as are the minority treaties.[1]

In 1921 the Ruthenes complained to the League that these guarantees had not been fulfilled. The Czechoslovak government replied that these had been embodied in the constitution but they could not now be put into effect because the local population was not yet prepared to take over the administration. The committee of the Council, investigating the matter, reported on January 14, 1922, and expressed its confidence that the Czechoslovak government would soon grant autonomy to this territory.[2] In March, 1924, the first general elections in the Ruthenian territory for representatives to the central parliament were held. The question has not been brought before the League since that time. Nevertheless the Czechoslovak government has from time to time furnished information to the League, showing the steps taken to fulfil the treaty of 1919.[3]

The Aaland Islands.—In the treaty of December, 1919, with the Allies, Roumania agreed to grant the Saxons and Czechlers in Transylvania local autonomy in school and religious matters, subject to the control of the Roumanian state.[4] Greece promised similar privileges to the Vlachs. The principle of autonomy was likewise invoked by the League in settling the Aaland island affair. As part of the Aaland island settlement, Finland undertook to amend her legislation so as to provide for the appointment of the governor of the Aaland islands by the President of Finland in agreement with the President of the legislature of the islands. If no agreement is possible, the Governor should be selected from a list of five candidates nominated by the local legislature. Finnish cannot be taught in the primary schools without the consent of the commune concerned. The Aaland islands are entitled to use fifty per cent of the land tax for their own needs. Some other provisions in regard to property and franchise are made, all of

[1] Cf. Art. 3, Czechoslovak constitution; and *Treaties of the U. S.*, Vol. III, p. 3703.
[2] *Monthly Summary*, League of Nations, Feb., 1922, p. 35.
[3] Cf. "The Autonomous Territory of the Ruthenians." C. 517. M. 151. 1928, I.
[4] Cf. the communication of the Czechoslovak government, C. 821, M. 310, 1923, I; and *Current History*, June, 1924, p. 506.

GUARANTEED AUTONOMY

which are placed under the supervision of the Council of the League.[1]

Memel.—Similarly, the League Council insisted on autonomy being granted to the city of Memel, inhabited by Germans but surrounded by Lithuanians who depend on Memel for access to the sea.[2] The Statute of the Memel Territory provides that it shall constitute, under the sovereignty of Lithuania, a unit enjoying legislative, judicial, administrative and financial autonomy. The Governor, who is appointed by the President of Lithuania, may veto laws passed by the local Chamber exceeding the powers granted by the Statute, or violating the international obligations of Lithuania. The executive power of the City is exercised by a Directorate of five Memel citizens, responsible to the Chamber of Representatives, a body elected by the inhabitants. The local authorities have competence over fifteen different matters, ranging from education to police.[3]

These different treaties providing for autonomy mark an advance over similar treaties before the War because they provide for a League guarantee—instead of the soft-and-loose diplomatic guarantee of a few great powers. While this guarantee is as defective as the minorities' guarantee,[4] nevertheless it possesses advantages, as was illustrated in the Carelia dispute between Finland and Soviet Russia. In the Dorpat treaty of 1920, Soviet Russia promised Finland that autonomy would be granted to the Finns in Eastern Carelia.[5] Since the League had not been intrusted with any duties under this treaty, Russia escaped from its jurisdiction in this dispute. If the Dorpat treaty had been placed under League guarantee, Russia could not have thus easily evaded its obligations. The advantage of a system of guaranteed autonomy

[1] *Minutes of the 13th Session of the Council*, p. 52.
[2] Cf. p. 132.
[3] Statute of the Memel Territory, *O. J.*, September, 1924, p. 1207. In awarding Eastern Galicia to Poland in May, 1923, the Council of Ambassadors imposed the condition of autonomy.
[4] Cf. p. 192.
[5] Erich, "La question de la Carélie Orientale," *R. D. I. L. C.*, 1922, p. 1, *ibid.*, 1923, p. 227.

One of the reasons why the eastern empires, such as China and India, remain so cohesive, despite continual disorder in the central government, is because of the great strength and autonomous powers of local communities. Cf. R. Mukerjee, *Democracies of the East* (1923), Part III. Cf. M. J. Bau, *Modern Democracy in China* (1923), Chs. XIV and XV.

was also illustrated in 1927 in the case of Memel. In that year the German government, in response to a petition from Memel citizens declaring that Lithuania was violating the autonomy of the territory, brought the matter to the attention of the League Council. The Lithuanian prime minister, M. Voldemaras, was obliged to go before the Council where he declared that Lithuania was fully conscious of its obligations and that it would hold the elections for the Diet in September.[1] As the question was not brought before the Council in the following year, this gentle reminder apparently was effective.

[1] *Monthly Summary of the League of Nations,* July 15, 1927, p. 201.

CHAPTER X

THE CONFEDERATION OF NATIONS

1. Confederations and Federations.—2. Their International Advantages.—3. Imperial Federation.—4. Balkan Federation.—5. The Little Entente.—6. Baltic Federation.—7. The New Russian Federation.—8. Pan-Europa.—9. Coöperation in Central America.—10. The Pan-American Movement—The Monroe Doctrine.—11. Regional Groups and the League of Nations.

Convinced that certain national interests can best be advanced by a policy of continuous coöperation rather than of either occasional conference or isolated independence, many nation-states have organized themselves into federations. The exact powers of these federations have perplexed jurists and statesmen, depending in fact on the agreements or "constitutions" bringing these federations into existence.

The most rudimentary form of coöperation, out of which more formal and extensive legal and political associations have sprung, has been the alliance.[1] In itself an alliance is merely a pledge for mutual military assistance in certain contingencies. But it is sometimes accompanied by economic agreements and other treaties which pave the way for closer coöperation in other than military activities, until the ground for a loose confederation has been made.[2]

1. CONFEDERATIONS AND FEDERATIONS

A confederation differs from an alliance chiefly in its organization. Objects of mutual concern are usually discussed by a common committee or Diet, with no power to enforce its decisions, but merely to make recommendations for the states, represented in the confederation, to carry out. The states remain not only equal but independent; nevertheless they accept certain restrictions upon their freedom of action, particularly in regard to foreign

---
[1] Cf. p. 505.
[2] Cf. P. S. Mowrer, *Balkanized Europe* (1920), p. 44.

affairs; each state usually promises not to go to war against other members of the confederation.¹ In the Germanic Confederation of 1815, each state promised to defend the others against attack. A confederation is not a super-state. It is a voluntary association, furnishing a means for carrying out certain measures in common.

In many cases, the policy of confederation has broken down because no authority existed which could oblige each nationality to conform its interests to those of the whole. The Germanic Confederation, which lasted from 1815 to 1866, came to an end because of this defect. The provisions of the constitution of the Confederation were violated by Prussia, when it declined to come to the aid of Austria in its war against Italy and France in 1859, and when Prussia made war on Austria in 1866. The Confederation itself came to an end as a result of this latter war; and it was eventually followed by the formation of the German Empire, establishing a federal form of government dominated by Prussia.²

A development somewhat similar took place in the United States. The thirteen states of the American revolution, who in modern parlance might be called "nationalities," associated themselves in the Articles of Confederation of 1787. While the Articles established a congress, this body could only make recommendations to the different states. "Nationalistic" differences led to obstacles in the way of commerce; taxes remained unpaid; state quotas for troops were not raised. A demand arose, consequently, for more complete subordination of state action, which terminated in the federal constitution, adopted in 1789.

The history of Switzerland illustrates an analogous tendency. In 1648 Switzerland was recognized as a confederation, having thirteen cantons. Although the Congress of Vienna altered the constitutions of 1791 and 1803, Switzerland remained a confederation resembling in some respects the German Bund. But the bonds were too loose for a people who had gradually grown closer together. The constitutions of 1848 and 1874 gave Switzerland a federal government.

A federation differs from a confederation in at least three re-

---

[1] Cf. G. Jellinek, *Allgemeine Staatslehre* (1905), pp. 720 ff.
[2] Cf. A. Debidour, *Histoire diplomatique de l'Europe* (1891), Vol. I, pp. 59–62; Vol. II, pp. 28–78; pp. 320–342. Also C. Dupuis, *Les rapports des grandes puissances avec les autres états* (1921), Ch. V.

spects. While a confederation is only an association of independent states, a federation establishes a super-state over its members. This leads, in the second place, to a difference in organization. A confederation sets up a loose organization of the representatives of equal states, whose decisions can be carried out only by and with the consent of these states. On the other hand, a federation has an organization of its own, with definite power to act, inside a limited sphere, upon individuals within the member states. Within a confederation, the members retain their sovereignty, which means that they may leave the confederation at their pleasure, and that they may interpret the powers delegated to it, as they please. Within a federation, on the other hand, there does not appear, ordinarily, to be a right of secession; while the federal government, or some branch of it—in the United States, the Supreme Court—interprets its own powers in relation to the states.[1]

2. THEIR INTERNATIONAL ADVANTAGES

As a solution of many of the problems of nationality, the policy of confederation or federation has much in its favor. Under either method of organization, each state or nation continues to govern itself in local affairs. In the confederation, a nation retains greater freedom than in a federation. But in either form of government, nations give up the right to go to war against each other, and agree to settle disputes, not by force, but by some form of adjudication. In most of these associations, high tariff walls are torn down and trade is made free. Economies are effected in administration, since one central government may perform certain interstate functions which hitherto had necessitated one government for each nation. Since federation removes suspicions, it stops propaganda originating in one state and directed against another; it leads to the reduction of armaments; it minimizes the chances of war. And at the same time, it allows the cultural characteristics of each nation to flourish unmolested; it gives each nation an opportunity to express itself politically in local affairs.

In some cases, the policy of autonomy, which was discussed in the last chapter, may satisfy the political aspirations of a nation.

[1] R. C. de Malberg, *Contribution à la théorie générale de l'État* (1920), Vol. I, pp. 92–95. There is a vast literature on the juristic differences between federations and confederations into which it is not necessary to go here.

But under such a policy the rights of a nation exist at the sufferance of an alien state. A nation never feels sure, therefore, in the absence of an international guarantee, that its autonomy will be respected. Under the policy of federation, however, the rights of one nation are guaranteed by the other and each nation has the same interest in maintaining the liberties and obligations granted to all. In a federation, the rights of each unit do not ordinarily depend upon the whim of a dominating power. The policy of autonomy may succeed in the case of a group which is of insignificant numbers, considering the state as a whole. It is not likely, however, to satisfy national aspirations as successfully as the policy of federation or confederation, when the national groups involved are more equal in strength.

Both in Europe and in America the federal principle has been frequently invoked. The particularism of Saxony and Bavaria was satisfied by the federal nature of the German Empire which came to an end in 1918. In the new German constitution, the hold of the central government has been strengthened so that many publicists doubt whether Germany is still a federation.[1]

In Switzerland, peoples of Italian, German and French extraction, differing in language and custom, have lived peacefully side by side by virtue of a constitution in which most local affairs are left to the cantons, while affairs of a wider interest are intrusted to the central government which the people directly control. In Latin America, Mexico, Brazil, Argentina and Venezuela have adopted federal forms of government.[2] The United States has held together forty-eight different localities,[3] by means of a federal type of government in which the states—during the last century, at least—were "sovereign" in local affairs, but in which a central authority controlled inter-state and foreign relations.

Within the British Empire the federal principle has also received wide application. In 1867 the British parliament passed an act which brought six colonies together into the federation of Canada. In 1901 six colonies were likewise joined in a federation—the Commonwealth of Australia. In 1909 five colonies of South

---

[1] Brunet, *The New Constitution of Germany* (1922), p. 70; McBain and Rogers, *The New Constitutions of Europe* (1922), p. 72.

[2] P. E. Martin and H. G. Janes, *The Republics of Latin America* (1923), pp. 146, 172, 273, 336 ff.

[3] E. Gruening (ed.), *These United States, a Symposium* (1923).

IMPERIAL FEDERATION

Africa were brought together into the Union of South Africa which has many federal features. Likewise, in the Crown colonies, a number of federal principles will be found. The Leeward Islands are a federation of five different islands in the British West Indies;[1] while nine states in British Asia are united in the Federated Malay States, also under British control. The act of 1919 organized India upon a federal basis, dividing the powers of government between fifteen provinces and the central authorities.

3. IMPERIAL FEDERATION

During the last fifty years, there has been a movement for the federation of the British Empire—of the Dominions with England. As we have seen, the present relationship of the Dominions with the Mother Country still rests upon a very tenuous and ill-defined basis. Canadians complain that in matters of foreign policy they are still autocratically controlled by the British foreign office, while Britishers complain that the Dominions are virtually independent. In order to clear up these uncertainties, a number of Englishmen have advocated the idea of Imperial federation. They would draw up a written constitution, providing for an Imperial cabinet, composed of ministers from Great Britain and the Dominions, responsible to an Imperial parliament, similarly constituted.[2]

Whatever the advantages of this system would be, its disadvantages are so numerous that the idea has made little headway. A federal form of government would reduce the present freedom and influence of the Dominions. If representation in an Imperial parliament should be based on population, New Zealand, for example, would have only five out of three hundred members. But at the present time—under the unanimity rule in Imperial Conferences—New Zealand's influence is immeasurably greater. In a federation, the Dominions would be bound by a majority vote in many cases where they are now free. They would probably be obliged to give up control over tariffs. It is extremely difficult, moreover, to define the powers to be allotted to the central government and those to be retained by the local units in any

---

[1] Cf. H. Wrong, *The Government of the British West Indies* (1923), Ch. IX.
[2] Cf. L. Curtis, *The Problem of the Commonwealth* (1916), chs. 12–18, 21.

federation. If India is granted dominion status, promised her in the act of 1919, she would probably demand the same representation as the Dominions in an Imperial parliament. As she has three-fourths of the population of the Empire, this demand could not possibly be fulfilled. The new status of India may be the final blow to the federal idea.[1]

4. BALKAN FEDERATION

While this policy may not be as satisfactory in the British Empire as the policy of autonomy, it has nevertheless been repeatedly advocated for different regions of Europe, and in fact for Europe as a whole. The application of self-determination to the Balkans has not led to permanent peace. Instead of hating their former master, the Turk, the Balkan states, once their independence had been gained, started to hate each other. Convinced of the necessity of coöperation so as to remove interminable boundary disputes, satisfy the demands of landlocked nationalities for harbors, and settle the ever-present minorities questions, many Balkan leaders have advocated the idea of federation. This was a favorite idea of such Serbian statesmen as Michel Obrenovitch, under whose auspices the representatives of a Bulgarian committee and the Serbian government signed a programme in 1868 for a "Serbo-Bulgarian" nation.[2] In 1828 it was advocated also by the Greek leader Capodistria and later by such Italians as Garibaldi and Mazzini. A large number of Balkan writers took up the idea; and in 1895 a League for Balkan Confederation was formed.

Following the World War, Bulgaria appeared to sponsor this idea. Its peasant prime minister, Stambulisky, assumed a very tolerant attitude toward Greece and Serbia, and relinquished Bulgaria's demands in regard to Macedonia and the Ægean. But he met the opposition of Greece as well as of extreme nationalists at home who eventually brought about his assassination.

So far the federal movement in the Balkans has been limited largely to talk. Apart from the negotiations of 1868, the alliance

---

[1] For an attempt to meet this problem by a system of limited representation, cf. W. B. Worsfold, *The Empire on the Anvil* (1916), p. 103.

[2] R. Pinon, *L'Europe et la jeune Turquie* (1911), p. 449. Cf. T. G. Djuvara, *Cent projets de partage de la Turquie* (1914), pp. 382, 405, 407; S. Panaretoff, *Near Eastern Affairs and Conditions* (1922), p. 190.

of 1912 between Greece, Bulgaria, Serbia and Montenegro marked the first tangible step in this direction; but it came to nothing because of the second Balkan war, fought between the allies. Each Balkan state has looked upon federation as a means of advancing its own interests and of becoming supreme over its neighbors. To the Greek it has meant Greek supremacy; to the Serb, it has meant Serb supremacy. In the past, the idea was supported by the great powers, such as Russia or Italy, as another means of furthering their own indirect control. Some of the Balkan states are republics; others are monarchies; in some the economic and financial condition is good; in others it is bad. It is difficult to decide what states belong to the Balkans and what states to Central Europe. Such are the perplexities confronting this regional movement, and which make prospects for success extremely remote.

5. THE LITTLE ENTENTE

In Central Europe, the idea of a Danubian federation received considerable support before the War. While the idea is still advanced,[1] responsible statesmen in the Succession States look upon it with disfavor. They regard it as a scheme for the restoration of the old Austro-Hungarian empire which so severely repressed the newly independent nationalities in the past.[2] While a federation of Central European states is not likely to become a reality for many years, nevertheless, some of these states have set up a loose system of coöperation called the Little Entente. The basis of this Entente is a series of agreements between Jugoslavia, Roumania and Czechoslovakia, entered into in 1920 and 1921. These agreements took the form of defensive alliances, military conventions stipulating military support in case of attack, and economic agreements facilitating exchange of trade.[3] More recently the prime ministers of these three countries held periodic

[1] O. Jaszi, "Dismembered Hungary and Peace in Central Europe," *Foreign Affairs*, December 15, 1923; A. Toynbee, *Nationality and the War* (1915), pp. 216–246, on a Balkan Zollverein. Cf. S. Muenz, "The Real Face Behind Hungary's Janus-Mask," *Current History*, Dec., 1923.
[2] A. Mousset, *La Petite Entente* (1923), pp. 11, 19.
[3] Convention of August 14, 1920, Jugoslavia and Czechoslovakia, *T. S.* 154. Convention of March 3, 1921, Poland and Roumania, *T. S.* 175; Convention of April 23, 1921, Roumania and Czechoslovakia, *T. S.* 155; cf. Mousset, cited, pp. 88 ff.

conferences, whether at Belgrade, Bucharest or Sinaia, at which matters of common interest were discussed with a view to formulating a joint policy. At the Genoa conference of 1922 between Russia and the Allies, the Little Entente was given representation in the different sub-committees; and following the signature of the German-Soviet treaty of Rappallo, they were given representation in the meetings of the Supreme Council. At the fourth Assembly of the League, the leading member of the Little Entente—Czechoslovakia, was elected to the League Council. Fear that Hungary would attempt to reëstablish its former control over Central Europe was the real force behind the formation of the Little Entente. It succeeded in preventing such a restoration and also in peacefully settling the quarrels between its different members. With the removal of the fear of Hungary, the ties between the members of the Little Entente may loosen. Already they have been strained by the dispute between Russia and Roumania over Bessarabia.[1] It would seem that if the Little Entente is to be permanent, it must develop into a closer political association.

6. BALTIC FEDERATION

Further north, proposals for confederation have also been vigorously made. As a result of the World War, five new states in the neighborhood of the Baltic came into existence—Finland, Lithuania, Latvia, Esthonia and Poland. Isolated from each other, these nations stand in constant fear of Russia. Combined, they would be reasonably secure since with a total population of 40,000,000, they would qualify as a first-class power.

In 1920 representatives of four Baltic countries discussed this question at a number of conferences. At Bulduri a number of conventions of a legal and commercial nature were drawn up, and also a political convention, providing for the arbitration of all disputes

---

[1] At the Congress of Berlin, Roumania was obliged to cede the remainder of Bessarabia, a northern province, to Russia. Following the Revolution of 1917 Bessarabia was reunited to Roumania—a union recognized by the Supreme Council in March, 1920. Russia, however, declined to recognize this disposition of Bessarabia, demanding a plebiscite, to which Roumania would not agree. "The Bessarabian Dispute," *Foreign Affairs*, June 15, 1924.

In 1927 and 1928 the Little Entente became aroused over the rapprochement of Hungary and Italy. Mussolini is on record as being in favor of the revision of the Treaty of Trianon. See "The Little Entente," *I. S.*, Vol. IV–No. 14.

between the Baltic states, the mutual protection of minorities, rights of transit, and military support in case of attack. The conference also provided for a permanent body—the Council of Delegates—which was to sit at Warsaw twice a month.[1]

Unhappily the Bulduri convention proved abortive partly because of the unsettled Vilna dispute between Lithuania and Poland.[2] But at a conference in 1922, the Accord of Warsaw was signed which repeated many of the provisions of the Bulduri agreement.[3] As Finland declined to ratify this agreement, the treaty did not go into effect. Further conferences, however, were held in 1923, mostly economic and financial in nature. In November, 1923, Esthonia and Lithuania signed a defensive alliance, and these two states together with Latvia and Poland signed a conciliation and arbitration convention in January, 1925.[4] In a number of trade agreements these states reserve for each other certain economic privileges.

While mutual good-will has been produced between many of these states as a result of these conferences, progress toward confederation has been slow. Finland has held aloof from this movement, being unable to decide whether to cast its lot with Scandinavia or with the Baltic states proper. If it should join the latter, it would stake its own future upon that of the new states. But many Finns hope to maintain their independence, regardless of the fate of the other Baltic nations. Likewise, Poland is an obstacle to confederation. It has a population of 27,000,000 as compared to the combined populations of 12,000,000 for the four other Baltic states. Naturally it will not enter an association which will place it under the control of lesser states; while these states are not anxious to enter an association dominated by Poland. Perhaps Lithuania, Latvia and Esthonia, may be able to form a federation without Finland and Poland. While the difficulties here also are

[1] W. Kamieniecki, "La Politique Balte," *L'Est Européen*, March 10, 1923.

[2] The Vilna dispute between Poland and Lithuania was over the possession of a district which in the historic past has been the capital of Lithuania, but which Poland now claimed to be inhabited by a majority of Poles. Disregarding the requests of the Council of the League, Poland annexed this territory in March, 1922, and has since occupied it. Lithuania, however, has never recognized this annexation, and periodically raises the question before the League.

[3] Convention March 17, 1922, *T. S.* 296.

[4] *T. S.* 578, 991.

many, it appears that some such association seems necessary if the Russian specter is to be mesmerized.¹ Perhaps the greatest enemy of all, is Soviet Russia. The establishment of a Baltic federation would be dangerous, in its opinion, to Russian security. Consequently Russia has declined to negotiate with the Baltic states as a whole but has insisted on making separate agreements with each such state. In 1927 Latvia and Russia signed a commercial agreement which was interpreted as a blow to the federation idea.²

7. THE NEW RUSSIAN FEDERATION

Soviet Russia is also experimenting with the federal principle. Dissatisfied with the autonomous policy described in the last chapter, the Soviet government signed a treaty, in December, 1922, with the nominally independent states of the Ukraine, White Russia and Transcaucasia, providing for confederation.³ In July, 1923, a constitution, elaborating the principles laid down in the treaty, was adopted.

According to this constitution, a Congress for the whole Union is set up, representing population rather than nationalities. It is composed of one delegate for each 25,000 city voters and one delegate for each 125,000 voters in the provinces. It meets once a year. Between its sessions, the highest authority is the Central Executive Committee, composed of two bodies, the Union Council and the Council of Nationalities. The former is composed of 371 members elected by the Congress. The latter represents the federal feature of the Union, each Soviet republic being represented by five members, and each of the autonomous provinces by one member. The Central Executive Committee meets at least three times a year. Its approval is necessary for decrees controlling the political and economic life of the Union. In case of disagreement between the two branches of the Executive Committee, the dispute

---

[1] Wuorinen, "The Efforts to Form a Union of Baltic States," *Current History*, July, 1924; Davies, "The Future of the New Baltic States," *Fortnightly Review*, June, 1924; and Lyon, "Baltic Alliances: Finland at the Cross Roads," *ibid.*, Vol. CXV (1924), 301.

[2] Cf. Buell, *Europe: A History of Ten Years*, p. 238.

[3] In August, 1922, Georgia, Armenia and Azerbaijan united into the Transcaucasian government. For the treaty of December, 1922, between Soviet Russia and the above governments, see *Current History*, March, 1923. Turkoman and Uzbek are now also members.

is referred, as a last resort, to the Congress. The Executive Committee has four presidents, one for each of the federated republics.

When this Committee is not in session, the highest authority is wielded by the "Præsidium," a body of twenty-seven members which has supreme power subject to the control of the Executive Committee. Still another organ exists—the Council of People's Commissars—really a cabinet of twelve members, under the control of the Præsidium. Matters such as foreign, military and naval affairs, transportation, foreign trade, are placed under the "exclusive" control of the Union commissars; other matters, such as food, labor and finance, are placed under "united" commissars, and are administered jointly by the central government and the local republics.

According to the constitution, each republic may secede from the Union, and with the exception of the powers delegated to the Union, each republic "enjoys its independent state power." A supreme court is established which will "enter protests" against decisions of local courts when they conflict with laws of the Union or the interests of other republics. This court has eleven members, including the chairman of each of the supreme courts of the allied republics.

Although this constitution purports to establish a federation, the federal principle is recognized only in the Council of Nationalities, in the presidents of the Committee, and in the Supreme Court. Apparently there are no limitations on the legislative power of the federal bodies, which so curiously combine legislative and executive functions; while all administrative affairs may indirectly be controlled from Moscow.[1]

While Russia seems to be traveling on the road of unification, it is hardly possible that either the old Tsarist policy of centralization or complete political independence for each nation, will prevail. A "Balkanized" Russia would be a calamity for the peace of the world. A federated or autonomous Russia is the best guarantee of the rights of its many nationalities, as well as of Russian peace.

---

[1] Nazaroff, "Soviet Russia's Advance toward Federation," *Current History*, March, 1923. For the text of the Russian constitution, of July 6, 1923, cf. *Soviet Russia*, British Foreign Office, 1924; *Nation*, August 15, 1923; *New York Times*, August 12, 1923, sec. 7.

8. PAN-EUROPA

Frequent suggestions have been made for the federation of all the states of Europe. Such a solution, if carried into effect, would of course solve a great number of problems which so sadly disturb the relations of its different nations. It would make really possible freedom of trade, the peaceful settlement of boundary disputes, the reduction of armaments, the protection of minorities, and the scrapping of some inefficient and inexperienced government machinery. President Masaryk of Czechoslovakia and Prof. Jaszi of Hungary are statesmen who have recently favored this idea.[1]

One writer believes that a federated Europe is essential if Europe is to maintain her past position in the world. The League of Nations, as at present constituted, cannot, in his opinion, satisfy European needs. Under it, non-European states interfere in the settlement of purely European disputes. Federations are already being formed in other parts of the world, the British Empire, the Pan-American Union, the Russian Empire, while a confederation between China and Japan may be formed in the future. The creation of a Pan-Europa is therefore also necessary. Otherwise, European states will stand in fear of Russia and Turkey, not to mention more distant foes. While the League of Nations should still exist, it should merely decide disputes between different regional groups. Since England is a world instead of a European power, it should not form part of Pan-Europa. But England should be bound with Pan-Europa by arbitration and armament agreements.

As a first step, a European conference should be convened to discuss the question of arbitration, guarantees, armaments, minorities, communications, tariffs, currencies, debts and culture. This conference should establish a Pan-European Bureau similar to the Pan-American Union. The second step would be the conclusion of treaties between European states providing for compulsory arbitration and a reciprocal territorial guarantee. This should be followed by the formation of a European tariff union and the gradual establishment of free trade. The culmination of the idea

---

[1] Jaszi, *Foreign Affairs*, cited. Cf. also A. H. Fried, *The Restoration of Europe* (1916), Ch. VI; P. V. Suchtelen, "The Only Solution—A European Federation," in *Toward an International Understanding*, Union of Democratic Control, No. 10. Hereafter cited, U. D. C.; also R. N. Coudenhove-Kalergi, *Pan-Europa* (1923).

COÖPERATION IN CENTRAL AMERICA

would be the constitution of a United States of Europe, with a Popular Assembly and a Chamber of States; the first body should be composed of three hundred representatives, one for each million people; while the second should represent equally each of the twenty-six states. As a result of such a Union, inter-European wars would be prevented, Europe would be neutralized in a world conflict and protected against a Russian invasion, while it could compete successfully against British, American and Asiatic industry.[1]

Many advocates of the federated Europe idea point to the example of the United States as one which Europe should have long since followed. Obviously, there is no basis of comparison.[2] The federation of the United States was formed out of thirteen small states, confronted by a wilderness on one side and greedy foreign powers on the other. These states spoke the same language, worshiped the same God, and had the same institutions. The cultural and historic differences which separate European nations to-day are far greater than those which separated the American states in 1789. Moreover, the economic and financial conditions in one country in Europe are so much better or worse than in other countries that any proposal for federation will be looked upon as a scheme whereby the weak countries may live upon the strong. The best hope of Europe is not in a close federation, but in the League where problems of mutual concern may be discussed and aid granted without necessitating elaborate readjustments in existing political machinery.

9. COÖPERATION IN CENTRAL AMERICA

If we turn to another hemisphere, we shall find that the federal principle is being advocated in Latin America. In that curious neck of land joining South and North America, called Central America, there are five independent republics: Guatemala, Honduras, Salvador, Nicaragua and Costa Rica. Of these the largest is Guatemala, which contains forty per cent of the popu-

[1] R. N. Coudenhove-Kalergi, *Pan-Europa* (1923), pp. 38, 53, 49, 152, 155. He also proposes a treaty where each European state should agree to teach English in the schools, so as to be able to cope with Anglo-Saxonism throughout the world.
[2] The winner of the Filene French Peace Award proposed a European League of Nations, with power to enforce its decisions. *N. Y. Times*, Sept. 1, 1924.

lation of Central America, while the smallest is Honduras with only 662,000. The federation of these different republics would result in a state of five million people.

Independent, each of these countries ekes out a feeble existence; joined in a federation, they could hope for progress which now seems impossible.

When under the rule of Spain, the countries of Central America were administered as a whole. Following their independence, they organized a federal government in 1825 which lasted until 1838, when each state threw aside these bonds in favor of complete independence. Renewed attempts to restore the federation of Central America in 1842, 1849, 1852, 1871, 1887, 1895 and 1907 met with no success, because of nationalistic jealousies, difficulties in communication, lack of leadership, and the old argument that while the idea is theoretically sound, "the time is not ripe."[1] In January, 1921, another such attempt was made in a treaty signed by Salvador, Guatemala, Honduras and Costa Rica, which provided for a "sovereign and independent nation" called "The Federation of Central America." Each state was to retain control of its internal affairs and all other powers not granted to the federal government. A federal council, after the Swiss model, was to be established composed of one councilor elected by each of the states, as well as a legislature of two houses; the senate being composed of three representatives from each state, and the house representing the people according to numbers. A supreme court was to be established.[2] The federation was not, however, established because of the refusal of Nicaragua to participate unless the other states recognized the Bryan-Chamorro treaty giving the United States a right to build a canal.[3] This they firmly declined to do. The attempts of El Salvador and Honduras to revive the idea at the Central American conference, held in Washington in 1922–1923, also failed.[4]

[1] For a history, see D. G. Munro, *The Five Republics of Central America* (1918), Ch. VIII. American diplomacy has consistently supported the federation idea in Central America, G. H. Stuart, *Latin America and the United States* (1922), Chs. XII, XIII. Cf. Cox, "The Movement for Independence in Central America," 53 *Bulletin of the Pan-American Union* (1921), 217.

[2] For text of treaty, cf. *T. S.* 113.

[3] "The United States and the Nicaragua Canal," *I. S.* Vol. IV, No. 6.

[4] Minutes, *Conference on Central American Affairs*, Washington, 1922–1923, p. 164.

COÖPERATION IN CENTRAL AMERICA

Although federation has not been realized, the five republics of Central America have signed a good many agreements looking toward a high degree of political and economic coöperation. In 1907 a conference of these states was held in Washington, under the good offices of the United States and Mexico, at which a number of these treaties were signed.[1] As a result of this conference, a Central American International Bureau was established in Guatemala, to carry out the decisions of the conference and to develop public education, commerce, agriculture, industry, monetary systems and sanitation. The Bureau was composed of one member from each government. But the treaty establishing it was to last only fifteen years; and as no attempt has been made to renew it, the Bureau is now defunct.

In 1922 a second Central American conference was held at Washington for the purpose of revising and extending the 1907 agreements. Twelve treaties and three Protocols and Declarations were signed, the most important of which was the General Treaty of Peace and Amity. In this treaty the five republics declared that they would not recognize any government in these republics resulting from a revolution, unless afterward the people freely sanctioned it. Even then, they would not recognize as President or Vice-President the leaders in the revolution. The republics promised not to intervene in case of civil war; and to maintain the principle of a single term for the President and Vice-President, to prohibit the organization of revolutionary movements against any recognized government in Central America, and not to enter into secret treaties with each other.[2]

In another treaty these republics resurrected the Central American Court of Justice, originally created in 1907, established "Bryan" commissions of inquiry, and provided for the limitation of armaments.[3] They likewise agreed to appoint a commission to prepare a general electoral law for the consideration of each government.[4] Equally important steps toward federation were taken in agreements establishing commissions on finance and communication for the purpose of drawing up plans for economic reform and

[1] *Treaties of U. S.*, Vol. II, pp. 2391–2430.
[2] Text, Treaty of Feb. 7, 1923, *Conference on Central American Affairs*, p. 287.
[3] Cf. pp. 562, 614, 625.
[4] Minutes, cited, p. 363.

for the construction of public works and communications in the five countries. The finance commission was to study tariff provisions with a view to the establishment of free trade, which was provided for in another agreement.[1] The republics also agreed to pass legislation improving labor conditions.[2] These treaties thus lay down certain common constitutional principles for the five republics; and they provide for similar electoral, tariff, labor and communication laws. They go far in clearing the ground for a closer form of coöperation in the future.[3]

10. THE PAN-AMERICAN MOVEMENT

Such patriots as Francisco de Miranda and Simón Bolívar long ago dreamed of a confederation of South America. An attempt to carry out this dream was made in the Congress of Panama of 1826, which recommended the formation of a South American League with an assembly meeting every two years. In 1846 a congress of five South American countries signed a treaty of confederation, which, however, was never ratified. In 1862 an "American Union Society" was formed in Chile. Three years later, seven states signed another treaty of union and alliance. A similar conference was held at Caracas in 1911. Although none of these treaties bore fruit, they kept alive the spirit of confederation.[4]

More restricted in character was the "A. B. C." movement which aimed to bring together Argentina, Brazil and Chile, so as to keep the peace between themselves and to increase their influence on the Latin-American continent.[5] In 1914 these powers tendered their good offices in the Vera Cruz dispute between Mexico and the United States which resulted in an armistice.[6] And in May, 1915, they signed a treaty providing for the compulsory arbitration of disputes among themselves. However, the A. B. C.

---

[1] Free trade does not, however, apply to Costa Rica, or to coffee and sugar. *Ibid.*, p. 388.

[2] Cf. p. 162.

[3] One Spanish writer asserts that the United States has secretly opposed Central American Federation. Calbó, "La intromisión norteamericana en Centroamerica," 29 *Cuba Contemporánea* (1922), 25.

[4] W. S. Robertson, *History of the Latin-American Nations* (1922), p. 439; *ibid.*, *Hispanic-American Relations with the United States* (1923), p. 387.

[5] C. A. Becú, *El "A. B. C." y su concepto político y jurídico* (1915), p. 10.

[6] *U. S. Foreign Relations*, 1914, pp. 489, 493. Cf. comments of J. B. Moore, *International Law and Some Current Illusions* (1924), p. 94.

movement did not progress beyond its elementary stage. In fact, naval rivalries appear to be endangering the good-will at one time existing between these three leading South American powers.[1]

A third development has been the Pan-American movement. Such noted Americans as Henry Clay, Stephen A. Douglas and James G. Blaine long advocated some form of association of American states. In 1889 the United States convened the first Pan-American conference, and since then six have been held, attended by the American republics.

In addition to these conferences the Pan-American Union, an administrative body, is located in Washington. Its duties relate primarily to the collection of information in regard to American countries and to conserving the archives and documents of the Pan-American conferences. The expenses are prorated among the different states according to population, the present quota being about a thousand dollars per million people. The Union is in charge of a director and sub-director, and is controlled by a Governing Board. Before 1925 this Board was composed of the diplomats of American republics at Washington, the chairman of which was always the Secretary of State of the United States.[2] As a result of the provision that only diplomatic representatives at Washington could be on this board, a state automatically lost its membership when its government was not recognized by the United States.

In addition to the regular conferences, a number of *ad hoc* conferences have been held. In 1915 an important Pan-American financial conference convened in Washington to consider the financial situation so sadly deranged by the War. It recommended uniform legislation in the different countries in regard to a large variety of commercial subjects. As a result of its recommendation there was established an International High Commission, of not more than nine members from each country, with power to suggest means of improving the commercial relations between the American countries. The fifth Pan-American conference of 1923 adopted a resolution requesting this Commission to coöperate in the preparation and execution of the programmes of these

[1] Cf. p. 562.
[2] Cf. p. 249.

conferences.[1] In 1920 the second Pan-American financial congress was held. In 1911, 1919, and 1927 Pan-American commercial conferences were convened under the auspices of the Pan-American Union. Likewise, Pan-American scientific congresses were held in 1907–1908, 1916 and 1925, while five Pan-American child welfare conferences have also been convened, the last in 1929.[2] In June, 1929, the second Pan-American highway conference was held.

All of these conferences, and the machinery set up to carry their decisions into effect, have performed a very high educational and cultural service, without which the political association of the American states would be impossible. But in the actual proceedings of the Pan-American conferences, political questions until recently have been studiously avoided. The conferences between 1889 and 1923 devoted themselves to discussing such subjects as uniform system of weights and measures, communications between American countries, sanitation, arbitration, and pecuniary claims. The first five Pan-American conferences produced a total of 21 treaties and conventions, and a large number of resolutions.[3] But apart from arbitration agreements, none of these treaties affected the really important political questions relating to the American continent.

In theory, Pan-Americanism is based on the idea that there is an American system of law and interests which is different from the European, African or Asiatic systems.[4] To the South American the Pan-American idea should mean a policy of complete political coöperation in the settlement of disputes between nations of the New World and in the protection of the New World against attack by the Old. The Pan-American ideal, to him, would mean that if intervention in a Latin-American country should become necessary, it should be authorized only by the joint approval of a Pan-American body.

[1] *Verbatim Record of the Plenary Sessions of the Fifth International Conference of American States*, Vol. I, Santiago, 1923, p. 193.
[2] There have also been conferences on journalism, standardization, etc.
[3] For a summary of the work of these conferences, cf. *Special Handbook for the use of the Delegates*, Fifth International Conference of American States, prepared by the Pan-American Union, 1922, Part I, and A. H. Fride, *Pan-Amerika* (2d ed., 1918), Chs. II–IV.
[4] A. Alvarez, *Le Droit international americain* (1910), pp. 251–277.

The Monroe Doctrine.—Such a conception of Pan-Americanism directly conflicts with the Monroe Doctrine of the United States. Originally employed to prevent the intervention of Europe in South American affairs, this doctrine has recently been used to justify the intervention of the United States at its own pleasure. Originally a doctrine of non-intervention, Latin-Americans believe that it is now one of hegemony. It is a unilateral doctrine to be invoked by the United States without regard to the approval or disapproval of the Latin-American countries. It is a doctrine which they must not be allowed to discuss.[1] In 1898 Mr. Olney declared, in the Venezuela dispute, that "the United States is practically sovereign on this continent and its fiat is law upon the subjects to which it confines its interposition." [2]

This attitude explains why the United States has prevented the Pan-American conferences from acting on political questions. This would mark the end, it is feared, of American dominance in the Western hemisphere. It would substitute a multilateral for a unilateral enforcement of the Monroe Doctrine. This attitude also explains why the Latin-Americans are coming to distrust the whole idea of Pan-Americanism.[3]

At the Santiago conference of 1923, two demands were made by Latin-American countries to strengthen the Pan-American principle. The first aimed to weaken the control of the United States over the Pan-American Union. The second aimed to establish an American League of Nations.

As a result of the efforts of Costa Rica, the conference recommended that the chairmanship of the Union be made elective instead of being permanently vested in the Secretary of State of the United States. In case a government was not recognized by the United States, it might appoint a special representative

---

[1] Cf. "C," "The Future of the Monroe Doctrine," *Foreign Affairs*, March 15, 1924. At the same time the Monroe Doctrine did not prevent France from blockading Mexico in 1838, England from blockading Brazil in 1861, war between Spain and Peru in 1864, or Germany from sending two warships to Haiti in 1897 in the Luder affair. Cf. H. Kraus, *Die Monroedoktrin* (1913), pp. 245–252.
[2] Moore, *Digest*, Vol. VI, p. 553.
[3] S. G. Inman, *Hacia la solidaridad americana* (1924), p. 94; F. C. Sotolongo, *El Imperialismo Norte-Americano* (1914), p. 195; I. Fabela, *Los Estados Unidos, contra la libertad* (Barcelona), p. 9. For a collection of documents, cf. A. Alvarez, *The Monroe Doctrine* (1924).

to sit upon the governing board. At the suggestion of Chile four permanent committees were created to assist the Pan-American Union in its work. Their purpose was to deal respectively with the best means of developing the commercial relations between the republics, international organization of labor in America, hygiene, and intellectual coöperation.[1] In each capital officials were to be appointed to look after Pan-American business.

An American League of Nations.—As early as 1919 Dr. Baltazar Brum, president of Uruguay, advocated an American League of Nations, based on the following principles: "All American countries will consider as an offense against themselves any attack on an American state by a non-American state, which they will resist by uniform and common action. This association should be constituted on the basis of complete equality of all its members; diplomatic intervention should not be employed in matters subject to the jurisdiction of the courts of a country; every child should have the nationality of the country of his birth; all controversies, of whatever nature, must be submitted to the arbitration of the League if they cannot be settled." [2]

By providing for the submission of all disputes to the League the Brum plan would prevent the intervention of the United States in the Caribbean and Central America until receiving the sanction of the League.

As a result of the pressure of the Latin-American countries, the Santiago conference contained on its agenda political subjects which "marks a distinct departure from the traditions of these conferences."[3] The agenda included the "consideration of measures tending toward closer association of the Republics of the American Continent with a view to promoting common interests,"

---

[1] Cf. "La Union Panamericana," *Tratado, Convenciones y resoluciones*, Quinta Conferencia internacional americana, 1923, p. 42.

[2] Cf. two addresses on "American Solidarity" and "World Solidarity," the latter published in English by the Buenos Aires *Nation*, Jan. 21, 1923. Proposals for a reciprocal territorial guarantee have been made by Latin-Americans upon several occasions in the past. When made by a South American diplomat in 1912, the United States instructed its diplomatic representatives "to belittle the idea." But President Wilson in a speech of January, 1916, came out in support of it. *U. S. For. Rel.*, 1912, p. 1; and Robinson and West, *The Foreign Policy of Woodrow Wilson* (1917), p. 301.

[3] *Bulletin of the Pan-American Union*, August, 1923, p. 11.

THE PAN-AMERICAN MOVEMENT 251

and "of the questions arising out of an encroachment by a non-American power on the rights of an American nation,"—which would include the Brum plan.[1]

But the Uruguay project met with failure at the Santiago conference because of the opposition of the United States.[2] Other plans to convert the existing Pan-American Union into a body similar to the Council of the League of Nations also failed. Costa Rica originally proposed separate representatives, other than the diplomats accredited to Washington, for the Pan-American Union. But although the proposal received the support of ten states, the United States succeeded in postponing its consideration.[3] Likewise the proposal for an international American court of justice was postponed. The only tangible results of the conference as far as political coöperations was concerned, were a treaty providing for the investigation of disputes,[4] and a resolution intrusting to the Governing Board of the Union the duty of studying proposals for a closer association between the American republics.[5]

At the sixth Pan-American conference held at Havana in January, 1928, vigorous debates took place over the status of the Pan-American Union, and over the questions of tariff and intervention. Mexico took the lead in attempting to reduce the influence of the United States in the Pan-American Union; Argentina took the lead in attacking indirectly the United States tariff; Argentina and Salvador led the campaign for non-intervention. In the convention drawn up in regard to the Pan-American Union, it was provided that the governments may appoint to the Governing Board such representatives as they desire, whether or not they are diplomats accredited to Washington. The Director-General of the Union may attend Pan-American conferences in an advisory capacity. The Pan-American Union shall not exercise any political functions. The conference imposed upon the Union the duty of calling in the future fourteen conferences, most of which are to be of an educational, cultural or commercial nature.

In the debate, Argentina declared that a statement should be

[1] *Special Handbook for the use of the Delegates*, p. 30.
[2] Inman, p. 87.
[3] *Report of the Delegates of the United States of America to the Fifth International Conference of American States* (1923), p. 6.
[4] See p. 626.
[5] *Tratado, Convenciones y resoluciones*, cited, p. 42.

made in the convention condemning excessive tariffs. This proposal was opposed by the United States and other governments, and the upshot was the resignation of M. Puerrydon, the Argentine representative.

Most vigorous controversy arose over the article in the proposed codification of public international law that no state should " intervene in the internal affairs " of the other. Peru proposed that this article which had been drafted by a body of jurists at Rio should be set aside in favor of a declaration of the rights and duties of nations. This was supported by the United States. Thirteen states, however, made strong declarations in favor of the principle of non-intervention. Agreement proving impossible, the question was postponed until the seventh conference.

Before adjourning the conference passed two important resolutions, the first of which declared that all aggression is considered illicit and is prohibited; and that the American states will employ all pacific means to settle conflicts which may arise between them. The second provided that the American republics would meet in Washington in a conference of conciliation and arbitration.

This Pan-American Arbitration and Conciliation Conference opened in Washington in December, 1928. It was immediately confronted with the threatened outbreak of hostilities between Bolivia and Paraguay over a boundary incident. As a result of telegrams from the League of Nations Council [1] and from the Pan-American conference hostilities were averted, and both governments agreed to sign a protocol drawn up at the Washington conference referring the dispute to a commission of nine members. Bolivia and Paraguay each appointed two delegates while the United States, Mexico, Colombia, Uruguay and Cuba appointed one delegate each.

Thus impressed with the necessity of some permanent conciliation machinery the Pan-American conference proceeded to draft and sign two very important treaties; the first is a Pan-American arbitration treaty providing for the arbitration of all legal disputes which are defined to include questions arising out of the interpretation of treaties and international law—an article based upon the optional clause of the World Court Statute. The only ex-

[1] See "Documentation concerning the Dispute between Bolivia and Paraguay," C. 619, M. 195, 1928 VI, cf. p. 638.

REGIONAL GROUPS: LEAGUE OF NATIONS

ceptions from arbitration are domestic questions and matters affecting states not party to the treaty. States may, however, make reservations at the time of signature. The conciliation treaty revises the Gondra Convention of 1923. It provides that the permanent diplomatic commissions at Montevideo and at Washington not only shall undertake the formation of *ad hoc* commissions of inquiry, authorized in the 1923 convention, but at their own discretion may themselves immediately undertake the task of conciliation in case of threatened conflict. In signing this treaty the United States recognizes that future interventions should be submitted to these bodies who will supposedly reflect the collective conscience of the Americas. In accepting such a provision the United States has apparently agreed to surrender, to this extent, the unilateral nature of the Monroe Doctrine.

11. REGIONAL GROUPS AND THE LEAGUE OF NATIONS

Such are the movements in Europe and America to bring about the coöperation of nations, whether in recurrent conferences, confederations or federations. Through these different forms of association, nations are trying to work out common policies, without sacrificing their independence in local and cultural affairs.

But the successful formation of these regional groups does not necessarily mean world peace. One European group may quarrel with another European group, or a confederated America may quarrel with a confederated Europe. The quarrel is likely to be more disastrous than a localized quarrel between two old-time nations because of the combined strength of each regional group. If world peace is to be secured, the coöperation of the whole world, whether of nations or of regional confederations of nations, is necessary.

Yet even if a League of Nations should become really effective, there would still be a legitimate sphere for regional groupings.[1] Nations in such regional groups, realizing the peculiar inter-

[1] Article XXI of the Covenant says, "Nothing in this Covenant shall be deemed to affect the validity of international engagements such as treaties of arbitration or *regional understandings* like the Monroe doctrine, for securing the maintenance of peace." The second Assembly (1921) took "note of the view expressed by the Committee that agreements between Members of the League tending to define or complete the engagements contained in the Cove-

ests they have in common, are likely to make greater concessions to each other than would nations entering into an association embracing the whole world. The conflict of interests in a world association is much greater than in a regional group. The coöperation of a few such nations will probably go further than that of the world as a whole.

For this very reason, an age of nationalism is likely to prevent the close confederation of regional groups. Experience has shown that federal governments tend to become centralized, suppressing the independence of local units even in domestic affairs. In a federation of the American type, nations must surrender very important powers to a super-state. In defining what powers should be thus granted and what powers should be retained many difficulties arise. A great nation—great in population and great in wealth—hesitates to enter a political association controlled by smaller nations. And smaller nations hesitate to enter a union dominated by a great power. In a world association, embracing every nation, great and small, where unanimity is the rule for important decisions, nations are not called upon to surrender such powers, but merely to accept some voluntary limitation particularly upon the exercise of the power to go to war. For this reason, more emphasis has been placed in recent years upon a world association of independent nations rather than upon regional confederations.[1] When such federations are established they should be welcomed. But they by no means fulfil the need of a larger and looser grouping of the powers. Both movements, however, have the same aim: the preservation of what is good in nationality and the removal of what is bad.

nant for the maintenance of peace or the promotion of international co-operation, may be regarded as of a nature likely to contribute to the progress of the League in the path of practical realisations.

"Such agreements may also be negotiated under the auspices of the League of Nations, for example, in special conferences, with its assistance."

[1] Cf. W. Schücking, "Ausbau des Haager Werkes," *Recueil des rapports*, Organization centrale pour une paix durable (1916), pp. 193-194.

CHAPTER XI

INTERNATIONAL ASPECTS OF THE DRUG AND LIQUOR TRAFFICS

1. The Drug Habit.—2. The World's Opium Supply.—3. Internal Attempts at Control—Poppy-Growing in India.—4. Opium Treaties.—5. The Hague Convention of 1912.—6. Opium and the League.—7. The Proposals of the United States.—8. Opium Smoking in the Far East.—9. The Opium Conferences of 1924-25.—10. Control of the Liquor Traffic in Africa and the North Sea.—11. Controversies between "Wet" and "Dry" Countries.—12. Liquor Smuggling.

During the last century there has been a growing recognition that the function of government is not only to maintain order and protect property, but also to improve in a positive manner the conditions of life of its citizens. Governments have long wrestled with the drug and liquor problems. Some of these have suppressed certain institutions, such as slavery, because of their unsocial nature. All of them pay attention to questions of public health and to the alleviation of suffering, particularly among the poor.

Ordinarily, these functions have been "domestic"—each government has determined for itself what attitude it would take toward any of these so-called humanitarian problems. One nation, it was said, could have no legitimate concern in the attitude of another nation toward such questions as liquor, opium or public health.

Yet because of the growing physical compactness of the world, this attitude is being modified. Whatever may be the status of a problem in international law, it may have international aspects which no nation can afford to ignore. New devices of transportation facilitate the ease with which disease may be transmitted from one country to another, and with which drugs and liquor may be smuggled from the outside world into a country prohibiting their use. Because of the problems arising out of these international contacts, a large number of treaties have been made and international institutions established.

1. THE DRUG HABIT

Perhaps no international humanitarian activity is more important than the regulation of the opium traffic. While the qualities of alcohol and tobacco have been hotly debated, there is fairly wide agreement that the use of opium and cocaine, except for medicinal and scientific purposes, is disastrous. Opium is a product of the poppy. Prepared opium is smoked primarily in China and other parts of the Far East. Medicinal opium and opium derivatives, such as morphine and heroin, may be used for legitimate purposes, and they are widely used as drugs in Europe and America. Cocaine, a product of the coca leaf, is a form of powder which may be inhaled several times a day through the nose. "Sniffing" is a popular indoor sport among dark-alley gangs in American cities. Sometimes cocaine may be inserted in the ear. Other drugs are dissolved in water or other beverages and then drunk. Heroin and morphine, opium derivatives, may be injected with the hypodermic needle, which means that the skin is punctured a number of times a day,—practices which may produce sores, abcesses and other disease.

Once the drug habit is formed, it is extremely difficult to break. Some medical authorities state that drug addiction is a form of disease. According to the annual report of the Narcotic Drug Control Commission of New York State, "The startling and significant result of taking drugs is not merely the wreck of bodily health, it is rather that once a person has become habituated to narcotic drugs, however small the amount, he is in the clutches of a cruel and unrelenting master, whose brutal grasp is almost never shaken off unaided. An intense craving for the drug has been developed with the corresponding loss of self-control and every miserable or distressing symptom that man has ever experienced can now be reproduced in the head, neck, chest, abdomen, and extremities, if the drug is withheld for so short a period as a day or part of a day. . . .

"Drug addiction is not like the habit of drinking alcoholic beverages. The worst drunkard can, if he will, make a sudden determination and quit his habit forever. . . . But the drug addict rarely, if ever, rids himself of his habit alone by force of determination or will. .... If his supply is in danger, he is just as nervous and anxious, just as ready to steal, to lie, to debase himself, to secure it, whether he is a respectable citizen, or a ruffian on the street. The life of every addict is dominated by the fear that his craving may not be satisfied. ...." [1]

Many of the crimes of violence in this country have been committed by drug addicts, particularly the users of heroin. A large number of medical authorities agree that the medical need of this drug is negligible compared with the damage that it does, and the Advisory Committee of the League of Nations has requested that governments inquire into the possibility of abolishing completely the manufacture and use of heroin.[2] The struggle against the drug traffic is of immediate concern to America. A recent report of the federal Public Health Service states that there are about 110,000 drug addicts in the United States [3]—victims who are not confined to the understratum of society, but who circulate among so-called respectable circles, where opium-smoking is the newest vice and where the use of dope sometimes results from the careless employment of opiates by the doctor. Dope peddlers solicit victims for commercial profit.

2. THE WORLD'S OPIUM SUPPLY

According to the estimates of the Secretariat of the League of Nations, the world production of opium is between 2,500 and 3,500 tons annually. Probably only a fifth of this amount is necessary for the scientific and medicinal purposes of the world. But no opium to speak of is produced in America or in Europe, with the exception of the Balkans. The world's opium comes from a number of Eastern and Balkan countries—China, India, Turkey, and Persia, Greece and Jugoslavia. Probably half of the

[1] *Second Annual Report, N. Y. Narcotic Drug Control Commission* (1920), p. 8.
[2] Cf. "The Case Against Heroin," Foreign Policy Association Pamphlet No. 24; and testimony of physicians, *Hearings before the Committee on Foreign Affairs, on Limiting Production of Habit-Forming Drugs and Raw Materials from Which They Are Made*, 67th Cong., 4th sess. H. of R. 1923, *passim*.
[3] "Extent and Trend of Drug Addiction in the United States," *Public Health Reports*, May 23, 1924. Cf. Dr. A. Lambert, "The Amount of Opiates Used in the Legitimate Practice of Medicine," *Hearings*, 25. (The use of heroin is prohibited in the United States.)

world's opium is grown in China. Until recently, at least, India has been the second largest producer.[1] The opium produced in India and China is practically all low-grade, and is almost entirely consumed in the Far East for eating and smoking purposes. The high-grade opium available for medicinal purposes and for drugs comes largely from Turkey and the Balkans. The production of coca leaves, on the other hand, is limited to Peru, Bolivia, the Dutch East Indies and Formosa. Considerable quantities of opium derivatives have been manufactured in Japan, Great Britain, the United States, France, Germany and Switzerland.

3. INTERNAL ATTEMPTS AT CONTROL

Originally, governments attempted to control the traffic in drugs by purely domestic legislation. Following a long struggle, the Chinese government issued an edict in 1906, ordering the suppression of poppy-growing within ten years.[2] In the United States, the problem has not been to suppress the production of opium at home, but to prohibit the importation of drugs and the manufacture of "dope" for illicit purposes. A large number of acts have been passed for this purpose, the most recent being the Jones-Miller Act of May, 1922, which established a Federal Narcotic Control Board with power to limit the importation of opium and coca to what it considers the "medical and legitimate uses" of the country.[3]

While the United States and China have followed the policy of prohibiting entirely the use of opium for illicit purposes, other countries attempt to regulate its use through a system of government monopolies. Such a policy is followed in many Asiatic colonies and in such independent countries as Siam, where the smoking of opium is widespread. Because of the extent of such practices, it is said that immediate prohibition could not possibly be enforced. When the Dutch government stopped the im-

[1] "Memorandum on the World Cultivation and Production of Opium," Annex 11, *Minutes of the 5th Session, Advisory Committee on Traffic in Opium and other Dangerous Drugs*, 1923. C. 418, M. 184, 1923, XI.

[2] Cf. N. B. Morse, *Trade and Administration of China* (rev. ed., 1913), Ch. XI; W. T. Dunn, *The Opium Traffic in Its International Aspects* (1920), 41.

[3] 42 Stat. 596; cf. *Opium and Narcotic Laws*, U. S. Government Printing Office, 1919.

portation of opium into Banka, 25,000 coolies went on a strike until their drug was restored.[1]

Poppy-Growing in India.—Until recently at least much criticism has been made of the British policy in India. Here the government annually fixes the total amount of opium to be raised. Poppy cultivators are licensed by the government and the native cultivator may be advanced money without interest. But he is bound to sell his product to the government at a fixed price. The government thus supervises production and monopolizes sale.

In defence of this policy, the British assert that the practice of eating opium is well-nigh universal among the Indians. In the malarial tracts it is used as a supposed prophylactic against fever, and is widely used for other ailments by Indians beyond the reach of medical care. In 1895 a British Royal Commission reported that such practices in India, while not strictly medicinal, were nevertheless legitimate. Although this Commission was charged with being "packed" with members interested in maintaining the drug traffic, some authorities still rely upon this report to justify the production of opium for uses which are not strictly medicinal.[2]

Such Indians as Gandhi and such acute observers as C. F. Andrews do not agree that the use of opium in this manner is legitimate. It is pointed out that while the whites of the Empire are protected by Dangerous Drug Acts, there is no such protection for Indians, and that while the Indians prescribe opium for their ills, these practices would be abolished if the British installed a competent medical service. One of the first acts of the Reformed Assam Council in 1919 was to curtail by 10% annually the amount of opium sold. Other Indians assert that the British are "drugging" India for the sake of revenue.[3]

It should be remembered, however, that the excise duties on

[1] H. Torchiana, *Tropical Holland* (1921), p. 195.
[2] G. G. Dixon, *Truth About Indian Opium* (1922), India Office, p. 5. An American commission once suggested the establishment of a government monopoly, as a transitory measure, for the Philippines, a suggestion which was not accepted by the American Congress, *Report of the Commission of Inquiry as to Opium in the Philippine Islands*, S. Doc. 265, 59th Cong., 1st sess., p. 53.
[3] Cf. C. F. Andrews, "The Opium Menace in India," *The Indian Review*, April, 1924. In 1924 the Indian National Congress passed a resolution criticising the government's opium policy.

opium comprise only three per cent of the total revenues of the country. In view of the great numbers and poverty of the peoples of India—which has a population three times as large as the United States—it is very difficult to establish adequate health service or to prohibit immediately the uses of drugs to which thousands have been accustomed.

Moreover, under the Government of India Act of 1919, provincial legislatures and ministries have control over the production and use of opium for internal purposes.

Nevertheless, the difficulties of non-opium countries were increased by the former practice of the British authorities in India of selling opium at public auction to the highest bidder, and no questions asked. Smugglers could purchase opium for the purpose of taking it to countries who were trying to keep it out. Since very little Indian opium is manufactured into morphia, most of these exports went to countries and colonies in the Far East where it was smoked. The British opium policy therefore concerned not so much the United States as the Orient.

4. OPIUM TREATIES

For these different reasons, international coöperation in suppressing the drug traffic has become essential if it is to be stamped out of any part of the world. The British government showed its good-will toward China in her anti-opium campaign, by making two agreements in 1907 and 1911,[1] promising gradually to stop all opium exports from India to China, at a loss of $8\frac{1}{2}\%$ in revenue to the Indian government. As a result of British coöperation, China's campaign against opium for the time being proved successful. Likewise, the British government has made agreements with foreign and colonial governments, such as the Straits Settlements, the Dutch East Indies, Siam and Hongkong, limiting opium exports to the amounts which these governments desire.[2] It has also abolished the system of auctions.

But since opium is a profitable source of income to many of

[1] For both, Cf. 104 *State Papers*, 140, 144. The agreements authorized China to send an official to observe the auctions at Calcutta. Cf. also "Correspondence respecting the Cultivation of Opium in China," Cmd. 1931 (1921). Cf. Cd. 3881 (1908).

[2] Dixon, 24. For the smuggling of opium into China from foreign leaseholds, cf. E. N. La Motte, *The Opium Monopoly* (1920), p. 39.

these Oriental governments, there is no incentive to cut down the amounts in these agreements.[1]

5. THE HAGUE CONVENTION OF 1912

Realizing that purely domestic efforts could not cope with the traffic in drugs, thirteen powers, under the leadership of the United States, appointed an opium commission which met in Shanghai in 1909. Out of the resolutions adopted by this body, came the first international opium conference, held at The Hague in 1912. In the Convention for the Suppression of the Abuse of Opium and other Drugs, at this conference, twelve governments promised "to enact efficacious laws or regulations for the control of the production and distribution of raw opium"—out of which smoking and medicinal opium, as well as "dope," are made.[2] But the convention did not say to what extent production should be limited. What was of great importance, however, the powers promised to prevent the export of raw opium to a country prohibiting its entry; that is, India would prevent such exports to the United States if the latter did not wish to receive them. Persia, while agreeing to the remaining parts of the convention, refused to be bound by this extremely important provision by which smuggling could be suppressed.

Recognizing impliedly at least that the smoking of prepared opium was harmful, the powers also agreed to take measures "for the gradual and efficacious suppression" of this traffic, "in so far as the different considerations peculiar to each nation shall allow of this." Another clause stated that "those nations which are not yet ready to prohibit the exportation of prepared opium at once, shall prohibit such exportation as soon as possible." The manufacture and sale of morphine and cocaine should be limited to "medical and legitimate purposes." And special measures should be taken to prevent the smuggling of opium from leased territories into China. Although the United States had suggested

---

[1] Opium furnishes 28.6% of the total revenue of British Malaya, 22.4% of that of Hongkong, 11.53% of that of the Dutch East Indies; 27.3% of that of French Indo-China, and 40% of that of Macao. R. L. Buell, *The International Opium Conferences*, World Peace Foundation Pamphlets, 1925, p. 63.

[2] Convention of January 23, 1912, *Treaties of the U. S.*, Vol. III, p. 302. For the protocols of the second and third conferences, cf. *ibid.*, pp. 3037, 3039.

that the treaty be carried out by an international commission,[1] this work was placed upon the Netherlands government.

While from the standpoint of formulating opinion, this convention marked great progress, the provisions limiting the production of raw opium and suppressing opium-smoking were too vague and contained too many exceptions to be effective. Each nation, moreover, was left the judge of what these exact conditions were and when they should be put into effect. The one concrete gain from the convention of 1912 was the agreement of opium-producing countries to prohibit the export of opium to countries forbidding its entrance.

Despite the vagueness of the 1912 convention, the governments most concerned hesitated to ratify. In 1913 and 1914 further conferences were held at The Hague to hasten ratification, but without much success. The war gave an excuse for further delay. But in the peace treaties of 1919–1920 all of the signatory powers agreed that the ratification of those treaties should automatically bring into force the convention of 1912.[2] Although Turkey agreed in the Treaty of Lausanne, to adhere to the Hague Convention she had not done so by the time the Opium Conference of 1924–1925 convened. Besides Turkey, Persia remained the only great opium-producing country, and Switzerland the only important manufacturing country, which had not put the convention into effect.

6. OPIUM AND THE LEAGUE

Since the League of Nations had been intrusted by the Covenant with the supervision of agreements in regard to the traffic in dangerous drugs, the Assembly of 1920 authorized the formation of an Advisory Committee, which is now composed of representatives of China, France, Great Britain, India, Japan, Netherlands, Siam, Portugal, Germany, Italy, Switzerland, Bolivia, Jugoslavia, and a United States observer, and three non-voting assessors.[3] The present struggle against the traffic is largely in the hands of this body.

As a result of the activities of the League, most of the states which were neutral during the War ratified the convention of 1912, there being 50 states bound by it in 1928. The League

[1] Circular of Sept. 1, 1909, *U. S. For. Rel. 1909*, p. 11.
[2] Cf. Art. 295, Treaty of Versailles; Art. 100, Treaty of Lausanne.
[3] Cf. *Minutes of the 12th Session.*

Secretariat dispatched several notes to Persia as to the advisability of ratifying without the original reservation, and Persia indicated that she would comply. As a result of opinion formulated by the League, Switzerland also finally ratified, a ratification of great importance because Switzerland had long been known as a center for smugglers.[1]

Through a system of questionnaires and annual reports the Advisory Committee collected a vast amount of information as to the production and use of opium. And in order to make more effective the provision that one state should not allow the exportation of raw opium to a state which did not wish to receive it, the Committee worked out an importation certificate system, whereby no person could export dangerous drugs without a license from the importing state certifying that such drugs were required for legitimate purposes. At the suggestion of the Assembly, the Committee inquired into the advisability of requesting the parties to the convention to prohibit all opium imports from countries which have not adopted the certificate plan. At present this system of certificates has been put into effect by 36 countries.[2]

Probably the most troublesome task before the League was the interpretation of the convention of 1912 and the elaboration of supplementary agreements to make the control of drugs really effective. At its thirteenth session, the League Council requested the Advisory Committee to report on the possibilities of an inquiry to determine the requirements of raw and prepared opium "for medicinal and scientific purposes."[3] This wording led to a debate in the second Assembly, in which the representative of India contended that these words were more strict than the words in the convention of 1912, and that opium was legitimately used for other than medical purposes. As a result of his suggestion, a recommendation was adopted omitting the word "strictly" and substituting the word "legitimate" for "medicinal and scientific" purposes.[4]

7. THE PROPOSALS OF THE UNITED STATES

This action aroused the ire of the American Congress which, on March 2, 1923, passed a resolution in effect condemning the

[1] *O. J.*, August, 1924, p. 1117. Persia had not ratified by 1929.
[2] *Progress Report.* O. C. 904, 1929.
[3] *Minutes of the 13th Session of the Council*, p. 278.
[4] *Records of the Second Assembly*, Plenary Meetings, p. 540.

League's terminology and requesting the President to urge upon the drug-producing states the necessity of limiting production as the only means of stopping illicit use.[1] Before January, 1923, the United States had declined to work with the Opium Committee of the League. But the Administration finally appointed Assistant Surgeon-General Blue to act as our "unofficial" representative at the fourth session of the Advisory Committee, while following the passage of the congressional resolution, the United States appointed three representatives to attend its sessions, as well as Assembly meetings, in an "advisory" capacity.

At the fifth session of the Advisory Committee on the Opium Traffic, the American delegation presented two resolutions, the first of which provided that if the purpose of the convention of 1912 was to be realized, the use of opium for other than medicinal and scientific purposes must be recognized as an abuse and not legitimate.[2] The second provided that in order to prevent these abuses, the amount of raw opium produced must be limited so that there will be no surplus available for illegitimate purposes. Congressman Porter argued that since the parties had agreed, in the 1912 convention, to control the production and use of raw opium, and since that convention had indirectly recognized that smoking opium and the use of dope was illicit, the production of opium should be limited to medicinal and scientific purposes.[3]

In attempting to base its propositions upon such an interpretation of the 1912 convention, the United States weakened its case materially. Each nation, under this convention, could decide for itself

[1] 42 Stat. 1431. The Jones-Miller Act of 1922 had itself used the words "medical and legitimate uses."

[2] *The Traffic in Habit-Forming Drugs*, Statement of the attitude of the U. S., Washington, 1923, p. 14.

[3] Statement of Congressman S. G. Porter, *Minutes, 5th session*, pp. 13 ff. The American delegation declined to discuss its proposals with the Committee and insisted on withdrawing while the Committee decided to accept or reject them. *Minutes*, p. 821. Mrs. Hamilton Wright, an assessor, attempted to amend a reservation made by India's representative, which finally brought forth the statement that "he alone had the right to accept the responsibility for the reservation, since he was the sole representative of the Government of India on the Committee. He thought he could assure Mrs. Hamilton Wright . . . that she had no responsibility whatsoever in the matter." *Ibid.*, p. 100.

when these provisions should be put into effect and just what measures should be taken. More ground would have probably been gained if this government had frankly recognized that the terms of the 1912 convention were inadequate to cover the situation.

As a compromise, the Advisory Committee finally recommended to the League the adoption of the American proposals, subject to a reservation made by all the powers, except China and the United States, that the use of prepared opium and the production of raw opium for that purpose are legitimate so long as that use is in accordance with Chapter II of the convention.[1] In plain language, this meant that until the powers prohibit the manufacture, importation and exportation of smoking opium, each may produce raw opium for that purpose as much as it pleases, as long as exports are controlled. Despite the adoption of the American resolutions, each power remained the judge of when smoking opium should be suppressed and the extent to which the production of raw opium should be controlled.

8. OPIUM-SMOKING IN THE FAR EAST

Nevertheless the 1912 convention had provided for the "gradual and efficacious suppression" of the use of prepared opium, "in so far as the different conditions peculiar to each nation shall allow of this." Notwithstanding, the smoking of opium has continued in the Orient, and in recent years has showed a tendency to increase.[2] Although the United States attempted to prohibit smoking in the Philippines, this policy was not entirely successful.[3] Most of the Far Eastern colonies relied upon India for their source of supply, and most of them derived a considerable revenue from the use of opium.

If any practical good was to come out of the great opium move-

---

[1] "Report to Council on work of Fifth Session," *Minutes*, p. 202. India also made a reservation saying that the use of raw opium in India, according to established practice, is not illegitimate.

[2] Cf. "Application of Part II of the Opium Convention with Special Reference to European Possessions and Countries in the Far East;" Annex 4, *Minutes*, cited, pp. 135 ff. Cf. E. N. La Motte, *The Ethics of Opium* (1924), Chs. II–XVI.

[3] Cf. Herbert L. May, *Survey of Smoking Opium Conditions in the Far East*, Foreign Policy Association, 1927, p. 15.

ment before the World War, further conventions were necessary to fill in the gaps of the agreement of 1912. Consequently the fourth Assembly of the League of Nations passed a resolution to the effect that two international conferences should be held. The first should be composed of governments having colonies in the Far East and should bring about a reduction of the amount of opium for the purpose of smoking in these colonies. The second conference should be composed of all the governments concerned, which should conclude an agreement limiting the production of raw opium and coca leaf for export to the amount required for "medicinal and scientific purposes." [1]

9. THE OPIUM CONFERENCES OF 1924–1925

As a result of these two Opium Conferences which were in session between November, 1924, and February, 1925, a number of agreements were adopted, none of which, however, provided for the international limitation of the production of drugs or of the poppy. The government of China was too weak to stop production; no opium was shipped out of India to countries which did not wish to receive it; the governments of Persia, Turkey and Jugoslavia contended that they could not limit production until other crops were substituted.[2]

In view of the unrestricted production of opium in China and the smuggling into neighboring territories, the powers would not unconditionally agree to terminate smoking. However, they did sign protocols providing for the complete suppression of opium-smoking within fifteen years after the poppy-growing countries have taken steps to prevent smuggling from constituting a "serious obstacle" to the suppression of smoking. A Commission appointed by the League Council is to determine whether these measures are effective. An agreement also provides for certain minor reforms, such as the abolition of opium farms and smoking by minors.

Apparently as a result of this conference, the government of India announced in February, 1926, that it would progressively reduce its exports so as to eliminate them altogether within a term

[1] For the draft proposals, cf. *Report of the Opium Preparatory Committee*, C. 348, M. 119, 1924, XI.

[2] For a review of the background, history, and results of these conferences, cf. my pamphlet, cited.

CONTROL OF THE LIQUOR TRAFFIC

of years except for strictly medical purposes.[1] In June, 1926, the government announced that the last exports would take place in 1935. Apparently this action has not decreased smoking in the Far Eastern colonies who are making arrangements to procure their opium elsewhere.

The 1928 Assembly recommended that the Council appoint a Commission to study the opium-smoking situation in the Orient. The United States has authorized this Commission to visit the Philippines.

The most practical gains of the 1925 opium agreement relate to the international control over the drug traffic which takes the form of the export and import certificate, and also of a Permanent Central Board of eight persons appointed by the League Council.[2] The parties to the convention agree periodically to send statistics to this Board. If it believes that there is a danger of a country becoming the center of illicit traffic, it may ask for explanations. If no satisfactory reply is given, the Board may call the attention of the other states and of the League Council to the matter, and may recommend that no further exports be made to such a country until the Board reports that the situation is satisfactory. The only power of the present Board, therefore, is the power of advice. Inasmuch as no limitation upon the production of opium or of drugs has as yet been imposed by treaty, it is improbable that these new agreements will wipe out the illicit drug traffic of the world. The members of the Board, including an American, Mr. Herbert L. May, were selected in 1928.

10. CONTROL OF THE LIQUOR TRAFFIC IN AFRICA AND THE NORTH SEA

Whatever may be the effect of alcohol upon the white man in the temperate zone, there is no argument as to its devastating effect upon colored peoples in the tropics. When the missionary-explorers of Africa opened it up to the outside world, white liquor sellers proceeded to pour strong drink in upon the natives in a way which threatened to demoralize a whole continent.[3]

---

[1] Cf. *The Opium Situation in India*, F. P. A. Pamphlet No. 39, 1926.

[2] The United States and Germany were invited to nominate a "person to participate in these appointments."

[3] Cf. A. J. MacDonald, *Trade, Politics and Christianity in Africa and the Far East* (1916), 62 ff. But as this book demonstrates, liquor was used in Africa long before the advent of the white man.

At the Brussels conference of 1889–1890 an effort was made to handle the liquor along with the slavery question in Africa. The Brussels Act provided that in those districts in Africa where the use of distilled liquors had not been developed, the importation or manufacture of such liquors should be prohibited. Each colonial power was to determine where these districts were, and "prohibited zones" were actually established in the Belgian Congo, Northern Nigeria and German East Africa, etc.[1] Elsewhere the powers agreed to impose a minimum import duty of about 11 cents a gallon on liquor, which was to be increased two-thirds after three years.[2] The slavery bureau at Brussels was authorized to collect information in regard to the liquor traffic also.

But this import duty was too low to stop effectively the importation of liquor. Consequently the powers held another conference at Brussels, in 1899, which agreed to increase the duties to about 51 cents a gallon.[3] But at the request of the British, another conference was held in 1906, where the duty was raised to about 75 cents.[4] These successive increases did not stop spirituous liquors from pouring into Africa. And another attempt was made to arrive at a more rigid agreement at a conference at Brussels in 1912; but this conference failed because of differences between France and England.[5]

At the Paris Peace Conference the powers had another opportunity to attack this problem; and in September, 1919, seven powers signed a treaty prohibiting the importation, sale or possession of "trade spirits" throughout the whole continent of Africa, with the exception of Algeria, Tunis, Morocco, Libya, Egypt and the Union of South Africa. Within this area the manufacture, whether by natives or whites, of distilled beverages is forbidden. A duty of 800 francs per hectolitre of pure alcohol is levied upon the importation of all distilled beverages not included in trade spirits. But several provisions of this convention do not apply to the Italian colonies. Each of the powers must publish an annual

---

[1] Cf. map, *Annexes to the Minutes of the Third Session*, Permanent Mandates Commission, A. 19, 1923, VI, 261.
[2] Act of July 2, 1890, *Treaties of the U. S.*, Vol. II, pp. 1964, 1992, 2205.
[3] Convention of June 8, 1899, 91 *State Papers*, 6.
[4] Convention of Nov. 3, 1906, 99 *State Papers*, 490.
[5] G. L. Beer, *African Questions at the Paris Peace Conference* (1923), Part III, Ch. IV.

report containing relevant statistics, which are transmitted to a Central International Office under the control of the League.[1]

While this convention marks a considerable advance, it so far has not effectively curbed the use of alcohol because the powers have been unable to agree upon the definition of "trade spirits."[2] Each government may decide what distilled beverages fall within this category; but if possible, agreements are to be made as to a uniform nomenclature and uniform measures against fraud.

A similar question has arisen in connection with the B and C mandates where each mandatory power is responsible for the "prohibition of such abuses as . . . the liquor traffic." New Zealand has interpreted this to mean, in her mandate in Samoa, complete prohibition for whites and natives alike. Australia prohibits the sale of liquor to natives in New Guinea, a policy which is followed in British Nauru and the Japanese mandate in the Pacific.[3] But in the West African mandates the sale of wines, etc., is merely controlled.[4]

There are a great many difficulties connected with the suppression of the liquor traffic in Africa. The liquor market is extremely profitable for certain countries in Europe whose zeal for the suppression of the traffic is consequently tempered. Even if the importation of foreign liquor should be stopped, native stills would continue to flourish, unless exceptionally vigilant measures were taken. "There is no corner of Africa where the manufacture of fermented beverages is unknown, whether made from grain, from fruit (bananas), from honey, from the sap of various palms, or from the green cocoanut. . . . We hear of whole villages being drunk for days together, and of intoxicants being given to young infants."[5] Moreover, many European colonial officials insist on having their whisky; and to allow its importation for their account and yet to prohibit its use by natives, would create an undesirable color bar.[6] Difficulties have also been created between

[1] Convention of Sept. 10, 1919, *Treaties of the U. S.*, Vol. III, p. 3746.
[2] Cf. F. Lugard, "The Liquor Traffic in Mandated Territories," *Annexes*, cited, p. 256.
[3] Report to the League of Nations, *Administration of New Guinea*, Australia, 1921–22, F. 15723, p. 130; *Report on Nauru*, 1922, No. 20, F. 295, Australia, p. 8; *Japanese Mandate Report*, 1922, p. 11.
[4] *Rapport Annuel du Gouvernment Français sur Cameroun*, 1922, p. 21.
[5] Lugard, cited, p. 257.
[6] This policy is, however, followed in British East Africa.

adjoining colonies which impose different duties upon imported liquors, resulting in smuggling from the low- to the high-duty colony.

The only other part of the world where European powers have agreed to enforce prohibition by international agreement is in the North Sea. A great many abuses arose out of floating cabarets in this region and the consequent drunkenness of fishermen, some of whom were accustomed to exchange their catches for liquor. In order to put a stop to this traffic, six governments signed a treaty in 1887 agreeing to forbid the sale of spirituous liquors to persons on fishing boats on the North Sea. The cruisers of the different powers should watch out for offenders, and when there were grounds for suspicion that vessels were violating this prohibition, they could be brought into port and turned over to the national authorities for trial.[1]

11. CONTROVERSIES BETWEEN "WET" AND "DRY" COUNTRIES

International complications have likewise arisen over prohibition in "white" countries. Finland has been the only country in Europe with full prohibition; although in Norway distilled liquors were for a time under the ban. A policy of liquor-control is followed in Sweden and Esthonia, and local option is followed in Scotland, Poland, Bulgaria and Lithuania. In the New World, the provinces of Canada control the sale of liquor, sometimes by government stores. Some South American countries follow the policy of local option,[2] as do all of the Australian states. In New Zealand, twelve districts have prohibition. The greatest prohibition country in the world, is, of course, the United States.

Following the World War, an over-production of alcoholic liquors in Europe led producers to bring pressure on their governments to increase the sale of drink abroad. As a result, small countries,

[1] Convention of Nov. 16, 1887, 79 *State Papers*, 694.

[2] For the prohibition campaigns in the Latin-American countries, cf. *Special Handbook*, 5th Pan-American Conference, cited, p. 162. This Conference considered "measures adapted to secure the progressive diminution in the consumption of alcoholic liquors." It passed a resolution recommending systematic taxation of the liquor traffic, propaganda in the schools against intemperance, and the prohibition of saloons in the vicinity of schools, and of the sale of liquor on holidays, etc. *Tratado, Convenciones y resoluciones*, cited, p. 53.

attempting to enforce prohibition, were subjected to extremely questionable forms of pressure. In 1921 the Spanish government asked the government of Iceland, which had adopted prohibition in 1915, to do away with this policy as far as the importation of Spanish wines was concerned; otherwise the duties charged by Spain on fish from Iceland would be trebled. Inasmuch as Spain constituted a valuable market, Iceland, a country dependent on the fish trade, was obliged to yield. And in April, 1922, it suspended its prohibition law for one year, a period which was later extended indefinitely.

In 1916 Norway adopted a law prohibiting the use of certain liquors, which again offended some of the wine-exporting states. France made such a vigorous protest that in correspondence of April, 1921, Norway was obliged to declare, "Whatever regulations may be adopted in Norway for the importation, and sale, transport and consumption of the above mentioned wines and sparkling wines, the Norwegian Government undertakes to allow private individuals as well as restaurant proprietors, hotel keepers and wine merchants, to obtain for their consumption or the purposes of trade, the importation and transport of all brands of French wines and sparkling wines referred to above, to an unlimited extent.

"These guarantees of the Norwegian Government shall, if necessary, prevail over any local regulations which may tend to hinder their application."[1] Spain similarly obliged Norway to import not less than 150,000 litres of liquors containing more than 14% of alcohol,[2] and Portugal followed with a demand of 850,000 litres. The Norwegian parliament refused to accede to the latter demand. A ministerial crisis followed, as a result of which prohibition was abolished.[3] Norway was obliged to give in to the demands of these wine-producing countries because they consumed large quantities of fish which constituted one-third of Norway's exports. Unless the adoption of prohibition violates the terms of commercial treaties, the threat of a trade embargo, while "legal" under international law, is certainly a most questionable

[1] Treaty of April 23, 1921, *T. S.* 386.
[2] Cf. *T. S.* 244.
[3] I am indebted to Dr. R. Hercod, Director-General of the International Bureau against Alcoholism, Lausanne, for this information.

procedure,[1] especially when followed by a powerful "wet" state against a small country attempting to enforce prohibition.

12. LIQUOR-SMUGGLING

While no "wet" country has threatened to boycott the United States because of its prohibition policy—the United States being too strong—foreigners have smuggled great quantities of liquor into America, unobstructed, and in some instances, apparently encouraged by their governments. In 1922 the government of the Bahama Islands was reported to have made $1,200,000 in duties on liquor shipped into the United States. Bahama officials would issue to rum-runners two sets of clearance papers in order to deceive American revenue officials. In many instances ships were transferred from American to British registry for bootlegging purposes.[2] Under international law, as interpreted by most foreign governments, the United States could not seize rum-runners, flying a foreign flag, outside the three-mile limit. Even inside this limit, apprehension was extremely difficult.[3]

On the other hand, foreign vessels could not bring liquor into American ports, although sealed up while in American territory.[4] This meant that these vessels must use up all their liquor before

---

[1] In a letter of December 28, 1922, the French Minister of Foreign Affairs declared to the Chamber of Commerce of Grenoble, "Every sovereign state has the right of regulating as it pleases the manufacture and the use of any product on its territory, without any foreign State being in any way authorized to protest on the subject."

In order to reconcile prohibition, etc., with the trade privileges of commercial treaties, the following clause was inserted in the treaty of commerce with Germany and the United States, Dec. 8, 1923: "Nothing in this treaty shall be construed to restrict the right of either High Contracting Party to impose, on such terms as it may see fit, prohibitions or restrictions of a sanitary character designed to protect human, animal or plant life or regulations for the enforcement of police or revenue laws," Art. VII.

In the Convention on the International Régime of Railways, Geneva, December, 1923, it was provided that "Nothing in this Statute shall affect the measures which one of the Contracting States is or may feel called upon to take in pursuance of general international conventions . . . relating to the transit, export or import of particular kinds of articles such as opium. . . ."

The Supreme Court of the United States has ruled that liquor cannot be shipped, in bond, across the United States from Canada to Mexico, despite the principle of "freedom of transit." *Grogan* v. *Walker*, 259 U. S. (1921) 79.

[2] *N. Y. Times*, Jan. 29, 1923.

[3] Cf. Corwin, "The Three-Mile Limit," *Forum*, Sept., 1923.

[4] *Cunard S. S. Co.* v. *Mellon*, 262 U. S. (1923) 100.

entering the three-mile limit and they must depart without any on board. In many cases, this meant a "dry" homeward voyage, as well as the violation of the laws of France, Italy and Spain, requiring ships flying their flags to carry a certain ration of liquor. Thus foreign powers aided the violation of the prohibition policy of America, while the United States forced prohibition upon foreign states! Such were the international problems created by what international law calls a purely "domestic" question.

A step toward settling these complications was taken by a series of treaties between the United States and foreign powers. The first was with the British Empire. In this treaty both countries declared that it was their firm intention to uphold the principle of the three-mile limit; but that for the purpose of stopping bootlegging into the United States, the British Empire would not object if the United States seized British vessels suspected of this offense, within one hour's distance offshore—probably twelve miles.[1] On the other hand, the United States agreed that British ships might bring liquor under seal into American ports, provided none of it was carried on shore. Similar treaties were negotiated with a number of other countries.

A new type of treaty was negotiated with the neighboring states of Mexico, Canada and Cuba, in which the parties promised to furnish information regarding clearance of vessels suspected of smuggling to each other. In the Cuba treaty the parties agree that clearance shall be denied shipments of articles prohibited by the country to which such shipment is destined.[2]

On August 19, 1925, Germany, Denmark, Esthonia, Finland, Latvia, Lithuania, Norway, Poland and the Free City of Danzig, Sweden and Soviet Russia signed a "smuggling" treaty aimed at small craft on the Baltic. Each party undertakes to prohibit a vessel of less than one hundred tons from exporting liquor from its territory, unless it has an official authorization from its country of origin. Vessels receiving permission to carry liquor must not engage in contraband traffic; and the master of the vessel must declare that the goods will really be shipped to the place of destina-

---

[1] Treaty of Jan. 23, 1924, *U. S. Treaty Series*, No. 685.
[2] Conventions of March 11, 1926, *U. S. Treaty Series*, No. 739. The only one of these smuggling treaties now in effect is the one with Cuba.

tion. The parties agree that they may apply their laws to vessels engaged in the contraband traffic within a zone extending twelve nautical miles from the coast.[1]

At the suggestion of the American delegation, the Pan-American Conference at Santiago (1923) recommended that the American States adopt "measures conducive to the prohibition of the shipment of intoxicating beverages to a country where their consumption is prohibited, without the special authorization of the competent authority of the country from which shipment is made." [2]

The 1928 League Assembly, at the initiative of the Finnish, Swedish and Polish delegations, passed a resolution to the effect that the Health Organization of the League should consider the consequence of the abuse of alcohol and that the Economic Committee should examine the terms of conventions for the prevention of smuggling.[3]

At the present time, however, it appears that few foreign governments, with the possible exception of Canada and Norway, have undertaken to prohibit the export of liquor to "dry" countries. The extension of this principle—already adopted in the case of the slave trade and opium—would appear necessary if prohibition is not to disturb the relations of the nations of the world. But an international treaty to this effect will probably not be negotiated until a larger number of strong governments are convinced that prohibition is a desirable policy.

[1] *T. S.* 1033.
[2] *Tratado, Convenciones y resoluciones*, cited, p. 54.
[3] *O. J.*, Supplement No. 63, p. 15.

CHAPTER XII

INTERNATIONAL HUMANITARIANISM

1. The Slave Trade—The Brussels Act—The League of Nations.—2. The Arms Traffic.—3. The Traffic in Women and Children.—4. Obscene Publications.—5. Catching Criminals.—6. Safety of Life at Sea.—7. International Protection of Animals.—8. International Health—The Health Organization of the League—The Red Cross and Rockefeller Foundation.—9. International Refugee Work—Disasters.—10. Free Legal Aid.—11. "National Interests" and Humanitarianism.

For many centuries Christian countries recognized the institution of slavery as legitimate,—an institution which was maintained by a slave trade of enormous proportions between Africa and America and Europe. In the treaty of Utrecht of 1713 Spain granted England a monopoly called the Assiento, for carrying slaves to the Spanish possessions, in which England agreed to supply 144,000 slaves within thirty years.[1] Even before the 18th century, however, different countries began to prohibit the slave trade and to abolish slavery. One of the last was the United States who did not do away with this form of bondage until 1865. While slavery as such is a domestic status, the slave trade is as a rule international in character. Some of the anti-slavery countries found themselves at a commercial disadvantage with countries who still maintained a profitable trade in human beings. Here also they had to cope with the problem of smuggling. An international conscience, moreover, soon arose to demand that concerted steps be taken to wipe out human trafficking.

1. THE SLAVE TRADE

For these different reasons, the slave trade soon became the object of treaties. Beginning in 1814–1815, European powers

---

[1] W. E. B. Dubois, *The Suppression of the African Slave Trade to the United States of America* (1896), pp. 3, 207; J. K. Ingram, *A History of Slavery and Freedom* (1895), Chs. VI–VIII.

condemned the traffic, while twenty-five or so binational treaties, providing for the limited right of visit of vessels suspected of engaging in the trade off the west coast of Africa, were signed by 1841.[1] In this year the first general treaty in regard to the trade was also signed at London, in which the five great powers of Europe promised to prohibit the slave trade, which they declared to be piracy. In order to stamp it out, they recognized a reciprocal right of search in certain waters.[2] The feeling in France, however, was so strong against the right of reciprocal visit, that France not only failed to ratify the convention but also terminated her previous agreements. In a new treaty with England of May, 1854, each state agreed to provide a fleet of 26 cruisers to stamp out the traffic, the commanders of which should "concert together" as to the most effective means "to prevent their respective flags from being usurped." But whenever it became necessary to use force to execute the treaty, the consent of both commanders was necessary.[3]

While in the treaty of December, 1814, Great Britain and the United States had agreed to promote the abolition of the trade, the United States too disapproved of the right of visit. However, in a treaty of August 9, 1842, both governments agreed to maintain on the coast of Africa a naval force to enforce the laws of their respective countries. Although each squadron was to be independent of the other, their officers were to coöperate.[4] Difficulty in suppressing the traffic finally led the United States to give up its objections to the visiting of American slavers by British ships. In a treaty with Great Britain of April 7, 1862, both parties agreed that certain vessels might visit merchant ships suspected of trading, within a limited zone off Africa and Cuba, and later extended to Madagascar, Porto Rico and San Domingo.[5]

---

[1] Fauchille, *Traité de droit international public*, Vol. I, p. 786. Many of these early treaties have only recently been denounced. Cf. *T. S.*, Vol. IX, *passim*.

[2] Treaty of Dec. 20, 1841, 30 *State Papers*, 269.

[3] Treaty of May 29, 1845, 33 *State Papers*, 4.

[4] *Treaties of the U. S.*, Vol. I., p. 655.

[5] *Ibid.*, pp. 674, 687. The treaty of 1862 provided for the establishment of three mixed courts of justice, to sit at Sierra Leone, the Cape of Good Hope, and New York, to try vessels suspected of trading. But these courts were abolished in the convention of June 3, 1870. *Treaties of the U. S.*, Vol. I, pp. 676, 693.

These international measures were directed to the suppression of the slave traffic at sea. In addition, Arab chieftains carried on an extensive trade in the heart of Africa, while native tribes encouraged many forms of domestic slavery. An attempt to suppress the slave traffic at its source was first made at the Berlin Conference of 1885. In the General Act, the powers promised to endeavor "to secure the complete suppression of slavery in all its forms and of the slave trade by land and sea." They agreed also that their colonies in the Congo region should not serve as a market or a means of transit for the slave traffic.[1]

The Brussels Act.—This convention did not, however, apply to the independent Arab chieftains who carried on slave raids in the Persian Gulf and the Red Sea. In order to handle this problem and to define measures against the traffic, an anti-slavery conference was convened in Brussels in 1889. In the Act of July 2, 1890, an attempt was made to stamp out this evil at its origin, its destination and in transit. The Act defined seven means as most effective in combating the traffic—such as the establishment of fortified stations and flying columns. In order to prevent the transportation of slaves, the powers undertook to exercise a close surveillance over the routes used by slave traders. The treaty also mapped out a zone extending from Baluchistan southward, including the Persian Gulf and the Red Sea. Within this zone, warships of the parties might verify the papers of a suspicious vessel. If in accordance with the convention, the commanding officer was convinced that a vessel was guilty of slaving, he could bring it into the proper port for trial. Countries still recognizing the existence of domestic slavery pledged themselves to prohibit the importation, transit and departure of slaves. Finally, the establishment of an international maritime bureau was authorized at Zanzibar to collect information about the traffic in the maritime zone.[2]

Apparently the elaborate provisions of the Brussels Act did not prove effective, for in September, 1919, the powers abrogated

[1] Art. 9, Act of Feb. 26, 1885, 10 Martens (2d series), 414.
[2] *Treaties of the U. S.*, Vol. II, p. 1964. The United States ratified this Act, with reservations, but failed to ratify the Act of Berlin. France ratified the Brussels Act only in part, rejecting the provisions in regard to the maritime zone out of fear they would enhance British maritime supremacy in a part of the world where British influence was already strong.

the anti-slavery provisions of both the Berlin and Brussels treaties. The only provision in the revised convention is that the powers will "endeavor to secure the complete suppression of slavery in all its forms and of the slave trade by land and sea." [1] In the mandates B and C, established in the Treaty of Versailles, the powers agree to prohibit such abuses as the slave trade, and also, eventually, to emancipate all slaves.

These obligations are not only vague, but their fulfillment depends, as in the case of the opium convention, upon the discretion of the power concerned. It is not surprising, therefore, that the slave trade and slavery still exist in some backward parts of the world. In 1922 Arabs were reported to be selling slaves in Morocco. Following the War, slave-deals were reported among the natives of Nigeria and the Sudan.[2] In the independent negro kingdom of Abyssinia, domestic slavery is still recognized, while the slave trade has flourished. Since the War, slave raiders from Abyssinia have raided British territory in Kenya and the Sudan, and made off with large numbers of British subjects. One writer saw with his own eyes, "a convoy of ten thousand slaves marching toward the great slave market of Jimma; and in the course of a single day's march along the trail he has counted the dead and dying bodies of more than fifty captives who have dropped by the roadside." [3]

Successive kings of Abyssinia,—the Emperors Theodoros, Johannes, Menelik, and the present sovereign, Ras Taffari, attempted to suppress the slave traffic. But because of the disorganized condition of the kingdom, local chieftains were able to flaunt the imperial will.

The League of Nations.—In 1923 Abyssinia applied for ad-

---

[1] Art. 11, Convention revising the Acts of Berlin and of Brussels, Sept. 10, 1919; *Treaties of the U. S.*, Vol. III, p. 3739.

[2] J. H. Harris, "Slavery and the Obligations of the League of Nations," Anti-Slavery and Aborigines Protection Society, March, 1923; F. Lugard, *Dual Mandate in British Tropical Africa* (1922), p. 388; "Slavery in Abyssinia," Cmd. 1858 (1923).

[3] Darley and Sharp, "Slave Trading and Slave Owning in Abyssinia," *Westminster Gazette*, January, 1922, reprinted by the Anti-Slavery Society. France now maintains a "Red Sea" naval station and England maintains 2 sloops in the Red Sea and 2 sloops and a special vessel in the Persian Gulf to wipe out the traffic. Cf. Debates, House of Commons, May 21, 1924, 173 *Parl. Debates*, H. C., p. 2169. Cf. "The Question of Slavery," A. 18, 1923, VI.

mission to the League of Nations. At the fourth Assembly, a vigorous debate took place over this application. Representatives of Switzerland, Holland and of the British Empire were inclined to doubt whether the government of Abyssinia could give effective guarantees that the slave and arms traffics would be wiped out.[1] Other nations, particularly France, supported Abyssinia's cause with the result that Abyssinia was finally admitted, upon making specific declarations adhering to the obligations in the convention of September, 1919, concerning slavery and the arms traffic. Abyssinia also promised to furnish the Council with whatever information it might desire, and to consider any recommendation the Council might make with regard to fulfilling these obligations.

In the League Covenant, the members undertook "to secure just treatment of the native inhabitants of territories under their control." On the basis of this obligation, the Assembly adopted a resolution in 1922 placing the question "of the recrudescence of slavery" on the agenda of the fourth Assembly in 1923. In September, 1922, the Council instructed the Secretary-General to request the various governments for information in regard to slavery. As only a small number of states adequately replied,[2] the League did not believe sufficient information had been secured; and the fourth Assembly requested the Council to authorize a competent body to continue the investigation and report to the fifth assembly.

In June, 1924, a Temporary Committee on Slavery was established, containing eight members.[3] In seeking information as to slavery, this Committee did not confine itself to government documents, but consulted every available private source of infor-

[1] Cf. Minutes of the 6th Committee, Records of the 4th Assembly, 1923, *O. J.*, Spec. Supplement 19, pp. 14–22. French writers assert that the British exaggerated the slavery charges against Abyssinia and opposed its entrance into the League because they wished to establish control over the country on account of the Blue Nile, upon which the irrigation system of the Sudan depends. Alype, "L'Empire Éthiopien," *Afrique française* (1922), p. 215; "L'Empire d'Éthiopie dans la Société des Nations," *ibid.* (1923), p. 499; Bruneau, "Les competitions des puissances autour de l'Éthiopie," *L'Europe Nouvelle*, May 24, 1924. Cf. "Règlement pour la Liberté des Esclaves," Addis-Abeba, 1924.

[2] Cf. "The Question of Slavery," A. 18, 1923, VI, and Grimshaw, Memorandum on Slavery and Labour in the Mandates, Annexes, *Minutes of Mandates Commission*, 1923, A. 19, 1923, VI, p. 262.

[3] *O. J.*, February, 1924, p. 331; April, 1924, p. 697; July, 1924, p. 909.

mation. While this may be a shocking deviation from the old ideas of "sovereignty," it is the only way of determining the truth, since in some countries official documents, whether purposely or not, hide facts damaging to the governmental authorities.

As a result of the work of this commission the 1926 Assembly was the scene of the signature of a new Slavery Convention. The parties to this convention promise to prevent and suppress the slave trade. And for this purpose they agree to negotiate a General Convention imposing upon them duties similar to those provided for in the 1925 Convention relative to the Arms Traffic (i. e., special control in special zones). They also promise to bring about as soon as possible the complete abolition of slavery in all its forms. Article 5 of the Convention provides, moreover, that "recourse to compulsory or forced labor may have grave consequences" and the parties agree that it shall be exacted only for public purposes. But in territories in which forced labor for other purposes still survives the parties shall "endeavor progressively and as soon as possible to put an end to the practice." This article does not go therefore as far as the League mandates in restricting forced labor.[1] Nevertheless, as a result of the Convention a number of governments, such as Abyssinia, Sierra Leone, India and Portuguese Africa, have promulgated new legislation in regard to slavery, the slave trade or forced labor.[2] The International Labor Office has also appointed a committee of experts to study the problem of colonial labor, and the question was discussed at the 1929 International Labor Organization Conference.[3]

2. THE ARMS TRAFFIC

Western firearms have been dumped by private traders into Africa along with western liquor, where they have been the deadly instruments of slave-raids, inter-tribal warfare and resistance to European rule. In an effort to stop this traffic, the powers agreed in the Brussels Act of 1890 to prohibit the sale of rifles and ammunition to natives in their African possessions, between 20

---

[1] Cf. p. 360.
[2] Goudal, "La Lutte Internationale contre l'Esclavage," *R. D. I. P.* September-October, 1928. Buell, "The Struggle in Africa," *Foreign Affairs*, October, 1927; *Annual Report of the Council*, A. 62. 1928. VI.
[3] Cf. *Forced Labor*, International Labor Office Publication, Geneva, 1928.

degrees north and 20 degrees south latitude.[1] Likewise France, Great Britain and Italy in 1906 attempted to stop gun-running into Abyssinia by a convention prohibiting the export of arms to Abyssinia through Somaliland or Eritrea, etc., except upon the special authorization of the Abyssinian government.[2] The Act of Algeciras of 1906 prohibited the unauthorized importation of war arms into Morocco.[3] In 1908 the Congo Free State, France, Germany, Portugal, Spain and Great Britain signed a protocol suspending for at least four years the importation of all firearms and ammunition for natives in a large zone within Eastern Equatorial Africa.[4] Similar international agreements were made in regard to Korea, when independent, and certain islands in the Pacific.[5] In 1919 twelve powers agreed to restrain their citizens from exporting arms and munitions to China "until the establishment of a government whose authority is recognized throughout the whole country."[6] This agreement was not enforced, however, and the whole subject of the arms traffic in China was discussed at the Washington Conference (1922), but without further action because of the opposition of Italy.[7] The agreement was terminated April 26, 1929.

As the provisions in the Brussels Act of 1890 in regard to Africa proved too lenient, a conference was held in 1908–1909 to extend the zones of prohibition and to set up some means of international control. Because of the opposition of France, however, no agreement proved possible, and no further steps toward prohibiting the arms traffic among "backward peoples" were taken until after the War.[8]

With the accumulation of great stores of surplus weapons during the World War, some new restrictions, imposed on the export of arms from Europe as well as import by Africa etc., were imperative.

[1] Ch. I. arts. 8–14, *Treaties of the U. S.*, pp. 1970–1973.
[2] Agreement of Dec. 13, 1906, *State Papers*, 252.
[3] Ch. II, Act of April 7, 1906, 99 *State Papers*, 141.
[4] Protocol of July 22, 1908, Cd. 4320.
[5] For citations, cf. Q. Wright, *Limitation of Armament*. Syllabus, Institute for International Education, No. XII, 1921, p. 13.
[6] *Treaties of the U. S.*, Vol. III, p. 3821; *China Year Book*, 1921–22, p. 530.
[7] Minutes, *Washington Conference on the Limitation of Armament*, pp. 733, 737, 744.
[8] G. L. Beer, *African Questions at the Paris Peace Conference* (1923), Part III, Ch. V.

Consequently, twenty-three powers, including the United States, signed an Arms Traffic convention at Saint Germain in 1919, which attempted to prohibit the sale of war arms to individuals and to control sales to governments by a system of license and publicity. Each power promised to publish annual reports about the traffic and to send them to an International Office established by the League.[1] If this convention had been put into effect, the shipment of arms by private firms to revolutionists in any country would have been prohibited; while native tribes would also have been prevented from obtaining instruments with which to carry on the slave trade or to cast off European rule.

Since the Covenant intrusted it with the "general supervision of the trade in arms and ammunition with the countries" where such control is necessary, the League undertook to secure the ratification of the Saint Germain convention. But the large arms-producing powers declared that they could ratify only if the convention would be accepted by the United States—one of the largest arms-manufacturing powers in the world.[2] After numerous inquiries from the League, the United States finally announced that it could not approve the convention. Both the Council and the third and fourth Assemblies of the League urged the United States to state its objections to the convention. Finally, in notes of August, 1922 and September, 1923, the United States declared that the convention would prohibit the export of arms to states not parties to the convention, such as Latin-American countries, that it did nothing to limit the traffic between governments,[3] and that the agreement was too closely intertwined with the League. The United States finally agreed to coöperate in framing a new agreement. This was done at a Conference on the International Trade in Arms held in Geneva in May–June 1925.[4]

[1] Convention of September 10, 1919. *Treaties of U. S.*, Vol. III, 3752.
[2] A. 124, X, 1922, p. 7.
[3] The U. S. is not opposed in principle to the regulation of the arms traffic. It ratified the Act of Brussels and of Algeciras containing such provisions, and signed a similar agreement in the case of China. The American Congress has expressly authorized the President to prohibit the export of arms to American countries where domestic violence prevails and to any country where the United States exercises exterritorial jurisdiction. Cf. 30 Stat. 739; 37 Stat. 630; 42 Stat. 361.
[4] See *Proceedings of the Conference for the Supervision of the International Trade in Arms and Ammunition and in Implements of War.* A. 13. 1925. IX.

According to the convention there signed, the trade in arms not suitable for military purposes may continue. But the governments promise not to allow the sale of war arms to individuals in foreign countries; and in case one government wishes to import cannon, machine guns or other war arms from manufacturers in another country it must present a written order to such manufacturers who must also hold a license from their own governments authorizing the export. In a special zone which includes Central Africa and a maritime zone covering the Red Sea, the Gulf of Aden, the Persian Gulf, etc., a more severe régime is established. No arms of any kind may be exported to the special zone without a license from the government of the exporter, which may be issued only in case the authorities governing the special zone are willing to have the arms admitted. Likewise the commander of warships may stop any native vessel of less than 500 tons in this zone which he feels is guilty of the illicit arms traffic and bring it into a port for trial. The purpose of these measures is to put an end to the traffic in rifles and ammunition which has been carried on by native tribes in Africa and Arabia. By means of these arms, it is said, tribes have carried on the slave trade.

Although it signed this arms convention in June, 1925, the United States had not ratified by July, 1929, and the convention was not in effect. Ratifications by fourteen governments are necessary; and the others seem to be awaiting American action.[1]

3. THE TRAFFIC IN WOMEN AND CHILDREN

For many years the white slave traffic has been organized upon an international basis. International white slave gangs have transported prostitutes from Berlin and Paris to the United States, South America and the Orient.[2] According to a League of Nations investigation, in some countries the majority of the inhabitants of brothels are foreign women.[3] Isolated national action cannot cope with the wide ramifications of this traffic. The

---

[1] Cf. "The United States and the Saint Germain Treaties," *I. S.*, Vol. IV. No. 22.

[2] R. Decante, *La Lutte contre la prostitution* (1909), pp. 215 ff.; A. Flexner, *Prostitution in Europe* (1914), p. 93.

[3] *Report on Traffic in Women and Children*, C. 52. M. 52. 1927. IV. Part I, p. 10.

284 INTERNATIONAL HUMANITARIANISM

procurers of these women may never enter the country to which their victims are sent.

Following the efforts of private international organizations, the French government called a conference in 1902 out of which came the White Slave Convention of 1904, signed by twelve states. This convention provided that any one engaging in the traffic should be punished and that the governments should exchange information in regard to it.[1] Difficulties arising out of this treaty in regard to the age of consent and rogatory commissions were cleared up in a new convention of 1910, to which sixteen states soon became parties.[2]

Upon the invitation of the Council of the League of Nations an International Conference on the Traffic in Women and Children was held in Geneva in the summer of 1921, attended by 34 states. A convention was drawn up to supplement the conventions of 1904 and 1910. It was agreed that all parties who had not ratified these conventions should ratify without delay. The convention of 1921 extends the offenses made punishable by the convention of 1910, raises the age of consent to 21 from 20, and provides for the licensing of employment agencies so as to protect women and children seeking work in a foreign country.[3] Governments promise to make annual reports to the League on measures taken to check the traffic. In 1921 the League Council set up a body now bearing the name of Advisory Commission for the Protection and Welfare of Children and Young People. Since 1925 it has consisted of two separate committees, the first dealing with the Traffic in Women and Children, and the second with Child Welfare. The latter committee has investigated the question of motion pictures, and has drafted conventions in regard to the repatriation of minors and for the relief of minors of foreign nationality. It has also studied the question of juvenile courts, recreation, and alcoholism.[4]

In 1923 the Council appointed a special body of experts to

---

[1] Convention May 18, 1904, *Treaties of U. S.*, Vol. II, p. 2131.

[2] Convention of May 4, 1910, 103 *State Papers*, 244.

[3] Convention of September 30, 1921, A. 124 (2) 1921. On June 12, 1920, about fifteen states signed a convention in regard to the Guardianship of Minors, 95 *State Papers*, 421, clearing up difficulties arising out of the fact that a guardian did not live in the same country as the minor.

[4] Cf. *Report on the Work of the Fourth Session*, C. 185. 1928. IV.

study the existence of the white slave traffic. In preparing its report, these experts interviewed 5000 persons connected with commercialized prostitution. Their report revealed the existence of a widespread traffic which affected practically every country of the world. "Many hundreds of women and girls—some of them very young—are transported each year from one country to another for purposes of prostitution." [1] It also declared that the existence of licensed houses of prostitution was an incentive to international traffic. It argued for the abolition of the licensed system in favor of prohibition. While the traffic existed, progress toward its termination had nevertheless been made. "Before the machinery of the League of Nations was established, no steps were taken nor could readily be taken to ascertain the results of international measures. The discussions of the Advisory Committee and the making of Annual Reports by the Governments have undoubtedly had a marked effect in informing public opinion and in stimulating active measures against the traffic." [2] The 1927 Assembly asked the Advisory Committee to consider the desirability of recommending all governments to abolish the system of licensed houses. In 1928 the Assembly supported the Committee's request that governments still following the system should investigate the question as soon as possible in the light of the Experts' Report.

In April, 1921, the League Council also appointed a Commission to rescue women and children in the Near East who had been deported by the Turks,—a body which was successful in restoring a large number of women to their relatives.

4. OBSCENE PUBLICATIONS

In 1910 a conference for the Suppression of the Traffic of Obscene Publications was held in Paris along with the White Slave Conference. It drew up two Acts (1) an "Arrangement" by which each of the parties agreed to appoint an authority charged with the duty of centralizing all information tending to check the importation of obscene literature; and (2) a draft convention, which, however, was never signed.

Because of the recent growth of this traffic in vicious literature

[1] *Report on Traffic in Women and Children*, Part I, p. 43.
[2] *Ibid.*, p. 40.

the third Assembly (1922) invited the French government to convene a new conference on the matter. This conference, which met in Geneva in August, 1923, drew up a convention—signed by 35 governments—which declared the traffic in obscene publications to be a punishable offense, provided for the enactment of national legislation for the searching of suspected premises, and for further conferences to revise the Convention, if necessary. The determination of what constitutes "obscene" literature is left to each government. The ratification of this convention also constitutes ratification of the agreement of 1910.[1]

Apparently this is the first international treaty in the history of diplomacy really to outlaw sordid literature. It not only prohibits the export of such literature but also punishes its possession for "purposes of trade."

5. CATCHING CRIMINALS

Because of the modern railway, automobile and airplane, it is now comparatively easy for a man who commits a crime in one country to flee to another, where, under the old ideas of "sovereignty," he would be free from arrest. The mutual advantages of coöperation in the return of such criminals have been so great that since the second half of the 19th century a large number of "extradition" treaties have been made.[2] However, with the exception of the Central American treaty of 1907, revised in 1923, no multilateral treaty for this purpose has as yet been ratified. It is not improbable, however, that in view of the desirability of a general international law of extradition, such a treaty will be negotiated in the future,—perhaps under League auspices.[3]

Even prisons have been brought into the field of world politics. Since 1846 congresses to discuss penitentiary administration and reform have been held periodically. These congresses discuss questions relating to the moral and physical improvement of prisoners as well as to the prevention of crime. In 1880 an international penitentiary commission was established to prepare the

---

[1] *O. J.*, October, 1923, p. 1151.
[2] Cf. index to *Treaties of the U. S.*; for the treaty of the five Central American Republics, cf. *Minutes*, Central American Conference, cited, p. 354.
[3] However, in 1902, 17 American countries signed a treaty for the extradition of criminals and for protection against anarchism. It was not, however, ratified. 6 Martens (3d series), 185.

work of these conferences. It is supported by twenty-two countries, including the United States.[1]

6. SAFETY OF LIFE AT SEA

Despite the vast expanse of the ocean, collisions between the vessels of different countries frequently occur, whether in the dark of night or in the midst of heavy fogs or storms. By providing for a uniform system of signaling, domestic law might prevent many such collisions between vessels of a single nation. The sea, however, is free to all. International provision must therefore be made, if common rules of the road are to be formulated and obeyed. The first International Marine Conference for this purpose was held at Washington in 1889, at which a resolution was adopted recommending rules for the prevention of collisions, and also for sound signals, lights, buoys, steering and sailing.[2] No further action was taken, however, until the signature of a convention in 1910 in which twenty-four powers agreed to certain uniform rules in regard to assistance and salvage at sea, and providing for equitable remuneration when such assistance is given.[3]

The great damage which those mavericks of the sea—icebergs—may do to human life was shown by the Titanic disaster in 1912 in which 1,490 lives were lost. As a result of this disaster, an international conference was held in London at which 13 countries signed a convention for Safety of Life at Sea. This convention provided for three services,—the destruction of derelicts, the

[1] Practically all of the international humanitarian activities of governments have been the result of the efforts of private and voluntary international organizations. At the present time eight such organizations are concerned with the protection of the "backward" peoples—the most important being the Anti-Slavery and Aborigines Protection Society of London. Nine organizations are fighting the liquor traffic; four are devoted to the protection of animal life; nine to the promotion of international philanthropy; twelve to sociological questions, such as the International Federation for the Observance of the Sabbath; twenty-five to the advancement of different kinds of education; five to the protection of children; eleven to the advancement of women; seventeen to the promotion of hygiene; five to moral questions, such as the Boy Scouts' International Bureau. There are seventeen international Christian organizations. Cf. Index analytique, *Handbook of International Organizations*, 1921, pp. 154 ff.

[2] "International Marine Conference," Dec. 31, 1889, 81 *State Papers*, 705.
[3] *Treaties of the U. S.*, Vol. III, p. 2943.

study of ice conditions and an ice patrol, two vessels being stipulated for these purposes. The United States was invited to undertake the management of these services, the expense was to be prorated between the parties, 30% being paid by Great Britain, 15% each by France, Germany and the United States, and lesser amounts by the other powers. The convention also made provision for international signals, life boats, safety certificates, and so forth.[1] A new conference on safety of life at sea was called in the spring of 1929. In June a new convention was signed, dealing with, among other subjects, life-saving appliances, radio-telegraphy, and helm or steering orders. Ocean-going liners must carry life-boats for all; they must be capable of being safely launched. Ships must be able to receive as well as to send out radio calls for assistance. Finally, since ships have to employ pilots of all nationalities, the system under which steering orders are given must be international.

7. INTERNATIONAL PROTECTION OF ANIMALS

Man is not the only species to be the subject of international benevolence. In 1900 the colonial powers of Africa held a conference in London out of which came a convention prohibiting the killing of certain wild animals, such as giraffes, gorillas and young elephants, within the zone in Africa established by the Brussels Act of 1890.[2] In 1902 twelve European powers signed an agreement prohibiting the killing of birds useful to agriculture.[3] In 1916 the United States and Great Britain signed a treaty, the preamble of which declared that many birds in their annual migrations from the United States to Canada are "in danger of extermination through lack of protection" of a uniform nature. To this end the treaty provided for a closed season in which these

[1] Convention of Jan. 20, 1914. Cd. 7246 (1914), LXX p. 183. In 1921 an International Hydrographic Bureau was put into operation. Its purpose is to coördinate the activities of different governments in their efforts to make the navigation of the sea more secure. In addition to the Bureau, conferences are held at least once every six years. Since 1902 an International Council for the Exploration of the Sea has carried on researches of a scientific nature and formulated international legislation for the protection of fisheries. *Handbook of International Organizations* (1921), pp. 45, 74.
[2] Convention of May 19, 1900, 94 *State Papers*, 715.
[3] Convention of March 19, 1902, 102 *State Papers*, 969.

PROTECTION OF ANIMALS

birds should be unmolested.[1] One result of the passage of the migratory bird treaty act, prohibiting spring shooting, was to increase the supply of wild fowl in the United States.[2]

Certain fisheries have likewise been placed under international protection. In order to prevent disputes arising between the fishermen of different nationalities interested in the North Sea, a convention was concluded in May, 1882, providing that any commissioned ship might seize fishing vessels violating the rules laid down in the treaty, but such a vessel must be delivered up for trial to the authorities of its own country.[3] Different countries have also made treaties regulating fishing on such rivers as the Danube and Pruth.[4] In order to preserve the halibut fisheries of the Pacific, the United States and Canada signed a treaty, in March, 1923, establishing a closed season of three months annually, and providing for an International Fisheries Commission to make recommendations as to the regulation of these fisheries.[5] Every person violating the provisions of the treaty may be seized except within the jurisdiction of the other party by duly authorized officers of either the United States or Canada; but the nation to which such person belongs alone may try him for the offense.

When the United States attempted to prevent the reckless destruction of seals in the Behring Sea, its efforts were blocked by Great Britain on the ground that the jurisdiction of the United States was limited to the three-mile limit—a contention which an arbitration court upheld.[6] However, the same end was accomplished—and perhaps more effectively—by a convention in 1911 between the United States, Great Britain, Russia and Japan, in which the powers agreed to prohibit their citizens from sealing in certain parts of the Pacific, to maintain a guard in the waters

---

[1] Treaty of August 16, 1916, *Treaties of U. S.*, Vol. III, p. 2645.
[2] *N. Y. Herald Tribune*, Dec. 5, 1924.
[3] Convention of May 6, 1882, 73 *State Papers*, 39.
[4] Fauchille, cited, p. 783.
[5] Treaty of March 2, 1923, *Treaties of the U. S.*, Vol. III, p. 2659. At least four international fisheries congresses have been held, the conference of 1908 being held in Washington, attended by delegates from 15 governments and a number of private organizations. *Organization and Sessional Business of the Fourth International Fishery Congress*, Washington, U. S. A., 1908, Bulletin of the Bureau of Fisheries, No. 726.
[6] For the Behring Sea arbitration of 1892, cf. J. B. Moore, *International Arbitrations* (1898), Vol. I, Ch. XVII.

frequented by herds, and to hand over to the other governments a certain percentage of the seals legally taken on their respective islands.[1] The sealing treaty contains the same provision for punishing offenders as is found in the halibut treaty.

8. INTERNATIONAL HEALTH

People may differ over politics but most of them do not differ over the necessity of expelling disease from the world. Out of a total population of about two billion people, 70,000,000 are sick all the time; and of these, 28,000,000 are needlessly sick.[2] Ordinarily, disease is considered as a matter for the doctor rather than the diplomat. But epidemics, starting in an isolated country, may spread throughout the world. An influenza wave originating in Spain may bring death to thousands of people in America. A rat infected with the bubonic plague, which climbs on board a ship at Calcutta, may carry the disease to Liverpool; while a man in South America bitten with a mosquito carrying yellow fever germs may bring the disease to New York. For hundreds of years, Europe has been inundated with plagues, carried along the trade routes from Asia. In the nineteenth century alone, six cholera plagues left their marks in European countries.[3] Following the World War, the struggling armies of Russia carried a typhus plague into Poland where it threatened to sweep over the whole of Europe.

For many years nations attempted to stop these epidemics by single-handed measures. Each would adopt a rigid quarantine policy in which commerce from infected states would be denied admission, and in which people and ships suspected of infection would be interned for uncomfortable lengths of time. But unless quarantine measures are immediately applied when disease breaks out in a foreign country, they are worthless; and the knowledge of the existence of such disease can be obtained only from foreign

[1] Convention of July 7, 1911, *Treaties of the U. S.*, Vol. III, p. 2966; this convention superseded the treaty between Great Britain and the United States of February 7, 1911, *Ibid.*, p. 2629.

[2] J. A. Tobey, "For the Health of the World," *Current History*, Nov., 1922.

[3] P. Manson, *Tropical Diseases* (3d ed., 1903), p. 345; cf. also F. G. Clemon, *The Geography of Disease* (1903); and F. Prinzing, *Epidemics Resulting from Wars* (1916); Whipple, "World Sanitation: A Twentieth Century Possibility," 1 *International Journal of Public Health* (1920), 38.

governments. Some form of international coöperation is therefore necessary, not only to reduce to a minimum obstructions to world intercourse, but to secure information as to the outbreak of disease.

Between 1851 and 1907 six international sanitation conferences were held in Europe to discuss common measures to be taken against epidemics. In 1893, 1894, 1897, 1903, 1907 and 1912 international health conventions were signed. In the 1912 convention each government promised to notify the others immediately of the first case of plague, cholera or yellow fever discovered in its territory. Measures must be taken to prevent the departure from the country of persons or goods thus contaminated until disinfected; while patients on ships infected with an epidemic must be landed and isolated. In order to prevent unnecessary obstructions, the convention provides that vessels from a contaminated port, which have been disinfected, and so forth, shall not be obliged to undergo the same process a second time in a new port, provided they have not touched at another contaminated port. Although no land quarantines may be established, persons showing symptoms of plague, cholera or yellow fever may be detained at frontiers.

Since many of the epidemics which sweep the world come out of Oriental and Far Eastern countries, the convention provides that special measures should be taken in regard to the Suez Canal, Egyptian ports, the Red Sea and Persian Gulf,—the thoroughfares between Europe and Asia. In these areas special precautions are taken to prevent the transmission of disease, by quarantines, observations and disinfection. Because the annual pilgrimages of thousands of Moslems to the Holy Places of the Hejaz have been breeding places for disease, the convention lays down special regulations for pilgrim ships.[1] In 1926 the international sanitary convention was thoroughly revised and its provisions extended to include typhus and smallpox.[2]

To supervise these prophylactic measures in Eastern countries, a Superior Health Council was established at Constantinople in 1838, while a Sanitary, Maritime and Quarantine Council of Egypt was established in Alexandria in 1881. Two other inter-

[1] Convention of Jan. 17, 1912, *Treaties of the U. S.*, Vol. III, p. 2972.
[2] Convention of June 11, 1926, *U. S. Treaty Series*, No. 762.

national health councils have functioned at Tangier in Morocco and at Teheran in Persia.

Although the Constantinople Council was presided over by the Turkish minister of foreign affairs and Turkey appointed four members, seventeen members were appointed by the foreign powers. Its expenses were met by quarantine fees, and it acted by majority vote. While nationalistic intrigues hindered the operations of the councils at Constantinople and Teheran, the Councils at Alexandria and at Tangier appear to have succeeded in keeping down disease.[1]

In 1907 an International Office of Public Health, authorized in a sanitary convention of 1903, was finally established.[2] This office is located at Paris, and its principal occupation is to collect information concerning public health and especially regarding infectious disease. The states participating in the office are divided into six classes, and each bears its share of the expenses according to these classes which range from 25 to 3 units. This office is under the supervision of a Committee of Delegates, one for each state. Each state is allowed a number of votes in the Committee inversely proportionate to the number of the class to which it belongs. In 1920, 37 countries participated in the work of this Office.

In the Americas international efforts to suppress disease have also been put forth, eight Pan-American sanitary conferences being held between 1902 and 1927. In 1905 a Pan-American sanitary convention was signed to prevent the appearance or spread of yellow fever, cholera or plague. It provides for notification and lays down the defensive measures which countries should adopt against infected areas.[3] At the first sanitary conference in 1902 a Pan-American Sanitary Bureau at Washington was authorized to collect all data relative to the protection of health. This Bureau was reorganized in 1920. Composed of seven members appointed by each sanitary conference, its expenses are borne according to the pro rata system employed in maintaining the Pan-American Union.[4]

[1] Woolf, *International Government*, pp. 234 ff.
[2] "Arrangement of Dec. 9, 1907," *Treaties of the U. S.*, Vol. II, p. 2214.
[3] Convention of Oct. 14, 1905, *ibid.*, p. 2144.
[4] The work of these conferences is summarized in *Handbook of Delegates*, cited, pp. 56–72.

INTERNATIONAL HEALTH

On November 14, 1924, the American states signed a new convention taking the form of a Pan-American Sanitary Code, which is regarded as one of the most successful international health agreements negotiated.[1]

In Africa tropical diseases have ravaged native tribes, resulting in thousands of deaths. One of the most deadly of these diseases is sleeping sickness—the germ of which is carried by the tsetse fly. In 1907 six colonial powers held a conference at London which adopted resolutions looking to the suppression of this disease. In the following year another conference was held to carry these resolutions into effect. It was proposed to give the initiative in these matters to a central bureau with national bureaus in each country. But the conference failed to arrive at definite results because of the objections of France and Italy to the location of this bureau at London.[2] However, in 1908 and 1911, the British and German governments signed agreements, providing for a mutual exchange of information as to sleeping sickness and preventing diseased natives from crossing colonial frontiers.[3] They also agreed to kill off certain crocodiles suspected of carrying disease.

The Health Organization of the League.—Inasmuch as the League members were obligated to "take steps in matters of international concern for the prevention and control of disease," the League Council summoned an international conference of health experts, which met in April, 1920. This conference would have built the League organization upon the existing international Health Office, if the United States, a member of this office, had not prevented such a step from being made. The League proceeded therefore to work out an organization which would be distinct from yet would coöperate with the Paris Office.

In 1923, the fourth Assembly established a permanent Health Organization, composed of (1) an Advisory Council, (2) a standing Health Committee, and (3) a Health Section, which is part of the Secretariat of the League of Nations. The Committee of the International Health Office Bureau acts as the Advisory Council. The Health Committee is composed of sixteen mem-

---

[1] *U. S. Treaty Series*, No. 714.
[2] Beer, *African Questions at the Paris Peace Conference*, pp. 242–248.
[3] Treaties of Oct. 22, 1908, 101 *State Papers*, 188; Treaty of Aug. 11, 1911, 104 *State Papers*, 155.

bers, the Chairman of the Committee of the International Health Bureau, nine members chosen by that Committee, and six members chosen by the League Council.[1] The Health Committee reports annually to the Advisory Council, while it has general charge of the health work of the League and acts as an advisory body for the Council and the Assembly. By means of this mixed organization, the League Committee coöperates with the Paris Office, both of which would have been merged, except for the opposition of the United States.

As a rule the League Health Committee does not carry on work apart from national health organizations. Its policy is to coördinate the work of these different national bodies and to make suggestions for the improvement of their work.

The League Health Organization acts as a clearing office for information in regard to epidemics and other health questions. Under its auspices, experts publish a large number of reports upon disease in various parts of the world. The League has brought about a large number of interchanges of public health personnel of different countries, public health officers from European countries coming together in Belgium, Italy, England, Austria, and the United States in order to study health methods used in these countries.[2]

In the past, scientists have been handicapped by various methods in testing different antitoxins in different countries. In order to bring about some uniformity, an agreement defining certain drug formulæ was signed at Brussels in 1906.[3] But by 1923 this agreement was antiquated; one German unit of tetanus antitoxin corresponded to 67 American and 2,500 French units. If a doctor should mistakenly administer German instead of French units, the consequences might be fatal. Under the auspices of the Health Organization, several conferences were held between 1921 and 1928, where new agreements respecting the unification of drug formulæ were worked out.

[1] Draft constitution, as approved by Council and Assembly, *O. J.*, Aug., 1923, p. 1050, Nov., 1923, p. 1318.
[2] Whipple, "The Education of Health Officers," 2 *International Public Health Review* (1921), pp. 263, 337.
[3] Agreement of Nov. 29, 1906, signed by 19 powers, respecting the Unification of the Pharmacopœial Formulas for Potent Drugs, *Treaties of U. S.*, Vol. II, p. 2209.

INTERNATIONAL HEALTH

Specifically, the Health Organization has organized the following commissions, (1) the Malaria Commission, under whose auspices an international malaria conference was held at Geneva in June, 1928, (2) a Cancer Commission, which is preparing the ground for a future Cancer Conference, (3) A Smallpox and Vaccination Commission, (4) a Permanent Standards Commission, under whose auspices a Laboratory Conference on the Serodiagnosis of Syphilis was held at Copenhagen in June, 1928, (5) an Opium Commission, (6) a Commission on Education in Hygiene.[1] In addition, under the auspices of the Health Committee, international conferences of experts on the subject of Child Welfare, on Syphilis and Cognate Subjects, and on Vaccination against Tuberculosis were held in 1928. Another International Conference on Child Welfare was held in Montevideo in June, 1927, while a Public Health Conference was held at Melbourne in December, 1926. Likewise two International Conferences on Sleeping Sickness have been held. The basis for these conferences was laid in studies of the League in regard to sleeping sickness in Africa.[2] The second International Conference on Sleeping Sickness was authorized to devote attention to the general health condition of the native population in Africa. In April, 1927, the first International Rabies Conference was held in Paris.

The object of these various conferences and committees is usually two-fold. The first is to devise joint means where necessary to combat disease; the second is to discuss the best methods applicable by individual countries for the promotion of public health. Through these meetings the officials in more experienced countries may lend their knowledge to officials in less experienced countries.

One of the most interesting examples of the aid which the Health Committee of the League may extend to governments is found in the study of Health Insurance prepared by this Committee in collaboration with the International Labor Office and the Uruguayan National Council of Health, on behalf of the Uruguayan government. With this international assistance a draft law revising the health legislation in Uruguay was prepared.

[1] *Health Committee*, Report to the Council on the work of the Thirteenth Session of the Committee, C. 555. M. 175. 1928. III.
[2] *Interim Report on Tuberculosis and Sleeping Sickness in Equatorial Africa*, C. 8. M. 6. 1924. III.

Securing Joint Action in Fighting Epidemics.—Following the World War, the sanitary conditions in the new states of central Europe, especially those which had been carved out of Russia, became very serious. Epidemics from Russia threatened to engulf the whole world. In order to coördinate the activities of the different countries fighting these plagues, the League organized a temporary Epidemics Commission. In April, 1920, it summoned a Health Conference at London, which recommended the organization of quarantine stations, the equipment of hospitals, certain disinfecting measures, etc. At the suggestion of the League Council the Polish government convened a second Health Conference in March, 1922, at Warsaw. As a result of this conference a number of binational treaties were signed, strengthening the sanitary defenses of each country. They are a departure from previous health treaties, principally in the fact that the Health Administration of each country communicates directly with the others in regard to disease, while formerly notification was made only through diplomatic channels. Moreover, if a difference should arise between two governments regarding the interpretation or application of these treaties, resort shall be had to the mediation of the Health Committee of the League.[1]

One of the most important methods of keeping the countries informed as to epidemics and disease generally is through the Eastern Bureau of the Health Organization at Singapore. In 1928 this Bureau received telegraphic information in regard to disease from 140 ports. Information thus received is broadcast every Friday to 124 public health administrations throughout the world. General information in regard to epidemiological intelligence is supplied by the Monthly Epidemiological Report of the League. It also publishes a valuable year book on Public Health, setting forth conditions in every country in the world.[2]

The Red Cross and the Rockefeller Foundation.—Private organizations have done as much perhaps as governments to advance the health of the world. Of these, the most important is the Red Cross, established in 1863. While the Red Cross is

---

[1] Cf. the Sanitary Convention between Poland and Roumania, Dec. 20, 1922, *T. S.* 458.

[2] The International Labor Office has likewise published an Encyclopedia of Industrial Hygiene in 3 volumes.

primarily national in character, an International Committee was established in Geneva in 1863, which ties together the 43 national societies. Between 1863 and 1928 thirteen international Red Cross Conferences were held.[1] Because of the belief that the International Committee of the Red Cross was devoted primarily to war work, and because of the need of carrying out a vast amount of refugee and reconstruction work following the World War, a League of Red Cross Societies was formed in Paris in May, 1919.[2] At present 32 national societies are affiliated with this body. In order to prevent conflicts between the League and the International Committee, a mixed commission was formed. It is probable that the two bodies will eventually be amalgamated.

In the United States, another private organization—the Rockefeller Foundation—has done much to promote international health. Through its International Health Board and the China Medical Board it has supported the League in several of its health activities, participated in attacks upon yellow fever, malaria, and hookworm in various parts of the world, and supported medical schools in a great number of different countries.[3]

Thus, as Pasteur said at an international scientific congress in Italy, "Science has no nationality because knowledge is the patrimony of humanity, the torch which gives light to the world. Science should be the highest personification of nationality because, of all the nations, that one will always be foremost which shall be first to progress by the labors of thought and of intelligence. Let us, therefore, strive in the pacific field of Science for the preëminence of our several countries." [4]

9. INTERNATIONAL REFUGEE WORK

No war in modern history left such a toll of human misery as did the World War. Prisoners of war, to the extent of half a million, still remained in confinement as late as April, 1920, waiting

[1] Cramer, "De l'activité des Croix Rouges en temps de paix," *Revue Internationale de la Croix Rouge*, 1919, p. 755. In 1923 the first Far Eastern Red Cross Conference was held, in Siam; Pan-American Red Cross Conferences are also held.
[2] For the Articles of Association, see *Bulletin of the League of Red Cross Societies* (1919), Vol. I, p. 3.
[3] *The Rockefeller Foundation*, Annual Report, 1923, pp. 7–9.
[4] Quoted, *ibid.*, p. 9.

to be sent to their homes. The governments in whose hands they were had no funds, while the prisoners themselves were destitute. In order to save the lives of great numbers of these prisoners, who were even threatened with starvation, the League Council appointed Dr. Nansen to coördinate all the efforts which had been previously made to secure the repatriation of these prisoners. By July 1, 1922, this task had been carried out. More than 427,000 prisoners, belonging to 26 different nationalities, had been taken to their homes, at a cost of about $2,000,000.

As a result of the revolutions which swept the world between 1917 and 1920, about a million and a half refugees were scattered about Europe without a state they could call their own, and in many cases without funds and without work. Following appeals from such charitable organizations as the Red Cross, the Council of the League also asked Dr. Nansen as a League High Commissioner to bring about a settlement of the refugee question. In August, 1922, an inter-governmental conference was held at Geneva, as a result of which the governments each appointed a special official to coöperate with Dr. Nansen. Through this agency, relief was extended to these refugees, and work eventually secured for them through employment agencies set up in several cities of Central and Eastern Europe. Under the auspices of this League organization, 25,000 refugees were evacuated from Constantinople to different countries in Europe and America. The position of the refugees was complicated by the fact that they had no passports since they were not subjects of the governments under whose jurisdiction they were temporarily placed. To meet this difficulty the League High Commissioner convened another conference at Geneva in 1922, at which a "standard" identity card, taking the place of a passport, was worked out, and which thirty-four governments have agreed to recognize.[1]

Further conferences on behalf of refugees were held in Geneva in 1926 and 1927, at which a refugee revolving fund was established. In 1928 the Assembly passed a resolution stating that a complete solution of the remaining refugee problem would be realized only by the repatriation of the refugees to their original countries or their naturalization in the countries giving them shelter. It asked the Council to establish an Advisory Refugee Com-

[1] Cf. Convention of July 5, 1922, *T. S.* 355.

INTERNATIONAL REFUGEE WORK

mission to report on the possibility of reaching a final solution of the refugee problem as soon as possible.[1]

As a result of the compulsory exchange of Greek and Turkish minorities [2] a million refugees—constituting about a fifth of the population—poured into Greece, which made the situation extremely difficult since Greece is not a rich country. Consequently Greece appealed to the League Council for a loan through which means could be derived whereby these refugees could make a living on Greek soil. In order to insure that the loan would be most effectively used, the Council drew up a plan whereby Greece should receive a loan of from $15,000,000 to $30,000,000 guaranteed by certain Greek revenues,[3] the expenditure of which is under the control of an international Refugees Settlement Commission of four members, two appointed by the Council and two by the Greek government with the approval of the Council. The chairman is an American. The Greek government transferred to this committee full control over land—amounting to 500,000 hectares —suitable for refugee settlement, which the committee is developing by means of the revenue from the loan.

In an agreement of September 15, 1927, a new loan on behalf of Greece for settlement, stabilization and debt purposes was authorized, not to exceed $45,000,000. As security the Greek government furnished the revenues under the control of the International Financial Commission, not already devoted to prior charges. The Greek government undertook to establish an independent bank to bring about the stabilization of currency, to keep the budget balanced, and not to issue short-term advances in excess of eight hundred million drachmas.[4]

As a result of the work of the Greek Refugee Commission the area of land under cultivation in Greece almost doubled between 1923 and 1928. More than 143,000 families were settled on the land during this period, while 76,000 houses were built.[5]

---

[1] *O. J.*, Supplement No. 63, p. 66. The 1928 Assembly also decided that the establishment of Armenian refugees in the Republic of Erivan should be carried out. Cf. *Scheme for the Settlement of Armenian Refugees.* C. 699. M. 264. 1926. IV., 1927. IV.
[2] Cf. p. 200.
[3] Cf. p. 425.
[4] *T. S.* 1622.
[5] *Ninth Yearbook of the League of Nations*, World Peace Foundation, p. 216.

In June, 1926, the Bulgarian government requested the aid of the Council in carrying out a scheme of settlement for 120,000 Bulgarian refugees. On September 8, 1926, a protocol authorizing a League-guaranteed loan of $25,000,000 for this purpose and the appointment by the Council of a Commissioner was drawn up.[1] Bulgaria assigns certain revenues for the payment of this loan. In 1928 a disastrous earthquake increased the burden of refugee settlement.

As a result of the ravages of the World War and of two bad harvests, the mountainous regions of Albania were reduced to a state of famine, with which the government was unable to cope. Following an appeal from Albania for outside aid, the Council appropriated 50,000 Swiss francs out of the "unforeseen expenditure" fund, and also requested the different members of the League and private organizations to come to Albania's aid.[2] As a result of this request six governments and a number of Red Cross societies responded. The expenditure of this money was placed in the hands of a League Administrator.

Disasters.—The world has been periodically scourged with famines, as in Albania or in India or in China; and with earthquakes, as in Sicily, in San Francisco or in Japan; and with other equally fearful disasters. In practically all of these cases, outside assistance has been freely granted. Nevertheless, in spite of the generosity and spontaneity of these gifts, much time has been lost and much work has been duplicated by the absence of any prearranged international relief organization. To meet this need, Senator Ciraolo, the president of the Italian Red Cross, conceived the idea of an International Federation for Mutual Assistance in the Relief of Peoples overtaken by Disaster, the aim of which should be "to provide in advance the permanent organs and the technical and financial resources necessary to bring automatically into immediate action prompt, adequate and appropriate relief for peoples collectively overtaken by disasters which, in view of the suddenness of the danger and the magnitude of the need, they cannot confront unaided with the means which are normally available on the spot and the ordinary resources of the State."[3] In

[1] T. S. 1375.
[2] O. J., April, 1924, p. 527.
[3] For the Draft Statute, cf. O. J., May, 1924, p. 770.

July, 1927, an international conference at Geneva, drew up a convention establishing an International Relief Union, based on the Ciraolo plan. Each state contributes to an initial fund in relation to its contribution to the League. States desiring to do so may be represented in the Union by their national Red Cross. Two of the nine members of the Executive Committee are chosen by the International Red Cross.[1]

10. FREE LEGAL AID

While most democracies have adopted the principle that men are equal before the law, the expense of taking a case to court has in many countries become so large that a poor person is often obliged to submit to injustice because he lacks funds to protect his rights. In order to remedy this defect, a movement has arisen to furnish the poor with free legal assistance. Strangely enough, this type of assistance has been made the subject of an international convention signed at The Hague in 1905,[2] which provided for national treatment as far as "gratuitious judicial assistance" was concerned, and also for certain "certificates of indigence." This development was furthered by the League of Nations, the fifth Assembly of which passed a resolution inviting the secretariat to prepare a list of agencies giving free legal assistance, inviting each government to appoint a person to answer inquiries as to such facilities, and requesting the Secretary-General of the League to find out if the various states would be disposed to become party to an international convention providing for free legal aid to the poor.

At a Conference on International Private Law held at The Hague in January, 1928, a new international convention on this subject was signed.

11. "NATIONAL INTERESTS" AND HUMANITARIANISM

As the last chapter shows, the coöperation of nations in the advancement of common sanitary and humanitarian ends, whe-

[1] Convention of July 12, 1927, *O. J.*, August, 1927, p. 997.

[2] Part IV, Convention of July 17, 1905, relative to Civil Procedure. 2 Martens (3d series), 243. This convention also contained certain provisions in regard to the communication of judicial and extrajudicial acts from one state to another, and rogatory commissions.

ther in the suppression of the slave trade, the arms traffic, the commerce in women and children, the protection of animal life, the promotion of international health, or the rescuing of refugees,— has been as genuine as it has been widespread. In all of these matters, the nations which have participated in these movements have agreed to shape or reshape their national and domestic legislation according to principles involved in an international treaty. In most of these cases, some form of international body has been created for the purpose of collecting information in regard to these activities, but also in some cases for the purpose of actively supervising administration. The establishment of the League has given marked impetus to the coördination of national and international activities to promote the welfare of mankind.

In some cases, international coöperation in humanitarian affairs has been delayed by so-called "national" interests. For a long time England held back from accepting the quarantine provisions of the international sanitary convention out of fear that its shipping would be harmed.[1] But after accepting it England found that whatever restrictions this convention had imposed were infinitely outweighed by the gains which it made to the health of England and of the world. Likewise, the United States hesitated at first to join the International Red Cross, because of the "Monroe Doctrine."[2] National intrigue in part defeated the success of some of the international health councils; while the insistence of France and Italy that the sanitary bureau for African health matters be set up in Paris rather than London defeated the signature of an African health convention. But in practically every case where international machinery of this nature has been created, fears lest national "independence" should be impaired or "sovereignty" tainted have not been realized. In place of injuring national interests, these international treaties have really contributed to their progress. The simple fact is that because of the growing dependence of one part of the world on another, the interests of each part can best be advanced by advancing the interests of the whole. A far-sighted national self-interest is one which promotes the interests of all mankind.

[1] Reinsch, *Public International Unions*, p. 59; Woolf, *International Government*, p. 227.
[2] W. E. Barton, *Life of Clara Barton* (1922), Vol. II, p. 150.

PART II
PROBLEMS OF IMPERIALISM

CHAPTER XIII

THE CAUSES OF IMPERIALISM

1. Nationalism and Imperialism.—2. Disputes Caused by Imperialism.—3. The Economic Cause of Imperialism.—4. Over-Population and Expansion.—5. The Military Cause of Imperialism.—Buffer States.—Troop Reservoirs.—6. The Nationalistic Spirit and Imperialism.—7. The White Man's Burden.—8. Missionaries and Imperialism.—9. Is Imperialism Justified?

1. NATIONALISM AND IMPERIALISM

It is very difficult to define the word "imperialism," despite the fact that it is one of the most frequently used words in international parlance. One is constantly hearing of British imperialism, French imperialism, German imperialism, Russian imperialism, Japanese imperialism, and American imperialism. To many people it is a word of reproach. They are inclined to agree that "Imperialism is a depraved choice of national life, imposed by self-seeking interests which appeal to the lusts of quantitative acquisitiveness and of forceful domination surviving in a nation from early centuries of animal struggle for existence."[1] Every unjustifiable demand made by one government upon another—every aggressive war—is called imperialistic. Imperialism is a word which indeed covers many sins. On the other hand, there are those who, using the word in a somewhat different sense, speak of imperialism in reverent terms. To them, the government of the "backward" regions of the world by the advanced peoples is a solemn duty. This is the White Man's Burden—the Imperialism of Responsibility.[2]

We also experience difficulty in drawing the line between nationalism and imperialism. As we have used the term, nationalism has caused a great number of international disputes, whether

---

[1] J. A. Hobson, *Imperialism, A Study* (1905), p. 324.
[2] E. Seillière, *La Philosophie de l'impérialisme* (1907), Vol. III, on "L'Impérialisme démocratique," pp. 3 ff.

over the question of minorities, self-determination, strategic frontiers or the control of certain economic resources. Although these disputes may be called "imperialistic," they are really disputes between nation-states over territory or peoples which they wish to incorporate integrally as part of themselves.

Historians have said that the 19th century was the age of nationalism. The disputes of this period arose very largely over the establishment and development of nation-states. Many of these disputes were caused by the autocratic control of subject nationalities, imposed and maintained through force by a government which represented either an alien nationality or merely an oligarchic or military clique. The efforts to establish and maintain such a control was one type of imperialism; but a type which was rigorously opposed by the forces of nationalism and which, with the establishment of the new map of Europe, following the World War, has to a certain extent come to an end.[1]

When we say that the 20th century is the age of imperialism, we do not refer to the subjection of one European nation by another, but rather to the control which modern nation-states have established or are seeking to establish, over the "backward" parts of the world. Unlike the old Roman imperialism, which sought to subject the whole world to the rule of a single power, modern imperialism does not object to the existence of separate nation-states of white men, but looks to the establishment of autocratic rule by such states over the colored peoples. Hitherto the white peoples inhabiting the British Empire, the United States, Germany, France and Russia, and the people of Japan, have been the strong peoples; and they, through their governments, have established some kind of control over the other peoples of Asia, Africa and parts of Latin America. At the present time, it is estimated that 283,000,000 Christian whites directly or indirectly interfere with the government and lives of 920,000,000 "backward peoples," whether Chinese, Indians, Polynesians, Persians, Arabs, Turks, Kurds or Negroes.[2]

While these primitive peoples have until recently lacked "na-

---

[1] Cf. P. S. Reinsch, *World Politics* (1900), Part I, on "National Imperialism."

[2] Sir Harry Johnston, *The Backward Peoples and our Relations with Them* (1920), p. 10.

tional" consciousness, they nevertheless differ as much from each other as a Britisher differs from an Italian. Some of these peoples, such as the Chinese and Indians, have fully as rich a cultural heritage—the art of great masters and the ideas of great thinkers—as has the West. Others, such as the tribal peoples of Africa and the Pacific, have little culture of their own. Spending their time in killing each other or in wandering between pasture and forest, they live the picturesque but perilous life of the Happy Savage, in a "brutish state of nature." Enervated by the boiling sun and the torrential rains of the tropics, the inhabitants of these regions have often lacked the initiative, the inventiveness and the persistence which an invigorating climate has stimulated in the western races. Nature has also robbed them of the incentive of necessity, by providing a lavish supply of food which may be had merely for the taking.[1] Held together only by tribal or family ties, subjected to the tenuous authority of chieftains, sultans or emperors, these peoples have lacked the cohesive organization which industry has given to western life; and they have lacked the military power which the terrible inventions of western science and the iron discipline of western militarism have given to the "advanced" nations of Europe and America.

2. DISPUTES CAUSED BY IMPERIALISM

Some of the most serious problems in the world have arisen out of the contact of the white with the darker races. When the latter peoples have a firm social organization, as in the case of Japan, China, Persia and Turkey, they may be strong enough to withstand subjugation by the whites; and their resistance may be strengthened by the vast extent and geographic situation of the territory which they occupy. But in the cases of such peoples as the African negro and the American Indian, the West has swiftly and surely established complete control; though not without wars, and subject to the ever-present fear of revolts and murmurings which, as in the case of the American aborigines, is terminated only when the natives become virtually extinct.

Imperialism produces a second type of disputes—those between imperialistic powers for the control of the backward regions. The history of the fifty years preceding the World War was a

[1] Cf. O. D. Von Engeln, *Inheriting the Earth* (1922), Chs. VIII, IX.

history of the struggle between European powers for the control of Africa and of Asia—a contest which the United States entered in 1898, as by a side door. While the initial struggle to occupy uncolonized territory has now come to an end, a second stage has set in—one that may last far into the future—in which one power will attempt to oust another from its possessions. Whether from the standpoint of the backward peoples or of the imperialistic powers, imperialism has thus been a fecund source of international controversy.

3. THE ECONOMIC CAUSE OF IMPERIALISM

While some people love to fight merely for the sake of fighting, this instinctive trait in itself does not explain most wars. Imperialism rests upon more practical considerations, the most fundamental of which is economic. The great powers have established control over the backward regions because they believe, not only that such control is a paying proposition, but that it is necessary if their people are to live. Nearly one-fifth of the trade of the world to-day is colonial trade, and it is increasing more rapidly than the trade between independent states.[1]

Due to the creation of foreign markets, the number of people reached by European trade increased during the 19th century about 400%.[2] At the present time, about 90% of the rubber and tin of the world comes from British possessions in the backward regions of southern Asia. In 1913–1914 the total foreign trade of India was nearly equal to two-fifths of that of the United States. More than one-half of the world's cocoa, tea, shellac, wool, camphor, and long-staple cotton comes from regions under imperial control.[3] French Indo-China is one of the world's greatest producers of rice. The Dutch East Indies have very valuable resources in rubber and oil; they also supply the world with about 90% of its quinine. Katanga—a part of the Belgian Congo—has fabulous copper fields, while the mines of Kimberley for a long time supplied the diamonds of the world.

[1] *Colonial Tariff Policies* (U. S. Tariff Commission, 1922), p. 19.
[2] N. D. Harris, *Intervention and Colonization in Africa* (1921), p. 13.
[3] *Colonial Tariff Policies*, p. 25; cf. G. L. Beer, *African Questions at the Paris Peace Conference* (1923), Part II, Chs. II and III. Cf. E. Lewin, *The Resources of the Empire and Their Development* (1924 British Empire Series, vol. 4).

ECONOMIC CAUSE OF IMPERIALISM

When placed in contact with the West, the natives of all of these regions buy European and American manufactured goods in return for the raw materials which the tropics so generously produce. As an Englishwoman once expressed it, "We want regions that will enable us to keep the very backbone of England, our manufacturing classes, in a state of healthy comfort and prosperity at home in England, in other words, we want markets."[1] When white emigrants settle in the backward regions, a demand for European goods is at once created.

Some self-styled moralists assert that a native population is warranted, in the name of "sovereignty," in locking up from the rest of the world resources placed in its possession by an accident of nature, not because it needs these resources for its own use, but merely because it is ignorant of or indifferent to their value. It is a queer sort of morality which would thus deify a tribe of cannibals who may have themselves conquered these resources from their "original" owners. Should such a standard be ethically sound, it could not possibly be respected by a practical world, parts of which are already confronted by fear of starvation.

Admitting that the resources of these regions should be unlocked for the benefit of the over-populated parts of the world, many people assert that this end could be accomplished without the establishment, in the ruthless manner of past history, of the political control which the great powers to-day maintain over Africa, Asia and Latin America [2]—a control made good against the wishes of the inhabitants and oftentimes after subjugation by force. In support of this contention, they point to the fact that trade between England and the United States greatly increased after the Declaration of Independence. The answer to the question whether or not political control is necessary for trade depends on local conditions. While trade may now take place freely between the United States, the Dominions, and Europe, it is safe to say that this trade would never have been created, had the colonial powers of the 17th and 18th centuries not established political control over regions at that time inhabited by wandering, fighting, improvident Red Men, having no desire to purchase western manufactures or to till their soil for European markets. For several

[1] Mary Kingsley, *West African Studies* (1899), p. 311.
[2] Cf. Ch. XIV.

hundred years even such civilized countries as China and Japan locked themselves up from all contact with the outside world. Once one grants that trade with these different regions is a world necessity, one also grants that the forcible establishment of political control is in some cases inevitable.

While the economic justification of imperialism may be theoretically sound, the importance of trade with the backward regions may be exaggerated. Despite our dependence on the tropics for certain raw materials, four-fifths of the trade of the world is between the independent civilized states of the world.[1] Moreover, the cost of administering colonies in many instances outweighs the returns. The average advances made by Germany to her colonies annually were about 60 million marks, while several powers have been obliged to subsidize their mandates.[2]

Furthermore, the existence of colonial empires has led to the establishment of great navies, designed to protect lines of communication, and in some cases to increased military expenditures for colonial wars. In holding the Philippines, the United States has expended between $500,000,000 and $700,000,000, a considerable fraction of which went to suppress the Aguinaldo rebellion. All of these sums constitute a direct burden, while, on the other hand, the economic returns from imperialism are indirect, and in case of monopolies, benefit a few traders far more than they do the people as a whole. Whether, therefore, imperialism in the past has profited in dollars and cents, it is impossible to say. Many of the original costs have been in the nature of capital investments, upon which returns are yet to be made. In other cases, these costs have been due to jealousies and fears which the abolition of war would remove. And willy nilly, the economic importance of the tropics yearly increases. Indeed, if it were not for "imperialism," Mr. Man-in-the-Street would

---

[1] *Colonial Tariff Policies*, p. 19.

[2] Beer, *African Questions*, p. 25. In 1855 John Bright said, that "with the exception of Australia, there is not a single dependency of the Crown which, if we come to reckon what it has cost in war and protection, would not be found to be a positive loss to the people of this country. . . . Wherever you turn, you will find that the opening of markets, developing of new countries, introducing cotton cloth with cannon balls, are vain, foolish, and wretched excuses for war, and ought not to be listened to for a moment by any man who understands the multiplication table, or who can do the simplest sum in arithmetic." *Bright's Speeches* (Everyman), p. 208.

have to go without automobiles, because the price of tires and of gasoline would be prohibitive; while the opening of China and of India has created a market for western manufactures which, though it is only in an incipient stage as yet, is of staggering possibilities.[1]

Nor are the economic gains from imperialism entirely one-sided. While the Bagdad railway in Turkey created a large number of controversies between European powers, it provided Turkey with a system of transportation which made it possible for the peasant to get from two to four times the price he had formerly received for his produce.[2] As a result of the British occupation of Egypt, the native government was able to borrow money at interest rates several per cent lower than when it was independent. "It is the same story in all backward countries that have come under the ægis of the progressive Powers, and is a vital fact that is usually ignored in discussions of this many-sided question."[3] As later chapters will show, there have been many cases of imperialism where the natives have been mercilessly exploited by the white man. There have been other cases where whatever economic gain has come to them has been more than offset by a deep-seated hatred of the white man. Whether or not these results are inherent in imperialism can only be determined after an examination of different methods which it may employ.[4]

4. OVER-POPULATION AND EXPANSION

In the second place, the fear of over-population has led some powers to expand. According to a German writer, "Because the German people nowadays increase at the rate of 800,000 inhabitants a year, they need both room and nourishment for the surplus."[5] As we have seen, emigration, whether to colonies or to independent countries, is not a permanent solution of the problem of over-population. Nevertheless, as long as this belief, erroneous though it may be, is held, wars may result between over-populated countries, each striving to gain control over under-populated territory;

[1] C. K. Hobson, *Export of Capital* (1914), p. 129.
[2] E. M. Earle, *Turkey, The Great Powers, and the Bagdad Railway* (1923), p. 230.
[3] Beer, *African Questions*, p. 312.
[4] Cf. Chs. XIV, XV.
[5] Quoted, H. Cox, *Growth of Population* (1920), p. 80.

and between an over-populated and an under-populated territory, the latter attempting to hold on to territory for the benefit of future generations, which an over-populated country may wish to use at once. In Australia and Canada to-day, there is a widespread suspicion that an over-populated Japan would like to annex the unoccupied lands of these dominions. Much of the recent diplomacy of the Pacific, whether in regard to the Australian Monroe Doctrine or the Four-Power treaty, is painted against this background.

5. THE MILITARY CAUSE OF IMPERIALISM

In the third place, imperialism is prompted by military considerations. Once backward territory is acquired, other territory is annexed to protect it or to establish a secure line of communications with the home country. Such was the justification of the acquisition of Morocco by France, of Tripoli by Italy, of Egypt by England. So important to her empire does England regard Egypt that, even after recognizing the independence of the latter in 1922, the British government declared that it would "regard as an unfriendly act any attempt at interference in the affairs of Egypt by another Power," and that it would "consider any aggression against the territory of Egypt as an act to be repelled with all the means at" its command.[1]

Buffer States and Naval Bases.—In order to prevent the invasion of colonial territory by a menacing power, some countries resort to the policy of establishing as "buffer states" nominally independent areas lying between the two territories in dispute, and under the control of one of the rival powers. Between 1840 and 1907 it was British policy to support the governments of Afghanistan, Persia and Tibet as buffer states so as to block the expansion of Russia toward India. This policy was sanctioned to a certain extent by Russia in the agreement of 1907, recognizing

[1] Declaration of March 15, 1922, Cmd. 1617. In a note of Oct. 7, 1924, Prime Minister Ramsay MacDonald said, "It is no less true to-day than in 1922 that the security of the communications of the British Empire in Egypt remains a vital British interest and that absolute certainty for the free passage of British ships is the foundation on which the entire defensive strategy of the British Empire rests." Cmd. 2269 (1924). Strategic considerations have increased Britain's desire to control Palestine and Mesopotamia; cf. P. Graves, *Palestine, Land of the Three Faiths* (1923), p. 246; Poidebard, "Mossoul et la route des Indes," *Asie française*, May, 1923, Doc. No. 8.

British interests in Tibet, Afghanistan, and southern Persia. Since the World War, however, the British have lost control over the two latter countries.[1]

Strategic considerations have led powers to acquire colonies as naval bases. Britain virtually controls the Mediterranean by virtue of such bases; while she has another string off Africa, India and Asia.[2] In the latter region, the most important in view of its recent fortification is Singapore. The French have an important base at Djibuti on the Red Sea lying on the way to Indo-China and Madagascar, which explains why France declined to cede it to Italy in 1919. German, French and Japanese designs upon different islands in the Pacific led Australia early to adopt an Australian Monroe Doctrine, which opposes the colonization of any foreign power within striking distance of her shores.[3] It was for strategic reasons that Japan demanded the German islands of the Pacific at the Paris Peace Conference, and it was for a similar reason that the United States insisted on the mandate principle—in full control of these islands, Japan could threaten the possessions of the United States.[4] For that matter, the whole Caribbean policy, as well as the Monroe Doctrine, of the United States has been motivated to a great extent by military fears.

Troop Reservoirs.—Perhaps the greatest military incentive for imperialism is the use to which colonies may be put as troop reservoirs. Although the Allies during the World War accused Germany of aiming to establish a black army to fight her European battles, as a matter of fact, the Allies have followed the same policy. During the World War, England made use of about 389,000 troops from India, while France employed 475,000 colonial troops, in addition to 220,000 colonials in labor battalions. In many of her colonies, France has now adopted as a permanent policy, the conscription of black African troops. Such a policy was advocated as far back as 1910 by General Mangin.[5] By a decree of July, 1919, conscription was imposed on the natives in French West and Equatorial Africa. It was later applied to

[1] Cf. pp. 470, 472.
[2] Cf. *The Dominions and Dependencies of the Empire*, (1924), pp. 335 ff.
[3] G. H. Scholefield, *The Pacific, Its Past and Future* (1919), p. 294.
[4] H. C. Bywater, *Sea Power in the Pacific* (1921), Ch. IX.
[5] Cf. his book *La France noire* (1910), p. 355.

Madagascar and the Pacific islands.[1] At the Paris Peace Conference and in the text of the mandates France reserves the right to drill natives to defend the home territory.[2] French statesmen, looking across the Rhine at a German population of 69,000,000, speak now of the Greater France, with a population, not of 39,000,000, but of 100,000,000, the majority consisting of the black and brown men of Africa and Asia. By using these natives for military purposes, France hopes to overcome the numerical superiority of Germany.

If one power uses its colonies as a military reservoir, other powers are likely to adopt the same practice. If the principle should become established that the use of colonial troops in European wars is legitimate, nations would have an added incentive to acquire territory, which in itself might lead to war. From the standpoint of the native, conscription for this purpose is another form of slavery—he is obliged to fight in a contest for which he is not even theoretically responsible and over which he has no control.

When engaged in European wars, natives must necessarily fight upon a basis of equality with white troops.[3] The spectacle of white men destroying each other is not particularly edifying to the black man from Africa; nor does it increase his respect for the white man's rule. If racial equality is good in time of war, it should be good in time of peace. When it is not forthcoming, the racial problem becomes more acute than ever. Out of fairness to the French, it should be said that they fraternize with colored peoples to a much greater extent than do Anglo-Saxons. Nevertheless, the policy of conscription of native troops for European service is sure to lead to disaster, not only because of international rivalries, but because of the complete disregard which such a policy involves of the interests and welfare of native populations.

In fact, the whole strategic argument in favor of the acquisition

---

[1] A. Girault, *Principes de colonisation et de législation coloniale* (1922), 2d pt., p. 380. Cf. also Buell, *The Native Problem in Africa*, Vol. II, Chs., 64, 76.

[2] R. S. Baker, *Woodrow Wilson and World Settlement* (1922), Vol. I, p. 428; Art. 3, Cameroons Mandate; Art. 3, Togo Mandate. Cf. p. 360.

[3] Some military experts assert that natives make inferior troops, cf. Levé, "La préparation de la guerre et l'armée indigène," 111 *Revue politique et parlementaire* (1923), 373.

of territory runs in a vicious circle. As a rule, territory is not seized originally to protect the home country. England did not establish control over the Suez Canal in order to protect herself, but in order to safeguard her communications with India. Once colonies are acquired, further territory is then seized to protect them. And a struggle ensues which is but one phase of the competition in armaments and of the institution of war. While the military cause of imperialism is only secondary, it produces a great deal of trouble in the world.

6. THE NATIONALISTIC SPIRIT AND IMPERIALISM

Paradoxical as it may seem, pure nationalism has forced governments into the path of imperialism. Writers since the time of Machiavelli have believed that after unifying itself a nation must reach out and become an empire if it is to live.[1] The time has not even yet passed when the rank and file in every country applaud the exploits of their army and navy in subjugating savage tribes, whether the Arabs of Morocco or the Moros of the Philippines. The hoisting of the flag on some bleak and unknown shore still commands newspaper headlines and leads to international rivalries. The romance of discovery has now been enhanced by the adventurous airplane. American Senators have become agitated over the occupation of Wrangel Island—a huddle of rocks in the Arctic Ocean—by British airmen; while a Secretary of the Navy has urged an aërial expedition to the North Pole to prevent its annexation by British prowlers!

In England the imperial spirit was literally created by historians such as Sir John Seeley, by poets such as Kipling, and by statesmen such as Disraeli and Chamberlain, the latter of whom said, "The Anglo-Saxon race is infallibly destined to be the predominant race in the history and civilization of the world."[2] A fatalistic nationalism has been invoked to justify the expansion of the

---

[1] Cf. the summary and criticism, Seillière, *La Philosophie de l'impérialisme*, 3 vols.; Estève, *Une nouvelle psychologie de l'impérialisme* (1913), and K. Renner, *Das Selbstbestimmungrecht der nationen*, p. 92.

[2] E. L. Godkin once wrote of Kipling, "I think most of the current jingoism on both sides of the water is due to him. He is the poet of the barrack-room cads." R. Ogden, *Life and Letters of E. L. Godkin* (1907), Vol. II, p. 30.

United States. According to the late Senator O. H. Platt, "every expansion of our territory has been in accordance with the irresistible law of growth. . . . We should rejoice that Providence has given us the opportunity to extend our influence, our institutions, and our civilization into regions hitherto closed to us, rather than contrive how we can thwart its designs." [1] The same sentiment has animated Italian and French Imperialism.[2] In view of the dwindling population of France, some writers assert that if France is not to decline to the level of Switzerland or Greece among the powers, she must colonize.[3]

These appeals to nationalistic sentiment have often been made by the groups in each country who would profit most from imperialism. Thus the capitalists and the military men frequently proclaim the "glories" of national expansion, the former in the hope of securing markets for goods or capital, the latter, in that of enhancing their importance in the community. Nevertheless, the public, regardless of all questions of profit and loss, has, as a rule, eagerly supported its government in a contest for the control of backward territory from motives akin to those which lead crowds to take sides at a prize-fight or a football game. Moreover, to withdraw from territory once occupied would be a national humiliation, no matter how much the cost of occupation may be. When the "virtues" of patriotism are thus enlisted in support of imperialism, governmental policy is apt to take the form of an exalted selfishness—a "sacred egoism," dominated not by reason but by Oriental conceptions of a fatalistic will. Controlled by such aberrations, a government will never be satisfied with international guarantees, no matter how strong they are, as to freedom of trade in colonies under the control of another power. It will insist on acquiring such territory in its own name, to satisfy some vague instinct of possession, which a nationalistic complex has made even more intense than in individuals. As

[1] Quoted, C. A. Beard, *Contemporary American History* (1918), p. 216. Cf. Von Holtz, *Constitutional History of the United States* (1881), Vol. III, p. 269, a passage which says history must judge imperialism by its results, and "the general interest of civilization."

[2] Cf. T. Barclay, *The Turko-Italian War* (1912), p. 52; W. M. Fullerton, *Problems of Power* (1914), p. 249.

[3] Cf. Leroy-Beaulieu, *Colonisation chez les peuples modernes* (3d ed., 1886), p. xiii; Girault, *Principes de colonisation et de législation coloniale*, 1st part, 4th ed., p. 49.

long as imperialism is dominated by such considerations, wars of expansion will be inevitable.

7. THE WHITE MAN'S BURDEN

Humanitarianism—the White Man's Burden—has been invoked along with nationalism to justify imperialism: the ignorance and savagery of the natives should be made to give way, if need be by force, to the enlightenment of the West. In his Uganda speech of 1893, Mr. Chamberlain said, "It is our duty to take our share in the work of civilization in Africa." [1] In criticising the establishment of control over the backward regions, people too frequently forget that particularly among the people of Africa and the Pacific, primitive life is by no means a happy existence. Among many such peoples, as in the Pacific islands, there has been practically no government beyond the sanctions enforced by secret societies, and by chieftains supposed to possess mystic powers of sorcery and witchcraft. Among other peoples, the processes of justice are still in the "trial by combat" stage of the Middle Ages. In some African tribes the guilt of a suspect has been determined by feeding him poison—if he survives he is innocent! [2] Throughout these regions human life has been valued at a negligible figure; cannibalism has been widespread; and other inhuman practices have prevailed, such as ear cutting, crucifixion, extraction of teeth, suspension by the thumbs, and slow starvation.[3] Before the British established control in the Malay peninsula, the natives were subject to "a system of taxation under which every necessity as well as every luxury of life was heavily taxed; law courts in which the procedure was the merest mockery of justice, the decisions depending solely on the relative wealth or influence of the litigants; a system of debt-slavery under which not only the debtor but his wife and their most remote descendants were condemned to hopeless bondage; an unlimited corvée, or forced labor for indefinite periods and entirely without remuneration; the right of the Raja to compel all female children to pass through his harem—such are some of the most flagrant exam-

---

[1] W. Boyd, *Mr. Chamberlain's Speeches* (1914), Vol. I, p. 345.
[2] *Rapport annuel du Gouvernement Français sur l'administration sous mandat des territoires du Cameroun*, p. 64. Cf. R. H. Lowie, *Primitive Society* (1920), Ch. XIV.
[3] De Cardi, in appendix to Kingsley, *West African Studies*, p. 535.

ples, although the list is by no means exhaustive, of administrative rule in a State within twenty-four hours of Singapore." [1] Among the tribes of Africa, the Pacific and Asia, disease is rife, whence it may spread to Europe and America. Venereal disease and sleeping sickness are in parts of Africa well-nigh universal.[2]

It would be a gross perversion of fact to say that European and American imperialism was originally inspired by a desire to better the lives of the peoples whom it forcibly subjugated. Monstrous brutalities have been committed by white men, whether private adventurers or officials. Nevertheless, there have been a number of instances where governments have established political control for humanitarian purposes, either out of self-protection or to establish restraints upon unprincipled white men.[3] France went into Algeria partly to stamp out the piracy which preyed upon western commerce. Thousands of Americans supported the war against Spain in 1898 because of their belief that Spain was pursuing a policy of oppression and exploitation in Cuba and Porto Rico. The abuses in the rule of India by a private corporation, the East India Company, were so great that the British government felt obliged to annex the country in 1857.[4] Following the occupation of New Zealand in 1814, unprincipled white men, uncontrolled by a government on the spot, wrought havoc with the natives, drugging them with liquor, liberally supplying them with firearms, and robbing them of their land. These outrages were brought to an end by the interference of the government in 1833.[5] Likewise, in order to stamp out the *kanaka* or "blackbirding" trade—a form of slave traffic in which natives were shipped from various islands into Australia wholesale to work on plantations—the British government, in 1872, passed the Pacific Islands Protection Act. As later amended, this act established a High Commissioner for the western Pacific who has jurisdiction over

[1] Quoted by A. Ireland, *Far Eastern Tropics* (1905), p. 111.
[2] Cf. "Public Health in Mandated Territories," *Mandates Commission*, A. 19 (annexes), 1923, VI.
[3] In Africa two communities were originally established for humanitarian reasons, Sierra Leone being settled as a home for free negroes, while Liberia was settled and controlled until 1846 by the American Colonization society, with a similar object in mind. In 1857 Liberia declared its independence. For the constitution, cf. Buell, *Native Problem in Africa*, Vol. II, p. 855.
[4] Cf. P. Kerr, in A. J. Grant (ed.), *International Relations* (1916), p. 157.
[5] E. Jenks, *History of the Australasian Colonies* (3d ed. 1912) p. 169 ff.

British subjects there outside of the Dominions.[1] As a result of such interventions, natives receive the "benefits of complete internal peace and order, improved industry, enlarged opportunities for learning, a better religion and a truer science;"[2] under colonial control they are, in theory, protected from the abuses of their own rulers and from renegade white men. While the welfare of the natives is seldom the reason for originally establishing control, it may become a reason for maintaining it.[3]

8. MISSIONARIES AND IMPERIALISM

In the 17th century the religious motive for imperialism was much stronger than it is to-day. The spreading of the Gospel was declared to be the chief cause for founding a colony by the Massachusetts Bay Company. As Captain John Smith put it, "The Reducing Heathen people to civilitie and true Religion, bringeth honour to the King of Heaven."[4] Even at the present time, Christian missionary interests in the backward regions are important. At the present time there are about 29,000 Protestant missionaries throughout the world and their converts number about 8,300,000. There are about 22,000 Roman Catholic missionaries with a total of about 13,500,000 converts.[5]

No western power now claims the right to force its religion upon unbelievers. However, the refusal of a backward people to come into contact with the ideas of the outside world has repeatedly provoked the intervention of the outside powers, particularly in China, Korea and Japan. A large amount of domestic legislation and a large number of treaties now recognize the right of missionaries to enter backward territories for the purpose of carrying on religious and educational work.[6] Once admitted to these regions, missionaries are as deserving of protection as business men; in fact, more so, since they have been responsible for

[1] 38 and 39 Vict., Ch. 51 (1875).
[2] Henry Sidgwick, *Elements of Politics* (1891), p. 298.
[3] Cf. Ch. XIV.
[4] G. L. Beer, *Origins of the British Colonial System* (1908), p. 28.
[5] Buell, *Native Problem in Africa*, Vol. II, p. 981.
[6] Cf. *Treaties, Acts and Regulations Relating to Missionary Freedom*, prepared by the International Missionary Council, London, 1923. Writing in the 16th century, the international jurist, Victoria, declared that Christians had the right to preach the gospel to the Indians. Cf. T. A. Walker, *History of the Law of Nations* (1899), p. 224.

most of the humanitarian work until recently done in the backward regions. While merchants are primarily interested in profits and officials in advancing the interests of the home country, the missionaries exist to serve the natives. Sometimes, however, missionaries have abused their position; sometimes they have become advance agents of imperialism. The Jesuits earnestly worked to bring about the annexation of Siam to France in the 17th century, while Dr. Peter Parker, a quondam missionary who turned diplomat, attempted to establish an American protectorate over Formosa in 1856.[1] In the words of a French writer, French missionaries do not neglect "our dear fatherland . . ., they show themselves . . . excellent servants of France"; the view of an Indian paper is that the white man "sends out his priest, his Bishop, and his missionary to foreign lands to pave the way for colonial dominion or exploitation of the native peoples and their lands."[2]

On many occasions governments have used the alleged necessity of protecting missionaries as a pretext for the annexation of territory. In 1897 two German missionaries were murdered in cold blood by a band of ruffians in Shantung, China. Despite the fact that the government had no connection with the crime and that the missionaries had been exiled from Germany, the German authorities used the incident as a pretext to demand not only the payment of a heavy indemnity, but the lease of Kiaochow, on terms which led to its becoming a virtual colony.[3] Moreover, governments sometimes retain control of territory to protect missionaries. It is probable that the British would have withdrawn from Uganda in 1891 had it not been for the entreaties of the Church Missionary Society and its contribution of £11,000 to aid the British East Africa Company in maintaining its position there.[4]

When missionaries abuse their position for political ends, they

[1] R. K. Douglas, *Europe and the Far East* (1913), p. 393; T. Dennett, *Americans in Eastern Asia* (1922), p. 286.

[2] *Asie française*, March, 1923, p. 73; *Living Age*, August 9, 1924, p. 247. In 1892 the Congo Free State authorized religious bodies to care for children liberated from slave traders. In 1905 grave charges were made by a Commission against the Roman Catholic missions who had undertaken this task, accusing them of flogging children, and prohibiting them from acquiring property, etc. *Peace Handbooks*, Vol. 99, p. 43.

[3] Cf. p. 464.

[4] L. Woolf, *Empire and Commerce in Africa* (1920), p. 297.

injure the cause of religion, as well as arouse native animosity. Experience has demonstrated that the missionaries who are most successful in their religious and social work have entirely divorced themselves from the favors of governments at home.[1] Within recent years, missionaries have been the foremost advocates of a policy of non-intervention in such independent areas as Central America and China, and of greater native self-government in colonies. They have been the first to expose abuse in Africa.

9. IS IMPERIALISM JUSTIFIED?

If the great powers should terminate their control over the backward regions and recognize their independence, the natives in many cases would fall a prey to the white adventurer, who could then carry on his activities subject to no effective governmental control. It would be impossible to prohibit the entrance of these adventurers into these areas. Unrestrained by European or American authorities on the spot, they would prove more than a match for the natives, or if not, bloodshed would be recurrent, in which the native would suffer as much as the white. Moreover, if the powers should withdraw entirely from these territories, in all probability natives would fight natives. India has a population of 315,000,000 people, divided into two great antagonistic religions, the Hindoo and Moslem faiths. In the past the British authorities have suppressed the animosities of one sect for the other only with the greatest difficulty.[2] Apparently, the strenuous efforts of Gandhi to establish a Hindoo-Moslem unity have also failed, as the Punjab massacres of 1920 showed. If the "protection of minorities" is a principle which is good for Europe, it should also be good for Africa and Asia.[3]

Imperialism has been evil primarily in the methods which it

[1] Dr. J. L. Barton, "Some Missionary Activities in Relation to Governments," *International Review of Missions*, July, 1924, an article which advises missionaries against calling upon their government for personal protection, except when the local government is virtually non-existent; and against carrying weapons, entering into commercial transactions or accepting government positions. As far as the writer knows, there is no case where a missionary society has demanded indemnities for the death of one of its missionaries. Cf. also T. Dennett, "Extraterritoriality and Missionaries in China," *Christian Century*, May 17, 1923, a plea that missionaries give up their special privileges under treaty.

[2] The Earl of Ronaldshay, *India: A Bird's-Eye View* (1924), Ch. XIX.

[3] Cf. Ch. VIII. Cf. Al. Carthill, *The Lost Dominion* (1924), Ch. IX.

has employed to establish control over a recalcitrant people, and in the methods it has followed in governing them. Whether or not control was originally established by abhorrent means is now a matter of history. The practical problem before the world is whether Europe and America should relinquish the control which they now exercise over these regions. Even the anti-imperialists draw back from the logical conclusion of their argument. Frederick Harrison was extremely bitter in his denunciation of the British Empire. "Nothing that England can gain, nothing that the world can gain from this empire is worth the frightful and increasing price that we pay for it year by year in guilt, and blood, and hatred." [1] Nevertheless, he realized that the Empire could not be deserted like a leaky ship. "We do not believe that the blind conquests of former ages can be settled in a day; or that we ought to fling off the tremendous responsibilities with which ages of history have burdened us." What he did demand was that the empire should be governed in the "sole interests of the countless millions who compose it."

Even the great "Little Englander," John Bright, did not believe that England could withdraw from India until the country had been made secure against discord and anarchy.[2] Lord Sydney Olivier, the socialist Secretary of State for India in 1924, wrote, "No true friend of primitive races would propose entirely to exclude or withdraw European intercourse and influence from them, or even to hand back to them, at this period, that unregulated and unsupported responsibility for their own governance under which slave-raiding, brigandage, and internecine violence were rampant." [3] Despite its anti-imperialist pretensions, the British Labor government, under Ramsay MacDonald in 1924, showed no disposition to relinquish control over any part of the Empire.

While the arguments of over-population, military necessity and pure nationalism are bogus causes of imperialism, economic necessity has made the interchange of raw materials and manufactured goods between every part of the world inevitable. This force is operating to-day, perhaps more strongly than half a century ago, and it has led to the establishment and to the main-

---

[1] *National and Social Problems* (1908), p. 254.
[2] *Speeches*, cited, p. 13.
[3] The *League of Nations and Primitive Peoples* (1918), p. 6.

IS IMPERIALISM JUSTIFIED?

tenance of political control over those parts of the world unable to stand by themselves. Likewise the inevitable contact between primitive peoples and individual white men and the whole scheme of industrial and military power in the west, has made the establishment of some form of control necessary for the protection of native interests themselves. Imperialism is not necessarily condemned because of the mere *existence* of such control in areas where native governments are demonstrably unable to maintain a certain standard of order and decency fixed by the civilized world. But imperialism does stand condemned when it follows certain methods and policies which ignore the interests of the natives and of the world at large for the benefit of a chosen few. These methods will be discussed in the next chapter.

CHAPTER XIV

THE POLICY OF EXPLOITATION

1. The Two Kinds of Colonies.—2. Colonial Empires of To-day.—3. Imperialism and the Native.—4. Forced Labor.—5. Imported Labor.—6. Confiscation of Native Lands.—7. Brutality and Discrimination.—8. Tariffs and the "Drain."—9. Debauchery.

Of the different methods open to imperialistic policy for the control of backward regions, the establishment of colonies is the most direct and probably the most important. When a government annexes territory in the backward regions, it acquires full legal power to do as it likes. In the absence of treaties, it has no legal obligations toward the outside world or toward native populations. It is absolutely supreme so far as international law is concerned.

1. THE TWO KINDS OF COLONIES

There are two general types of colonies, the settlement colony and the exploitation colony. The first type is established by settlers from the home country and thus acts as a population outlet. The second is held for economic rather than settlement purposes. At the present time there are few settlement colonies left in the world.[1] In a sense, the Spanish and Brazilian possessions in Latin America were settlement colonies, but they are now independent states. The French possessions in Canada and Louisiana were likewise settlement colonies in the 18th century before they passed to Great Britain in the Treaty of Paris of 1763. The only approach to settlement "colonies," existing in the world to-day, are the self-governing dominions of the British Empire, which, however, cannot be called colonies in any true sense. Settlement colonies are limited in number because European peoples can live comfortably only in the temperate zones, which are already occupied by independent states. The settlement

---

[1] For attempted settlement colonies in Africa, cf. p. 67.

colonies which were planted in such zones have all demanded and obtained a real or virtual independence after attaining a certain point of growth. Applied to this type of colony, there is much truth in Turgot's remark that a colony is like a fruit which when ripened falls from the mother tree.

Practically all of the colonies in the world to-day are exploitation colonies, colonies held for economic and commercial purposes, most of them being in the tropics. Originally, colonies were bled for the financial benefit of the colonizing government. Between 1870 and 1874 the Dutch government made a direct net profit from the island of Java of more than 22,000,000 guilders a year.[1] Cuba, when a dependency of Spain, turned over to the home government a surplus of about $6,000,000 annually. At the present time, however, colonial powers seldom indulge in this form of exploitation. Most of the natives are too impoverished to pay taxes into the coffers of a foreign government. Humanitarian reasons also prohibit this type of "drain." To-day colonial officials are satisfied if they can balance their budget, while surpluses are ordinarily held for the benefit of the local administration.[2] As a matter of fact, many governments have been obliged to subsidize their colonies. The modern idea of exploiting a colony does not mean direct profit for the government as such, but for individual merchants and indirectly perhaps for the individual consumer in the home country. On the one hand, colonies are exploited for their natural resources, such as rubber or tin; on the other, they may be valuable as trading ports, such as Hongkong and Singapore.

2. COLONIAL EMPIRES OF TO-DAY

Through colonies or the imperfect colonial form known as a protectorate, European countries with a total population of 286,608,000 govern backward regions containing more than 550,000,000 people—covering nearly twenty times the area of the colonizing powers.[3] The colonial empires of the world are nearly three times the size of Latin America and have eight times

[1] Cf. A. G. Keller, *Colonization* (1908), pp. 336, 481.
[2] One exception is Formosa which has made an annual contribution to the treasury of Japan for the last 18 years. Hayden, "Japan's New Policy in Korea and Formosa," *Foreign Affairs*, March 15, 1924.
[3] *Colonial Tariff Policies*, p. 5.

its population. India alone has an area nearly two-thirds as large as the United States, and a population three times as large. Dutch Java is larger than the state of Louisiana; Dutch Borneo is larger than the whole of Germany; British Nigeria is larger than the United Kingdom and France combined.

There are three great colonial powers in the world to-day—Great Britain, France and Holland. Six other powers,—Japan, the United States, Belgium, Italy, Portugal and Spain also possess colonies of less importance.

Of the colonial empires of the world, the British Empire is the most interesting and the most important. Having an area of nearly 13 million square miles, it touches every corner of the globe and embraces every type of civilization, race and government. Eight of its units are self-governing in local affairs: the five Dominions, as well as the Irish Free State, Ulster and Southern Rhodesia.[1] Two of its possessions, India and Malta, have semi-responsible governments. About 75 crown colonies and protectorates, with varying types of government, are controlled by the Colonial Office in London. The total population of the Empire is about 450,000,000—a quarter of the population of the world. Of this number, only about 65,000,000 are white men, including the inhabitants of the United Kingdom and the Dominions. The remaining 385,000,000 of whom 315,000,000 live in India, belong to dark-skinned races. As a result of the World War, Great Britain made some indirect colonial gains in the form of mandates under the League of Nations, such as German East Africa, part of German Togo and Cameroons, and Palestine. Mesopotamia also came under her control.[2] Meantime, in 1914, she had annexed Cyprus, which had been occupied by her since 1878. On the other hand, Great Britain has, since the war, lost control of Egypt, Persia and Afghanistan, and in 1924 she was obliged to cede Jubaland to Italy.[3]

France has the second most important colonial empire in the world, extending over about 4,500,000 square miles of territory

[1] See p. 205.
[2] See p. 388.
[3] See p. 330. For a description of the Empire, cf. *Oxford Survey of the British Empire* (1914), 6 Vols.; *Dominions and Dependencies of the British Empire*, by a number of writers (1924); Sir G. Lagden, *Native Races of the Empire* (1924), ("The British Empire Series," Vols. 1 and 9).

and containing together with the home population, 100,000,000 people—the "Greater France." [1] This empire falls into four groups: (1) northern Africa, comprising Algeria which was annexed in 1830 and is administered as an integral part of France; Tunis and Morocco, both of the latter being nominally protectorates, which came under French control in the treaties of 1883 and 1912. (2) French West Africa, a group of 7 colonies on the west coast, under a governor-general at Dakar. (3) French Equatorial Africa,—a group of four colonies similarly controlled. (4) French Asia, principally Indo-China, which has a population of about 16 millions. Inhabited by three different peoples, the Annamites, the Cambodians, and the Thai, Indo-China is divided into the colony of Cochin China and the four protectorates of Tonkin, Loas, Annam and Cambodia. The colony is presided over by a lieutenant-governor, while a resident superior is found in each protectorate. All five districts are under the control of the French governor-general of Indo-China.[2] A direct gain from the World War was the recovery of 100,000 square miles of territory in Equatorial Africa, which France had ceded to Germany in 1911 in return for recognition of her Moroccan protectorate.[3] France also gained three mandates—the greater part of Togo and the Cameroons, and Syria. As a partial offset, she ceded certain territory to Italy along the Tripoli frontier.

Strange as it may seem, the little country of Holland has the third most important colonial empire in the world—an empire which contains a population eight times as great and an area 62 times as large as the home country. With the exception of several tiny possessions, such as Dutch Guiana, this empire lies off south-

[1] Hauser, "Greater France," *Foreign Affairs*, December 15, 1923.

[2] For a brief description of the French colonial empire, cf. A. Sarraut, *La Mise en valeur des colonies françaises* (1923), Ch. IV; A. Megglé, *Le domaine colonial de la France* (1922); Busson, Févre and Hauser, *La France d'aujourd'hui et ses colonies* (1920), Part IV.

[3] In Article 125 of the Treaty of Versailles, Germany renounced all her rights relating to Equatorial Africa. Although this article was similar to Article 119 in regard to her "overseas" possessions, France interpreted it to mean the unconditional retrocession of Equatorial Africa, although the other German possessions were placed under mandate. France likewise attempted to annex ex-German Togo and Cameroons, instead of accepting a mandate. Cf. speech of M. Simon, French minister of colonies, Chamber of Deputies, Sept. 17, 1919, *Afrique française*, 1919, Renseignements Coloniaux, p. 161.

ern Asia, and is ordinarily called the Dutch East Indies, or "Insulinde." Inhabited by Malays and Papuans, the first of which are of Asiatic and the second of Polynesian origin, these islands have a population of some 47 millions. From the administrative standpoint, they are divided into two groups, the first containing Java and Madura, and the second, called the Outposts, including the remaining islands. The Dutch East Indies are governed by a governor-general, assisted by residents.[1]

Japan has a colonial empire which, from the international standpoint, is important because it includes Formosa and Korea. The former island was taken from China in 1895, while Korea was annexed in 1910 as an aftermath of the Russian war. Korea is now governed as an integral part of Japan, under a governor-general; and Formosa is under a similar régime.[2] The southern part of the island of Sakhalin was annexed by Japan in 1905; while in 1920 Japan occupied the northern part of the island—Russian territory—in retaliation for the massacre at Nikolaevsk. However, she agreed to withdraw from this part of the island in the Russo-Japanese treaty of January, 1925. In the Treaty of Versailles, Japan received the German islands in the northern Pacific under mandate.

As a result of the war with Spain in 1898, the United States became the fifth largest colonial power in the world, governing 12,000,000 subject people. Our dependencies are found in two parts of the globe—in the Caribbean and in the Pacific. Porto Rico, an "unincorporated territory" in the Caribbean, is under a governor appointed by the President with the consent of the Senate. The Virgin Islands, purchased from Denmark in 1917 for $25,000,000, are governed by a naval captain, while the Philippines, the most important possession of the United States, are under a governor-general. Hawaii and Alaska are not dependencies in the proper sense of the word since they have a prospect of becoming states in the Union.

The little country of Belgium has a single but immense colony in the Belgian Congo. In 1885 an "international" association

[1] Cf. H. A. V. C. Torchiana, *Tropical Holland* (1921), Chs. IV and X; A. Cabaton, *Java, Sumatra and the Dutch East Indies*, Chs. IV and IX.

[2] Hayden, *Foreign Affairs*, cited. For a description of the Japanese Empire, cf. F. Wertheimer, *Die Japanische Kolonialpolitik* (1910); N. Asami, *Japanese Colonial Government* (1924).

which came to be known as the Congo Free State, the president of which was King Leopold of Belgium, was recognized as sovereign over this territory. By rather questionable diplomacy, Belgium annexed this territory in 1908 and has since retained it.[1] As a result of the World War, Belgium was also allotted one mandate—part of German East Africa, called Ruanda-Urundi.

Italy—as well as Germany—was busy setting up housekeeping at home when the older powers were snapping up all the bargains in the backward regions. When Italy had time to look about, all she was able to secure was a barren stretch of territory along the coast of the Mediterranean and the Red Sea, with an area only of 591,000 square miles. Eritrea and Somaliland were occupied about 1880–1890; while following a frankly imperialistic war against Turkey in 1911, Italy secured Tripoli, now called Libya. In the secret treaty of London of 1915, France and Britain promised Italy that in case they should increase their territories in Africa at the expense of Germany, Italy could "claim some equitable compensation, particularly as regards the settlement in her favor of the questions relative to the frontiers of the Italian colonies of Eritrea, Somaliland and Libya and the neighboring colonies belonging to France and Great Britain."[2]

Also, she was to have the Dodecanese Islands, Turkish territory in the Ægean which she had occupied since the war of 1911. This promise, moreover, was formally fulfilled in the unratified treaty of Sévres of August, 1920; but at the same time Italy signed another treaty promising to hand over these islands to Greece, because they are inhabited by an indisputably Greek population.[3] With the defeat of Greece by Turkey, however, and the advent of the nationalistic Mussolini government, Italy declined to fulfil this promise, and so remains in possession of these islands to-day. At the Paris Peace Conference Italy suggested that France cede to her the port of Djibuti on the Red Sea—a port on the way to French

---

[1] A. B. Keith, *Belgian Congo and the Berlin Act* (1919); P. Daye, *L'Empire colonial belge* (1923).

[2] Art. 13, Treaty of April 26, 1915, Cmd. 671 (1920).

[3] For the abortive Tittoni-Venizelos agreement of July 29, 1919, cf. A. Gannini, *I Documenti Diplomatici della Pace Orientale* (1922), p. 27. The Treaty with Greece provided, however, that Rhodes should remain with Italy for 15 years when a plebiscite would be held, or as long as England kept Cyprus. 113 *State Papers*, 1078.

Indo-China. Although this demand was refused, France ceded certain territory along her Tripolitan frontier.[1] Negotiations between Italy and Great Britain also took place in regard to the cession of a portion of Jubaland—part of British East Africa, adjoining Italian Somaliland. The demands of Italy were increased here upon the advent of the Mussolini government; and a settlement was delayed by the insistence of Great Britain that the Jubaland and Dodecanese questions be settled together. When Ramsay MacDonald came to power, England agreed to dissociate the two questions, while Italy receded from part of her territorial demands. Upon this basis, Jubaland was finally ceded to Italy.[2]

Little remains of the magnificent colonial empire which Portugal ruled so proudly in the 17th century. Her most important possession to-day is the African colony of Angola, which is larger than Germany, France, Holland, Belgium, Denmark and Switzerland combined. In East Africa, Portugal has the colony of Mozambique —larger than Texas—while it also rules a number of very small islands off Africa, India and in the East Pacific, such as Timor.

The Spanish Empire of to-day is even more reduced than the Portuguese. It consists only of a barren zone in Morocco and a few minor colonies. Spanish Morocco is a mountainous district— called the Riff—which is inhabited by very savage Berber tribes. Spain has a nominal protectorate over this region, where she was represented by a High Commissioner and three military commandants, the Sultan of Morocco being represented by a khalifa, chosen by him from a list of two candidates nominated by Spain.[3] The natives, however, have never accepted Spain's rule; and between 1921 and 1925 Spanish troops suffered a series of disasters which gradually forced them down to the coast.[4] As a result of these reverses, England and France negotiated as to concerted action to keep this ferment from spreading throughout the whole of North Africa. It is not improbable that Spanish Morocco will eventually fall into French hands.

[1] Agreement of Sept. 12, 1919, *Afrique française*, 1920, p. 88. Cf. Tittoni's speech of Sept., 1919, *New Europe*, Oct. 23, 1919, p. 44.
[2] Anglo-Italian treaty of July 15, 1924, Cmd. 2194.
[3] Art. 1, Treaty of Nov. 27, 1912, between France and Spain, 106 *State Papers*, 1025.
[4] A. Mousset, *L'Espagne dans la politique mondiale* (1923), pp. 252 ff.

3. IMPERIALISM AND THE NATIVE

Inasmuch as the colonial empires of to-day are held primarily for economic exploitation, the question arises whether, in advancing the economic interests of the outside world, colonial powers also promote the material and moral interests of the natives, or whether they disregard these native interests and establish monopolies for the benefit of a few privileged outsiders. In this chapter colonial policies will be discussed from the internal standpoint—their effect on the native. In another chapter—on the Open Door—they will be examined in relation to the outside world.

Probably the greatest economic problem in colonial empires is the problem of securing a labor supply, without which their territorial resources could not be developed. While capital may come from the outside world, labor must come, for the most part, from the natives. But the native is not always impressed with the value and the dignity of labor. He would much rather recline under a banana tree than labor under a broiling sun. Necessity—the mother of industry—brings no action to bear upon him, since all his wants in the way of food may be supplied in the neighboring forests, while he needs no silks to clothe his wives. According to one theory, if you double his wages, you soon discover that he will work only half as long![1]

In order to secure a labor supply, colonial powers may follow one of two policies: (1) the policy of exploitation, or (2) the policy of development, which, in its larger aspects, is called trusteeship. Under the first policy, natives are literally forced to work as wage-earners for the white man. Under the second policy, they are encouraged to work for themselves. In the past the vast

---

[1] Cf. A. Ireland, *Far Eastern Tropics*, p. 115, "As far as my own observation extends, I should say that the Malay of the Peninsula is the most steadfast loafer on the face of the earth. His characteristics in this respect have been recognized by every one who has come in contact with him. He will work neither for himself, for the Government, nor for private employers. He builds himself a house of bamboo and attaps, plants enough rice to fill out the menu which stream and forest afford him, and for nine tenths of his waking hours, year in and year out, he sits on a wooden bench in the shade and watches the Chinaman and the Tamil build roads and railways, work the mines, cultivate the soil, raise cattle, and pay taxes. As all his desires are completely satisfied by this kind of life, you can make no appeal to him for industry." For the opposing point of view, cf. p. 346.

majority of the colonial powers have at one time or another followed the exploitation policy on the theory that the native is incorrigibly lazy. White men have gone into these colonies upon this theory, staked out huge plantations, and proceeded to make the laborers till the soil. At least four different methods have been followed to bring about this end: (1) slavery, (2) forced and imported labor, (3) excessive taxation, (4) land confiscation.

4. FORCED LABOR

Despite its wide prevalence in the 18th century, open slavery is not tolerated to-day in any colonial empire, with the exception of household slaves held by native chieftains.[1] But this institution has, in many colonies, been replaced by various systems of forced labor. Sometimes natives have been forced to work for the government; and sometimes for private employers—European settlers. One of the most notorious forms of forced labor was the "culture system" followed by Holland in the Dutch East Indies after 1830. In order to pay off a colonial debt, the Dutch government introduced a system whereby natives were compelled to plant one-fifth of their land and give one-fifth of their time to growing crops or "cultures" for the benefit of the Dutch government. While this system proved very profitable to the mother country, it worked disastrously as far as the natives were concerned. The safeguards originally set up to protect them were violated, and the natives were compelled to give more than one-fifth of their time to the government, at grossly insufficient remuneration, and subject to mistreatment of the most cruel sort. So great did the opposition in Holland become, that the culture system was, for the most part, abolished about 1870.[2]

The Belgian Congo.—A still more flagrant example occurred in the Belgian Congo. Despite the provisions of the Berlin Act of 1885, providing for the humane treatment of the natives in the Congo, King Leopold introduced a system of compulsory labor, under which the less the natives were paid for gathering rubber, the more the Belgian officials personally received. Natives were

---

[1] Cf. p. 275.
[2] Cf. J. W. B. Money, *Java, or How to Manage a Colony* (1861), 2 vols.; Clive Day, *The Dutch in Java*, (1904), Chs. VII–IX; A. Ireland, *Tropical Colonization* (1899), Ch. VI; Keller, *Colonization*, pp. 473 ff.

FORCED LABOR

penalized for not working by having their families placed in "hostage" houses. Non-rubber producing districts were required to provide food for rubber-producing districts and for the soldiers. When the natives refused to submit to this system, thousands were killed and the dead mutilated. From the standpoint of a few foreign trading concerns the policy was very profitable, one of them making a net profit in six years of $3,600,000 on a paid-up capital of $46,000. But in order to make the system "work," an army was necessary, while 10,000 people passed through the "hostage houses" annually.[1] Following the protest of the various governments and other forms of pressure, this system was finally abolished in 1910–1911.

The Cocoa Islands.—Conditions of virtual slavery also existed for a number of years in the "Cocoa" islands of Portugal. The extraordinary development of the cocoa industry in the islands of San Thomé and Principe led the Portuguese government to bring in natives from the African interior under contracts or "apprenticeships," which amounted to enslavement. Between 1888 and 1909 nearly 68,000 Africans were carried from the mainland to these islands.[2] While they were supposed to come of their own free will, they were compelled to enter into contracts, many being ignorant of what they signed. They were taken to the islands under the harshest conditions, thousands of them dying on the way. Labor contracts were entered into for a term of five years, but the planter had the option of renewal. The laborer was thus bound indefinitely. In return, he was to be supplied with board, lodging and wages; but despite the "regulations" of the Portuguese government, these were below the minimum required for a decent existence. As a result of the great outcry in Great Britain against this type of forced labor, the Portuguese government in 1913 brought about a number of reforms.[3]

In many colonies natives have been indirectly forced to labor

[1] Cf. the Casement Report, Dec. 11, 1903, Cd. 1933 (1904), pp. 21–69; also Cd. 3880 (1908); E. D. Morel, *King Leopold's Rule in Africa* (1905), Parts II and III; A. B. Keith, *The Belgian Congo and the Berlin Act*, Ch. XI.
[2] J. N. Harris, *Portuguese Slavery* (1913); H. W. Nevinson, *A Modern Slavery* (1906), Chs. IV–X.
[3] Decree 154, Oct. 1, 1913, printed in Cd. 7279 (1914), p. 16; these reforms were so satisfactory to the British cocoa firms that thereafter they resumed business with the islands. Cd. 8479 (1917).

by a number of means. Native laborers have been persuaded to enter into labor contracts with white employers, which in many cases deliver them body and soul to the employer. Although white men could "jump" a contract, subject only to the academic fear of a fine or damages, a native who thus broke it might be put in jail. The flogging of natives to hurry their labor also accentuated their hatred of the white man.

In many colonies, a poll or hut tax has been imposed on the native which could be paid only by working for a white employer. According to the so-called Glen Grey Act of 1894, all adult natives in South Africa who were not landholders were liable to an annual tax of ten shillings, unless they could show that they had regular employment for at least three months a year.[1] Every government in Central Africa resorts to forced labor for certain public works. In British East Africa and in the Belgian Congo, the labor exactions are limited by law to sixty days a year. In other colonies the limit to forced labor is usually the discretion of the local administration. A French decree has recently established a labor army in French West Africa and in Madagascar whereby natives may be conscripted as laborers for public purposes for three years.[2]

Even where there is no statute authorizing forced labor, government officials have often recruited such laborers through native chieftains. While there has been no open compulsion about furnishing these laborers, chieftains realize that their position with the authorities depends upon furnishing such a supply.[3] The abuses of such indirect pressure were so great that in 1921 the British government ruled that officials should take no part in recruiting labor for private employment.[4]

Compulsion of this sort has not stimulated qualities of initiative or discipline in the native. Instead of awakening his energies, it deadens every incentive he may have. Just as slavery proved inefficient in the United States, forced labor in the backward

[1] P. S. Reinsch, *Colonial Administration* (1905), p. 359.
[2] Buell, *Native Problem*, Vol. II, p. 186.
[3] Sir F. D. Lugard, *The Dual Mandate in British Tropical Africa* (2d ed., 1923), p. 392; cf. Cmd. 873 (1920).
[4] Cmd. 1509 (1921). In Southwest Africa, now controlled as a mandate by the Union of South Africa, there is an ordinance to the effect that a magistrate may sentence a native culprit to a term of service on public works or *to employment by a private person*, other than the complainant, in lieu of imprisonment. *Minutes, Mandates Commission*, 3d sess., A. 19, 1923, VI, p. 112.

countries has proved, in the long run, to be a money-losing proposition.[1]

Under certain circumstances, a limited form of forced labor may be necessary for the government. When essential public works need to be constructed, such as roads, bridges and railways, governments may be obliged to draft native labor. It should always be accompanied, however, by an adequate wage.

Trouble over forced labor has arisen primarily in those tropical colonies which the whites have tried to adapt for settlement purposes—such as Kenya and South Africa. If these whites are to make a go of it, they must secure a supply of native workmen. "The requirements of the settlers, to put it bluntly, are incompatible with the interests and the advancement of the agricultural tribes."[2]

5. IMPORTED LABOR

When all measures of force have failed to secure a suitable native supply, or where the country is under-populated, the policy of imported labor has been frequently employed. This labor usually comes from over-populated countries, such as India and China, or it may come from neighboring colonies. Thus large numbers of natives from Portuguese Mozambique have been imported to work in the mines of British South Africa. Ordinarily, imported labor is placed under an iron-bound contract, running from three to five years. During this period, the laborer, under the old style contract at least, was a virtual slave so far as his freedom was concerned, although in return for his services his employer provided him with food, housing, wages and medical care. In the Malay peninsula the British have relied upon Chinese coolies to work the tin mines, one million of the total 3,500,000 inhabitants of the colony being Chinese. In the Union of South Africa a large number of East Indians have been imported to work in the mines and in British East Africa to construct the railways. In its Samoan mandate, New Zealand has brought in some 3,000 Chinese laborers under three-year contracts from Hongkong.

While the policy of importing labor is not as objectionable as that of compelling natives to work for private employers, it

[1] Cf. Sir Sydney Olivier, *White Capital and Colored Labor* (1906), Ch. VIII.
[2] Lugard, p. 397.

presents many abuses. Such laborers may be exploited by employers, unless safeguards are erected by the governments concerned. The presence of alien labor in a community creates grave political questions, such as in British East and South Africa, where the Indians have demanded political and economic equality with the whites.[1] Grave social abuses may likewise arise. Detached from the social restraints of their home communities and separated ordinarily from their wives, these laborers frequently degenerate into the basest types of corruption and immorality.[2] Imported labor, moreover, does an injustice to the native populations, who by its presence are deprived of every stimulus to work for themselves.[3] Because of the evils of this system, India is prohibiting the emigration of indentured labor altogether.[4]

6. CONFISCATION OF NATIVE LANDS

Many colonial powers have also adopted the policy of confiscating native lands or breaking up time-honored tribal holdings, either in order to force the natives, thus deprived of their source of livelihood, to work for the white men, or because of a mistaken idea of the values of private property. Among most of the "backward peoples" of the world, landed property is held in what amounts to common ownership. So that while there may be an individual right of user, not even the chieftain may alienate the title.[5] Ignorant of these land usages, colonial authorities have often signed agreements with chieftains which the latter had no power to make, instituting a system of private property. Beginning with the law of 1873 the French authorities thus divided up the lands in Algeria. While the natives were theoretically left with individual holdings, they were so unaccustomed to western conceptions of property that scheming white men soon acquired their titles, and thousands of natives were thus reduced to laboring for the white men.[6]

Other powers have gone further than to institute a system of

[1] Cf. p. 63.
[2] Cf. L. E. Neame, *The Asiatic Danger in the Colonies* (1907), Ch. II.
[3] Olivier, cited, Ch. XI.
[4] *Emigration and Immigration*, cited, p. 53.
[5] W. C. Willoughby, *Race Problems in the New Africa* (1923), pp. 91 ff. Cf. Lowie, *Primitive Society*, Ch. IX.
[6] Reinsch, *Colonial Administration*, p. 317.

CONFISCATION OF NATIVE LANDS

private property. They have adopted a system of confiscating native lands outright. One of the most frightful examples of this policy was in the Congo Free State under King Leopold II. Along with his policy of forced labor he nationalized nine-tenths of the land in the territory, the natives being allowed to retain as "reserves" only the area upon which they lived or actually had under cultivation. In order to exploit the rubber resources thus taken away from the natives, he formed "concessionaire" companies, the king himself having half the capital in each company, the other half usually being held by Belgians. The natives were even forbidden to wander through the uninhabited forests to gather "sylvan" products for themselves—all such products being the property of the white monopolists.[1] In 1899 the French government adopted a similar policy in the French Congo, the land of which was placed under the control of some forty corporations who had the exclusive right of exploiting the natural products of the soil. The French government went so far as to impose a direct tax upon the natives, payable in rubber, which was handed over to these companies. Many officials in the French government profited by this policy, one French minister of colonies being a director of six concession companies. As a result of outside protests, the Belgian system was done away with in 1910–1911; while the French government also terminated the concessions of the companies monopolizing the French Congo.[2]

In British territory, similar offences against the natives have been perpetrated. In 1888 King Lobengula of the Matabele—the dominant tribe in Southern Rhodesia—made a concession to the South Africa Trading Company, granting it "the complete and exclusive charge over all metals and minerals" in the country. This and a later concession were interpreted by the company to give it the ownership of all of the land. It thereupon proceeded to make large grants to stockholders and white settlers and to oblige natives living on "alienated" lands to pay a tax to the company and also to the white occupant. As a result, the natives were deprived of all ownership in the land which they had held until the advent of the white man; and many of them were obliged

---

[1] Buell, *Native Problem*, Ch. 82. For a defense of French policy, cf. J. Massiou, *Les grandes concessions au Congo français* (1920).

[2] C. Humbert, *Œuvres française aux colonies* (1913), pp. 60 ff.

to become wage-earners of the European over-lord. The irony of the case was increased by the fact that the Judicial Committee of the Privy Council ruled in 1918 that the claims of the Company, based on the so-called Lippert Concession, were without validity.[1]

In British East Africa—called Kenya—the authorities have not gone quite so far. But the government alienates from 300,000 to 600,000 acres of land a year, which is sold and leased, not to natives, but to Britishers. Certain "reserves" have been set aside for the native tribes, but which are inadequate for future, native needs.[2] It happened that the Masai tribe had been guaranteed certain grazing lands, by treaty with the British authorities, through which a railway had been constructed. The location of the land made it attractive to the white settlers who finally succeeded in pressing the government to drive the Masai tribe off, the treaty to the contrary notwithstanding. In 1913 the tribe brought an action against the colonial government for violation of its pledge. But the Judge of the local court quoted a decision involving an Indian case, "If a wrong has been done, it is a wrong for which no Municipal Court can afford a remedy."[3] Since these agreements were treaties—and not contracts—the court could not enforce them against the government if it chose to violate them. Such a violation was an Act of State against which the natives have no judicial redress.

In Southwest Africa the Germans followed the same policy of driving the natives off the land. And such a policy was followed to a certain extent in Korea by Japan; in the Five Rivers case, some 15,000 Koreans were dispossessed of their homes.[4] Soon after acquiring Porto Rico, the United States enacted a law limiting land holdings by corporations engaged in agriculture there to 500 acres.[5] But the statute has never been enforced and the Organic Act of 1917 provided that the Governor should report on excess holdings. As a result of this investigation it was found that 432 partnerships and 45 corporations, two-thirds of which

[1] Report of the Judicial Committee of the Privy Council, July 29, 1918, Appendix I, Cmd. 547 (1920). Cf. J. H. Harris, *The Chartered Millions* (1920).
[2] Buell, *Native Problem in Africa*, Vol. I, Ch. 20.
[3] Judgment of the High Court at Mombasa, May 26, 1913, Cd. 6939 (1913).
[4] J. A. McKenzie, *Korea's Fight for Freedom* (1919), p. 84.
[5] Act of May 1, 1900, 31 Stat. 716.

were American, held 765,000 acres of land in excess of the amount authorized by law.[1] To-day Porto Rico is an appanage of the American business houses.

7. BRUTALITY AND DISCRIMINATION

Under the policy of exploitation, which aims to convert the native into a wage-earner and to deprive him of his lands, colonial governments have been guilty of brutal treatment of the most inhuman nature. In the German colonies white men carried around whips as naturally as they did handkerchiefs.[2] In many of the French and British possessions, the flogging of natives has also been a common spectacle. The German adventurer, Dr. Karl Peters, beat his concubines to death, and Frenchmen in the New Hebrides twisted the flesh of their servants with pinchers.[3]

This policy has likewise been accompanied by a policy of discriminatory social and political treatment of the natives in favor of the whites. In many colonies, alcoholic liquors are prohibited to the natives but not to the whites. In the Union of South Africa, natives are required to carry identification cards—under the notorious Pass Laws.[4] White labor unions not only refuse to admit natives as members, but Color Bar Legislation prohibits negroes from becoming skilled laborers in the mines of the Transvaal. In the French colonies, a special body of rules, applicable only to the natives, called the *Indigénat*, exists.[5] Those who violate these rules are liable to a summary type of punishment. In French West Africa the rules of this character cover some forty subjects, prescribing punishments for natives who refuse to pay taxes, or who carry firearms without permission, or who practice sorcery, and so forth. Until 1919 special taxes were levied on the Arabs in Algeria,[6] while in German Southwest Africa natives were forbidden to own stock. In Korea flogging was employed by the Japanese authorities but only against Koreans. Principals of the

---

[1] S. Doc., No. 165, 65th Cong., 2d sess.
[2] Cf. Beer, *African Questions at the Paris Peace Conference*, pp. 33 ff.; E. Lewin, *The Germans and Africa* (1915), Ch. 17.
[3] Cf. G. Murray, in *Liberalism and the Empire* (1900), p. 153.
[4] Buell, *Native Problem in Africa*, Vol. I, p. 68.
[5] Piquet, *La Colonisation française dans l'Afrique du Nord* (1914), p. 226.
[6] Humbert, *Œuvre française*, p. 219; Piquet, p. 236.

common schools in Korea had to be Japanese. Penal codes were especially severe toward Koreans, while a disproportionate part of the revenue for schools was expended for the benefit of Japanese instead of Korean children. Following the Revolution of 1919, an Imperial Rescript abolished many of these discriminations, particularly flogging. Koreans also became eligible as principals of schools.[1]

8. TARIFFS AND THE "DRAIN"

While tariff policies are ordinarily considered of external importance, they may also be manipulated so as to impose great hardships on the natives. A protective tariff generally increases prices to the consumer, and where a tariff is charged only on foreign goods, and not on goods from the home country, a colony is deprived of an easy source of revenue. While tariffs may be charged on imports from other countries, these imports amount to very little since the home country has virtually monopolized the trade. Instead of taxing imports, colonies are forced to resort to more direct taxes on the natives, which are particularly burdensome in a new country.[2]

In India, the charge has been made that "free trade" is an instrument by which Great Britain exploits the Indian people. Unobstructed by tariff duties, the Lancashire cotton manufacturers have had a market of 315,000,000 people. Because of the impossibility of erecting tariffs, Indian industries were unable to receive any protection which infant industries need if they are to compete with established ones. In 1894 a 5% tariff on imports was imposed by the British authorities in India, with the exception of cotton goods. Two years later, a $3\frac{1}{2}\%$ import duty on cottons was levied, in order to meet a continuing deficit; but at the same time an excise of $3\frac{1}{2}\%$ on all cotton manufactured in Indian mills was also imposed, so that they could not benefit by these duties. It was not until 1917 that Indian cotton goods received any protection against British goods—at that time a net duty of 4% was imposed. The Indians assert, with some reason, that the British insisted on free trade throughout this period in

---

[1] *Annual Report on Reforms and Progress in Chosen* (1918–1921), pp. 25, 172. Cf. H. H. Cynn, *The Rebirth of Korea* (1920), p. 94.

[2] Cf p. 447.

order to prevent the growth of Indian competitors to British manufacturers.[1]

Lord Salisbury once said that "India must be bled"; and there is no doubt that under the East India Company, it was robbed right and left. Even under the existing British régime, the Indians assert that they pay tribute, denominated the "Drain." The exports of India since 1850 have annually been a couple of million pounds greater than imports; this excess, Indians assert, goes to England in the form of salaries, interest on capital which India has borrowed from England, and advances for government supplies. Englishmen say that India got her money's worth in return for these payments. Money borrowed from England at $3\frac{1}{2}\%$ is now earning 7% for the Indian government.[2] But the Indians reply that the cost of administration is much higher than it would be in Indian hands and that the rule was forced upon India against her wishes.

While the defence of the Dominions has long been recognized as a duty of the imperial government, 60,500 British troops and 137,000 native soldiers have been maintained in India—and officered by Englishmen—at a cost to India in 1922–23 of about $200,000,000.[3] Moreover, it is charged [4] that the cost of a large number of wars, beginning with the first Afghan war of 1838 down to the Sudan war of 1885, including wars in Egypt, Abyssinia, Persia and China, has been assessed by British authorities against the Indian budget. Whatever truth there may have been in these charges, the Government Act of 1919 placed such matters as tariff in the hands of an Indian legislature, while Indians were made eligible as officers in the Indian army. The gradual replacement of British officials by Indians and the industrialization of India will diminish the occasion for exporting silver, which India has called the "Drain."

9. DEBAUCHERY

Finally, the policy of exploitation has resulted, in some cases, in debauching the natives. In a former chapter we have seen how

[1] *Colonial Tariff Policies*, p. 333; H. M. Hyndman, *The Awakening of Asia* (1919), p. 227.
[2] L. F. Rushbrook Williams, *India in 1921–22*, statement prepared for presentation to Parliament, Calcutta, 1922, p. 119.
[3] *India Office List*, 1924, p. 3792.
[4] L. Rai, *England's Debt to India* (1920), Ch. IV.

widespread the liquor and the drug traffic is in the tropical parts of the world. In Africa hundreds of children have been pawned in order to secure gin; and some governments have aided the process by requiring that fines should be paid in liquor. One-half of the revenue of the colonies in West Africa once came from excises largely on strong drink.[1] Smoking opium and gambling have been encouraged in many colonies in the Far East.[2]

Such are the methods of exploitation: forced or imported labor; the confiscation, total or partial, of the natives' land; brutality, discrimination and debauchery. The policy of exploitation has been responsible for recurrent anti-white movements.[3] In German Southwest Africa, the Germans were obliged to launch twenty-nine punitive expeditions against the natives to suppress discontent;[4] while the Matabele wars, the revolts in the Portuguese possessions, as well as the chronic unrest in other colonies, show that the continuance of the exploitation policy tends to keep the world unsettled. This policy is also shortsighted from the material standpoint. Instead of producing a labor supply, it has led in Africa to under-population and to a labor shortage.

If imperialism means exploitation of this type, it is surely an evil thing. Peoples have tolerated it in the past partly because of ignorance. Until recently parliaments have taken little interest in colonial affairs. Moreover, many colonial abuses were committed by governments which were at the same time abusing their subjects at home. With the growth of democracy, some of these abuses have been destroyed. But in many countries, colored men are not yet regarded as human beings entitled to the same rights as whites; and in other countries democracy has not lifted its head above home frontiers. But if governmental in-

[1] A. J. MacDonald, *Trade, Politics and Christianity in Africa and the East* (1916), p. 99.
[2] Cf. p. 257. A large number of charges were made in 1919–20 against the British North Borneo Company in regard to vice and forced labor. Cf. Cmd. 1060 (1920), "Correspondence on the subject of Allegations against the Administration of the British North Borneo Co."; also E. A. Powell, *Where the Strange Trails End* (1919), p. 191. These charges were sweepingly denied by the Company. Cf. *Report on the 75th Half-Yearly Meeting of the British North Borneo* (Chartered), *Company*, July 27, 1920, p. 13; *ibid.*, 77th Meeting, Nov., 1921, p. 17.
[3] Cf. pp. 85 ff.
[4] Lewin, *The Germans and Africa*, p. 271.

tervention has proved necessary to suppress abuses at home, it is doubly necessary in the tropical regions where whites lose the restraints which a temperate climate and a social heritage impose upon them in their native countries. Fortunately for the native, for the peace of the world, and for the honor of western civilization, the policy of exploitation, as outlined in this chapter, is gradually giving way to the policy of trusteeship which will now be discussed.

CHAPTER XV

THE POLICY OF TRUSTEESHIP

1. Adolescent Peoples.—2. The Trusteeship Principle Applied to Land.—3. Native Farms in West Africa.—4. Coolie Treaties.—5. The Basel Trading Company.—6. Education of Native Peoples.—7. The Berlin Act.—8. The Mandates.—9. Their Legal Status.—10. Guarantees to the Natives.—11. The Mandates Commission.—12. The Ruanda Frontier.—13. The Bondelzwarts Affair.—14. The Extension of the Mandate Principle.

For many years the colonial powers have recognized, in theory at least, that they owe an obligation to the backward peoples under their control, which in many respects is analogous to the obligation of a guardian to his ward. They have recognized that if the advanced powers of the world are entitled to exploit the great resources of the backward regions, they must give value received; and they must accept the obligation to promote the spiritual and material interests of the natives.

1. ADOLESCENT PEOPLES

Apparently the theory is growing that the peoples inhabiting the tropical and sub-tropical parts of the world are in the "adolescent" stage of development, reached by the white peoples thousands of years ago, and that with proper encouragement and assistance the time will come when the darker peoples will reach an adult stage in international society.[1] "The most unfortunate and unfair of all the misunderstandings is to the effect that the African people do not give promise of development sufficient to warrant efforts in their behalf. The endeavor to prove the inferiority or the equality of Africans in comparison with other peoples of the world is of little value in determining policies concerned with their development. Biological and other researches may show the differentiation of social groups, both within and

[1] Cf. G. Stanley Hall, *Adolescence* (1905), Ch. XVIII on "Adolescent Races."

without Africa, but their results can never be used to justify the denial of educational or other opportunities to any group. The present distribution of the African groups through the various stages of human society, whether that stage be cannibalistic, barbaric, primitive, or civilized, is a natural condition that has been almost completely duplicated at some time with all civilized races. . . . An adequate study of the tribal customs and capacities of those who are still in barbaric and primitive stages will more and more reveal the fact that the present condition of the masses of the African people is normal and comparable with other peoples of the same stage of development. Their folklore, their handicrafts, their native music, their forms of government, their linguistic powers, all are substantial evidences of their capacity to respond to the wise approaches of civilization so that they may share in the development of the African continent."[1] In other words, the tropics may be inhabited by backward, but not necessarily inferior peoples. Even if one should accept the opposite theory that the African negro is in a permanent stage of arrested development, the obligations of the European powers toward him would still be equally great, if of a different nature.

As early as 1821 a special commissioner reported to the Secretary of War that the United States should consider itself to be a guardian over the Indians and that its government of them "should be in its nature parental—absolute, kind, and mild." In the report of the British Parliamentary Committee on Aboriginal Tribes of 1837 the "responsibility" and "obligation" of Great Britain toward these peoples was expressed, because of "the ability which we possess to confer upon them the most important benefits," and because of "their inability to resist any encroachments, however unjust, however mischievous, which we may be disposed to make."[2] In 1879 Mr. Chamberlain said, "Our rule over these territories can only be justified if we can show that it adds to the happiness and prosperity of the people." And upon another occasion he said that their government was a "trust" of the British people.[3] When the United States acquired the Philippines as a result of the war of 1898, it promised to promote the

[1] *Education in Africa*, cited, pp. 5–6.
[2] Quoted in A. H. Snow, *The Question of Aborigines* (1921), pp. 32, 39.
[3] *Speeches*, cited, Vol. II, p. 3.

"well-being, the prosperity and the happiness of the Philippine people, and their elevation and advancement to a position among the civilized peoples of the world." [1]

In 1923 the British Colonial Office declared, "Primarily Kenya is an African territory, and His Majesty's Government think it necessary definitely to record their considered opinion that the interests of the African natives must be paramount, and that if, and when, those interests and the interests of the immigrant races should conflict, the former should prevail. . . . In the administration of Kenya His Majesty's Government regard themselves as exercising a trust on behalf of the African population, and they are unable to delegate or share this trust, the object of which may be defined as the protection and advancement of the native races. . . . There can be no room for doubt that it is the mission of Great Britain to work continuously for the training and education of the Africans toward a higher intellectual, moral and economic level than that which they had reached when the Crown assumed the responsibility for the administration of this territory. . . ." [2]

2. THE TRUSTEESHIP PRINCIPLE APPLIED TO LAND

As the last chapter demonstrated, in many colonies this obligation of trusteeship has not, in practice at least, been realized. But in other colonies, serious attempts have been made to convert the theory into reality. Probably the most fundamental difference between the old idea of exploitation and the newer idea of trusteeship is in labor and land policy. Opinion is by no means unanimous that the African native is incorrigibly lazy and that he must be driven to work. In the past, the uncertainty of the future took away an incentive to labor. A large number of authorities agree that, given the proper incentive, the native will voluntarily work for himself and in many cases for the white man.[3] Under the proper educational influences, he will learn the advantages of a higher standard of living and the value of property.

---

[1] President McKinley's instructions to the second Philippines Commission.
[2] "Indians in Kenya," Cmd. 1922 (1923).
[3] Lugard, cited, pp. 401, 404 ff.; Olivier, Chs. VIII and X; J. Harmand, *Domination et Colonisation* (1910), Ch. VI; Willoughby, *Race Problems in the New Africa*, pp. 189 ff.

Impelled by such considerations, his labor will be far more productive than if coerced.

When the policy of trusteeship is intelligently applied, tribal customs in regard to land are not ruthlessly violated out of false notions as to the universal value of private property in land, or in order to turn over plantations to white settlers. After readjusting themselves to the impact of western industrialism, it is probable that primitive peoples will eventually adopt, as a matter of course, the institution of private property. But if the trusteeship principle is actually applied, the colonial power will not force this transition. As in the case of the French practice in Morocco, the transition from tribal to private property should be gradual. Individual titles should be made secure. And even if they are freely granted, some land should always be reserved for the use of the community as a whole.[1] In colonies where white settlers have entered, particular care should be taken to delimit and to protect adequate native "reserves," upon which the white man cannot encroach.

In many colonies, natives are forbidden to transfer their land to non-natives, except with the consent of the government authorities. By this means white men are prevented from duping chieftains into the "sale" of their land for a string of beads or a case of gin. In the Dutch East Indies, the ownership of land by a non-native is forbidden altogether.[2] In Natal, a province in British South Africa, an institution called the Natal Native Trust has been established to supervise and to safeguard native property rights. In British West Africa, "the acknowledged general principle is that all the land in the Colony belongs to the native community." [3]

Wherever geographic conditions and the nature of crops make it possible, colonial governments, inspired by the trusteeship principle, will encourage natives to acquire individual farms, and —under the "development" or small-farm system—to raise crops of their own. Instead of being a slave driver, forcing negroes to work on huge plantations under threat of the whip, the white

[1] Cf. P. S. Reinsch, *Colonial Administration*, p. 321; and Leclere, "Les Terres collectives de tribu au Maroc," *Afrique française* (1922), Rene Col., p. 33.
[2] Torchiana, *Tropical Holland*, p. 249.
[3] Statement of British Colonial Office, *Anti-Slavery Reporter and Aborigines' Friend*, January, 1923.

man under this system becomes a middleman, while the native becomes a peasant farmer. The white man may lend money to the natives; but his chief profit will come from selling native produce in western countries and western goods to the natives. By encouraging the native to work for himself and by elevating his standard of living through education, the demand of the natives for European goods will be stimulated and an incentive given to native industry, which is impossible under the system of exploitation. Under the trusteeship system, government officials instruct natives as to the best methods of agricultural production. Such a system of development does away with highly-paid, numerous European directors; it implants in the native a real incentive to work for himself; in so doing, it tends to remove the bitterness which the system of exploitation has created between white and black.

3. NATIVE FARMS IN WEST AFRICA

That this system has long passed out of the domain of philanthropic theory, is shown by the experiments in the British West Indies and in British Africa. In the West Indies, a great sugar company did away with the large-estate plan in favor of a system of the small farm worked by negro owners. As a result of this change, sugar production increased three hundred per cent. A still better example will be found in British West Africa—by far the most important of the British possessions in Africa[1]—where a number of native export industries, particularly the palm oil and cocoa industries, have flourished. The production of palm oil, a commodity which has a large number of industrial uses, involves the exploitation of more than 25,000,000 trees annually. And the striking feature of this industry in Africa is that it is in the hands, not of European planters, but of natives, working for themselves. During the seven years preceding the War, the natives of southern Nigeria produced, and handed over to white men for exploitation, palm oil and kernels to the value of $120,000,000. The record of the cocoa industry, also in native hands, is equally remarkable. In 1891 the output of cocoa on the Gold Coast

---

[1] British West Africa has an area of 488,677 square miles, a population of 21,800,000, and trade of about £49,000,000 a year. British East Africa has an area of 2,139,821 square miles, a population of 16,149,000, and trade of only £26,759,126.

NATIVE FARMS IN WEST AFRICA

was 80 pounds, valued at $20. In 1919 the output equaled 176,151 tons, valued at $41,392,500. This little colony, with a population of only two million, produces about half the cocoa in the world. Following the adoption of this system in British West Africa, the yield of cocoa increased seven times in seven years. In the adjoining Cameroons, the Germans followed the opposite policy of large plantations. But despite the use of more advanced industrial equipment, production increased less than half as rapidly as in British West Africa during the same period.[1] In British East Africa, the natives also grow cotton, without the assistance of white men. It appears that many of the French colonies now encourage the development system. If such a system could become general, the world would be adequately supplied with the raw materials which it needs, while the natives would receive a legitimate return for voluntary labor. At the same time they would acquire the qualities of initiative and independence which are necessary if they are to stand on their own feet.

It is not likely, however, that the small-farm system can be universally applied. It is easily adaptable to such a crop as cocoa, which grows with little attention. But even in Nigeria, difficulties have arisen which indicate that the universal application of the small-farm system throughout Africa is improbable in the near future.[2]

In those cases where white management is necessary to the development of tropical resources, experience has demonstrated the possibility of securing a supply of native labor not by resorting to force but by paying attractive wages and guaranteeing suitable working conditions. In 1926 the Belgian Congo administration went so far as to adopt the principle that not more than five per cent of the able-bodied men could be taken away from home at one time to work, at a distance,[3] for European employers. The Aborigines' Protection Society suggested, in a Memorial to the Foreign Office of January 22, 1917, that only civil and not criminal penalties be attached to the violation of labor contracts and that a maximum employment term of six months be prescribed for

---

[1] J. H. Harris, in Marvin, *Western Races and the World* (1922), Ch. X; E. D. Morel, *The Black Man's Burden*, pp. 182 ff.; Lugard, *The Dual Mandate*, p. 398.
[2] Lugard, p. 399.
[3] Buell, *Native Problem*, Vol. II, cited, p. 548.

contracts to work in the mines and three years for contracts covering agricultural labor.[1] The appointment of Labor Inspectors is the only assurance that laws protecting natives in labor contracts are being enforced.[2]

4. COOLIE TREATIES

When it is necessary to resort to imported labor, precautions and safeguards become all the more desirable. This aspect of the labor question is essentially international—Portuguese Mozambique has supplied about 100,000 natives for work in the Rand mines in British South Africa, and China and India have likewise furnished thousands of laborers for the tropical regions of the world. In order to reduce to a minimum the evils of this system, a number of international agreements have been made. In 1860, and again in 1904, England and China entered into treaties concerning the recruiting of Chinese workers for employment in the British protectorates and colonies. According to the convention of 1904, the British minister at Pekin must notify the Chinese authorities when the British wish a supply of laborers. The Chinese government then appoints an Inspector who, together with the British consular representative, works out the text of the contract, defining carefully the terms and conditions of employment. No Chinese may embark without a permit signed by this inspector and the British authority, and without submitting to a medical examination. In colonies where these laborers are employed, the Chinese government may appoint a Consul approved by the British government, to watch over the interest and well-being of these laborers. Emigrants are guaranteed free access to the courts, while provision is also made for the return of laborers to their home country.[3] In the New Hebrides agreement of 1906 France and Great Britain established certain safeguards for the recruiting of native labor, contracts being limited to three years.[4] In 1909 Portuguese Mozambique and the

[1] Beer, *African Questions*, p. 187. An international agreement to this effect was advocated.
[2] Cf. Ordinance of Oct. 20, 1919, providing for Labor Inspectors in Kenya; Cmd. 873 (1920), p. 26.
[3] Convention of May 13, 1904, 97 *State Papers*, 20.
[4] 99 *State Papers*, 242.

THE BASEL TRADING COMPANY

Transvaal made an agreement concerning the recruiting of labor in Mozambique for the Rand mines. If an employer fails to comply with the obligations imposed, the Portuguese government may prohibit him from employing laborers. Licenses to recruit laborers are granted only by the Mozambique authorities, the first contracts being limited for one year. A Portuguese official—the *Curator*—protects native interests in the Rand.[1] A somewhat similar treaty was signed between Spain and Liberia in 1914 and between Portugal and Southern Rhodesia in 1925.[2]

5. THE BASEL TRADING COMPANY

Backward countries will always need a certain amount of foreign capital if they are to be developed. But in order to safeguard native interests, the conditions surrounding the advancement, use and repayment of such foreign capital need particularly to be controlled. An extremely interesting application of the trusteeship principle in the matter of capital in colonies was found in the case of the Basel Mission Trading Company, founded in 1859. This company—a white man's organization—carried on a large trade on the Gold Coast and also in India. Dividends were limited to five per cent, profits above that amount being handed over to a Committee of Trustees to be expended for religious work among the natives. For a number of years this company handed over to the Basel Mission about $100,000 annually. As this company was composed largely of Germans, the British government expelled it from the African coast during the War. But in view of the great value of its work, the British government established as its successor the Commonwealth Trust, Limited, based upon the same principle of a limited dividend, the excess being handed over to a trustee, to be expended for the benefit of the natives in the colony concerned.[3]

---

[1] Convention of April 1, 1909, 102 *State Papers*, 110.
[2] *Emigration and Immigration*, cited, p. 337. Buell, *Native Problem in Africa*, Vol. I, p. 227.
[3] Cf. Prospectus, *Commonwealth Trust, Limited*. In 1928 the Gold Coast government appropriated £250,000 to the Basel Mission Company as well as restored to it the property in possession of the Commonwealth Trust as a full settlement. The government also appropriated £55,000 to the Commonwealth Trust in return for the properties which it surrendered to the

Under the trusteeship theory, colonial powers are under a strict obligation to combat tropical diseases and to promote public health in the colonies, and to stamp out the opium and liquor habits which ravage native populations.[1] The promotion of education is most important of all. From the material standpoint, education will increase the native standard of living; it will raise the native birth rate; it will automatically stamp out the indecencies and inhumanities which sometimes mark the religious practices of primitive peoples. In raising the standard of living, the wants of the native will be increased along with his own productivity, thus enlarging the demand for European and American goods. Educational progress must be the basis of political development. Until the native possesses the rudiments of an education, he cannot be expected to govern himself. The right sort of education will lead to inter-racial understanding and prepare the ground for real racial equality.

6. EDUCATION OF NATIVE PEOPLES

While education is thus fundamental, it has been sadly neglected by colonial governments. In India and Egypt to-day 90% of the people cannot read or write any language. Even in the British colonies on the West Coast, probably the best administered colonies in the world, the appropriations for education absorb only between one and four per cent of the total expenditures. On the Gold Coast only one-tenth of the children of school age are in school. Even in the Union of South Africa only 20% of the children are being educated, and only 10% of the school appropriations go to the natives, although they constitute 80% of the population. The United States has probably made more progress than any other colonial power. About ten per cent of the population in the Philippines is in school, compared with only one and a half per cent of the population of the neighboring Dutch East Indies. In Porto Rico the number of pupils in schools has increased from 18,000 in 1900 to 240,000 in 1924. About 40% of the Porto Rican budget and about 30% of the Philippine budget

---

Basel Company. This settlement was an admission that the government had made a mistake in treating the Basel Company, technically a Swiss society, as an enemy concern. Cf. *Gold Coast Leader*, November 7, 1928.

[1] Cf. p. 255.

goes for education. It should be remembered, however, that these sums are contributed, not by the United States, but by the inhabitants. Despite these efforts about 40% of the people of Porto Rico are still illiterate.

When governments have established schools, they have usually installed educational systems, which instead of increasing the value of an educated native to the community and inculcating in him ideas of character and discipline, have created a gulf between him and the remainder of the community, making labor distasteful to him, and making him rebellious to all authority. A "literary" education unfits the African or Indian for service to his people. Among these peoples, education should rather aim at the development of vocations and of character. As a distinguished authority says, "Among the primitive tribes ethical standards must be created—among few are they a vital and potent force. If, for instance, in his village home the African boy perceives that self-indulgence and lack of self-control excite no reprobation; that thrift, ambition and incentive are conceptions as foreign to his associates as an alien tongue, for which his language has no appropriate terms; if justice, fair-play, truthfulness, and mutual obligation have no influence in guiding the actions of those around him,—then these conceptions must be created and built up. . . . If then, it is admitted that it is inevitable that education should produce a ferment of new and progressive ideas, subversive of the old order, the function of a sound system must be to guide these tendencies so that they may conduce to the betterment of the body politic and not to its disintegration. . . ."[1]

Governments have often excused their negligence on the ground that educational work is being carried on by the missionaries. It is true that eighty per cent of the educational work in these regions, in addition to strictly religious and humanitarian activities, have come from the missionaries. Because of their independent position, they have been able to emphasize the moral as well as the strictly intellectual aspect of training.[2] There are no more exciting tales of modern adventure than the exploits of such men as Livingstone and Dr. Krapf in Africa; and there is no

---

[1] Lugard, p. 432.
[2] Cf. Mrs. L. Creighton, *Missions, Their Rise and Development* (1912), Ch. IX.

better example of a supreme devotion to duty, in many cases at the cost of life itself, than the career of these men, as well as of Alexander Mackay, Dr. Grenfell or Cardinal Lavigerie.[1] As Sir Charles Lucas has said, "To the various missionary bodies is due the advancement, industrial as well as spiritual, of the native races of Africa."[2] Many abuses in colonial administration have been brought to the attention of the outside world by missionaries, as in the case of forced labor in the Congo and later in Kenya, and of the division of the tribes of Ruanda.[3] But while it is difficult to give too much credit to the humanitarian and religious activities of these private organizations, in the future governments must take over at least the educational burden, which is too heavy for unofficial bodies to carry alone.

7. THE BERLIN ACT

If imperialism of any sort is to be morally justified, the principle of trusteeship must be actually put into effect. In a few colonies, such as British West Africa, French Morocco and the Philippines, a sound beginning has been made. But the isolated action of the colonizing power in applying this principle is subject to much the same limitations which restrict the effectiveness of any single power in many other matters, such as the protection of minorities, labor legislation, or the suppression of the liquor and drug evils. Consequently, the principle of trusteeship can best be promoted by international means.

This fact was recognized as far back as 1885, when at a conference held in Berlin a General Act was signed by the powers in which the governments holding colonies in Africa bound themselves "to watch over the preservation of the native tribes, and to care for the improvement of the conditions of their moral and material well-being"—a statement which was virtually repeated in the Revised Act of Berlin, signed at Saint Germain in September, 1919.[4] The importance of writing such a principle into an international treaty is that it converts what is otherwise a "domestic" question into an international obligation, the violation of which gives other powers the right to protest. But as we have

[1] Cf. Sir H. H. Johnston, *Colonization of Africa* (1913), Ch. X.
[2] *Partition and Colonization of Africa* (1922), p. 75.
[3] Cf. p. 364.
[4] *Treaties of the U. S.*, Vol. III, p. 3744.

seen, the 1885 treaty was ruthlessly violated by the forced labor system and land policy of King Leopold in the Congo and by the concessionaire policy followed by the French in the adjoining colony. The Belgian government declined the request of Great Britain that these questions be referred to arbitration—partly on the ground that no such obligation had been accepted by the other parties to the Act.[1] Since no impartial body had the power to enforce and to interpret these provisions, the Act of Berlin virtually became a dead letter.

8. THE MANDATES

At the Paris Peace Conference a new opportunity arose to put the trusteeship principle into effect. About 6,500,000 Arabs had been taken away from Turkey, while about 11,000,000 natives of Africa and of the Pacific islands had been taken away from Germany. After a struggle in which the attempt of particular Allied powers to annex these peoples was definitely defeated, the so-called Mandate system was set up.

Germany transferred her colonies to the five Allied powers, and Turkey recognized the disposition which these powers had made of the territory outside of the frontiers drawn by the Treaty of Lausanne.[2] Nevertheless, in governing this territory, certain definite obligations had to be fulfilled. As the Covenant of the League of Nations states, "To those colonies and territories which as a consequence of the late war have ceased to be under the sovereignty of the States which formerly governed them and which are inhabited by peoples not yet able to stand by themselves under the strenuous conditions of the modern world, there should be applied the principle that the well-being and development of such peoples form a sacred trust of civilization and that securities for the performance of this trust should be embodied in this Covenant."

To give effect to this principle, the tutelage of such peoples should be intrusted to "advanced nations who by reason of their resources, their experience or their geographical position can best undertake this responsibility," if they are willing to accept it; but "this tutelage should be exercised by them as Mandatories

---

[1] Cf. Belgian Memorandum, March 15, 1909, Cd. 4701 (1909), p. 8.
[2] Art. 125, Treaty of Versailles; art. 16, Treaty of Lausanne.

on behalf of the League."[1] There were established fourteen different mandated territories, divided into three groups.

Class A Mandates—in the Near East
1. Syria and the Lebanon.....................France
2. Palestine and Transjordania................Great Britain
3. Mesopotamia (Iraq).......................Great Britain [2]

These communities have "reached a stage of development where their existence as independent nations can be provisionally recognized subject to the rendering of administrative advice and assistance by a Mandatory until such time as they are able to stand alone."

Class B Mandates—Africa
4. Togo....................................France
5. Togo....................................Great Britain
6. Cameroons..............................France
7. Cameroons..............................Great Britain
8. Tanganyika.............................Great Britain
9. Ruanda-Urundi.........................Belgium

These territories are in a more backward stage where "the Mandatory must be responsible for the administration of the territories," subject to certain guarantees.

Class C Mandates—the Pacific and Africa
10. Southwest Africa........................Union of South Africa
11. Samoa..................................New Zealand
12. Nauru island...........................British Empire
13. German islands south of the equator.........Australia
14. German islands north of the equator.........Japan

These are territories which, "owing to the sparseness of their population, or their small size, or their remoteness from the centres of civilisation, or their geographical contiguity to the territory of the Mandatory, and other circumstances, can be best administered under the laws of the Mandatory as integral portions of its territory," subject to certain guarantees.

These mandates were allocated between the different powers at two meetings of the Supreme Council, the first held on May 7, 1919, at Paris, when the Class B and C mandates were allocated; and the second at San Remo, in 1920, where a similar disposition was made of the Class A mandates. The total area of the man-

[1] Article 22, Covenant.
[2] For the special status of Iraq, cf. p. 388.

dated territory is 1,244,000 square miles, the total population 17,815,000 and the total trade, about $166,000,000.[1] While the population of the Class B mandates is 10,600,000 compared with a population of only 746,000, for the Class C mandates, the trade of the Class C mandates is about 4 million dollars more annually than that of the B mandates. By far the most valuable mandate from the standpoint of trade is Iraq, which does an annual business of about $95,000,000. The mandates with the largest populations are Tanganyika and Ruanda-Urundi, each with 3,500,000 people, while the population of French Syria is 3,000,000.

9. THEIR LEGAL STATUS

There is as yet no agreement as to the legal status of mandated territory, in regard to which four different theories have been advanced. There are those who believe that each mandatory has annexed the territory allocated to it;[2] others assert that mandated territory is held jointly by the five Principal Allied and Associated powers; a report to the League Council stated that the legal title "must be a double one: one conferred by the Principal Powers and the other conferred by the League of Nations;"[3] still others make a strong argument to the effect that the League of Nations has complete control over these territories.[4]

This question was brought before the League by a frontier agreement between Portuguese Angola and the Union of South Africa which stated that the Union, "subject to the terms of the said mandate, possesses sovereignty over the territory of Southwest Africa."[5] The Mandates Commission expressed doubt whether this terminology was correct; and in September, 1927, a rapporteur of the Council stated that the legal relationship between the mandatories and the mandates "is clearly a new one in international law, and for this reason the use of some of the time-honored terminology in the same way as previously, is perhaps sometimes inappropriate to the new conditions."[6]

[1] Cf. Table, *Colonial Tariff Policies*, p. 269.
[2] Rolin, "Le Système des mandats coloniaux," *R. D. I. L. C.* (1920), Nos. 3–4, p. 329.
[3] The Hymans Report, *O. J.*, Sept., 1920, p. 376.
[4] Schücking and Wehberg, *Satzung des Völkerbundes* (2d ed., 1924), pp. 688–703.
[5] Agreement of June 22, 1926, *T. S.* 1642.
[6] *O. J.*, 1927, p. 1120.

This legal question may become of great importance. Upon its determination may rest the status of mandates in time of war; and the power of the League to transfer a mandate from one government to another, when it fails to fulfill its obligations or resigns or is excluded from the League, or to recognize the independence of peoples held under mandate when they show themselves capable of governing themselves.[1]

The mandatory power may constitute an administrative union between a neighboring colony and a mandate, subject to the observance of the mandate guarantees.[2]

Under authority of this provision the mandates of British Togo and British Cameroons are administered as part of adjoining territories, while the Belgian mandate of Ruanda-Urundi has become a fifth province in the Belgian Congo. The Mandates Commission retains its power over the mandate which may thus be indirectly extended to the whole administrative union.

While the juridical status of the mandates cannot be discussed here because of its complex legal nature, decisions already taken by the League Council and the mandatory powers show that the mandates are not regarded in practice as annexed territories. The principle appears to have been established in the case of the Urundi frontier that once a mandate has been approved by the Council, no part of it can be ceded away without the consent of the Council.[3] After a careful examination into the question of whether lands in the mandated territories were being held in trust for the natives or regarded as property of the mandatory power, the Mandates Commission passed a resolution to the effect that the mandatory powers do not possess "any right over any part of the territory under mandate other than that resulting

---

[1] Cf. Wright, "Sovereignty of the Mandates," *A. J. I. L.*, Oct., 1923, p. 691. Another important question from the economic standpoint is the security of loans made to mandated territory. The Mandates Commission declared that in some quarters the belief was held that the mandate was revocable, which would raise the question of security. At its third session the Commission asked the Council to consider the advisibility of a pronouncement to the effect that in the event of a transfer the mandatory power would be held responsible for all guarantees for loans, etc. A declaration to this general effect was made by the Council in September, 1925. *O. J.*, Oct. 1925, p. 1365.

[2] Art. 9, Mandate for the French Cameroons.

[3] Cf. *Minutes of the Third Session*, Mandates Commission, A. 19, 1923, p. 138. Cf. p. 364.

from their being entrusted with the administration of the territory."[1] Local laws in regard to land tenure leading to contrary conclusions should be modified. Each of the mandates is financially autonomous; and if the budget produces a surplus, it must be held in trust for local purposes.[2] Moreover, the Council ruled in April, 1923, that the nationality of the natives in the B and C mandates was distinct from that of the mandatory power.[3] All of these examples go to show that the mandatory system is by no means a system of disguised annexation.

10. GUARANTEES TO THE NATIVES

There are two distinctive features of the mandate system, the first of which consists of the obligations which each mandatory power assumes toward the native and toward the outside world. The second is the system of international administration established to supervise the fulfillment of these obligations. Each B and C mandatory guarantees (a) freedom of conscience and religion, subject only to the maintenance of public order and morals, (b) the prohibition of abuses such as the slave trade, and the arms and liquor traffic, (c) the prevention of the establishment of fortifications or military bases and of military training of the natives for other than police purposes, "and the defense of territory." This attempt to prevent the mandated territories from being used as military reservoirs was strengthened in the actual texts of the mandates themselves, where the use of troops was limited to the defence of the "local" territory. But as far as the French mandates were concerned, France sturdily opposed such a limitation both at the Peace Conference and in the League. In

[1] *Minutes of the Fourth Session*, Mandates Commission, A. 13, 1924, VI, p. 157.
[2] *Minutes of the First Session*, C. 416, M. 296 (1921), VI, p. 14.
[3] *O. J.*, 1923, p. 604. At the same session, the Council approved a declaration of the representative of South Africa to the effect that South Africa wished to confer British nationality on the German inhabitants of its mandate, provided that each inhabitant should be allowed to decline such nationality (cf. *Ibid.*, p. 659). Germany agreed to such action in a Memorandum of Oct. 23, 1923, which also provided that Germans in Southwest Africa and their children should not be liable for military service against the German Reich for a period of thirty years; it contained other guarantees in regard to language, schools, churches and coöperatives. Cf. Cmd. 2220 (1924). That the inhabitants of the Class A mandates have a distinct nationality is implied from the terms of the Covenant. Cf. p. 356.

the mandates for Togo and Cameroons, France made a reservation insisting on the right to train natives in order "to repel an attack or for the defense of the territory, outside of that subject to mandate."[1] Under this provision, she may ship negro troops from her mandates to fight along the Rhine. France has not, however, made use of this reservation to conscript natives in the Mandates. If this right is to be exercised at all, it will be apparently only in case of war.[2]

In addition to the obligations defined in the Covenant, the actual texts under which each mandatory holds its territory establishes four definite obligations. Each power promises not only to prohibit the slave trade, but eventually to emancipate the slaves in its mandated territory. As a safeguard against the abuses arising out of contract labor, the League insists that mandatory powers protect natives against fraud in labor contracts. Likewise, the mandates prohibit all forced labor, except for essential public works. They also provide that no land shall be transferred from natives to non-natives without governmental consent.[3]

Despite the extent of these obligations, the mandatory powers have gone beyond them in putting the trusteeship principle into effect. The British have made witchcraft punishable in Tanganyika, where they have also established auction markets to do away with grasping middlemen.[4] Education in the mandated territories is free, and in at least one mandate, Nauru, it is compulsory.[5] In Syria, the French increased the number of schools from 14 to 1,609 between 1919 and May, 1921. Japan provides dormitories for some native children in her Pacific mandate and grants a subsidy to Christian missions established there.[6]

11. THE MANDATES COMMISSION

Important as are the obligations assumed by the mandatory powers, the distinctive feature of the mandate system is the accountability of each mandatory to an impartial international

---

[1] Cf. Art. 3, French mandate for the Cameroons.
[2] Buell, *Native Problem in Africa*, Vol. II, p. 281.
[3] Cf. Art. 5, British Mandate for East Africa.
[4] *Report on Tanganyika*, p. 12.
[5] *Report on the Administration of Nauru* (1922), No. 20, F. 295, p. 10.
[6] Buell, "Backward Peoples Under the Mandate System," *Current History*, June, 1924.

THE MANDATES COMMISSION

body. Because of the absence of such accountability the Berlin Act proved a failure.[1] In an effort to overcome this defect, the revised Berlin Act of 1919 provided for the compulsory arbitration of disputes relating to the application of the convention.[2] But these obligations to promote the "well-being of backward peoples" are scarcely more justiciable in a court of law than the question of what constitutes a "fair price" or a "reasonable return" in ordinary municipal jurisprudence.[3] These questions have accordingly led in America to the creation of a new type of administrative tribunal, such as the Interstate Commerce Commission and state public utility boards. Similarly, the League of Nations has established a new type of semi-administrative tribunal, composed not of lawyers but of colonial experts—called the Mandates Commission.

In establishing the mandate system, the Council of the League "confirmed" and "defined" the degree of authority as well as the obligations of each mandatory power.[4] It supervises not only the execution of the obligations definitely assumed by these powers, but also the whole administration of the mandated territory.[5] To advise the Council, the Covenant provides for a permanent Commission which shall examine the annual reports which each mandatory is obliged to make. This Commission is composed of

[1] Even in this Act an attempt was made to create some form of machinery. Art. 8 provided that in all the territory covered by the Convention where no power exercises the rights of sovereignty or of a protectorate, "The International Navigation Commission of the Congo, established by virtue of Article 17, will be charged to watch over the application of the principles proclaimed and consecrated by this Declaration [which include the provisions in regard to the protection of the natives, etc.]. In every case where difficulties relative to the application of the principles established by the present declaration should arise, the interested government could appeal to the good offices of the International Commission, deferring to it the examination of the facts which have given rise to difficulties." Act of Feb. 26, 1885, 14 De Clercq, *Recueil des traités de la France*, 462.

[2] Art. 12, Act of Sept. 10, 1919, *Treaties of the U. S.*, Vol. III, p. 3740.

[3] *International Harvester Co.* v. *Kentucky*, 233 U. S. (1913), 216.

[4] According to article 22, "the degree of authority," etc., shall, "if not previously agreed upon by the Members of the League," be defined by the Council. It was the contention of some members of the Assembly, notably Lord Robert Cecil, that the words "Members of the League" should be interpreted to mean the Assembly. But the Council, following the Hymans Report, decided that it meant merely the principal Allied and Associated Powers.

[5] The Hymans' Report, *O. J.*, Sept., 1920, pp. 334, 339.

ten members, five of whom must come from countries which do not hold mandates, and none of whom may be a governmental representative at the time of his appointment. A representative of the International Labor Office also serves in an advisory capacity in regard to labor matters.[1]

This Commission meets annually in Geneva, at present in the latter part of June. Its members meanwhile are kept in touch with the operations of the system through the mandates section of the League Secretariat. Special sessions may also be called. Each of the fourteen mandatories is required to submit to the League an annual report, which is carefully examined by the Commission. In order fully to explain these reports, representatives of the mandatory powers attend the sessions of the Commission. In 1924 South Africa was represented by the administrator of Southwest Africa while France was represented by the former Secretary-General of the French High Commissioner for Syria. In studying these different reports the Commission is frequently obliged to interpret the obligations which the mandatory governments have assumed. It has expressed the opinion that the establishment of religious spheres of influence is not a violation of the religious freedom guaranteed in the mandates if necessary to stop missionary quarrels. On the other hand, it believed that the voluntary enlistment of a native of a mandated territory in an adjoining body violates the military obligations of the mandatory power.[2] At last, a system has come into existence whereby obligations may really be interpreted and applied.

As part of its supervisory tasks, the Mandates Commission

[1] Constitution, *O. J.*, Nov.–Dec., 1920, p. 87. A German was appointed in 1927.
[2] Cf. Report of Work of the Third Session, Annex 13, *Minutes of the Third Session*, cited. As the Commission is only an advisory body to the Council, its opinions have no legal weight as such. At the third Assembly, the representative of New Zealand declared that New Zealand "is willing and anxious to receive suggestions and advice from either the Permanent Mandates Commission or the Council of the League, but she cannot admit that the Permanent Commission has power to interpret for her the meaning of the Covenant, or to dictate to her what procedure she should adopt in her endeavours to perform her duties to the League." *Records of the Third Assembly*, Plenary Meetings, p. 147. As in the case of the Minority treaties, the Mandates also provide that disputes between a mandatory and another member of the League which cannot be settled by negotiation, shall be referred to the World Court. One case has already arisen, cf. p. 461.

inquires into the entire spirit of the administration of these regions. As a woman member of the Commission declared to the third Assembly, "We feel it our duty to be watchful; we have to safeguard the interests of men and women who are not capable of defending themselves, who have very little knowledge of our ways and methods, and who very often do not understand those ways and methods, even when they are unquestionably meant for their benefit. We must try, as far as we can, to look with their eyes and feel with their hearts, and sometimes both their eyes and their hearts are suspicious. We have to scrutinize every decree and every ordinance given by the diverse administrations, and see if there may not possibly be some loophole that will permit abuse. We have to look to it that the good and useful dispositions laid down in the ordinances are also well and justly applied, for the application of the law is, indeed, still more important than the law itself." [1]

Upon its own initiative, the Commission may make inquiries into the whole sphere of mandatory administration. Under this authority, it has prepared excellent surveys in regard to land tenure, public health, education, and labor.[2] It has called attention to the dangers arising out of the presence of Chinese indentured labor in Samoa, although such labor is not forbidden by the mandate.[3] On the other hand, natives may petition the Commission in regard to alleged abuses in administration. All such petitions must be sent to the Secretariat of the League through the mandatory government concerned. To these petitions the government concerned should attach its comments. While this procedure has been criticised on the ground that some governments will pigeonhole petitions, the Council and Assembly believed this means was necessary to restrict petitions originating from irresponsible agitators.[4] However, sources other than the inhabitants of mandated territories, such as anti-slavery societies, may petition directly to the chairman of the Mandates Commis-

[1] The late Mme. Wicksell, who was delegated by the Commission to attend the Assembly. *Records of the Third Assembly*, Plenary Meetings, p. 144.
[2] Cf. the annexes to the Third Session, cited.
[3] Report on Second Session, *O. J.*, Nov., 1922, p. 1267.
[4] Cf. the remarks of the Haitian delegate at the 1922 Assembly, to which Dr. Nansen replied that because of the great strength of public opinion, no government could secretly withhold a complaint. *Records*, cited, p. 156.

sion who should decide whether such petitions are deserving of attention. If so, they shall be communicated to the governments concerned for their comments. Petitions correctly submitted to the League are examined at the meeting of the Mandates Commission [1] which decides what petitions should be circulated to the Council and the Members of the League.

Government representatives have been allowed to participate in meetings of the Commission where these petitions were being considered, but this right so far has been denied to the petitioners. In September, 1926, the Commission asked the League Council, (a) to give its opinion as to whether the Commission should grant audience to petitioners in exceptional cases, and (b) to request the mandatory powers to submit in future fuller accounts of their administration to the Mandates Commission. The mandatory governments objected to these proposals and the Council decided against both of them.[2]

12. THE RUANDA FRONTIER

In bringing out the facts of mandatory administration, the Commission calls attention to abuses and to the violation of the obligations which the powers have assumed. The Commission is only an advisory body, and neither the Council nor the Assembly, both of which discuss mandate matters, is a super-state. Nevertheless, these bodies can organize a powerful moral pressure, as was forcefully illustrated in the case of the Ruanda-Urundi frontier. In December, 1921, Belgium and Great Britain drew a boundary line between their mandates in former German East

[1] Cf. Council Resolution, *O. J.*, March, 1923, pp. 211, 298. In passing upon the merits of these petitions, the Mandates Commission is usually obliged to accept the accompanying comments of the Government. To quote a member in the case of the Adjigo petition, "The Mandates Commission, not having the data necessary for a proper appreciation of the claims of the two families, could only bow before the decision of the responsible local Government. . . ." The Chairman took the same ground, since the Mandates Commission "was not in a position to make an inquiry upon the spot." The Commission finally adopted a resolution stating that from "the information given by the mandatory Power," the decision in question was justified, but saying that the "Commission has no doubt that the local authorities will abstain from taking any severe measures which are not absolutely necessary for the maintenance of public order." *Minutes of the Fourth Session*, A. 13, 1924, VI, pp. 41, 140.

[2] *O. J.*, February, 1927, p. 153; *O. J.*, April, 1927, p. 348.

Africa, in such a manner as to give the British a right of way for the Cape-to-Cairo railway. As a result of this division, however, the tribes of the native kingdom of Ruanda were cut in two, which brought about great hardship and suffering.[1] Missionaries drew the attention of the Mandates Commission to this frontier at the 1922 meeting [2] and asked that the boundary be modified. After inquiring into the matter, the Commission placed the question before the League Council which in turn placed the facts before Belgium and England.[3] Following correspondence between the governments of these two countries, the Council authorized the rectification of the frontier.[4] This action was the outcome, not of any diplomatic haggling nor of ambitious maneuvers by either power, but solely of a desire to advance the interests of the natives themselves. In fact, Great Britain sacrificed the right of way for the Cape-to-Cairo railway out of consideration of the trusteeship principle.[5]

13. THE BONDELZWARTS AFFAIR

A more difficult question arose with the Bondelzwarts rebellion of 1922 in the mandate of Southwest Africa, administered by the Union of South Africa, a British Dominion. In 1921 the South African Administrator imposed an excessive dog tax—$5 for the first dog and $50 for five dogs—which the Bondelzwarts tribe was unable to pay. Native agitators took advantage of the tax to stir up a "rebellion," which the South African authorities suppressed with a force of 390 men, four machine guns and two bombing planes. Sixteen bombs were dropped by the planes the first day, and more than a hundred men, women and children were killed.[6] A black delegate from Haiti brought the incident to the

[1] Described in *Rapport sur l'administration Belge du Ruanda-Urundi* (Chambre des Représentants) (1922–23), p. 6.
[2] *Minutes of the Second Session*, Mandates Commission, cited, pp. 97–99.
[3] *O. J.*, Nov., 1922, p. 1178; Nov., 1923, p. 1273.
[4] "Correspondence regarding the modification of the Boundary between British Mandated Territory and Belgian Mandated Territory in East Africa," Cmd. 1974, and 1794 (1923).
[5] At its 1923 session the Commission also called attention to the frontier between the British and French Cameroons which had injured certain tribes. At the 1924 session the British and French representatives declared that their governments were ready to make adjustments. *Minutes of the Fourth Session*, p. 133.
[6] *Minutes of the Third Session*, cited, pp. 118, 123.

attention of the Assembly of the League at its meeting in September, 1922.[1] The Assembly unanimously passed a resolution calling on the Mandates Commission to look into the matter. The South African government also promised to investigate. But when the commission began its inquiry at its meeting of August, 1923, it found that the South African government had failed to present an official report, and the only data before the commission was a report of a local commission of inquiry—both a majority and a minority report—the former of which the South African government had disavowed. Consequently the commission had no authoritative material upon which to base its study.

After a rigorous examination of the representatives of South Africa, Major Herbst and Sir Edgar Walton, the Mandates Commission presented a report to the Council which severely criticised the South African government for its failure to keep the promise it had made to the Assembly. The majority of the commission believed that the dog tax and other measures taken by the South African authorities were unduly severe, and the report implied that no rebellion would have occurred had a more intelligent policy been followed. The Bondelzwarts affair was "such an incident as has occurred in the same territory at other periods." But a new principle—that of trusteeship—had come into existence under the mandate system.[2] In a statement made by the Chairman of the Commission, Marquis Theodoli, it was said, "As far as the mandated territories are concerned, the Covenant of the League of Nations, in general, and Article 22 in particular, has profoundly and substantially altered colonial law and colonial administration," because of the acceptance of the "trusteeship" principle. "This principle involves the adoption of an attitude toward the various interests and administrative practices very different from the former. First in importance come the interests of the natives, secondly the interests of the whites. The interests of the whites should only be considered in relation to the direct or indirect

---

[1] Minute 31, *Records of the Third Assembly,* Plenary Meetings. Before this, however, the South African representative had informed the Assembly that a special commission had been appointed to investigate the affair. Minute 18, *ibid.* It is significant that such representatives of the darker peoples as India and Haiti have taken the lead in defending the position of mandated inhabitants at the Assembly.

[2] "Report on the Bondelzwarts Rebellion," Annex 8 b, Annexes, cited.

EXTENSION OF MANDATE PRINCIPLE 367

exercise of protection over the natives."[1] While the majority of the commission would not express themselves so strongly, there is no doubt that the mandate system and the League have advanced the trusteeship principle much further than ever before. The obligations accepted under the mandates are much more strict and definite than the obligations in the Act of Berlin; and for the first time in history, a system of international machinery is carrying these obligations into effect.

While the Mandates Commission did nothing spectacular in the Bondelzwarts affair, while it did not prevent the rebellion nor secure the immediate adoption of all the remedies proposed, it none the less established the responsibility of a mandatory power to the outside world.[2] As in the case of the Corfu affair,[3] the machinery of the League was used to concentrate the burning light of world opinion on powers which otherwise might disregard their obligations with impunity.

14. THE EXTENSION OF THE MANDATE PRINCIPLE

Perhaps the membership of the Commission might be enlarged. The Pan-African Congress has suggested the addition of a negro member; while Sir Frederick Lugard, a distinguished colonial administrator and now a member of the Mandates Commission, has suggested that a representative from the United States would be valuable because of our experience with the negro in the South.[4] The growing practice of sending the officials actually in charge

---

[1] Annexes, cited, p. 296.
[2] In 1925 a rebellion broke out in Syria which was repressed by the French authorities with the utmost severity. The Mandates Commission had not been able to remove the causes of this rebellion or to prevent it from taking place. But it did hold the French authorities responsible and brought about an improvement in administration. Miss E. P. MacCallum, who has made the most careful study of the question, says, "Without the Permanent Mandates Commission the Syrian rebellion . . . might have been as barren of achievement as the Moroccan rebellion. But with the publicity attendant upon the work of the Commission serving to intensify the public demand for fulfilment of the spirit of the mandate, France has not cared to force Syrian Nationalists to renounce the chief principles for which they fought. Military defeat was not accompanied by moral defeat." *The Nationalist Crusade in Syria*, p. 248.
[3] Cf. p. 630.
[4] "The Mandates Commission," 242 *Quarterly Review* (1924).

of mandatory administration to the meetings of the Mandates Commission will increase their feeling of responsibility. It is to be hoped, moreover, that the Commission will soon be allowed to send its own representatives to inspect mandated territories. At present it is virtually obliged to accept the statement of governments, especially when they come in conflict with complaints from the natives. The Commission has no way of independently checking the facts. The greatest improvement of the mandate system would be its extension to all parts of the colonial world. Already international obligations have been assumed under the Act of Berlin for most of the African possessions. Article XXIII of the Covenant also requires all members "to secure just treatment of the native inhabitants of territories under their control." But these obligations are as yet ineffective because they have not been vitalized by having them placed under the supervision of a body such as the Mandates Commission. One of the greatest steps toward world peace would be a treaty signed by the ten leading colonial powers, guaranteeing the Open Door in their colonies and just treatment for the natives, as provided in the mandates, subject to the supervision of the Mandates Commission. Such a treaty is at the present time perhaps beyond the scope of practical politics, especially since the present disposition of the League Council appears to be to confine strictly the activities of the Commission. At its meeting of December, 1923, the Council declined to consider the possibility of placing the question of slavery in the hands of the Commission out of fear of extending its power.[1] But if political and especially nationalistic feeling prevents the immediate extension of these principles, it should at least be possible to carry out the suggestion made by Sir Harry Johnston several years ago, to establish a great International Council of Advice which would recommend colonial policies for the powers to follow.[2] The assumption of such advisory duties by the

[1] *O. J.*, Feb., 1924, p. 331. Cf. also p. 364.
[2] "International Interference in African Affairs," 18 *Journal of the Society of Comparative Legislation*, 26. The French minister of colonies, M. Albert Sarraut, said in 1923, "Reforms accomplished in one place will inevitably penetrate elsewhere. Whether we like it or not, colonial questions have ceased to be purely national; they have become international, placed under the eyes of the world." *Afrique française*, 1923, p. 254. The Mandates Commission has already exercised an indirect influence on colonies proper.

EXTENSION OF MANDATE PRINCIPLE

Mandates Commission would be an important step in making really effective the trusteeship principle—the only policy which morally justifies the continuance of imperialist control over the backward parts of the world.[1] Moreover, the League and the International Labor Office may contribute to the improvement of conditions in backward areas through the conclusion of international conventions safeguarding native rights, such as the Slavery Convention of 1926.[2]

Many mandates such as the Cameroons and Togo are administered as integral parts of adjoining colonies. In criticising mandatory administration, the Commission thus criticises colonial administration. At the fourth session, the liquor policy in the British colonies in West Africa was criticised by Sir Frederick Lugard, *Minutes of the Fourth Session*, p. 137.

[1] The open door in relation to the mandate system is discussed on p. 453.
[2] Cf. p. 280.

CHAPTER XVI

SELF–DETERMINATION AND BACKWARD PEOPLES

1. Imperialism and Force.—2. The Demand for Independence.—3. The Attempt at Assimilation.—4. Autonomy and Indirect Administration.—5. Colonial Legislatures.—6. Communal Representation.—7. Prevention of Deadlocks.—8. The Peaceful Emancipation of Colonies.—9. The Example of Mesopotamia.—10. The Example of Syria.—11. International Intervention.

1. IMPERIALISM AND FORCE

It is a striking fact that the colonial empires of the world have been established for the most part by force—that the backward peoples under the direct control of the whites have submitted to this rule only at the flourish of the sword. Imperialism has thus violated the principle of democracy. Troubled by this inconsistency, some imperialistic powers have made a show of obtaining the consent of the natives to the establishment of European and American control. In a declaration made to the United States (as well as to European powers), the Independent Association of the Congo based its territorial claims in Africa upon "treaties with the legitimate sovereigns" in the regions concerned.[1] Elsewhere, dozens of agreements were made between adventurers or military officials and natives, in which the latter "voluntarily" accepted the white man's control.

However logical such methods of recognizing the principle of self-determination might be in international law, from the moral point of view they were a mere sham,—a legalistic salve for the conscience of European foreign offices. In the case of ignorant African chieftains, these treaties were often the product of fraud, attended by no consideration except a pair of boots or a few bottles of gin. In the case of more advanced native kingdoms, such as Korea, Tunis and Morocco, they were signed by the local sover-

---

[1] Declaration of April 22, 1884, Hertslet, *Map of Africa by Treaty* (2d ed.), Vol. I, p. 244.

THE DEMAND FOR INDEPENDENCE 371

eigns under duress. It is a curious type of morality which, while shocked at the open violation of the principle of self-determination, sanctions such an artificial pretense of adhering to its letter. It would be much better if the great powers frankly admitted that the principle of self-determination could not be respected in the case of peoples chronically unable or unwilling to recognize certain minimum obligations to the outside world.[1]

There is no doubt that unnecessary bloodshed and deception were used by imperial powers in fastening their control upon Africa, America and Asia. Until recently many governments attempted to shift the responsibility for many of these incidents on to private Chartered Companies. Subject to slight governmental control, these companies often neglected the interests of the natives, partly because they attempted to combine governmental administration with commercial profit—a mixture which usually ends in disaster.[2] But from the narrow point of view of imperialism, the chartered company system was advantageous, in that the acts of these companies could be disavowed by governments when necessary, while their territorial acquisitions still remained under the national flag.

At the present time, the chartered company has nearly passed out of existence. Within the British Empire, there remains the British North Borneo Company, against whose rule at one time charges were made.[3] In the neighboring territory of Sarawak, an Englishman of the House of Brooke holds kingly sway, subject to the protection of the Empire. The control of the South Africa Company over Southern Rhodesia was terminated in 1923 and over Northern Rhodesia in April, 1924. Several chartered companies operate in Portuguese Mozambique. As a rule, however, colonial territories are now directly controlled by governments.

2. THE DEMAND FOR INDEPENDENCE

Great as the abuses in establishing control over such territories have been, most of these unsavory incidents have now become

[1] For further treaties, cf. Hertslet, *Map of Africa by Treaty*, passim. For the disregard of the principle of self-determination in the case of native peoples by the United States, cf. p. 33.
[2] For a discussion of these companies, cf. P. S. Reinsch, *Colonial Government* (1902), Ch. V; Lugard, cited, pp. 18 ff.
[3] Cf. p. 342.

past history. The practical problem to be decided is to what extent the principle of self-determination should affect the administration of these territories at the present time and in the future.

It is all very well to say, as did Senator Hoar in opposing the annexation of the Philippines, that the principle of the "consent of the governed" should apply to the backward peoples of the world as well as to the whites. This conception, however, appears to be unknown to many parts of the tropical world. There are few instances where native governments in these regions have been based on the democratic principle.[1] Native chieftains have ruled because they were strong. In some cases the ruler would be an alien conqueror, as in North Africa, where the Arab invader had subjected the native Berber. In other cases, he would be a native despot, as in Benin, Uganda, Dahomey, Zululand, or in many of the native states of India, oppressing his subjects in ways undreamt of by white invaders.[2] In still other cases, native tribes carried on bitter internecine wars, in which there was no security for life or property belonging to the native, not to mention the foreigner.

If the backward regions should immediately and indiscriminately be given their freedom in the name of self-determination, there is a practical certainty that the old order of things would be restored,—that the masses of the population would be oppressed by native rulers and exploited by white adventurers, subject to no governmental control.[3] When natives replaced Americans in the administration of the Philippine government, governmental efficiency underwent a slump.[4] As a result of the partial withdrawal of British control from Egypt in 1922, the different branches of the government were thrown into almost anarchical confusion from which they are only beginning to emerge.[5]

Nevertheless, if a plebiscite should be taken among the back-

---

[1] Some Oriental scholars allege that the ancient communal organization of India, etc., was upon a democratic basis. Cf. R. Mukerjee, *Democracies of the East* (1923), Chs. XI and XII.
[2] Lugard, cited, p. 17.
[3] Cf. p. 317.
[4] Wood-Forbes Report (1919), H. R. 325, 67th Cong., 2d sess., p. 45. Cf. D. R. Williams, *The United States and the Philippines* (1924), Chs. VII, VIII.
[5] "Egypt and the Sudan," *Round Table*, Sept., 1924.

THE DEMAND FOR INDEPENDENCE

ward peoples ruled by white administrators to-day, it is probable that the vote for "independence" would be overwhelming. In any country, and especially among Oriental peoples, such questions would be decided not upon a basis of reason but of sentiment. In making the decision, the inhabitants would pay little attention to the question of whether the rule of the colonial power has been good or bad. It is significant that movements for independence, whether in India or Egypt, become strongest when the material prosperity in these countries, which has resulted from European rule, has been greatest. The fundamental paradox of the trusteeship principle is that the more education and the more prosperity a backward people derives from its colonial status, the more importunate become its demands for independence. "They see a freedom and power of which their fathers never dreamt, and they want it." [1] Usually education and prosperity increase the vociferousness of this demand out of all proportion to the peoples' capacity for self-government.

As a result of the World War and of the gospel of self-determination, which accompanied it, the colored peoples of the world have become more insistent than ever upon obtaining their freedom. If this gospel was good for the oppressed nationalities of Europe, why should it not be good for the oppressed peoples of Africa and Asia? The non-coöperative movement in India under the leadership of Gandhi; the agitation in Egypt against British rule; the Korean revolution of 1919 against Japan; the revolts in Syria and Mesopotamia; the nationalistic movements in Lybia, Tunis and West Africa; the establishment of the "Republic of the Riff" in Spanish Morocco; the military defeats of Italy and Spain in North Africa, and the demands for independence in the Philippines and Porto Rico are indications of the mutterings of this other-world—mutterings which are not based so much on economic considerations as upon the mere sentimental desire to be "free."

In the face of such demands, a colonial power animated by the trusteeship principle is placed in a serious dilemma. Should it recognize the demands for independence at once, the masses in these colonies would probably suffer and their welfare would be neglected. At the same time, it cannot be definitely determined whether a people can really govern itself unless full responsibility

[1] Willoughby, *Race Problems in the New Africa*, p. 234.

is placed upon it—a boy cannot learn to swim without getting in the water. At the present stage of knowledge, we do not know whether the difficulties which the non-whites frequently have with their governments are due to racial incapacity or merely to social inexperience. The question whether the outside world is justified in complaining of bad government in any country depends upon the point of view. Even if one should answer the question, "Am I my brother's keeper?" in the negative—especially when the brother does not want to be "kept"—it would not necessarily follow that the principle of self-determination should be universally applied. As we have seen, native governments may not only fail to protect their own subjects but they may fail to fulfill those international obligations upon which the world now insists, before a government can be recognized.

On the other hand, if a colonial power assumes the attitude that it knows what is best for its dependent peoples, and if it believes that they will never be able to govern themselves, it is bound to have chronic revolts on its hands, which will violate the trusteeship principle and prevent the economic development of the territory for the benefit of the world. Government by force is one way out—but it is a policy which democracies can indefinitely maintain only with the greatest difficulty. A more hopeful alternative would be to assume, tentatively at least, that the backward peoples will eventually be able to govern themselves. Acting upon this assumption, a colonial power would adopt educational and political policies designed to fit its colonials gradually for the task of self-government. This is the policy adopted by the United States in the Philippines. The policy of gradual emancipation is by no means simple. The greater the liberty subject peoples acquire, the greater their capacity for criticism becomes. Once given autonomy, a long period of time will be necessary to determine whether or not the natives are capable of self-government—a period in which the colonizing power must exercise infinite patience and sympathy. If three centuries were necessary to teach the whites democracy, the colored peoples cannot learn it in a day. After a long period of time, it may be demonstrated that the colored peoples cannot govern themselves. But it should be reiterated that this question can be determined only by imposing responsibility upon their own shoulders. It would be unfair, moreover, to exact more severe standards from such peoples—as we are too often wont to do—than we require of ourselves. The native may not make the same demands on government as a westerner. The world is justified in forcing its standards of "efficiency" on the backward regions, only when its real interests are legitimately involved.

3. THE ATTEMPT AT ASSIMILATION

Colonial empires follow two conflicting systems in their government of backward peoples, (1) the policy of assimilation, or (2) the policy of autonomy. Either policy may be inspired by the sentiment of trusteeship, but the application of the one leads to very different results than the other. The policy of assimilation aims to impress the culture, language, and institutions of the home country upon the native groups which happen to fall under its control. It is the old policy of nationalism applied to the darker parts of the world. It means brusquely overturning native customs and tribal institutions, and the sudden transplanting of new institutions from the European world. Such appears to be the aim of Japan to-day in Korea—an aim sincerely held even by those Japanese who wish to be liberal toward Korea. One Japanese statesman has said, "The Korean people will be absorbed by the Japanese. They will talk our language, live our life, and will be an integral part of us. There are only two ways of colonial administration. One is to rule over the people as aliens. This you British have done in India, and therefore your Empire cannot endure. India must pass out of your rule. The second way is to absorb the people. This is what we will do. We will teach them our language, establish our institutions and make them one with us." [1]

From the administrative standpoint, the policy of assimilation means the direct administration of a colony by officials from the home government immediately responsible to the home authorities. It sometimes means that legislation enacted at home automatically applies to the colonies, regardless of different conditions; while the home parliament may at any time dictate the policies to be followed. It means that the actual conduct of

[1] Quoted, Buxton and Conwil-Evans, *Oppressed Peoples and the League of Nations*, p. 190.

colonial administration is in the hands of a home colonial office. Ordinarily, it means a policy of tariff assimilation; while it may mean the representation either appointive or elective of the natives in the home government.

In Algeria.—Due to the well-known centralizing tendencies of the French government it is natural that France should have originally followed the policy of assimilation and centralization in the government of her colonies. The most important experiment in this respect was in the case of Algeria—territory which is now considered as a prolongation of France. Between 1880 and 1895 Algeria was governed under the policy of *rattachements*—a policy of complete assimilation in which the governor-general was a mere figurehead. The system worked so badly, however, that in 1896 it was in part abandoned. In 1900 a law was passed giving Algeria financial autonomy. The control of many ministerial duties, hitherto administered in Paris, was likewise vested in the governor-general. Nevertheless, at the present time, he is still subject to the close supervision of the French Minister of the Interior; while certain services, connected with religion, justice and education are still controlled directly from Paris.[1] In February, 1919, the ballot was given to the natives above twenty-five who could meet certain property or educational qualifications.[2]

Colonial Representation.—In an effect to democratize this policy of assimilation, France has given some of her colonies representation in the Chambers at Paris. The French colonies in America, the possessions in India, Cochin China and Senegal have a total of ten representatives in the Chamber of Deputies and four in the Senate.[3] Algeria is also represented by six deputies and three senators. France is the only great power to follow this system of colonial representation. Not even the British Dominions send representatives to the London parliament.[4] Colonial repre-

---
[1] C. Humbert, *L'Œuvre française aux colonies*, Chs. V and VI; V. Piquet, *Colonisation française dans l'Afrique du Nord* (2d ed., 1914), Ch. IV.

[2] Girault, *Principes de colonisation et de législation coloniale*, 3d part, p. 149. For the situation before the reforms, cf. Piquet, *Les Réformes en Algérie* (1919), Parts I, II.

[3] Girault, *Principes de colonisation*, Part II, p. 677.

[4] Spain and Portugal, however, follow the French policy; the United States uses a compromise system, in which the Philippines, Porto Rico, Hawaii and Alaska are allowed to send commissioners or delegates who may speak but not vote in Congress.

THE ATTEMPT AT ASSIMILATION 377

sentation is too small to give the colonies a positive influence upon the colonial legislation of the home parliament; but it is large enough to give the colonial deputies a disproportionate influence in home politics with which they have no legitimate concern. These reasons have led to a demand in France for the abolition of this representation.[1]

A more satisfactory method of representing local interests is through Colonial Councils—advisory bodies to the ministries of colonial affairs in the home government. In 1883 a Superior Council of Colonies was established in France for this purpose—a body which, however, soon ceased to meet. In an effort to revive such an institution, three new bodies, containing colonial representatives and experts, a High Colonial Council, an Economic Council, and a Council of Colonial Legislation, were established in September, 1920.[2] The same system of advisory councils is followed in Belgium, Portugal and in England as far as India is concerned; while the establishment of a similar African Council in England has been proposed.[3]

The policy of assimilation has failed, not only in the case of colonial representation, but in its other aspects as well. Administrative centralization leads to bureaucracy and inefficiency, which is increased tenfold when the administration of distant dependencies, inhabited by strange peoples, is attempted. Under the policy of assimilation, the commerce of Indo-China and the Pacific Establishments, as well as of the French West Indies, has languished, while natives have become disorganized and rife with discontent. Although the sentiment of nationalism may not have the same foundation in the backward regions that it has in the Western world, the policy of assimilation is more unlikely to succeed with the former than with the latter, because the customs and institutions of the backward peoples are even more dissimilar to those of the west than are the differences between the dominant nationalities themselves. The attempt to break down native institutions will therefore provoke dissatisfaction, as it has done in Algeria and Korea. In destroying native institutions by in-

[1] J. Harmand, *Domination et colonisation*, Ch. 14; L. Vignon, *Une Programme de politique coloniale* (2d ed., 1919), p. 546; M. Ipranossain, *La Colonisation et le législateur colonial français* (1916), pp. 187–188.
[2] Girault, cited, Part II, p. 224.
[3] Lugard, *Dual Mandate in Tropical Africa*, p. 174.

troducing an entirely new system of officials from the home country, the only basis upon which native self-government can be erected is cast aside. Such is the situation confronting the British in India to-day. In order to establish an "efficient" government, the British originally introduced a foreign civil service, ignoring local institutions; and now that they are forced to give India self-government, there is no sound basis upon which to build.

4. AUTONOMY AND INDIRECT ADMINISTRATION

An opposite policy, colonial autonomy, or what the French call "la politique du protectorat" has been followed more successfully by the British Empire, Holland and, in her more successful colonies, by France herself.[1] This policy does not attempt to make Frenchmen or Britishers or Dutchmen out of blacks or Malays. It does not attempt to establish brand new institutions of government or to supplant native officials with armies of white men, controlled by a bureaucratic and centralized system, overloaded with authority at the top. On the contrary, the policy of autonomy aims gradually to mold native institutions so that they will readjust themselves to the demands of western moral and material life. While it stamps out practices which are incompatible with western standards of decency, such as the burning of widows in India or the pledging of wives for the payment of debt in Africa, it keeps the framework or cadres of native society as the soundest framework upon which to build up native communities capable of standing on their own feet. Instead of eliminating native rulers, as the French did in Algeria and as the Japanese have virtually done in Korea, it makes use of them in the government of the country. From the administrative standpoint, the policy of autonomy means, in the first place, the reduction of the authority of the home government and the increase of the power of the colonial authorities on the spot. Such is the policy followed in the British Empire, where the powers of colonial legislatures and governors are comparatively great.[2] As a result of experience

---

[1] Humbert, cited, Ch. V and pp. 107, 114, 175 and 205. However, the assimilation policy has been modified in Indo-China.

[2] Cf. Keith, *Constitution of the British Empire*, cited, pp. 120–136; 265–301.

AUTONOMY: INDIRECT ADMINISTRATION

with the opposite policy, France has also come to appreciate the advantages of decentralization. In at least three groups of colonies, she has delegated part of the supervisory work of the French colonial office to governors-general, who preside over federations of colonies, each of which is administered by a lieutenant-governor or a similar official. This system is followed in West Africa and Equatorial Africa and in Indo-China.[1] By this means colonial offices are relieved of much detail; instead of actively administering colonies, they merely exercise control.

As far as non-Europeanized natives are concerned, colonial autonomy or the "protectorate" policy usually means "indirect administration"—the government of tribes through their own native chieftains and institutions. Under the system of indirect rule the European government recognizes and develops the native authority. In Nigeria native courts try the majority of cases to which natives are parties. The Moslem courts of Northern Nigeria may even impose the death penalty, subject to review by the British governor. Natives are confined in prisons in charge of native wardens. Perhaps the most important feature of indirect rule is the Native Treasury. The British authorities turn over half the taxes to native treasuries of which there are 61 in Northern Nigeria having an income of about $3,500,000. These funds are administered by chiefs and their councils, in accordance with a budget drawn up in consultation with the British authorities. These funds are used to pay salaries to native officials and to European engineers or doctors who work for the native administration. They are also used for the construction of schools, roads and native agriculture. All of these activities are controlled by the British authority; but the aim of indirect rule is to place real administrative responsibility upon native institutions. This system is applied in Nigeria, Uganda and Tanganyika, and to a certain extent in the Belgian Congo.[2]

In Egypt, a country of a more advanced civilization, the British also applied the same principle of working through native authorities.[3] English "advisers" were found in the different Egyptian

[1] Cf. P. Charmeil, *Les gouverneurs généraux des colonies françaises* (1922).
[2] Cf. Buell, *Native Problem in Africa*, Ch. 42.
[3] For Egypt's status, cf. p. 478; cf. The Earl of Cromer, *Modern Egypt* (1908), Vol. II, Ch. 39.

ministries, and also throughout the provinces. The actual administration remained in the hands of the Egyptians, subject to this type of control, the British consul-general being the final authority to which the Egyptian government was responsible. It was the tendency of these English "advisers" to interfere directly with the Egyptian administration—instead of merely supervising it—which increased the growing dissatisfaction with British rule before the War. The internal administration of Egypt is now in native hands except for British financial and judicial advisers.

While other countries do not appear to have placed undivided authority upon local officials to as great an extent as have the British, they have nevertheless undertaken to secure the collaboration of the natives. In the Dutch East Indies, an important native official, called the Regent, assists in the administration of each district.[1] France follows a similar policy in her protectorates of Tunis and Morocco, where the traditional forms of government are in most respects retained. Legislation takes the form of royal decree, countersigned, however, by the French resident-general who has general supervision over the government. Certain native affairs are controlled by native ministers, subject to French "advice." In many matters affecting Europeans, however, French officials have full responsibility. Likewise there are two systems of courts, one for natives and one for foreigners.[2]

By making use of native officials in this manner, a colonial power may administer territory much less expensively than if it were obliged to place a white man in every office. Such a system in the long run will probably prove more efficient than the assimilative system, since native officials are more familiar with the intimate details of local government and the characteristics of native peoples than foreigners can possibly be. By developing native institutions, the policy of indirect administration gradually paves the way for ultimate native self-government which is extremely difficult to achieve where native institutions have been forcibly uprooted by the direct rule of the white man.

The chief danger from indirect administration is that the colo-

---

[1] Torchiana, *Tropical Holland*, pp. 166 ff.; Hayden, "Political Progress in the Netherlands Indies," *Atlantic Monthly*, Sept., 1924.

[2] V. Piquet, *Le Maroc* (3d ed., 1920), Chs. XV, XVI.

nial power will tolerate conditions of ignorance or oppression by local chiefs which direct administration would attempt to remove. This fact has been recognized by the Belgians in their mandate in regard to which it was declared that while the maintenance of native institutions was an indispensable instrument to all progress, indirect administration would result in sterility, unless it were accompanied by a "serious and patient education" of the natives.[1]

In some communities, where tribal institutions have disintegrated because of western ideas, indirect administration may be impossible. In such circumstances many colonial powers train natives to fill minor administrative positions which Europeans originally occupied. Moreover, they also encourage the functioning of native judicial tribunals, on the theory that such courts constitute a step toward representative institutions. Finally they establish advisory assemblies, which later may be converted into legislatures.

5. COLONIAL LEGISLATURES

Probably the British Empire has gone further than any other power in the policy of establishing colonial legislatures, about 25 of which exist in the crown colonies to-day. France has established a large number of advisory bodies, under different names, which must be consulted in regard to certain matters defined in the decrees establishing them.[2] A few of these bodies, such as the Councils-General in the "old colonies," the Financial Delegations of Algeria and Madagascar, and the Grand Council of Tunis have limited powers over finance. The Colonial Councils of Cochin China and of Senegal have certain legislative powers in regard to public works. As a rule, however, all of these bodies are under strict executive control. Advisory bodies with

[1] *Rapport sur l'Administration Belge du Ruanda et de l'Urundi*, Chambre des Représéntants, No. 384 (1922), p. 18. A severe criticism of the policy of indirect rule was made by Fitzpatrick, "Nigeria's Curse, The Native Administration," *National Review*, Dec., 1924, an article which brought forth a reply from the government in the House of Commons.

[2] These bodies are (1) Council-General, in the "old" colonies such as in the French West Indies, (2) Council of Administration, found in many African colonies, (3) Council of Government, found in each of the federations, (4) Colonial Council, in Senegal and Cochin China, (5) Financial Delegations in Algeria and Madagascar, (6) Grand Council in Tunis. There is no representative body in Morocco. For a survey cf. *Documents parlementaires, Chambre des Députés* (1922), 12 leg. sess., ord., pp. 3831 ff.

native members have been established in the Italian, Dutch and Japanese colonial empires, while the United States has established legislatures in the Philippines and Porto Rico.[1]

If the natives are really given adequate representation upon such bodies, these colonial assemblies should serve as valuable schools of self-government. For example, there was no native political assembly when Tunis was under the independent rule of the Bey. But in 1896, about ten years after the establishment of the French protectorate, France created a Consultative Conference, which was given a native section in 1907. In 1922 a sweeping innovation took place when this body was supplanted by a Grand Council with more extended powers, while in each district a caidat council was also established.[2] By such progressive steps, the natives may be gradually trained in the art of self-government.

Although in most of these colonial assemblies, the majority is composed of white residents, either appointed or elected, there is a growing tendency to include native elected members. Such a policy has been adopted in India, Nigeria, the Dutch East Indies, the Philippines, Porto Rico, Senegal, Algeria, Tunis and Cochin China, as well as elsewhere.[3] The native population is so backward in Central Africa that the elective principle is seldom used. Apparently the first British colony in this part of the world to authorize the election of natives to the Legislative Council, is Nigeria, in its constitution of 1922.[4] The principle has since been adopted in the Gold Coast and Sierra Leone.

---

[1] For the decree establishing the Italian "parliaments" in Tripoli, cf. *Bolletin Ufficiale*, Ministero delle Colonie, Maggio, 1920. But it was abrogated later, cf. *Afrique française* (1923), p. 206.

[2] For the text of this constitution, cf. *Afrique française* (1922), Sup., p. 247.

[3] In the Philippines and Porto Rico, the legislatures are made up wholly of natives. The Colonial Council of Senegal has 40 members, 20 elected by the French of Senegal, and 20 native chiefs indirectly elected. Most of the native section (21 members) of the Financial Delegations of Algeria, and also of the Grand Council of Morocco (18 members), are elected indirectly. In Cochin China, there are six Asiatic members of the Colonial Council, elected by native electoral colleges. In India two-thirds of the assembly is elected.

[4] Cf. Art. 20, Nigeria (Legislative Council), Order in Council (1922). The natives of Lagos and Calabar, having a gross annual income of 100 pounds, elect four members to the Legislative Council. *Statutory Rules and Orders* (1922), p. 291.

PREVENTION OF DEADLOCKS

6. COMMUNAL REPRESENTATION

As a rule, the representatives of the European population still outweigh the natives in the colonial assemblies of France, the British Empire, and Holland. If the natives were given the same numerical representation, they would hopelessly outnumber the whites and paralyze government effectiveness. Moreover, the native is much less fitted to serve in such a body than the white man. Consequently, many colonial powers have adopted the principle of "communal representation"—the representation of *groups* rather than of individuals. In the new government of India, voters select candidates according to race or religion, such as that of the Moslems or Sikhs; or according to economic or educational status, such as the landlords, university graduates, and industrial men, each voting for their own candidates. In many of their colonies, the French and British grant a certain number of seats to chambers of commerce and agriculture. The Legislative Council of the British colony of Kenya contains five elected Indian members, eleven elected Europeans, and one elected Arab, each chosen by the community concerned. The British government also nominates an unofficial member, a Christian missionary, to advise on matters concerning the natives, until they are fitted for direct representation.[1] The Indians who outnumber the Europeans two to one have declined to elect their members to the Kenya Council. They demand a common franchise. The principle of communal representation in Ceylon was recently condemned by a commission on the ground that it tended to magnify racial differences rather than develop a common inter-racial point of view.[2]

7. PREVENTION OF DEADLOCKS

As the history of government for the last three hundred years has shown, the mere grant of representative government—through an elected legislature—to a people, whether white, brown, or black, will not satisfy their desire to govern themselves. As long as actual executive power is retained in the hands of alien officials, responsible to outside authority, a representative legislature will

[1] Cmd. 1922 (1923), p. 13.
[2] "Report of the Special Commission on the Constitution" of Ceylon. Cmd. 3131 (1928), p. 99.

increase rather than diminish popular criticism. In the Philippines, the United States has established a native legislature with "general legislative power," subject to certain exceptions; but an American governor-general retains "supreme executive power." The governor-general is circumscribed by legislation passed by the native legislature; while the acts of this body may in turn be vetoed by the governor. Likewise, appointments of the governor-general must be confirmed by the Philippine Senate before they are effective. If the Philippine legislature refuses to vote the budget recommended by the governor-general, appropriations of the previous year automatically continue in force. But on other matters deadlocks are likely to occur, as soon as the American governor-general and the native legislature disagree, as they did during the administration of General Wood.[1] A representative legislature gives the natives a forum for criticism which becomes the more violent because they are not obliged, and in fact are unable, to carry into effect the policies which they advocate. When a representative legislature is once established, the natives are not likely to remain satisfied until *responsible* government is also granted—i. e., until they are also given some control over the administration.

In France and in the British Empire, colonial administrators have been alert to the difficulties inherent in the nature of mere representative governments. In the case of the Dominions, Great Britain has overcome them by a grant of responsible government in local affairs.[2] It has been impossible, however, to go this far in colonies inhabited by black and brown men who have had none of the experience of the white settlers of Canada or Australia. The danger of a representative legislature and an independent executive was forcibly illustrated by a rebellion in Jamaica, as a result of which, in 1866, the British authorities abolished the old constitution, and established a system which would not produce deadlocks between the two elements involved.[3]

"**Official Majorities.**"—In order to preserve the advantages of native representation and at the same time to prevent deadlocks,

---

[1] Buell, "What About the Philippines?" *Atlantic Monthly*, March, 1924. "America and the Philippines," *Round Table*, Dec., 1924.

[2] Cf. p. 204.

[3] Wrong, *Government of the West Indies*, pp. 44, 75.

PREVENTION OF DEADLOCKS

the first policy which the British Empire follows is that of "official majorities." At present, real representative legislatures, elected entirely by the local population, exist in only three crown colonies. Elsewhere, while they may have an elective element, legislatures usually contain a majority appointed, either from the local officials or the natives, by the Crown. As the government may require the official members to vote in its favor, deadlocks are easily broken, if indeed they ever arise.[1] A second development has recently come in the constitution of Ceylon. The demand for an elective majority in this colony was so strong that in 1923 the British government established a legislative council with only 12 official and 37 unofficial members, 29 of the latter being elected by the local inhabitants. Nevertheless, in order to prevent deadlocks, the constitution provides that if the governor is of opinion that the passage of a certain bill is of "paramount importance to the public interest," only the votes of the official members are counted. If a majority of such members approve a bill, it is passed.[2]

In 1928 a Royal Commission reported that this system had not worked satisfactorily because the Council, although it had power to block the actions of officials, was not responsible for administration. To train the Council in such responsibilities it proposed that it be divided up into seven executive committees, each responsible for the oversight of an administrative department,[3] and each committee headed by a Ceylonese minister responsible to the committee. The governor would retain his certificate power and would also have the right to refer measures back to the Council for reconsideration.

Diarchy.—A third means of breaking deadlocks in colonies not able fully to govern themselves is the means used in Malta and India, and known as diarchy. In Malta, the legislature has control over a native ministry and local affairs; but its power does not extend to "reserved" matters, "touching the public safety and defense of Our Empire and the general interests of Our subjects not resident in Malta. . . ." If the governor certifies that a bill concerns a reserved subject, the legislature can take no

---

[1] Cf. the famous dispatch of the Duke of Buckingham, August 17, 1868, quoted in C. Bruce, *Broad Stone of Empire* (1910), Vol. I, p. 234.
[2] Cf. Article XVI, *Statutory Rules and Orders* (1923), p. 1035.
[3] Cmd. 3131, cited.

further action.[1] Thus "two clearly defined concurrent systems of government" exist in Malta, the first relating to local affairs under the control of the people, the second, involving imperial matters, which are retained in British hands.

In the government of India, set up in the Act of 1919, the idea of diarchy is carried still further. In eight provinces native legislatures are given legislative power, except that they cannot withhold consent to such matters as the appropriation of salaries for British officials. They also have control over a native ministry, the members of which must be elected members of the legislature. This ministry is responsible for the administration of certain "transferred" subjects, such as education, and local self-government.[2] But the British governor retains control over "reserved" subjects, such as land laws, famine-relief, and the administration of prisons and justice. The provincial governor may certify that a law in regard to a "reserved" subject is necessary, and it thereupon goes into effect regardless of the wishes of the legislature. But the governor may not thus legislate in regard to the "transferred subjects" which are in native hands. In the provinces, therefore, the natives have representative legislatures, with native majorities; and they have a responsible government over certain "transferred" subjects, but subject to general British control. While this system marks an advance over a representative but irresponsible government, it has not yet worked satisfactorily in India. Indians assert that it is impossible to divide responsibility between an Indian legislature and a British governor, and that under this system, the British have retained control of the purse strings.[3] In the central government, no attempt has yet been made to introduce the principle of parliamentary responsibility. Deadlocks may be broken between the native legislature and the British executive by the power of the governor-general to certify that the passage of legislation is necessary, whereupon it goes into effect. The governor-general so far has used this power frequently to certify financial legislation.

In many respects, the Indian experiment is one of the most

[1] Malta constitution of April 14, 1921, Statutory Rules and Orders (1921), p. 1464.
[2] Government of India Act, 1919, 9 and 10 Geo. V, Ch. 101, p. 519.
[3] Chakravarty, "Ministerial Responsibility"; Sapru, "Way to Responsible Government," *The Indian Review*, January, 1924.

tremendous experiments which the world has ever beheld in the government of colored peoples. It is an attempt gradually to prepare a people for the time when they can govern themselves. The diarchy plan, however, has not had a fair trial in India because of the "non-coöperative" movement. In so far as it does not give provincial legislatures control over the executive services, it has the defects of such a government as we have established in the Philippines, except that they are not so numerous. It is the intention of the India Act gradually to transfer the remaining "reserved" subjects to the provincial legislatures. This Act also provided that after ten years the British government should appoint a commission to inquire into the desirability of further extending self-government in India. In January, 1928 a Statutory Commission, headed by Sir John Simon, sailed for India for this purpose. Diarchy therefore is planned to be a transitional system —a school of education—which will only have attained success when it is discarded.

8. THE PEACEFUL EMANCIPATION OF COLONIES

Under the trusteeship principle, imperialism should be merely a stage in the development of backward peoples, who are to be given their independence, either complete or qualified, when they have demonstrated their ability to govern themselves. In the past, a number of colonial powers have promised that their control would be relinquished as soon as these peoples could stand on their own feet. England before the World War repeatedly promised to withdraw from Egypt, and the United States has repeatedly, through one mouthpiece or another, promised the Philippines their independence when the requisite conditions are fulfilled. Hitherto, however, a colonial power has been the sole judge of what these conditions shall be and when they shall be regarded as fulfilled. Consequently, as its judgment is likely to be biased by self-interest, the promise may never be kept. In the past, brute force has been the chief test of a people's capacity to govern itself. If it has been strong enough to throw off outside control it has become free. Transition from subjection to independence, instead of being a gradual process, has been as abrupt as it has been violent. As long as such conditions prevail, the question of imperialism will always trouble the world.

This problem was definitely thrust upon the League of Nations in the peace treaties, in regard to Mesopotamia, Syria and the Lebanon, and Palestine and Transjordan. According to article XXII of the Covenant, "certain communities belonging to the Turkish Empire have reached a stage of development where their existence as independent nations can be provisionally recognised subject to the rendering of administrative advice and assistance by a Mandatory until such time as they are able to stand alone. The wishes of these communities must be a principal consideration in the selection of the Mandatory."

9. THE EXAMPLE OF MESOPOTAMIA

Though there is no indication that a popular consultation was held before the mandatory powers—France and England—were selected,[1] these powers, under League supervision, have nevertheless taken steps to recognize the provisional independence of some of the countries named. They have gone farthest in the case of Mesopotamia. Although a draft mandate for Mesopotamia was drawn up, it was never approved by the Council, and Great Britain did not attempt to apply to Mesopotamia this form of control. Instead she recognized Feisal as king of Iraq.[2] In 1921, a report was submitted to the Council of the League stating that "the recognition of a local Sovereign modified to some extent the position of the Mandatory Power," and led the British government to believe that its obligations could best be fulfilled through a treaty. But such an agreement "is not intended as a substitute for the Mandate, which will remain the operation document defining the obligations undertaken by His Majesty's Government on behalf of the League of Nations."[3] On October 10, 1922, the British government signed a treaty of alliance with the King of Iraq, which provided that Great Britain should be represented in Mesopotamia by a High Commissioner; the British should have control over the appointment of foreign advisers, and over financial and

---

[1] The King-Crane Report indicated quite the contrary. Cf. *Editor-Publisher*, Sup., Dec. 2, 1922.
[2] Cf. p. 89.
[3] The Fisher Report, *O. J.*, Dec., 1921, p. 215.

foreign affairs; the king of Iraq should draw up an Organic Law insuring protection of minorities; the open door should be guaranteed; Mesopotamia should have the right of diplomatic representation abroad as agreed upon with Great Britain; Great Britain should undertake to secure the admission of Mesopotamia as a member of the League as soon as possible. Differences in interpretation of the alliance should be submitted to the World Court.[1] In an announcement accompanying the treaty, Great Britain declared that as soon as the frontiers of Iraq were determined and the treaty ratified, Great Britain would endeavor to secure the admission of Iraq to the League "which affords," in its opinion, "the sole means by which the mandatory relation can be legally terminated." This alliance was followed by a protocol of April 30, 1923, which declared that the treaty of alliance would be terminated as soon as Iraq became a member of the League, "and in any case not later than four years from the ratification of peace with Turkey."[2] So far, however, the powers of the League of Nations over the British position in Mesopotamia remained undefined. It was finally clarified by the Council in September, 1924, in approving a communication from the British government in which the latter (a) assumed responsibility for the fulfillment by Mesopotamia of the pledges given in the treaty of alliance; (b) agreed to report annually to the Council as to the measures taken to carry out the terms of the alliance, (c) bound itself not to modify the alliance except with the Council's consent, and (d) consented to submit disputes between Great Britain and a member of the League as to whether the provisions of the alliance were being fulfilled, to the World Court.[3] As a result of this method of settlement, it appears that the League has about as much power of supervision of the British in Mesopotamia as of the French in Syria. At the same time, it also appears that the autonomy of Mesopotamia is greater than that of either Syria or Palestine. This does not seem to be due, however, to pressure from the

[1] Text, *O. J.*, Dec., 1922, pp. 1505, 1509. Cf. "Great Britain and the Iraq: An Experiment in Anglo-Asiatic Relations," *Round Table*, December, 1923.

[2] *O. J.*, July, 1923, p. 729. For the text of the Organic Law of July 10, 1924, cf. C. 412, 1921, VI. As part of the Mosul case the Council decided in 1925 that Iraq should remain under British mandate for 25 years. Cf. p. 55.

[3] *O. J.*, Oct., 1924, p. 1346.

League, but rather to pressure from the natives and the desire of the British public to withdraw.

10. THE EXAMPLE OF SYRIA

In Palestine, the situation has been complicated by the question of Zionism.[1] Here political independence would mean death to the political aspirations of the Jews. Consequently, the mandate makes fewer promises to the natives than in Syria and the Lebanon, where the mandate obliges France to frame an Organic Law within three years, and also "to enact measures to facilitate the progressive development of Syria and the Lebanon as independent States." Making allowances for religious and sectional differences, the French authorities divided up the country into four autonomous states—Damascus, Aleppo, the Alaouite State and the Jebel Druze. Each of these possessed a Council. Lebanon, the home of a Christian sect—the Maronites—was doubled in size and made independent of the rest of the country under the name of Greater Lebanon. In June 1922 a federation of the first three states was provisionally organized, but this was superseded in 1925 by yet another arrangement whereby Damascus and Aleppo were united to form the unitary state of Syria, while the Alaouite State and the Jebel Druze still remained separate political entities. Greater Lebanon in 1926 was recognized as an independent republic with a native president. France is represented throughout the mandated territories by a High Commissioner, whose function is not to govern, except in some exceptional cases, but to supervise native officials, "according to the necessities which have inspired Article 22 of the Covenant of the League of Nations." The police, navigation, mail and telegraph services have been under native control since January, 1924; while shortly all of the local administration will be in native hands, except the customs and matters affecting foreigners.[2]

In 1925 a serious revolt broke out in Syria; it was caused by misrule and lasted for two years.[3] In June, 1928, the French government finally allowed a Syrian Constituent Assembly to meet and

[1] Cf. p. 216.
[2] *Rapport sur la situation de la Syrie et du Liban*, Ministère des Affaires Étrangères, July, 1922–July, 1923, pp. 5, 12. Cf. A. Samné, *La Syrie* (1920), Chs. XX, XXI; J. Luquet, *Le Mandat A et l'organisation du mandat français en Syrie* (1923).
[3] Cf. p. 367.

draft a constitution. This body decided to establish a republic (rather than a kingdom), and made demands which were regarded as being incompatible with French mandatory control. The Constituent Assembly was therefore prorogued. (February, 1929.)

Inasmuch as the Class A mandates did not go into effect until the fall of 1922, the supervision of the League and the Mandates Commission has not yet had time to become effective. The Mandates Commission examined reports from these mandates for the first time at its fifth session in the fall of 1924. Complaints against the French in Syria have been bitter. Demanding independence, the Syrian nationalists insist that only a selfish imperialism retains France in Syria. But whatever selfish motives led France and Great Britain to establish their control over this part of the East, it seems obvious that had Syria and Palestine and Mesopotamia been given their independence in 1918, they would soon have been ground under the iron heel of Mustapha Kemal. While the establishment of this control may have been originally justified, the League, if it is to be effective, must eventually exert pressure upon Great Britain and France, to follow policies in Mesopotamia and Syria which are best suited to train the people for self-government, according to a reasonable standard, and to relinquish control, when, according to the impartial opinion of a body such as the Mandates Commission, the time has come for such a step.

11. INTERNATIONAL INTERVENTION

The world is confronted with the problem not only of freeing backward peoples from external control, when desirable, but also of extending such control should it become necessary in the future. As previous chapters have indicated, intervention in independent countries may be justified to suppress nuisances and to correct conditions which violate certain minimum standards exacted of every government by mankind. But intervention when exercised by a single power, responsible only to itself, is likely to be abused. There have been a number of cases where governments have seized upon the murder of an isolated subject in a backward country as a justification for its annexation. It is also a frequent occurrence for strong governments, when their subjects are thus murdered, to exact indemnities out of all proportion to the monetary value of the lives lost. The United States has, however, started a happy precedent of devoting part of such payments to the education in America of students from the country concerned—indemnities exacted from China and Persia now being used for that purpose.[1]

Thus in the past, legitimate grievances have been often used as pretexts to advance illegitimate ends. So far no clearly defined principles of intervention have been written into international law. What is of even more importance, no international agency has the power to decide whether or not these principles have been really violated, and whether or not an outside power is justified in intervening. No international organization has had the power to control such intervention to prevent its original justification from being used as a mere pretext for fastening on a backward country a permanent and unjustified form of control.

With the establishment of a League of Nations, however, a start has been made in establishing some form of international control over intervention. The League guarantees to all its members, including the "backward" governments of Ethiopia, Siam, or Liberia, territorial integrity and independence. If France should become involved in an altercation with Ethiopia the dispute would have to go before the League. If France intervened in Ethiopia without thus submitting the dispute, it would have violated the Covenant.[2] While the League guarantees its members against aggression, it will not protect them from wrongdoing. In case of the chronic unwillingness or inability of a backward government to fulfil its obligations to the world, the League would undoubtedly decide that intervention under its

---

[1] The indemnity exacted by England from Egypt for the Stack murder was $2,500,000; that exacted by the United States from Persia as a result of the fatal attack on Vice Consul Imbrie in July, 1924, was $60,000, to go to his widow, and about $110,000 to reimburse the expense incurred in sending an American man-of-war to Persia for the Vice Consul's remains. It is this latter sum that was devoted to the education of Persian students in the United States. There is a difference, however, between the Stack and the Imbrie murders; Stack was a high official who had been attacked by the Egyptian authorities; while Imbrie was a subordinate who apparently went out of his way to intrude upon a semi-fanatic religious spectacle. The indemnity paid by Greece to Italy for the Janina murder in 1923 was 50,000,000 Italian lire, which at current exchange, would be somewhat over $2,500,000.

[2] Following the British demands on Egypt in the Stack affair, when the British occupied the customs at Alexandria, the Egyptian parliament sent an appeal to the Secretary-General of the League, asking the League to in-

authority was not "aggression" within the meaning of the Covenant.[1]

Sometimes it may be necessary to act immediately to prevent great interests from being irretrievably damaged. Emergencies may arise, such as the necessity of preventing the loss of life, which will prevent a prior appeal to the League.[2] If such actions are *bona fide*, they are not necessarily prohibited by the Covenant. The Committee of Jurists, who interpreted this document in connection with the Corfu affair, stated that "coercive measures which are not intended to constitute acts of war may or may not be consistent with the provisions of Articles 12 to 15 of the Covenant, and it is for the Council, when the dispute has been submitted to it, to decide immediately, having due regard to all the circumstances of the case and to the nature of the measures adopted, whether it should recommend the maintenance of or the withdrawal of such measures."[3] This interpretation would appear to authorize a state to take coercive measures, corresponding to an injunction in municipal law, which an emergency may justify. But such action will be subjected to subsequent examination by

tervene "to defend against arbitrariness an innocent nation." Following a principle previously established (cf. p. 635), it was decided that a non-member could not invoke the services of the League. However, under article 11, it was the "friendly right" of any member to call the attention of the League to any circumstance threatening international relations. No member, however, undertook to defend Egypt's cause. If the latter country had been a member she could have sought its protection. Whether or not the League would have intervened in this case is doubtful in view of the British reservations in the recognition of Egypt's independence in 1922. Cf. p. 635.

[1] Cf. p. 589. Cf. E. Stowell, *Intervention in International Law* (1921), Ch. II; A. H. Snow, *The Question of the Aborigines*, Ch. XIV.

[2] International law draws a distinction between *non-political intervention*—the use of armed force for the protection of immediately endangered life and property; and *political intervention* which has wider purposes and which results in the establishment of political control over the territory concerned. The latter type of intervention, such as the United States has carried out in Haiti and Santo Domingo, seems to be more questionable than non-political intervention. It is probable, however, that sooner or later both types of intervention will be placed under international control. Cf. *Right to Protect Citizens in Foreign Countries by Landing Forces.* Memorandum of the Solicitor for the Department of State, October 5, 1912. R. L. Buell, "The Protection of Foreign Lives and Property in Disturbed Areas," *Annals of the American Academy of Political and Social Science*, July, 1929.

[3] *O. J.*, April, 1924, p. 524.

a relatively impartial international body. If this body finds that the measures were unjustified they should be withdrawn and compensation made.[1]

As we shall see elsewhere, the League has been very effective in preventing international control from being abused as in the case of the financial reconstruction of Austria and Hungary.[2] It may be said generally that the League offers the best means of working out a system of international intervention, which will establish a law of intervention, decide when the law is violated, and then, when there is no other possible alternative, give a "mandate" to some power to intervene. But it must supervise the acts of the intervening power just as it supervises the administration of the present mandatory powers. From one standpoint, the supervision will be more strict, for it will be the duty of the League to secure the withdrawal of the intervening "mandatory" as soon as the legitimate objects of its intervention have been attained.

Of course, there is the same danger from international intervention as from an international trust. Some people fear lest the great, selfish powers will control the League for their own advantage. This, naturally, is possible. But if the League takes intervention out of the field of policy by building up a code of law defining when intervention may take place, intervention for any other purpose will be extremely difficult, if not impossible to justify. As a matter of fact, the League is not controlled by a few great powers. Through their membership in the Assembly, the small countries, most likely to be the object of imperialist aggression, are now able to combine their joint strength in summoning to their

---

[1] In the convention of December 13, 1906, in regard to Abyssinia, France, Great Britain and Italy agreed that no government could intervene in any manner or extent, except after an entente with the others. Cf. p. 473.

In deciding upon the justification of intervention, the probable effects of foreign intrusion must also be weighed. Instead of improving local conditions in some countries, intervention may simply make them worse, and delay a fundamental solution brought about from within. In the case of a country as large as China, foreign intervention against the wishes of Chinese opinion is almost bound to fail because of the vast extent of the country. This may also be true of a country such as Mexico. On the other hand, in the case of countries as small as the Central America and Caribbean countries or some of the Balkan states, intervention may be effective in achieving the desired end. The question whether intervention will succeed in any given country can be decided only as the case arises.

[2] Cf. p. 426.

aid the moral opinion in every country of the world.[1] Even the Council, designed originally for the benefit of the great powers, is now controlled by the smaller nations who have nine out of fourteen members. Under any system of government, trust must be imposed somewhere. Certainly a League-controlled intervention is less likely to be abused than intervention by the unrestrained "authority" of a single government.

[1] One of the first acts of Santo Domingo, following the evacuation of the American troops in 1924, was to apply for membership in the League.

CHAPTER XVII

CAPITAL AND THE BACKWARD REGIONS

1. Foreign Investments.—2. Concessions.—3. Capitalistic Abuses in Backward Regions—the Putumayo Affair.—4. The Revolt Against Foreign Capital.—5. Disputes over Vested Interests.—6. The Control of Foreign Investments—American Policy.

1. FOREIGN INVESTMENTS

Since the desire for markets is one of the principal causes of imperialism, business men and financiers have been particularly interested in the economic exploitation of the undeveloped regions of the world, whether of colonies or independent countries. In such regions, capital has a very legitimate function to perform. The railroads of China, Russia, Mexico, Turkey and South America, by means of which these countries are being unified and the wants of their inhabitants fulfilled, have been built very largely by foreign capital and foreign engineers. It is foolish to believe that foreign investments are always forced on the people who live in these regions. In Soviet Russia, where anti-capitalistic doctrine has been so vigorously preached, Leonid Krassin, the Soviet trade commissioner, has said, "We are now devoting attention to a great international loan, without which it will be impossible to rebuild Russia economically in a short time."[1] At the Lausanne conference of 1923, the Turkish delegates announced that, "fully alive to their country's need of foreign capital," they would seek as much capital as possible.[2] China and the countries of the Caribbean have likewise made repeated efforts to obtain funds from foreign bankers.

Pushed by the economic law of diminishing returns, European capitalists sought out the untouched regions of the world long before the World War. In 1914 the foreign investments of Euro-

---

[1] *Soviet Russia*, 1921, p. 202.
[2] *Minutes*, Cmd. 1814, p. 612.

pean countries totalled 40 billion dollars, of which Great Britain held about 20 billion, France 8 billion, and Germany about 7½ billion dollars.[1] Following the War, the United States took the lead in making foreign investments. Between 1914 and 1924 Americans purchased about $6,800,000,000 of foreign securities. While in 1914 the United States was a debtor country to the extent of $2,000,000,000, in 1928 it was a creditor nation to an extent (excluding the inter-allied debts) of $15,000,000,000.

In the case of private loans between countries with strong governments, few problems in international relations arise. On the other hand, in the case of loans to backward countries having governments inclined to frequent change and of uncertain character, the situation is quite different. For the most part, such loans are not made by a government but by individual bankers who may loan money to a government in a backward country or may invest it in connection with the development of a concession. Loans to governments in these regions may be for (a) industrial purposes, such as the construction of a railroad or a port, (b) for administrative purposes, such as for the funding of a debt or the payment of old obligations, (c) for war or indemnity purposes, such as the loan China was obliged to make in order to pay Japan the indemnity exacted following the war of 1894.[2]

From the international standpoint, capital in the backward regions creates two types of problems: (1) those which arise between foreign investors and borrowing governments—problems discussed in this chapter, (2) those which arise between different groups of foreign investors and their governments over the opportunity for investments abroad—problems discussed in the chapter on the Open Door.

2. CONCESSIONS

Because of the industrial inexperience of "backward" governments, foreign investors often insist upon controlling the expenditure of money lent for industrial enterprises. This control usually takes the form of a concession, which is a privilege granted by a government to an individual or group, of developing certain re-

[1] *Report on Coöperation in American Export Trade*, Federal Trade Commission (1916), pp. 71 ff.
[2] Cf. Willoughby, *Foreign Rights and Interests in China*, p. 487.

sources or of constructing certain public works. Ordinarily such enterprises are carried out at the expense of the concessionnaire who receives in return the profits from exploiting these concerns, such as a mine or a railway, for a certain number of years. Sometimes, he is exempt from taxation. In some concessions, he may even receive a subsidy from the government. For example, the Turkish government subsidized the construction of certain of its railways by the payment of "kilometric guarantees," in one case amounting to $55,000 for each kilometer constructed.[1] In other concessions, the foreign capitalists may be obliged to pay the government granting the concession a royalty or percentage on their profits. At the end of a certain period, such as 99 years, the rights of such capitalists usually revert to the government without compensation. By means of a concession, therefore, it is possible for a government to secure the construction of a railway or similar enterprises without direct cost; while foreign investors are willing to build such systems in return for the profits of operation over a long period of years.[2]

Concessions of this general type have been granted by governments in the Balkan countries, in the Near East, in China, in Mexico, and throughout Latin America. Their effect is to give foreigners actual administration over the expenditure of capital invested abroad. In cases where loans are not accompanied by concessions, foreign "control" may be exercised through "advisers" in the management of such enterprises as a railway. In many cases, loans are made with the stipulation that the mate-

[1] Earle, *Turkey*, p. 77.

[2] A concession which aroused great popular interest in the United States was a concession granted January 23, 1923, by the Turkish government to Admiral Chester, representing certain American interests. This concession granted an American company the privilege of building three railway systems in Turkey, which would cost about 200–300 million dollars. In return for constructing at its own expense these roads, the American company could operate them at its own profit and risk for 99 years. Materials necessary for construction were exempt from duty. Within a zone of twenty kilometers on each side, it might develop the mines, including oil lands—resources valued at ten billion dollars. At the end of thirty years the Turkish government might redeem the roads and ports, upon paying a sum equal to the average revenue received during the previous five years—a sum to be paid annually until the expiration of the concession. At the termination of the 99-year period, the government acquires all rights. Thirty per cent of the net profits, after payment of a 12% dividend, goes to the government. Cf. *Current History*, June, 1923, for text. This concession has since been terminated.

CAPITALISTIC ABUSES

rials to be used in construction should be purchased only in the country making the loan.

3. CAPITALISTIC ABUSES IN BACKWARD REGIONS

Unfortunately many foreign investments have been made and concessions obtained for illegitimate purposes and by illegitimate means. Unscrupulous or unwary bankers have lent large sums of money to governments or individuals in backward countries for political or unproductive purposes, and at handsome profits to themselves. The Khedive of Egypt nominally raised some $480,000,000 from foreign money-lenders to pay his debts, but secured actual possession of only $270,000,000, the remainder being absorbed in interest and commissions. Although he spent this sum on Oriental luxuries to gratify purely personal desires, the poor people of Egypt have still to pay the banking interests that first made the loans.[1] The Czar of Russia was able to suppress the revolution of 1905 by money lent him by France. Revolutions in Nicaragua have been financed by loans made in New Orleans, and General Huerta was able to maintain his murderous régime in Mexico by the aid of a foreign loan made in 1913. The Tuchuns of China were financed by foreigners, such as the mysterious Nishihara loans of $110,000,000, in return for concessions which these Tuchuns—usurping military generals—had no right to grant, but the validity of which foreign governments have supported.[2]

In Central America, governments have been extremely reluctant to repay public debts because of the circumstances under which they were originally contracted. "The bonds, bearing heavy rates of interest, were usually purchased in the first place at a considerable reduction from their face value, and the speculators who floated them took advantage of the ignorance or the cupidity of the agents with whom they negotiated to defraud the borrowing governments of large sums. A large part of the product

---

[1] W. S. Blount, *Secret History of the Occupation of Egypt*, (new ed., 1922), p. 15; Woodhouse, "New Understanding with Mexico," *Current History*, Sept., 1922.

[2] T. Millard, *Democracy and the Eastern Question* (1919), p. 182.

of the issue, in fact, seems in many cases to have been retained by the underwriters or divided by them with the Central American officials. Subsequent administrations were naturally unwilling to repay sums from which the country as a whole had never received the benefit, especially as the service of the loan involved a heavy and in some cases intolerable burden upon the impoverished treasury and deprived the government of resources which were sorely needed for the maintenance of order and the promotion of internal improvements."[1] In many countries concessions have been secured by bribery, while "friends" of the authorities have received choice favors.[2]

Foreign capitalists have been particularly anxious to exploit these regions because of a labor supply which is as a rule extraordinarily cheap. In the continent of Asia there are about 570 million cheap laborers—twice the number in Europe and America combined. China alone has seven times as many workers as the United States.[3] The same type of abuses arises in exploiting labor in these independent countries as in colonies, except that they are usually greater. In colonies such abuses may be controlled and abolished by governments, under the influence of an enlightened public opinion. In nominally independent but backward countries, governments are ordinarily too weak and local opinion too inarticulate, effectively to control foreign capital.

Almost all of the factories of China are operated by foreign capital; and they employ child labor, and compel men, women, and children to work inordinately long hours.[4] Throughout Latin America a system of semi-slavery called peonage has existed by which foreign capital has made large profits.[5] Life and labor are cheap in India, where before the international labor treaties, the 16-hour day was the rule.

[1] Munro, *The Five Republics of Central America*, p. 295.
[2] G. W. Crichfield, *American Supremacy* (1908), Vol. I, p. 454; cf. *Mexican Year Book*, 1921–1922 (R. G. Cleland, ed.), p. 222.
[3] S. Eddy, *The New World of Labor* (1923), p. 13. Cf. Chs. I–III.
[4] Tayler and Zung, "Labor and Industry in China," 8 *International Labor Review* (1923), 1. Since so many factories are located in settlements under foreign control, it would appear extremely difficult because of exterritoriality for China to apply protective legislation to the plants most needing it. Cf. p. 485.
[5] Cf. J. K. Turner, *Barbarous Mexico* (1911), Chs. 1–7.

The Putumayo affair.

—One of the most disgraceful examples of foreign exploitation occurred in the Putumayo district in South America a number of years ago. The Putumayo is a very rich district in the Amazon, the jurisdiction of which Peru and Colombia disputed. For a number of years the Peruvian Amazon Rubber Company, controlled by British capital, exploited its rubber resources by a system of virtual slave labor. Under the direction of 200 foremen and armed assistants, about 10,000 Indian laborers were kept in a system of slavery on the plantations. The foremen were usually illiterate men, some of them ex-criminals—who were guilty of the most outrageous conduct in the treatment of their men. When an Indian fled, an armed expedition would go in pursuit. In one instance, when a woman's work was hindered by the presence of her child, a foreman dashed its brains out against a tree before the mother's eyes. Other natives were decapitated, and still others were flogged to death.[1] The company actually employed in its service local government officials; and by this and other means had such influence over the Peruvian government that its atrocities were unhindered. The sentiment of the outside world—particularly the American and British governments—was finally aroused to these conditions, as a result of which Peru and Colombia signed agreements appointing a mixed commission to fix an indemnity for the victims, and to bring the guilty to trial.[2] While it does not appear that these agreements were put into effect, Peru brought about certain reforms in 1913.[3] Such abuses can best be restricted by some form of international control of capital; and the international labor system, discussed in another chapter, is a promising beginning.

While in theory foreign investments should benefit a backward country, many investments and concessions have been made upon the most extravagant terms. Not only is the interest rate exorbitant, but in some railway concessions, the projected route, as in the case of Turkey, has meandered throughout the whole

---

[1] Cf. "Slavery in Peru," *U. S. For. Rel.*, 1913, pp. 1248 ff.; Cd. 6266 (1912); W. E. Hardenburg, *Putumayo, The Devil's Paradise* (1912).

[2] 102 *State Papers*, 400; 103 *State Papers*, 401.

[3] *Putumayo Red Book* (1913), p. 136; for the decree, cf. G. S. Paternoster, *The Lords of the Devil's Paradise* (1913), p. 299. Another case recently arose in regard to the ill-treatment of British West Indian laborers in Cuba, which brought forth several protests from the British government. Cf. Cmds. 2158, 2245 (1924).

country in order to increase the "kilometric guarantees" and also to include as many mines and oil wells as possible.[1] Theoretically, foreign firms should build railways in backward countries more cheaply than the natives. But in China the average cost of foreign-built roads is said to have been $45,000 gold a mile; while it is said that roads constructed without foreign assistance can be built for between $20,000 and $30,000 a mile.[2]

Since economic control frequently leads to political control, governments of backward countries possessing great natural wealth have been obliged to contend against the political pressure of foreign interests. American financial interests were accused of backing the revolution against Diaz in 1910 because the latter had been partial to British oil interests.[3] British oil men were accused of similarly backing Huerta against Madero in 1914 and de la Huerta against Obregon in 1924, in order to secure concessions and other privileges which had been going to Americans under the established régime. In 1916 the Tinoco government in Costa Rica was placed in power largely because of the efforts of an American oil company, in order that the government might grant it concessions which previous administrations had refused to make.[4] In Central America, governments are "almost powerless to protect themselves against the oppression and greed of foreign interests, for corporations like the great fruit companies and the railway companies are able to bring to the support of their projects financial resources which far exceed those of the local governments or of any group of natives. . . ."[5]

4. THE REVOLT AGAINST FOREIGN CAPITAL

Foreign governments may also bring indirect forms of pressure on backward countries to grant favors to capitalists. In 1914

[1] Earle, p. 251.
[2] M. C. Hsu, *Railway Problems in China* (1915), p. 179.
[3] A Mr. Converse, a captain in the Madero army, testified that Madero told him that as soon as the rebels made a good showing, "several leading bankers in El Paso stood ready to advance" funds; other Mexicans testified that no funds had been placed at the disposal of Madero. Senate Hearings, *Revolutions in Mexico* (1913), For. Rel. Com., 62d Cong., 2d sess., pp. 104–105. For the belief that the British interests were backing Huerta, cf. B. J. Hendrick, *Life and Letters of Walter Hines Page* (1922), Vol. I, p. 180; cf. "D," "The Presidential Dilemma in Mexico," *Foreign Affairs*, Sept. 15, 1924.
[4] Cf. the special articles, *N. Y. Herald*, Nov. 18–23, 1918.
[5] Munro, *Five Republics of Central America*, p. 314.

REVOLT AGAINST FOREIGN CAPITAL

the United States signed a treaty with Colombia, agreeing to pay the latter country the sum of $25,000,000 in compensation for the loss of Panama in 1901.[1] The Senate withheld its approval of this treaty until 1922, when it finally agreed to its terms following assertions that American interests could not secure oil concessions from Colombia unless the treaty was ratified.[2]

In order to protect themselves from the abuses of foreign capitalism, backward countries sometimes resort to violent measures. The struggle for leases and concessions between foreigners in China provoked the Boxer uprising of 1900, while the second great struggle for such rights between 1908–1911, was a major cause of the Chinese revolution of the latter year. Different Chinese provincial assemblies even threatened to boycott the trade with nations who made further loans to China.[3]

In some cases, foreign property operating in such countries has been confiscated. Such was the policy of the Soviet government of Russia which nationalized all property, whether domestic or foreign. In other cases, governments have repudiated their foreign debts. In a decree of January, 1918, the Soviet government repudiated "unconditionally and without any exception" all foreign loans, including $187,000,000 loaned by the United States to the preceding Kerensky government. In 1914 the Mexican government went into default because of revolutionary disturbances, and paid neither interest nor principal on its foreign debt of more than half a billion dollars until 1923.[4] In 1920 about ten billion dollars of foreign loans had for some reason or other been repudiated by different governments throughout the world, about 8 billion of which was owed by Russia.[5]

Many backward countries, without going this far, have at-

---

[1] The treaty finally omitted all reference to this incident. *Treaties of the U. S.*, Vol. III, p. 2538. At the request of the Senate, the State Department published the correspondence in regard to this treaty, which showed, however, that the State Department proposed an amendment to the effect that Columbia should pass no retroactive oil legislation, etc. S. Doc. 64 68th Cong., 1st sess., March 14, 1924.

[2] Cf. the Fall letter of March 21, 1921, 61 *Cong. Record*, 167.

[3] M. J. Bau, *The Open Door Doctrine* (1923), p. 73; T. W. Overlach, *Foreign Financial Control in China* (1919), p. 237.

[4] Cf. p. 414.

[5] *48th Annual Report*, the Council of the Corporation of Foreign Bondholders, 1920, p. 370.

tempted to work out a system which would secure the advantages of foreign capital and at the same time subject it to domestic control. Some countries have passed a general concession law, regularizing the procedure for obtaining concessions, which thus diminishes the element of personal favoritism. China's unfortunate experiences with foreign capitalists have been partly due to the absence of a general concession law. A number of countries now insist on the "mixed" company, as the instrument for developing resources. The mining laws of China require that 50% of the stock in mining companies must be Chinese.[1] The Chester concession provided that one-half of the stock of the stock company to be constituted should be offered to Turkish investors for a period of thirty days, after which the company could dispose of it. In Soviet Russia, foreign grants are controlled by a Central Concessions Committee. Some of the concessions provided for "mixed companies" where the Soviet government retained a share of the profits.[2]

Some South American countries, such as Ecuador and Venezuela, have inserted the "Calvo" clause in their constitutions to the effect that no concession shall be made to a foreigner unless he agrees not to invoke the aid of his government in case of a dispute in regard to the concession.[3] In 1917 Mexico adopted a constitution, article 27 of which provided that the ownership of all minerals, including oil, is vested in the nation—a provision designed to keep the control of such resources out of the hands of foreigners. In granting concessions to develop these resources, the government should favor Mexicans over foreigners; monopolies are prohibited; and foreign concessionnaires are not to be exempt from taxation. Moreover, all contracts and concessions made by former Mexican governments after 1876 "which shall have resulted in the monopoly of lands, waters and natural resources of the Nation by a single individual or corporation, are declared subject to revision, and the Executive is authorized to declare those null and void which seriously prejudice the public interest."

[1] *China, An Economic Survey,* American Bankers' Association (1923), p. 7.

[2] Cf. regulations for "Foreign Firms in Soviet Russia," *Russian Review,* Oct. 1, 1923; also the decree of August 21, 1923, reorganizing the Chief Concessions Committee; *ibid;* and Statement of M. Litvinov, Assistant Commissar of Foreign Affairs, *Manchester Guardian Weekly,* Jan. 11, 1924.

[3] Art. 38, constitution of Ecuador; art. 124, constitution of Venezuela; E. M. Borchard, *Diplomatic Protection of Citizens Abroad* (1915), p. 856.

DISPUTES OVER VESTED INTERESTS

By virtue of this clause large foreign properties were offered for sale by the government.[1]

5. DISPUTES OVER VESTED INTERESTS

Theoretically, the strong powers do not object to policies adopted by backward countries in regard to foreign capital, as long as these policies only *apply to the future*. But they do protest when backward countries infringe upon "vested interests" of foreigners. In a note of June 8, 1921, the American government stated that "Mexico is free to adopt any policy which she pleases with respect to her public lands, but she is not free to destroy without compensation valid titles which have been obtained by American citizens under Mexican laws."

A large number of disputes have arisen over whether or not vested interests are impaired by certain legislation and the extent to which they are impaired. It appears that the United States government protested against the imposition of certain taxes on American oil companies in Mexico, and that the companies refused to pay these taxes, on the ground that they were confiscatory.[2] But where is the line to be drawn between a tax which is and one which is not confiscatory? In 1913 the United States protested against the Chinese mining law which provided that companies should contain 50% Chinese capital, on the ground that it violated a treaty of 1903, in which China promised the United States to "offer no impediment to the attraction of foreign capital."[3] The United States also protested against article 27 of the Mexican constitution on the ground that it was retroactive in effect. This contention was denied by Mexico, five decisions of the Mexican supreme court being cited to that effect. This statement would not, however, satisfy the State Department of the United States, which at first demanded that Mexico sign a treaty expressly safeguarding American rights. Mexico naturally refused to accept such a demand, and it was later withdrawn. Instead, at a conference at Mexico City in the summer of 1923, the United States accepted the statement of the Mexican govern-

---

[1] *Mexican Year Book*, 1922–1924, p. 51. For an English translation of the constitution, cf. Branch's translation, *Year Book*, 1921, cited, p. 122.

[2] C. Beals, *Mexico, an Interpretation* (1923), p. 275.

[3] *U. S. For. Rel.*, 1914, p. 134.

ment that the constitution was not retroactive—an assurance written into the minutes of the Conference.[1] A vigorous disagreement arose between the United States and Mexico over the interpretation of the 1923 agreement, and during 1926–1927 relations between the two governments became strained. Following the appointment of Mr. Dwight W. Morrow as Ambassador to Mexico, an agreement was reached in March, 1928. In that agreement the United States consented that American oil companies should surrender their titles in return for concessions from the Mexican government without limit in time. The Mexican government agreed to waive the Calvo clause in its Constitution. The United States also accepted the Mexican doctrine of "positive acts," namely that an owner holding land before 1917 had to perform certain acts in order to retain it. These acts, however, are not very burdensome.

Whether or not a government should come to the support of its citizens in disputes over capital invested abroad is a question which has been hotly debated. Some so-called "liberals" take the position that under no circumstances should a government thus lend its support—human life should never be sacrificed for propertied interests. (A theory which if pushed too far would lead to the abolition of policemen!) Some writers make a distinction between the commercial exchange of goods, which they advocate, and the export of capital, which they abhor. They assert that while a backward country profits from an exchange of goods, it suffers from the import of capital.[2] It is difficult to see any logical basis for this distinction. Ordinarily, exported capital takes the form of goods, whether railway rails or steam derricks. Oftentimes backward countries cannot exchange their products for foreign goods until foreign capital has brought raw wealth into a productive stage. There seems to be little more truth in the statement that "it is to the advantage of a trader to have his customer prosperous, while to the banker or loan shark the bankruptcy of his client may be his most profitable transaction,"[3]

[1] Cf. Secretary Hughes' letter, "Mexican Claims Convention," Report of Committee on Foreign Relations, No. 1, 68th Congress, 1st sess., *Informe Presidencial Parte Relativa al Ramo de Relaciones Exteriores* (1923), p. 18.
[2] H. N. Brailsford, *War of Steel and Gold* (1915), pp. 63 ff.
[3] Lovett, "American Foreign Policy: A Progressive View," *Foreign Affairs*, Sept. 15, 1924.

CONTROL OF FOREIGN INVESTMENTS

since the history of bankrupt countries has shown that foreign creditors are usually obliged, when a government goes into default, to scale down claims which, if the country had remained solvent, might have been paid in full.

If one grants that the export of capital is legitimate from the standpoint of international solidarity, it follows that the protection of such capital may also under certain circumstances be legitimate. A government which habitually robs subjects or aliens of property, or which is chronically unable to prevent its destruction by brigands or mobs, and from the courts of which no redress may be obtained, cannot expect indefinitely to protect itself from the outside world, by the shield of "sovereignty." As the American State Department has declared, "When a nation has invited intercourse with other nations, has established laws under which investments have been lawfully made, contracts entered into and property rights acquired by citizens of other jurisdictions, it is an essential condition of international intercourse that international obligations shall be met and that there shall be no resort to confiscation and repudiation."[1] In some cases, the exercise of some form of intervention in territory in which capital has been legitimately invested may become inevitable. Of the two types of control, temporary intervention is more desirable from the standpoint of the backward region than open or disguised annexation.[2]

6. THE CONTROL OF FOREIGN INVESTMENTS

None the less, while the doctrine of the sanctity of contracts, whether governmental or private, may be perfectly "moral," and while it may be fundamental to membership in the family of nations, it has, as we have seen, been greatly abused. Under the present system, there is no international law of bankruptcy. There is no means of telling whether contracts and debts were as "sanctified" when originally entered into as they later became. Stories are numerous that when a government goes into default foreign speculators buy up its foreign obligations at an extremely low figure—ten or twenty cents on the dollar—and then persuade their governments to collect the par value of these obligations,

[1] Letter of Secretary of State Hughes, Report, Mexican Claims Conventions, cited.
[2] Cf. Ch. XX.

making a handsome profit of five hundred or a thousand per cent for imperialism.[1]

As Dr. A. N. Young, late economic adviser of the State Department, has said:

"Agreements for the flotation of foreign loans are essentially of a public character. . . . One country might borrow in the United States to build a warship or to equip its army for aggression against a friendly neighbor. A Government which states it is unable to make payments upon its indebtedness to the Government of the United States might seek to borrow for unproductive purposes. Or American interests might propose arrangements involving the possibility of economic exploitation and which would be likely to prejudice good relations between the United States and a particular country." [2]

There are two means of preventing such abuses. The first is the settlement of disputes after they arise by some form of judicial process—arbitration or otherwise—a practice frequently resorted to in the past.[3] In 1912 the Honduras government accepted the Chief Justice of the Supreme Court of the United States as "supreme arbitrator" of disputes arising out of a foreign loan, and a similar provision has recently been made in regard to Salvador.[4] The question of the validity of concessions has also been arbitrated by the Chief Justice of the United States. An interesting development in this respect was embodied in an agreement between the government of Czechoslovakia and Baring Brothers, a great London investment house, of April 5, 1924,[5] in which both parties notified the Council of the League of Nations that if the Government did not fulfil its obligations under a loan just made by the

[1] For Senator Borah's charges in regard to the proposed loan to Liberia and the denial of these charges, as far as the American firms were concerned, cf. 62 *Cong. Record*, 12574, Sept. 14, 1922; for similar charges in regard to the Ethelburga bonds, issued by the Nicaraguan government, bought up by New York bankers at 25 cents on the dollar, which were added to the public debt of Nicaragua at par, cf. *N. Y. Nation*, May 31, 1922, p. 647; J. K. Turner, *Shall It Be Again* (1922), p. 357.

[2] Williamstown address, August 26, 1924.

[3] For a discussion of the whole question of interposition, the settlement of claims, etc., cf. any standard work on international law, particularly Borchard, *The Diplomatic Protection of Citizens Abroad*, Part II.

[4] Cf. *U. S. For. Rel.*, *1912*, p. 615, and cf. p. 400. Cf. the arbitration between Great Britain and Costa Rica, Oct. 18, 1923, over concessions awarded by the Tinoco government. *A. J. I. L.*, January, 1924, p. 147.

[5] *O. J.*, June, 1922, p. 688.

bank, the Council should make the best arrangements possible for the protection of the bondholders, subject to their consent.[1]

In the second place, the acquisition of concessions and the making of foreign investments should be controlled when they are originally contracted. If individuals may freely enter these countries and acquire holdings by illegitimate means, establishing what the diplomats call "accomplished facts," it will be very difficult to determine, when a dispute arises, whether or not they were illegitimately acquired. Such interests are likely to be supported by their respective governments, under the pressure of individual capitalists or pure nationalist sentiment. As Secretary of State Knox stated in January, 1912, "a leading Government should deter its nationals from making loans not of a sufficiently broad purpose to secure the approval of said Government in consultation with the other interested powers." [2]

At the present time, it appears that France, Belgium and Italy are the only countries of importance which officially supervise the floating of foreign loans. No foreign security can be listed on the Paris Bourse without the consent of the French Ministry of Foreign Affairs.[3] While ostensibly this provision is designed to protect investors against fraud, it has been used in the past to control finance for political purposes. When the Krupps, a German concern, were awarded an artillery contract by the Argentine government which a French firm had wanted, the French authorities refused to authorize the sale of Argentinian bonds in France. Likewise the French government threatened to treat Danish government bonds similarly when the Danish government proposed to increase duties on French wines.[4]

While the British government does not go as far as France, it

---

[1] Foreign investors usually form organizations to bring pressure upon their governments to protect their interests abroad. Probably the most notable is the Corporation of Foreign Bondholders in England. Similar bodies exist in France and Belgium, while in the United States an Association for the Protection of American Interests in Mexico once had considerable influence. For the European organizations, cf. A. Wuarin, *Essai sur les Emprunts d'États et la protection des droits des porteurs des Fonds d'États Étrangers* (1907), Ch. VII.

[2] *U. S. For. Rel.*, 1912, p. 108.

[3] For the decree, cf. Wuarin, cited, p. 268.

[4] Lasswell, "Political Policies and the International Investment Market," 31 *Journal of Political Economy* (1923), 380.

exercises an informal control which is nearly as effective. It is understood that investment houses wishing to secure the support of the government in case of difficulties arising out of a foreign loan, must consult and secure the informal approval of the Foreign office in regard to the issue.[1] When Crispi and Company attempted in 1912 to float a Chinese loan in England without such approval, this form of control was so effective that the company was able to dispose of only 40% of the amounts offered to the public.[2]

American Policy.—Following the World War, the United States adopted the British practice. In a statement issued in March, 1922, it was declared,

"At a conference held last summer between the President, certain members of the cabinet and a number of investment bankers, the interest of the Government in the public flotation of issues of foreign bonds in the American market was informally discussed, and the desire of the Government to be duly and adequately informed regarding such transactions before their consummation, so that it might express itself regarding them if that should be requested, or seem desirable was fully explained. Subsequently the President was informed by the bankers that they and their associates were in harmony with the Government's wishes and would act accordingly. . . . The flotation of foreign bond issues in the American market is assuming an increasing importance and on account of the bearing of such operations upon the proper conduct of affairs, it is hoped that American concerns that contemplate making foreign loans will inform the State Department in due time of the essential facts and subsequent developments of importance. . . . Responsible American bankers will be competent to determine what information they should furnish and when it should be supplied. . . . The Department of State cannot of course require American bankers to consult it. . . . The Department believes that in view of the possible national interests involved it should have the opportunity of saying to the underwriters concerned, should it appear advisable to do so, that there is or there is not objection to any particular issue."

While the State Department may not be able to compel the submission of proposed contracts for its scrutiny, the rule might

[1] "The Council of Foreign Bondholders cannot consider any proposal unless submitted and approved by the British Foreign Office," *U. S. For. Rel.*, 1913, p. 562.

[2] Willoughby, *Foreign Rights and Interests in China*, p. 498.

easily be adopted to support no contract which had not thus been submitted to it, in case it later became the subject of a controversy. If the bankers, as at present, are under no clear-cut obligation to submit to this type of supervision, some of them, sooner or later, will probably ignore the "hopes" of the State Department. The worst criticism, however, of the present financial policy of the American State Department is that it declines to make public the terms thus submitted to it.[1] The government even undertakes certain obligations in regard to some foreign loans, without gaining legislative approval or without informing the public as to what these obligations are.[2] While bankers are inclined to regard all business dealings as private, these transactions become invested with a public interest as soon as the support of the government is or may in the future be invoked.

While no serious accusations have been made against the integrity of the State Department, scandals have occurred in other departments of the government, which shows that Washington is not immune from the illegitimate influence of the money power. In view of the huge amounts involved in foreign loans, and of the pressure which financial interests may bring upon government officials, the utmost publicity is desirable so that the public will know that its government is acting as a just mediatory between creditor and debtor rather than as financial agent for corporate wealth.

In October, 1927, Senator Carter Glass voiced the objections of many bankers and others to the loan supervision policy of the United States. He declared that such supervision was illegal and that the State Department had no facilities to examine adequately whether or not a given foreign loan was undesirable. If the department vetoed a loan to a foreign government, the latter might become antagonized. An example of this possibility arose in the fall of 1927 in regard to a proposed American loan to the South Manchuria Railway. Many observers believed that any such loan would imply American approval of the Japanese position in South Manchuria that the Nationalist Government in China had

[1] The State Department declined to make known the exchange of notes with Salvador, cf. p. 419. For the "confidential circular," cf. 117 *Nation* (1923), 452.

[2] Cf. pp. 419, 421. Cf. Hyde, "The Negotiation of External Loans with Foreign Governments," 16 *A. J. I. L.* (1922) 523.

challenged. Yet if the State Department failed to approve such a loan, the Japanese government might be offended.[1] Another difficulty with supervision is that a loan disapproved by one country may be taken by another. Thus when the State Department disapproved a German potash loan on the ground that it might develop a monopoly abroad to the detriment of the American farmer, the loan was placed elsewhere. The history of the Brazilian coffee valorization loan, vetoed because of fears of a foreign coffee monopoly, is similar.

The loan policy of the United States is also open to the criticism that it is exercised with a view to advancing the self-interest of the United States, rather than with a view to protecting undeveloped countries from exploitation. The most notable example of failure to safeguard the interests of a borrowing country is in the case of the 1927 loan to Liberia.[2] The State Department not only approved this loan, but used its good offices to induce the Liberian government to accept it.

Many of these disadvantages arising out of the supervision of loans by a single government could be overcome by a form of international supervision in which standards of legitimate foreign investments are defined by common agreement, and administered by some international authority. A beginning in this type of supervision has already been made in the League of Nations loans to Austria, Hungary, Esthonia, and other countries.[3]

[1] Public opinion was so outspoken that the proposed loan was not made.
[2] Cf. p. 420.
[3] Cf. p. 426.

CHAPTER XVIII

FINANCIAL CONTROL

1. Non-Recognition of Defaulting Governments.—2. Temporary Intervention.—3. Financial Control.—4. Cuba, Haiti, Santo Domingo, Nicaragua.—5. Bolivia and Salvador.—6. Liberia and Persia.—7. Dangers of this Type of Control.—8. International Financial Control.—Egypt—Turkey—Greece—China.—9. The League Plan in Austria and Hungary.—10. The International Adviser.—11. Merits and Demerits of International Control.

No matter what safeguards are set up to control foreign investments, it is conceivable that governments will go into default, sometimes because of the rascality or chronic incapacity of their agents. Whether or not a capitalist government should intervene for the purpose of collecting debts or protecting the property of its nationals, in such cases, is a matter for each government to determine for itself. British policy was laid down as early as 1848 in a circular issued by Lord Palmerston and reaffirmed by later ministries, in which it was declared that capitalists could not consider intervention as a matter of international law but entirely as a "question of discretion."[1] The American State Department, in its letter of July, 1923, stated that the government was not bound to defend the validity of concessions, "but that it would deal with questions affecting nationals as they arise, as international courtesy, equity and justice justify."[2]

1. NON-RECOGNITION OF DEFAULTING GOVERNMENTS

When creditor governments believe that their nationals have been wronged by backward countries, and when diplomacy fails to bring about a settlement, they may choose from four policies to make the debtor countries pay their bills. The first is refusal

[1] Cf. C. Dupuis, *Les Rapports des puissances grandes avec les autres états* (1920), p. 275.
[2] Cf. p. 441n.

to recognize new governments until they admit such obligations. This policy was pursued for a number of years toward the Soviet government of Russia. At the Cannes conference of January, 1922, the Allies adopted a resolution stating that foreign loans could be floated only if the investor was assured that his rights would be respected. This assurance depended on (1) the recognition of debts contracted by past governments, (2) the indemnification of foreigners for confiscated property, (3) a legal system which would impartially execute contracts.[1] At the Genoa conference of May, 1922, an attempt was unsuccessfully made to settle the debt question as a condition precedent to the recognition of Russia. With the advent of liberal governments in England and France, the Soviet government was recognized, the subject of debts being left for later discussion. In August, 1924, a treaty was signed between Russia and England in which Russia recognized, in principle, her liability to foreign bondholders, in return for a guaranteed loan.[2] The opposition of the Liberal and Conservative parties to the conditions of the treaty was so strong that the Labor government was obliged to call a new election in which it was defeated. Consequently the treaty was not ratified. This experience apparently strengthened the position of the American State Department in its refusal to recognize the Soviet government until it admitted its liability for the Kerensky loan made by the United States to Russia in 1917—an admission which had not been made by 1929.

In a similar manner, the United States withheld recognition from the Obregon government of Mexico, which came to power in 1920, until the government came to an agreement with the International Committee of Bankers in regard to the resumption of debt payments, suspended in 1914; and until an agreement in regard to article 27 of the Mexican constitution could be made.[3] Following a conference in the summer of 1923 and the signature

[1] Minutes, "Conference Économique Internationale," *Documents Diplomatiques*, 1922, p. 15.
[2] Cmd. 2216. In recognizing the Soviet, the French government, in the note of October, 1924, expressly reserved "the rights which French citizens hold in respect of obligations entered into by Russia or her nationals under the former régimes, obligations respect for which is guaranteed by the general principles of law which remain for us the rule of international life."
[3] Cf. "Agreement between the Mexican Government and the International Committee of Bankers on Mexico," *International Conciliation*, No. 187, p. 30.

of two claims conventions, the United States recognized the Obregon government.¹

Until a new government is recognized, it is virtually impossible for it to secure foreign loans, and it is difficult for its nationals to engage in foreign trade. Contracts made under its authority have a dubious standing in foreign courts. Withholding recognition may be, therefore, a very effective club. On the other hand, rich commercial results may accrue to the power which recognizes the government of a country before other powers are willing to do so. As a result of the recognition of the Soviet government by Germany at the Genoa conference, the Soviet government granted Germany more concessions than any other group of foreigners. On the contrary, all of the 80 odd French requests for concessions in 1923–24 were rejected, apparently because of the rigid opposition of the Poincaré government to Russia.²

2. TEMPORARY INTERVENTION

In the second place, powers may resort to temporary intervention—the use of force for police purposes. In 1861 France, Great Britain and Austria intervened in Mexico on the ground that the government had defaulted in its foreign obligations.³ In 1838 a French fleet bombarded Chile to enforce the collection of debts; in 1902 three European powers established a pacific blockade against Venezuela for a similar purpose. In 1913 Great Britain threatened to send a warship to Guatemala if the latter government continued to misappropriate the coffee duties which in an agreement of 1895 it had promised to set aside as security for a British loan.⁴ Upon half a dozen occasions, the United States has landed troops in the Caribbean in order to restore order and liquidate bankruptcy. In 1914 it landed troops in Vera Cruz, and took over the customs to secure "unequivocal amends for affronts and indignities committed against the United States." ⁵

South American countries have long contended that the use of

[1] Cf. the General Claims convention of September 8, 1923, *Treaty Series*, No. 678; Special Claims convention of September 10, 1923, *Treaty Series*, No. 676.
[2] The Litvinov statement, *Manchester Guardian Weekly*, Jan. 11, 1924.
[3] Cf. p. 593.
[4] *U. S. For. Rel.*, 1913, p. 568.
[5] Cf. *ibid.*, 1914, p. 483.

force for the collection of debts should be made illegal under international law; this is the substance of the Drago and Calvo doctrines.¹ A modified form of these doctrines was adopted at the Hague conference in 1907, in a convention the parties to which agreed "not to have recourse to armed force for the recovery of contract debts claimed from the Government of one country by the Government of another country as being due its nationals." ² Nevertheless, this undertaking does not apply "when the debtor State refuses or neglects to reply to an offer of arbitration, or after accepting the offer, prevents any 'compromis' from being agreed on, or, after the arbitration, fails to submit to the award." In the case of a government which is financially unable or unwilling to pay debts adjudicated by an international tribunal, this convention apparently offers no protection. At any rate, it has not prevented the United States from intervening in Haiti and Santo Domingo or from maintaining troops in Nicaragua.

Intervention may be temporary, or it may result in some permanent sort of control. The financial difficulties of the Khedive of Egypt led to the establishment of foreign control in 1882; while similar financial difficulties of native sovereigns led to the French occupation of Tunis and Morocco.

3. FINANCIAL CONTROL

A more indirect form of control than the establishment of a protectorate or annexation, is financial control, which may be established by governments or by foreign financiers, indirectly supported by governments. In 1891 a foreign group acquired a tobacco monopoly from Portugal, part of the proceeds of which were used to pay off a loan they had previously made to the Portuguese government. Bulgaria and Peru have followed similar plans.³

Strange as it may sound, the United States exercises financial control over more backward countries than any other power. This does not necessarily mean that the United States is more

¹ Cf. Drago, "State Loans in Their Relation to International Policy," 1 *A. J. I. L.* (1907), 692.
² Convention Respecting the Limitation of the Employment of Force for the Recovery of Contract Debts, *Treaties of the U. S.*, Vol. II, p. 2254.
² Wuarin, *Essai sur les emprunts d'États*, pp. 50, 84; *West Coast Leader*, (Peru), Nov. 15, 1922; *Peruvian Year Book* (1921), p. 49.

imperialistic than the rest of the world; it may mean that it is less imperialistic. While other powers might have used the same pretext to annex territory, the United States has satisfied itself merely with the establishment of financial control. Although the United States opposes the use of force by European powers to collect debts and protect lives in Latin America, it has felt obliged itself to use force for this purpose. There is nothing inconsistent with this attitude. Before the war, the bulk of foreign interests in Latin America was European. When these interests were unjustly impaired, the United States could not logically insist on a policy of non-interference by Europe unless it undertook itself to prevent a Latin-American country from escaping obligations which it had voluntarily contracted.

4. CUBA, HAITI, SANTO DOMINGO, NICARAGUA

The finances of four Latin-American countries are under the control of the United States government. By virtue of the "Platt amendment" Cuba can make no loan without adequate revenue. The American representative in Havana has had considerable informal control over Cuban finances.[1] In 1920 Cuba underwent a financial depression which might have put the country in bankruptcy, had it not been for American assistance. At present the United States has no control over the administration of Cuban finance. The treaty of 1915 with Haiti authorizes the United States to "nominate" a General Receiver of Customs in Haiti, and also a Financial Adviser. The revenues collected by the Receiver go, first, to pay the salary of American officials; second, to pay the interest and sinking fund of the public debt; third, to pay for the maintenance of an American-controlled police force; the remaining revenues, if any, go to the Haiti government.[2] In 1922 the Haitian government floated a loan, after consultation

[1] On August 15, 1912, Secretary Knox said that the Platt amendment entitles the United States "to caution the Cuban government against adopting an improvident or otherwise objectionable fiscal policy on the ground that such policy might ultimately, either by itself or in connection with general conditions in Cuba, produce a situation requiring intervention." *U. S. For. Rel.*, 1912, p. 315.

[2] Arts. II–VIII, Treaty of Sept. 16, 1915, *Treaties of U. S.*, Vol. III, p. 2673. Cf. *Haiti Customs Receivership*, 6th fiscal period, 1922, Republic of Haiti. Haiti is also governed by American officials. Cf. p. 477.

with the State Department, upon much more favorable terms than if this financial control had not existed. In fact, it is doubtful whether any foreign loan would have been possible as long as Haiti remained financially disorganized.

Santo Domingo—the home of chronic revolutions—was the third country to fall under this type of control. In 1907 the annual obligations of this republic amounted to $3,900,000 while its revenues equaled only $1,850,000. In order to forestall possible European intervention, President Roosevelt entered into an executive agreement, later converted into the treaty of February, 1907, which empowered the United States to appoint an American General Receiver of the customs of Santo Domingo.[1] In 1916 the American government intervened to establish military rule over the island, on the ground that Santo Domingo had violated or was going to violate the treaty of 1907 by increasing her debt without the consent of the United States. Our intervention was accompanied by a demand for a new treaty, providing for an American financial adviser and the control of the police.[2] The Dominican republic refused to accept such a treaty, as a result of which the United States marines governed the republic, apparently in defiance of the wishes of the people, until 1924. Troops were then withdrawn after an agreement under which Santo Domingo allows American "advisers" to assist the government.[3] Between 1905 and 1922 an American receiver collected $67,000,000 in customs duty, $33,000,000 of which went to foreign bankers for loans they had at one time made.[4]

In 1910 Nicaragua—a fourth Latin-American country—got into financial difficulty, as a result of which the United States established an extra-legal receivership. This position was finally regularized by a very ingenious means in the Bryan-Chamorro treaty of August 5, 1914. In this agreement, the United States

[1] Treaty of Feb. 8, 1907, *Treaties of the U. S.*, Vol. I, p. 418.
[2] Cf. *Inquiry into the Occupation and Administration of Haiti and Santo Domingo*, Hearings before a Select Committee, 67th Cong., 1st and 2d sess., pursuant to S. Res. 112, Vols. I and II.
[3] Cf. Appendix B, *Dominican Customs Receivership*, 16th Fiscal Period, 1922, Dominican Republic.
[4] Cf. the agreement of evacuation, as in the Convention of June 12, 1924. *U. S. Treaty Series* 729. Cf. also the Convention of December 27, 1924 revising the 1907 Convention for the collection of customs. *U. S. Treaty Series* 728.

agreed to pay Nicaragua $3,000,000 for the exclusive right to construct a canal across Nicaragua, and for the lease of certain islands as naval bases. In return Nicaragua gave the United States power to supervise the expenditure of this money which was "to be applied by Nicaragua upon its indebtedness or other public purposes for the advancement of the welfare of Nicaragua in a manner to be determined by the two high contracting parties." [1]

5. BOLIVIA AND SALVADOR

Other Latin-American countries have fallen under the control, not of official representatives of the American government, but of American banking institutions. In May, 1922, Bolivia borrowed $33,000,000 from a number of banks in New York City, at 8% interest. As security for this loan, Bolivia set aside the import and export duties; 90% of the revenues from the tobacco monopoly; the tax on mining claims; the Republic's majority stock interest in the National Bank; and a large number of other taxes. If these revenues do not equal one and a half times the interest and sinking fund charges of the loan, additional revenues will be pledged. As long as the loan is outstanding, the collection of these revenues is to be supervised by a Permanent Fiscal Commission composed of three commissioners, two of whom are recommended by the Bankers, and one of these two is to be Chairman. [2]

In July, 1923, the little country of Salvador submitted itself to a similar type of control, except that under certain circumstances the government of the United States is related to the loan. In return for a loan of $8,000,000 at 8% interest, Salvador allows the collection of her revenues to be supervised by New York banking representatives, and 70% of the collections go to the service of the loan. In case of disagreement between the Republic and the fiscal agent of the bankers, the difference will be referred for settlement to the Chief Justice of the Supreme Court of the United States. Should Salvador default, the United States State Department will aid the bankers in selecting two individuals, one of whom Salvador shall name as Collector General, who is to act as a sort of receiver. But if he "interferes in the political

---

[1] Art. III, *Treaties of the U. S.*, Vol. III, p. 2740.
[2] Article Fifth, Trust Contract, May 31, 1922.

affairs of the Republic," Salvador may recommend his removal, which will be carried out in case Salvador submits "sufficient proof"—of which the American bankers and State Department are presumably to be the judges.[1]

Within recent years, American financial experts have been employed, following consultations with the American State Department, by Colombia, Cuba, Guatemala, Honduras, Panama and Peru, in addition to Liberia and Persia, shortly to be discussed. The governments of Bolivia, China, Ecuador, Hungary,[2] Mexico and Paraguay have also engaged Americans as financial experts, without the assistance of the American State Department. Thus the finances of about fifteen "backward" countries have at one time or another been supervised by Americans. In six countries, these financial experts have been informally aided by American military forces on the spot.[3]

6. LIBERIA AND PERSIA

The financial hegemony of America extends also to Africa and middle Asia. In 1908 Liberia appealed to the United States for assistance in maintaining its independence, asking for a guarantee of its territory and political integrity. While this request was declined, President Roosevelt sent a commission of investigation to this negro republic, and thereafter brought about the negotiation of a loan contract between Liberia and an international banking group, in 1912. In addition to a loan, this contract provided that the government of the United States should appoint a General Receiver of Liberian Customs, to be assisted by a German, a French, and a British Receiver.[4] As a result of the World War, it appears that these foreign receivers were withdrawn and that Liberia fell under the exclusive financial control of the United States. In order to reorganize Liberian finances and apparently in order to strengthen American influence, the American State Department asked Congress to appropriate a loan of $5,000,000 to Liberia, in return for which an American Financial Councilor

---

[1] Articles IX, XIX, XXI of the loan contract.
[2] This expert, Mr. Jeremiah Smith, is, however, responsible to the League of Nations. An American is also adviser to Poland.
[3] Inman, "Imperialistic America," *Atlantic Monthly*, July, 1924.
[4] *U. S. For. Rel.*, 1910, pp. 699 ff.; *Ibid.*, 1912, p. 675.

would be given great powers over the Liberian budget. The Councilor was to have been assisted by a Finance Commission nominated by the President of the United States.¹ The American House of Representatives passed a bill appropriating the money, but because of the belief that it was to be used to pay up Liberian bonds held by speculators, the Senate declined to pass the Bill.²

In 1927 the Liberian government entered into an agreement with Mr. H. S. Firestone, in connection with a million-acre rubber concession, whereby the 1912 5% loan agreement which would have expired in 1952 was refunded with a 7% $5,000,000 loan agreement which will not expire until 1967. This new agreement increases interest charges about $170,000 a year and extends these charges for about 15 years. Most of the proceeds of the issue were used for refunding purposes. In some cases European traders who had acquired Liberian bonds at a heavy discount made a profit of 100% by their refunding operations. Despite the obviously unfavorable terms of this agreement, the Liberian government accepted it because it believed that by so doing it would secure the aid of the United States against France in a boundary dispute.³

Apparently in an effort to escape from the clutches of Russia and England, the Persian government in 1910 asked the American State Department to recommend a financial adviser to put its affairs in order. From a list nominated by the Department, Persia appointed Mr. Morgan Shuster who, however, was unable successfully to carry out the duties of his office because of an ultimatum from Russia to the Persian government.⁴ Following an abortive agreement with England of 1919, by which the British apparently attempted to establish a protectorate, the Per-

¹ Cf. Buell, *Native Problem in Africa*, Vol. II, p. 803.
² For the French attack, cf. Thierry, "L'emprunt américain du Libérie," *Afrique française*, 1922, p. 141. Cf. also R. C. F. Maugham, *The Republic of Liberia* (1920), pp. 91 ff.
³ For details, cf. Buell, *Native Problem in Africa*, Vol. II, Chs. 102, 103. Under the 1927 agreement Americans occupy the positions of Financial Adviser, Supervisor of Customs, Supervisor of Internal Revenue, Auditor, and Assistant Auditor. The American State Department designates the Financial Adviser and recommends military officers to be appointed to the Frontier Force. It also under certain contingencies arranges for the arbitration of disputes arising out of the Firestone and loan agreements.
⁴ *U. S. For. Rel.*, 1911, pp. 679-683; M. Shuster, *The Strangling of Persia* (1912).

sian government again turned to the United States, employing Dr. A. C. Millspaugh, who had been an official of the American Department of State, as "Administrator General of the Finances of Persia." This official, an appointee of the Persian government, had general charge of the finances of Persia, including full authority to prepare the budget, the right to be consulted in regard to all concessions, the right to approve all financial obligations and expenditures of the government, and the right to approve the employment of foreign experts.[1] In 1927 Dr. Millspaugh resigned and his place was taken by German and Swiss experts, all of whom were to be subject to the Persian Minister of Finance.[2]

7. DANGERS OF THIS TYPE OF CONTROL

In rendering this financial assistance to backward countries, the United States in many cases has performed a useful service. In perhaps the majority of cases, this assistance, whether in the form of advisers or of loans, has been requested by the "backward" government. In some instances, it is true, financial control has been forcibly imposed. We have felt forced to act to forestall European intervention: it is much easier to establish financial control over Nicaragua than to dislodge Germany or France, once it may have landed troops in Nicaragua. Thus the Caribbean policy of the United States has been dominated as much by strategic as by economic reasons.

Whether because of present financial conditions or of past financial insolvencies, many backward countries find themselves in a position where if they really wish a new foreign loan, they must accept some form of external administrative control. It is no more immoral for a nation to mortgage certain revenues to pay its debts than it is for a man to mortgage his house, provided, in both cases, value is received. By means of foreign financial assistance, backward countries have reduced their foreign debts, balanced their budgets and put into effect necessary public improvements. They have been able to make loans when previously loans were impossible at any terms. In 1923, American financial experts dramatically averted a panic in Colombia by setting up a new national bank, which was supplied with banknotes by airplane.

---

[1] Letter of October 23, 1923, from Imperial Legation of Persia.
[2] *I. S.*, Vol. III, No. 26.

INTERNATIONAL FINANCIAL CONTROL

While the principle of financial assistance and control may therefore be legitimate, the system followed by the United States has many dangers. As long as one government remains the sole judge when to establish financial control over a backward country, it is conceivable that it will abuse its power. The inhabitants of such countries will inevitably believe that such intervention is being abused for selfish purposes and that America is being moved more by motives of aggrandizement than a desire to establish justice. Moreover, national financial advisers have frequently exerted their influence in favor of their own country. In Persia, the American financial adviser had to be consulted in regard to concessions; and it is not surprising that American investments and concessions there greatly increased following his control.[1] At one time, the United States protested that foreign advisers in Siam were turning government contracts toward their co-citizens.[2] Some of Liberia's difficulties before 1910 were also caused by such advisers.[3] Since the World War, the United States has encouraged Central American countries to refund European obligations with American loans. While some economies may have resulted from such consolidations, the practice inevitably increases the influence of this government over Latin America.

The great danger of national financial control over a defaulting country, therefore, is that it may be abused. For this reason, and in order to terminate the feverish competition of nationalist capitalists, international financial control has frequently been established.

8. INTERNATIONAL FINANCIAL CONTROL

At one time international financial control was imposed on Tunis and Morocco, a control which was, however, brought to an end with the establishment of the French protectorates. It was temporarily imposed upon Mexico by France and England in 1864.

Egypt.—European powers imposed it upon Egypt in 1876 when they virtually forced the Khedive to establish the Caisse de la

---

[1] *N. Y. Times*, August 10, 1924; *Isvestiya*, the official organ of the Russian government, on August 31, 1924, charged that the American adviser in Persia was engaging in "aggressive activities," aimed against Russia. Fischer, "Persia the Victim of Russo-British Rivalry," *Current History*, Feb., 1925.

[2] *U. S. For. Rel.*, 1910, p. 846.

[3] *Ibid.*, p. 706.

Dette Publique under the control of an International Debt Commission, which came to be composed of representatives of German, French, English, Austrian and Italian bondholders nominated by their respective governments and irremovable except with their consent. In 1880 the Khedive was also obliged to issue the Law of Liquidation, which assigned certain revenues for the service of the debt. Hereafter the Egyptian government could not issue new loans or change taxes, etc., except with the consent of the Commission.[1]

In 1885 the powers not only consented to but guaranteed a loan to Egypt;[2] while five years later, they consented to the conversion of some of the more onerous debts. But particularly France continued to place obstacles in the way of increasing the revenues of Egypt because of her hostility to the British position there. As the consent of the Commission to new loans and taxes was necessary, the British administration was greatly hampered by this type of international control. However, as a result of the Entente Cordiale of 1904, France withdrew her opposition. A decree of the Egyptian government was thereupon issued declaring that the Commission would exist until the debt was paid off, but saying that hereafter the Egyptian government would freely change taxes, make loans and dispose of reserves so long as the return did not fall below the amount necessary for the service of the debt.[3] Upon this basis, the International Debt Commission has continued to function.

In 1905 the powers imposed a number of financial reforms upon Turkey in Macedonia. These reforms were to be administered by a commission acting in the name of the Turkish government, but composed of four European members, together with agents of Austria-Hungary and Russia.[4]

Turkey.—The Turkish Empire proper fell under European financial control as early as 1855, when foreign bankers refused to lend further sums without guarantees. In 1881 foreign governments virtually forced the Sultan to issue the Decree of Mouharrem, which gave a Council of Administration power to collect the "Five Principal Revenues" for the purpose of satisfying

---

[1] Law of July 17, 1880, 71 *State Papers*, 557.
[2] Convention of March 18, 1885, 14 *De Clercq*, 488.
[3] Cf. the Declaration of April 8, 1904, 22 *De Clercq*, 509.
[4] Réglement of Nov. 13, 1905, Lippert, *Finanzrecht*, p. 945.

INTERNATIONAL FINANCIAL CONTROL

foreign debts. In 1914 this Council was composed of one representative each of the bondholders of France, Great Britain, Holland, Germany, Austria-Hungary, Italy and Turkey—a total of seven.[1] But the representatives of the German, Austrian and Hungarian bondholders were excluded from the Council in the Treaty of Lausanne.[2]

In the abortive Treaty of Sèvres of August, 1920, an attempt was made to place all of the revenues of Turkey, not already in the hands of the Council of Administration, at the disposal of a Financial Commission, whose status would thus be guaranteed by an international treaty, instead of a mere decree of the Sultan. The severity of these financial terms led in part to the rejection of this treaty by the Turks. These provisions were omitted from the treaty of July, 1923. Despite the existence of the Council of Administration, Turkey defaulted in the payments on account of the Ottoman Public Debt at the end of the World War. In July, 1927, an agreement was reached providing for resumption of payments the collection of which is now partly in Turkish hands.

Greece.—Greece is also under international financial control. At the end of a disastrous war in 1897 between Turkey and Greece the powers agreed to mediate on condition that Greece accept financial control.[3] This was made all the more imperative because Turkey insisted on an indemnity of four million Turkish pounds. In order to safeguard previous creditors, Greece undertook to establish an international commission, containing a representative of each of the six powers, to supervise Greek finances and administer certain taxes and monopolies.[4] In 1923 and 1927 the Council of the League of Nations approved new loans to Greece to be used in part for refugees, guaranteed by certain revenues, also to be administered by the International Financial Commission.[5]

China.—International financial control has to a certain extent been established in China. Some six foreign loans have been

---

[1] *Council of Foreign Bondholders,* cited p. 148.
[2] Article 56, Treaty of July 24, 1923, Cmd. 1929.
[3] Dupuis, *Les Rapports des grandes puissances,* pp. 296–297.
[4] Greek Law of Control, Feb. 26, 1898; K. Strupp, *Documents pour servir à l'histoire du droit des gens* (1923), Vol. II, p. 26. This law cannot be modified except with the consent of the six powers (Art. 38). The actual collection of the taxes is in the hands of a Greek company, the *Société de Régie des monopoles,* under the control of the Commission.
[5] Cf. p. 299.

guaranteed by the customs revenue, five by the likin (an internal transit tax), and thirteen by the salt revenue; others have been based on similar security. As long as British trade predominates in China, a Britisher is to be at the head of the Maritime Customs.[1] In the administration of the salt tax, the Chinese government is assisted by a foreign Associate Chief Inspector (now British), called "Adviser of the Central Salt Administration." In case payments on the Reorganization loan of 1913 go into default, the salt administration shall be incorporated with the Maritime Customs and administered for the benefit of the bondholders.[2]

Thus, as one writer informs us, "if we except Mexico . . . international control and quasi-control have succeeded in their work of restoring the finances of the defaulting state. . . . Through such control, financially dead States have regained a new life."[3]

9. THE LEAGUE PLAN IN AUSTRIA AND HUNGARY

An entirely new type of international financial control was worked out by the League of Nations in the case of Austria and Hungary. As a result of the World War, Austria went into virtual bankruptcy. Her government expenditures were twice the amount of revenue. The crown had dropped to one-fifteen-thousandth of its gold value. The government had no resources in the winter of 1922 with which to purchase foreign food necessary to keep the people alive, a condition which led Austria to appeal to the Allied governments for a loan. Although they advanced her about 30 million dollars, this sum was soon expended, without any steps being taken to place the country on its feet. When Austria appealed to the powers a second time in August, 1922, the Allied Supreme Council replied that the powers could spare no further funds "unless the League were able to propose such a programme of reconstruction . . . as would induce financiers in our respective

[1] Willoughby, *Foreign Rights and Interests*, pp. 136, 265, 570; MacMurray, *Treaties*, Vol. II, p. 1009. The Maritime Customs Service remains, however, a branch of the Chinese government.
[2] Cf. p. 480.
[3] F. Deville, *Les Contrôles financiers internationaux et la souveraineté de l'État* (1912), p. 239. Of course, the above statement does not apply to China where international financial control has not fully existed.

countries to come to the rescue of Austria."[1] At the request of the Supreme Council, the League Council asked its Financial Committee to investigate, and as a result of the League's study, three protocols were signed on October 4, 1922, by Austria and Great Britain, France, Italy and Czechoslovakia. Under the plan therein set up, Austria agreed to commence a programme of reforms which would balance her budget by the end of 1924. The deficit in the meantime—estimated at 650,000,000 gold crowns—would be met from the proceeds of a foreign loan. In view of the precarious situation of Austria, a double security was necessary. In the first place, the loan was guaranteed by the gross receipts of the Austrian customs and of the tobacco monopoly, and in case the Commissioner General deemed it necessary, by other assets. In the second place, the loan was guaranteed by a number of foreign governments. Great Britain, Italy, France and Czechoslovakia each guaranteed 20%, and other governments the remainder. However, as long as the Austrian assets were forthcoming, these guarantor governments had no liability. By means of this loan, Austria could now cut through the vicious circle created by a paper money régime. She could now inaugurate reforms, with the assistance of sympathetic outsiders, which would soon balance her budget and restore her to a healthy condition.

This Austrian plan is notable for the precautions taken to prevent international financial control from injuring Austria's interests. In one of the protocols of October, 1922, the British, French, Italian and Slovak governments, "acting solely in the interests of Austria and of the general peace, and in accordance with the obligations which they assumed when they agreed to become Members of the League of Nations,

"Solemnly declare:
"That they will respect the political independence, the territorial integrity and the sovereignty of Austria;
"That they will not seek to obtain any special or exclusive economic or financial advantage calculated directly or indirectly to compromise that independence;
"That they will abstain from any act which might be contrary to the spirit of the conventions which will be drawn up in common with a view

[1] Cf. "The Financial Reconstruction of Austria," *Monthly Summary*, League of Nations, Supplement, Oct., 1922.

to effecting the economic and financial reconstruction of Austria, or which might prejudicially affect the guarantees demanded by the Powers for the protection of the interests of the creditors and of the guarantor States;

"And that, with a view to ensuring the respect of these principles by all nations, they will, should occasion arise, appeal, in accordance with the regulations contained in the Covenant of the League of Nations, either individually or collectively to the Council of the League, in order that the latter may consider what measures should be taken, and that they will conform to the decisions of the said Council." [1]

When the Council is considering Austria's affairs, Austria is entitled to be represented upon it as a member—an additional safeguard.

For its part, Austria

"Undertakes . . . not to alienate its independence; it will abstain from any negotiations or from any economic or financial engagement calculated directly or indirectly to compromise this independence.

"This undertaking shall not prevent Austria from maintaining, subject to the provisions of the Treaty of St. Germain, her freedom in the matter of customs tariffs and commercial or financial agreements, and in general, in all matters relating to her economic régime or her commercial relations, provided always that she shall not violate her economic independence by granting to any State a special régime or exclusive advantages calculated to threaten this independence."

In the second place, this plan is notable because of the system of control established to safeguard the expenditure of the loan. If the purpose of this loan—the restoration of Austria—was to be realized, it was necessary to carry out a large number of reforms. Foreign investors demanded some assurance that these reforms were being realized and that their funds were not being wasted. Consequently the Austrian government agreed not to dispose of any funds derived from loans without the consent of a Commissioner General appointed by the League Council; but the only conditions he could impose were to insure the "progressive realisation of the programme of reforms and of avoiding any deterioration in the assets assigned for the service of the loan."

[1] Cf. Protocol No. I, *O. J.*, Nov., 1922, p. 1471. The powers, however, made simiiar declarations when they intervened in Lebanon and also in Mexico and Greece.

The office of Commissioner General was very important. By virtue of his control over the loan, he supervised the programme of Austrian reforms. He could not be a national of any of the principal guaranteeing countries or of any country bordering on Austria.

If the Austrian government considered that the Commissioner General had abused his authority, it might appeal to the League Council. And this body could terminate his duties whenever it believed that the financial stability of Austria had been restored. Austria, moreover, agreed not to grant concessions which, in the opinion of the Commissioner General, might compromise the execution of the reforms.[1]

In addition to the Commissioner, a "Committee of Control of the Guaranteeing Governments" was set up, composed of representatives of the British, French, Italian and Czechoslovak governments, each having 20 votes. Those governments guaranteeing the remainder of the loan held votes proportionate to the sums which each guaranteed. This Committee approved the conditions of the loan subscription and of the payments to be made from it to the Austrian government. Decisions in these matters required a two-thirds vote; but other questions could be decided by majority. While the Commissioner General looked after Austrian interests primarily, the Committee of Control safeguarded the interests of the foreign investor. The committee could not communicate with the Austrian government, but only with the commissioner. It had the right of appeal, however, as did each guaranteeing state, to the Council.[2]

In short, the League plan called for Austria to carry out reforms, involving economies in expenditure, the stabilizing of the currency and the dismissal of surplus officials, which would balance the budget by the end of 1924. In the meantime, it would be tided over by a foreign loan, guaranteed by European governments and certain Austrian revenues—the whole plan being supervised by a Commissioner General of the League. It also surrendered its right to issue paper money and to conclude loans except in conformity with the programme.

As a result of this system—which the fourth Assembly called

[1] Protocol No. III, *ibid*, p. 1477.
[2] Protocol No. II, *ibid.*, p. 1472.

the "most notable effort of economic reconstruction since the war"—both the short-term and long-term loans for Austria were over-subscribed by investors in Europe and America—a striking contrast with the situation before the establishment of such control when foreign investors refused to consider making further advances to Austria. Under the supervision of the Commissioner General, Dr. Zimmerman, the Austrian crown was stabilized, Austria's credit restored, unemployment and the cost of living decreased, and savings banks deposits increased 500% in three months. A deficit in the budget which in the first half of 1923 averaged 339,000,000,000 paper crowns per month, declined to 79,100,000,000 in January, 1924. Only once in 1924 did the government request the Commissioner General to place at its disposal part of the loan kept in reserve to meet possible budgetary deficits.

Despite these successes a number of difficulties appeared. While the revenues were in excess of those contemplated in the League plan, the Austrian government failed to effect the economies which the plan had contemplated. By June 15, 1924, only 67,101 of the over-numerous state officials had been dismissed, although the Government had agreed to dismiss 100,000.[1] On the other hand, further expenditures were caused by salary increases voted by the Austrian parliament. The Austrian government took the position that this increased expenditure was immaterial as long as revenues had also proportionately increased. It asserted that the figure originally agreed upon, at which the budget should be balanced—350,000,000 gold crowns—was too low and should be increased.[2] While the Council authorized this increase to 495,-000,000 crowns, it insisted that further economies were necessary.[3]

In September, 1924, an agreement between the Council and the Austrian government was signed, providing for the adoption of a less vigorous form of control in view of the balancing of the budget. If developments did not warrant relaxing this control, it could be fully reëstablished. On the contrary, if the economic and financial situation in Austria continued to improve, it would, after a period

[1] 18th Report of the Commissioner General, *ibid.*, August, 1924, p. 1101.
[2] *O. J.*, April, 1924, p. 683.
[3] *Ibid.*, July, 1924, p. 917.

of transition, be entirely suppressed.[1] Thus while the finances of Austria were not entirely restored by the end of 1924, the Council showed its willingness to modify too stringent terms and to bring about a gradual relinquishment of control when Austria had performed her part of the bargain. Although in 1924 the financial situation was as good as could be expected, the economic condition of Austria continued to be unsatisfactory, largely because the country was too small to be self-supporting.

In 1925 Mr. W. T. Layton and Professor Charles Rist made a study of the economic situation of Austria in which they declared that the economic life of the country was showing slow but definite signs of improvement.[2]

Following this report, the League control over Austrian finances was terminated—on June 30, 1926. Nevertheless the Committee of Control still sees to it that the proper Austrian revenues are assigned to the service of the League loan.[3]

In 1923 the government of Hungary requested that the League assist it in a similar way, as a result of which protocols, based on the Austrian model, were adopted in March, 1924,[4] and placed under the administration of an American, Mr. Jeremiah Smith, as Commissioner General. The situation in Hungary was not as acute as it had been in Austria, partly because Hungary was an agricultural and comparatively self-sufficient country. While in the case of Austria, the powers had surrendered all claims for reparations and so forth for twenty years, in the case of Hungary the Reparations Commission merely reduced reparation payments to an annual average of 10,000,000 gold crowns for 20 years, which is equivalent to one shilling per capita compared with the 41 shillings per capita demanded as reparations from Germany.[5] Moreover, the assets of Hungary were considered sufficient to secure the loan of $2,500,000—itself small compared with the Austrian loan—without the guarantee of the outside powers.

[1] *O. J.*, October, 1924, p. 1557.
[2] "The Economic Situation of Austria," C. 440 (1), M. 1. (1), 162. 1925. II.
[3] Cf. " Financial Reconstruction of Austria. General Survey and Principal Documents." C. 568. M. 232.
[4] For the Protocols, cf. *O. J.*, May, 1924, p. 802.
[5] "The Financial Reconstruction of Hungary," *Monthly Summary of the League of Nations, Supplement*, May, 1924.

In place of the Committee of Control of the Guaranteeing Powers, a Committee of Control, named by the Reparations Commission, watched the progress of the reforms. Trustees named by the Council also safeguard the special interest of the bondholders. The Commissioner General was withdrawn in June, 1926.

Both of these plans for financial control call for the rigid reduction of government expenditures, which means discharging non-essential officials from office and the abolition of subsidies to the unemployed. These economies, it is urged, strike the hardest at the poor and laboring classes,[1] for the benefit of foreign bondholders. The ghost of the international banker has again been invoked to damn the League's reconstruction work in these countries. Little evidence has been presented, however, to show that the workingman has unduly suffered from these reconstruction plans. In fact, under them unemployment has decreased and the cost of living has declined—certainly more wholesome methods of improving the condition of labor than artificial and unproductive subsidies which must sooner or later have to come to an end.

While the economic and humanitarian benefits of the League's work in Austria and Hungary have been of the utmost importance, the political consequences of this work are perhaps even more important still. As Count Bethlen, the prime minister of Hungary, declared to the fifth Assembly, the reconstruction of Austria and Hungary has "succeeded in bringing about friendly collaboration, for the first time since the war, between all countries involved in the political life of that part of Europe."[2] Before the League plan went into operation, there were about a hundred questions outstanding between Hungary and her neighbors which were later settled, for the most part, because of the mediating action of the League.

In addition to loans made to Austria, Hungary, Bulgaria, and Greece under League auspices, there should also be mentioned the League loan to Danzig of $7,500,000 in 1925 and the loan of $6,500,000 to Esthonia in 1926. Loans issued under League supervision have proved profitable to the investor. An investor pur-

---

[1] Peffer, "Austria: Saved or Duped?" 35 *New Republic* (1923), 91.
[2] 15th Plenary meeting, Sept. 11, 1924, *Verbatim Record*, 5th Assembly, pp. 2–3.

chasing a $1,000 League bond received a return averaging 7.79%
and (up to 1928) an appreciation in his principal amounting to
$123.30 per bond. Moreover, issues not sold under League auspices
proved more expensive to borrowing governments than the issues
just mentioned.[1]

10. THE INTERNATIONAL ADVISER

In order to establish a financial system, which would be independent of political manipulation, the League also worked out a plan for a Bank of Issue in Austria and also in Hungary. The parliaments of these countries enacted the necessary legislation to set up such a bank the directors of which, with the exception of the president, were not government officials but were elected by the stockholders. The League appointed a Financial Adviser to aid in the operation of this bank. This type of adviser marks an advance over the national adviser, who is tempted to abuse his power so that as a result many countries which might profit by such services will not accept them. As the provisional economic and financial committee of the League declared, "Some countries which would be unwilling on grounds of prestige, to apply for advisers to particular governments, may be willing and anxious to utilize the services of an international and impartial body like the League of Nations for this purpose, and in view of the fact that the financial administration of certain States is at the present very critical time in the hands of relatively inexperienced officers, we venture to think that an experiment in the direction indicated may be fruitful of good results."[2] The League appointed financial advisers not only to Austria and to Hungary, but also to the little kingdom of Albania. This latter official was of especial interest because Albania occupies a status which in many respects is similar to that of the independent countries in more tropical parts of the world. In April, 1923, the League Council appointed Mr. J. D. Hunger, formerly a colonial official in the Dutch East Indies, as adviser on a five-year contract with the Albanian government. He was obliged to report to the Council quarterly.[3] The

---

[1] Winkler, "The Investor and League Loans," *I. S.* Vol. IV. Special Supplement No. 2, 1928.

[2] "Report to the Council on certain Aspects of the Raw Materials Problem," A. 112, 1921 (II).

[3] *O. J.*, June, 1922, p. 523; June, 1923, p. 560.

contract allowed the Albanian government to cancel it after one year, upon three months' notice. In February, 1924, such a notice was served on Mr. Hunger by an acting minister in a government which had resigned office a few days previously.[1] In his report to the Council, Mr. Hunger stated that the Albanian government had failed to live up to his advice, granting a concession to foreigners without consulting him. This action of the Albanian government irritated not only Mr. Hunger but also the government of the Netherlands which had been asked by the League Council to propose a candidate for the position in question. In a letter to the Secretary-General of the League, the Netherlands government stated that "this question is one in which the prestige of the League of Nations is involved. . . ." The Netherlands government had "on all occasions urged its nationals to place themselves at the disposal of the League of Nations whenever an appeal for their services has been made; it would have some hesitation in doing so in future, however, if, after they have entered upon their duties, candidates nominated by the League of Nations cannot continue to rely on its support." [2]

11. MERITS AND DEMERITS OF INTERNATIONAL CONTROL

As the reluctance of the Albanian government to coöperate wholeheartedly with the League shows, the type of international financial control established by the League has some disadvantages. Unlike the control established in some places in Latin America by the United States and in North Africa by European powers, it is not imposed by force; it is based upon voluntary coöperation. The governments of some small and backward countries, with governments none too representative of the people, may desire outside help only long enough to right internal troubles, but not long enough to pay off foreign obligations. In such cases, the League can only appeal to the principle of the validity of contracts. At present, however, it is an appeal backed, not by the force of arms which a single power may muster in establishing financial control, but only of "moral opinion." While this "soul-force" may influence the actions of countries

[1] Cf. 4th Annual Report to Council, *O. J.*, April, 1924, p. 727.
[2] *O. J.*, July, 1924, p. 1018.

which play an important part in international life, it is not apt to have as much influence over illiterate and unscrupulous bandit-leaders in regions out of contact with the main currents of the world.

But whether or not the League should resort to stronger sanctions, discussed elsewhere,[1] the system of financial control which it has established possesses many advantages over previous systems. An imperialistic power may, as we have seen, use the device of national financial control as a pretext to bring about the economic and political subjugation of a debtor country. Private financial control, such as established by American bankers in Bolivia and Salvador, lends itself to even greater abuses. As long as bankers assume such powers, uncontrolled by their governments, they may exact guarantees out of all proportion to the need of the loan, which may severely handicap the legitimate expenditures of a debtor country. Bankers in control of the revenues of a debtor country may also become involved in political intrigues, especially since their activities are carried on in the dark, which may make the intervention of their own government inevitable.

While international control may likewise be abused, it is less apt to be abused than national control. The system established by the League in Austria and Hungary was open and above-board. It was accompanied by no hidden agreements; a detailed report of the progress of the control was made every month by the Commissioner General to the Council. The League system is scientifically applied by skilled and impartial experts, not interested in advancing the political interests of a particular government or the economic interests of a particular bank. It is now possible to make use of experts from such small countries as Denmark and Holland, who in the old days of the great powers were ignored in the performance of such services. Of even greater importance, the League system of control may be carefully scrutinized by the Assembly, dominated by non-capitalist countries, and by the Council upon which the debtor country may sit as a member while its interests are discussed. It is not without significance that following the acceptance of international financial control by Austria, Hungary and Germany,[2] some Chinese advocated a

[1] Cf. p. 595.
[2] For the control over Germany, cf. pp. 542 ff.

"Dawes" Plan for China. If European powers may accept this control with profit, the Latin-American and Oriental countries in chronic bankruptcy may possibly modify their traditional position that such control works only to the advantage of the "imperialistic" powers. At any rate, countries unable to obtain foreign loans without granting guarantees will receive the best assurance that these guarantees will not be abused and that they will really receive their money's worth, through the procedure which the League has established.

CHAPTER XIX

THE OPEN DOOR

1. Economic Rivalries of Governments.—2. The Navy and Business.—3. The Closed Door.—4. Effect of the Closed Door.—5. The Open Door Defined.—6. Open Door Agreements.—7. Ineffectiveness of These Agreements.—8. International Coöperation and the Open Door.—9. Necessity of International Control.

Imperialism has caused disputes not only between native peoples and foreign governments but also between capitalistic or industrially developed powers. Once political control is established over a backward region, it becomes possible for a government to establish an economic monopoly to the detriment of the outside world. This is the fundamental reason why imperialism has become bitterly competitive and bitterly nationalistic. Some nations such as France and Russia have attempted to gain control over nominally independent countries and to set up colonies, in order to close the door to the traders from all nations except their own.[1] Other nations, such as England, dependent particularly upon foreign trade because of their insular position, have felt obliged to become colonial powers in order to prevent the door in such regions from being slammed in their faces.

1. ECONOMIC RIVALRIES OF GOVERNMENTS

Although private business men, and not officials, have been immediately interested in the commercial development of the backward regions, they have usually been supported in their efforts by their respective governments. Economic rivalry between groups of private business men at home is usually settled by non-political competition or coöperation, the government remaining an impartial umpire. But when governments come to the support of their business men in such contests in the back-

[1] Cf. Pradier, and Besson, *La guerre économique dans nos colonies* (1916), Chs. I–III.

ward regions of the earth an economic competition is converted into political rivalry; behind the competitors looms the political strength of governments. Disputes are no longer considered on their economic merits; under the ægis of national prestige, they become political quarrels which may ultimately have to be settled by force.

Governments have supported their business men abroad, and have even annexed territory at their behest, not only because of the influence which these interests have in government circles, not only because of nationalistic sentiment, but also because of the belief that the trade resulting from such control will benefit the country as a whole. Thus Senator Lodge advocated the annexation of the Philippines because of the "vast commercial and trade interests, which I believe we have a right to guard and a duty to foster." [1]

Many of the great incidents of modern diplomacy have been contests between different groups of business men, supported by their respective governments. While such disputes of course engender ill-will between the participants, of even greater importance is the effect they have upon the rank-and-file at home. A German who was a true "patriot" would at once become angry at Great Britain if a British concern secured certain trading privileges which a German concern wanted. The differences between the French, British and German business men over the Bagdad railway were practically settled in 1914; but the international ill-feeling which had been aroused in part by this economic struggle could not so easily be appeased, as the outbreak of the World War shortly afterward showed.

Between 1895 and 1905 the history of China was marked by a "Battle for Concessions," during which foreigners constructed four systems of railways, largely for political and strategic purposes.[2] In 1896 China granted a concession to an organization later known as the Russo-Asiatic bank, a Russian concern dominated, however, by French capital, to construct the Chinese Eastern railway, linking the trans-Siberian to the sea. The bank established for this purpose a company the shareholders of which

---

[1] Cf. J. S. Reyes, *Legislative History of the Economic Policy of the U. S. toward the Philippines* (1923), p. 40.
[2] Hsu, *Railway Problems in China*, p. 33.

could only be Russian or Chinese. As a result of the collapse of Russia during the World War, a scramble took place for the control of this road. Partly in order to prevent it from falling into the hands of the Japanese and also to provide for a uniform system of military transportation, the Allied expeditionary forces in Siberia established an Inter-allied Board of Control in 1918. After negotiations with Soviet Russia in 1920, China announced that it would assume provisionally "supreme administration." Nevertheless, the Washington Conference apparently did not regard this as a Russo-Chinese affair, since it adopted a resolution saying that the administration of the road should be dealt with through diplomatic channels. The American government thereupon dispatched a note to China saying that it could not approve of a change in the status quo which did not protect the rights of all creditors. China and Soviet Russia nevertheless declined to discuss the matter with the outside world; and in May, 1924, they signed a treaty providing that the future of the road would be determined by them "to the exclusion of any third party or parties."[1] The long duel between France, Russia, Great Britain and Germany over the control and construction of the Bagdad railway was a similar controversy, which early passed beyond its purely commercial stages, and became a political and strategic game of governments for the control of the Near East.[2]

Following the World War, the United States which already produced 70% of the world's annual oil supply embarked on a struggle for concessions out of fear that its oil reserves would be exhausted. While the State Department did not seek out concessions for American companies, it supported the attempts of American firms, such as the Standard Oil and the Sinclair interests, to secure such grants from foreign countries, as a result of which it became involved in a number of contests over the question of exclusive concessions. The United States accused Great Britain of slamming the door in the face of American concession hunters in Mesopotamia, and in the British colonies. A controversy with Holland over the Djambi fields in the East Indies also took place. The American entrance into this race for concessions was by a different door than the one used by the old-style diplomacy. While

[1] Deane, "The Chinese Eastern Railway," *Foreign Affairs*, Sept. 15, 1924.
[2] Earle, *Turkey*, Chs. VI, XII.

the American government did not officially take part in negotiations for concessions, it did ask that our private business interests should not be excluded—which amounted nearly to the same thing.[1]

With the progress of state socialism, competition for concessions will probably take on more and more of a political aspect. The state operation of the oil business at home, as in Poland and Roumania, may be harmless. But when state-operated companies enter foreign markets and strive for concessions and for trade, political quarrels are likely to be intensified. The Anglo-Persian company—the majority stock of which is held by the British government—recently drove an American firm out of the Belgian market in a rate war.[2] Instead of making for peace, this sort of state enterprise may increase irritations unless some form of international control is established.

Sometimes backward countries grant concessions and trading privileges to foreign business men purely for political purposes. It appears that the Soviet government granted Americans oil concessions in Siberia and Sakhalin in order to embroil the United States with Japan who claimed prior rights in this territory. In fact, the Soviet government provided for cancellation of the Sinclair concession if the United States had not recognized the Russian government within five years; and in the treaty of January, 1925, Russia calmly handed over these rights to the Japanese. The majority of the oil wells in Poland are operated by French companies—a fact which is not surprising in view of the political alliance between France and Poland. Following the British support of the Greeks in their war against Turkey in 1920, Greece granted British oil companies a monopoly in Macedonia.[3] When political considerations thus control commercial policy, every government, anxious to maintain its place as a great power and to secure for its people a share of the resources of the backward regions, is tempted to embark upon the road of imperialism.

Many governments are so anxious to secure commercial privi-

---

[1] Cf. P. L. De la Tramerye, *The World Struggle for Oil* (1924), Part III; G. Spies, *Zwei Denkschriften zum Petroleum-Monopol* (1913), pp. 16 ff.; F. W. Möller, *Die Versorgung der Welt mit Petroleum* (1910); Apostol and Michelson, *La Lutte pour le pètrole et la Russie* (1922).

[2] For a discussion, cf. E. H. Davenport and S. R. Cooke, *The Oil Trusts and Anglo-American Relations* (1924), Ch. XIX.

[3] Buell, "Oil Interests in the Fight for Mosul," *Current History*, March, 1923.

leges for their nationals in backward countries that they negotiate for such privileges through treaties and agreements. In the famous Twenty-One Demands of 1915, the Japanese government demanded mining and other concessions from China for Japanese subjects, most of which were granted.[1] In the Angora agreement of October, 1921, the French government likewise secured for Frenchmen certain concessions in Asia Minor.[2] While the Turkish Petroleum Company was supposedly a business man's affair, the agreement of March 19, 1914, determining the participation of each group, was signed not only by business men, but by diplomats.[3]

2. THE NAVY AND BUSINESS

According to the official statement of the American State Department, the American government does not follow the European and Japanese practice of negotiating with backward countries for concessions for American business men.[4] Nevertheless agents of the American government have used political influence, even if of an indirect nature, to aid American business interests abroad. This following quotation is from an official publication of the United States navy:

"The Navy frequently has to land men in Mexico to protect the hemp trade and great oil trade from Tampico. . . . There is also a tremendous trade in sugar throughout Cuba and the other islands, and Navy men are frequently landed and sent to sugar plantations. The maintenance

[1] MacMurray, *Treaties and Agreements with and concerning China*, Vol. II, pp. 1224, 1229 and 1231.
[2] 114 *State Papers*, 774.
[3] Earle, "The Turkish Petroleum Company—A Study in Oleaginous Diplomacy," *Political Science Quarterly*, June, 1924, which contains the text.
[4] In a letter to the National Popular Government League of July 3, 1923, in reference to the Chester concession, the State Department declared, "The reply to your second question as to whether the concessionnaires had been promised moral or political endorsement or have received assurances that in the event of any dispute this Government would be bound to defend the validity of the concession is in the negative. It is not this Government's practice to give such assurance, or 'to give implied future guarantees.' . . .
"For your further information it may be added that neither the department nor its officers in the field took part in the negotiations for the concession. . . . The department believes that this Government should deal with questions affecting nationals as they arise, as international courtesy, equity and justice justify." For the activities of the State Department in connection with the Firestone agreements in Liberia, cf. Buell, *Native Problem in Africa*, Vol. II, Chs. 102, 103.

of these ships which are not suitable for the first line of battle costs the Navy some $3,000,000 a year.

"We have extensive interests in the Near East, especially tobacco and petroleum. . . . The possible development of the economic resources of this part of the world was carefully investigated by representatives of American commercial interests. These representatives were given every assistance by the Navy, transportation furnished them to various places, and all information of commercial activities obtained by the naval officers in their frequent trips around the Black Sea, given them. The competition for trade in this part of the world is very keen, the various European countries using every means at their disposal to obtain preferential rates, etc. The Navy not only assists our commercial firms to obtain business, but when business opportunities present themselves, American firms are notified and given full information on the subject.

"One destroyer is kept continuously at Samsun, Turkey, to look after the American tobacco interests at that port. A large percentage of the Turkish tobacco used in the Cigarettes made in this country is obtained in the vicinity of Samsun, and the American tobacco companies represented there depend practically entirely on the moral effect of having an American man-of-war in port to have their tobacco released for shipment."[1]

Within recent years the United States Department of Commerce has developed a system of foreign trade promotion which has been criticized on the ground that it is improper for a government to assist in procuring markets for its business men.

3. THE CLOSED DOOR

When a government annexes territory in the backward regions, or when it establishes indirect control over nominally independent governments, it is tempted to establish an economic monopoly in behalf of its own nationals,—a policy popularly known as the Closed Door. In such backward countries as Turkey and China, different foreign governments have thus endeavored to set up the Closed Door. In the Black Sea Agreement of 1900, the Sultan of Turkey was obliged to promise not to grant further railway concessions in northern Turkey except to Russians approved by the Tsarist government.[2] In an alleged convention of Febru-

[1] *The United States Navy as an Industrial Asset* (1923), Office of Naval Intelligence, U. S. Navy, pp. 4–5.
[2] Earle, p. 149.

ary, 1901, China was obliged to promise that she would not employ foreign advisers other than Russians in northern Manchuria, and that she would not, without the consent of Russia, grant to other nations, mining or other interests in Mongolia or Manchuria.[1]

Colonial Tariff Policies.—Whatever may be the legal character of such attempts in nominally independent countries, within colonial empires a power may follow what economic and commercial policy it likes, as far as abstract international law is concerned. At the present time, most colonial powers follow policies which aim to reserve these colonies as a preserve for the home merchants. The closed door may take three aspects within colonial empires (1) tariffs, (2) shipping, (3) concessions. The Closed Door in tariffs does not mean necessarily a high tariff; it means discrimination in favor of the home country. At the present time, three different tariff systems are followed in the colonies: The first is the Open Door, in which goods from the mother country are given no privileges not accorded goods from any other country. At the present time, only the Netherlands, Belgium, and a majority of the British Crown colonies follow this policy. The second policy is tariff assimilation, under which trade between the mother country and the colony is absolutely free, while the tariff system of the mother country is applied to the colony as far as outside trade is concerned. For example, trade between the United States and Porto Rico is free to Americans, but the American tariff rates apply to foreign goods wishing to enter Porto Rico. A like policy is followed by France and Japan.

The third policy is tariff preference. Under this system, the mother country and the colony have different tariffs, but they each may grant a partial or complete exemption in duties on goods coming from the other. Thus trade between the United States and the Philippines is free, but the Philippine legislature may enact a tariff law of its own, subject to the approval of the President of the United States. The policy of tariff preference is also followed by Italy, Spain, Portugal and the Dominions of the British Empire. Between 1898 and 1907 all of the Dominions granted tariff preference in favor of goods coming from Great Britain, while maintaining protective walls against the outside

[1] MacMurray, p. 330.

world. New Zealand granted a preference to the whole Empire in 1903; but the other Dominions extended such favors to each other only after negotiations and mutual concessions. Until 1919 Great Britain did not grant preferences to goods imported from the Dominions; but in the Finance Act of that year, this policy was partially deserted, and a reduction of one-sixth of the regular duty was given to twelve kinds of goods coming from within the Empire. At the economic conference of the Dominions, held in 1923, an extension of the preference principle was recommended.

Even in the crown colonies, which are under the strict control of London, and where the policy of the Open Door was followed long before 1914, a change appeared, largely as a result of the World War. In twenty-six of these colonies, the Closed Door was adopted, in the form of (1) preferential import or (2) preferential export duties. In 1920 Cyprus adopted a tariff schedule which charges enumerated British goods only two-thirds of the duty charged foreign goods. In 1912 and in 1920 the British West Indies entered into trade agreements with Canada, granting a similar preference ranging from $33\frac{1}{3}$ to 50%. As far as preferential export taxes are concerned, since 1903 the Federated Malay states have levied an export tax of 10% on tin, except when it is to be smelted in certain parts of the Empire. In September, 1919, India imposed an export duty of 15% on untanned hides and skins, but with a rebate of two-thirds when they were to be tanned within the Empire. Originally advocated as a war measure, Great Britain imposed in 1919 an export tax on palm-kernels in West Africa, but granted a rebate in case they were shipped to England.[1] The avowed purpose of this act was to kill the German palm-oil industry, for the benefit of English concerns, one of which has never paid a dividend of less than 20% since 1912. The criticism against this tax was so great that it was abolished in the summer of 1922.

Shipping and Concessions.—In addition to tariff discriminations of this nature, the Closed Door may also apply to colonial shipping. Some countries extend their definition of coastwise trade to include trade between the home country and the colonies, which is, therefore, reserved to home vessels. Spain and the United

[1] Cf. *Colonial Tariff Policies*, pp. 32 ff., p. 818.

States are the only countries in the world to follow this policy in their dependencies as a whole,[1] although France applies it to Algeria. The United States and Spain also bar foreign vessels from the carrying trade between their dependencies.[2]

Finally, the Closed Door relates to concessions—the privilege of developing resources or building certain public works in backward regions.[3] A large number of colonies reserve all such rights to citizens of the home country, barring foreigners. Sometimes such a limitation is prescribed openly by law. At other times, no discrimination against foreigners may exist on the statute books; but full discretion may be vested in the hands of the administrative officials, who may discriminate in practice in favor of their own subjects.

In the French colonies, oil concessions are apparently granted to aliens only when they form part of a French joint-stock company, two-thirds of the directors of which are Frenchmen. In the Dutch East Indies no concessions are granted to non-resident alien companies. While this law does not on its face discriminate against foreigners, the American State Department in May, 1921, protested that it was being administered to the disadvantage of Americans. Within the British Empire, no uniform policy appears to be followed in regard to concessions. In Canada and Trinidad some restrictions upon foreigners exist, but foreign firms have evaded them by participating in domestic companies. In India prospecting or mining leases have in practice been granted only to British subjects. In four dominions and six crown colonies no nationality restrictions exist.[4]

In nominally independent, backward countries, such as China, Turkey or Siam, the Closed Door means monopolistic grants of public resources or concessions to build public works, or other commercial discriminations in favor of one foreign country against another, granted because of political influence. In colonies, it

---

[1] The Merchant Marine Act of 1920 authorized the President to extend the coastwise laws to the Philippines; but no President so far has exercised this power because of the opposition of the Philippines to this extension of the Closed Door. Cf. Sec. 21, 41 Stat. 997.

[2] "National Restrictions on Marine Transportation," cited.

[3] Cf. p. 397.

[4] "Restrictions on American Petroleum Prospectors in Certain Foreign Countries," Sen. Doc. 11, 67th Cong., 1st session, May 16, 1921, p. 10; "Memorandum on the Petroleum Situation." Cmd. 1351 (1921).

means discrimination against foreign trade, either through tariff assimilation or tariff preference, and discrimination against foreign capital by refusing to grant it opportunities for employment.

4. EFFECT OF THE CLOSED DOOR

In its purpose of monopolizing the resources of colonies or regions under some form of external control, for the benefit of an imperialistic power, the Closed Door has succeeded notably in some instances. In Algeria four-fifths of the exports go to France; while about 90% of the trade of Porto Rico is with the United States. America's share in the Philippine trade has increased from 13% in 1894 to 61% in 1921, while the share of the trade carried in American ships has increased from less than 4% in 1909 to 32% in 1919. The following table shows the gains of certain commodities in detail:

COMMODITY	% OF IMPORTS FROM U. S. TO PHILIPPINES	
	1899	1923
iron and steel	8.	80.
cotton goods	.51	58.78
leather	2.32	90.28
wheat flour	17.47	80.24
machinery	.15	89.
fish & products	3.	85.
silk manufactures	.19	42.18

These great increases cannot be explained on wholly natural grounds. They have been due largely to the exclusion of foreign traders by the tariff policy of the United States. Trade carried on under the Closed Door tends to be a monopolistic trade, which means higher prices to the consumer in every country for the gain of a few men. Preference arrangements badly hit the flour trade between the United States and the British West Indies; and because of the export tax on tin in the Straits Settlements an American smelting factory was obliged to close. As a result of the export leather tax in India, Americans are obliged to pay 10% more for their shoes when made of the same leather, than Britishers.[1] If Japan and other neighboring countries could freely trade with the Philippines, there would be no economic reason why these countries should want to annex the islands; but as long as the United

---

[1] *Colonial Tariff Policies*, pp. 339, 356.

THE OPEN DOOR DEFINED

States maintains the Closed Door, these countries are confronted with a political obstruction to very rich markets, which may in the future lead to war. From the standpoint of the consumer, the Closed Door means high prices; from the standpoint of a native, it is but one more phase of the policy of exploitation; [1] from the standpoint of the world at large, it means the perpetuation of the worst forms of nationalistic imperialism. Excluded from markets because they are under the political control of one power, a capitalist state, dependent on foreign markets for the essentials of existence, will attempt to annex colonies of its own. A hundred years ago, this might have been possible without provoking war, except with the natives, because of the great stretches of unappropriated territory in the world. To-day, however, such a policy will lead to conflicts between the powers already in possession and those which wish to enter such territory. Germans are at present clamoring for the return of their colonies; and Germany has negotiated for certain interests in the Dutch East Indies.[2] The United States has become increasingly vigilant in seeking out opportunities for its subjects in backward countries. As long as the Closed Door is followed in such countries, governments will always be involved in business disputes, regardless of their merits; colonies will always be a potential cause of war. The continuance of this policy will eventually result in the destruction of colonial empires, just as the empires of the 17th and 18th centuries were destroyed by the Mercantilist system of which the Closed Door is a lineal descendant. Only the adoption of the opposite policy of the Open Door throughout the world will destroy this cause of war and ensure peace in the backward regions as far as capitalist powers are concerned.

5. THE OPEN DOOR DEFINED

The Open Door simply means "equality of opportunity." As far as independent countries, such as China, are concerned, it has come to mean most-favored-nation treatment.[3] Whether in re-

---

[1] Cf. p. 340.
[2] H. Schnee, "Die Notwendigkeit eigenen Kolonialbesitzes," *Handbüch der Politik* (1922), Vol. V, p. 249; Besson, "Le revanche colonial d'Allemagne," 120 *Revue politique et parlementaire* (1924), 23.
[3] Dennett, *Americans in Eastern Asia*, p. 110.

gard to such countries or to colonies, the Open Door means that goods from any outside country should enter upon the same terms as any other goods; that products may be freely exported from the country to any market without discrimination; that there should be complete freedom of navigation on the rivers; that foreign merchants should have an unrestricted right to enter such a country to settle and trade. From the financial standpoint, the Open Door policy means equal opportunities for subjects of all foreign countries to secure contracts for public works, to furnish government supplies and to obtain concessions.[1]

It was once the glory of the British Empire that it was open to the trade of the whole world. While this policy has been partially deserted in the Dominions and in some of the crown colonies, the British Empire still remains more open to outside countries, as far as trade is concerned, than the colonial empires of France or the United States. Although nationalism has been largely responsible for the Closed Door, nations who recognize the theoretical advantages of the opposite policy have been reluctant to adopt the Open Door because of the monopolistic policies of other countries. When one nation opens its colonies to all comers, and yet finds itself barred from trading with the colonies of other powers, it confers advantages on foreign traders without obtaining reciprocal advantages for itself. Another field has therefore arisen where treaties are necessary. A large number of Open Door agreements have been consequently made which apply (1) to nominally independent countries, such as China and Turkey, (2) to colonies proper.

6. OPEN DOOR AGREEMENTS

As early as 1844 China assured the United States that Americans would receive the same trading concessions as had just been given to the British in consequence of the Opium War.[2] When the European powers took advantage of China's weakness following her struggle with Japan in 1899, to seize a number of leaseholds,[3] discrimination against outside trade would probably have occurred, had it not been for the notes dispatched in the fall of 1899 by Hay,

---

[1] Cf. Beer, *African Questions at the Paris Peace Conference*, p. 215.
[2] M. J. Bau, *The Open Door Doctrine in Relation to China* (1923), p. 2.
[3] Cf. p. 464.

the American Secretary of State, who asked the powers holding spheres of interest in China to declare that in their spheres they would not discriminate in tariff charges, harbor dues or railway rates—a declaration finally accepted by the powers with certain reservations.[1] In Hay's note of July 3, 1900, the scope of the Open Door policy was broadened to include the preservation of "Chinese territorial and administrative entity." Subsequently, some ten treaties and agreements were made by foreign powers upholding the principle of the Open Door in China.[2] The original Hay note was restricted in scope. It did not alter existing interests; it applied only to future policies in regard to certain limited areas; it was silent as to concessions. Seizing upon this omission at the Washington Conference, the Japanese government contended that the Open Door policy did not apply to concessions;—a contention which was successfully challenged by the United States, on the ground that subsequent negotiations had extended the Open Door policy to include concessions.[3] In the Open Door treaty of 1922 any "general superiority of rights" is prohibited.[4] This is the first international Open Door treaty to be signed in regard to China—and it is the first treaty in which China herself has definitely accepted the obligation of the Open Door. In this treaty, the nine powers promise to respect the sovereignty, independence, and the territorial and administrative integrity of China, and to use their influence to maintain the principle of equal opportunity for commerce and industry. No spheres of influence shall be created; monopolies are prohibited; and China agrees not to permit unfair discrimination on the railways.

Turkey.—In Turkey a number of agreements have been made in favor of the Open Door. An agreement between German interests and the Turkish government in 1903 prohibited preferential treatment on railways constructed by these interests. In the famous Potsdam agreement of 1910 both Russia and Germany promised to follow the Open Door in their respective spheres in

[1] Note of Sept. 6, 1889, *U. S. For. Rel.*, 1899, p. 129.
[2] Cf. index, "Far East, Interests and Policies," MacMurray, *Treaties and Agreements with and concerning China.* For the French-British agreement in regard to Siam, of Jan. 15, 1896, cf. MacMurray, p. 54.
[3] Minutes, *Conference on the Limitation of Armament*, pp. 1250 ff.
[4] Treaty relating to the Principles and Policies in Matters Concerning China, Feb. 6, 1922, *ibid.*, p. 1621.

Turkey and Persia.[1] When a French company was given a railway concession in Turkey in 1910 it was obliged to promise not to grant preferential rates, a declaration which was repeated in regard to later railway concessions.

Abyssinia.—In 1906, France, Great Britain and Italy signed a treaty in regard to Abyssinia, in which they agreed that when requests were made for agricultural, commercial or industrial concessions there, the diplomatic representatives of these countries would take action to prevent such a concession granted in the interest of one of these states from being detrimental to the interests of the other. Moreover, the French government undertook to secure the appointment of an English and an Italian representative on the managing board of French railways being constructed in Abyssinia. "Absolute equality of treatment" was guaranteed on the railways and in certain ports.[2]

In December, 1925, the British and Italian governments exchanged notes in which the Italian government promised to support the British effort to secure from the Abyssinian government a concession for the construction of a barrage at Lake Tsana with a view to storing its waters for use in the Blue Nile; in return the British government promised to support the Italian effort to secure from Abyssinia a concession to construct a railway from the frontier of Eritrea to the frontier of Italian Somaliland. The British government was also prepared to recognize an "exclusive Italian economic influence" in the territory crossed by this railway in Abyssinia.

In June, 1926, the Abyssinian government protested to members of the League that it could not accept this agreement, which had been concluded without its knowledge. Italy and Great Britain were attempting to "exert pressure" upon Abyssinia. Throughout their entire history the people of Abyssinia "have seldom met with foreigners who did not desire to possess themselves of Abyssinian territory and to destroy their independence." The Abyssinian government declared that it would like to hear from "the Members of the League whether they think it right that means of pressure should be exerted upon us which they themselves would doubtless never accept." In reply the British and Italian

---

[1] Earle, *Turkey*, pp. 125, 240, 246, 253.
[2] Treaty of Dec. 13, 1906, 99 *State Papers*, 487.

governments declared that their agreement was not binding upon Abyssinia or upon third parties. In this agreement the British government simply promised not to compete with the Italian government in parts of Abyssinia, and vice versa.

The Secretary General of the League asked the Abyssinian government if it wished to place the matter on the agenda of the next Council. In reply the Abyssinian government declared that the agreement must be deemed null and void and it asked that its protest be sent to all members of the League.[1]

Morocco.—In 1904 France and Great Britain agreed that no differential treatment either in import duties or railway rates should exist in Egypt or Morocco.[2] The Act of Algeciras of 1906 provided for "economic liberty without inequality" in Morocco—an Act which the United States signed because of its desire to maintain this principle throughout the world.[3] The Act also provided that concessions should be controlled by the "principle of public awards on proposals, without preference of nationality," and that the specifications should "not contain, either directly or indirectly, any condition or provision which may be prejudicial to free competition and which may give advantage to competitors of one nationality over those of another;" likewise, bids for the opium monopoly should be awarded without preference of nationality.

As a condition of her acceptance of the American plan for financial control over Liberia in 1910, France insisted upon "the maintenance of absolute economic equality for all the powers in Liberia."[4] In 1914 the United States declared that its chief interest in Mexico was the maintenance of the Open Door.[5]

Colonial Treaties.—A large number of Open Door treaties have also been made in regard to colonies proper. The earliest international treaty of this nature was the General Act of Berlin of 1885, part of which provided for the Open Door in the basin of the

[1] *O. J.*, November, 1926, p. 1517.
[2] Hertslet, *New Map of Africa by Treaty* (3d ed.), Vol. II, p. 1820.
[3] Cf. the Declaration of the U. S., *Treaties of the U. S.*, Vol. II, p. 2183. Cf. Arts. 74, 109, 121, and Ch. VI of the Act of Algeciras. For the Open Door in Tangier, cf. p. 492.
[4] *U. S. For. Rel.*, 1911, p. 344. The Firestone interests have in effect now established the Closed Door. See Buell, *Native Problem*, Vol. II, p. 830.
[5] *U. S. For. Rel.*, 1914, p. 444.

Congo, territory which embraced the British colonies in East Africa, part of Somaliland, the Belgian Congo, and parts of the Cameroons, Portuguese Angola, and French Equatorial Africa.[1] The imposition of any tariff duties within this district was prohibited. But to provide colonial governments with a revenue, a new agreement in 1890 removed this limitation, authorizing a duty of ten per cent.[2] In the revised Act of Berlin of September, 1919, all limitations on the height of duties were abolished, although discriminations even in favor of the mother country are still prohibited.[3]

Other parts of Africa have also been subjected to the Open Door régime by international agreement. Not only was such a régime applied to the independent countries of Morocco and Abyssinia,[4] but also to certain colonies in West Africa. In 1885 England and Germany reciprocally guaranteed equality of treatment in their possessions in the Gulf of Guinea,[5] while in a treaty of 1898 France and England made a similar pledge in their possessions in West Africa.[6]

In the Pacific the same rule has been laid down. In 1886 Germany and England made an agreement, guaranteeing the Open Door in their Pacific possessions, except the Dominions[7]—a principle accepted in the treaty of 1899 between Great Britain, Germany and the United States, in regard to Samoa.[8] In the Treaty

[1] Arts. I–V, Act of Feb. 26, 1885; Hertslet, *Map of Africa by Treaty*, Vol. II, pp. 471–73.
[2] Declaration of July 2, 1890, *ibid.*, p. 517.
[3] *Treaties of U. S.*, Vol. III, p. 3742.
[4] In 1912 France established a protectorate over Morocco. But she was obliged to continue the Act of 1906. In the Treaty of Versailles, Germany renounced all her rights there under previous agreements; and the day following the time when the treaty went into effect—January 11, 1920—France imposed discriminatory duties on German goods entering Morocco. It was contended by some Frenchmen that since 25 governments signed the treaty along with Germany, this indirectly waived their rights also. But the powers have not accepted this reasoning. *Colonial Tariff Policies*, p. 207. While it appears that France is willing to maintain the Open Door in this protectorate, she wishes to escape other limitations imposed by the Act in regard to tariffs, taxation, and so forth.

The Open Door is also recognized in Tangier. Art. 7, Convention regarding the Organization of the Statute of the Tangier Zone, Dec. 18, 1923, Cmd. 2096.

[5] Arrangement of April–June, 1885, Hertslet, Vol. III, p. 873.
[6] Art. IX, Convention of June 14, 1898, Hertslet, Vol. II, p. 789.
[7] Declaration of April 10, 1886, 77 *State Papers*, 44.
[8] Art. III, Convention of Dec. 2, 1899, *Treaties of the U. S.*, Vol. II, 1596.

of Paris, the United States undertook to grant Spain equality of treatment in the Philippines for ten years.¹ The New Hebrides agreement of 1906 insured similar treatment to French and British traders.² Upon the annexation of Korea in 1910 Japan promised equality of treatment for ten years.³ Even in the arctic part of the world—in Greenland—the Open Door was guaranteed in a convention between Norway and Denmark of January, 1924.⁴

Probably the most widesweeping declarations in favor of the Open Door have been inserted in the League of Nations mandates. Any foreigner whose government belongs to the League may enter and reside in a mandated territory of the A. and B. variety, acquire property and pursue a profession or trade upon exactly the same basis as a subject of the mandatory power. He has "complete economic, commercial and industrial equality," whether in taxation or commerce. There can be no discrimination in granting concessions, except for essential public works, while monopolistic concessions are rigorously forbidden.⁵ A series of treaties extends these rights to the United States, although it is not as yet a member of the League.⁶

Unfortunately nationalist sentiment was strong enough to prevent the establishment of the Open Door régime in the Class C. mandates. To-day the opposite policy is being followed in Nauru

---

¹ Art. 4, Treaty of Dec. 10, 1898, *ibid.*, p. 1691.
² Art. 1, Convention of Oct. 20, 1906, 99 *State Papers*, 231.
³ Declaration quoted in *Colonial Tariff Policies*, p. 440.
⁴ F. Castberg, "Le Conflit entre le Danemark et la Norvège concernant le Groenland," *R. D. I. L. C.*, 1924, No. 3.
⁵ Cf. Art. 6 in the four Togo-Cameroon mandates; and Art. 7 in the Belgian and British East Africa mandates. The Open Door provisions in the Syrian mandate (Art. 11), are somewhat weaker; while the Palestine mandate (Art. 18), omits the concessions provision.
⁶ Cf. "Correspondence between His Majesty's Government and the United States Ambassador respecting Economic Rights in Mandated Territories," Cmd. 1226 (1921); Batsell, "The United States and the System of Mandates," *Revue de Droit International*, July–Sept., 1924. Cf. also Treaty of Feb. 11, 1922, between the United States and Japan, *Treaties of the U. S.*, Vol. III, p. 2723. These treaties provide that a copy of the annual mandate report, made to the League Council, should be sent to the United States. No treaties have yet been made in regard to the British mandates in the Pacific, apparently because the New Zealand tariff preferences conflict with the Open Door provisions of the Samoan treaty of 1899 to which the U. S. and Germany are a party. Cf. Blakeslee, "The Mandates of the Pacific," 1 *Foreign Affairs* (1922), 98.

island, where the British have monopolized the production of phosphate,[1] and in Samoa where the principle of tariff preference has been applied by New Zealand. While these examples are bad, the League's success in extending the Open Door to the A. and B. mandates is considerable, in view of the present trend in the opposite directions. In defiance of the Act of Berlin, Italy has abolished the Open Door régime in Somaliland; in the tariff act of 1909 the United States established the Closed Door in the Philippines and in 1920 Japan did likewise in Korea. The attempt in 1919 to extend the Open Door to the parts of Africa not covered by the Berlin Act was defeated. Apparently the Treaty of Versailles terminated the Open Door agreement between Germany and Great Britain in the Pacific. The efforts of the League in the mandates and of the Washington Conference as to China did something to check this tendency.

7. INEFFECTIVENESS OF THESE AGREEMENTS

Although the Open Door principle has been accepted by many nations, so many difficulties in application have arisen that in practice it has usually been nullified. The diplomatic history of China shows that the Closed Door has been the rule, despite the verbal acceptance of the Open Door, which applies only "to the future." The difficulty with such agreements is that they do not affect vested interests. The United States has protested not only against the violations of the Open Door in China, but also in Morocco and Siam.[2] Probably the worst violations occurred in the Belgian and French Congo. The famous concessionnaire policies adopted by these states established virtually a governmental monopoly of great natural resources to the exclusion of outside traders, and despite the Open Door provisions in the Berlin Act.[3] A monopolistic policy also appears to have been followed by the Royal Niger Company.[4]

While nationalism has dimmed the enthusiasm for the Open

---

[1] The Empire purchased the rights of a German company and the products of the monopoly are allocated, 42% each to England and Australia, and 16% to New Zealand.

[2] *U. S. For. Rel.*, 1914, p. 912.

[3] Cf. p. 451.

[4] H. H. Johnston, *Colonization of Africa*, p. 231.

INTERNATIONAL COÖPERATION

Door, the doctrine itself has been subject to two limitations which have done much to prevent its own enforcement. In the first place, the Open Door has been considered as a doctrine, authorizing a form of laissez-faire cut-throat competition, rather than a system of international coöperation subject to governmental control. In the second place, there has been no impartial body to determine differences in regard to the application of the Open Door.

Although the Open Door policy is a very simple matter so far as tariff and railway rates are concerned, it becomes very intricate in the case of investments and concessions. The mere verbal acceptance of the policy does not lead, in these cases, to satisfactory results. It does not of itself avoid international quarrels. No foreigner will build a railroad at his own expense in a backward region without assurance that no other railway will be built in the same territory which his road is designed to serve. In the case of certain "natural" monopolies, competition becomes disastrous. An interpretation of the Open Door compelling such a type of competition would merely intensify ill-will, especially if the prize is as large as railway and public works concessions usually are.[1]

8. INTERNATIONAL COÖPERATION AND THE OPEN DOOR

For this reason, a number of attempts have been made to substitute some form of international coöperation in place of cut-throat competition. Instead of awarding a large concession to one national group, after receiving bids from all competitors, this plan would award such concessions to a single international group, in which the resources of the various national groups would be pooled.

International coöperation in such matters has been attempted in the Near East, in Morocco, and in China. In 1899 an agreement was made regarding the Bagdad Railway, in which the German and French bankers received 40% of the capital stock,

[1] In 1912 the British government declared against the "dangerous policy of unprofitable international competition in China, which only enables the Chinese government to obtain money without adequate guarantees, and rendered it impossible for the governments interested to exercise the necessary control over the terms of any loans." Quoted, Overlach, *Foreign Financial Control in China*, p. 246.

the remainder being offered to Turkish investors.[1] Although British capitalists were invited to participate, the nationalism of the Balfour government blocked their coöperation. In the Anglo-Turkish agreement of 1913, the Ottoman government agreed that two British citizens should be elected to the Board of Directors of the Bagdad Railway.

Plans for international financing were also worked out for Morocco. In the Act of Algeciras of 1906 a State Bank was established, for a period of 40 years, to act as the financial agent of the Moroccan government. It was to be controlled by a Moroccan High Commissioner; a General Assembly of Stockholders; a Board of Directors, representing the different national groups in proportion to the stock held by each, and four censors, appointed by the Banks of Germany, England, Spain and France respectively.[2] In 1912 the Fez-Tangier railway was financed by a plan in which French interests took 60% and Spanish, 40%. Upon the Board of Directors were nine Frenchmen and six Spaniards.

In 1910 Mr. Knox, the American Secretary of State, proposed a far-reaching plan for international coöperation in concessions and investments in connection with the railways of Manchuria. The American Department of State declared that the "complete commercial neutralization of Manchuria" would be a large contribution toward world peace; and it believed that this could be done and the Open Door maintained, by placing the railways of Manchuria "under an economic and impartial administration by vesting in China the ownership of its railroads; the funds for that purpose to be furnished by the nationals of such interested powers as might be willing to participate and who are pledged to the policy of the Open Door and equal opportunity, the powers participating to operate the railway system during the period of the loan and enjoy the usual preferences in supplying materials."[3] By this means the railways of Manchuria would be built by a pool of foreign interests.

The Chinese Consortium.—While the Knox plan was defeated primarily because of the opposition of Russia and Japan, the same idea was revived in the proposed Six Power Consortium of 1912,

[1] Earle, *Turkey*, pp. 59, 92, 256.
[2] Ch. III, Act of Algeciras, cited; V. Piquet, *Maroc* (1920), p. 349.
[3] *U. S. For. Rel.*, 1910, pp. 243 ff.

in which six foreign banking groups agreed to participate equally in future administrative loans to China. The agreement was not carried out, however, because of the opposition of President Wilson, who felt that such an arrangement might lead to the "forcible interference in the financial, and even the political, affairs of that great Oriental state." [1] These objections, however, were later waived; and in October, 1920, a second China Consortium agreement was signed by banking groups in Japan, France, Great Britain and the United States. In this agreement the parties promised to finance existing and future loans to the Chinese central or provincial governments upon the basis of "complete equality in every respect." Each of the parties shall "take an equal share in all operations and sign all contracts and shall bear an equal share of all charges in connection with any business." [2] If put into effect, the China Consortium will represent a very important application of the Open Door, inasmuch as it applies not only to political and industrial loans, but also to concessions upon which no progress has been made, or which may be granted in the future.[3]

So far, however, none of these efforts at international coöperation has really succeeded. In Turkey and Morocco, pure nationalism defeated the attempt. Even the Chinese Consortium has done nothing constructive because of China's fear that she will become subjected to the control of a great international trust, and because of political disturbances which have made a foreign loan impossible. At the same time, the Consortium has prevented loans being made to China by a single government or group, in return for political favors.

These methods of coöperation have been defective, also, in that ordinarily no provision has been made for representation of the debtor country. In the absence of such a representative, the creditor's interests alone obtain a hearing. The methods employed by the League in the financial reconstruction of Austria and Hungary remedy this weakness since the Covenant provides for representation of each of these countries as a full member when

[1] *Ibid.*, 1913, pp. 170, 187.
[2] Art. 4, Consortium Agreement, Oct. 15, 1920, *Treaties of U. S.*, Vol. III, p. 3822.
[3] Bau, *Open Door Doctrine*, p. 178.

the Council discusses its affairs. Moreover, a Consortium is ordinarily composed of only a limited number of private banking groups, who are subject to little governmental control.[1] An unrestrained international trust may be guilty of exploitation to a greater extent even than a national trust. Three or four national groups may settle disputes between themselves as to the Open Door, but they may slam it all the tighter in the face of capitalists and bankers not a party to the combination. To insure real equality of opportunity, some means must be found which will give business interests in every country a chance to participate. This can only be done by some form of governmental and intergovernmental coöperation and control.

9. NECESSITY OF INTERNATIONAL CONTROL

If supervision is not established over the activities of capitalists abroad, it is not unlikely that individuals may defeat the foreign policies of governments. For instance in March, 1923, the National City Company of New York made a loan of $19,900,000, yielding 6.62%, to the Oriental Development Company, a concern under the control of the Japanese government, which guaranteed the loan. This company operates in Korea and Manchuria, and it was widely believed that the loan was used to consolidate exclusive Japanese interests in South Manchuria, and thus violate the spirit of the Consortium and the Open Door.[2] This may not be so in the case of this particular loan; nevertheless in the absence of control over and publicity concerning foreign investments, bankers are left free to finance monopolistic concessions abroad, and thereby perpetuate the régime of the Closed Door which the American government is attempting to overthrow.

Many governments accept in theory the principle of the Open Door, but violently disagree as to its meaning; and in the past, there has been no satisfactory means of settling such disputes. Both Belgium and France justified the establishment of a monopo-

[1] In the preamble of the China Consortium, it is stated that the governments have undertaken to give their "complete support" to their banking groups. But this is more a pledge of support than control, although governments will presumably exercise both. For the international agreements between private oil companies, cf. p. 113.

[2] Buell, "International Capitalism and Its Control," *Current History*, Dec., 1923.

NECESSITY OF INTERNATIONAL CONTROL

listic régime in the Congo, in spite of the Open Door provisions in the Treaty of Berlin, on the ground that the treaty did not apply to the particular acts involved.[1] Both powers rejected the suggestion of Great Britain that such a difference in interpretation be settled either by arbitration or by a conference. The Berlin Act provided merely for "mediation" in case of disagreement.[2] Between 1920 and 1923, the United States was involved in at least three important diplomatic disputes as to the meaning of the Open Door.[3] In the spring of 1920, France and England entered into the San Remo oil agreement, in which French interests were given one-quarter of the oil rights in Mesopotamia.[4] The United States protested that this agreement monopolized the oil of this region in the hands of the French and the British, and that, therefore, the Open Door had been violated. The British government denied the charge, saying that the concessions in question had been granted in 1914 by Turkey to the Turkish Petroleum Company, a quarter of which was German, and that the San Remo agreement merely transferred the German interest to the French. A deadlock thus arose over the application of a principle which both governments in theory accepted.[5] Likewise, in April, 1921, the United States and Holland disagreed as to the meaning of the Open Door in certain oil concessions in the Dutch East Indies. The Netherlands government had granted what

[1] Cf. the Delcassé dispatch of Feb. 11, 1903; A. Tardieu, *Le Mystère d'Agadir* (1912), pp. 209–220.

[2] Art. 12.

[3] In 1915 the South Manchurian Railway, under the control of the Japanese government, granted certain reduced rates on through goods imported into Manchuria from Japan but not from Shanghai. "Although apparently not in violation of the literal wording of the undertaking concerning equality of opportunity . . . such an arrangement would seem to be clearly contrary to the spirit of that undertaking" since only Japanese goods were shipped via Japan. Reinsch note of June 27, 1914, *U. S. For. Rel.*, 1915, p. 595. Here was another difference in interpretation which could merely be argued about through diplomatic correspondence.

[4] F. Delaisi, *Oil, Its Influence in Politics* (1920), Ch. V.

[5] This controversy was finally settled by negotiations, not of governments but of the private oil companies concerned. In March, 1925, it was announced that an agreement with the Iraq government for 75 years had been made, which provided that the chairman of the Turkish Petroleum Company should always be British but that the stock should be divided equally between the Anglo-Persian, Royal Dutch-Shell, the Standard Oil and six other American companies, and 65 French companies. Thus British interests have surrendered majority control. Cf. *Manchester Guardian*, March 17, 1925.

the United States considered to be an exclusive oil concession in Djambi to a company controlled by the Royal Dutch-Shell, and had refused to consider bids for this concession from American oil interests. The United States declared that this refusal to accept the American bid was a violation of the Open Door, particularly as this was the only valuable concession in the colony. But Holland replied that the Standard Oil had neglected to bid when tenders were originally opened, and that the concession granted was by no means exclusive.[1]

A similar difference in interpretation arose between the United States and Japan in 1921–23 over the Federal Wireless Telegraph contract in China. In this controversy the Japanese government took the position that previous contracts of the Mitsui firm entitled it to a monopoly, without which it could not make a profit, and that the Federal contract should therefore be set aside. In a statement distributed to the Far Eastern newspapers, in March, 1923, the Japanese legation in Peking stated that the nine-power Open Door treaty of February, 1922, provided only "for the future" and that "there is absolutely no doubt that the existence of monopolies and its necessity has been admitted and recognized at the Washington Conference."[2] The United States declined to accept the argument, and continued to support the Federal Wireless contract.[3]

While monopolies have generally been considered as violating the Open Door, some types of monopolies, as we have seen, are necessary if concessions are to be profitably developed.[4] This fact was recognized in the Open Door treaty of Washington which

[1] Cf. "Oil Prospecting in Foreign Countries," 67th Cong., 1st sess., Sen. Doc. No. 39; *Foreign Ownership in the Petroleum Industry*, Report of the Federal Trade Commission (1923), Sen. Com. print; 67th Cong., 4th sess., p. 53.

[2] Cf. p. 471 n. 2.

[3] "Le Litigie relatif à le radio télégraphie en Chine," *Revue du Pacifique* (1924), p. 412, an article which says that the United States forced China to spend $26,000,000 unnecessarily, since the same service was already being supplied by the Japanese company. The case was pending in 1929.

[4] In its note of May 12, 1920, the United States suggested an agreement with Great Britain providing that "no exclusive economic concessions covering the whole of any mandated region or sufficiently large to be virtually exclusive shall be granted," and that "reasonable provision shall be made for publicity of application for concessions" so that American firms should not be placed at a disadvantage with nationals of the mandate nation. Cmd. 1226, p. 3.

NECESSITY OF INTERNATIONAL CONTROL 461

states that the Open Door provisions do not "prohibit the acquisition of such properties or rights as may be necessary to the conduct of a particular commercial or financial undertaking. . . ."[1] Unfortunately the treaty does not say who is to interpret what rights are "necessary." While the original Berlin Act of 1885 contained a provision against monopolies, the revised Act of 1919 provided that "Each State reserves the right to dispose freely of its property and to grant concessions for the development of the natural resources of the territory, but no regulations on these matters shall admit of any differential treatment between the nationals of the Signatory Powers. . . .,"[2] a provision which apparently authorizes monopolies. The B. mandates prohibit concessions having the character of a general monopoly. But monopolies of a purely fiscal nature or for the purpose of controlling the development of natural resources may be created.[3]

These illustrations show how hard it is to draw the line between concessions which violate and those which do not violate the Open Door. Obviously it is extremely difficult to settle such differences by diplomatic correspondence. If left to the decision of the governments involved, a deadlock will probably arise, because each government is not only a judge but a party to the dispute, in which its application of the principle of the Open Door is likely to be controlled by self-interest rather than by law.

In an attempt to remedy this weakness and to provide for some impartial means of settling such controversies and of defining the meaning of the Open Door, the revised Act of Berlin of 1919 provides that such disputes which cannot be settled by negotiation shall be settled by compulsory arbitration.[4] Such a provision is also inserted in the mandates. In the summer of 1924 the Greek government invoked such a clause to bring before the Permanent Court of International Justice a dispute between it and the British government over a concession in Palestine.[5] In 1914 a Greek contractor, M. Mavrommatis, had obtained, or was about to obtain, certain concessions from the Turks in Palestine, in regard to

[1] Art. 3, *Treaties of U. S.*, Vol. III, p. 122.
[2] Art. IV, *ibid.*, p. 3742.
[3] Cf. Art. 7, British mandate for East Africa.
[4] Art. 12.
[5] The Mavrommatis Palestine Concessions, Judgment No. 2, Series A. August 30, 1924.

electric tramway lines, etc. At the end of the war, Mavrommatis requested of the British government that these concessions be readapted to new economic conditions—but in vain. After the failure of negotiations to bring about an agreement, Greece laid the dispute before the World Court. In August, 1924, the Court decided that it had jurisdiction over the case.[1] In March of the following year it held that while the concession was valid, the claim for an indemnity should be dismissed, since no loss to Mavrommatis from expropriation had been proved.

While the settlement of these differences by judicial procedure is a great step forward, many of the obligations arising out of Open Door treaties are scarcely justiciable in an ordinary court of law, but may more suitably be dealt with by an administrative tribunal. For this reason, the Mandates Commission of the League may be successful in settling disputes over the Open Door without the necessity of invoking the jurisdiction of the World Court.[2]

Another step in this direction was taken at the Washington Conference. While the Open Door treaty did not provide for compulsory arbitration, a resolution was adopted providing for the establishment of a Board of Reference "to which any questions arising in connection with the execution of the Open Door provisions of the treaty" may be referred for investigation and report.[3] This Board has no compulsory powers and as a matter of fact it has never been established. Nevertheless, the recognition of the principle of an international administrative tribunal for the settlement of such questions is of far-reaching importance. One of the greatest possible steps toward world peace would be a treaty signed by the ten leading colonial powers, guaranteeing the Open Door, not only in their own colonies but in the independent countries of the world, such as China, Turkey, Mexico, Siam, Liberia, Abyssinia, Persia and Afghanistan, and placing the supervision of such an agreement in the hands of some impartial international tribunal.

[1] Cf. Art. 26 of the Palestine Mandate: "The Mandatory agrees that, if any dispute whatever should arise between the Mandatory and another Member of the League of Nations relating to the interpretation or the application of the provisions of the Mandate, such dispute, if it cannot be settled by negotiation, shall be submitted to the Permanent Court of International Justice."

[2] Cf. p. 361.

[3] *Treaties of the U. S.*, Vol. III, p. 3138.

CHAPTER XX

INDIRECT FORMS OF IMPERIALISM

1. Danger Zones.—2. The Leasehold.—3. The Sphere of Influence.—4. Protectorates.—5. Semi-protectorates.—6. Financial Control.—7. Tariff Control.—8. Exterritoriality.—9. Informal Control.—10. Joint Government.—11. National *v.* International Control.

1. DANGER ZONES

Because of the disfavor into which the old-style imperialism has fallen, the outright annexation of backward regions is less frequent than formerly. While most of the backward regions of the world were appropriated as colonies a half-century ago, a number of nominally independent countries nevertheless remain as tempting morsels for the imperialist. In Africa, such countries are Abyssinia, Liberia and Egypt; in the Near East,—Turkey, Mesopotamia, Persia and Afghanistan; in the Far East,—China and Siam; in the Americas, the Caribbean countries—Cuba, Haiti and Santo Domingo, the five Central American republics, and some of the weaker states of South America. These countries together with other regions are still "free," whether because of the rivalry of different imperialist powers, their own geographic position which makes invasion difficult, or their inherent strength. Nevertheless, most of these countries have fallen under some indirect form of foreign control, which may possibly be converted in the future into more permanent and far-reaching subjugation. As a rule, these countries possess valuable resources which attract the foreigner. Many of them, as we have seen, have borrowed money from outside bankers who naturally demand that their interest be paid. Some of them have archaic forms of government, oftentimes too weak or too corrupt to protect the lives either of natives or foreigners. In these "danger zones" of imperialism, chronic incompetence has, in some cases at least, justified foreign intervention, often resulting in the establishment of some more or less permanent and indirect means of foreign control, converting these countries into what Professor Lawrence calls "client states."[1] However innocent these forms of control may look, they usually give the government possessing them a hidden influence of far-reaching political and economic importance.

2. THE LEASEHOLD

One of the most interesting and hitherto important forms of indirect control is the leasehold. An imperialistic power may wish to acquire control over certain territory in a backward country which is particularly valuable for commercial or strategic reasons. Instead of annexing it outright, the power makes a treaty with the government of the backward country—a treaty often imposed by a show of force—whereby it is given a lease over such territory for a period, usually of ninety-nine years. To salve the prestige of the backward country, the lease may say, as did the lease of the Manchurian ports by China to Russia in 1898, that it "in no way violates the sovereign rights" of the local government.[2] In other words, the leasing power technically retains its sovereignty over the region, but transfers all powers of jurisdiction to the foreign government.[3] Thus in the Port Arthur lease, the "entire military command of the land and naval forces and equally the supreme civil administration" were handed over to the Russian authorities. For all practical purposes, therefore, a leasehold is a colony until the lease expires.

China.—In China the leasehold has had an important political influence. The habit of leasing was started by Germany when she, in 1898, because of the murder of two missionaries, obliged China to lease the valuable port of Tsingtau for 99 years. In 1914 Japan drove Germany out of this lease, and in agreements of 1915 and 1918 China agreed to give full assent to the disposition which Japan and Germany should agree to make of Shantung.[4] At the Paris Peace Conference China declared that these agreements had been extorted by force and that these German interests should be returned to her. Nevertheless despite the efforts of the United

---

[1] T. J. Lawrence, *The Principles of International Law* (7th ed., 1923), p. 56.
[2] Lease of March 27, 1898, MacMurray, *Treaties and Agreement with and concerning China* (1921), p. 119.
[3] Oppenheim, *International Law* (2d ed., 1920), Vol. I, p. 223.
[4] Treaty of May 25, 1915, MacMurray, Vol. II, p. 1216.

THE LEASEHOLD

States, all of Germany's rights in Tsingtau were transferred in the Treaty of Versailles to Japan. But at the same time, Japan orally promised to return Tsingtau to China at some time in the future.[1] This promise was eventually carried out, partly because of the pressure of the United States. During the Washington Conference—in February, 1922—Japan signed a treaty with China, withdrawing her administration from Tsingtau but retaining certain valuable economic interests.[2]

At the present time, the only lease held by Japan in China is of the ports of Port Arthur and Dairen. China originally leased these ports to Russia in 1898 for twenty-five years, a period which would have expired in 1923. As a result of the Russo-Japanese war of 1905, Russia was obliged to transfer these leases to Japan.[3] In order to forestall their expiration in 1923, Japan, as part of the famous Twenty-One Demands of 1915, obliged China to extend them to 1997.[4] At the Washington Conference of 1921-1922, Japan refused to give up these rights, and she also declined to consider the protest of the Chinese parliament in January, 1923, that the treaties extending these leases were invalid because they had not been approved by it, as required by the Chinese constitution, and also because they had been secured under duress.

Great Britain has held two leases in China, the most important of which is located across the bay from Port Arthur—Wei-hai-wei. This lease was made in 1898 "for so long a period as Port Arthur shall remain in the occupation of Russia."[5] However, the transfer of the lease to Japan in 1905 led Great Britain to stay in Wei-hai-wei until the Washington Conference when she agreed to negotiate in regard to withdrawal. Negotiations having failed, Great Britain was still in Wei-hai-wei in July, 1929. But at the Washington Conference, she would not agree to withdraw from her second lease at Kowloon—also made in 1898 for 99 years—on the ground that its occupation was necessary to protect Hongkong.[6]

[1] J. Tumulty, *Woodrow Wilson as I Know Him* (1921), p. 390; Arts. 156-58, Treaty of Versailles.
[2] Treaty of Feb. 4, 1922, T. S. 277. Cf. Ge-Zay Wood, *The Shantung Question* (1922), Chs. XVIII and XIX; cf. Willoughby, *Foreign Rights and Interests in China*, Ch. VIII.
[3] MacMurray, Vol. I, p. 523.
[4] *Ibid.*, Vol. II, p. 1221.
[5] *Ibid.*, Vol. I, p. 152.
[6] *Conference on the Limitation of Armament*, p. 1066.

France, the last power to hold a lease of Chinese territory, leased the port of Kwang-chow-wan in 1898 for a period of 99 years.[1] At the Washington Conference, while France was willing to "join in the collective restitution of the leaseholds," this suggestion did not appeal to Great Britain or Japan, and so fell through. As a result of this Conference, therefore, the two leaseholds of Tsingtau and Wei-hai-wei were to be returned to China; Japan still retains her leases of Port Arthur and Dairen, Great Britain that of Kowloon, and France that of Kwang-chow-wan, all of which expire in 1997.[2] While the United States has no leases in Asia, its possession of the Philippines serves to offset European influence in the Orient to some degree.[3]

Panama.—In the western hemisphere, the United States has followed European practice in exacting leaseholds from the backward countries. The construction of a canal, uniting the Atlantic and the Pacific, was a task of great service to the world, but it was a task the importance of which the republic of Colombia, through whose territory the canal needed to go, did not realize to the same degree as did the United States. Despite protracted negotiations, Colombia refused to authorize the United States to construct such a canal through the Panama isthmus, except on what the United States regarded as exorbitant terms. A revolution thereupon broke out, resulting in the establishment of the Panama republic which the United States hastened to recognize; and in the Hay-Bunau-Varilla treaty of 1903, the United States guaranteed the independence of this suspiciously-born republic in return for a lease of territory for the canal. Within a zone five miles wide on each side, the United States has "all the rights, powers and authority" which it would "possess and exercise if it were sovereign of the territory" within which the canal zone is located, "to the entire exclusion of the exercise by the republic of Panama of any such" rights.[4]

Moreover, the republic of Panama grants to the United States "in perpetuity the use, occupation and control of any other lands and waters outside the zone, which may be necessary or conven-

---

[1] MacMurray, Vol. I, p. 218.
[2] *Conference on the Limitation of Armament*, pp. 1064, 1518. W. W. Willoughby, *China at the Conference, A Report* (1922), Ch. XIV.
[3] Cf. Dennett, *Americans in Eastern Asia*, p. 622.
[4] Treaty of Nov. 18, 1903, *Treaties of the U. S.*, Vol. II, p. 1349.

ient" for the construction, maintenance, operation, sanitation and protection of the canal, or other works necessary and convenient for its construction. Apparently the United States is to judge what additional territory is thus "convenient," and a literal interpretation of the treaty would authorize the extension of its control over the whole territory of Panama if it chose to do so. The United States may also use its military forces "at all times and in its discretion" for the safety and protection of the canal; and in case the cities of Panama and Colon do not comply with the sanitary ordinances of the United States or maintain order, the Panama republic grants the United States the right to enforce such ordinances whenever it judges necessary.[1]

In return for this lease which, unlike the Chinese leases, is made in perpetuity, the United States paid to Panama the sum of $10,000,-000 outright, which is supplemented by an annual subsidy of $250,000. Moreover, the "Taft Agreement" of 1904 allowed Panama to import goods through the ports of Ancon and Cristobol, which are within the Zone, and further provided that no duties should be imposed by the American authorities upon goods passing from the republic of Panama into the Zone.[2] Following the abrogation of the Taft Agreement by the American Congress in 1922 on the ground that the Canal had now been constructed, the two countries proceeded to negotiate a new treaty. In the course of these negotiations, as well as previously, Panama asserted that the United States had taken advantage of past agreements to discriminate in favor of American as opposed to Panama trade, contrary to the spirit of the lease.[3] On July 28, 1926, a new treaty was finally signed, but the National Assembly was so dissatisfied with its terms that it asked the government to reopen negotiations. The question was unsettled in July, 1929.[4]

[1] The Panama Constitution (Art. 136), also provides, "The Government of the United States of America shall have the power to intervene in any part of the Republic of Panama to reëstablish public peace and constitutional order, in the event of their being disturbed, if the said nation, by public treaty, assumes the obligation of guaranteeing the independence and sovereignty of this Republic." H. F. Wright, *The Constitutions of the States at War* (1918), p. 476.
[2] *Treaties of the U. S.*, Vol. III, p. 2758.
[3] Cf. G. W. Goethals, *Government of the Canal Zone* (1915), pp. 28 ff.
[4] Cf. "Mexico, the Caribbean, and Tacna-Arica," *I. S.*, Vol. III, No. 23. If the United States went to war, the territory held under lease would pre-

Within the Canal Zone the United States maintains undisputed sway, the Zone being governed by an American army officer. Although the United States has no direct control over the internal affairs of Panama proper—merely guaranteeing its independence—it has to a certain extent influenced domestic policy. It has objected to certain concessions on the ground that they would interfere with the defence of the Canal.[1] It has warned the Panama government against "any unwise or ill-advised" use of the annuities paid under the treaty of 1903; while upon two occasions—in 1908 and 1912—it has supervised elections at the request of the Panama government.[2] Thus by virtue of the canal lease acquired in 1903, a semi-protectorate has been established.[3]

3. THE SPHERE OF INFLUENCE

Inasmuch as leaseholds have in many cases been acquired over important ports, they give great indirect control over the trade of the hinterland. For even though this territory is not included in the leased area, it may be dependent upon it as an outlet to the sea. Thus, a "sphere of influence" may be based upon a leasehold. But unlike a lease, which gives certain political rights, the sphere of influence as a rule gives only economic rights.[4] A sphere of

sumably be belligerent territory although the state possessing ultimate sovereignty might not wish to go to war, and if a member of the League, might not legally be able to go to war. Cf. p. 580.

[1] *U. S. For. Rel.*, 1913, p. 1091.
[2] *Ibid.*, p. 1103; *ibid.*, 1914, p. 1035; *ibid.*, 1912, p. 1141.
[3] The United States has also leased in perpetuity certain coaling and naval stations from Cuba, and several islands, for 99 years with a right of renewal from Nicaragua. Cf. *Treaties of the U. S.*, Vol. I, p. 358; Vol. III, p. 2740. For the Nicaragua canal lease, cf. p. 419. About a dozen leases of ports, etc., have been made between European colonial powers in Africa, which are more of the European category (cf. p. 130); while the United States has leased certain islands to the North Borneo Company. *Treaties of the U. S.*, Vol. III, p. 2605; *U. S. For Rel.*, 1907, p. 548. Great Britain has also leased territory from native states along the Indian frontier. Cf. index "leases," *Map of Africa by Treaty.*
[4] There is a technical difference between the sphere of influence and sphere of interest. The former may give a power certain vague political rights, short of a protectorate; while the latter is merely economic. According to this distinction, the sphere of influence is found in Africa, while the sphere of interest is found in Asia. But if conditions had been favorable, there is no doubt that the powers holding spheres of interest would have acquired political authority also. Cf. Willoughby, *Foreign Rights and Interests in China*, p. 270.

this nature may be granted to an imperialist power by a backward government; or imperialist powers may divide up nominally independent backward countries into such spheres, without asking the consent of the latter. Within a sphere of influence, the power holding it has preferential or exclusive rights to make loans, construct railways, operate mines, or develop public works.[1] In dividing up the economic resources of a backward country into such zones, the powers have adopted one means of compromising economic rivalries. But since there are ordinarily not enough spheres to go around—the United States had no sphere in China—outside powers will complain. Monopolies of any sort exploit the native; and powers will disagree as to the extent of their respective spheres. Consequently this form of control has probably led to more disputes than it has settled.

Asia.—In Asia, Africa and the Pacific, the sphere of influence has been a common instrument of imperialism. In China, six European powers have held spheres. Russia had such a sphere in Manchuria from which she was evicted by Japan following the war of 1905. She maintained, however, a sphere of influence in Outer Mongolia.[2] In an agreement entered upon in 1898 Great Britain and Germany mapped out respective spheres, the former in the Yangtze valley and the latter in Shantung province—back of the Tsingtau leasehold.[3] It appears that as a result of the World War Japan has succeeded to the German sphere. France also has had a sphere of influence in the Chinese provinces north of Indo-China.[4] Parts of the kingdom of Siam were placed under the respective spheres of influence of Great Britain and France in an agreement of 1896 renewed in 1904.[5]

The sphere of influence has also been established in Central Asia. In the Anglo-Russian agreement of 1907 Persia was divided up into three zones; England was given a sphere in the south, Russia in the north; while the central zone was neutral. Although

[1] Willoughby, *Foreign Rights and Interests in China*, p. 274.
[2] Cf. Agreement of Nov. 3, 1916, Mongolia and Russia, MacMurray, Vol. II, p. 992; in treaties of 1907 and 1910 Japan and Russia came to an agreement which virtually guaranteed their respective spheres. MacMurray, Vol. I, pp. 657, 803.
[3] Cf. Anglo-German Bankers' Arrangement Regarding Spheres of Interest in Railway Construction, Sept. 2, 1898, MacMurray, Vol. I, p. 266.
[4] For summary of treaties, cf. Willoughby, cited, pp. 275 ff.
[5] Franco-British agreement of Jan. 15, 1896, MacMurray, Vol. I, p. 54.

the "special interests" of England in the foreign affairs of Tibet, were recognized, neither England nor Russia could obtain concessions there.[1] Great Britain apparently had designs on the whole of Persia. For in March, 1915, Russia assented to the inclusion of the neutral zone within the British sphere; while in the Anglo-Persian agreement of August 9, 1919, Great Britain obtained the right to furnish Persia with advisers and to make a loan. But the government of the Shah declined to put this agreement into effect, turning instead to the United States for help.[2]

Likewise in Turkey the sphere of influence has been used as a means of compromising the economic rivalries of the great powers. In 1914 a Franco-German agreement mapped out spheres of influence for railway construction, the French being given a monopoly in northern Anatolia and Syria.[3] During the World War, some six secret agreements were made by the Allies, dividing up the Turkish Empire into spheres;[4] while in 1920 France, Great Britain and Italy made a new agreement, to which Turkey was not a party, providing that in their respective spheres France and Italy had a "preferential claim" to supply advisers to the Turkish government, if the latter desired such assistance; and recognizing a monopoly of concessions by the powers holding such spheres.[5] Because of the protests of the United States and Turkey this agreement did not go into effect.

Africa and the Pacific.—About thirty treaties involving practically all the great European powers have been made recognizing spheres of influence in Africa.[6] When the French government in 1912 demanded that the customs receiver nearest the French frontier be a Frenchman, it was suspected of wishing to divide Liberia up into spheres.[7] In the Pacific, Germany and Great Britain mapped out their respective spheres in the agreement of 1886.[8]

[1] 1 Martens (3d series), 8.
[2] Cf. 112 *State Papers*, 760; J. M. Balfour, *Recent Happenings in Persia* (1922), Chs. IX–XIV. Cf. p. 421.
[3] Earle, *Turkey*, p. 248.
[4] Baker, *Woodrow Wilson and World Settlement*, Ch. III.
[5] 113 *State Papers*, 797.
[6] Cf. index, "sphere of influence," Hertslet, cited.
[7] *U. S. For. Rel.*, 1912, p. 700. However, the French government denied any such purpose. For spheres in Abyssinia, cf. p. 450.
[8] Cf. p. 452.

In the case of Africa and the Pacific, the sphere of influence has been the first step in the establishment of political control, which has taken the form either of a protectorate or annexation. That the sphere has not led to such results in Asia is due primarily to the greater strength of the countries exploited, but in part also to the opposition of the United States, who held no such spheres. Indeed as far as China is concerned, the Open Door treaty, signed at the Washington Conference, provided that the powers would not support any agreements "designed to create Spheres of Influence" in China.[1] Apparently this treaty does not invalidate existing spheres, but merely prevents their establishment in the future.[2]

4. PROTECTORATES

There is no single type of protectorate, but in all of them an imperialist power controls the foreign affairs of the protected community; and usually it has some control over internal finance and other matters of domestic administration. Within Europe there are such protectorates as Monaco, the independence of which is guaranteed by France, in return for which Monaco promises to exercise its independence in perfect conformity with the political, military, naval and economic interests of France.[3] But the most important protectorates are the "colonial" protectorates established over backward regions, in which the powers also have a high degree of control in internal affairs.[4] The administration of the twenty-odd protectorates in the British Empire is much the same as that of the crown colony, except that the chief British official is called a High Commissioner.[5] Among the French protectorates, however, local institutions have been preserved to a greater extent than among the French colonies. Thus, in the treaty of June, 1884, between the King of Cambodia and France, establishing a French protectorate, the King of Cambodia agreed

[1] Treaty of Feb. 6, 1922, *Treaties of the U. S.*, Vol. III, p. 3123.

[2] Cf. statement of Japanese legation at Peking, *Weekly Review* (Shanghai), April 7, 1923, p. 193.

[3] Treaty of July 17, 1918, 11 Martens (3d series), 313; cf. also Willoughby and Fenwick, *Types of Restricted Sovereignty and of Colonial Autonomy* (1919); and Fenwick, *Wardship in International Law* (1919).

[4] Cf. F. Despagnet, *Éssai sur les protectorats* (1896), pp. 137 ff.; Dupuis, cited, Ch. VIII.

[5] H. Jenkyns, *British Rule and Jurisdiction Beyond the Seas* (1902), p. 173.

to accept all the administrative, judicial, financial and commercial reforms which the French government might judge to be useful, although the King retained general direction of administration. Nevertheless the levy and collection of taxes, tariffs, indirect contributions, public works and services, needing European experts, were to be in hands of French agents, and the King could not contract a loan without French consent.[1] As far as the outside world is concerned, the internal native administration of a protectorate may be assimilated to that of a colony, but from the international standpoint, there are important differences. When a previously independent country is annexed, its past treaties are automatically extinguished, while in the case of protectorates, the protecting power must respect all such treaties which affect the rights of foreign states. For this reason, powers which object to the annexation of backward regions may acquiesce in the establishment of a protectorate. Likewise in a protectorate the protecting power does not ordinarily have jurisdiction over foreigners, unless it is granted by treaty.

Fauchille lists twenty-eight different countries as having been under protectorates, national or international.[2] In some cases, these protectorates have been terminated by annexation. This was the case of Georgia which was a protectorate under a treaty of 1783, but was annexed by Russia in 1801; and of Madagascar, which was a protectorate under the treaty of 1885 between the Queen of Madagascar and France, but was annexed in 1896. In other cases, protectorates have terminated in independence. In treaties of 1879, 1893 and 1907 Afghanistan accepted the protection of Great Britain, receiving a British subsidy; however, in the Dobbs treaty of November, 1921, the British were forced to terminate this control.[3] Likewise, the British protectorate over Egypt, proclaimed in 1914, was terminated in February, 1922.[4]

[1] Treaty of June 17, 1884, 12 Martens (2d series), 637.
[2] Fauchille, *Traité*, Vol. I, pp. 268 ff.
[3] Soviet Russia thereupon made a treaty with Afghanistan, promising it a subsidy of a million roubles gold, annually. Both parties agreed not to make political or military conventions injurious to the other. Cf. Marin, "L'entrée en relations indépendantes de l'Afghanistan avec les Puissances," *L'Aise française*, No. 211, March, 1923; also Castigne, "La politique extérieure de l'Afghanistan depuis 1919," 48 *Revue du Monde Musulman* (1921); cf. treaty of Nov. 22, 1921, 12 Martens (3d series), 587.
[4] Cf. p. 478.

International Protectorates.—Several attempts in modern history have been made to establish international protectorates. In the Act of Algeciras, the powers attempted to impose such a status upon Morocco. The administration of the customs was placed in the hands of two international bodies; provision was made for an international state bank; while a native police force was to be organized under French and Spanish instructors, subject to Swiss inspection. The Swiss inspector was to make an annual report, transmitted to the diplomatic corps as to whether the police were acting in conformity with the decisions of the Conference.[1] Nevertheless, this plan gave the foreign powers no positive means of control, and the assassination of foreigners and chronic revolts continued.[2] Consequently, following negotiations with Germany, France in 1912 modified the international régime and established a protectorate.

The idea of international protection was applied to the kingdom of Abyssinia—which had been the object of rivalries between different European powers. As a result of the battle of Adowa of 1895 in which Abyssinia definitely defeated Italy, the latter government recognized Abyssinia's complete independence. In order to prevent further rivalries, France, Great Britain and Italy signed a convention, on December 13, 1906, in which they agreed to protect the integrity of Abyssinia, and to prevent rivalries in regard to concessions.[3] While this convention gave Abyssinia "protection" against external aggression, it does not appear until recently at least to have been used to interfere with her internal affairs.

5. SEMI-PROTECTORATES

A number of small countries have been obliged to grant a right of intervention to great powers and to submit to a form of control, which is neither complete nor continuous, even in foreign affairs, but which acts as a constant negative check upon the action of such governments, out of fear of the consequences of wrongdoing. Such is the type of control which Great Britain now exercises

[1] Ch. I, Act of April 7, 1906, *Treaties of the U. S.*, Vol. II, p. 2157.
[2] Piquet, *Maroc*, pp. 197 ff.
[3] 35 Martens (2d series), 556. Previous to the battle of Adowa, Italy had claimed a protectorate over Abyssinia, by virtue of a dubious article in the Treaty of Ucciali, of May, 1889. For Abyssinia and the League cf. p. 278.

over Egypt and Mesopotamia, and which the United States exercises in Cuba and Haiti—two republics in the Caribbean Sea—as well as in Panama, already discussed. These countries are at least partially independent in foreign affairs. Cuba, Haiti and Panama are members of the League of Nations. Mesopotamia and Egypt are expected to join shortly. All of these countries are entitled to some diplomatic representation abroad; while they may make certain treaties in their own name. They cannot therefore properly be called protectorates.

Cuba.—Nevertheless, they are subject to a number of important limitations upon their independence, as illustrated by the treaty of 1903 between Cuba and the United States. This treaty, embodying what is known as the Platt amendment, provides that Cuba shall never enter into any treaty with foreign powers which will impair its independence, or permit a foreign power to obtain control over any part of the island, either through colonization or by establishing military bases; and accords the United States the right of intervention to preserve the independence of Cuba and to sustain a government capable of protecting life, property, and individual liberty.[1]

Attempts of diplomatic and consular officials of the United States in Cuba to depart from diplomatic channels in influencing local administration were resisted by the Cuban government in 1902; and when the Cuban government protested against the landing of American marines, for the purpose of sounding certain waters, the American Secretary of State offered his apologies and asked Cuba to authorize such landing. Also when an American consul protested against certain insanitary conditions in Santiago, on the ground of the Platt amendment, the Cuban government ended the matter by telling the State Department that it would receive such protests only through diplomatic channels.[2]

The first intervention of the United States under the Platt amendment was in 1906. A revolution had broken out, to suppress which President Palma requested the aid of the United States.[3] The president thereupon resigned; the Cuban congress

---

[1] Convention of May 22, 1903, *Treaties of the U. S.*, Vol. I, p. 362.
[2] Leuchsenring, "La Enmienda Platt. Su interpretacion primitiva y su aplicaciones posteriores," 29 *Cuba Contemporánea* (1922), 197, 305.
[3] *U. S. For. Rel.*, 1906, Pt. 1, pp. 479, 480.

SEMI-PROTECTORATES 475

failed to select a successor; and conditions became so turbulent that the United States intervened with an army of 6,000 men, and established a provisional government at first under Secretary of War Taft and later under C. E. Magoon, a government which lasted two years and four months.[1] In creating this government, the United States issued a proclamation stating that "in so far as is consistent with the nature of a provisional government established under authority of the United States, this will be a Cuban government conforming, as far as may be, to the constitution of Cuba. The Cuban flag will be hoisted as usual over the government buildings of the island. All the executive departments and the provincial and municipal governments, including that of the city of Havana, will be continued to be administered as under the Cuban Republic. The courts will continue to administer justice, and all laws not in their nature inapplicable by reason of the temporary and emergent character of the Government will be in force."[2] Despite this professed moderation, Cubans charged American authorities with expending government balances, issuing pardons wholesale, and granting Americans a large number of concessions. One of the first acts of the Cuban government, upon being restored, was to cancel some of these contracts on the ground that they had been granted because of favoritism.[3]

In 1912 Cuba again got into difficulty. In an attempt to stamp out an independence movement among the negroes, the Cuban congress passed a law prohibiting the organization of political parties whose members were only of one race. This led to a revolution which, despite the assertions of President Gomez to the contrary, soon got beyond the control of the Government, as a

[1] The United States first attempted to effect a reconciliation between the factions. *U. S. For. Rel.*, 1906, p. 490.

[2] *U. S. For. Rel.*, p. 491.

[3] Leuchsenring cited, p. 325. While the reports of the provisional government are silent as to these charges, they show that although there was $13,625,000 on hand at the beginning of the American occupation, there was only $2,860,000 on hand at the end. These expenditures were defended on the ground that they went to pay existing obligations, and expenses of the occupation and to build roads. Cf. Supplementary Report, Dec. 1, 1908–Jan. 28, 1909, of the provisional government, S. Doc. 80, vol. 9, 61st Cong., 1st sess.; cf. also the Annual Report of C. E. Magoon, provisional governor of Cuba, 1907, S. Doc. 155, 60th Cong., 1st sess., vol. 6. *U. S. Foreign Relations* for 1907 and 1908 contain no material in regard to this government.

result of which the United States landed four companies of marines to protect the lives and property of Americans, but not, according to official pronouncements, to put down the insurrection which was a duty of Cuba.[1]

Four years later a bitterly contested election was held in Cuba; and after the votes were cast, it was charged that the government in power interrupted the communications of Havana with the rest of the country so that the ballots could be opened and changed to favor the government. The leaders of the Liberal party—the party out of power—asked the American State Department to appoint witnesses to watch the verification of the elections. When this suggestion was not acted upon, a revolution broke out against the Menocal government, charging that it had illegally controlled elections.[2] Despite these charges, the United States came to the support of the existing government. And when Cuba entered the War, the United States declared that the revolutionists menaced sugar production, necessary to the Allied cause, and that they were therefore enemies. In order to suppress the insurgents, the United States landed troops in Cuba in October, 1917, who remained there until 1921. Meantime—in 1919—General Crowder went to Cuba at the "invitation" of President Menocal to study the Cuban electoral system, apparently in an attempt to bring about honest elections. He was followed by other Americans who took a census of the island, and by an American financial adviser who, it is charged, put in a bill of $50,000 for 15 days' work.[3] None of these officials, it appears, were approved by the Cuban congress. Later the position of General Crowder was put on a more regular basis—for in 1923 he was sent to Cuba as an "Ambassador," an official as a rule sent only to the great powers. Within recent years the American government apparently has returned to a strict interpretation of the Platt amendment; i. e., it does not interfere with Cuban affairs, although the Machado administration seems to be a ruthless dictatorship.

Throughout the history of the Platt amendment, Cuba and the United States have differed as to its scope. Following a protest

---

[1] *U. S. For. Rel.*, 1912, pp. 243 ff.

[2] Leuchsenring, "La ingerencia notreamericana en los asuntos interiores de Cuba," 30 *Cuba Contemporánea* (1922), 41 ff.

[3] *Ibid.*, 61. The Cuban government, however, paid him only $15,000.

of the United States in regard to the Zapata Swamp concession, President Gomez declared that the Platt amendment "does not authorize or signify meddling in internal affairs, subjecting the acts of the administration to control or tutelage."[1] The United States has not claimed that the "Platt amendment gave this nation a right to do more than protest" against enterprises to which it was opposed.[2] In the case of the Caibarien-Neuvitas railway project, in which British capitalists were interested and asking a subsidy from the Cuban government, the United States exercised this right by expressing its vigorous disapproval of the burden which "it would impose on the Cuban Treasury in favor of capital which is neither American or Cuban."[3]

Haiti.—American presidents have attempted to extend the principle of the Platt amendment to other countries. In 1911 treaties to this effect were negotiated with Honduras and Nicaragua, but rejected by the Senate. Although a treaty was again negotiated with Nicaragua including such an "amendment" in 1913, this clause was later stricken out. Partly because of the hysterical fear of German aggressions in Haiti, the United States literally forced a "Platt amendment" treaty on the black republic of Haiti in 1915, a country which had been torn by internal dissension and faced with the prospects of bankruptcy. This treaty gives the United States financial control over the country and provides that Haiti shall not increase its public debt without the consent of the President of the United States; and shall not assume any financial obligation unless the ordinary revenues are adequate to pay interest and provide a sinking fund. Haiti further agrees to organize a constabulary "organized and officered by Americans," nominated by the President of the United States, while American engineers are to assist the country in the development of its natural resources. "Should the necessity occur, the United States will lend an efficient aid for the preservation of Haitian independence and the maintenance of a government adequate for the protection of life, property and individual liberty."[4]

Since 1915 United States marines have been stationed in Haiti

[1] *U. S. For. Rel.*, 1912, p. 312.
[2] *Ibid.*, 1914, p. 380.
[3] *Ibid.*, p. 381.
[4] *Treaties of the U. S.*, Vol. III, p. 2673.

where they have maintained order, except for an outbreak in 1919, organized the local gendarmerie, introduced a sanitary system, and begun the construction of roads. In order to unify American activities in the island, the United States appointed a High Commissioner to Haiti, in the early part of 1922. He is assisted by five "Treaty Officials,"—the financial adviser, and the heads of the gendarmerie, public works, the agricultural department and a medical service. Altogether there are about 100 Americans in the Haitian government, in addition to a brigade of marines.

Egypt.—A similar form of control has been exercised by Great Britain over Egypt and Mesopotamia. As a result of the resentment against the British protectorate of December, 1914, Great Britain was obliged, in a unilateral declaration of February, 1922, to recognize the independence of Egypt, maintaining, however, the status quo until further negotiations in respect to (1) the security of communications, (2) the defence of Egypt against foreign interference, (3) protection of foreign interests and minorities, (4) the Anglo-Egyptian Sudan. This was followed by an announcement that Egypt could now establish a Ministry of Foreign Affairs and that hereafter Great Britain would not accord protection to Egyptians in foreign countries. However, since "the welfare and security of Egypt are necessary to the peace and safety of the British Empire . . . the British government will regard as an unfriendly act any interference in the affairs of Egypt by another Power, and it will consider any aggression against the territory of Egypt as an act to be repelled with all the means at their command." [1]

Between 1922 and the fall of 1924 negotiations between Egypt and England took place in regard to the four reserved subjects, particularly the Sudan, it being England's wish to effect some form of alliance with Egypt similar to that with Mesopotamia.[2]

---

[1] Cmd. 1592 (1922), p. 29, and Cmd. 1617.

[2] In a dispatch of Oct. 7, 1924, Ramsay MacDonald said, "The effective co-operation of Great Britain and Egypt in protecting those communications might in my view have been ensured by the conclusion of a treaty of close alliance. The presence of a British force in Egypt provided for by such a treaty freely entered into by both parties on an equal footing would in no way be incompatible with Egyptian independence, whilst it would be an indication of the specially close and intimate relations between the two countries and their determination to co-operate in a matter of vital concern to both. It is not the wish of His Majesty's Government that this force should in any

But the Egyptians stood out against any compromise, Zaghlul Pasha, the Egyptian prime minister, even refusing to accept the Declaration of 1922. He stated before the Egyptian parliament in May, 1924, that a foreign officer in command of the Egyptian army was inconsistent with the dignity of an independent Egypt. Apparently as a result of the anti-British campaign in Egypt, Sir Lee Stack, a Britisher who was Governor General of the Sudan and Commander in Chief of the Egyptian army, was assassinated on Nov. 19, 1924. While the Egyptian government expressed its regret at the murder and while there was no evidence that it had been directly implicated, the British government nevertheless sent a stern ultimatum to the Egyptian government, stating that the assassination was the inevitable consequence of the anti-British attitude of the Egyptian government, and demanding an apology, an indemnity, and certain rights in regard to British advisers and the Sudan.[1] Following the occupation of the Customs House at Alexandria by British troops, Egypt acceded to most of these demands. While it does not appear that the murderers of Sir Lee Stack were apprehended, the situation in Egypt became more quiet. The British continue to be represented there by a High Commissioner, a Counselor and other advisers to the Egyptian government—a status which some Egyptians call a "disguised protectorate." [2] In 1927 a treaty of alliance between England and Egypt was drafted but not signed. Mesopotamia is in a similar position, except that its relations with Great Britain have been regularized by an alliance placed under the supervision of the League.[3]

way interfere with the function of the Egyptian Government or encroach upon Egyptian sovereignty. It is not the intention of His Majesty's Government to assume any responsibility for the actions or conduct of the Egyptian Government or to attempt to control or direct the policy which that Government may see fit to adopt." Cmd. 2269.

While the Cuban constitution embodies the Platt amendment as an appendix, the only relevant provision in the new Egyptian constitution of April 19, 1924, is article 154 which says, "The application of the present Constitution cannot have the effect of injuring the obligations of Egypt toward foreign states, nor the rights which foreigners may have acquired in Egypt by virtue of laws, treaties, or recognized usage." For the text of the constitution of April 19, 1923, cf. *Afrique française* (1923), sup. p. 167.

[1] Cf. p. 489.
[2] L. Himaya, *La Condition Internationale de l'Egypte* (1922), pp. 214 ff.
[3] Cf. p. 388.

480 INDIRECT FORMS OF IMPERIALISM

6. FINANCIAL CONTROL

In a number of cases, capitalist countries, either through government officials or representatives of bankers, control the revenues and expenditures of the governments of backward countries, who are otherwise independent. This control may be international, as in the case of Turkey, Greece, Tunis, Morocco, Egypt, China, Austria and Hungary. Or it may be national, such as the United States, officially or unofficially, has exercised in about eight Caribbean and Central American countries, as well as in Liberia and Persia.[1]

7. TARIFF CONTROL

The western powers have also obliged a number of backward countries to accept limitations upon the height of tariff duties affecting western imports. These countries have been Japan, China, Turkey, Morocco, Siam and Persia. As early as 1858 Japan was obliged to limit her tariff duties, and it was not until the treaties of 1911 that full tariff autonomy was given to Japan by the European powers.[2]

China.—In the Treaty of Nanking of 1842 China agreed to limit the duty on goods coming in or going out of the country to 5% ad valorem.[3] It was understood that the price schedules upon which this 5% was levied should be constantly modified so as to agree with existing prices. But notwithstanding a constant increase in price levels, there were no tariff revisions between 1858 and 1902, or between 1902 and 1918. Despite the revision of the latter year, prices continued to rise in China so that in 1922 she was receiving only an effective three and a half per cent duty instead of the 5% to which she was entitled.[4] At the Washington Conference of 1921–1922, China asked the powers to restore her tariff autonomy. Although they refused to meet this demand, a resolution authorizing revision of schedules so as to make the tariff an effective 5% was adopted; as well as a customs treaty

---

[1] Cf. Ch. XVIII.
[2] Cf. Regulation VII, Treaty between Great Britain and Japan, August 26, 1858, 48 *State Papers*, 37.
[3] Tariff Schedule, Treaty between Great Britain and China, August 29, 1842, 30 *State Papers*, 394.
[4] Wellington Koo, *Conference on the Limitation of Armament*, p. 920.

which provided that a Special Conference of the powers could authorize a surtax of $2\frac{1}{2}\%$ generally and 5% on luxuries. If China abolished the internal transit tax (likin), the Special Conference should increase the ordinary tariff rate to $12\frac{1}{2}\%$.[1] While China's schedules were revised so as to give her a 5% effective tariff, France, until 1925, withheld ratification of the Tariff Treaty, because of a dispute with China in which she insisted that China pay the Boxer indemnity with gold. Hence the resources of the central government remained meager. The Special Tariff Conference was convened finally in October, 1925, but it soon adjourned because there was no recognized government in China with which foreign delegates could deal. In July, 1928, the United States took the lead in concluding a new treaty providing for tariff autonomy upon a most-favored-nation basis.[2] Other powers followed suit, with the exception of Japan, and on February 1, 1929, the Chinese government put into effect a new tariff schedule aimed to foster infant industries.

Turkey.—As part of the Capitulations—the exterritorial rights first granted by Turkey to France in 1535—the powers secured the right to fix maximum tariff duties in Turkey. A protocol signed in 1907 between Turkey, Great Britain, Austria-Hungary, France, Germany, Italy and Russia increased the rate from 8% to 11%, presumably in order that Turkey might finance further railroad construction by foreign firms.[3] In 1914 the Sultan abrogated the capitulation by unilateral decree; and the Treaty of Lausanne of July, 1923, recognizes Turkey's freedom in this respect.

Siam.—The powers have gone even further in Siam than in China or Turkey. Beginning with the British Treaty of 1855, tariff duties in Siam were limited to 3%.[4] The United States was the first government voluntarily to recognize that the principle of "national autonomy" should apply to Siam. However, Siam may not impose a higher tariff on American than other foreign goods because of the most-favored-nation clause.[5] In the peace treaties, the Central Powers were obliged to terminate all their rights in

[1] Treaty of Feb. 6, 1922, *Treaties of U. S.*, Vol. III, p. 3125.
[2] For the treaty of July 25, 1928, see *A. J. I. L.*, Oct. 1928, p. 170.
[3] Protocol of April 25, 1907, 1 Martens (3d series), 790.
[4] Art. 8, Treaty of April 18, 1855, 46 *State Papers*, 138.
[5] Art. VII, Treaty of Dec. 16, 1920, *Treaties of U. S.*, Vol. III, p. 2828.

this country.¹ In a treaty of July 14, 1925, Great Britain recognized the fiscal autonomy of Siam.²

Morocco.—While still independent, the Sultan of Morocco made a number of treaties with foreign powers limiting duties on imports to 10%, increased to $12\frac{1}{2}\%$ by the Act of Algeciras. These limitations, which the Moroccan officials regard as irksome, France is still obliged to observe, except in regard to the Central Powers.³

Persia.—This "backward" country has been subject to similar restrictions accepted in such treaties as those of 1828 with Russia and of 1857 with Great Britain. In 1903 Persia and Great Britain revised their treaties with the result that the tariff rates which Persia might charge on British imports were fixed in a schedule providing for the free admission of some products and low duties on others. Moreover, Persia could levy no export taxes, with certain exceptions.⁴ On May 10, 1928, Great Britain signed an agreement granting Persia customs autonomy.⁵ Other governments in a similar position followed this example.

Haiti and Santo Domingo.—In exercising financial control over Haiti and Santo Domingo, the United States has insisted that tariff duties there should be modified so as to reduce revenues only with its assent.⁶ Otherwise it would be possible to decrease duties so that no revenues would exist for the payment of foreign obligations. The United States has interpreted such a clause to mean that its consent is necessary not only for a decrease but for an increase of duties.⁷

However great the advantage of free trade may be, its forcible and one-sided imposition by the powers on the different backward regions appears to be animated by a desire to dump foreign goods into these countries so as to prevent them from developing industries of their own.

---

¹ Cf. Art. 135, Treaty of Versailles.
² *T. S.* No. 1175.
³ *Colonial Tariff Policies*, p. 208.
⁴ Treaty of Feb. 9, 1903, 96 *State Papers*, 51. For the Persian Tariff Law of February 26, 1903, cf. 31 Martens (2d series), 514.
⁵ *European Economic and Political Survey*, July 15, 1928, p. 689.
⁶ Cf. Art. 9, Treaty of 1915 with Haiti, *Treaties of the U. S.*, Vol. III, p. 2675.
⁷ *U. S. For. Rel.*, 1911, p. 150.

8. EXTERRITORIALITY

This means the right of a foreign government to use its own courts and law in the trial of cases involving its subjects in those countries whose standards of justice have been at radical variance with those of the west. When a government possesses such rights, its consuls usually act as judges of offenses involving its citizens in exterritorial countries. For example, if an American commits murder in China, he is tried not by a Chinese but by an American court in China.[1] Such a system has been followed by foreign governments in practically all Mohammedan countries, because their law is based on a religion which accords few rights to Christians. It has also been exercised in such Oriental countries as Korea, Japan, China and Siam, as well as in the native kingdoms of the Pacific.[2] In these countries judicial procedure was originally regarded by western countries as unfair and punishments inhumane.

When such countries adopt western standards of justice, it is customary for the powers to relinquish their exterritorial powers. The United States surrendered her rights in Japan in the Treaty of 1894.[3] The powers have gradually relinquished their rights in Siam. As far back as 1909 Great Britain agreed that her subjects should come under the jurisdiction of the ordinary courts of Siam, with the exception of those who had registered previous to 1909, who should be tried in special Siamese courts, called the international courts;[4] but a European legal adviser may still be present at these trials in either court, where his voice has considerable weight. France has agreed to place her Asiatic subjects in Siam under ordinary Siamese jurisdiction; while in five northern provinces all Frenchmen are subject to the international court.[5] In 1920 the United States accepted the jurisdiction of the Siamese court, without insisting, as did the French and British, on the

---

[1] For the procedure, cf. Willoughby, *Foreign Rights and Interests in China*, pp. 28 ff.; Thayer, "The Capitulations of the Ottoman Empire," 17 *A. J. I. L.* (1923), 215; F. E. Hinckley, *American Consular Jurisdiction in the Orient* (1906), Ch. IV.

[2] For a summary of the treaties, cf. Hinckley, cited, p. 38.

[3] Art. I, XVII, Treaty of Nov. 22, 1894, *Treaties of the U. S.*, Vol. I, p. 1028.

[4] Convention of March 10, 1909, 102 *State Papers*, 126.

[5] James, "Jurisdiction over Foreigners in Siam," 16 *A. J. I. L.* (1922), 585; Chassigneux, "Le Siam et la France," *L'Asie française*, March, 1923.

international court procedure. However, for a period of five years, representatives of the United States could "invoke" any case before the lower Siamese courts, whereupon it should be transferred to an American court for trial.[1]

China.—Encouraged by the examples of Japan and Siam, China has repeatedly attempted to rid herself of these exterritorial restrictions. In the treaties of 1902, 1903 and 1908 the powers agreed that they would be removed as soon as China reformed her judicial system, and at the Washington Conference China asked that a date be definitely fixed when these rights would be extinguished. But despite the previous efforts of China to modernize her judicial system, the Washington Conference decided that no change could be made until China's judicial system had been investigated, which should be done by a commission within three months.[2] At the request of China herself, however, the work of the Commission was postponed. The Commission finally met in China in January, 1926, and after nine months' investigation made a report, stating that when the Chinese government had complied with its recommendations exterritoriality should be relinquished. While no great power has yet agreed to abolish these rights, China negotiated treaties in 1929 with Belgium, Denmark, Italy and Portugal providing for such abolition. The Belgian treaty provides that Belgian subjects shall become amenable to Chinese jurisdiction as soon as the majority of the powers relinquish their rights. The Portuguese treaty provides for the immediate surrender of exterritoriality.[3]

The Middle East.—Both in 1856 and 1897 Turkey attempted unsuccessfully to cast off the judicial restrictions resulting from the Capitulations; and at the outbreak of the war, in September, 1914, she abrogated them outright, though this action was denounced as illegal by the Allies, the Central Powers, and the United States.[4] Despite the fact that the exterritorial system was rein-

---

[1] *Treaties of the U. S.*, Vol. III, p. 2835.

[2] *Ibid.*, p. 3131. Foreigners also have "settlements" and "concessions" in some Chinese cities, the government of which is almost entirely in their hands. It is charged that these foreign settlements protect Chinese revolutionists from the government. G. E. Sokolsky, "Foreign Concession and Chinese Intrigue," *Trans-pacific*, July 21, 1923.

[3] The texts of some of these treaties are printed in *L' Europe Nouvelle*, January 5, 1929.

[4] *U. S. For. Rel.*, 1914, p. 1090.

forced in the Treaty of Sèvres, Turkey proved strong enough to maintain her position; and in the Treaty of Lausanne, the European powers accepted the "complete abolition of the Capitulations in Turkey in every respect." However, in a unilateral declaration, the Turkish government proposed to appoint for at least five years, a number of European legal counselors, from a list prepared by the Permanent Court of International Justice and composed of jurists from countries which were neutral during the World War. These jurists are engaged as "Turkish officials," serving under the Turkish minister of justice. It is their duty to observe the working of the judicial system but "without interfering in the performance by the magistrates of their duties."[1] While they may receive complaints against the administration of justice, with a view to placing them before the minister of justice, they have only advisory power.

Since 1828 Persia has exempted foreigners of certain nationalities from the jurisdiction of its courts. In May, 1927, it gave notice that the capitulations would be renounced on May 10, 1928. Provisional treaties to this effect were signed by Persia and a number of other powers.[2]

In Abyssinia there are eight consular tribunals and a mixed court which try foreigners. On the latter tribunal the consul of the foreigner concerned in a case sits as a judge, along with Abyssinian judges.[3]

Although exterritorial jurisdiction in backward countries has had a legitimate basis, European and American powers have abused their privileges. Foreigners in such countries as China, Turkey and Egypt have claimed exemption, not only from local courts, but from local taxation. Since the industry and commerce of these countries is largely monopolized by foreigners, it has been very difficult for a local government, under the exterritorial system, to provide itself with revenue.[4] Exterritoriality has also made the enforcement of local laws against the foreigner difficult. If he commits a crime the local authorities cannot try him, but

[1] Cf. XI, Treaty of July 24, 1923, Cmd. 1929, p. 201.
[2] "Abolition of Capitulations in Persia," *European Economic and Political Survey*, July, 15, 1928.
[3] Gardiner, "La juridiction concernant les étrangers en Ethiopie," *R. G. D. I. P.*, November, 1928.
[4] V. Chirol, *The Egyptian Question* (1922), pp. 57 ff.

486 INDIRECT FORMS OF IMPERIALISM

must ordinarily turn him over to a foreign court which may or may not fairly try the case. In such countries as Turkey and Morocco, European and American powers have adopted certain natives as their "protégés," who thereupon have obtained the same privileges as foreigners, and who have often plotted against the native government without restraint—and under foreign protection. In times past, foreign powers have freely sold such rights to natives in Turkey, where in 1808 Russia had 120,000 Greek protégés. In order to limit the number of protégés the powers might have in Morocco, a conference was held in Madrid in 1880, at which a treaty was signed stipulating what natives should be entitled to foreign protection.[1] In China, natives have put the title to their property in foreign hands to escape local taxation.[2] Such abuses of exterritoriality—which are really abuses arising out of imperialism—have naturally increased the desire of the backward countries to throw off this means of control.

9. INFORMAL CONTROL

For want of a better name, this is the type of control which great powers exercise over smaller ones in an extra-legal or backstairs manner. In the case of many backward countries, the powers follow the practice of collectively recognizing a government, only after it has accepted certain conditions laid down by the diplomats.[3] In October, 1923, the diplomatic corps at Peking declined to recognize General Tsao Kun as president until he had promised to meet the demands of the powers in the Lincheng affair—bandit raids in which foreigners were kidnapped. It is doubtful whether a president more patriotic and more representative of the will of the people would have acquiesced in such demands. The United States actively aids governments in Latin-American countries by supplying them with arms from government stores with which to suppress revolutions, as it did to the Obregon government in Mexico in the winter of 1923–1924, and to the Zayas government of Cuba in April, 1924. At the same time, it imposes embargoes preventing revolutionaries from obtaining arms from private manufacturers in the United States.[4]

[1] Convention of July 3, 1880, *Treaties of the U. S.*, Vol. I, p. 1220.
[2] Cf. Liu, "What Japan is doing to China," *Current History*, July, 1921.
[3] For the case of China, cf. *U. S. For. Rel.*, 1912, p. 68.
[4] Cf. p. 282, n. 2.

INFORMAL CONTROL

Marines.—Between 1912 and 1925 the United States maintained a Legation Guard of marines in Nicaragua. By this means it is said that unrepresentative governments were maintained in Nicaragua—a charge to which credence was given when the Nicaraguan government expressed the hope that American troops would not be withdrawn.[1] Moreover, in 1926–1927 the United States sent 5000 marines and blue jackets to Nicaragua in order to suppress a revolution. In April, 1927, the United States induced leaders of the two parties to accept the Stimson agreement under which they promised to stop fighting, while in return the United States agreed to supervise the elections in order to prevent the Diaz government from controlling them unfairly. The elections were finally held under American supervision in November, 1928. General Sandino did not accept the Stimson agreement and American marines unsuccessfully attempted to capture him. American officers are drilling a local constabulary, called La Guardia.[2] The United States has also been accused of keeping unrepresentative or corrupt governments in office in Cuba.[3] Whether or not such charges are true, a government kept in power by the aid of a foreign country is apt to submit to its advice.

The military arm of the United States government has gone even further than in Nicaragua. Between 1898 and 1902 it maintained a government in Cuba, under General Leonard Wood. In 1906 the United States established, with the consent of the Cuban president, a provisional government in Cuba, which lasted until 1909. In 1915 the American marines occupied Haiti, and the United States established a government, headed by a former marine officer, which in effect governs Haiti to-day.[4]

The United States maintained troops in Santo Domingo between 1916–1924, and ruled the island through a military government. In June of that year an Agreement of Evacuation was

---

[1] Cf. D. G. Munro, *Five Republics of Central America*, p. 245, and the Nicaraguan note of Jan. 7, 1925.

[2] Cf. "Mexico, the Caribbean and Tacna-Arica," *I. S.*, Vol. III, 23. W. W. Cumberland, *Nicaragua, An Economic and Financial Survey*, State Department, 1928. *A Brief History of the Relations between the United States and Nicaragua*, 1909–1928. State Department, 1928. I. J. Cox, *Nicaragua and the United States*, World Peace Foundation, 1927, No. 7.

[3] Cf. Leuchsenring, "Analisis y consecuencias de la intervención notreamericana en los asuntos interiores de Cuba," 32 *Cuba Contemporànea* (1923), 138.

[4] Cf. p. 447.

made, by which the United States agreed to withdraw, as soon as the constituent assembly adopted certain reforms to the Constitution. When these reforms were inadopted in July, 1924, American troops were withdrawn.[1]

The United States maintains a force of gunboats on the Yangtze river in China, at the expense of $3,000,000 a year. A Caribbean patrol has likewise been maintained. "In case of a threatened revolution, the mere arrival of an American cruiser, flying our flag, is usually sufficient to quiet the disturbance."[2] Americans have supervised the elections in Panama, Haiti, Santo Domingo, Cuba and Nicaragua.

Advisers.—Moreover, as we have seen especially in the realm of finance, advanced countries have influenced backward countries by the means of advisers, who may be technically private citizens but who, in some cases, have had the interests of their own country at heart more than the one which employed them. Military advisers have probably had more influence over politics than financial advisers. France has maintained a military mission in Peru since 1895, which, according to *El Tiempo*, a Peruvian journal, has succeeded in stimulating great French sentiment in Peru.[3] French officers have instructed the armies of Serbia, Bulgaria and Greece; while French advisers in the new governments of Europe have been numerous and powerful. In the famous Twenty-One Demands of 1915 Japan demanded that China employ Japanese advisers in the Chinese government in political, financial and military affairs. In the agreement of 1919, Great Britain made the same demand of Persia. England still maintains a large number of advisers in Egypt and Mesopotamia.[4] As we have seen the United States controls, through advisers, whether official or unofficial, the police of Liberia, Nicaragua, and Haiti. In 1912 Congress authorized an American army officer to become "instructor" for the Chilean government.[5] In an act of May 19, 1926, Congress authorized the President of the United States to detail officers and enlisted men to assist Latin-American govern-

---

[1] *Annual Report of the Secretary of the Navy*, 1924, p. 51.
[2] *Ibid.*, 1923, p. 15.
[3] General Maitrot, *La France et les Républiques Sud-Américaines* (1920), pp. 359 ff.
[4] Cf. pp. 388–478. A Frenchman is adviser to the Abyssinian government.
[5] 37 Stat. 1346.

JOINT GOVERNMENT

ments in military and naval matters.[1] Americans and Europeans have long advised the Siamese government. The United States has maintained a naval mission in Peru; and in 1923 great feeling was stirred up in South American countries when the Navy Department dispatched a naval mission to Brazil.

The purpose of these advisers may be legitimate: new and backward countries may need administrative advice from the more experienced nations of the world. Nevertheless, the opportunity for giving such advice has frequently been abused. From the theoretical standpoint the international adviser would do away with many of these evils.[2]

10. JOINT GOVERNMENT

In order to compromise colonial rivalry, joint or binational control over disputed territory has frequently been established in the past. Under this system, which has been attempted at various times in Moresnet, Samoa, Albania, Schleswig-Holstein and Spitzbergen,[3] officials of different nations have attempted to divide up the work of administering disputed territory between themselves. While in these particular cases the experiment with joint government has been abandoned, three examples still remain.

The Sudan.—The Anglo-Egyptian Sudan—a vast district south of Egypt controlling the headwaters of the Nile—has been technically under the joint control of Egypt and Great Britain. The Governor-General is appointed by Egypt on the recommendation of the British government; the British and Egyptian flags are both used; and all laws promulgated by the Governor-General are notified to the British consulate at Cairo.[4] Between 1922

---

[1] *U. S. Statutes at Large*, Vol. XLIV, p. 2057.
[2] Cf. p. 433.
[3] The Samoan attempt came to an end with the treaty of 1899, by dividing the islands between Germany and the United States. In 1912 the Conference of Ambassadors proposed that Albania be governed by a European prince elected by the European powers. He should be assisted by an international commission of control, composed of one delegate from each power and from Albania. For the Organic Statute of July 29, 1913, cf. 9 Martens (3d series), 650. In 1909 a conference was held to internationalize the island of Spitzbergen; this plan was given up in the treaty of Feb., 1920, which gave the island to Norway, subject to certain guarantees; cf. 113 *State Papers*, 789.
[4] For the convention of Jan. 19, 1889, cf. *Peace Handbooks*, No. 98, p. 165. Cf. Cromer, *Modern Egypt* (1908), Chs. XXXIII and LX.

and 1924 Egypt demanded the withdrawal of the British from the Sudan on the ground that it was an integral part of Egypt. Hidden behind this political argument was the fact that the Sudan controls Egypt's water supply. The population of Egypt increases at the rate of 200,000 a year. As it is wholly an agricultural country, cultivation must constantly be expanded, for which water is necessary. Egypt "cannot exist without drawing water from a river which rises far beyond her borders."[1] A dam must be constructed in the Sudan. On the other hand, there are British cotton interests in this region which also wish the water.[2] As part of the ultimatum after the Stack murder, Great Britain demanded that Egypt withdraw all officers and units from the Sudan and increase the area in the Gezira irrigation project. However, the belief that Great Britain had taken advantage of the Stack affair virtually to annex the Sudan by these means, did not prove to be well founded; for in December, 1924, Mr. Austen Chamberlain informed the House of Commons that the British government "had no desire to terminate the Condominium," and that it would invite the Egyptian government to join in an inquiry as to what water is available for the Sudan "after making full allowance for Egypt." A commission with a neutral chairman should be selected to look after these matters.[3]

In May, 1929, an agreement in regard to the Nile waters was announced. In this agreement the Egyptian government promises to allow waters to be taken from the Nile for irrigation purposes in the Sudan, on the understanding that this does not "infringe upon Egypt's natural and historical rights in the waters of the Nile and its requirements of agricultural extension." Both governments reserve their full liberty in regard to the political status of the Sudan.[4]

Tangier.—Perched over the entrance of the Mediterranean, the city of Tangier has been a potential center of international rivalry

---

[1] Crabitès, "Egypt, the Sudan and the Nile," *Foreign Affairs*, Dec. 15, 1924.
[2] Cf. the Gezira Irrigation Project, Cmd. 2171 (1924).
[3] *Manchester Guardian*, Dec. 16, 1924. In an editorial, the *Manchester Guardian* had suggested that if Great Britain insisted on pressing its claims to the Sudan, it take over the territory as a mandate from the League of Nations. *Manchester Guardian Weekly*, Nov. 28, 1924.
[4] "The Nile Waters Agreement," *Bulletin of International News*, May 25, 1929.

because of its great strategic and commercial importance. In order to forestall disputes, agreements made in 1904, 1906 and 1912 recognized that regardless of the status of Morocco, Tangier should have a special status of its own. Just before the War a plan for the international government of the city was worked out,[1] the adoption of which, however, was prevented by the outbreak of the World War. Meanwhile Tangier was extra-legally governed by a curious and unsatisfactory international body— the Conseil Sanitaire—composed of representatives of the diplomatic corps.[2] Because of her position in Morocco, France felt she had special interests in Tangier, and after the War attempted to gain exclusive control.[3] After a long period of negotiations, this attempt was checked by England and Spain. And the convention of December, 1923,[4] established a joint form of government, in which, however, France has a certain preponderance. The Sultan of Morocco retains "sovereignty" over the city, being represented there by a "mendoub" who looks after the natives—a provision which increases French influence since France controls the Sultan. The government of Tangier is in the hands of a Committee of Control and an International Legislative Assembly. The first body is composed of the eight consular officers of the powers who signed the Act of Algeciras. This body has the duty of insuring the observance of the statute, having power to veto legislation by a majority vote. The International Assembly, which has legislative power over natives and foreigners, is composed of 26 members, representing European countries and natives, the latter, however, having only nine appointive representatives. France and Spain have four members each, while England has only three. Other signatories of the Act of Algeciras including the United States may also be represented.

The Assembly approves all administrative officials, with the exception of the Administrator and his two assistants. But for six years, the Administrator will be French; while his two assist-

[1] D. P. Myers, "Tangier, An International City," 4 *National Municipal Review* (1915), 60.
[2] Tangier, "A Study in Internationalisation," *Round Table*, No. 38 (1920), 348.
[3] Piquet, *Maroc*, p. 456; *Manchester Guardian Weekly*, Dec. 21, 1923.
[4] "Convention regarding the Organization of the Statute of the Tangier Zone," Dec. 18, 1923. Cmd. 2096.

ants will be British and Spanish, the first being in charge of finance and the latter in charge of health and relief. The commander of the gendarmes is a Belgian assisted by French and Spanish cadres. The head of the customs is nominated by the Sultan of Morocco—which means France. But the Committee of Control may demand his dismissal by three-fourths vote. The convention also provides for the Open Door, neutralization and non-fortification. Nevertheless, French or Spanish troops may pass through the port on the way to their respective zones in Morocco. Under the convention France secured control of the administration of the natives and of the Customs, as well as of the Administrator. The proposal to put Tangier under some form of supervision by the League of Nations was defeated. As a result, a system of government was set up which has only a semi-international character.

For some reason Italy did not become a party to the original Tangier convention—a fact which later led to a misunderstanding between Italy and France. As a result of representations of the Mussolini government, the parties revised the Tangier Statute in 1928 recognizing Italy as a contracting party; and granting her the right to three Italian members on the International Legislative Assembly, an Italian assistant administrator for the administration of justice and an Italian magistrate on the Mixed Court. An exchange of notes promised to Italian capital and labor a fair distribution in the execution of public works at Tangier and a fair participation in the personnel of the administration.[1]

New Hebrides.—In the New Hebrides islands the system of joint government or condominium has also been tried. Determined to settle their rivalry over these islands, France and England signed an agreement in 1906 (modified in March, 1922), establishing in the New Hebrides "a region of joint influence, in which the subjects and citizens of the two signatory Powers shall enjoy equal rights of residence, personal protection, and trade, each of the two powers retaining jurisdiction over its nationals" and over its corporations, "and neither exercising a separate authority over the Group." Each power is represented on the islands by a High Commissioner, each commanding one-half of the island police

---

[1] "Final Protocol for the Amendment of the Tangier Statute," July 25, 1928. Cmd. 3216.

force. Legislative power and the number of public services is vested in the High Commissioners jointly. There is a French and an English Court for French and English cases respectively; there is also a Joint Court to hear cases between natives and foreigners, composed of one English and one French judge, with one neutral judge who acts as president and who is appointed by the King of Spain. A Joint Naval Commission coöperates in the maintenance of order. Municipal Councils may be established at the request of a certain number of non-natives. No fortifications may be erected.[1]

Ever since the establishment of this government there have been bitter conflicts between the French and British, while the native, it is said, has fared badly.[2] The French demand annexation on the ground that the majority of the inhabitants of the islands are French.[3] But Australia is likely always to oppose this solution for strategic reasons.[4]

11. NATIONAL v. INTERNATIONAL CONTROL

In this discussion of imperialism the different methods of controlling the backward regions by the imperial powers may be reduced to these catagories: (1) complete or partial; (2) national or international. It is of course difficult if not impossible to say what type of control is best. Conditions peculiar to the country concerned must be the determining factor. Nevertheless, where it is possible to satisfy the legitimate demands of the outside world by partial control, whether through the means of a semi-protectorate or financial control, that means is perhaps preferable to complete control, which tends to stamp out all the liberties of the peoples concerned. At the same time, the indirect means of control established in Cuba and Nicaragua present many difficulties. The Platt amendment gives the United States a negative check over Cuban affairs, to be utilized apparently at its pleasure, but does not impose any definite and positive responsibility upon the United States for the condition of affairs in Cuba. Cuba lives

[1] Convention of Oct. 20, 1906, 1 Martens (3d series), 523. For the Protocol signed on August 6, 1914, but not ratified until March 18, 1922, cf. Cmd. 1681. Cf. A. Brunet, *Le Régime international des Nouvelles Hebrides* (1908), Ch. IV.
[2] Cf. editorial, *The Continent*, Nov. 20, 1924, p. 1429.
[3] Pelleray, "Les Nouvelles Hebrides," *Revue du Pacifique*, April, 1923.
[4] This question was discussed at the Imperial Conference of 1923, Cmd. 1987, p. 15. In 1920 there were 317 British and 300 French on the islands.

with a club held over her head; Cubans are likely to feel that they are no longer responsible for their government, because of the United States; while the United States itself assumes no responsibility. When the United States repeatedly interferes in the internal affairs of Cuba, coming to the support of corrupt and unpopular governments, this feeling on the part of the Cuban people becomes stronger than ever.[1] If the semi-protectorate idea is to work successfully, it must be strictly limited to cases which really and immediately involve foreign interests. If it is desirable to control the internal government, some more direct and responsible means must be found. As Professor Coolidge says, "There is no logical stopping place, no halfway house which will make a permanent home on the road to equality, and those who have once got well started on that road grow increasingly impatient and resent every effort to delay them on their way to their final goal." [2]

In the vast majority of cases where the advanced powers have established their control over the backward regions, each has acted independently of the other, and has been responsible to no one in the administration of territory thus acquired. This system of national imperialism possesses the advantage of swiftness and unity of action; but it possesses the disadvantage of fostering quarrels with other nations and the exploitation of the natives for the material interests of a few people in the home country. These disadvantages are theoretically removed by the system of international control or accountability. Quarrels in ordinary life are settled not by the parties to the dispute but by an impartial judge. And quarrels in international life will not be settled justly and permanently so long as they remain in the hands of the parties to the dispute, especially when one party is weak and the other is strong. On the other hand, international control introduces an element of impartiality which is more likely to secure the observance of pledges than national imperialism.

Three types of international control over territory have been attempted. The first is the condominium, discussed above. This

[1] Cf. Machado, "El Derecho de Intervención," 29 *Cuba Contemporánea* (1922), 337.

[2] A. C. Coolidge, "Ten Years of War and Peace," *Foreign Affairs*, Sept. 15, 1924.

system has failed in every place where it has been attempted, because it is based on the principle of divided responsibility. The officials on the executive side must act under the instructions of their own foreign officers and therefore become, as Lord Cromer says, "the political agents of their country of origin," [1] who instead of considering questions on their merits, consider them in the light of political advantage. "Any action often involves a presumed advantage accorded to some rival nation, and it is a principle of internationalism, which is scornfully rejected in theory and but too often recognized as a guide for practical action, that it is better to do nothing, even though evil may ensue, than to allow good to be done at the expense of furthering the interests, or of exalting the reputation of an international rival. For all purposes of action, therefore, administrative internationalism may be said to tend towards the creation of administrative impotence." [2]

There is the second type of international government—such as is established in the Saar—which gets away from these difficulties by adopting, in theory, the principle of undivided responsibility to an international body—the Council of the League. But as we have seen, the League is not yet capable of making this responsibility effective enough, to warrant extending the principle to the backward parts of the world.[3] Because of the weaknesses of these two principles, the Paris Peace Conference attempted to work out a third, which would preserve the advantages of a unified national responsibility with the advantages of accountability to an international body. This was done through the creation of the Mandate system, whereby each nation, while it has complete administrative freedom and independence in governing backward territory, is obliged to accept and live up to certain obligations imposed for the good of the outside world.[4]

[1] *Modern Egypt*, Vol. II, p. 441.
[2] *Ibid.*, p. 304. For the same difficulty in the Albanian commission, cf. A. Chekrezi, *Albania Past and Present* (1919), p. 127.
[3] For this example, cf. p. 118.
[4] Cf. p. 360.

PART III
THE SETTLEMENT OF INTERNATIONAL DISPUTES

CHAPTER XXI

WAR, ALLIANCES AND ARMAMENTS

1. Material and Spiritual Costs of War.—2. Warfare in the Future.—3. "Defensive" Alliances.—4. The Balance of Power.—5. Secret Diplomacy.—6. Competition in Armaments—Naval Rivalry—Aircraft and Submarines.—7. The Private Manufacture of Arms.—8. Force and International Society.

It may sound very disagreeable to say that the most important and most frequently used means for settling international disputes has been the weight of arms. Such a statement nevertheless appears to be true. "Each state in the last resort has had to rely for its safety, its rights, and the rights of its nationals, not upon an appeal to law, but upon its own physical strength, upon armaments, and upon a diplomacy founded on force."[1]

1. MATERIAL AND SPIRITUAL COSTS OF WAR

If you look at the history books, you will find that wars occupy most of the pages. Between 1470 and 1721 some part of Europe was visited with a war a year. Between 1721 and 1814 Europe was involved in such general conflagrations as the War of the Austrian Succession, the Seven Years' War, and the Wars of the French Revolution and Napoleon. In the 19th century a lull came, no general war engulfing the world after Waterloo until 1914. Nevertheless little wars were recurrent, whether between European or Asiatic countries, or between the so-called advanced and backward peoples.

Holland and Sweden are apparently the only countries in Europe who have been able to stay out of war for a period of fifty years. England has been at war during 419 years out of the last eight centuries.[2] Between South American countries, however, there has been no war since 1883; and, except for the World War,

---

[1] Kepi, "Versailles—Before and After," *Foreign Affairs*, Dec. 15, 1923; cf. Admiral Mahan, *Armaments and Arbitration* (1912).

[2] Woods and Baltzly, *Is War Diminishing?* (1915), pp. 43, 64, 103.

there has been no war between South American and European powers since 1865.[1] The problem of South America is not so much ridding itself of international wars as doing away with internal revolutions, with which a large number of Latin countries are chronically afflicted.

Despite the great number of wars fought in the last century—40 being fought between 1821 and 1914,[2]—it seems that wars are becoming less numerous than they were in ancient times. Between 1450 and 1600 about 65% of the time was spent in fighting; during the last half century, however, the per cent fell to twenty-two.[3] Nevertheless if wars are decreasing in duration, they are increasing in intensity and in the suffering which they cause. Twice as many men were killed in the last war as in all of the other wars since the time of the French Revolution.

LOSS OF LIFE IN 19TH CENTURY WARS

Wars	Duration	Dead
Napoleonic, 1790–1815	9,000 days	2,100,000
Crimean, 1854–1856	730	785,000
Prussian-Danish, 1864	135	3,500
Prussian-Austrian, 1866	40	45,000
American Civil, 1861–1865	1,350	700,000
Franco-Prussian, 1870–1871	210	184,000
English-Boer, 1899–1902	995	9,800
Russo–Japanese, 1904–1905	548	160,000
Balkan, 1912–1913	238	462,000
		4,449,300
World War, 1914–1918	1,750	10,000,000 [4]

In an attempt to limit human slaughter, international lawyers at one time drew a distinction between civilian and military populations. But such a distinction has now become fictitious because modern warfare, to be effective, demands the absorbed attention of every man, woman, and child. While men fight in the trenches,

[1] S. C. Vestal, *The Maintenance of Peace* (1920), p. 27.
[2] A. Ponsonby, *Wars and Treaties* (1918).
[3] Woods and Baltzly, p. 28, Chart D.
[4] E. L. Bogart, *Direct and Indirect Costs of the Great World War* (1919), pp. 270 ff. Cf. Dumas and Vedel-Petersen, *Losses of Life Caused by War* (1923); also Villard, "Losses from Disease in the World War Armies," *Current History*, Sept., 1924, an article which says that while in past wars disease brought more deaths than direct fighting, the contrary was true in the last war because of the progress of preventive medicine.

MATERIAL AND SPIRITUAL COSTS OF WAR 501

women and children fight in the rear, working feverishly to supply the front line not only with munitions but with food. When a nation is blockaded civilians suffer as much as soldiers. The World War brought death to at least 10,000,000 men and it wounded 20,000,000 more. It also brought death to some ten millions of civilians, through privation, pestilence, and actual gunfire. It left fatherless 9,000,000 orphans; it created 5,000,000 widows; it made destitute 10,000,000 refugees. Instead of insuring the survival of the fittest, war kills off or disables the best, leaving the physically unfit as fathers of the race.[1]

War has been costly also from the standpoint of the destruction of property. The direct cost of the last war—expenditures on ammunition and so forth—came to more than 186 billion dollars; while the indirect cost—the capitalized value of the lives lost and property destroyed—came to about 151 billion dollars—making a total war cost of 337 billion. This means of settling international disputes cost the world the sum of 9 million dollars an hour. In sixty minutes' time, the war consumed an amount equal to the endowment of the University of California.[2]

The effect of the War was to increase national debts in Allied countries as follows:

NATIONAL DEBTS

	1913	1920
United States	$1,188,000,000	24,298,000,000
British Empire	6,897,000,000	31,803,000,000
France	6,598,000,000	22,871,000,000 [3]

When the armistice of 1918 was declared the ordnance department of the United States army was consuming every month labor and raw material equal to the cost of the Panama Canal—a total effort which was equivalent to rebuilding New York City once a year.[4] In 1920 most of the European states found them-

---

[1] Cf. V. Kellogg, *Military Selection and Race Deterioration* (1916), pp. 199-200, particularly in regard to racial deterioration in France following the Wars of the Revolution.

[2] K. Page, *War: Its Causes and Cure* (1923), p. 38. Cf. G. Bodart, *Losses of Life in Modern Wars: Austria-Hungary; France* (1916).

[3] H. E. Fisk, *The Inter-ally Debts* (1924), pp. 324, 341; these are dollars at exchange.

[4] Address of Col. J. L. Walsh, *N. Y. Times*, Feb. 6, 1924. Cf. his article, *ibid.*, March 30, 1924.

selves spending far beyond their income—largely because of the disorganization caused by the War.

While neutrals may develop a brisk war trade, they too must suffer whenever such tremendous amounts of wealth are unproductively destroyed. With the increasing economic interdependence of the world, it is more than ever impossible to localize the devastating effects of war. Even if the Allies repay the 11 billions they borrowed from the United States, the American people will be worse off because of the war having been fought—since the total cost to the government of America's participation came to 32 billion dollars.

These tremendous expenditures might be justified if war ever settled international disputes as they should be settled, and if no other means of settling them could be found. But it is very seldom that a war ever settles a dispute between nations according to principles of justice and of law. As a result, the vanquished come to believe that the only basis of peace is force, and thereupon proceed to drill large armies in order to overturn by force the settlement imposed upon them. Thousands were tragically disappointed at the results of the Paris Peace Conference of 1919. Here was an opportunity to create a new and better world. But it was expecting altogether too much of a group of belligerent statesmen and peoples who had been hating intensely an enemy for four long years, to let him off easily. During the course of the war Allied peoples may have been absolutely sincere in believing that they were fighting to make the World Safe for Democracy,—fighting a War to end Wars for all time. But the intoxication of victory deadens the ears of "peacemakers" to past promises. As long as the institution of war exists, peace settlements are likely to be vindictive. Instead of reconstructing a world upon a stable basis, victors in a campaign of unrestrained bloodshed are inclined to use their power over a prostrate enemy to wreak revenge.

War looses the bands of morality. When men are taught to hate and kill each other in the trenches, some of them will not hesitate to commit acts of violence upon returning home. War also breeds falsehood. The enemy is always wicked—guilty of all crimes. Sole responsibility for the war rests upon his shoulders,—

a principle which the Allies wrote into the Treaty of Versailles.[1] Many of the charges made against the Germans during the last war are now known to be false, whether it be in regard to cutting off babies' hands in Belgium, or U-boat atrocities. Rear Admiral Sims has said that "most of the accounts of atrocities popularly attributed to them [the Germans] were untrue; that, barring the case of the hospital ship, Llandovery Castle, I did not know of any case where a German submarine commander deliberately fired upon the boats of a torpedoed vessel. . . ."[2] Possibly this organized campaign of falsehood, of which Germany was perhaps even more guilty than the Allies, was a necessity. If popular support of a war is only lukewarm, disaster is likely to result. While an individual American did not hate an individual German, by means of nation-wide propaganda "America" could be stirred up to hate "Germany." But the price paid for this type of popular support is ultimate disillusion and loss of faith in governments.[3] The propagandist methods employed by governments in time of war are in time of peace turned against them by economic or political groupings which wish to use the government to promote their private ends. The effect of war upon democracy and liberty, we need not discuss, since these effects are primarily domestic rather than international. Nevertheless, the suppression of all popular criticism in war-time makes the establishment of dictatorships comparatively easy in the reconstruction period—a fact which hinders the establishment of real peace, since no sound international coöperation can exist between governments which do not rest upon a democratic basis.

2. WARFARE IN THE FUTURE

If international relations are based on the same foundations in the future as they have been in the past, further wars are probably inevitable. Because of the "progress" which science continually

---

[1] Article 231 of the Treaty says: "The Allied and Associated Governments affirm and Germany accepts the responsibility of Germany and her allies for causing all the loss and damage to which the Allied and Associated Governments and their nationals have been subjected as a consequence of the war imposed upon them by the aggression of Germany and her allies."

[2] "The Truth About the German Submarine Atrocities," *Current History*, June, 1923.

[3] Cf. J. Duhelly, *Philosophie de la guerre* (1921), Chs. III, XIV.

makes, and of the growing interdependence of the world, they will necessarily be more frightful in their consequences than any wars of the last century. Just as the discovery of gunpowder revolutionized warfare in the 14th century, so the inventions of chemistry to-day bid fair to revolutionize the warfare of the future.[1] Gas, the submarine, and the airplane have already challenged the supremacy of the capital ship and the Remington rifle. To-day the man in the laboratory has become more important than the man with a gun.

"Almost any chemical known can be made a war gas if desired."[2] The Chemical Warfare Service of the United States is reported to have invented a liquid three drops of which, applied to any part of the skin, will cause a man's death. One plane carrying two tons of this liquid could, it is said, deposit in one trip material enough to kill every person in an area a hundred feet wide and seven miles long.[3] This Service has also developed apparatus for sprinkling a smoke curtain from airplanes, the possibilities of which are almost unlimited. In the future, there is no technical reason why the civil populations of great cities should not be attacked with poison gas from long-range guns. No means of protecting such populations has yet proved effective. "It may be said that such a development of warfare would be too horrible for use and that the conscience of mankind would revolt at it. It may be so, but in view of the fact that in modern wars such as the last one the whole population of a country is more or less directly engaged, it may well be that an unscrupulous belligerent may not see much difference between the use of poison gas against troops in the field and its use against the centres from which those troops draw the sinews of war."[4]

[1] Cf. G. Maitrot, *La prochaine guerre* (1921), p. 7.
[2] *Annual Report of the Chief of Chemical Warfare Service* (1924), p. 3. Cf. A. A. Fries and C. J. West, *Chemical Warfare* (1921), Chs. XXIII, XXVI; V. Lefebure, *The Riddle of the Rhine* (1921), Chs. VIII–XII.
[3] Cf. D. B. Bradner, of the Chemical Warfare Service, quoted in *The Staggering Burden of Armament*, A League of Nations, April, 1921.
[4] *Report of the Temporary Mixed Commission for the Reduction of Armaments*, League of Nations, A. 16, 1924, IX, p. 30. The danger is increased by the use of bacteria to pollute drinking water, to propagate plague, and to poison weapons. For a further discussion of gases, cf. the reports in *Conference on the Limitation of Armament*, Washington, November 12, 1921–February 6, 1922, pp. 730 ff. For a defence of chemical warfare, cf. Haldane, "Chemistry and Peace," *Atlantic Monthly*, Jan., 1925.

Similar developments are taking place in increasing the terrible effectiveness of tanks—a modern adaptation of the armor of ancient knights. While the first tanks could advance at a speed of only four or five miles an hour, in 1924 the American Ordnance Department produced a tractor which could go thirty miles an hour, up a 45-degree slope, and through water up to the driver's chin.[1] The United States has also devised a 75-millimeter gun with nearly twice the range of the famous "Soixante-quinze"; while its new 155-millimeter gun outranges the French G. P. F. by nearly five miles. A new machine gun shoots a bullet weighing four times as much as the 30-calibre Browning—one direct hit of which will almost certainly demolish a plane—going nearly three times as far. In the development of the bombing plane—the best agency for the distribution of gas—science is also reaping the rewards of research. The American Ordnance Department has perfected an aërial bomb of 4,000 pounds, which is fourteen feet in length and ten times as heavy as the largest aërial bomb used in the World War.

No laws of war are likely to prevent the use of such weapons by belligerents in a contest fought, as they believe, for national existence. It is not too much to say that "If mankind does not end war, war will end mankind."[2]

3. "DEFENSIVE" ALLIANCES

When war is the chief means of settling international disputes, one nation standing by itself may be overwhelmed by another nation with greater resources and man-power. In order to offset this superiority of a potential enemy, one nation may enter into an alliance with another nation having similar interests or fearing the same foe. While "offensive" alliances may be conceivably negotiated, it appears that all of the alliances of the 19th and 20th centuries have been in theory "defensive." In their military convention of 1892, France and Russia, "being animated by an equal desire to preserve peace, and having no other object than to meet the necessities of a defensive war, provoked by an attack of the forces of the Triple Alliance against the one or the other of them,"

---

[1] Col. Walsh, cited, *N. Y. Times*, March 30, 1924.
[2] G. L. Dickinson, *War: Its Nature, Cause and Cure* (1923), p. 11.

agreed to support each other with military forces.¹ In the first Triple Alliance of 1882, Austria-Hungary, Germany and Italy concluded a treaty which, "by its essentially conservative and defensive nature, pursues only the aim of forestalling the dangers which might threaten the security of Their States and the peace of Europe." ² In case one party, "without direct provocation," should chance to be attacked by two or more powers, the other members of the alliance would come to its aid. Article I of the Anglo-Japanese Alliance of 1902 declared that the parties "were entirely uninfluenced by any aggressive tendencies in either country"; and the Alliance was operative only in case the interests of each party were attacked. While all of these alliances have, therefore, been called "defensive," they have not prevented nations from engaging in aggression. Consequently, the outside world has justly come to fear that an alliance, regardless of avowed "defensive" ends, may be used for this purpose. The distinction between "defensive" and "offensive" alliances has been as unsubstantial as the distinction between "defensive" and "offensive" wars.

In an alliance one party may promise to bring military support to the other party in all cases in which it is attacked. Thus in the alliance of February 19, 1921, between France and Poland, it is declared, "If, notwithstanding the sincerely pacific views and intentions of the two Contracting States, either or both of them should be attacked without giving provocation, the two Governments should take concerted measures for the defense of their territory and the protection of their legitimate demands. . . ." ³ In other alliances, one ally may promise merely to remain neutral in a contest where the other ally is involved with a third power, and "to use its efforts to prevent other Powers from joining in hostility against its Ally." However, in case another power should enter the war against the ally involved, the second ally must then come to its defence. This type of undertaking was embodied in the Anglo-Japanese Alliance of 1902, but it was supplanted by the broader undertaking of mutual help against a

¹ A. F. Pribram and A. C. Coolidge, *The Secret Treaties of Austria-Hungary, 1879–1914* (1921), Vol. II, p. 215.
² Pribram, Vol. I, p. 67. The *casus fœderis* would also arise if Italy should be attacked by France.
³ *T. S.* 449.

single outside power, in the revised alliance of 1905.[1] In the third place, some alliances mention specifically the enemy against whom they are directed. Under the alliance of 1892, Russia would come to the aid of France only in case France was attacked by Germany, or by Italy supported by Germany; while France would come to the aid of Russia in case it was attacked by Germany, or by Austria supported by Germany. The alliance between Austria-Hungary and Germany of 1879 became operative only in case one of the two Empires was attacked by Russia. Likewise, the abortive alliance of 1919 between the United States and France provided for military aid to the latter country "in the event of any unprovoked movement of aggression against her being made by Germany."[2] When an alliance directly names the enemy feared, it naturally increases international ill-will. When it does not name the enemy, it arouses international suspicion. Thus in either case, an alliance intensifies an atmosphere of distrust.

Many alliances do not content themselves merely with a blanket promise of military aid in case of attack; they frequently specify the exact form such aid shall take. These specifications may be included in the body of the alliance itself, as in the convention of 1892 with Russia in which France promised in case of war to employ 1,300,000 men against Germany, while Russia promised to use 700,000 or 800,000 men. "These forces shall engage to the full, with all speed, in order that Germany may have to fight at the same time on the East and the West." Likewise, the General Staffs of the Armies of the two countries were to coöperate with each other at all times in the preparation and facilitation of the execution of these measures. Or an alliance may be accompanied by separate technical naval and military agreements. In 1912 France and Russia entered into a convention providing for the monthly exchange of information between their navies.[3] In 1913 Austria-Hungary, Germany and Italy made a naval agreement, providing that the naval forces of the Triple Alliance should unite in time of war to gain control of the Mediterranean, the Supreme Command of which should be intrusted to an Austro-

---

[1] J. V. A. MacMurray, *Treaties and Conventions with and concerning China*, Vol. I, pp. 324, 516.
[2] *Treaties of the U. S.*, Vol. III, p. 3210.
[3] Pribram, Vol. II, p. 223.

Hungarian or Italian Flag Officer. The plan of operations should be prepared in peace time by the Admiralty Staffs. A supplementary agreement defined in detail the main bases for operations, the vessels to be employed, and so forth.[1] By means of such agreements, each nation may know precisely what support it may expect from an ally in case war should break out.

4. THE BALANCE OF POWER

Most alliances have been concluded in the name of the principle, called the Balance of Power, or of *L'équilibre politique européen*. Since it is impossible to divide the world into states equal to each other in military and industrial power, the principle of Balance would group states into opposing alliances so that no state would be able, standing alone or in alliance, to impose its will upon the rest of the world. While territorial readjustments and compensations, weakening some states and strengthening others, have been made in order to establish this Balance of Power, ordinarily the principle is sustained by the system of alliances and coalitions—a system known even to the ancient world. Polybius tells us that Hanno of Syracuse sent help to Carthage in one of her civil wars, even though he was an ally of Rome, "esteeming it requisite, both in order to retain his dominions in Sicily, and to preserve the Roman friendship, that Carthage should be safe; lest by its fall the remaining Power should be able, without contract or opposition, to execute every purpose and undertaking. . . ." Vattel defined the idea of Balance of Power as "such a disposition of affairs that no power can ever find itself in a position to enjoy undisputed predominance and to impose the law on others." [2] This principle was expressed in the Peace of Westphalia of 1648 and in the Treaty of Utrecht of 1713—treaties which attempted to make territorial readjustments which would prevent any one state from having undue power.[3] In 1855 several powers virtually guaranteed the integrity of Norway "to prevent all complications of a nature to trouble the equilibrium of Europe." [4]

[1] Pribram, Vol. I, p. 282.
[2] Cf. *The Balance of Power*, Union of Democratic Control, No. 14.
[3] Cf. E. Nys, "Théorie de l'équilibre européen," *R. D. I. P.*, Vol. XXV (1893, 1st series), p. 34. Cf. O. Hoijer, *La Théorie de l'équilibre et le droit des gens* (1917); A. de Stieglitz, *de l'Équilibre politique* (1897), 3 vols.
[4] Cf. p. 584.

THE BALANCE OF POWER

Since the time of the Napoleonic wars, European powers have entered into about twenty great coalitions, ententes and alliances. Between 1792 and 1815 five coalitions were formed against France. In 1800 four Baltic Powers entered into an alliance, known as the Armed Neutrality, to maintain the freedom of the seas against the pretensions of England. Following the Napoleonic Wars, European monarchs formed the Holy Alliance and the Quadruple Alliance, directed against France; they also established a system of intervention in favor of monarchical institutions in Europe.[1] In a protocol adopted at Troppau in 1820, the members of the Quadruple Alliance promised to employ "coercive force" whenever necessary to suppress internal revolutions against any one of the Allied Governments.[2] At a later period the leading powers of Europe signed three "pacification" agreements, in 1827, 1834 and 1840, by which they jointly undertook to remove conditions in Greece, Portugal and Turkey which threatened to disturb their interests.[3] In 1854 Great Britain, France and Turkey signed an alliance aimed at Russia, the preamble of which declared "that Their Majesties are fully persuaded that the existence of the Ottoman Empire in its present limits is essential to the maintenance of the balance of power between the States of Europe."[4]

With the establishment of the German Empire in 1871 readjustments became necessary if the balance of power was not to be upset. After much hesitation as to Russia, the German Empire finally decided to cast its lot with Austria-Hungary and Italy.[5] In 1882 these three powers signed the Triple Alliance, which was renewed with changes in 1887, 1891, 1902 and 1912, and to which Roumania adhered in 1883. Bulgaria and Turkey also adhered to the Central Powers during the World War. The opposing group of powers was composed of France, Russia and Great Britain. In 1892 France and Russia entered into a defensive alliance directed against Germany and Italy, and in 1904 France and Great Britain signed a number of agreements

[1] W. A. Phillips, *The Confederation of Europe* (1914), Pts. II and IV; 3 *State Papers*, 211, 273; W. P. Cresson, *The Holy Alliance* (1922).
[2] Martens, *Recueil des traités conclue par la Russie*, Vol. IV, p. 281.
[3] *State Papers*, 22: 134; 28: 342; 14: 632.
[4] 44 *State Papers*, 5.
[5] Pribram, cited, vol. I, *passim*. For the Balkan alliances, cf. p. 236.

settling their political disputes and creating an atmosphere of friendly coöperation which gradually grew into a common bond against Germany. In 1907 Great Britain and Russia settled their differences in the Near East. To the Entente group, Japan was also pledged, because of the Anglo-Japanese Alliances of 1902, 1905 and 1911 in which Japan virtually undertook to safeguard the interests of the Entente in the Far East.[1] Following the entrance of England into the war, Great Britain, France and Russia entered into an agreement of September, 1914, in which they promised "not to conclude peace separately during the present war. The three Governments agree that, when terms of peace come to be discussed, no one of the allies will demand terms of peace without the previous agreement of each of the other allies."[2] During the World War, these terms were defined in a number of notable declarations and secret treaties parceling out enemy territory, despite the fact that the alliance between France and Russia as well as the understanding with England was "defensive" in character.[3] Deserting the Central Powers, Italy joined the Entente in 1915, while Roumania and Greece likewise adhered to the Allied cause in 1916.

Following the defeat of Germany by combined Allied arms, attempts were made to reëstablish the Balance of Power. Austria and Hungary were virtually forbidden to join Germany. In proposed agreements signed June 28, 1919 between France, Great Britain and the United States, the two latter powers promised to come "immediately" to the aid of France in the event of unprovoked German aggression. When the United States declined to ratify this treaty, France resorted to a policy of forming alliances with the new and smaller states of Europe, so as to surround Germany, and to establish a cordon along the Russian frontier. By this means, France hoped to protect herself from Germanism and Bolshevism, while the smaller states received in return a pledge of French aid in case their newly acquired independence was threatened. Such motives prompted France to sign a Military Understanding with Belgium in September, 1920;[4]

---

[1] A. L. P. Dennis, *The Anglo-Japanese Alliance* (1923); R. L. Buell, *The Washington Conference*, Ch. IV.
[2] Cd. 7737; for the adhesion of Italy, cf. Cd. 8107 (1915).
[3] Cf. F. S. Cocks, *The Secret Treaties and Understandings* (2d ed., 1918).
[4] *T. S.* 56.

and alliances with Poland in February, 1921,[1] with Czechoslovakia in January, 1924,[2] with Roumania in June, 1926, and with Jugoslavia in November, 1927.[3] French influence, for a time at least, appeared to be predominant in the Polish-Roumanian alliance of March, 1921,[4] and in the Little Entente.[5]

Temporarily the system of alliances and of the Balance of Power may succeed in keeping the world in a nervous state of armed "peace," in which one group of powers is afraid to attack another group but stands in constant fear of itself being attacked. Yet as the history of the last century shows, the principle of Balance of Power, while it may postpone war, cannot permanently maintain peace. It is a principle which does not aim at the establishment of treaties upon principles of justice. It aims only to prevent the hypothetical preponderance of one power or group of powers over another. Coalitions were necessary to prevent soldiers like Charles V, Philip II, Louis XIV and Napoleon Bonaparte, and Kaiser Wilhelm II from establishing a hegemony over the world. Nevertheless, as soon as an alliance destroys an opposing power, the balance is upset and jealousies and divergent interests inside the victorious group arise. The Balance of Power principle is "incapable not only of insuring justice, but of dictating clear solutions."[6] It is a policy which aims at finding out the strongest state and then attacking it with the purpose of reducing it to the level of weaker states. "A formula which elevates a proportion of power into a principle of politics, and contains within itself no criterion of justice as between nation and nation, necessarily rests international relations on the idea of force. It makes the condition of antagonism the normal relationship between nations, and if it sometimes prevents that antagonism from expressing itself in actual war, it does so simply by the purely physical threat of a greater war. The Balance of Power in modern Europe necessarily implies its division into two hostile camps. It cramps the free interplay of moral and political ideas in a purely mechanical

---

[1] T. S. 449.
[2] T. S. 588.
[3] *Arbitration and Security*, C. 653. M. 216, 1927, V. p. 325.
[4] T. S. 175.
[5] Cf. p. 237. Also *Postwar Political Alignments* (League of Nations, Vol. II, No. 2, 1923).
[6] C. Dupuis, *Le Principe d'équilibre et le concert européen* (1909), p. 97.

mold, and has thus a natural affinity with some of the principles that have made European militarism. If it prevents small wars, it makes war more general and more and more devastating when it does come. It inoculates against measles with the serum of plague." [1] It is a system which creates universal suspicion and a general deadlock. Even from the military standpoint, one party to an alliance, as experience shows, cannot depend upon the assistance promised by its ally. Italy pulled out of the Triple Alliance and joined the Allies in the last war, as did Roumania. In fact, it appears that Germany and France were the only states in Europe brought into the war by existing alliances.[2] Nevertheless, the Balance of Power system—the conception that Europe should be divided into two great armed camps, each waiting to spring at the throat of the other—created and perpetuated an atmosphere which made permanent peace quite impossible.

5. SECRET DIPLOMACY

If military conventions and alliances were to be effective, the Old Diplomacy believed that they should be kept secret: the enemy should be kept in ignorance of the strength of his foe. Consequently the institution of secret diplomacy became an integral part of the institution of war.[3] The alliance between Germany and Austria-Hungary was signed in 1879 but its terms were not published until 1888. The League of the Three Emperors of 1881, the Austro-Serbian alliance of 1881, the Reinsurance treaty between Germany and Russia of 1887, the British-Italian agreement of 1887, all were kept secret after they had been signed. Most of the colonial gains of France since 1878 have been made by secret ententes. The exact obligations of England to France created by the Entente Cordiale of 1904 were never known to the outside world until after the outbreak of the World War.[4]

Great as the evils of secret diplomacy are from the standpoint of democracy,[5] they are even greater from the standpoint of

---

[1] *The Balance of Power*, cited, p. 7.
[2] A. C. Coolidge, "Ten Years of War and Peace," *Foreign Affairs*, Sept. 15, 1924.
[3] Cf. for a defence, J. Barthélemy, *Démocratie et politique étrangère* (1917), pp. 224 ff.
[4] Cf. Earl Loreburn, *How the War Came* (1919), Ch. IV.
[5] Cf. p. 745.

international relations. When a secret treaty is made, the fact usually leaks out to the world. Nevertheless, since its actual terms remain hidden, rumors and suspicions arise which may be altogether unwarranted, but which produce fear on the part of one country as regards another, and in general create an international atmosphere of an unhealthy nature. In 1887 a rumor that England and Italy had signed an alliance pushed France into alliance with Russia. The Allied secret treaties of the World War not only led to the distrust of the Allies by the neutrals, but also to disputes between the Allies, some of whom felt that they had been slighted in the division of spoils.

6. COMPETITION IN ARMAMENTS

The institution of war has been responsible for a third peace time policy—standing armies and great armaments. When war breaks out, the best armed nation has a great initial advantage which in many cases may be decisive. Moreover, since preparedness is a relative matter, each nation desires greater armies and defences than those of its neighbor, and when its neighbor increases its armaments, rivalry ensues. While economic disputes are fundamental as a cause of international irritation, competition in armaments may be even more important, since it arouses the instinctive fear of masses of people, ignorant of more complex and distant economic controversies, that they will be attacked. Originally established for reasons of defence, armaments may nevertheless become an instrument of aggression. Originally adopted as a means to an end— the furtherance of certain policies—armaments become an end in themselves. Nations come to seek great armies and fleets without regard for their use; they seek power merely because of power. As a result, armament rivalries themselves constitute a cause for war.

To European states land frontiers have been more important than sea frontiers, and they have been less easy to defend. Most of the fighting since 1815 has been between armies on the land. Man-power has therefore been the basis of military power. With the exception of Great Britain and the United States, practically every nation in the world has, for this reason, followed the policy of conscription. This is true not only of monarchies such as the former German Empire or the present Empire of Japan, but also of such democratic countries as Belgium, France, Holland, Switzerland, Canada, Australia, and the new states of Europe.[1] While the Central Powers followed the policy of conscription before the war, as a result of the peace treaties Germany, Austria, Hungary and Bulgaria were obliged to abandon this policy. Those powers which follow the conscription policy usually employ either the Swiss military system, which requires every young man to spend a few weeks out of every year in a training camp; or the French system which obliges men between certain ages to spend a year or so in active military service, and a longer period in reserve.[2]

The growth of standing armies from 1800 to 1921 may be seen from the following table:[3]

GROWTH OF STANDING ARMIES

	1800	1854	1870	1880	1900	1906	1921
Great Britain	169,428	417,046	302,405	307,494	513,863	445,731	425,000
France	160,230	260,000	393,500	609,983	672,565	677,581	735,000
Austria	280,000	539,000	800,000	291,876	375,291	409,638	22,000
Russia	433,000	677,000	733,000	947,000	1,119,000	1,225,000	1,500,000
Germany	220,000	127,000	315,000	427,000	495,000	610,000	150,000
United States	5,000	10,000	54,000	25,000	65,000	67,000	222,000

The twelve largest armies in the world in 1927 were as follows:[4]

1. France.................623,171
2. Russia.................562,000
3. Great Britain...........512,801
4. Italy..................250,470
5. Poland.................263,405
6. Japan..................198,800
7. Roumania..............149,769
8. United States..........134,914
9. Czechoslovakia.........127,012
10. Jugoslavia.............115,942
11. Spain..................113,434
12. Germany...............100,000

[1] In October, 1924, a bill was placed before the parliament of Denmark, providing for the abolition of the army and the navy, the War Office and the Admiralty, in favor of a "constabulary" of 7,000 frontier guards and a few armed vessels to police Danish waters. In supporting the bill, the government said that a small military force merely invited attack, and that since Denmark could not possibly maintain a large establishment, it would be better to disarm altogether. While the bill passed the lower house it was rejected by the Senate in June, 1927.

[2] The most authoritative description of the different military systems of the world will be found in the *Armaments Year-Book* (2d ed., 1924), League of Nations, C. 601. M. 209. 1924, IX; for the French and Swiss systems, cf. pp. 431, 744. This volume is published annually.

[3] War Department figures, *Staggering Burden of Armament*, cited.

[4] *Armaments Year-Book*, 1927, pp. 437, 107, 536, 698, 785, 597, 743, 903, 763. China claims an army of 1,607,400 (p. 332), but in view of the internal situation there it can hardly be listed above.

COMPETITION IN ARMAMENTS

Naval Rivalry.—Particularly for the British Empire, the United States and Japan, navies have also constituted a vital factor in national defence, and an essential instrument for the prosecution of wars abroad. By means of ships great armies may be transported to foreign battlefields. While modern wars are seldom won by the actual fighting of battleships, sea power is nevertheless decisive, because it may interrrupt the supplies of the enemy and safeguard the transportation of millions to distant battlefields. The influence which a nation plays in international politics has often been dependent upon the strength of its navy. "The problem of maintaining the balance of power and preserving the liberties of the world has ever been, as it is to-day, the problem of preventing the control of the seas from passing into the hands of the most powerful continental European state, which, if it were free to traverse the sea, would impose its rule upon all nations."[1] Navies have kept open trade and political communications between the mother country and her colonies. It has been by the instrumentality of the navy and the marines that the United States has carried out its interventions in Latin America, and other powers have intervened in China and the Near East. Navies have been the bulwark of imperialism.

Naval rivalry has probably been the most bitter form of armament competition in modern history. The command of the seas has been a prize for which many battles have been fought by Spain, Portugal, Holland, France and England.[2] However, between 1588 and 1921 the British Empire commanded the seas—a command justified, under the Old Diplomacy, by the far-flung dominions of the Empire and the fact that England imports four-fifths of her food and one-half of her meat.

In 1888 Germany determined to challenge this supremacy by creating a navy; and by 1900, the German government was asserting that Germany "must have a battle fleet so strong that even for the adversary with the greatest sea power, a war against us would involve such dangers as to imperil his own position in the world."[3] British policy had aimed to maintain a Two-Power

[1] S. C. Vestal, *The Maintenance of Peace* (1920), p. v.
[2] A. T. Mahan, *The Influence of Sea Power upon History*, 1660–1783 (1890); also his *The Influence of Sea Power upon the French Revolution and Empire*, 1793–1812 (1894).
[3] B. E. Schmitt, *England and Germany*, 1740–1914 (1916), p. 176.

standard—a navy equal in strength to that of any other two European powers. But German competition was so strong that this standard could not be maintained. In 1902 Great Britain negotiated the Anglo-Japanese Alliance, which had a direct bearing upon this naval rivalry. As a result of the alliance England could now withdraw her fleet from Asiatic Waters to the North Sea where they confronted the German squadrons.

Another power next arose to challenge the supremacy of the British navy. This was the United States. Before the World War, this country was a poor third to England and Germany. But aroused by fears of the German submarine and the World War generally, the Congress of the United States passed a Naval Appropriation Act in 1916 which called for the construction within three years of ten first-class battleships, six battle cruisers, and a large number of smaller vessels. The execution of the "1916" programme was delayed by America's entrance into the war and the diversion of building facilities to submarines and merchantmen. At the close of the war, however, the construction of the vessels was resumed. The avowed purpose of American policy was the creation of a "navy equal to the most powerful maintained by any other nation in the world." [1] If the American programme had been completed, the American navy would have been actually stronger than the British navy in 1924.[2]

In view of the fact that American opinion had frequently objected to the expansion of Japan in Asia, the Japanese government became alarmed at the expansion of the American fleet. In order to prevent the naval intervention of America in the Orient, it adopted an "eight-eight" programme, in July, 1920, which by 1928 would have given Japan a navy of 16 capital ships, compared with 33 such ships in the American navy at that time. In order to achieve this programme, Japan would have been obliged to expend about $400,000,000—as great a sum as that being expended by the United States, despite the fact that the population of the latter country is twice as great.

Aircraft and Submarines.—Following the World War naval rivalry shifted from so-called capital ships to aircraft and sub-

[1] Report of General Board of Navy, Sept. 24, 1920.
[2] R. L. Buell, *Washington Conference*, p. 144.

marines. In the opinion of many naval authorities, these new weapons of warfare may displace the old battleship-types; while practically all authorities are agreed that sea power will be fatally handicapped unless it is protected adequately by planes.[1] "Efficiency of sea-power in European waters is dependent primarily upon command of the air."[2] As a result of an air-fleet partly accumulated during the World War, France soon had a superiority in planes over the British, which some writers estimated to be as 15:1. Alarmed lest French air supremacy would be used with terrible effect against England because of its proximity to France and because its population is concentrated in easily bombed cities, the British government in June, 1923, announced that it would be necessary to build a force "of sufficient strength adequately to protect us against Air attack by the strongest Air Force within striking distance of this country."[3] This announcement was followed by increased air appropriations of the French parliament; while the Italian prime minister said, "If others arm in the air, Italy must arm in the air."

Competition in submarines also became serious. On the ground that such craft were necessary to safeguard her communications with Africa, which otherwise might be intercepted by a Spanish-Italian fleet, France declined to limit submarines at the Washington Conference.[4] At this failure, some of the powers, diverted their funds to the construction of submarines, cruisers and other non-treaty vessels.

Following the Washington Conference and up to 1929 the British government laid down or appropriated for naval tonnage to the amount of 393,274 tons, while Japan laid down or appropriated for a tonnage of 415,252 tons. The United States, however, laid down only 156,900 tons.[5] Before the passage of the 15-cruiser bill by the United States in January, 1929, Great Britain had 56 first-line cruisers in comparison with 18 for the United

[1] Cf. Report of General Board, U. S. Navy, cited; H. Bywater, "Japan: A Sequel to the Washington Conference," *Atlantic Monthly*, Feb., 1923, *ibid.*, "The Dismal Prospects for Limiting Armaments," Nov., 1924.
[2] Brig. Gen. P. R. G. Groves, "For France to Answer," *Atlantic Monthly*, February, 1924.
[3] Prime Minister Baldwin, 65 *Parl. Debates, H. C.* (1923), 2142.
[4] Cf. p. 560.
[5] Cf. Senator Hale's table, *Congressional Record*, Jan. 3, 1929, p. 1083.

States. If the 15 cruisers authorized in 1929 are completed the United States will have a total cruiser tonnage (first line) of 305,000 tons in comparison with 380,800 for the British Empire. While the British Empire will be ahead in small cruisers, the United States will have 23 8-inch gun cruisers in comparison with 18 for the British.[1] Taking all factors into consideration it is believed that with the construction of the 15 cruisers by the United States the American and British fleets will be substantially equal. It should therefore be feasible to conclude an agreement providing for the naval status quo.

Between 1900 and 1920 the eight leading naval powers of the world constructed a total of 2,861 warships. During the same period the fourteen leading powers expended sixty-one and a half billion pounds for war-like expenditures, compared with only 46,000,000 pounds for all other purposes, social or otherwise. Thus the peace time expenditures on armaments during this period were nearly twice that of the direct cost of the World War. In 1900 the total national debts of these fourteen powers stood at 4 billion pounds, while in 1920 they had increased to more than 53 billion pounds, an increase of 13 times, due largely to military outlays, including the costs of war.[2] Despite the impoverishment brought about by the World War, the military expenditures of most European powers were greater in 1922 than they had been in 1913 on account of the feeling of insecurity prevailing everywhere.[3]

Inasmuch as standing armies withdraw men from productive enterprise, the economic reconstruction of Europe was undoubtedly delayed by the fact that some six million men were toting guns instead of hoes. As the invitation of the American government to the Washington Conference stated, "It is idle to look for stability, or the assurance of social justice, or the security of peace, while wasteful and unproductive outlays deprive effort of its just reward and defeat the reasonable expectation of progress."[4]

Of still more importance, competition in armaments is a "constant menace to the peace of the world." In 1870 Lord Clarendon,

[1] Cf. "The Disarmament Deadlock," *I. S.*, Vol. IV–No. 20, p. 395.
[2] A. G. Enock, *The Problem of Armaments* (1923), pp. 30 ff.
[3] *Budget Expenditures on National Defence, 1913 and 1910–22*, Sept., 1922, League of Nations, A. 31 (a) 1922.
[4] Note of August 11, 1921.

THE PRIVATE MANUFACTURE OF ARMS 519

the British Foreign Secretary, protested against the "enormous standing armies that now afflict Europe by constituting a state of things that is neither peace nor war, but which is so destructive of confidence that men almost desire war with all its horrors in order to arrive at some certainty of peace—a state of things that withdraws millions of hands from productive industry and heavily taxes the people to their own injury and renders them discontent with their rulers. . . . This system is cruel, it is out of harmony with the civilization of our age, and it is pregnant with danger." [1]

Out of fear of Germany, France arms. Out of fear of France, Italy arms. Out of fear of Italy and France, England arms. It is a vicious circle—in which rivalry engenders jealousy and in which jealousy engenders hate. It is a policy which ends only in war. The existence of arms—of guns and battleships—tempts nations to their use.

7. THE PRIVATE MANUFACTURE OF ARMS

An immense amount of capital and business enterprise is necessarily devoted to the maintenance of military establishments. Soldiers must be equipped; battleships, aircraft, submarines and munitions must be provided. In most countries, this business is in the hands of private interests, who sell their wares to the state.

---

[1] Quoted by Fisher, *The Common Weal*, p. 245.

In its note convening the Hague conference of 1899, the Russian government similarly said, "The ever-increasing financial expense touches public prosperity at its very source; the intellectual and physical powers of the people, labor and capital, are, in a great measure, turned aside from their natural functions and consumed unproductively. Hundreds of millions are used in acquiring fearful engines of destruction, which, to-day considered as the highest triumph of science, are destined to-morrow to lose all their value because of some new discovery in this sphere.

"It is true also that as the armaments of each power increase in size they succeed less and less in accomplishing the result which is aimed at by the governments. Economic crises, due in great part to the existence of excessive armaments, and the constant dangers which result from this accumulation of war material, make of the armed peace of our day an overwhelming burden which it is more and more difficult for the people to bear. It therefore seems evident that, if this state of affairs continues it will inevitably lead to that very cataclysm which we are trying to avoid, and the horrors of which are fearful to human thought." Note of August 12, 1898, Moore, *Digest*, VII, p. 79.

Under such a system, private munition firms are tempted to increase the sale of armaments by every possible means.[1]

As the size of armaments depends upon the fear that war is imminent, unscrupulous men may go so far as to stimulate international animosity. If the armament interests worked in the open, their purpose would be defeated. Consequently they frequently make use of "patriotic" organizations and support "preparedness" campaigns, really in the interest of business profits. Before the World War, the executive committee of the British National Service League was composed of nine men who were at the same time officers in armament firms.[2]

Armament firms may also make use of distorted information to create war scares. The Dreadnaught panic of 1909 in England was caused by the false report that the German fleet would outdistance the British fleet in 1912 by 9 dreadnaughts. This information was innocently given to parliament by Lord Balfour from a "secret" source which later proved to be an armament firm. Although the information was false, this fact was not established until parliament had passed the desired appropriations.[3]

Likewise direct bribery has been employed to increase the gun business. Perhaps the most notorious instance was the Krupp Scandal of 1913. An official named Brandt was employed by this firm to purchase from government officials all secret documents

---

[1] The trade in arms in the world for 1920–1925 is as follows:

	1920	1921	1922	1925
	Millions of dollars			
Total exports	139.8	48.4	42.3	55.7
Total imports	32.6	26.9	26.9	45.2

Statistical Information on the Trade in Arms, Ammunition, and Material of War, C. 26 M. 13, 1928, IX. It is evident from the excess of recorded exports that a great deal of smuggling is taking place. Cf. p. 283.

[2] "Est-il souhaitable que la fabrication des armes et autres matériels de guerre soit confiée à l'État et cette situation favoriserait-elle effectivement la limitation des armaments?" By La Commission Neérlandaise d'Étude, *Recueil de Rapports, Organisation Centrale pour une paix durable* (1916), Vol. II, p. 322.

[3] H. Wehberg, *Die Internationale Beschränkung der Rüstungen* (1919), p. 35. For the famous Poutiloff affair, in which a German firm attempted to secure the publication in a Paris paper that the number of machine guns in the French army had been doubled, cf. *ibid.*, p. 354. For the rivalry between the Krupp and Schneider firms, supported respectively by the German and French governments, for orders in Argentina, cf. General Maitrot, *La France et les Républiques Sud-Américaines*, pp. 12–25.

relating to armaments which might interest the company, including the bids of competitors. When his activities were discovered, a number of officials of the German government and of Krupps were punished. In 1914 a similar scandal occurred in Japan where, in the notorious Siemens affair, a number of Japanese naval officers were charged with accepting bribes from a German armament firm in return for orders.[1]

Moreover, armament orders may be influenced by the presence in parliaments of men who are stockholders in armament firms. Before the war, twelve members of the British House of Lords and nine of the Commons were thus interested.[2]

Although armament firms have advocated preparedness upon the basis of national necessity, they have not hesitated to form international trusts to advance the interests of foreign and domestic firms, whether "enemy" or not. The most important of these trusts was the Powder Cartel, which was composed of seven different munition enterprises in different countries. In 1901 another trust, called the Harvey United Steel Co., Ltd., was formed containing representatives of six British, two German, two French, one Italian and one American firms. The Nobel Dynamite Trust Company, originally a British concern, was also interested in four German companies. In 1868 the Krupps were so brazen as to offer to sell guns to France, which might have been used in the Franco-German war.[3]

Obviously, the private manufacture of arms and munitions, if uncontrolled, will seriously disturb international relations. The tendency under such a system is for private munition interests, whether or not in collusion with the press or government officials, to stimulate the fear of war in order to increase armament orders. The result of such a tendency is to accelerate international animosity for the sake of private gain.

8. FORCE AND INTERNATIONAL SOCIETY

Terrible as are war and its by-products—alliances, secret diplomacy, competition in armaments and the private manufac-

---

[1] 61 *Japan Weekly Mail* (1914), 213, 648.
[2] *Recueil*, p. 321.
[3] Wehberg, p. 349. *Recueil*, p. 335. *The International Industry of War*, U. D. C. No. 7, p. 5. The Bethlehem Steel Co. of the U. S. was a large stock-

ture of arms—nations have clung to this institution because of the belief that, in the last analysis, their existence or independence depended upon force. They have been loath to give up physical preparedness until some certain means of settling international disputes upon a basis of justice has been established. Even then a certain type of force—internationally controlled—may be necessary.[1] In a domestic community the policeman's billy has been used to enforce generally recognized law. On the other hand, the army's bayonet has in the past been used as the instrument of national "interests" which violated accepted rules of international law or as to which there were no such rules. Although there may have been "righteous" wars in the past, no machinery existed to determine this question before the war began. Moreover, a war righteously started, usually ended in unrighteous peace demands. In the domestic community, force is the instrument of law; in the international community it has been the instrument of non-juristic interests, in much the same way as privateering and duelling were several hundred years ago. While international machinery is being developed to make and interpret international law, machinery must also be established to enforce the law when wilfully violated. The use of force, thus controlled, will probably be as necessary, in exceptional cases, in international as it is in domestic relations. Whether machinery will be developed to give a sanction to law before or after the legislative and judicial processes of international society have been perfected is a question now before the world.[2] Before discussing the progress made toward the establishment of machinery for the pacific settlement of international disputes, the next chapter will deal with another important by-product of the war system—the question of Reparations.

holder in the Harvey United Steel Company, Ltd. This latter company was dissolved in 1913.

[1] Cf. p. 595.
[2] For the Protocol, cf. p. 645.

CHAPTER XXII

REPARATIONS AND INTER-ALLIED DEBTS

1. Reparations and the Peace Treaty.—2. The Reparations Commission and Germany's Bill.—3. Germany's Failure to Pay.—4. The Legality of the Occupation of the Ruhr.—5. Germany's Capacity to Pay.—6. The "Dawes Plan" (1924).—Raising Reparations—Getting the Money out of Germany—Foreign Control over Germany—Arbitration and Default.—7. The Inter-Allied Debts.—8. The "Young Plan" (1929).—9. The Bank for International Settlement.

In ancient times it was the custom of the victor in war to walk off with as much booty as he could conveniently carry, and to burn what he was obliged to leave behind. With the progress of civilization, such practices, at least when carried on in the open, came to be frowned upon. It is no longer the fashion to impose punitive damages upon a vanquished foe. When "reparations" are exacted, they should in theory be limited to the cost of the war or to the damage done by the war to the civilian population. As a matter of fact this distinction between "reparations" and "indemnities" has become largely fictitious, since the damage to a civilian population in a modern war fought upon a world-wide scale is incalculable.

In wars ending in a draw, the question of reparations is passed over in silence. In the three most important wars in the 20th century—before 1914—the Russo-Japanese war, the Turkish-Italian war, and the Balkan wars of 1912-1913, no monetary indemnity or reparations were imposed upon the defeated power. Following her victories over Greece in 1921-1922, Turkey was able to sign a peace treaty in which she was not obliged to pay any reparations to the Allied powers.

Reparations have been, nevertheless, exacted at the end of about fifteen wars fought between 1815 and 1914.[1] The sums in

---
[1] *Indemnities*, Peace Handbooks, No. 158, vol. 25.

each case, however, were relatively small, the largest being the billion dollars exacted by Germany from France as a result of the war of 1870. While she did not exact a monetary sum, Chile, as victor in the "War of the Pacific," secured from Peru and Bolivia very rich nitrate deposits worth a billion dollars.[1]

1. REPARATIONS AND THE PEACE TREATY

It was a foregone conclusion that the victor in the World War of 1914–1918 would, if strong enough, impose some form of exaction upon the vanquished. However, the exactions foreseen were limited by President Wilson in his Fourteen Points, where it was declared merely that "invaded territories must be restored as well as evacuated and freed." This principle was accepted by the Allies and Germany in the pre-armistice negotiations, subject to the understanding that "compensation will be made by Germany for all damage to the civilian population of the Allies and their property by the aggression of Germany by land, by sea, and from the air." The acceptance of this principle meant that Germany would not have to pay for the costs of the war—for munitions, soldiers' pay, and so forth—but only for damage actually done to civilians.

In the actual armistice agreement, however, it was provided that Germany would make reparation for "damage" done, with the reservation "of any future concessions and claims by the Allies and United States."[2] The inclusion of this clause in regard to future claims was seized upon by certain of the Allied governments to open up the whole question of "war costs" at the Peace Conference. It was contended that because of this clause the Allies were no longer bound by the Fourteen Points and that Germany should be compelled to pay for the whole cost of the war.[3]

President Wilson wished to limit Germany's liability to civilian damage, partly because the total cost of the war, including damages to property and persons, reached the tremendous figure of three trillion francs,[4]—a sum obviously impossible for any government

[1] Cf. *The Case of Peru*, Peru-Chile arbitration, 1923, p. 96.
[2] Armistice Convention of Nov. 11, 1918, *Treaties of U. S.*, Vol. III, p. 3310.
[3] B. M. Baruch, *The Making of the Reparation and Economic Sections of the Treaty* (1920), pp. 24 ff.
[4] A. Tardieu, *The Truth About the Treaty* (1921), p. 290. According to Lord Sumner, a British delegate at the Conference, war costs were demanded

REPARATIONS AND THE PEACE TREATY 525

ever to pay. Moreover, if the principle should become established that a victor could exact from the vanquished all the expenses incurred by hostilities, war might become a paying proposition which would be an added, if indirect, incentive for nations to fight.

Despite this reasoning and the pre-armistice pledge, nationalistic considerations and election pledges caused some of the Allies to reiterate the demand that Germany pay for the whole cost of the war. A compromise was finally reached by inserting a provision in the Treaty of Versailles declaring that Germany was responsible "for causing all the loss and damage to which the Allied and Associated Governments and their nationals have been subjected as a consequence of the war imposed upon them by the aggression of Germany and her allies." Nevertheless, the Allies recognized that the resources of Germany were not adequate to make complete reparation for this damage. For this reason Germany's liability was limited to damage done to the civilian population of the Allies and their property during the war.[1]

An annex of the treaty defines what is meant by "civilian damage," enumerating ten different types of obligations falling within this class, such as the reparation of devastated regions and compensation for forced labor. A controversy arose at the Peace Conference over whether pensions to soldiers and allowances to their families should be considered "civilian damage." It was the contention of the American delegation that civilian damage meant "direct physical damage to property of non-military character and direct physical injury to civilians."[2] Once pensions were included in this category, the whole costs of the war could be called civilian damages, since they must ultimately be borne by the taxpayer. Despite the soundness of this argument, the Conference finally voted to include pensions in the sums for which Germany is liable.[3]

As a result of this decision, the amount of the reparations was

by the Allied powers from France in 1815 (700 million francs); by Austria from Sardinia in 1849 (25 millions); by Prussia from Austria in 1866 (40 millions); by Prussia from France in 1871 (5,000 millions), *ibid.*, p. 287.

[1] Articles 231–232. But Germany also undertook to pay the sums Belgium had borrowed from the Allies during the war, "as a consequence of the violation of the Treaty of 1839."

[2] Baruch, p. 19.

[3] The "Big Four" was won over by the argument of General Smuts; for the latter's memorandum, cf. Baruch, p. 29.

about doubled. The actual damage to English civilian property had been small. But British pensions and allowances were nearly as large as those of France. The inclusion of pensions, therefore, worked to increase British claims, although the French unwittingly supported the pension demand.[1]

The Conference was confronted not only with the problem of how much Germany *should* pay but also of what she was financially and economically *able* to pay. No agreement was possible upon either problem. France was unwilling to name a definite sum on the ground that she could not determine what her exact losses were. Official estimates of what Germany should or could pay ranged from $30,000,000,000 named by the American Delegation to $125,000,000,000 made by Lord Cunliffe of the British Delegation; while unofficial estimates, made for campaign purposes, ranged higher. These figures were so divergent and the fear that Germany would be "let off" was so great that it was impossible to agree upon a definite sum which the Allies should exact.

2. THE REPARATIONS COMMISSION AND GERMANY'S BILL

The Treaty of Versailles did not therefore fix the total sum which Germany should pay. It merely provided that an Inter-Allied body—the Reparations Commission—should fix this sum not later than May 1, 1921, a sum which should be paid within thirty years.[2] However, before May 1, 1921, Germany was obligated to advance on account 20 billion gold marks to the Allies.[3]

For a time the Reparations Commission was the most important of the administrative bodies set up to enforce the treaties of peace. It was to have been composed of representatives of France, Great Britain, the United States, Italy, Japan, Belgium and Jugoslavia. However, the delegates of Japan and Jugoslavia could attend only in certain defined cases, when they replaced Belgium.[4]

---

[1] The United States waived its claims to pensions against Germany in the exchange of notes, August 10, 1922, *Treaties of the U. S.*, Vol. III, p. 2603.

[2] Art. 233.

[3] Out of this sum the expenses of the armies of occupation, etc., were to be paid. Art. 235.

[4] The United States, after the failure to ratify the treaty, was represented by an "unofficial" delegate, except for a short time between February and May, 1921. *Report on the Work of the Reparation Commission from 1920 to 1922*, V, Reparation Commission, H. M. Stationary Office (1923), p. 9.

THE REPARATIONS COMMISSION

The refusal of the United States to appoint the delegate to which it was entitled, destroyed the independence of the Commission and led to a struggle between France and England for control, which resulted in French ascendancy. The administration of the whole reparations question was in the hands of this Commission. It was obliged to fix the total sum which Germany must pay. Once this sum was fixed, it could be reduced only by the unanimous vote of the members of the Commission and their respective governments. Unanimity was also required to interpret the reparation clauses.[1]

The first duty of this Commission was to define the amount of damage done by Germany and inform her of this figure by May 1, 1921. In estimating this amount, the Commission was not obliged to take into consideration Germany's capacity to pay, but only the actual damage caused by Germany during the war which represented "the extent of that Government's obligations."[2] After May 1, 1921, the Commission should consider Germany's resources, being empowered to modify the forms of payment, but not to cancel any part except with the consent of the governments represented on the Commission. These provisions were defective, first because the actual extent of Germany's obligation was not made known until nearly two years after the treaty was signed, and in the meantime, Germany had no incentive to go to work. Of more practical importance, the total reparations sum was to be drawn up *without consideration of Germany's capacity to pay*. This failure to relate Germany's obligations to Germany's capacity was at the bottom of the whole reparations controversy which

---

[1] It appears that the Commission interpreted most questions in favor of the Allies and against Germany. *Report, passim.* So many difficulties in interpretation arose that this part of the treaty was amended to the effect that by unanimous agreement the Commission could submit differences to an arbitrator. But these provisions have been superseded by the 1924 plan; cf. p. 544. The reparation clauses of the treaty could be amended by the States on the Reparation Commission. Par. 22, Annex II, Part VIII, Treaty of Versailles. The work of the Reparation Commission was done through a number of Services, chief of which were the Finance Service, the Service of Restitution, and the Maritime Service. Cf. *Report*, p. 9.

[2] Article 233. A great number of other duties were laid on the Commission by different peace treaties, i. e., the appointment of persons to conduct the liquidation of the Austro-Hungarian Bank and the distribution of the pre-war Austrian and Hungarian debts among the Succession States. Cf. *Report*, cited, pp. 5–6.

disturbed the peace of the world for six years after the end of the war.

The Allies were uncertain as to the procedure to be followed in drawing up Germany's bill. Although the treaty said that this task should fall upon the Reparations Commission, the Allied prime ministers soon took it into their hands. Six or seven conferences of the Supreme Council were held before May, 1921, for this purpose. Of these the most important was at Spa in 1920. Although the original purpose of this conference was to work out a "lump sum settlement," its time was fully consumed in discussing the basis of dividing reparations among the Allies. It was finally agreed that France should receive 52%, the British Empire 22%, Italy 10%, Belgium 8%, Greece, Roumania and Jugoslavia 6.5%; Japan and Portugal each .75%.[1]

Just four months before the total had to be fixed, the problem was turned back to the Reparations Commission.[2] Confronted with the extremely difficult task of estimating within a short three months the extent of Germany's obligations, the Commission adopted a system by which it received from the governments concerned claims for damages which were then transmitted to the *Kriegslastenkommission*—the German body appointed to administer questions arising out of the treaty. The Germans contested some 300 claims thus submitted, and hearings of the German government before the Reparations Commission lasted over ninety hours. On April 27th, the Commission finally announced the total sum for which Germany was liable—132 billion gold marks. This sum was at least 50 billions lower than the claims submitted by the Allied governments.[3]

In determining the time and the manner by which this sum should be paid, the Reparations Commission provided that Germany should issue three series of bonds, the first, called Class A bonds, for the amount of 12 billion gold marks; the second, called Class B bonds, for 38 billion gold marks, and the third, called Class C bonds, for 82 billion gold marks, making a total of 132 billion. However, the Class C bonds were not to be issued until

---

[1] Agreement of July 16, 1920, 114 *State Papers*, 550.
[2] *Report*, cited, pp. 26 ff.
[3] The claims of France alone came to $218\frac{1}{2}$ billion francs; cf. Appendix VII, *Report*.

the Commission was satisfied that Germany could meet payments upon them. By this means, the Commission attempted to make some allowance for Germany's ability to pay. Thus Germany was obliged to pay interest of 5% plus 1% for sinking fund only upon the first two classes of bonds, totaling 50 billion gold marks. The annual payments of Germany to the Allies would, at this rate, equal 3 billion gold marks a year. However, instead of requiring the payment of this sum outright, the London settlement provided that Germany should pay 2 billion gold marks a year, plus 26% of the value of her exports,[1] thus adding another element of flexibility to the plan.

3. GERMANY'S FAILURE TO PAY

Although Germany promised to meet these payments, the promise was not kept in whole. By May, 1922, Germany owed 965 million gold marks of the sums fixed by the Commission as due.[2] She claimed that she could not meet these payments because the sums were excessive and because the financial situation at home was demoralized. Consequently she asked for a moratorium or delay. Throughout the fall of 1922 the Allied governments conferred as to Germany's request. Great Britain believed that Germany should be given a breathing space, enabling her to reorganize her finances and to restore her foreign trade, without which the payment of reparations would be impossible. France theoretically recognized the necessity for a moratorium, but took the position that Germany had wilfully depreciated her currency and had deliberately evaded her obligations through the fraudulent sale of the mark and the export of capital. She accordingly urged that if a moratorium was granted, the Allies should first secure "productive" guarantees—the control of German customs and finance, and the further occupation of German territory.[3]

The distrust of France toward Germany had been heightened

---

[1] Schedule of Payments London Settlement of May 5, 1921, *Documents Officiels relatifs au montant des versements a éffectuer par l'Allemagne au Titre des Réparations*, Commission des Réparations (1922), Vol. I, p. 1.

[2] *État des obligations de l'Allemagne, etc., à la date du 30 Avril, 1922*, Commission des Réparations, p. 34.

[3] Cf. *Minutes of the London Conference on Reparations*, August, 1922, Cmd. 2258; *Inter-Allied Conferences on Reparations and Inter-Allied Debts*, Cmd. 1812.

by the alleged failure of Germany to pay the 20 billion gold marks she was obliged to advance before May, 1921. Germany claimed to have paid the whole value of this sum in goods, public property and so forth, surrendered to the Allies. But the Reparations Commission declined to accept Germany's valuation of the property, declaring that she still owed 12 billion gold marks.[1] Upon the failure of Germany to pay this balance and to meet other provisions of the treaty, the Allied governments occupied the towns of Duisburg, Düsseldorf and Ruhrort in March, 1921, establishing a special customs régime which was maintained until July, 1922.[2]

In January, 1922, another inter-Allied conference was held in Paris where a deadlock between the British and the French attitudes toward Germany was reached. On December 26, 1922, the French, Italian and Belgian members of the Reparations Commission had voted that Germany had gone into default in timber deliveries.[3] On January 6, 1923, the Commission recorded a similar default for coal. On the basis of these decisions, France and Belgium proceeded to occupy the Ruhr—a district which is the industrial heart of Germany, containing 80% of its coal supply. By occupying it, France hoped to exploit German resources directly and thus secure sums from Germany which Germany herself had failed to deliver. If this proved impossible, France at least hoped to make Germany feel that France was really in earnest in her demands for reparation; that if Germany would not pay, France would by this occupation ruin the industrial organization of Germany. In entering this territory French and Belgian troops were accompanied by engineers and experts who not only took over the railways, but eventually the local government itself. In the nine months of the occupation, 31,000 Germans who opposed the French were evicted from the territory. Prison sentences, in addition to ten death penalties, were imposed which aggregated fifteen hundred years; 209 school buildings were requisitioned for military purposes; while 173 newspapers were suspended. Nevertheless, this policy did not immediately break

---

[1] *Report*, cited, p. 23.
[2] *Reparation*, Part II, A League of Nations, Vol. V, No. 2 (1922), p. 74.
[3] *Report*, cited, p. 260. It was reported that the default was only 5–10% of the total sum originally demanded.

the passive resistance of the Germans. Backed by funds from the Berlin government, the inhabitants of the Ruhr refused to coöperate in any way with the French.

But this exhausting campaign could not endure indefinitely. In May, 1924, the German government made an offer to pay the Allies a total sum of 30 billion gold marks, which was rejected. Germany now made a second offer (June 7) in which she repeated her willingness to submit the question of the amount to be paid to an impartial international body of experts—an idea advanced by the American Secretary of State, Mr. C. E. Hughes, in a speech at New Haven in December, 1922. In the same note, the German government also offered to place at the disposal of the Allies the returns of the railways, a general property tax, and customs duties on luxuries, etc., which were estimated to yield, after 1926, the annual sum of 1,800,000,000 gold marks.[1]

4. THE LEGALITY OF THE OCCUPATION OF THE RUHR

Whether or not the French occupation of the Ruhr was justified by law or by facts has been a hotly debated question. The Treaty of Versailles contains certain definite provision as to the guarantees for the execution of the treaty. For a period of fifteen years "from the coming into force of the present treaty" Allied troops may occupy the German territory west of the Rhine, together with the bridgeheads, which are of great strategic importance.[2] While this occupation is limited to fifteen years, Germany under the treaty is given at least thirty years in which to pay reparations, leaving fifteen in which the Allies will not be allowed to occupy German territory.[3] This discrepancy greatly alarmed

[1] "Correspondence with the Allied Governments Respecting Reparation Payments by Germany," Misc. No. 5 (1923), Cmd. 1943, p. 2.

[2] At the end of five years, a certain district would be evacuated, and at the end of ten years other districts would be evacuated, provided Germany had faithfully carried out the terms of the treaty. Article 429. Cf. p. 565. No limitation upon the number of Allied troops in the Rhine was imposed in the treaty; but on June 16, 1919, Wilson, Clemenceau and Lloyd George signed a declaration to the effect that "as soon as the allied and associated powers concerned are convinced that the conditions of disarmament by Germany are being satisfactorily fulfilled, the annual amount of the sums to be paid by Germany to cover the cost of occupation shall not exceed 240,000,000 marks (gold)." Cmd. 240 (1919).

[3] Art. 233, Treaty of Versailles.

France who insisted that the Rhine should not be given up until the reparations had been paid in full. This demand was finally granted in January, 1921, when the Supreme Council, by a strained interpretation of the treaty, ruled that "the date from which will begin to run the term of occupation of the Rhine territories will be that on which satisfaction is given to the Allies." [1]

Within the German territory occupied by the Allied troops, a Rhineland Commission was established, composed of three members, representing Belgium, France and Great Britain.[2] This Commission was "the supreme representative" of the Allies in a territory inhabited by six million Germans. It had power to issue ordinances "so far as may be necessary for securing the maintenance, safety, and requirements" of the Allied troops. These ordinances were binding on the German authorities, although in the absence of such ordinances, the ordinary civil German administration continued to exist. All new German laws had to be submitted to the Rhineland Commission for its approval before being effective.[3] The Commission exercised its power so as to veto the appointment of German officials; to order deportations of Germans from the territory; to grant immunity to Allied officials so far as the jurisdiction of German courts was concerned, and to prohibit public meetings. While apparently the Rhineland Commission performed its duties with a minimum of friction, the existence of a virtual foreign government upon Germany's soil did nothing to diminish the hostility of the French and German peoples.[4]

Germany made no legal objection to the military occupation of the Rhine, the Rhineland Commission, or the Reparations Commission, which had been provided for by the Treaty of Ver-

[1] *Reparation*, A League of Nations, Part II, p. 61.

[2] "Agreement with regard to the Military Occupation of the Territory of the Rhine, between the United States, Belgium, British Empire, France, and Germany," July 28, 1919. *Treaties of U. S.*, Vol. II, p. 3524. The United States was entitled to membership on the Commission; because of the failure to ratify the treaty, she was represented merely by an "unofficial observer," Major General H. T. Allen, who took part in discussion but did not vote.

[3] Ireton, "The Rhineland Commission at Work," *A. J. I. L.*, July, 1923; J. Rousseau, *La haute commission interalliée des territoires Rhénans* (1923), pp. 87–214. Cf. Arts. 7–8, Ordinance No. 1, Ordinances and Instructions issued by the Inter-Allied Rhineland High Commission (1920), Cmd. 591.

[4] A third body was set up by an amendment to the treaty, on May 27, 1921, the Committee of Guarantees. It administered certain revenues assigned by Germany for reparations, etc. Cf. Chapter X of the *Report*.

LEGALITY OF OCCUPATION OF THE RUHR 533

sailles. But she did contend that the military occupation of the Ruhr by France and Belgium was illegal. This position was also taken by the British government in its note of August 11, 1923.[1] The occupation of the Ruhr had been based on the following paragraphs of annex II of the Reparations section of the treaty (Part VIII):

17

In case of default by Germany in the performance of any obligation under this Part of the present Treaty, the Commission will forthwith give notice of such default to each of the interested Powers and may make recommendations as to the action to be taken in consequence of such default as it may think necessary.

18

The measures which the Allied and Associated Powers shall have the right to take, in case of voluntary default by Germany, and which Germany agrees not to regard as acts of war, may include economic and financial prohibitions and reprisals and in general such other measures as the respective Governments may determine to be necessary in the circumstances.

It was the contention of the German and British governments that paragraph 18 did not justify the further occupation of territory but that the only measures which the Allies could take were measures, *collectively* agreed upon, and similar *in kind* to the economic and financial prohibitions stated above. The British government stated its willingness to submit this difference in interpretation to the World Court, a request which France declined. The British government also stated that the limits of military occupation were restricted in the treaty to the west bank of the Rhine, and that if the French contention was correct, this limitation would become meaningless, and the French government could send troops throughout the whole of Germany whenever in its opinion the treaty provisions were not complied with.

The British position was weakened because it was not advanced until August, 1923, whereas the occupation had begun in the previous January. England's opposition to further military sanctions was also inconsistent with her former position in March,

[1] Cmd. 1943. Cf. also Schuster, "The Question as to the Legality of the Ruhr Occupation," *A. J. I. L.*, July, 1924. McNair, "The Legality of the Occupation of the Ruhr," *British Year-Book of International Law, 1924.*

1921, when Mr. Lloyd George, the British prime minister, sanctioned the occupation by Allied troops of the towns of Duisburg, Ruhrort and Düsseldorf on the right bank of the Rhine. From the strictly legal standpoint, it is clear that Germany did not meet the obligations imposed upon her by the Reparations Commission. It is not so clear that France was entitled to occupy the Ruhr in order to force Germany to live up to these obligations. However, legal considerations were not fundamental to the controversy. The fundamental question was whether or not the demands made upon Germany by the Allies were humanly possible for any nation under the best of circumstances to meet, and whether or not the Allies, as well as Germany, were following policies which would allow Germany to make any reparation payments at all.

5. GERMANY'S CAPACITY TO PAY

France was entitled to the sympathy of the outside world because despite the great extent of her devastated regions and the cost of reconstruction which she was bearing by loans, she had received comparatively little cash (144 million gold marks) from Germany up to January, 1923. Out of the 8 billion gold marks advanced by Germany to the Reparations Commission by the end of 1922, two and a half billion went to pay the cost of the armies of occupation and the control commissions.[1] Certain priorities were also given to Belgium. Furthermore, much of the payments of Germany was in the form of ceded property and deliveries in kind which, when detached from the German economic system, became of little worth, although at the same time the loss of this property impaired Germany's capacity for production.

[1] *État des Obligations de l'Allemagne*, Vol. IV, Commission des Réparations, Table XI. Charges were made that the upkeep of the Allied troops on the Rhine and of the control commissions in Germany was extravagant. Moreover, it was charged that up to October, 1923, Germany was obliged to expend some 802,000 marks on brothels for the use of Allied soldiers. F. Nitti, *The Decadence of Europe* (1923), p. 128.

Germany claimed to have advanced to the Allies, by the end of 1922, the sum of 55 billion gold marks. This excessive figure was partly due to the fact that it included certain property which the Reparation Commission had not yet evaluated and also to different systems of valuation—the Germans taking pre-war values, while the Commission took present values. Cf. *Report*, pp. 15 ff.

GERMANY'S CAPACITY TO PAY

Of the deliveries in kind, coal was perhaps the most important. The Allies finally, in the Spa agreement of 1920,[1] fixed the amount that Germany should deliver to France at 2,000,000 tons a month. Even this quantity proved to be more than French industry could absorb. France stopped buying coal from England, with the result that British coal mines shut down and British miners were thrown out of work. Moreover, French merchants adopted the policy of reselling German coal to Belgium, Holland and Central European countries which in turn, sold the coal back to Germany! Pushed to this extreme, deliveries in kind diverted coal from the channels in Germany where it was greatly needed to channels where it was not needed at all. Payment in kind was supported, as in the Wiesbaden agreement of 1921 and the Lubersac-Stinnes agreement, on the ground that it relieved Germany of the necessity for making cash payments.[2] While exchange difficulties were thus averted, the German miners had to be paid—an obligation which weighed upon the German government. So close to bankruptcy was Germany that in the Spa agreement the Allies undertook to advance 5 gold marks a ton, to be used for food for the miners. In the first six months following the Spa agreement, the Allies actually advanced for this purpose nearly 361 million gold marks—more than twice what Germany had paid to France in cash up to 1923.

Great as these objections were to the demands of the Allies upon Germany, the greatest objection of all was that the sums originally demanded from Germany bore little relation to Germany's capacity to pay. The extent of this capacity depended upon two distinct processes, raising funds by taxation in Germany and transferring such funds to foreign countries. It was impossible for Germany to pay the reparations in gold. The total world production of this metal since 1492 would pay only for half the total sum which the Allies demanded.[3] But foreign countries could not use German marks. The only way, therefore, to pay reparations was by an export balance of goods or by services.

[1] *Report*, p. 98. For the provisions in the Treaty of Versailles, cf. Annex V of Part VIII.
[2] Cf. M. Auboin, *Les Prestations en nature de l'Allemagne et le problème des réparations* (2d ed., 1923), Part II. Cf. *Treaty of Versailles* (*Deliveries in Kind*), Cmd. 1547 (1921).
[3] Moulton and McGuire, p. 10.

Instead of having such a balance following the war, Germany was obliged to import more than she exported. Even in 1913, when Germany was producing at full capacity, she imported more than she exported.

This so-called "invisible balance," which amounted to 2,100 million gold marks, consisted of returns from foreign investments, remittances of immigrants, returns from shipping, tourist expenditures, and so forth. Even if Germany could have applied this "invisible balance" to the payment of reparations, it would have paid only half the sums demanded in the London agreement of 1921.[1] And at that time, Germany's invisible balance had been virtually wiped out. It was, moreover, impossible for Germany materially to reduce her imports because these were essential to feed her people and to provide her factories with raw materials.

Germany's capacity to pay was further reduced by the peace treaties which deprived Germany of two-thirds of her iron, 26% of her coal, 13% of her territory, 7% of her population, a million square miles of colonies, 40% of her blast furnaces, 30% of her steel mills, and 28% of her rolling mills.[2] These facts inevitably reduced Germany's productive power and made more necessary than ever imports of raw materials.

The occupation of the Ruhr still further delayed reparation payments. In the nine months of the occupation, France took out of the Ruhr only 2,375,000 tons of coal compared with 11,460,000 tons voluntarily delivered by Germany in a corresponding period in 1922. The occupation cost the French government 700,000,000 francs as against 525,000,000 francs in receipts. As a result of the occupation, coke exports to France from the Ruhr fell off, the production of French blast furnaces decreased 35%, while the bonds of "La Grosse Metallurgie" declined 30 points.[3] The occupation also severely injured the trade of such countries as England and Holland, dependent on foreign markets, while it increased the economic and financial chaos in Germany, postponing still further the payment of real reparations. The incident

---

[1] *Ibid.*, p. 48; J. M. Keynes, *A Revision of the Treaty* (1922), Ch. III.
[2] Moulton and McGuire, p. 114.
[3] *Current History*, Nov., 1923, p. 327; A. Chevalley, "France and the Ruhr," *Atlantic Monthly*, June, 1923; *Manchester Guardian Weekly*, March 9, 1923.

demonstrated that it is psychologically impossible to force a nation to work at the point of a bayonet.

England was interested in the industrial restoration of Germany for the sake of British markets and also for the sake of reparation payments. On the other hand, France, a nation which was nearly self-supporting with the exception of coke, feared a strong industrial Germany, believing that a strong economic organization would lead to a strong political and military organization. Security was more important to her than reparations. Though many Frenchmen realized that the occupation of the Ruhr would be economically harmful to France, they nevertheless supported it upon political grounds. Some of them believed that it would give France an opportunity to establish an independent Rhineland and Palatinate—a buffer state against Germany under French control. It appears that movements with these aims were supported by the French troops of occupation, after the Ruhr had been seized. Similar demands had been made during the Paris Peace Conference.[1] This movement ended, however, in a dismal failure. Other Frenchmen supported the Ruhr occupation in order to gain control of coke necessary for the Alsatian blast furnaces and also to kill off the competition of German steel.[2]

The official purpose of the French government in occupying the Ruhr came to be this: "We occupied the Ruhr in order to induce Germany to settle with us and to conquer the stubborn resistance of the German magnates."[3] There is no doubt that the industrial leaders of Germany had escaped the obligations which a stronger government would have imposed. But the British government said, "the will to pay is useless without the power." There was no incentive for Germany to pay when the demands made upon her far exceeded her capacity.

6. THE "DAWES PLAN" (1924)

For some six months following the occupation of the Ruhr, the British government followed a policy of neutrality. But because of the intolerable economic and political conditions for which the occupation was responsible, the Baldwin ministry attempted to

---

[1] R. S. Baker, *Woodrow Wilson and World Settlement*, Chs. XXV, XXIX.
[2] See p. 112.
[3] Note of February 25, 1924.

reopen the reparations question. Notes were exchanged during the summer of 1923, in which the British government suggested that a body of impartial experts investigate Germany's capacity to pay—a suggestion made originally by Mr. Hughes—and that the Ruhr be evacuated. France insisted that before negotiations with Germany could be resumed, passive resistance must come to an end; but even then, troops would not be entirely withdrawn from the Ruhr until reparations had been paid. France also rejected an inquiry into Germany's capacity, arguing that this was variable; that while Germany was financially weak to-day she might be strong to-morrow. In an extremely sharp note of August 11, 1923, the British government replied, challenging the legality of the Ruhr occupation and saying that if France stayed in the Ruhr, the peace of the world would be threatened, as envisaged by Article XI of the Covenant of the League.[1]

Unable to finance the opposition of the Germans in the Ruhr to French rule, which cost the government about 8 billion marks a week, Germany announced the abandonment of the policy of passive resistance in September, 1923. This action, which was hailed as a triumph for French policy, did not lead at once to the resumption of relations between France and Germany. As a condition to negotiations, France demanded the resumption of payments in kind. In the latter part of October Germany announced to the Reparations Commission her willingness to resume these payments, but declared that it was impossible to finance them.

Meanwhile the British government had continued its efforts to bring about an impartial investigation. In a note of October 13, 1923, Lord Curzon, the British Secretary of State, asked that the United States participate in such an inquiry as Mr. Hughes had proposed in the previous December. In reply, Mr. Hughes stated that the United States would be "entirely willing" to participate in an inquiry to determine Germany's capacity to pay and an appropriate financial plan for securing payments. But the French government not only insisted that this inquiry should not question the legality of the Ruhr occupation, but that it should limit its inquiry to Germany's present capacity and should not reduce the

[1] "Correspondence with the Allied Governments respecting Reparation Payments by Germany," Misc. No. 5 (1925), Cmd. 1943.

total obligations of Germany. Believing that an inquiry subject to such limitations would be fruitless, the American government declined to proceed.[1]

The French government now quickly shifted its position. Dissatisfaction was growing in some circles in France on account of the economic failure of the Ruhr policy; while France's allies, Belgium and Italy, were becoming restive. On November 30, 1923, the Reparations Commission voted to name two committees of experts, (1) to study the means of balancing the German budget and stabilizing the currency, (2) to determine the amount of German capital abroad and means for recovering it. Since in balancing the budget the Commission would have to consider Germany's capacity in connection with her reparation obligations, it was empowered to go to the very heart of the problem. Consequently, the American government, on December 11, 1923, approved the "unofficial" participation of Americans in the work of these commissions; and three financial experts, with practical business experience, were appointed for this purpose.

After deliberations lasting between January and April, 1924, the experts representing the different powers presented two reports, one estimating the amount of German capital abroad at 6,750,000,000 gold marks and stating that the only way to prevent this flight and bring about the return of this capital was permanently stopping inflation; the second, working out a plan by which Germany would pay reparations.[2] To become effective, these reports had to be accepted by the Allied governments and Germany. After negotiations, a conference for this purpose was held in London in July and August, 1924, which was attended by representatives of ten governments, including the United States.[3] As a

[1] For this correspondence, cf. World Peace Foundation Pamphlet, *Reparation*—Part V—the Dawes Report (1923), Vol. VI, No. 5.

[2] The Reparations Committee was presided over by General Dawes of the United States. The other committee, by Reginald McKenna of England. For the report of the latter, cf. *Report of the Second Committee of Experts*, Annexe 2076 de la Commission des Réparations.

[3] This was the first European conference of a political nature since the war in which the United States was "officially" represented. But even here the representatives of the United States government had "specifically limited powers." At the last moment they decided not to sign the final protocol.

For the programme of the Conference, cf. Cmd. 2191. For the Agreements of August 30, 1924, cf. Cmd. 2259.

result of this conference a number of agreements were signed putting the experts' plan into effect.

This plan attempted to solve four main problems: (1) the problem of raising reparations in Germany; (2) the problem of transferring such reparations to Allied governments; (3) the problem of guaranteeing specific assets to meet Germany's obligations; (4) the problem of foreign intervention in case Germany voluntarily defaulted.

Raising Reparations.—In determining the amount of reparations which Germany should pay, the experts' plan proceeded upon the principle of "commensurate taxation"—Germany's burden of taxation and debt should at least equal that of the Allied countries, a principle first enunciated in the Treaty of Versailles. Since Germany's domestic debt had been virtually extinguished by inflation, budget payments for debt could be confined to reparations. But the productivity of Germany, upon which the payment of reparations depends, could not be restored unless the Allied governments terminated the restrictions which had been imposed on the fiscal and economic unity of Germany by the occupation of the Ruhr. Although the military aspect of the problem was beyond the jurisdiction of the experts, they nevertheless believed that if the military occupation of Germany was to continue, it must not impede the free exercise of economic activities.

If reparation payments were to be forthcoming, the German currency should be stabilized and the budget balanced. With this end in view the experts' plan called for a foreign loan of 800,000,000 gold marks, the establishment of a Bank of Issue independent of government control, and a limited moratorium. That is, reparation payments should be made on a sliding scale, beginning with 1,000,000,000 gold marks in the first year and reaching 2,500,000,000 gold marks in the fifth year—or in 1928—and thereafter. While in the first year no payments whatever were to be made from the budget, other sources such as the foreign loan and interest on certain railroad bonds were to provide revenue. In the third year, the budget should pay 110 million gold marks for reparations.[1] Even after the fifth year only half of the annual sum of 2,500,000,000 gold marks was to come out of the budget,

---

[1] *Report of the First Committee of Experts*, Annexe 2075 de la Commission des Réparations, p. 18.

i. e., from direct taxes. The remaining half was to come from the interest on railway bonds and on industrial debentures, and from a transport tax. Bonds to the extent of 11 billion marks at 5% were to be issued against the German railways and of 5 billion marks, paying 5% after the fourth year, against German industries. The Allied governments would receive the interest from these bonds which, together with the transport tax, should amount to 1,250,000,000 gold marks a year. After careful investigation, the experts came to the conclusion that German industry could meet these charges upon the basis of pre-war earnings. In other words, only half of the annual payment of reparations was to be borne directly by the German budget and the German taxpayer. The other half was to be borne by German industry—by which, however, it probably would be shifted to the consumer. The experts' plan also called for an "index of prosperity." If this index showed that German prosperity increased over the average prosperity, reparations should be proportionately increased.[1] But these sums embraced all the amounts for which Germany was liable to the Allies, including the costs of the armies of occupation. Moreover, deliveries in kind might continue where Allied countries are dependent upon German goods, but they were to be paid for out of balances in the Bank.

The summary of the schedule for treaty payments by Germany was as follows:

Budget Moratorium Period

1st year, 1924–1925: from foreign loan and part interest (200 millions) on railway bonds..........1,000,000,000 gold marks
2d year, 1925–1926: from interest on railway bonds (including 130 millions balance from first year) and interest on industrial debentures and budget contribution...............................1,222,000,000 " "

Transition Period

3d year, 1926–1927: from interest on railway bonds, and industrial debentures, from transport tax and from budget...............................1,200,000,000 " "
4th year, 1927–1928: from same sources...........1,750,000,000 [2] " "

Standard Year

5th year, 1928–1929: from same sources...........2,500,000,000 [3] " "

[1] Cf. Annex 2, *Report of the First Committee of Experts.*
[2] In the third and fourth years, the total may be added to or reduced, according to the yield of certain German taxes.
[3] *Report of the First Committee*, p. 23.

Getting the Money Out of Germany.—As we have seen, it is one thing for the German people to raise money in the form of taxes for reparations. But it is altogether another thing to transfer this money to foreign countries in an acceptable form. The Allies cannot use German marks. Germany cannot pay gold. Some means must be devised whereby German marks can be converted into francs and sterling. This will be possible only in case Germany has an export balance, which in turn depends upon whether or not foreign countries are willing to receive German goods or services. The experts' plan did not attempt to solve this problem. Following a plan worked out by the League in the reconstruction of Austria and Hungary, it merely provided for the establishment of a Transfer Committee, composed of an Agent for Reparation Payments (a post now held by an American, Mr. S. Parker Gilbert), and five other representatives, coming from the Allied and Associated countries, appointed by the Reparations Commission. This Transfer Committee controlled "the transfer of cash to the Allies by purchase of foreign exchange and generally acts so as to secure the maximum transfers, without bringing about instability of currency." [1] If the payments by Germany to the Bank on reparation account exceeded the sums that the Committee could transfer, they would accumulate in the Bank. But when this sum exceeded 5 billion gold marks, the reparation charges were to be reduced until this surplus had been reduced by transfers to foreign countries. It was to the interest of Germany therefore to increase this surplus, while it was to the interest of the Allies, if they wished to receive reparation payments, to encourage German export trade.

Foreign Control over Germany.—France and Belgium would not agree to withdraw from the Ruhr until they were given guarantees that Germany would observe her pledges as to reparations. The experts' plan, therefore, provided for the maintenance of certain kinds of foreign control over German industry and finance. While the new Bank of Issue, established to stabilize the currency and to receive reparation payments, was administered by a German Managing Board, the interests of foreign creditors were safeguarded by a General Board of fourteen members, one-half of whom was

---

[1] *Ibid.*, p. 27; cf. Annex No. 6. Cf. Sir J. A. Salter, "The Reconstruction of Austria," *Foreign Affairs*, June 15, 1924; also Prof. A. A. Young, *N. Y. Times*, August 28, 1924.

foreign and one-half was German. This General Board elected a foreign bank commissioner by a majority of nine, six of which should be foreign members. This commissioner enforced the provisions of the plan in regard to note issues, and so forth. Moreover, one-half of the Board of Directors of the German railways was appointed by the German government, but the other half was appointed by a Trustee, representing the Reparations Commission. The latter official insured the service of the railway and industrial bonds. A majority of the foreign members of this Board appointed a railway commissioner who inspected the whole railway system to see that it met the charges imposed upon it by the experts' plan.[1]

Foreign control was not only established over the bank and the railways, but to a certain extent over the German budget. To insure the budget payments on reparations, revenues from alcohol, tobacco, beer, sugar and customs were pledged as security. The experts estimated that the customary returns from these so-called "controlled revenues" would much more than equal the 1,250,000-000 marks required of the budget annually. The excess was returned to the German government. The administration of these revenues was supervised by an Allied Commissioner of Controlled Revenues. Thus the internal affairs of Germany were supervised by three Allied Commissioners as well as a Trustee. Over these officials was the Agent for Reparations Payment who linked them with the Reparations Commission. The latter body was, as a result of these different provisions, reduced to a position merely of control.[2]

Before the experts' plan could be put into effect, some agreement had to be made in regard to the question of Germany's default in the future. British and American bankers would not agree to float the proposed loan of 800,000,000 marks if a single Allied government could decide, as France virtually did in 1923, that Germany had violated her reparations pledges, and thereupon proceed to disrupt German industry by the force of arms. At the

[1] Cf. Annexes Nos. 1, 4 and 5, also pp. 54 ff.; *Report of the First Committee*, cited.
[2] On Nov. 12, 1924, the Commission practically abolished the organization it had previously maintained. Henceforth the representatives of the Commission would serve without salaries, receiving only their expenses. *N. Y. Times*, Nov. 13, 1924.

same time, France would not agree to give up military control over the Ruhr unless some provision was made for forcing Germany, if necessary, to live up to her obligations.

Arbitration and Default.—This problem was finally solved at the London Conference by providing for the arbitration of all questions arising out of the application of the experts' plan. All disputes arising between the Reparations Commission and Germany were to be submitted to three arbitrators, one chosen by the Commission, one by Germany, and a third by agreement, or failing such agreement, by the President of the World Court.[1]

While, with the withdrawal of the United States from Europe, the Reparations Commission fell under French control, the London Conference restored it to a position of comparative independence by providing that when it was deliberating upon any point connected with the experts' plan, an American citizen should have a vote. In case the Commission could not agree on the person the President of the World Court would make this appointment.

It was conceivable that Germany, having accepted the experts' plan, would deliberately refuse to carry it out. The London Conference nevertheless believed that the determination of such a question should not be left to a single government or even to the Reparations Commission. It provided that the question whether or not Germany has gone into default, should be decided by majority vote of the Commission. But any member, in such a case, might appeal to the arbitration of three persons, appointed for five years by the Commission, or when it could not agree by the President of the World Court. The President of this arbitration board should be an American. No military or other form of intervention in Germany should take place unless a default was established by this procedure.

But even if this board decided that Germany had gone into default, no single government could proceed against Germany in disregard of the other Allies. In such a case, the Allied governments, "acting with the consciousness of joint trusteeship for the financial interests of themselves and of the persons who advance money upon the lines of the said plan, will confer at once on the nature of the sanctions to be applied and on the

---

[1] Agreement No. 1, Clause 1, Cmd. 2259. This provided also for other arbitrations.

THE "DAWES PLAN"

method of their rapid and effective application."[1] In case intervention was decided upon, the revenues set aside to guarantee the foreign loan had to be respected. Finally, the French and Belgian governments, in a declaration of August 16, 1924, promised to evacuate their troops from the Ruhr within one year, "provided the agreements of London are freely entered into and are applied in the spirit of loyalty and pacification which has inspired the deliberations of the conference." Economic control of the Ruhr, however, was terminated immediately after the plan went into effect on October 13, 1924. Shortly after the Conference adjourned, French troops also evacuated a few German towns.

There were two great advantages to the reparations settlement of 1924. (1) The responsibility for getting reparations out of Germany, once the sums were collected there, was transferred from Germany to the Allies. (2) Disputes as to whether or not Germany was fulfilling her obligations were to be settled by at least eight different arbitrations. If it was decided that Germany had gone into voluntary default, intervention apparently had to be joint.

On the other hand, the settlement possessed certain disadvantages. Germany's total liability was not fixed, and no limit was placed upon the number of annual payments which Germany had to make.

During the first four years under the experts' plan, Germany promptly and fully met all of the payments required. During the same period German industry and municipalities, etc., borrowed, largely from the United States, sums totalling about five billion marks or more than Germany paid out in reparations. These sums were invested in the reconstruction of German industry. Placing these credits in foreign banks automatically created the foreign exchange which Germany needed to meet her annuities. And it was generally agreed that during the past five years Germany could not have met all of these annuities without the aid of such loans. While "Germany might continue for some length of time to pay reparation and at the same time resort to extensive foreign borrowing, it should nevertheless be observed that as long as this process continues, Germany is not liquidating any portion of her total obligations, but merely transferring them from public

[1] Art. 2 of the Inter-Allied Agreement, *Proceedings of the London Reparations Conference*, Cmd. 2270, p. 354.

to private obligations. A true conception of capacity to pay, therefore, requires that Germany raise and transfer these sums unaided." [1]

7. THE INTER-ALLIED DEBTS

The solution of the reparations question was delayed partly because of the problem of the inter-Allied debts, the debts contracted by the Allied governments from the United States and Great Britain during the war.[2] The debt owed to the United States by such governments amounted to $11,600,000,000—a sum one-third as large as that which the Allies originally demanded from Germany, and the interest on which was nearly as great as the annual payments which Germany was to make under the experts' plan. It was natural that the peoples in these debtor countries should demand that Germany pay sums sufficient not only to reconstruct devastated regions but also to meet these debts which they owed to Great Britain and the United States.[3]

Despite the legal obligation of this debt, no Allied country until 1923 even paid interest to the United States, a sum amounting to $400,000,000, which was borne by the American taxpayer. But in 1922 the American Congress passed the Foreign Debt Funding Act establishing a Debt Commission to refund or convert the payment of this debt, and providing that the time of maturity should not extend beyond 1947 and the rate of interest should not be less than $4\frac{1}{4}\%$.[4] The passage of this act showed that the United States was not disposed to cancel the inter-Allied debt. It was the position of Secretary of State Hughes that the "capacity of Germany to pay is not at all affected by any indebtedness of any of the Allies to us. That indebtedness does not diminish Germany's capacity, and its removal would not increase her capacity." In other words, the American position was that there was no connection between reparations and inter-Allied debts.

---

[1] "The Financial Liquidation of the War," *I. S.*, Vol. IV—No. 21. Cf. C. Bergman, *The History of Reparations*, London, 1925. G. P. Auld, *The Dawes Plan and the New Economics*, New York, 1927.

[2] Thirty per cent of the money loaned the Allies by the United States was loaned after the armistice.

[3] Legally, there was no basis for this claim, since war costs had been excluded from the German obligations. Yet it was inevitable that the reparations should be linked with the debts by the public.

[4] 42 Stat. 363.

It was soon evident that the terms laid down by the American Congress in the Debt Funding Act were altogether too severe. Great Britain offered to fund her indebtedness to us, provided she were granted more liberal terms. And in January, 1923, an agreement was signed between the two countries, later embodied in an act of Congress, in which England agreed to pay her debt of $4,600,000,000 within 62 years—or by 1985—annual payments on the principal of the debt gradually increasing from $23,000,000 in 1923 to $175,000,000 in 1984. For the first ten years, interest is at the rate of 3%, after which it is 3.5%.[1] Although in accepting this agreement the United States reduced her claims upon England about $820,000,000, the British government was severely criticized for entering upon it not only by Englishmen but by Europeans generally. It imposed a tremendous burden upon the English treasury, and in proceeding to settle the question independently of other Allied countries it was said the British government had weakened the bargaining power of Europe with America. Much ill-will in England over the "debt" was due to a misconception. According to the famous Balfour note of 1922, the policy of the British government was to ask in reparation from Germany and in payment on the war debt of France and Italy only as much as was necessary to satisfy the British war debt to the United States. This meant, therefore, that, taking the period as a whole, the British people would not themselves pay the debt to America—this debt would be paid largely by the German taxpayer. And if the United States should reduce its claims upon Great Britain, the British government, according to the Balfour note, would be obliged to reduce its claims upon its Allies and upon Germany.

By July, 1929, fourteen principal debtors of the United States had entered into funding agreements based upon the principles contained in our agreement with England. In each agreement we maintained intact the capital sum, but we reduced the interest rate in accordance with what we regarded as the capacity of each debtor to pay. For some reason the United States charged the heaviest rate—3.3%—to Great Britain. Italy received the best terms—an interest rate of 0.4%. If one regards 4.25% as a fair interest rate, the United States, by thus reducing the interest rate in these settlements, canceled 75% of the Italian debt and 17%

[1] 42 Stat. 1325; cf. also Cmd. 1912 (1923).

of the British debt. If 3% is regarded over a long period as a fair interest rate for governments, it will be seen that the United States overcharged eight out of the fourteen principal countries with which it made an agreement.[1]

Under the Experts' Plan Germany was required to pay to the Allies a net sum of $595,000,000 a year. The United States under the debt-funding agreements is to receive from the four leading Allies sums ranging from $204,333,750 in 1929 to $406,000,000 in 1983. In considering whether to fix German payments at ten or fifteen years or more the Allied governments were confronted by the fact that they were obliged to make payments on the war-debt to the United States until 1988. Thus to their minds the questions of debts and reparation were integrally related.

8. THE "YOUNG PLAN" (1929)

The last stage of the reparation question began with the announcement of the principal Allied and German governments, at Geneva, on September 16, 1929, that they had decided to establish a new committee of experts to work out a "complete and definite settlement" of the reparation problem.

In February, 1929, experts from Belgium, France, Germany, Great Britain, Italy, Japan and the United States met in Paris.[2] After long and difficult negotiations, a report was finally signed on June 7. Its acceptance by the respective governments was unanimously recommended by the experts, and a diplomatic conference to consider the adoption of the report, as a substitute for the 1924 plan, was called for in the following August.

The chief features of the new plan are as follows. In the first place, the number of German annuities was definitely fixed at 58. In other words, the financial settlement of the World War will be

[1] In a statement to the Ways and Means Committee of the House of Representatives on May 20, 1926, Mr. Andrew Mellon defended the 3% rate. See L. W. Jones, "The United States and the War Debts," *I. S.*, Vol. III, Supp. No. 1. Also Moulton and Pasvolsky, *World War Debt Settlements*, New York, 1926.

[2] The Belgian, British, French, Italian and Japanese experts were appointed by the Reparation Commission upon the nomination of their respective governments. The German experts were appointed by the German government. The American experts, Mr. Owen D. Young and Mr. J. P. Morgan, were appointed by the Reparation Commission conjointly with the German government.

THE "YOUNG PLAN"

definitely liquidated in 1987-1988. During the first thirty-seven years, or until 1965-1966, the average German annuity will be 2,051,000,000 marks or $473,700,000, which is a considerable reduction in the normal annuity of $595,000,000 in the 1924 plan. During the last twenty-two years it will be considerably reduced. The present value of the new annuities over the total period of 58 years is about 36,996,000,000 marks or $8,879,040,000. The value for the first 37 years is about 32,886,000,000 marks or $7,826,868,000. This total sum marks a reduction in the capitalized value of the 1924 plan which amounted to about $12,000,-000,000, or in the $31,000,000,000 envisaged by the London schedule of May, 1921.

Of this average annuity of $473,700,000, Germany is unconditionally liable only for 660,000,000 marks or $157,000,000. This sum is to be met out of a tax on the German railways, similar to the 1924 tax. The remainder of the annuity is to come from the German budget. The German revenues pledged by the 1924 plan will continue to be assigned to reparation payments. Nevertheless, the payment of this second annual portion, amounting to about $320,000,000 is conditional upon the ability of Germany to transfer this sum into foreign currencies. The experts' report recommended that the German government shall have the right, upon giving ninety days notice, to postpone the transfer of the conditional share of the annuity for a period not exceeding two years. The German government must, however, continue to pay the sum in marks to the Reichsbank to the credit of the creditor governments, who may invest such sums in Germany or employ them in arranging German deliveries in kind to the creditor governments. If economic conditions warrant it, the German government may, moreover, suspend for one year payment to the Reichsbank up to 50% of the amount due.

When the German government makes a declaration of postponement, the Bank of International Settlement, described below, shall convene a special advisory committee. This committee shall consider the circumstances and conditions which led up to the necessity for postponement or which created the situation in which Germany considers her exchange and economic life to be seriously endangered by further transfer. The committee shall satisfy itself that the German authorities have used every effort in their power to fulfil their obligations, and it shall recommend to the governments and banks what measures should be taken.

The report recommends that the foreign control set up over German finances and industry by the Dawes plan come to an end. The Reparation Commission will be supplanted by a new international bank, divorced from politics. Germany accepts complete responsibility for raising and transferring reparation payments, subject to the provisions in regard to the conditional payments above; in return she recovers complete financial and industrial autonomy.[1] Moreover, the "index of prosperity" is abolished.

9. THE BANK OF INTERNATIONAL SETTLEMENT

Perhaps the most interesting feature of the new plan is the proposed "Bank for International Settlement." Its purpose, according to the experts' report, is "to provide additional facilities for international movement of funds and to afford a ready instrument for promoting international relations. In connection with German reparation annuities, it shall perform as trustee for creditor countries the entire work of external administration of this plan, shall act as agency for receipt and distribution of funds and shall supervise and assist in the commercialization and mobilization of certain portions of the annuities." Germany will pay the annuities into an annuity trust account of the bank. After deducting its expenses, the bank shall distribute the remainder to the Allies, roughly in accordance with the percentages drawn up in the Spa Agreement of 1920, except that France is to receive 500,000,000 out of the 660,000,000 marks in the unconditional part of the annuity.[2] The bank is expected to be of great assistance to Germany in making transfers of reparation payments. It may give to Germany temporary credits, or in agreement with the Reichsbank it may invest marks currently accruing to the reparation account in Germany. By such measures, the bank will be able to ease any strain "until such time as the discount rate and other corrective measures have had an opportunity to exert themselves."

Capital stock for the international bank to the amount of $100,000,000 is authorized, and at least 55% of the shares shall be issued in the seven countries represented on the expert committee. The

[1] She promises, however, to continue the system of assigned revenues.
[2] In return France must make certain deposits with the bank.

control of the bank shall be vested in a board of directors. The governor of each central bank in the seven countries, such as the Bank of England, the Banque de France, and the Reichsbank, shall be a director,[1] and each governor shall name another director from his country. France and Germany each will be entitled to an additional director. These sixteen directors shall choose nine others, making a total of 25.

Through the new bank, it will be possible to have Germany issue bonds representing the capital value of the unconditional annuity, the present value of which amounts to about $2,960,000,-000.

It is intended that the Bank for International Settlement shall have even larger functions than the handling of the reparation problem. Central banks may for ordinary exchange purposes find it advantageous to make use of the bank. The experts' report declares, "As a stabilizing factor in foreign exchange, its advantages are obvious, and if in due time arrangements provided for any international settlement fund are put into effective operation, the bank should go far to eliminate the costs and risks now incurred in shipping and reshipping gold." The bank will not interfere with, but rather supplement existing institutions. In the natural course of time it is expected that the bank will furnish "to the world of international commerce and finance important facilities hitherto lacking. Especially it is to be hoped that it will become an increasingly close and valuable link in the coöperation of central banking institutions generally—coöperation essential to the continuing stability of the world's credit structure."

Finally, the reparation settlement is linked up to the inter-allied debts. The unconditional part of the first 37 annuities is earmarked to cover reconstruction costs of the Allies, particularly France; the conditional part is framed to cover the sums owed by the Allies to each other and to the United States. At the end of 37 years the reconstruction claims of the Allies upon Germany will come to an end. But for the next 22 years, or until 1987–1988—the last year in which Allied payments to the United States are to be made,—Germany is to pay a reduced annuity approximately large

[1] Provision is made for representation of the Federal Reserve Bank or some other bank in the United States. Secretary Stimson has declared that the Federal Reserve Bank will not be permitted to be represented.

552 REPARATIONS AND INTER-ALLIED DEBTS

enough to cover what the Allies still owe the United States. If these so-called "outpayments" are reduced, during the first 37 years, i. e., if the United States agrees to cancel all or part of the debt, two-thirds of the reduction will accrue to the benefit of Germany, and one-third to the allied governments.[1] But if the United States makes any reduction applying to the last 22 years the whole of the benefit shall accrue to Germany.

Moreover, the profits of the bank are to go in part toward payment of these inter-allied debts. After making provision for a legal reserve fund and for an annual dividend, the plan provides that one-half of the remaining profits of the bank shall go into a general reserve fund until it equals the paid-in capital. Seventy-five per cent of the remainder shall go to the creditor governments and to Germany in proportion to the size of their deposits in the bank. The remaining 25% will be set aside as a special fund to aid Germany in paying the last 22 annuities, subject to the condition that Germany makes a long-term deposit with the bank of 400,000,000 reichmarks.

By this ingenious provision it is hoped that a fund will be built up large enough by 1966 to meet the remaining debt payments to the United States. If the fund does not meet this expectation, Germany remains liable.[2]

* * *

Looking at the reparations and debt question as an incident to the institution of war, the conclusion is inevitable that victors and defeated, the guilty and the innocent, must suffer in its consequence. Even if Germany pays up to the extreme limit of her capacity, she will not repair the damage done by the last war. Even if the Allied countries pay up to the extreme limit of their capacity, the United States will not be repaid in full.[3] War and its aftermath are a losing proposition to all parties concerned.

---

[1] However, as long as Germany remains liable for any annuity after 1966 the creditor will retain annually only one-fourth part of the net relief, the balance being paid to the bank to be applied to the last 22 annuities.

[2] Other provisions of the report are to the effect that ordinary deliveries in kind shall end after ten years; that governments should make no further use of their right to seize the property of German nations; that Germany should waive past claims against the Allies; and that the joint liability of Germany on the one hand, and of Austria, Hungary and Bulgaria on the other for reparation, should be dissolved.

[3] In its special treaty of August 25, 1291, with Germany, the United States

BANK OF INTERNATIONAL SETTLEMENT

retained the right to receive reparation payments under Part VIII of the Treaty of Versailles. On August 10, 1922, an agreement established a Mixed Commission to determine the amount Germany should pay to the United States. But the United States stated it would not press claims for pensions (*Treaties of the U. S.*, Vol. III, pp. 2596, 2601, 2603).

On May 25, 1923, the United States and the Allied governments signed an agreement in which the latter agreed to the reimbursement of the United States for the cost of maintaining American troops on the Rhine (cf. Cmd. 1973, 1923). In January, 1925, an agreement was reached between the United States and the Allied governments by which the United States would be paid $240,000,000 for its Rhineland army costs, out of certain advances under the May agreement and also out of the receipts from the experts' plan. It is believed that these sums will have been paid by 1943 or 1944. Secondly, this agreement limited the private claims of American citizens against Germany to $350,000,000, in payment for which the United States will receive $2\frac{1}{4}\%$ of the annuities under the experts' plan. In order to assist the Paris experts in finding the basis for a reparation settlement the United States government in May, 1929, agreed to allow the payment of the expenses of the Army of Occupation to be extended over 37 years rather than to be made in 18 years. It is estimated that this concession amounted to a reduction of about ten per cent or $30,000,000.

CHAPTER XXIII
THE LIMITATION OF ARMAMENTS

1. Limitation of Armaments before the War—The Rush-Bagot Agreement—The Argentina-Chile Agreement.—2. The Washington Conference.—3. The Moscow and Latin-American Conferences.—4. The Geneva Conference.—5. The Disarmament of Germany.—6. The Demilitarization of Territory.—7. The Control of Private Manufacture of Arms.—8. Armaments and the League.—9. Obstacles to Disarmament.—10. The Limitation of Alliances.

For the last century attempts have been made to do away with the abuses of modern warfare without, at the same time, doing away with war. Of these abuses, competition in armaments has been regarded as one of the greatest—as being in itself a cause of war. Despite the burden which armaments have imposed, no great nation has believed that it could disarm alone. If a power should adopt the policy of absolute disarmament at a time when its neighbors continued to arm, its very existence would be threatened. However, should nations disarm by agreement, the comparative security of each would remain as it was before. In one sense, a nation would be more secure because its knowledge of the strength of its neighbors would be definite—a fact which would inspire confidence—while under the old competitive system, it could only guess at the strength of other establishments, which was sometimes kept secret, and which fluctuated in accordance with the military programmes of the respective powers.

1. LIMITATION OF ARMAMENTS BEFORE THE WAR

A number of attempts have been made on a small scale to limit the size of armaments in the past. An unsuccessful attempt was made following the Seven Years' War and also the Congress of Vienna.[1] In 1831 and 1863 France attempted, but without results,

[1] These attempts are traced in Hans Wehberg, *Die internationale Beschränkung der Rüstungen* (1919); especially pp. 253 ff. Cf. the same author, *Limitation of Armaments* (1921). Cf. also R. Picard, *La Question de la Limitation des Armements* (1911).

LIMITATION OF ARMAMENTS BEFORE THE WAR

to bring about an international limitation of armament. As part of the plan to neutralize the Black Sea, Russia and Turkey made an agreement to limit the number of warships to ten each on this body of water,[1] a convention which was later denounced. The Straits Convention of 1923 imposes new limitations upon this area, by providing that while any power may send at least three ships, not exceeding 10,000 tons, into the Black Sea, the number of vessels above this figure must not be greater than that of the most powerful fleet of the littoral powers. While no limitation is placed upon the size of the fleets which these latter powers may maintain, the Turkish garrison at Constantinople is limited to 12,000 men.[2]

In its famous invitation to the first Hague Conference of 1899 the Russian government, pointing out the oppressive burdens of armaments, proposed that an agreement should be made in regard to the "non-augmentation" of the armies and navies, as well as the war budgets, of the respective powers, for a term to be agreed upon. The first commission of the Conference rejected a more concrete proposal of Russia that the powers should not increase their armies and military budgets for a period of five years and that they should limit the size of their naval budgets for three years.[3] The only result of the first Hague Conference, as far as armaments was concerned, was a resolution saying that the "restriction of military charges, which are at present a heavy burden on the world, is extremely desirable for the increase of the material and moral welfare of mankind;" and a *vœu* that the governments examine "the possibility of an agreement" limiting armaments and budgets in the future.[4] At the second Hague Conference (1907), the resolution of 1899 was merely reaffirmed; while it was also declared that "inasmuch as military expenditure has considerably increased in almost every country . . . it is eminently desirable that the Governments should resume the

---

[1] Convention of March 30, 1856, 46 *State Papers*, 22.

[2] Sec. 2 of the Annex, Straits Convention of July 24, 1923, Cmd. 1929, pp. 115, 125.

[3] *The Proceedings of the Hague Peace Conferences*, Conference of 1899 (translation of official texts, 1920, ed. by J. B. Scott), pp. 89–90.

The proposal to limit the size of budgets was defeated because some governments declared that they could not bind their parliaments as to future appropriations.

[4] *Ibid.*, p. 233.

serious examination of this question."[1] No further action was possible because of the opposition of Germany.

The Rush-Bagot Agreement.—The only successful attempts to limit armaments before the World War took place in the Americas. In 1817 the United States and Great Britain entered into the Rush-Bagot agreement which limited the number of warships on the Great Lakes to three vessels for each power, none of them to exceed one hundred tons burden and each to be armed with one eighteen-pound cannon.[2] To suppress revolutionists known as the "Canadian Patriots," the British government between 1838 and 1841, increased its naval armaments on the Great Lakes beyond that provided for in the agreement—which led to a protest from the United States. Similarly the United States increased its armaments there, during the Civil War, to suppress insurgents. A number of resolutions have been introduced into Congress providing for the termination of the agreement, one of which was passed but later withdrawn. At the present time, the United States maintains eleven vessels on the Great Lakes instead of three. It appears therefore that neither party has lived up to the agreement, largely because it has not been revised in accordance with modern conditions. Nevertheless, the negotiation of the agreement did much to calm the feelings of the two countries following the War of 1812.

The Argentina-Chile Agreement.—In 1902 Argentina and Chile made an agreement promising to "desist from acquiring the vessels of war which they have in construction, and from henceforth making new acquisitions." Moreover, they promised not to increase their naval armaments for five years without previous notice and also to reduce their fleets within a year.[3] In 1903 the two governments signed a protocol agreeing to sell or otherwise dispose of ships under construction; while Chile agreed to scrap one

---

[1] *The Proceedings of the Hague Peace Conferences*, Conference of 1907, Vol. I, p. 689.
[2] *American State Papers*, For. Rel., Vol. IV, pp. 202, 207; 11 Stat. 766. Cf. "Limitation of Armament on the Great Lakes," Report of J. W. Foster, Sec. of State, Sen. Ex. Doc. No. 9, 52d Cong., 2d sess., reprinted, Carnegie Endowment for International Peace, Division of International Law, Pamphlet No. 2, 1914.
[3] Convention of May 28, 1902, 95 *State Papers*, 762. Differences as to reduction were to be referred to arbitration in accordance with the general arbitration treaty drawn up at the same time.

battleship and Argentina, two.[1] This treaty was not renewed at the end of the five-year period, apparently because Brazil continued to increase her armaments, thus threatening both of her neighbors.[2] The example shows that to be successful the limitation of armaments must be generally applied.

At the end of the World War, it was hoped that armaments would generally be reduced by international agreement.[3] But because of the animosities aroused by the war, the members of the League of Nations merely recognized "that the maintenance of peace requires the reduction of national armaments to the lowest point consistent with national safety and the enforcement by common action of international obligations."[4] There were many reasons why the League could not put this principle immediately into effect, one of the most important being the fact that the leader in naval competition—the United States—was not a member. Although Great Britain—owing largely to financial exigencies—had stopped building battleships at the end of the war, the United States had continued such construction, which, sooner or later, would have forced the British Empire to retaliate, unless some agreement were made.

2. THE WASHINGTON CONFERENCE

In the midst of this competition, the American government issued an invitation to the four other leading naval powers of the world—Great Britain, Japan, France and Italy—to participate with it in a conference for the Limitation of Armaments.[5] This

[1] Protocol of Jan. 9, 1903, 96 *State Papers*, 311.
[2] Wehberg, *Beschränkung*, p. 282.
[3] Beginning with 1911, British statesmen proposed the exchange of naval information with Germany, and also a naval holiday upon a 16:10 basis, but without effect. These attempts are reviewed in Wehberg, *Limitation of Armament*, Ch. IX.
[4] Art. 8, Covenant.
[5] The agenda called for
    I. Limitation of Naval Armament, under which shall be discussed:
        (a) Basis of limitation.
        (b) Extent.
        (c) Fulfillment.
    II. Rules for control of new agencies of warfare.
    III. Limitation of land armaments.
The Conference also dealt with certain Pacific and Far Eastern Questions. When the Conference discussed these latter subjects, it was attended by China, Holland, Portugal and Belgium, in addition to the five other powers.

Conference, which was convened in Washington, opened on November 12, 1921. At the opening session, Mr. Hughes, the American Secretary of State, laid before the Conference a concrete programme for the reduction of armaments which provided a working basis for negotiation. The guiding principle of the American programme was that "regard should be had to the existing naval strength of the powers concerned,"—in other words, the status quo. To carry this principle into effect, it was proposed that the powers discard building programmes and scrap certain older ships. This meant that the United States would give up its "1916 programme," and that Japan would give up its "Eight-eight programme," with the result that the British fleet would approach equality with the American, while the Japanese fleet would be about sixty per cent as strong.[1]

After a month's negotiations, an agreement was reached as to "capital ships," both battleships and battle cruisers, according to which the three naval powers agreed to scrap a total of 70 ships, built or projected, having a total tonnage of about 1,650,000 tons. The status of the navies of the five powers, until 1931, is as follows:

NAVIES UNTIL 1931

	Capital Ships	Tons
United States	18	527,850
British Empire	20	558,950
Japan	10	301,320
France	10	221,170
Italy	10	182,800 [2]

In accepting this agreement, the United States sacrificed fifteen new vessels, to seven for Japan and four for Great Britain. While the British navy, until 1931, is slightly larger than the American navy in number and tonnage of capital ships, after 1931 replacements of old tonnage may begin, which will eventually place the United States and the British Empire on a basis of equality, as the following table shows:

Conference on the Limitation of Armament (Minutes) (1922), p. 10. The minutes of many of the sub-commissions are also published in *La Conférence de Washington*, La Documentation internationale, 3 vols.

[1] *Minutes*, cited, p. 60.
[2] Ch. II, Part I of the Treaty of Feb. 6, 1922, *Minutes*, cited, p. 1573.

NAVIES IN 1942

	Capital Ships	Tonnage	Ratio
United States	15	525,000	5
British Empire	15	525,000	5
Japan	9	315,000	3
France	5	175,000	1.67
Italy	5	175,000	1.67 [1]

This treaty, which is the most important international agreement for the limitation of armaments ever signed, remains in force until 1937; and in case none of the contracting parties shall have given notice two years before this date of its intention to terminate the treaty, it shall continue in force until two years after such notice has been given.[2]

As a result of this agreement, the British and American navies, as far as capital ships are concerned, will be theoretically on an absolute equality—both powers giving up their claims to the naval supremacy of the world. Japan has the third strongest navy—60% as strong as the British or American—and strong enough probably to prevent the naval intervention of America in the Orient.[3] France and Italy are fourth and fifth naval powers—at a ratio of 1.67 to 5. The position of France is really weaker than that of Italy, since she must divide her fleet between the Mediterranean and the Atlantic, while Italy may concentrate her fleet in the Adriatic,[4] where it may threaten French communications with Morocco.

Successful as the Washington Conference was in limiting capital ships, it failed to put an end to competition in the building of

---

[1] Sec. 2, Part III, and Article IV, *ibid.* France and Italy reserve the right to employ this tonnage as they consider desirable. The number of ships to be built by the United States, British Empire, and Japan is as given in 1942, after replacements have been made.

[2] However, in August, 1931, a conference is to be held to consider technical developments.

[3] Buell, *Washington Conference*, pp. 163 ff.

[4] Thus the fact that France's position as a naval power was fixed below that of Japan delayed the ratification of this treaty by France until July, 1923. It was accompanied by a declaration of the French government to the effect that "The French Government considers and always has considered that the ratios of total tonnage in capital ships and aircraft carriers allowed to the several Contracting Powers do not represent the respective importance of the maritime interests of those Powers and cannot be extended to the categories of vessels other than those for which they were expressly stipulated." *Procès verbal*, U. S. Treaty Series No. 671.

submarines, light cruisers and aircraft; while it left totally untouched the problem of disarmament on land. The limitation of armies was blocked by France, who took the ground that she required a large army to carry out the Treaty of Versailles and defend herself against Germany. The same power also blocked the limitation of submarine building, contending that a submarine tonnage of at least 90,000 tonnage was essential to the defence of the French colonies and to the protection of their communications with the mother country. Great Britain took the opposite position. Arguing that the submarine was a hideous means of warfare, and implying, at least, that the possession of such a large fleet by France would be particularly dangerous to England, the British delegation attempted, but unsuccessfully, to secure the absolute prohibition of its use or construction.[1] As a result of this conflict in points of view, no limitation whatever in regard to submarines was formulated. As a concession to the British position, however, a treaty was signed in which the powers recognized the "practical impossibility of using submarines as commerce destroyers without violating . . . the requirements universally accepted by civilized nations for the protection of neutrals and non-combatants." They therefore agreed not to use the submarine as a commerce destroyer. Moreover, any person violating the principle of international law that merchant vessels cannot be seized without warning or sunk without providing for the safety of passengers and crew—is liable to punishment "as if for an act of piracy."[2] The order of a superior officer is no defence.

[1] For the submarine debate, cf. *Minutes*, cited, pp. 475, 520, 532, 554 ff.

[2] Arts. I–IV, Treaty of Feb. 6, 1922, *Treaties of U. S.*, Vol. III, p. 3118. This treaty has been severely criticized, particularly the punishment to be meted out to a person for violating international law, etc. Cf. Rear Admiral Sims, "Changing Methods of Submarine Warfare," *Current History*, Sept., 1923. France has not yet ratified the submarine treaty, July, 1929. This treaty also declared that the use of asphyxiating gas is prohibited, a provision also inserted in the Central American treaty of Feb. 7, 1923 (Art. V), and "recommended" to the respective governments at the Pan-American conference at Santiago. Resolution on "Limitacion de Armamentos, Quinto Acuerdo," *Quinta Conferencia Internacional Americana*, p. 59. In June, 1925, was drawn up at Geneva a Poison Gas Protocol in which the parties agreed, "so far as they are not already parties to Treaties prohibiting such use," to accept the prohibition in regard to the use of poison gas, and "agree to extend this prohibition to the use of bacteriological methods of warfare and agree

In view of the failure of the Conference to limit the number of submarines, Great Britain would not agree to the limitation of light cruisers on the ground that they were the most effective means of combatting submarine attack. Also, attempts to limit the construction of aircraft failed because of the belief that to prohibit the use of military craft would impede the development of commercial aviation.[1] The only action of the Conference in this respect was to limit the tonnage of aircraft carriers to 135,000 tons each in the case of the United States and Great Britain, 60,000 tons in the case of France and Italy, and 81,000 tons in the case of Japan. Consequently, as far as the Washington Naval Treaty is concerned, there is no restriction upon the number of submarines, light-cruisers, or airplanes the powers may build, or the number of troops they may maintain. Moreover, when war breaks out, the obligations of this treaty shall not apply if notice to that effect is given to the signatory powers.[2] As a previous chapter indicated, competition in armaments between the great powers has now shifted away from battleships to these new weapons of warfare.

3. THE MOSCOW AND LATIN-AMERICAN CONFERENCES

Following the Washington Conference a number of other attempts were made to bring about the regional limitation of armaments. In December, 1922, the Soviet government of Russia called a disarmament conference at Moscow of the Baltic states—Finland, Poland, Estonia, Latvia and Lithuania. Russia proposed to reduce by one-quarter the size of its own army, that is, to 200,000 men, provided the border states would make similar reductions. It also proposed to limit military budgets to a certain sum per soldier and to establish a neutral zone along the frontier. After prolonged debate, the border states rejected these proposals

to be bound as between themselves according to the terms of this declaration." C. C. I. A. 1 (1) p. 33. Although the United States urged the adoption of this protocol and although a number of other states have ratified, the United States has not done so (July, 1929).

[1] Cf. the Report of the Subcommittee on Aircraft, *Minutes*, Washington Conference, p. 752.

[2] When notice is given the powers shall consult together as to what temporary modifications should be made; but if no agreement is reached, the power concerned may suspend the treaty. At the close of hostilities another conference, however, shall be held. Article XXII.

on the ground that their armies were already disproportionately small, and that a treaty of non-aggression and arbitration should precede disarmament.[1]

One of the aims of the Central American Conference of 1922–1923 at Washington was to adopt "effective measures for the limitation of armaments in Central America." As a result of the good offices of the United States, these five republics signed a Convention for the Limitation of Armaments in which they agreed to limit for five years their armies to the following figures:

> Guatemala..............................5,200
> El Salvador............................4,200
> Honduras...............................2,500
> Nicaragua..............................2,500
> Costa Rica.............................2,000

None of the parties may have more than ten war aircraft or acquire any war vessels.[2]

When the fifth Pan-American Conference opened in March, 1923, the governments in the American hemisphere were devoting, on the average, about 20% of their budgets to military purposes.[3] In an effort to reduce this expense, a number of proposals for the limitation of armaments were made at the Conference. Brazil proposed to limit capital ships in the case of the three leading South American powers—Argentina, Chile and Brazil—to 80,000 tons each, for a period of five years. Inasmuch as this tonnage was much larger than Argentina then possessed, the latter power declared the limitation too high—a view which Chile also shared. Brazil, on the other hand, contended that in view of the extent of her territory and population, this was the minimum to which she could agree. Consequently no agreement was reached.[4] Apparently competition in armaments between these "A B C" powers has since been resumed.[5] The only action of the Conference on

[1] *Conférence de Moscou pour la Limitation des Armements* (Moscow, 1923), Édition du Commissariat du Peuple aux Affaires Étrangères, pp. 47, 207.

[2] Articles I and IV, Treaty of February 7, 1923, *Conference on Central American Affairs*, p. 339.

[3] *Special Handbook for the Use of the Delegates*, Pan-American Union, 1922, p. 142.

[4] *Report of the Delegates of the United States of America to the Fifth International Conference of American States* (1923), pp. 23 ff.

[5] *N. Y. Evening Post*, July 24, 1923; *Christian Science Monitor*, Sept. 18, 1924. Argentinians charged that this failure was due to the support given

THE GENEVA CONFERENCE

this subject was a resolution "condemning armed peace," and recommending, among other things, that the South American powers adhere to certain provisions of the Naval Treaty of Washington.[1]

4. THE GENEVA CONFERENCE

As an outgrowth of the disarmament work of the League of Nations, President Coolidge called a three-power naval conference[2] of the United States, Great Britain and Japan at Geneva in June, 1927. The Conference broke up on August 4 without agreement. The chief differences were over (1) the ratio of naval strength between Great Britain and the United States in cruisers, (2) whether the number of 10,000 ton eight-inch gun cruisers, within the total tonnage for cruisers should be limited, (3) the amount of tonnage and the number of ships. Although Great Britain had agreed to parity in capital ships at the Washington Conference, her delegation seemed loath to accept the principle of mathematical parity with the United States in cruisers. Much of the confusion over the question of parity arose over the difficulty of defining it. Even if the tonnage of each navy should be fixed at the same figure, one country might use its tonnage in the construction of a few powerful vessels which in a contest could worst a larger number of small vessels constructed by the other within the same tonnage total. The American delegation at first insisted on placing no limitation on the number of 10,000 ton cruisers which the United States might construct within the tonnage totals; while the British attempted to limit such large cruisers. The American delegation toward the end of the Conference finally agreed to discuss the number of 10,000 ton cruisers, but no agreement could be reached. Finally a difference arose over the total tonnage which each state should have. The United States proposed a maximum of 300,000 tons for cruisers, and a total tonnage in auxiliary craft of 640,000, while the British insisted on a tonnage which would allow them to have a minimum of 70 cruisers which would bring their total tonnage requirements to 875,000 tons. The United States declared that

Brazil by the United States, which maintained a naval mission in that country. Cf. p. 489.

[1] "Limitación de Armamentos," *Quinta Conferencia Internacional Americana*, 1923, p. 57. The minutes of the 7th commission are published in the *Revista de Politica Internacional*, Nov., 1923.

[2] France and Italy declined to attend.

a naval limitation based upon the British tonnage figure would require the United States to build 30 new cruisers at an expense of $450,000,000. The Conference really failed because Great Britain insisted on a minimum of 70 cruisers, while the United States insisted upon retaining freedom to mount large or small cruisers with eight-inch guns.[1]

5. THE DISARMAMENT OF GERMANY

Armaments have not only been limited by voluntary agreement, but they have been limited by force—disarmament has been imposed by a victorious upon a conquered power. In 1808 Napoleon obliged Prussia to limit her army to 42,000 men for a period of ten years;[2] while in a treaty of 1830 Tripoli promised France not to increase her naval forces.[3] The greatest example of disarmament by compulsion, however, came in 1919 when the Allies forced Germany and the other defeated powers to make sweeping reductions in armaments and radical changes in military policy.

According to the Treaty of Versailles, the German army is limited to 100,000 men, the German General Staff is abolished, and all establishments for the manufacture of munitions, with certain exceptions, must be closed. In order to prevent the accumulation of a large body of trained soldiers in reserve, conscription is done away with and voluntary enlistments must be for a term of twelve consecutive years; while discharges must not exceed five per cent of the total effectives in any year. Likewise the German navy is restricted to six small battleships, six light cruisers, twelve destroyers, and no submarines; Germany can maintain no military or naval air-forces.[4] Similar provisions are incorporated in the peace treaties with Austria, Hungary and Bulgaria. The army of Austria is limited to 30,000 men, that of Hungary to 35,000, that of Bulgaria to 33,000. Compared with Germany's army, these armies are proportionately large; but compared with the Czechoslovakian army of 147,000 men, the Greek army of 250,000 men, the Jugoslavian, of 200,000, and the

---

[1] "The International Naval Situation," *I. S.*, Vol. III, Nos. 21–22.
[2] "Articles Séparés," Treaty of Sept. 8, 1808; De Clercq, *Recueil de Traités de la France*, Vol. II, p. 272.
[3] Art. II, Treaty of August 11, 1830, 19 *State Papers*, 1053.
[4] Part V, Treaty of Versailles, especially articles 173–210.

THE DISARMAMENT OF GERMANY 565

Roumanian, of 160,000, the armies of Austria, Hungary and Bulgaria are small.[1]

Whatever the justification for compulsory disarmament may be, it is not a policy which in the past has proved effective from the standpoint of the peace of the world. When disarmament is one-sided, there is every incentive for a disarmed power to evade the limitations imposed upon it. Prussia evaded the limitations of the treaty of 1808 by the secret training of troops and by frequent discharges, thus building up a large reserve. At the battle of Waterloo in 1815, Prussia had an army of 150,000 men instead of 42,000.[2]

In the treaties of 1919 an attempt was made to prevent such evasions by establishing Military, Naval and Aeronautical Inter-Allied Commissions of Control to supervise the disarmament provisions of these treaties. Apparently these commissions were to go out of existence as soon as these provisions had been complied with. Nevertheless, according to Article 213 of the Treaty of Versailles, "so long as the present Treaty remains in force, Germany undertakes to give every facility for any investigation which the Council of the League of Nations, acting if need be by a majority vote, may consider necessary."

Owing to great practical difficulties in reducing armaments immediately, and because of Germany's fear of communism, the Allied governments granted Germany certain delays in executing the treaty. Despite these concessions, Germany failed to live up to the Allied demands. In June, 1920, the Supreme Council pointed out to the German government that her regular army, instead of being 100,000, was 200,000 and that certain irregular police forces, such as "protection police" (sicherheitspolizei) and the "home guards" (einwohnerwehr) had not yet been dissolved as the Allies had demanded. At the conference of Spa, however, in July, 1920, the Allies relented in their demands and consented to prolong until January 1, 1921, the reduction of the army to 100,000 men, on condition that the German government abolish the irregular forces, deliver over military supplies as provided for in the treaty, and immediately abolish conscription. If these

---

[1] Temperley, *History of the Peace Conference*, Vol. IV, p. 170.
[2] H. Treitschke, *History of Germany in the Nineteenth Century* (1915), Vol. I, p. 336.

measures were not carried out, the Allies would occupy further German territory. Although Germany had not complied with these demands by January, 1921, further delays were granted by the Allies,[1] but as a result of additional obstruction by Germany the Allies finally occupied Düsseldorf and other towns in March, 1921.[2] The German parliament thereupon voted a law reducing the army to 100,000 men.

After further steps carrying the disarmament provisions of the treaty into effect, German ministers began to say that since disarmament was now effected the Control Commissions should be terminated and the right to investigate German armaments be transferred, according to Article 213 of the treaty, to the League. Opposition to the Control Commissions became so strong among the German people and progress in disarmament had reached such a point that in September, 1922, the Allied governments informed Germany that as soon as all of these disarmament clauses had been fulfilled, the Commission of Control would be replaced by a less inquisitorial Committee of Guarantees.[3] But before negotiations on this subject were completed, the French invaded the Ruhr—in January, 1923—a fact which the German government put forward as a pretext to escape from all military control. The work of these Commissions was now suspended, since the Germans were so embittered that the lives of the Allied representatives would have been endangered. In June, 1923, the Allied governments attempted to reëstablish military control, but the German government refused to accept a commission containing French and Belgian members. This invidious discrimination was rejected by the Allies who, in November, 1923, informed the German government that the Control Commission would commence its activities at once. Diplomatic correspondence continued in which Germany contended that only the League Council was entitled to undertake an inquiry. However in June, 1924, the German government finally agreed to the resumption of inter-Allied con-

[1] Cf. A. Honnorat, *Le Désarmement de l'Allemagne* (1924), Part I. For the popular agitation in favor of increasing armaments, cf. Part II; cf. also Lucien Graux, *Histoire des Violations du Traités de Paix* (1923), Vol. III, Chs. X and XI.
[2] This occupation was also to enforce reparation payments; cf. p. 530.
[3] In 1922, the Naval and Aeronautical Commissions were withdrawn, but in its place a Committee of Guarantees was established.

DEMILITARIZATION OF TERRITORY

trol, provided that it should be a step toward the assumption of these powers by the League Council. The Council thereupon began to study how to exercise its duties in this respect. In September, 1924, it approved a plan for investigating armaments in Germany, Austria, Hungary and Bulgaria, through Commissions of Investigation.

Each government represented on the Council may name thirty-four military experts who constitute a panel that may be called upon to undertake an investigation by the Council upon the complaint of some state. While each commission has a permanent president, its members are selected ad hoc from the panel of experts. At least three experts of different nationalities must conduct the investigation, and the state under investigation cannot be represented on the investigating body.[1] The Allies dissolved their commission in Germany in January, 1927, following the establishment of this form of League control. In the case of Hungary, Allied control was removed in May, 1927; in Bulgaria, in June, 1927; and in Austria, in February, 1928.

Despite the establishment of control commissions, the enforcement of compulsory disarmament is very difficult. The supervision of such provisions by an inquisitorial commission inevitably increases international ill-will. Disarmament that has been imposed by force will probably have to be maintained by force. Unless political grievances are wiped out and unless the limitation of armaments becomes general, one-sided disarmament, as imposed on Germany, may be an added provocation to war.

6. THE DEMILITARIZATION OF TERRITORY

Territory has frequently been deprived of its strategic value, and the fears of nations have been frequently composed, by agreements limiting the erection of fortifications upon certain territory. A succession of treaties has provided that fortifications should not exist in the city of Luxemburg,[2] on the Straits of Magellan,[3] in certain parts of Bulgaria and Montenegro, below the Iron Gates on the Danube,[4] in a ten-mile zone along the frontier between

[1] League of Nations, *Rules on the Exercise of the Rights of Investigation* (C. 729, 1926, XI), and also *O. J.*, 1924, p. 1592.
[2] Arts. III–IV, Convention of May 11, 1867, 18 Martens (1st ser.) 445.
[3] Cf. p. 134.
[4] Arts. II, XXIX, LII, Treaty of July 13, 1878, 69 *State Papers*, 749.

Burma and Tibet,[1] on the island of Sakhalin,[2] on the Moroccan coast across from the Straits of Gibraltar,[3] in a zone along the frontier between Sweden and Norway,[4] on the Aaland islands,[5] or on Spitzbergen.[6] According to the Treaty of Versailles, all fortifications within fifty kilometers east of the Rhine must be dismantled and the construction of new fortifications there is forbidden. Likewise German fortifications in certain regions of the Baltic must be demolished, while no fortifications may be erected in the Saar.[7] The Straits Convention of 1923 demilitarized both shores of the Dardanelles and Bosporus, with the exception of Constantinople where a base and garrison may be maintained.[8] In order to prevent this demilitarization from endangering Turkey, France, Great Britain, Italy and Japan agree to meet any act of war or threat of war in regard to the Straits "by all the means that the Council of the League of Nations may decide for this purpose." The frontier separating Turkey from Bulgaria and from Greece is also demilitarized to a depth of 30 kilometers; all fortifications must be removed, while the number of troops in these zones is limited to 5,000 for Turkey, 2,500 for Greece and 2,500 for Bulgaria.[9] In the territories held under B and C mandates, the establishment of fortifications or bases is prohibited.[10]

Probably the most important non-fortification agreement from the political standpoint is found in the Naval Treaty of Washington, involving the naval bases of the Pacific. Without bases a navy cannot operate in foreign waters. While the United States has a large number of islands in the Pacific capable of becoming

[1] Art. VII, Convention of March 1, 1894, MacMurray, *Treaties with China*, Vol. I, p. 5.
[2] Art. IX, Treaty of Aug. 23, 1905, 98 *State Papers*, 735.
[3] Art. 3, Tangier convention, Dec. 18, 1923, Cmd. 2203, being the last.
[4] Art. II, Convention of Oct. 26, 1905, 98 *State Papers*, 821.
[5] Art. 3, Non-fortification agreement of Oct. 20, 1921, *T. S.* 255; this treaty also excludes military forces from entering the Aaland island zone.
[6] Art. 9, Treaty of Feb. 9, 1920, Cmd. 2092. The Treaty of Dorpat between Finland and Russia, of Oct. 14, 1920 (*T. S.* 91) also limited the number of warships and bases that Finland could maintain in the Arctic Ocean.
[7] Arts. 115, 180, para. 30 of Ch. I of Annex to Art. 50, Treaty of Versailles.
[8] Arts. 6–8, Convention cited, Cmd. 1919, p. 123.
[9] Cf. Convention Respecting the Thracian Frontier, July 24, 1923, Cmd. 1929, p. 133.
[10] Cf. Art. 3, Cameroons mandates; Art. 4, Pacific mandate.

CONTROL OF MANUFACTURE OF ARMS

good bases, it had neglected to fortify them before 1921. Without such bases, it would be virtually impossible for the United States successfully to attack Japan. Consequently at the Washington Conference Japan took the position that it would limit its armaments only if the United States would agree not to fortify its Pacific possessions, a demand to which the United States finally acceded. Article 19 of the Naval Treaty therefore provides for the status quo in fortifications and bases in the possessions of the United States, the British Empire, Japan in the Pacific, east of 110 degrees east longitude, a region which does not include the important British base at Singapore.[1] Moreover, the limitation does not apply to Hawaii and to the islands lying off the coasts of the contracting powers, including Canada and Australia. Since Great Britain may fortify Singapore and the United States may fortify Hawaii, it will be very difficult for Japan ever to attack either power; while in consenting to the status quo in the Pacific, the United States virtually surrenders the possibility of attacking Japan in Oriental waters.

The effect of these non-fortification agreements is altogether wholesome. They remove bits of territory, having only strategic value, from the domain of war. Consequently such agreements deprive nations of an incentive to establish control over territory for strategic reasons. They thus remove one incentive, if a minor one, to international military competition.

7. THE CONTROL OF PRIVATE MANUFACTURE OF ARMS

Attempts are also being made to do away with the evils arising out of the private manufacture of arms. These evils are recognized by the Covenant of the League of Nations which states that "the manufacture by private enterprise of munitions and implements of war is open to grave objections;" and the Council is to advise how these evil effects may be prevented, "due regard being had to the necessities of those Members of the League which are not able to manufacture the munitions and implements of war necessary for their safety."

---

[1] Art. 19, Naval Treaty of Feb. 6, 1922, *Treaties of the U. S.*, Vol. III, p. 3105.

Two means have been advocated for the solution of these evils,[1] the first of which is the limitation of private enterprise.

In its report of July, 1924, the Temporary Mixed Commission for the Reduction of Armaments, submitted a majority and a minority report on private manufacture. The majority report recommended the adoption of certain principles to this effect: (1) no company should be allowed to manufacture armaments without a license from the government, which may thereby subject it to control; (2) no director or manager of such a company should be in a position to influence a newspaper, (3) no director or manager should at the same time be a member of parliament. It was believed that such control would prevent all improper and corrupt practices in armament deals. The minority of the Commission, however, objected to this solution on the ground that the enforcement of control was left with each individual government; that the problem had an international character and should, therefore, be submitted to some form of international supervision.[2]

While control of the private manufacture of arms is better than unrestricted production, indirect means can usually be found of circumventing governmental restrictions. For this reason, the minority of the Commission believed that the best solution would be absolute prohibition of the private manufacture of arms in favor of manufacture by the state. Before the War, this policy was followed by Russia and Holland, and to a certain extent by Germany. The policy of the United States has also been to secure armaments from government arsenals, as long as they can fill the need.[3] If the state monopolized the manufacture of arms, the reduction of armaments would not necessarily follow. If a government is militaristic, it will manufacture arms to its heart's content, as the case of Russia and Germany before the war shows. But since state manufacture eliminates the factor of private profit, the government would not be subject to the pressure of private interests.

---

[1] The Jury of the Bok Peace Award (January, 1924) made a proposal, scarcely meriting attention, as follows: "It is the unanimous hope of the Jury that the first fruit of the mutual counsel and coöperation among the nations which will result from the adoption of the plan selected will be a general prohibition of the manufacture and sale of all materials of war."

[2] Report of July 30, 1924, A. 16, 1924, IX, p. 20.

[3] *Navy Ordnance Activities, World War,* 1917–1918 (1920), U. S. Navy, pp. 27 ff., Ch. XVII.

In December, 1928, a League commission examined a draft convention on the supervision of the private manufacture and publicity for the manufacture of arms.

8. ARMAMENTS AND THE LEAGUE

Inasmuch as the limitation of armaments to be effective must be universal, the League of Nations is the logical body to undertake the task. In the Covenant, the League members recognize "that the maintenance of peace requires the reduction of national armaments to the lowest point consistent with national safety and the enforcement by common action of international obligations." And the Council, "taking account of the geographical situation and circumstances of each State, shall formulate plans for such reduction for the consideration and action of the several Governments." Once adopted, the limitations therein fixed shall not be exceeded except with the Council's consent, though they are to be reconsidered every ten years. The members of the League also agree to interchange "full and frank information as to the sale of their armaments, their military, naval and air programmes, and the conditions of such of their industries as are adaptable to warlike purposes." Such an exchange would remove the distrust created when military spies seek out, by underhanded means, the military plans of the enemy. It would establish authentic information which would make alarmist campaigns of the jingo press as to the secret designs of foreign powers less effective than at present, when there is no certain knowledge of such military preparations. It would "improve the political atmosphere by creating confidence."[1]

In order to advise the Council as to these military questions, the Covenant provided for the establishment of a permanent Commission, now known as the Permanent Advisory Commission. It is composed of a naval, military and air representative from each of the countries represented on the Council.[2] But as this was a purely technical body composed solely of military experts, the first Assembly believed that a temporary commission largely of civilians should also be appointed to work out plans for the

[1] *Report of Temporary Mixed Commission for 1923*, A. 35 (Part A), 1923, IX, p. 8.
[2] *O. J.*, June, 1920, p. 134.

general reduction of armaments. Consequently the Council appointed a Temporary Mixed Commission, of six persons of recognized authority in political, social and economic matters, as well as representatives of the permanent Advisory Commission, the Economic and Financial Committees, and the Governing Body of the International Labor Office. The Temporary Mixed Commission ceased to exist after the fifth Assembly (1924), but was succeeded by the Coördination Commission, which consists of the Council acting as a committee and two members each of the Economic, Financial and Transit Organizations, representatives from the Governing Board of the International Labor Office, members competent to deal with questions connected with industry and transport, and other experts.[1]

League Commissions have attacked such questions as the control of the arms traffic and the private manufacture of arms, and at their suggestion the first four Assemblies adopted recommendations asking members to limit military expenditures.[2] Through these commissions the League Secretariat has also collected and published a large amount of information in regard to armaments and different methods of warfare. This information is now annually published in a voluminous *Armaments Year Book* which gives detailed information in regard to the Military Forces, Budget Expenditures on National Defence, and Industries capable of being used for War Purposes, of practically every country in the world.[3]

Having laid the basis for action through the collection of information, the different organizations of the League next attempted to attack the real problem of armament reduction. As a minor step, the 1922 Assembly requested the Council to recommend that members of the League adhere to the Washington treaty concerning the use of asphyxiating gases and submarines. In an effort to secure the adoption of the principle of the Washington Naval Treaty by non-signatory states, the Permanent Ad-

[1] *O. J.*, Oct., 1924, p. 1380.
[2] In 1920, 1921 and 1923, the Assembly recommended that members should not exceed in the future expenditures for the present year. In 1922 it recommended the reduction of military expenditures to what they were in 1913.
[3] Cf. *Armaments Year Book*, Geneva, Sept., 1924, First Year, 2d ed., C. 601, M. 209, 1924, IX; cf. also *Statistical Enquiry into National Armaments*, Parts I and II, A. 20, 1923, IX.

ARMAMENTS AND THE LEAGUE 573

visory Commission also convened a conference of experts from 17 countries at Rome, in February, 1924. Although a draft convention was signed in which the parties agreed to a naval holiday, it was accompanied by so many reservations that no further progress has been made.[1]

The League was no more successful originally in bringing about a limitation of land armaments. The principal plan was that submitted to the Commission by Lord Esher in 1921. It attempted to limit the size of armies in each country to units of 30,000 men, the number of units of each country to be determined by its population, strength, needs, and so forth. Lord Esher proposed to give France six units, Italy and Poland, four each; Great Britain, Czechoslovakia, Greece, Jugoslavia, Netherlands, Roumania and Spain, three each; Belgium, Denmark, Norway, Sweden and Switzerland, two; Portugal, one. However, this plan failed of adoption, partly because of difficulties in deciding how many units each state should have.[2]

Finally, the Council established the Preparatory Commission for a Disarmament Conference in September, 1925, consisting of representatives of states on the Council, certain other members of the League, and Soviet Russia, Turkey, and the United States.[3]

---

[1] The tonnage of the different powers was to be limited in the case of Brazil and Chile each to 80,000 tons; Denmark, 18,000 tons; Greece, 36,000 tons; the Netherlands, 26,550 tons; Norway, 16,048 tons; Spain, 105,000 tons; Sweden, 60,000 tons; Russia, 490,000 tons. Cf. Report to the Council on Extension to Non-signatory States of the principles of the Treaty of Washington, *O. J.*, April, 1924, p. 699.

[2] Report of *The Temporary Mixed Commission on Armaments*, A. 31, 1922, p. 12. One means of restricting armaments which the Assembly has not yet used very rigorously is in prescribing regulations for each new member "in regard to its military, naval and air forces and armaments" as a condition of membership. In each case the Permanent Advisory Committee and the Assembly Committee have investigated the armaments of the applicants. In many cases the examination has been perfunctory, and it does not appear that the League organs have asked any state actually to reduce its armaments before entering the League. However, in the case of Hungary, the Allied Military Committee at Versailles found that Hungary had only partially executed the military clauses of the Treaty of Trianon, but nevertheless the Assembly Committee reported in favor of its admission after receiving the undertaking of the Hungarian representative that these provisions would be fulfilled. *Records of the Third Assembly, Plenary Meetings*, Vol. 2, p. 122; Hudson, "Membership in the League of Nations," *A. J. I. L.*, July, 1924.

[3] *O. J.* Feb., 1926, p. 164.

During the first five sessions of the Preparatory Commission a divergence gradually developed between a group led by France, and other continental powers following the conscription system, and a second group, led by Great Britain and the United States. The French group maintained that land, sea and air armaments form an interdependent whole which must be considered together, that any agreement must be universal, and that a single standard must be applicable to the world. The French maintained, moreover, that trained reserves could not be limited. The British on the other hand stood out for limitation of trained reserves, until the Anglo-French naval accord of 1928.[1] France also contended that international supervision of a limitation agreement was necessary. But this idea was opposed by Great Britain and the United States on the ground that supervision would foment suspicion. Russia represented a yet different point of view. At the meeting of December, 1927, the Russian delegate proposed the complete abolition of armies and navies. These differences have been so great that the Commission has not yet been able to ask that a League Disarmament Conference be called. The sixth meeting of the Commission was scheduled for April, 1929.

9. OBSTACLES TO DISARMAMENT

As this description of the various attempts to limit armament in the past shows, progress has been slow—difficulties innumerable. In the first place, one power has been willing to limit its armaments only on condition that all of its neighbors in a position to attack it accept proportionate limitations. This fact was demonstrated at the Pan-American Conference where no one of the "A B C" powers would agree to limit armaments unless limitations were accepted by the others; and also at the Rome Conference where Sweden would limit her navy only on condition that all the other states on the Baltic should not exceed her tonnage. The abstention of one state from accepting such a limitation may defeat the whole plan. No nation feels like disarming if its neighbor goes unrestrained. Although the League has, so far, because of political reasons, been unsuccessful in limiting armaments, it offers the best means—when it becomes universal—of bringing about a world-wide limitation. The Washington Conference, convened by the

[1] Cf. "The Disarmament Deadlock," *I. S.*, Vol. IV, No. 19.

United States and attended by four other naval powers, was a success. Five months, however, were required to convene and organize the Conference, and after the signature of the treaties, the Conference adjourned, leaving many questions, such as the limitation of submarines, untouched. No administrative machinery was established to follow up its work, to supervise the administration of the treaties effected at the Conference, or to prepare the ground for periodic conferences in the future, where new phases of the armaments question might be discussed.[1] The first Hague Conference passed a resolution saying that the governments should examine the possibility of an armament agreement, taking into consideration the proposals made at the Conference. But when the Conference met in 1907, nothing had been done to carry this resolution into effect.[2] The existence of the League organization—a permanent and continuous body—provides administrative machinery whereby such resolutions may be effectively executed.

In the second place, difficulties arise over the interpretation and enforcement of armament treaties. Following the Washington Conference the United States Congress passed an appropriation to increase the gun-levels on American battleships. Great Britain protested that such an increase violated the Naval Treaty. A difference of interpretation arose, in regard to the settlement of which the treaty was silent. The great advantage of international treaties negotiated under League auspices is that such differences are finally settled by the World Court. Moreover, difficulties may also arise over whether or not a government is actually living up to its obligations under a treaty. As Allied experience in Germany showed, international inspection presents many difficulties. Perhaps it might be possible for one power to complain to an international armaments tribunal, as it may in regard to labor treaties, to the International Labor Organization.[3] But the most practical means of handling this aspect of the armament problem, at the present time, would be by the submission of annual arma-

[1] However, at the end of eight years, the United States shall convene a conference to consider what changes may be necessary. Likewise in case a power believes that requirements of national security are affected by a change of circumstances, the parties will meet in conference.
[2] Schücking and Wehberg, *Satzung des Völkerbundes* (2d ed., 1924), p. 397.
[3] Cf. p. 166.

ment reports by each power to the Permanent Advisory Commission of the League.

In the third place, it is difficult to secure an agreement as to the standard by which armaments are to be measured, and according to which limitations are to be imposed. The first standard is that of the status quo: armaments should be limited to their present relative size. This standard offers a definite and practical means of measuring armaments. The Washington Conference succeeded because it proceeded upon this principle. But the principle of the status quo will be rejected by those nations who in the past, whether because of pacific intentions or lack of resources, have failed to maintain a military establishment as strong as that maintained by other nations of similar potential strength. It was only with great difficulty that the powers at the Washington Conference succeeded in persuading France to accept the status quo in regard to capital ships—which placed her beneath Japan as a naval power. She argued that she had been forced to postpone building on account of the War, while Japan, on the other hand, had increased her programme during the same period. When it came to submarines, France absolutely refused to accept the status quo. Consequently, a second principle has been advocated according to which armaments should be limited,—the principle of "national security," based on the special geographical and political conditions of each state. This principle was written into the League Covenant, since it provided that in formulating plans for the reduction of armaments the Council should take into account "the geographical situation and circumstances of each State."[1]

But as the Rome Conference showed, the reduction of armaments according to such vague principles is very difficult to achieve. The geographic position of one state may differ so radically from another that it is virtually impossible to agree upon a common measure for armaments. "National security," moreover, depends not so much upon geographic as upon political conditions,—upon the existence of political controversies between different states.

[1] The Central American treaty limiting land armaments stated that the Contracting Parties had taken into consideration "their relative population, area, extent of frontiers and various other factors of military importance." A more vague resolution of the fifth Pan-American Conference provided that armaments should be limited to the "necessities of domestic security and of the sovereign independence of the States."

The number of troops France requires in order to enforce the Treaty of Versailles is much greater than if the Treaty of Versailles did not exist.

This leads to the fourth and, until it is removed, an insuperable difficulty to disarmament. Nations are not likely to disarm unless the institution of war is outlawed. As long as one nation may freely declare war upon another nation, in order to secure the redress of alleged grievances or for purely selfish purposes, neither power will do away with military establishments. Nations will not give up the means of protecting themselves unless they secure an equally certain guarantee that they will not be attacked. In other words, before disarmament can be achieved, the problem of security must be solved.[1] Once this question is settled, differences over standards for armament limitation will become relatively unimportant. The establishment of the League and the conclusion of the Anti-War Pact should eventually facilitate armament limitation.

9. THE LIMITATION OF ALLIANCES

Recognizing that there is something inconsistent between the old idea of Balance of Power and of the League, the Covenant (Article XX) provides as follows:

> The Members of the League severally agree that this Covenant is accepted as abrogating all obligations or understandings inter se which are inconsistent with the terms thereof, and solemnly undertake that they will not hereafter enter into any engagements inconsistent with the terms thereof.
>
> In case any Member of the League shall, before becoming a Member of the League, have undertaken any obligations inconsistent with the terms of this Covenant, it shall be the duty of such Member to take immediate steps to procure its release from such obligations.

It was the intention of the framers of this article to prohibit only aggressive alliances, "defensive" agreements not being, in

---

[1] In theory, the proportionate reduction of armaments should be capable of accomplishment regardless of the question of security, because when reduction is proportionate, the armaments of the states are in the same *relative* position as before. However, in the case of armies, armaments may be increased overnight, and a super-sensitive nation, in constant fear of attack, is not likely to trust other nations to limit their armaments when it is at the same time expecting them to attack it on account of political causes.

their opinion, inconsistent with the Covenant.¹ It might be contended that no alliance is an engagement "inconsistent" with the Covenant, under Article XX, because of Article XXI, which reads as follows:

> Nothing in this Covenant shall be deemed to affect the validity of international engagements such as treaties of arbitration or regional understandings like the Monroe doctrine, for securing the maintenance of peace.

But in view of the express obligation of the members of the League to submit disputes to arbitration or investigation, it would appear that the provisions of alliances must conform to the provisions of the Covenant. Otherwise they would not fit the formula, "for the maintenance of peace." In case of a conflict between the two, the Covenant is supreme. The interpretation of what constitutes engagements mentioned either by Article XX or XXI apparently rests with each government, although the World Court might be asked for an advisory opinion upon the matter.²

Consequently, the terms even of defensive alliances should conform to League procedure. For example, an alliance which provided for military aid in case of a dispute, regardless of whether or not this dispute had been referred to arbitration or investigation under the Covenant, would be inconsistent with the Covenant. The proposed Franco-American alliance of June, 1919, "must be recognized by the Council, acting if need be by a majority, as an engagement which is consistent with the Covenant of the League." ³ Some of the European alliances made since the World War state that the parties are "resolved to maintain the peace . . . provided for by the Covenant of the League of Nations," which may mean that the obligations under them will be interpreted to conform with those of the Covenant.⁴ Likewise an article is inserted in many international treaties, negotiated under League auspices,

[1] Lord Robert Cecil, Conference of Neutrals, March 20, 1919, Schücking and Wehberg, p. 667.
[2] Cf. p. 617.
[3] *Treaties of the U. S.*, Vol. III, p. 3710.
[4] Cf. Preamble of Alliance of August 14, 1920, Czechoslovakia and Jugoslavia, *T. S.* 154; cf. the Czech-Roumanian alliance of April 19, 1921, *T. S.* 155. However, some alliances say nothing of the League. Cf. Polish-Roumanian alliance, March 3, 1921, *T. S.* 175.

THE LIMITATION OF ALLIANCES 579

for freedom of transit, etc., providing that the provisions of the treaty concerned do not "impose upon a Contracting State any obligations conflicting with its rights and duties as a Member of the League of Nations." [1]

It appears that two international agreements have been recognized as being inconsistent with the obligations of the Covenant, the Anglo-Japanese Alliance, and the Norway Guarantee Treaty of 1907. On July 8, 1920, Japan and Great Britain informed the League Secretariat that the Anglo-Japanese Agreement, "though in harmony with the spirit of the Covenant," was not entirely consistent with the letter of the Covenant, and if it should be continued, "it must be in a form which is not inconsistent with the Covenant." [2] Likewise an exchange of notes took place in 1924 announcing the denunciation of the treaty of 1907 in regard to the integrity of Norway.[3] While the note itself did not mention the cause for the denunciation, it is understood that Norway regarded this treaty as unnecessary in view of the provisions in the Covenant and, in some respect, incompatible with the obligations which Norway had assumed thereby.[4]

While the League Covenant has not terminated defensive alliances, it has put them under control. They may not be invoked until after the peaceful procedure of the Covenant is exhausted. From the idealistic standpoint, the abolition of all special agreements may be desirable. But in the absence of international sanctions, it is improbable that special sanctions will be willingly surrendered. In subjecting these alliances to a form of control, the Covenant has taken a step toward removing the evils of the Balance of Power. Where it cannot abolish the Old Diplomacy, it

---

[1] Cf. Art. 9, Barcelona Statute on Freedom of Transit, April 20, 1921, *T. S.* 171.

[2] *O. J.*, July–August, 1920, p. 252. According to the *Monthly Summary of the League of Nations*, August, 1921, p. 64, these governments sent a second note of July 7, 1921, stating that, pending further action, they would follow the procedure prescribed by the Covenant when it conflicted with the procedure prescribed by the Alliance, in case of a dispute. However, it does not appear that this note has been published officially either in the Official Journal or in the League Treaty Series.

[3] Exchange of notes of Jan. 8, 1924. While the denunciation would not take effect until Feb. 6, 1928, the Norwegian government did not intend to avail itself of this treaty before that time. *T. S.* 576.

[4] Cf. *R. G. D. I. P.*, 1924, p. 300. For the registration of the anti-war pact, cf. p. 668.

may temper its defects.[1] Nevertheless, from the political standpoint, these alliances may create trouble in the League Council. If one member of the Council has an ally which is also a member, it may prevent a unanimous vote (except for the parties to the dispute) which is usually necessary before the Council can act.

An interesting question, similar to those just discussed, is the validity of certain agreements between great powers and nominally independent but small countries. In 1921 Albania was admitted as a member of the League of Nations. But on November 9, 1921, the British Empire, France, Italy and Japan agreed that if Albania should at any time find it impossible to maintain her territorial integrity intact she should be free to address a request to the League Council for assistance. In this event the British, French, Italian and Japanese governments agree to instruct their representatives on the Council to recommend that the restoration of the territorial frontiers of Albania should be entrusted to Italy.[2] If Italy is the state that threatens the territorial integrity of Albania, must the other governments give Italy a free hand? And if so, does this declaration infringe upon the obligations of these states under the Covenant and upon the rights of Albania as a member of the League? On November 27, 1926, Italy and Albania signed a treaty recognizing that any disturbance directed against the status quo, political, juridical and territorial, of Albania, was contrary to their reciprocal interests. And for the protection of these interests the parties pledged themselves to "lend their mutual support and their cordial coöperation." This treaty was interpreted by some observers as virtually establishing a protectorate over Albania and thus diminishing the independence which is requisite to states members of the League of Nations.

From the theoretical standpoint, even greater difficulties have arisen out of agreements between a non-member of the League, the United States, and two member states, Panama and Cuba. On July 28, 1926, the United States and Panama signed a treaty, in which (Art. XI) Panama agreed to "consider herself in a state of war in case of any war in which the United States should be a belligerent." This article was criticised on the ground that Pan-

---

[1] Cf. Zimmern, "The League and the Old Diplomacy," *Contemporary Review*, Feb., 1924. For the relation of alliances to the Protocol, cf. p. 651.
[2] Cf. "Albania: The Problem of the Adriatic," *I. S.* Vol. III–No. 8.

ama might be obliged, in violation of its obligations under the Covenant, to take the side of the United States in a war against a League member. Panama representatives defended this provision on the ground that in case the United States went to war, its opponent would immediately attempt to capture the Panama Canal Zone—Panama territory; in resisting such attack Panama would be acting in self-defense, which the Covenant allows.

A similar question may arise in connection with the Platt Amendment. In accordance with this amendment, Cuba has leased to the United States coaling and naval stations at Guantanomo. If the United States goes to war it may use Cuban territory as a base for operations. Would this not automatically make Cuba a belligerent, in possible violation of its obligations under the Covenant?

CHAPTER XXIV

SECURITY AND SANCTIONS

1. Neutralization Agreements.—2. "Territorial Integrity" Agreements. —3. Agreements as to the Status Quo.—4. Non-Aggression Agreements.—5. The Demand for "Guarantees."—6. Article Ten.—7. Four Kinds of Sanctions.—Trial of the Kaiser—Blockades.—8. The Sanctions of the League Covenant, Economic, Military, Political.—9. The Attack against the Sanctions.—10. Financial Assistance in Case of Aggression.

Throughout the history of international relations more attention has been paid to the question of security than of the limitation of armaments. In fact, standing armies and alliances were regarded as the only sure form of security upon which nations could rely. Even when experience demonstrated that armaments, instead of bringing security, invited attack, nations were reluctant to disarm until they received some satisfactory guarantee that their soil or their rights would not be imperiled by a foreign power. This fact was recognized at the Washington Conference. The limitation of armaments was linked up not only with the non-fortification agreement, but with the Four-Power Treaty of the Pacific in which the parties agreed to refer disputes over the Pacific to some peaceful form of mediation.[1]

1. NEUTRALIZATION AGREEMENTS

With a view to guaranteeing the security of certain states or territories, a large number of treaties have been made, which may be divided into four general types, (1) neutralization agreements, (2) treaties guaranteeing the political independence or territorial integrity of certain states, (3) treaties in regard to the status quo, (4) non-aggression agreements.

In a neutralization agreement, the powers usually promise to "respect" the neutral status of the territory concerned, which

[1] Cf. p. 587.

NEUTRALIZATION AGREEMENTS

means that they will not attack it. In return, the neutralized state promises not to engage in wars of an aggressive nature.[1] This type of agreement has been employed to bring security to small states unable to stand on their feet, and also to establish small buffer states between larger powers. During the last hundred years neutralization in one form or another has been applied to such states as Cracow, Switzerland, Belgium, Luxemburg, the Congo Free State, Honduras and Albania. In addition Iceland is neutralized by a unilateral act;[2] while a large number of neutralization treaties have applied to certain regions, such as some provinces along the Swiss-French frontier, the islands of Corfu and Paxo, the Samoan islands, a zone along the frontier between Norway and Sweden, the Aaland islands, as well as the Black Sea and certain waterways.[3]

In the past, neutralization agreements were usually limited to states unable to protect themselves—to secure the protection of a neutralization agreement was a sign of weakness. This type of treaty was, therefore, altogether exceptional. It did not attempt to prevent attacks against all national frontiers; it did little to outlaw the institution of war. Moreover, the great powers really

---

[1] Opinions differ as to the acts forbidden to a neutralized state. Germany contended that Belgium could not send troops as part of the international force which was sent to China at the time of the Boxer rebellion, on account of its neutralized status. Cf. Fauchille, *Traité*, No. 355 ff.

[2] *Cracow*—Art. I, VI, Treaty of April 21, 1815, 2 *State Papers*, 74; Cracow was incorporated with Austria in 1846; *Switzerland*—Declaration of March 20, 1815, 2 *State Papers*, 142; *Belgium*—Art. VII, annex, Treaty of April 19, 1839, 27 *State Papers*, 994; *Luxemburg*—Convention of May 11, 1867, 18 Martens, 2d series, 448. Unlike Switzerland, Luxemburg is forbidden to maintain fortifications. *Congo Free State*—The Act of Berlin of 1885 provided that the powers would respect the neutrality of African territories as long as the powers in control fulfilled the duties of neutrality, following which Leopold II proclaimed the neutrality of the Congo Free State. Act of Feb. 26, 1885, 76 *State Papers*, 11. Fauchille, p. 715. *Honduras*—Art. III, Central American treaty of Dec. 20, 1907, *Treaties of the United States*, Vol. II, p. 2393. This provision was omitted from the revised treaty of 1923. *Albania*—cf. the Declaration of Nov. 9, 1921, *T. S.* 333. *Iceland*—Danish Act of Nov. 30, 1918, 111 *State Papers*, 706.

[3] *Haute-Savoie*—Act of Nov. 20, 1815, Annexe, 3 *State Papers*, 360. *Corfu*—Protocol of Jan. 25, 1864, 54 *State Papers*, 34, limiting the neutralization provisions of 1863 in regard to the Ionian islands. *Samoa*—Treaty of June 14, 1889, *Treaties of U. S.*, Vol. I, p. 1576, terminated in 1899, p. 1596. *Norway-Sweden*—cf. p. 584. *Aaland islands*—cf. p. 50. The Black Sea was neutralized between 1856 and 1870.

"respected" the neutralized status only when it was in conformity to their interests and "policy" to do so.[1] Prussia accused France of violating the neutrality of Luxemburg in 1870, while Germany flagrantly and confessedly violated the neutrality of Belgium and Luxemburg during the World War.

The Treaty of Versailles provided for the termination of the neutralized status of Belgium, Luxemburg and the zone along the Swiss-French frontier, while the revised Act of Berlin omitted the provisions for the optional neutrality of Central Africa.[2] Thus the neutralization agreement lost ground following the War, partly because of the strengthening of the belief that security could rest only upon alliances and the force of arms.

2. "TERRITORIAL INTEGRITY" AGREEMENTS

Agreements guaranteeing the political independence or the territorial integrity of states differ from neutralization agreements very slightly. While the neutralization agreement has been applied to the small states of Europe, the "integrity" agreement has been applied largely to countries in the backward regions. About eight such agreements have been made in regard to China.[3] Japan and France have respectively promised to guarantee the integrity of Korea and Annam;[4] and other similar treaties have been made regarding Persia, Tibet and Abyssinia.[5] Likewise, in the Treaty of Paris of 1856 the powers promised to respect the independence and territorial integrity of the Ottoman Empire;[6] while a year earlier, France and Great Britain had virtually guaranteed the territory of Norway and Sweden against attack by Russia. Although the latter guarantee came to an end following

[1] G. G. Wilson, "Neutralization in Theory and Practice," 4 *Yale Review* (1915), 474.
[2] Arts. 31, 40, 435, Treaty of Versailles. In regard to Belgium, Germany promised to recognize whatever conventions might be made; no agreement, however, appears to have been entered into, and Belgium has not formally agreed to the termination of neutrality. Nevertheless, in making an alliance with France, she has apparently accomplished the same end. Fauchille, p. 712n.
[3] Cf. index, MacMurray, *Treaties and Agreements with and concerning China*—"territorial integrity."
[4] Treaty of June 6, 1884, 75 *State Papers*, 103; Art. XV, Protocol of Feb. 23, 1904, 98 *State Papers*, 842.
[5] Cf. p. 470.
[6] Art. VII, Treaty of April 15, 1856, 46 *State Papers*, 26.

AGREEMENTS AS TO THE STATUS QUO

the separation of Norway from Sweden in 1905, the powers in 1907 signed a new agreement guaranteeing the independence of Norway, which in turn was denounced in 1924 at Norway's behest.[1] In 1846 the United States guaranteed the "rights of sovereignty" of Colombia over the isthmus of Panama; and when the republic of Panama was established, its independence was also guaranteed by the United States.[2]

Despite their great number, these treaties have not succeeded in really preserving the independence or the integrity of the countries that were designated beneficiaries. They did not, for instance, prevent the powers from encroaching upon Korea, Annam, China or Turkey. The truth is, such treaties are made largely for the purpose of compromising the rivalries of the parties to them, and not at all for the good of the countries which are the ostensible objects of their solicitude. It is not surprising that no one seriously proposed before the War that the European powers reciprocally guarantee the territorial integrity of each other.[3]

3. AGREEMENTS AS TO THE STATUS QUO

Finally, agreements have been made in regard to the status quo, which bind the parties to respect existing territorial boundaries. Beginning with 1887 a number of "Mediterranean agreements" were made by littoral powers; while in 1907 and 1908 different powers made new declarations resolving to "preserve intact" their rights in the Mediterranean, the North, and the Baltic Seas.[4] A development of this principle came in the Four-Power Treaty of the Pacific, signed in 1921 by the British Empire, France, the United States and Japan. "With a view to the preservation of the general peace and the maintenance of their rights in relation

[1] Treaty of Nov. 21, 1855, 45 *State Papers*, 33; Treaty of Nov. 2, 1907, 1 Martens (3d series), 14; cf. p. 579.

[2] Art. 35, Treaty of Dec. 12, 1846, *Treaties of the U. S.*, Vol. I, p. 362; Art. 1, Treaty of Nov. 18, 1903; *ibid.*, Vol. II, p. 1348.

[3] The Interparliamentary Union, however, proposed an international neutralization convention, while proposals for an American guarantee of territorial integrity were made.

[4] Pribram, *Secret Treaties of Austria-Hungary*, Nos. 9, 11, 12, 14; Declaration of May 16, 1907, 1 Martens (3d series), 30 Declaration of April 23, 1908, 1 Martens (3d series), 17. Cf. Floeckner, "La question de la mer Baltique et de la mer du Nord," "La convention relative à la Baltique," 15 *R. G. D. I. P.* (1908), 125, 271.

to their insular possessions and insular dominions in the region of the Pacific Ocean," the four powers "agree as between themselves to respect their rights" in these possessions.[1]

4. NON-AGGRESSION AGREEMENTS

A new type of agreement has recently come into existence called the non-aggression agreement. In it the parties promise not to attack or invade the territory of each other, and in no case to resort to war against each other. This principle was laid down in the Locarno agreement of Mutual Security. The 1928 League Assembly, acting upon the recommendations of a Committee on Arbitration and Security, drafted a model convention containing this provision.[2] The 1927 Assembly declared that all wars of aggression are prohibited; and the anti-war pact enunciated the same principle in a different form.[3]

Russia has made a number of non-aggression agreements. In its treaty of September 28, 1926, with Lithuania, both parties promise to refrain from any act of aggression whatsoever against the other party.[4] Russia has a similar treaty with Persia.[5] On November 28, 1927, Persia and Afghanistan signed an agreement promising to abstain from proceeding to aggression against each other.[6]

5. THE DEMAND FOR "GUARANTEES"

The mere promise to "respect" the neutrality, the independence or the status quo of certain countries has rarely been deemed an adequate form of security in international relations. Consequently in some of these agreements, the parties have also promised to "guarantee" that the terms of the treaty shall not be violated. In other words, in guaranteeing the neutrality of Switzerland, Cracow and Luxemburg, the powers not only promised to "respect" this neutrality themselves, but also to prevent other pow-

---

[1] Treaty of Dec. 13, 1921, *Treaties of the U. S.*, Vol. III, p. 3094. In a supplementary treaty, the "insular possessions and insular dominions" of Japan were limited to Formosa, the Pescadores, southern Sakhalin, and the mandated islands. *Ibid.*, p. 3098. This definition set aside the "homeland" interpretation. Buell, *Washington Conference*, p. 180.
[2] *O. J.*, Spec. Sup. No. 63, p. 40.
[3] Cf. p. 659.
[4] *T. S.*, 1410.
[5] *European Economic and Political Survey*, Vol. III, p. 67.
[6] *Ibid.*, Vol. III, p. 432.

ers from violating it. The agreements of 1907–1908 provided that the powers would consult as to the measures considered useful to maintain the status quo, in case it was threatened; while in the Four-Power Treaty, it was provided that in case a controversy should arise between any of the four powers out of a Pacific question involving their insular rights, a conference should be held. If any outside power threatened "said rights," the parties should communicate with each other "in order to arrive at an understanding as to the most efficient measures to be taken, jointly or separately, to meet the situation." [1]

While some of these treaties therefore provided for a "guarantee," it was, as a rule, too vague to be effective. No provision was made under which the guaranteeing power could be definitely asked to fulfil an obligation, except possibly to confer. Under the neutralization agreements, the obligation to guarantee the neutrality of Belgium and Luxemburg was regarded by some statesmen merely as a "moral" guarantee, to be fulfilled at the complete discretion of each power.[2]

6. ARTICLE TEN

With the establishment of the League of Nations in 1919, an attempt was made to extend these principles, so imperfectly developed before the War, and to give a moral guarantee of security to every member of the League, great and small. According to the famous Article X of the Covenant:

> The Members of the League undertake to respect and preserve as against external aggression the territorial integrity and existing political independence of all Members of the League. In case of any such aggression or in case of any threat or danger of such aggression the Council shall advise upon the means by which this obligation shall be fulfilled.

---

[1] "Domestic questions" are excluded from these conferences, *Treaties*, p. 3097. The Senate of the U. S. made a reservation to the effect that the Treaty imposes "no commitment to armed force, no alliance, no obligation to join in any defence." *Treaties of the U. S.*, Vol. IV, p. 3096. While Holland and Portugal are not parties to the treaties, the four powers in an exchange of notes promised also to respect their rights. *Treaties, ibid.*, p. 3097.

[2] In January, 1923, the German government suggested that the German, British, French and Italian governments promise not to make war among themselves for thirty years, unless after popular vote. France refused to consider it on the ground that Germany wished to divert attention from the reparations question.

Article X does not necessarily perpetuate the territorial status quo established at the Paris Peace Conference, since it does not prevent states from making territorial changes by peaceful means. In fact, when they are necessary to the maintenance of peace, the Assembly or Council may, under Articles XI and XIX of the Covenant,[1] suggest such changes. The words "existing political independence" apparently mean "existing" at the time of a dispute, and not "existing" at the time the Covenant was drawn up, in 1919. Article X simply means that no annexations should result from warlike action—a principle that must be accepted before a real international community can be established.[2] Moreover, under Article X, the territorial integrity and political independence of each state is guaranteed only "as against external aggression"—i. e., the attack of an outside power. Internal revolts are disputes within the "domestic jurisdiction" of each state, over which the League has no jurisdiction.[3]

Just what "external aggression" means is more difficult to determine. Does any use of armed force by one state against another constitute a violation of its territorial integrity or political independence? If such an interpretation should be adopted it would be virtually impossible to apply military sanctions against a state which had violated international law or refused to perform a positive obligation which it owed to another state. That such an interpretation is unreasonable is indicated by the Protocol adopted by the fifth Assembly, which provides that "in view of Article X of the Covenant, neither the territorial integrity nor the political independence of the aggressor State shall in any case be affected as the result of the application of the sanctions. . . ."[4] Additional support for the interpretation that territory may be temporarily invaded without violating Article X is furnished by the fact that the proposal of the Belgian delegate at the Paris Peace

---

[1] Cf. p. 628.

[2] For this interpretation cf. Report of Jurists, A. 24 (1), 1921, p. 12; also *Records of the Second Assembly*, First Committee, p. 191. Cf. W. Schücking, *The International Unions of the Hague Conferences* (tr., 1918), pp. 283 ff.

[3] Such was the interpretation made by the fifth Committee of the first Assembly in regard to the threatened separation of Voralberg from Austria. *Procès-Verbaux of the Committees*, First Assembly, No. 12, Dec. 10, 1920, p. 4; for the Aaland island case, cf. p. 46.

[4] Art. 13; cf. p. 651.

Conference that Article X guarantee the "inviolability" as well as the "integrity" of the state, was rejected.[1] Apparently Article X simply means that the invasion of territory shall not result in permanent annexation or the establishment of permanent control of a lesser form such as a protectorate, but that territory may be invaded for other purposes, provided that the attacking state has not violated the provisions of the Covenant in regard to pacific procedure.[2] This interpretation may give rise to a number of technical difficulties. For example, a state may invade territory, stating that it does not intend to annex it but continuing in indefinite occupation. Under the above interpretation, the League could not act until after the armed occupation had taken on the character of permanency when it would be very difficult for the League to dislodge the trespasser. To prevent such abuses, the invasion of territory, for purposes not prohibited by Article X, should not take place unless with the authorization of either the Council or the Assembly.[3]

In exacting a pledge from each member of the League to "respect" the territorial integrity and independence of the others, the Covenant follows out a development started in the different treaties before the War. While such a pledge not to acquire territory by forcible means in the future marks a distinct advance toward world peace, the Covenant believes that it must be supported by a positive sanction—that is, that a penalty should be imposed

---

[1] Schücking and Wehberg, p. 459. Cf. A. A. H. Struycken, "La Société des Nations et l'intégrité territoriale," *Bibliotheca Visseriana* (1923), p. 93; Rolin, "L'Article 10 du Pacte de la Société des Nations," in *Les Origines et l'Œuvre de la Société des Nations* (1924), Vol. II, p. 453, ed. by P. Munch.

[2] The Committee of Jurist in the Corfu affair reported that acts of coercion may or may not violate articles 12–15; cf. p. 393. However, the Committee of Jurists (A. 24, cited, p. 14) said that the ultimate intention of the aggressor did not affect the issue.

[3] Apparently the first case where a nation appealed to the League under Article X was Persia's appeal in 1920, following an invasion by Russian troops. The Council decided that before advising as to how the obligations in the Covenant should be fulfilled, it should await the outcome of negotiations then in progress between Russia and Persia. But it expressly stated that the Persian government had acted in the best interests of peace and had rightly appealed to the principle of international coöperation. No further action on the part of the Council appeared necessary because the negotiations resulted in the withdrawal of Soviet troops. Cf. *O. J.*, July, 1920, pp. 216 ff. In most of the disputes placed before the Council the parties have not invoked Article X, but rather Articles XI, XII and XV. Cf. pp. 628 ff.

upon any state that violates this or other pledges laid down in the Covenant.¹

7. FOUR KINDS OF SANCTIONS

To impose sanctions against a state which commits an aggression or which refuses to live up to its other international obligations, the establishment of a super-state is not necessary. The same end may be attained by the agreement of the remaining states to take common measures against such a state for the purpose of bringing it to terms. With this aim, at least four types of sanctions may be employed.²

1. Diplomatic sanctions—such as the suspension of diplomatic relations or the withdrawal of the exequaturs of consuls—a frequent practice between states.

2. Judicial sanctions—suspending all commercial treaties of a defaulting state, and thereby the right of its nationals to engage in trade or to have access to the courts of the suspending states.

3. Economic sanctions.

4. International military sanctions.

Trial of the Kaiser.—In the Treaty of Versailles an attempt was made to apply one type of judicial sanction—in the trial of the Kaiser. The Allied and Associated Powers publicly arraigned William II of Hohenzollern, formerly German Emperor, "for a supreme offence against international morality and the sanctity

[1] One jurist says, "Just as the task accomplished in the period before this war consisted in the main of the creation of a system of *international law procedure*, so now the *new* task to be faced by reason of this war consists in devising a system of coercive measures based on international law for the application of this procedure. . . ." O. Nippold, *The Development of International Law After the War* (tr., 1923), p. 57. The widespread demand among publicists for coercive sanctions is summarized in this book on pp. 58–72. Cf. also J. Dumas, *Les Sanctions de l'arbitrage international* (1905). While the federal government has not hesitated to enforce Supreme Court judgments against individuals, there has been some doubt expressed as to its power to enforce judgments against states. However, in *Virginia* v. *West Virginia*, 246 U. S. (1918) 566, the Court hinted that such a power existed in the federal government, although it did not exercise it. For an interesting discussion of the power of opinion in regard to such decisions, and the analogy to an international court, see Charles Warren, *The Supreme Court and Sovereign States* (1924), Chs. III and IV. Also J. B. Scott, *The United States of America: a Study in International Organization* (1920).

[2] This classification was used in the French plan submitted to the Paris Conference; cf. p. 598.

of treaties." The treaty provided that a special tribunal should be appointed, composed of five judges representing the United States, Great Britain, France, Italy and Japan, to try the accused. "In its decision the tribunal will be guided by the highest motives of international policy, with a view to vindicating the solemn obligations of international undertakings and the validity of international morality." The German government "recognized" the right of the Allies to try before military tribunals persons accused of having committed acts in violation of the laws of war and promised to hand over to the Allies all persons thus accused.[1]

At the Paris Peace Conference the American delegation protested against the proposed trial of the Kaiser on the ground that the proposed tribunal would not be neutral and that the head of a state is not responsible to any other state for his acts.[2] Regardless of the wording of the treaty, the German people would not believe that the Kaiser was guilty of the crimes thus charged to him. His execution would have made the Kaiser a martyr, which would have further intensified European bitterness. The little country of Holland prevented this part of the treaty from being carried into effect by declining to give up the Kaiser, who had taken refuge there, on the ground that such an act would violate her neutrality. The Allied governments were no more successful in securing the delivery of German officers, charged with violating the laws of war, to Allied courts. As a compromise it was finally agreed in 1920 that a list of 45 officers, submitted by the Allied governments, would be tried in the German courts.[3] These War Criminals' Trials, which occurred at Leipzig in 1921, resulted in the conviction of six officers.[4] While the attempt to prevent wars by punishing individuals for "starting" them [5] has many difficulties in principle, in the case of the Germans the principle was especially defective because there had been no international law defining the offense and prescribing the punishment, and because no really

---

[1] Arts. 227–230, Treaty of Versailles.
[2] "Violations of the Laws and Customs of War," Report of Majority and Dissenting Reports of American and Japanese Members of the Commission of Responsibilities, Conference of 1919, *Pamphlet No. 32*, Carnegie Endowment, p. 77.
[3] "German War Trials," Cmd. 1450, p. 17.
[4] C. Mullins, *The Leipzig Trials* (1921), p. 199.
[5] For the Outlawry of War plan, cf. p. 656.

impartial tribunal existed to determine whether or not the law had been violated.

The purpose of the economic sanction internationally applied is to cut off the economic and commercial life of the offending state from the outside world. This purpose may be accomplished either through (a) the boycott, or (b) the blockade, the former being a passive, and the latter an aggressive means of injuring trade.

In a boycott the citizens of a foreign state are forbidden to patronize the goods of an offending country. Boycotts may be officially imposed by governments. In 1808 the American Congress passed a Non-Intercourse Act, authorizing the President to place an embargo on goods coming from France. During the World War, too, embargoes were imposed on trade of certain types. Nor do boycotts always await the approval of governments. Thus the Chinese boycotted the United States over the administration of the exclusion laws in 1905, while in 1922 they boycotted Japan over the Shantung affair. At the annexation of Bosnia, the Turks boycotted Austria, and they have also boycotted Greece.

Blockades.—When states blockade a power, they attempt by forceful means to stop all imports and exports of the state concerned. During modern history, altogether about twenty-two "pacific" blockades have been imposed, usually upon smaller states, ten of which have been executed by international fleets as, for example, when an international fleet blockaded Montenegro in 1913.[1] Such blockades are "pacific." They may also be imposed by belligerents during the course of a war.[2] The blockade of the South by the North during the American Civil War prevented the South from purchasing essential European manufactures and from disposing of her cotton abroad. During the World War, the Allies also shut the Central Powers off from the outside world; while Germany attempted, by means of submarine warfare, to blockade England.[3]

[1] H. P. Falcke, *Le Blocus pacifique* (1919), Part I; Nippold, cited, pp. 73 ff.; S. Cheou-Wei, *Essai sur l'organisation juridique de la société internationale* (1917), p. 74.

[2] The rules of blockade are discussed in any treatise on international law. The question whether the blockade under Article 16 of the Covenant would be pacific or belligerent was discussed at the first Assembly. Shücking and Wehberg, p. 630.

[3] Cf. M. Parmelee, *Blockade and Sea Power* (1924), Part I.

FOUR KINDS OF SANCTIONS

The effectiveness of the economic sanction will depend upon the economic situation of the state against which it is used. If a state is economically self-sufficient, such as are the United States and France, the boycott would be comparatively ineffective. Nor is it impossible that in the future states will deliberately erect high tariff walls with a view to protecting themselves from the imposition of an international economic sanction. Moreover, because of the growing economic interdependence of the world, a boycott or blockade is likely to hurt those states which impose it, particularly such small states as Holland, Denmark and Switzerland, as much as the states against which it is imposed. The damage will be increased if the blockaded state contains a monopoly of certain raw materials needed by the outside world. In view of these considerations, the value of the economic sanction in international relations is dubious. Emphasis has consequently been placed upon a fourth means of enforcing international law—international military sanctions.

In a number of instances in past history, various powers have agreed jointly to employ force, apart from war, to impose their wishes upon recalcitrant states. In the "pacification" agreement of 1840 Great Britain undertook to employ her naval force in combination with Spanish and Portuguese troops, to suppress a revolt in Portugal.[1] In order "to aid the Sultan to restore order" in the Lebanon, the convention of 1860 authorized the organization of an international expeditionary force of 12,000 men.[2] In the same year a French-English force occupied certain ports in China, while in 1861, France, England and Spain agreed to send a joint force to occupy certain positions in Mexico.[3] In 1896 an international force, representing six nations, landed in Crete.[4] To protect foreigners in the Boxer rebellion, twelve powers, including the United States, sent a police force to China.[5] In 1913 the powers decided to ask "one of the smaller neutral Powers" to organize a gendarmerie for the policing of Albania.[6] Following the World

[1] Cf. p. 509. [2] Cf. p. 223.
[3] Convention of Oct. 31, 1861, 51 *State Papers*, 63.
[4] R. Robin, *Des occupations militaires en dehors des opérations de guerre* (1913), p. 489.
[5] *U. S. For. Rel.*, 1900, p. 236.
[6] Cf. Sir Ed. Grey, 56 *Parl. Debates H. C.* (1913), 2283; for the policing of Morocco, cf. p. 473.

War, inter-Allied troops occupied disputed territory and policed several plebiscites.¹

Strange to say, the demand for military sanctions at one time was strong in the United States. In 1910 Congress passed a resolution authorizing the appointment of a commission to consider the expediency of utilizing existing international agencies for the purpose of limiting armaments of the world, "and of constituting the combined navies of the world, an international force for the preservation of universal peace. . . ." ² In his message of Dec., 1904, President Roosevelt anticipated this resolution, by declaring that under any circumstances, "sufficient armament would have to be kept up to serve the purposes of international police." ³ In his Nobel Prize Speech of May 5, 1910, he declared that the supreme difficulty in developing the work of The Hague "arises from the lack of any executive power, of any police power to enforce the decrees of the court." Secretary of the Navy von Meyer in 1910 also wrote that "under the most favorable circumstances it will be necessary for at least five or six of the nations to maintain navies which will be able to enforce the decrees of the international court against any single nation that might object to its decision." ⁴ President Taft is reported to have expressed a similar sentiment.⁵ Likewise, Senator Henry Cabot Lodge, in a speech at Union College in 1915, said that "if we were to promote international peace at the close of the present terrible war, if we were to restore international law as it must be restored, we must find some way in which the united forces of the nations could be put behind the cause of peace and law." In the following year he said, "I think the next step . . . is to put force behind international peace." ⁶ These different examples indicate a belief that the enforcement of certain international decisions depends, in some cases, upon the joint force of arms.

[1] Cf. Cavaré, "Quelques notions sur l'occupation pacifique," *R. G. D. I. P.*, Sept.—Oct., 1924.
[2] Res. 43, June 25, 1910, 36 *Stat.* 885.
[3] *Messages and Documents* (abridgment), 1904, Vol. I, p. 38.
[4] *Ibid.*, 1910, Vol. II, p. 1289.
[5] *War Obviated by an International Police* (1915), p. 205.
[6] *Enforced Peace*, Proceedings of the First National Assemblage of the League to Enforce Peace (1916), p. 164.

8. THE SANCTIONS OF THE LEAGUE COVENANT

Drawing upon the rudimentary experience of the past, the Covenant attempts to provide guarantees against the illegal acts of states. It is significant that, with the exception of the Norwegian plan, almost all of the drafts for a League submitted to the Paris Peace Conference contained some provision for sanctions.[1] In the final Covenant, sanctions may be employed in five cases:

1. When Article X is violated.
2. Under Article XI, in case of any war or threat of war.
3. When a member fails to carry out an arbitral award under Article XIII.
4. When a member resorts to war without submitting a dispute to the Council or Assembly in accordance with Articles XII–XV of the Covenant.
5. When a non-member of the League, which has refused to accept the obligations of League membership, under Article XVII, resorts to war against a member.

These sanctions may be divided into two general classes, first, those which compel a state to perform a positive obligation toward another state. If a state fails to carry out an arbitral award under Article XIII, "the Council shall propose what steps *should* be taken to give effect thereto." But no sanction at all is provided to enforce a recommendation of the Council.[2] For example, Hungary and Roumania become involved in a minorities dispute, which is referred to the Council. That body makes a unanimous recommendation which Hungary accepts, but which Roumania rejects, continuing the while to mistreat Hungarian minorities. Under the Covenant, the Council has no power to ask the members of the League to act against Roumania. However, it appears that it may authorize Hungary to declare war on Roumania, provided such a war does not result in annexation, in violation of Article X.[3]

[1] Schücking and Wehberg, p. 602.
[2] In the original draft of the Covenant such a provision was inserted, but it was later stricken out. Cf. A. 24 (1), 1921 V, p. 10; cf. Committee of Jurists, cited.
[3] In case of a war or a threat of war under Article XI, "the League *shall* take any action that may be deemed wise and effectual to safeguard the peace of nations." Presumably it may take, under this article, the economic and military sanctions elsewhere mentioned. Cf. p. 645.

Secondly, those which may be imposed to suppress an illegal war. In case Articles X, XII, XIII or XV of the Covenant are violated, more definite sanctions are authorized; they may be economic, military or political.

Economic sanctions.—Should any Member of the League resort to war in disregard of its covenants under articles 12, 13, or 15, it shall *ipso facto* be deemed to have committed an act of war against all other Members of the League, which hereby undertake immediately to subject it to the severance of all trade or financial relations, the prohibition of all intercourse between their nationals and the nationals of the covenant-breaking State, and the prevention of all financial, commercial or personal intercourse between the nationals of the covenant-breaking State and the nationals of any other State, whether a Member of the League or not.

It appears that under this provision diplomatic representatives of the boycotted state in foreign countries would have to be withdrawn, including its representatives at the League.

In order to prevent the weight of this boycott from falling too heavily upon certain states more closely dependent upon the boycotted states than others, the Covenant also provides:

The Members of the League agree, further, that they will mutually support one another in the financial and economic measures which are taken under this Article, in order to minimize the loss and inconvenience resulting from the above measures, and that they will mutually support one another in resisting any special measures aimed at one of their number by the covenant-breaking State. . . .[1]

While this article imposes the definite obligation on each member of the League to impose a boycott against a state illegally going to war, each member judges for itself when this obligation comes into existence, and how it shall be fulfilled. No international body is authorized to lay down a binding interpretation or, except by advice, to coördinate different national activities.[2]

Military sanctions.—In case of any threat or danger of aggression, under Article X, "The Council shall advise upon the means" by which the members of the League shall fulfil their ob-

---

[1] Art. 16.
[2] G. Scelle, *Le Pacte des Nations et sa liaison avec le Traité de Paix* (1919), pp. 321 ff.

ligation to guarantee the territorial integrity and political independence of each state. According to Article XVI, "It shall be the duty of the Council in such case [when a member resorts to war in disregard of Articles XII, XIII or XV] to recommend to the several Governments concerned what effective military, naval or air force the Members of the League shall severally contribute to the armed forces to be used to protect the covenants of the League." Moreover, the members agree "that they will take the necessary steps to afford passage through their territory to the forces of any of the Members of the League which are co-operating to protect the covenants of the League."

It is clear from these articles that each member is under some form of obligation to impose a sanction in case a state illegally goes to war. The mere existence of a territorial guarantee, such as is given in Article X, implies an obligation to enforce it. Although the Council has the duty of "advising" or "recommending" what measures to take, here also each state interprets for itself what its obligations are.[1]

Political sanctions.—Exclusion from membership in the League. "Any Member of the League which has violated any covenant of the League may be declared to be no longer a Member of the League by a vote of the Council concurred in by the Representatives of all the other Members of the League represented thereon."[2] This apparently means, by all the regular members of the Council together with the states represented on the Council during the discussion of matters affecting their interests. However, the state accused of violating the Covenant should not be allowed to vote on the question of its exclusion from the League.[3]

9. THE ATTACK AGAINST THE SANCTIONS

These military and economic sanctions of the Covenant were attacked from two conflicting points of view. Those nations fearing attack, such as France, complained that the sanctions

[1] While under Article X, the members of the League are under no obligation to accept the "advice" of the Council, some powers have agreed to follow it in the protection of the Aaland islands, Albania, and the Straits, in case these are threatened with an attack. For the powers of the Council in the Locarno agreement. Cf. p. 653.
[2] Art. XVI.
[3] Schücking and Wehberg, p. 637.

were not strong enough. As long as each state judged for itself the existence and the extent of its obligations, France could not disarm. On the other hand, such nations as the United States and Canada, complained that the sanctions were too strong. At the Paris Peace Conference, the French illustrated their point of view by proposing to establish an international police force, under an international General Staff, which should inspect different national armies and make suggestions as to modifications in national recruiting systems which the governments should accept. Also, by the same proposal, the Council might entrust a mandate to enforce decisions of the League to one or more powers.[1] This plan was rejected because it was believed that it would oblige every country to adopt conscription at the behest of the international staff, substituting, according to President Wilson, "international for national militarism." [2] Difficulties would also arise over the control and location of an international military force.[3] While the French proposal was thus open to many objections, its defeat increased sentiment in France in favor of alliances and armaments as the only certain means of security.

On the other hand, some countries believed that the obligations imposed on League members to resist aggression were too severe. In the United States, the opinion was expressed that this country should not go to the aid of a European power in a dispute not primarily of American concern. This argument, however, missed the significance of the League procedure under which any war was considered of world concern, regardless of the issue involved. A tiny match struck in a distant part of the world might start a conflagration which would engulf humanity. Opinion in many countries, whether members of the League or not, nevertheless inclined to the belief that the Covenant over-emphasized sanctions. Some countries did not wish to assume the obligation to defend the status quo, because in some instances it might be based on rank injustice, and because the League machinery did not guar-

---

[1] For the French plan, cf. D. N. Hadjicos, *Les sanctions internationales de la Société des Nations* (1920), p. 233. The British also suggested the possibility of establishing a League Naval Staff. Baker, *Woodrow Wilson*, Vol. I, p. 382.

[2] Baker, cited, Vol. I, p. 368.

[3] Cf. also *War Obviated by an International Police*, pp. 56 ff.

antee peaceful changes in it. They would not agree to defend nations from attack so long as they could commit acts which would provoke attacks. It was impossible, in their opinion, to do away with war until the causes of war had been removed—a fact which the policy of military sanctions ignored.

During the early years of the League the anti-sanction school appeared to predominate. At the first Assembly the Canadian delegation proposed the repeal of Article X, guaranteeing members against aggressive attack. At the third Assembly this proposal was withdrawn; but the exact meaning of Article X continued to be an objection of discussion.[1] At the fourth Assembly (1923) an interpretative resolution was proposed by the First Juridical Committee as follows:

"It is in conformity with the spirit of Article 10 that, in the event of the Council considering it to be its duty to recommend the application of military measures in consequence of an aggression or danger or threat of aggression, the Council shall be bound to take account, more particularly, of the geographic situation and of the special conditions of each State.

"It is for the constitutional authorities of each Member to decide, in reference to the obligation of preserving the independence and the integrity of the territory of Members, in what degree the Member is bound to assure the execution of this obligation by employment of its military forces.

"The recommendation made by the Council shall be regarded as being of the highest importance, and shall be taken into consideration by all the Members of the League with the desire to execute their engagements in good faith."

Twenty-nine states voted in favor of this interpretation, thirteen abstained, and one state—the little country of Persia surrounded by three menacing countries who did not belong to the League—voted no. As a resolution interpreting the Covenant must be passed unanimously, it failed of passage. The President of the Assembly, however, declared that, according to precedent, the motion should not be considered as rejected since the Assembly had not declared in favor of a contrary interpretation.[2]

---

[1] For a summary, cf. Schücking and Wehberg, pp. 451 ff.
[2] *Records of the Fourth Assembly*, Plenary Meetings, p. 86.

Similar steps to make more elastic the provisions of Article XVI in regard to an economic boycott [1] were taken by the second Assembly. In the first place a resolution was passed making a distinction between an "act of war" and a "state of war." It appears that the framers of Article XVI contemplated the immediate establishment of an economic boycott against a state which illegally went to war.[2] Such an interpretation would have required the instant imposition of such a boycott by all the members of the League. But according to the resolution of the second Assembly,

"the unilateral act of the defaulting State cannot create a state of war; it merely entitles the other Members of the League to resort to acts

[1] The original Article 16 adopted the "nationality" principle; the system of blockade therefore did not apply to nationals of states imposing the blockade who could continue economic relations with their co-nationals resident in the Covenant-breaking state. The system was too rigid, on the other hand, because it would suddenly suspend all the economic and personal relationships between the nationals of the Covenant-breaking state and nationals of the state imposing the blockade, *living together within the borders of the latter state, etc.* The second Assembly consequently proposed an amendment to Article 16, adopting the "territorial" principle, namely, that the blockade should apply only to persons living in the territory of the Covenant-breaking state. The question thereupon arose whether under the proposed amendment a state could, in addition, prohibit relationships between aliens and its nationals, living within its borders, etc. In order to make possible the *optional* combination of the two methods, the British government proposed a new amendment to Article 16, which the fifth Assembly approved in lieu of the previous amendment, as follows:

"Which hereby undertake immediately to subject it to the severance of all trade or financial relations and to prohibit all intercourse at least between persons resident within their territories and persons resident within the territory of the covenant-breaking State and, if they deem it expedient, also between their nationals and the nationals of the covenant-breaking State, and to prevent all financial, commercial or personal intercourse at least between persons resident within the territory of that State and persons resident within the territory of any other State, whether a Member of the League or not, and, if they deem it expedient, also between the nationals of that State and the nationals of any other State whether a Member of the League or not."

According to the sub-committee of the First Committee, "such a combination which there can be no question of rendering obligatory, ought to be possible wherever it can be organized in practice. It has the great advantage of rendering particularly complete the blockade of the State which has violated the Covenant by preventing nationals of the latter State residing in the territory of States not participating in the infliction of economic penalties from provisioning their country with war materials despatched by nationals of a State participating in the blockade." *Records of the Fifth Assembly*, Minutes of the First Committee, p. 103.

[2] Schücking and Wehberg, p. 621.

THE ATTACK AGAINST THE SANCTIONS 601

of war or to declare themselves in a state of war with the Covenant-breaking State; but it is in accordance with the spirit of the Covenant that the League of Nations should attempt, at least at the outset, to avoid war, and restore peace by economic pressure."

This resolution apparently means that each member of the League may disregard the "acts of war" of a defaulting state; so if it does not choose to regard such acts as creating a state of war, it is not obliged to impose an economic boycott. In other words, instead of being automatic, the boycott is optional.

In the second place, the resolution provided:

"It is the duty of each Member of the League to decide for itself whether a breach of the Covenant has been committed. The fulfilment of their duties under Article 16 is required from Members of the League by the express terms of the Covenant and they cannot neglect them without breach of their Treaty obligations."

If the Council believes that a state has been guilty of a breach, it transmits its opinion to the members of the League. But apparently they are under no obligation to accept this opinion, since each member judges for itself whether the Covenant has been violated.

Finally, the Council may in the case of particular members "postpone the coming into force of any of these measures for a specified period where it is satisfied that such postponement will facilitate the attainment of the object of the measures . . . or that it is necessary to minimize the loss and inconvenience which will be caused to such Members." [1] In other words, those states which would suffer by the imposition of a boycott might indefinitely delay action, if authorized to do so by the Council. The effect of these resolutions weakened still further the sanctions of Article XVI. Since each member is to judge whether or not the Covenant is violated, the situation may arise in which a defaulting state is subjected to penalties by one member, but not by others.

[1] Some of these resolutions were put in the form of a proposed amendment to Article XVI; meanwhile they were to be regarded as "rules of guidance." One commentator states that some of these resolutions adopted at the second Assembly in regard to Article XVI violate the Covenant, and that the Assembly does not have the power to amend the Covenant by interpretative resolution. M. Gonsiorowski, *Société des Nations et Problème de la Paix*, Vol. II, p. 417.

Difficulties may also arise when the economic weapon is imposed so as to affect the trade of a non-member state, such as the United States,—witness a similar controversy between England and the United States in the early years of the World War. Because of these limitations, the Economic Weapon is not apt to be effective in restraining aggression in the future.

In February, 1921, the Council established an International Blockade Committee to study the means by which Article XVI could be fulfilled.[1] To date it does not appear that the Council has recommended the use of military or economic sanctions on the part of any member of the League, under Articles X or XVI.[2]

Fearful of invoking these sanctions because of delicate political considerations, the Council in the first nine years of its existence relied to a large extent upon the weight of public opinion to force states to live up to the terms of the Covenant. In some cases this was effective,—in the Corfu case, the Italian government was literally obliged to withdraw from Corfu because of the indignation of the world, concentrated in the Council and particularly in the Assembly.

But despite its great strength, the exact weight of moral opinion is never demonstrable. It is improbable that moral suasion will in itself be any more effective in permanently maintaining the peace among nations than among individuals. Under exceptional cir-

[1] *O. J.*, March—April, 1921, pp. 116, 120. Cf. Report of International Blockade Committee, A. 28, 1921, V.

[2] In 1920 the Council authorized the establishment of a military force to be sent to Vilna during the proposed plebiscite. The troops were to be furnished by France, Great Britain, Belgium and Spain; and if they wished to contribute, by Denmark, Holland, Norway and Sweden. Each state was to finance its own contingent, but was to be reimbursed by Poland and Lithuania later. *O. J.*, January–February, 1921, p. 5. Switzerland declined, however, to permit the passage of these troops through her territory because of her neutralized position, which had been recognized in the Declaration of Feb. 13, 1920. But this police force was not to carry out Article XVI of the Covenant, which was not in question here, but merely to police the plebiscite. *O. J.*, March–April, 1921, p. 170. The British government requested the Council to use Article XVI when Serbia invaded Albania in 1921, but Serbia withdrew her troops without this action becoming necessary.

Certain suggestions were made in regard to stopping the hostilities between Turks and Armenians in 1920, but nothing appears to have come of them. *O. J.*, Nov.–Dec., 1920, p. 90. When General Zeligowski invaded Vilna in October, 1920, the Lithuanians asked that the Council apply Article XVI. But the Council took no action involving this Article. *Ibid.*, Special Supplement, No. 4, p. 135.

THE ATTACK AGAINST THE SANCTIONS

cumstances, force must come to the aid of morality. Consequently, when the Assembly weakened the sanctions of Articles X and XVI of the Covenant, France and the new states of Europe came to believe that they could not rely on the League for security. Also the distrust of some states was increased by the failure of the Council to come to the aid of wronged parties, such as Armenia, Lithuania, and Egypt. Nations could not disarm, it was said, until they received a guarantee of outside help proportionate to the extent of disarmament. If the League would not build up sanctions which would guarantee the security, particularly of the new states of Europe and of France, these nations would be obliged, in their opinion, to cling to the old military system of alliances and standing armies.[1] In other words, the questions of disarmament and security were indissoluble.

Many states, however, took the attitude that the military sanctions proposed by France could never permanently maintain peace, simply because the sanctions policy ignored the question whether France or any other state invoking protection in a particular dispute was right or wrong. According to this opinion, the best guarantee against attack was the universal acceptance of the obligation to submit all disputes to some form of arbitration. If nations actually agreed to this principle and to abide by arbitral decisions, war would be automatically outlawed. On the other hand, the unflinching insistence on the status quo and on the guarantee of a state against attack, regardless of its acts which might have provoked the attack, would not insure peace. According to this point of view, the principles of Disarmament and Security depended for their validity and their fulfillment upon Compulsory Arbitration.

---

[1] President Wilson and Lloyd George recognized the strength of the French argument at the Peace Conference when they agreed to an alliance promising to come to the assistance of France "in the event of any unprovoked aggression against her by Germany." While the United States failed to ratify the agreement, French and British prime ministers carried on further negotiations with this end in view between 1920 and 1923. Cf. *Documents relatifs aux négociations concernant les Garanties de Sécurité contre un agression de l'Allemagne.* French Yellow Book (1924).

10. FINANCIAL ASSISTANCE IN CASE OF AGGRESSION

Meanwhile the movement within the League for the strengthening of the sanctions seems to have revived, despite the defeat of the Geneva protocol.[1] This movement has taken a new form. Instead of working out a general scheme of military support, this movement proposes to place international credit immediately at the disposition of a state which is the victim of aggression or which is threatened by aggression. One of the first effects of war is to weaken the credit of belligerents. An international plan whereby a state unjustly attacked could immediately rely upon outside financial support would strengthen its position by allowing it to import supplies of which it was in need; and would be a powerful deterrent against the outbreak of aggressive war.

Originally proposed by Finland, the plan was studied by the Financial Committee of the League. It worked out a scheme for guaranteeing credit to a victim of aggression as follows. Each state interested in the scheme should deposit with the League non-interest-bearing "General Guarantee Bonds," of an amount equal to, say, 50 times its annual contribution to the League expenses. This would provide the League with a potential sum of about $250,000,000. In case an attacked state appealed for financial assistance, the Council would decide to what extent the request should be granted and would fix the amount of the loan. The other states would guarantee the interest and amortization of such loan in the ratio of their participation. When their quota is decided the League would ask them to exchange their non-interest-bearing "General Guarantee Bonds" for "Special Guarantee Bonds" guaranteeing service on the loan, up to the amount of their guarantee.[2] This scheme was also studied by a joint committee of the League Committee on Arbitration and Security and the Financial Committee.[3] The Joint Committee recommended that these principles be embodied in a convention and that financial assistance should be given not only after war broke out but when war was threatened, "if such action were deemed wise and effectual to safeguard or re-establish the peace of nations." In other words,

[1] Cf. 649.
[2] Cf. "Financial Assistance to States Victims of Aggression," A. 57. 1927. IX.
[3] "Committee on Arbitration and Security," A. 20. 1928. IX, p. 57.

FINANCIAL ASSISTANCE IN CASE OF AGGRESSION

this type of *preventive* sanction would be less severe than the sanctions of Article XVI of the Covenant and might make the application of the more severe sanctions of this Article unnecessary.

One of the principal difficulties in such a scheme is in deciding which state is the victim of aggression and thereby entitled to secure financial aid. Under the Covenant as at present interpreted, the Council may make recommendations as to which state has violated its obligations but each state determines for itself the question.[1] The Joint Committee recommended, however, that the Council by unanimous vote except for the parties should have the power to determine which state was entitled to financial aid.[2] The 1928 Assembly passed a resolution requesting that a draft Convention embodying these principles be submitted to the governments for their observations and then be placed before the tenth Assembly.[3]

---

[1] Cf. p. 601.

[2] The Third Committee of the Assembly recommended that a state signing this convention should waive its right under Article 4, para. 5 of the Covenant to send a representative to the Council when its interests were involved. A. 60. 1928. IX.

[3] O. J., Spec. Sup. No. 63, p. 60.

CHAPTER XXV
WORLD COURTS

1. Voluntary and Compulsory Arbitration.—2. Arbitration and "Vital Interests."—3. The Permanent Court of Arbitration at the Hague.—4. The Central American Court.—5. The Permanent Court of International Justice.—6. The United States and the World Court.—7. The Settlement of "Non-Legal" Disputes.—8. "Non-Legal" Disputes and the League Covenant.—9. Conciliation Commissions.

Despite the frequency of wars in the past, nations have often resorted to peaceful means in settling their disputes. Thousands of international controversies have been settled by the silent processes of negotiation and diplomacy; and when negotiation has failed in devising a compromise acceptable to both parties, governments have often resorted to a second method, called arbitration. They have attempted to apply to disputes between nations the procedure used to settle disputes between individuals. But the establishment of international courts is more difficult than that of domestic courts because, unlike individuals, nations are subject to no common government which enforces the law. Their consent—at some stage of the process—is therefore necessary if international adjudication is to take place.

1. VOLUNTARY AND COMPULSORY ARBITRATION

When nations decide to arbitrate a dispute, they submit it to an impartial tribunal, composed of one or more judges, for a decision which they, impliedly at least, agree to accept.[1] Dating back to ancient Greece, arbitration has been used many times especially

[1] Article 37, Convention for the Pacific Settlement of International Disputes, Oct. 18, 1907, provides, "International arbitration has for its object the settlement of disputes between States by judges of their own choice and on the basis of respect for law.
"Recourse to arbitration implies an engagement to submit in good faith to the award." *Proceedings of the Hague Peace Conferences*, Conference of 1907, Vol. I, p. 562.

VOLUNTARY AND COMPULSORY ARBITRATION 607

in the 19th century. Statistics have been compiled to show that about 240 cases were submitted to arbitration between 1794 and 1910.[1] Moreover, more than one hundred and twenty arbitration treaties of a general nature were signed between 1899 and 1918.[2]

There are two kinds of arbitration, (1) voluntary, (2) compulsory. Under the first system, nations are not obliged to submit disputes to arbitration, but after a dispute has arisen, they may voluntarily agree to submit it to a tribunal already in existence or created ad hoc. Under the second system, two or more governments sign a "general" arbitration treaty in which they agree to submit to arbitration all future disputes of a certain type defined in the treaty concerned, which cannot be settled by diplomacy. In other words, when such a dispute arises, the parties to the treaty are obliged to submit it to a tribunal and abide by the award. The weakness of voluntary arbitration is that a special agreement must be concluded submitting each dispute to arbitration, after it has arisen, and at a time when the parties to the dispute may be in a bad mood. Indeed, it is improbable that under this system nations will refer any really important disputes to a court. For this reason, the only effective system is compulsory arbitration—based on a general agreement providing for the automatic reference of all disputes of the classes defined in the agreement, to some form of international tribunal, as soon as a deadlock in diplomacy has been reached.

A number of states have recognized the value of compulsory arbitration. Before 1917 thirty-six treaties had been signed, providing for the arbitration of any dispute whatever between the parties; while thirteen others provided for the arbitration of any

---

[1] A. F. Fried, *Handbuch der Friedensbewegung* (2d ed., 1911), p. 191. Estimates, however, vary. According to W. E. Darby, *International Tribunals* (4th ed., 1904), there were 534 cases of arbitration between 1783 and 1904, a list which, however, includes settlement by mixed commissions, etc. According to H. La Fontaine, *Pasicrisie internationale* (1902), p. viii, there were 177 arbitrations between 1794 and 1900. Cf. Lapradelle and Politis, *Recueil des arbitrages internationaux*, Vol. I, 1798–1855 (1905); Vol. II, 1856–1872 (1923).

[2] For the general arbitration treaties since 1899, cf. Annex A, *Traités généraux d'arbitrage communiqués au Bureau International de la Cour Permanente d'Arbitrage* (3d series, 1921). Cf. also N. Politis, *La Justice internationale* (1924), Chs. I, III.

dispute not involving constitutional questions.[1] But no general treaty of this character had been signed by two of the great powers. Sometimes a great power has made a such treaty with a lesser power, such as the treaty of 1907 between Italy and Argentina, or that of 1909 between Italy and the Netherlands.[2] More frequently, small powers have made treaties providing for the general arbitration of disputes between themselves. Apparently the first compulsory arbitration treaty in modern times covering all disputes was signed on May 28, 1902, between Argentina and Chile— accompanying the armament agreement of that date.[3] In 1907 the five Central American Republics agreed to arbitrate all disputes among themselves, an obligation, however, which was terminated in 1923.[4] At the first Hague Conference of 1899 the Russian delegation advocated the signature of a treaty providing for obligatory arbitration in disputes relating to pecuniary claims or to the interpretation of certain types of treaties.[5] At the Conference of 1907 the Portuguese delegation submitted a similar list of cases which should be submitted to compulsory arbitration; while the United States proposed that "differences of a legal nature or relating to the interpretation of treaties," shall be submitted to arbitration, on the condition that they do not involve either the vital interests or independence or honor of any of the said states, and that they do not concern the interests of third parties.[6] While these various propositions were defeated, primarily because of the opposition of Germany,[7] the 1907 Conference adopted a resolution unanimously "admitting the principle of compulsory arbitration," especially in

[1] D. P. Myers, *Arbitration Engagements now Existing in Treaties*, World Peace Foundation (1915), Vol. V, No. 5, Pt. III, p. 34. Cf. also Sir Thomas Barclay, *New Methods of Adjusting International Disputes and the Future* (1917), p. 109.

[2] Agreement of Sept. 18, 1907, 101 *State Papers*, 239; Agreement of Nov. 20, 1907, 102 *State Papers*, 462.

[3] Agreement of May 28, 1902, 95 *State Papers*, 759. Questions affecting the principles of the constitution of either state are excepted. Cf. p. 556.

[4] Cf. p. 614.

[5] For the Russian memorandum, see *Proceedings of the Hague Peace Conferences*, cited, Conference of 1899, p. 170.

[6] *Ibid.*, *Conference of 1907*, Vol. II, Annexes 19, 20, 21 and 37.

[7] The German delegates declared that a world arbitration treaty would hinder the development of bilateral treaties, from which greater progress could be expected. For a summary of the debates, cf. W. I. Hull, *The Two Hague Conferences* (1908), pp. 297–348.

regard to disputes over the interpretation of international treaties. However, neither of the Conventions for the Pacific Settlement of International Disputes, whether of 1899 or of 1907, provided for compulsory arbitration. Even in regard to disputes over questions of a legal nature, the powers bound themselves to have recourse to arbitration only "in so far as circumstances permit." [1]

2. ARBITRATION AND "VITAL INTERESTS"

Nevertheless, because of growing sentiment in favor of the principle of arbitration, many great powers, in the year following these conferences, signed so-called general arbitration treaties, the scope of which, however, was limited to comparatively unimportant questions.

Most of the general arbitration treaties between the great powers were modeled after the Anglo-French treaty of October 14, 1903.[2] This treaty limited arbitration to differences of a legal nature, or relating to the interpretation of treaties, which had not been settled by diplomacy—provided neither the vital interests, nor the independence nor honor of the two contracting parties, nor the interests of a third state, were involved. In 1908 the United States entered into some twenty-five treaties of this character, which were renewable every five years; of these, at the present time, only nineteen remain in force.[3] (March, 1929.)

Obviously, an arbitration treaty exempting such questions as "vital interests" will be abused, simply because this term has never been defined. Consequently, such exemptions enable any nation which may feel that its case is weak, to withhold it from arbitration on the ground that it affects a "vital interest." Several attempts have been made to do away with the abuses to which such a doctrine may give rise. In the first place, some treaties enumerate specifically the disputes which do not fall into such a category. In 1902 nine Latin-American governments signed an arbitration treaty exempting from arbitration questions of na-

[1] Art. 38, Convention of Oct. 18, 1907. Cf. the declaration in the Final Act of Oct. 18, 1907, *Proceedings*, Conference of 1907, Vol. I, p. 689. However, compulsory arbitration was provided for in the convention restricting the use of force in collecting debts; cf. p. 416.

[2] 96 *State Papers*, 35.

[3] Cf. the treaty of April 4, 1908, between United States and Great Britain. *Treaties of the U. S.*, Vol. I, p. 814.

tional independence or honor, but at the same time providing that disputes arising out of diplomatic privileges, boundaries, navigation rights, and the validity, interpretation and fulfillment of treaties are not such disputes, and are therefore subject to arbitration.[1] Likewise, the French-Danish treaty of 1911 defined four classes of disputes, those arising out of pecuniary claims, contractual claims, and the interpretation of commercial treaties, and eleven other types of agreements in regard to such subjects as industrial property, as not being included within "vital interests." [2]

In the second place, it has been suggested that an impartial tribunal be invested with the power to decide whether a given dispute falls within a class, such as "vital interests," which is not subject to arbitration. In the proposed arbitration treaty of 1911 between Great Britain and the United States, it was provided that in case a difference of opinion should arise as to whether or not a dispute fell within the scope of the treaty, this difference should be referred to a Joint High Commission, composed of three members from each country, whose decision should be final.[3] The Senate of the United States refused to accept this provision, on the ground that such a commission would infringe upon the sovereignty of the United States. A similar attitude on the part of the Senate prevented the ratification, in a desirable form, of compulsory arbitration treaties of 1897, 1904, and 1908.[4] In the latter treaties, the Senate made a reservation requiring the conclusion of a special agreement before a given dispute could be arbitrated. By withholding its consent from such an agreement the Senate could prevent any arbitration it disapproved.

A more successful plan of impartially interpreting the meaning of non-justiciable questions was established in the arbitration treaty of August, 1911, between France and Denmark, which authorizes the arbitral tribunal to determine whether or not a dispute falls within one of the classes subject to arbitration.[5] Likewise, the

---

[1] W. R. Manning, *Arbitration Treaties Among the American Nations* (1924), p. 307, Treaty of Jan. 29, 1902. The same principle is followed in the Pan-American Arbitration Treaty of 1929. Cf. p. 252.
[2] Treaty of August 9, 1911, 104 *State Papers*, 907.
[3] Sen. Doc. 476, 62d Cong., 2d sess., Vol. 37.
[4] Cf. Sec. Hughes' letter to Senator Lodge, Feb. 17, 1923, 64 *Cong. Record*, 4508.
[5] Treaty of August 9, 1911, 104 *State Papers*, p. 907.

Optional Clause in the Statute for the Permanent Court of International Justice, established in December, 1920, provides that "in the event of a dispute as to whether the Court has jurisdiction, the matter shall be settled by the decision of the Court." [1]

3. THE PERMANENT COURT OF ARBITRATION AT THE HAGUE

Recourse to arbitration has been hindered, not only by the "vital interests" bug-a-boo, but also by the absence of a real international court of justice. Before 1899 there was no tribunal of a permanent nature to which an international dispute might be referred. When nations wanted to arbitrate a dispute, they were obliged to establish a special court for each dispute, which was done by choosing a number of judges or by selecting a single arbitrator. The Treaty of Washington between England and the United States provided for a court of five arbitrators; one chosen by each party, and one each by the King of Italy, the President of Switzerland and the Emperor of Brazil.[2] The treaty between Chile and Peru of 1922, in regard to the Tacna-Arica controversy, referred the dispute to the arbitration of the President of the United States.

Realizing the necessity of a real international court, the Hague Conference of 1899 drew up a convention for the Pacific Settlement of International Disputes in which 26 powers undertook to establish a Permanent Court of Arbitration. Under this convention, each power appointed four recognized international lawyers, for a period of six years, whose names were inscribed upon a list, called a panel. When two governments wished to arbitrate, they could select out of this panel from three to five "members" who would thereupon proceed to The Hague to hear the case. According to the amended convention of 1907, three of the five judges had to be neutrals. An International Bureau established at The Hague handled the administrative work connected with the court.[3]

[1] Article 36, Statute of December 16, 1920, *T. S.* No. 170.
[2] Treaty May 8, 1871, *Treaties of the U. S.*, Vol. I, p. 700.
[3] Cf. Arts. 42–45, 87, Convention of 1907. This Bureau is under the control of a Permanent Administrative Council, composed of the diplomatic representatives of the contracting parties at The Hague, and the Dutch minister of foreign affairs (Art. 49). The expenses of the Bureau are borne on the same basis as the International Postal Union (Art. 50).

While this arrangement was better than none at all, it did not establish a really "permanent" court, despite its title. The only permanent feature was a list of names—numbering 148 in 1924. The tribunal would vary with each case. It was not a continuous body profiting by experience or building up a body of international law. As Mr. Choate, the delegate of the United States at the Conference of 1907, said,

"The fact that there was nothing permanent or continuous or connected in the sessions of the court, or in the adjudication of the cases submitted to it, has been an obvious source of weakness and want of prestige in the tribunal. Each trial it had before it has been wholly independent of every other, and its occasional utterances, widely distant in point of time and disconnected in subject-matter, have not gone far toward constituting a consistent body of international law or of valuable contributions to international law, which ought to emanate from an international tribunal representing the power and might of all the nations. In fact, it has thus far been a court only in name,—a framework for the selection of referees for each particular case, never consisting of the same judges. It has done great good so far as it has been permitted to work at all, but our efforts should be to try to make it a tribunal which should be the medium of vastly greater and consistently increasing benefit to the nations and to mankind at large." [1]

Between 1899 and the present time (1929), the Permanent Court of Arbitration has decided only nineteen cases, most of which have been of relatively unimportant matters.[2]

At the second conference in 1907 an attempt was made to create a Court of Arbitral Justice of a limited number of permanent judges, meeting periodically at The Hague, which would overcome the weaknesses of the older tribunal. In electing the judges of this tribunal, the small powers, insisting on the doctrine of equality of states, demanded the same vote as the great powers. The latter would not, however, agree to a court which would be controlled

---

[1] *Proceedings*, Conference of 1907, Vol. II, p. 314.

[2] There is some question whether the eighteenth question—the Norway Arbitration of October, 1922—over shipping claims, was really before the Hague court, or whether another court merely used its administrative facilities. For the list of cases, the judges of the court, and the governments adhering to it, cf. *Rapport du Conseil administratif de la Cour Permanente d'Arbitrage*, 23d year (1924). For the nineteenth case, relative to the island Palmas, cf. 22 *A. J. I. L.*, 867.

by the small states, which naturally outnumber the large ones.[1] This difference was so irremovable that the 1907 Conference merely drew up a draft convention for a Court of Arbitral Justice, leaving the selection of the judges to a later agreement, which, however, was never arrived at.[2] In drawing up a plan for an international prize court, the Conference was more successful in devising a method of selection. While each state was entitled to appoint a judge, the judges appointed by Germany, the United States, Austria-Hungary, France, Great Britain, Italy, Japan and Russia were always to be summoned to sit, while the judges of the other states were to be summoned by a system of rotation.[3] But this convention departed so widely from existing conceptions as to the equality of states, that it was not ratified.

4. THE CENTRAL AMERICAN COURT

The only other international tribunal in existence before the War was the Central American Court of Justice, established in 1907 by a treaty between the five republics of Central America.[4] This court was composed of five judges, one elected by the legislature of each state. It had compulsory jurisdiction over all questions arising between the parties "of whatsoever nature and no matter what their origin may be." A number of disputes were referred to the court, the decisions of which led to the belief that it was subject to domestic political influences.[5] It finally passed out of existence following the ignoring of its decision by the United

[1] The German, British and American Delegations proposed that the court should have 17 judges, eight of which should be selected by the eight "large powers"; while the remaining powers should each appoint a judge, they should sit for periods of one, two, four or ten years, so that the court should never be composed of more than 17 judges. The "smaller" powers were divided into four classes, as above, according to differences in population, language and jurisprudence, etc. Annex 81, also p. 609, Vol. II, of the *Proceedings*, Conference of 1907.

[2] Cf. Final Act of Oct. 18, 1907, the first *vœu*. *Proceedings*, Vol. I, 1907, p. 689.

[3] Cf. Art. 15, Convention Relative to the Creation of an International Prize Court, October 18, 1907, *Proceedings* (1907), Vol. I, p. 660.

[4] Convention of Dec. 20, 1907, *Treaties of the U. S.*, Vol. II, p. 2399.

[5] D. G. Munro, *Five Republics of Central America*, pp. 218, 222; M. C. Ramirez, *Cinco Años en la Corte de Justicia Centroamericana* (1918), Ch. IV. For the judgment of Sept., 1916, in regard to Salvador, Nicaragua and the Bryan-Chamorro treaty, cf. *Anales de la Corte de Justicia Centroamericana*, Vol. VII (1917), p. 7.

States and Nicaragua to the effect that the treaty of 1914 between these two governments violated the rights of other Central American countries.

At the Central American Conference, held at Washington in 1922–23, an attempt was made to give the Central American Court of Justice a new lease of life. Deserting the old plan of a permanent court, the new treaty provides for a panel of thirty judges. Each of the five governments names six judges for this panel, one of whom shall be chosen from a list nominated by the United States, and one from a list nominated by a South American republic.[1] When two governments wish to resort to the court, each selects one arbitrator from the panel, outside of the judges they themselves have nominated. In case the two governments cannot agree, the two arbitrators already selected choose a third by agreement. While the new system may produce a court less dominated by politics than was the 1907 court, it now has the same weaknessess as the old Hague tribunal. Its jurisdiction is limited by the exception from arbitration of questions affecting the "sovereign and independent existence" of the parties; and its composition is always shifting.

5. THE PERMANENT COURT OF INTERNATIONAL JUSTICE

So many problems confronted the Paris Peace Conference of 1919 that very little attention was given to the establishment of a new international court. The only definite provision in this respect was contained in Article XIV of the Covenant of the League which provided that the Council of the League should draw up plans for a Permanent Court of International Justice. In accordance with this article, the Council appointed a committee of jurists, which met at The Hague in the summer of 1920 where it produced a "draft scheme."[2] Subject to a number of amendments, this plan was approved by the Council and by the Assembly on December 13, 1920, when a Protocol promulgating the Statute was submitted to the signature and ratification of the different

---

[1] II, *Conference on Central American Affairs* (1923), p. 296.
[2] *Procès-Verbaux of the Proceedings of the Committee*, June 16th–July 24th, 1920, Permanent Court of International Justice, Advisory Committee of Jurists (1920), p. 673.

PERMANENT COURT OF INTERNATIONAL JUSTICE 615

states. By September, 1921, a majority of the members of the League had ratified, thereby bringing the Statute into effect. By the fall of 1928 fifty-two states had signed and forty-one states have ratified.[1]

Both in respect to composition and to jurisdiction, the new World Court is superior to the old Hague Tribunal. It is composed of eleven regular and four deputy judges, elected for a term of nine years, but eligible for reëlection. The Court holds its regular session in June of each year, while the president of the Court may convene it in extraordinary session. The procedure of the Court is defined in Chapter III of the Statute and in its Body of Rules.

Candidates for the Court are nominated by the national groups of the old Court of Arbitration, each of which may nominate four judges. Eighty candidates were nominated before the first election in September, 1921. Judges are elected by a majority vote of the Council and of the Assembly, each voting separately. In electing this Court, the Council and Assembly should bear in mind that the "whole body should represent the main forms of civilization and the principal legal systems of the world." [2] In case the Council and Assembly fail to agree, a joint conference may be set up to propose a single candidate. If a deadlock should again arise, those members of the Court already chosen may elect the remaining members "from among those candidates who have obtained votes either in the Assembly or in the Council." [3] By this means of election the small powers participate equally with

[1] Cf. "Progress of Certain International Conventions and Engagements," A. 6 (a) 1928, Annex, September 3, 1928.

[2] Art. 9, Statute. The Rules are printed in *The Permanent Court of International Justice*, Statute and Rules (International Intermediatory Institute, 1922), pp. 74–114.

[3] Arts. 10–12. At the first election of judges, in September, 1921, the joint conference was resorted to only in the case of the fourth deputy-judge. Only one ballot of the Assembly and Council was necessary in September, 1923, to elect Judge Pessoa (Brazil) as the successor of Judge Ruy Barbosa who died in the previous March.

In addition to the full Court, there are three different Chambers, (1) The Chamber of Summary Procedure, composed of three judges, annually appointed, (2) the Chamber on labor questions, (3) the Chamber on questions of communications, both of five judges, which deal with technical questions arising particularly out of the peace treaties. The judges of the two latter Chambers are appointed for three years and sit at the request of the parties. Arts. 26–29, Statute.

the great powers, since they control the Assembly, while the latter control the Council. The existence of the League has made possible for the first time in history a real international tribunal of a limited number of permanent judges. Moreover, the interests of a state which has no regular judge on the court is specially protected by the provision that it may select a judge for any case to which it is a party.[1]

In many respects, the powers of the new World Court are more extensive than the old. According to Article XIV of the Covenant, the Court is competent to hear and determine any dispute of an international character which the parties thereto submit to it. The Court may also give an advisory opinion upon any dispute or question referred to it by the Council or by the Assembly. Moreover, according to Article XIII, the members of the League agree that whenever any dispute shall arise between them which they recognize to be suitable for submission to arbitration, which cannot be settled by diplomacy, they will thus submit it. Disputes as to (1) the interpretation of a treaty, (2) any question of international law, (3) the existence of any fact which if established would constitute a breach of any international obligation, and (4) the extent and nature of the reparation to be made for such a breach, are declared to be among those which are generally suitable for submission to arbitration.

In its draft, the Committee of Jurists proposed to give to the World Court compulsory jurisdiction over these four types of disputes. But the Council struck out this provision on the ground that it went beyond the Covenant. Instead, the Statute contains what is called an Optional Clause. If a government signs this Clause "it accepts as compulsory, *ipso facto* and without special Convention," the jurisdiction of the World Court in these disputes. The obligation may be conditional or it may be made subject to the condition of reciprocity on the part of other states.[2] By 1928, 29 states, including France, Germany, China and Brazil, had signed the Optional Clause agreeing to this type of compulsory arbitration, while 16 had ratified. Moreover, the members of the League agree that in case of a dispute not otherwise settled

[1] Art. 31, Statute.
[2] Art. 36, Statute. For a similar article in the Pan-American Arbitration agreement cf. p. 252.

PERMANENT COURT OF INTERNATIONAL JUSTICE 617

they will refer it either to arbitration or to the investigation of the Council—a provision which will probably increase the duties of the Court.

A large number of international treaties likewise confer compulsory jurisdiction upon the Court. It may be called upon to decide about fifty different questions arising out of the peace treaties, particularly in regard to ports, waterways, and railways. The minorities treaties, the mandates, the international conventions for the control of the arms and liquor traffic, the regulation of air navigation, the freedom of transit, and a number of other similar agreements provide that any difference over the interpretation of the treaty concerned shall be decided by the Permanent Court. The custom seems to be growing to insert such a provision in many bilateral political treaties, such as the agreement between Finland and Sweden over the Aaland islands, the agreement of December, 1921, between Czechoslovakia and Austria, the Upper Silesia agreement between Poland and Germany, and the alliance between Great Britain and Iraq.[1]

In addition to deciding disputes proper, the World Court may give advisory opinions upon any dispute or question referred to it by the Assembly or Council.[2] This practice of giving advisory opinions upon disputed legal questions is followed by the courts in some eleven states in the United States and in Canada.[3] By this means, the Council may ask the opinion of the Court upon semi-judicial matters within the Council's jurisdiction. For example, Article XV of the Covenant says that if the Council finds that a dispute arises out of a matter which by international law is solely within the jurisdiction of one of the parties, it shall so report. Before determining such a matter, the practice of the Council has been to ask the opinion of the Court, as illustrated in the opinion as to the Tunis-Morocco nationality decrees, decided in February, 1923. Moreover, by means of an advisory opinion,

[1] Cf. *Extracts from International Agreements Affecting the Jurisdiction of the Court* (2d ed., June, 1924), Publications of the Permanent Court of International Justice, Series D, No. 4.

[2] Article 14, Covenant.

[3] Cf. Hudson, "The Second Year of the Permanent Court of International Justice," *A. J. I. L.*, January, 1924. There has been some question whether giving advisory opinions is a proper judicial function. Cf. Hudson, "Advisory Opinions of National and International Courts," 37 *Harvard Law Review* (1924), p. 970.

the Court may also pass upon a question arising between a state and a private organization or such a body as the League of Nations which, under customary international procedure, would have no standing before it because one of the parties did not have the status of a state. For example, in 1921–1922, the labor unions of Holland disagreed with the Dutch government over the interpretation of the labor provisions of the Treaty of Versailles.[1] While it would have been impossible for a Dutch labor union to bring an action against its own government in an international tribunal, it was possible for it, acting through the International Labor Office and the Council of the League, to ask the Court for an advisory opinion. Although advisory opinions have no binding force, they have ordinarily been accepted by the Council. However, the World Court is under no obligation to give an advisory opinion when requested to do so by the Council, as was illustrated in the Eastern Carelia case.[2]

Between 1922 and 1928 the Court handed down thirteen judgments and sixteen advisory opinions, which are listed below:

JUDGMENTS

1. The S. S. Wimbledon. (August 17, 1923.)
2. The Mavrommatis concessions in Palestine (jurisdiction). (August 30, 1924.)
3 and 4. Treaty of Neuilly. (September 12, 1924 and March 26, 1925.)
5. The Mavrommatis concessions at Jerusalem (merits). (March 26, 1925.)
6. Certain German interests in Polish Upper Silesia (jurisdiction). (August 25, 1925.)
7. Certain German interests in Polish Upper Silesia (merits). (May 25, 1926.)
8. Claim for Indemnity in respect of the Factory at Chorzow (jurisdiction). (July 26, 1927.)
9. Case of the *Lotus*. (September 7, 1927.)
10. Case of the re-adaptation of the Mavrommatis Jerusalem concessions (jurisdiction). (October 10, 1927.)
11. Interpretation of Judgments Nos. 7 and 8. (December 16, 1927.)
12. Case relating to certain rights of minorities in Upper Silesia (minority schools). (April 26, 1928.)
13. Case concerning the Factory at Chorzow (Merits). (Sept. 13, 1928.)

[1] Cf. p. 160 n.
[2] Cf. p. 189.

ADVISORY OPINIONS

1. Nomination of the workers' delegate for the Netherlands at the third session of the International Labour Conference. (July 31, 1922.)
2. Competence of the International Labour Organization in regard to Agriculture. (August 12, 1922.)
3. Competence of the International Labour Organization in regard to agricultural production. (August 12, 1922.)
4. Nationality decrees in Tunis and Morocco. (February 7, 1923).
5. The status of Eastern Carelia. (July 23, 1923.)
6. German Settlers in Poland. (September 10, 1923.)
7. Acquisition of Polish Nationality. (September 15, 1923.)
8. Delimitation of the Polish and Czechoslovak frontiers (the Jaworzina question). (December 6, 1923.)
9. Question of the Monastery of Saint-Naoum. (September 4, 1923.)
10. The Exchange of Greek and Turkish Populations. (February 21, 1925.)
11. The Polish Postal Service at Danzig. (May 16, 1925.)
12. Interpretation of the Treaty of Lausanne (Mosul question). (November 21, 1925.)
13. Competence of the International Labour Organization to regulate incidentally the personal work of the employer. (July 23, 1926.)
14. Case relating to the jurisdiction of the European Commission of the Danube between Galatz and Braila. (December 8, 1927.)
15. Jurisdiction of the Courts of Danzig. (March 3, 1928.) [1]
16. Interpretation of the Greco-Turkish Agreement of December 1, 1926. (August 28, 1928.)

The expenses of the Court form a regular item in the League budget voted annually by the Assembly, contributions to which are made according to a fixed scale.[2]

The decisions of the Court are made by majority vote and are without appeal.[3] However, in case a party discovers a new fact,

---

[1] Cf. *Fourth Annual Report of the Permanent Court of International Justice.* Series E. No. 4, p. 140.
The Court has also issued an order defining interim measures to be followed by China pending the decision whether or not the Belgian treaty of November 2nd, 1865 had been validly terminated. Cf. *Collection of Judgments,* Series A, No. 8. An Order of the Court seems to be similar to an injunction.

[2] Cf. p. 715.

[3] However, the proposed arbitration treaty between England and the United States of 1897 provided that certain cases decided in an original arbitration court might be taken to a court of appeal of five judges, two selected by each party and one by agreement of these four. Moore, *Digest,* Vol. VII, p. 76.

it may ask for a revision of judgment, provided it uses this right within six months after the discovery of the fact and within ten years after the judgment.[1] A judge cannot be removed from office except upon the unanimous opinion of the other members that he has ceased to fulfil the required conditions.[2]

One difficulty confronting any international tribunal arises out of the law to be applied. The Statute provides that the World Court shall apply (1) international conventions, whether general or particular, establishing rules expressly recognized by the contesting states; (2) international custom, as evidence of general practice accepted by law; (3) the general principles of law recognized by civilized nations; (4) judicial decisions and the teachings of the most highly qualified publicists of the various nations, as subsidiary means for the determination of the rules of law.[3]

6. THE UNITED STATES AND THE WORLD COURT

Although Mr. Elihu Root was a member of the Committee which drafted the World Court Statute, and although another American, Professor John Bassett Moore, was elected a judge in 1921, the United States has not as yet (July, 1929) adhered to the Protocol of Signature. In February, 1923, President Harding recommended to the Senate that the United States ratify this Protocol, subject to a number of conditions. President Coolidge repeated this recommendation in December, 1924. On January 27, 1926, the Senate finally passed a resolution in favor of adherence to the Court, subject to five reservations: (1) that such adherence does not involve any legal relation of the United States to the League of Nations, (2) that the United States may participate with members of the Council and Assembly of the League in the election of judges, (3) that the United States will pay a fair share of the Court's expenses, (4) that the United States may at any time withdraw its adherence to the Protocol, and that the Statute of the Court shall not be amended without the consent of the United States, (5) "That the Court shall not render any advisory opinion except publicly after due notice to all states adhering to the Court and to all interested states and after public

At the ninth Assembly it was proposed that an appeal might be taken from an arbitral award, in case the arbitrators are not unanimous, to the World Court. *Journal*, p. 91.

[1] Arts. 55, 60–61, Statute. [2] Art. 18, Statute. [3] Art. 38, Statute.

hearing or opportunity for hearing given to any state concerned; nor shall it, without the consent of the United States, entertain any request for an advisory opinion touching any dispute or question in which the United States has or claims an interest."

The State Department now wrote 44 notes asking the states which had already accepted the Court Statute if they would accept these reservations. These states decided to hold a conference in regard to the subject in Geneva, and invited the United States to attend. The United States declined on the ground that the reservations were "plain and unequivocal." The conference met in Geneva in September, 1926, and accepted the first four reservations and the first half of the fifth.[1]

In regard to the last reservation concerning advisory opinions, the conference made a distinction between advisory opinions in the case of a dispute to which the United States is a party and of a dispute to which the United States is not a party but claims an interest. As far as the first type of opinion was concerned, the World Court had already decided in the Eastern Carelia case [2] that it would not take jurisdiction without the consent of both parties to the dispute. As far as the second type of opinion was concerned, it was declared:

> The Conference understands the object of the United States to be to assure to itself a position of equality with states represented either on the Council or in the Assembly of the League of Nations. This principle should be agreed to. But the fifth reservation appears to rest upon the presumption that the adoption of a request for an advisory opinion by the Council or Assembly requires a unanimous vote. No such presumption has, however, so far been established. It is therefore impossible to say with certainty whether in some cases, or possibly in all cases, a decision by a majority is not sufficient. In any event the United States should be guaranteed a position of equality in this respect; that is to say, in any case where a state represented on the Council or in the Assembly would possess the right of preventing, by opposition in either of these bodies, the adoption of a proposal to request an advisory opinion from the Court, the United States shall enjoy an equivalent right. . . .[3]

---

[1] In July, 1926, the Court revised its rules (Arts. 73, 74) so as to conform with the wishes of the first half of the fifth reservation of the United States.
[2] Cf. pp. 189, 229.
[3] For the text of the Final Act and other relevant documents, cf. M. O. Hudson, *The World Court, 1922–1928*, World Peace Foundation.

The United States remained silent for three years. Finally the 1928 Assembly adopted a resolution recommending that the Council study the question whether requests for advisory opinions required unanimity or merely a majority; it also asked that since a new election for World Court judges would be held in 1930, a group of jurists reëxamine the Statute of the Court in order to recommend possible amendments. Finally the Assembly elected as successor to Professor Moore, who had resigned from the Court, Mr. Charles Evans Hughes. The Council now appointed this committee of jurists, and asked Mr. Elihu Root to serve—an invitation which was accepted. The situation was aided by a note from Secretary Kellogg of February 19, 1929, addressed to the Secretary-General of the League, stating that the United States "desires to avoid in so far as may be possible any proposal which would interfere with or embarrass the work of the Council of the League." But there were some elements of uncertainty in the suggestions made by the Geneva Conference which seemed to require further discussion; these proposals did not give "adequate protection to the United States." [1]

The Committee of Jurists convened on March 4, and adopted with certain amendments a formula presented by Mr. Root to meet the American position in regard to advisory opinions. According to this formula, the Secretary-General of the League shall inform the United States of any proposal for obtaining an advisory opinion; thereupon, if desired, an exchange of views as to whether an interest of the United States is affected shall proceed with all convenient speed between the Council or Assembly of the League and the United States. Whenever a request for an advisory opinion comes to the Court, the registrar shall notify the United States, among other states, giving a reasonable time-limit within which a written statement by the United States concerning the request will be received. If for any reason no sufficient opportunity for an exchange of views upon such request should have been afforded and the United States advises the Court that the question affects the interests of the United States, proceedings shall be stayed for a period sufficient to enable such an exchange of views between the Council or the Assembly and the United States to take place. If after this exchange of views, no agreement is reached

[1] *O. J.*, April, 1929, p. 779.

and the United States is not prepared to forego its objection, the withdrawal of the United States from the Court will follow "without any imputation of unfriendliness or unwillingness to coöperate generally for peace and goodwill." [1]

7. THE SETTLEMENT OF "NON-LEGAL" DISPUTES

In regard to many international disputes over important political questions, there is no international law to be applied. Consequently before the War, at least, no great power was willing to submit these so-called "non-legal" disputes to arbitration. Sometimes these disputes were said to involve "national honor," "independence," or "vital interests." [2] Whatever the terminology, no state was inclined to grant a tribunal, which it did not control, the power to decide such controversies; albeit most of the wars of history have arisen out of these non-legal disputes, out of conflicts of national policy which international law does not control. Nevertheless, while the submission of such disputes to a judicial tribunal appears impossible until international legislation covering these questions is developed, some nations have found it possible to submit non-political disputes to the investigation of an impartial body to find out the exact facts, and even in some cases to make a recommendation as to a settlement.

In the convention for the Pacific Settlement of International Disputes of 1899 (amended in 1907), it was provided that International Commissions of Inquiry might be established to investigate international differences involving "neither honor nor essential interests, and arising from differences of opinion on points of fact." [3] The attempt to make the establishment of these fact-finding commissions obligatory was defeated primarily because of the opposition of the little state of Roumania. While the convention sanctioned the principle of impartial investigation, it was defective, not only because these commissions were established

[1] Report of the Committee of Jurists, C. 142. M. 52. 1929. V. The American government has not as yet (July, 1929) acted upon this formula.
[2] Cf. H. Lammasch, "Über die Begrenzung der internationalen Schiedsgerichtsbarkeit," *Recueil des rapports*, cited, p. 294; J. Westlake, "International Arbitration," 7 *International Journal of Ethics* (1896), p. 1.
[3] Cf. Part III, Convention of October 18, 1907, cited. Part I contains provisions in regard to good offices and mediation.

only with the consent of both parties and after the breakdown of diplomacy, but also because they could make no recommendation as to settlement. Moreover, the parties to a dispute were under no obligation not to go to war while the investigation was being made. Resort to such commissions has been had only three times.[1]

The Bryan Peace Commission Treaties.—Just before the World War the United States carried this idea further, in the so-called Bryan Peace Commission treaties, which embodied four principles: (1) The principle of investigation applies to *all* disputes not settled by diplomacy or arbitration, whether they involve national honor or not. (2) These disputes are to be investigated by a *permanent* commission of five members, the majority of which is neutral.[2] While in most of these treaties, the commission may investigate a dispute only at the request of one of the parties, in some treaties, such as that with Honduras, the commission may "act upon its own initiative." [3] (3) Each party retains the right of independent action at the close of the investigation—it is under no obligation to accept the recommendation of the commission. (4) During the course of the investigation, which must be concluded within a year, the parties promise not to go to war.[4]

Altogether thirty Peace Commission treaties were signed; twenty-nine were consented to by the Senate; and twenty-one were actually proclaimed. Nine of the treaties in effect are with European powers; eleven with Latin-American countries, and one with China. None was entered into with Japan apparently because of the dispute over the California land laws. Although the United States has appointed commissioners to 18 of the com-

[1] The Doggerbank case between Great Britain and Russia of 1906; a shipping dispute between France and Italy of 1912—here apparently the commission never met; the case of the Tubantia in 1917.

[2] Each party names one national and one non-national; the two governments agree upon a fifth neutral member. Treaty of Sept. 15, 1924, British Empire and United States, Art. II, *Treaties of U. S.*, Vol. III, p. 2642.

[3] Treaty of November 3, 1913, Art. III, *ibid.*, p. 2691.

[4] In some of the treaties, an attempt was made to provide that the powers should not increase their military or naval programmes, pending the investigation of the commission, unless danger from a third power should compel such an increase, whereupon the other party to the dispute would be released from its obligation. This provision, however, was rejected by some of the powers and by the Senate of the United States. Cf. J. B. Scott, *Treaties for the Advancement of Peace* (1920), p. xliii.

SETTLEMENT OF "NON-LEGAL" DISPUTES

missions thus authorized, no case has yet arisen demanding investigation.[1]

If the procedure adopted in these treaties for the advancement of peace is universally followed, wars caused by hot-headedness and unfounded suspicions would cease to arise. The great advantage which these treaties possess is that they provide for the investigation of every dispute, not settled by diplomacy or arbitration; and they afford a "cooling-off" period during which a commission may try to find an impartial solution of the difficulty, which, however, either party may reject.[2] Thus the Bryan treaties constituted a step in advance over the Hague conventions just as the League of Nations procedure, shortly to be discussed, constitutes a further development toward the pacific settlement of all international controversies.

Although the Bryan treaties were limited to disputes between the United States and another power, the principle has been applied to international treaties—and apart from the League. In a treaty of May 25, 1915, Argentina, Brazil and Chile undertook to submit controversies arising between them to the investigation and report of a commission, containing a representative of each state.[3] At the Central American Conference at Washington of 1922–1923, the United States and the five republics of Central America signed a treaty applying the principle of investigation and report to disputes between the Central American Republics or between any such republic and the United States. But for some mysterious reason, investigation is limited to disputes which arise out of differences of opinion as to the failure to comply with treaties and which "affect neither the sovereign and independent existence of any of the Signatory Republics, nor their honor or vital interests." Each of the six states shall nominate five of its nationals to form a permanent list of commissioners. When the need for a commission arises, each government may name one of its nationals on this list. The commissioners thus chosen select as chairman a person on the list appointed by a government not interested in the dispute. The commissioners must report within

---

[1] For the Commissioners, cf. *U. S. Daily*, June 2, 1928.
[2] Wicksell, "Einige Bermerekungen über den ständigen internationalen Untersuchungs und Vermittlungsrat," *Recueil*, cited, p. 351.
[3] Text in Scott, cited, p. 146.

three months, and, at the request of either party, they may fix the status in which the parties must remain pending the report. However, the parties are under no obligation to accept the report or to refrain from war after it is made.[1]

At the fifth Pan-American Congress, held at Santiago in March–May, 1923, a continental treaty was signed extending the Bryan principle to the American Republics. As originally drafted, the treaty provided for commissions of inquiry, and also for the settlement of a dispute by arbitration in case the report of the commission was not acceptable, and in case the dispute did not involve the sovereignty, honor, vital interests or constitutional provisions of the parties, or the interests of a third party.[2] But the arbitration clause was too strong for some of the states, and the final treaty provides that all controversies between American states not settled by diplomacy or arbitration, shall be submitted to a Commission of Inquiry which shall report within one year. During this time the parties cannot concentrate troops on the frontier or engage in hostile acts. After the report is made, another six months is available for negotiations; at the end of the eighteen months' period, each party recovers its entire liberty of action.[3] Two permanent bodies are constituted—one in Washington and the other in Montevideo—for the purpose of receiving requests for the convocation of the Commissions of Inquiry, which they shall notify to the other party. These two bodies are composed of the three American diplomatic agents longest accredited at these capitals.

The Commission of Inquiry is composed of five members, all nationals of American states, two being appointed by each of the governments involved in a controversy; only one of whom, however, may be a national of the appointing power. The four members thus chosen select by common agreement a president who shall likewise be a neutral party.

[1] XIII, Convention for the Establishment of International Commissions of Inquiry, February 7, 1923, *Conference on Central American Affairs*, p. 392.

[2] *Report of the Delegates of the U. S. to the 5th International Conference*, 1923, cited, p. 22. This treaty is called the Gondra Convention.

[3] Tratado para evitar o prevenir conflictos entre los estados americanos, May 3, 1923. *Quinta Conferencia internacional Americana* (1923), p. 1. However, in disputes arising between nations having no general arbitration treaties, the investigation shall not take place in issues affecting constitutional questions or those already settled by other treaties.

SETTLEMENT OF "NON-LEGAL" DISPUTES

Unlike the Bryan treaties, the 1923 Pan-American treaty did not provide for a permanent Commission, but merely for ad hoc bodies [1] which were convened only after one party made a request, via the diplomatic committee at Washington or Montevideo, upon the other party. If one party failed to name its commissioners the procedure broke down. At the 1929 American Arbitration Conference this defect was remedied by a new agreement which stated that the Diplomatic Committees in Washington and in Montevideo are "bound to exercise conciliatory functions either on their own motion when it appears that there is a prospect of disturbance of peaceful relations, or at the request of a party to the dispute" until the ad hoc commission is established. [2]

By means of these different commissions, some of which may only investigate the facts, but others of which may recommend a solution, non-legal disputes have been submitted to an international forum. [3] By the two means of arbitration and of compulsory

[1] Since this treaty provides for the investigation of *all* disputes not otherwise settled, and since it was signed by the five Central American Republics, it would supposedly supersede the convention of 1923. But this is apparently not the case, because Article VIII of the Pan-American treaty provides that the present treaty shall not abrogate any similar treaties which exist or which may exist between one or more of the High Contracting Parties, although they contain particular circumstances or conditions which differ from those stipulated in this treaty. This provision would apparently, therefore, exempt the Central American Republics from the compulsory investigation of all disputes, although such an obligation has been imposed on the other American states.

[2] Cf. p. 252.

[3] Other international commissions have also been established having semi-judicial or semi-administrative power. An International Joint Commission of six members, three appointed by the President of the United States and three by the British Crown on recommendation of the Canadian government, has jurisdiction over cases involving the use of boundary waters between the United States and Canada, and any other questions involving interests along the common frontier. Decision is by majority. Treaty of Jan. 11, 1909, *Treaties of U. S.*, Vol. III, p. 2611.

In 1859 a boundary commission was established by the United States and Mexico also to settle differences arising out of the boundary. If both commissioners agree, decision is binding on the two governments, unless one of them disapproves it within one month. Treaty of March 1, 1899, *Treaties of U. S.*, Vol. I, p. 1167. In a speech at Montreal in 1923, Secretary Hughes suggested the appointment of another Canadian-American commission to investigate so-called "domestic questions," which nevertheless affected both countries. In June, 1923, the American-Japanese Relations Committee of Tokyo also recommended the appointment of a Joint High Commission to investigate and recommend a solution of the Japanese question in America.

investigation, the world, before the outbreak of the World War in 1914, had planted the seeds for the pacific settlement of international controversies. There was no obligation, however, to arbitrate even legal questions. Among the twenty odd nations which accepted the Bryan treaties, there was no obligation to accept the recommendation of the investigating committee. At the same time, these nations, so far as their disputes with the United States were concerned, were obliged not to go to war until after the report of this committee had been made. Nevertheless, despite the establishment of the Permanent Court of Arbitration and despite the Bryan treaties, neither the principle of compulsory arbitration nor even of compulsory investigation had been accepted by the great powers before the War. When the Serajevo murder took place in 1914, neither Austria nor Serbia was under any obligation to submit the dispute to impartial investigation. We shall now see how these ideas concerning the pacific settlement of international disputes have developed under the aegis of the League of Nations.

8. "NON-LEGAL" DISPUTES AND THE LEAGUE COVENANT

According to the preamble of the Covenant, the express purpose of the League of Nations is "to promote international coöperation and to achieve international peace and security by the acceptance of obligations not to resort to war." This purpose was carried out, as far as the adjudication of purely legal disputes is concerned, by the establishment of the Permanent Court of International Justice. While the framers of the Covenant realized that in the present stage of international relations, the powers would not agree to submit "non-legal" [1] disputes to such a court, they nevertheless did provide that such disputes should be submitted to the mediation or the investigation of the political branches of the League—the Council or Assembly—during which time war could not be declared. In most of the Bryan treaties, the Commission could investigate a dispute only at the request of a party to the dispute. Under Article XI of the Covenant, however,

[1] "Only in lay circles is the opinion held that it would be possible to-day to submit all international disputes to one and the same court of arbitration." Schücking and Wehberg, *Satzung des Volkerbundes*, p. 580.

Any war or threat of war, whether immediately affecting any of the Members of the League or not, is hereby declared a matter of concern to the whole League, and the League shall take any action that may be deemed wise and effectual to safeguard the peace of nations. In case any such emergency should arise the Secretary-General shall, on the request of any Member of the League, forthwith summon a meeting of the Council.

It is also declared to be the friendly right of each Member of the League to bring to the attention of the Assembly or of the Council any circumstance whatever affecting international relations which threatens to disturb international peace or the good understanding between nations upon which peace depends.

This article does not authorize the Assembly or the Council to impose a solution upon either party to a dispute.[1] But it does legalize the intervention or the mediation of the League in any dispute which threatens peace. It also authorizes the League to call attention to domestic practices which may result in war. In case the parties should decline to submit a dispute to the Assembly or Council as provided in Article XV, any member of the League may, under Article XI, place such dispute before either body. By virtue of Article XI, Great Britain referred the dispute between Sweden and Finland over the Aaland islands to the Council of the League.[2] The Allied powers acting jointly through the Supreme Council of the Conference of Ambassadors also utilized this Article to refer several disputes arising out of the peace treaties, such as the dispute over Upper Silesia and Memel, to the Council.[3]

While Article XI authorizes any member of the League to invoke the good offices of the League to stop a war, Article XV defines, in more precise terms, the duties of members who become involved in a dispute.

If there should arise between Members of the League any dispute likely to lead to a rupture, which is not submitted to arbitration in accordance with Article 13, the Members of the League agree that they will submit the matter to the Council.

It appears that this provision would prevent one member from

[1] Cf. Report of the First Committee, Fifth Assembly, on the Protocol.
[2] Cf. p. 49.
[3] Cf. pp. 41, 132.

breaking off diplomatic relations with, or dispatching an ultimatum to, another member without first invoking the procedure of Article XV.[1] While the consent of both parties is necessary to refer a dispute to arbitration under Article XIII, one party to the dispute may place it before the Council of the League, even without the consent of the other,—a feature in the procedure for the pacific settlement of disputes which is unique. The Council is not obliged to inquire whether or not a dispute is really "likely to lead to a rupture." It takes account of the gravity of the dispute only in choosing the method to effect a settlement. No reservations in regard to "national honor" or "vital interests" can be pleaded as a bar to the proceedings before the Council.[2]

The Council and the Conference of Ambassadors.—However, if a dispute has already been submitted by the parties to arbitration or some other means of settlement, the Council apparently must postpone action as long as the dispute is thus being considered. This situation arose in connection with the so-called Corfu affair. In August, 1923, the Italian members of the boundary commission, sent by the Conference of Ambassadors to delimit the frontier between Albania and Greece, were killed by unknown persons in Greece a few miles from the Albanian frontier. The Conference of Ambassadors immediately began to investigate the case, since it was the body established to carry out these provisions in a peace treaty which both Greece and Italy had signed. During the course of the investigation, the Italian government occupied Corfu in reprisal for the murder, action which led Greece to appeal to the Council of the League under Articles XII and XV of the Covenant. The Italian member of this body, however, claimed that the Council could not deal with the question as long as it was before the Conference of Ambassadors.[3] Meanwhile, the Conference sent a communication to the League Council, informing it as to the progress of its deliberations,[4] while the Council

---

[1] Schücking and Wehberg, p. 507.

[2] Advisory Opinion No. 4, Feb. 7, 1923, Permanent Court of International Justice. Report of the Committee of Jurists, Corfu affair, O. J., April, 1924, p. 525; Visscher, "L'Interpretation du Pacte au lendemain du différend Italo-Grec," R. D. I. L. C., 1924, No. 3. Cf. also K. Strupp, "L'incident de Janina entre la Grèce et l'Italie," R. G. D. I. P., May–August, 1924.

[3] O. J., Nov., 1923, pp. 1278, 1287.

[4] Ibid., p. 1294.

communicated to the Conference suggestions for a settlement, which to a certain extent were adopted by the Conference and accepted by Greece and Italy.[1]

The question whether the Council was bound to submit to the jurisdiction of the Conference of Ambassadors in a dispute voluntarily referred to the latter body by the parties was referred to a Committee of Jurists and answered as follows:

> Where, contrary to the terms of Article 15, paragraph 1, a dispute is submitted to the Council on the application of one of the parties, where such a dispute already forms the subject of arbitration or of judicial proceedings, the Council must refuse to consider the application.
>
> If the matter in dispute, by an agreement between the parties, has already been submitted to other jurisdiction before which it is being regularly proceeded with, or is being dealt with in the said manner in another channel, it is in conformity with the general principles of law that it should be possible for a reference back to such jurisdiction to be asked for and ordered.[2]

---

[1] *Ibid.*, p. 1305. In this settlement Italy agreed to evacuate Corfu, while Greece agreed to make formal apologies and to pay Italy the sum of 50 million lire. The original settlement of September 7 had merely provided that the Greek government should deposit with the Swiss National Bank the sum, "to be paid over, in whole or in part, to the Italian Government, upon the decision of the Permanent Court of International Justice at The Hague—" a body which should determine the amount of the indemnity. However, following the investigation of the crime, the Conference changed this provision, and required Greece to pay over to Italy the entire sum, without asking the decision of the Court as to what size the indemnity should actually be. Cf. Lowell and Hudson, *The Corfu Crisis* (World Peace Foundation Pamphlets, Vol. VI, No. 3, 1923). This decision was criticized on the ground that the payment was a bribe to secure the withdrawal of Italy from Corfu. Whatever the legal relation of the Conference to the Council may be, the incident shows that the affairs of small countries will fare better at the hands of the Council on which they may be represented than of the Conference of Ambassadors, representing only the four Allied powers.

[2] The question asked the Jurists was as follows: "Is the Council, when seized of a dispute in accordance with Article 15, paragraph 1, of the Covenant, at the instance of a Member of the League of Nations, bound, either at the request of a party or on its own authority, to suspend its inquiry into the dispute when, with the consent of the parties, the settlement of the dispute is being sought through some other channel?" *O. J.*, April, 1924, p. 525. Cf. Visscher's Article, cited.

A similar ruling was made by the Council in the "Salamis" case. This was a dispute between Greece and Germany over the liability of the Greek government to complete contracts made in 1914 for the construction of certain warships in Germany. The question was pending before the Greco-German Mixed Arbitral Tribunal. And the Council adopted the report of a Committee of

In other words, the same principle applies here as in the case where two parties agree to refer a controversy to an arbitration tribunal. The Council cannot intervene without the consent of both parties until the findings of this body have been made.

When one party to a dispute notifies the Secretary-General of its wish to submit it to the Council, he must convene the Council in an emergency session. Following the Serajevo murder of 1914, Lord Grey attempted frantically to call a conference of the interested powers. At that time, however, there was no obligation to submit such a dispute to a conference and no machinery to make the necessary preparations for such a meeting. In the opinion of many students and statesmen, if such obligations and such machinery had existed, the World War would have never occurred. By establishing a Secretariat and imposing the obligation to submit such disputes to investigation, the Covenant has remedied two vital defects in the old international régime.

When a dispute is placed before the Council for investigation it may do one of four things, (1) keep it in its own hands, (2) submit it, if of a legal nature, to the World Court for an advisory opinion, (3) refer it to "commissions of conciliation," later described, (4) refer it to the Assembly.[1] If the Council finds it impossible to effect a reconciliation between the parties, it is obliged to publish a report containing a statement of the facts and making such recommendations as "are deemed just and proper." This report must be made within six months after the submission of the dispute. Any member of the Council may also make a statement, including the parties to the dispute. If the report is not unanimous (except for the parties to the dispute) "The Members of the League reserve to themselves the right to take such action as they

---

Jurists part of which declared: "as a general principle and in the absence of some special attribution of competence, the Council should not intervene in a question pending before another international organ such as a Mixed Arbitral Tribunal when (a) the request for the Council's intervention is made by only one of the parties, and (b) the case is being dealt with by that international organ with the consent of both parties and is regarded by it as within its competence. If this rule were not followed as a general principle, the position of all international tribunals would be prejudiced and an intolerable burden would be imposed on the Council of the League of Nations. . . ." *O. J.*, Feb. 1928, p. 179.

[1] Cf. "Covenant of the League of Nations with a Commentary Thereon," Cmd. 151, 1919, p. 16.

shall consider necessary for the maintenance of right and justice."
In no case, however, may a member resort to war until three
months after the report.[1] On the other hand, if the report is unanimous (except for the parties) and is accepted by one party to the
dispute, the other party—while it is not obliged to accept the terms
of the report—agrees that it will not go to war. The procedure
laid down in the League Covenant is therefore a development of
the ideas formulated before the war—the idea of arbitration and
compulsory investigation. But the Covenant goes much further
than any previous international agreement in that members of
the League agree to *submit all* disputes either to arbitration or
investigation, and—unlike the Bryan treaties where each party
eventually recovered its freedom of action—not to go to war in
case of a unanimous report of the Council.

"**Domestic Questions.**"—There is only one type of question in
regard to which the Council can make no recommendation—
"domestic questions." If a dispute is claimed by one of the parties
and is found by the Council to arise out of a matter "which by
international law is solely within the domestic jurisdiction of
that party," the Council shall so report. Thereupon each party
retains its freedom of action, subject only to Article XI.[2] Such
questions as immigration, the status of minorities, especially of
aliens, tariffs, the internal production of liquor and opium, and
armaments, have, in the absence of treaties, been generally regarded as "domestic." In 1923 the World Court declared, "the
words 'solely within the domestic jurisdiction' seem rather to
contemplate certain matters which, though they may very closely
concern the interests of more than one state, are not, in principle,
regulated by international law. As regards such matters, each
state is the sole judge. The question whether a certain matter is
or is not solely within the jurisdiction of a state is an essentially
relative question; it depends upon the development of international
relations." [3] In other words, a domestic question, such as the
size of armaments or the status of minorities, may be converted
into an international question, over which the League may take

[1] Article XIII, Covenant.
[2] Cf. p. 628.
[3] Tunis-Morocco Nationality Decrees, Advisory Opinions, Series B, No. 4,
Feb. 7, 1923, p. 23.

jurisdiction, by the signature of a treaty in which the parties freely undertake certain obligations in regard to these subjects. Nevertheless, as long as a subject is "domestic," i. e., as long as no international customs or treaties apply to it, the Council cannot proceed, in its semi-judicial capacity, to make a recommendation. On the other hand, either the Council or the Assembly, may "discuss" such questions if they threaten the peace of the world.[1]

If each state could interpret for itself what constitutes a "domestic question" it would tend to use this provision as a pretext to withdraw from arbitration a dispute which it believed it might lose. In a similar way, the doctrine of "national honor" had been abused before the War. Under the Covenant, this practice has been made impossible by empowering the Council to decide whether or not a dispute involves a domestic question. Since the determination of this question is properly a judicial task, the practice of the Council has been to request the World Court for an advisory opinion upon such a subject.[2]

Within fourteen days after the submission of a dispute to the Council, either party may request it to be referred to the Assembly, while the Council on its own motion may so refer it. In investigating a dispute the Assembly has the same powers as the Council, except that a report made by the Assembly, to be binding to the same extent as a unanimous Council report, must be approved by the Representatives of those members of the League represented on the Council and a majority of the other members of the League, exclusive of the parties to the dispute. While the Assem-

[1] Cf. p. 628.
[2] In the Aaland island case, this question was referred to a special committee of jurists, since the World Court had not as yet been established. The following reservation received 49 yeas to 35 nays in the United States Senate, "The United States reserves to itself exclusively the right to decide what questions are within its domestic jurisdiction and declares that all domestic and political questions relating wholly or in part to its internal affairs, including immigration, labor, coastwise traffic, the tariff, commerce, the suppression of traffic in women and children and in opium and other dangerous drugs, and all other domestic questions, are solely within the jurisdiction of the United States and are not under this treaty to be submitted in any way either to arbitration or to the consideration of the Council or of the Assembly of the League of Nations, or any agency thereof, or to the decision or recommendation of any other Power," March 19, 1920, 59 *Cong. Record*, 4599. As this resolution failed to receive the two-thirds majority and as the Treaty of Versailles was not ratified, it is of value only in showing American opinion at that time toward so-called "domestic questions."

bly has discussed a number of disputes placed before it under Article XI, it does not appear that any party to a dispute has invoked this provision to transfer a dispute from the Council to the Assembly.

At the suggestion of the German government, the 1928 League Assembly adopted a model treaty "to strengthen the means of preventing war." The purpose of this treaty is to facilitate the task of the Council under Article XI and other provisions of the Covenant. Those states which undertake to accept this treaty promise in the event of a dispute being brought to the Council, to accept provisional recommendations by the Council. If the Council recommends that forces be withdrawn from certain territories or demilitarized zones they agree to carry such recommendations into effect. These provisions are modelled after similar provisions in the Locarno security agreement.[1] It is not proposed to make an international convention, but merely to encourage regional agreements to this effect. The League has also taken steps to facilitate telegraphic communications with Geneva.

Non-Members.—While the League aims to embrace every nation in the world, a number of powerful states still remain aloof from its membership who may come in conflict with members of the League. In order to extend the League arbitral procedure to non-members, Article XVII of the Covenant provides that when a dispute breaks out between a member and a non-member, the latter shall be invited to accept the obligations of membership for the purposes of the dispute. If the non-member refuses to accept such obligations and if it resorts to war against a member, the provisions of Article XVI in regard to sanctions become applicable. Thus Finland and Lithuania were invited, while non-members of the League, to submit their disputes to the Council. On the other hand, a non-member is not entitled to invoke this article or Article XI on its own authority. When Hungary, while a non-member of the League, appealed to the Secretariat to convene a Council meeting because of the threatening attitude of the Little Entente, the Secretariat replied that it was powerless to convene such a meeting without the request of a member of the League.[2]

[1] Cf. p. 635. For the model treaty to strengthen the means of preventing war. See "Committee on Arbitration and Security," A. 20. 1928. IX.
[2] *O. J.*, Dec., 1921, p. 1218; Feb. 1922, p. 130 ff.

In 1922 the Esthonian government invited the Soviet government of Russia to submit a dispute with Finland over Eastern Carelia,[1] to the Council on the basis of Article XVII. Although the Soviet government declined to accept this request, the Council, in April, 1923, asked the World Court for an advisory opinion on whether or not the provisions of the Dorpat treaty between Finland and Russia constituted obligations of an international character; but, as we have seen, the Court declined to render an opinion.[2] This "opinion" was noted by the Council which, however, declared that it could not exclude the possibility of further action by the Council in the case of a non-member state, if circumstances make such action "necessary to enable the Council to fulfill its functions under the Covenant in the interests of peace."[3] Following the ultimatum dispatched by the British to the Egyptian government as a result of the Stack murder in the fall of 1924, the Egyptian parliament sent an appeal to the Secretariat asking the League of Nations to intervene. But as Egypt was not a member of the League, and the appeal was made by a parliament instead of by a government, no action was taken in regard to it.

Article XVII will become unimportant when Russia, Turkey and the United States enter the League. Until then, however, great difficulties may arise in case of disputes between member and non-member states. Especially in view of its historic opposition to compulsory arbitration, the United States is not likely to submit any of its disputes to the League in accordance with Article XVII. While the members of the League would be under no obligation to use force against the United States until the latter declared war, the refusal of America and other non-members to use the arbitral procedure of the League might create a gulf which would be dangerous to the existence of the League and to the peace of the world.

Disputes over the Monroe Doctrine.—Article XXI of the Covenant states,

> Nothing in this Covenant shall be deemed to affect the validity of international engagements, such as treaties of arbitration or regional understandings like the Monroe doctrine, for securing the maintenance of peace.

[1] Cf. the memorandum of the Secretariat, *O. J.*, March, 1923, p. 343.
[2] *Advisory Opinion*, No. 5, July 23, 1923, pp. 27–29.
[3] *O. J.*, 1923, p. 1336.

In view of the special mention of the Monroe Doctrine in this article, it has been contended that the League has no jurisdiction over disputes on the American continent. In the dispute between Bolivia and Chile over the treaty of 1904, Chile sent a communication to the League as follows:

"A second consideration of a legal nature shows also, beyond any manner of doubt, that it is not within the competence of the Assembly to deal with Bolivia's claim. This claim concerns an *exclusively* American affair.

"The use, however, of the expression 'regional understandings, like the Monroe Doctrine,' in Article 21 of the Covenant, amounts to a formal recognition of the principle of American International Law, according to which the non-American States, and consequently the Assembly, cannot interfere in questions exclusively affecting countries of the New World." [1]

Before 1928, the League avoided the settlement of inter-American disputes. Although in 1920 Peru placed a dispute with Chile over Tacna-Arica before the Assembly, it was withdrawn and submitted to the arbitration of the President of the United States.[2] While a dispute between Panama and Costa Rica in 1921 was being considered by the League Council, the United States offered its good offices to these parties, which were accepted. In a telegram from the League Secretary-General, it was stated that the President of the League Council was glad to learn that the parties had accepted the mediation of the United States, and trusted that "final arrangements between the two Members of the League will be successfully reached in accordance with the spirit of the Covenant." [3]

These instances strengthened the belief that because of Article XXI League members in the western hemisphere could not place disputes with each other before the Permanent Court or the League Council. The belief had also been expressed that because of Article XXI Latin-American states could not appeal to the League

[1] *Bolivia's Claim against Chile for the revision of the Treaty of Peace of 1904*, A. 33, 1921, p. 3. In its reply, Bolivia declared the claim "specious," because members had recognized the universal competence of the League in international disputes, and because the Monroe Doctrine had hitherto never been employed to prevent the arbitration of South American disputes by European arbitrators. Cf. A. 73, 1921, VII, p. 4; also J. Carrasco, *La Bolivie devant la Société des Nations* (1921), pp. 178 ff.

[2] Cf. p. 38.

[3] *O. J.*, March, 1921, p. 218.

in case the United States should make threatening demands upon them.[1]

Apparently having these fears in mind, Costa Rica who had withdrawn from the League in 1926 informed the League Council in July, 1928, that she would return to the League, provided the Council gave its interpretation of Article XXI.[2] In reply the Council stated that it could not define the "regional understandings" mentioned in Article XXI; this was a task only for the parties to such understandings. Nevertheless Article XXI "neither weakens nor limits any of the safeguards provided in the Covenant." The Covenant confers upon "all the members of the League equal obligations and equal rights . . ."[3] Apparently this interpretation means that the Latin-American members of the League may invoke the aid of Geneva or the Hague in case of a dispute with each other, or even with the United States.

In December, 1928, a dispute between Bolivia and Paraguay broke out, when the Council was meeting in Lugano and when a Pan-American Arbitration Conference was meeting in Washington.[4] Upon the receipt of the news to this effect, the President of the Council immediately (December 11) sent a telegram to both governments saying that the Council "does not doubt that the two States, which by signing the Covenant have solemnly pledged themselves to seek by pacific means the solution of disputes arising between them, will have recourse to such methods as would be in conformity with their international obligations and would appear, in the actual circumstances, to be the most likely to ensure, together with the maintenance of peace, the settlement of their dispute."[5] On the next day Paraguay replied stating that it had asked for the summoning of the Commission provided for in the Pan-American conciliation treaty of 1923.[6]

[1] Cf. R. L. Buell, "The Monroe Doctrine and the League," *New Republic*, November 21, 1928. "The Monroe Doctrine and Latin America," *I. S.* Vol. IV–No. 20.

[2] *O. J.*, October, 1928, p. 1607.

[3] Telegram of September 1, 1928, *O. J.*, cited, p. 1608.

[4] The Bolivia-Paraguay dispute involves the Chaco district which has been the subject of diplomatic correspondence for many years. "Averting a Latin American War." *News Bulletin*, F. P. A. December 14, 1928. "El litigio Paraguayo-Boliviano," *Revista Chileana*, January, 1928.

[5] "Dispute between Bolivia and Paraguay," C. 619. M. 195. 1928. VII, p. 3.

[6] Cf. p. 626.

At the same time Bolivia replied declaring that Paraguay had been the aggressor in the incident and that "it is impossible to accept anything so preposterous as that an aggressor State should not only commit the act of aggression but claim the intervention of a conciliation tribunal which is intended to prevent disputes and not to repair the effects afterwards. . . . It is impossible to consider such a procedure when forts are in ruins, when lives are being sacrificed and soldiers conducted as prisoners of war into the defences of the aggressor. What preventive or investigating tribunal can deal with an attack of this kind which compromises the sovereignty, honour and dignity of a country?" The conciliatory attitude which Bolivia had shown in the past had merely encouraged Paraguay to commit bellicose acts. On December 14, the Council decided to forward the telegrams of each party to the other. On the same day the Council received a second telegram from Bolivia stating that "Bolivia will not depart from the principles and obligations contained in the Covenant of the League." Nevertheless, Paraguay had violated Articles X and XIII of the Covenant and had committed an act of aggression; while Bolivia had no other alternative than to take measures of a "defensive" nature. Paraguay again telegraphed that she did not refuse conciliation procedure.

On December 15, the Council once more telegraphed Bolivia and Paraguay noting that both states were attached to the principles and obligations of the Covenant. The Council accordingly hoped "that the parties will carefully abstain from any act which might aggravate the situation. . . . " The President of the Council declared that he had been charged with following events, after the Council's adjournment. The Secretary-General was then authorized to communicate copies of the telegrams to the Ministers of the United States and Brazil at Berne and to the Ministers of Costa Rica, Ecuador and Mexico at Paris. Copies also went to members of the League.

On December 15, Bolivia telegraphed the League Council that "in conformity with its international obligations," it "hastened to inform the Council of the League" of a new attack by Paraguay. On the 16th, M. Briand sent another telegram from Lugano intimating that Bolivia should withdraw its troops from the boundary so as to prevent such clashes. On the 17th, Paraguay telegraphed a protest "against the unheard-of-distortion of the truth contained in the Bolivian Government's assertions. . . . " Paraguay demanded an inquiry, but Bolivia "rejects any enquiry as if she feared it. This alone shows on what side is the truth and reveals the aggressor." Paraguay stated that it had just accepted the good offices of the Pan-American Arbitration Conference.

The Council meeting now adjourned and M. Briand, its president, together with several members of the League Secretariat, journied to Paris. Bolivia having failed to agree to an investigation, M. Briand handed, on December 18, an aide-mémoire to the chargé d'affaires of Argentina and of the United States in Paris, in which he said that if the two governments did not " in some form or other accept" mediation, the Council could hardly avoid holding an extraordinary session. The Council had reason to believe that Argentina and the Pan-American Arbitration Conference were attempting to bring about a peaceful settlement. "The Council has not, however, received any official information from either of these parties." It thought it was essential that the efforts of all those engaged in securing a settlement "should be completely co-ordinated." The President of the Council therefore felt it would be of the greatest importance that Argentina and the United States "should inform him what measures" could be "the most advantageously taken by all who are working to bring about a pacific settlement of the dispute." On December 18th, Bolivia wired M. Briand that "in accordance with the nobly inspired suggestions of the Council" it had accepted the good offices of the Pan-American Arbitration Conference.[1] M. Briand telegraphed on the 19th, that the "Council, all of whose efforts were directed . . . toward . . . facilitating a peaceful settlement by any possible method," could not but be gratified at the cessation of the conflict, "and at the favourable reception given to the generous initiative of the Pan-American Arbitration Conference."

Commenting on this settlement, the Uruguay government telegraphed, "The Uruguayan Government is happy to possess this evidence of the Council's valuable action on behalf of peace which brings into prominence the exalted rôle of the League and the ad-

[1] The Arbitration Conference appointed a Commission of nine members to proceed to fix responsibility for the clash. Two members each were appointed by Bolivia and Paraguay; and five by the Conference. Cf. p. 252.

"NON-LEGAL" DISPUTES AND LEAGUE COVENANT 641

mirable spirit of co-operation and concord that animates the distinguished members of its Council, who have so definitely, and by such well-chosen means, upheld the prestige and illuminated the lofty aims of the League of Nations. . . . "

In reading these documents, one should remember that no state asked that the Bolivia-Paraguay dispute be placed before the Council. Nevertheless the Council took the initiative in firmly upholding the obligations of the Covenant; and it is evident from the record that its influence had weight. At no time did the Council ask that the dispute be settled in Geneva. It followed the principle which the League had previously upheld that the Council did not care what procedure of pacific settlement was followed so long as the dispute did not lead to war.[1]

The Bolivia-Paraguay dispute is the first instance of an approach to coöperation between the League Council and the United States in the settlement of a Latin-American dispute. It may have established a precedent which will be developed in the future.

The Council's Record.—More than twenty-five disputes were considered by the Assembly and Council during the first eight years.[2] When one considers that during the entire period of their existence only two disputes were referred to the Hague commissions and none to the Bryan commissions, the League record is rather remarkable. The great majority of these disputes have been handled by the Council because of its limited size and the consequent rapidity with which its members may be assembled. In most of these disputes, the Council did not go so far as to make a formal report, but merely attempted to effect a reconciliation. The mere consideration of some of these cases led the parties to settle the dispute "out of court." By means of this procedure, the Council settled amicably the dispute between Finland and Sweden over the Aaland islands, between Jugoslavia and Albania over a frontier, between Lithuania and the Allied powers over Memel, between Poland and Germany over Upper Silesia, between Turkey and England over the Mesopotamian frontier, and between Greece and Bulgaria.[3] It was also instrumental to some extent in settling the Corfu dispute between Italy and Greece. While it was unable

---

[1] For the recognition of regional understandings, cf. p. 253.
[2] Cf. the list in Schücking and Wehberg, pp. 469–501.
[3] Cf. p. 665. For the Bolivia-Paraguay dispute, cf. above.

to bring about a settlement between Poland and Lithuania over Vilna, it did prevent one government from declaring war on the other. On the other hand, a large number of disputes arising out of the peace treaties, such as the reparations question and the occupation of the Ruhr, were not submitted to the Council or the Assembly, on the theory that the Treaty of Versailles had established separate machinery for these disputes, such as the Reparations Commission and the Conference of Ambassadors. Sometimes, when this machinery broke down, the League, upon invitation, took over such disputes, as in the case of Upper Silesia and Memel, and effected a settlement. Moreover, disputes involving Russia and Turkey could not be brought before the Council or Assembly as long as they remained in a technical state of war.

Some of the recommendations of the Council have been attacked on the ground that they unfairly favored the cause of the former Allied powers.[1] Some basis for this belief existed in the case between Hungary and Roumania over the Optant question.[2] Even if one should admit that these charges are true, it would not follow that a court could have effected more "just" settlements. The disputes arising out of the reconstruction of Europe following the War have been, for the most part, non-legal disputes—in which considerations of policy and law are intertwined. They have been "political questions" over which, in the United States, the Supreme Court has consistently declined to assume jurisdiction. If the Paris Peace Conference had provided for the submission of these disputes to a single court composed of irremovable judges deciding by a majority vote, such a tribunal would have been a "judicial oligarchy," which would probably not have survived a single European boundary dispute.

While from the standpoint of juridical precision and abstract justice, the mediatory functions of the Council and the Assembly may be defective, it is just this flexibility which has enabled these bodies to hear non-legal disputes without antagonizing disputants to the extent that they would refrain from all pacific forms of procedure. When international law has reached the present stage of municipal law, the semi-judicial functions of the Council and Assembly will probably be transferred to a system of purely judi-

[1] Cf. F. Kellor, *Security against War* (1924), Vol. I.
[2] Cf. p. 193.

cial courts. Before this transfer is effected, however, a great body of international law must be developed which will give the courts a basis upon which to proceed.

9. CONCILIATION COMMISSIONS

Moreover, the mediatory functions of the Council and Assembly may be delegated, in the first instance, to decentralized and binational commissions of conciliation, removed from the immediate influence of the Council. At the first Assembly, Norway and Sweden proposed an amendment to the Covenant whereby the judicial powers of the Council could be "decentralized" or delegated to other bodies. While the suggestion of an amendment was rejected as being unnecessary,[1] the third Assembly adopted a resolution recommending that members place their disputes before binational conciliation commissions, the organization of which should follow the Hague convention of 1907. It was recommended that neighboring states should form such commissions, each state appointing two members, one a national and one a neutral. The two states should then agree upon a neutral chairman, making a total membership of five. Upon notifying the chairman and the other party, either party could refer a dispute to this commission, though the notification should also be communicated to the Secretariat of the League. The investigation of the commission should be completed within six months, unless the time is extended by mutual consent; and decisions are by majority vote. These commissions are to exercise their duties "subject to the rights and obligations mentioned in Article 15 of the Covenant." Several powers have made treaties establishing such commissions to mediate disputes between themselves. In a treaty of March 26, 1920, Sweden and Chile signed a treaty, promising not to have recourse to the Council of the League, without first referring disputes, which are not arbitrated, to a joint commission. Likewise, a treaty providing for a Permanent Board of Conciliation was signed in December, 1920, between Germany and Switzerland.[2] An interesting development of these

[1] Cf. the British Commentary, Cmd. 151; de Visscher, "La procèdure de conciliation devant la Société des Nations," R. D. I. L. C. (1923), IV, No. 1.
[2] T. S. 111, 320. The latter provides that disputes affecting national honor shall be referred to conciliation.

ideas came in the treaty between Italy and Switzerland, signed in September, 1924, establishing a Permanent Commission of five members. All disputes of whatever nature are to be submitted to this commission if they cannot be settled by diplomacy. If one party does not accept the recommendations of the commission, either may demand that the dispute be referred to the World Court, which shall decide whether or not the dispute is of a judicial nature. If not, the parties will settle it "ex aequo et bono." [1]

The 1928 Model Treaties.—By encouraging the formation of these conciliation commissions the League of Nations is extending the plan started by the United States with its twenty Bryan peace commission treaties, and accepted by the Central American Republics in 1922 and by the Pan-American nations in 1923 and 1929. Eventually, the League commissions for the investigation of non-legal disputes should cover the whole world, being linked together by the Council as a final court of appeal.

While under a water-tight system of compulsory arbitration and investigation, all wars would become illegal, the Covenant still contains some "gaps." Even now war is apparently "legal" in case (1) of disputes over domestic questions, (2) of a report of the Council which is not unanimous, (3) of a report which is unanimous but which is not accepted by either party to the dis-

---

[1] *Feuille Fédérale,* No. 1890, Oct. 28, 1924.

Before 1919 Switzerland made reservations as to honor, independence, etc., but in 1919 the Swiss parliament decided to do away with reservations as to "honor," and to examine each particular case as it arose. Thereafter a series of treaties was negotiated combining the ideas of conciliation with arbitration. In the German treaty, conciliation was resorted to only in case one state refused to arbitrate on account of a "question of independence" being involved; on June 18, 1924, Switzerland and Hungary signed a treaty also providing for conciliation and arbitration. If one party does not accept the recommendation of the conciliation commission, constituted for each case, it will be arbitrated by a tribunal. If the parties do not agree as to setting it up within six months, the dispute will be addressed to the World Court who shall pass upon it if it is of a legal nature as defined in Article 36 of its Statute. The Italian treaty goes furthest of all in providing for the arbitration of all disputes, in case of failure of the conciliation process. On June 23, 1924, Switzerland made an agreement with Brazil for compulsory adjudication by the World Court of all differences excepting those affecting the constitutions of each state. Other treaties are being negotiated. "La Suisse et l'arbitrage," *Journal de Genève,* Sept. 25, 1924; C. H. Gossweiler, *L'Arbitrage international avant 1914 et après 1919* (1923), pp. 132 ff.

pute, (4) the Council does not report within six months.[1] In the first three cases, however, war cannot take place until three months after the report of the Council has been made. Thus a "cooling off" period is insured. According to one theory of interpretation, even if the Council fails to settle a dispute under Article XV, it will have the duty of taking jurisdiction over it under Article XI, and the parties will not therefore be free until after the procedure authorized by this article is exhausted. Article XI authorizes the Council or the Assembly to take "any action that may be deemed wise and effectual to safeguard the peace of nations." And it may therefore impose sanctions against states who might embark upon a war legal under Article XV.[2] Even if this theory is sound, Article XI is not likely to be employed in this manner simply because of the necessity of securing the consent of the two parties to the dispute to any decision made under Article XI.

The 1928 Assembly invited states whether members of the League or not to become parties to one of two groups of model treaties which had been prepared by the Committee on Arbitration and Security. The Assembly declared that these engagements were not to be interpreted as impeding the right of the Council to intervene, under Articles XV and XVII of the Covenant.

The first model treaty took the form of a General Act which any number of states may sign. It provides that (1) all disputes with regard to which the parties are in conflict as to their respective rights shall, subject to reservations, be submitted to the Permanent Court or to an arbitral tribunal; (2) all other disputes not settled by diplomacy must be submitted to conciliation commissions. If the parties do not within a month after the report of the commission reach an agreement, the dispute *may* be brought before an arbitral tribunal.

The second model treaty is a bilateral convention for the pacific settlement of all international disputes. This treaty goes further than the General Act in providing that if the parties have not reached an agreement within a month after the termination of the

---

[1] The use of force is authorized also when necessary to carry into effect an arbitral award or a unanimous report of the Council. Cf. p. 589.
[2] Cf. M. Gonsiorowski, *Société des Nations et Problème de la Paix*, Vol. II, pp. 326 ff.

proceedings of the Conciliation Commission, the question *shall* be brought before an arbitral tribunal.

The third model treaty is a bilateral convention which merely provides for the conciliation of non-legal disputes subject to appeal to the League under Article XV, together with the adjudication of legal disputes. The fourth model treaty provides only for conciliation. It shall "not be interpreted as restricting the duty of the League to take, at any time, whatever action may be deemed wise and effectual to safeguard the peace of the world."

If members of the League should accept the first type of bilateral agreement, the "gap in the Covenant" would, as far as they are concerned, be closed. A positive method for the settlement of all kinds of disputes, whether legal or non-legal, would be established. But these agreements are not yet in effect.[1] The Covenant proper does not in every case provide its members with the "moral" security which arises out of the pacific settlement of all disputes. Moreover, it is extremely vague about the enforcement of arbitral decisions and about resistance to aggression. As long as certain types of war are still legal and as long as each nation feels obliged to rely upon its own arms to enforce its rights and to resist aggression, nations cannot disband their armies. Disarmament is therefore linked to security. While to a certain extent security is dependent upon sanctions, to a greater extent it is dependent upon compulsory arbitration for all international disputes, without any loopholes by which a state may escape. The next chapter will outline the attempt of the League Assembly to tie together these three great principles of Disarmament, Security and Arbitration, and the effect upon this movement of the negotiation of the anti-war pact.

[1] The 1928 Assembly also drafted (a) a Collective Treaty of Mutual Assistance, similar to the Locarno treaty, and (b) a Collective Treaty of Non-Aggression, which contains no guarantee, (c) a Bilateral Treaty of Non-Aggression. Cf. p. 586. These agreements provide also for the adjudication of legal disputes and the conciliation of non-legal disputes.

CHAPTER XXVI
THE RENUNCIATION OF WAR

1. The Geneva Protocol.—2. The Locarno Agreements.—3. Germany and the League.—4. The "Outlawry of War."—5. History of the Anti-War Pact.—6. What Wars are Renounced?—7. The Greco-Bulgaria Case.—8. The Anti-War Pact and the League.

During the five years following the Peace Conference the idea that security could be gained only by military guarantees struggled with the idea that it could be gained only by compulsory arbitration. For a time the idea of military guarantees lost ground— both Articles X and XVI of the Covenant were attacked and weakened by the adoption of resolutions in the Assembly. But the effect of these attacks was rather unexpected. Instead of diminishing the emphasis on militarism, it exaggerated it. France and other countries in similar political situations began to increase their armaments and to contract alliances.

This fact was recognized by the third Assembly of the League when it adopted the famous resolution XIV stating that disarmament depended upon security and that a guarantee of security could be obtained through an agreement in which states bound themselves to provide "immediate and effective assistance in accordance with a pre-arranged plan in the event of one of them being attacked, provided that the obligation to render assistance to a country attacked shall be limited in principle to those countries situated in the same part of the globe. . . . "

Various proposals looking toward this end were worked over by the Temporary Mixed Commission and finally embodied in the Draft Treaty of Mutual Assistance, placed before the fourth Assembly in 1925.[1] This treaty obligated all the powers located on the same continent to give military aid to a nation when attacked, as the Council should direct. The determination of which state was the aggressor was placed in the hands of the Council.[2]

[1] For the Cecil and Requin drafts, see *Report of the Temporary Mixed Commission for the Reduction of Armaments.* A. 35, pp. 361–66.
[2] For the replies of the British and Soviet governments, see *O. J.*, May, 1924, p. 752; July, 1924, p. 1037.

Such was the situation when the fifth Assembly opened at Geneva in September, 1924. One point of view insisted that security could only be assured by an all-inclusive League of Nations, the members of which agreed to compulsory arbitration—the settlement of all international controversies by some form of international tribunal whose decision would be binding. The other point of view insisted that security must rest upon some sanction of force, and that even if compulsory arbitration is accepted, some sanction must be established to restrain a nation which, in violation of its promises, illegally resorts to war. This contrast was vividly portrayed in the speeches of Ramsay MacDonald, prime minister of England, and of Edouard Herriot, prime minister of France, at the fifth Assembly. The former declared that the only real security lay in compulsory arbitration. "History is full of invasions, full of wars and of aggressions and there have always been pacts, always military guarantees and always military security. The history of the world is a history which shows the nations always ready for war and always at war, and the one is absolutely essentially and organically connected with the other. History is full of the doom of nations which have trusted that false security." [1] Edouard Herriot, on the other hand, declared that while France accepted the principle of compulsory arbitration, she regarded it as inseparably linked up with the questions of security and disarmament. If necessary a great nation could protect itself unaided against attack, but a small nation could not. A nation which accepted compulsory arbitration had a right to be secure. He quoted Pascal—"Justice without might is impotent. Might without justice is tyranny. Justice without might is unavailing, for the wicked are ever with us. Might without justice stands condemned. We must therefore mate justice with might and to that end we must ensure that what is just is mighty and that what is mighty is just." [2]

Both points of view had now come to realize that real security must rest upon the principle of compulsory arbitration. But differences still existed as to the sanctions to be imposed against a power which refused to arbitrate and went to war, and as to the different forms which arbitration should take.

[1] *Verbatim Record*, 6th plenary meeting, p. 5.
[2] *Ibid.*, 8th plenary meeting, p. 3.

1. THE GENEVA PROTOCOL

Stimulated by this discussion, the 1924 Assembly drew up the famous Geneva Protocol. The preamble of this Protocol declared that "war of aggression" was an "international crime." The Protocol provided in the first place for the pacific settlement of nearly every kind of international dispute. States should accept the Optional Clause of the Statute of the Permanent Court of International Justice, subject if necessary to reservations. In case disputes were not referred to the Court or to arbitration they had to be referred to the Council. In case the Council did not arrive at a unanimous decision, it had to submit the dispute to a Committee of Arbitrators whose decision would be binding. If a state declined to live up to a decision, the Council should invoke economic and financial sanctions but not military. "It had not appeared possible to go further and to employ force against a State which is not itself resorting to force. The party in favor of which the decision has been given might, however, employ force against the recalcitrant party if authorized to do so by the Council." [1] However, in certain kinds of disputes, the Council or Committee of Arbitrators could not lay down a decision. The most important of these disputes were those over "domestic questions." If the World Court should decide at the request of the Council that a dispute involved a "domestic question," the arbitrators could not consider the case further. But the question could be brought before the League under Article XI of the Covenant. This article "confers no right on the Council or on the Assembly to impose any solution of a dispute without the consent of the parties." [2] The Council had no power to settle disputes arising out of the peace treaties. The First Committee of the fifth Assembly declared that the new system would not apply to "disputes which aim at revising treaties and international acts in force, or which seek to jeopardize the existing territorial integrity of signatory States." If it was desired to change treaties, Article XIX of the Covenant should be employed. [3]

---

[1] *General Report of the First and Third Committees*, Arbitration, Security and Reduction of Armaments, 5th Assembly, A. 135, 1924, p. 10.

[2] *Report*, cited, p. 12.

[3] Cf. p. 700. And speech of M. Politis, *Verbatim Record*, Fifth Assembly, October 1, 1924, p. 4.

Parties to the Protocol promised "in no case to resort to war" except to resist an act of aggression and to employ force with the consent of the Council or Assembly. The Protocol thus closed the "gap in the Covenant," by abolishing so-called private wars. A state might apply force, however, with the authorization of the League to enforce an arbitral decision in its favor. Under the Protocol states also agreed to "abstain from any act which might constitute a threat of aggression against another State."

If a state should go to war it would automatically be *presumed* to be the aggressor, until the contrary had been established by the Council (1) in case it refused to accept the procedure of pacific settlement and to submit to a decision, or (2) in case it violated the provisional measures which the Council might enjoin. In case a dispute should arise the two parties pledged themselves not to mobilize, etc. If the Council by a two-thirds majority decided that it had violated such measures, the state would be declared to have violated the Covenant and Protocol. A state was also presumed to be an aggressor in case it disregarded a decision recognizing that the dispute arose out of a "domestic question" and went to war without first submitting the question to the Council or the Assembly.[1]

[1] The Japanese delegate on the First Committee proposed to add to the original article in the Protocol saying that the arbitrators shall confine themselves to declaring in their award that a dispute is domestic, this provision: "Without prejudice to the Council's duty of endeavoring to conciliate the parties so as to assure the maintenance of peace and good understanding between nations." (Sept. 25th.) M. Adatci withdrew the amendment the following day, because of opposition, but made "every possible express reservation as to the whole system" set up in the Protocol. Further negotiations having failed, he made a statement on the 28th to the effect that the "League of Nations should not remain indifferent to the fact that the most flagrant acts of injustice are being committed under the purely technical and juridical cover of the alleged domestic jurisdiction of a State which is a Member of the League." He declared that it was "illogical, and unjust" that any party "should incur the risk of being declared the aggressor because it takes action when flagrant injustice has given rise to disputes between the Members of the League and the latter has categorically refused, in virtue of purely technical and juridical considerations, to deal with the matter. . . . The League should not threaten to declare guilty any party which takes action, precisely when the League offers no solution, when a dispute has arisen between that party and another State which threatens to disturb international peace or the good understanding between nations." Consequently, the Japanese delegation proposed the deletion of the provision making a state an aggressor who went to war over a "domestic question." As a compromise the above provisions

Apart from these three cases, the Council was obliged to try to determine the aggressor in each particular case. If it was unanimous, sanctions had to be applied. If unanimity was impossible, the Council had to enjoin upon the belligerents an armistice, the terms of which should be fixed by a two-thirds majority. Any belligerent refusing to accept the armistice would be deemed an aggressor.[1] The existence of aggression was thus determined by (1) presumption, (2) unanimous vote of the Council, (3) refusal to accept an armistice.

If the Council was unanimous, states had to apply sanctions under Article XVI; in doing so they were entitled to exercise the rights of a belligerent. Under the Covenant each state was not only judge of the method of fulfilling its obligations to apply sanctions but also of when these obligations came into existence. These loopholes were closed by the Protocol. If the Council branded a state as an aggressor, the parties to the Protocol were to carry out their obligations "loyally and effectively." When one party was considered the aggressor, military sanctions might be applied. When both parties were considered the aggressors, only economic measures were to be taken.[2] Each state continued to define what measures it should take against the aggressor. The parties agreed that the whole cost of any operations undertaken for the repression of aggression should be borne by the aggressor state "up to the extreme limit of its capacity."[3] The sanctions should not affect the territorial integrity or political independence of the aggressor state—in other words, no annexation should result.

To make more certain the guarantees against aggression, the Protocol authorized defensive alliances; but they were to become operative only after the Council had called upon the states to apply sanctions and they were to be used only against the aggres-

were adopted, to the effect that such a state should be presumed an aggressor only in case it refused to refer the dispute to the Council or the Assembly under Article 11. *O. J.*, Spec. Supplement No. 24, *Records of the 5th Assembly*, Minutes of the First Committee, pp. 45, 57, 80, 85, 90. Cf. M. Adatci, "Les 'amendments japonais' au Protocole de Genève," *Revue de Droit International*, July–Sept., 1924. For a general discussion, cf. D. H. Miller, *The Geneva Protocol* (1925).

[1] Article 10, Protocol.
[2] Article 11.
[3] Article 15.

sor. The Protocol required that these alliances be registered and published by the League. Perhaps the most striking provision in regard to these "controlled" alliances was that "they should remain open to all States Members of the League which may desire to accede thereto." By such means potential enemies and friends could be united in a common bond, as was later done in Locarno.[1]

With the strengthening of the principles of compulsory arbitration and of sanctions the chief incentive for large armaments—the thirst for security—is diminished. The Protocol therefore provided that in case it was ratified by May 1, 1925, by a majority of the permanent members of the Council and ten other League members—a total of thirteen—an International Armaments Conference should be held, and until a disarmament plan was actually adopted, the Protocol should not go into effect. Thus the Protocol was a magnificent attempt to prohibit all forms of aggressive war; to arbitrate all disputes except over domestic questions and the peace treaties; automatically to determine the existence of aggression; to extend the obligation to apply sanctions, and finally to bring about the reduction of armaments. Such was the attempt to solve the three joint problems of security, arbitration and disarmament.

Following the fifth Assembly, the MacDonald government in England fell, and was succeeded by a conservative ministry, under Mr. Baldwin. The new British government finally decided it could not ratify the Protocol. In a statement to the Council, Mr. Austen Chamberlain, the Secretary of State for Foreign Affairs, declared his government objected to the principle of compulsory arbitration and to the scope of the sanctions, which might lead to trouble with non-members of the League, such as the United States. The best means of obtaining security was to make supplementary agreements between the nations most immediately concerned.[2]

2. THE LOCARNO AGREEMENTS

As early as 1922, Dr. Cuno, the German Chancellor had advanced the idea of a Rhineland pact, and the Luther Cabinet in February, 1925, again proposed this idea to France, Italy, Ger-

[1] Cf. p. 653.
[2] Cmd. 2368, Statement made March 12, 1925.

many and Great Britain. Following long negotiations, representatives of these governments, together with representatives from Belgium, Poland and Czechoslovakia, met at Locarno and there initialled five historic treaties. The first of these is a Treaty of Mutual Guarantee. In this treaty Germany, Belgium, France, Great Britain and Italy "collectively and severally guarantee the maintenance of the territorial *status quo*" in the Rhineland. Germany and Belgium and also Germany and France agree "in no case to attack or invade each other or resort to war against each other," [1] except in case of the exercise of the right of legitimate defence which includes resistance to a flagrant breach of Articles 42 or 43 of the Treaty of Versailles [2]; action under Article XVI of the Covenant; and action as the result of a decision taken by the Assembly or Council of the League. If the League Council is satisfied that the above pledge is violated, the parties to the Locarno pact agree that "they will each of them come immediately to the assistance of the Power against whom the act complained of is directed." In case of a flagrant breach, each party "hereby undertakes immediately to come to the help of the party against whom such a violation or breach has been directed as soon as the said Power has been able to satisfy itself that this violation constitutes an unprovoked act of aggression," and that immediate action is necessary. Nevertheless, the League Council will later pass upon the question and the parties agree to act in accordance with its recommendations, provided the Council is unanimous except for the parties to the dispute.

This pact applied only to the western frontier of Germany. Nevertheless on the same day Germany entered into compulsory arbitration treaties with Poland and with Czechoslovakia, while France entered into guarantee treaties with these states extending to them French aid in case of attack. On June 23, 1927, Herr Stresemann declared in the German Reichstag, "There does not exist in Germany any responsible man who would be criminal enough to drag Germany into a war with any power whatsoever, neither in the west nor in the east."

---

[1] This terminology is much more precise than the "renunciation of war as an instrument of national policy" later used in the anti-war pact. Cf. p. 659.
[2] Cf. p. 568.

The Rhineland Pact was followed by a series of arbitration treaties between Germany and France and Belgium, in addition to the treaties with Poland and Czechoslovakia. These provide for the reference of "all disputes of every kind" with regard to "which the parties are in conflict as to their respective rights," either to an arbitral tribunal or to the Permanent Court of International Justice. Before resorting to the latter tribunal the parties may place the dispute before a Permanent Conciliation Commission, three of whose members are neutral. Moreover, all questions not falling within the above category shall be submitted to this Commission; and if the parties do not accept the findings, the question shall be referred to the Council of the League which shall handle it in accordance with Article XV of the Covenant.

In case the Council is not unanimous or rules that a dispute involves a domestic question, will Germany be free to go to war? If under such circumstances Germany goes to war against Poland, may France attack Germany across the Rhineland, despite the guarantee of the Rhine frontier by the five powers? Are the Allies barred from attacking Germany in case Austria should unite with Germany without the consent of the League Council?[1] Such are some of the legal questions left obscure by the Locarno agreement. Nevertheless the real importance of this agreement was political—it made possible peace between France and Germany—it paved the way for Germany's entrance to the League.

3. GERMANY AND THE LEAGUE

These Locarno agreements were not a repudiation of the League. They did for a limited area what the Geneva Protocol attempted to do more elaborately for the world. The Locarno Guarantee treaty went into force only when Germany entered the League. And the agreement stated that it should not be interpreted "as restricting the duty of the League" to act to safeguard the peace of the world. The original text of the Locarno agreement was deposited with the League at Geneva; and the treaty remains in force until the League Council decides that the League "insures sufficient protection" to the parties.

It was understood that following the approval of the Locarno

[1] Cf. Politis, N., *Les Accords de Locarno R. D. I. L. C.* 1925, Vol. VI, p. 713.

agreements Germany would enter the League of Nations, and that Germany should be given a permanent seat upon the Council. In February, 1926, such an application was made. Before making application Germany had negotiated with the other governments in regard to her obligations to impose sanctions against an aggressor. Apparently Germany did not wish to impose an economic boycott in the case of a war in which the League Council ruled that Russia was the aggressor against Poland. The imposition of an economic boycott according to the German government would create a state of war and subject Germany to attack. In view of her disarmed condition, Germany would find this risk "unbearable." Germany believed, therefore, that in joining the League she should be left free to determine the extent to which an economic boycott should be applied. Germany received apparent satisfaction when in a note written at Locarno in October, 1925, the Allied governments stated that as far as they were concerned each member of the League was bound to coöperate in support of the Covenant under Article XVI "to an extent which is compatible with its military situation and takes its geographical position into account."

A special Assembly to pass upon the German application for League membership was called for March, 1926. But it failed to act because of the demands of Spain, Brazil and Poland for permanent seats on the Council in return for a German seat. Germany declined to accept this form of trade. The Assembly was forced to adjourn without action. When the next Assembly met in September a plan had been worked out to compromise these demands. Germany was the only state to be made a permanent member on the Council, but the number of non-permanent seats was increased from six to nine and three of these seats were made semi-permanent, in the sense that the occupants could be declared reëligible. Despite this compromise, Spain and Brazil both served notice of resignation from the League. Spain returned, however, in 1928.[1]

Such was the situation in 1927. The League Covenant had made a large number of wars illegal and provided a rather vague system of sanctions. The Locarno pact made war in the Rhineland illegal and provided concrete sanctions for this area. Both the Covenant and Locarno established machinery for the pacific settlement of disputes.

[1] Cf. p. 697.

4. THE "OUTLAWRY OF WAR"

The United States did not participate in any of these efforts to make war illegal. Nevertheless a movement having much the same object arose in America, called the "outlawry of war." Its proponents advocated an international treaty making war a "public crime under the law of nations" except in the case of self-defence. Every nation should "indict and punish its own international war breeders or instigators." An international court should be established with power to decide all "purely international controversies," in accordance with a code of international law. The classes of disputes to be exempted from the jurisdiction of the Court were to be enumerated; and, for the United States, these exemptions included questions arising out of the Monroe Doctrine, conservation, immigration, the right to expel aliens, tariff, military establishments, coaling stations, fortification of the Panama canal, discrimination against foreigners—in fact, some of the most irritating factors in international relations. The international court with compulsory jurisdiction over all "purely" international controversies, was to have the same power "for the enforcement of its decrees as our Federal Supreme Court, namely, the respect of all enlightened nations for judgments resting upon open and fair investigations and impartial decisions and the compelling power of enlightened public opinion." [1]

Commendable as was the underlying purpose of the American plan, it was somewhat naïve to expect nations to punish their own "War breeders" for a war which the parliament of such a nation had declared. As will be pointed out later, it is impossible to draw up at one stroke a code of international law, applicable to every conceivable type of dispute. Moreover, it is a contradiction in terms to advocate compulsory arbitration as a substitute for war and then except from arbitration the most important questions out of which international disputes arise. Likewise, it is misleading to imply that the only sanction of the decisions of the Supreme Court of the United States is the force of public opinion. Supreme Court decisions are enforced, regardless of

---

[1] Cf. Senator W. E. Borah's resolution, Senate Resolution, No. 101, 67th Cong., 4th session. The originators of this plan included not only Senator Borah, but S. P. Levinson, Raymond Robbins, John Dewey, J. R. Clark, and the late Senator P. C. Knox.

public opinion, by the executive branch of a real government. If decisions of an international court, especially when made in the case of a party that has been unwillingly haled before its jurisdiction, are not to be disobeyed, "moral opinion" may not always prove an effective sanction. The most impracticable feature of the American Outlawry of War plan, at least as advocated by Senator Borah and his group, was the demand for the establishment of brand new machinery—and of an imperfect character—instead of utilizing machinery already in existence.[1]

Nevertheless the slogan "outlawry of war" took hold of the imagination of American organizations, which got behind a definite "anti-war movement." The outgrowth of this movement was the anti-war pact.

5. HISTORY OF THE ANTI-WAR PACT

This pact was first proposed by M. Briand,[2] Foreign Minister of France, upon the tenth anniversary of the entrance of the United States into the World War, on April 6, 1927. He suggested that France would be willing to make a treaty with the United States "tending to 'outlaw war'. The renunciation of war as an instrument of national policy is a conception already familiar to the signatories of the Covenant of the League of Nations and of the Treaties of Locarno. . . . " On June 20, the French government presented a draft treaty embodying the above principle to the State Department. The Department did not, however, answer the proposal for six months, but finally did so, on December 28, following an energetic campaign of opinion in favor of the treaty. On this date Secretary Kellogg expressed sympathy with M. Briand's suggestion; but suggested that it include all the principal powers. France stated that this proposal which would convert a bilateral into a multilateral treaty affected its original suggestion. It could afford to renounce war with the United States because the possibility of applying the sanctions of the Covenant and of Locarno against the United States was only

[1] For a statement in favor of the American plan, cf. F. Kellor, *Security Against War* (1924), Vol. II, Ch. XXIX, and C. C. Morrison, *The Outlawry of War*, (1927); for a criticism, cf. W. Lippmann, "The Outlawry of War," *Atlantic Monthly*, August, 1923.

[2] It is understood at the suggestion of Prof. James T. Shotwell of Columbia University.

theoretical. But it could not afford to sign an agreement embracing every state which might weaken its obligations to enforce sanctions. Consequently it would have to restrict the renunciation to "wars of aggression." The United States objected to this term on the ground that it would destroy the "true significance" of the end in view. In a note of March 30, France agreed to drop the phrase "war of aggression" but declared that in case one state violated its promises to renounce war, the other signatories should be released from their obligations with reference to that state; that the pact should not deprive states of the right of "legitimate defence," and that it should not prejudice obligations contracted under the Covenant, the Locarno agreements and treaties guaranteeing "neutrality." Moreover, such a treaty should go into effect only after receiving universal acceptance.

On April 13, 1928, the United States transmitted a draft treaty to the leading powers. And the French government, a week later, presented its own draft stating in the text of the treaty the above exceptions. On April 28, Secretary Kellogg made an address to the American Society of International Law in which he declared that the right of self-defence could not be restricted by any treaty; and that the obligations under the Locarno agreements and the French "neutrality" treaties would become operative only after a party had gone to war in violation of its pledges. In case such a state was also party to the anti-war pact, the other parties would then be free to proceed against it. The United States was willing that the parties to the Locarno agreement should sign the anti-war pact. Mr. Kellogg declared that the League Covenant "authorized war in certain circumstances," but "it is an authorization and not a positive requirement." In view of these considerations it was unnecessary to make any changes in the draft. In other words, he accepted the substance of the French reservations while declining to incorporate them in the treaty.

On May 19, the British Government accepted the treaty subject to the French exceptions and Mr. Kellogg's interpretations, and subject also to the following interpretation:

"The language of Article 1, as to the renunciation of war as an instrument of national policy, renders it desirable that I should remind your excellency that there are certain regions of the world the welfare and integrity of which constitute a special and vital interest for our peace

HISTORY OF THE ANTI-WAR PACT

and safety. His Majesty's Government have been at pains to make it clear in the past that interference with these regions cannot be suffered. Their protection against attack is to the British Empire a measure of self-defense. It must be clearly understood that His Majesty's Government in Great Britain accept the new treaty upon the distinct understanding that it does not prejudice their freedom of action in this respect. . . ."

This has been popularly called the British Monroe Doctrine. But unlike the Monroe Doctrine, the British government placed no geographic limits upon its doctrine. Apparently it wished to state expressly its right to defend from attack territories where British sovereignty was uncertain, such as the Anglo-Egyptian Sudan, the League of Nations mandates, and other areas where British influence has been great, such as Egypt, certain parts of the Red Sea, and the Persian Gulf. In Arabia there are a number of tiny kings who were not invited to adhere to the anti-war pact and hence do not enjoy its protection. If a party to the anti-war pact should attack an Arab state of this type, England could not legally go to war against such a party without an understanding to the contrary.[1] What the British Government also feared was, for example, an agreement between Afghanistan and Russia under which Russia would be allowed to build in Afghanistan military roads and fortifications aimed at the Indian frontier. Great Britain apparently wishes the right to interfere to prevent the execution of such agreements before India is actually attacked.

As a result of further negotiations, in which the preamble of the pact was modified, the parties accepted the treaty subject to the above interpretations. On August 27, 1928, representatives of fifteen states [2] met at Paris and affixed their signatures to the following treaty:

GENERAL PACT FOR THE RENUNCIATION OF WAR.—SIGNED AT PARIS, AUGUST 27, 1928

. . . Deeply sensible of their solemn duty to promote the welfare of mankind;

Persuaded that the time has come when a frank renunciation of war as an instrument of national policy should be made to the end that the peace-

[1] This account follows "The Anti-War Pact," *I. S.* Vol. IV–No. 18.
[2] France, United States, Great Britain, Germany, Italy, Japan, Belgium, Poland, Czechoslovakia, Canada, Australia, South Africa, India, New Zealand, Irish Free State.

ful and friendly relations now existing between their peoples may be perpetuated;

Convinced that all changes in their relations with one another should be sought only by pacific means and be the result of a peaceful and orderly process, and that any signatory Power which hereafter seeks to promote its national interests by resort to war should be denied the benefits furnished by this Treaty;

Hopeful that, encouraged by their example, all the other nations of the world will join in this humane endeavor and by adhering to the present Treaty as soon as it comes into force bring their peoples within the scope of its beneficent provisions, thus uniting the civilized nations of the world in a common renunciation of war as an instrument of their national policy;

Have decided to conclude a Treaty and for that purpose have appointed as their respective Plenipotentiaries. . . .

Article 1

The High Contracting Parties solemnly declare in the names of their respective peoples that they condemn recourse to war for the solution of international controversies, and renounce it as an instrument of national policy in their relations with one another.

Article 2

The High Contracting Parties agree that the settlement or solution of all disputes or conflicts of whatever nature or of whatever origin they may be, which may arise among them, shall never be sought except by pacific means.

Article 3

The present Treaty shall be ratified by the High Contracting Parties named in the Preamble in accordance with their respective constitutional requirements, and shall take effect as between them as soon as all their several instruments of ratification shall have been deposited at Washington.

This Treaty shall, when it has come into effect as prescribed in the preceding paragraph, remain open as long as may be necessary for adherence by all the other Powers of the world. Every instrument evidencing the adherence of a Power shall be deposited at Washington and the Treaty shall immediately upon such deposit become effective as between the Power thus adhering and the other Powers parties hereto.

It shall be the duty of the Government of the United States to furnish each Government named in the Preamble and every Government subsequently adhering to this Treaty with a certified copy of the Treaty and of every instrument of ratification or adherence. It shall also be the duty of the Government of the United States telegraphically to notify such Governments immediately upon the deposit with it of each instrument of ratification or adherence. . . .

On August 28, the United States extended an invitation to 48 governments to adhere to the pact. Because the United States had not recognized the Soviet government, Russia was invited by France. In a note of August 31, 1928, the Soviet government vigorously criticized the treaty because of its silence in regard to disarmament, because of its indefiniteness, and because of its "reservations." Nevertheless it was willing to adhere. By December 1, about 60 states had adhered or signified their intention of doing so. Of these states, the Egyptian, Persian and Turkish governments declared that they could not accept the reservations to the treaty, particularly in regard to the British Monroe Doctrine. By July, 1929, neither Argentina nor Brazil had signified their intention in regard to the anti-war pact apparently because of uncertainty as to its relation to the Monroe Doctrine.

6. WHAT WARS ARE RENOUNCED?

As a result of the interpretative notes, the leading parties to the anti-war pact made it clear that the renunciation of war as an instrument of national policy did not apply in the following cases:

1. In self-defence, which may include acts taken to enforce the Monroe Doctrine or the British Monroe Doctrine.
2. Against any state which breaks the treaty.
3. In execution of obligations under the League Covenant.
4. In execution of obligations under the Locarno agreements.
5. In execution of obligations under treaties guaranteeing neutrality.[1]

These exceptions may be reduced to wars of "self-defence" or "coöperative defence." If it is legitimate for one state to defend itself, why is it illegitimate for other states jointly to come to its aid—the principle embodied in the Covenant? Without such sanctions it is argued that the reduction of armaments by each state is impossible. The sanctions do not constitute a primary

[1] This probably covers the international agreement of 1815 guaranteeing the neutrality of Switzerland, (cf. p. 586) and conceivably the French alliances. (Cf. p. 510.)

right to go to war. They may be invoked only on behalf of a state which is illegally attacked and which is acting in the name of self-defence.

While the principles of self-defence and of coöperative defence may be perfectly valid, the application of these principles may lead to difficulties. In private law a court and jury decide whether the doctrine of self-defence may be applied; but in international law each state has decided for itself whether the doctrine may be legitimately invoked. The European system of alliances was made in the name of "self-defence"; [1] many wars, including the World War, were fought in the name of that principle and competition in armaments has also been carried on in the name of "self-defence." Under the anti-war pact, several extreme forms of the doctrine were advanced. Thus the British Monroe Doctrine was based on the principle of self-defence. While the United States Government was silent in regard to the Monroe Doctrine it was suggested that it would regard the use of force under the Monroe Doctrine as an act of self-defence.

The use of force by the United States under the Monroe Doctrine is conceivable under at least three circumstances:

(1) To repel the military invasion of a Latin-American State by a non-American power.

(2) To intervene in Latin-American countries where disorders threaten foreign interests.

(3) To prevent the execution of agreements between Latin-American and non-American powers providing for the establishment of naval bases, etc., which in the opinion of the United States might endanger its security.

If, under the anti-war pact, state X should invade a Latin-American state, and assuming that both states were parties to the anti-war pact, the United States would recover its freedom under the pact with reference to state X. There would be no conflict between the treaty and this aspect of the Monroe Doctrine. The same consideration would apply to the execution of the treaty of November 3, 1903, between the United States and Panama. In this treaty the United States "guarantees and will maintain the independence of the Republic of Panama." It may be argued that

[1] Cf. 505.

WHAT WARS ARE RENOUNCED? 663

the obligations of the United States vis-à-vis Panama under this treaty are similar to the obligations of other states under the Covenant and the Locarno agreement. In case Panama is attacked, the United States, under this treaty, would presumably be obliged to lend it military support. If both Panama and the attacking power are parties to the anti-war pact, the United States would be free to act with respect to the attacking power which had thus violated the anti-war pact. If Panama should not become a party to the pact,[1] the United States would apparently have to justify the use of force against a signatory to the pact in behalf of Panama, on the ground of self-defence; i. e., of defending the Panama Canal Zone. The United States holds this zone under perpetual lease and for the purposes of the treaty it would probably be regarded as part of the territory of the United States.

But will the pact prevent the United States from continuing its policy of military intervention in Central American countries? The United States delegation at Havana vigorously opposed a non-intervention resolution at the time when the United States was carrying on its anti-war negotiations.[2] The government of the United States has frequently carried on military operations without any direct authorization of Congress, although that body under the Constitution has the power to declare war.[3] Moreover, a number of governments have landed marines or other troops in disorderly countries for the purpose of protecting foreign interests without regarding such an act as necessarily creating a state of war.[4]

It may be argued, therefore, that the anti-war pact does not affect the right of temporary intervention by the United States or other powers. Nevertheless, if the anti-war pact does not prohibit the United States from intervening in Latin America, it does not prevent European governments from doing so for the same reason. The question therefore arises, how may the United States, under the anti-war pact, forcibly prevent European intervention in Latin America, unless it justifies the use of force for this purpose on the ground of self-defence?

[1] Panama has, however, signified its intention of adhering to the pact.
[2] Cf. *Pan American Conference, Part I, I. S.*, Vol. IV, No. 4, p. 67. Cf. p. 252.
[3] Cf. *The Powers of the President as Commander-in-Chief, I. S.*, Vol. IV, No. 10.
[4] Cf. Hyde, *International Law*, Vol. I, p. 117; Fauchille, *Droit International Public*, Vol. I, p. 538 ff. Cf. p. 393.

Any such definition of self-defence has been regarded with wide misgivings.[1] The solution of the difficulty is in placing all intervention under some form of international control which will prevent the abuse of intervention for the ends of a single power.[2]

Will the pact prevent the United States from using force to prevent a Latin American state from granting naval bases, etc., to a non-American power? Hitherto any such agreement has been regarded as a danger to the security of the United States, and it is possible to argue that any preventive acts to forestall such a danger would be "self-defence" within the meaning of the pact. Nevertheless, if all the parties to the pact should support this doctrine of "preventive" wars, it is difficult to conceive of any war which the pact actually prohibits.[3] Thus it would seem possible to give the term "self-defence" perhaps as many divergent interpretations as the term "aggressive war." There are at least two ways by which the discretion of individual states in this respect may be narrowed and disputes over the meaning of self-defence removed. One is by the adoption of an interpretation of the term self-defence, restricting it to repelling the actual invasion of territory. Such an interpretation might take the form of a protocol annexed to the treaty. It is doubtful, however, if in view of the wide interpretation of "self-defence" employed in the past any important state would accept such a limited definition. Whatever the definition may be, any attempt to define the meaning of "self-defence" is likely to be as unsuccessful in international law as it has been in private law.

[1] The Soviet note of August 31 declared: "In the opinion of the Soviet Government there must be a ban not only on war in its formal juridical sense (such as normally follows a declaration of war), but also such military actions as a blockade or the occupation of foreign territory. . . ."

[2] Cf. Buell, Raymond L., *The United States and Latin America, A Suggested Program, I. S.*, Vol. III, Supp. No. 4.

[3] Somewhat the same question arises under Article 80 of the Treaty of Versailles which provides that Germany and Austria shall remain independent unless the League Council consents otherwise. May France legally go to war under the anti-war pact in case these two states unite in defiance of the Council? Likewise Articles 42–44 of the Treaty prohibit Germany from maintaining fortifications or troops in the Rhineland. If Germany violates this provision, "she shall have been regarded as committing a hostile act" against the Powers. *Le Temps* (July 17, 1928) states that if Germany violates this demilitarized zone, the other parties to the anti-war pact could regard such an act as "the first step in preparing for a war as an instrument of national policy", and therefore a violation of the anti-war pact.

THE GRECO-BULGARIAN CASE

A second method of preventing the abuse of the doctrines of self-defence and coöperative defence is by establishing some international means of determining in a particular case whether or not a nation is justified or would be justified in acting in self-defence. Mr. Kellogg hinted at some such possibility when he stated before the Society of International Law that if a state has "a good case" in invoking the doctrine of self-defence, "the world will applaud and not condemn its action."

The League and Self-Defence.—The fact should be emphasized that international means for this purpose already exist in the case of a vast majority of the states which have signed or adhered to the anti-war pact. A member of the League of Nations cannot legally go to war simply by invoking the doctrine of self-defence. All disputes in which members of the League are involved must be submitted, as we have seen, to some form of arbitration or conciliation; and any resort to war without first invoking this procedure, except possibly to repel actual invasion, is a violation of the Covenant. This fact was clearly illustrated in the Greco-Bulgarian frontier incident of 1925.

7. THE GRECO-BULGARIAN CASE

In this case a Greek soldier crossed the frontier and fired on a Bulgarian sentry. The sentry replied and killed the Greek. General firing resulted and Bulgaria telegraphed the Council, invoking Articles X and XI of the Covenant. The Council met hurriedly at Paris. Its first act was not to determine which of the two states was the aggressor,—which of the two states was in the wrong. Its first act was to request *both* governments to withdraw their troops behind their respective frontiers within sixty days. When this invitation had been accepted by both parties, the Council then heard each party state its case. The Greek government said that in invading Bulgarian territory it had acted in "legitimate defence." Bulgaria replied that it was an act of aggression.[1] Commenting on the fact that Greek troops had actually invaded Bulgarian territory, M. Briand, Acting President of the Council, declared that "it was essential that such ideas [of legitimate defence] should not take root in the minds" of League Members "and become a kind of jurisprudence, for it would be extremely

[1] *O. J.*, November, 1925, p. 1696.

dangerous." Under the pretext of legitimate defence, disputes might arise which, though limited in extent, were extremely unfortunate owing to the damage they entailed. These disputes, once they had broken out, might assume such proportions that the government, which started them under a feeling of legitimate defence, would be no longer able to control them.

"The League of Nations, through its Council, and through all the methods of conciliation which were at its disposal, offered the nations a means of avoiding such deplorable events. The nations had only to appeal to the Council." The Council appointed a commission of inquiry and both Bulgaria and Greece agreed to accept its findings after a visit to the spot. It reported that in invading Bulgarian territory the Greek government although it had believed that invasion was imminent had acted upon false or exaggerated information. The Council ruled that Greece had violated Bulgarian territory without sufficient cause and should therefore pay an indemnity of 30,000,000 levas in reparation for the loss of Bulgarian life and property, deduction having been made for the initial murder of the Greek soldier. The commission recommended that neutral officers be appointed to take control of the Greek and Bulgarian frontier forces and that certain measures be taken to remove the difficulties arising out of the local minorities and the "comitadjis" problems. This case is of striking interest not only as an example of the effectiveness of the conciliating procedure of the League, but also because it shows that so far as its own wars are concerned, a member of the League is not free to define the meaning of self-defence. If it should attempt to do so, it might act upon false information and aggravate a dispute which otherwise might be kept within modest bounds and quietly settled. This case also shows that if the danger of war is to be really removed, the underlying political difficulties between states must be solved.

This international control over the question of self-defence applies to the British government and any action under the British Monroe Doctrine just as it applies to boundary disputes between Greece and Bulgaria.[1] The principal states to which this control

[1] Article 14 of the British Draft of an Anglo-Egyptian Alliance of July 28, 1927, provided that "nothing in the present treaty is intended to or shall in any way prejudice the rights and obligations which devolve or may devolve

does not apply are the United States and Russia. The same international machinery also controls the application of the principle of coöperative defence whether under the Covenant or the Locarno agreement, or the French alliances.[1]

8. THE ANTI-WAR PACT AND THE LEAGUE

More than three centuries ago, Albericus Gentilis wrote in his *De Jure Belli:* "In the absence of a supreme tribunal charged with passing judgment on international disputes, and in the absence of a super-state charged with the power to carry out the judgments of such a tribunal, States have no other alternative than to resort to force in order to have their rights recognized and their interests respected."

The movement in favor of international organization during the last few years has usually assumed that if war is to be effectively banned, some peaceful means for settling disputes must be established.

During the negotiation of the anti-war pact, the French, Polish and Czechoslovak governments, all of which have profited from the 1919–1920 peace treaties, stressed the belief that the anti-war pact would, to quote the French note, perpetuate "pacific and friendly relations under the contractual conditions on which they are today established." [2]

Freezing the Status Quo.—Does this statement mean that the states regard the anti-war pact as one more step in freezing the *status quo?* Do they regard the pact as an added guarantee that the boundaries established in the peace treaties shall not be changed by force? In a note of October 6, 1928, the Hungarian government, which lost territory as a result of the World War, informed the United States that it adhered to the anti-war pact "under the supposition that the Government of the United States as well as the governments of the other signatory powers will seek to find the means of rendering it possible that in the future injustices may be remedied by peaceful means."

upon either of the high contracting parties under the Covenant of the League of Nations." Cmd. 3050, p. 13.

[1] Those states which have accepted the optional clause of the statute of the permanent court may have to submit this question of whether or not a violation of the anti-war pact has occurred to the permanent court.

[2] Cf. French note of July 14, 1928, Polish note of July 17, 1928, Czechoslovak note of July 20, 1928.

Article 2 of the anti-war pact declares:

"The High Contracting Parties agree that the settlement or solution of all disputes or conflicts of whatever nature or of whatever origin they may be, which may arise between them, shall never be sought except by pacific means."

This article does not seem to create a positive obligation to *settle* disputes by pacific means. It merely provides that they shall not be settled by non-pacific means. Neither does this article define the procedure to be followed. In his address of August 27, 1928, M. Briand, declared, "Peace is proclaimed. That is well; that is much. But it still remains necessary to organize it. In the solution of difficulties, right and not might must prevail. That is to be the work of to-morrow."[1]

The argument that the pact freezes the *status quo* and hence is undesirable is weakened by the fact that Germany who is vigorously opposed to the freezing of the *status quo* was among the first to support the anti-war treaty. Germany does not like some of the provisions of the Treaty of Versailles, but Germany does not wish to change them by force. Apparently Germany believes that the conclusion of the anti-war pact will make for a better international feeling and that this feeling will lead to voluntary readjustments in the peace treaties of immensely more value than any attempted readjustments by force.

The Treaty for the Renunciation of War and the Covenant of the League both have the same object—the elimination of war. But the anti-war pact confines itself to a verbal renunciation, while the Covenant provides for machinery to remove the cause of disputes. Likewise the Covenant embodies the principle of sanctions, and all the leading parties to the anti-war pact made it clear that the renunciation of war as an instrument of *national* policy did not affect their obligations under the Covenant. On August 4, 1928, the British government transmitted to the League of Nations Secretariat copies of the notes setting forth the British interpretation of the Kellogg Pact. In

[1] Mr. Reed Smoot, member of the United States Senate, recently declared: "The Kellogg agreement for renunciation of war is a great and basic step toward lasting peace. Yet it is clear that the agreement must be supplemented by other steps, such as additional arbitration treaties or international courts . . . " *Foreign Relations and Peace*, New York *Herald-Tribune Magazine*, September 23, 1928, p. 3.

a covering letter it was declared: "in examining these proposals the British government have been very anxious, in view of the provisions of Clause 20 of the League Covenant, to ascertain whether there exists any incompatibility between their acceptance and the obligations resulting from the Covenant. As appears from the enclosed Notes the Government has acquired the conviction that its signature of the proposed treaty would not be in opposition to its obligations resulting from its position as a member of the League. . . . " [1]

On the other hand, the anti-war pact may have the effect of closing the "gap in the Covenant." That is, it may make illegal wars which under the Covenant were not prohibited.[2] Speaking of the relation between the pact and the League, M. Politis declared at the Assembly on September 7, 1928, "The great merit of the Paris treaty, as compared with the League Covenant, is that it fills the chief gap in the last named instrument. . . . It realizes a reform which for the last five years we have sought in vain. It lays down as a rule of positive law the essential principle, the fundamental principle of the Geneva Protocol of 1924 . . . the principle of which I speak is the prohibition of what we have always called here 'wars of aggression.'"

Unlike the Covenant, the anti-war pact contains no sanctions. If one party violates the pact, the other states do not promise to do anything about it; they simply are relieved of their obligation not to go to war against the guilty state. Nevertheless, in the case of wars prohibited by the Covenant, the violation of the pact by a League member would encounter the sanctions imposed by members of the League. The main sanction provided for in the Covenant is an economic boycott. The opinion has been frequently expressed that the League could not successfully apply such a boycott against a violator of the Covenant, so long as the United States, whose commercial interests would be immediately affected by such a boycott, insisted upon adhering to the old laws of neutrality which had been based on the legality of war. [3]

[1] *Monthly Summary of the League of Nations*, September 15, 1928, p. 219.
[2] Cf. p. 644.
[3] In view of the fact that the United States has always recognized the law of contraband and blockade, the fear that the United States would obstruct belligerent sanctions if imposed by the League seems to have been exaggerated. Cf. *American Neutrality and League Wars, I. S.*, Vol. IV, No. 2.

Several attempts to waive these traditional neutral rights of the United States in the case of an aggressor have been made. The original Burton resolution introduced December 5, 1927, declared that the policy of the United States was to prohibit the export of arms to an aggressor country, as determined by the President.[1] Objection to the original resolution was made on the ground that in prohibiting the export of arms to one belligerent and not to another, the United States would be violating the rules of neutrality. This objection would now seem to have been met by the anti-war pact; i. e., if a state goes to war in violation of the pact, the United States is under no obligation to treat it as a neutral but as a state which has violated its obligations.

While the United States has not undertaken any obligations to apply sanctions against a state which violates the anti-war pact, it is argued that the United States will feel morally bound to support the pact of which it is the author by waiving its "neutral rights" in case the League members should attempt to impose an economic boycott against a state which violates the pact and the Covenant at the same time.[2] On July 30, 1928, Sir Austen Chamberlain declared in the House of Commons that the importance of the anti-war treaty depended on "how the rest of the world thought the United States was going to judge the action of the

---

[1] The resolution was later amended to prohibit arms exports to *any* nation. On February 11, 1929, Senator Capper introduced a resolution stating that whenever the President determines that "any country has violated the multilateral treaty for the renunciation of war" it shall be unlawful "to export to such country arms, munitions, implements of war, or other articles. . . ." A second section provided, "It is declared to be the policy of the United States that the nationals of the United States should not be protected by their Government in giving aid and comfort to a nation which has committed a breach of the said treaty." For a discussion, cf. J. P. Chamberlain, "The Embargo Resolutions and Neutrality." *International Conciliation*, June, 1929; also P. C. Jessup, *American Neutrality and International Police*, World Peace Foundation, 1928.

[2] The preamble of the treaty states that any signatory Power "which shall hereafter seek to promote its national interests by resort to war should be denied the benefits furnished by this Treaty." Professor James T. Shotwell argues that there is a "moral duty expressed or implied in this phrase, that the signatories to the treaty do not become the silent partners of an aggressor; but no formal obligation is entered into to put down the aggression." *The Pact of Paris*, International Conciliation, October, 1928, p. 451. He adds: "We are inclined to accept the view, almost universally held outside the United States, that the principle involved in this single phrase is at least equal in importance with that in the heart of the treaty."

aggressor, and whether they would help or hinder him in his aggression."

M. Briand declared on August 27 that a guilty state "would run the positive risk of seeing all of them gradually and freely gather against it with redoubtable consequences that would not long be ensuing."

Senator Borah in an interview in the New York *Times* of March 25, 1928, declared:

"Another important result of such a treaty [the anti-war treaty] would be to enlist the support of the United States in coöperative action against any nation which is guilty of a flagrant violation of this outlawry agreement. Of course, the Government of the United States must reserve the right to decide, in the first place, whether or not the treaty has been violated, and second, what coercive measures it feels obliged to take. But it is quite inconceivable that this country would stand idly by in case of a grave breach of a multilateral treaty to which it is a party."

At present the League of Nations Council has been given the authority to conciliate disputes arising among the great majority of the states of the world and the action of the Council may therefore be of importance in bringing about or preventing war; or of stigmatizing as an aggressor a state which goes to war. Obviously such a decision may vitally affect the interests of the United States and it is argued that the anti-war pact will morally oblige the United States to accept the conditions thus created whereas otherwise it could protest against it. It is possible therefore as a result of the anti-war pact that the United States may agree to consult with the League Council whenever two states threaten to go to war. If the United States should agree to throw the weight of its prestige upon the side of the League Council in causing states to find a pacific settlement of their differences, it is doubtful whether war would take place. This form of coöperation between the United States and the League could take place without committing the United States to the use of sanctions, or any form of alliance.[1]

As far as sanctions are concerned, the anti-war pact is important from another angle: it would seem to prevent a state from re-

[1] Cf. R. L. Buell, "Sea Law under the Kellogg Pact," *The New Republic*, May 15, 1929.

sorting to self-help to enforce a claim against another state. Suppose, for example, that the United States and state X submitted a dispute to an arbitral tribunal and that the tribunal decided in favor of the United States. Suppose also that state X refused to execute the award. Under the anti-war pact it may be argued that the United States would be prohibited from going to war against state X to compel execution. The anti-war pact would not, however, seem to prohibit the use of *international* sanctions for this purpose, since the pact prohibits merely war as an instrument of *national* policy. An international sanction does not necessarily mean an international force, but it may mean merely international authorization and control over the action of a single state.

9. MORAL ASPECTS OF THE PACT

The legal aspects of the anti-war pact have now been discussed. It has been necessary to determine the actual legal effect of the pact upon the right to go to war, and the relation of this pact to other factors in international relations. But this document should be judged fundamentally, not by technical criteria, but by the moral and spiritual effect it may have upon world opinion and upon the future conduct of diplomacy and international relations.

Until very recent times groups in every important country have glorified the institution of war. It was not many years ago that von Moltke wrote: "War is an element in the order of the world ordained by God. In it the noblest virtues of mankind are developed; courage and the abnegation of self, faithfulness to duty, and the spirit of sacrifice; the soldier gives his life. Without war the world would stagnate and lose itself in materialism." In every great state the army and navy have occupied a high social position and have had great influence upon policy.

Moreover, the history of European diplomacy and international relations generally seems to demonstrate that most great powers have regarded war as sooner or later inevitable. They have relied for their safety and their rights upon physical strength.

Diplomats formed combinations and made bargains to postpone the evil day; but down in their hearts they believed the day would come. In 1914 Europe was ridden with war psychology. The international system was built upon a conviction of war's inevitability. No state dreamed of renouncing war as an instrument of national policy.

Ever since the Congress of Berlin of 1878 the great powers followed a policy of threats. They did not intend that war should occur as a result of their demands, but they did believe in backing up these demands with a show of force; they believed that the states upon which they made these demands were weak and would therefore have to give way.[1]

Friends of the anti-war pact state that it will have a revolutionary effect upon international relations as they have existed in the past. It is argued that the anti-war pact will eventually abolish war psychology, and force governments and peoples to think in terms of peace; that it will no longer be possible for Foreign Offices to advance their ends by a policy of threats—whether open or veiled; that it will no longer be possible for demagogues to whip up popular enthusiasm in favor of wars on behalf of "national destiny" or "national honor." Disputes will continue to arise between nations; and they may or may not be positively settled by peaceful means. But it is contended that as a result of the new peace psychology produced by the pact, peoples will take the view that no matter how serious the dispute, there is no justification for solving it by force, unless the question of self-defence is involved. Some opponents state that the pact has no positive value since it does nothing which the League of Nations has not done. Nevertheless, while the League has made great progress toward organizing the machinery of peace, the "gap in the Covenant" still exists. This gap will be filled by the pact, it is argued, and, what is of equal importance, the United States, which has declined to accept the obligations of League membership, for the first time commits itself not to embark upon aggressive war.

Other opponents argue that the pact is useless without machinery for the pacific settlement of disputes, without disarmament, without the modification of peace-time policies which in the past

---

[1] Cf. a Foreign Office memorandum on British Relations with France and Germany, written in 1907 by Eyre Crowe, who later became the permanent head of the British Foreign Office. *British Documents on the Origins of the War,* Vol. III (1928), p. 397.

have led to war. But in reply it is declared that if governments take the pact seriously, if in a high act of faith they really believe their neighbors have renounced war, they will soon translate this belief into acts. The occupation of the Rhineland, the prohibition of the union of Germany and Austria, the demand for large navies and high tariff walls rest largely upon the fundamental fear of war. If nations now really trust each other's promise, the justification for these and for other policies will, it is contended, come to an end.

If despite the ratification of the anti-war pact, governments decline to change their policies, if they construct large navies in the name of self-defence, and if they follow policies which unnecessarily irritate their neighbors, they may be charged with hypocrisy and the international situation will become more critical than if no anti-war pact existed. But even if governments pay only lip service to the ideal, the anti-war pact will become a formidable weapon in the hands of public opinion. If the British government introduces a large navy bill into Parliament, members will ask, does this bill conform to the spirit of the pact? If the government of the United States should land troops in Nicaragua, public opinion will ask, does this intervention conform to the spirit of the pact? Legal arguments upon these points may be made. But whatever the result of these arguments may be, the moral fact of the existence of the pact may constitute an overpowering obstacle to any peace-time policy which disturbs international friendship. Viewed from this standpoint, the pact contains really immense possibilities.

All of these agreements, the Geneva Protocol, Locarno and the anti-war pact in a sense guarantee the *status quo* and prevent it from being changed by force. Some of these agreements provide for arbitration. By itself, however, arbitration is no adequate substitute for law. Courts of law, domestic or international, cannot change unjust laws; they can only apply and enforce them. If the League is to become a living agency for peace, it must provide some means for revising treaties whose terms are inequitable and for developing international law in those realms of international relations where so far each state has been a law unto itself. The League cannot maintain peace simply by preventing the forceful change in a status quo which may be unjust. Without justice, no real peace can endure.¹ While the anti-war pact and similar agreements are welcome as the beginnings of an international régime based upon law, they must be supplemented by the development of the quasi-"legislative" activities of the League and other international organizations, which will be discussed in the next two chapters.

¹ Apparently M. Politis had this in view when he said, at the fifth Assembly, while the Protocol would check wars, it could not be certain of preventing all wars "because there are certain disputes which cannot be settled by the application of rules of law." *Verbatim Record*, 25th Plenary meeting, p. 5. Cf. also Prof. J. L. Brierly, "The Shortcomings of International Law," *British Yearbook of International Law*, 1924, p. 4.

CHAPTER XXVII
INTERNATIONAL CONFERENCES

1. The Making of International Law.—2. International Legislation before the War.—3. The Supreme Council.—4. International Legislation and the Equality of States.—5. Modifications in the Equality Doctrine.—6. The Lack of a Conference System.

1. THE MAKING OF INTERNATIONAL LAW

Until recent years, advocates of world peace have concentrated their attention upon the development of judicial or semi-judicial machinery for the settlement of international disputes. Important as this development has been, it has taken cognizance of disputes only after they have arisen; it has done nothing to prevent them from coming into existence. Removing the causes of disputes involves the making of new law—the determination of new policies. This is ordinarily a task for an institution known as the legislature.[1] In international relations, such a body is called a conference; being composed of representatives of presumably equal and independent states, it proceeds by a set of rules which differ radically from the rules which bind a domestic legislature. Nevertheless, the function of both bodies is the same—remedying old wrongs by new laws, or erecting new legal fences about fields in which men or nations hitherto have roamed without restraint.

That there is an important difference between the judicial and legislative functions in international society is emphasized in the following statement:

"The primary function of government is not to decide disputes

[1] In Anglo-Saxon countries, the courts have built up a large body of judge-made law. Cf. R. Pound, *The Spirit of the Common Law* (1921), Ch. VI. But in continental countries the courts have never exercised such liberty. It is doubtful whether the world, dominated by the Roman idea of law, would allow the World Court to create new international law by judicial decision as freely as did the common-law courts of England. This possibility is already hindered by Article 59 of the Statute which provides that a decision of the World Court "has no binding force except between the parties and in respect of that particular case."

THE MAKING OF INTERNATIONAL LAW

when they have arisen, but to settle relations between sections and persons on lines so just and clear that a conflict of interest may never arise. . . . Boards of conciliation and courts of arbitration may compose disputes which would otherwise inflame international relations. . . . They can remove dust capable of causing dangerous friction in bearings. But where heat is due to faults in the design or workmanship of the bearings they can do nothing. Judges are menders, not fitters or engineers. . . . The overemphasis placed by jurists on conciliation and on arbitration arises from a failure to distinguish occasions of conflict from the causes of war. In domestic policy their whole training limits their view to occasion of conflict, and hence the notorious failure of the legal mind in the sphere of statesmanship. In foreign affairs they are even more dangerous advisers. Machinery for conciliating and adjudicating disputes—for dealing, that is, with occasions of conflict—has its uses. . . . But machinery for handing the real causes from which great conflicts arise is of infinitely greater importance." [1]

What a few of these causes are, has been pointed out in the first two sections of this book, where it was demonstrated that many of the really important sources of international conflict have not yet been subjected to the regulatory influence of international legislation. Moreover, the history of the world has been filled with treaties imposed on defeated powers at the end of wars, the injustices of which have been remedied only by the use of force when the vanquished power has sufficiently recuperated. The anti-war pact discussed in the last chapter, takes the position, and perhaps wisely, that the use of force is not justified even to right existing injustices. If this is so, it becomes all the more necessary to establish some peaceful means of revising treaties whose terms are recognizably unfair.

Many international lawyers, and some states, have upheld a doctrine called *rebus sic stantibus*—that when conditions change, a state is relieved from observing a treaty which is no longer applicable.[2] A good case may be made out for this doctrine just as a

---

[1] "The World in Conference," Sept., 1920, *Round Table*, No. 40, pp. 732–734.
[2] For a summary of the different writers, cf. C. G. Fenwick, *International Law*, pp. 345 ff. Cf. also Sir J. F. Williams, "The Permanence of Treaties," *A. J. I. L.* Jan. 1928.

good case may be made out for the doctrine of humanitarian intervention. Nevertheless, as long as each state remains the sole judge of whether a treaty should be terminated, the doctrine of *rebus sic stantibus* will be abused. For example, Germany invaded Belgium in 1914, in violation of the treaty of 1839, on the ground of self-defence, a justification which other powers regarded only as a pretext. The only means of linking up this doctrine with justice is by submitting the question of whether or not a treaty should be changed to an international body.

In the past, international law has been largely derived from a body of customs which has arisen out of the practice of the different nations.[1] Although no regular international legislative body existed for the purpose of formulating international law, nevertheless a growing number of conferences were held during the nineteenth century, to draft treaties which—when ratified—became new international law, and to carry on other kinds of international business.

2. INTERNATIONAL LEGISLATION BEFORE THE WAR

During the last century international conferences were held in regard to technical, economic, commercial and humanitarian subjects which produced about fifty international conventions that may be called international law.[2] In 1874 the powers signed a convention establishing the Universal Postal Union; in 1875 they sim-

[1] Cf. *Paquete Habana*, 175 U. S. (1899) 677, 708.

[2] The following is a list of the chief multinational conventions produced by this type of "law-making":
  1. Conventions regarding the protection of submarine cables—1884, 1886, 1887.
  2. Convention regarding the international circulation of motor cars—1909.
  3. Agreement regarding the sealing of railway trucks subject to customs inspection—1907.
  4. Agreement regarding the standardization of railways—1886.
  5. Convention establishing an International Union for the publication of Customs Tariffs—1890.
  6. Convention regarding the unification of commercial statistics—1913.
  7. Convention raising the Turkish customs tariff—1907.
  8. Convention for the redemption of toll dues on the Sound and Belts—1857.
  9. Convention for the redemption of the Stade Tolls on the Elbe—1861.
  10. Convention for the redemption of the toll dues on the Scheldt—1863.
  11. Convention guaranteeing the free use of the Suez Canal—1888.
  12. Convention unifying regulations regarding collisions at sea—1910.
  13. Convention for the safety of life at sea—1913.

INTERNATIONAL LEGISLATION BEFORE THE WAR 679

ilarly established a Telegraphic Union; fifteen years later they set up an International Union for the publication of Customs Tariffs; while in 1905 they established the International Institute of Agriculture. During this period were formulated the two Berne labor conventions. Conferences were also held in 1899 and 1907 which produced the conventions in regard to the pacific settlement of international disputes. In response to the moral sense of the world, conferences similarly met to make international law aimed at the white slave, opium and liquor traffics. In 1885 and 1890 two great conferences laid down new international law for the continent of Africa.

Before the War about twenty-five different types of conferences were periodically held, at which the multinational conventions on

14. Convention exempting hospital ships from port charges—1904.
15. Convention regulating tonnage measurements of vessels—1898.
16. Convention suppressing nightwork for women—1906.
17. Convention suppressing the use of white phosphorus in matches—1906.
18. Conventions suppressing the White Slave Traffic—1904, 1910.
19. Convention suppressing obscene publications—1910.
20. Sanitary conventions—1892, 1893, 1894, 1897, 1903.
21. Convention regarding the unification of the metric system—1875.
22. Convention regarding the unification of drug formulae—1906.
23. Convention regarding the establishment of a concert pitch—1885.
24. Convention establishing the International Agricultural Institute—1905.
25. Conventions regarding precautionary measures against phylloxera—1881, 1889.
26. Convention protecting birds useful to agriculture—1902.
27. Convention as to the protection of minors—1902.
28. Conventions as to the Universal Postal Union—1874, 1891, 1897, 1906.
29. Conventions in regard to the International Telegraphic Union—1875, 1908.
30. Convention in regard to wireless telegraphy—1912.
31. Conventions regulating fisheries in the North Sea—1882, 1889.
32. Conventions regulating the North Sea liquor traffic—1887, 1893, 1894.
33. Conventions protecting industrial, artistic and literary property—1883, 1886, 1908, 1911, 1914.
34. Convention relating to civil procedure—1905.
35. Conventions in regard to the slave traffic—1841, 1885, 1890.
36. Convention in regard to the opium traffic—1912.
37. Conventions in regard to the arms traffic—1890, 1906, 1908.
38. Convention protecting seals—1911.
39. Conventions restricting the liquor traffic—1890, 1906.
40. Conventions establishing the Permanent Court of Arbitration—1899, 1907.
41. Conventions in regard to the laws of war—1856, 1864, 1868, 1907, 1909.
42. Convention in regard to weights and measures—1875.

these different subjects could be revised. More spectacular, perhaps, have been the conferences held at the close of every great war, such as the Conference of Vienna of 1815, the Congress of Berlin of 1878, and the Paris Peace Conference of 1919.[1] On the American continent, the Pan-American Union holds periodic conferences, the last being held in 1928, and the next to the last in 1923. The Central American Republics have held two conferences at Washington—in 1907 and in 1922–1923. The only international political conference on American soil in which European and Asiatic powers have participated was the Washington Conference on Armament and Pacific questions, held in 1921–1922, and attended by nine European and Asiatic powers.

The Concert of Europe.—During the early part of the 19th century, a serious effort to dictate European policy was made by a loose association of the great powers, called the Concert of Europe. Following the Napoleonic wars, Austria, Prussia, and later, France, held a number of conferences for this purpose, not only at Vienna in 1815, but also at Aix-la-Chapelle in 1818, Troppau and Laibach in 1820–1821, and at Verona in 1822.[2]

[1] The most important international political conferences before the World War are as follows:

Date	Place	Subject
1820	Troppau	Peace of Europe
1821	Laibach	" "
1822	Verona	" "
1826	Panama	Peace of America
1827	London	Greek affairs
1847	Lima	Peace of America
1855	Vienna	Crimean War
1858	Paris	Danubian Principalities
1860	Paris	Syrian question
1864	London	Schleswig-Holstein
1867	London	Luxemburg
1869	Paris	Crete
1871	London	Black Sea question
1876	Constantinople	Balkan question
1878	Berlin	" "
1900	Peking	Chinese affairs
1906	Algeciras	Morocco
1913	London	Balkan affairs

Cf. E. Satow, *Guide to Diplomatic Practice* (2d ed., 1924), paras. 460 ff., also Satow, *International Congresses and Conferences*, Peace Handbook, No. 151; P. Potter, *Introduction to International Organization*, p. 322; L. Woolf, *International Government*, p. 159.

[2] Cf. W. A. Phillips, *The Confederation of Europe* (1914), Pts. V, VI.

INTERNATIONAL LEGISLATION BEFORE THE WAR 681

While this combination failed in its purpose to guarantee the constitutional status quo of Europe, its failure was due, not to the principle of coöperation, but to a policy which violated the principles of nationalism and of democracy, which no Concert could possibly enforce. In settling Near Eastern affairs, the great powers were more successful. During the critical period of Greek independence, they did not hesitate to "arrange" the affairs of Greece and Turkey, compelling both parties to accept the settlement, in the interest of the "peace of Europe," of which the Concert regarded itself as trustee. The influence of the Concert was later extended to other Near Eastern disputes, until it assumed a "collective authority" to supervise the solution of the whole Eastern question—an authority which was tentatively exercised after 1826, and systematically exercised after 1856; and which was successively applied to Greece, Egypt, Syria, the Danubian principalities and the Balkan peninsula generally.[1] In 1880 the powers held a conference at Berlin where it was declared "an object of European interest" to put an end to the delay of Greece and Turkey in agreeing as to a boundary. Consequently, by a majority vote, they determined upon a frontier which, despite the mobilization of her troops, Greece was obliged to accept.[2]

In 1867 Holland contemplated the sale of the Duchy of Luxemburg to France. From the narrow standpoint of "sovereignty," this sale was nobody's affair, except the parties immediately concerned. If consummated it would have nevertheless led to war between France and Prussia because of the strategic location of the territory. Consequently the powers intervened in support of the peace of Europe; and a conference was held in London of Austria, France, Belgium, Holland, Great Britain, Italy, Prussia and Russia, at which the sale was blocked and Luxemburg placed under a collective guarantee.[3] The same principle of a conference of the great powers was used to settle the Moroccan question at Algeciras in 1906. By invoking this principle, the European Concert prevented a European war not only over the Balkan

[1] T. E. Holland, *The European Concert in the Eastern Question* (1885), p. 2.
[2] Cf. C. 2611 (1880), Vol. LXXXI, p. 901.
[3] A cardinal policy of the Concert of Europe was, if it could not prevent a war, to localize it, i. e., prevent powers not immediately involved in the controversy, from entering it. Cf. Sir Edward Grey, on the Balkan question, 56 *Parl. Debates*, H. C. (1913), 2283.

question, but also over the Belgian question in 1831, over Mehemet Ali in 1840, over the Luxemburg question in 1867, and over the Moroccan question in 1905–06. While many of these different conferences were controlled by considerations of expediency rather than of justice, and while they were composed only of a few great powers, some of which had autocratic governments, they did constitute a rudimentary attempt to establish an international "legislature" to formulate European policy, without recourse to war.

Despite these conferences, diplomatic business before the War was conducted for the most part by negotiation. When conferences were convened they were attended, not as a rule by responsible cabinet ministers, but by diplomats. "If a difficult question arose it was unusual for the responsible Ministers from the countries concerned to meet and discuss the matter face to face. Almost the invariable practice was to deal through intermediaries—skilled, tactful and experienced intermediaries, but not those persons on whom the ultimate responsibility rested." [1] Consequently, the decisions of these conferences were in constant danger of being rejected when subjected to the scrutiny of ministry and parliament at home.

3. THE SUPREME COUNCIL

As a result of the necessity for coöperation during the World War, the Allied governments resorted to a new and improved type of conference, a conference of the principal ministers and experts concerned. The first meeting of Heads of Governments took place in July, 1915—a meeting at Calais, which accomplished, we are told, more in a single day than ordinary diplomatic correspondence could have accomplished in weeks.[2] In 1916 the Supreme War Council was formed of the Allied Prime Ministers, each accompanied by one colleague, selected according to the subject under discussion.[3] The Allied Naval Council, the Maritime Transport Council, and the Blockade Council which "covered every sphere of inter-allied activity, and constituted a veritable

---

[1] Sir Maurice Hankey, "Diplomacy by Conference," reprinted, *Round Table* (1921), No. 42, p. 288.
[2] *Ibid.*, p. 291.
[3] P. E. Wright, *At the Supreme War Council* (1921), Ch. I; *The Supreme War Council*, A League of Nations, Vol. I, No. 7 (1918).

organ of international government," were also created.[1] These different councils, however, were purely advisory. They were councils, not of diplomatic representatives with delegated authority, but of ministers and experts responsible for carrying out the advice they themselves had agreed upon in conference. In other words, the type of international administration employed during the war influenced and in many instances controlled national governments, but it did not replace them. It succeeded in this purpose because it followed the principle of direct contact—bringing together experts in the different national administrations, instead of diplomats, and developing among these national experts an international point of view. Thus the French wool official dealt with British and Italian wool officials, but only on the subject of wool. "The Members of these Committees were essentially national officers who met in conference, or in constant association, for international work. In their own departments they represented the international point of view; in Allied meetings they represented the national point of view." [2]

Although about twenty-five powers had taken part in the war against Germany, it would obviously have been as unfair as it was impossible to give them each an equal share in the decisions of the Peace Conference. Consequently, this important gathering was rigorously controlled by the Supreme Council—composed of the five great powers each of which had two representatives—under the name of the Council of Ten. In February, 1919, a Supreme Economic Council was also established with a view to alleviating the dreadful economic condition of Europe.[3] Since the Council of Ten proved too large for effective work, the main decisions of the Peace Conference were made by the Council of Four—the President of the United States, and the Prime Ministers of Great Britain, France and Italy.[4] For more than three weeks this body met only with an interpreter and without a secretary. After January, 1920, the date when the Treaty of Versailles went into effect, the Supreme Council—the Allied Prime Ministers—brought

[1] Hankey, cited, p. 299.
[2] Sir J. A. Salter, *Allied Shipping Control, An Experiment in International Administration* (1921), pp. 251, 253 ff.
[3] Cf. Baker, *Woodrow Wilson and World Settlement*, Ch. XL.
[4] Cf. Temperley, *A History of the Peace Conference at Paris*, Vol. I, pp. 247 ff.; Vol. III, Appendix IV.

to an end its permanent sittings. But periodic sessions were held from time to time until December, 1923, when they appear to have ended altogether, following the French occupation of the Ruhr.

In the reconstruction period following the War, the Supreme Council acted as the arbiter of Europe. Its authority was not derived from any legal document—at least before the ratification of the peace treaties; but it resulted from the military power which the Allies had acquired as a result of their victory. With the disorganization of Russia and the disintegration of the Austro-Hungarian Empire, a large number of responsibilities fell upon the Allies, which the Supreme Council was obliged to assume. In those cases where the peace treaties merely provided for the transfer of certain territory to the principal Allied and Associated Powers, such territory had to be governed temporarily by the Supreme Council, which was also obliged to make some permanent disposition of it.[1] In some instances, as in the case of the Polish occupation of Eastern Galicia, the trouble between Hungary and Roumania in Transylvania, and the seizure of Fiume by d'Annunzio, the Supreme Council was unable to act effectively, because of lack of troops and of differences of opinion between the governments concerned. Moreover, since the Supreme Council was a body representing only the principal Allied powers, its decisions in a dispute between a defeated and an Allied government were naturally tinged with favoritism.

In the opinion of some critics, the Supreme Council should have transferred its functions to the League of Nations. The latter body, it was urged, could have settled the disputes arising out of the reconstruction of Europe more fairly and more effectively than a body composed of a few victorious powers. But manifestly this was impossible. The League lacked the force and the resources to carry the peace treaties into effect. It had no power

---

[1] Some of its tasks, particularly that of drawing new boundaries, the Supreme Council delegated to the Conference of Ambassadors, the diplomatic representatives of the principal Allied governments at Paris, a body which held about 285 meetings up to January, 1924. For its relation to the League, cf. p. 630. Sometimes the old Concert of Europe worked through a Conference of Ambassadors, particularly at Constantinople, where they were called *Elchis*, controlling both foreign and internal affairs in Turkey between 1839 and 1867. Lord Eversley, *The Turkish Empire* (2d ed., 1923), Ch. X. The Diplomatic Corps at Peking has also frequently intervened in Chinese affairs.

INTERNATIONAL LEGISLATION

to change the terms of the treaties. Neutral members of the League would have disliked to assume any obligations in connection with such treaties, some of the provisions of which were regarded as unjust. If the League had immediately attempted to settle all of the problems arising out of the Treaty of Versailles, it would probably have been torn by dissensions over the liquidation of a war for which it was in no way responsible.[1]

4. INTERNATIONAL LEGISLATION AND THE EQUALITY OF STATES

Such is the rudimentary machinery which the powers have from time to time set up to formulate and administer international legislation, either in regard to non-political subjects or to policies which the great powers wished to impose upon the remainder of the world. As we have seen, the fruit of these conferences has been a large body of international law. As yet, however, this body of law has only touched upon the really important problems out of which international conflicts arise. While a misconceived nationalism and imperialism have been largely responsible for this backwardness in international society, there have been three defects in international machinery which also prevented conferences, numerous as they were before the War, from building up a real international spirit and accomplishing results of a more far-reaching nature. These defects arose out of (1) the doctrine of equality of states, (2) the lack of a regular conference system, (3) the lack of permanent administrative machinery.

Ordinary domestic legislation is usually adopted by a mere majority vote of the legislative body concerned, the minority being bound without its consent. International legislation, on the other hand, becomes binding upon each power only with its own consent—a corollary from the doctrine of Equality of States.[2]

[1] "The Supreme Council," *The Round Table* (1920), No. 39, "The World in Conference," *ibid.*, No. 40.

[2] The American Institute of International Law, December, 1915, adopted a resolution, part of which declared, "Every nation is in law and before law the equal of every other nation belonging to the society of nations, and all nations have the right to claim and, according to the Declaration of Independence of the United States, to assume, among the Powers of the earth, the separate and equal station to which the laws of nature and of nature's God entitles them." Cf. E. Root, "The Declaration of the Rights and Duties of Nations Adopted by the American Institute of International Law," 10 *A. J. I. L.* (1916), 211.

Applied to international conferences, this doctrine has been interpreted to mean, first, equality of voting power—thus in an international conference Costa Rica has the same vote as the United States; and second, unanimity before any decision can be taken. At the first Hague conference Roumania defeated the principle of compulsory investigation; while at the fourth Assembly, Persia defeated the adoption of a resolution voted for by all the other members present.[1] Indeed, in some conferences, the principle of unanimity has been applied, not only to formal voting, but also to the mere discussion of subjects. At the Conference on Central American Affairs, Secretary of State Hughes, the presiding officer, said, "When nations are invited as sovereign powers to engage in a conference, of course no nation can be bound without its consent. Unanimity is a part of the consequences of the status of States in international law. They must consent. Now, it is usual, therefore, when a conference is called, for the Government calling the conference to propose the questions to be discussed, because if those invited do not want to discuss the questions, then of course they will refuse. . . ." Therefore, as to new questions unanimous consent, formally or informally, is required.[2] In the third place the principle of equality carries with it the requirement of unanimity in ratification before an agreement signed at a conference may go into effect. A state cannot be bound by a convention which it does not ratify. In some cases, this doctrine has gone so far as to prevent the execution, between themselves, of a convention by those states who have ratified, as long as one power which has signed the convention withholds its ratification. The treaties of the Washington Conference provided that they should "take effect on the date of the deposit of *all* the ratifications. . . ."[3] The failure of France to ratify the submarine treaty has consequently prevented this treaty from going into effect even among the powers ratifying it.

At the two Hague Conferences of 1899 and 1907 the doctrine of equality of states was rigorously adhered to. Twenty-six states were represented at the first conference, and forty-four states at

---

[1] Cf. p. 599.
[2] *Minutes*, cited, p. 80.
[3] Cf. Art. 24, Naval Treaty; Art 6, Submarine Treaty; Art. 9, Open Door Treaty. [Italics ours.]

MODIFICATIONS IN THE EQUALITY DOCTRINE 687

the second, making the difficulty of securing unanimity unusually great. In the 1907 Conference each state was given one vote,[1] and unanimity on all important decisions was required. Because of this rule, agreement as to the establishment of a Court of Arbitral Justice and of an International Prize Court proved impossible. The power wielded by the small states under this system aroused a great deal of criticism, especially in the press.[2]

5. MODIFICATIONS IN THE EQUALITY DOCTRINE

So great have been the defects in the equality of states principle, that even before the War, the rule was being modified. First of all, in the case of some non-political bodies, states have agreed to be bound without their specific consent. The Congress of the International Postal Union decides by majority vote.[3] Certain fundamental articles in the convention can be amended only by unanimous vote; but 13 other articles may be amended by two-thirds vote, while the convention may be interpreted by a simple majority. In the old sugar commission, decisions were by majority. A state was actually bound to change its tariff against its wishes if a majority so decreed.[4] The International Board of Health at Constantinople and the Danube Commission also decide many questions by majority vote.[5] In fact, it appears that in the most successful international administrative unions, the unanimity requirement has been displaced by the rule of the majority.[6]

In the second place, the equality of states rule has been modified, as far as non-political conferences are concerned, by according increased representation to the large states. Eight international administrative unions give separate representation to colonies.[7]

---

[1] Cf. Art. 8, Regulations, *Proceedings, Conference of 1907*, cited, p. 58. Cf. Hicks, "The Equality of States and the Hague Conferences," 2 *A. J. I. L.* 530.

[2] Cf. summary in E. D. Dickinson, *Equality of States in International Law* (1920), pp. 287 ff.

[3] Art. 18, Convention of Oct. 9, 1864, 65 *State Papers*, 13.

[4] Convention of March 5, 1902, 95 *State Papers*, 6, 10.

[5] Art. 12, "Règlement fixant l'ordre des travaux de la Commission Européene du Danube," Nov. 10, 1879; D. Sturdza, *Recueil de documents relatifs à la liberté de navigation du Danube* (1904), p. 130.

[6] F. Sayre, *Experiments in International Administration* (1920), p. 158.

[7] The Universal Postal Union, the International Telegraphic Union, the International Union of Weights and Measures, the International Union for the

Other international organizations divide their members into groups, the members in each being given a certain number of votes, according to the strength of the group. This plan is followed in the International Office of Public Hygiene and in the International Institute of Agriculture. The members of the latter body are divided into five groups, members of the first group being given 5 votes and 16 units of assessment for expenses; the second group, 4 votes and 8 units; the third group, 3 votes and 4 units; the fourth group, 2 votes and 2 units; the fifth group, 1 vote and 1 unit.[1] In the Air Navigation convention of 1919, an International Commission was established, composed of two representatives each for the United States, France, Italy and Japan; one for Great Britain and one for each of the Dominions and India; and one for each of the remaining states. While representatives are thus allocated, the convention provides (in effect) that each of the five great powers (Great Britain, the Dominions and India constituting for this purpose one state) shall have five votes; while the remaining powers—twenty-two in number—shall each have one. By this means the five great powers have a majority.[2]

In the third place, the expenses of many organizations are borne, not according to equality, but according to capacity. Contributions to a number of bodies, such as the Pan-American Bureau and the Bureau of Weights and Measures, are made by member states in proportion to their population.[3] Eight other bodies divide members into classes and apportion units of assessment among each class according to the ability of each class to pay such assessments.[4] These examples show that in the case of certain non-

Publication of Customs Tariffs, the International Institute of Agriculture, the International Wireless Telegraphic Union, the International Sanitary Conference, and the International Conference on Expositions; D. P. Myers, "Representation in Public International Organs," *A. J. I. L.* (1914), 81.

[1] Art. 10, *Treaties of the U. S.*, Vol. II, p. 2140; cf. Art. I, convention for the International Office of Public Hygiene, *ibid.*, p. 2216.

[2] *Treaties of the U. S.*, Vol. III, p. 3778.

[3] *Ibid.*, Vol. II, p. 1927.

[4] International Bureau of Industrial Property, the International Telegraphic Union, the Universal Postal Union, the International Union for the Protection of Literary and Artistic Works, the International Wireless Telegraphic Union, the International Institute of Agriculture, the International Office of Public Hygiene, the International Bureau of the Permanent Court of Arbitration at The Hague. Dickinson, *Equality of States in International Law*, pp. 313–321.

MODIFICATIONS IN THE EQUALITY DOCTRINE

political activities, independent states have been willing, for the purpose of forwarding national interests as well as international solidarity, to modify the old doctrine of equality of states, whether in waiving the rule in regard to unanimity, or to equality of votes and contributions.

While states have been willing to surrender their prerogatives in certain non-political international activities, they have been very reluctant to be bound in political matters without their express consent. In order to overcome the obstacle which an extreme application of the equality of state doctrine opposed to international coöperation, the tendency before the War was to confine important political conferences to the great powers immediately concerned and to limit the agenda to subjects upon which agreement was possible. Nevertheless, some of the most important political conferences avowedly discarded the equality of state doctrine. At the Congress of Vienna of 1815, the European powers were divided into four classes: (1) the four great powers—Prussia, Russia, Austria and England—which reserved for themselves the initiative and the decision in questions affecting the whole of Europe; (2) France and Spain, which were admitted to present their views on European subjects; (3) Sweden and Portugal, which, as signatories of the treaty of Paris of 1814, nominally participated in the work of the Conference, but actually had less influence than France or Spain; (4) the remaining states which could present opinions only on questions directly interesting them. At the protest of Portugal, all eight powers which signed the Treaty of Paris were finally admitted to the committee which prepared the work of the Conference. But the most important decisions, such as the disposition of Poland, Saxony and Naples were made by the five great powers. Not more than 17 out of the 67 Protocols were signed by Portugal, Spain and Sweden. Although the Final Act of June 9, 1815, was signed only by five powers—Sweden, Portugal and Spain having declined to adhere—this did not prevent it from becoming the law of Europe. [1]

At the Paris Peace Conference of 1919 the rule of equality of states was similarly modified. In the preamble of the peace treaties, a distinction was made between the Principal Allied and Associated Powers—the British Empire, France, Japan, Italy,

[1] C. Dupuis, *Les Rapports des grandes puissances avec les autres états*, p. 47.

and the United States [1]—and the lesser Allies. At the conference, each of the five Principal Powers was entitled to five plenipotentiary delegates; Belgium, Brazil and Serbia, three; Australia, Canada, South Africa, India, China, Greece, Hejaz, Poland, Portugal, Roumania, Siam and Czechoslovakia, two; Cuba, Guatemala, Haiti, Honduras, Liberia, Nicaragua, Panama, Bolivia, Ecuador, Peru, Uruguay and New Zealand, one. This grouping was arranged by the Supreme Council; following the rule of every important conference, the real work was done in a number of commissions—fifty-eight technical commissions being appointed, which held a total number of 1,646 meetings.[2] For purposes of representation on these commissions, the powers were grouped as follows: (1) belligerent powers with general interests— the five Allied and Associated Powers, representatives of which attended all sessions and all commissions; (2) belligerent powers with particular interests—the lesser Allies, representatives of which attended sessions only when matters concerning them were discussed; (3) powers which had only broken off diplomatic relations with the Central Powers—such as Bolivia, Ecuador, Peru and Uruguay, representatives of which attended sessions only when matters concerning them were discussed; (4) neutral powers which might be heard at sessions devoted to questions in which they were directly concerned.[3]

While in the plenary sessions of the Conference, each power had a single vote and the rule of unanimity was followed, only six plenary sessions, largely formal in character, were held. The real decisions were taken in the commissions referred to, which were dominated by the great powers. When disagreement appeared between these great powers, one usually submitted to the wishes of the majority without the formality of a vote, or mutual compromises were effected which made agreement possible. The rule of unanimity, strictly construed, was ignored when, despite the refusal of China to sign the treaty because of the Shantung award, the Treaty of Versailles was nevertheless put into effect.[4] Moreover, the text of the treaty provided that it should become

[1] The United States was known as an "Associated" Power.
[2] Baker, W. *Wilson and World Settlement*, Vol. I, p. 188.
[3] "Rules of the Preliminary Peace Conference at Paris, 1919," 13 *A. J. I. L.* (1919), sup., 109. Cf. Temperley, cited, Vol. I, pp. 247 ff.
[4] Cf. p. 465.

binding in its provisions, upon being ratified by Germany and *three* of the Principal Allied and Associated Powers, despite the fact that a total of 27 powers had signed it. In the commissions established by the different peace treaties, for the purpose of delimiting frontiers, administering certain territories, conducting plebiscites, controlling armaments, reparations and waterways and so forth, the principal Allied and Associated Powers were given a preponderant voice.[1]

This domination of political conferences by the great powers has been the subject of much hostile criticism, not only because of the violation of the academic doctrine of equality of states, but also because of the belief that these powers dictate settlements to suit selfish interests, and enforce such settlements upon smaller states, in disregard of their wishes and their needs. Undoubtedly this is a danger which, in some cases, has been realized. On the other hand, the opposite extreme—in which a tiny country such as Panama would have the same voice in an international conference as the British Empire—is perhaps more dangerous and impracticable. As long as the strictly construed doctrine of equality of states is followed, the progress of international coöperation may be blocked by a tiny country having an unrepresentative government.

6. THE LACK OF A CONFERENCE SYSTEM

Again, international conferences have not been as successful as they might have been in the past, because they did not meet periodically and because they were not world-wide in membership. Political conferences were often held just after a war or to prevent the outbreak of a war, at a time when the atmosphere was not conducive to the advancement of peace or the supremacy of reason. As a rule, conferences met only upon invitation—a fact which gave the nation extending the invitation an initial advantage. It could control the subjects under discussion and it could limit membership in the conferences as it desired.[2] Since conferences were exceptional, diplomats attempted to limit their

[1] Cf. Arts. 81, 86, 87, 93, 95, 109, 110, 118, 119, 203, 428, Treaty of Versailles; Armstrong, "The Doctrine of Equality of Nations in International Law and the Relation of the Doctrine to the Treaty of Versailles," 14 *A. J. I. L.* (1920), 540.

[2] P. Potter, *Introduction to the Study of International Organization* (1922), p. 327.

activities to ratifying proposals tentatively arrived at by previous negotiations.[1] Discussion—an essential of international legislation—was consequently restricted. There was no obligation regularly to confer in an international conference, with the exception of the non-political conferences mentioned above. Powers regarded an international gathering as people regard a major operation,—something to be submitted to as a last resort.

Finally, with the exception of the administrative bureaus elsewhere discussed, there was no administrative machinery preparing the ground for these conferences or supervising the administration of agreements which they should adopt. Six months were required to perform the administrative work necessary for the convening of the Washington Conference. While an efficient Secretariat served the Conference during its sessions, it was dissolved at its close.[2] To act intelligently and efficiently, an international conference must be supplied with impartial, accurate, and carefully digested information—a task for a permanent secretariat to perform. If international legislation is to develop progressively, international agreements must be carefully and continuously scrutinized by administrative agencies. In the next chapter, we shall see to what extent the League of Nations has established a conference system which, while maintaining unimpaired the independence of its members, has escaped the three limitations which we have just discussed of the conference system as it existed before the War.

[1] Woolf, *International Government*, p. 55.
[2] The resolution regarding Existing Commitments in China provided that the powers should "at their earliest convenience" file with the Secretariat General a list of concessions held by their nationals in China. *Treaties of the U. S.*, Vol. III, p. 3135. While the task of collecting such a list would take several months, the Secretariat was dissolved at the close of the conference, virtually rendering this part of the resolution nugatory.

CHAPTER XXVIII

THE LEAGUE OF NATIONS

1. The "Legislative" Function of the League.—2. Membership in the League.—3. The Assembly: Organization and Powers.—4. The Council: Organization and Powers.—5. Relation of the Council to the Assembly.—6. The League's Finances.—7. The League and the Equality Doctrine.—8. The Secretariat.—9. The Amendment and Interpretation of the Covenant.

In creating the League of Nations as an integral part of the peace treaties of 1919, the authors of the Covenant wished to insure the establishment of a permanent international organization which should serve two main purposes: (1) the pacific settlement of international disputes, a judicial function which has been previously discussed;[1] (2) the formulation of international policies, new international law, by periodic international conferences, so that disputes between nations should not arise—a legislative function.

1. THE "LEGISLATIVE" FUNCTION OF THE LEAGUE

Of these two objects, the latter is, perhaps, the more difficult to achieve. Decisions of courts are made by majority vote, and they follow prescribed principles of law. Parties to such decisions are supposed to carry them out in good faith. On the other hand, legislative conferences act only by unanimous vote, subject to the ratification of each government concerned. In bringing about the establishment of the World Court, the League of Nations has laid a judicial foundation for an international society. But if it is to succeed in bringing about a peaceful and a happy international world, it must construct a firm legislative framework, unhampered by those obstacles which have made the progress of international legislation so difficult in the past.

[1] Cf. Ch. XXV.

In fulfilling its legislative aim, the Covenant of the League of Nations does not attempt to establish a super-state. "It is not a separate organization existing apart from and above the States of which it is composed. It is international, not supernational. . . . It seeks agreement, in which it may or may not be successful, but failure to accept its decisions or recommendations involves no penalty. . . . The League is, in fact, a body of States working together on a common basis, seeking to promote their common interests in one co-operative effort for the purpose of which they have voluntarily agreed beforehand to observe certain rules of conduct, and, in the mutual interest, to limit their freedom of action in certain directions." [1] Whatever the sanctions against aggression may be,[2] no member of the League may be obliged to accept any legislative proposal of either the Council or the Assembly.

2. MEMBERSHIP IN THE LEAGUE

There are two kinds of members of the League, (1) original, (2) non-original. The original members are those states—42 in number—actually named in the Covenant.[3] "Any fully self-governing State, Dominion or Colony not named in the Annex" may become a non-original member, "if its admission is agreed to by two-thirds of the Assembly, provided that it shall give effective guarantees of its international obligations, and shall accept such regulations as may be prescribed by the League in regard to its military, naval, and air force and armaments." [4] Fourteen non-original members were elected by the first seven Assemblies of the League, making the total membership, in 1929,

---

[1] *The League of Nations: Its Constitution and Organization* (1923), Information Section, p. 6.
[2] Cf. p. 595.
[3] The annex of the Covenant listed 32 states signatories of the treaties of peace as original members, and listed 13 other states who were invited to accede. Three signatories of the treaties of peace—the United States, Ecuador and the Hejaz—did not ratify. Cf. M. O. Hudson, "Membership in the League of Nations," *A. J. I. L.*, July, 1924, p. 436, also Schücking and Wehberg, *Satzung des Völkerbundes*, pp. 164–255; Scelle, "L'admission des nouveaux membres de la Société des Nations par l'Assemblée de Genève," 28 *R. G. D. I. P.* (1921), 122.
[4] Article 1. "Fully self-governing State" apparently means a state independent of outside control. For the membership of the British Dominions, cf. p. 208.

MEMBERSHIP IN THE LEAGUE 695

fifty-four.[1] The chief difference between original and non-original membership is that only non-original members are obliged to give effective guarantees as to their international obligations and to accept regulations prescribed by the League in regard to armaments.[2] The application of a number of states such as Armenia, Azerbaijan and Lichtenstein for membership has been rejected on the ground that they are too small to assume the obligations of the Covenant.[3] Only one state thus far has been admitted without fully accepting the obligations prescribed by the Covenant—Switzerland. In declarations made to the Council in 1919 and 1920 the Swiss government declared that Switzerland, as a member of the League, could not take part in any military action or allow foreign troops to pass through its territory, on account of its neutralized status; although it would fulfil the obligation to impose an economic boycott under Article XVI. In February, 1920, the Council adopted a resolution recognizing Switzerland's unique position and accepting its declaration in regard to military troops.[4]

Of the fifty-four members of the League, 26 are European and 29 are non-European states. The following states are not members:[5]

Afghanistan	Iraq
Brazil	Mexico
Ecuador	Russia
Egypt	Turkey
Nejd	United States

[1] Two states resigned. Cf. p. 697.

[2] This provision in regard to international obligations has been interpreted very liberally. Most of these states have been virtually required to make Declarations protecting Minorities, although, in the absence of treaties, such protection has not been considered an international obligation.

[3] The first Committee of the first Assembly suggested the possibility of three lesser forms of membership for small states: (1) association with the League but without a vote; (2) representation by some other state, a member of the League, (3) "limited participation,"—admission to membership with privileges only to be invoked when its special interests are concerned. Cf. *Records of Second Assembly* (1921), Plenary Meetings, p. 687.

[4] *O. J.*, March, 1920, p. 57; for the German position cf. p. 655. However, the government of Colombia adhered to the Covenant but did not desire to recognize ipso facto the republic of Panama which was a signatory to the Covenant. *Procès-Verbaux*, Conseil, II, p. 41. Ottlik, *Annuaire*, 1920–1927, p. 204. Since then the treaty of April 6, 1914, between Colombia and the United States in which the United States pays an indemnity of $25,000,000 to Colombia, and in which Colombia recognizes the Panama Republic, has been ratified. March, 1922. *Treaties of the U. S.*, Vol. III, p. 2538.

[5] For Brazil and Costa Rica, cf. p. 697.

The status of Argentina is uncertain. The executive acceded to the pact, but this accession has not yet been approved by the Argentine parliament. The delegate of Argentina withdrew from the first Assembly following its failure to adopt certain Argentine proposals. But the Argentine government continued to pay its dues and has attended meetings of League Committees.

Bolivia and Peru have been absent from the Assembly since 1921 because of the election at that time of the Chilean delegate as president.[1]

If the ideal of international coöperation is to achieve its greatest measure of success, the League must become universal. As long as such powerful states as Russia, Turkey and the United States remain aloof and in a position of active opposition, conflicts between non-members and members of the League may arise.[2]

This possibility has, however, been diminished by the willingness of non-members to coöperate in certain League activities. Soviet Russia has coöperated with the League in its health and disarmament activities. It attended the International Economic Conference. During the last eight years the United States has materially changed its attitude toward the League. It gradually adopted the policy of sending representatives "in an advisory and consultative capacity" and observers to various meetings, such as the Brussels Financial Conference of 1920, the Transit Conference of 1923, the Customs Formalities Conference of 1923, and the Obscene Publications Conference of 1923. Its present practice is, however, to send delegates with full powers to all ad hoc League conferences of a humanitarian and economic nature, and also to disarmament meetings. American private citizens are represented on the Opium, Health, White Slave, and Economic Committees. An American is also a member of the League Narcotic Control Board.[3] In January, 1928, the United States paid to the Secretariat $16,748.60, as its share of the secretariat expenses in connection with certain conferences attended by the United States. The United States also transmits its treaties to the Secretariat for

[1] Howard-Ellis, *The Origin, Structure and Working of the League of Nations*, p. 104. For the Tacna-Arica dispute, cf. pp. 37, 39.

[2] Cf. p. 635.

[3] For the list of League meetings in which the United State has participated, cf. G. Ottlik, *Annuaire de la Société des Nations*, 1928 p. 455.

publication.¹ Such treaties are not, however, registered but given a special numbering.

In a confederation of independent states, a member state may secede from the association whenever it wishes to do so.² In the Covenant, however, the members voluntarily agree to restrict the right of secession so that it shall not be used to escape their obligations and to keep the League upon a permanently unstable basis. According to the Covenant, any member "may, after two years' notice of its intention to do so, withdraw from the League, provided that all of its international obligations and all its obligations under this Covenant shall have been fulfilled at the time of its withdrawal." While the Covenant is silent in regard to the matter, the Council or the Assembly apparently determines whether or not a member wishing to withdraw has fulfilled its obligations, although the World Court may no doubt be asked for an advisory opinion.³

Three states have given notice of withdrawal. The first was Costa Rica who, following a request to pay up back dues, served notice on January 1, 1925, and ceased to be a member, December 31, 1926. Following correspondence in regard to the Monroe Doctrine,⁴ the Costa Rican government in September, 1928, said that it would ask its Congress for funds so that it might return to the League.

Brazil and Spain gave notice of withdrawal from the League in June and September, 1926, as a result of the struggle over permanent seats on the Council at the time of the admission of Germany.⁵ In reply to a communication from the Council, March, 1928, Spain announced that she would remain in the League.⁶ Brazil ceased being a member June 13, 1928. In a note of April 9, 1928, the Brazilian government informed the Council that it would be "one of the most devoted collaborators of the League of Nations."⁷ One question which is not finally settled is whether or

---

[1] Cf. M. O. Hudson, "The United States and the Registration of Treaties," *A. J. I. L.*, 1928, p. 853.

[2] Cf. p. 231.

[3] In the United States Senate, a reservation was proposed making the United States the sole judge of whether or not its obligations had been fulfilled. 59 *Cong. Record* (1920), 4599.

[4] Cf. p. 638.

[5] Cf. p. 655.

[6] *O. J.*, May, 1928, p. 603.

[7] *O. J.*, June 1, 1928, p. 778.

not non-members of the League may participate in certain activities of the League, and thus receive League advantages without assuming the corresponding responsibilities.

Moreover, no amendment to the Covenant shall bind any member which signifies its dissent therefrom, but in that case it shall cease to be a member of the League. To withdraw in this case it is not necessary, apparently, to give the two years' notice otherwise required.[1] Furthermore, "Any Member of the League which has violated any covenant of the League may be declared to be no longer a Member of the League by a vote of the Council concurred in by the Representatives of all the other Members of the League represented thereon."[2] In other words, a member that violates the Covenant may be expelled.

3. THE ASSEMBLY: ORGANIZATION AND POWERS

In order to provide for a permanent conference system, in which a legitimate distinction between the great and small powers would be recognized, the Covenant provided for the establishment of a Council and an Assembly. "At meetings of the Assembly each Member of the League shall have one vote, and may have not more than three representatives." Since each member is thus equally represented, the Assembly is a body controlled by the small powers. This body regularly meets the first Monday of every September at Geneva, while special assemblies may be held at the request of a member, approved by a majority. The agenda of each meeting is drawn up by the Secretary-General of the League with the approval of the President of the Council; but any question proposed by a former Assembly, by the Council, or by a member of the League is included. Under exceptional circumstances the Assembly may add new questions to the agenda; but it cannot pass upon them until four days after they have been reported by a Commission, unless the Assembly shall decide otherwise by a two-thirds vote.

The "Bureau" of the Assembly is composed of a president, and twelve vice-presidents, six specially elected, and the six presidents of the general committees. For the most part, the work of the

[1] Schücking and Wehberg, p. 254.
[2] Arts. 1, 26, 16 of the Covenant.

THE ASSEMBLY: ORGANIZATION AND POWERS

Assembly is done through Committees, upon each of which every state may have one delegate. At present these Committees are as follows:

> First Committee: Constitutional Questions
> Second Committee: Technical Organizations
> Third Committee: Reduction of Armaments
> Fourth Committee: Budget and Financial Questions
> Fifth Committee: Social and General Questions
> Sixth Committee: Political Questions.

While all important questions are debated in these Committees, an opportunity for final debate is given in the Plenary Assembly, where the final vote on questions is taken. The official languages of both the Council and the Assembly are English and French, speeches delivered in one language being interpreted into the other.[1]

Three kinds of power are exercised by the Assembly: (1) The *powers of an electoral college*—the Assembly admits new members to the League, elects non-permanent members of the Council, and participates in the election of the judges of the Permanent Court. (2) The *constituent power*—that of discussing and proposing amendments to the Covenant.[2] (3) The *deliberative power*. According to Article III of the Covenant, "The Assembly may deal at its meetings with any matter within the sphere of action of the League or affecting the peace of the world." Then, according to Article XI, "It is also declared to be the friendly right of each Member of the League to bring to the attention of the Assembly or of the Council any circumstance whatever affecting international relations which threatens to disturb international peace or the good understanding between nations upon which peace depends." This latter article not only authorizes the League to use its good offices to bring about the settlement of a dispute, but it also sanctions the unlimited discussion of policies out of which disputes may in the future arise.

Finally, according to Article XIX,

[1] "Rules of Procedure of the Assembly," *Records of the First Assembly*, Plenary Meeting, 1920, p. 236; for the Revised Rules containing the amendments of the second, third and fourth Assemblies, cf. C. 356 (1) M. 158 (2) 1923.

[2] Cf. p. 723. Cf. Rougier, "La Première Assemblée de la Société des Nations," *R. G. D. I. P.* (1921), p. 200.

"The Assembly may from time to time advise the reconsideration by Members of the League of treaties which have become inapplicable and the consideration of international conditions whose continuance might endanger the peace of the world."

Revision of Treaties.—Under this Article the Assembly may merely give "advice." Since the League is not a super-state, it cannot compel states to modify treaties against their own consent. As a result of the War of the Pacific, Bolivia in 1904, finally signed a treaty with Chile, ceding territory which had given her access to the sea. Believing that this treaty was unjust, Bolivia invoked Article XIX of the Covenant, in 1920, with a view "to obtaining from the League of Nations the revision" of the treaty of 1904.[1] While the first Assembly of the League postponed the consideration of this question, the second Assembly referred Bolivia's request to a Committee of Jurists, which reported that "in its present form," the request of Bolivia was not in order, because the Assembly "cannot of itself modify any treaty, the modification of treaties lying solely within the competence of the contracting States." In other words, Bolivia's request was thrown out on the technical ground that it had been framed improperly.

While this was sufficient cause for rejecting Bolivia's appeal, the Committee did not stop here. But it went further and declared that while the Assembly may "advise" as to the reconsideration by members of their treaties, such advice "can only be given in cases where treaties have become inapplicable—that is to say, when the state of affairs existing at the moment of their conclusion has subsequently undergone, either materially or morally, such radical changes that their application has ceased to be reasonably possible." It appears that this definition would thus prevent the Assembly from advising as to the reconsideration of treaties whose terms were *originally* unjust. Thus interpreted, the value of Article XIX is very restricted. However, this article also says that the Assembly may advise consideration in case of the "existence of international conditions whose continuance might endanger the peace of the world," a clause which is not subject to the limitations imposed on the reconsideration

---

[1] *Records of the First Assembly*, Plenary Meetings, pp. 580, 595. Peru also asked the Assembly to "revise" the Treaty of 1883 with Chile, a request later dropped. Cf. p. 39.

THE ASSEMBLY: ORGANIZATION AND POWERS

of treaties. According to the Committee of Jurists, it is for the Assembly to determine, in each case, "whether one of these conditions did in point of fact exist." [1] Since this question is only one of "advice," it appears that it may be decided by a majority vote, and that, therefore, an interested party cannot block action distasteful to it.[2] Thus, while by virtue of Article XIX, the Assembly has no power to alter treaties, no matter how unjust their terms may be, it does have the power to focus the opinion of the world upon conditions which threaten to disturb world peace. If world opinion is virtually unanimous that a change in these conditions should be made, it would be very difficult for a power to decline the recommendations of the Assembly.

The deliberative powers of the Assembly, thus derived from Articles III, XI and XIX of the Covenant may in turn be distinguished as (1) judicial, (2) legislative, (3) administrative. The judicial powers of the Assembly have already been discussed.[3] The "administrative" power of the Assembly is the power of surveying the work of the other organs of the League. This is done not only through the committees, but also through the debate on the Report on the Work of the Council which occurs during the first six to ten plenary sessions of the Assembly. Usually 20 or 30 member states are represented in the debate, and they may discuss any point raised in the report. The "legislative" power of the Assembly is merely the power to discuss any matter of concern to two or more members of the League. While the different arbitral bodies established by the Covenant or the Protocol may not determine disputes arising out of so-called "domestic questions," such questions may be discussed by the Assembly under Article XI. The result of this discussion may take the form of a treaty which, when ratified, converts a domestic into an international question, so far as the powers ratifying the treaty are concerned. Legal restraints may thus be gradually imposed upon those actions of states which hitherto have led to serious international conflict.[4]

[1] *Records of the Second Assembly*, Plenary Meetings, p. 466.
[2] Cf. p. 718.
[3] Cf. p. 634.
[4] In their report on the Protocol, the First and Third Committees said, "This reference to Article 11 in two of the articles of the Protocol (Articles 5 and 10) has advantages beyond those to which attention is drawn in the commentary on the text of those articles. It will be an incitement to science to clear the

Through these processes the formulation of new international legislation and the codification of existing international law is gradually taking place. In the first eight years of its existence, the following conventions and agreements have been negotiated under the auspices of the League of Nations:

League Agreements

16 international labor conventions.
15 amendments to the Covenant, 4 of which have been adopted.
13 agreements in regard to mandates.
 8 communication and transit conventions.
 8 sanitary conventions, binational in character.
 2 conventions and 2 protocols in regard to opium.
A convention suppressing the traffic in women and children.
A convention suppressing the traffic in obscene literature.
A convention in regard to arms traffic.
A convention in regard to the simplification of customs formalities.
An arrangement in regard to identity certificates for Russian refugees.
A protocol in regard to the settlement of refugees in Greece.
Protocols providing for the financial reconstruction of Austria and Hungary.
The statute establishing the Permanent Court of International Justice.
A draft protocol for the outlawry of war.
A protocol on arbitration clauses in commercial matters.
A convention relating to the non-fortification and neutralization of the Aaland islands.
The German-Polish convention relating to Upper Silesia.
Agreements regulating the status of the Saar and Danzig.
A convention guaranteeing the status of Memel.
Certain resolutions of the Assembly concerning legal assistance for the poor.[1]
Protocol concerning the settlement of Refugees in Bulgaria.
Protocol for the stabilization of the Currency of Greece.
A convention in regard to slavery and forced labor.
A convention on the Execution of Foreign Arbitral Awards.
Conventions for the abolition of Import and Export Prohibitions and Restrictions.
International Agreement relating to the Exportation of Hides and Skins.

ground for the work which the League of Nations will one day have to undertake with a view to bringing about, through the development of the rules of international law, a closer reconciliation between the individual interests of its Members and the universal interests which it is designed to serve." A. 135, cited, p. 12; cf. H. Triepel, *Le Droit international et le droit interne* (1920).

[1] For references to these agreements consult the Index.

THE ASSEMBLY: ORGANIZATION AND POWERS

Protocol regarding Currency and Banking Reform in Esthonia.
Protocol regarding the Bulgarian Stabilization Loan.
Convention establishing an International Relief Union.
General Act and Model Treaties in regard to the pacific settlement of disputes, mutual assistance, nonaggression and the strengthening of the means of preventing war.

The first eight Assemblies adopted a total of 296 resolutions and recommendations. During the same period the Council held 53 sessions and handled 2,400 items of business.[1] By means of such periodic conferences and conventions a great body of international legislation is being accumulated. A beginning only has been made. Nevertheless, for the first time in history, semi-legislative machinery exists for the purpose of furthering the systematic development of international law.

If the Assembly or the Council had restricted the discussion of all of these international subjects to its own sessions, the League would have been doomed to failure. The world is too large and too intricate for any single "legislative" body to supply all of its international needs. The Assembly and Council have wisely avoided the dangers of over-centralization by making use of the following "Technical Organizations":

1. The International Labor Organization.
2. The Communications and Transit Organization.
3. The Economic and Financial Organization.
4. The Health Organization.[2]

These organizations "are established for the purpose of facilitating the task of the Assembly and the Council by the setting up of technical sections on the one hand and on the other to assist the Members of the League, by establishing direct contact between their technical representatives in the various spheres, to fulfill their international duties."[3] The first three of these organizations hold periodic conferences of their own where international treaties relating to each organization are drafted and referred to the different states for ratification. The internal working of these organ-

[1] Cf. G. Ottlik, *Annuaire de la Société des Nations*, 1928, p. 614; D. P. Myers, *Nine Years of the League of Nations*, 1920–1928, p. 26.
[2] The three last Organizations have been established by resolutions of the Assembly.
[3] Council Resolution, *O. J.*, June, 1920, p. 151.

izations should be independent; but their relations with the members of the League should be under control.[1] Thus before any communications of the proposals of these organizations, with the exception of the Labor Organization, is made to the members, the Council of the League must be informed. It should be added that the conferences held by these technical organizations are composed, not of diplomats or even of political representatives, but of experts in the particular subject under discussion.

Moreover, in the formation of international policy in regard to the reduction of armaments, opium, mandates, intellectual coöperation, and the white slave traffic, the League has the services of a number of standing commissions.[2]

International progress depends upon a well-informed and vigorous public opinion; and not the least value of the League is the world-wide interest it has stimulated in foreign affairs.[3] But the League has not only stimulated public opinion; it has worked out a new and scientific technique in the holding of conferences and the formulation of agreements. One example may be found in the negotiation of a European railway convention. In 1922 the Third Assembly voted the League budget which contained an appropriation for a railway conference in 1923. The first step toward this conference was taken by the Transit Section of the League Secretariat, who collected information as to existing facts. Private railway experts and government railway officials were next consulted. The Transit Section now submitted to the Transit Committee of the League information and schemes drawn from the best sources. And the Transit Committee then drew up a draft railway convention which was sent to all the governments together with a report of the Committee. Governments were given three months in which to make up their minds as to the draft before the conference was held. Because of such careful groundwork, which is periodically checked up by the League Council, such conferences, coming as the last act in a long process, are usually a success.[4]

[1] *Ibid.*
[2] Cf. p. 721.
[3] Cf. C. Howard-Ellis, *The Origin, Structure and Working of the League of Nations*, p. 453.
[4] Howard-Ellis, cited, p. 480. The League has also frequently utilized the questionnaire as a method of finding out the attitude of governments toward pending international proposals.

THE ASSEMBLY: ORGANIZATION AND POWERS

Codification.—While the League of Nations has properly recognized that international legislation can best be developed by a series of periodic ad hoc conferences, it has also paid some attention to what is called the codification of international law. Properly understood, this does not mean the making of new law, but merely the formulation in a code of existing law. The purpose of codification is therefore merely to improve the form of law "by getting rid of apparent ambiguities or conflicts, by bringing customary law and statutory law together into one coherent and consistent whole. . . ." [1] It would be extremely difficult, if not impossible, to codify the whole system of international law simply because so many branches are in an undeveloped stage. The objection oftenest made to codification is that it would cut off the spontaneous growth of law, imposing upon the world a static system which practical conditions would soon outgrow. But this would not appear to be a necessarily valid objection, if a code could be drafted in flexible terms so that it would be a better starting point for new development than a mass of incoherent and contradictory precedents.

Realizing that some features of international law may lend themselves to codification, the fifth Assembly (1924) unanimously passed a resolution, requesting the Council,[2]

"To convene a committee of experts, not merely possessing individually the required qualifications but also, as a body, representing the main forms of civilisation and the principal legal systems of the world. This committee, after eventually consulting the most authoritative organisations which have devoted themselves to the study of international law, and without trespassing in any way upon the official initiative which may have been taken by particular States, shall have the duty:

[1] Baker, "The Codification of International Law," *British Year Book of International Law*, 1924; cf. the remarks of M. Rolin, Sept. 22, 1924, *Verbatim Record*, Fifth Assembly, 17th Plenary Meeting.

[2] In passing this resolution, the Assembly was apparently influenced by the popular demand in the United States for "codification" of international law. The fifth Assembly also invited the Council to accept an offer of the Italian government to found an International Institute for the Unification or the Assimilation and Coördination of Private Law, under the direction of the League of Nations, according to principles laid down for the control of the International Institute for Intellectual Coöperation at Paris. This body was established at Rome in May, 1928. Some concern has been expressed at the establishment of such bodies, under the influence of single governments, located at cities other than Geneva.

" (1) To prepare a provisional list of the subjects of international law the regulation of which by international agreement would seem to be most desirable and realisable at the present moment; and

" (2) After communication of the list by the Secretariat to the Governments of States, whether Members of the League or not, for their opinion, to examine the replies received; and

" (3) To report to the Council on the questions which are sufficiently ripe and on the procedure which might be followed with a view to preparing eventually for conferences for their solution."

At the December meeting, the Council appointed such a committee of jurists, including an American.[1]

After considering the reports of this Committee in 1927 the Assembly voted to hold the first Codification Conference at the Hague in 1929, at which would be examined the following questions, (a) Nationality, (b) Territorial Waters, (c) Responsibility of States for Damage done in their Territory to the Person or Property of Foreigners.[2]

The Independence of League Members.—Although the Assembly may thus exercise a great influence in developing international legislation, the independence of each member of the League is safeguarded by three different checks. In the first place, the Assembly can make no decision without the unanimous vote of the members represented at the meeting.[3] Secondly, the representatives at the Assembly act as representatives, not of the League, but of their respective states, and are therefore subject to instructions from their foreign offices. The first Assembly established this principle by adopting a resolution stating that the "representatives sitting on the Council and the Assembly render their decisions as the representatives of their respective States, and in rendering such decisions they have no standing except as such representatives."[4] In the third place, no state can be bound

[1] Mr. G. W. Wickersham is the American member.
[2] By June, 1928, the Committee of Experts for the Progressive Codification of International Law had held four sessions. Cf. *Report*, Committee of Experts, etc., C. 196. M. 70. 1927 V. *Second Report*. A 15. 1928. V. For the Pan-American codification, cf. "The Sixth Pan American Conference, Part II." *I. S.* Vol. IV. No. 9.
[3] Cf. Art. 19, Revised Rules of Procedure.
[4] *O. J. Spec. Sup.*, Jan., 1921, p. 10. The first Assembly adopted a committee report as follows, "In our opinion, the Assembly and the Council should be considered to have complete authority on all matters which the

THE ASSEMBLY: ORGANIZATION AND POWERS

by an agreement drawn up by a League body unless it expressly ratifies it. The procedure of the Assembly, and of conferences held under League auspices, is to draft an agreement, open it for the signature of the states represented, and then submit it to each state for ratification. The Assembly does not even adopt amendments to the Covenant, but merely submits them to the consideration of each member of the League. While the Covenant thus preserves the independence of each state, it has succeeded in establishing periodic world conferences where international affairs may be intelligently and sympathetically discussed. If these discussions lead to international agreements which are ratified by the different members of the League, new international law will have been made.

The advantages of the League system over the old conference system are manifold. While under the old system a prolonged diplomatic correspondence was necessary before holding a conference, any power at present may present a proposal to the Council or the Assembly whereupon it will be discussed. Indeed, in some cases, the initiative comes from the standing commissions.[1] Moreover, while the old conference system was embarrassed by the difficulty of getting preliminary agreement upon the main principles of the desired convention, this work is now undertaken by experts, who submit preliminary drafts to their governments. Conferences are now called, not by a single state, but by the Council and are paid for out of the League budget. The pressure of the Council, the Assembly and the Secretariat in securing the signature and ratification of agreements also explains the remarkable success of the "legislative" activities of the League during the last nine years.[2]

Covenant or the Treaties have committed to them for decision. There are, however, matters referred to in the Covenant which are not within the competence of these organs, but require the concurrence and action of the Governments concerned in the form of international conventions. . . . In these matters one must not forget that the responsibilities of the Governments represented at the Assembly, which is external to the Assembly, cannot be engaged. The action of the Assembly should accordingly take the form of a recommendation or invitation leading up to agreement between the Governments." *Records of the First Assembly*, Plenary Meetings, p. 319.

[1] Baker's article, cited.

[2] Cf. this resolution, passed by the Fifth Assembly (1924): "The Assembly expresses its regret that so few States have as yet ratified the International Convention of 1921 [in regard to the White Slave Traffic], and recommends

A number of suggestions have been made to improve this machinery. In order to create greater international interest, the final discussion and actual signature of conventions drawn up at ad hoc, technical conferences might take place in the Assembly— a procedure which has been tried in the case of a number of conventions.[1] Moreover, the ratification by each power of a convention which its representatives had signed might be assumed, unless within a certain period it notified the other powers that it did not wish to ratify. Furthermore, it may eventually be possible to adopt the practice followed by the Labor Organization in which every government agrees to present a convention adopted by a League Conference to the proper ratifying authority at home for discussion, resulting either in adoption or rejection.

4. THE COUNCIL: ORGANIZATION AND POWERS

While the Assembly represents equally every member of the League, the Council—the second great organ—was originally designed to represent the great powers. This body has three different kinds of members, (1) permanent, (2) non-permanent, (3) special. The four principal Allied powers and Germany are permanent members;[2] while, with the approval of a majority of the Assembly, the Council may name additional states as permanent members, a provision which would authorize the admission of Russia to the Council upon the same basis as France or the British Empire.

Non-permanent Members.—According to the Covenant, the Assembly shall select four members of the Council—"from time to time in its discretion,"—the non-permanent members. This number may be increased by the Council with the approval of the Assembly. In fact, the Council decided in September, 1922, to increase the non-permanent members from four to six, an action

that those States which have not yet adhered to or ratified the Convention should be invited to give the reasons which have prevented their doing so."

[1] The Statute of the Permanent Court of International Justice, the Optional Protocol for Obligatory Jurisdiction, the White Slave Convention of 1921, the Protocol on Commercial Arbitration Clauses of 1923, the Slavery Convention of 1926, and the model arbitration treaties of 1928.

[2] The United States was also entitled to permanent membership. Cf. Art. 4, Covenant.

approved by the third Assembly.[1] In September, 1926, this number was increased to nine. Since the latter are elected by the Assembly, that body, in turn controlled by the small powers, may technically dominate the Council. But as the Council pointed out, "this objection can hardly be considered a serious one, since by Article V of the Covenant, the decisions of the Council are—except where otherwise provided—taken unanimously." [2]

Although the Covenant gives the Assembly complete freedom in choosing non-permanent members of the Council and in determining the time for which they shall serve, members of the first Assembly believed that rules should be laid down which would prevent these positions from being monopolized by a few powers. Switzerland advocated a system of rotation, giving every member an opportunity to serve on the Council, while China proposed that the non-permanent members be divided into a European-American group and an Asia-Pacific-African group, the first being given three seats, and the second being given one. Neither of these plans was adopted partly because of a doubt whether, under the original Covenant, the Assembly could constitutionally impose any limitations of this character.[3] To remove this doubt, the second Assembly (1921), adopted a resolution of amendment, providing that the Assembly, by a two-thirds majority, could fix the rules dealing with the election of non-permanent members.[4] The third Assembly (1922) passed a resolution saying that non-permanent members should be chosen, on the first ballot, by absolute majority of the Assembly, and if a further ballot was necessary, by a plurality. It also declared that it was desirable in electing these members that the Assembly should make its choice "with due consideration for the main geographical divisions of the world, the great ethnical groups, the different religious traditions, the various types of civilization and the chief sources of wealth." The latter recommendation was reiterated by the Assemblies of 1923 and

---

[1] This proposal was opposed by representatives of the Swiss and Dutch delegations in the third Assembly on the ground that an enlarged membership would weaken the efficiency of the Council, and that it would diminish its political influence so that the great powers would hesitate to place disputes before it. The debate is summarized in Schücking and Wehberg, p. 311.
[2] *O. J.*, Nov., 1922, p. 1197, also Annex 423.
[3] *Records of the First Assembly* (1920), Plenary Meetings, pp. 414 ff.
[4] In effect July, 1926.

1924. Following the difficulties arising out of the admission of Germany into the League,[1] the Council appointed a Committee on the Composition of the Council. As a result of its report, the 1926 Assembly passed a resolution stating that it would annually elect three non-permanent members of the Council, to serve for three years. Such a member is not eligible for reëlection unless the Assembly decides by a two-thirds majority that such member is reëligible. This vote may be taken at the expiration of the member's term or in the course of the three year period.[2] The Assembly has declared Poland and Spain reëligible. In 1928 the non-permanent members of the Council were: Canada, Chile, Cuba, Finland, Persia, Poland, Roumania, Spain and Venezuela. Thus four such members are from the western hemisphere. A total of 19 states served as non-permanent members between 1920 and 1928. In order to do away with the difficulties arising out of the differences between permanent and non-permanent members of the Council, the proposal has frequently been made that all Council members should be periodically elected by the Assembly.[3]

"Special" Membership.—According to the Covenant, "Any Member of the League not represented on the Council shall be invited to send a Representative to sit as a Member at any meeting of the Council during the consideration of matters specially affecting the interests of that Member of the League."[4] Since, according to the English text, such a state may sit "as a member," it would, it appears, be entitled to take part in debate and vote. However, it would be unfair to give it a vote in cases where a regular member could not vote, such as when it is a party to a dispute. When the League Council was determining the members of the League of greatest industrial importance, the question arose whether India, which claimed to be such a state and was consequently admitted to special membership, should be given the right to vote. It was decided that India could not be judge and party to the question and that therefore India should simply be allowed to state her case preferably in writing, and then with-

[1] Cf. p. 655.
[2] Resolutions and Recommendations of the Assembly . . . 1926, *O. J.*, Spec. Sup. No. 43, p. 9.
[3] Howard-Ellis, cited, p. 154.
[4] Art. 4, para. 5, Covenant. The French text omits the words "as a member."

THE COUNCIL: ORGANIZATION AND POWERS 711

draw.[1] The same rule was followed in the case of the dispute between Roumania and Hungary in April, 1923.[2] The principle appears to be established, therefore, that "special" members may not vote when the Council sits as an arbitral body for the purpose of deciding a dispute in which such a "special" member is involved.[3] Organizations also have representatives at Council sessions dealing with matters in which they are concerned. For example, the High Commissioner of Danzig sits when Danzig is concerned. But only representatives of states may vote. In fifteen sessions between 1925 and 1928 a total of 120 states and 58 committees thus participated in Council sessions.[4]

According to its rules of procedure, the Council now holds four regular meetings a year, but special meetings may be called upon the demand of any member represented on the Council, or of three members not thus represented. Thus emergency sessions may be held to consider any dispute which threatens international relations. At the beginning of each session, the Secretary-General presents a report upon the steps taken to carry out previous decisions of the Council. The President and Vice-president of the Council are elected by secret ballot and by majority vote. They serve for one year and are not immediately reëligible.[5]

As a rule the Council does its work through a system of *rappor-*

[1] *O. J.*, Nov., 1922, p. 1160.
[2] *O. J.*, June, 1923, p. 611; cf. also the dispute between Czechoslovakia and Hungary, *ibid.*, p. 599. On the other hand, it was stated that both parties in a case coming up under a minorities treaty were entitled to vote. *O. J.*, August, 1923, p. 908.
[3] The determination of what states are "specially affected" by a question before the Council and therefore entitled to representation, is apparently decided by the Council, and since it is a question of procedure, apparently by a majority vote. However, the Council may consult a committee of jurists on the point. Thus when Roumania, Jugoslavia, Bulgaria, Greece, Austria and Hungary asked to sit on the Council when it was considering the control of armaments over the defeated powers, since they were "specially affected," the Council referred the question of their admission to a committee of jurists. After examining the particular clauses in the treaties concerned, the Committee reported that in this particular question the Council should be "constituted in its ordinary manner without the addition of the representatives of other States." It stated, however, that this was not a general opinion as to paragraph 5 of Article 4 of the Covenant. *O. J.*, July, 1924, p. 902; *ibid.*, Oct., 1924, p. 1316.
[4] Myers, *Nine Years of the League of Nations*, p. 31.
[5] Rules of Procedure of the Council, adopted May 17, 1920, *O. J.*, July-Aug., 1920, p. 272.

teurs. That is, a member of the Council is delegated to study and report upon a problem. *Rapporteurs* are chosen from representatives of states neutral to the dispute. The Council now draws up annual lists of *rapporteurs.* Thus the representative of Cuba is *rapporteur* on financial questions; Italy on international law, Canada on child-welfare, and so on.

The "legislative" powers of the Council correspond to those of the Assembly. It may deal with "any matter within the sphere of action of the League." The Council and the Assembly, or their members, perform certain tasks jointly—such as the election of the judges to the World Court; the appointment of future Secretaries-General; increasing the number of members on the Council; the amendment of the Covenant; or under certain conditions the settlement of international disputes.[1]

On the other hand, the Covenant and a growing number of international treaties impose on the Council a large number of duties, a fact which is rapidly making it an integral part of the international system, particularly of Europe. So important have its manifold duties become that—entirely apart from its purely judicial functions—the disappearance of the League would have very serious consequences upon international life.[2]

[1] Cf. p. 634.

[2] For example, the Council has exclusive power to change the seat of the League from Geneva, to formulate plans for the reduction of armaments and for the establishment of a World Court, to advise as to the fulfillment of obligations under Articles 10, 16, and 17 of the Covenant, to define the terms of the mandates and to receive the annual reports from the Mandatory Powers, and to authorize certain expenditures in connection with international bureaus. The independence of Hungary and of Austria is inalienable except with the consent of the Council (Art. 80, Treaty of Versailles; Art. 88, Treaty of St. Germain; Art. 73, Treaty of Trianon). Duties are also imposed upon it in regard to maintaining the independence of Albania, the neutralization of the Aaland Islands, and the security of Constantinople (cf. p. 568). It may exercise certain powers in regard to the disarmament of the defeated powers (cf. p. 567). The Council has certain duties in connection with the Ottoman Public Debt assigned to territories detached from Turkey (Art. 48, Treaty of Lausanne). It appoints a commissioner to secure freedom of transit on railways across the Greek-Turkish frontiers (Art. 107, Treaty of Lausanne). It also performs certain functions under the Statutes of the International Régime of Railways and of Maritime Ports (Art. 36, Statute of Railways, Art. 22, of Ports). It has certain control over the tariff régime of the defeated powers; and over the transfer of insurance in ceded territory, and ports, waterways and railways (Arts. 280, 312, 378, Treaty of Versailles). The Council has certain duties in connection with the safeguarding of the Holy Places and the

5. RELATION OF THE COUNCIL TO THE ASSEMBLY

What the exact relationship of the Council to the Assembly should be is not defined in the Covenant. At the first Assembly it was argued that since the Assembly includes all the members of the League and since it is always named before the Council in the Covenant, it had a superior authority.[1] This argument, however, failed to receive the support of the Assembly as a whole. Nevertheless, because of its power in naming the 9 non-permanent members of the Council, its control over the League budget, and its examination of an annual report from the Council, the Assembly may exercise an indirect pressure upon this body. The Assembly frequently "recommends" that the Council take certain action, a request with which the Council usually complies. Because of its restricted size, it is easier for the Council to meet than for the Assembly. For this reason, and also because of the provisions in the Covenant in regard to the settlement of disputes, the Council has occupied itself largely with semi-judicial and administrative work, while the Assembly has devoted its time largely to questions of "legislative" policy. It is possible that in the future the Council will

fulfillment of financial obligations in Syria and Palestine (Art. 28, British mandate, Art. 19, French mandate). It has other duties relating to the settlement of Greek refugees. It may decide that certain conventions, such as the Arms Traffic convention, need revision (Preamble, Convention of Sept. 10, 1919, cf. p. 282). The Council may be called upon, in at least ten cases, to decide differences of opinion arising out of a number of treaties, such as differences between the Poles and Danzig, or differences over the question of what states are of greatest industrial importance. The Council is authorized to appoint arbitrators, failing the agreement of the interested parties, in regard to the use of waterpower (Arts. 309, 310, Treaty of St. Germain). It has certain powers in connection with appointments to the Mixed Arbitral Tribunals (Art. 304, Treaty of Versailles) as well as of other officials, such as members of the Emigration Commission set up in the Bulgar-Greek convention of 1919 (cf. p. 200) Schücking and Wehberg, p. 315. It has a large number of duties in connection with the meetings of the Assembly; it exercises general control over the Technical Organizations of the League; it chooses the Governing Commission of the Saar; it is the organ of the League as regards Danzig. Important duties are imposed on it in regard to the financial reconstruction of Austria and Hungary. It investigates disputes over minority treaties.

[1] Cf. M. Politis, *Records of the First Assembly*, Plenary Meetings, p. 291.

evolve into a sort of international ministry responsible to the Assembly.[1]

According to the Covenant, either the Assembly or the Council may "deal at its meetings with any matter within the sphere of action of the League or affecting the peace of the world." Does this mean that the Assembly may discuss matters which are specifically placed in the hands of the Council by the Covenant, such as the supervision of the mandates or the limitation of armaments? Or may the Assembly undertake to discuss a matter which the Council already has under consideration? At the first Assembly Lord Balfour proposed that mixed commissions should be established to settle conflicts in jurisdiction between the two bodies,—a suggestion which was not adopted, partly because it would establish a body higher than either the Assembly or the Council.[2] The first Assembly (1920) finally adopted a resolution stating that "The Council and the Assembly are each invested with particular powers and duties. Neither body has jurisdiction to render a decision in any matter which by the Treaties and the Covenant has been expressly committed to the other organ of the League. Either body may discuss and examine any matter which is within the competence of the League."[3]

6. THE LEAGUE'S FINANCES

One of the knottiest problems connected with the League has been that of finance. Since the League cannot tax individuals, it must rely for support upon the contribution of member states. According to the original Covenant, the expenses of the Secretariat shall be borne by members of the League in accordance with the apportionment of the expenses of the International Bureau of the Universal Postal Union.[4] Although this classification did not cause much complaint because of the small contribu-

---

[1] Cf. the remarks of Lord Robert Cecil, *Records of the First Assembly*, Plenary Meetings, p. 286. However, the first Assembly rejected the comparison of the Council to the upper house of a legislature or to a parliamentary ministry.

[2] Rougier, cited, p. 258. *Records*, cited, p. 318.

[3] The first Assembly voted down this proposal: "The Assembly has no power to reverse or modify a decision which falls within the exclusive competence of the Council. The same respect must be shown by the Council for the decision of the Assembly." *Records*, cited, pp. 284, 303.

[4] Cf. p. 140.

tions asked of each state for postal services, when applied to the League, which required much larger sums from its members, the plan proved unsuitable.[1] During the first Assembly (1920) the question was debated whether or not an amendment to the Covenant would be necessary before the allocation system of the Postal Union could be set aside. The second Assembly finally decided the question in the affirmative by adopting a resolution for amendment as follows: "The expenses of the League shall be borne by the Members of the League in a proportion decided upon by the Assembly," an amendment which was ratified and went into force in August, 1924.

At present the value of a single unit amounts to about $5,289; and the number of units assessed against each state is based upon its public revenue in 1913 and its population in 1919. Thus Great Britain pays 105 units, Japan, 60, Netherlands, 23, and Albania, 1.[2]

[1] Thus under the Postal system, the Dominions and India pay the same sums as Great Britain, France, Japan and Italy. Liberia pays one unit to Great Britain's 25, although in population and revenue Great Britain has fifty times as many people as Liberia and 4,250 times as much revenue. Sir Herbert Ames, *Financial Administration and Apportionment of Expenses*, League of Nations Information Section (1923) p. 26.

[2] For 1929–32 the allocation is as follows:

Abyssinia	2	Haiti	1
Albania	1	Honduras	1
Argentina	29	Hungary	8
Australia	27	India	56
Austria	8	Irish Free State	10
Belgium	18	Italy	60
Bolivia	4	Japan	60
Bulgaria	5	Kingdom of Serbs, Croats, and Slovenes	20
Canada	35	Latvia	3
Chile	14	Liberia	1
China	46	Lithuania	4
Colombia	6	Luxemburg	1
Costa Rica	1	Netherlands	23
Cuba	9	New Zealand	10
Czechoslovakia	29	Nicaragua	1
Denmark	12	Norway	9
Dominican Republic	1	Panama	1
Esthonia	3	Paraguay	1
Finland	10	Persia	5
France	79	Peru	9
Germany	79	Poland	32
Great Britain	105	Portugal	6
Greece	7	Roumania	22
Guatemala	1		

Deductions, however, are made in the case of countries which severely suffered from invasion during the War—France, Italy, Roumania, Jugoslavia and Belgium. As an expression of sympathy for Japan in her earthquake disaster, the fourth and fifth Assemblies granted her a temporary reduction of 12 units.

During the first four years of its existence, only 70% of the expected sums reached the League Treasury during a given financial period. In 1926, Bolivia, China, Honduras, Liberia, Nicaragua, and Peru were still in arrears in payments, to the amount of 4,487,000 francs.[1] To make allowance for delinquent assessments, the League has built up a Working Capital Fund, from which each organization of the League may draw funds in case its regular appropriations are not forthcoming. If these are finally paid in, the Working Capital Fund must be reimbursed.

Although the Covenant is silent as to the control of finances, the Council, following the democratic principle that appropriations should originate in the most popular body, left the establishment of a financial system to the Assembly. According to the Regulations for the Financial Administration of the League of Nations, a Supervisory Commission, appointed by the Council, minutely examines a draft budget prepared by the Secretariat.[2] It is then circulated to the members, with the comments of the Commission, three months before the meeting of the Assembly, a provision which insures full publicity. No proposal to increase the budget can be made in the Assembly without being first reported upon by the Fourth Committee, whose judgment the Assembly has rarely reversed.

The average budget of the League for the years, 1921–1929, was between $4,000,000 and $5,200,000 a year—the cost of one-eighth

Salvador	1	Sweden	18
Siam	9	Switzerland	17
South Africa	15	Uruguay	7
Spain	40	Venezuela	5
			986

Cf. "Allocation of the Expenses for the tenth Financial Period" (1928), C. 526. M. 184, 1927. X. *Verbatim Record*, 5th Assembly, 20th Plenary Meeting, p. 12.

[1] Supervisory Commission. Report on 18th and 19th Sessions. A. S. 1926. X, p. 11.

[2] For the regulations, cf. *O. J.*, Jan., 1924, Pt. I, p. 79. An Internal Control Office and an Auditor control the internal expenditure of this money.

of a modern battleship. A little over half of this sum goes to the Secretariat, about one-third to the International Labor Office, and about one-tenth to the World Court. Another tenth of the budget goes for printing bills, which are especially high because of the necessity of printing every document in French and English. The first Assembly cost $180,000, but the Secretary-General was able to cut this sum down one-half, so that the League now holds a conference of delegates from 55 states, sitting continuously for a month, at the cost of $86,000. Great credit is due to the financial administration of the League for its ability to work with limited funds in a time of great stringency. But students now declare that the work of the League is hampered by parsimony, and that the Supervisory Commission has altogether too much influence upon policy.[1]

7. THE LEAGUE AND THE EQUALITY DOCTRINE

In providing for periodic conferences, the League of Nations has fulfilled the first great need of a system of international conferences. We shall now determine to what extent it has modified, if any, the old obstacle of equality and unanimity of votes. The World Court decides by a majority vote; and the International Labor Conferences may adopt recommendations and draft conventions by a majority of two-thirds.[2] As for the Assembly and Council, the Covenant provides (Art. V):

"Except where otherwise expressly provided in this Covenant, or by the terms of the present Treaty, decisions at any meeting of the Assembly or of the Council shall require the agreement of all the Members of the League represented at the meeting.

All matters of procedure at meetings of the Assembly or of the Council, including the appointment of Committees to investigate particular matters, shall be regulated by the Assembly or by the Council and may be decided by a majority of the Members of the League represented at the meeting."

While the Covenant contains no provision as to a quorum, meetings of the Council can be held only when a majority of the

[1] Cf. C. Howard-Ellis, cited, Ch. XI.
[2] Cf. p. 162.

members are present.[1] A majority is one-half of the members plus one. When representatives refrain from voting in the Assembly they are regarded as not being present.[2]

Although unanimity is ordinarily the rule, the Assembly may depart from it in some seven classes of questions and the Council in twelve.[3] Since only a majority is needed to decide questions of procedure,[4] it is now impossible for a single state to block the appointment of a committee to investigate a distasteful subject. Moreover, amendments to the Covenant may be adopted by the members of the League represented on the Council and by a majority of the members represented on the Assembly. Under the Covenant unanimity is restricted to actual "decisions." It does not necessarily apply therefore to recommendations, invitations or advisory opinions. In "advising" as to the consideration of treaties under Article 19, the Assembly apparently may act by majority vote.[5]

The Covenant recognizes that at the present stage of international relations, sovereign states are not ready to be bound in important matters by majority decisions. While preserving intact the sovereignty of each state in these matters, the Covenant has nevertheless made certain modifications in the strict interpretation of the equality-of-state doctrine, so that international progress

[1] Art. 6, Rules of the Council, which says a majority of the representatives of Members, designated in the first two paragraphs of Article IV of the Covenant.

[2] Article 19, Rules of the Assembly.

[3] *Assembly:* (1) election of non-permanent members of the Council—majority; (2) of new members of the League—two-thirds majority; (3) of judges of the World Court—majority; (4) approval of additional Council members—majority; (5) of future Secretaries-General—majority; (6) report in regard to international disputes; (7) questions of procedure—majority.

The Council: (1) questions of procedure—majority; (2) settlement of international disputes; (3) questions relating to the Saar—majority; (4) military control of defeated powers—majority; (5) Albania's independence—majority; (6) the Aaland islands convention—two-thirds majority; (7) protocols relating to the financial reconstruction of Hungary and Austria—majority; (8) Memel—majority; (9) the Greek Refugee Settlement Commission—majority; (10) the Oriental railway—majority; (11) Germany's obligations toward Allied nationals—majority; (12) changes of provisions in minority treaties—majority.

[4] Whether or not a given question relates to procedure is apparently determined by the Assembly (or the Council, as the case may be) by unanimous vote. Cf. the remarks of M. Schanzer, *Records of the First Assembly*, Plenary Meetings, p. 426.

[5] Schücking and Wehberg, p. 336.

will probably be more rapid in the future than in the past. In the first place, a legitimate distinction between the great and the small powers has been made in creating the Council and the Assembly of the League.[1] Secondly, a single state may no longer bar the discussion of any subject of world concern in either the Council or the Assembly. Thirdly, matters affecting the internal organization of the League, and not directly affecting states as such, may usually be decided by a majority. Fourthly, while no treaty may be presented to the members of the League for ratification until it is unanimously adopted by the conference concerned, and while each state may or may not ratify as it chooses, the refusal of a single state does not now prevent an international treaty from going into effect as far as those states which have ratified are concerned. The League has thus sanctioned the doctrine that a state shall not use its freedom to prevent coöperation between states that are willing to accept the obligations to which the first state may be opposed. Fifthly, when a resolution adopted by the Council or the Assembly fails of unanimity, but receives a majority vote, it becomes a recommendation under which any state may act.[2] A resolution interpreting the Covenant which does not receive a unanimous vote is not rejected, it is merely *not adopted*.[3] While under the Covenant the independence of each state has been safeguarded, it thus appears that a large number of improvements over the old conference system have been made.

8. THE SECRETARIAT

Before the War no international civil service collected facts for the consideration of international conferences, arranged the countless details connected with their organization, followed up the ratification of agreements negotiated, or supervised their execution. Not the least important of the provisions of the League Covenant is the article establishing a Secretariat to per-

[1] For the importance of this distinction, as far as the election of the judges of the World Court is concerned, cf. p. 615.
[2] Cf. Point of Order on Article 18 of the Covenant, *Records of the Second Assembly*, Plenary Meetings, p. 895.
[3] Cf. the ruling of the President of the Assembly on the vote on the proposed interpretation of Article 10, *Records of Fourth Assembly*, Plenary Meetings, p. 87.

form these services. The first Secretary-General, named in the annex of the Covenant, is Sir Eric Drummond who apparently holds office indefinitely. Hereafter Secretaries-General are to be named by the Council with the approval of the majority of the Assembly. The secretaries and other members of the staff are appointed by the Secretary-General with the approval of the Council.[1]

The Secretariat prepares and keeps all records of the League. It performs the work necessary for the meetings of the Council and the Assembly. It transmits all League documents and reports to members. When a state wishes to invoke the services of the League, it transmits the request to the Secretary-General who forwards it to the proper authority. However, the Secretariat is more than a piece of machinery. It is constantly preparing data and making suggestions as to current international problems. Composed of about 600 people of 36 nationalities, the Secretariat has acquired a detachment which gives serious weight to its studies. No member of the Secretariat may accept any honor or decoration during the term of his appointment.[2] As Lord Balfour has said, "The members of the Secretariat once appointed are no longer the servants of the country of which they are citizens but become for the time being the servants only of the League of Nations. Their duties are not national but international."[3] Much of the progress of the last nine years in international legislation has been due to the follow-up work of the Secretariat. In addition to being an extremely important piece of machinery without which the periodic conferences of the League could not be held, the Secretariat has really become a permanent adviser on international affairs.[4] The Secretary-General who presides over the

---

[1] Arts. 6, 7, Covenant. All positions in the League are open equally to men and women. Representatives of the members of the League and officials of the League when engaged on its business enjoy diplomatic privileges and immunities. The property of the League shall be inviolable. For the Secretariat personnel, cf. "Staff List of the Secretariat," *O. J.*, Oct., 1923, p. 1232.

[2] Resolution of the Council, *O. J.*, June, 1920, p. 139.

[3] *Ibid.*, p. 137.

[4] "By its composition, its functioning and its permanent character, the Secretariat General constitutes one of the most interesting institutions and one of the most original creations of modern political history." Krabbe, "Le Secrétariat Général de la Société des Nations et son Activité," *Les Origines et L'Œuvre de la Société des Nations*, cited, Vol. II, p. 264.

Secretariat, is assisted by four Under-Secretaries-General. Each section is usually headed by a director and assisted by a "member of section." Within the Secretariat, a Bureau for Latin America has likewise been established to handle the relations between the Secretariat and the Central and South American countries.

Recently the Secretariat has been criticized on the ground that it is losing its international character. Each of the great powers has come to feel entitled to an Under-Secretary-Generalship, and a number of positions have come to be filled not by independent experts but by career diplomats. Promotions to the high posts are not always made from within the ranks, but the plums are given to diplomats who temporarily leave their respective services for a turn at Geneva. The system, unless checked, will be bad for the morale of the Secretariat, and will cast doubt upon the impartiality of its officials.[1] Thus the Nationalist government of China has been confronted by the fact that the director of the political section of the Secretariat is a Japanese diplomat. These developments came to the attention of the 1928 Assembly which passed a resolution asking the Secretary-General and Council to follow out the principles of the Balfour report.

A number of standing commissions have also been established which exercise an important influence not only upon administration but upon international policy. Two of these commissions—the Permanent Advisory Commission on Armaments and the Mandates Commission—are provided for in the Covenant. The first Assembly authorized the establishment of a Temporary Mixed Commission on Armaments and also the Opium Commission. The Geneva Conference of 1921 in regard to the White Slave Traffic established a Commission on the Traffic in Women and Children. The second Assembly authorized the establishment of the Committee on Intellectual Coöperation. In June, 1924, the Council established a Slavery Committee. Moreover, each of the so-called Technical Organizations has a committee, such as the Economic and Finance Committee, the Communications and Transit Committee, and the Health Committee, which advise in regard to these subjects and act as semi-executive bodies for the organizations. When questions concerning these different matters come up before the League, it is customary to refer them to the

[1] C. Howard-Ellis, *cited*, p. 202.

appropriate commission, which makes a thorough study and recommendation to the Council or the Assembly.[1]

According to Article XXIV of the Covenant, "all international bureaux already established by general treaties," shall be placed under the direction of the League, if the parties consent. All bureaux hereafter constituted shall likewise be placed under the League. By this means unnecessary duplication and expense will be saved. In considering the meaning of Article XXIV, the League Council decided that when a bureau was placed under the League, the latter should not interfere with its purely internal affairs. It was also decided that private international organizations (of which there are about 500) might be placed under the League.[2]

[1] The Secretariat is divided up into Sections as follows:

1. *The Political Section*—which studies political questions, especially those placed before the League by members under Articles 11, 15, 16, 17, and 19 of the Covenant.

2. *The Information Section*—which keeps the public informed as to the activities of the League, through such publications as the *Monthly Summary*, published in 12 different languages.

3. *The Legal Section*—which studies questions arising out of the interpretation of the Covenant and other instruments, relating to the competence of the League, etc.

4. *Financial Administration*—which studies and collects information in regard to the financial problems of the League.

5. *The Economic and Financial Section*—a section which has investigated such problems as the distribution of raw materials, the economic boycott, and the financial reconstruction of Austria and Hungary; and which serves the Economic and Finance Committees.

6. *Section for Administrative Commissions and Minorities Questions*—which studies questions relating to Danzig, the Saar, and alleged violations of the minorities treaties.

7. *Transit Section*—which studies the problems intrusted to the League by Article 23 of the Covenant and which serves the Communications and Transit Organization.

8. *The Mandates Section*—which serves the Mandates Commission.

9. *The Section for Intellectual Coöperation and International Bureaux*—which studies matters connected with Article 24 of the Covenant, and which serves the Committee on Intellectual Coöperation.

10. *Section for Social Questions*—which studies questions connected with the opium and white slave traffics and which serves the Opium and Slavery Committees.

11. *Armaments Section*—which serves both the Standing and Temporary Mixed Armament Commissions.

12. *Health Section*—which studies the international aspects of disease and serves the Health Committee.

[2] *O. J.*, Sept., 1921, p. 759. Up to 1925, five organizations—the International Hydrographic Bureau, the International Office for the Control of the

AMENDMENT: INTERPRETATION OF COVENANT 723

There are two types of administrative activities in which the League is engaged. The first is directed toward coördinating certain activities of independent states—already discussed. The second is more strictly of a supra-national nature—duties engaged in by the League as such.

The League agencies undertaking the latter class of duties may be listed as follows:

1. The Governing Commission of the Saar.
2. The League High Commissioner for Danzig.
3. The General Commissioners of the League in regard to the reconstruction of Austria and Hungary.[1]
4. The Financial Adviser to Albania.[1]
5. The High Commissioner for the repatriation of prisoners of war and of the Russian refugees.
6. The Commissioner for Bulgarian Refugees and the Autonomous Office for Greek Refugees.

By means of these different administrative officials, whether in the Secretariat proper or out in the field, a new system of international machinery is gradually being built up which, merely by throwing individuals of different nationalities together, should prepare the way for a better international spirit.

9. THE AMENDMENT AND INTERPRETATION OF THE COVENANT

In order to meet the needs of a growing experience, the interpretation and amendment of any constitution, domestic or international, is necessary. In the vast majority of domestic constitutions, amendments may be enacted without the necessity of a unanimous vote of the constituent power. If the rule of unanimity is followed, change becomes well-nigh impossible, as our experience with the Articles of Confederation showed. At the same time, as we have seen, in international affairs states refuse to be bound in important matters without their consent. Realizing these two

Liquor Traffic in Africa, the International Committee for Air Navigation, the International Association for the Promotion of Child Welfare, and the International Relief Bureau had been placed under the League. By virtue of Article 24, the Secretariat publishes an annual *Handbook of International Organizations* and a *Quarterly Bulletin of Information on the Work of International Organizations.*

[1] Now terminated. Cf. p. 431.

conflicting difficulties, the authors of the Covenant worked out a practicable means of amendment without binding a state to a change to which it could not agree. Article XXVI of the Covenant attempts to reconcile the needs of progress with the doctrine of independence by providing,

"Amendments to this Covenant will take effect when ratified by the Members of the League whose Representatives compose the Council and by a majority of the Members of the League whose representatives compose the Assembly.

"No such amendment shall bind any Member of the League which signifies its dissent therefrom, but in that case it shall cease to be a Member of the League."

While the Covenant is silent as to the means of proposing amendments, the second Assembly passed a resolution saying that no amendment should be proposed for ratification unless it received a three-fourths vote of the Assembly, including the votes of all members represented on the Council—a provision which prevents the submission of amendments which have no chance of adoption. It also proposed an amendment to the Covenant to the effect that if the required ratifications are not received in 22 months, the proposed amendment shall remain without effect—a provision similar in nature to the clause in the 18th amendment of the Constitution of the United States, stating that it would be inoperative unless ratified by the necessary number of states within seven years. Moreover, the Covenant is not clear as to whether the members belonging to the Council which must approve the amendment, means those members of the Council at the time the amendment is *proposed* or when it is *adopted*. In order to clear up this ambiguity the second Assembly also proposed in its resolution for amendment that amendments must be ratified by states represented on the Council "when the vote was taken" by the Assembly. In the first six Assemblies, sixteen proposals for amendments to the Covenant were adopted. Up to the present, five amendments [1] have received the necessary ratifications. The amending process is thus still slow, primarily because of the necessity of securing the ratification of all the members on the Council.[2]

[1] To Articles IV, VI, XII, XIII and XV.
[2] The ratification of some of these amendments was delayed so long because of a single member on the Council—Spain. *Report of British Delegates, Fourth*

AMENDMENT: INTERPRETATION OF COVENANT

Every constitution needs interpretation, and in federal constitutions the question has arisen whether they should be interpreted by the states or by some branch of the federal government. Although a large number of questions of interpretation have arisen under the League Covenant, the League Council or Assembly has not referred them to the World Court, apparently on the theory that since the power to amend the Constitution is vested in the states members of the League, the power to interpret the Constitution must also be placed there. Moreover, these questions, it is urged, are "political" and "general" in nature; the Court should limit itself to the determination of concrete cases.[1]

When a question in interpretation arises before the Council or the Assembly, the practice ordinarily has been to refer the question to a committee of jurists, the report of which is not binding unless approved. At the fifth Assembly, M. Ador of Switzerland, in discussing the Jurists' Report on the dispute over the Covenant arising out of the Corfu affair, said, "the document cannot be regarded as an authentic interpretation of the Covenant or as binding in character. The Assembly must remain the supreme authority in so far as concerns the interpretation of the Covenant." Similarly, M. Politis declared, "The interpretation of the Covenant falls within the sovereign competence of the States Members of the League of Nations." [2] In adopting this principle, the League is following the rule of a confederation instead of a super-state—the rule unsuccessfully advocated by the Virginia and Kentucky Resolutions of 1798.

Assembly, Cmd. 2015 (1924), p. 11. On February 21, 1921, the Council appointed a Committee on Amendments to study the means of proposing amendments and other questions connected with this part of the Covenant. *O. J.*, March–April, p. 110.

[1] Cf. the remarks of M. Salandra in regard to the proposal to submit the disputed interpretation over the Covenant at the time of the Corfu affair to the World Court. *O. J.*, Nov., 1923, p. 1330. At the first Assembly, Mr. Millen of Australia proposed that some authority, such as the World Court, should interpret the Covenant in cases of doubt. But M. Schanzer said that the Assembly had full power to interpret questions by unanimous vote. *Records of the First Assembly*, Plenary Meetings, p. 425.

[2] *Verbatim Record of the Fifth Assembly*, 12th Plenary Meeting, p. 3; *ibid.*, 14th Plenary Meeting, p. 6. The fifth Assembly passed a resolution placing on the agenda of the 6th Assembly, the proposal that, "considering that certain points" in the Jurists' Report on the Covenant "require elucidation, the First Committee should consider how far such elucidation would be desirable."

As this discussion shows, the establishment of international machinery is of great importance. The demand for World Peace will always remain a vain platitude unless it is accompanied by the establishment of permanent international machinery which must necessarily impose certain definite sacrifices upon every nation interested in its maintenance. It is possible, perhaps, to make out an argument for the "Supremacy of National Interests" and "National Freedom of Action." But it is obvious that if each of the fifty-five states of the world should follow these doctrines, international conflicts would be inevitable. The purpose of any international machinery must be to effect a compromise between these conflicting interests. States which refuse to accept these compromises—which refuse to subordinate the principle of national sovereignty to the principle of international solidarity—will obstruct the peace of the world.

The League of Nations is a mere instrumentality which will serve the cause of peace or of war according to the spirit which actuates its members. At the same time, the mere existence of international machinery will elevate this spirit, simply by bringing the nations of the world together in periodic conferences, out of which an international point of view will inevitably be evolved. The adoption of this point of view will not lead to the destruction of nationality. On the contrary, by removing the fear of war and by promoting mutual coöperation, it will facilitate a development of the finest fruits of nationality, a thing which has been impossible in the past.

CHAPTER XXIX
THE CONTROL OF INTERNATIONAL POLICY

1. Are Democracies Pacific?—2. Control of Foreign Affairs in Japan.—3. Constitutional Checks on the Conduct of Foreign Affairs.—4. Legislative Checks on Foreign Policy.—5. Political Checks on Foreign Policy.—6. Democracy and Secret Treaties.—7. Committees on Foreign Affairs.—8. Public Opinion and Foreign Affairs.—9. A "League of Peoples."—10. The American Constitution and Foreign Affairs.

Unprofitable as war has proved to peoples as a whole, it sometimes yields a selfish advantage to a few individuals. For this reason, economic or military groups may conceivably instigate wars in order to pile up profits, acquire monopolies as the fruit of conquest, or to increase their importance in the community. One writer states that "military men cannot admit to be unnecessary that which forms the object of their activity in time of peace. . . . As a chief factor tending to preserve the system of militarism the existence of a professional military class must be considered."[1] While the importance as well as the motives of such a class may be incorrectly estimated, nevertheless a democracy must be ever vigilant to prevent foreign policy from falling under the control of groups who would be tempted to enhance their fortunes or prestige at the expense of the people. If such groups should also dominate an international organization, the welfare of the weaker parts of the world might be more endangered than if such an international organization did not exist. The League of Nations is a system of machinery whose increasing strength may be used for good or evil depending upon the motives of the men in control.

1. ARE DEMOCRACIES PACIFIC?

If an international organization is to promote peace, the members composing it should be agreed upon certain common ideals.

[1] J. de Bloch, *The Future of War* (1899), p. 349.

States which believe that the end of government is only to serve the interests of a privileged class, whether military, social, clerical or economic, will find it difficult to coöperate with really democratic governments whose ostensible object is to advance the social welfare. When Ramsay Macdonald and Edouard Herriot became the respective heads of the British and French governments in 1924, an atmosphere was created which immeasurably purified European politics—and largely because they believed in common liberal principles. The success of international coöperation depends in part upon the diffusion of really democratic ideals throughout the world.

There is a widespread belief that democracies are more pacific than monarchies. Absolutist courts are usually surrounded by a military class, bred in the traditions of war, and a statesman-class, consecrated to the service of Machiavelli. A monarchy may also be consumed with dynastic ambitions which do not trouble democracies. Lord Bryce has pointed out that more liberal views of the American Civil War, the Turkish massacres of 1876, and the Boer War of 1901, were held by the British workingman than by the aristocratic classes—views which were later sustained by history.[1] While the "best people" may be better informed, they are usually more cynical than the "common people"—more inclined to rely upon *force majeur* than upon justice. As a rule, democracies do not harbor the petty suspicions and silly jealousies which have marked the courts of absolutist monarchs in the past. In his message of April, 1917, President Wilson said, "Self-governing nations do not fill their neighbour states with spies or set the course of intrigue to bring about some critical posture of affairs which will give them an opportunity to strike and make conquest. Such designs can be successfully worked out only under cover and where no one has the right to ask questions. . . . They are happily impossible where public opinion commands and insists upon full information concerning all the nation's affairs." He also believed that "no autocratic government could be trusted to keep faith" with the League of Nations.[2]

---

[1] Bryce, *Modern Democracies* (1921), Vol. II, pp. 377–379.

[2] According to Bismarck, "A Republic would find it more difficult to obtain allies than a monarchy." Consequently he supported the Republican movement in France. C. G. Robertson, *Bismarck* (1919), p. 347.

The bitter rivalries between the so-called democracies of the Balkans and Central Europe indicate that there are many exceptions to Mr. Wilson's thesis. But if intrigues do exist in democracies, this may partly be due to the fact that foreign policy is still conducted in the dark. Moreover, the mere change of governmental forms does not alter the fundamental causes of war. People will fight when they believe war is necessary for self-preservation. In fact, nationalistic passions may go to greater excesses in a democracy than in a country where absolutist authority may restrain, when it wishes, jingoism and demagogy.

At the same time, when people realize that war is unprofitable to them as a whole and that, moreover, it is likely to destroy civilization, their willingness to be led into battle by false cries of patriotism will decline. If they are actually in control of government, their pacifism will be reflected in governmental policy. On the other hand, if the people do not control their government, military and economic cliques may attempt, regardless of popular feelings, to incite wars at the expense of the people but for personal gain.[1] As an American statesman says, "Irresponsible governments may fight without being in the least degree mistaken about their rights and duties. They may be quite willing to make cannon fodder of their own people in order to get more territory or more power; but two democracies will not fight unless they believe themselves to be right. They may have been brought to their belief by misrepresentation as to facts, by a misunderstanding of rules of right conduct, or through having the blank of ignorance filled by racial or national prejudice and passion to the exclusion of inquiry and thought; but they will fight not because they mean to do wrong but because they think they are doing right. When foreign affairs were ruled by autocracies or oligarchies the danger of war was in sinister purpose. When foreign affairs are ruled by de-

[1] The Covenant of the League of Nations provides that "any fully self-governing State, Dominion or Colony" is eligible for membership. "Fully self-governing" does not mean democratic, as the admission of Abyssinia, an absolutist kingdom, shows. Japan and Siam, both of which are non-democratic, were original members. Some of the drafts for the Covenant provided that membership should be limited to democratic governments—a proposal which, as the above examples show, was defeated. Schücking and Wehberg, p. 181. "Fully self-governing" means freedom from outside interference in internal affairs. Cf. p. 694.

mocracies the danger of war will be in mistaken beliefs. The world will be the gainer by the change, for, while there is no human way to prevent a king from having a bad heart, there is a human way to prevent a people from having an erroneous opinion. That way is to furnish the whole people, as a part of their ordinary education, with correct information about their relations to other peoples, about the limitations upon their own rights, about their duties to respect the rights of others, about what has happened and is happening in international affairs, and about the effects upon national life of the things that are done or refused as between nations; so that the people themselves will have the means to test misinformation and appeals to prejudice and passion based upon error." [1] If democratic governments indulge in wars peoples have only themselves to blame. The one advantage of democracy over autocracy is that it provides a machinery which the people can control to prevent war as soon as they realize its folly. While the establishment of democratic government is therefore important from the international standpoint, the education of peoples as to the policies which governments should follow is more important still.

2. CONTROL OF FOREIGN AFFAIRS IN JAPAN

That the conduct of foreign affairs by an irresponsible government may have harmful results to the peace of the world, is shown by the constitutional system of Japan. According to the constitution of 1889, the Japanese Emperor may declare war, make peace, and conclude treaties, subject to the advice of the Privy Council which is also under the Emperor's control.[2] In England, the Crown has similar powers but they are exercised only in conformity with the wishes of a ministry responsible to parliament. In Japan, the Emperor has, perhaps, little more power than the British Crown; but his powers are controlled by an extra-constitutional

---

[1] E. Root, "A Requisite for the Success of Popular Diplomacy," I *Foreign Affairs* (1922), p. 5. On the other hand, some writers such as Homer Lea in the United States and Charles Maurras in France take the position that successful diplomacy on the part of democracy is impossible. For a discussion of this issue which gives a verdict in favor of democracy, cf. J. Barthélemy, *Démocratie et Politique Étrangère* (1917), Ch. I; Bryce, *Modern Democracies*, Vol. II, Ch. XVII.

[2] Arts. XI–XIII, Constitution of Feb. 11, 1889.

body, which is responsible only to itself, called the Genro or Elder Statesmen.[1] This body has named prime ministers and decided fundamental questions of foreign policy. It decided whether Japan should enter into an alliance with Russia or with England in 1902, and whether the war with Russia should come to an end when it did in 1905. Owing to the death of two prominent members in 1922–24, Princes Yamagata and Matsukata, it appears as if the power of the Genro is on the wane, and as yet it appears uncertain what body, if any, will take its place.[2]

Certain clans have also had great influence upon Japanese foreign policy. For a long time, the Satsuma clan controlled the navy and the Chioshu clan, the army.[3] Although the influence of these clans has apparently decreased, the control of parliament or even the civilian ministers over the army and navy has not yet been established. The ministers of war and of marine must be military officers. Moreover, the supreme military command is exercised by the Emperor through the chiefs of the General Staffs of the Army and Navy who are responsible only to the Emperor. "Japan is the only large country in the world where the military authorities are not subject to civil control."[4] The chiefs of these staffs have the right of private audience with the Emperor upon all matters concerning national defence. When decisions are reached in conference with the Emperor, they are presented to the Cabinet

---

[1] H. Byas, "The Gods behind the Machine," 23 *Asia* (1923), 753; also "The Elder Statesmen," *Asia*, Feb., 1924. According to one authority, "There is not a single instance on record of the Emperor Mutsuhito of Japan taking any state matter into his hands, independently of the Ministers of State." Uyehara, *The Political Development of Japan* (1910), p. 195.

[2] In 1923 the House of Peers and the Privy Council engaged in a tilt in which the latter body apparently attempted to abrogate to itself the influence of the Genro. The contest reached its climax over the ratification of the Chinese Postal Convention in December, 1922. The Privy Council not only protested that this treaty had been ratified without its consent—which is required by Japanese constitutional practice—but it also protested against the whole China policy of the Kato cabinet. This is the second time in Japanese history where the Privy Council has dared to criticize cabinet policy. Cf. J. Hart, "The China Question in the Politics of Japan," 24 *Weekly Review* (Shanghai, 1923), 82. Cf. also "Constitutional Problems," *Japan Weekly Chronicle*, Jan. 17, 1924, p. 85; "The Choosing of the Premier," *ibid.*, March 6, 1924, p. 320.

[3] For the renewal of clan rivalry, cf. *Japan Weekly Chronicle*, Jan. 10, 1924, p. 55.

[4] T. Nakano, *Ordinance Power of the Japanese Emperor* (1923), p. 155.

as an accomplished fact. It would be an offense against the Emperor to criticize a measure which he has sanctioned. Because of these constitutional arrangements, including the fact that the Japanese parliament cannot withhold military appropriations, the Japanese army and navy are really a law unto themselves. Their families have intermarried with the families of the great commercial interests—resulting in a combined military and economic group whose desire for war may become too strong for a civilian cabinet to control. The establishment of parliamentary and civilian control over the military branch of the government is consequently a reform which recurrently agitates Japanese politics.

Even under supposedly democratic governments, the same problem of subjecting the military to the civil arm still exists. Military dictatorships were established in some European countries following the World War, which became aggressive in foreign policy.[1] In the United States, military men have frequently led campaigns for preparedness and compulsory military service, while some of them have condemned as "pacifist" and "bolshevik," movements for disarmament. Following the Washington Conference, the Navy Department circulated literature criticizing the work of the conference. In 1922 the Navy Department created considerable ill-will in South America by sending a Naval Mission to Brazil—an act taken without the authorization of Congress. In the fall of 1924, the War Department sponsored the celebration of Mobilization Day, one of the purposes of which was apparently to stimulate the drooping militarist sentiment in the country. As citizens, military and naval officials are entitled to their opinions. Whether or not they should be allowed to circulate these opinions by means of governmental machinery, is another question.

3. CONSTITUTIONAL CHECKS ON THE CONDUCT OF FOREIGN AFFAIRS

Even in presumably democratic countries, the control of foreign policy has not yet been subjected to responsible popular control. In every government of the world—with the possible exception

[1] For the intrigues of French military officers in Hungary following the Armistice of 1918, cf. Baker, *Woodrow Wilson and World Settlement*, Vol. II, p. 29.

CHECKS ON CONDUCT OF FOREIGN AFFAIRS

of Turkey—the conduct of foreign affairs is in the hands of an executive department, usually called the Foreign Office, or, in the United States, the State Department. The official at the head of such an office usually formulates the foreign policy of his government. In this respect he has much greater power than the ordinary cabinet minister who merely carries into effect a policy which the legislature has prescribed.[1] While the conduct of foreign affairs must necessarily be left in executive hands, some means of controlling this power must be established, if the danger of its control by a few influential groups for selfish purposes is to be overcome. In an effort to establish a democratic control, governments have set up three kinds of checks over the executive—the first being imposed by constitutional provisions; the second by legislation, and the third by usage.[2]

In England.—In England, there are no constitutional checks upon the power of the Crown over foreign policy. The power to make war and peace and ratify treaties is part of the prerogative of the Crown—which Parliament has never taken away.[3] The Crown also makes treaties without being obliged to obtain legislative consent, as in the United States. While the Crown ratified

---

[1] Cf. A. Ponsonby, *Democracy and Diplomacy* (1915), p. 45.

[2] S. R. Chow, *Le Contrôle parlementaire de la politique étrangère en Angleterre, en France et aux États-Unis* (1920), p. 275.

[3] There are four types of treaty-making power throughout the world: (1) where the executive makes treaties without formal legislative approval, as in the British Empire, Japan and Sweden. In 1919 Senator Giolitti unsuccessfully proposed a constitutional amendment to the Italian Constitution requiring approval of parliament to all treaties and to declarations of war; (2) where certain types of treaties require legislative consent, as in France, Belgium, Bulgaria, Denmark, Italy, and the new constitutions of Europe; (3) where all treaties must be subjected to one branch of the legislature, as in the United States, Mexico and Cuba; (4) where all treaties must be approved by both branches, as in Switzerland, Portugal and the republics of the New World, with the exceptions above.

The power to declare war is (1) an executive function in about 15 governments, including the British Empire and Belgium. In some cases the power to declare an offensive war is limited by the necessity of securing legislative consent; (2) a joint executive and legislative function, as in France, Portugal and 15 of the American republics; (3) an exclusive legislative function as in the United States, Switzerland, and several Central American Republics. Cf. E. D. Dickinson, *Equality of States in International Law* (1920), pp. 193 ff., 201 ff. However, in the United States Congress has never declared war except on the recommendation of the Executive. J. M. Mathews, *The Conduct of American Foreign Relations* (1920), pp. 257 ff.

the Anglo-Russian treaty in August, 1907, it was not even discussed in the House of Commons until the following February.[1] The day before the ratification of the Anglo-Japanese Alliance of 1905, the House of Commons was prorogued, which made parliamentary discussion of these treaties impossible.[2] Only two of the five treaties of the Washington Conference were submitted by the British government to parliament for its approval.[3]

In France.—In contrast with the British system, the constitution of France imposes certain checks upon the conduct of foreign policy. The power of the French President to declare war is dependent upon the consent of Parliament.[4] But if another power declares war on France, the President may repel attack without awaiting the authorization of parliament. Thus France did not declare war on Germany in 1914. Moreover, military expeditions against backward peoples are not considered wars, with the result that the President may embark upon such enterprises without parliamentary consent. Before ratifying certain classes of treaties, such as treaties of peace, finance, commerce, and those involving the status of persons and property rights of Frenchmen abroad, the French President must secure the consent of a majority of both houses of parliament; but he may ratify all other classes of treaties upon his own authority, submitting them to parliament "as soon as circumstances permit."[5] Apparently the interpretation of what treaties fall within each class rests with the President. Treaties involving finance have been interpreted to mean only treaties which cannot be entirely executed without voting a finance law.[6] There is no obligation to submit alliances, arbitration treaties, etc., to parliament. The Treaty of Berlin of 1878, the Franco-Russian alliance of 1897, the Hague convention of 1899, and the treaties relative to freedom of navigation on the Danube and

[1] Ponsonby, p. 75.
[2] On August 11, 1905, 151 *Parl. Debates*, H. C., 4th series, 993.
[3] 156 *Parl. Debates*, H. C. (1922), 717, 1010. Cf. the Treaties of Washington Act, 1922, 12 and 13 Geo. 5, c. 21.
[4] Art. 8, Law of Feb. 25, 1875.
[5] H. Esmein, *Éléments de droit constitutionnel français et comparé* (7th ed., 1921), Vol. II, pp. 192, 196 ff. Cf. E. Villey, *Les Vices de la constitution française* (1918), p. 131; L. Michon, *Les traités internationaux devant les chambres* (1901); J. Sapira, *Le Rôle des Chambres au point de vue diplomatique* (1920).
[6] Esmein, *Droit constitutionnel*, Vol. II, p. 185.

through the Suez Canal were not approved by the French parliament before ratification.[1]

Moreover, French foreign officials have entered into "understandings" with foreign governments which do not even require the signature of the President—let alone parliamentary approval. Thus the "understanding" with Spain over Morocco of October, 1904, was signed merely by the French Minister of Foreign Affairs. During the World War, the French government advanced 20 million francs to Greece, and concluded agreements with Belgium and England in regard to the jurisdiction of their respective armies—all without the signature of the President or the approval of Parliament. The Declaration signed by the Allies in September, 1914, by which they promised not to make a separate peace, was not approved by any parliament. A great number of "declarations" were made by diplomatic representatives during the War, in regard to future peace terms, etc., without legislative approval.

In the United States.—In the United States, constitutional checks on the conduct of foreign policy are more rigid than in France. Here the power to make treaties is invested in the President subject to the advice and consent of two-thirds of the Senate. The appointment of public ministers is likewise vested in the President and a majority of the Senate. Power to declare war, however, rests with Congress.

Many of these checks, the President of the United States has at times been able to evade. In case the United States is attacked, whether by foreign or domestic foes, he may declare a blockade and commit other acts of war without waiting upon Congress.[2] As commander-in-chief of the army and navy, President McKinley sent troops to China in 1900, President Roosevelt sent the fleet around the world in 1907, President Wilson sent troops to Archangel in 1918, and President Coolidge sent three warships to Honduras in 1923—all without the authorization of Congress. As commander-in-chief of the military forces, the Presidents of the United States have also intervened repeatedly in Caribbean and Latin-American countries, upon their own authority. The determination of whether or not intervention should take place under the Platt amendment with Cuba has also rested with the

---

[1] Barthélemy, *Démocratie et la politique étrangère*, pp. 107 ff.
[2] *The Prize Cases*, 2 Black (1865), 635.

executive; in no case has Congress been consulted. While the use of troops without congressional authorization may sometimes be justified because of the necessity of protecting American interests abroad, the President may obviously create a situation by such practices which will make war inevitable.

By means of "executive agreements," the President has also evaded some of the restrictions imposed upon the treaty-making power. Theoretically these agreements are a mere expression of foreign policy, the control of which is in executive hands. Consequently these agreements are never submitted to the Senate for approval. They do not therefore constitute the "supreme law" of the land which the courts will enforce, and their terms may, if the President wishes, be kept secret.[1] Since these agreements are only expressions of foreign policy, they may be terminated by a succeeding administration. For example, in 1923, President Harding terminated the Lansing-Ishii agreement made by the Wilson administration in 1917.[2]

Although the executive agreement has supposedly been only an expression of the President's foreign policy, it has in many cases been used to accomplish the same purpose as a treaty. The Gentlemen's Agreement of 1908, negotiated by President Roosevelt with Japan, regulated Japanese emigration to the United States.[3] Most of the "Resolutions" adopted at the Washington Conference in regard to China were not embodied in treaties and were not consequently submitted to the United States Senate, although they provided for the withdrawal of foreign post-offices from China and the establishment of a Board of Reference.[4] The

[1] Cf. Secretary Hughes' letter in re the Gentlemen's Agreement, to Mr. Johnson, chairman of the House Committee on Immigration, August 16, 1921, "Labor Problems in Hawaii," Hearings before House Committee on Immigration, 67th Cong., 1st sess., pt. 2, p. 928.

[2] *Treaties of the U. S.*, Vol. III, pp. 2720, 3825.

[3] The full text of this agreement has never been published. Cf. House Report 350, House Committee on Immigration, 68th Cong., 1st session.

[4] At the sixth Plenary session of the Washington Conference, Feb. 4, 1922, the Chairman made this statement respecting the form and time of the validity of these resolutions: "It will be observed that certain of the resolutions adopted by the Committee, and on its recommendation adopted by the Conference, are put in treaty form, and other resolutions are not put in that form. The distinction is that those engagements which it is deemed require the sanction of a treaty are put in the form of a treaty and proposed for execution by the Powers. In other cases, the Resolutions are of a character not requiring such

CHECKS ON CONDUCT OF FOREIGN AFFAIRS 737

executive agreement has even been used to annex territory to the United States. By such a means the United States secured the Horse-Shoe Reef from England in 1850. It has also been used to make armistices and peace preliminaries, in some cases defining the terms of peace.[1] Sometimes, the executive agreement has brought about a definitive settlement, as in the case of the Protocol of 1901 ending the Boxer Rebellion which was ratified by President McKinley without the approval of the Senate. Financial control has been established over backward countries by the United States without consulting either branch of Congress. Originally President Roosevelt negotiated a treaty for this purpose with Santo Domingo, but when he found that the Senate would not approve it, he accomplished the same end, in 1905, by means of an executive agreement.[2]

Despite the constitutional provision that the Senate must approve the appointment of "public ministers," Presidents since the time of Washington have appointed special diplomatic agents and peace commissioners without asking the consent of the Senate. Many agents of this character have been appointed by the President alone, for the purpose of negotiating treaties.[3] The American delegates to the Hague Conferences of 1899 and 1907, to the Paris Peace Conference of 1919, and to the Washington Conference of 1921–1922 were appointed by the President without the approval of the Senate. In order to evade the obstructions of the "bitter-

sanction in the form of a treaty, and are deemed to be binding upon the Powers according to their tenor when adopted by the Conference." Official Minutes, *Conference on the Limitation of Armament*, p. 286. On July 29, 1905, a representative of President Roosevelt and the Prime Minister of Japan held a conversation in which the American stated that while the United States could not enter into an alliance or "even to any understanding amounting in effect to a confidential informal agreement, without the consent of the Senate," he felt sure that Japan and Great Britain could count on "appropriate action" of the United States to maintain the peace in the Far East in conjunction with Japan and Great Britain. President Roosevelt is said to have approved this statement. While this may have been "an executive agreement," it appears too vague in terms to constitute a binding obligation. This "secret pact" is first published in Dennett, "President Roosevelt's Secret Pact with Japan," *Current History*, October, 1924.

[1] For the armistice with Germany of Nov. 11, 1918, cf. *Treaties of the U. S.*, Vol. III, p. 3307.

[2] *U. S. For. Rel.*, 1905, p. 378. This agreement was later supplanted by a treaty; cf. p. 399. For the Liberian and Salvador loans cf. pp. 400–401.

[3] Q. Wright, *The Control of American Foreign Relations* (1922), p. 249.

enders" to international coöperation, the State Department during the Harding-Coolidge administration, appointed "unofficial observers" to the committees of the League on Anthrax, Opium, Health, Traffic in Women and Children, and so forth, and also to the Rhineland Commission, the Reparations Commission, and to different conferences, such as the Barcelona conference on transit, the conference on customs formalities.[1] Secretary of State Hughes was bold enough to say that these "unofficial observers" represented this country as fully as "official observers," a statement which is hardly correct, since they had no power to sign agreements upon the same basis as other representatives.[2] Different Presidents have justified the practice of appointing such commissioners without the approval of the Senate on the ground that they are not really public ministers, but mere agents of the President acting in his capacity to conduct foreign affairs. The President, however, would be more likely to secure the approval of treaties negotiated by such commissioners, if he had originally submitted their names to the Senate.

When it becomes necessary to embody some principle of international policy in a treaty, the President or his agent must not only negotiate and sign it, but he must then present it to the Senate for its approval or rejection. The Senate is at perfect liberty to reject the treaty as a whole or suggest amendments or reservations. Altogether the Senate has made about 70 reservations to the 650 or so treaties to which the United States has been a party.[3] It has rejected about 20 treaties, including such important treaties as those providing for the annexation of Texas, Hawaii, Santo Domingo and the Virgin Islands. It has insisted upon reservations or amendments so drastic as to defeat the arbi-

[1] Hudson, *American Coöperation with the League of Nations*, cited. The extent to which a minister may bind a government in foreign affairs has arisen recently in a controversy between Norway and Denmark over Greenland. In 1919 the Norwegian Minister of Foreign Affairs said that the Norwegian government would not put any difficulty in the way of the acquisition of Greenland by Denmark. A later government, however, would not recognize this ministerial statement as binding. Cf. Castberg, "Le Conflit entre le Danemark et le Norvège concernant le Groenland," *R. D. I. L. C.*, 1924, No. 3. The Norwegian government said that a minister could engage his government only in so far as the constitution of the country allowed.

[2] Speech of April 13, 1924, *N. Y. Times*, April 16, 1924.

[3] Q. Wright, *The Control of American Foreign Relations*, p. 252.

tration treaties of 1897, 1904 and 1911, and the Treaty of Versailles of 1919. It has amended fifty-seven treaties which were afterward accepted and ratified by the President.[1]

Desirable as a constitutional check upon making treaties may be, the American method has very serious defects which arise out of the doctrine of the separation of powers. The President is free to negotiate any treaty he likes and the Senate is free to reject it. Since the time of President Washington, Presidents have, with few exceptions, ignored the Senate in the process of negotiating such treaties.[2] Partly because of this neglect the Senate throughout its history has been hypercritical of executive proposals. One Secretary of State, John Hay, went so far as to say that "no treaty on which discussion was possible, no treaty that gave room for a difference of opinion, could ever pass the Senate."[3] Whether or not this statement is true, the procedure of the Senate is such that treaties may lie pigeon-holed for months and even years without any action being taken. This was particularly true during the Harding and Coolidge administrations where, despite the fact that the President and the Senate were of the same party, the Senate declined for months to act upon such agreements as the commercial treaty with Germany and the arrangement by which the United States would adhere to the World Court. Oblivious to the blasts of public opinion, a handful of Senators may follow a path of relentless obstruction from which there is no constitutional escape. Confronted with such a leviathan, Presidents have seized upon every possible device to evade the constitutional provisions in regard to the treaty-making power.

While there is no obligation to ratify a treaty following its signature, foreign countries are likely to become impatient with a government which repeatedly fails to ratify treaties which have been signed in good faith by the President.[4] In 1919 President Wilson signed an alliance promising to help France in case she

[1] Tansill, "The Treaty-making Powers of the Senate," *A. J. I. L.*, July, 1924.
[2] For President Washington's disagreeable experience with the Indian treaty, see R. Hayden, *The Senate and Treaties* (1920), pp. 16–31.
[3] W. R. Thayer, *The Life and Letters of John Hay* (1915), Vol. II, p. 273.
[4] It is customary for the United States to insert the following provision in its treaties, "It shall be ratified in accordance with the constitutional methods of the high contracting parties." Art. V, American-Canadian treaty of March 2, 1923, *Treaties of U. S.*, Vol. III, p. 2661.

was attacked by Germany. In return for this promise, France gave up her demand for the left bank of the Rhine, the Treaty of Versailles omitting such a provision. But the American Senate did not approve the alliance and France was left without a legal hold on the Rhine and at the same time without the moral guarantee of the United States which it had agreed to accept as a substitute. In these circumstances, it was natural for many people in France to believe that the United States had not lived up to its obligations. If President Wilson had kept in touch with the Senate throughout the Peace Conference, he would probably have never signed this alliance. On the other hand, he might have disarmed the Senate's opposition.

As a result of this literal interpretation of the separation of powers, followed by both Presidents Wilson and Roosevelt, a reaction set in after the World War, which led the American Congress to impose a large number of limitations even upon executive initiative in foreign policy. The special treaty with Germany of August, 1921, contains a Senate reservation to the effect that the United States shall not be represented in any body established under the treaty without the authorization of an act of Congress.[1] In the Debt Funding Act of February, 1922, Congress defined the bounds within which the negotiation for funding the Allied debt should be kept.[2] When Congress authorized the participation of representatives in the League Opium Conferences of 1924, it stipulated that they should not sign any treaty not containing certain anti-opium provisions. When the hands of the executive are tied by these means, it is impossible to confront special conditions as they arise, without violating such limitations. This fact was early demonstrated by the agents sent to England to negotiate the treaty of peace of 1783 under rigid instructions from the Congress of the Confederation, which they were obliged to violate before they could reach an agreement. Likewise, the Debt Funding Commission in 1923 exceeded the limitations prescribed

[1] This reservation has been challenged on the ground that it violates the constitutional provision authorizing the President to appoint officers with the consent of the Senate, not of Congress. Cf. Wickersham, "The Senate and our Foreign Relations," *Foreign Affairs*, Dec. 15, 1923. But the precedents appear to be the other way. Cf. E. S. Corwin, *President's Control of Foreign Relations* (1917), p. 66.

[2] 42 Stat. 363.

by Congress, in negotiating an agreement with England, for the approval of which a subsequent act of Congress was necessary.[1] Moreover, by the passage of legislation Congress may also defeat the policy of a President who wishes to handle the same subject by diplomatic means, which was illustrated by the termination of the Gentlemen's Agreement by an act of Congress, over the protest of the President of the United States, in the spring of 1924.[2]

Under a literal system of separation of powers, where no continuous contact between executive and legislature exists, the control of foreign relations thus becomes halting in nature. Occasionally the President succeeds in running away with the Senate. But when this body, supported by the House, succeeds in putting on the brakes, the machinery sometimes stops so suddenly that everybody gets a frightful jolt.

4. LEGISLATIVE CHECKS ON FOREIGN POLICY

If the constitutional checks upon foreign policy in the United States are awkward, they are, as we have seen, non-existent in England and quite inadequate in France. This defect in the two latter countries is remedied to a certain extent by legislative checks. In Great Britain, a treaty is not the "supreme law of the land" as in the United States. Consequently, before a treaty affecting internal affairs in England can become operative, it must be enacted into law by parliament. For example, such an act is necessary to give effect to treaties of commerce, extradition and arbitration. Although the British parliament did not approve the Treaty of Versailles as a whole, it did pass a Treaty of Versailles Act which authorized the Crown to make such appointments and orders as appeared necessary to carry the treaty into effect.[3] While parliament did not pass upon the Open Door and Four Power treaties of the Washington Conference, since they involved only international obligations, it did pass an act carrying the

---

[1] Cf. p. 546.
[2] For President Coolidge's efforts, cf. Buell, *Japanese Immigration*, cited, p. 309.
[3] 9, 10 Geo. V, Ch. 33; cf. Treaty of Peace Order, *Statutory Rules and Orders* (1919), Vol. II, p. 198.

Naval and Submarine treaties, which affected internal affairs, into effect.[1]

A further legislative check upon treaties was proposed in a resolution introduced in parliament in 1873, providing that all future treaties ought to be laid on the table of both houses of parliament before ratification "in order that an opportunity may be afforded to both Houses of expressing their opinion upon the provisions of such treaties."[2] At the instance of Mr. Gladstone the resolution was dropped. Influenced by the programme of the Union for Democratic Control, the MacDonald government, in April, 1924, announced that in the future parliament would be given an adequate opportunity for the discussion of all treaties before their final ratification. With this end in view, the government would lay on the table of the house every treaty, when signed, for a period of twenty-one days, which would give parliament an opportunity for discussion, before such treaties were ratified. This proposal included "all agreements, commitments, and understandings which might in any way bind the nation. . . ."[3] If this practice is continued by subsequent ministries, secret treaties in England will be impossible, and responsibility in foreign affairs will be more firmly established than in the past.[4]

In theory, legislatures may check ministerial policy through withholding appropriations,—a check which, however, is seldom used. While the American Congress has never withheld appropria-

[1] The Parliamentary Secretary to the Admiralty said the Government "at the present time does not possess powers to prevent any private citizen or firm building ships of any size. . . ." 156 *Parl. Debates*, H. C., 718.

[2] 214 *Parl. Debates*, H. C. (1873), 448, 469; cf. also p. 1309.

[3] Statement of the Under-Secretary of State for Foreign Affairs, Mr. Arthur Ponsonby, April 1, 1924, 171 *Parl. Debates*, H. C., 2001. At the time of the Chanak crisis, 100 members of parliament sent a communication to the Dominion parliaments, pointing out that Lloyd George had, without consulting any parliament, nearly involved the Empire in war. The members pledged themselves to a resolution providing that no act of war shall be committed, directly or indirectly, without the consent of parliament; no international treaty whatever shall be ratified without parliamentary approval; no diplomatic arrangements or verbal or written understandings with a foreign state, involving any military obligations shall be concluded without parliamentary consent; and no preparations for war between different naval staffs shall be lawful without such sanction. For text of the communication, cf. *Foreign Affairs* (London), August, 1923.

[4] It appears, however, that the succeeding Conservative Government did not follow this innovation.

tions necessary to give effect to a treaty or to prosecute a war, the Senate did defeat the Liberian policy of the State Department in 1922 by refusing to sanction a proposed loan.[1] In the same year, the Japanese Diet blocked the attempt of the Cabinet to send a diplomatic representative to the Vatican by refusing to vote the necessary appropriations.[2] Despite this legislative control of the purse, the executive as commander-in-chief of the military forces may create a situation in which legislatures will feel obliged to appropriate money or declare war in order to defend the "interests" or the "honor" of the country.

5. POLITICAL CHECKS ON FOREIGN POLICY

While the constitutional checks upon foreign policy in the United States, as we have seen, are strong, the political checks are weak. On the other hand, in such countries as England and France where constitutional checks are weak, political checks are theoretically strong. In these two countries, the Cabinet is responsible to parliament for all of its acts, including foreign policy. If parliament disapproves of these acts it may vote the ministry immediately out of power. In 1782 the British ministry was obliged to bring the war with the American colonies to an end because of the opposition of the House of Commons. However, when in 1857 the House of Commons condemned the war with China, Palmerston appealed to the country which decided in his favor.[3] In 1922 Lloyd George resigned largely because of popular disapproval of his Near Eastern policy, while Ramsay MacDonald resigned in 1924 partly because of opposition to the Russian treaty. In France, Aristide Briand was obliged to resign as prime minister in 1921 because of the opposition of parliament to his concessions to England made at the conference of Cannes. Thus while initiative in foreign policy, under the parliamentary system, is taken by the executive, the Foreign Secretary is constantly responsible to parliament which may at any time vote him out of office. In practice, however, this responsibility has often been fictitious. Especially before the War, foreign ministers were a law unto themselves, escaping from

[1] Cf. p. 420.
[2] Cf. p. 14.
[3] Sir William Anson, *Law and Custom of the Constitution* (3d ed., 1908), Vol. II, p. 102.

parliamentary control, for three reasons: (1) the irresponsible power of the Crown or the President; (2) secret diplomacy, as a result of which parliament was kept in ignorance of the most important foreign affairs; (3) the absence of parliamentary committees and of debate on foreign affairs.

Both in England and in France, the Crown and the President are supposed to be figureheads, acting only upon the advice of ministers responsible to parliament. Nevertheless, both the British Crown and the French President have exercised considerable personal influence in diplomacy. Queen Victoria insisted that Lord Palmerston keep her minutely informed as to foreign policy and not to make any changes "arbitrarily" in measures which had obtained her sanction.[1] The King's influence upon the Irish question in 1914 was also very great.[2] In France, the President has usually taken a prominent part in foreign negotiations. Presidents Carnot and Faure helped to bring about the Franco-Russian alliance; Casimir Perier resigned in 1894 because of disagreement with the cabinet as to foreign policy; the negotiations with Bismarck closing the war of 1870 were personally conducted by President Thiers; President Grévy intervened to settle peacefully the Schnaebele affair with Germany; President Poincaré was active in the negotiations leading up to the outbreak of the World War and in establishing unity of military command during the war.[3] As long as the titular and irresponsible heads of states personally exercise such powers, the parliamentary control of foreign affairs will not be complete.

6. DEMOCRACY AND SECRET TREATIES

Under the old Balance of Power system, cabinets as well as parliaments regarded secrecy as a necessity of statecraft. If the text of an alliance, and especially of military agreements, should be published, the enemy would know exactly the strength of the opposition upon the outbreak of war, and plan accordingly. If secret treaties were confidentially submitted to parliaments, their terms would inevitably leak out to the world. Since parliaments be-

[1] L. Strachy, *Queen Victoria* (1921), p. 232.
[2] G. Wallas, *Our Social Heritage* (1921), p. 234; also McBain and Rogers, *New Constitutions of Europe* (1922), pp. 144 ff.
[3] Esmein, Vol. II, p. 177; also Raymond Poincaré, "La Présidence et la politique extérieure," *Temps*, Sept. 27, 1920.

lieved that secret diplomacy was necessary for national existence, they were obliged to leave practically all the important questions of foreign policy to the unfettered discretion of the ministry. Under such a system, parliament had no means of telling whether or not ministers followed a policy which it would approve; and when the pledges undertaken by ministers were finally revealed, as at the outbreak of the World War, they were found in many cases to be contrary to the desires of the people. In 1913 and 1914 the Ministry informed the House of Commons that England was under no obligation to France; yet upon the outbreak of the war, it informed the Commons that England was really bound to come to the aid of France, because of the *Entente Cordiale*.[1] When diplomats are drawn into a secretive game of hide and seek, they are likely to make moves which popular opinion would never tolerate, if informed of what is going on. Secret diplomacy not only intensifies international distrust, but it makes the democratic control of foreign policy impossible.

On the other hand, "publicity has for a long time been considered as a source of moral strength in the administration of National Law. It should equally strengthen the laws and engagements which exist *between Nations*. It will promote public control. It will awaken public interest. It will remove causes for distrust and conflict. Publicity alone will enable the League of Nations to extend a moral sanction to the contractual obligations of its members. It will, moreover, contribute to the formation of a clear and indisputable system of International Law." [2]

A distinction should be made, however, between secrecy in negotiations and secrecy in final results. President Wilson never intended that his phrase "open covenants of peace openly arrived at," should mean complete publicity during the discussion of delicate matters, but simply that "no secret agreements should be entered into, and that all international relations, when fixed, should be open, above board, and explicit." Commenting further on this phrase, Mr. Wilson said, "If we announced partial results, or one decision at a time, it might easily result in bloodshed. We must do nothing that will incite more war, we must do everything

[1] Cf. the criticism, Earl Loreburn, *How the War Came* (1919), pp. 183, 286 ff.
[2] Memorandum in regard to Article 18, approved by the Council, May 19, 1920, *O. J.*, June, 1920, p. 154.

to get a speedy peace. When we reach real decisions everything must be made known to the world." [1] Compromise is an essential element in dealings between nations as between men. As President Lowell has pointed out, privacy of negotiation is essential to juries, if a fair verdict is to be arrived at. And the same considerations apply to the negotiation of international agreements.[2] No statesman can shift his ground when the glaring eyes of publicity are focused upon him. If negotiations were carried on in public, few agreements would be possible. Consequently, the abolition of secret diplomacy does not necessarily mean the abolition of secret negotiations, but merely the publication of all agreements, once they have been arrived at.[3]

Secret treaties may be forbidden by the provisions of either internal or international law. Since all treaties must be submitted to the Senate, secret treaties in the United States are virtually impossible.[4] Should the practice instituted by Ramsay MacDonald be followed, secret treaties in England would likewise be impossible. Secret treaties may also be forbidden by treaty. The

[1] Baker, *Woodrow Wilson and World Settlement*, Vol. I, p. 138.
[2] *Public Opinion in Peace and War* (1923), pp. 69, 154.
[3] DeWitt C. Poole, *The Conduct of Foreign Relations under Modern Democratic Conditions* (1924), Ch. VI. On the other hand, there is a danger that agreements may be perfected in secrecy which are extremely difficult to alter, even should they be opposed by the public, after publication. Cf. P. S. Reinsch, *Secret Diplomacy* (1922), Ch. X.

The Paris Peace Conference was severely criticized for excluding the newspapers from the important committee sessions. Cf. Baker, cited. The Washington Conference issued more full communiqués of committee meetings than did the Paris Conference; and the minutes of the two Committees of the Conference were published immediately after the Conference had closed. The minutes of the Paris Peace Conference have not as yet been officially published. It is the custom of most conferences to hold "plenary sessions" in public, but they usually are limited to the ratification of decisions taken in secret committee meetings. Publicity has proceeded further in the bodies of the League of Nations than in previous international conferences. As a rule each body determines for itself whether sessions shall be held in public or private. The practice has been to hold public meetings of the Council and Assembly; although private council sessions are held to discuss extremely delicate matters and also appointments. Whether these sessions are public or private, the minutes of the meetings of the League bodies are published immediately. While this was not true of the minutes of the first eleven sessions of the Council, they have now been published, so that there is no act of the League organizations which is not publicly recorded.

[4] However, executive agreements and loan contracts under which the United States has assumed certain obligations may be kept secret.

Five Central American Republics have obligated themselves "not to conclude with each other from any motive whatever, secret pacts, conventions or agreements."

Effect of the Covenant.—What is of more importance, Article XVIII of the League Covenant provides:

"Every treaty or international engagement entered into hereafter by any Member of the League shall be forthwith registered with the Secretariat and shall as soon as possible be published by it. No such treaty or international engagement shall be binding until so registered."

In 1920 the French and Belgian governments came to an agreement respecting common action against Germany. The governments declined to publish the terms of this agreement on the ground that it related to the movement of troops, and so forth, which would lose its value if known to the world. However, the two governments finally registered with the League Secretariat an exchange of letters stating that a Military Understanding had been approved by the two governments concerned,[1] although the actual terms of the Understanding were not disclosed. This incident at once raised the question whether military agreements were included under the "treaties or international engagements" to be registered under Article XVIII. The first Assembly (1920) authorized a special committee of jurists to study the question. And in a report, approved by the first committee of the second Assembly, it was proposed that under Article XVIII only treaties which *create* international obligations should be registered, and that an amendment should be adopted to the effect that "instruments which consist merely of technical regulations defining without in any way modifying an instrument already registered, or which are only designed to enable such an instrument to be carried into effect," need not be registered.[2] Thus while an alliance had to be registered, a military agreement defining the alliance could be kept secret, an interpretation which would support the practice followed in the French-Belgian Understanding. But the Assembly rejected the proposal of Lord Balfour

---

[1] *T. S.* 56.
[2] *Records of 2d Assembly*, Plenary Meetings, p. 704. Great Britain wished particularly to exempt confidential financial agreements from registration. Cf. Lord Balfour, *Records*, cited, p. 848.

that, pending further action, each member should be at liberty to interpret Article XVIII in conformity with the proposed amendment. Later Assemblies were no more successful in agreeing upon a change. One method of meeting the difficulty is suggested by the Protocol for the Pacific Settlement of International Disputes, which provides that all military agreements should be registered and published by the Secretariat of the League.[1] Thus interpreted, the League Covenant would eliminate all secret treaties as far as they define international obligations which the outside world is obliged to recognize.[2] To carry the publication feature of Article XVIII into effect, the League Secretariat publishes an invaluable treaty series which, in its first eight years, filled 73 volumes and contained 1800 treaties and agreements.[3]

7. COMMITTEES ON FOREIGN AFFAIRS

Partly because of the belief that foreign affairs should be kept secret, parliaments in the past paid comparatively little attention to questions of foreign policy. The treaty of 1874 establishing a protectorate in Annam was approved by the French National Assembly without discussion, and little attention was given to the Act of Berlin of 1885. In 1907, a year of great diplomatic importance, there were only ten interpellations on foreign policy in the French Chamber; while in England foreign office votes, before the War, were frequently passed without debate or with a debate of less than a day.[4] Since the War parliaments have been more

[1] Article 13.

[2] According to the Memorandum of May 19, 1920, "As no Treaties or International Engagements will be binding until registration with the International Secretariat has taken place, the latest date at which they should be presented for registration will be the date when, so far as the acts of the Parties *inter se* are concerned, they receive binding force, and are intended to come into operation." At the first Assembly the Roumanian delegate said that the principle in the Covenant that treaties are only valid after registration is in contradiction with many constitutions, an argument which impressed the committee to such an extent that they proposed that when a treaty is registered within the three months following the conclusion of the treaty, the treaty is considered valid from the time of its conclusion. *Records of the Second Assembly*, Plenary Meetings, p. 839.

[3] Non-member states were invited to register treaties, an invitation accepted by Germany, *O. J.*, October, 1920, p. 44. Cf. the Treaty of August 25, 1921, between Germany and the United States, *T. S.* 310. For the United States policy. Cf. p. 697.

[4] Barthélemy, p. 132; Chow, p. 198; Ponsonby, p. 50.

COMMITTEES ON FOREIGN AFFAIRS 749

interested in foreign affairs. But their ability to gain information in some countries has been hampered by lack of proper machinery. An attempt to remedy this defect was made in France by the establishment of Commissions of Foreign Affairs, the Commission of the Chamber being established in 1902 and that of the Senate in 1915. These Commissions hold secret sessions at which Cabinet ministers may talk freely. Moreover, the French Committees on Finance have considerable influence on foreign policy, the reporter of the Committee having free access to the Quai d'Orsay.[1] The French Commissions on Foreign Affairs have claimed the right to warn and advise the foreign office in every stage of negotiations. In the United States similar committees of a more partisan nature may be found—the Committee on Foreign Relations in the Senate and the Committee on Foreign Affairs in the House. While in England no parliamentary committee on foreign affairs has existed, in May, 1918, a motion was introduced into the House of Commons to the effect that a "standing committee on foreign affairs should be appointed, representative of all parties and groups in the House, in order that a regular channel of communication may be established between the Foreign Secretary and the House of Commons which will afford him frequent opportunities of giving information on questions of foreign policy and which, by allowing Members to acquaint themselves more fully with current international problems, will enable this House to exercise closer supervision over the general conduct of foreign affairs."[2] Be-

[1] T. S. Chien, *Parliamentary Committees, A Study in Comparative Government* (Harvard University thesis, 1923), pp. 444 ff. However, a speaker in the House of Commons in 1918 said that the French Committee on Foreign Affairs "has been intensely expansionist and Jingoist, to use a broad word. . . . The Foreign Affairs Committee deals extraordinarily little with foreign affairs, and almost entirely with colonial affairs. . . . All it has dealt with practically has been colonial affairs, oversea trade affairs, and in those affairs there has been no body that I know that has been more expansionist and more penetrating in its attempts to introduce French methods, French trade, and French influence in other countries than the Foreign Affairs Committee of the French Chamber," Captain Lloyd, 104 *Parl. Debates*, H. C., 866.

[2] 104 *Parl. Debates*, H. C. (1918), 841, 901; for the reply of Mr. Balfour, Secretary of State for Foreign Affairs, cf. p. 867. However, according to one writer, "It is beyond doubt that even in foreign politics it [the Cabinet] gives the House of Commons and the public far more information as to what has actually taken place and been done than the Government of any other great nation in Europe." J. Redlich, *Proceedings of the House of Commons* (1908), Vol. II, p. 42.

cause of the plea of the government that such a committee would handicap the workings of parliamentary government, the proposal was voted down.

In 1921 Sweden established a new parliamentary Committee of Foreign Affairs, chosen by both chambers of parliament. A conference of this Committee takes place before the ministry comes to a decision on foreign affairs of importance.[1] The new German constitution of 1919 contains an interesting provision for a *permanent* Committee on Foreign Affairs. Parliaments are only in session a few months out of the year; and during the remainder of the time, the ministry has a free hand, particularly in foreign policy. In order to fill in this gap, the new German constitution provides for the appointment of a "standing committee on foreign affairs which may act between sessions of the Reichstag and after the end of the legislative term, or between the dissolution of the Reichstag and the convening of a new Reichstag." [2] The sittings are in private unless the Committee, by two-thirds majority, decides otherwise. So far, this committee appears to have influenced policy largely in a negative manner. Further coöperation with the foreign ministry has been retarded by the leakage of confidential information.[3] Nevertheless, this committee is said to have had considerable influence in bringing about the acceptance by the German government of the "Dawes Report." In Czechoslovakia a Committee of Twenty-Four—16 from the Chamber and 8 from the Senate—has been established to act on all matters of "immediate urgency" while parliament is not in session.[4] Several Latin-American constitutions provide for similar committees.[5] Through such an instrument parliaments may keep in

[1] Brusewitz, "Parliamentary Control of Foreign Affairs in Sweden," *Foreign Affairs*, Jan., 1922. In Norway a special committee of both parties was also appointed during the War, Pederson, "Foreign Policy Control in Norway," *Foreign Affairs*, Dec., 1921. In 1919 the Netherlands constituted a Standing Committee on Foreign Affairs. Cf. a British White Paper containing reports from His Majesty's representatives abroad on the methods adopted in the parliaments of foreign countries for dealing with international questions. Cmd. 2282 (1924). For an earlier report on the same subject, cf. "Treatment of International Questions by Foreign Parliaments," Cd. 6102 (1912).
[2] Art. 35, Constitution of August 11, 1919.
[3] D. C. Poole, *The Conduct of Foreign Relations* (1924), p. 52.
[4] Art. 54, Constitution of Feb. 29, 1920.
[5] Art. 78, Constitution of Mexico, January 31, 1917; for other constitutions cf. James and Martin, *Republics of Latin America* (1923), p. 218.

constant touch with foreign policy, even though they are not in session.

8. PUBLIC OPINION AND FOREIGN AFFAIRS

Despite the defective structure of governments for the conduct of foreign relations, public opinion has indirectly exercised considerable influence upon international affairs. Practically all of the great humanitarian movements of the world, such as the anti-slavery and anti-opium movements, originated with the activities of private associations. In England the Anti-Slavery and Aborigines Protection Society has exercised great influence in exposing the evils of British colonial policy. The Union of Democratic Control, established in 1914, has not only demanded the establishment of parliamentary checks upon the conduct of foreign affairs, but has also taken a stand on current political questions.[1] More than 350 bodies of organized labor, with an aggregate membership of a million, are affiliated with the Unions which maintain some 40 branches in England, and conduct conferences and week-end schools on foreign policy. In the United States, the church organizations have carried on effective work for peace,[2] while such bodies as the Foreign Policy Association and the Council for the Prevention of War have been instrumental in educating public opinion.

Whether or not the influence of the press upon foreign policy is benign has been a matter of controversy. In their discussion of foreign affairs and in their interpretation of foreign news, certain journals have systematically catered to jingoism. In some cases, their attitude has not been disinterested. It has been the practice of European governments to subsidize influential newspapers in foreign countries in order to create a favorable diplomatic atmosphere. To pave the way for the support of France, the Tsar of Russia expended in the single year of 1905 nearly 4 million francs on the Paris press, continuing these "subsidies" until the revolution of 1917.[3] While no such charges have been

[1] C. Trevelyan, *The Union of Democratic Control* (1921); H. M. Swanwick, *Builders of Peace* (1924).
[2] Cf. p. 13.
[3] Gannett, "The Secret Corruption of the French Press," *Nation*, Feb. 6, 1924.

brought against the American press, it has been frequently criticized for its ignorance as well as its irresponsibility in regard to foreign questions. But in their denunciation of the action of Congress in passing the Japanese exclusion legislation of 1924, the great majority of the outstanding papers of the country showed that these criticisms are not always just.

In some countries accustomed to direct legislation in domestic affairs, the demand has arisen for the referendum on questions of foreign policy. So far, however, this demand has taken root only in Switzerland. In May, 1920, this country held a referendum to determine whether to join the League of Nations. Eleven and a half cantons voted for, and ten and a half voted against, the proposal; indeed a change of 94 votes in a particular canton would have reversed the outcome.[1] In January, 1921, the Swiss people adopted a constitutional amendment providing that "Treaties with foreign powers which are concluded without limit of time or for a period of more than fifteen years shall also be submitted to the people for acceptance or rejection upon demand of 30,000 Swiss citizens qualified to vote, or of eight cantons." The referendum was first invoked under this provision in the case of the convention abolishing the free zones with France, which was rejected by a vote of four to one. The French government protested against the failure to ratify this treaty because of the referendum on the ground that the treaty had been made before the referendum provision had been adopted. It also declared that "there would be in reality no equality between Switzerland, whose international engagements could be annulled by a referendum" and states which followed orthodox methods of ratification. This latter argument, however, does not seem very impressive, since in principle a referendum does not differ from the legislative approval of a treaty required by most countries.

In the United States the use of the referendum was advocated in the 1924 platform of the Democratic party on the question of war, "except in case of actual or threatened attack," and also on the question of the League of Nations. In order to "lift this question out of party politics," the party would hold a referendum

---

[1] Brooks, "Swiss Referendum on the League of Nations," 14 *American Political Science Review* (1920), 479; also "Swiss Treaty Initiative," 15 *ibid.* (1921), 423.

election, advisory to the government, to be held officially under act of Congress, upon the question whether the United States should become a member of the League with such reservations or amendments to the League Covenant as the President and Senate should agree upon.[1] The Progressive platform of 1924 also declared in favor of "referendums [sic] on peace and war."

Such a referendum as the Democratic platform proposed would scarcely decide the issue, since the original defeat of the Treaty of Versailles was due to a difference between the President and the Senate as to reservations which the proposed referendum would not solve. Moreover, a referendum on war would be distinctly out of place when war is definitely outlawed by international agreement. In some cases referenda on broad questions of foreign policy may have an educational value; and they may break down the resistance of unrepresentative legislatures. At the same time, questions of foreign policy are so intricate and, when irresponsibly discussed, tinged with so much demagogy, that many of the new constitutions since the War have exempted matters of foreign affairs from the questions to which the referendum may apply.[2] Disputes which might be solved by delicate negotiations become insoluble when subjected to the bitterness of irresponsible and misinformed debate.

9. A "LEAGUE OF PEOPLES"

With the establishment of the League of Nations the democratic control of international policy has become more important than ever. If the League should fall under the control of diplomats irresponsible to public opinion it would be in danger of becoming an agent of exploitation rather than of good. Each member of the League is entitled to three "representatives" on the Assembly, while each state which is a member of the Council may have one representative on that body. As a rule, these "representatives" have been diplomats or cabinet ministers appointed by their respective governments, without consulting parliamentary bodies. Under a system of parliamentary government, where cabinets are actually responsible to legislatures for the conduct of affairs, such

[1] For the view of the originator of the idea, see Lucking, "A National Vote on the League," *Our World*, May, 1923.
[2] Cf. Article 34, Constitution of Esthonia, June 15, 1920.

representatives on the League would ultimately be subject to a form of legislative control. Representatives would act under instructions from Foreign Offices in turn subject to parliaments. Thus in 1923 the debate in the British House of Commons, anent French policy in the Saar, virtually forced the British representative on the Council, to ask for an inquiry.[1] Yet, especially in the case of diplomatic representatives on the Assembly or the Council, this form of legislative control is only indirect. A diplomat never appears before parliament and, ordinarily, he is out of touch with popular opinion. At least the older diplomats are schooled in the belief that the state is above the moral standards exacted of individuals; hence they make unreasonable demands for their states and look with suspicion upon the demands of other states, which makes the development of international solidarity difficult to achieve. Moreover, diplomatic considerations may control the actions of a diplomatic representative on a League body. For example, the Japanese Ambassador at Paris, who is also the representative of Japan on the League Council, might hesitate to vote in favor of a measure opposed there by France because it might prejudice his diplomatic position in Paris. The German Bund, which was in existence between 1815 and 1866, failed to build up a national spirit in Germany, partly because it was a conference of diplomats rather than a gathering of peoples.[2] World solidarity will probably not be achieved until a League of Diplomats and a League of Governments is converted, at least as far as the Assembly is concerned, into a League of Nations or of Peoples.[3]

In appointing responsible cabinet ministers to League positions, an improvement has been made. In England a special cabinet

[1] 163 *Parl. Debates*, H. C. (1923), 2643, 2666.
[2] Schücking and Wehberg, p. 139.
[3] Cf. Jacks, "A League of Nations or a League of Governments?" 131 *Atlantic Monthly* (1923), 161; Williams, "Technique of the League of Nations," *International Journal of Ethics*, January, 1924. An unofficial gathering of members of parliament is periodically held by the Interparliamentary Union, founded in 1899. This organization, which had held 18 meetings before the War, is composed of groups from national parliaments, in 1914, there being 24 groups and about 3,500 members; (in 1920 there were only 14 groups and 2,000 members). The United States is represented in the Union, which makes careful studies of current international problems. *Handbook of International Organizations*, 1921, p. 123; *L'Union interparlementaire, son œuvre et son organisation* (3d ed., 1922), Bureau International.

minister devotes his entire time to League affairs. The Prime Ministers of England, France, Belgium, Denmark, Austria and Hungary, attended the fifth Assembly at which about one hundred other cabinet ministers were also present. It is now the practice of the leading European governments to be represented by their Ministers of Foreign Affairs at Council meetings. Cabinet ministers are also tempted to regard themselves as agents of a strict national interest rather than servants of an international good. If the League of Nations is to enter into the life of the peoples, they should be directly represented. The German plan for a League of Nations provided for a World Parliament (in addition to a Congress of States), composed of representatives of the parliaments of the states members of the League. Other plans called for the direct election of such representatives, according to population. While practical difficulties, among other considerations, prevented the adoption of any of these proposals, President Wilson pointed out that each member would be free to select its three representatives on the Assembly in any manner it preferred.[1] This liberty was utilized by Norway, Sweden and Denmark to appoint members of parliament on their delegations to the Assembly, while the representatives of Denmark and Sweden are nominated by the different parties; the Norwegian delegation has contained two outstanding men, Dr. Nansen and Dr. C. Lange, neither of whom is in active politics.[2] If the Scandinavian practice should become general, the Assembly would be converted into a real World Parliament.

10. THE AMERICAN CONSTITUTION AND FOREIGN AFFAIRS

Because of the nature of the American constitutional system, based as it is on the theory of the separation of powers, the problem of participating in an international organization is more difficult than in countries having a parliamentary system of government. While treaties drafted by League bodies must be ratified by home governments, certain actions for the purpose of protecting the world against war must be immediately taken by the League Council which it would be difficult to submit to formal

[1] Mrs. C. A. Kluyver, *Documents on the League of Nations* (1920), p. 12.
[2] R. Williams, *The League of Nations at Work* (1923), p. 162.

parliamentary approval.[1] In the case of parliamentary countries, having adequate committee systems, parliament may keep a constant check on the decisions of such representatives. But under the American system of separation of powers, the President may act in complete independence of Congress. While he cannot declare war or make a treaty, he could send the fleet to Europe, and otherwise create a situation which would make war inevitable. As long as this gulf exists between the President and the legislature, Congress is not likely to give to the American executive the same initiative in such questions of international policy as executives in parliamentary countries may safely exercise.[2]

Three means of solving this problem have been proposed. The first is by reservation. In 1919 the Senate of the United States insisted on a number of reservations restricting the independent action of the President. They provided that the United States should not accept a League mandate, that no person should be appointed to represent the United States on any body established by the League or treaty, and that the United States should not contribute to the expenses of the League, except under the authority of an act of Congress. Moreover, the Senate refused to assume any obligations of a military or economic character, under Articles X and XVI of the Covenant.[3]

In the second place, the League has attempted to preserve the discretion of the legislature by providing, in the proposed resolution in regard to Article X, that "It is for the *constitutional authorities* of each member to decide, in reference to the obligation of preserving the independence and the integrity of the territory of

[1] Cf. p. 623.
[2] As we have seen, the League Council recommended that legislatures empower the executive to impose immediately an economic boycott when the occasion should arise. The Congress of the United States has the power to delegate such power to the President, as it did in the Non-Intercourse Act of 1807, which provided that no clearance be furnished to any ship bound for any foreign port except vessels under the immediate direction of the President. 2 Stat. 452. Cf. also the case of *Field* v. *Clark*, 143 U. S. (1891) 649. But it is doubtful whether Congress would delegate such a wide power to be exercised in case of any war throughout the world, to the President, as long as he may act in complete disregard of its wishes.
[3] Cf. the resolution of March 19, 1920, 59 *Cong. Record*, pt. 5, p. 4599. Of course these reservations are not in effect, as they did not receive two-thirds majority in the Senate and as the Treaty of Versailles was not ratified.

members, in what degree the member is bound to assure the execution of this obligation. . . ."¹

As far as the United States is concerned, we shall be able to play an active part in world affairs only if we establish certain "understandings" between the executive and the legislature which will prevent the deadlocks which have marred our conduct of foreign relations in the past. The first steps in this direction would be to admit the Secretary of State to the floor of either house, where he would virtually be obliged to answer questions from the floor. At the present time, the State Department frequently refuses requests for information on the ground that "it is incompatible with the public interest," and when it does divulge information, it gives out only what it chooses, and the legislature has no opportunity to ferret out the truth by cross-examination. In the second place, some curb should be placed on the Senate's treaty-making power. As long as one-third of the Senate has its present power, an unrepresentative minority will always be able to block a treaty which the country may overwhelmingly desire. In the vast majority of cases, treaties are of no more importance than domestic legislation which is passed by bare majority vote of both houses. No other important government in the world requires the overwhelming legislative consent which our constitution demands for treaties. At one time in our history, deadlocks over treaties made little difference. But with the growing complication of international affairs, the obstructive nature of the American constitution may become increasingly harmful.² Until the approval of treaties is transferred from the Senate to a majority of both houses, this country will always be in danger of the dominance of a minority.

Finally, the creation of an Advisory Committee of Foreign Affairs, composed of representatives of both parties in Congress and of the public, which the President should consult on all important negotiations and questions of policy, might be feasible—

[1] Cf. p. 599. An alliance is undemocratic because the executive always decides when to send troops to the aid of an ally, in accordance with its terms. This was one difficulty with the proposed Draft Treaty, under which the Council could apparently *require* the assistance of certain nations. Art. 5 (c) of the Draft Treaty of Mutual Assistance.

[2] Cf. the presidential address of Mr. J. W. Davis, Report of 46th *Annual Meeting of the American Bar Association Proceedings* (1923), p. 202.

a committee combining the advantages of the Swedish and German systems. If a foreign policy is to be successful, full play should be given to executive initiative. At the same time the actions of the executive should be subject to continuous and sympathetic legislative control. Perhaps the foremost problem in American government is the problem, not of decreasing the President's power, but of increasing its accountability.[1]

[1] Cf. H. J. Ford, *Representative Government* (1924), Chs. VI–VIII.

APPENDIX

COVENANT OF THE LEAGUE OF NATIONS

WITH AMENDMENTS IN FORCE APRIL 1, 1928

The High Contracting Parties,

In order to promote international coöperation and to achieve international peace and security

by the acceptance of obligations not to resort to war,

by the prescription of open, just and honorable relations between nations,

by the firm establishment of the understandings of international law as the actual rule of conduct among Governments, and

by the maintenance of justice and a scrupulous respect for all treaty obligations in the dealings of organized peoples with one another,

Agree to this Covenant of the League of Nations.

Article 1

Membership and Withdrawal

1. [1] The original Members of the League of Nations shall be those of the Signatories which are named in the Annex to this Covenant, and also such of those other States named in the Annex as shall accede without reservation to this Covenant. Such accessions shall be effected by a declaration deposited with the Secretariat within two months of the coming into force of the Covenant. Notice thereof shall be sent to all other Members of the League.

2. Any fully self-governing State, Dominion or Colony not named in the Annex may become a Member of the League if its admission is agreed to by two-thirds of the Assembly, provided that it shall give effective guarantees of its sincere intention to observe its international obligations, and shall accept such regulations as may be prescribed by the League in regard to its military, naval and air forces and armaments.

3. Any Member of the League may, after two years' notice of its intention so to do, withdraw from the League, provided that all its inter-

[1] Paragraphs numbered in accordance with Assembly resolution of September 21, 1926.

national obligations and all its obligations under this Covenant shall have been fulfilled at the time of its withdrawal.

ARTICLE 2

Executive Organs

The action of the League under this Covenant shall be effected through the instrumentality of an Assembly and of a Council, with a permanent Secretariat.

ARTICLE 3

Assembly

1. The Assembly shall consist of representatives of the Members of the League.
2. The Assembly shall meet at stated intervals and from time to time, as occasion may require, at the Seat of the League, or at such other place as may be decided upon.
3. The Assembly may deal at its meetings with any matter within the sphere of action of the League or affecting the peace of the world.
4. At meetings of the Assembly each Member of the League shall have one vote and may have not more than three Representatives.

ARTICLE 4

Council

1. The Council shall consist of representatives of the Principal Allied and Associated Powers [United States of America, the British Empire, France, Italy and Japan], together with Representatives of four[1] other Members of the League. These four[1] Members of the League shall be selected by the Assembly from time to time in its discretion. Until the appointment of the Representatives of the four Members of the League first selected by the Assembly, Representatives of Belgium, Brazil, Greece and Spain shall be Members of the Council.
2. With the approval of the majority of the Assembly, the Council may name additional Members of the League, whose Representatives shall always be Members of the Council;[2] the Council with like approval may increase the number of Members of the League to be selected by the Assembly[2] for representation on the Council.[1]

[1] The number of Members of the Council selected by the Assembly, by application of the second clause of Art. 4, par. 2, was increased from four to six on September 25, 1922, and from six to nine on September 8, 1926.

[2] By application of this clause Germany was designated as a permanent Member of the Council on September 8, 1926, the appropriate action of the Council having been taken on September 4.

2 bis.[1] *The Assembly shall fix by a two-thirds majority the rules dealing with the election of the non-permanent Members of the Council, and particularly such regulations as relate to their term of office and the conditions of reëligibility.*

3. The Council shall meet from time to time as occasion may require, and at least once a year, at the Seat of the League, or at such other place as may be decided upon.

4. The Council may deal at its meetings with any matter within the sphere of action of the League or affecting the peace of the world.

5. Any Member of the League not represented on the Council shall be invited to send a Representative to sit as a member at any meeting of the Council during the consideration of matters specially affecting the interests of that Member of the League.

6. At meetings of the Council, each Member of the League represented on the Council shall have one vote, and may have not more than one Representative.

Article 5
Voting and Procedure

1. Except where otherwise expressly provided in this Covenant, or by the terms of the present Treaty, decisions at any meeting of the Assembly or of the Council shall require the agreement of all the Members of the League represented at the meeting.

2. All matters of procedure at meetings of the Assembly or of the Council, including the appointment of Committees to investigate particular matters, shall be regulated by the Assembly or by the Council and may be decided by a majority of the Members of the League represented at the meeting.

3. The first meeting of the Assembly and the first meeting of the Council shall be summoned by the President of the United States of America.

Article 6
Secretariat and Expenses

1. The permanent Secretariat shall be established at the Seat of the League. The Secretariat shall comprise a Secretary-General and such secretaries and staff as may be required.

2. The first Secretary-General shall be the person named in the Annex; thereafter the Secretary-General shall be appointed by the Council with the approval of the majority of the Assembly.

3. The secretaries and the staff of the Secretariat shall be appointed by the Secretary-General with the approval of the Council.

---

[1] This paragraph came into force on July 29, 1926, in accordance with Art. 26. The regulations were adopted by the Assembly on September 15.

4. The Secretary-General shall act in that capacity at all meetings of the Assembly and of the Council.

5.[1] *The expenses of the League shall be borne by the Members of the League in the proportion decided by the Assembly.*

Article 7
Seat, Qualifications of Officials, Immunities

1. The Seat of the League is established at Geneva.
2. The Council may at any time decide that the Seat of the League shall be established elsewhere.
3. All positions under or in connection with the League, including the Secretariat, shall be open equally to men and women.
4. Representatives of the Members of the League and officials of the League when engaged on the business of the League shall enjoy diplomatic privileges and immunities.
5. The buildings and other property occupied by the League or its officials or by Representatives attending its meetings shall be inviolable.

Article 8
Reduction of Armaments

1. The Members of the League recognize that the maintenance of peace requires the reduction of national armaments to the lowest point consistent with national safety and the enforcement by common action of international obligations.
2. The Council, taking account of the geographical situation and circumstances of each State, shall formulate plans for such reduction for the consideration and action of the several Governments.
3. Such plans shall be subject to reconsideration and revision at least every 10 years.
4. After these plans shall have been adopted by the several Governments, the limits of armaments therein fixed shall not be exceeded without the concurrence of the Council.
5. The Members of the League agree that the manufacture by private enterprise of munitions and implements of war is open to grave objections. The Council shall advise how the evil effects attendant upon such manufacture can be prevented, due regard being had to the necessities of those Members of the League which are not able to manufacture the munitions and implements of war necessary for their safety.

[1] This paragraph came into force as an amendment on August 13, 1924, in accordance with Art. 26. The original provision was as follows:
"The expenses of the Secretariat shall be borne by the Members of the League in accordance with the apportionment of the expenses of the International Bureau of the Universal Postal Union."

6. The Members of the League undertake to interchange full and frank information as to the scale of their armaments, their military, naval and air programs, and the condition of such of their industries as are adaptable to warlike purposes.

Article 9
Permanent Military, Naval and Air Commission

A permanent Commission shall be constituted to advise the Council on the execution of the provisions of Articles 1 and 8 and on military, naval and air questions generally.

Article 10
Guaranties Against Aggression

The Members of the League undertake to respect and preserve as against external aggression the territorial integrity and existing political independence of all Members of the League. In case of any such aggression or in case of any threat or danger of such aggression, the Council shall advise upon the means by which this obligation shall be fulfilled.

Article 11
Action in Case of War or Threat of War

1. Any war or threat of war, whether immediately affecting any of the Members of the League or not, is hereby declared a matter of concern to the whole League, and the League shall take any action that may be deemed wise and effectual to safeguard the peace of nations. In case any such emergency should arise, the Secretary-General shall, on the request of any Member of the League, forthwith summon a meeting of the Council.

2. It is also declared to be the friendly right of each Member of the League to bring to the attention of the Assembly or of the Council any circumstance whatever affecting international relations which threatens to disturb international peace or the good understanding between nations upon which peace depends.

Article 12 [1]
Disputes to Be Submitted for Settlement

1. The Members of the League agree that, if there should arise between them any dispute likely to lead to a rupture they will submit the matter

[1] The text as printed came into force as an amendment on September 26, 1924, in accordance with Art. 26. The original text was as follows:
"The Members of the League agree that, if there should arise between them any dispute likely to lead to a rupture, they will submit the matter either to arbitration or to inquiry by the Council, and they agree in no case to resort

either to arbitration *or judicial settlement* or to inquiry by the Council and they agree in no case to resort to war until three months after the award by the arbitrators *or the judicial decision*, or the report by the Council.

2. In any case under this Article, the award of the arbitrators *or the judicial decision* shall be made within a reasonable time, and the report of the Council shall be made within six months after the submission of the dispute.

ARTICLE 13 [1]

Arbitration or Judicial Settlement

1. The Members of the League agree that, whenever any dispute shall arise between them which they recognize to be suitable for submission to arbitration *or judicial settlement*, and which can not be satisfactorily settled by diplomacy, they will submit the whole subject-matter to arbitration *or judicial settlement*.

2. Disputes as to the interpretation of a treaty, as to any question of international law, as to the existence of any fact which, if established, would constitute a breach of any international obligation, or as to the extent and nature of the reparation to be made for any such breach, are declared to be among those which are generally suitable for submission to arbitration *or judicial settlement*.

to war until three months after the award by the arbitrators or the report by the Council.

"In any case under this Article the award of the arbitrators shall be made within a reasonable time, and the report of the Council shall be made within six months after the submission of the dispute."

[1] The text as printed came into force as an amendment on September 26, 1924 in accordance with Art. 26. The original text was as follows:

"The Members of the League agree that, whenever any dispute shall arise between them which they recognize to be suitable for submission to arbitration and which can not be satisfactorily settled by diplomacy, they will submit the whole subject-matter to arbitration.

"Disputes as to the interpretation of a treaty, as to any question of international law, as to the existence of any fact which if established would constitute a breach of any international obligation, or as to the extent and nature of the reparation to be made for any such breach, are declared to be among those which are generally suitable for submission to arbitration.

"For the consideration of any such dispute the court of arbitration to which the case is referred shall be the court agreed on by the parties to the dispute or stipulated in any convention existing between them.

"The Members of the League agree that they will carry out in full good faith any award that may be rendered and that they will not resort to war against a Member of the League which complies therewith. In the event of any failure to carry out such an award, the Council shall propose what steps should be taken to give effect thereto."

APPENDIX 765

3. *For the consideration of any such dispute, the court to which the case is referred shall be the Permanent Court of International Justice, established in accordance with Article 14, or any tribunal agreed on by the parties to the dispute or stipulated in any convention existing between them.*

4. The Members of the League agree that they will carry out in full good faith any award *or decision* that may be rendered, and that they will not resort to war against a Member of the League which complies therewith. In the event of any failure to carry out such an award *or decision*, the Council shall propose what steps should be taken to give effect thereto.

ARTICLE 14 [1]
Permanent Court of International Justice

The Council shall formulate and submit to the Members of the League for adoption plans for the establishment of a Permanent Court of International Justice. The Court shall be competent to hear and determine any dispute of an international character which the parties thereto submit to it. The Court may also give an advisory opinion upon any dispute or question referred to it by the Council or by the Assembly.

ARTICLE 15 [2]
Disputes Not Submitted to Arbitration or Judicial Settlement

1.[3] If there should arise between Members of the League any dispute likely to lead to a rupture, which is not submitted to arbitration *or judicial*

[1] The first sentence of this article has been fulfilled. The Council on February 13, 1920, appointed an Advisory Committee of Jurists to report a scheme to it. The draft Statute, prepared by the Committee June 16–July 24, 1920, was revised and finally approved by the Council on October 28. It was then submitted to the First Assembly for consideration of representatives of Members of the League. The plan, called a Statute, is attached to a protocol of signature of December 16, 1920, the ratification of which constitutes adoption of the plan by Members of the League and other states.

The stipulations of the second sentence are carried out by Art. 36 of the Statute. Cognizance is taken of the third sentence in Arts. 71–74 of the Rules of Court.

[2] On interpretations of pars. 1 and 8, see *Official Journal*, V, p. 524, and for the replies of the Governments, Document 1926. V. 12.

[3] The text of the first paragraph as printed came into force as an amendment on September 26, 1924, in accordance with Art. 26. The original text was as follows:

"If there should arise between Members of the League any dispute likely to lead to a rupture, which is not submitted to arbitration in accordance with Article 13, the Members of the League agree that they will submit the matter to the Council. Any party to the dispute may effect such submission by giving notice of the existence of the dispute to the Secretary-General, who will make all necessary arrangements for a full investigation and consideration thereof."

settlement in accordance with Article 13, the Members of the League agree that they will submit the matter to the Council. Any party to the dispute may effect such submission by giving notice of the existence of the dispute to the Secretary-General, who will make all necessary arrangements for a full investigation and consideration thereof.

2. For this purpose the parties to the dispute will communicate to the Secretary-General, as promptly as possible, statements of their case, with all the relevant facts and papers, and the Council may forthwith direct the publication thereof.

3. The Council shall endeavor to effect a settlement of the dispute and, if such efforts are successful, a statement shall be made public giving such facts and explanations regarding the dispute and the terms of settlement thereof as the Council may deem appropriate.

4. If the dispute is not thus settled, the Council, either unanimously or by a majority vote, shall make and publish a report containing a statement of the facts of the dispute and the recommendations which are deemed just and proper in regard thereto.

5. Any Member of the League represented on the Council may make public a statement of the facts of the dispute and of its conclusions regarding the same.

6. If a report by the Council is unanimously agreed to by the Members thereof other than the Representatives of one or more of the parties to the dispute, the Members of the League agree that they will not go to war with any party to the dispute which complies with the recommendations of the report.

7. If the Council fails to reach a report which is unanimously agreed to by the members thereof, other than the Representatives of one or more of the parties to the dispute, the Members of the League reserve to themselves the right to take such action as they shall consider necessary for the maintenance of right and justice.

8. If the dispute between the parties is claimed by one of them, and is found by the Council, to arise out of a matter which by international law is solely within the domestic jurisdiction of that party, the Council shall so report, and shall make no recommendation as to its settlement.

9. The Council may in any case under this Article refer the dispute to the Assembly. The dispute shall be so referred at the request of either party to the dispute, provided that such request be made within 14 days after the submission of the dispute to the Council.

10. In any case referred to the Assembly, all the provisions of this Article and of Article 12 relating to the action and powers of the Council shall apply to the action and powers of the Assembly, provided that a report made by the Assembly, if concurred in by the Representatives of

those Members of the League represented on the Council and of a majority of the other Members of the League, exclusive in each case of the Representatives of the parties to the dispute, shall have the same force as a report by the Council concurred in by all the members thereof other than the Representatives of one or more of the parties to the dispute.

ARTICLE 16

Sanctions of Pacific Settlement

1.[1] Should any Member of the League resort to war in disregard of its covenants under Articles 12, 13 or 15, it shall *ipso facto* be deemed to have committed an act of war against all other Members of the League, which hereby undertake immediately to subject it to the severance of all trade or financial relations, the prohibition of all intercourse between

[1] The Assembly has voted in favor of the following amendments to Art. 16, to replace paragraph one, and the Members are now deciding upon their ratification:

"Should any Member of the League resort to war in disregard of its covenants under Articles 12, 13 or 15, it shall *ipso facto* be deemed to have committed an act of war against all other Members of the League, *which hereby undertake immediately to subject it to the severance of all trade or financial relations and to prohibit all intercourse at least between persons resident within their territories and persons resident within the territory of the covenant-breaking State and, if they deem it expedient, also between their nationals and the nationals of the covenant-breaking State, and to prevent all financial, commercial or personal intercourse at least between persons resident within the territory of that State and persons resident within the territory of any other State, whether a Member of the League or not, and, if they deem it expedient, also between the nationals of that State and the nationals of any other State whether a Member of the League or not.*"

[N. B. — The above amendment was voted by the Fifth Assembly on September 27, 1924, to supersede an amendment voted by the Second Assembly and which was being ratified in the following form: " . . . *which hereby undertake immediately to subject it to the severance of all trade or financial relations, the prohibition of all intercourse between persons residing in their territory and persons residing in the territory of the covenant-breaking State, and the prevention of all financial, commercial or personal intercourse between persons residing in the territory of the covenant-breaking State and persons residing in the territory of any other State, whether a Member of the League or not.*"]

"*It is for the Council to give an opinion whether or not a breach of the Covenant has taken place. In deliberations on this question in the Council, the votes of Members of the League alleged to have resorted to war and of Members against whom such action was directed shall not be counted.*

"*The Council will notify to all Members of the League the date which it recommends for the application of the economic pressure under this Article.*

"*Nevertheless, the Council may, in the case of particular Members, postpone the coming into force of any of these measures for a specified period where it is satisfied that such a postponement will facilitate the attainment of the object of the measures referred to in the preceding paragraph, or that it is necessary in order to minimize the loss and inconvenience which will be caused to such Members.*"

their nationals and the nationals of the covenant-breaking State, and the prevention of all financial, commercial or personal intercourse between the nationals of the covenant-breaking State and the nationals of any other State, whether a Member of the League or not.

2. It shall be the duty of the Council in such case[1] to recommend to the several Governments concerned what effective military, naval or air force the Members of the League shall severally contribute to the armed forces to be used to protect the covenants of the League.

3. The Members of the League agree, further, that they will mutually support one another in the financial and economic measures which are taken under this Article, in order to minimize the loss and inconvenience resulting from the above measures, and that they will mutually support one another in resisting any special measures aimed at one of their number by the covenant-breaking State, and that they will take the necessary steps to afford passage through their territory to the forces of any of the Members of the League which are coöperating to protect the covenants of the League.

4. Any Member of the League which has violated any covenant of the League may be declared to be no longer a Member of the League by a vote of the Council concurred in by the Representatives of all the other Members of the League represented thereon.

Article 17

Disputes Involving Nonmembers

1. In the event of a dispute between a Member of the League and a State which is not a Member of the League, or between States not Members of the League, the State or States not Members of the League shall be invited to accept the obligations of Membership in the League for the purposes of such dispute, upon such conditions as the Council may deem just. If such invitation is accepted, the provisions of Articles 12 to 16, inclusive, shall be applied with such modifications as may be deemed necessary by the Council.

2. Upon such invitation being given, the Council shall immediately institute an inquiry into the circumstances of the dispute and recommend such action as may seem best and most effectual in the circumstances.

3. If a State so invited shall refuse to accept the obligations of Membership in the League for the purposes of such dispute, and shall resort to war against a Member of the League, the provisions of Article 16 shall be applicable as against the State taking such action.

---

[1] The Assembly on September 21, 1925, adopted a resolution providing that the words "in such case" shall be deleted. The amendment has been submitted to Member States for ratification.

4. If both parties to the dispute, when so invited, refuse to accept the obligations of Membership in the League for the purposes of such dispute, the Council may take such measures and make such recommendations as will prevent hostilities and will result in the settlement of the dispute.

Article 18
Registration and Publication of Treaties

Every treaty or international engagement entered into hereafter by any Member of the League shall be forthwith registered with the Secretariat and shall as soon as possible be published by it. No such treaty or international engagement shall be binding until so registered.

Article 19
Review of Treaties

The Assembly may from time to time advise the reconsideration by Members of the League of treaties which have become inapplicable, and the consideration of international conditions whose continuance might endanger the peace of the world.

Article 20
Abrogation of Inconsistent Obligations

1. The Members of the League severally agree that this Covenant is accepted as abrogating all obligations or understandings *inter se* which are inconsistent with the terms thereof, and solemnly undertake that they will not hereafter enter into any engagements inconsistent with the terms thereof.

2. In case any Member of the League shall, before becoming a Member of the League, have undertaken any obligation inconsistent with the terms of this Covenant, it shall be the duty of such Member to take immediate steps to procure its release from such obligations.

Article 21
Engagements that Remain Valid

Nothing in this Covenant shall be deemed to affect the validity of international engagements, such as treaties of arbitration or regional understandings like the Monroe doctrine, for securing the maintenance of peace.

Article 22
Mandatory System

1. To those colonies and territories which as a consequence of the late war have ceased to be under the sovereignty of the States which formerly

governed them and which are inhabited by peoples not yet able to stand by themselves under the strenuous conditions of the modern world, there should be applied the principle that the well-being and development of such peoples form a sacred trust of civilization and that securities for the performance of this trust should be embodied in this Covenant.

2. The best method of giving practical effect to this principle is that the tutelage of such peoples should be intrusted to advanced nations who, by reason of their resources, their experience or their geographical position, can best undertake this responsibility, and who are willing to accept it, and that this tutelage should be exercised by them as Mandatories on behalf of the League.

3. The character of the mandate must differ according to the stage of the development of the people, the geographical situation of the territory, its economic conditions and other similar circumstances.

4. Certain communities formerly belonging to the Turkish Empire have reached a stage of development where their existence as independent nations can be provisionally recognized subject to the rendering of administrative advice and assistance by a Mandatory until such time as they are able to stand alone. The wishes of these communities must be a principal consideration in the selection of the Mandatory.

5. Other peoples, especially those of Central Africa, are at such a stage that the Mandatory must be responsible for the administration of the territory under conditions which will guarantee freedom of conscience and religion, subject only to the maintenance of public order and morals, the prohibition of abuses such as the slave trade, the arms traffic and the liquor traffic, and the prevention of the establishment of fortifications or military and naval bases and of military training of the natives for other than police purposes and the defense of territory, and will also secure equal opportunities for the trade and commerce of other Members of the League.

6. There are territories, such as Southwest Africa and certain of the South Pacific islands, which, owing to the sparseness of their population or their small size, or their remoteness from the centers of civilization, or their geographical contiguity to the territory of the Mandatory, and other circumstances, can be best administered under the laws of the Mandatory as integral portions of its territory, subject to the safeguards above mentioned in the interests of the indigenous population.

7. In every case of mandate, the Mandatory shall render to the Council an annual report in reference to the territory committed to its charge.

8. The degree of authority, control or administration to be exercised by the Mandatory shall, if not previously agreed upon by the Members of the League, be explicitly defined in each case by the Council.

9. A permanent Commission shall be constituted to receive and examine the annual reports of the Mandatories, and to advise the Council on all matters relating to the observance of the mandates.

Article 23

Social and Other Activities

Subject to and in accordance with the provisions of international conventions existing or hereafter to be agreed upon, the Members of the League:

(a) will endeavor to secure and maintain fair and humane conditions of labor for men, women, and children, both in their own countries and in all countries to which their commercial and industrial relations extend, and for that purpose will establish and maintain the necessary international organizations;

(b) undertake to secure just treatment of the native inhabitants of territories under their control;

(c) will intrust the League with the general supervision over the execution of agreements with regard to the traffic in women and children and the traffic in opium and other dangerous drugs;

(d) will intrust the League with the general supervision of the trade in arms and ammunition with the countries in which the control of this traffic is necessary in the common interest;

(e) will make provision to secure and maintain freedom of communications and of transit and equitable treatment for the commerce of all Members of the League. In this connection, the special necessities of the regions devastated during the war of 1914–1918 shall be borne in mind;

(f) will endeavor to take steps in matters of international concern for the prevention and control of disease.

Article 24

International Bureaus

1. There shall be placed under the direction of the League all international bureaus already established by general treaties, if the parties to such treaties consent. All such international bureaus and all commissions for the regulation of matters of international interest hereafter constituted shall be placed under the direction of the League.

2. In all matters of international interest which are regulated by general conventions but which are not placed under the control of international bureaus or commissions, the Secretariat of the League shall, subject to the consent of the Council and if desired by the parties, collect and dis-

tribute all relevant information and shall render any other assistance which may be necessary or desirable.

3. The Council may include as part of the expenses of the Secretariat the expenses of any bureau or commission which is placed under the direction of the League.

Article 25

Promotion of Red Cross and Health

The Members of the League agree to encourage and promote the establishment and coöperation of duly authorized voluntary national Red Cross organizations having as purposes the improvement of health, the prevention of disease and the mitigation of suffering throughout the world.

Article 26[1]

Amendments

1. Amendments to this Covenant will take effect when ratified by the Members of the League whose Representatives compose the Council and by a majority of the Members of the League whose Representatives compose the Assembly.

2. No such amendment shall bind any Member of the League which signifies its dissent therefrom, but in that case it shall cease to be a Member of the League.

---

[1] The Assembly voted in favor of the following amendments to replace Art. 26, in 1921, and the Members are now deciding upon its ratification:

"*Amendments to the present Covenant the text of which shall have been voted by the Assembly on a three-fourths majority, in which there shall be included the votes of all the Members of the Council represented at the meeting, will take effect when ratified by the Members of the League whose Representatives composed the Council when the vote was taken and by the majority of those whose Representatives form the Assembly.*

"*If the required number of ratifications shall not have been obtained within twenty-two months after the vote of the Assembly, the proposed amendment shall remain without effect.*

"*The Secretary-General shall inform the Members of the taking effect of an amendment.*

"*Any Member of the League which has not at that time ratified the amendment is free to notify the Secretary-General within a year of its refusal to accept it, but in that case it shall cease to be a Member of the League.*"

APPENDIX

ANNEX

I. Original Members of the League of Nations, Signatories of the Treaty of Peace

- *United States of America
- Belgium
- Bolivia
- *Brazil
- British Empire
  - Canada
  - Australia
  - South Africa
  - New Zealand
  - India
- China
- Cuba
- *Ecuador
- France
- Greece
- Guatemala
- Haiti
- *Hedjaz
- Honduras
- Italy
- Japan
- Liberia
- Nicaragua
- Panamá
- Perú
- Poland
- Portugal
- Roumania
- Serb-Croat-Slovene State
- Siam
- Czechoslovakia
- Uruguay

States Invited to Accede to the Covenant

- Argentine Republic
- Chile
- Colombia
- Denmark
- Netherlands
- Norway
- Paraguay
- Persia
- Salvador
- Spain
- Sweden
- Switzerland
- Venezuela

II. First Secretary-General of the League of Nations

The Honorable Sir James Eric Drummond, K.C.M.G., C.B.

States Admitted to Membership

- Abyssinia
- Albania
- Austria
- Bulgaria
- *Costa Rica
- Dominican Republic
- Esthonia
- Finland
- Germany
- Hungary
- Irish Free State
- Latvia
- Lithuania
- Luxemburg

* Not a Member state.

BIBLIOGRAPHY[1]

CHAPTER I

BOOKS

ACTON, LORD, *History of Freedom and other Essays*, 1909. New York: Macmillan.
BEAULIEU, L., *The Empire of the Tsars and the Russians*, 1893. New York: Putnam.
BEYENS, BARON, *L'Avenir des petits états*, 1919.
BOUTMY, E., *The English People*, 1904. New York: Putnam.
BRAILSFORD, H. N., *Macedonia*, 1906. London: Methuen.
BRYCE, JAMES, *South America*, 1912. New York: Macmillan.
——, *Modern Democracies*, 1922. New York: Macmillan.
COOKE, R. J., *The Church and World Peace*, 1920. New York: Abingdon Press.
COUTURAT AND LEAU, *Histoire de la langue universelle*, 1903.
DOMINIAN, LEON, *Frontiers of Language and Nationality in Europe*, 1917. New York: Holt.
DRINKWATER, JOHN, *Patriotism in Literature*, 1924. New York: Holt (H. U. L.).
FAIRGRIEVE, J., *Geography and World Power*, 1915. New York: Dutton.
FAUCHILLE, P., *Traité de droit international*, 8th ed., 1920.
FENWICK, C. G., *International Law*, 1924. New York: Century.
FILMER, SIR ROBERT, *Observations on Grotius* (in *The Freeholders*), 1699. Dixon, W. H., Col. of Pamphlets, No. 406. London, 1652.
FISHER, H. A. L., *The Common Weal*, 1924. New York: Oxford Press.
——, *Studies in History and Politics*, 1920. New York: Oxford Press.
FLEURE, H. J., *Human Geography in Western Europe*, 1919. London: Williams & Norgate.
FRANCKE, K., *The German Spirit*, 1916. New York: Holt.
FREEMAN, E. A., *The Historical Geography of Europe* (3rd ed.), 1903. New York: Longmans.
GUÉRARD, A. L., *Short History of the International Language Movement*, 1922. New York: Boni & Liveright.
GULICK AND MACFARLAND, *The Church and International Relations*, 1917. Missionary Educ. Movement.
HAMERTON, P. G., *French and English*, 1889. London: Macmillan.
HERBERT, S., *Nationality and Its Problems*, 1919. New York: Dutton.
HOLCOMBE, A. N., *The Foundations of the Modern Commonwealth*, 1923. New York: Harper.
HUNTINGTON, E., *World Power and Evolution*, 1919. New Haven: Yale Press.
MACKINDER, H. J., *Democratic Ideals and Reality*, 1919. New York: Holt.
MARTIN, E. D., *The Behavior of Crowds*, 1920. New York: Harper.

[1] Students wishing another bibliography on this subject and also a syllabus should not fail to consult Parker Thomas Moon's *Syllabus on International Relations*, Macmillan, 1925.

BIBLIOGRAPHY

MARVIN (ed.), *Western Races of the World*, 1922. New York: Oxford Press.
MAWSON, *Geographical Manual and New Atlas*, 1917. New York, Doubleday Page.
MAZZINI, *The Duties of Man and Other Essays* (Everyman), 1907. New York: Dutton.
MEILLET, A., *Les Langues dans l'Europe Nouvelle*, 1918.
MUIR, R., *Nationalism and Internationalism*, 1917. Boston: Houghton Mifflin.
NEWBIGIN, M. I., *Geographical Aspects of Balkan Problems*, 1915. New York: Putnam.
NICOLAI, G. F., *The Biology of War*, 1918. New York: Century.
OTLET, P., *Les Problèmes Internationaux et les Guerres*, 1916.
PEARSON, KARL, *National Life and Character, a Forecast*, 1893. New York: Macmillan.
PERLA, L., *What is "National Honor"?*, 1918. New York: Macmillan.
PERRY, R. B., *The Present Conflict of Ideals*, 1918. New York: Longmans.
RAMBAUD, A., *Histoire de la Russie* (7th ed.), 1918.
RIHBANY, A. M., *Wise Men from the East and from the West*, 1922. Boston: Houghton Mifflin.
PILLSBURY, W. B., *The Psychology of Nationality and Internationalism*, 1919. New York: Appleton.
RUSSELL, B., *The Problem of China*. New York: Century, 1922.
SANTAYANA, G., *Winds of Doctrine*, 1913. New York: Scribner.
SCOTT, J. F., *Patriots in the Making*, 1916. New York: Appleton.
STOCKS, J. L., *Patriotism and the Super-State*, 1920. New York: Harcourt, Brace & Co.
TAGORE, R., *Creative Unity*, 1922. New York: Macmillan.
TURNER, F. J., *The Frontier in American History*, 1920. New York: Holt.
VAN GENNEP, A., *Traité comparatif des nationalités*, 1922, Vol. I.
VON JHERING, R., *The Evolution of the Aryan*, 1897. New York: Holt.
VIGNON, L., *L'Expansion de la France*, 1891.
YOUNG, G., *Nationalism and War in the New East*, 1915. New York: Oxford Press.
ZIMMERN, A. E., *Nationality and Government*, 1918. New York: McBride.

ARTICLES

BUCK, "Language and the Sentiment of Nationality," 10 *Pol. Sci. Review*, 1916.
COOLIDGE, A. C., "Nationality and the New Europe," 4 *Yale Review*, 1915.
FORD, H. J., "The Anglo Saxon Myth," *American Mercury*, 1924.
GOYAU, G., "Sur l'Horizon du Vatican," *Revue des Deux Mondes*, 1922.
HART, A. B., "School Books and International Prejudices," *International Conciliation*, 1911.
LANGEROCK, H., "The Flemish Demand for Autonomy," *Current History*, 1923.
MAZZINI, "Europe: Its Condition and Prospects," 1852.
RENAN, ERNEST, "Qu'est-ce Qu'une Nation?" *Discours et Conférences*, 1887.
RUSSELL, BERTRAND, "If we are to Prevent the Next War," *Century*, May, 1924.
STEPHENS, H. M., "Nationality and History," 21 *American Historical Review*, 1916.

BIBLIOGRAPHY

PAMPHLETS

Amerika Esperanto, organ of the Esperanto Association of North America.
"The Churches of America Mobilizing for World Justice and World Peace," and "The Churches of America and the World Court of Justice," issued by the Commission on International Justice and Goodwill.
"Paris Peace Conference," *Eleven Year Survey of the Activities of the American School Peace League*, 1919.

CHAPTER II

BOOKS

BLAGOYÉVITCH, V., *Le Principe des nationalités et son application dans les traités de paix de Versailles et Saint-Germain.*
BOEHM, M. H., *Europa Irredenta*, 1923.
BRUN, L., *Le Problème des minorités*, 1923.
BRUNHES AND VALLAUX, *La Géographie de Histoire*, 1921.
BUTLER, R., *The New Eastern Europe*, 1919. New York: Longmans.
DUPARC, F., *La Protection des Minorités de race, de langue, et de religion*, 1922.
FAWCETT, C. B., *Frontiers, A Study in Political Geography*, 1918. New York: Oxford Press.
FREEMAN, E. A., *History of Federal Government from the Foundation of the Achaian League to the Disruption of the United States*, 1863. London: Macmillan.
GALITZA, T., *Du Droit de voter dans les plébiscites contemporains*, 1921.
GEORGE, H. B., *The Relations of Geography and History* (4th ed.), 1910. New York: Oxford Press.
GIROUD, J., *Le Plébiscite international*, 1920.
GONSSOLLIN, E., *Le Plébiscite dans le droit international actuel*, 1921.
HAUSER, H., *Principe des Nationalités*, 1916.
HERBERT, SIDNEY, *Nationality and its Problems*, 1920. New York: Dutton.
HOLDICH, T. H., *Boundaries in Europe and the Near East*, 1918. New York: Macmillan.
IORGA, N., *Les Hongrois et la nationalité roumanie*, 1909.
KALLEN, H., *Culture and Democracy in the United States*, 1924. New York: Boni & Liveright.
KELLOR, F. A., AND A. HATVAMY, *Security Against War*, 1924. New York: Macmillan.
LANSING, R., *The Peace Negotiations*, 1921. Boston: Houghton Mifflin.
LAVERGNE, B., *Le Principe des nationalités et les guerres*, 1921.
MATTERN, J., *The Employment of the Plebiscite in the Determination of Sovereignty*, 1920. Baltimore: Johns Hopkins Press.
MILL, J. S., *Representative Government*, 1861, 1905. New York: Dutton.
MITSCHERLICH, W., *Des Nationalismus Westeuropas*, 1920.
MOORE, J. B., *Digest of International Law*, 1906. Washington: Supt. of Documents.
MUIR, R., *Nationalism and Internationalism*, 1917. Boston: Houghton Mifflin.
OSBORNE, S., *The Saar Question: A Disease Spot in Europe*, 1923. London: Allen & Univen.
PHILLIPS, W. A., *Poland*, 1916. New York: Holt.

PHILLIPSON, C., *Alsace-Lorraine*, 1918. New York: Dutton.
RENNER, K., *Das Selbstbestimmungsrecht der nationen in besonderer Anwendung auf Oesterreich*, 1918.
SEIGNOBOS, C. (ed.), *Les Aspirations autonomistes en Europe*, 1913.
TEMPERLEY, H. W. V. (ed.), *History of the Peace Conference at Paris*, 1924. New York: Oxford Press.
VALLAUX, *Le Sol et l'État*, 1911.
VAN GENNEP, *Traité comparatif des nationalités*, Vol. I.
VESTAL, *The Maintenance of Peace*, 1920. New York: Putnam.
VIATOR, S. (R. W. SETON-WATSON), *Racial Problems in Hungary*, 1908. London: Constable.
WAMBAUGH, S., *A Monograph on Plebiscites with a Collection of Official Documents*, 1920. New York: Oxford Press.
WITTMANN, E., *Past and Future of the Right of National Self-determination*, 1919. Amsterdam: Van Holkema & Warendorf.
YOUNG, G., *Nationalism and War in the Near East*, 1915. New York: Oxford Press.

ARTICLES

ARMSTRONG, "Forces of Disunion in Canada," *Current History*, July, 1924.
CORCORAN, T., "The Language Campaign in Alsace-Lorraine," *Studies* (an Irish quarterly), 1924.
CURZON, LORD, "Frontiers," *The Romanes lecture*, 1907.
DUGDALE, "Eupen and Malmedy: The League's Responsibility," 16 *New Europe*, 1920.
GILFILLAN, S. C., "European Political Boundaries," 39 *Pol. Sci. Quarterly*, 1924.
HALLAYS, A., "En Alsace et Lorraine, la protestation contre les lois laiques," *Revue des Deux Mondes*, Aug., 1924.
HEADLAM-MORLEY, "Plebiscites," 236 *Quarterly Review*, 1921.
JOHNSTONE, "The German Problem in Czechoslovakia," *Foreign Affairs*, June, Sept., 1923.
LIEBER, F., "De la valeur des plébiscites dans le droit international," 3 *R. D. I. L. C.*, 1871.
PHILLIPS, W. A., "Self-Determination," *Encyclopedia Britannica*, new vols., 1922.
RAGLAN, LORD, "Armaments and Frontiers," 92 *Nineteenth Century*, 1922.
RICE, "The Free Isle of St. Louis," *N. Y. Times Magazine*, Aug. 24, 1924.
WAMBAUGH, S., "Frontiers by Plebiscite," 107 *Century*, 1923.
"British Foreign Office," *Peace Handbooks*, 1920.
"The Case of Peru," *Arbitration between Peru and Chile*.
"Documents Préliminaires," *IIIme Conférence des Nationalités*, June, 1916.
"The Question of the Pacific," *Arbitration between Peru and Chile*, 1923.

CHAPTER III

BOOKS

EAST, E. M., *Mankind at the Cross Roads*, 1924. New York: Scribner.
—— AND JONES, D. F., *Inbreeding and Outbreeding*, 1919. Philadelphia: Lippincott.
HUNTINGTON, E., *Civilization and Climate*, 1915. New Haven: Yale Press.

OLDHAM, J. H., *Christianity and the Race Problem*, 1924. New York: Doran.
PITKIN, W., *Must we Fight Japan?* 1921. New York: Century.
STODDARD, T. L., *The Rising Tide of Color*, 1920. New York: Scribner.
WALLAS, GRAHAM, *Human Nature in Politics* (3rd ed.), 1921. New York: Knopf.

ARTICLES

BUELL, "Some Legal Aspects of the Japanese Question," *A. J. I. L.*, Jan., 1923.
BRYCE, JAMES, Creighton Lecture, *Race Sentiment as a Factor in History*, 1915.
MCCAUGHEY, "Race Mixture in Hawaii," *Journal of Heredity*, Jan. and Feb., 1919.
MCCLATCHEY AND BUELL, "Shall we Naturalize the Japanese?" *Forum*, Sept., 1924.
MCGOVNEY, "Race Discrimination in Naturalization," *Iowa Law Bulletin*, 1923.
RICE, "The Indian Question in Kenya," *Foreign Affairs*, Dec. 15, 1923.

PAMPHLETS

BUELL, R. L., "Japanese Immigration," *World Peace Foundation*, 1924, Vol. VI.
CHEN, "Chinese Migrations with Special Reference to Labor Conditions," *Bulletin of the U. S. Bureau of Labor Statistics*, 1923.
"Emigration and Immigration: Legislation and Treaties," *International Labor Office, Geneva*, 1922.
JONES, T. S., *Education in Africa* (Phelps-Stokes Fund), 1922, African Education Commission.
MADISON, JAMES, *The Federalist*, No. 10.
MOORE, J. B., *Digest of Int. Law*, Vol. LV, 1906. Washington: Supt. of Documents.
Y. TAKENOB (ed.), *Japan Year Book*, 1923. Dixie Bus. Book Shop.
WILLIAMS, L. F. RUSHBROOK, *India in 1922-23*, a statement presented to Parliament, 1923.

CHAPTER IV

BOOKS

AALL, H., *Das Schicksal des Nordens*, 1918.
ABD AL-KĀHIR, *Moslem Schisms and Sects* (tr. by K. C. Seelye), 1920. New York: Columbia University Press.
ARCHER, W., *Gems of German Thought*, 1917. New York: Doubleday.
BEER, GEORGE L., *The English-Speaking Peoples*, 1917. New York: Macmillan.
BERENGUER, F., *El Hispano-Americanismo*, 1918.
"Berentning om Den Danske, Den Norske Og Den Svenske Forening 'Nordens'," 1922.
BOAS, F., *The Mind of Primitive Man*, 1911. New York: Macmillan.
BURGESS, J. N., *Political Science and Comparative Constitutional Law*, 1890. Boston: Ginn.
BURR, C. S., *America's Race Heritage*, 1922. New York: Nat. Hist. Soc.

BIBLIOGRAPHY

CHAMBERLAIN, H. S., *The Foundations of the Nineteenth Century* (English translation, 1910). New York: Lane.
CHÉRADAME, A., *The Pan-German Plot Unmasked*, 1917. New York: Scribner.
CLEMENTS, P. H., *The Boxer Rebellion*, 1915. New York: Longmans.
CONKLIN, E. G., *The Direction of Human Evolution*, 1921, 1922. New York: Scribner.
DEMOLINS, E., *Anglo-Saxon Superiority*, 1898. New York: Fenno.
DUNNING, W. A., *History of Political Theories, Recent Times*, 1924. New York: Macmillan.
DE GOBINEAU, LE COMTE, *Essai sur L'Inequalité des Races Humaines* (2d ed.), 1884.
DENIKER, J., *The Races of Man* (2d ed.). New York: Scribner.
DRAGE, G., *Austria-Hungary*, 1909. New York: Dutton.
DUBOSEQ, A., *L'Evolution de la Chine*, 1911–1921. 1922.
FINOT, JEAN, *Race Prejudice* (new ed.), 1924. New York: Dutton.
GARRIGO, R. E., *America para los Americanos*, 1910.
GIBBONS, H. A., *World Politics*, 1922. New York: Century.
GOULD, C. W., *America, A Family Matter*, 1922. New York: Scribner
GRANT, MADISON, *Racial Realities in Europe*, 1924. New York: Scribner.
———, *The Passing of the Great Race* (new ed.), 1918. New York: Scribner.
GROUSSET, R., *Le Reveil de l'Asie* (3d ed.), 1924.
HÖIJER, O., *Le Scandinavisme*, 1919.
HUNTINGTON, ELLSWORTH, *The Character of Races*, 1924. New York: Scribner.
INSABATO, E., *L'Islam et la politique des Alliés*, 1920.
JAMAL, AHMED, PASHA, *Memories of a Turkish Statesman*, 1922. London: Hutchinson.
JOHNSTON, H. H., *Views and Reviews, From the Outlook of an Anthropologist*, 1912. London: Williams & Norgate.
JOSEY, C. C., *Race and National Solidarity*, 1923. New York: Scribner.
KEANE, A. H., *Man: Past and Present*, 1899. New York: Putnam.
LEA, HOMER, *Day of the Saxon*, 1912. New York: Harper.
LEACH, H. G., *Scandinavia of the Scandinavians*, 1916. New York: Scribner.
LE BON, G., *The Psychology of Socialism*, 1899. New York: Macmillan.
LE FUR, *Races, Nationalités, États*, 1922.
LEGER, L., *Le Panslavisme et le intérêt français*, 1917.
MARGOLIOUTH, D. S., *Early Development of Mohammedanism*, 1914. New York: Scribner.
MOUSSET, A., *L'Espagne dans la Politique Mondiale*, 1923.
NAUMANN, F., *Central Europe*, 1917. New York: Knopf.
NIEDERLE, L., *La Slave Race* (2d ed.), 1916.
OAKESMITH, J., *Race and Nationality*, 1919. New York: Stokes.
POOLEY, A. M., *Japan's Foreign Policies*, 1920. New York: Dodd, Mead.
POWELL, E. A., *Struggle for Power in Moslem Asia*, 1923. New York: Century.
REUTER, B. A., *Anglo-American Relations during the Spanish-American War*, 1924. New York: Macmillan.
RIPLEY, W. Z., *The Races of Europe*, 1899. New York: Appleton.
STODDARD, T. L., *The New World of Islam*, 1922. New York: Scribner.
———, *Revolt Against Civilization*, 1922. New York: Scribner.
———, *Rising Tide of Color*, 1920. New York: Scribner.
USHER, R., *Pan-Germanism*, 1914. Boston: Houghton Mifflin.

WEALE, B. L. P., *The Conflict of Color*, 1910. New York: Macmillan.
WERTHEIMER, M. S., *The Pan-German League, 1890–1914*, 1924. New York: Columbia Press.
WILLOUGHBY, W. C., *Race Problems in the New Africa*, 1923. New York: Oxford Press.
ZWEMER, REV. S. M., *The Disintegration of Islam*, 1916. New York: Revell.

ARTICLES

"La approximacion Latin-Americana," *La Nueva Democracia*, March, 1924.
"The Anti-Religion Movement," 53 *Chinese Recorder*, 1922.
BALFOUR, "English Speaking Union," *The Landmark*, June, 1923.
BARRÈS, M., "Les Liens spirituels de la France et de l'Espagne," *Revue des Deux Mondes*, June 15, 1924.
BOWMAN, I., "Moslem state relations," *New World*, 1921.
Pan-African Congress, *Crisis*, Jan. and Feb., 1924.
DEAKIN, F. B., "Spain and Hispano-Americanism," *Contemporary Review*, May, 1924.
DELAFOSSE, "Le Congrès Panafricain," *Afrique française*, 1919.
———, "Les points sombres de l'horizon en Afrique Occidentale," *Afrique française*, 1922.
DUBOIS, W. E., "Back to Africa," 105 *Century*, 1923.
EXPERTUS, "Neutralisiergun Deutsch-Osterreichs?" 6 *Sudöst*, 1919.
GARVEY, M., "The Negro's Greatest Enemy," *Current History*, Sept., 1923.
"Norden", *American-Scandinavian Review*, Aug., 1923.
OLIVIER, "Colour Prejudice," 124 *Contemporary Review*, 1923.
OSSENDOWSKI, "King of the World," *Century*, Nov., 1923.
"Pan-Turanianism," *Encyclopedia Britannica*, 12th ed.; vol. 33.
PEARSON, "The Problem of Anthropology," *Scientific Monthly*, Nov., 1920.
PICKENS, W., "The Emperor of Africa," *Forum*, Aug., 1923.
RIPPY, "Pan-Hispanic Propaganda in Hispanic America," 37 *Political Science Quarterly*, 1922.
SAROLEA, "Bolshevism and World Revolution," *Current History*, Feb., 1924.
SHIH-YI, LIANG, "China Faces the Modern World," *Current History*, Sept., 1924.
SNOUCK-HURGRONJE, "L'Islam et le problème des Races," 50 *Revue du Monde Musulman*, 1922.
SNOUCK-HURGRONJE, "Islam and Turkish Nationalism," *Foreign Affairs*, Sept. 15, 1924.
STODDARD, "Pan-Turanism," 11 *Am. Pol. Sci. Review*, 1917.
VON SOSNOSKY, "The New Pan-Germanism," 240 *Quarterly Review*, 1923.
DE WARNAFFE, "Le mouvement pan nègre aux États-unis et ailleurs," *Congo*, May, 1922.
WUORINEN, "The Efforts to Form a Union of Baltic States," *Current History*, July, 1924.
"X," "Le Panislamisme et le Pan-Turquisme," 22 *Revue du Monde Musulman*, 1913.

PAMPHLETS

BUELL, "Japanese Immigration," *World Peace Foundation*, 1924. Vol. VI.
OTLET, M., "Documents préliminaires, IIIme Conference des Nationalités," Lausanne, June 27, 1916.

CHAPTER V

Books

ASHLEY, P., *Modern Tariff History* (3rd Ed.), 1920. New York: Dutton.
BANERJEA, P., *Fiscal Policy in India*, 1922. Calcutta: Macmillan & Co., Ltd.
BURNS, C. D., *Government and Industry*, 1921. New York: Oxford University Press.
CULBERTSON, W. S., *Commercial Policy in War Time and After*, 1919. New York: Appleton.
ECKEL, E. C., *Coal, Iron and War*, 1920. New York: Holt.
P. FAUCHILLE, *Traité de Droit International Public* (8th Ed.), 1922. Vol. 1.
FISK, G. M., AND PEIRCE, P. S., *International Commercial Policies*, 1923. New York: Macmillan.
FRIEDMAN, E. M., *International Commerce and Reconstruction*, 1920. New York: Dutton.
GOOCH, G. P., *History of Modern Europe*, 1923. New York: Holt.
GREGORY, T. E. G., *Tariffs: A Study in Methods*, 1921. Philadelphia: Lippincott.
KEYNES, J. M., *Economic Consequences of the Peace*, 1920. New York: Harcourt, Brace.
MCCLURE, W. M., *A New American Commercial Policy*, 1924. New York: Columbia University Press.
NOURSE, E. G., *American Agriculture and the European Market*, 1924. New York: McGraw Hill.
OTLET, *Les Problèmes Internationaux et les Guerres*.
SMITH, G. O. (Ed.), *The Strategy of Minerals*, 1919. New York: Appleton.
SOMBART, W., *Krieg und Kapitalismus*, 1912.
SPURR, J. E., *Political and Commercial Geology and the World's Mineral Resources*, 1920. New York: McGraw Hill.
TAUSSIG, F. W., *Tariff History of the U. S.* (7th Ed.), 1922. New York: Putnam.
TELEKI, P., *The Evolution of Hungary and its Place in European History*, 1923. New York: Macmillan.
TITTONI, T., *Modern Italy*, 1922. New York: Macmillan.
DE LA TRAMERYE, P. E., *The World-Struggle for Oil*, 1924. New York: Knopf.
VINER, J., *Dumping: A Problem in International Trade*, 1923. Chicago: University Press.
WOOLF, L., *International Government*, 1916. New York: Brentano.
YOUNG, G., *Portugal, Old and Young*, 1917. New York: Oxford Press.

Articles

ANDERSON, B. M., "Annual Financial Survey and Business Forecast," *The Annalist*, Jan. 5, 1925.
CULBERTSON, W. S., "Raw Materials and Foodstuffs in the Commercial Policies of Nations," *Annals of the Amer. Acad. of Pol. and Soc. Sci.*, March, 1924.
CURTIS, "Fertilizers: The World Supply," *Foreign Affairs*, March 15, 1924.
DELAISI, F., "The Comité des Forges de France, and its Pre-war and Post-war Policy," *Reconstruction in Europe*, May 31, July 12, 1923.
ESTEP, "The New Balance of Power in European Iron and Steel," *Reconstruction in Europe*, Sept. 7, 1922.

BIBLIOGRAPHY 783

HODAC, "The Tariff Arrangements of the Succession States," *Reconstruction in Europe*, July 27, 1922.
HURD, A., "Open Seas and Closed Ports," *Fortnightly Review*, Jan. 1924.
LEITH, "The World Iron and Steel Situation," *Foreign Affairs*, 1923.
" Nouveau tarif douanier turc pour L'Anatolie," *L'Asie francaise*, April, 1923.
REW, "The World's Grain Supplies as Affected by the Situation in Russia," *Reconstruction in Europe (Manchester Guardian Commercial)* August 17, 1922.
TODD, "The World Crisis in Cotton," *Foreign Affairs*, Dec. 15, 1923.
TOWER, "The Coal Question," *Foreign Affairs*, Sept., 1923.
WHITFORD, "The Crude Rubber Supply," *Foreign Affairs*, June 15, 1924.

PAMPHLETS

AMERICAN BANANA COMPANY V. UNITED FRUIT CO., 213 U. S., 1909.
BAIN AND MILLIKEN, "Nitrogen Survey," Part 1, *Trade Information Bulletin No. 170*, 1924, *Supplement to U. S. Commerce Reports.*
11th Annual Report, "The Baltic and White Sea Conference," 1921.
"Colonial Tariff Policies," *U. S. Tariff Commission*, 1922.
Congressional Digest, May, 1924.
"Department of Commerce Reports," July 31, 1923.
"Constitution of the Commission for the Gov't of Saar," Council of the League of Nations, O. J., March, 1920.
"Co-operation in Amer. Export Trade." *Report of the Federal Trade Commission*, 1916.
CROSETTE, L., "Sisal," *Trade Information Bulletin*, No. 200.
"Crude Rubber Survey," Part 1, *Trade Information Bulletin*, No. 180.
GINI, "Report on the Problem of Raw Materials," *The League of Nations.*
"National Restrictions on Marine Transportation," *International Chamber of Commerce*, Brochure No. 28, March, 1923.
"Reciprocity and Commercial Treaties," *U. S. Tariff Commissions*, 1919.
"Report on Tariff Wars between certain European States," 1904, *Cd.* 1938.
RUTTER, F. R., "Tariff Systems of South American Countries." *U. S. Tariff Series* No. 34, 1916.
STRONG, H. M., "Distribution of Agricultural Exports from the U. S." *Trade Information Bulletin* No. 177.
"Valorization of Brazilian Coffee," *Trade Information Bulletin* No. 73.

CHAPTER VI

BOOKS

AGRESTI, O. R., *David Lubin*, 1922. Cambridge, Mass.: A. D. Little.
CHAMBERLAIN, J. P., *The Régime of the International Rivers: Danube und Rhine*, 1923. New York: Longmans.
The League of Nations (S. P. Duggan Ed.), 1919. Boston: Atlantic Press.
DEVAUX, J., *Les Télégraphie sans fil dans les rapports internationaux*, 1914.
EGER, G., *Das Internationales ubereinkommenuber den Eisenbahn-Frachtverkehr*, 1909.
LIPPERT, G., *Das Internationale Finanzrecht*, 1912.
MCCLURE, W. M., *A New American Commercial Policy*, 1924. New York: Columbia Press.
MCPHERSON, L. G., *Transportation in Europe*, 1910. New York: Holt.

MOUSSET, A., *La Petite Entente*, 1923.
PELLETIER AND VIDAL-NAQUET, *La Convention d'Union pour la protection de la propriété industrielle*, 1902.
REINSCH, P., *Public International Unions*, 1911. Boston: Ginn.
SALTER, J. A., *Allied Shipping Control, an Experiment in International Administration*, 1921. New York: Oxford Press.
SAYRE, F. B., *Experiments in International Administration*, 1920. New York: Harper.

ARTICLES

"Die serbische freizone in Saloniki," *Neue Zurucher Zeitung*, Jan. 30, 1924.
HOSTIE, "Les actes du Danube et de l'Elbe," *R. D. I. L. C.*, 1923.
KAZANSKY, "Théorie de l'administration internationale," 1902. (*Reprinted from R. G. D. I. P.*)
PANTARO, "L'Istituto Internazionale d'Agricoltura. La sia vita ed. I. suoi Problemi," *Nuova Antologia*, Maggio, 1924.
PAULUS, "Les Zones franches autour de Geneve," *R. D. I. L. C.*, 1924.
DE VISSCHER, F., "Le Régime nouveau des Détroits," *R. D. I. L. C.*, 1923.
ZIMMERN, "Fiscal Policy and International Relations," *Journal of the British Institute of International Affairs*, Jan., 1924.

PAMPHLETS

"Actes de la Septième Assemblée Générale," 1924.
"Case of the S. S. Wimbledon," *Series A, Collection of Judgments, No. 1, Permanent Court of International Justice*, 1923, (Pub. by).
"Convention and Statute on Freedom of Transit, Barcelona," April 20, 1921. *T. S.* 171.
"Annex to Art. 16—Convention of Feb. 2, 1920, between Lithuania and Russia," *T. S.* 289.
HERTSLET, *Map of Africa by Treaty*, Vol. II.
Handbook of International Organizations, 1921.
"International Economic Conference at Genoa," April–May, 1922, *Cmd.* 1667.
KAECKENBEECK, G., "International Rivers, 1920," *Peace Handbooks No. 149*, Art. 331, Treaty of Versailles.
"Minutes, Lausanne Conference," *Cmd.* 1814 (1923).
MOORE, J. B., *Digest of International Law*, Vol. V.
"The Portorose Conference," *International Conciliation*, 1922, No. 176.
"The Proceedings of the International Railway Congress—8th Session," 1911.
"Report on Palestine Administration," 1920-1921.
"Report to the Fifth Assembly, etc.," A. 8, 1924.
"Saar Basin and Free City of Danzig," *Information Section, League of Nations*, 1924.
"Art. 35, Statute on the International Régime of Railways," *O. J.*, Jan., 1924 (Part II).
WHITTUCK, E. A., "International Canals," *Peace Handbooks*, No. 150.

CHAPTER VII

BOOKS

The American Labor Year Book, 1923–1924.
CARR-SAUNDERS, A. M., *The Population Problem*, 1922. New York: Oxford Press.

COOLIDGE, M. R., *Chinese Immigration*, 1909. New York: Holt.
Cox, H., *The Problem of Population*, 1923. New York: Putnam.
EAST, E. M., *Mankind at the Cross Roads*, 1923. New York: Scribner.
FOERSTER, R. F., *The Italian Emigration of Our Times*, 1919. Cambridge: Harvard Press.
JOHNSTON, G. A., *International Social Progress*, 1924. London: Allen & Unwin.
LEROY-BEAULIEU, *Colonisation chez les peuples modernes*, Vol. II.
LOWE, B. E., *The International Protection of Labor*, 1921. New York: Macmillan.
PICQUET, V., *Colonization française dans Afrique du Nord*, 1914.
POSTGATE, R. W., *The Workers' International*, 1920. New York: Harcourt, Brace.
WRIGHT, H., *Population*, 1923. New York: Harcourt, Brace.

ARTICLES

"Alleged instructions of Soviet Government to English Communists," *Manchester Guardian Weekly*, Oct. 31, 1924,
FAUCHILLE, P., "The Right of Emigration and Immigration," 9 *International Labor Review*, 1924.
FEIS, "The Attempt to Establish the Eight-hour Day by International Action," 39 *Political Science Quarterly*, 1924.
"The Fourth Session of the International Labor Conference," 6 *International Labor Review*, 1922.
GUERREAU, M., "Une nouvelle institution du droit des gens," *L'Organisation permanente du Travail*, 1923.
"Immigration report of the Imperial Economic Council of Japan," *Japan Weekly Chronicle*, June 15, 1924.
MCNAIR, H. F., "Treaty Rights of Chinese Merchants and Free Laborers Abroad," *Chinese Social and Political Science Review*, Jan., 1924.
"The Migration of Races," 42 *Round Table*, 1921.
SAROLEA, C., "Bolshevism and the World Revolution," *Current History*, Feb., 1924.
VILALLONGA, "The Legal Character of the International Labor Organisation," 9 *International Labor Review*, 1924.
WAGNER, "The Economic International," *The International Trade Union Review*, Jan.–March, 1924.

PAMPHLETS

"Four Years' Work of the International Labor Organization," *League of Nations Union*, Part I, 1924.
"Industrial and Labor Information," *International Labor Office*, May 26, 1924.
LAUGHLIN, Dr. H. H., "Europe as an Emigrant-Exporting Continent and the United States as Immigrant-Receiving Nation," *Hearings before the House Committee on Immigration and Naturalization*, 68 Congress, 1st Session, 1924.
"Methods of Compiling Emigration and Immigration Statistics," *I. L. O.*, 1922.
Report of the International Emigration Commission, 1921.
"Report of the British Ambassador, Sir Eric Geddes, on Conditions at Ellis Island Immigration Station," *Cmd.*, 1940, 1923.

CHAPTER VIII

Books

BUXTON, N. E., AND CONWIL-EVANS, T. P., *Oppressed Peoples and the League of Nations*, 1922. London: Dent & Sons.
DRAGE, G., *Austria-Hungary*, 1909. New York: Dutton.
DUPARC, J. F., *La Protection des Minorités de race, de langue et de religion*, 1922.
GOOCH, G. P., *History of Modern Europe*, 1923. New York: Holt.
LUCIEN-BRUN, J., *Le Problème des Minorités*, 1923.
MANDELSTAM, A., *Le Sort de l'Empire ottoman*, 1917.
MIGNOT, P., *Le Problème juif et le principe des nationalités*, 1923.
DE MORGAN, J., *Histoire du Peuple Arménien*, 1919.
TEMPERLEY, H. W. V. (editor), *A History of the Peace Conference of Paris*, 1922, Vol. V. New York: Oxford Press.
TOYNBEE, A. J., *The Western Question in Greece and Turkey*, 1923. New York: Oxford Press.
WOLF, L., *Notes on the Diplomatic History of the Jewish Question*, 1919. London: Spottiswoode, Ballantyne.

Articles

BLOCISZEWSKI, "La constitution polanaise du 17 Mars," 1921, *Revue des sciences politiques*, 1922.
DÄNEMARK, *Neue Zürucher Zeitung*, May 12, 1924.
DÄNEMARK, *Neue Zürucher Zeitung*, May 15, 1924.
"Das Völkerbundsregime in Oberschlesien," *Neue Zürucher Zeitung*, Dec. 20, 1923.
DELL, R., "Fascist Terrorism in the Tyrol," *Nation*, May 28, 1924.
DUPARC, "L'état de la protection des minorités à la veille de l'assemblée de la société des Nations," *R. D. I. L. C.*, 1923.
HEYKING, "Racial Minorities and the League," *Foreign Affairs*, June, 1924.
KLIMOV, "The Jewish Commissiariat in Soviet Russia," 5 *Soviet Russia*, 1921.
LANE, "Why Greeks and Turks Oppose Being Exchanged," *Current History*, March and April, 1923.
LUDWIG, "Le Sort des Minorités en Hongrie et en Tchéo-Slovaque," and "La Tchéo-Slovaque, La Grande Roumanie, La Yougoslave, Que Seraient-Elle sans la signature des traités de Minorités," *Revue de Hongrie*, Jan. 16, April 15, 1923.
MANDÉLSTAM, A., "La Société des Nations et les puissances devant le problème arménien," *R. G. D. I. P.*, 1922.
MAXWELL, F., "The Treatment of Hungarian Minorities," *Fortnightly Review*, July, 1924.
MESTRÉ, A., "Le protectorat catholique de la France en Orient," *Europe Nouvelle*, August 9, 1924.
MUNZ, S., "Czechoslovakia under Masaryk," 123 *Contemporary Review*, 1923, 598.
"Polish voting qualifications," *Manchester Guardian Weekly*, March 28, 1924.
"Count Toggenburg, a South Tyrol deputy," *Neue Zürucher Zeitung*, Dec. 7, 1923.
"Turkish attempts to segregate minorities," *N. Y. Times*, April 5, 1924.

BIBLIOGRAPHY

Pamphlets

"Affairs in Southeastern Europe," *Cd.* 1532, 1903.
"Clemenceau to Paderewski, covering letter to the Polish Minority Treaty," June 28, 1919.
"Collection of Advisory Opinions," *Publications of the Permanent Court of International Justice, Series B*, No. 6, Sept. 10, 1923.
"Convention Concerning the Exchange of Greek and Turkish Populations," Jan. 30, 1923, *Cmd.* 1929.
"The German Minority in South Jutland," *Danish Ministry for Foreign Affairs*, 1924.
"Interparliamentary Union," August, 1923, *Bulletin Interparlementaire*, July-August, 1923, Part IV.
"The League of Nations and Minorities," *Information Section, League of Nations Secretariat*, 1923.
"Art. 151, Traité de paix entre les puissances alliées et associés et la Turquie," *Minutes, Lausanne Conference, Cmd.* 1814, 1923.
"Report of the International Commission to Inquire into the Causes of the Balkan Wars," 1914.
"Report on Questions of Jewish Interest at the Fourth Assembly," *Board of Deputies of British Jews*, 1923.
"La situation des minorities en Slovaquie et en Russie-Subcarpathique," *Mémoire à la Société des Nations*, 1923.
ZEKERIA, "Solving Greco-Turkish Blood Feuds by Migration," *Current History* March, 1923.

CHAPTER IX

Books

BAU, M. J., "Modern Democracy in China," 1923. Shanghai: Commercial Press.
BRACQ, J. C., *The Evolution of French Canada*, 1924. New York: Macmillan.
COHEN, E., *La Question juive devant le droit international public*, 1922.
DARESTE, F. R., *Les Constitutions modernes*, 1883, Vol. II.
DEAKIN, F. B., *Spain Today*, 1924. New York: Knopf.
DRAGE, G., *Austria-Hungary*, 1909. New York: Dutton.
GJERSET, K., *History of Iceland*, 1924. New York: Macmillan.
DE HEVESY, A., *Nationalities in Hungary*, 1919. London: T. F. Unwin.
JEBB, R., *The Imperial Conference, a History and a Study*, 1911. 2 vols. New York: Longmans.
JEBB, R., *Studies in Colonial Nationalism*, 1905. New York: Longmans.
JOHNSON, C. R., *Constantinople Today*, 1922. New York: Macmillan.
JOUPLAIN, *La Question du Liban*, 1908.
KEITH, A. B., *The Constitution, Administration and Laws of the Empire*, 1924. London: Collins.
——, *Imperial Unity and the Dominions*, 1916. New York: Oxford Press.
——, *Responsible Government in the Dominions*, 1912. New York: Oxford Press.
——, *War Government of the British Dominions*, 1921. New York: Oxford Press.
LYBYER, A. H., *The Government of the Ottoman Empire in the Time of Suleiman the Magnificent*, 1913. Cambridge: Harvard Press.
MARQUIS DE OLIVART, *La Questión Catalana ante el derecho internacional*, 1909.
MUKERJEE, R., *Democracies of the East*, Part III, 1923. London: King.

PASHA, A., *Le Liban après la guerre*, 1919.
PHILLIPS, W. A., *Poland*, 1916. New York: Holt.
RAMBAUD, A., *Histoire de la Russie*.
REDSLOB, R., *Abhängige Länder*, 1914.
TARRING, C. J., *Laws Relating to the Colonies* (4th ed.), 1913. London: Stevens & Haynes.
TEMPERLEY, *History of the Peace Conference*, 1922, Vol. IV. New York: Oxford Press.
TOYNBEE. A. J., *The Western Question in Greece and Turkey*, 1922. New York: Oxford Press.
WILLIAMS, R., *The League of Nations To-day*, 1923. New York: Holt.

ARTICLES

ALLIN, "International Status of the British Dominions," *Amer. Pol. Science Review*, Nov., 1923.
CAMPBELL, "South Africa Before the Elections," *Foreign Affairs*, June 16, 1924.
CASTAGNÉ, "Le Bolchevisme et le Islam," 51 *Revue du Monde Musulman*, 1923.
"Catalonian Appeal to League of Nations," *Le Courrier Catalan*, July 15, 1924.
CHAMBERLAIN, "Asiatic States in the Soviet Union," *Current History*, June, 1924.
"Communication of Liberal and Labor M. P.'s to members of Dominion parliament," *Foreign Affairs*, August, 1923.
"Constitution for the autonomous republic of the Kirghizes," 51 *Revue du Monde Musulman*, 1923.
"Correspondence between British Govt. and Irish Free State re *inter se* relations of the various Dominions," *Manchester Guardian*, Dec. 16, 24, 1924.
DAVIES, "Spain and the Basques," *Fortnightly Review*, Jan., 1924.
ERICH, "La question de la Carélie Orientale," *R. D. I. L. C.*, 1922, 1923.
"The Geneva Protocol: An Analysis," *Round Table*, Dec., 1924.
"The Imperial Conference," 13 *The Round Table*, 1923.
JOAD, "The Spanish Separatists," *Foreign Affairs*, May, 1924.
LENGYEL, E., "The New Gandhi of the Balkans," *Nation*, June 4, 1924.
LOWELL, "Canada's Treaty-Making Power," *Foreign Affairs*, Sept., 1923.
MARRIOTT, "Empire Foreign Policy," 119 *Fortnightly Review*, 1923.
MITRANY, "The New Roumanian Constitution," *Journal of Comparative Legislation and International Law*, Feb., 1924.
NAZAROFF, "Soviet Russia's Advance toward Federation," *Current History*, March, 1923.
"The New Imperial Problem," 13 *Round Table*, 1923.
"Roumanian Treaty with the Allies," *Current History*, June, 1924.
"Text of New Roumanian Constitution," *Current History*, Sept., 1923.
TRACQUAIR, "The Canadian Type," *Atlantic Monthly*, August, 1923.

PAMPHLETS

"Bericht Über die Verwaltung von Bosnien und Der Hercegovina," 1913. *Ministry of Finance*, Vienna.
"Colonial Tariff Policies," *U. S. Tariff Commission*, 1922.

BIBLIOGRAPHY 789

"Documents relatifs aux négoçiations concernant les garanties de sécurité contre une aggression de l' Allemagne," 1924. *Documentes Diplomatiques, Ministère des Affaires Étrangerès.*
"Halibut Fisheries Treaty," *Canadian Sessional Paper*, No. 111a, 31 Geo. V. A. 1923.
"Corres. with the Palestine Arab Delegation and the Zionist Organization," *Cmd.* 1700, 1922.
"Report of Canadian Delegate, Conference on Limitation of Armament," *Sessional Paper*, No. 47, 12 Geo. V. A., 1922.
"Statute of the Memel Territory," *O. J.*, Sept., 1924.
"Treaty of April 3, 1911, British Empire and Japan," 104 *State Papers*, 159.
"Zionism," *Peace Handbook*, No. 162.

CHAPTER X

Books

ALVAREZ, A., *Le Droit International Americain*, 1910.
ALVAREZ, A., *The Monroe Doctrine*, 1924. New York: Oxford Press.
BECÚ, C. A., *El " A. B. C." y su concepto politico y juridico*, 1915.
BRUNET RENÉ, *The New German Constitution*, 1922. New York: Knopf.
COUDENHOVE-KALERGE, *Pan-Europa*, 1923.
CURTIS, L., *The Problem of the Commonwealth*, 1916. New York: Macmillan.
DEBIDOUR, A., *Histoire Diplomatique de l'europe*, Vol. I & II, 1891.
DJUVARA, T. G., *Cent Projets de Partage de la Turquie*, 1914.
DUPUIS, C., *Les rapports des grandes Puissances avec les autres États*, 1921.
FABELA, I., *Los Estados Unidos, contra la libertad.* Barcelona.
FRIED, A. H., *The Restoration of Europe*, 1916. New York: Macmillan.
FRIED, A. H., *Pan-Amerika* (2nd edition), 1918.
GRUENING, E., (Ed.) *These United States, A Symposium*, 1923. New York: Boni and Liveright.
INMAN, S. G., *Hacia la solidaridad americana*, 1914.
JELLINEK, G., *Allgemeine Staatslehre*, 1905.
KRAUS, H., *Die Monroedoktrin*, 1913.
MCBAIN AND ROGERS, *The New Constitutions of Europe*, 1922. New York: Doubleday, Page.
DE MALBERG, R. C., *Contribution à la Théorie générale de l'État*, Vol. I, 1921.
MARTIN, P. AND JAMES, H. G., *The Republics of Latin America*, 1923. New York: Harper.
MOORE, J. B., *International Law and Some Current Illusions*, 1924. New York: Macmillan.
MOUSSET, A., *La Petite Entente*, 1923.
MOWRER, P. S., *Balkanized Europe*, 1920. New York: Dutton.
MUNRO, D. G., *The Five Republics of Central America*, 1918. New York: Oxford Press.
PANARETOFF, S., *Near Eastern Affairs and Conditions*, 1922. New York: Macmillan.
PINON, R., *L'Europe et la Jeune Turquie*, 1911.
ROBERTSON, W. S., *Hispanic-American Relations with the U. S.*, 1923. New York: Oxford Press.
——, *History of the Latin-American Nations*, 1922. New York: Appleton.

ROBINSON AND WEST, *The Foreign Policy of Woodrow Wilson*, 1917. New York: Macmillan.
SOTOLONGO, *El Imperialismo Notre-Americano*, 1914.
STUART, G. H., *Latin America and the United States*, 1922. New York: Century.
TOYNBEE, A., *Nationality and the War*, 1915. New York: Dutton.
WORSFOLD, W. B., *The Empire on the Anvil*, 1916. London: Smith, Elder.
WRONG, H., *The Government of the West Indies*, 1923. New York: Oxford Press.

ARTICLES

"The Bessarabian Dispute," *Foreign Affairs*, June 15, 1924.
"C.", "The Future of the Monroe Doctrine," *Foreign Affairs*, March 15, 1924.
CALBÓ, "La intromisión norte americana en Centroamerica," 29 *Cuba Contemporánea*, 1922.
DAVIES, "The Future of the New Baltic States," *Fortnightly Review*, June, 1924.
"Filene French Peace Award," *New York Times*, Sept. 1, 1924.
JASZI, O., "Dismembered Hungary and Peace in Central Europe," *Foreign Affairs*, Dec. 15, 1923.
KAMIENIECKI, W., "La Politique Balte," *L'Ést Européen*, March 10, 1923.
LYON, "Baltic Alliances: Finland at the Cross Roads," *Fortnightly Review*, June, 1924.
MUENZ, "The Real Face Behind Hungary's Janus-Mask," *Current History*, Dec., 1923.
NAZAROFF, "Soviet Russia's Advance Toward Federation," *Current History*, March, 1923.
"Text of Russian Constitution of July 6, 1923," *Nation*, August 15, 1923.
"Treaty of Dec., 1922, between soviet Russia and Ukraine, White Russia, and Transcaucasia," *Current History*, March, 1923.
"World Solidarity," *Buenos Aires Nation*, Jan. 12, 1923.
WUORINEN, "The Efforts to Form a Union of Baltic States," *Current History*, July, 1924.

PAMPHLETS

Bulletin of the Pan-American Union, August, 1923.
Conference on Central American Affairs, Washington, 1922–23.
"Convention of August 14, 1920, Jugoslavia and Czechoslovakia," *T. S.*, 154.
"Convention of March 3, 1921, Poland and Roumania," *T. S.* 175.
"Convention of April 23, 1921, Roumania and Czechoslovakia," *T. S.*, 155.
Cox, "The Movement for Independence in Central America," 53 *Bulletin of the Pan-American Union*, 1921.
"Report of the Delegates of the U. S. of America to the Fifth International Conference of American States," 1923.
"Soviet Russia," *British Foreign Office*, 1924.
"Special Handbook for the use of the Delegates Fifth International Conference of American States," Part I, *Prepared by the Pan-American Union*, 1922.
SUCHTELEN, P. V., "The Only Solution—A European Federation," in "Toward an International Understanding," *Union of Democratic Control*, No. 10.
"La Union Panamericana Tratado, Convenciones y resoluciones," *Quinta Conferencia internacional americana*, 1923.
Verbatim Record of the Plenary Sessions of the Fifth International Conference of American States, Vol. I, Santiago, 1923.

BIBLIOGRAPHY

CHAPTER XI

Books

BEER, G. L., *African Questions at the Paris Peace Conferences*, 1923. New York: Macmillan.
BUELL, R. L., *The International Opium Conference*, 1925, Boston: World Peace Foundation.
DUNN, W. T., *The Opium Traffic in Its International Aspects*, 1920. New York: Columbia University (Thesis).
LA MOTTE, E. N., *The Opium Monopoly*, 1920. New York: Macmillan.
——, *The Ethics of Opium*, 1924. New York: Century.
MACDONALD, A. J. M., *Trade, Politics and Christianity in Africa and the Far East*, 1916. New York: Longmans.
MORSE, H. B., *Trade and Administration of China* (rev. ed.), 1913. New York: Longmans.
TORCHIANA, H., *Tropical Holland*, 1921. Chicago: University Press.

Articles

ANDREWS, C. F., "The Opium Menace in India," *The Indian Review*, April, 1924.
CORWIN, "The Three-Mile Limit," *Forum*, Sept., 1923.

Pamphlets

"Administration of New Guinea, Australia," *Report to the League of Nations*, F. 15723.
"Annexes to the Minutes of the Third Session Permanent Mandates Commission," A. 19, 193.
"The Case Against Heroin," *Foreign Policy Association Pamphlet*, No. 24.
"Correspondence respecting the Cultivation of Opium in China," *Cmd.* 1931. 1921.
Cunard S. S. Co. v. Mellon, 262 U. S., 1923, 100.
DIXON, G. G., "Truth About Indian Opium," *India Office*, 1922.
"Extent and Trend of Drug Addiction in the United States," *Public Health Reports*, May 23, 1924.
"Hearings before the Committee on Foreign Affairs, on Limiting Production of Habit-Forming Drugs and Raw Materials from which they are made," *67th Cong., 4th sess. H. of R.* 1923, passim.
"International Control of the Traffic in Habit-Forming Narcotic Drugs," *4th International Conference*.
LAMBERT A., "The Amount of Opiates Used in the Legitimate Practice of Medicine," *Hearings before the Committee on Foreign Affairs, etc., 67th Cong., 4th sess. H. of R.* 1923, passim.
LUGARD, F., "The Liquor Traffic in Mandated Territories," *Annexes to the Minutes of the Third Session, Permanent Mandate Commission*, A. 19, 1923.
"Memorandum on the World Cultivation and Production of Opium," *Annex 11, Minutes of the 5th Session Advisory Committee on Traffic in Opium and other Dangerous Drugs*, 1923 C. 418, M. 184.
"Opium and Narcotic Laws," *Government Printing Office*, 1919.
"Rapport Annuel du Gouvernment Français sur Cameroun," 1922.

"Report of the Commission of Inquiry as to Opium in the Philippine Islands," *S. Doc. 265, 59th Cong., 1st sess.*
"Report on Nauru, 1922," *No. 20, F. 295, Australia.*
"Report of the Opium Preparatory Committee," *C. 348, M. 119*, 1924.
"Second Annual Report," *N. Y. Narcotic Drug Control Commission*, 1920.
"Siam's Case for Revision of Obsolete Treaty Obligations," 1919.
"Statement of Congressman S. G. Porter," *Minutes 5th session, Opium Advisory Committee, League of Nations.*
"The Traffic in Habit-Forming Drugs," *Statement of the Attitude of the United States, Washington*, 1923.
"The Traffic in Habit-Forming Narcotic Drugs Hearings before the Committee on Foreign Affairs," *House of Representatives, 68th Cong., 1st sess., H. Doc. 380*, 1924.

CHAPTER XII

Books

BARTON, W. E., *Life of Clara Barton*, Vol. II, 1922. Boston: Houghton Mifflin.
BEER, G. L., *African Questions at the Paris Peace Conference*, 1923. New York: Macmillan.
CLEMON, F. G., *The Geography of Disease*, 1903. New York: Putnam.
DECANTE, R., *La Lutte contre la Prostitution*, 1909.
DUBOIS, W. E. B., *The Suppression of the African Slave Trade to the United States of America*, 1896. New York: Longmans.
FAUCHILLE, *Traité de Droit International Public*, Vol. I.
FLEXNER, A., *Prostitution in Europe*, 1914. New York: Century.
INGRAM, J. K., *A History of Slavery and Serfdom*, 1895. New York: Macmillan.
LUGARD, SIR F. D., *Dual Mandate in British Tropical Africa*, 1922. London: Blackwood.
MANSON, P., *Tropical Diseases* (3d ed.), 1903. New York: Wood.
MOORE, J. B., *International Arbitrations*, 1898, Vol. I. Washington: Government Printing Office.
PRINZING, F., *Epidemics Resulting from Wars*, 1916. New York: Oxford Press.
REINSCH, P. S., *Public International Unions*, 1916. Boston: World Peace Foundation.
WOOLF, L. S., *International Government*, 1916. New York: Brentano.

Articles

ALYPE, "L'Empire Éthiopien," *Afrique française*, 1922.
BRUNEAU, "Les competitions des puissances autour de l'Éthiopie," *Europe Nouvelle*, May 24, 1924.
CRAMER, "De l'activité des Croix-Rouges en temps de paix," *Revue Internationale de la Croix Rouge*, 1919.
DARLEY AND SHARP, "Slave Trading and Slave Owning in Abyssinia," *Westminster Gazette, Jan., 1922* (reprinted by the Anti-Slavery Society).
"L'Empire d' Éthiopie dans la Société des Nations," *Afrique française*, 1923.
TOBEY, J. A., "For the Health of the World," *Current History*, Nov., 1922.
WHIPPLE, "The Education of Health Officers," 2 *International Public Health Review*, 1921.
———, "World Sanitation: A Twentieth Century Possibility," *International Journal of Public Health*, 1920.

BIBLIOGRAPHY

PAMPHLETS

Bulletin of the League of Red Cross Societies, Vol. I., 1919.
China Year Book, 1921–22.
GRIMSHAW, "Memorandum on Slavery and Labour in the Mandates," *Annexes, Minutes of Mandates Commission*, 1923, A. 19 VI.
Handbook of International Organizations, 1921.
HARRIS, J. H., "Slavery and the Obligations of the League of Nations," *Anti-Slavery and Aborigines Protection Society*, March, 1923.
"International Marine Conference," Dec. 31, 1889, 81 *State Papers*, 75.
Minutes, Washington Conference on the Limitation of Armament.
"Organization and Sessional Business of the Fourth International Fishery Congress, Washington, U. S. A.," 1908. *Bulletin of the Bureau of Fisheries*, No. 726.
"The Question of Slavery," A. 18, 1923, VI.
"Règlement Pour la Liberté des Esclaves Addis-Abeba," 1924.
The Rockefeller Foundation Annual Report, 1923.
"The Sanitary Convention between Poland and Roumania," Dec. 20, 1922. T. S., 458.
"The Settlement of Greek Refugees," *Monthly Summary League of Nations, Supplement*, Nov., 1924.
"Slavery in Abyssinia," *Cmd.*, 1858, 1923.
WRIGHT, Q., "Limitation of Armament," *Syllabus, Institute for International Education*, No. XII.

CHAPTER XIII

BOOKS

BAKER, R. S., *Woodrow Wilson and World Settlement*, Vol. I, 1922. New York: Doubleday Page.
BARCLAY, T., *The Turko-Italian War*, 1912. London: Constable.
BEARD, C. A., *Contemporary American History*, 1914. New York: Macmillan.
BEER, G. L., *African Questions at the Paris Peace Conference*, 1923. New York: Macmillan.
——, *Origins of the British Colonial System*, 1908. New York: Macmillan.
BOYD, W., *Mr. Joseph Chamberlain's Speeches*, Vol. I, 1914. Boston: Houghton Mifflin.
Bright's Speeches, New York: Dutton.
BYWATER, H. C., *Sea Power in the Pacific*, 1921. Boston: Houghton Mifflin.
CARTHILL, A., *The Lost Dominion*, 1924. Edinburgh: Blackwood.
COX, H., *Problem of Population*, 1923. New York: Putnam.
DENNETT, T., *Americans in Eastern Asia*, 1922. New York: Macmillan.
DOUGLAS, R. K., *Europe and the Far East*, 1913. New York: Putnam.
EARLE, E. M., *Turkey, The Great Powers and the Bagdad Railway*, 1923. New York: Macmillan.
ESTÈVE, *Une nouvelle psychologie de l'impérialisme*, 1913.
FULLERTON, W. M., *Problems of Power*, 1918. New York: Scribner.
GIRAULT, *Principes de colonisation et de législation coloniale*, 1st part, 4th ed., 1922.
GRAVES, P., *Palestine, Land of the Three Faiths*, 1923. New York: Doran.
HARRIS, N. D., *Intervention and Colonization in Africa*, 1914. Boston: Houghton Mifflin Co.

BIBLIOGRAPHY

HARRISON, F., *National and Social Problem*, 1908. New York: Macmillan.
HOBSON, C. K., *Export of Capital*, 1914. New York: Macmillan.
HOBSON, J. A., *Imperialism, A Study*, 1905. New York: Pott (Gorham).
VON HOLST, E., *Constitutional and Political History of the United States*, Vol. III, 1881. Chicago: Cullaghan.
IRELAND, A., *Far Eastern Tropics*, 1905. Boston: Houghton Mifflin.
JENKS, E., *History of the Australasian Colonies* (3d ed.), 1912. New York: Putnam.
JOHNSTON, SIR HARRY, *The Backward Peoples and Our Relations with Them*, 1920. New York: Oxford Press.
KERR, P., in A. J. Grant (ed.) *International Relations*, 1916. New York: Macmillan.
KINGSLEY, MARY, *West African Studies, 1899*. New York: Macmillan.
LEROY-BEAULIEU, *Colonisation chez les peuples modernes* (3d ed.), 1886.
LEWIN, E., *The Resources of the Empire and Their Development* (British Empire Series), Vol. 4, 1924. New York: Holt.
LOWIE, R. H., *Primitive Society*, 1920. New York: Boni & Liveright.
MANGIN, GENERAL, *La France Noire*, 1910.
MAUGHAM, R. C. F., *Republic of Liberia*, 1920. New York: Scribner.
Missiones Catholicæ cura S. Congregationis de Propaganda Fide, 1922.
OGDEN, R., *Life and Letters of E. L. Godkin*, Vol. II, 1907. New York: Macmillan.
OLIVIER, SIR SYDNEY, *The League of Nations and Primitive Peoples*, 1918. London: Oxford Press.
REINSCH, P. S., *World Politics*, Part I, 1900. New York: Macmillan.
RENNER, K., *Das Selbstbestimmungrecht der nationen*.
RONALDSHAY, THE EARL OF, *India: A Bird's-Eye View*, 1924. Boston: Houghton Mifflin.
SCHOLEFIELD, G. H., *The Pacific, Its Past and Future*, 1919. New York: Scribner.
SEILLIÈRE, *La Philosophie de l'impérialisme*, 3 vols., 1907.
SIDGWICK, HENRY, *Elements of Politics*, 1891. New York: Macmillan.
VON ENGELN, O. D., *Inheriting the Earth*, 1922. New York: Macmillan.
WALKER, T. A., *History of the Law of Nations*, 1899. New York: Putnam.
WOOLF, L., *Empire and Commerce in Africa*, 1920. New York: Macmillan.

ARTICLES

BARTON, Dr. J. L., "Some Missionary Activities in Relation to Governments," *International Review of Missions*, July, 1924.
DENNETT, T., "Extraterritoriality and Missionaries in China," *Christian Century*, May 17, 1923.
LEVE, "La préparation de la guerre et l'armée indigène," 111 *Revue politique et parlementaire*, 1923, 373.
POIDEBARD, "Mossoul et la Route des Indes," *Asie Française*, May, 1923, Doc. 8.

PAMPHLETS

"Colonial Tariff Policies," *U. S. Tariff Commission*, 1922.
Peace Handbooks, Vol. 99.
"Public Health in Mandated Territories," *Mandates Commission A.* 19 (annexes) 1923.

BIBLIOGRAPHY

"Rapport annuel du Gouvernment Français sur l'administration sous mandat des territoires du Cameroun."
"Treaties, Acts and Regulations Relating to Missionary Freedom," *International Missionary Council*, London, 1923.
Year Book of Missions, 1924.

CHAPTER XIV
Books

ASAMI, N., *Japanese Colonial Government*, 1924. New York: Columbia University (Thesis).
BEER, G. L., "African Questions at the Paris Peace Conference," New York: Macmillan.
BUSSON, FÈVRE AND HAUSER, *La France d'aujourd'hui et ses colonies*, 1920.
CABATON, A., *Java, Sumatra and the Dutch East Indies*, 1914. New York: Scribner.
CYNN, H. H., *The Rebirth of Korea*, 1920. New York: Abingdon Press.
DAY, CLIVE, *Policy and Administration of The Dutch in Java*, 1904. New York: Macmillan.
DAYE, P., *L'empire colonial belge*, 1923.
GRANNINI, A., *I Documenti Diplomatici della Pace Orientale*, 1922.
HARRIS, J. H., *The Chartered Millions*, 1920. London: Swarthmore Press.
———, *Portuguese Slavery*, 1913. London: Methuen.
HUMBERT, *Œuvres française aux Colonies*, 1913.
HYNDMAN, H. M., *The Awakening of Asia*, 1919. New York: Boni & Liveright.
IRELAND, A., *Tropical Colonization*, 1899. Philadelphia: Am. Acad. of Pol. and Soc. Sci.
———, *Far Eastern Tropics*, 1905. Boston: Houghton Mifflin.
KEITH, A. B., *Belgian Congo and the Berlin Act*, 1919. New York: Oxford Press.
KELLER, A. G., *Colonization*, 1908. Boston: Ginn.
LAGDEN, SIR G., *The Native Races of the Empire*, (The British Empire Series), vol. 9, 1924. New York: Holt.
LEWIN, P. E., *The Germans and Africa*, 1915. New York: Stokes.
LOWIE, R. H., *Primitive Society*, 1920. New York: Boni & Liveright.
LUGARD, SIR F. D., *The Dual Mandate in British Tropical Africa* (2nd ed.), 1923. London: Blackwood.
MACDONALD, A. J., *Trade, Politics and Christianity in Africa and the East*, 1916. New York: Longmans.
MCKENZIE, F. A., *Korea's Fight for Freedom*, 1919. New York: Revell.
MASSIOU, J., *Les Grandes concessions au Congo français*, 1920.
MEGGLÉ, A., *Le Domaine colonial de la France*, 1922.
MONEY, J. W. B., *Java or How to Manage a Colony*, 2 vols., 1861. London: Hurst & Blackett.
MOREL, E. D., *King Leopold's Rule in Africa*, 1904. London: Heinemann.
MOREL, E. D., *The Black Man's Burden*, 1920. New York: Huebsch.
MOUSSET, A., *L'Espagne dans la Politique Mondiale*, 1923.
MURRAY, G., *Liberalism and the Empire*, 1900. London: R. B. Johnson.
NEAME, L. E., *The Asiatic Danger in the Colonies*, 1907. New York: Dutton.
NEVINSON, H. W., *A Modern Slavery*, 1906. New York: Harper.
OLIVIER, SIR SYDNEY, *White Capital and Coloured Labor*, 1906. London: Independent Labour Party.

Oxford Survey of the British Empire, 1914 (6 vols.).
PIQUET, *La Colonisation française dans l'Afrique du Nord*, 1914.
POWELL, E. A., *Where the Strange Trails Go Down*, 1921. New York: Scribner
RAI, LAJPAT, *England's Debt to India*, 1917. New York: Huebsch.
REINSCH, P. S., *Colonial Administration*, 1905. New York: Macmillan.
SARRAUT, A., *La Mise en valeur des colonies françaises*, 1923.
TORCHIANA, H. A. V. C., *Tropical Holland*, 1921. Chicago: University Press.
WERTHEIMER, F., *Die japanische Kolonialpolitik*, 1910.
WILLOUGHBY, W. C., *Race Problems in the New Africa*, 1923. New York: Oxford Press.
WOOLF, L. S., *Empire and Commerce in Africa*, 1920. New York: Macmillan.

ARTICLES

HAUSER, "Greater France," *Foreign Affairs*, Dec. 15, 1923.
HAYDEN, "Japan's New Policy in Korea and Formosa," *Foreign Affairs*, March 15, 1924.
"Speech of M. Simon, French minister of colonies, Chamber of Deputies," Sept. 17, 1919, *Afrique française* 1919, *Renseignements Coloniaux*.
"Tittoni's speech of Sept. 1919," *New Europe*, Oct. 23, 1919.

PAMPHLETS

"Anglo-Italian treaty of July 15, 1924." *Cmd.* 2194.
"Annual Report on Reforms and Progress in Chosen," 1918–1921.
"Casement Report," Dec. 11, 1903. *Cd.* 1922, 1904.
"Correspondence on the subject of Allegations against the Administration of the British North Borneo Co," *Cmd.* 1060, 1920.
"Judgment of the High Court at Mombasa," May 26, 1913, *Cd.* 6939.
"Treaty of Nov. 27, 1912, between France and Spain," 106 *State Papers*, 1025.
WILLIAMS, L. F. RUSHBROOK, "India in 1921–22, statement prepared for presentation to Parliament," Calcutta, 1922.

CHAPTER XV
BOOKS

BEER, G. L., *African Questions at the Paris Peace Conference*, 1923. New York: Macmillan.
CREIGHTON, MRS. L., *Missions, Their Rise and Development*, 1912. New York: Holt.
HALL, G. STANLEY, *Adolescence*, 1904. New York: Appleton.
HARMAND, J., *Domination et Colonisation*, 1910.
J. H. HARRIS, in MARVIN, F. S., *Western Races and the World*, 1922. New York: Oxford Press.
JOHNSTON, SIR H. H., *Colonization of Africa*, 1905. Cambridge, Eng.: University Press.
LUGARD, SIR F. D., *The Dual Mandate in British Tropical Africa*, 1922. London: Blackwood.
MILLOT, A., *Les Mandats Internationaux*, 1924.
MOREL, E. D., *The Black Man's Burden*, 1920. New York: Huebsch.
LUCAS, C., *Partition and Colonization of Africa*, 1922. New York: Oxford Press.

BIBLIOGRAPHY

SCHÜCKING AND WEHBERG, *Satzung des Völkerbundes* (2d ed.), 1924.
SNOW, A. H., *The Question of Aborigines*, 1921. New York: Putnam.
TORCHIANA, H. A. V. C., *Tropical Holland*, 1921. Chicago: University Press.
WILLOUGHBY, W. C., *Race Problems in the New Africa*, 1923. New York: Oxford Press.

ARTICLES

BUELL, "Backward Peoples Under the Mandate System," *Current History*, June, 1924.
LECLERE, "Les Terres collectives de tribu au Maroc," *Afrique française*, 1922. *Renseignements Coloniaux*.
ROLIN, "Le Système des Mandats coloniaux," *R. D. I. L. C.*, 1920, Nos. 3–4.
"Statement of British Colonial Office," *Anti-Slavery Reporter and Aborigines Friend*, Jan., 1923.
WRIGHT, "Sovereignty of the Mandates," *A. J. I. L.*, Oct., 1923.

PAMPHLETS

"Colonial Tariff Policies," *U. S. Tariff Commission*. Washington, D. C.: Supt. of Documents.
"Corres. regarding the modification of the Boundary between British Mandated Territory and Belgian Mandated Territory in East Africa," *Cmd.* 1974, 1794, 1923.
"The Hymans Report," *O. J.*, Sept., 1920.
"Indians in Kenya," *Cmd.* 1922, 1923.
International Harvester Co. *v.* Kentucky, 234 U. S. 1913, 216.
"Ordinance of Oct. 20, 1919, providing for Labor Inspectors in Kenya," *Cmd.* 873, 1920.
"Prospectus, Commonwealth Trust, Limited."
"Rapport sur l'administration Belge du Ruanda-Urundi," (Chambre des Représentants), 1922–23.
VALLINI, A. A., "I Mandati Internazionali della Società delle Nazione," 1923.

CHAPTER XVI

BOOKS

BRUCE, C., *Broad Stone of Empire*, 1910, Vol. I. New York: Macmillan.
BUXTON, N. E., AND CONWIL-EVANS, T. P., *Oppressed Peoples and the League of Nations*, 1922. London: Dent.
CHARMEIL, P., *Les gouverneurs généraux des colonies françaises*, 1922.
THE EARL OF CROMER, *Modern Egypt*, 1908. Vol. II. New York: Macmillan.
GIRAULT, *Principes de colonisation et de législation coloniale*.
HARMAND, J., *Domination et colonisation*.
HERTSLET, SIR EDWARD, *Map of Africa by Treaty* (2d ed.), Vol. 1, 1896. London: Harrison & Sons.
HUMBERT, *L'Œuvre française aux colonies*.
IPRANOSSIAN, M., *La Colonisation et le législateur colonial français*, 1916.
LUGARD, SIR F. D., *Dual Mandate in British Tropical Africa*, 1922. London: Blackwood.
LUQUET, J., *Le Mandat A et l'organisation du mandat française en Syrie*, 1923.
MUKERJEE, R., *Democracies of the East*, 1923. London: King.
PIQUET, V., *Colonisation française dans l'Afrique du Nord* (2d ed.), 1914.

PIQUET, V., *Le Maroc* (3d ed.), 1920.
———, *Les Réformes en Algérie*, 1919. Parts I, II.
REINSCH, P. S., *Colonial Government*, 1902. New York: Macmillan.
RIHBANY, A. M., *Wise Men from the East*, 1922. Boston: Houghton Mifflin.
SAMNÉ, A., *La Syrie*, 1920.
SNOW, A. H., *The Question of the Aborigines*, 1921. New York: Putnam.
STOWELL, E. C., *Intervention in International Law*, 1921. Washington: Byrne.
TORCHIANA, H. A. V. C., *Tropical Holland*, 1921. Chicago: University Press.
VIGNON, L., *Un Programme de politique colonial* (2d ed.), 1919.
WILLIAMS, D. R., *The United States and the Philippines*, 1924. New York: Doubleday, Page.
WILLOUGHBY, W. C., *Race Problems in the New Africa*, 1923. New York: Oxford Press.
WRONG, H., *Government of the West Indies*, 1923. New York: Oxford Press.

ARTICLES

"America and the Philippines," *Round Table*, Dec., 1924.
ARSLAN, "Syrian Opposition to French Rule," *Current History*, May, 1924.
BUELL, "What About the Philippines?" *Atlantic Monthly*, March, 1924.
CHAKRAVARTY, "Ministerial Responsibility," *Indian Review*, Jan., 1924.
"Egypt and the Sudan," *Round Table*, Sept., 1924.
HAYDEN, "Political Progress in the Netherlands Indies," *Atlantic Monthly*, Sept., 1924.
"International Interference in African Affairs," 18 *Journal of the Society of Comparative Legislation*.
"The Mandates Commission," 242 *Quarterly Review*, 1924.
"Nigeria's Curse, The Native Administration," *National Review*, Dec., 1924.
SAPRU, "Way to Responsible Government," *The Indian Review*, Jan., 1924.

PAMPHLETS

"Bolletin Ufficiale, Ministero delle Colonie," Maggio, 1920.
"Documents parlementaires, Chambre des Députés," 1922, 12 leg. sess., ord.
"The Fisher Report," *O. J.*, Dec., 1921.
"Government of India Act, 1919," 9 and 10 *Geo. V.*
"Malta constitution of April 14, 1921," *Statutory Rules and Orders*, 1921.
"Rapport sur la situation de la Syrie et du Liban," *Ministère des Affaires Étrangères*, July, 1922–July, 1923.
"Rapport sur l'Administration Belge du Ruanda et de l'Urundi," *Chambre des Représentants*, No. 384, 1922.
"Wood-Forbes Report, 1919," *H. R.* 325, 67th *Cong.*, 2d sess.

CHAPTER XVII

BOOKS

BAU, M. J., *The Open Door Doctrine in Relation to China*, 1923. New York: Macmillan.
BEALS, C., *Mexico, an Interpretation*, 1923. New York: Huebsch.
BLUNT, W. S., *Secret History of the Occupation of Egypt* (new ed.), 1922. New York: Knopf.
BORCHARD, E. M., *The Diplomatic Protection of Citizens Abroad*, Part II, 1915. New York: Banks Law Pub. Co.
BRAILSFORD, H. N., *War of Steel and Gold*, 1915. New York: Macmillan.

BIBLIOGRAPHY

CRICHFIELD, G. W., *American Supremacy*, 1908, Vol. I. New York: Brentano.
EARLE, E. M., *Turkey, the Great Powers and the Bagdad Railway*, 1923. New York: Macmillan.
EDDY, S., *The New World of Labor*, 1923. New York: Doran.
HARDENBURG, W. E., *Putumayo, The Devil's Paradise*, 1912. London: T. F. Unwin.
HENDRICK, B. J., *Life and Letters of Walter Hines Page*, Vol. I, 1922. New York: Doubleday, Page.
HSU, M. C., *Railway Problems in China*, 1915. New York: Longmans.
MILLARD, T., *Democracy and the Eastern Question*, 1919. New York: Century.
MUNRO, D. G., *The Five Republics of Central America*, 1918. New York: Oxford Press.
OVERLACH, T. W., *Foreign Financial Control in China*, 1919. New York: Macmillan.
PATERNOSTER, G. S., *The Lords of the Devil's Paradise*, 1913. London: S. Paul & Co.
TURNER, J. K., *Barbarous Mexico*, 1911. Chicago: Kerr.
——, *Shall it Be Again?* 1922. New York: Huebsch.
WILLOUGHBY, W. W., *Foreign Rights and Interests in China*, 1920. Baltimore: Johns Hopkins Press.
WUARIN, A., *Essai sur les Emprunts d'États et la protection des droits des porteurs de fonds d'états étrangers*, 1907.

ARTICLES

"Arbitration between Great Britain and Costa Rica," Oct. 18, 1923, *A. J. I. L.*, Jan. 1924.
"Confidential circular," of State Department concerning Salvador, 117 *Nation*, 1923.
"D.," "The Presidential Dilemma in Mexico," *Foreign Affairs*, Sept. 15, 1924.
"Foreign Firms in Soviet Russia," *Russian Review*, Oct. 1, 1923.
HYDE, "The Negotiation of External Loans with Foreign Governments," 16 *A. J. I. L.*, 1922, 523.
KRASSIN, LEONID, "An International Loan to Russia," *Soviet Russia*, 1921.
LASSWELL, "Political Policies and the International Investment Market," 31 *Journal of Political Economy*, 1923.
LITVINOV, M., "Business Concessions in Russia," *Manchester Guardian Weekly*, Jan. 11, 1924.
LOVETT, R. M., "American Foreign Policy: A Progressive View," *Foreign Affairs*, Sept. 15, 1924.
"The Nicaraguan Bond Issue," *Nation*, May 31, 1922.
"Slavery in Peru," *U. S. For. Rel.*, 1913.
TAYLOR AND ZUNG, "Labor and Industry in China," 8 *International Labor Review*, 1923.
"Text of Turkish railway concession to Admiral Chester," Jan., 1923. *Current History*, June, 1923.
WOODHOUSE, "New Understanding with Mexico," *Current History*, Sept., 1922.

PAMPHLETS

"China, An Economic Survey," *American Banker's Association*, 1923.
CLELAND, R. G. (ed.), *Mexican Year Book*.
Putumayo Red Book, 1913.

BIBLIOGRAPHY

"Report on Coöperation in American Export Trade," *Federal Trade Commission*, 1916.
"Revolutions in Mexico," *Senate Hearings*, 1913, *For. Fel. Com.*, 62d Cong., 2d sess.
DR. A. N. YOUNG, economic adviser of the State Department, Williamstown address, August 26, 1924.

CHAPTER XVIII
Books

DEVILLE, F., *Les Contrôles financiers internationaux er la souveraineté de l'État*, 1912.
DUPUIS, C., *Les Rapports des puissances grandes avec les autres états*, 1920, *Education in Africa*, 1922. New York: Phelps-Stokes Fund.
MACMURRAY, J. V. A., *Treaties and Agreements with and concerning China*, Vol. II, 1921. New York: Oxford Press.
MAUGHAM, R. C. F., *The Republic of Liberia*, 1920. New York: Scribner.
SHUSTER, M., *The Strangling of Persia*, 1912. New York: Century.
WILLOUGHBY, W. W., *Foreign Rights and Interests in China*, 1920. Baltimore: Johns Hopkins Press.
WUARIN, *Essai sur les Emprunts d'États*.

Articles

DRAGO, "State loans in their relation to international policy," *A. J. I. L.*, 692, 1907.
FISCHER, "Persia the Victim of Russo-British Rivalry," *Current History*, Feb., 1925.
INMAN, "Imperialistic America," *Atlantic Monthly*, July, 1924.
"Litvinov statement," *Manchester Guardian Weekly*, Jan. 11, 1924.
PEFFER, "Austria: Saved or Duped," 35 *New Republic*, 1923.
THIERRY, "L'emprunt américain du Libérie," *Afrique française*, 1922.

Pamphlets

"Agreement between the Mexican Government and the International Committee of Bankers on Mexico," *International Conciliation*, No. 187.
"The Financial Reconstruction of Austria," *Monthly Summary, League of Nations, Sup.*, Oct., 1922.
"The Financial Reconstruction of Hungary," *Monthly Summary of the League of Nations, Sup.*, May, 1924.
"General Claims Convention of Sept. 8, 1923," *Treaty Series*, No. 678.
"Haiti Customs Receivership, 6th fiscal period, 1922," *Republic of Haiti*.
"Inquiry into the Occupation and Administration of Santo Domingo," *Hearings before a Select Committee, 67th Cong., 1st and 2d sess.*
Peruvian Year Book, 1921.
"4th Annual Report to Council," *O. J.*, April, 1924.
"Special Claims Convention of Sept. 10, 1923," *Treaty Series*, No. 676.
STRUPP, K., *Documents pour servir L'histoire du droit des gens*, 1923, Vol. II.

CHAPTER XIX
Books

APOSTOL AND MICHLESON, *La Lutte pour le pétrole et la Russie*, 1922.
BAU, M. J., *The Open Door Doctrine in Relation to China*, 1923. New York: Macmillan.

BIBLIOGRAPHY

BEER, G. L., *African Questions at the Paris Peace Conference*, 1923. New York: Macmillan.
DAVENPORT, E. H., AND COOKE, S. R., *The Oil Trusts and Anglo-American Relations*, 1924. New York: Macmillan.
DELAISI, F., *Oil, Its Influence on Politics*, 1922. London: Labour Publishing Co.
DENNETT, T., *Americans in Eastern Asia*, 1922. New York: Macmillan.
DE LA TRAMERYE, P. L., *The World Struggle for Oil*, Part III, 1924. New York: Knopf.
EARLE, E. M., *Turkey, The Great Powers, and the Bagdad Railway*, 1923. New York: Macmillan.
HERTSLET, SIR EDWARD, *Map of Africa by Treaty*, Vol. II, Vol. III (3rd Ed.), 1909. London: Harrison.
HSU, M. C., *Railway Problems in China*, 1915. New York: Longmans.
JOHNSTON, SIR H. H., *A History of Colonization of Africa*, 1905. Cambridge, Eng.: University Press.
MACMURRAY, J. V. A., *Treaties and Agreements with and concerning China*, Vol. II, 1921. New York: Oxford Press.
MÖLLER, F. W., *Die Versorgung der Welt mit Petroleum*, 1910.
OVERLACH, T. W., *Foreign Financial Control in China*, 1919. New York: Macmillan.
PIQUET, V., *Maroc*, 1920.
PRADIER AND BESSON, *La Guerre économique dans nos colonies*, 1916.
REYES, J. S., *Legislative History of the Economic Policy of the United States toward the Philippines*, 1923. New York: Longmans.
SPIES, G., *Zwei denkschriften zum Petroleum-Monopol*, 1913.
TARDIEU, A., *Le Mystère d'Agadir*, 1912.

ARTICLES

BESSON, "Le revanche colonial d'Allemagne," 120 *Revue politique et parlementaire*, 1924.
BLAKESLEE, "The Mandates of the Pacific," 7 *Foreign Affairs*, 1922.
BUELL, "International Capitalism and Its Control," *Current History*, Dec., 1923.
BUELL, "Oil Interests in the Fight for Mosul," *Current History*, March, 1923.
CASTBERG, F., "Le Conflit entre le Danemark et la Norvège concernant le Groenland," *R. D. I. L. C.*, 1924, No. 3.
DEANE, "The Chinese Eastern Railway," *Foreign Affairs*, Sept. 15, 1924.
EARLE, "The Turkish Petroleum Company—A study in oleaginous diplomacy," *Political Science Quarterly*, June, 1924.
"La Litigie relatif à le radio télégraphie en Chine," *Revue du Pacifique*, 1924.

PAMPHLETS

"Corres. between His Majesty's Government and the United States Ambassador respecting Economic Rights in Mandated Territories," *Cmd.* 1226, 1921.
"Foreign Ownership in the Petroleum Industry," *Report of the Federal Trade Commission, Sen. Com. print,* 67 *Cong.*, 4th sess. 1923.
"The Mavromatis Palestine Concessions Judgment," *No. 2, Series A*, August 30, 1924.
"Memorandum on the Petroleum Situation," *Cmd.* 1351, 1921.

"Oil Prospecting in Foreign Countries," *67th Congr., 1st sess., Sen. Doc. No. 39.*
"Restrictions on American Petroleum Prospectors in Certain Foreign Countries," *Sen. Doc. 11, 67th Cong., 1st sess.,* May 16, 1921.
SCHNEE, H., "Die Notwendigkeit eigenen Kolonialbesitzes," *Handbüch der Politik,* Vol. V, 1922.
"Act of Algeciras," *Treaties of the U. S.,* Vol. II.
"The United States Navy as an Industrial Asset," *Office of Naval Intelligence, U. S. Navy,* 1923.

CHAPTER XX

Books

BAKER, R. S., *Woodrow Wilson and World Settlement,* 1922. New York: Doubleday, Page.
BALFOUR, J. M., *Recent Happenings in Persia,* 1922. London: Blackwood.
BRUNET, A., *Le Régime International des Nouvelles Hebrides,* 1908.
CASTIGNÉ, *La politique extérieure de l'Afghanistan depuis 1919.*
CHEKREZI, C. A., *Albania, Past and Present,* 1919. New York: Macmillan.
CHIROL, V., *The Egyptian Problem,* 1920. London: Macmillan.
CROMER, EARL OF, *Modern Egypt,* 1908. New York: Macmillan.
DENNETT, T., *Americans in Eastern Asia,* 1922. New York: Macmillan.
DESPAGNET, F., *Essai sur les protectorats,* 1896.
EARLE, E. M., *Turkey, the Great Powers, and the Bagdad Railway,* 1923. New York: Macmillan.
FENWICK, C. G., *Wardship in International Law,* 1919. Washington: Government Printing Office.
GOETHALS, G. W., *Government of the Canal Zone,* 1915. Princeton: Princeton Press.
HIMAYA, L., *La Condition Internationale de l'Egypte,* 1922.
HINCKLEY, F. E., *American Consular Jurisdiction in the Orient,* 1906. Washington: Lowdermilk.
JENKYNS, H., *British Rule and Jurisdiction Beyond the Seas,* 1902. New York: Oxford Press.
LAWRENCE, T. J., *The Principles of International Law* (7th ed.), 1923. Boston: Heath.
MACMURRAY, J. V. A., *Treaties and Agreement with and Concerning China,* 1921. New York: Oxford Press.
GENERAL MAITROT, *La France et les Républiques sud-Américaines,* 1920.
MUNRO, D. G., *Five Republics of Central America,* 1918. New York: Oxford Press.
OPPENHEIM, L. F. L., *International Law* (2d ed.), 1920, Vol. I. New York: Longmans.
TUMULTY, J. P., *Woodrow Wilson as I Know Him,* 1921. New York: Doubleday, Page.
WILLOUGHBY, W. W., *Foreign Rights and Interests in China,* 1920. Baltimore: Johns Hopkins Press.
———, *China at the Conference, A Report,* 1922. Baltimore: Johns Hopkins Press.
———, AND FENWICK, *Types of Restricted Sovereignty and of Colonial Autonomy,* 1919. Washington: Government Printing Office.

Wood Ge-Zay, *The Shantung Question*, 1922. New York: Revell.
Wright, H. F., *The Constitutions of the States at War*, 1918. Washington: Government Printing Office.

Articles

Castigné, "La politique extérieure de l'afghanistan depuis 1919," 48 *Revue du Monde Musulman*, 1921.
Chassigneux, "Le Siam et la France," *L'Asie française*, March, 1923.
Coolidge, "Ten Years of War and Peace," *Foreign Affairs*, Sept. 15, 1924.
Crabités, "Egypt, the Sudan and the Nile," *Foreign Affairs*, Dec. 15, 1924.
"France's attempts to control Tangier," *Manchester Guardian Weekly*, Dec. 21, 1923.
"Jurisdiction Difficulties in the New Hebrides," *The Continent*, Nov. 20, 1924.
Leuchsenring, "La Enmienda Platt. Su interpretacion primitiva y su aplicaciones posteriores," 29 *Cuba Contemporánea*, 1922.
——, "La ingerencia notreamericana en los asuntos interiores de Cuba," 30 *Cuba Contemporánea*, 1922.
——, "Analisis y consecuencias de la intervención notreamericana en los asuntos interiores de Cuba," 32 *Cuba Contemporánea*, 1923.
Liu, "What Japan is doing to China," *Current History*, July, 1921.
Machado, "El Derecho de Intervención," 29 *Cuba Contemporánea*, 1922.
Marin, "L'entrée en relations indépendantes de l'Afghanistan avec les Puissances," *L'Aise française* No. 211, March, 1923.
Myers, D. P., "Tangier, An International City," 4 *National Municipal Review*, 1915.
Pelleray, "Les Nouvelles Hebrides," *Revue du Pacifique*, April, 1923.
Sokolsky, G. E., "Foreign Concessions and Chinese Intrigue," *Transpacific*, July 21, 1923.
"Statement of Japanese Legation at Peking," *Weekly Review* (Shanghai), April 7, 1923.
Tangier, "A Study in Internationalisation," *Round Table*, No. 38, 1920.
Thayer, "The Capitulations of the Ottoman Empire," 17 *A. J. I. L.*, 1923, 215.

Pamphlets

"Annual Report of the Secretary of the Navy," 1924.
"Convention regarding the Organization of the Statute of the Tangier Zone, Dec. 18, 1923," *Cmd.* 2096.
"Gezira Irrigation Project," *Cmd.* 217, 1924.
"Imperial Conference of 1923," *Cmd.* 1987.
James, "Jurisdiction over Foreigners in Siam," 16 *A. J. I. L.*, 1922.
"Ramsay MacDonald dispatch of Oct. 7, 1924," *Cmd.* 2269.
"Treaty between Great Britain and Japan, August 26, 1858," 48 *State Papers*, 37.
"Annual Report of C. E. Magoon, provisional governor of Cuba, 1907," *S. Doc. 155, 69th Cong., 1st sess.*, Vol. 6.
"Tariff Schedule, Treaty between Great Britain and China, August 29, 1842," 30 *State Papers*, 394.

CHAPTER XXI

Books

BARTHÉLEMY, J., *Democratie et Politique Étrangère*, 1917.
BODART, G., *Losses of Life in Modern Wars: Austria-Hungary; France*, 1916. New York: Oxford Press.
BOGART, E. L., *Direct and Indirect Costs of the Great World War*, 1919. New York: Oxford Press.
BUELL, R. L., *The Washington Conference*, 1922. New York: Appleton.
COCKS, F. S., *The Secret Treaties and Understandings* (2d ed.), 1918. London: Union of Democratic Control.
CRESSON, W. P., *The Holy Alliance*, 1922. New York: Oxford Press.
DENNIS, A. L. P., *The Anglo-Japanese Alliance*, 1923. Berkeley: University Press.
DICKINSON, G. L., *War: Its Nature, Cause and Cure*, 1923. New York: Macmillan.
DUHELLY, J., *Philosophie de la Guerre*, 1921.
DUMAS, S., AND VEDEL-PETERSEN, *Losses of Life Caused by War*. 1923. New York: Oxford Press.
DUPUIS, C., *Le Principe d'Équilibre et le Concert Européen*, 1909.
ENOCK, A. G., *The Problem of Armaments*, 1923. New York: Macmillan.
FISHER, H. A. L., *The Commonweal*, 1924. New York: Oxford Press.
FRIES, A. A., AND WEST, C. J., *Chemical Warfare*, 1921. New York: McGraw-Hill.
HOIJER, O., *La Théorie de l'Équilibre et le Droit des Gens*, 1917.
KELLOGG, V., "Military Selection and Race Deterioration," 1916, in Bodart, G., *Losses of Life in Modern Wars*. Oxford: Clarendon Press.
LEFEBURE, V., *The Riddle of the Rhine*, 1921. New York: Dutton.
LOREBURN, EARL, *How the War Came*, 1919. New York: Knopf.
MACMURRAY, J. V. A., *Treaties and Agreements with and concerning China*, Vol. I, 1921. New York: Oxford Press.
MAHAN, A. T., *Armaments and Arbitration*, 1912. New York: Harper.
———, *The Influence of Sea Power upon History*, 1660–1783, 1890. Boston: Little, Brown.
———, *The Influence of Sea Power upon the French Revolution and Empire*, 1793–1812, 1894. Boston: Little, Brown.
MAITROT, GENERAL, *La France et les Républiques Sud-Américaines*.
———, *La Prochaine Guerre*, 1921.
PAGE, K., *War: Its Causes and Cure*, 1923. New York: Doran.
PHILLIPS, W. A., *The Confederation of Europe*, 1914. New York: Longmans.
PONSONBY, A., *Wars and Treaties*, 1918. New York: Macmillan.
PRIBRAM, A. F., AND COOLIDGE, A. D., *The Secret Treaties of Austria-Hungary, 1879–1914*, Vol. II, 1921. Cambridge: University Press.
SCHMITT, B. E., *England and Germany, 1740–1914*, 1916. Princeton: Princeton Press.
DE STIEGLITZ, A., *de l'Équilibre Politique*, 1897, 3 vols.
VESTAL, S. C., *The Maintenance of Peace*, 1920. New York: Putnam.
WEHBERG, H., *Die internationale Beschrankung der Rustungen*, 1919.
WOODS, F. A., AND BALTZLY, A., *Is War Diminishing?* 1915. Boston: Houghton Mifflin Co.

BIBLIOGRAPHY

ARTICLES

BYWATER, H., "Japan: A Sequel to the Washington Conference," *Atlantic Monthly*, Feb., 1923.
COOLIDGE, "Ten Years of War and Peace," *Foreign Affairs*, Sept. 15, 1924.
"The Dismal Prospects for Limiting Armaments," *Atlantic Monthly*, Nov., 1924.
GROVES, P. R. G., "For France to Answer," *Atlantic Monthly*, Feb., 1924.
HALDANE, "Chemistry and Peace," *Atlantic Monthly*, Jan., 1925.
KEPI, "Versailles—Before and After," *Foreign Affairs*, Dec. 15, 1923.
NYS, E., "Théorie de l'équilibre européen," *R. D. I. P.*, Vol. XXV, 1893, 1st series.
SIMS, ADMIRAL, "The Truth About the German Submarine Atrocities," *Current History*, June, 1923.
VILLARD, "Losses from Disease in the World War Armies," *Current History*, Sept., 1924.

PAMPHLETS

"Annual Report of the Chief of Chemical Warfare Service 1924."
"Armaments Year-Book," (2d ed.) 1924, *League of Nations*, C. 61, M. 29, 1924, IX.
"The Balance of Power," *Union of Democratic Control*, No. 14.
BRADNER, D. B., quoted in "The Staggering Burden of Armament," found in *A League of Nations*, April, 1921.
MARTENS, *Recueil des traités conclue par la Russie*, Vol. IV.
"Postwar Political Alignments," *League of Nations*, Vol. II, No. 2, 1923.
"Prime Minister Baldwin," 65 *Parl. Debates, H. C.*, 1923, 2142.
"Recueil de Rapports Organisation Centrale pour une paix durable," Vol. II, 1916, *La Commission Neerlandaise d'Étude*.
"Report of the Temporary Mixed Commission for the Reduction of Armaments," *League of Nations*, A, 16, 1924.
"Statistical Information on the Trade in Arms, Ammunition, and Materials of War," A. 30, 1924, IX.

CHAPTER XXII

BOOKS

AUBOIN, M., *Les Prestations en nature de l'Allemagne et le Problème des Réparations*, 2d ed., 1923.
BAKER, R. S., *Woodrow Wilson and World Settlement*, 1922. New York: Doubleday, Page.
BARUCH, B. M., *The Making of the Reparation and Economic Sections of the Treaty*, 1920. New York: Harper.
BASS, J. F., AND MOULTON, H. G., *America and the Balance Sheet of Europe*, 1921. New York: Ronald Press.
CASSINELLI, R., *Les Dettes Interalliées*, 1923.
KEYNES, J. M., *A Revision of the Treaty*, 1922. New York: Harcourt, Brace.
MOULTON, H. G., *The Reparations Plan*, 1924. New York: McGraw-Hill.
MOULTON, H. G., AND McGUIRE, C. E., *Germany's Capacity to Pay*, 1923. New York: McGraw-Hill.
NITTI, F., *The Decadence of Europe*, 1923. New York: Holt.
ROUSSEAU, J., *La haute Commission Interalliées des Territories Rhenans*, 1923.
TARDIEU, A., *The Truth About the Treaty*, 1921. New York: Bobbs-Merrill.

Articles

CHEVALLEY, A., "France and the Ruhr," *Atlantic Monthly*, June, 1923.
COOLIDGE, A. C., "Ten Years of War and Peace," *Foreign Affairs*, Sept. 15, 1924.
"The French Occupation of the Ruhr," *Manchester Guardian Weekly*, March 9, 1923.
IRETON, "The Rhineland Commission at Work," *A. J. I. L.*, July, 1923.
"Results of French Occupation of the Ruhr," *Current History*, Nov., 1923.
SALTER, SIR J. A., "The Reconstruction of Austria," *Foreign Affairs*, June 15, 1924.
SCHUSTER, "The Question as to the Legality of the Ruhr Occupation," *A. J. I. L.*, July, 1924.
YOUNG, A. A., "War Debts, External and Internal," *Foreign Affairs*, March 15, 1924.

Pamphlets

"Agreement with regard to the Military Occupation of the Territory of the Rhine, etc.," July 28, 1919, *Treaties of the U. S.*, Vol. II.
"Armistice Convention of Nov. 11, 1918," *Treaties of U. S.*, Vol. III.
British Year-Book of International Law, 1924.
"The Case of Peru," (*Peru-Chile arbitration*), 1923.
"Ordinances and Instructions issued by the Inter-Allied Rhineland High Commission, 1920," *Cmd.*, 591.
"Correspondence With the Allied Governments respecting Reparation Payments by Germany," *Mis. No. 5*, 1925, *Cmd.* 1943.
"Programme of the Conference July and August, 1924, at London," *Cmd.* 2191.
"État des Obligations de l'Allemagne," Vol. IV, *Commission des Réparations*, Table XI.
"Indemnities," *Peace Handbooks*, No. 158, Vol. 25.
"Inter-Allied Conferences on Reparations and Inter-Allied Debts," *Cmd.* 1812.
"Minutes of the London Conference on Reparations," *Cmd.* 2258, August, 1922.
"Reparation," *A League of Nations*, Part II, Vol. V, No. 2, 1922.
"Report of the First Committee of Experts," *Annexe 2075 de la Commission des Réparations*.
"Report of the Second Committee of Experts," *Annexes 2076 de la Commission des Réparations*.
"Report of the Work of the Reparation Commission from 1920 to 1922," V, *Reparation Commission, H. M. Stationary Office*, 1923.
"Documents Officiels relatifs au Montant des Versements a Éffectuer par l'Allemagne au Titre des Réparations," *Commission des Réparations*, Vol. I, 1922.
"World Peace Foundation Pamphlet," *Reparation—Part V—the Dawes Report*, 1923, Vol. VI, No. 5.
"World War Foreign Debt Commission and Obligations of Foreign Governments," *Report of Secretary of Treasury*, 1924 (extract).

BIBLIOGRAPHY

CHAPTER XXIII

Books

BUELL, R. L., *Washington Conference*, 1922. New York: Appleton.
DE CLERCQ, *Recueil de Traités de la France*, Vol. II.
GRAUX, LUCIEN, *Histoire des Violations du Traités de Paix*, Vol. III, 1923.
HONNORAT, A., *Le Désarmenemt de l'Allemagne*, Part I.
MACMURRAY, J. V. A., Art. VII, Convention of March 1, 1894. *Treaties and Agreements with and concerning China*, Vol. I, 1921. New York: Oxford Press.
PICARD, R., *La Question de la Limitation des Armements*, 1921.
TEMPERLEY, H. W. V., *History of the Peace Conference*, Vol. IV, 1920–24. New York: Oxford Press.
TREITSCHKE, H., *History of Germany in the Nineteenth Century*, 1915, Vol. I. New York: McBride.
WEHBERG, HANS, *Die internationale Beschränkungen*, 1919.

Articles

"Armament Competition Between the ABC Powers of South America," *Christian Science Monitor*, Sept. 18, 1924.
"Minutes of the 7th Commission of 'Conferencia Internacional Americana,'" *Revista de Politica Internacional*, Nov., 1923.
SIMS, "Changing Methods of Submarine Warfare," *Current History*, Sept., 1923.

Pamphlets

"Conference of 1899," *The Proceedings of the Hague Peace Conferences* (translation of official texts, 1920, ed. by J. B. Scott).
"Conference on the Limitation of Armament," *Minutes*, 1922.
"Conference de Moscou pour la Limitation des Armements," Moscow, 1923. *Edition du Commissiariat du Peuple aux Affaires Étrangères*.
"Limitation of Armament on the Great Lakes," *Report of J. W. Foster, Sec. of State*, Sen. Ex. Doc. No. 9, 52d Cong., 2d sess. Reprinted, *Carnegie Endowment for International Peace, Division of International Law, Pamphlet, No. 2*, 1914.
"Non-fortification agreement of Oct. 20, 1921," *T. S.*, 255.
"Report of the Delegates of the United States of America to the Fifth International Conference of American States, 1923."
"Resolution on Limitacion of Armamentos, Quinto Acuerdo," *Quinta Conferencia Internacional Americana*.
"Special Handbook for the use of the Delegates Pan-American Union, 1922."
"Treaty of Dorpat between Finland and Russia, of Oct. 14, 1920," *T. S.*, 91.

CHAPTER XXIV

Books

BAKER, R. S., *Woodrow Wilson and World Settlement*, 1922. New York: Doubleday, Page.
BUELL, R. L., *Washington Conference*, 1922. New York: Appleton.
CHEOU-WEI, S., *Essai sur l'organisation juridique de la société internationale*, 1917.

DUMAS, J., *Les Sanctions de l'arbitrage international*, 1905.
FALCKE, H. P., *Le Blocus Pacifique*, 1919.
HADJISCOS, D. N., *Les sanctions internationales de la Société des Nations*, 1920.
MACMURRAY, J. V. A., *Treaties and Agreements with and concerning China*, 1921. New York: Oxford Press.
MULLINS, C. W., *The Leipzig Trials*, 1921. London: Witherby.
NIPPOLD, O., *The Development of International Law after the War* (tr. 1923). New York: Oxford Press.
PARMELEE, M., *Blockade and Sea Power*, 1924. New York: Crowell.
PRIBAM, *Secret Treaties of Austria-Hungary*, 1920. Cambridge; Harvard Press.
ROBIN, R., *Des occupations militaires en dehors des opérations de guerre*, 1913.
ROLIN, *L'Article 10 du Pacte de la Société des Nations, in Les Origines et l'Œuvre de la Société des Nations*, 1924, Vol. II, ed. by P. Munch.
SCELLE, G., *Le Pacte des Nations et sa liaison avec le Traité de Paix*, 1919.
SCHÜCKING, W., *The International Unions of the Hague Conference*, tr. 1918. New York: Oxford Press.
SCOTT, J. B., *The United States of America: a Study in International Organization*, 1920. New York: Oxford Press.
STRUYCKEN, A. A. H., *La Société des Nations et l'intégrité territoriale*, Bibliotheca Visseriana, 1923.
War Obviated by an International Peace, 1915. The Hague: Nijkoff.
WARREN, CHAS., *The Supreme Court and Sovereign States*, 1924. Princeton: Princeton Press.

ARTICLES

CAVARÉ, "Quelques notions sur l'occupation pacifique," *R. G. D. I. P.*, 1924.
FLOECKNER, "La Question de la mer Baltique et de la mer du Nord, La convention relative à la Baltique," *15 R. G. D. I. P.*, 1908.
WILSON, G. G., "Neutralization in Theory and Practice," 4 *Yale Review*, 1915.

PAMPHLETS

"German War Trials," *Cmd. 1450.*
"Conference of 1919," *Pamphlet No. 32, Carnegie Endowment.*
"Documents relatifs aux négociations concernant les Guaranties de Sécurité contre un agression de l'Allemagne, 1924," *French Yellow Book.*

CHAPTER XXV

BOOKS

BARCLAY, SIR THOMAS, *New Methods of Adjusting International Disputes and the Future*, 1917. London: Constable.
CARRASCO, J., *La Bolivie devant la Société des Nations*, 1921.
DARBY, W. E., *International Tribunals*, 4th ed., 1904. Washington: American Peace Society.
FRIED, A. F., *Handbuch der Friedensbewegung*, 2d ed. 1911.
GOSSWEILER, C. H., *L'arbitrage international avant 1914 et après 1919*, 1923.
HULL, W. I., *The Two Hague Conferences*, 1908. Boston: Ginn.
KELLOR, F., *Security against War*, 1924. New York: Macmillan.
LA FONTAINE, H., *Pasicrisie internationale*, 1902.

BIBLIOGRAPHY

LAPRADELLE AND POLITIS, *Recueil des arbitrages internationaux*, Vol. I, 1905; II, 1923.
MANNING, W. R., *Arbitration Treaties among the American Nations*, 1924. New York: Oxford Press.
MUNRO, D. G., *Five Republics of Central America*, 1918. New York: Oxford Press.
MYERS, D. P., *Arbitration Engagements now Existing in Treaties*, 1915. Boston: World Peace Foundation.
POLITIS, N., *La Justice internationale*, 1924.
RAMIREZ, M. C., *Cinco Anos en la Corte de Justicia Centosmericana*, 1918.
SCHÜCKING AND WEHBERG, *Satzung des Völkerbundes*.
SCOTT, J. B., *Treaties for the Advancement of Peace*, 1920. New York: Oxford Press.

ARTICLES

HUDSON, "The Second Year of the Permanent Court of International Justice," *A. J. I. L.*, 1924.
———, "Advisory Opinions of National and International Courts," 37 *Harvard Law Review*, 1924.
STRUPP, K., "L'incident de Janina entre le Grèc et l'Italie," *R. G. D. I. P.*, 1924.
"La Suisse et l'arbitrage," *Journal de Genève*, 1924.
VISSCHER, "L'Interpretation du Pacte au lendemain du différend Italo-Grec," *R. D. I. L. C.*, 1924.
WESTLAKE, J., "International Arbitration," 7 *International Journal of Ethics*, 1896.

PAMPHLETS

"Anales de la Corte de Justicia Centoamericana," Vol. VII, 1917.
ANNEX, A., "Traités généraux d'arbitrage communiqués au Bureau International de la Cour Permanente d'Arbitrage," 1921.
"Bolivia's Claim against Chili for the Revision of the Treaty of Peace of 1904," A. 33, 1921.
"Conference on Central American Affairs," 1923.
"Feuillé Fédérale," No. 1890, 1924.
LAMMASCH, H., "Über die Begrenzung der internationale Schiedsgerichtsbarkeit," *Recueil des Rapports*.
LOWELL AND HUDSON, "The Corfu Crisis," *World Peace Foundation Pamphlets*, 1923.
"Proceedings of the Hague Peace Conference," 1907.
"Rapport du Conseil Administratif de la Cour Permanente d'Arbitrage," 23d year, 1924.
"Report of the Delegates of the U. S. to the 5th International Conference," 1923.
WICKSELL, "Einige Bermerkungen über den stä٦digen internationalem untersuchungs und vermittlungsrat," *Recueil des Rapports*.

CHAPTER XXVI

BOOKS

KELLOR, F., *Security against War*, 1924. New York: Macmillan.
MILLER, D. H., *The Geneva Protocol*, 1925. New York: Macmillan.
SCHÜCKING AND WEHBERG, *Satzung des Völkerdundes*.

BIBLIOGRAPHY

ARTICLES

ADATCI, C., "Les 'amendments japonais' au Protocole de Genève," *Revue de Droit International*, 1924.
ERICH, R., "Les rapports entre le pacte de la Société des Nations et le projet de traité d'assistance mutuelle," *R. D. I. L. C.*, 1924.
"The Geneva Protocol: An Analysis," *Round Table*, December, 1924.
LIPPMANN, W., "The Outlawry of War," *Atlantic Monthly*, Aug., 1923.
"Should We Guarantee a European Settlement?" *Round Table*, June, 1924.

PAMPHLETS

BRIERLY, J. L., "The Shortcomings of International Law," *British Yearbook of International Law*, 1924.

CHAPTER XXVII

BOOKS

BAKER, R. S., *Woodrow Wilson and World Settlement*, 1922. New York: Doubleday, Page.
DICKINSON, E. D., *Equality of States in International Law*, 1920. Cambridge: Harvard Press.
DUPUIS, C., *Les Rapports des grandes puissances avec les autres états*.
EVERSLEY, LORD, *The Turkish Empire*, 2d ed., 1923. New York: Dodd, Mead.
FENWICK, C. G., *International Law*, 1924. New York: Century.
HOLLAND, T. E., *The European Concert in the Eastern Question*, 1885. New York: Oxford Press.
PHILLIPS, W. A., *The Confederation of Europe*, 1914. New York: Longmans.
POTTER, P., *Introduction to the Study of International Organization*. New York: Century.
POUND, R., *The Spirit of the Common Law*, 1921. Boston: Marshall Jones.
SALTER, SIR J. A., *Allied Shipping Control, An Experiment in International Administration*, 1921. New York: Oxford Press.
SATOW, E., *Guide to Diplomatic Practice*, 2d ed., 1924. New York: Longmans.
SAYRE, F. B., *Experiments in International Administration*, 1920. New York: Harper.
STURDZA, D., *Recueil de documents relatifs à la liberté de navigation du Danube*, 1904.
TEMPERLEY, H. W. V., *A History of the Peace Conference at Paris*, 1920–24. New York: Oxford Press.
WOOLF, L. S., *International Government*, 1916. New York: Brentano.
WRIGHT, P. E., *At the Supreme War Council*, 1921. New York: Putnam.

ARTICLES

HANKEY, SIR MAURICE, "Diplomacy by Conference," *Round Table*, No. 42, 1921.
HICKS, "The Equality of States and the Hague Conferences," 2 *A. J. I. L.*, 530.
MYERS, D. P., "Representation in the Public International Organs," *A. J. I. L.*, 1914.
ROOT, E., "The Declaration of the Rights and Duties of Nations Adopted by the American Institute of International Law," 10 *A. J. I. L.*, 1916, 211.

"The Supreme Council," *The Round Table*, 1920, No. 39.
"The World in Conference," *Round Table*, Sept., 1920.
"The Supreme War Council, A League of Nations," Vol. I, No. 7, 1918.
Satow, E., "International Congresses and Conferences," *Peace Handbook*, No. 151.

PAMPHLETS

Report of Sir Edward Fry, *Cd.* 3857, 1908.

CHAPTER XXVIII
Books

Schücking and Wehberg, *Satzung des Völkerbundes*.
Triepel, H., *Le Droit international et le droit interne*, 1920.

Articles

Hudson, M. O., "Membership in the League of Nations," *A. J. I. L.*, July, 1924.
Rougier, "La Première Assemblée de la Société des Nations," *R. G. D. I. P.*, 1921.
Scelle, "L'admission des nouveaux membres de la Société des Nations par l'Assemblée de Genéve," 28 *R. D. I. P.*, 1921.
Triepel, H., *Le Droit international et le droit interne*, 1920.

Pamphlets

Ames, Sir Herbert, "Financial Administration and Apportionment of Expenses," *League of Nations Information Section*, 1923.
Baker, "Codification of International Law," *British Year Book of International Law*, 1924.
Krabbe, "Le Secrétariat Général de la Société des Nations et son Activité," *Les Origines et L'Œuvre de la Société des Nations*.
Records of the First Assembly, Plenary Meetings.

CHAPTER XXIX
Books

Anson, Sir Wm., Law and Custom of the Constitution (3d ed., 1908). New York: Oxford Press.
Baker, R. S., *Woodrow Wilson and World Settlement*, 1922. New York: Doubleday, Page.
Barthélemy, J., *Démocratie et Politique, Étrangère*, 1917.
de Bloch, J., *The Future of War*, 1899. Boston: Ginn.
Bryce, J. W., *Modern Democracies*, 1921. New York: Macmillan.
Chien, T. S., *Parliamentary Committees, A Study in Comparative Governments* (Harvard University Thesis, 1923).
Chow, S. R., *Le Controle parlementaire de la politique étrangère en Angleterre, en France, et aux États-Unis*, 1920.
"Clan Rivalry in Japan," *Japan Weekly Chronicle*, Jan., 1924.
Corwin, E. S., *President's Control of Foreign Relations*, 1917. Princeton: Princeton Press.

BIBLIOGRAPHY

DICKINSON, E. D., *Equality of States in International Law*, 1920. Cambridge: Harvard Press.
ESMEIN, H., *Éléments de droit constitutionnel français et comparé*, 1921.
FORD, H. J., *Representative Government*, 1924. New York: Holt.
HAYDEN, R., *The Senate and Treaties*, 1920. New York: Macmillan.
JAMES, H. G., AND MARTIN, P. A., *Republics of Latin America*, 1923. New York: Harper.
KLUYVER, MRS. C. A., *Documents on the League of Nations*, 1920. Leiden: Sijthoff.
LOREBURN, EARL OF, *How the War Came*, 1919. New York: Knopf.
LOWELL, A. L., *Public Opinion in Peace and War*, 1923. Cambridge: Harvard Press.
MCBAIN, H. R. AND ROGERS, L., *New Constitutions of Europe*, 1922. New York: Doubleday, Page.
MATHEWS, J. M., *The Conduct of American Foreign Relations*, 1922. New York: Century.
MICHON, L., *Les traités internationaux devant les chambres*, 1901.
NAKANO, T., *Ordinance Power of the Japanese Emperor*, 1923. Baltimore: Johns Hopkins Press.
PONSONBY, A., *Democracy and Diplomacy*, 1915. London: Methuen.
POOLE, DEWITTE C., *The Conduct of Foreign Relations under Modern Democratic Conditions*, 1924. New Haven: Yale Press.
REDLICH, J., *The Proceedings of the House of Commons*, 1908. New York: Dutton.
REINSCH, P. S., *Secret Diplomacy*, 1922. New York: Harcourt, Brace.
ROBERTSON, C. G., *Bismarck*, 1919. New York: Holt.
SAPIRA, J., *Le Rôle des Chambres au point de vue diplomatique*, 1920.
STRACHEY, L., *Queen Victoria*, 1921. New York: Harcourt, Brace.
SWANWICK, H. M., *Builders of Peace*, 1924. London: Swarthmore Press.
THAYER, W. R., *Life and Letters of John Hay*, 1915. Boston: Houghton, Mifflin.
TREVELYAN, C., *The Union of Democratic Control*, 1919. London: Simson.
UYEHARA, *The Political Development of Japan*, 1910. New York: Dutton.
VILLEY, E., *Les Vices de la constitution française*, 1918.
WALLAS, G., *Our Social Heritage*, 1921. New Haven: Yale Press.
WILLIAMS, R., *The League of Nations Today*, 1923. New York: Holt.
WRIGHT, Q., *The Control of American Foreign Relations*, 1922. New York: Macmillan.

ARTICLES

BROOKS, "Swiss Referendum on the League of Nations," 14 *American Political Science Review*, 1920; *ibid*: "Swiss Treaty Initiative," 1921.
BRUSEWITZ, "Parliamentary Control of Foreign Affairs in Sweden," *Foreign Affairs*, Jan., 1922.
BYAS, H., "The Gods behind the Machine," 2 *Asia*, 1923.
CASTBERG, "Le Conflit entre le Danemark et le Norvège concernant le Groenland," *R. D. I. L. C.*, 1924.
"The Choosing of the Premier," *Japan Weekly Chronicle*, Mar. 6, 1924.
"Constitutional Problems," *Japan Weekly Chronicle*, Jan., 1924.
DAVIS, J. W., *Report of 46th Annual Meeting of the American Bar Association Proceedings*, 1923.

DENNETT, "President Roosevelt's Secret Pact with Japan," *Current History*, Oct., 1924.
"The Elder Statesman," *Asia*, Feb., 1924.
GANNETT, "The Secret Corruption of the French Press," *Nation*, Feb. 6, 1924.
HART, J., "The China Question in the Politics of Japan," 24 *Weekly Review*, Shanghai, 1923.
JACKS, "A League of Nations or a League of Governments?" 131 *Atlantic Monthly*, 1923, 161.
LUCKING, "A National Vote on the League," *Our World*, May, 1923.
PEDERSON, "Foreign Policy Control in Norway," *Foreign Affairs*, Dec., 1921.
POINCARÉ, RAYMOND, "La Présidence et la politique extérieure," *Temps*, Sept. 27, 1920.
ROOT, E., "A Requisite for the Success of Popular Diplomacy," *Foreign Affairs*, 1922.
TANSILL, "The Treaty-making Powers of the Senate," *A. J. I. L.*, July, 1924.
WICKERSHAM, "The Senate and Our Foreign Relations," *Foreign Affairs*, Dec. 15, 1923.
WILLIAMS, "Technique of the League of Nations," *International Journal of Ethics*, Jan., 1924.

PAMPHLETS

BUELL, R. L., *Japanese Immigration*, World Peace Foundation, 1924. Vol. VI.
Handbook of International Organizations, 1921.
LLOYD, CAPTAIN, 104 *Parl. Debates, H. C.*
PONSONBY, ARTHUR, April 1, 1924, 171 *Parl. Debates, H. C.* 2001.
Records of the 2d Assembly, Plenary Meetings.
"L'Union interparlementaire, son oeuvre et son organisation," 3d ed., 1922, *Bureau International.*

SUPPLEMENTARY BIBLIOGRAPHY OF BOOKS, 1925-1929

ADAMI, C. V., *National frontiers in relation to international law* (Tr.). London, 1927.
ALLEN, H. T., *The Rhineland occupation*. Indianapolis, 1927.
AMERICAN TRADE UNION DELEGATION, *Russia after ten years*. New York, 1927.
AUGUR, pseud. for POLIAKOFF, VLADIMIR, *Peace in Europe*. New York, 1928.
AULD, GEORGE P., *The Dawes plan and the new economics*. New York, 1927.
AULNEAU, J., *Histoire de l'Europe centrale*. Paris, 1926.
BAIN, H. F., *Ores and industry in the Far East: the influence of key mineral resources on the development of Oriental civilization*. New York, Council on Foreign Relations, 1927.
BAKER, D. J. N., *Disarmament*. London, 1926.
——, *The Geneva protocol for the pacific settlement of international disputes*. London, 1925.
BALCH, E. G., and others, *Occupied Haiti*. New York, 1927.
BALLESTER, RAFAEL, *Histoire de l'Espagne*. Paris, 1928.
BANERJEE, D. N., *The Indian constitution and its actual working*. New York, 1926.
BARNES, G. N., *History of the international labour office*. London, 1926.
BATSELL, W. R., *The debt settlements and the future*. Paris, 1927.
BEARD, C. A., and G. RADIN, *The Balkan pivot: Yugoslavia*. New York, 1929.
BERGMANN, CARL, *The history of reparations*. London, 1927.
BIRKENHEAD, F. E., EARL OF, *International law*. London, 1927.
BLAKESLEE, GEORGE H., *The recent foreign policy of the United States*. New York, 1925.
BOLDUR, ALEXANDRE, *La Bessarabie et les relations Russo-Roumaines*. Paris, 1927.
BOWMAN, ISAIAH, *The new world: problems in political geography*. Yonkers, 1928.
BRAILSFORD, H. N., *Olives of endless age*. New York, 1928.
BRANDENBURG, ERICH, *From Bismarck to the World War: a history of German foreign policy 1870-1914*. London, 1927.
Brassey's naval and shipping annual, 1928. Edited by A. Richardson and A. Hurd, London, 1927.
BRIERLY, J. L., *The law of nations*. Oxford, 1928.
British yearbook of international law, 1927. London, Oxford University Press, 1927.
BUELL, R. L., *The native problem in Africa*. 2 vols. New York, 1928.
BUSTAMANTE, A. S., DE, *The world court*. New York, American Foundation, 1925.
CABOT, J. M., *The racial conflict in Transylvania: a discussion of the conflicting claims of Rumania and Hungary to Transylvania, the Banat, and the eastern section of the Hungarian Plain*. Boston, 1926.

SUPPLEMENTARY BIBLIOGRAPHY

CALMETTE, GERMAIN, *Les dettes interalliées*. Paris, 1926.
CARTER, JOHN, *Man is war*. Indianapolis, 1926.
CHAPMAN, C. E., *A history of the Cuban republic: a study in Hispanic-American politics*. New York, 1927.
CHIDELL, FLEETWOOD, *Australia—white or yellow*. London, 1926.
CHURCHILL, WINSTON S., *The aftermath 1918–1928*. New York, 1929.
CIPPICO, ANTONIO, *Italy, the central problem of the Mediterranean*. New Haven, Yale University Press, 1926.
CLARK, C. U., *Bessarabia: Russia and Roumania on the Black Sea*. New York, 1927.
CLYDE, P. H., *International rivalries in Manchuria, 1689–1922*. Columbus, Ohio State University Press, 1926.
COOLIDGE, A. C., *Ten years of war and peace*. Cambridge, Harvard University Press, 1927.
CORNISH, L. C. comp., *The religious minorities in Transylvania*. Boston, 1925.
COTTON, W. A., *The race problem in South Africa*. London, Student Christian Movement, 1926.
COUNCIL ON FOREIGN RELATIONS, *Political handbook of the world, 1929*. New Haven, Yale University Press, 1929.
COX, ISAAC JOSLIN, *Nicaragua and the United States, 1909–1927*. Boston, World Peace Foundation, 1927.
CULBERTSON, W. S., *International economic policies: a survey of the economics of diplomacy*. New York, 1925.
DAVIS, H. P., *Black democracy*. New York, 1929.
DEÁK, FRANCIS, *The Hungarian-Rumanian land dispute*. New York, Columbia University Press, 1928.
DEALEY, JAMES QUAYLE, *Foreign policies of the United States*. New York, 1926.
DELAISI, FRANCIS, *Political myths and economic realities*. New York, 1927.
DELLE-DONNE, O. *European tariff policies*. New York, 1928.
DENNIS, A. P., *The romance of world trade*. New York, 1926.
DENNY, LUDWELL, *We fight for oil*. New York, 1928.
DEXTER, P., and J. H. SEDGWICK, *The war debts: an American view*. New York, 1928.
DIRECTORATE OF THE CHAMBER OF PRINCES' SPECIAL ORGANISATION, *The British Crown and the Indian states*. London, 1929.
DONALDSON, JOHN, *International economic relations*. New York, 1928.
DRIAULT, EDOUARD, ET L'HERITIER, MICHEL, *Histoire diplomatique de la Grèce de 1821 à nos jours*. Paris, Les Presses Universitaires de France, 1925.
DUNN, F. S., *The practice and procedure of international conferences*. Baltimore, 1929.
DUNN, R. W., *American foreign investments*. New York, 1926.
DURAND, RAPHAEL, *Le problème de Tangier*. Paris, Société Anonyme du Recueil Sirey, 1926.
DUTCHER, G. M., *The political awakening of the East: studies of political progress in Egypt, India, China, Japan, and the Philippines*. New York, 1925.
EAGLETON, CLYDE, *The responsibility of states in international law*. New York, New York University Press, 1928.
EDWARDS, G. W., *Investing in foreign securities*. New York, 1926.
EGGLESTON, HON. F. W. (Ed.), *The Australian mandate for New Guinea*. Melbourne, 1928.

SUPPLEMENTARY BIBLIOGRAPHY 817

EVANS, IFOR L., *The British in tropical Africa.* Cambridge, Cambridge University Press, 1929.
FACHIRI, A. P., *The Permanent court of international justice.* London, Oxford University Press, 1925.
FAY, S. B., *The origins of the world war.* 2 vols. New York, 1928.
FISCHER, LOUIS, *Oil imperialism: the international struggle for petroleum.* New York, 1926.
FORBES, W. C., *The Philippine islands.* 2 vols. Boston, 1928.
FRASER, H. F., *Foreign trade and world politics.* New York, 1926.
FÜLÖP-MILLER, RENÉ, *The mind and face of Bolshevism.* New York, 1928.
GARNER, J. W., *American foreign policies.* New York, New York University Press, 1928.
——, *Recent developments in international law.* Calcutta, University of Calcutta, 1925.
GARRATT, G. T., *An Indian commentary.* London, 1928.
GAVIT, J. P., *Opium.* New York, 1927.
GIDEONSE, H. D., *Transfert des réparations et le plan Dawes.* Lausanne, 1928.
GLASGOW, GEORGE, *From Dawes to Locarno: being a critical record of an important achievement in European diplomacy, 1924-1925.* New York, 1926.
GONSIOROWSKI, MIROSLAS, *Société des Nations et problème de la paix.* Paris, 1927.
GOOCH, G. P., and TEMPERLEY, HAROLD, eds., *British documents on the origins of the war, 1898-1914.* London, H. M. Stationery Office, 1927.
GRAHAM, M. W., *New governments of eastern Europe.* New York, 1927.
GREER, GUY, *The Ruhr-Lorraine industrial problem: a study of the economic interdependence of the two regions and their relation to the reparation question.* New York, 1925.
GRUENING, E., *Mexico and its heritage.* New York, 1928.
HARING, C. H., *South America looks at the United States.* New York, 1928.
HARRIS, JOHN H., *Slavery or "sacred trust"?* London, 1926.
HARRIS, N. D., *Europe and the east.* Boston, 1926.
HARRIS, W. B., *France, Spain and the Rif.* New York, 1927.
HAYES, C. J. H., *Essays on nationalism.* New York, 1926.
HEADLAM-MORLEY, AGNES, *The new democratic constitutions of Europe.* London, Oxford University Press, 1928.
HERFORD, C. H., *The case of German South Tyrol against Italy.* London, 1927.
HERRE, PAUL, *Die Südtiroler frage.* Munich, 1927.
HERVEY, J. F., *Legal effects of recognition in international law.* Philadelphia, University of Pennsylvania Press, 1928.
HEYKING, ALPHONSE DE, *L'exterritorialité.* Paris, 1926.
HILL, NORMAN, *The public international conference.* Stanford, Stanford University Press, 1929.
HUDSON, M. O., *Current international coöperation.* Calcutta, Calcutta University, 1927.
——, *The permanent court of international justice.* Cambridge, Harvard University Press, 1925.
HUGHES, C. E., *Our relations to the nations of the western hemisphere.* Princeton, Princeton University Press, 1928.
INSTITUTE OF PACIFIC RELATIONS, *Problems of the Pacific; proceedings of the second conference of the Institute of Pacific Relations, Honolulu, Hawaii, July 15 to July 29, 1927,* edited by J. B. Condlife. Chicago University Press, 1928.

818   SUPPLEMENTARY BIBLIOGRAPHY

Ise, John, *The United States oil policy.* New Haven, Yale University Press, 1926.
Jenks, Leland H., *Our Cuban colony.* New York, 1928.
Johnson, K. C., and Frankland, J. M., *Aspects of Anglo-American relations.* New Haven, Yale University Press, 1928.
Jones, Robert, and Sherman, S. S., *The League of Nations from idea to reality.* London, 1927.
Joûhaux, Leon, *Le désarmement.* Paris, 1927.
Keeton, G. W., *The development of extraterritoriality in China.* New York, 1928.
Kenworthy, J. M., *Peace or war?* New York, 1927.
Knight, Melvin M., *The Americans in Santo Domingo.* New York, 1928.
Kuczynski, R. R., *American loans to Germany.* New York, 1927.
Laski, H. G., *Communism.* New York, 1927.
Latané, John Halladay, *A history of American foreign policy.* New York, 1927.
Latourette, K. S., *A history of Christian missions in China.* New York, 1929.
Lay, T. H., *The foreign service of the United States.* New York, 1925.
Leys, Norman, *Kenya.* London, 1925.
Long, R. C., *The mythology of reparations.* London, 1928.
Macedo Soares, Jose Carlos de, *Le Brésil et la Société des Nations.* Paris, 1927.
McGuire, Constantine E., *Italy's international economic position.* New York, 1926.
McKenzie, R. D., *Oriental exclusion.* New York, American Group of the Institute of Pacific Relations, 1927.
MacNair, H. F., *The Chinese abroad: their position and protection.* Shanghai, 1925.
Madariaga, Salvador de, *Disarmament.* New York, 1929.
Mair, L. P., *The protection of minorities.* London, 1928.
Martin, Charles E., *The politics of peace.* Stanford, Stanford University Press, 1929.
Mears, E. G., *Resident Orientals on the American Pacific coast: their legal and economic status. Preliminary report prepared for the July 1927 conference of the Institute of Pacific Relations in Honolulu.* New York, American Group of the Institute of Pacific Relations, 1927.
Miller, D. H., *The drafting of the Covenant . . .* New York, 1928.
——, *The peace pact of Paris.* New York, 1928.
Mitrany, D., *The problem of international sanctions.* London, Oxford University Press, 1925.
Monroe, Paul, *China: a nation in evolution.* New York, 1928.
Moon, P. T., *Imperialism and world politics.* New York, 1926.
Morrison, C. C., *The outlawry of war: a constructive policy for world peace.* Chicago, 1927.
Moulton, H. G., and Lewis, C., *The French debt problem.* New York, 1925.
Moulton, H. G., and Pasvolsky, Leo, *World war debt settlements.* New York, 1926.
Morley, Felix, *Our Far Eastern assignment.* New York, 1926.
Nearing, Scott, and Freeman, J., *Dollar diplomacy.* New York, 1925.
Norton, Henry Kittredge, *China and the powers.* New York, 1927.
Ottlik, Georges, ed., *Annuaire de la Société des Nations, 1920–1927,* 1928. Geneva, 1927, 1928.

SUPPLEMENTARY BIBLIOGRAPHY 819

PAGE, KIRBY, *Dollars and world peace.* New York, 1927.
PASVOLSKY, LEO, *Economic nationalism of the Danubian states.* New York, 1928.
PEFFER, NATHANIEL, *The white man's dilemma: climax of the age of imperialism.* New York, 1927.
Question de Mossoul de la signature du traité d'armistice de Mourdrois (30 Octobre 1918) au 1re Mars 1925, La. Constantinople, 1925.
QUIGLEY, HAROLD S., *From Versailles to Locarno.* Minneapolis, University of Minnesota Press, 1927.
RALSTON, JACKSON H., *International arbitration from Athens to Locarno.* Stanford, Stanford University Press, 1929.
———, *The law and procedure of international tribunals.* Stanford, Stanford University Press, 1926.
RECKE, WALTHER, *Die polnische frage als problem der europäische politik.* Berlin, 1927.
REMER, C. F., *The foreign trade of China.* Shanghai, 1926.
RIPPY, J. F., *Latin America in world politics.* New York, 1928.
———, *The United States and Mexico.* New York, 1926.
RODICK, B. C., *The doctrine of necessity in international law.* New York, Columbia University Press, 1928.
ROMIER, LUCIEN, *Who will be master? Europe or America?* New York, 1928.
ROOSEVELT, NICHOLAS, *The Philippines: a treasure and a problem.* New York, 1926.
RUTTER, OWEN, *The new Baltic states and their future: an account of Lithuania, Latvia and Estonia.* New York, 1926.
SACK, A. N., *Les effets des transformations des états sur leurs dettes publiques.* Paris, 1927.
SCHACHT, HJALMAR, *The stabilization of the mark.* New York, 1927.
SEARS, L. M., *A history of American foreign relations.* New York, 1927.
SERING, MAX, *Germany under the Dawes plan.* London, 1929.
SEYMOUR, CHARLES, *The intimate papers of Colonel House.* Boston, 1926.
SHEEAN, VINCENT, *The new Persia.* New York, 1927.
SIMONDS, F. H., *How Europe made peace without America.* New York, 1927.
SLOSSON, P. W., *Twentieth century Europe.* Boston, 1927.
SMITH, D. H., *The Panama canal: its history, activities and organization.* Baltimore, Johns Hopkins Press, 1927.
SPAIGHT, J. M., *Pseudo-security.* New York, 1928.
STEGEMANN, HERMANN, *The struggle for the Rhine.* New York, 1927.
STICKNEY, E. P., *Southern Albania or Northern Epirus in European international affairs, 1913-1923.* Stanford, Stanford University Press, 1926.
STIMSON, H. L., *American policy in Nicaragua.* New York, 1927.
STOREY, MOORFIELD, and LICHAUCO, M. P., *The conquest of the Philippines by the United States, 1898-1925.* New York, 1926.
STOYANOVSKY, J., *The mandate for Palestine.* New York, 1928.
STRUPP, KARL, *Das werk von Locarno.* Berlin and Leipzig, 1926.
SZASZ, DE ZSOMBOR, *The minorities in Roumanian Transylvania.* London, 1927.
TAUSSIG, F. W., *International trade.* New York, 1927.
THORN, W. T., JR., *Petroleum and coal.* Princeton, Princeton University Press, 1929.
TOYNBEE, ARNOLD J., *The conduct of British Empire foreign relations since the peace settlement.* London, Oxford University Press, 1928. *Survey of in-*

ternational affairs, 1920–1924. London, Oxford University Press, 1925–1926; also annually.

TRIBOLET, LESLIE B., *The international aspects of electrical communications in the Pacific area.* Baltimore, Johns Hopkins Press, 1929.

VAN MAANEN-HELMER, ELIZABETH, *The mandates system in relation to Africa and the Pacific Islands.* London, 1929.

VINACKE, HAROLD M., *Problems of industrial development in China.* Princeton, Princeton University Press, 1926.

WALTER, H. C., *Foreign exchange and foreign debts.* London, 1926.

WELLES, SUMNER, *Naboth's vineyard.* 2 vols. New York, 1928.

WHEELER-BENNETT, J. W., and LANGERMANN, F. E., *Information on the problem of security (1917–1926).* London, 1927.

———, *Information on the reduction of armaments.* London, 1925.

———, *Information on the renunciation of war (1927–1928).* London, 1925.

WHITE, FREDA, *Mandates.* London, 1926.

WILLIAMS, BENJAMIN H., *Economic foreign policy of the United States.* New York, 1929.

WILLIAMS, BRUCE, *State security and the League of Nations.* Baltimore, Johns Hopkins Press, 1927.

WILLIAMS, EDWARD THOMAS, *China yesterday and today.* New York, 1927.

WRIGHT, S. F., *The collection and disposal of the maritime native customs revenue since the revolution of 1911 with an account of the loan services administered by the Inspector General of Customs.* Shanghai, Statistical Department of the Inspectorate General of Customs, 1927.

YÜ, T. C., *The interpretation of treaties.* New York, Columbia University Press, 1927.

ZIMMERN, ALFRED, *America and Europe and other essays.* New York, Oxford University Press, 1929.

———, *The third British empire.* London, Oxford University Press, 1926.

INDEX

A. B. C. powers, 246, 625; armaments, 556
Aaland Islands, 46, 48, 228, 583, 629, 634, 641
Abdul Hamid, 87
Aborigines' Protection Society, 349, 751
Abyssinia, 394, 473, 584; courts, 485; Open Door agreements, 450; slavery, 278; and League, 451
Access to the sea, 129
Act of war, 601
Acton, Lord, 20
Adolescent peoples, 344
Advisers, 380, 388, 398; financial, 420, 433; military, 470, 488
Advisory opinions, 579, 617, 636; list of, 619
Ægean Sea, 129, 132, 329
Afghanistan, 312, 341, 472, 586, 659
Africa, 308, 313, 317, 339, 679; Equatorial, 327; liquor traffic, 268; native farms, 347; North, 327; Open Door, 452; slave trade, 277; spheres of influence, 470; tropical diseases, 293
"Africa for the Africans," 85
African troops, 313
Aggression, 393, 507, 588, 653, 658; American, prohibited, 252; financial assistance, 604; determination of, 647, 650, 665
Agreements. See Treaties
Agriculture, coöperation in, 146
Air Navigation, convention of 1919, 144, 688
Aircraft, 517, 561
Aircraft carriers, 561
Albania, 489, 593; agreement with Italy, 580; and League, 580; financial adviser, 433; refugees, 300
Alcohol. See Liquor
Algeciras, Act of, 280, 456, 473, 681
Algeria, 70, 336, 339; French policy in, 376, 382

Aliens. See Smuggling
Alliances, 237, 239, 388, 509, 511; and Geneva Protocol, 651; Defensive, 505, 662; versus League, 577
Alpine race, 77
Alsace-Lorraine, 6, 28, 30, 43, 117, 203
Ambassadors. See Conference of Ambassadors
American Institute of International Law, Equality of States, 685
American League of Nations, 250
Andrews, C. F., 259
Anglo-American coöperation, 81
Anglo-American debt agreement, 547
Anglo-Egyptian Sudan. See Sudan
Anglo-French Treaty of 1903, 609
Anglo-Japanese Alliances, 506, 516, 579, 734
Anglo-Saxonism, 75, 81
Angola, 330
Animals, International protection, 288
Anti-dumping laws, 116, 147
Anti-War Pact, 653; analysis, 661; history, 657; text, 659
Appeal. See World Court
Arabs, 89; Palestine and, 217; slave raids, 277
Arbitration, 252; declined, 354; of loan disputes, 408; of Open Door disputes, 461; "vital interests" and, 609; voluntary and compulsory, 607; weakness of, 674, 676
Argentina, 641; and League, 695; Anti-War Pact, 661; armament agreement, 556; arbitration, 608; and Pan-American Conference, 251
Argol Agreements, 107
Armament, competition in, 513; attempts before the World War, 555; conferences subsequent to Washington Conference, 561; cost of, 518; demilitarization of terri-

821

tory, 567; disarmament of Germany, 514, 584; League of Nations and, 557, 571; naval rivalry, 515, 557; private manufacture, 520, 569; standing armies, 514; unlimited classes, 560. *See* Washington Conference
Armaments Year Book, 572
Armed Neutrality, 509
Armenians, 31, 184, 603
Arms, private manufacture, 519, 570
Arms Embargo, 486
Arms traffic, 280, 359, 520
Arms Traffic Convention (1925), 283
Article X of the League Covenant, 587, 595, 639, 665, 756; 1923 resolution, 599, 756
Article XI of the League Covenant, 49, 192, 538, 588, 595, 628, 633, 635, 645, 649, 665, 699
Article XIII of the League Covenant, 595, 639
Article XV of the League Covenant, 595, 617, 629, 654
Article XVI of the League Covenant, 596; 2nd Assembly and, 600
Article XVII of the League Covenant, 595, 635
Article XVIII of the League Covenant, 747
Article XIX of the League Covenant, 588, 649, 699
Article XX of the League Covenant, 577, 669
Article XXI of the League Covenant, 253, 578, 636
Article XXII of the League Covenant, 388
Article XXIII of the League Covenant, 128
Aryanism, 74
Asbestos, 98
Asia, 308; spheres of influence in, 469
Asquith, H. H., 34
Assembly of the League of Nations, 698; committees, 699; deliberative powers, 701; revision of treaties, 699; settlement of disputes, 634
Assiento, 275
Assimilation, 29; backward peoples, 375; failure of the policy, 377
Atlantic Shipping Trust, 113

Australia, 234, 312, 384, 493; dictation test for immigrants, 65; Monroe Doctrine, 312
Austria, 36, 43, 394, 628; Italy and, 52; League reconstruction, 426; union with Germany, 79
Austria-Hungary, autonomy in, 221
Authors, protection, 145
Automobiles, international driving, 143, 150
Autonomy, 203; guaranteed, 227. *See* Chapter IX

Backward peoples. *See* Part II
Bagdad railway, 311, 438, 455
Bahama Islands, 272
Balance of Power, 508, 579, 744; a false principle, 512
Baldwin government, 652
Balfour, Lord, 82, 714, 720, 747
Balfour Declaration (1917), 216
Balfour note of 1922, 547
Balkans, 20, 31; federation idea, 236
Baltic Conference, 112; Agreements, 585
Baltic States, 238; minorities, 188; smuggling treaty, 274
Banat, 120
Bank, International, 139
Bankers' Conference, 139
Bank of International Settlement, 549
Bankruptcy, international law and, 407
Barcelona conference (1921), 129
Baring Brothers and Czechoslovakia, 408
Barrès, Maurice, 10
Basel Mission Trading Company, 351
Basques, 227
Beer, G. L., 82
Behring Sea, 289
Belgian Congo, 328, 349, 379; new labor policy, 374. *See* Congo Free State
Belgium, 11, 510, 583, 678; colonies, 328; Eupen and Malmedy, 39. *See* Belgian Congo
Berlin Act of 1890–1919, 277, 354, 361, 451, 459, 584
Berlin labor conference (1890), 159, 679

Berne Labor Conference (1906), 159
Bessarabia, 29, 238
Bethlen, Count, 432
Birds, protection, 288
"Blackbirding," 318
Black Sea, neutralized, 555, 583
Black Star Steamship Line, 86
Black troops, 313
Blockades, 592; Pacific, 415. *See* Article XVI of the Covenant, and Boycotts
Bolivia, finances, 419; League and, 636, 696, 700
Bolivia-Paraguay dispute, 252, 638
Bolsheviks. *See* Russia
Bondelzwarts affair, 365
Borah, W. E., 408, 657, 669
Bosnia-Herzegovina, 221, 592
Bosphorus. *See* Straits
Boundaries, 41, 42; agreements to preserve, 585
Bounties, 147
Boxer revolt, 91, 403, 593, 737
Boycotts, 403, 592, 597, 669
Brazil, 107; and Anti-War Pact, 661; and League, 655, 697; and U. S. naval mission, 732; coffee, 110; immigration treaty with Italy, 171; reciprocity with U. S., 125
Briand, Aristide, 657, 665, 668, 671, 743
Bright, John, 322
British characteristics, 6
British Empire, 205, 326, 381; colonial possessions, 310; Dominion governments and foreign policy, 207; federal principle, 234; federation movement, 235; racial equality and, 65; Russia Trade Agreement of 1921, 156; sea power, 515; trade policy, 444
British Monroe Doctrine, 659, 666
British North America Act, 225
British North Borneo Company, 342, 372
British West Africa, industries and natives, 348
Brooke, Rajah, 371
Brum, Baltazar, 250
Brussels Act of 1890, liquor, 268; arms, 280; on the slave trade, 277
Brussels Financial Conference, 151

Bryan Peace Commission treaties, 245, 624, 628, 632
Bryce, Lord, 21, 58, 728
Buffer states, 312
Bulduri convention, 238
Bulgaria, 417; and sea, 129, 132; refugees loan, 300; *See* also Greco-Bulgarian dispute
Burton resolution, 670

Cabinet ministers and the League of Nations, 755
Cables, 141
Cacao beans, 110
Calendar Reform, 150
California and the Japanese, 63
Caliph, 87
Calvo Doctrine, 404, 416
Cambodia, 471
Cameroons, 349, 360
Camphor, 110
Canada, 203, 308, 312, 322, 384; Japanese and, 66; pulp-wood, 109. *See* British Empire
Canals, internationalized, 133
Cannes, Conference (1922), 414
Cape-to-Cairo railway, 365
Capital, abuses in backward regions, 399; government protection of foreign investments, 406; revolt against foreign, 402
Capper resolution, 670
Caribbean policy, U. S., 313
Cartels, International, 111
Catalan State, 203, 227
Cecil, Viscount, 361
Celtic language, 10
Central America, 321; arbitration, 608, 625; arms limitation, 562; Conference, unanimity, 686; co-operation, 243; debts, 399; foreign capital, 399, 402; free trade, 136; labor convention, 168
Central American Conference (1907), 245; (1922–23), 245, 614
Central American Court of Justice, 245, 613
Central American International Bureau, 245
Central Europe, 103, 135, 237
Ceylon, 383, 385
Chamberlain, Austen, 652, 670

824　INDEX

Chamberlain, H. S., 74
Chamberlain, Joseph, 84, 315, 345; Uganda speech, 317
Chartered company system, 320, 371
Chemical Warfare Service, 504
Chester concession, 398, 404, 441
Child labor, 163, 400
Chile, 31, 42, 401, 524, 608, 643, 700; and Monroe Doctrine, 637
China, 69, 310, 692; American gunboats in, 488; anti-foreign sentiment, 91; arms embargo, 281; battle for concessions in, 403; Board of Reference, 462; courts, 484; foreign capital, 399; international financial control, 425; labor regulation, 164; labor treaties, 350; leasehold, 464; mining law protested by the United States, 405; Open Door, 449; poppy-growing, 260; spheres of influence, 584; tariff control, 400, 426, 480, 481
Chinese, 57; imported labor, 350
Chinese Consortium, 456
Chinese Eastern railway, 438
Chinese exclusion laws, 61, 170
Chino-Japanese relations, 92
Chioshu clan, 731
Choate, J. H., 612
Christ as a black man, 86
Church Missionary Society, 320
Churches, 13, 751
Ciraolo, Senator, 300
"Civilian damage," 525
Clarendon, Lord, 519
Client states, 464
Closed Door, 442; aspects in colonies, 443; concessions, 445; effect, 446; in tariffs, 443; and Imperialism, 447; shipping, 444
Clothing, 99
Coal, 98; British trust, 111; German payments after the World War, 535; Germany, 117
Coast lighting, 150
Coasting trade, 114
Cocaine. *See* Opium
Cocoa industry, 308, 348
Cocoa Islands, 333
Codification of international law, 705
Coffee, 107; Brazil "valorization," 110

Colmar trial, 30
Colombia, 585; finances, 422; United States and, 403, 695
Colonial Councils, 377
Colonial empires, 325
Colonial legislatures, 381
Colonial policies, 331
Colonial powers, 326
Colonial representation in France, 376
Colonial trade, 308
Colonies, 322; peaceful emancipation, 387; tariff policies, 443; two kinds, 322. *See also* Capital, Conscription, Imperialism, Open Door
Color Bar, 339
Commercial treaties, 106, 123
Common law, 21
Commonwealth Trust, Limited, 351
Communal representation, 383
Communications, international control, 139
Communications and Transit Committee, 143, 149
Communists, 154
Competition, unfair, 114, 144, 151
Compulsory arbitration. *See* Arbitration
Concert of Europe, 680
Concessions, 397, 415; Closed Door policy, 442; competition for, 438; China, 449; Congo, 337; Mexico, 404; United States and, 413
Conciliation commissions, 643; Pan American, 252
Condominium, 489
Confederations, 69, 75, 231; federations and, 233; international advantages, 234
Conference of Ambassadors, 630, 684
Conferences. *See* International Conferences
Conferences on Education, 24
Confiscation of native lands, 336
Congo Free State, 329, 332, 337, 359, 583
Congress of Panama of 1826, 246
Congress of Vienna of 1815, 232, 689
Conscription, 513; and Central Powers, 514; Colonial, 313
Constantinople, Greek patriarch at, 201, 223; health council, 291

INDEX

Contracts, labor, 333, 349
Conventional duties, 105, 135
Coolidge, A. C., 494
Coolidge, Calvin, 620, 735
Coolies, treaties regarding, 350
Copper, 99, 308
Copra, 99
Copyright convention, 144
Corfu affair, 367, 589, 602, 630, 641, 725; neutralized, 583
Corporation of Foreign Bondholders, England, 409, 410
Costa Rica, 249, 402; and League, 697
Cotton, 99, 308
Cotton industry and India, 340
Council for the Prevention of War, 731
Council of Four, 683
Council of Ten, 683
Council of the League of Nations, 238, 389, 495, 605; and Albania, 580; and armaments, 565, 569, 571; and Art. XVI, 601; and Council of Ambassadors, 630; duties, 712; loans, 408; and Locarno, 653; mandates and, 357, 361; minorities, 188, 228; non-permanent members, 655, 708; procedure and meetings, 708; provisional measures, 635; refugees, 298; settlement of disputes, 633, 641; special membership, 605, 710; and Straits, 568; and United States, 671
Counterfeiting treaty, 151
Court of Arbitral Justice, 613; relation to Council, 713
Covenant, League, text, 759; amendment, 362; gap in, 644, 650, 669, 673. See Articles
Crete, 593
Criminals, catching, 286
Crispi Loan, 409
Croatia, 221, 227
Cromer, Lord, 495
Crowder, General, 476
Cruisers, 517, 563
Cuba, 8, 318, 326, 401; finances, 417; reciprocity, 108; United States relations, 474, 487
Cultural internationalism, 23
Culture system, 332

Cunliffe, Lord, 526
Currencies, 103, 139
Curzon, Lord, 538
Customs Formalities Convention, 135
Customs unions, 136
Cypress, 326, 329
Cyrillic alphabet, 6
Czechoslovakia, 80, 227, 242; free zones, 131

D'Annunzio, Gabriele, 73
Dairen, 465
Dandurand, Senator, 199
Danger zones of imperialism, 463
Danish West Indies, 37
Danube, 133
Danzig, 120, 130
Dardanelles, 134
Davis, N. H., 132
Dawes Plan, 537, 750
Deadlocks, 383, 386
Debauchery of natives, 341
Debt Funding Act, U. S., 547, 740
Debts, national, 501; repudiation of, 403. See also Inter-allied Debts
Decatur, Stephen, 19
Dedeagatch, 129
Defaulting governments, 403, 407
Defensive alliances. See Alliances
Demilitarization of territory, 567
Democracy and Imperialism, 342, 370; and League, 729; in inter-racial communities, 70; pacific character, 727; secret treaties and, 744
Diarchy, 385
Dictation Test, 65
Dictators, Native, 372
Dingley tariff, 102
Disarmament. See Armaments
Disasters, relief for, 300
Disease, 290, 318
Disputes, commercial, 120; non-legal and the League of Nations, 628. See Arbitration; World Court
Disraeli, 315
Djambi concession, 460
Djemal Pasha, 90
Djibuti, 313, 329
Dodecanese Islands, 329
Domestic questions, 354, 587, 627; League Council and, 633; Protocol

826 INDEX

and, 649; Japanese amendment, 650
Dominions, British, 205, 215, 377; Imperial treaties and, 210
Dorpat treaty, 229, 631, 636
Double Taxation, 151
Draft Treaty of Mutual Assistance, 647
Drago Doctrine, 416
"Drain, The," 340
Dreadnaught panic of 1909, 520
Drug formulæ, 294
Drug traffic, 256, 267, 342
Drummond, Sir Eric, 720
Duisburg, 530, 534
Dumping, 114, 147
Düsseldorf, 530, 534
Dutch East Indies, 328, 332, 347, 380; oil concessions, 460

East Carelia case, 189, 229, 636
East India Company, 318, 341
Eastern question, and Concert of Europe, 681
Economic Committee of the League of Nations, 109, 144, 149. *See also* League of Nations
Economic internationalism. *See* Chapter VI
Economic nationalism. *See* Chapter V
Economic rivalries of governments, 437
Economic sanctions. *See* Sanctions
Economic self-sufficiency, 96
Education, 18, 24; of native peoples, 352
Educational conferences, 24
Egypt, 352, 372, 636; and Anti-War Pact, 659, 661; and League, 392, 667; British policy, 312, 379; British semi-protectorate, 472, 478; international financial control, 423; Khedive's loans, 399; Sudan government, 467
Eight-hour day convention, 163
Elchis, 684
Elections, supervision of, 476
Electric power, 129
Electrical communications, 139; Inter-American, 142
Emancipation of colonies, 387

Embargoes, 109; arms, 281. *See also* Boycotts
Emigration, 56; over-population and, 175. *See also* Immigration
Empires, Colonial, 325
Empire Settlement Act, 176
Ems dispatch, 8
Enclaves, 47
England, 52. *See also* British Empire
English-speaking peoples, 81
English Speaking Union, 82
Entente Cordiale, 510, 744
Epidemics, 290; securing joint action, 296
Equality of states, 685; League of Nations and, 717; modifications of the doctrine, 687
Eritrea, 329
Esher, Lord, army plan, 573
Esperanto, 23
Esthonia, 189, 636
Ethelburger bonds, 408
Eupen-Malmedy, 39
Exchange of minorities, 200
Executive agreements, 735
Experts, conferences, 683, 704
Export-controls, 110
Export Prohibition Convention, 138
Export taxes, 108, 136, 138, 444
Exterritoriality, 483; abuses, 485
Extradition treaties, 286

Fauchille, M., 472
Federal Wireless Telegraph Co., 460
Federated Malay States, 235
Federations, 230; confederations and, 230; international advantages, 233
Feisal, King, 89, 388
Filmer, Sir Robert, 5
Financial assistance in case of aggression, 604
Financial control, 480; of African and Asiatic countries by the United States, 416, 417; dangers, 422; international, 423
Finland, 22, 46, 81, 328, 635; Russia and, 219, 239
Firestone loan, 421
Fisher, H. A. L., 21
Fisheries, international protection, 289

loans, 299; minorities exchanged with Turkey, 200; refugees in, 201, 299
Greenland, 453, 738
Grenoble, 272
Grey, Lord, 632
Group Consciousness, 203
Guarantees, 586
Guatemala, 243
Gunboats, China, 488
Guns, machine, 505

Hague Conference of 1899, 555, 575, 608; of 1907, 555, 608, 643, 679, 686, 737; Permanent Court of Arbitration, 611
Hague Conference in 1912, on opium, 261
Hague Debt Collection Convention, 416
Haiti, Finances, 417; League, 365; tariff control, 482; United States relations, 477, 487
Halibut fisheries, 289
Halibut treaty, 208
Harding, W. G., 620
Harrison, Frederic, 322
Hawaii, 33, 62, 569; reciprocity agreement, 107
Hay, John, 65, 449, 466, 739
Hayashi, Baron, 92
Health, conferences, 299; councils, 299; international, 290; tropics, 352
Health Organization, League, 293, 296
Hejaz, 87, 91
Heroin, 257
Herriot, Edouard, 648, 728
Hertzog native policy, 70
Herzl, Theodor, 216
Hides, India, 321, 444
Hides and Skins Convention, 139
Hindoos, 66, 335
History, influence of, 15
Hlinka, Father, 226
Hoar, G. F., 372
Holland, 327, 332, 608, 619, 681; refusal to surrender the Kaiser, 591
Holy Alliance, 509
Holy Places, 87
Honduras, 624; arbitration, 408; neutralized, 583
Huerta, General, 399, 402
Hughes, C. E., 156, 531, 538, 546, 627; and unanimity rule, 686
Hungary, 43, 54, 595, 635; and Anti-War Pact, 667; Land dispute, Roumania, 192; League financial control, 394, 431. *See also* Austria-Hungary
Hunger, J. D., 433
Hussein, 90

Ibn Saud, 90, 91
Ice patrol, 287
Iceland, Denmark and, 224; neutralized, 583; prohibition, 271
Identity cards, 298
Imbrie, Vice Consul, 392
Immigration, discriminatory laws, 61; international aspects, 169; treaties, 176
Imperial Conferences, 209, 214
Imperial Federation, 235
Imperial Preference, 443
Import duties. *See* Tariffs
Imported labor, 335
Indemnities, 321, 391, 397
Independence, 28, 204; agreements guaranteeing, 584; demand for, from backward peoples, 370, 386; economic, 97; where to draw the line, 44
India, 235, 311, 313, 315, 318, 326, 336, 352, 378, 383, 400; British Empire and, 64; British goods in, 444; diarchy plan, 386; "Drain," 340; Hindoo and Moslem, 321; League of Nations Council and, 710; poppy-growing, 260; status of Indians in the British Empire, 66, 335; tariffs, 340; trade, 308; troops, 340
Indians, American, 62, 309. *See* Hindoos
Indigénat, 339
"Indirect Rule," 379
Indo-China, 327, 377
Industrial property, protection, 144
Informal control, 486
Integrity agreements, 584
Intellectual Coöperation, Committee, 25, 705
Inter-allied debts, 546; and reparations, 548, 551

INDEX

Fiume, 72, 120, 131, 684
Flags, 6
Flanders, 11
Flogging of natives, 334, 339
Food supply, 100, 176
Force, 122; imperialism and, 370; justification of, 522
Forced labor, 332, 360
Ford, Henry, 78
Fordney tariff, 101, 125
Foreign affairs, committees, 748, 757; control in England and France, 733; newspapers and, 751; public opinion and, 751; U. S. Constitution and, 755
Foreign investments, 396; government control, 409; government protection, 413; international control, 412; United States policy, 410. *See* Debts
Foreign Policy Association, 751
Foreign trade, 96; trusts and, 111
Formosa, 320, 328
Fortifications, prohibited, 567
Four Power Treaty of the Pacific, 312, 582, 585, 587
Fourteen Points, 108, 524
France, 18, 313, 316, 359, 526, 597; alliances in Central Europe, 511; checks on foreign policy, 734; colonial possessions, 327; colonial representation in Paris, 376; influence of Presidents on foreign policy, 744; submarine treaty, 686; Washington Conference reservation, 559
Franchise, native, 376, 382
Franco-American Tariff dispute, 105
Franco-American Alliance (1919), 506, 510, 578, 603, 739
Franco-Belgian Understanding, 510, 747
Franco-Danish arbitration treaty, 610
Franco-Polish Alliance, 506, 511
Franco-Russian Alliance, 505
Free trade, 121, 136; within the United States, 136
Free zones, 131; Franco-Swiss controversy, 137
Freedom of navigation, 132
Freedom of transit, 128
French-Canadians, 225

French colonies, 327
French Congo, 337, 454
French West Africa, 327
Frontiers, 9, 120; arbitra economic and strateg toric, 51; natural and a problem of, 51

Galicia, 120, 221
Gallicism, 75
Gandhi, Mahatma, 259, 3
Garvey, Marcus, 85
Geneva. *See* League of N
Geneva Arms Conference,
Geneva Protocol, 649
Genoa Conference, 127, 41
Genro, 731
Gentilis, A., 667
Gentlemen's Agreement, 6
Geography, influence of, 9
Georgia, 472
German Bund, 754
German colonies, 338, 339,
German marks, 536
German settlers' case, 191
German Zollverein, 136
Germanization, 30
Germany, 311, 592, 608, and Anti-War Pact, 668; 464; coal and iron, 117; ment by compulsion, nomic system, 100; forei committee, 750; and Lea and Locarno, 652; minori 230; navy, 515; payment 535; United States, treaty 8, 1923, 123; World Wa hoods, 503. *See* Reparati
Gex-Savoy, 137
Gilbert, S. Parker, 542
Gladstone, W. E., 742
Glass, 99
Glass, Carter, and foreign 411
Gobineau, Comte de, 74
Gold Coast, 348, 351, 352, 38
Gomez, President, 475
Gondra convention, 626, 638
Grant, Madison, 75
Greco-Bulgaria dispute, 641,
Greece, 316, 326, 637, 681; tional financial control, 425;

INDEX

Intermarriage, 59
International Bank. *See* Bank of International Settlement
International bureaus, 140, 722
International commerce, 113
International Commissions of Inquiry, 623
International Conference on the traffic in women and children, 283
International Conferences, 680; expenses divided, 688; lack of system, 691; majority decisions, 681; voting systems, 688
International Council of Advice, Africa, 368
International Economic Conference, 151
International Educational Cinematographic Institute, 26
International Emigration and Immigration Conference at Rome, 1924, 173; at Havana, 1928, 174
International Federation for Mutual Assistance, etc., 300
International financial advisers, 433
International financial control, 424; case of Austria and Hungary, 426; merits and demerits, 434
International High Commission, 247
International Hydrographic Bureau, 288
International Institute of Agriculture, 146, 152
International Institute of Refrigeration, 148
International Institute for Unification of Private Law, 705
International intervention. *See* Intervention
International Joint Commission, 627
International labor bank, 157
International labor conferences, 159
International labor legislation, before the war, 158
International Labor Office, 159, 163; duties, 161; enforcement of treaties, 166
International Labor Organization, 159, 575; accomplishments, 162; Washington Conference, 162
International languages, 23
International law, codification, 705;
conventions, list, 678; making of, 676; principle of self-determination and, 33; tariffs and, 162
International legislation, before the World War, 678
International Marine Conference, 286
International Office of Public Health, 292
International opium conference, 266
International organizations, 287; method of voting, 687
International police force, 593, 602
International Régime of Railways, 142
International Telegraphic Union, 141
International trade federations, 157
International Union and Bureau for the Publication of Customs Tariffs, 135
Internationals, Labor, 157
Inter-racial communities, 70
Intervention, 187, 321, 735; and Anti-War Pact, 663; international, 391, 664; justification, 393; temporary for debt collection, etc., 393, 407, 415
Intervention and War, 504
Investments, foreign. *See* Foreign investments
Iraq. *See* Mesopotamia
Irish Free State, 212; minister to the United States, 216
Iron, 98
Iroquois, 50
Islam, 87
Italianization, 81
Italy, 608, 631, 644; Austria and, 52; colonies, 329; emigration treaty with Brazil, 171; over-population problem, 175. *See* Corfu affair

Jamaica, 384
Japan, 8, 57, 310, 592, 624; and China, 465; colonies, 328; control of foreign affairs, 730; Gentlemen's Agreement, 67, 741; naval programme, 516; over-population problem, 92, 176, 312; United States relations, 63, 68
Japanese, 58, 62; British treatment, 65
Japanese Exclusion Law of 1924, 61, 752

Java, 325, 328
Jesuits, 320
Jews, 28, 216; in Roumania, 65
Jhering, Rudolf von, 74
Johnston, Sir Harry, 368
Joint government, 489
Jubaland, 330
Judicial Sanctions, 590

Kaiser, trial of, 590
Kanaka trade, 318
Karahan, 93
Kavala, 129
Kellogg, F. B., 622, 657, 665
Kemal, Mustapha, 391
Kenya Colony, 338, 346, 383; status of Indians, 67
Kerensky loan, 403
Kiaochow, 464
Kiel Canal, 133
Kilometric guarantees, 398, 402
King of the World, 93
Kipling, R., 315
Knox, P. C., 408, 417, 456
Kollár, Jan, 80
Korea, 328, 453, 584; Japanese in, 338, 377, 379, 399
Kowloon, 465
Krassin, Leonid, 396
Krijanitcha, 80
Krupps, 409; scandal of 1913, 520
Ku Klux Klan, 78
Kwang-chow-wan, 466

Labor, 154; colonial, 163, 280, 331; conferences, 161; emigration conferences, 173; enforcement of labor treaties, 166; exploitation in backward regions, 400; forced, native, 332; important treaties, 153, 350; imported, in colonies, 335; inspectors, 350; legislation, 158; overpopulation problem, 174
Labor Internationals, 154
Labor Office. *See* International Labor Office
Land, backward peoples and, 336; private ownership, 347; trusteeship principle, 347, 360
Landlocked States, 129
Lange, C., 754
Language, 7; ethnic minorities, 187;
influence of, 9; international, 23; number of languages, 11
Lansing-Ishii agreement, 735
Lapointe, Ernest, 208
Lake Tsana barrage, 450
Lassiter report, 39
Latin America, 234, 325; arbitration, treaty of 1902, 609; United States financial control, 420
Latin-American League, 84
Latin-American Union, 84
Latin race, 83
Law, Bonar, 213
Lawrence, T. J., 464
League of Nations, 253; administrative activities, 723; Advisory Committee on Traffic in Women and Children, 283; agreements made, 702; and Alliances, 577; amendment and interpretation of the Covenant, 698, 723; American League, 250; and Anti-War Pact, 668; armament investigation, 566; armament limitation and, 571; Arms Traffic, 282; Austria and Hungary, financial control, 426, 431; Dominions and, 214; equality doctrine and, 717; expulsion, 698; finances, 714; health organization, 293; humanitarian work, 302; independence of members, 706; inter-American disputes, 636; intervention and, 392; legislative function, 693; liquor traffic, 273; loans, 433; membership, 694; minorities and, 191, 201; non-members, 595, 635, 696; opium traffic, 263; Ruthenes, 228; Secretariat, 632; settlement of disputes, 632; slavery and, 278; standing Commissions, 704, 721; Straits, 134; technical organizations, 703; unanimity rule, 717; undemocratic nature, 753; unfair competition, 146; United States and, 634; withdrawal, 697; women and children, 284. *See also* Assembly, Council, Economic Committee, Health Organization, Intellectual coöperation, Mandates, Sanctions
League of Peoples, 753
League of Races, 95

INDEX 831

League of Red Cross Societies, 297
Leaseholds, 464
Lebanon, 223, 593
Leeward Islands, 235
Legal aid, free, 301
Leopold II. *See* Congo Free State
Liberia, 89, 743; financial control, 408, 412, 420
Libya, 329
Lichtenstein, 136, 695
Limitation of armaments. *See* Armaments
Lincheng affair, 486
Lippert Concession, 338
Liquor traffic, 267, 339, 342, 352, 359; African control, 268; Brussels conferences, 268; international problems, 270; smuggling liquor into the United States, 272
Literary property, 145
Literature, historic and poetic, 16
Lithuania, 228, 230, 586, 633
Little Entente, 237, 511
Little Protocols, 196
Lloyd George, David, 13, 83, 534, 743
Loans, backward countries, 311, 397, 407; League of Nations, 151, 412; in Mandates, 358
Lobengula, King, 337
Locarno arbitration agreements, 653
Locarno Security Agreement, 635, 653; and Anti-War Pact, 658
Lodge, H. C., 437, 594
London Conference of 1924, 539
London, Treaty of (1915), 329
Lowell, A. L., 746
Lugard, Frederick, 367
Luther Cabinet, 652
Luxemburg, 136, 583, 587, 681

MacDonald Government, 322, 330, 648, 728, 742, 743
Macedonia, 20; finances, 424
McNary-Haugen bill, 111
Madagascar, 314, 334, 472
Madero, Francisco, 402
Magna Charta Day Association, 82
Magoon, C. E., 475
Magyarization, 30
Malay peninsula, 317, 335
Malmedy, 39
Malta, 385

Malthus, T. R., 177
Manchuria, Knox plan for railways, 456, 459, 462; loan proposed, 411
Mandates, 326, 328, 355; classes, 356; extension, 368; legal status, 357; liquor policy, 269; military policy, 314; obligation of mandatories, 359; open door, 453; origin, 359
Mandates Commission, 361, 391, 462; enlargement, 368
Mandatory powers, responsibility to the World, 367
Mangin, General, 313
Marines, informal control by, 487
Maritime Flag, right to, 129
Maritime Transport Council, 149
Markets, 309, 311
Marx, Karl, 154
Masai tribe, 338
Masaryk, President, 242
Matabele, 337, 342
Mavrommatis Palestine concession, 461
May, H. L., 261
Mazzini, Giuseppe, 21, 32, 237
Mediterranean Sea, 313; agreements, 585
Memel, 120, 132, 229, 641, 642
Menocal, President, 476
Mercury, control of, 113
Mesopotamia, 54, 89, 356; example of, 388; oil rights, 460
Metals, 99
Mexico, 82, 403, 451; American rights in, 404; 1861 intervention, 593; boundary commission, 627; oil export tax, 109
Meyer, G. von L., 594
Michelet, Jules, 7
Middle East, British policy, 312
Military advisers. *See* Advisers
Military agreements, 507
Military class, 727; in Japan, 731
Military fears, as cause of imperialism, 312
Military sanctions, 592
Military Systems, 513; colonial, 313; mandates, 359
Mill, J. S., 70
Millspaugh, A. C., 422
Milton, John, 7
Minerals, 99

Minorities, 46; exchange of, 200, 298; protection of, 179, 321; German farmers in Poland, 191; internal guarantees, 180; League of Nations and, 191; "Little Protocols," 195; principle criticised, 192; procedure, 199; treaties before the war, 184
Minorities Office, 196
Missionaries, 352; imperialism and, 319; numbers, 319
Mixed Companies, 404
Model Treaties, League (1928), 645
Mohammedans, 87, 321
Monaco, 471
Monopolies, 116, 447, 469; Open Door and, 445, 461. See also Closed Door
Monroe Doctrine, 248, 253, 302, 313; and Anti-War Pact, 661, 662; Australian, 312; interpretation, 637; League Council and, 636
Moore, J. B., 620
Moresnet, 52
Morocco, 330, 347, 380, 452, 473; finances, 456; Open Door, 451, 456; tariff control, 482
Morphine. See Drug habit
Morrow, D. W., 406
Moscow Conference (1922) on Armaments, 561
Most-favored-nation treatment, 108, 124, 126, 447
Mosul case, 54
Mozambique, 330, 335, 350, 371
Müller, Max, 73
Mussolini, Benito, 329, 330
Mutual Assistance, Treaty of, 757

Nansen, Fridtjof, 298, 753
Narcotic Drug Control Commission, 267
Natal Land Trust, 347
National characteristics, 6
National debts. See Debts
National Education Association, 25
"National interests," 301, 743
National treatment, 127
Nationalities, international conference of, Paris, 34
Nationalization of property, 403
Native officials in colonies, 379
Natives, 383; customs, 316, 378; discrimination and brutality toward, 341; education, 336; and imperialism, 331; labor, 332; land, 336. See also Mandates
Naturalization, 61
Nauru, 360, 453
Naval bases, 312, 359, 664; Pacific, status quo, 569
Navies, capital ships of chief powers, status, 558; gun levels on battleships, 575; ratios of the chief powers, 559; rivalry, 515. See Washington Conference
Navigation, freedom of, 132
Navy, U. S., business and, 441; militarism and propaganda, 733
Near East, Concert of Europe and, 681
Negroes, 71, 85. See also Natives
Neuilly, treaty of, 618
Neutrality, 502, 513, 669
Neutralization agreements, 582
New Hebrides, 339, 350, 453; joint government, 492
New Zealand, 65, 66, 318, 335. See also British Empire
Newspapers and foreign affairs, 752
Nicaragua, 321; Canal, 244, 419; finances, 349, 419
Nigeria, 348; native policy, 379
Nile Agreement (1928), 490
Nitrates, 100, 113
Nobel Dynamite Trust Company, 521
Non-aggression agreements, 586
Non-fortification agreements, 492, 493
Non-Intercourse Act, 592, 756
Non-legal disputes, 623; League of Nations and, 628
Non-recognition of defaulting governments, 413
Norden movement, 80
Nordic race, 61, 75
North Pole, 315
North Sea, control of liquor traffic, 270; fisheries, 289
Norway, 643; integrity guaranteed, 508, 579, 585; prohibition, 271

Obregon government and the United States, 403
Obrenovitch, Michel, 236

INDEX

Obscene publications, 289
Official majorities, 384
Oil, 99; concessions, scramble for, 402, 439; Dutch East Indies, 460; Mesopotamia, 460; trusts, 113
Okuma, Count, 91
Olivier, Lord Sydney, 322
Open Door, 368, 437, 447, 492; agreements, 448; agreements violated, 453; colonial treaties, 457; definition, 447; governmental disagreement over, 459; international cooperation and, 455; League declarations, 452; settlement of disputes, 459
Open Door Treaty—China, 449, 460, 471
Opium, 257; India, use, 259; League of Nations and, 262; smoking in the Far East, 266; treaties, 260; United States proposals, 264; world production, 257
Opium Conferences of 1924–1925, 266
Optant question, 193
Orange Free State, 21
Oriental Development Company, 458
Orientals, 58; abroad, 69; living in white countries, 68; treatment, 59; in the United States, 61
Outlawry of war, 656. See also Anti-War Pact
Over-population problem, 174; expansion and, 311

Pacific Islands, 313
Pacific Ocean, 69; Four Power Treaty, 312; naval bases, 569; Open Door, 452; spheres of influence, 470
Pacific Protectorate Act, 318
Pacific Settlement of International Disputes, convention of 1899. See Hague Conferences
Palestine, 356, 390; Jewish home in, 216
Palm oil, 348, 444
Palma, President, 474
Palmerston, Lord, 413, 743, 744
Pan-African Congress, 87
Pan-African movement, 85
Pan-American Arbitration Conference, 252, 627, 638

Pan-American Conferences, 246, 249; armament limitation, 562, 574; Fifth, 626; Sixth, 261
Pan-American Sanitary Code, 293
Pan-American sanitary conferences, 293
Pan-American Union, 246
Pan-Angle movement, 81
Pan-Arab movement, 89
Pan Asiatic Conference, Baku, 92
Pan-Asiatic movement, 91
Pan-Europa, 242
Pan-German League, 78
Pan-Germanism, 78
Pan-Hispanism, 83
Pan-Islam Society, 87
Pan-Latinism, 83
Pan-nationalism, 73
Pan-Slavism, 79
Pan-Turanian movement, 88
Panama, republic of, 403, 466, 695; Costa Rica dispute, 637; 1926 treaty with U. S., 580; independence guaranteed, 585, 663
Panama Canal, 133, 501
Paris Peace Conference, 503; plenary sessions and commissions, 690; rule of equality of states at, 210, 689. See also Self-determination; Minorities
Parker, Peter, 320
Parliament, British, 205
Pascal, on justice, 648
Passport Conferences, 150, 198
Pasteur, Louis, 297
Peace Commission treaties, 624, 628, 633
Pearson, Karl, 8
Peonage, 400
Permanent Court of Arbitration, 611
Permanent Court of International Justice, 192, 201, 389, 461, 485, 628, 631, 632, 633, 644, 725; advisory opinions, 579, 617, 619; compulsory jurisdiction, 654; judgments handed down, list, 618; law to be applied, 620; and League, 615; organization, 615; Optional Clause, 611, 616, 649, 667; problem of appeal, 619; and United States, 620
Persia, 586; and Article X, 589, 599, 686; courts, 312, 485; finances, 421;

spheres of influence and, 469, 584; tariff control, 482
Peru, 42, 401, 416, 524, 696
Peruvian Amazon Rubber Company, 401
Peters, Karl, 339
Petitions, mandates, 363; minorities, 190
Petroleum. *See* Oil
Philippines, 310, 315, 328, 345, 352, 372, 382, 384, 466; Closed Door in, 104, 443; opium, 265
Phosphate, 453
Phosphorus Conventions, 158
Phylloxera, 148
"Pig War," 107
Pirating, literary, 145
Platinum, 99
Platt, O. H., 316
Platt Amendment, 417, 493, 735; and League, 581; extension of principle, 477; history, 474
Plebiscites, 37, 372, 587, 594, 602; abuses, 38; disadvantages, 40; practical benefits, 42
Poincaré, 744
Poison gas, 504, 560, 572
Poland, 37, 239; German farmers in, 191; Russia and, 219. *See also* Danzig
"Political Questions," 250
Political sanctions, 597
Politis, M., 669, 725
Pope, 14
Poppy. *See* Opium
Population, 2, 104; tariffs and, 104. *See also* Over-population
Port Arthur lease, 464
Porter, S. G., 264
Porto Rico, 318, 328, 352, 382; land, 338
Portorose Conference, 128
Ports, freedom of access, 129; internationalization, 130; maritime convention, 127
Portugal, 114, 416; colonies, 330, 332, 342; revolt crushed, 593
Postal Union, 140, 678, 715
Potash agreement, 113
Powder Cartel, 521
Preparatory Commission on Armament, 574

Press Experts Conference, 26
Principe, 333
Prison Conferences, 286
Private International Law, 301
Prohibition, international enforcement, 270; "wet" and "dry" countries, controversies, 272
Propaganda, military, in U. S., 733; treaties with Russia against, 156; and war, 503
Prostitutes, 283
Protective tariff system, 102
Protectorates, 325, 421, 471; international, 473; policy of, 378; semi-protectorates, 473
Protégés, 486
Protestantism, 13, 75
Protocol for the Pacific Settlement of International Disputes, 649
Protocols, Little, 196
Publicity, at international conferences, 746
Pulp-wood, 109
Punjab affair, 321
Putumayo affair, 401

Quadruple Alliance, 509
Quarantine, health, 290; veterinary, 135
Quebec, Canada and, 225
Quinine, 112, 308
"Quota" system, 61

Race Prejudice, 57, 77; causes, 58
Race relations, 50, 352; colored troops in war, 314; demand for equality, 62; democracy in inter-racial communities, 70; racial segregation, 59. *See also* Gentlemen's Agreement; Kenya
Radio monopoly, 142
Radio Telegraphic Union, 142
Raditch, Stephen, 226
Railroads, in backward countries, 398, 402; convention, 142, 704
Raw materials, 98, 309; monopolies, 116; two kinds, 99
Rebus sic stantibus, 667
Reciprocity treaties, 107
Recognition of Governments, 413
Red Cross, 296, 301
Red Sea, arms traffic, 283

INDEX

Referendum, Switzerland, 752; United States, proposed, 753
Refugees, 201, 501; international work for, 297
Regional groups, 253
Regional understandings. *See* Article XXI, Covenant
Religion, 12; backward peoples and, 319; religions of the world, 12; toleration, 13. *See also* Minorities
Renan, Ernest, 16
Renner, Karl, 223
Renovación, 85
Reparations, Chapter XXII; arbitration and default, 544; "civilian damage," 525; Commission and Germany's bill, 526; Dawes plan, 537; German failure to pay, 530; Germany's capacity, 527, 534; in 19th century, 523; passive resistance, 530; Ruhr occupation, 530; Transfer Committee, 542, 549; Young Plan, 548
Revolution, 29, 33; in colonies, 373; foreign aid, 402; in Latin America, 500; Holy Alliance and, 509
Rhine, Allied troops on, 534; American troops on, 553; Commission, 532; occupation, costs, 531; Versailles Treaty, 531, 653
Rice, 308
Riff, 330
Rivers, 52; navigation, international, 133
Rockefeller Foundation, 297
Roman Catholic Church, 14
Roosevelt, Theodore, 67, 594, 735; "alliance" with Japan, 737
Root, Elihu, 620, 729
Roumania, 30, 595, 623, 686; Jews, 65; land disputes with Hungary, 110; minorities, 226
Roumanization, 30
Royal Dutch Shell Co., 112
Royal Niger Company, 454
Ruanda-Urundi frontier, 329, 356, 364
Rubber, 100, 308; Congo, 332; Liberia, 421; price control, 111. *See* Putumayo affair
Ruhr occupation, 530, 566, 642; evacuation, 545; legality, 531
Ruhrort, 530, 534

Russell, Bertrand, 20
Russia, 31, 35, 312, 398, 399, 509, 561, 636; and Anti-War Pact, 659, 661; autonomy of Finland and Poland, 208; Hague conference, 519; nationalization of property, 403; non-aggression agreements, 586; non-recognition, 414; oil concessions, 440; recognition of liability, 413; Soviet government and autonomy, 219; Soviet Russian federation, 240; United States and, 414
Russification, 31, 220
Russo-Asiatic bank, 438
Rush-Bagot agreement, 556
Ruthenes, 227

Saar valley, 40, 118, 495, 754; discontent, 120; French influence, 119
Safety at sea, convention, 287
St. Germain Conventions, 282, 354
Sakhalin, 328
Salamis case, 631
Salisbury, Lord, 341
Salonika, 131
Salvador, 243; finances, 419
Samoa, 335, 452, 466
San Remo oil agreement, 459
Sanctions, 590; and Anti-War Pact, 669; German and Swiss reservations, 654, 695; League Covenant and, 595; sanctions attacked, 597; under the Geneva protocol, 651
Sanitation conferences, 291
San Thomé, 333
Santayana, George, 20
Santo Domingo, 395; American troops, 488; finances, 418; Tariff control, 482, 487
Sarawak, 371
Satsuma clan, 731
Scandinavians, 80
Schleswig, 6, 37, 40
School histories, 19
Sea, free access to, 129; freedom of, 669; safety of life at, 287
Sealing treaty, 289
Secession, 233
Secret treaties, 512; covenant of the League and, 747; democracy and, 744; of the World War, 510, 513

Secretariat, League, 632, 635, 719
Security, 582
Seely, Sir J., 315
Self-defense and Anti-War Pact, 661; and League, 665
Self-determination, 28; backward peoples and, 370, 386. *See* Chapter II
Self-government, capacity for, 374
Semi-protectorates, 473
Senate, U. S., and reservations, 741, 756; and treaties, 739
Serajevo murder, 628, 632
Settlement colonies, 332, 335
Sèvres, treaty of, 187, 329, 425, 485
Shantung, 320, 690
Shipping, 127; conference, 112; national aid, 114. *See* Open Door
Shotwell, J. T., 657
Shuster, Morgan, 422
Siam, 258, 320; Courts, 483; tariff control, 481
Siemens affair, 521
Silk, 99
Silver, price, 112
Simon Commission, 387
Sims, Admiral, 503
Singapore, 313; base, 569; Health Bureau, 296
Sisal, 108, 110
Six Power Consortium, 456
Slave trade, 275, 318; treaties about, 276
Slavery, 261, 275, 332; present status, 278, 317, 360
Slavery convention, 279, 369
Slavs, 79
Sleeping sickness, 299, 318
Small-farm system, 347
Smith, Adam, 97
Smith, Jeremiah, 431
Smith, Captain John, 319
Smuggling, aliens, 170; of liquor, 272; treaties, 273
Somaliland, 329
South Africa, 70, 234, 335, 339, 352; Indians, 67; native policy, 71
South Africa Trading Company, 337, 371
Southern Rhodesia, 205, 337, 351, 371
Sovereignty, 308, 318, 407
Spa agreement of 1920, 528, 535, 550

Spain, 83, 203; and League, 655, 697; colonies, 330; wines in northern countries, 270
Spanish-speaking peoples, 83
Sphere of influence, 449; religious, 362
Spitzbergen, 136
Stack murder, 392, 479, 490, 636
Stambulisky, Alexander, 236
Standard Oil Co., 113, 460
State of war, 600
Statistics Convention, 151
Status quo, agreements as to, 585; freezing, 667, 674
Steel, 97; European cartel, 113
Stevenson Restriction Act, 111
Stimson agreement, 487
Straits, international, 111, 134; convention, 1923, 555, 568
Stresemann, H., 201, 653
Submarine cables, 141
Submarines, 517, 560
Subsidies, 113, 175, 398; colonial, 323; newspapers, 751
Sudan, 341, 478, 659; joint government, 489; mandate, 490
Suez Canal, 133, 216, 315
Sugar Convention, 140, 147, 152
Sulphur, 112
Sultanate, 87
Supreme Court, U. S., 408, 419, 656
Supreme War Council, 682
Sweden, 6, 22, 80, 643; Aaland Islands and, 48
Switzerland, 22, 234, 316, 583, 587, 643; League of Nations and, 602, 695; referendum, 752
Syndicates, 111
Syria, 89, 357; example of, 390; rebellion, 367

Tacna-Arica, 31, 37, 39, 611, 636
Taft Agreement, 467
Tagore, Rabindranath, 20
Tanganyika, 356, 379
Tangier, status, 490
Tanks in warfare, 505
Tariff Act of 1897, 107
Tariff Act of 1922 (sec. 317), 125
Tariff control of backward countries, 480

Tariffs, 102, 153, 251, 340; changes in rates, 109; changes, publication, 135; colonial policies, 390, 443; discriminations and "Wars," 105; elimination of discriminations, 125; limitations, 137; as taxes on natives, 340
Taylor, Isaac, 74
"Tea council," 112
Technical Organizations, League, 149, 702
Telegraphic Union, 141, 679
Territorial integrity agreements, 584
Teschen, 120
Teutonism, 75
Theodoli, Marquis, 366
Third International (Labor), 155
Thomas, Albert, 161
Three-mile limit, 272
Tibet, 312, 470
Tin, 99, 308
Tinoco government, 402
Tittoni, M., 181
Tokutomi, Mr., 91
Tolstoy, Leo, 20
Trade, colonial, 308; obstructions, 123; political control and, 309
Trade Internationals, 157
Trade promotion, 111, 437, 442
Trade spirits, 268
Trade unionists, 157
Transcaucasia, 240
Transit, freedom of, 128
Transkei, 71
Transport Council, 149
Transylvania, 226
Treaties, British Empire and the Dominions, 210; registration, 652, 748; revision by Assembly, 700. *See also* Commercial Treaties
Treaty-making power, 733; British Dominions, 207; British Parliament, 741; proposed changes, U. S., 757
Treitschke, Heinrich von, 74
Trentino, 181
Triple Alliance, 506, 509
Triple Entente, 509
Tripoli, 329
Troop reservoirs, 313
Tropical diseases, 352
Trusteeship, 345, 387

Trusts, foreign markets, 111; international, 112
Tsetse fly, 299
Tsingtau, 464
Tunis, 380
Tunis-Morocco case, 617
Turanian race, 88
Turkey, 31, 87, 555, 681; anatomy in, 223; Chester concession, 398; European financial control, 425; exterritoriality, 484; minorities, 187, 229; minorities exchanged with Greece, 200; Open Door agreements, 449; spheres of influence, 470, 584; tariff control, 481
Turkification, 30, 223
Turkish Petroleum Company, 441, 459
Turner, F. J., 10
Twenty-One Demands, 441, 465
Twenty-One Points, 155

Uganda, 320, 379
Ukraine, 221
Unanimity in international conferences, 686, 710, 717
Union of Democratic Control, 751
Union of Kalmar, 80
United States, 19, 316, 397; and military sanctions, 594, 598, 652, 669; arbitration policy, 609, 610, 624, 739; arms embargo, 282; checks on foreign policy, 735; commercial interests abroad, 100; concession policy, 420; Constitution and foreign affairs, 755; dependencies, 328; economic sufficiency, 101; federal government, 232; financial control of Latin-American countries, 420; financial control of Liberia, 420; financial control of Persia, 421; International Labor Office, 161; League of Nations and, 634, 696; Naval power, 517; racial status quo, 61; reparation commission, 532; State Department's financial policy, 410; tariff bargaining, 107; treaty-making powers, 735; unofficial observers, 738. *See* Monroe Doctrine
United States of Europe. *See* Pan-Europa

Universal Negro Improvement Association, 85
Unredeemed territory, 29
Upper Silesia, 40, 120, 641, 642; free trade, 137; minorities, 195, 199
Uruguay, 250, 640
Utrecht treaty, 275

Valorization, coffee, 110
Vatican, 14, 743
Venezuela dispute, 249
Vera Cruz, 246
Versailles, Treaty of, 35, 39, 577, 584, 685, 690, 741, 753; Articles 42 and 43, 653, 664; Article 80, 664; Article 213, 565; Article 231, 503; occupation of Ruhr and, 533; reparation and, 525
Vested interests, 405
Veterinary questions, 135
Victoria, Queen, 744
Vilna dispute, 239, 602, 642
Vineyards, 148
Virgin Islands, 328
Visit, right of, 276
"Vital interests," 623; and arbitration, 609
Vlachs, 187
von Moltke, 672
Vorarlberg, 47

Wallas, Graham, 57
War, 13, 311, 316; and democracy, 728; and food supply, 97, 105; costs, material and spiritual, 499; economic nationalism and, 116; future warfare, 503; laws of, 505; legal types, 644; loss of life in 19th century, 500; outlawry. *See* Outlawry of war, and Aggression
War Criminals' Trials, 591
War guilt, 502, 503
War of the Pacific, 524. *See also* Tacna-Arica
Washington Conference of 1921, 13, 281, 449, 465, 480, 484, 517, 557, 692, 737; agreements made, 449, 465, 558, 582; British Empire and, 211
Webb-Pomerene Act, 114
Wei-hai-wei, 465
West Indies, native farms, 348
Wheat, 100
Wheat Executive, 149
White Man's Burden, 305, 317
White Peril, 91
White Slave Traffic, 283
Wickersham, G. W., 706
Wicksell, Mme., 363
Will to peace, 26
William II of Hohenzollern, 590
Wilson, Woodrow, 34, 598, 728, 735; on access to the sea, 128; on economic barriers, 127; Fourteen Points, 524; "open covenants" etc., 745; reparation, 524; secret treaties, 745; on self-determination, 35, 38, 272; Senate and France and, 740
Wimbledon case, 134
Wireless telegraphy, 141
Witchcraft, 360
Women, night work, 159; traffic in, 283
Wood, Leonard, 384
Wool, 99
World Court. *See* Permanent Court of International Justice
World Island, 3
World War, 16, 34, 307; cost, 500; treaties following, 38, 41
Wrangel Island, 315

Young, A. N., 408
Young Plan, 548
Young Turks, 89
Yucatan, 108, 110

Zaghlul Pasha, 479
Zaleski, M., 199
Zanzibar, 277
Zimmerman, Dr., 430
Zionism, 216